A Companion to the Early Middle Ages

WILEY-BLACKWELL COMPANIONS TO HISTORY

This series provides sophisticated and authoritative overviews of the scholarship that has shaped our current understanding of the past. Defined by theme, period and/or region, each volume comprises between twenty-five and forty concise essays written by individual scholars within their area of specialization. The aim of each contribution is to synthesize the current state of scholarship from a variety of historical perspectives and to provide a statement on where the field is heading. The essays are written in a clear, provocative, and lively manner, designed for an international audience of scholars, students, and general readers.

WILEY-BLACKWELL COMPANIONS TO BRITISH HISTORY

A Companion to Roman Britain
Edited by Malcolm Todd
A Companion to Britain in the Later Middle Ages
Edited by S. H. Rigby
A Companion to Tudor Britain
Edited by Robert Tittler and Norman Jones
A Companion to Stuart Britain
Edited by Barry Coward
A Companion to Eighteenth-Century Britain
Edited by H. T. Dickinson
A Companion to Nineteenth-Century Britain
Edited by Chris Williams
A Companion to Early Twentieth-Century Britain
Edited by Chris Wrigley
A Companion to Contemporary Britain
Edited by Paul Addison and Harriet Jones
A Companion to the Early Middle Ages: Britain and Ireland c.500–c.1100
Edited by Pauline Stafford

WILEY-BLACKWELL COMPANIONS TO EUROPEAN HISTORY

A Companion to Europe 1900–1945
Edited by Gordon Martel
A Companion to Eighteenth-Century Europe
Edited by Peter H. Wilson
A Companion to Nineteenth-Century Europe
Edited by Stefan Berger
A Companion to the Worlds of the Renaissance
Edited by Guido Ruggiero
A Companion to the Reformation World
Edited by R. Po-chia Hsia

A Companion to Europe Since 1945
Edited by Klaus Larres
A Companion to the Medieval World
Edited by Carol Lansing and Edward D. English
A Companion to the French Revolution
Edited by Peter McPhee

WILEY-BLACKWELL COMPANIONS TO WORLD HISTORY

A Companion to Western Historical Thought
Edited by Lloyd Kramer and Sarah Maza
A Companion to Gender History
Edited by Teresa A. Meade and Merry E. Wiesner-Hanks
A Companion to the History of the Middle East
Edited by Youssef M. Choueiri
A Companion to Japanese History
Edited by William M. Tsutsui
A Companion to International History 1900–2001
Edited by Gordon Martel
A Companion to Latin American History
Edited by Thomas Holloway
A Companion to Russian History
Edited by Abbott Gleason
A Companion to World War I
Edited by John Horne
A Companion to Mexican History and Culture
Edited by William H. Beezley
A Companion to World History
Edited by Douglas Northrop
A Companion to Global Environmental History
Edited by J. R. McNeill and Erin Stewart Mauldin
A Companion to World War II
Edited by Thomas W. Zeiler, with Daniel M. DuBois

For further information on these and other titles in the series please visit our website at

www.wiley.com.

A COMPANION TO THE EARLY MIDDLE AGES

Britain and Ireland c.500–c.1100

Edited by

Pauline Stafford

A John Wiley & Sons, Ltd., Publication

This paperback edition first published 2013
© 2013 Blackwell Publishing Limited

Edition history: Blackwell Publishing Ltd (hardback, 2009)

Blackwell Publishing was acquired by John Wiley & Sons in February 2007. Blackwell's publishing program has been merged with Wiley's global Scientific, Technical, and Medical business to form Wiley-Blackwell.

Registered Office
John Wiley & Sons Ltd, The Atrium, Southern Gate, Chichester, West Sussex, PO19 8SQ, UK

Editorial Offices
350 Main Street, Malden, MA 02148-5020, USA
9600 Garsington Road, Oxford, OX4 2DQ, UK
The Atrium, Southern Gate, Chichester, West Sussex, PO19 8SQ, UK

For details of our global editorial offices, for customer services, and for information about how to apply for permission to reuse the copyright material in this book please see our website at www.wiley.com/wiley-blackwell.

The right of Pauline Stafford to be identified as the author of the editorial material in this work has been asserted in accordance with the UK Copyright, Designs and Patents Act 1988.

Library of Congress Cataloging-in-Publication Data

A companion to the early Middle Ages : Britain and Ireland c.500–c.1100 / edited by Pauline Stafford.
    p. cm. – (Wiley-Blackwell companions to British history)
    Includes bibliographical references and index.
    ISBN 978-1-4051-0628-3 (hardcover : alk. paper) — 978-1-118-42513-8 (pbk.). 1. Great Britain–History–To 1066.   2. Ireland–History–To 1172.   3. Great Britain–Civilization–To 1066.
4. Ireland–Civilization–To 1172.   5. Civilization, Medieval.   6. Middle Ages.   I. Stafford, Pauline.

DA152.C6975 2009
941.01–dc22

2008032202

A catalogue record for this book is available from the British Library.

Cover image: St. John's Gospel, carpet page from Lindisfarne Gospels, 710-21.
Cover design by Richard Boxall Design Associates

Set in 10/12.5pt Galliard by Toppan Best-set Premedia Limited

1   2013

Contents

List of Maps   viii

Notes on Contributors   ix

List of Abbreviations   xiii

Maps   xv

PART I INTRODUCTORY MATTER   1

1 Introduction   3
  Pauline Stafford

2 Historiography   9
  Pauline Stafford

3 Sources   23
  Pauline Stafford

PART II BRITAIN AND IRELAND, C.500–C.750   39

4 Britain and Ireland, c.500   41
  Barbara Yorke

5 Economy   57
  Howard B. Clarke

6 Kings and Kingship   76
  Barbara Yorke

7 Communities and Kinship   91
  David E. Thornton

8 Social Structure   107
  Thomas M. Charles-Edwards

9 Britain, Ireland, and Europe, c.500–c.750   126
   Paul Fouracre

10 Conversions to Christianity   143
   Huw Pryce

11 Church Organization and Pastoral Care   160
   Thomas Pickles

12 Latin Learning and Christian Art   177
   Martin J. Ryan

PART III BRITAIN AND IRELAND IN THE LONG NINTH CENTURY,
c.750–c.900   **193**

13 Viking Raids and Conquest   195
   Dawn Hadley

14 Scandinavian Settlement   212
   Dawn Hadley

15 Britain, Ireland, and Europe, c.750–c.900   231
   Janet L. Nelson

PART IV BRITAIN AND IRELAND, c.900–c.1100   249

16 Scotland   251
   Alex Woolf

17 Ireland, c.900–c.1000   268
   Edel Bhreathnach

18 Ireland, c.1000–c.1100   285
   Seán Duffy

19 Northumbria   303
   William M. Aird

20 Southumbria   322
   Charles Insley

21 Wales and West Britain   341
   John Reuben Davies

22 Britain, Ireland, and Europe, c.900–c.1100   358
   Simon MacLean

23 The Institutional Church   376
   Catherine Cubitt

24 Pastoral Care and Religious Belief   395
   Catherine Cubitt

25 Nobility   414
   Julia Crick

26 Settlement and Social Differentiation   432
    Sally Crawford

27 Localities   446
    David E. Thornton

28 Queens and Queenship   459
    Pauline Stafford

    Bibliography   477

    Index   524

List of Maps

Map 1   Ireland in the Early Middle Ages   xv

Map 2   Southern Britain in the Early Middle Ages   xvi

Map 3   West Britain in the Early Middle Ages   xvii

Map 4a Northern Britain in the Early Middle Ages: Early Christian
        Period   xviii

Map 4b Northern Britain in the Early Middle Ages: Viking Age
        and after   xix

Map 5   Continental European links to Britain and Ireland   xx

Map 6   Economically advantaged and disadvantaged areas in Britain
        and Ireland   60

Notes on Contributors

William M. Aird lectures on medieval history at Cardiff University, Wales. He was awarded his PhD by Edinburgh University. With a particular interest in the history of the Normans in the eleventh and twelfth centuries, he is the author of a number of articles and monographs including, *St. Cuthbert and the Normans: The Church of Durham, 1071–1153* (1998) and *Robert Curthose, Duke of Normandy, c.1050–1134* (2008). His current research concerns the medieval *Life of St. Margaret of Scotland* and the career of Edward A. Freeman.

Edel Bhreathnach is the Academic Project Manager at the Mícheál Ó Cléirigh Institute for the Study of Irish History and Civilisation, University College Dublin. She has published on many aspects of medieval Ireland, including the royal complex of Tara, Co. Meath, and edited the interdisciplinary volume *The Kingship and Landscape of Tara* (2005). Her current interests include royal sites in Ireland and the intellectual history of the Franciscan order in late medieval and early modern Ireland.

Thomas M. Charles-Edwards is Jesus Professor of Celtic, University of Oxford. His main field of research is early medieval Irish and Welsh history and literature. He was a Scholar of the School of Celtic Studies in the Dublin Institute of Advanced Studies and has held posts in Oxford since 1969. He was elected a Fellow of the British Academy in 2001 and an Honorary Member of the Royal Irish Academy in 2006. His main publications are *Bechbretha* (1983, with Fergus Kelly), *The Welsh Laws* (1989), *Early Irish and Welsh Kinship* (1993), *Early Christian Ireland* (2000), and *The Chronicle of Ireland* (2006), and he edited *After Rome* (2003). He is currently writing volume 1 of the *Oxford History of Wales*.

Howard B. Clarke is a graduate of the University of Birmingham and spent most of his working life teaching in the former Department of Medieval History at University College, Dublin. Having retired in 2005 as Associate Professor of Medieval Economic and Social History, he served for four years as secretary of the Royal Irish Academy. He has published widely on medieval urban history, especially that of Dublin but including also the Provençal town of Draguignan. He is currently editing the two cartularies of Evesham Abbey, which will provide a basis for further publications on a variety of twelfth-century surveys.

Sally Crawford is an Honorary Senior Research Fellow at the Centre for the History of Medicine at the University of Birmingham, and an Honorary Research Associate at the Institute of Archaeology, Oxford. She has written extensively on Anglo-Saxon archaeology, burial ritual, childhood and medicine, and has directed excavations on medieval sites in the UK. Published books include *Childhood in Anglo-Saxon England* (1999) and *Daily Life in Anglo-Saxon England* (2008). She is a founder of the Society for the Study of Childhood in the Past; a founder and general editor of the *Journal of Early Medicine*; and co-editor of *Anglo-Saxon Studies in Archaeology and History*. Current projects include *The Handbook of Anglo-Saxon Archaeology* and *The Encyclopedia of Childhood*, vol. 1: *Ancient and Medieval*.

Julia Crick was educated at the University of Cambridge in the Department of Anglo-Saxon, Norse and Celtic and the Faculty of History. She is currently Associate Professor of History at the University of Exeter. Her research interests include property, power, and gender before 1100, aspects of paleography, and the transmission of texts, monastic culture, and the uses of the past. Her most recent book, *Charters of St. Albans*, appeared in 2007 in the Royal Historical Society/British Academy series "Anglo-Saxon Charters." She has published a number of studies of landholding practices and family solidarity before the Norman Conquest.

Catherine Cubitt is Senior Lecturer in Early Medieval History at the University of York. She is the author of *Anglo-Saxon Church Councils, c.650–c.850* (1995) and has published articles on many aspects of Anglo-Saxon religious history. She has just completed a study of penance and confession, *Sin and Society in Tenth- and Eleventh-century England*, and is currently working on the introduction to a translation of the 649 Lateran Council.

John Reuben Davies gained his PhD from the University of Cambridge, and is Research Assistant in the Department of History at the University of Glasgow. He is the author of *The Book of Llandaf and the Norman Church in Wales* (2003), co-author of the online *Database of Dedications to Saints in Medieval Scotland*, and co-editor of *Saints' Cults in the Celtic World* (2009). He has also published on the Latin hagiography of Wales and Scotland, as well as on the broader ecclesiastical history of Wales, Scotland, and Ireland in the early and central Middle Ages.

Seán Duffy is Senior Lecturer in Medieval History and a Fellow of Trinity College Dublin. His primary research interests are currently the history and archaeology of Dublin from the Viking Age to the early modern period; medieval Irish relations with Wales, Scotland, and the Isles; and Anglo-Irish relations, particularly the historiography of the English colony in medieval Ireland. He has published widely on Irish history generally, and medieval Ireland in particular. He is Chairman of the Friends of Medieval Dublin, and since 1999 has organized an annual interdisciplinary conference on medieval Dublin, the proceedings of which are published.

Paul Fouracre taught at Goldsmiths College, London from 1984 before becoming Professor of Medieval History at the University of Manchester in 2003. His research area is Francia under the Merovingian and Carolingian dynasties, and he is presently working on the cost of lighting rituals. He is the author of *The Age of Charles Martel* (2000), the editor of *The New Cambridge Medieval History*, volume 1 (2005) and, up to 2008, the coordinating editor of the journal *Early Medieval Europe*.

Dawn Hadley is Reader in Historical Archaeology at the University of Sheffield. She gained a degree in History from the University of Hull, and her PhD at the University of Birmingham focused on the Scandinavian impact on the social and ecclesiastical organization of the Danelaw. She has published widely on the Scandinavian settlements in England, on the construction of masculinity in Anglo-Saxon society, and on Anglo-Saxon and medieval funerary practices. She is currently working on the construction of masculinity through the material culture of medieval drinking and on the archaeology of childhood.

Charles Insley is Senior Lecturer in Medieval History at Canterbury Christ Church University; formerly, he was County Editor of the *Victoria County History of Northamptonshire*. He was an undergraduate and postgraduate student at Worcester College Oxford, where he received a DPhil for his thesis on the pre-Conquest charters of Exeter Cathedral. He has published a number of articles on Anglo-Saxon history, as well as papers on twelfth- and thirteenth-century Wales. He is currently finishing an edition of the Exeter charters and is writing a biography of England's first king, Æthelstan.

Simon MacLean studied at the universities of Glasgow and London. He was a Research Fellow at Trinity Hall, Cambridge, from 2000 to 2002, before becoming Lecturer in History at the University of St. Andrews. His research focuses on the Carolingian Empire and its successor kingdoms. Major publications include *Kingship and Politics in the Late Ninth Century: Charles the Fat and the End of the Carolingian Empire* (2003) and *History and Politics in Late Carolingian and Ottonian Europe: The Chronicle of Regino of Prüm and Adalbert of Magdeburg* (2009). He was awarded a Philip Leverhulme Prize in 2008.

Janet L. Nelson is Emeritus Professor of Medieval History at King's College London. Her interests in the earlier medieval period have ranged across Anglo-Saxon as well as Frankish topics, with a major focus on rulership, politics, and government. She has published four collections of her papers, as well as a biography of Charles the Bald. She currently co-directs the Prosopography of Anglo-Saxon England Database project at King's, and is working on a biography of Charlemagne.

Thomas Pickles is a Fellow by Special Election and Lecturer in Medieval History at St. Catherine's College, Oxford. His research focuses on the history of the Anglo-Saxon church. He takes an interdisciplinary approach that combines texts with stone sculpture, archaeology, place-names, and landscape analysis. His forthcoming publications include a study on the date, distribution, and significance of the Old English place-names *biscopes-tūn*, *muneca-tūn*, and *prēosta-tūn* and an investigation of images of angel veneration on Anglo-Saxon stone sculpture. He is currently writing up his doctoral thesis as a book called *The Church in Anglo-Saxon Yorkshire: "Minsters" in the "Danelaw."*

Huw Pryce is Professor of Welsh History at Bangor University, where he has taught since 1981. He has wide research interests in medieval Wales, and also works on aspects of modern Welsh historiography. His publications include *Native Law and the Church in Medieval Wales* (1993), *Literacy in Medieval Celtic Societies* (editor, 1998), *The Acts of Welsh Rulers 1120–1283* (with the assistance of Charles Insley, 2005), and *Power and Identity in the Middle Ages: Essays in Memory of Rees Davies* (co-editor with John Watts, 2007).

Martin J. Ryan is a Teaching Fellow in Early Medieval History in the School of Arts, Histories, and Cultures at the University of Manchester. He received his PhD from the same institution with a thesis on land tenure in pre-Viking England, and is currently working on a revised version of this study for publication as a monograph. He is also researching theories of violence and inequality in the biblical commentaries of the Venerable Bede. He is co-editor, with Alan Deyermond, of *Early Medieval Spain: A Symposium* (2009), and co-author, with Nicholas Higham, of *The Anglo-Saxon World* (forthcoming).

Pauline Stafford is Professor Emerita at Liverpool University, previously Professor of Medieval History. She is a specialist in the history of Anglo-Saxon England and of women and gender in England and Europe from the eighth to the twelfth century. Her previous publications include *Queens, Concubines and Dowagers: The King's Wife in the Early Middle Ages* (1983, 1998), *Unification and Conquest: A Political and Social History of England in the Tenth and Eleventh Centuries* (1989), *Queen Emma and Queen Edith: Queenship and Women's Power in Eleventh-century England* (1997, 2001), *Law, Laity and Solidarities* (2001), *Gender, Family and the Legitimation of Power: England from the Ninth to Early Twelfth Century* (2006), and the jointly edited *Gendering the Middle Ages* (2000).

David E. Thornton read History at the University of York, has an MA in Welsh History from the University of Wales, and a PhD from the University of Cambridge. He worked as a postdoctoral researcher at the School of Celtic Studies, Dublin, and at the Unit for Prosopographical Research, Oxford. Since 1997, he has been Assistant Professor in European History at Bilkent University, Turkey, where he is also Library Director. His research interests include early medieval Britain and Ireland, and Anglo-Norman England, and he is currently working on Irish anthroponymy before 1100 and the geographical origins of religions in the late medieval diocese of Worcester.

Alex Woolf was educated at Bexhill County Grammar School and the University of Sheffield. He is a lecturer in the School of History at the University of St. Andrews and has published on a wide range of topics in early insular history. His monograph *From Pictland to Alba 789–1070*, volume II of the "New Edinburgh History of Scotland," was published in 2007.

Barbara Yorke is Professor of Early Medieval History at the University of Winchester. She has worked, and published papers, on many different topics relating to the history of Anglo-Saxon England, with a particular interest in royal houses and the interrelationship of ecclesiastical and secular authority. Her books include *Kings and Kingdoms of Early Anglo-Saxon England* (1990), *Wessex in the Early Middle Ages* (1995), *Nunneries and the Anglo-Saxon Royal Houses* (2003), and *The Conversion of Britain: Religion, Politics and Society c.600–800* (2006).

Abbreviations

AC A *Annales Cambriae*, version A: E. Phillimore, "The *Annales Cambriæ* and Old-Welsh genealogies from *Harleian MS 3859*," *Y Cymmrodor*, 9 (1888), 141–83.

AC B, C *Annales Cambriae*, versions B and C: J. Williams (ab Ithel) (ed.), *Annales Cambriae*, Rolls Series, 20 (London, 1860).

AFM *Annals by the Four Masters*: J. O'Donovan (ed. and trans), *Annála Rioghachta Éireann: Annals of the Kingdom of Ireland by the Four Masters from the Earliest Period to the Year 1616*, 7 vols. (Dublin, 1851; 3rd edn. 1990).

AI *The Annals of Inisfallen*: S. Mac Airt (ed.), *The Annals of Inisfallen* (Dublin, 1944, repr. 1951, 1977).

ASC (A–G) *The Anglo-Saxon Chronicle*, many editions: see D. N. Dumville and S. D. Keynes (gen. eds.), *The Anglo-Saxon Chronicle: A Collaborative Edition* (Cambridge, 1983–); see also *EHD*, vol. I: *c.500–1042*; vol. II: *1042–1189*.

AT *The Annals of Tigernach*: W. Stokes (ed. and trans.), *The Annals of Tigernach* (reprinted from *Revue Celtique*, 1895–7; repr. Felinfach, 1993).

AU *The Annals of Ulster*: S. Mac Airt and G. Mac Niocaill (eds. and trans.), *The Annals of Ulster (to AD 1131)*. Part I: *Text and translation* (Dublin, 1983).

ByS *Brenhinedd y Saesson*: T. Jones (ed.), *Brenhinedd y Saesson, or The Kings of the Saxons* (Cardiff, 1971).

ByT **(Pen 20)** *Brut y Tywysogion* (Peniarth MS 20 version): T. Jones (trans.), *Brut y Tywysogion or the Chronicle of the Princes, Peniarth MS 20 Version* (Cardiff, 1952).

ByT **(RB)** *Brut y Tywysogion* (Red Book of Hergest version): T. Jones (ed.), *Brut y Tywysogion or the Chronicle of the Princes, Red Book of Hergest Version* (2nd edn., Cardiff, 1973).

EHD *English Historical Documents*: I: D. Whitelock (ed. and trans.), *English

Historical Documents, vol. I: *c.500–1042*, 2nd edn. (London, 1979). II: D. C. Douglas and G. W. Greenaway (eds.), *English Historical Documents*, vol. II: *1042–1189*, 2nd edn. (London, 1981).

HE Bede, *Historia ecclesiastica gentis Anglorum* (*The Ecclesiastical History of the English People*), various editions.

MGH *Monumenta Germaniae historica*: SRG, *Scriptores rerum Germanicarum*; SRL, *Scriptores rerum Langobardorum*; SRM, *Scriptores rerum Merovingicarum*; SS, *Scriptores*

S (Sawyer) Charter no. in P. Sawyer, *Anglo-Saxon Charters: An Annotated List and Bibliography* (London, 1968).

Map 1 Ireland in the Early Middle Ages

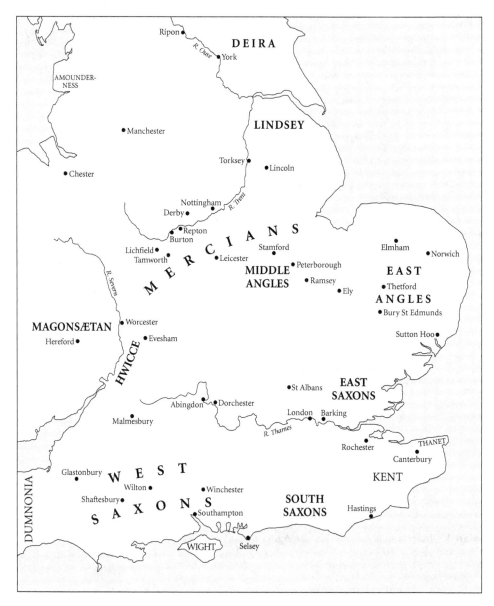

Map 2 Southern Britain in the Early Middle Ages

Map 3 West Britain in the Early Middle Ages

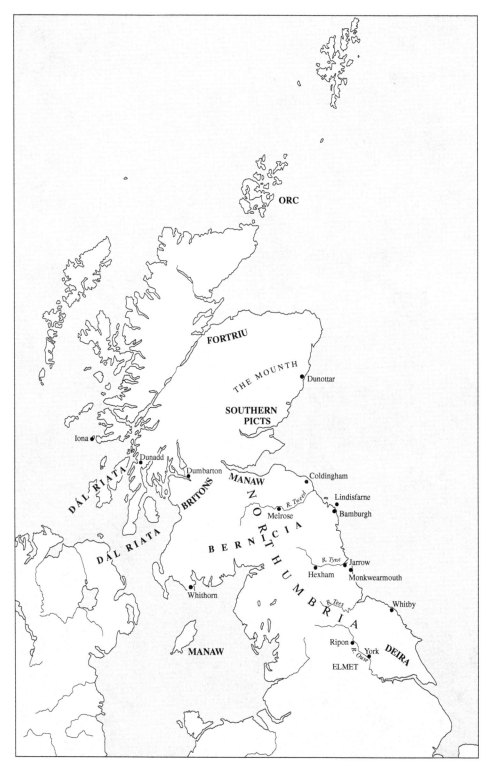

Map 4a Northern Britain in the Early Middle Ages: Early Christian Period

Map 4b Northern Britain in the Early Middle Ages: Viking Age and after

Map 5 Continental European links to Britain and Ireland

PART I

Introductory Matter

CHAPTER ONE

Introduction

PAULINE STAFFORD

This volume is a collaborative history of Britain and Ireland from c. AD 500 to c.1100. It gives special attention to areas of recent historiographical development and advance. It does not set out to provide a narrative, though it will attempt to provide a new historical account and overall picture of these critical centuries. It covers Britain and Ireland at an arguably significant, if not formative period. This task is both a huge challenge and a pressing need. Britain-wide, let alone Britain and Ireland-wide, history poses problems at any period, but acute ones for these centuries. The historiographies of these islands are divergent and make comparison difficult; the demands on any scholar who tries to range across them are high. Their political geography was far more complicated at this period than at any later date. Thus, the core political story, which holds together so many historical surveys of later periods, cannot easily be written.

The focus is on Britain and Ireland. Ireland is, of course, not a part of Britain, either as defined in the early Middle Ages or now. "Britain" is the biggest island of what might be described as the "Atlantic Archipelago," and early medieval writers, following classical geographers, already used the term "Britannia" in this way. Britain thus includes what we would now call Scotland, England, and Wales. Any inclusion of Ireland or any part of Ireland within it is a result of centuries of English imperialism. But Ireland is to be given all due attention in this volume. The reasons are simple. What is now Ireland was at this date linked to, as much as separate from, much of the development of Britain, and was, in many respects, crucial to that development. It would be impossible, for example, to tell the story of English conversion to Christianity, or of Scottish kingship, without reference to Ireland. As these conversion and political stories would illustrate, the Irish Sea joined as much as, if not more than, it separated those around its shores at this date. They experienced common problems, such as Scandinavian attacks during the ninth century, and, at times, formed close political links; for example, between the north of Ireland and the west of what is now Scotland throughout much of the period, or between Dublin and York in the later ninth and tenth centuries. The political boundaries within what is now Britain and Ireland were far from fore-ordained c.500, or even much later. One aim of this volume is to see the early Middle Ages in the Atlantic Archipelago as it developed, rather than teleologically, that is, from the viewpoint of its later shape. That aim necessitates the inclusion of Ireland.

The inclusion of Ireland also has the effect of de-centering England, or rather southern England. One of the potential pitfalls of British history is Anglo-centricity, a history of England with additions. This danger is compounded in this early period by the poverty of sources for northern and western Britain vis-à-vis southern England. Ireland, by contrast, has extremely rich sources, if in some ways markedly different from English ones (see chapter 3). Ireland cannot and should not be taken as representative of Scotland or Wales at this date: it is thus not being seen here as providing the "Celtic" alternative picture. But its inclusion sets up comparisons that ensure a wider focus, and one from which the study of southern England should itself benefit.

Even these most preliminary statements about a history of Britain and Ireland run into a fundamental problem, that of political terminology. It is a problem that dogs a volume of this type, and its organization. "Ireland," "Scotland," "Wales," "England" represent modern political entities. They find some expression within this period, but they correspond very imperfectly to the political geography, or to the identities, of the centuries between 500 and 1100. All these terms were in use during or soon after this period, but none describes or does justice to the complex and shifting politics within it. That complex and shifting situation is partly revealed by the bewildering variety of names used for groups and political entities within Britain and Ireland over these centuries. A range of Latin and vernacular terms was in use. Some denoted apparently wide groups or areas: for example, Scotti, Hibernia, Érenn, Alba, Picts, Angli, Englisc, Angelcynn, Englalond – very rarely Anglo-Saxon – Britannia, Britones, Cymry. Yet alongside these, others remained in use and appear to describe much more limited groups: West Saxons, East Saxons, Northumbrians, Leinstermen, Ulstermen/Ulaid. Some of these terms have recently been the subject of much productive scholarship, though their meaning and significance are still hotly debated. Their variety underlines the fluid politics, if not identities, of this period. Study of them has certainly highlighted potential differences between cultural and political identities. But it has also raised problems of change in the use and meaning of some of them, and emphasized their ideological deployment; for example, in the making of claims to political control. Such debates, plus the fact that these terms are far from consistently used over the whole period, mean that they cannot easily be substituted for the modern terms.

The modern terms will thus be used here to describe the geographical areas that they now cover, since it is necessary to give the modern reader some purchase on these remote centuries. But we must be aware from the beginning of the problems that this use entails. The aim of this volume is to approach this period without assumptions about its eventual political shape, with no sense that any one of them was fated – or bound – to develop, retaining an eye for a range of political possibilities, rather than putting on blinkers which lead the historical gaze firmly forward to a known future. Chapter 2 will consider the nationalist historiographies that have profoundly influenced the study of this period, and alert us to their power. Yet the very use of these terms may carry an insidious because silent teleology. It is almost impossible to avoid them, but we must be fully aware of their dangers. These same historiographies have produced other terminological sensitivities among modern historians, particularly over such terms as "nation" and "state." The authors in this volume are especially alert to the problems of these terms. Many of them have preferred the more neutral "polity," a synonym for any political unit, which avoids questions about whether and when any of these might be described as "states"; the more general usage in this volume is "kingdom," which describes the nature of almost all the political systems with which they are dealing.

There are certainly other ways in which historians have divided the areas to be considered here. The distinction between upland and lowland Britain – that is, north and west and south and east, respectively, of an imaginary line from the Humber to the Severn – may seem a useful one.[1] That line has a very rough correspondence with economic distinctions between pastoral and arable-based farming, though there are many significant micro-patterns either side of it. In Ireland, the fertile plain of Brega has some of the same economic significance as lowland Britain. Historians have pointed out the significant coincidences of such geographical divisions and political development: southern English and southern Scottish power, for example, centered on control of these lowland areas. These divisions are discussed more fully by Howard Clarke in chapter 5.

These divisions are crude, even when refined to allow, for example, for the particular geography of Wales, with a highland center separating coastal strips. Like Howard Clarke, we should be aware of the importance of other, more regional and local divisions. Important as the wider geographical divisions are, they too have not formed the basis of the organization of this volume which eschews any straightforward geographical or economic determinism. We should, nonetheless, be aware of geography and its influence, and of other geographical features such as the Mounth, the highland area acting as a significant barrier between northern and southern Scotland, or the combination of deep estuary and extensive marshland that made the Humber a more formidable barrier to travel in the early Middle Ages than it is now. On the other hand, the Irish Sea, as has been noted, should be seen as a highway as much as a divider. Its routeways and links took Patrick there in the fifth century, and the southern English nobles fled across it after defeat by the Normans in 1066. They explain the strong political and cultural links that bound Ireland and western Scotland. The kingdom and *Chronicle* of Man demonstrate that sea kingdoms should not be ruled out as possible lines of development, including ones that might have encompassed areas of what are now Wales and west and northern England, though it should also be remembered that the Irish Sea's unity long had a darker incarnation as a slaving lake.

We must be wary of how we divide, yet also aware that contemporaries themselves were divided and made divisions. The Northumbrian monk Bede, in the early eighth century, divided the inhabitants of Britain by languages, those of the Angles, Britons, Scots, and Picts and Latin. The divisions within the period may have varied, and were almost certainly even more complex. The Germanic language of the "English" differed between, for example, Anglian and the Late West Saxon in which most of our surviving vernacular texts are written. In what is now north-west England, the "Cumbrians" and ultimately "Cumberland" shared a name very similar to the Welsh self-designation as "Cymry" and probably spoke a Brittonic language whose status vis-à-vis Welsh is much debated. The incoming Scandinavian settlers of north-west as of eastern England spoke a different Germanic tongue from the one in local use by the ninth century, though recent work has suggested the possibility of mutual comprehension. As Barbara Yorke points out in chapter 4, for Bede, as for many others in the early Middle Ages, peoples were defined at least in part by language. But we should not assume it was any more simple a barrier or definer than geography.

The date limits of this volume, c.500–1100, are to a degree arbitrary. They correspond roughly to the end of Roman Britain and the arrival and first impact of the Normans. These are processes that have long been seen as significant. For example, another division that could be made within these islands is between areas that had been Romanized or felt Roman influence before AD 500 and those that had not, although Roman influence was felt much more widely than simply in Romanized areas, and the whole Atlantic Archipelago was, in some senses, a peripheral area to the Roman world (see chapter 9). The end date is deliberately not taken as 1066, the year of the Norman victory at Hastings. That date has more immediate relevance for England than for the rest of the area under consideration here. And an end date of 1100 allows consideration of the Normans' immediate impact, throughout Britain and Ireland, without focusing a spotlight upon them which then defines their arrival as a turning point.

Within this period, no simple narrative has been attempted; the chapters, especially pre-800, have not been organized to produce this. There are some obvious lineaments and themes which give it shape: the end of Roman Britain and the arrival of a new set of Germanic inhabitants at the beginning, both processes well under way, and Roman withdrawal complete, before AD 500, but with continuing significance into the sixth century. Conversion to Christianity, already under way in fifth-century Ireland and technically complete in Wales and west Britain by 500, was a phenomenon of the sixth and seventh centuries among the Picts and in England. The vikings – a term that describes a particular type of Scandinavian activity – were active throughout most of the Atlantic Archipelago during the long ninth century, and continued to be important into the later tenth and eleventh centuries. They receive due attention here, especially in the first stages of their activity, not least because they dominate the historiographies of this period. Those historiographies have also placed center stage some of the "hero kings" who are known for their responses to the vikings: Máel Sechnaill in Ireland, Cinaed/Kenneth in Scotland, Rhodri "Mawr" in Wales, Alfred "the Great" in England. In England and Scotland, these kings have been seen to mark a crucial step on the road to monarchy and unity. All four find their place in this volume, though their reigns are not used to organize its coverage. It is linear political narrative in particular that has been largely omitted here.

The prime reason for this is a recognition of the limits of the volume, which covers such a wide chronology and geographical area at a time of great political complexity. Any linear political narrative would be sketchy and would threaten to simplify the story around a series of "great kings," so judged, in most cases, by the very historiographies that entrench the views of inevitable developments which is one of the interpretations that this volume seeks to scrutinize. Linear political history lends itself to the painting of a heroic past beloved of particular types of nationalist historiography, though cultural history has its own pitfalls, not least of Golden Ages that can console the political "failures." Good political narrative of this period needs to allow for the range of outcomes that was still possible, placing and understanding political action within its full contemporary context, ideally with very detailed coverage of that context. So complex a story is clearly impossible for this date range within this compass. The chapters that deal with the structures of politics and political society – with, for example, nobility, kingship, communities, courts and law, kinship – give some idea of the nature and parameters of political activity, and highlight similarities and differences here. A number of chapters do nonetheless attempt an overall narrative for particular parts of Britain and Ireland at certain dates. This is especially the case where such a story is hard to find in existing historiography and/or where its establishment is still a pressing need or is contested, and thus central to current historical endeavors – thus for Scotland, Wales, and, to a lesser extent, Ireland in the tenth and eleventh centuries. For England in this period, the lineaments of such a story are readily available. Here, the opportunity has been taken to subject a particularly influential picture of precocious English unity to scrutiny, especially by separating coverage of Southumbria and Northumbria in their post-900 development, though separating England/Britain north and south of the Humber still lumps together West Saxons and Mercians post-900. In all these cases, treatment is responding in different ways to the state of existing work. Inevitably, however, there have been many omissions.

Three chapters (9, 15, and 22) deal with "Britain, Ireland, and Europe." They are a deliberate reminder that these islands were far from isolated from, albeit by some definitions peripheral to, continental Europe. Events and developments there, and especially in Francia (covering large parts of modern France, Germany, and the Low Countries), were of significance for Britain and Ireland. And, as these chapters make clear, influence was not a one-way traffic.

This volume has thus been structured by a number of aims and questions. Some are well-established ones – for example, Christianization or the arrival and impact of the vikings – and here the volume seeks to provide both an update on recent rethinking and a new synthesis. Many are broadly sociopolitical, much concerned with the building blocks of political society and with the question of how it worked. But behind these questions also lurks an older question, or rather an older question reframed: were there substantial and fundamental differences across these islands? In its older form, this question often seemed to take divergence for granted and to seek its origins. We hope that our reframing is different. We do not begin from an assumption of difference and divergence, especially not by 1100. That remains an overall question.

The question "How did it work?" is not the same as "Why, if at all, did it change?" Attention to structures may highlight factors producing possible change. And treatment of the economy, Christianization, vikings may be critical here. But the chapter structure deliberately avoids giving priority to any particular historical explanation of change – whether, for example, economic or ideological – preferring to allow room for all, for interactions, and for long-term continuities.

Three final notes on the approach in this volume are needed here. First, the treatment of women: one of the great advances in recent historiography has been the study of women (see chapter 2). Any broad treatment has to decide how to include this. With the exception of chapter 28 on queens and queenship, the deliberate decision here was against specific chapters on women. Rather, the brief was to be alert to women throughout. The danger is that they may disappear again in such a broad sweep of history; the hope is that they thus become, as they should be, part of the mainstream of historical writing. Second, the treatment of names: preference throughout is for the non-anglicized form of names. Some familiar names may thus appear – at least to English readers – in unfamiliar forms: Kenneth as Cinaed, Malcolm as Máel Coluim. Writing British and Irish history makes us acutely aware of English imperialism, including its linguistic forms. This nomenclature also reflects significant shifts in recent Scottish historiography (see chapter 2). Third, divergences of interpretation: no systematic attempt has been made to iron out differences of interpretation between authors. Given the problems of sources and historiography, differences among historians on this period have been, and sometimes still are, both significant and legitimate. It is to that historiography and those sources that attention must now turn.

Note

1   Frame, *Political Development*, p. 13.

Bibliography

Frame, R., *The Political Development of the British Isles, 1100–1400* (Oxford, 1990).

Chapter Two

Historiography

Pauline Stafford

History is not simply what happened in the past, but the answers to questions that historians pose about what happened in the past. The questions posed largely determine the answers that can or will be given. If we are to understand and work with the history we have, we must identify those questions and have some understanding of the contexts in which they were produced. This is one, if not the main, task of historiography. Historiography is the study of the writing of history. As we would now define it, history is technically what professional historians produce, trained in the techniques of their craft. So it is their context and questions that are especially significant. But non-professionals have also turned to the past, and their use of it and concern with it can be part of the professional historian's environment. Questions are never asked or defined in a vacuum: previous traditions, assumptions, and contemporary concerns are always a context, as well as – especially in the case of professional historians – changing theoretical models and concepts. Knowledge of, and engagement with, historiography should be part of all historical writing. It is arguably of particular importance in a volume of this type, which aspires, in some part, to be comparative, since one of the problems of comparative history is the often non-comparability of historiographies.[1] Historians in different traditions have not necessarily asked the same questions, or started with the same set of assumptions; the answers that they have produced do not necessarily lend themselves to comparative use. Many of the individual chapters that follow will give topic-specific historiographical guidance and discussion. This second introductory chapter is concerned with the larger trends, especially those within different national historiographies of the various components of Britain and Ireland.

A period as remote in time as c. AD 500–c.1100 inevitably has a long historiography. The historical baggage that it carries is often substantial. It will not be the task of this chapter to deal in detail with some of the hoariest contents of its suitcases. Questions, for example, such as those about feudalism and 1066 are arguably now best left to gather dust, forgotten in the lost luggage department. But those hoary questions date back to periods whose interests formed them – in this case the sixteenth and seventeenth centuries – and those periods and the history they produced have left a legacy of assumptions and questions that still require some attention. Indeed, any study of the historiography of this period should reach back at least to the twelfth century, and arguably earlier. Some of the "primary sources" that have been used to study this period are in truth "histories" of parts of it. This was long ago defined as a time of "origins," and the earliest years and centuries of the period were already so seen and used before, let alone after, 1100. Such periods are peculiarly susceptible to rewriting from later viewpoints; their history is especially likely to be exploited for various purposes. Historiography, then, important for all periods, is essential as an approach to this one.

Historiography, Nations, and Nationalism

As noted in chapter 1, modern nations are not necessarily the best starting-point for an understanding of these centuries. They are, however, essential to an understanding of its historiography. Since the nineteenth century, and before, the history of nations and its more engaged form, nationalist history, have played a central role in European historiography.[2] Britain and Ireland are no exceptions here. Many recent studies of Welsh and Irish history in this period are aware of this and of its impact, some addressing it specifically.[3] In both countries, the nationalist movements of the late nineteenth and early twentieth centuries had significant repercussion on the presentation of these centuries and have left a legacy of assumptions and approaches, if not questions. Some of the founding fathers (sic) of modern study not only lived at this time of strong nationalist feeling, but were actively involved in nationalist movements. John Edward Lloyd, for example, author of *A History of Wales from the Earliest Times to the Edwardian Conquest* (London, 1911), became a member of a patriotic nationalist group in the late 1870s at the recently founded University College of Wales, Aberystwyth, participated in the Liverpool Eisteddfod of 1884, and would later be a member of the Council for the Society for Utilizing the Welsh Language. For such a man, the chief use of history was "the task of nation building."[4] Eoin MacNeill, to whom historians of early Ireland still look back as a pioneer and agenda setter,[5] was from 1920 to 1921 a political prisoner in the Mountjoy where, as Binchy noted, he read the five volumes of the *Ancient Laws of Ireland*,[6] a reading likely to be affected by these circumstances.

These were professional historians, writing with professional standards. But the context that formed them was a strongly nationalist one, and arguably a Romantic nationalist one, where the language and culture were important elements of the nation. Its concerns permeated their history, and that of many others. So, for example, for MacNeill the question of nationality in pre-Norman Ireland was important, and it was a contemporary political question. Early Irish nationality had not necessarily found political expression – and for MacNeill, as arguably for G .H. Orpen, successful political expression was defined essentially in terms of the late Victorian (English) state[7] – but it had had a clear cultural one in, for example, the "national" law.

This nationalist historiographical moment had a much wider intellectual context. Movements such as evolutionism exerted influence not only on history-writing, but also on philology, and many nineteenth-century historians of this period – like some of their later successors (see below) – were, perforce, philologists, too.[8] The results were some abiding assumptions, some entrenchment of stereotypes, some setting of questions and frameworks, which were to be very influential for much of the twentieth century. Both Ireland and Wales were characterized as "tribal," often within an evolutionary view that placed tribalism as an early stage of development. This played to notions of static if not archaic societies, and sat easily alongside Romantic nationalist ideas of a mysterious, poetic, Celtic past. Indo-European origins and parallels were often stressed, with Ireland, especially, just as likely to be compared with ancient India as early medieval Europe. A strong sense of Irish difference marked Ireland out from imperialist England, but also from much of Europe, though early Ireland was also felt to represent a survival of a common Indo-European past. It was presented as a world of undeveloped sacral kingship, without institutions, its traditions in the hands of a pagan mandarin class, the *filid*, who could be variously seen as obscurantist pedants or keepers of a deep, specifically Irish, cultural tradition, but who were, and this was critical, Celtic and different. "Tribal" and, even more, "Celtic" were often vague and unexamined but highly charged terms, and remain so even in some recent historiography.[9]

Modern students of early Ireland are acutely aware of this legacy. It still held some sway in the 1970s and 1980s, including in the work of Binchy and Byrne.[10] A seminal article by Donnchadh Ó Corráin in 1978 fundamentally questioned many aspects of it; and individual elements – for example, the nature of the *filid* and their relationship and that of their alleged traditions to the Christian church – have been essentially overturned.[11] Ó Corráin, significantly, sought parallels to early medieval Ireland in early medieval Europe. And Europe is now the normal referent for the excellent work in early Irish studies, perhaps not surprisingly given the new political context of a resurgent Ireland. This current political context and the historical work produced within it are far from simply linked, but they suggest the continued reaction of historical questions and assumptions to the wider context, whether consciously or unconsciously.

The writing of the history of early medieval Wales has followed in some ways a parallel trajectory. In a recent excellent survey of developments, Wendy Davies has identified a series of themes and questions that have dominated study since the 1880s, many of which will be familiar to students of Ireland.[12] A concern with peoples, migration, settlement, and race was linked to a focus on language as what makes "a people" before – or in the absence of – political expression, and in particular on (Celtic) racial identity, with an acceptance, overt or assumed, of distinct racial characteristics. In political history, there was little or no interest in institutions, parliamentary developments, or similar attempts to limit royal power, but on kings as heroes and on heroic activity such as warfare. Sanctity has absorbed, in Davies's view, a disproportionate amount of historical effort, especially given a rather static picture of a "Land and Age of Saints" changing little after the sixth century.

Succession and kinship have engrossed attention both at the structural level and as the stuff of detailed political narrative. The central place given to kinship in political history reflects a much wider historiographical concern with it, one which is rooted in a persistent view of this as a tribal society, where "tribal" signifies its basis in blood and kinship links. Inheritance patterns have thus been more important than the study of land exploitation and of the elites that controlled it. The picture this produced was, as in the history of sanctity, a static one, largely, in this case, because it relied on normative legal texts. The study of early Wales rested here on more dubious foundations since the legal texts that are its sources are, unlike the Irish laws, late. But, as in the Irish case, evolutionary ideas influenced their interpretation. The apparent fit of the later Welsh texts with a presumed earlier stage in models of Indo-European development seemed to vindicate their dubious application to sixth-century society.

Unlike the recent situation in Ireland, archaeology has been much less exploited, and the more dynamic picture it could provide is thus still largely missing. But Irish scholars will recognize the parallel centrality of textual study. The importance of the vernacular in both cases suggests how far this centrality, too, has some of its roots in Romantic cultural nationalism, though there are other issues here (see below). Davies's stress on a Welsh concern with enemies seems to be a function of a national identity defined in terms of resistance. There is a parallel in the Irish sources, and thus the earlier historiography, where the most definitive ingredient of medieval Irish sources from c.800 (vikings) to c.1600 (Elizabethans) was a bi-polar Gael versus Gall perspective. So, not merely enemies and resistance, but a world inhabited by just two groups: one the (perfect?) Gael; the other the utterly alien Gall. Ireland's insular status may have contributed to the potency of this division.

Wendy Davies provides not only an important survey of a century or more of work on Welsh history, but one that makes clear the abiding questions and perspectives of the nationalist legacy. Hers is, however, also the particular perspective of a materialist, if not Marxist, historiography to which we shall return. And its referent is here explicitly England and English historiography, by which yardstick Welsh historiography, if not Wales itself, is implicitly deemed to have failed. England has long been a presence, shadowy or explicit, in the historiographies of Ireland and Wales, and rarely without some implicit or explicit idea of value. Orpen, for example, castigated pre-Norman Ireland as tribal, anarchic, and archaic, lacking the strong state structures that the (Anglo-)Normans brought.[13] Davies's denigration is arguably far more a critique of Welsh historiography, Orpen's of Ireland itself. But the picture of England, and the English historiography that has produced it, are, in each case, arguably unexamined.

English and Scottish historiography both appear at first sight less affected by this nationalist legacy. Nationalist political movements have, at least until recently, played a less significant role in either modern nation. The rather different relationships of these nations are reflected in their historiographies. In spite of exiguous sources, some historians of early Scotland have been more interested in the themes that have dominated early English history, particularly, for example, royal power and its institutional forms and bases.[14] This picture of a Scotland parallel in development to England, if not "doing it better," has recently been rivaled by a strong tendency to place Scottish history in a "Celtic" or "Gaelic" Irish Sea context.[15] If a major strand in recent Irish history has been to Europeanize it, a significant current in recent work on early Scottish history has been to Gaelicize it. Ireland has become the referent, and one by-product of this, namely the Gaelicization of the nomenclature of early Scottish history, has already been remarked. One might be forgiven for seeing here some reflection of the current political struggle for Scotland's soul; and yet another example of the implication of these periods of origins in the definition of such "souls" (below).

Early medieval Irish studies, at least as seen from an English perspective, currently appear to be very self-reflexive and historiographically aware.[16] In fact, Irish, Welsh, and Scottish history-writing have all been subject to much recent self-examination.[17] Such historiographical reflexivity or reflection is far less apparent in early English history. There has been considerable general work by modern historians on English historiography, and especially its nineteenth-century developments.[18] All of this has made clear how far similar concepts of national identity and evolutionism influenced this formative period of English historical writing. It is clear how far the agenda of questions that Wendy Davies sees as characterizing English historiography emerged then: the story of parliament and the struggle for liberty plus the limitation of royal power (though these trends have much deeper roots), and the institutional expression of both. These agendas are as much the reflections and products of a national self-image and stereotype as the mysterious, poetic Celt. In the nineteenth century, they were, like the definition of "Celt," partly fed and nourished by racial theories and by particular valuations of the Aryan Teutonic race, though there was already a strong sense of English difference and divergence. But these insights on the part of historians of nineteenth- and twentieth-century historiography have not always been applied by working historians of early England to their own work. One honorable exception must be made in the case of James Campbell, especially his work on Stubbs.[19] It should, however, be noted that he is also the most powerful and influential exponent of the view of English exceptionalism, and of an exceptionalism expressed particularly in the nature and precocious development of the English state, an exceptionalism defined precisely in the terms established by this long-standing historiography.

The late and much-lamented Rees Davies was shrewdly aware of how far England, and English historiography, needed to become the basis for questions rather than assumptions. It is notable that some of the most perceptive commentary on English historiography has come from those whose work has been largely outside it: Rees Davies himself, but also Karl Leyser.[20] The latter saw England from a European, specifically an early medieval German, standpoint. Rees Davies's awareness arose from the perspective of a wider British history, in which England was a constant conscious or unconscious comparison. Assessments of England and its historiography are central not only to its study, but also to that of its neighbors in these islands. And, in turn, study of them can perhaps open up questions about England. It is hoped that this volume might be in some ways a small contribution to this endeavor.

The intellectual and political contexts of the later nineteenth and early twentieth centuries were clearly of great importance in setting patterns of questions and themes. But English interest in our period certainly did not begin then. Early English histo-riography may have been unaffected by national liberation struggles, but it was far from untouched by questions of nation and nationalism. As early as the twelfth century, Englishness and civilization were being defined together in dialogue with a definition of Celtic barbarism.[21] This was one of the first great periods of English historical writing, and it is no coincidence that it was also a time when national identity was a pressing question in the aftermath of the Norman Conquest.[22] During the sixteenth and seventeenth centuries, another period of English national definition, prompted now especially by the Reformation break with Rome and continued into the political struggles between king and parliament, saw renewed interest in the early medieval and particularly the pre-1066 past. Although interest in these early centuries was lively at other periods in English historiography, these were defining moments. Both had a major impact in entrenching the period before 1066 as one of peculiar significance in English history and in the making of the English.[23] Here were the origins of the English, defined against the foreign/French invaders of 1066 and a foreign/European papacy in the sixteenth and seventeenth centuries. Those origins were thus firmly located in the period of the arrival of "the English" in Britain (an arrival which must thus perforce have replaced indigenous, native elements) and in a period characterized by the use of the vernacular Old English tongue as opposed to pan-European Latin, not least in the church. (This characterization has had long-term and baleful results, producing, for example, a relative attention to vernacular sources of early English history vis-à-vis Latin out of all proportion to their relative scale and survival.)

This is the stuff of origin myth as much as of history, and it raises the peculiar problems of studying a period long defined as a time of "origins." Origins are potent. They play a crucial role in defining and legitimating groups or individuals, a heightened function of the more general use of the past.

> Origins are where "we" came from, what "we" first were, offering particularly convincing answers to deeper questions about who "we" are and what we should be. The past is a source of identity and legitimation, most powerfully of both combined: that power is never felt so strongly as when the past in which both identity and legitimation are sought is seen as "origins." But where are origins to be located? They speak deeply to the sense of the natural – what we first were, what we truly are – and therein lies much of their seduction. Yet they are no more natural and obvious than any other division of the past. Origins are themselves chosen, constructed and contested. Arguably they are to be sought as early as possible: the earlier the better; the older the more venerable, the more powerful. But lines are always drawn, and specific origins defined. In this use of the past as in all uses of the past, the origins which define us are themselves defined by us.[24]

The year 1066 has provided such a demarcation point of origins for the English since the sixteenth – even from the twelfth – century.

The coming of the Normans has had some significance in defining "origins," or periods of particular significance in the telling of national stories, throughout Britain and Ireland. The arrival of the (Anglo-)Normans – though a century or so later – has some of the same significance in shaping Irish historical memory as 1066 does in English. The vernacular here may as a result have assumed an even greater role in a culturally defined national identity whose political expression the invaders are seen as effectively aborting. In Wales, the Edwardian Conquest of the late thirteenth century has arguably been of greater moment in articulating the national story, and the world of heroic princes stretches up to that point, though the coming of the Normans is seen as very significant. In Scotland, the coming – or rather the influence of – the Normans has been important in historiographical periodization. Here, however, it has been a question of the activities of Normanizing native kings rather than invaders. But the result was, as in England, a pre-Norman period seen as peculiarly Celtic and as defining what was Scottish. The Scots' experience of Reformation in some ways paralleled that of the English. Here, too, the period defined as that of national origins was used to justify reforming activity, and that justification in turn entrenched the view of it as "truly Scottish," as witness the nineteenth-century Presbyterian myth of a "Celtic" bishop-less church.[25]

Twentieth-century Trends

The use of the vernacular in the literature of early England – and Ireland, if not Wales – was an important component of the appeal of the early period to definers of the nation, in the sixteenth as in the nineteenth century. That use of the vernacular (obviously in forms – Old English and Old and Middle Irish – no longer intelligible to modern speakers) continues to have an influence on the shape and nature of study of the insular early Middle Ages. A number of scholars have emphasized the proportion of intellectual effort that is invested in textual study in Wales and Ireland,[26] and vernacular textual study accounts for much of this. All are aware of the importance of such work. But there is also a recognition of its potential problems, which apply also to England. The vernacular, which ironically places these periods at the origins of culturally defined nations, is now an extra barrier to modern study. All students of the Middle Ages face the problem of mastering Latin; for those who would study early Ireland or England, to this is added the formidable task of learning Old Irish or Old English. The hurdle has sometimes been set unnecessarily high. And it has been defended by sharp and often vituperative criticism which easily deters all but the most intrepid assailants of this Castle Perilous.[27] One obvious effect of this is partial ownership of work on this period by the philologically trained, and the absorption of much effort in the editing of texts, an entirely necessary and important task. But, as Wendy Davies has pointed out, such editing is not history. It could and can be the history of ideas or mentalités, but is not always thus conceptualized.[28] This may be a symptom of a wider question of the relative historiographical insulation of this early period.

Combined with the cultural and political agendas of nationalist history, the rooting of some study of the period in the skills and training of students of literature and philology, rather than those of history, may account for the relatively limited impact of some of the great currents of twentieth-century historiography on the study of this period. One of these was the influence of the social sciences on history, and Wendy Davies has noted and lamented the lack of substantial developments in the social and economic history of early medieval Wales but also of Ireland. That lack, she feels, applies to Scotland, but is less marked in the case of England, where the recent work of, among others, Rosamond Faith and Robin Fleming, along with that based on archaeological and especially numismatic evidence, represents an important, but not rich, tradition.[29] Davies excludes studies of kinship from the definition of social history, no doubt because, as the study of structures, it does not provide an explanation of change – essential to part, at least, of history's task. This is a substantial criticism, though one that applies to much recent history in general, which has been more concerned with questions about the working of societies than about change in them. It also implies that socioeconomic – if not solely economic – factors are the major, if not only, stimuli to change, not a premise on which this book has been planned. Ironically, given Wendy Davies's critique, the sort of kinship studies and concern with succession that have long characterized the study of Irish and Welsh society are beginning to have more impact on England. This is in part at least a result of a greater concern with women and thus family (see below), but in part a response to a shift away from debates about "feudalism." Family and kin are now rightly seen as central concerns of early medieval people, and thus meriting major historical attention. And debates about feudalism and 1066 were stifling and proved ultimately sterile. Feudalism in its Marxist sense, however, with its questions about rent and the control of labor, is part of an economic model of change, and Davies is right to bemoan the relatively limited concern of early medieval historians of Britain and Ireland with these questions. Her critique remains a very important comment on recent historiography, and a challenge to further work.

Recent historiography, or rather historiographies, will, as suggested above, be dealt with throughout this work; this is not the place to comment on them in detail. As will become apparent, there have been some major shifts in thinking, and new areas and questions have been opened up. "Celtic" is a label subjected to increasing scrutiny; as chapters 10 and 11 make clear, for example, the "Celtic church" is a notion that has had its day, and "Celtic kingship" should arguably follow it (see chapter 6). Viking studies are perennially popular, sometimes perhaps with pernicious effects in the determination to discover their impact, as has been argued for Irish urban archaeology.[30] Recent study of vikings has, however, been increasingly in the context of new paradigms. Debate has shifted from one about numbers and violence, with an approach to contemporary written sources that turned on acceptance or rejection, to one about cultural contact, assimilation, and resistance, in which the contemporary sources, written and material, are read as much with an eye to what they reveal about authors, patrons, and audience as for the brute facts they convey (see chapter 14). This new approach is much more concerned with identity than numbers, and employs a much more fluid and situational reading of it.

It is an approach that is arguably part of the much wider phenomenon of new cultural history, and it has characterized a swathe of important work on this period across Europe. It is central, for example, to the work on ethnogenesis that has dominated study of the late antique and earliest medieval centuries since World War II. Encouraged by, if not simply beginning from, a revulsion against the racial theories that fed Nazi Germany and the history of population groups and migrations that utilized them, this work replaced the notion of "race" with "ethnicity." Ethnicity raises questions about group and individual identity, and emphasizes this as malleable, fluid, situational, and subjective. Its impact has been felt on all studies of group formation and movement, and is clear in this volume in chapters on the arrival of "Anglo-Saxons" as well as vikings (see chapters 4, 13, and 14). It has been a key element in the rethinking of the "transformation of the Roman World" (see chapter 9). Ethnicity as a concept is still hotly debated, not least as far as the degree of malleability and the possibilities of conscious molding are concerned. Given the critique of nineteenth- and early twentieth-century nationalist history offered above, however, it is only fair to note how far this shift too has contemporary contexts in post-Auschwitz and, in Britain, in post-Windrush generations.

In its attention to identity and its construction, and in its re-reading of texts in a less straightforwardly empiricist way, this recent work is all loosely "postmodern," though very few early medievalists would be happy simply to categorize themselves or their work in this way. Historians would say, and rightly, that they have always been sensitive to the reading of texts and to the influence of texts one on another – postmodernism's intertextuality. But there can be little doubt that new attitudes to textual reading are becoming widely apparent, and ones that betray the influence, however indirect, of postmodernism. The recent historiography of early Britain and Ireland has not been immune, though the impact is not as thoroughgoing as, for example, in British Carolingian studies.[31] Increasingly, the facts that we take from texts are not merely those contained in their overt messages, but also those they impart about their creators, patrons, and audiences; not only the nuggets of information about people, dates, and events for which they can be quarried, but the purposes, mentalities, and ideologies to which their very existence and previously discarded "verbiage" attest. This has huge potential for all texts, including many that have often seemed unpromising, such as Irish genealogical material, which may in some respects parallel the English charters if read in this way.[32] It is very apparent in the re-reading of saints' lives. And, as this has shown, it allows "normal" questions to be asked of "non-normal" texts (the categorization is in part that of Edel Bhreathnach); for example, political questions asked of literary texts.[33] This approach has, rightly, complemented rather than replaced older textual skills and methods; as so often, the historian has been adding new tools to the kit and refashioning older ones. It is, however, having a transforming effect on the way we read narrative histories produced at this date – and deserves to have more.

Some of this work on the "uses of history" is postmodern also in its concern with power and authority and how they are exercised. To shape the past is to exercise power; or, more neutrally and less consciously, the past is powerful and the shape it takes of great potential significance. The past is a source of authority, and also of identity. Writing or rewriting history, genealogies, and charters is thus not merely recording fact, but selecting and presenting it in ways that have an impact on the receivers. Awareness of this underlies the modern studies of ethnogenesis. These are "technologies of power" in a loosely Foucauldian sense. Rethinking power has been a major contribution of postmodernist, but also of later Marxist work, as witness the central Gramscian notion of hegemony. Power and authority do not lie simply in physical force or economic control – important as both are. Their sources are much more diverse and include ideas and beliefs; their exercise is much more all-encompassing and not always consciously planned. The most effective power is often one whose messages are absorbed and internalized, and the authority with which those messages come is critical to that process. These approaches do not overturn or replace the study of institutions, so central to English historiography, though they do probe much deeper into the question of how and why institutions work. They place less emphasis on innovation – new institutions – and more on intangibles such as iteration, doing it often enough and for long enough, becoming part of a Bourdieuian "habitus." And they undermine the crude antitheses of a Hobbesian reading of politics. They reinstate the sacred, ideas and values as sources and techniques of power and authority. This is an approach that is capable of generating its own model of change, though it is unlikely to be a simple one.

These insights are beginning to have an important impact on our understanding of early medieval politics, though again this is clearest in the work of Carolingian scholars such a Jinty Nelson, Rosamund McKitterick, and Matthew Innes.[34] But they have already encouraged work on saints' cults and the fashioning, use, and functioning of political identities such as "Angelcynn" or "Alba," and their future potential for our understanding of early Britain and Ireland is huge. This volume, of necessity, reflects the state of historiography now, and thus the as-yet fairly limited impact of this thinking. But here, as elsewhere, it may make some contribution to future study.

The study of women and gender has been one of the great growth areas of later twentieth-century historiography in general. This has had an influence, albeit patchy, on the study of early medieval Britain and Ireland. Scotland pre-1100 is poorly served with written sources, and there has been little advance here. But Viking Age archaeology, in Scotland and elsewhere, has been very alert to both women and the wider gender questions (see chapter 14). The same source problems have inhibited work on Welsh women, though here archaeology has done less to redress the balance. There has been more substantial work on women in both England and Ireland, and the work done on women and marriage, kinship, status, and identity informs many chapters. As stated in chapter 1, the volume has been constructed on the premise that women should and will feature throughout.

In almost all the recent work on women, old conceptual frameworks that generalized women have been rejected; we have gone beyond the earlier historiography that generalized women's experience, often as Golden Ages of freedom in the case, for example, of early England, or of sharp turning points. Neither the generalization of "women," nor the modern individualistic definitions of "freedom" involved here are defensible. Women's history has its own historiography, and one which, inevitably, tells as much about the periods that produced it as about the experience of early medieval women. During and after the Enlightenment, "the condition of women" was seen as an important marker of civilization. Women's history in the nineteenth and early twentieth centuries proved peculiarly susceptible to ideological rewriting.[35] This is, in fact, an interesting example not so much of women's history as of gender history. Women were often used "to think with"; their significance was symbolic: it signified things quite other than the experience of women themselves. Symbolic women have often proved useful in national and nationalist thought.[36] The early Middle Ages is no exception, but as yet their symbolic use in early medieval writing about nation or political legitimacy has been little exploited.[37] Gender as a way of conceptualizing, describing, and normalizing power and other relationships has been even less covered. Similarly, outside archaeology, gender as the study of masculinity and the masculine as opposed to femininity and the feminine is barely in its infancy in the study of this period. Yet these were societies dominated by warrior elites, where land and status were transmitted by birth and blood, face to face with a Christian ideology in which asceticism and celibacy were central. There is clearly a potential awaiting exploitation here.

This chapter has been concerned with a number of major historiographical trends, past and present. There is a danger of seeing the motes in the eyes of earlier historiographies – of seeing them as children of their time from our lofty eminence – whilst missing the beams in recent ones. It is certainly important to recognize how far some rethinking has its obvious context in current preoccupations. All historiographies are in some sense partial, all are certainly situated; the questions we ask are from our present, our point in time. Awareness of historiography in this sense is itself an arguably postmodern approach, and for many a disturbing experience. It seems to threaten dangerous relativism. Historiographical awareness is a prerequisite of good history, but good history offers an antidote to total relativism. The past has many answers to many questions. Some questions are more fruitful than others; some questions are products of concepts or ideas that can be shown to be wrong or at least very dubious. But no answer can be right unless it is secured through the rigorous methods of history, including the most traditional methods of source criticism. It is to these sources that we now turn.

Notes

1   Wickham, *Problems in Doing Comparative History.*
2   Donovan et al. (eds.), *Writing National Histories.*
3   See, e.g., Etchingham, "Early medieval Irish history"; Ó Corráin, "Nationality and kingship"; Pryce, "Modern nationality and the medieval past"; Wormald, "Celtic and Anglo-Saxon kingship."
4   Pryce, "Modern nationality and the medieval past," pp. 15–19.
5   Bhreathnach, "Medieval Irish history," p. 261; Etchingham, "Early medieval Irish history," p. 124; Johnston, "Early Irish history," p. 342; Ó Corráin in MacNeill, *Celtic Ireland* (1981).
6   Binchy, "Irish history and Irish law: II," p. 32.
7   Ó Corráin, "Nationality and kingship."
8   Charles-Edwards, "The lure of Celtic languages."
9   Cowan, "The invention of Celtic Scotland"; Sims-Williams, "Celtomania and Celtoscepticism" and "The visionary Celt."
10 See, e.g., Binchy, *Celtic and Anglo-Saxon Kingship* and "Irish history and Irish law: I and II"; Byrne, *Irish Kings and High-kings.*
11 Ó Corráin, "Nationality and kingship"; see also, Etchingham, "Early medieval Irish history," discussing the work of James Carney and others.
12 Davies, "Looking backwards."
13 Orpen, *Ireland under the Normans.*
14 See, e.g., Grant, "The construction of the early Scottish state"; cf. Campbell, "The united kingdom of England," p. 47, for the admittedly controversial statement, "it is almost as if there are two Englands, and one of them is called Scotland."
15 Broun, *Irish Identity of the Kingdom of the Scots*; Woolf, *From Pictland to Alba*; cf. Irish approaches in Herbert, "Sea-divided Gaels?"
16 Bhreathnach, "Medieval Irish history"; Etchingham, "Early medieval Irish history"; Johnston, "Early Irish history."
17 *Scottish Historical Review*, 76, nos. 201–2 (1997) was devoted to "Writing Scotland's history: what have historians made of the nation's past?"
18 See, e.g., Burrow, *Liberal Descent*; Donovan et al. (eds.), *Writing National Histories.*
19 Campbell, *Stubbs and the English state*; cf. also Stafford, "Women and the Norman Conquest."
20 Davies, personal comment and cf., e.g., *The Matter of Britain*; Leyser, "The Anglo-Saxons 'at home.'"
21 Gillingham, "The beginnings of English imperialism."
22 See, e.g., Thomas, *The English and the Normans.*
23 Stafford, "Introduction."
24 Ibid., pp. 6–7.
25 Hammond, "Ethnicity and the writing of medieval Scottish history," 26.

26 Bhreathnach, "Medieval Irish history"; Davies, "Looking backwards"; Etchingham, "Early medieval Irish history"; Johnston, "Early Irish history."
27 Cf. the comments of Etchingham, "Early medieval Irish history," pp. 141–3.
28 Cf. Davies, "Looking backwards," 205.
29 Faith, *English Peasantry*; Fleming, "Acquiring, flaunting and destroying silk," "The new wealth," and "Rural elites and urban communities."
30 Ryan in McCone and Simms (eds.), *Progress in Medieval Irish Studies*, p. 163.
31 See Hen and Innes, *Uses of the Past*, introduction and essays, for careful utilization of these techniques.
32 Bhreathnach, "Medieval Irish history," 263–4.
33 Ibid., p. 264.
34 See, e.g., the essays collected in de Jong and Theuws (eds.), *Topographies of Power*, and Nelson, *Politics and Ritual*; see also Innes, *State and Society*; McKitterick, *History and Memory*.
35 Stafford, "Women and the Norman Conquest."
36 Cf. the essays in the collection, *Gendered Nations*, edited by Blom et al.
37 Though see Geary, *Women at the Beginning*; Stafford, "Chronicle D, 1067 and women" and "The meanings of hair in the Anglo-Norman world."

Bibliography

Bhreathnach, E., "Medieval Irish history at the end of the twentieth century: unfinished work," *Irish Historical Studies*, 32: 126 (2000), 260–71.

Binchy, D. A., *Celtic and Anglo-Saxon Kingship* (Oxford, 1970).

Binchy, D. A., "Irish history and Irish law: I and II," *Studia Hibernica*, 15 and 16 (1975 and 1976), 7–36 and 7–45.

Blom, I., Hagemann, K., and Hall, C. (eds.), *Gendered Nations: Nationalisms and Gender Order in the Long Nineteenth Century* (Oxford, 2000).

Broun, D., *The Irish Identity of the Kingdom of the Scots* (Woodbridge, 1999).

Burrow, J. W., *A Liberal Descent: Victorian Historians and the English Past* (Cambridge, 1981).

Byrne, F. J., *Irish Kings and High-kings* (London, 1973).

Campbell, J., *Stubbs and the English State*, Stenton Lecture (Reading, 1989).

Campbell, J., "The united kingdom of England: the Anglo-Saxon achievement," in A. Grant and K. J. Stringer (eds.), *Uniting the Kingdom? The Making of British History* (London, 1995), pp. 30–47.

Charles-Edwards, T. M., "The lure of Celtic languages, 1850–1914," in M. Costambeys, A. Hamer, and M. Heale (eds.), *The Making of the Middle Ages* (Liverpool, 2007), pp. 15–35.

Cowan, E. J., "The invention of Celtic Scotland," in E. J. Cowan and R. A. McDonald (eds.), *Alba: Celtic Scotland in the Middle Ages* (East Linton, 2000), pp. 1–23.

Davies, R., *The Matter of Britain and the Matter of England* (Oxford, 1996).

Davies, W., "Looking backwards to the early medieval past: Wales and England, a contrast in approaches," *Welsh History Review*, 22 (2004), 197–221.

de Jong, M. and Theuws, F. (eds.), *Topographies of Power in the Early Middle Ages* (Leiden, 2001).

Donovan, M., Passmore, K., and Berger, S. (eds.), *Writing National Histories: Western Europe since 1800* (London, 1999 and 2005).

Etchingham, C., "Early medieval Irish history," in K. McCone and K. Simms (eds.), *Progress in Medieval Irish Studies* (Maynooth, 1996), pp. 123–53.

Faith, R., *The English Peasantry and the Growth of Lordship* (London, 1997).

Fleming, R., "Acquiring, flaunting and destroying silk in late Anglo-Saxon England," *Early Medieval Europe*, 15: 2 (2007), 127–58.

Fleming, R., "The new wealth, the new rich and the new political style in late Anglo-Saxon England," *Anglo-Norman Studies*, 23 (2001), 1–22.

Fleming, R., "Rural elites and urban communities in late-Saxon England," *Past & Present*, 141 (1993), 3–37.

Geary, P., *Women at the Beginning: Origin Myths from the Amazons to the Virgin Mary* (Princeton, NJ, 2006).

Gillingham, J., "The beginnings of English imperialism," *Journal of Historical Sociology*, 5: 4 (1992), 392–409, reprinted in J. Gillingham, *The English in the Twelfth Century: Imperialism, National Identity and Political Values* (Woodbridge, 2000), pp. 3–18.

Grant, A., "The construction of the early Scottish state," in J. R. Maddicott and D. M. Palliser (eds.), *The Medieval State: Essays Presented to James Campbell* (London, 2000), pp. 47–71.

Hammond, M. H., "Ethnicity and the writing of medieval Scottish history," *Scottish Historical Review*, 85: 1, no. 219 (2006), 1–27.

Hen, Y. and Innes, M., *Uses of the Past in the Early Middle Ages* (Cambridge, 2000).

Herbert, M., "Sea-divided Gaels? Constructing relationships between Irish and Scots c.800–1169," in B. Smith (ed.), *Britain and Ireland 900–1300: Insular Responses to Medieval European Change* (Cambridge, 1999), pp. 87–97.

Innes, M., *State and Society in the Early Middle Ages: The Middle Rhine Valley, 400–1000* (Cambridge, 2000).

Johnston, E., "Early Irish history: the state of the art," *Irish Historical Studies*, 33: 131 (2003), 342–8.

Leyser, K., "The Anglo-Saxons 'at home,'" in D. Brown, J. Campbell, and S. C. Hawkes (eds.), *Anglo-Saxon Studies in Archaeology and History*, 2, British Archaeological Reports, British series, 92 (Oxford, 1981), pp. 237–42; reprinted in K. Leyser, *Communications and Power in Medieval Europe: The Carolingian and Ottonian Centuries*, ed. T. Reuter (London, 1994), pp. 105–10.

McCone, K. and Simms, K., *Progress in Medieval Irish Studies* (Maynooth, 1996).

McKitterick, R., *History and Memory in the Carolingian World* (Cambridge, 2004).

MacNeill, E., *Celtic Ireland* (Dublin, 1921, reissued Dublin, 1981, with contribution by D. Ó Corráin).

MacNeill, E., *Phases of Irish History* (Dublin, 1919).

Nelson, J. L., *Politics and Ritual in Early Medieval Europe* (London, 1986).

Ó Corráin, D., "Nationality and kingship in pre-Norman Ireland," in T. W. Moody (ed.), *Nationality and the Pursuit of National Independence* (Belfast, 1978), pp. 1–35.

Orpen, G. H., *Ireland under the Normans 1169–1333* (Oxford, 1911, reissued with an introduction by S. Duffy, Dublin, 2005).

Pryce, H., "Modern nationality and the medieval past: the Wales of John Edward Lloyd," in R. R. Davies and G. H. Jenkins (eds.), *From Medieval to Modern Wales: Historical Essays in Honour of K. O. Morgan and R. A. Griffiths* (Cardiff, 2004), pp. 14–29.

Reuter, T., "The making of England and Germany, 850–1050: points of comparison and difference," in A. P. Smyth (ed.), *Medieval Europeans: Studies in Ethnic Identity and National Perspectives in Medieval Europe* (Basingstoke, 1998), pp. 53–70.

Scottish Historical Review, "Writing Scotland's history: what have historians made of the nation's past?," 76 (1997), nos. 201–2.

Sims-Williams, P., "Celtomania and Celtoscepticism," *Cambrian Medieval Celtic Studies*, 36 (1998), 1–35.

Sims-Williams, P., "The visionary Celt: the construction of an ethnic preconception," *Cambrian Medieval Celtic Studies*, 11 (1986), 71–96.

Stafford, P., "Chronicle D, 1067 and women: gendering conquest in eleventh-century England," in S. Keynes and A. P. Smyth (eds.), *Anglo-Saxons: Studies Presented to Cyril Roy Hart* (Dublin, 2006), pp. 208–23.

Stafford, P., "Introduction," in M. Costambeys, A. Hamer, and M. Heale (eds.), *The Making of the Middle Ages* (Liverpool, 2007), pp. 1–14.

Stafford, P., "The meanings of hair in the Anglo-Norman world: masculinity, reform, and national identity," in M. van Dijk and R. Nip (eds.), *Saints, Scholars, and Politicians: Gender as a Tool in Medieval Studies. Festschrift in Honour of Anneke Mulder-Bakker on the Occasion of her Sixty-fifth Birthday*, Medieval Church Studies, 15 (Turnhout, 2005), pp. 153–71.

Stafford, P., "Women and the Norman Conquest," *Transactions of the Royal Historical Society*, 6th series, 4 (1994), 221–49.

Thomas, H. M., *The English and the Normans: Ethnic Hostility, Assimilation and Identity 1066–c.1220* (Oxford, 2003).

Wickham, C., *Problems in Doing Comparative History*, Reuter Lecture 2004 (Southampton, 2005).

Woolf, A., *From Pictland to Alba 789 to 1070* (Edinburgh, 2007).

Wormald, P., "Celtic and Anglo-Saxon kingship: some further thoughts," in P. E. Szarmach and V. D. Oggins (eds.), *Sources of Anglo-Saxon Culture*. Papers from the Symposium on the Sources of Anglo-Saxon Culture held in conjunction with the Eighteenth International Congress on Medieval Studies at Western Michigan University, May 5–8, 1983; Studies in Medieval Culture, 20 (Kalamazoo, MI, 1986), pp. 151–83.

CHAPTER THREE

Sources

PAULINE STAFFORD

The primary source material for the centuries between c. AD 500 and c.1100 is peculiarly sparse, and its use and interpretation are fraught with difficulties. It is no surprise
that study of the primary texts themselves has long been central to work on this period.
The abiding refrain from historians, including the authors of this volume, is a lament
at the paucity of written material, though this sometimes masks historians' preference
for certain categories of source, a preference determined as much by historiographical
tradition as by scale of survival. The pattern of sources, or at least source survival,
across Britain and Ireland is extremely varied, both regionally and chronologically.
There is certainly a fairly intractable problem of mismatches between type and date
of evidence which render the whole enterprise of comparison more difficult. There
are, however, important similarities, including ones that have been obscured.
Considerable changes are underway in the way in which historians approach written
sources, and these are already provoking major rethinking. The full fruits of this are
still to be harvested. Non-written sources play a larger part in the writing of the history
of this period than of most subsequent ones. They pose their own problems as well
as offering major opportunities. What is clear is that no history of this period can be
written – or, for that matter, read – without attention to these questions.

The surviving sources may be divided into a number of major categories:

- *historical writing*, mainly annals and chronicles, but also material such as king-
  lists, genealogies, and pedigrees, plus rare biographical sources, which are often
  difficult to separate clearly from hagiography.
- *hagiography*, not only saints' *Lives* but also other documentation concerned with
  the cult of saints.
- *liturgical material*, which may overlap with hagiography in its celebration of the
  saints.
- *theological, exegetical, and pastoral material*, including, for example, homilies and
  glosses.
- *legal material*, from general statements to specific documentation of cases and
  disputes, the latter often classified as charters, a wider range of texts associated
  with landholding and transfer.
- *literature*, though this may shade into historical writing.

Some material is difficult to classify in our categories. Computistical material, a substantial body of work concerned with the reckoning of time, is by our standards scientific or mathematical, but for contemporaries intimately bound up with the cycle of the Christian year, and may sometimes have provided a vehicle for annalistic writing. Old English charms and remedies look sometimes like medicine, sometimes like magic; to call them "folklore"[1] risks inappropriate distinctions between "learned" and "popular" culture, belied by the fact that they appear in manuscripts alongside a variety of ecclesiastical material. As these and other examples make clear, contemporary categories would not necessarily have been ours. We are also alerted to the importance of manuscript study; among other things, it has much to tell us about which texts contemporaries associated together and how they read some in relation to others.

Some of the sources are easy to define, if unfamiliar: for example, liturgical material, covering details of the celebration of Christian rituals, or exegetical texts, expounding the meanings of Christian writings, especially the books of the Bible. Some pose obvious, and not so obvious, problems. Literature, for example, is widely used as a source for social history, and this period produced some of the great vernacular works: *Beowulf, Táin Bó Cúailnge, Y Gododdin*. All raise the obvious questions of how far literary works simply reflect the world that produced them, a question compounded by the fact that none can be dated precisely. Others look deceptively simple, but turn out to be complex and problematic. Annals, for example, could be distinguished from chronicles as historical material entered in a year-by-year format, as opposed to organized thematically by a later author. It is a distinction which, consciously or unconsciously, can affect judgments of the relative veracity and reliability of the two. But annals, which form the overwhelming bulk of historical writing in this period, were often compiled retrospectively. Even if compiled on a year-by-year basis, the selection of material for inclusion was a choice, albeit often constrained by traditions.

Few sets of annals survive in their original form. Annals are an essentially open-ended form, which could be added to or incorporated into compilations. They were copied and recopied, continued and edited. It is sometimes possible to establish particularly important compilations or sets of annals which seem to have then become the basis for much later development. The annals produced at the court of King Alfred in late ninth-century Wessex are one such set, and became the basis for the vernacular chronicles that were produced in England during the tenth and eleventh centuries, usually known, a little misleadingly, as "the" *Anglo-Saxon Chronicle*.[2] A now lost text, the so-called *Chronicle of Ireland*, existed by the early tenth century, but can now be reconstructed only from the various surviving "daughter" chronicles which grew out of it or made use of it; for example, the annals of Clonmacnoise, Ulster, Inisfallen, and Tigernach.[3] Historians have sometimes seemed especially interested in the first version of such chronicles, and the establishment of a text such as the lost *Chronicle of Ireland* or Alfred's chronicle is a necessary quest. But neither of these was the first stage of development of the material they used, and Alfred's own reputation has affected the attention paid to his annals. Every decision to copy annals – let alone to compile them from existing material, to continue or collate them – is significant in itself. It is important to establish where and when each section was written, as well as each compilation made. But it is also important to ask who wanted a history/set of annals – including "mere" copies of earlier ones – where and when. The historiographical concerns of the early Middle Ages must be identified.

Historians work with what they term primary evidence produced at the time (sources) and secondary comment and discussion (historiography). As discussion in chapter 2 made clear, the issues that each raise are not clearly separable. Historiographical traditions have evolved in response to the sources available, which have to some extent determined which questions have been seen as "askable." But historiographical traditions have other roots. Those traditions have themselves had considerable influence on how sources have been approached, and how different categories of source have been perceived, interpreted, valued – and published. Moreover, the history of this period was being written from the twelfth century, and in many ways long before. Its historiographical traditions are deep, and blur the apparently simple distinction between primary source and historiography. Early historiographical concerns had a major impact on what sources were once produced and which now survive. The "use of history," and the writing, rewriting, and sifting that result from it, did not begin in the sixteenth and seventeenth centuries. The past is powerful, never more so than in societies that set great store by tradition. The function and significance of "origins," seen (in chapter 2) to have such an impact on later historiography, already affected works produced during these centuries and just after. Some sources which we now use as primary are, in fact, themselves early stages of historiographical development.

The past in general, and origins in particular, provide important answers to questions about identity and legitimacy. "What we are" is deeply affected by the view of "what we once were, where we came from, what we origin-ally were." Argument about how things should be now often involves precedent, the venerable authority of age and tradition, lines of unbroken descent, but also, paradoxically, claims of return to (lost) origins. The present from which such questions are asked reshapes the past which is turned to for answers – nostalgically and unconsciously, as for example in "Golden Ages," usually defined in terms of present concerns, but sometimes consciously and deliberately. The early Middle Ages was being defined and redefined in these terms well before 1100, and certainly immediately afterward.

The twelfth and thirteenth centuries were important in the writing of history and in wider uses of the recent past throughout these islands. From the late eleventh century onward, for example, early Irish history was rewritten from the perspective of the great kingships that existed by that date, projecting back monarchy, over-interpreting earlier overkingships as monarchical.[4] Thirteenth-century Scottish political myth-making produced seven kingdoms of sons of Cruithne.[5] Some later historians took this thirteenth-century Scottish myth-making as a description of early political geography – which it is not. The antiquarianism that was such a feature of the twelfth century onward is evident here, elaborating, inventing, but also archaizing and conventionalizing. In England, the Norman Conquest of 1066, with the longer-term questions it left about both legitimacy and national identity, had enormous impact on the production of historical writing for a century or more.[6] That outpouring of historical writing was instrumental in defining the period pre-1066 as *the* period of English origins, a status which, as we saw in chapter 2, was reinforced by the questions of identity and Englishness raised during the confessional strife of the sixteenth and seventeenth centuries.

Turning to the past for legitimacy not only produced new documentation, including forgery, but also collected, preserved, sifted, and edited existing documentation. This was occurring after 1100, but also before. Documentation obviously concerned with the legitimation of kings, such as genealogies, pedigrees, and king-lists, was not only collected and preserved, but certainly manipulated and altered in the interests of particular claimants or dynasties within our period itself.[7] Control of the past was an exercise of power, and it could involve forgetting or even erasing, as when the kingship of Harold II in 1066 was systematically, and almost successfully, expunged from *Domesday Book* in 1086. It can be very difficult to recover any information about dynasties that were replaced or lost power. The ethos and concerns of an entire movement could affect documentation. For example, as MacLean and Cubitt argue below (see chapters 22 and 23), the English ecclesiastical "reform" movement of the tenth and early eleventh centuries claimed its innovations as a return to original practices. It not only spurred the collection but also the forgery of documentation on landholding, an issue central to its concerns; as a result, the bulk of such documentation in England is determined by its horizon of memory. It also rewrote the more remote ecclesiastical past as a means of blackening the unreformed present, potentially misleading later historians both of remote past and tenth-century present. Attention to these questions can be very revealing, though usually about the concerns of the time and place of writing or collection and not about the past purportedly recorded. The danger for historians of the early medieval period is the use of texts thus produced or reworked as evidence for earlier centuries.

The differences across Britain and Ireland are often stressed. It is thus instructive to begin with some of the similarities; some of these apply across early medieval Europe, others are peculiar to, or are especially marked in, these islands. The first is the fact that, in comparison with later periods, much less was written down. This is a bold and debatable statement. Recent work has stressed that literacy was much more widespread than once believed.[8] In addition, as we shall see, there has certainly been loss of documentation, probably on a large scale, and not merely due to the passage of many centuries and the fragility of the written document. But a number of arguments point to societies in which the written word was less common than in later periods. Figures produced by Michael Clanchy, although much discussed as to interpretation, remain very telling:

> From Anglo-Saxon England about 2000 charters and writs (including originals and copies and an indefinite number of forgeries) survive. From thirteenth-century England, on the other hand, tens of thousands of such charters and writs survive; this estimate is no more precise because the documents have never been systematically counted. How many documents once existed (as distinct from how many now survive), either in the Anglo-Saxon period or in the thirteenth century, is a matter for conjecture and inevitably therefore for different opinions. An estimate . . . suggests that eight million charters may have been written in the thirteenth century alone for smallholders and serfs.[9]

Documents were expensive, written, for example, on pages produced from animal skin. Literacy, although more common than once thought, and requiring careful definition, was nonetheless restricted. Much was done orally and never committed to writing, including, for example, in judicial cases. The loss of the world of gesture, ritual performance, and oral styles is thus a major loss, though some efforts are now being made to recover it.[10] We cannot make any simple link between written form and contemporary perception of significance. Important things were not necessarily written down. One corollary of this first generalization is a second: we should not take the written form for granted. For this period, the historian's key questions – who was writing this and why – have a particular sharpness.

The answers to the "who" would be, overwhelmingly, churchmen and women throughout the period and across Britain and Ireland, though there is little clear evidence of women writing in Ireland. Clearly, conditions for preservation have played a part in influencing our picture here. The archives and libraries of ecclesiastical institutions are much more likely to survive, since those institutions were themselves often long-lived and had well-developed attitudes toward documentary preservation. Their history has often been disrupted, and these disruptions account for some of the major losses which we can be certain have occurred – though also, as we shall see below, for production and preservation. The impact of viking invasions on churches, and thus on documentary survival, has often been stressed, and the loss, for example, of what was clearly once an outstanding early library at York is probably due to this. The destruction and dispersal of monastic archives in parts of Britain and Ireland at the Reformation was a tragedy. And, as a result, a lot of the surviving Irish material ended up in continental libraries. But it is still the case that documents in ecclesiastical hands had a far greater chance of long-term survival than those in the hands of lay people. Yet the dominance of churchmen and women in the production of documents of all sorts in this period was real, and not just an accident or function of preservation.

This is not, of course, to say that nothing was produced or survives that was of any relevance to lay people. Indeed, it can be dangerous to speak in too sharply differentiated lay/clerical terms. Clerics had "secular" interests, including the literature they read and enjoyed,[11] and the laity's religious commitment and belief should never be underestimated. Churchmen, if not women, frequented royal courts and legal ones, and were involved in the recording of activities there, including the production of documents concerning the landholding of lay people; there is no sign of the notarial activity still found elsewhere in early medieval Europe. Some lay people undoubtedly read and certainly wrote, though recent work on the law experts of early Ireland has stressed that what was once seen as a straightforwardly lay group was in fact working within an ecclesiastical milieu.[12] We need to be alert to the laity as audience, even probably for the ornate "hermeneutic" Latin that characterizes some early insular texts (see chapter 12). At the end of the tenth century, for example, a lay noble, Æthelweard, translated a vernacular Anglo-Saxon chronicle into a Latin that has clear signs of this style.[13] A layman translating a vernacular text into Latin is a warning against any simple alignment of vernacular/Latin with lay/cleric. Nonetheless, the clerical dominance of the initial production as well as the preservation of our texts is a third generalization that holds good throughout the period.

It is thus not surprising that clerical concerns are evident in the overall pattern of texts, and in the content of libraries and manuscripts, whether lost or surviving. This content is not always obvious from the balance of texts used and highlighted by historians. The content of Anglo-Saxon libraries was, for example, determined by their principal purposes: "the interpretation of Scripture and the regulation of the Church."[14] The reader of many historical works, including this one, would be forgiven for not realizing how large patristic texts and scriptural exegesis, for example, bulk in the surviving evidence (but see chapter 12). Textual study, of course, has maintained a much broader and more catholic remit, though, interestingly, it has tended to show a bias toward vernacular rather than Latin texts.[15] This is in part a reflection of language problems. Very few scholars now have competence in Old Irish or Old English. Editions, often with translation, are part of a laudable desire to make texts available. This bias is also, however, a legacy of the significance of the vernacular in the national and nationalist historiographies discussed in chapter 2. It is a sharp reminder of how far historiography and its concerns have shaped even the editing and publication of texts.

This is arguably even more marked in historians' approaches, and in which texts they use or recognize. Later twentieth-century interest in mentalities has widened their perspectives. The study of saints' *Lives*, for example – such a significant element in the quantity of material surviving – is enjoying a renaissance. They were once largely dismissed, not least because they are by definition formulaic: their central requirement, proof of sanctity, militates against stress on individuality. A half-grudging empiricist rehabilitation would use them for incidental detail, but now increasingly sophisticated readings of these *Lives* are revealing what they can tell us about the contexts that produced them, including the political contexts (see, for example, chapter 24). The writing – or rewriting – of a saint's *Life* gives insight, for example, into the community for which it was done and its intended audience beyond that, as well as the circumstances that prompted it and the perceptions of those circumstances by authors, patrons, and audience. As with annals, historians are increasingly aware that what matters is not merely novelty – what does this text add in rewriting? – but that the text was created at all, that someone wanted to have it. But, as this suggests, renewed interest is as much about our questions and concerns as those of the texts' authors. In general, "reading against the grain" – for what a text was not designed to tell us – has become a central methodology. In the dialogue between past and present, historians ask the questions. Their interest – in the nineteenth and twentieth centuries – in state formation, nations, social change, and religious history in its more institutional forms, for example, tended to mean that only some voices from the past were fully heard, and, in spite of recent developments, this is often still the case. Historians' control of the past is both defensible and to some extent inevitable, but their questions should not be solely the result of an imperialist dialogue of the deaf. Even, perhaps especially, in our approach to sources, awareness of historiography – and the scrutiny of our own questions and perspectives that should result – is essential.

If we turn from similarities to differences in the written evidence, we are immediately aware of some of the divergences within the Atlantic Archipelago, but also that they may have been overstressed, over-interpreted, or oversimplified. Most remarkable are differences in quantity. England and Ireland are marked by the relative wealth of surviving evidence, Wales and Scotland by its paucity. Modern boundaries are misleading here. In fact, the contrast is between England south of the Trent/Humber and southern, especially south-eastern, Ireland, on the one hand, and northern England, Wales, and Scotland and Ireland's northern half, on the other. Further enquiry reveals even more regional diversity. In southern England, for example, the Fenlands and western East Anglia are an island of more detailed documentation in the later tenth and eleventh centuries. Little has survived that was originally written in northern England after c.900. Yet in the eighth century this same area was home to Bede, and a wide range of exegetical, computistical, hagiographical, and historical writing was produced there.

As these examples show, there are shifts across the period. Early Ireland, that is, pre-800, has a greater wealth of material than early England. The quantity and variety of early Irish sources, including, for example, extensive legal material, means that Irish society can be examined from the sixth century onward in a way that is more difficult for England and Wales, and – at least on the basis of written material – virtually impossible for Scotland. The wealth of the Irish evidence continues into the tenth and eleventh centuries, in annals, genealogies, saints' *Lives*, prophetic texts, topographical poetry, and pseudo-historic prose and poetry. Legal material continued to attract commentary, though only very careful textual excavation can uncover its different layers. Tenth- and eleventh-century southern England is also richly served with surviving sources, though often in later manuscripts. Of pre-1066 charters, the bulk dates from after 900, the vast majority from after 800. Most of the laws belong after 870. It is from the tenth century that most writing in Old English survives. This includes homilies, laws, saints' *Lives*, and a developing tradition of vernacular annal writing. In Ireland, too, vernacular writing seems on the surviving evidence to grow in scale from the ninth century. Again, the manuscript evidence is late, sometimes here very late; but the shift is marked in, for example, annalistic writing, which from the tenth if not ninth century onward is increasingly in Irish.[16] The early flowering of historical writing in northern England, by contrast, and its eighth- and ninth-century continuations, seem to have been in Latin.

Different patterns of survival also involve different types of evidence. One alleged difference is that between England, with a relative abundance of surviving charters, and the rest where there are virtually none. Again, northern England and southern England diverge; this is a southern England/rest pattern, and even more localized than this, since large areas of central England/Mercia and East Anglia have few or no charters. Conversely, both Ireland and England are rich in legal material – probably Wales, too, if the earlier elements of later legal material could be disentangled.[17] But, again, the evidence is of very different types. If such early Welsh material could be confidently identified, it would almost certainly be akin to the Irish. The latter consists of texts that can be compared with the lawyers' books of later Welsh law. These are fairly systematic and full statements of custom, or of legal practice on a particular topic, for example, surety, designed for the use of lawyers. The English laws, by contrast, survive as texts issued in the name of southern kings. There are a handful of texts more akin to the Irish, but these are vastly outweighed in the manuscripts by royal laws.[18]

These patterns are potentially of considerable significance, and could be used to argue many things. It is tempting to read them straightforwardly as reflecting real differences: most significantly, broad political and cultural differences between southern England and the rest of Britain and Ireland. But they need to be handled with great care. It is already apparent that the patterns are more complex than they seem at first sight, and we need to be very alert to the possibility that our historiographical concerns have distorted them. So we need, first, to be sure what the pattern is, and that it is accurate. Second, we must ensure that we are interpreting categories of evidence correctly one in relation to another. And, third, we need to take into account questions of production and survival; we need to establish what was probably once there as well as what now survives, and the factors that determined production, loss, and preservation. The answers, if we could once establish them, would still be very instructive. But they might not paint quite the same broad-brush picture. In a chapter such as this, only preliminary considerations and cautions can be indicated.

The more these broad patterns are examined, the more complicated they become. Thus, for example, most southern English charters that survive are post-900, but the

period from c.1016 to 1066 is a relative hiatus,[19] and regional variations are very
sharp. The original production of English vernacular texts peaks in the later tenth
and early eleventh centuries, but if we were to consider manuscripts (and thus use)
as opposed to composition, the picture might look different, though there are problems of precise dating. Moreover, concentration on the vernacular has, until recently,
tended to obscure the wealth of Latin hagiography, especially that produced in the
later eleventh century.[20] The bulk of English vernacular legal material dates from the
tenth and eleventh centuries, but to be more precise from the period pre-1023.
Apparent similarities, such as the production of vernacular annals in southern England
and Ireland, mask significant differences. The English vernacular annalistic tradition
was born at the court of King Alfred, and remained, if not court-centered, at least
tied to the politics of the expanding Southumbrian kingdom, even when annals were
produced outside the court. The Irish tradition, on the other hand, was, like Bede
and his Northumbrian heirs, firmly monastic in origin and continuation, though in
neither case insulated from political concerns or without political agendas.

These differences may have much to tell us about the differences between early
Ireland and southern England, but not without careful thought about questions
of transmission and preservation. First, there is a remarkable difference between
early Irish material surviving *within* and *outside* Ireland. There are whole categories
of material about which we would know virtually nothing were we to be dependent
on manuscripts surviving within Ireland: thus, for example, early Irish theology, biblical commentary, Latin penitentials, canon law, or liturgy; our knowledge of early
saints' *Lives* would also be greatly impoverished.[21] We owe our knowledge of this
important material to manuscripts from continental Europe, connected with the
work of early Irish scholars and churchmen, especially in Francia. By contrast, we are
plentifully supplied with genealogies, sagas, and law tracts from manuscripts within
Ireland, though notably from very late manuscripts, in many cases as late as the sixteenth and seventeenth centuries. This highlights the importance of different patterns
of transmission – that is, of collection and preservation – in producing the pattern
we now have. In Ireland, for example, secular learned families played an important
role, at least from the high Middle Ages onward. The English pattern of transmission,
by contrast, is overwhelmingly determined by long-surviving ecclesiastical institutions, in particular those that flourished from the late eleventh and twelfth centuries
onward. We need to be alert to the distortions of evidence that these patterns of
transmission have imposed, including perhaps a greater interest not only in certain
sorts of text but also in the preservation of vernacular material in Ireland as opposed
to England. Patrick Wormald's awareness of the "extremely misleading impression
of pre-Norman Ireland" that indigenous channels of transmission give is worth
repetition,[22] though that insight should be extended to the distortions inherent in
English channels, too.

The potential impacts of such differences in transmission are wide-ranging. Irish
material preserved in continental Europe may fill gaps in some areas of ecclesiastical
history, as, for example, in theology, liturgy, and canon law, which were common
ecclesiastical concerns across Europe, although the Irish material on the continent
relating to these topics is often peculiarly Irish, whether in the approach taken or in
its use of Latin. But it is very unlikely to fill gaps in other areas; for example, early
landholding or land transactions specific to local Irish churches, which are the

building blocks of institutional history. Yet this is precisely the type of document that a range of events and developments in southern England were preserving – and producing, at least for a limited number of ultimately successful churches. This highlights the potential significance of these events and developments within southern England. But it should also warn of the dangers of taking those same documents and arguing from them to a different narrative of, for example, state development or English dynamism. This danger is magnified when a powerful and long-standing historiography, like that of English precociousness and state development, provides both a distorting lens through which to read the evidence and a ready-made story to fill in the gaps between its dots.

Charters, for example, appear to mark out southern England from the rest of Britain and Ireland by the tenth century, if not before. Indeed, if we add the differences between southern English and Irish annals, royally centered vis-à-vis monastic, plus English royal laws, the divergence is reinforced. The strong and precocious English (more correctly, southern English) state easily emerges. But there is need for real caution in how we interpret this evidence, as deeper consideration of the charter evidence reveals.

"Charter" is the term used to cover a wide range of documents concerned with recording land transactions – grants, gifts, exchanges, legal disputes, immunities. What these have in common is their involvement with the range and intersecting levels of power and control over the labor of others that landholding in the early Middle Ages entailed. "Charter" is sometimes extended to include other documents, recording, for example, the results of criminal legal cases, though in general these only survive if the judgment had implications for landholding; for example, forfeiture on the part of the accused. As a class, they are often perceived as "record" sources. That perception consciously or unconsciously gives them a truth status rather different from that accorded to other sources, especially narrative ones. It also, consciously or unconsciously, aligns them with the products of bureaucratic state apparatuses in other periods. Both perceptions are dangerous, at least without further examination.

Charters from early England survive almost exclusively in ecclesiastical, especially monastic, archives. A number of major events or developments had an impact on this survival: most notably the so-called (monastic) reform movement of the tenth and early eleventh centuries, and the Norman Conquest of 1066 and its aftermath; but also others, less often stressed, for example, the early ninth-century "reforming" activities of the Archbishop of Canterbury in relation to the southern English church.[23] At first sight less apparent are the significant losses: most obviously because of the disruption to ecclesiastical institutions caused by viking invasions; more generally and insidiously by the fluctuations and shifts in the history of such institutions across the period. In the musical chairs of early ecclesiastical institutional history, the final pattern was very largely determined by who was in their seats, if not when the music stopped, at least at a significant end of movement in the late eleventh and especially twelfth century; the largely Benedictine houses with an earlier history, which consolidated their position now, are those whose archives predominate.

For the rest of Britain and Ireland, surviving charters are much more sparse, though chance comments in other sources suggest that much has been lost. Some early Welsh charters were copied into the *Book of Llandaff*, and there is charter-type material in the marginalia to the *Lichfield Gospels*.[24] A few Scottish land transactions were copied into the *Book of Deer*.[25] For Ireland, there is charter-type material in the late seventh-century *collectanea* of Bishop Tírechán relating to churches and property, and eleventh-century memoranda in the *Book of Kells*.[26] These are scant when set against the southern English evidence. But there is much to suggest very significant losses which have affected the picture. A northern English charter tradition is now known only from inferences which can be made from references in historical works.[27] Early Ireland had a charter tradition which is known almost exclusively from indirect evidence: the references to the use of writing in relation to buying and selling land in the eighth-century *Hibernensis*, and the fact that such places as St. Gall or Salzburg, Irish foundations or places where their presence was important, were early centers for the production and preservation of charters.[28] It is significant that where so-called "Celtic" charters have survived, they share important features with the well-documented early English tradition, and are different from continental European development: for example, the lack of outward signs of validation, such as seal or autograph signatures, and the frequent entry in gospel books and/or use of the script – uncial/half uncial – considered appropriate for such sacred texts. Like the exclusively religious sanctions for infringement found in English charters, this underlines their religious and ecclesiastical context.[29]

The relationship of these documents to royal power, let alone early state development, requires very careful handling. Most surviving English charters are royal in the sense that they are written in the name of kings and cover, among other things, dues payable to kings. Again, we should be wary of overstressing difference: eleventh-century entries in the *Book of Armagh* and the *Book of Kells* record similar grants or immunities in kings' names. But there are more insidious issues of interpretation. It is by no means clear that the English documents should be seen as "royal" in the straightforward sense of instruments of the state and its activities; the terminology of royal "issuing" should be used very cautiously, if at all. There are no central records of them, no secular sanctions were involved in their infringement. We know that the earliest of them were produced by their ecclesiastical beneficiaries. There has been a long debate over the existence or not of an English royal chancery or writing office producing them before the mid-eleventh century. It is far from closed: recent work on the charters of the major abbey of Abingdon has cast that existence once more into doubt.[30]

There is real danger that the evidence of the English charters is being read within an existing historiographical tradition that takes a strong, precocious – and bureaucratic – English state for granted. There is probably some link with royal power. But that link requires careful investigation. It is likely to be at the level of ideological expression rather than bureaucratic procedures.[31] On surviving evidence, the major flowerings of English royal laws and charters coincide – as does their apparent wilting. The major surviving charter form, the solemn diploma, goes into rapid decline from the early eleventh century, at a date similar to the last surviving laws, from the early 1020s. Both may have much to tell us about the ideological nature and reach of the southern English court, and the importance of a Carolingian interaction of churchmen and kings in tenth-century England. It is arguably better to pursue the interpretation of both in the context of Carolingian models of royal power and its exercise. That might still underline differences within Britain and Ireland, but focus them on questions of reception, or not, of these Carolingian models – models that, ironically, owed much to early Irish influence, especially regarding royal authority and abuses – rather than on questions of "strength," "weakness," "precociousness," and similar value-laden terms.

And "might" is still important, since the issues of transmission remain central. Any rethink must take these into account, just as it must also carefully consider function and form. Charters, for example, act as title deeds and, more broadly, as legitimation, which is the major reason for their survival as well as production. Irish genealogies, which survive in large numbers, may once have had the same function.[32] If so, that would raise questions about the different documentary forms that parallel functions took. These are precisely the interesting questions that could emerge from a new historiographical orientation toward these sources.

Charters have been given very full treatment, partly because of their difficulty, but also because at first sight they offer such a sharp distinction and one that leads readily to major assumptions about divergent development. They may indeed tell us about such divergence. But not before we have fully considered the questions of loss and preservation, asked more questions about what they do and whether they are the only way of doing it, and questioned *what* precisely they can tell us about *whose* power and authority. Above all, they will not yield their potential until seen, if not without the lenses of historiography, at least without some of its traditional blinkers.

Laws need equally careful handling. English royal laws vis-à-vis Irish and Welsh statements of custom have fed a view of English dynamism – the law reacting to change – vis-à-vis "Celtic" immemorial custom. Customary law inevitably looks static. Yet careful excavation of the texts reveals its dynamic relationship to changing situations.[33] Such excavation is extremely difficult, and was not necessarily encouraged by Irish historiography fertilized by cultural nationalism. Customary law is often a statement about a "people." It can also be seen as a witness to their immemorial existence. The English laws look rather different if we take a wider comparative view of them. Laws in kings' names are rare in early Europe; tenth-century England and late eighth- and ninth-century Carolingian Francia are odd. Such texts virtually disappear in England after c.1020, including from the allegedly powerful and increasingly bureaucratic twelfth-century state. Irish and Welsh customary laws are arguably more comparable to the lawyers' laws of, for example, Glanvill and Bracton than to the early English ones, though, again, what has been committed to writing and survived has almost certainly under-represented royal involvement in the law in Wales or Ireland. More insidiously, difference is exaggerated by historiographies that either prioritize vernacular over Latin – and especially Latin ecclesiastical – laws or pursue parallel but, until recently, rarely intersecting courses. But the interrelationships between both are significant in Ireland and England.[34] And it is, for example, in the Latin canonical collection, the *Hibernensis*, that evidence for Irish royal involvement in law is to be found.

The nature of the surviving evidence has affected historiography in specific instances as well as in broad ways. Kinship, for example, is central to customary law, and is thus stressed in Irish and Welsh collections. English laws take it for granted, but their nature means that there are virtually no systematic statements of it. Customary law gives a picture of kinship as a series of rules and norms. Until recently, this had a deep impact on the way in which Irish royal succession was discussed; it was seen as deeply affected by such rules of kinship and similar norms, which obscured the impact of political circumstances that have recently been stressed.[35] Conversely, lack of such legal statements fed a tradition of discussing English royal succession in almost entirely political terms, seeing English succession in a realpolitik framework, whereas recent study has shown that it, too, operated in a context of normative argument that parallels Ireland.[36] The view of Irish succession was fed by a tendency, at least up to the mid-twentieth century, to pay more attention to laws than to annals. It was also the result of a historiography far more influenced by anthropological approaches, itself a product of the centrality given to customary law. In both cases, we are again confronted by historiography profoundly shaped by cultural nationalism.

The paucity of the written evidence has meant that historians of this period have made considerable use of non-written forms. Archaeology and material evidence more generally have played a particularly important role throughout the period. It is the one form of evidence that is constantly increasing in quantity, both as a result of new excavation, but also as a consequence of new questions applied to material remains, such as sculpture or coins, whose value for religious or political history, for example, is increasingly realized. It is a form of evidence that offers the possibility of exploring lives other than those of the small elite who produced and preserved our written sources, and has enormous potential for social and economic history, sometimes now reframed as questions about lifestyle and consumption. There are obvious problems, most fundamentally the danger of argument from absence when excavation has never been systematic: absence of evidence is not evidence of absence. Problems of interpretation are more subtle, especially when archaeological material is used to answer historians' questions rather than its own, and in particular when it is applied to questions of belief or subjectivity. But even here sophisticated questions and methods are bringing together historians and archaeologists in their interest, for example, in ethnicity and identity, as witness recent shifts in the study of the vikings, away from questions of numbers arriving and settling and toward others about situational ethnicity and assimilation. Dawn Hadley's chapter on Scandinavian settlement (see chapter 14) is typical of these new approaches, although their impact – and discussion of the problems of interpretation they pose – can be found throughout this volume.

Another body of non-written evidence is that of language and the related study of place and personal names. Like archaeological material, this offers tempting possibilities of probing beyond the elite to the population more generally. Much has been deduced from it about population movements, though the potential of naming practices, for example, for studies of kinship, ethnicity, and identity are being realized.[37] Although in one sense this material is non-written evidence, it can only be accessed via written sources, and often much later ones. The same questions of production and preservation that apply to written evidence in general are relevant here too. Many older arguments about language change, and the numbers needed to produce it, have been so hotly debated that progress in this field seemed to have stalled. But recent careful reworking has shown its continuing potential.[38]

Careful attention to sources is fundamental to the historian's training, and this is apparent throughout this volume. This third introductory chapter has done no more than indicate broad problems and lines of enquiry, and subjected a few key categories to more detailed analysis. A general volume of this type cannot discuss all the issues that the evidence raises. Ironically, it is contributions like that of Alex Woolf on northern Britain (chapter 16), where the written sources are thinnest, that have the scope to bring out the ambiguities in reading and translation that affect all historical interpretation. The sources of the early Middle Ages seem particularly problematic for the sort of reasons laid out here. Paucity of sources may appear to allow particular scope to interpretation and assumptions, though these are problems in all periods. The paucity of written sources certainly allows historians of this period to subject their sources to the detailed scrutiny that all historical sources require. That attention is something that the reader, too, must be ready to pay.

Notes

1   As, e.g., Ker, *Catalogue of Manuscripts*, p. 523.
2   *EHD*, I and II; Dumville and Keynes (gen. eds.), *Anglo-Saxon Chronicle*.
3   Charles-Edwards (ed. and trans.), *Chronicle of Ireland*, and cf. the ground-breaking edition of *The Annals of Ulster*, edited and translated by Mac Airt and Mac Niocaill.
4   Ó Corráin, "Nationality and kingship."
5   Broun, "The seven kingdoms."
6   Gillingham, *The English in the Twelfth Century*; Thomas, *The English and the Normans*; Williams, *The English and the Norman Conquest*.
7   Dumville, "Kingship, genealogies and regnal lists"; Thornton, *Kings, Chronologies and Genealogies*.
8   Kelly, "Anglo-Saxon lay society"; Keynes, "Royal government."
9   Clanchy, *From Memory to Written Record*, pp. 1–2.
10 Halsall, *Humour, History and Politics*; Rosenwein, *Anger's Past*, and *Emotional Communities*.
11 Wormald, "Bede, *Beowulf* and the conversion."
12 Etchingham, "Early medieval Irish history," pp. 124–5, citing extensive work by L. Breatnach, J. Carney, K. McCone, and D. Ó Corráin.
13 Campbell (ed.), *Chronicle of Æthelweard*, pp. xlv–lx.
14 Lapidge, *Anglo-Saxon Library*, p. 129.
15 Cf. Lapidge, *Anglo-Latin Literature*, p. vii.
16 Dumville, "Latin and Irish in the *Annals of Ulster*."
17 Charles-Edwards, *Welsh Laws*.
18 Wormald, *Making of English Law*.
19 Insley, "Where did all the charters go?"
20 Love and Lapidge, "England and Wales (600–1550)."
21 Wormald, "Celtic and Anglo-Saxon kingship," pp. 155–8 and esp. n.21.
22 Ibid., p. 157.
23 On these reforms, see Brooks, *Early History of the Church of Canterbury*.
24 Davies, *Llandaff Charters*, cf. eadem, "Charter-writing and its uses" and "The Latin charter-tradition"; Jenkins and Owen, "The Welsh marginalia."
25 Broun, *Charters of Gaelic Scotland and Ireland*; Jackson, *Gaelic Notes in the Book of Deer*.
26 Mac Niocaill, *Notitiae as Leabhar Cheanannais* (translations via CELT website).
27 Chaplais, "Who introduced charters into England?"
28 Flanagan, *Irish Royal Charters*, pp. 11–12.
29 Chaplais, "The origin and authenticity"; Flanagan, *Irish Royal Charters*.
30 Chaplais, "The Anglo-Saxon chancery"; Keynes, *Diplomas of King Æthelred "the Unready"*; and now Kelly, *Charters of Abingdon Abbey*, esp. pp. cxv–cxxxi.
31 Insley, "Assemblies and charters"; Stafford, "Political ideas in late tenth-century England."

32   Bhreathnach, "Medieval Irish history," pp. 264–5.
33   Breatnach, in McCone and Simms (eds.), *Progress in Medieval Irish Studies,* surveys recent work.
34   Breatnach, "Canon law and secular law"; Kelly, *Guide to Early Irish Law.*
35   Cf., especially, Jaski, *Early Irish Kingship and Succession;* Ó Corráin, "Irish regnal succession" and "Nationality and kingship."
36   Stafford, *Queen Emma and Queen Edith.*
37   Beech et al. (eds.), *Personal Names Studies;* Clark, *Words, Names and History.*
38   Abrams and Parsons, "Place-names and the history of Scandinavian settlement"; Townend, *Language and History.*

Further Reading

Even in a period of relatively exiguous sources, it is impossible to list all available editions. Special reference can, however, be made to important online resources and sources, which provide both texts and bibliography. Thus CELT, "the Corpus of Electronic Texts, [which] brings the wealth of Irish literary and historical culture to the Internet, for the use and benefit of everyone worldwide. It has a searchable online textbase consisting of 11 million words, in 961 contemporary and historical documents from many areas, including literature and the other arts." It is based at the University of Cork (http://www.ucc.ie/celt/index.html) and includes a huge range of translations of Irish texts from Old Irish and Latin, plus important web links. Dublin Institute for Advanced Studies' publications catalogue for Irish, Welsh, and related texts is available at: http://www.celt.dias.ie/publications/cat/. Professor Simon Keynes's homepage (http://www.trin.cam.ac.uk/sdk13/asindex.html#bibliog) provides an invaluable portal with a range of links to sources and bibliography on English history, but also more widely, including, for example, the Electronic Sawyer (http://www.trin.cam.ac.uk/sdk13/chartwww/eSawyer.99/eSawyer2.html), listing all known Anglo-Saxon charters, with commentary. For access to texts of most of them, see: http://www.anglo-saxons.net/hwaet/. PASE, the ongoing Prosopography of Anglo-Saxon England, is at: http://www.pase.ac.uk/.

Bibliography

Abrams, L. and Parsons, D. N., "Place-names and the history of Scandinavian settlement in England," in J. Hines, A. Lane, and M. Redknap (eds.), *Land, Sea and Home.* Proceedings of a Conference on Viking-period Settlement, Cardiff, July 2001 (Leeds, 2004), pp. 379–431.

Beech, G. T., Bourin, M., and Chareille, P. (eds.), *Personal Names Studies of Medieval Europe: Social Identity and Familial Structures* (Kalamazoo, MI, 2002).

Bhreathnach, E., "Medieval Irish history at the end of the twentieth century: unfinished work," *Irish Historical Studies,* 32: 126 (2000), 260–71.

Breatnach, L., "Canon law and secular law in early Ireland: the significance of *Bretha Nemed,*" *Peritia,* 3 (1984), 439–59.

Breatnach, L., *A Companion to the Corpus Iuris Hibernici.* Early Irish Law Series 5 (Dublin, 2005).

Brooks, N., *The Early History of the Church of Canterbury* (Leicester, 1984).

Broun, D., *The Charters of Gaelic Scotland and Ireland in the Early and Central Middle Ages* (Cambridge, 1995).

Broun, D., "The seven kingdoms in *De situ Albanie*: a record of Pictish political geography or imaginary map of ancient Alba?," in E. J. Cowan and R. A. McDonald (eds.), *Alba: Celtic Scotland in the Middle Ages* (East Linton, 2000), pp. 24–42.

Campbell, A. (ed.), *The Chronicle of Æthelweard* (London, 1962).

Chaplais, P., "The Anglo-Saxon chancery: from the diploma to the writ," *Journal of the Society of Archivists*, 3: 4 (1966), 160–76, reprinted in F. Ranger (ed.), *Prisca Munimenta*, (1973), pp. 43–62.

Chaplais, P., "The origin and authenticity of the royal Anglo-Saxon diploma," *Journal of the Society of Archivists*, 3: 2 (1965), 48–61; reprinted in F. Ranger (ed.), *Prisca Munimenta* (1973), pp. 28–42.

Chaplais, P., "Who introduced charters into England? The case for Augustine," *Journal of the Society of Archivists*, 3: 10 (1969), 526–42; reprinted in F. Ranger (ed.), *Prisca Munimenta* (1973), pp. 88–107.

Charles-Edwards, T. M. (ed. and trans.), *The Chronicle of Ireland*, 2 vols. Translated Texts for Historians, 44 (Liverpool, 2006).

Charles-Edwards, T. M., *The Welsh Laws* (Cardiff, 1989).

Clanchy, M., *From Memory to Written Record, England 1066–1307*, 2nd edn. (Oxford, 1993).

Clark, C., *Words, Names and History: Selected Writings of Cecily Clark*, ed. P. Jackson (Cambridge, 1995).

Davies, W., "Braint Teilo," *Bulletin of the Board of Celtic Studies*, 26 (1976), 123–33.

Davies, W. "Charter-writing and its uses in early medieval Celtic societies," in H. Pryce (ed.), *Literacy in Medieval Celtic Societies* (Cambridge, 1998), pp. 99–112.

Davies, W., "The Latin charter-tradition in western Britain, Brittany and Ireland in the early mediaeval period," in D. Whitelock, R. McKitterick, and D. Dumville (eds.), *Ireland in Early Mediaeval Europe: Studies in Memory of Kathleen Hughes* (Cambridge, 1982), pp. 258–80.

Davies, W., *The Llandaff Charters* (Aberystwyth, 1979).

Dumville, D. N., "Kingship, genealogies and regnal lists," in P. H. Sawyer and I. N. Wood (eds.), *Early Medieval Kingship* (Leeds, 1977), pp. 72–104.

Dumville, D. N., "Latin and Irish in the *Annals of Ulster*, AD 431–1050," in D. Whitelock, R. McKitterick, and D. Dumville (eds.), *Ireland in Early Mediaeval Europe: Studies in Memory of Kathleen Hughes* (Cambridge, 1982), pp. 320–41.

Dumville, D. N. and Keynes, S. D. (gen. eds.), *The Anglo-Saxon Chronicle: A Collaborative Edition*, 7 vols. to date, various vol. eds. (Cambridge, 1983–).

Etchingham, C., "Early medieval Irish history," in K. McCone and K. Simms (eds.), *Progress in Medieval Irish Studies* (Maynooth, 1996), pp. 123–53.

Flanagan, M. T., *Irish Royal Charters: Texts and Contexts* (Oxford, 2005).

Gillingham, J., *The English in the Twelfth Century: Imperialism, National Identity and Political Values* (Woodbridge, 2000).

Halsall, G. (ed.), *Humour, History and Politics in Late Antiquity and the Early Middle Ages* (Cambridge, 2002).

Insley, C., "Assemblies and charters in late Anglo-Saxon England," in P. S. Barnwell and M. Mostert (eds.), *Political Assemblies in the Earlier Middle Ages* (Turnhout, 2003), pp. 47–59.

Insley, C., "Where did all the charters go? Anglo-Saxon charters and the new politics of the eleventh century," *Anglo-Norman Studies*, 24 (2002), 109–27.

Jackson, K. H., *The Gaelic Notes in the Book of Deer* (Cambridge, 1972).

Jaski, B., *Early Irish Kingship and Succession* (Dublin, 2000).

Jenkins, D. and Owen, M. E., "The Welsh marginalia in the Lichfield Gospels," *Cambridge Medieval Celtic Studies*, 5 (1983), 37–66.

Kelly, F., *A Guide to Early Irish Law* (Dublin, 1988).

Kelly, S. E. "Anglo-Saxon lay society and the written word," in R. McKitterick (ed.), *The Uses of Literacy in Early Mediaeval Europe* (Cambridge, 1990), pp. 36–62.

Kelly, S. E., *Charters of Abingdon Abbey*, part 1 (Oxford, 2000).

Ker, N., *Catalogue of Manuscripts Containing Anglo-Saxon* (Oxford, 1957), plus "A supplement to *Catalogue of Manuscripts containing Anglo-Saxon*," *Anglo-Saxon England*, 5 (1976), 121–31.

Keynes, S., *The Diplomas of King Æthelred "the Unready" 978–1016: A Study in their Use as Historical Evidence* (Cambridge, 1980).

Keynes, S., "Royal government and the written word in late Anglo-Saxon England," in R. McKitterick (ed.), *The Uses of Literacy in Early Mediaeval Europe* (Cambridge, 1990), pp. 226–57.

Lapidge, M., *Anglo-Latin Literature, 900–1066* (London, 1993).

Lapidge, M., *The Anglo-Saxon Library* (Oxford, 2006).

Love, R. and Lapidge, M., "England and Wales (600–1550)," in G. Philippart (ed.), *Hagiographies: histoire internationale de la littérature hagiographique latine et vernaculaire, en Occident, des origines à 1500*, vol. 3 (Turnhout, 2001), pp. 203–325.

Mac Airt, S. and Mac Niocaill, G. (eds. and trans.), *The Annals of Ulster (to AD 1131)*. Part I: *Text and Translation* (Dublin, 1983).

Mac Niocaill, G., *Notitiae as Leabhar Cheanannais, 1033–1161* (Dublin, 1961).

McCone, K. and Simms, K., *Progress in Medieval Irish Studies* (Maynooth, 1996).

Ó Corráin, D., "Irish regnal succession: a reappraisal," *Studia Hibernica*, 11 (1971), 7–39.

Ó Corráin, D., "Nationality and kingship in pre-Norman Ireland," in T. W. Moody (ed.), *Nationality and the Pursuit of National Independence* (Belfast, 1978), pp. 1–35.

Rosenwein, B. H. (ed.), *Anger's Past: Social Uses of an Emotion in the Middle Ages* (Cornell, 1998).

Rosenwein, B. H., *Emotional Communities in the Early Middle Ages* (Cornell, 2006).

Stafford, P., "Political ideas in late tenth-century England: charters as evidence," in P. Stafford, J. L. Nelson, and J. Martindale (eds.), *Law, Laity and Solidarities: Essays in Honour of Susan Reynolds* (Manchester, 2001), pp. 68–82.

Stafford, P., *Queen Emma and Queen Edith: Queenship and Women's Power in Eleventh-century England* (Oxford, 1997).

Thomas, H. M., *The English and the Normans: Ethnic Hostility, Assimilation and Identity, 1066–c.1220* (Oxford, 2003).

Thornton, D. E., *Kings, Chronologies and Genealogies: Studies in the Political History of Early Medieval Ireland and Wales*. Occasional Publications of the Oxford Unit for Prosopographical Research, 10 (Oxford, 2003).

Townend, M., *Language and History in Viking Age England: Linguistic Relations between Speakers of Old Norse and Old English* (Turnhout, 2002).

Williams, A., *The English and the Norman Conquest* (Woodbridge, 1995).

Wormald, P., "Bede, *Beowulf* and the conversion of the Anglo-Saxon aristocracy," in R. T. Farrell (ed.), *Bede and Anglo-Saxon England*. Papers in Honour of the 1300th Anniversary of the Birth of Bede, given at Cornell University in 1973 and 1974. British Archaeological Reports, British series, 46 (Oxford, 1978), pp. 32–95.

Wormald, P., "Celtic and Anglo-Saxon kingship: some further thoughts," in P. E. Szarmach (ed.), *Sources of Anglo-Saxon Culture* (Kalamazoo, MI, 1986), pp. 151–83.

Wormald, P., *The Making of English Law: King Alfred to the Twelfth Century*, vol. I: *Legislation and its Limits* (Oxford, 1999).

PART II

Britain and Ireland, c.500–c.750

CHAPTER FOUR

Britain and Ireland, c.500

BARBARA YORKE

Sources and Approaches

"The peoples and kingdoms of Britain [are] divided among the speakers of four different languages, British, Pictish, Irish and English."[1] Bede, in his *Ecclesiastical History of the English People*, which was completed in 731, introduces the four main ethnic groupings of Britain and Ireland in c.500. To go beyond Bede to delineate the exact geographical deposition or political arrangements of the four groups within the islands is a difficult task. The main problem is the shortage of contemporary written sources. In the post-Roman world literacy was linked with the spread of Christianity, and by 500 that religion was only widespread among the British who had been introduced to it when they had been part of the Roman Empire. The main surviving works of British authorship produced in the fifth and sixth centuries are limited to St. Patrick's *Confession* and *Letter to Coroticus*,[2] and Gildas's *De Excidio Britanniae* ("The Ruin of Britain"), which was probably written in the first half of the sixth century.[3] Gildas provides a brief résumé of recent history, but his main aim in writing was to make his Christian audience aware of their responsibilities as the new Chosen People of God; his work, like many other early medieval writings from Britain and Ireland, is suffused with Old Testament imagery and parallels.

There were undoubtedly Christians in Ireland by 500, but the earliest surviving native Irish writings (other than inscriptions) are of late sixth-century date. That was the period at which the conversion of the Anglo-Saxons and Picts began, but, although there are relatively extensive Anglo-Saxon written sources of various types from the seventh century onward, virtually no written records have survived from Pictland, though there is every reason to believe that they once existed. There are also some observations from writers in mainland Europe that throw light on the situation in Britain and Ireland, but the number of contemporary sources is limited compared to later centuries. The medieval peoples of Britain were concerned about the apparent lack of information for the period in which they seemed to have originated, but later sources purporting to describe what occurred in the fifth and sixth centuries often had to resort to myths rather than hard fact to fill the gap. An extreme example is provided by King Arthur who probably began life as a British folk-hero, or even as a god, and was given a bogus historical reality in the ninth-century *Historia Brittonum* when he was fitted into an historical format and assigned the achievements of others, such as the victory at *Mons Badonicus* c.500 which Gildas appears to attribute to a British leader called Ambrosius Aurelianus.[4]

Historians can appear to have expended much energy over the past 30 years or so in reducing the number of sources that can be deemed reliable for the reconstruction of Britain and Ireland c.500; archaeologists, meanwhile, have increased them by the recovery and study of a wide range of sites and artifacts. Many examples can be found in the following pages of a constructive interplay of written and archaeological source material. But there are also currently major differences of opinion about how evidence should be interpreted amongst archaeologists as well as between archaeologists and experts in other disciplines. Archaeologists and linguists, for instance, have reached very different conclusions about the scale of migration needed to have brought about the changes in culture and language apparent in eastern Britain in the fifth and sixth centuries. One of the problems in interpreting archaeological evidence is that not all sites seem to tell the same story, and there is an important broader lesson to be drawn from this. In spite of what general histories such as this volume encourage us to do, not all the British, Irish, Anglo-Saxons, and Picts had identical histories within this period; experiences may have varied between regions within their territories. Therefore, although the historian of this period has to try to bring out the major trends, allowance must also be made for regional variation.

Ideally, all potential sources of evidence should be reconciled, but major areas of contention need to be recognized and cannot always be smoothed over in our present state of knowledge. When using written sources, those produced closest in date are potentially the most valuable, but are not necessarily any more straightforward than later accounts. Inevitably, with a shortage of written records, one has to project back to a certain extent from the better recorded periods of the seventh century or later, but this is a risky process which may not make sufficient allowance for rapidly changing conditions. Above all, in focusing on the period around 500 one is trying to discover how the transition was made from late Roman Britain to the world of the numerous Anglo-Saxon and Celtic kingdoms that was known to Bede and his contemporaries. As will become apparent from the discussion that follows, the political geography of the period around 500 was very different from that with which we are familiar from the later medieval period onward. The boundaries of England, Wales, and Scotland are not meaningful entities for understanding the fifth and sixth centuries, but reference is made to them in the following discussion to assist the orientation of the modern reader.

The Late Roman Background

Although books and courses on the early history of Britain often draw a firm dividing line between the Roman and early medieval periods, the reality was not that clear cut. The inclusion of the greater part of Britain within the Roman Empire had a profound effect upon its development and on the post-Roman structures that emerged subsequently. Ireland and Scotland north of the Forth–Clyde isthmus (the later territories of the Dál Riata and the Picts) were not included within the Roman province of *Britannia*, but were nevertheless in its sphere of influence. Irish and northern Scottish traders are likely to have visited the Roman province, and some of their countrymen may have found employment in other spheres including the army; a monument to an Irishman, possibly early fifth century in date, has been recovered from the Roman town of Silchester. The monument provides another indicator of the range of Roman influence even in areas of Britain not directly controlled from Rome because its inscription is carved in ogham, a script of incised lines around a central staff that was developed as a means of recording simple inscriptions in Old Irish, and is believed to have been inspired by Roman scripts. Pictish symbols that are found carved in stone and on metalwork and other materials may also have functioned as a form of script and been developed in similar circumstances, though the date of the earliest symbols and their exact significance remain controversial.

The Roman authorities tried to keep the peoples on their borders quiescent through treaties and gifts, and often encouraged small, diverse groups to coalesce into larger units with which it was more convenient for them to negotiate, but relations were not always harmonious. In the fourth century, raids from the north and west by the Picts and Scots became a major problem. The people Roman writers referred to as the Scots (*Scotti*) were Irish-speaking (Gaelic) raiders from Ireland and the west coast of Scotland. (In the ninth century, rulers of the west coast *Scotti* became kings of much of the area we know as Scotland which is why it has that name still today rather than being known as Pictland or similar.) A third group of raiders that afflicted *Britannia* in the fourth century were the Saxons, a catch-all Roman term for Germanic peoples from the North Sea coastal areas of Germany and southern Scandinavia. These peoples were also outside the Roman Empire, but had a history of interaction with it similar to that of the Celtic areas bordering Britain. "Saxons" too were involved in trade with the empire and were recruited into its army; they also developed their own linear script of runes for inscriptions in Germanic dialects. In 367, these three "barbarian" groups are recorded as having joined forces and inflicted a major defeat on the military forces of the Roman province.[5]

By 400, the Roman diocese of *Britannia* was divided into four, or possibly five, provinces, whose major units of more local government were the *civitates* based on older tribal territories. One of the major questions is how far these Roman administrative units continued to be relevant in the new polities that had begun to form by 500. The degree of Roman influence within the major provinces varied. The north of England and southern Scotland had originally formed part of a militarized frontier zone delineated by the Hadrian and Antonine walls. The Antonine Wall, which controlled the land between the firths of the Clyde and the Forth, had only intermittently been occupied by Roman forces, but the area between it and Hadrian's Wall probably remained in the Roman sphere of influence through treaties with the local peoples.[6] Although native rather than Roman culture predominated, considerable finds of Roman artifacts have been made from sites like Traprain Law (Lothian), a hillfort of the Votadini, which may be either the fruits of diplomatic treaties with Rome or, alternatively, the profits that could be made from raiding once Roman military control began to slip. In contrast, the area based around Hadrian's Wall, the northern frontier of the Roman province of *Britannia Secunda* in the fourth century, was more intensively occupied and large civilian settlements grew up around the forts. Inscriptions show that the wall's garrison was widely recruited from within the Roman Empire.

Many Roman soldiers are likely to have married local women and settled in its vicinity with their descendants still serving as frontier troops (*limitanei*) in the fourth century. St. Patrick's family may have owned an estate close to one of the civilian settlements linked to the forts if the *Bannavem Taburniae* that Patrick refers to in his *Confessio* has been correctly identified as being in the vicinity of Birdoswald (*Banna*).

In other highland areas of England and Wales one finds that overt signs of Romanization were limited to a few controlling settlements. Roman authorities were keen to exploit the mineral resources of areas like Cornwall and north Wales, but the upland farming did not yield sufficient profits to attract the type of agri-business and exploitation that transformed the lowland regions through the introduction of many of the classic features of Roman control – towns, villas, roads, temples, and the like. But, increasingly, archaeologists have begun to question how deep the Romanization of even lowland Britain went.[7] There are signs well before the end of the fourth century that many towns were not functioning as they should have been in a stable Roman society; public buildings were not being kept up, and stone build-ings were replaced by simpler, timber-framed ones. Villas were beginning to go out of use or were adapted for simpler living. But the picture is not uniform throughout the whole country. In the west of England, in the province of *Britannia Prima*, substantial new villas with mosaics were erected in the fourth century, suggesting that the nobility of this area were doing well at a time when in the centre and east, the provinces of *Flavia Caesariensis* and *Maxima Caesariensis*, there was greater retrenchment. Such variations make it hard to grasp the overall picture, and as a result there are major differences in interpretation about what exactly was happening in late Roman Britain. But one interpretation that seems to be gaining increasing acceptance is that many aspects of the transformation from Roman to early medieval society were already apparent in the fourth century. It can be seen, for instance, in changing burial rituals, including the reuse of prehistoric monuments, and the building of what may have been the timber residences of local leaders in former official buildings, such as the bath-house at Wroxeter or the Roman forts at Birdoswald and South Shields. The key to many of the differences observable in Britain and Ireland in 500 lies in the Roman past.

The Break with Rome

The sixth-century Byzantine historian Zosimus, drawing on an earlier written source, ascribed the final rupture between Britain and Rome, in 409 or 410, to the deter-mination of the British to manage their own affairs and to organize their own defense against the "barbarians" who were attacking them.[8] Although British leaders may have taken the final decision, it is likely to have been provoked by the failure of Rome adequately to provide for the province while at the same time exacting increasingly large payments from its inhabitants. The discontent of the main Roman forces serving in Britain must have exacerbated the situation. Armies stationed in the province had raised a series of emperors within Britain and then left with them to support their claims, probably leaving the country with only locally raised defensive forces such as the *limitanei* of Hadrian's Wall. The failure to defend the borders adequately encour-aged the Scots, Picts, and Saxons to be increasingly bold in their raiding, though their actions may also have been stimulated by a downturn in traditional forms of revenue if trade and diplomatic payments were no longer flowing freely to leaders who had come to rely on them to underpin their status.

How well the British coped with their independence is one of the areas where the greatest differences of opinion exist between specialists of the period. A continental chronicle records a serious Saxon incursion in 408–9, but Zosimus implies that this was successfully dealt with by British leaders. Further than that, much depends on how much reliance one places on the narrative of Gildas. This lacks specific dates, though he has a crucial reference to an appeal to Rome for help made in the third consulship of Aetius in 446–7 after which, he says, a decision was made to recruit Saxons to fight as federate forces against the Picts. Such a decision would have been very much in line with what was happening in other areas of Europe in this period. When adequate defense from Rome was not forthcoming, local leaders were obliged to try to reach favorable terms with their invaders. And, as in other areas of Europe, those with the greater military power eventually got the upper hand, or as Gildas rather more vividly puts it, "they first of all fixed their dreadful claws on the east side of the island . . . the mother lioness learnt that her first contingent had prospered, and she sent a second and larger troop of satellite dogs."[9] Bede and various Kentish sources were later to adapt Gildas's account to present the invitation as resulting in the arrival of Hengist and Horsa, founders of the royal house of Kent, but the historical validity of this material is doubtful. However, a variety of sources suggests that at least part of eastern England came under Germanic control at some point in the decade 440–50. Against this tense background of raiding and rival groups bidding for power as Roman order and culture rapidly dwindled, we can attempt an overview of Britain and Ireland c.500.

The Irish

The internal structure of Ireland had not been affected by Roman rule in the sense that it had not been invaded or had Romanized structures imposed upon it, but the stasis, if not stagnation, that seems to be apparent in the archaeological record for the first to fourth centuries AD may suggest that the Roman presence across the Irish Sea had a repressive effect.[10] However, in the fourth century, a new period of settlement expansion seems to have begun. This coincides with the successful raiding of British territory, though there may have also been other, more peaceful, contacts with the apparently prosperous west of Britain and with further afield: with the Channel affected by Saxon raiding, the western route to mainland Europe via the Irish Sea and the Bristol Channel came to have increasing importance as finds of imported goods in eastern Ireland and western Britain suggest.

One commodity that seems to have passed from the west of Britain to some areas of Ireland in the fourth and fifth centuries was Christianity. By 431, Christians in Ireland were sufficiently numerous for the pope to dispatch a mission led by Palladius, and later tradition suggests that he was based in Leinster.[11] Other Christians in Ireland came less willingly – converts from Britain who had been captured in raiding and sold into slavery. Patrick, of course, is the best known of these. He escaped from captivity, but subsequently returned, probably in the latter part of the fifth century, to bring Christianity to other areas of Ireland, including the far west where he had served his time as a slave. Patrick says that large numbers were captured with him.

Rulers who could command successful raiding or trading fleets (not necessarily the same people for both activities) had access to new sources of wealth and so to the means to develop their power bases. Contemporary annals were not kept in Irish religious houses until the seventh century, but the annals compiled retrospectively for the period around 500 suggest a period of considerable aggression between the more powerful kingdoms. What is more difficult to assess is whether this was a new development after a period of relative peace. It is possible that the opportunities provided by the decline of Roman control stimulated new political developments within Ireland, such as the development of provincial overkingships; it does appear to be in the period around 500 that new dynasties, like those of the Cenél Conaill in the north and the Eóganachta in the south which would dominate early Christian Ireland, came to prominence. The sources do not permit a simple overview of the organization of the country c.500, and even for 700 this can only be achieved in part.[12] However, it is likely that the complexity of small kingdoms and peoples visible at the latter date was also a dominant feature of Ireland two centuries earlier.

Gaelic-speaking Irish were not only to be found in Ireland, for by 500 there were settlements of Irish people in Britain. The presence of Irish settlers in western parts of Wales and the south-west of England is indicated by place-names, personal names, and ogham inscriptions.[13] The greatest concentration is in Dyfed in the south-west of Wales whose royal house appears to have been of Irish origin. Later sources, both Irish and British, contain somewhat muddled descriptions of how an Irish dynasty came to be ruling in Wales. The ninth-century *Historia Brittonum* claimed that a branch of the Déissi from Munster moved to Wales when expelled by their enemies. Historians might be inclined to be suspicious of the Irish origin of the kings of Dyfed were it not for the supporting information from memorial stones such as that inscribed in both Latin and Irish to Voteporix "Protector." Voteporix may either be the King Vortipor of Dyfed who was one of the "tyrants" addressed by Gildas in *De Excidio Britanniae* or, perhaps more likely, a kinsman of his. The use of an Irish ogham inscription on the stone implies that Voteporix was likely to have been a speaker of Irish, and the spread of ogham inscriptions in general suggests that Irish was widely spoken in south-western Wales in the fifth and sixth centuries by an elite at least. But the use of Latin, including the title "Protector," and the retention of the British name of the province (Dyfed derives from Demetae, the name of the Iron Age inhabitants and their subsequent *civitas*) suggests a certain amount of assimilation to native society, and it does not appear that the kings of Dyfed remained actively involved in the political affairs of Ireland. Gildas draws no distinction between them and their British contemporaries, about whom he is equally critical.

Until recently, it would have been normal to present Scottish Dalriada, the Irish province of Argyll and the southern Hebrides, as a comparable example of colonization from Ireland. An entry for 501 in one of the Irish annals records that "Fergus Mór, mac Erc, with the nation of Dál Riata, took [or held] part of Britain, and died there," and this has been traditionally taken as evidence of a Dalriadic conquest of the area around the turn of the century. However, this annal may be no earlier than the tenth century in date, and the archaeological record provides no support for a major invasion or settlement.[14] Yet it is undoubtedly the case that Argyll was a Gaelic-speaking province and ruled in the sixth century by Dalriadic kings whose family also held territory in Antrim in the north of Ireland. The Irish orientation of the province is made abundantly clear in Adomnán's *Life* of St. Columba of Iona (d.597), and Bede knew an earlier foundation legend concerning an eponymous King Reuda who had crossed from Ireland. The solution may be that the Dalriadic lands in northern Ireland and western Scotland had been a united kingdom for some considerable time before the sixth century.[15] It is not uncommon to find provinces united rather than divided by sea in prehistoric and early medieval periods. There therefore may have been no Irish conquest of western Scotland c.500, though there could have been significant opportunities for its rulers to develop their powers at around this time as the creation of the fort at Dunadd may suggest. The later interest in Fergus Mór may be explained by the fact that the later kings of all Scotland claimed descent from him, but he may also have been a significant ruler who took advantage of the new opportunities available in the post-Roman world to increase the prospects of his dynasty. Gildas saw the *Scotti* who oppressed the British as coming from the north-west, perhaps implying it was the Argyll province he had in mind.

The Picts

The Picts were at one time seen as a rather mysterious people with customs and language that were different from those of other areas of Britain,[16] and there are enthusiasts in Scotland who continue to see matters in this way. However, the name of the Picts is not of great antiquity and may have been bestowed by Roman writers around the turn of the fourth century to describe a new coalition of peoples whose earlier recorded names appear to be British in origin. It has been suggested that the name means "the painted ones" and refers to a custom of tattooing, but other explanations are also possible. The Picts belonged to the same broad cultural grouping as the other non-Irish peoples of Scotland and seem to have spoken predominantly the same variant of the Celtic language (British-Welsh P-Celtic as opposed to the Gaelic-Irish Q-Celtic).

However, within the territory of the Picts there may have been significant subdivisions. Roman authorities often refer to two major peoples in the area (though not always by the same names) and this may have been perpetuated into the historic period when there are indications of a division into northern and southern Picts either side of the Moray Firth. The situation may have been even more complex, though the alleged seven Pictish provinces, interpreted as the remnants of once independent peoples, have at very least been subject to some later reworking.[17] In the seventh century, the province of Fortriu, which recent research suggests was the province of the northern Picts,[18] seems to have been dominant and may well have been establishing the seeds of that power in the fifth century when Pictish fleets were raiding the eastern coasts. However, it is difficult to know whether the territory of the Picts had reached its full extent by 500, and in particular whether Orkney, Shetland, and some other areas of the Atlantic north and west, which appear culturally rather different in the late prehistoric and Roman periods, were integrated into it. Adomnán records that in the late sixth century Orkney had its own ruler, but that he recognized the overlordship of the chief Pictish king.[19]

Around 500 the Picts were probably still progressing from being disparate groups to becoming a more united people under common leadership. A common identity among the nobility was an important element of this, and is most readily visible through the distribution of Pictish symbols on stone and other media. Finds come from the whole of Pictland, including Orkney and Shetland, but are not generally dated as early as 500, though there are speculations that earlier examples tattooed on skin or carved in wood may once have existed. The earliest symbols we have may date from later in the sixth century, but the whole question of their date and genesis is a controversial one on which several different opinions exist.[20] One of the most exciting suggestions to emerge from recent discussion is that some symbols may have functioned as a form of writing and were used in a similar way to ogham inscriptions.[21] Others like the splendid bulls from Burghead may have been linked with Pictish religious beliefs or were totems associated with powerful families.

The British

There were variations in the way in which the different provinces and geographical zones of Roman Britain reacted to the severance of links with empire in c.410. In the provinces of *Britannia Prima* (Wales and the south-west), *Britannia Secunda* (the north), and the military zone, north of Hadrian's Wall, in southern Scotland, kingdoms had developed by 500 or soon after, and local "big men" may have begun a consolidation of power as Roman effectiveness waned in the latter part of the fourth century. In these areas, there is little sign in the archaeological evidence of any major disruption or shift of settlement between 400 and 500. It is even possible that in the west, and perhaps elsewhere, Magnus Maximus, who held the military command in Britain before he declared himself emperor in 383 and plays a prominent role in later Welsh traditions about the period, ceded defense of the area to local chiefs.[22] The earliest references to kings are the five contemporary rulers of the south-west and Wales who are castigated by Gildas in his *De Excidio Britanniae* and who seem to have been at least the second generation in power at the time he wrote, probably in the early sixth century.[23] Three of his rulers, or tyrants as he prefers to call them, Constantine of Dumnonia (the south-west peninsula), Vortipor of Dyfed, and Maglocunus of Gwynedd, controlled areas than can be identified with specific Roman *civitates*. The areas controlled by the other two, Aurelius Caninus and Cuneglasus, are the subject of some debate, but the medieval kingdoms of Wales can broadly be seen as evolving out of the Roman political geography of the region.[24] Aurelius may have been a kinsman of Ambrosius Aurelianus, "the last of the Romans," who led a major victory over the Saxons at the unidentified *Mons Badonicus* in c.500 which kept the western areas of Britain free from Saxon incursion up to the time that Gildas was writing.

By 500 there were probably also kingdoms that had developed from administrative units of the Roman period in the area between the Hadrian and Antonine walls, though reliable contemporary evidence for them is limited. This was the area of the "Old North" whose rulers were much celebrated in later Welsh poetry, some of which, including *Υ Gododdin*, may have had its origins in the sixth and seventh centuries. From these poems and occasional references in other sources we can identify various northern British kingdoms whose origins may go back to around 500. The three most prominent in the poetry and genealogies are those of the Gododdin, of Dumbarton and of Rheged, but there may have been other smaller or short-lived kingdoms of which even less is known. The name of the Gododdin is derived from that of the Votadini, the people who lived in the same area of south-eastern Scotland in the later Iron Age and Roman periods; Edinburgh appears to have been their significant royal center in the sixth century. The impressive rocky fortification of Dumbarton (*Alt Clut*, "the rock of the Clyde") was used to identify the rulers of a kingdom based in this area, the land of the northern Dumnonii, which was known later as the kingdom of Strathclyde and survived into the tenth century. The kingdom of Rheged is in many ways the most shadowy, but at its full extent at the end of the sixth century under King Urien, it may well have dominated both sides of the Solway Firth, including the northern part of *Britannia Secunda*. There are other possible candidates for British kingdoms c.500 within the former province of *Britannia Secunda*, including Bernicia and Deira, the kingdoms based in Northumbria and eastern Yorkshire respectively that by 600 were in the hands of Anglo-Saxon dynasties. A British kingdom in Elmet, in western Yorkshire, is known to have been in existence c.600.[25]

It is more difficult to say what happened in the two predominantly lowland provinces of *Flavia Caesariensis* and *Maxima Caesariensis* in the east and south, but we have no evidence of the formation of British kingdoms in these areas. Gildas depicts councilors meeting under the aegis of "a proud tyrant" (identified in other sources as Vortigern) to decide to use Saxons as federate forces which could suggest continuation of the Roman structures of civil government, a conclusion that receives some support from an account of the visit of Bishop Germanus to *Verulamium* (St. Albans) in 429.[26] The figure of Vortigern, if his historicity can be accepted, suggests circumstances in sub-Roman Britain in which a supreme ruler could have emerged over some of the provinces, as Syagrius did in Gaul, but Gildas implies that the decision to recruit Saxon federates put an end to any such ambitions.

Archaeological evidence does not readily reveal "events," and radically different interpretations have been made based on it for the history of the British between 400 and 500. The rapid decline of towns, villas, and other accoutrements of Romanization has led some to argue for a complete "systems collapse" in fifth-century Britain.[27] The changes may appear more rapid than was actually the case because the latest buildings were in timber rather than stone and so leave less trace, and the sudden cessation of imports of coin and pottery meant the loss of some of the foremost indicators of occupation. Other archaeologists have preferred to stress the continuity in farming and use of many sites; villas and their owners may have vanished, but ordinary people had to stay put and support themselves. The same evidence can be interpreted in quite different ways. A decline in the amount of cultivatable land, particularly the more marginal areas, has been seen by the first school of thought as evidence for a major collapse of the population in a time of chaos, while the second would see contraction because it was no longer necessary to produce such a large surplus to pay Roman taxes. These differences in interpretation have quite major implications for the question of whether the later Anglo-Saxon kingdoms were able to draw on a Roman infrastructure of local government and communities.

The study of the British in the south and east is made difficult because of an apparent lack of diagnostic archaeological evidence for a specifically British presence in the fifth and sixth centuries. New Germanic forms of pottery and metalwork dominate the small finds and, coupled with Gildas's remarks about inhabitants fleeing in the face of Saxon advance, led to the conclusion in the nineteenth and early twentieth centuries that any remaining British were annihilated. The advent of scientific forms of dating and analysis can help make them more visible. In the Thames valley, in the midst of an area of early Saxon settlement, radio-carbon dating has shown that at Queensford Farm, near Dorchester-on-Thames, a cemetery of unfurnished graves that began life in the fourth century was still in use in the sixth century. Continuity can also be found at sites away from the earliest concentrations of Anglo-Saxon material. Particularly interesting is the case of *Verulamium*–St. Albans. We know from material associated with Germanus of Auxerre that, when he visited *Verulamium* in 429, he found the cult of St. Alban flourishing. Gildas believed the cult was still active in his day, and St. Alban and the place of his martyrdom survived to be revered by the Anglo-Saxons after their conversion. There are no Anglo-Saxon cemeteries in the vicinity of St. Albans, and few finds of Germanic material culture. There seems to be a general continuity of land use in this part of Hertfordshire and the local governmental units of the Anglo-Saxon period may well be based on similar Roman units of the *pagi*, insofar as these can be identified.[28]

In 500 there were areas that fell between the Anglo-Saxon controlled communities on south and east coasts and the upper Thames and the known British kingdoms of the west and north. But we have very little indication of how these middle-zone areas were managed and remarkably few archaeological sites in them where occupation has been dated to the fifth and sixth centuries. Possibly, Roman local government structures still functioned in this area, and it has been suggested that the *judices* whom Gildas castigated along with his tyrant kings could be some sort of locally appointed magistrates.[29] These problematic middle areas were absorbed into the expanding Anglo-Saxon provinces in the course of the sixth and seventh centuries.

The Anglo-Saxons

Finds of distinctive burial forms, weaponry, dress-assemblages, and building traditions make it clear that there was migration from Germanic-speaking areas of northern Europe to eastern and southern England during the fifth century.[30] Gildas's account of the recruitment of some Germanic people as federates may help to explain the origins of settlement in eastern England, but is unlikely to give us the whole story. The fifth century was a time of movement of Germanic peoples within Europe from homelands that had the ability to support a limited population to the more fertile former areas of the Roman Empire, and movement to Britain has to be seen as part of this wider trend. The Germanic settlement was not a single event, as nineteenth-century authors liked to present it, but a more complex movement of peoples in a range of circumstances spread over many years. Fifth-century finds of Germanic material are very varied in nature and suggest that settlers came from many different Germanic areas, including Norway and Francia, even if the bulk was from the North Sea areas of modern Germany and Denmark. The numbers involved are difficult to estimate, and this is one of the topics of current debate on which very different conclusions have been reached. Changes in language and culture might seem to suggest that migration must have been substantial, but there is a need to distinguish the initial fifth-century impact from the results of centuries of dominance by Anglo-Saxon rulers. For instance, although the place-names of England are predominantly of Old English origin (except in the western extremities), only a small proportion of these names go back to the fifth century; rather, they were bestowed during a much longer period of Anglo-Saxon rule. The archaeological evidence suggests regional variation in the scale of settlement even in the south and east. There seems to have been heavier settlement in East Anglia and Lincolnshire, where large cremation-only cemeteries have been found, than in the areas of the Thames valley and further south with smaller mixed or inhumation-only cemeteries. Some areas such as the Chilterns are notable for an absence of any evidence of Germanic settlement in the fifth and sixth centuries.

Bede says that the Germanic settlers were divided into three main groups of Angles, Saxons, and Jutes. The names of later kingdoms give an indication of the division between the Anglian areas of eastern England and those of the Saxons in the Thames valley and to the south. The division between Saxon and Anglian areas broadly follows that between the two late Roman provinces of *Flavia* and *Maxima Caesariensis*. It is probably the case that settlers from Saxony dominated in the Saxon areas and settlers from Angeln (roughly the area of Schleswig-Holstein) were in the majority in eastern England, but, as already noted, the origins of Germanic peoples coming to Britain were more diverse than this. "Saxon" and "Anglian" identities must have deepened and been consolidated after settlement within the two different British provinces. Bede goes on to explain that the people of Kent, the Isle of Wight, and the part of Hampshire opposite the island claimed to be of Jutish descent by which a link with the Jutland area of Denmark is usually presumed, though the history of the name "Jutland" is complex and not fully understood. The Jutes controlled the shortest crossing points between southern England and Francia, and presumably for this reason considerable Frankish influence can be traced within them in the sixth century, especially in Kent.[31]

That by 500 the division into Anglian, Saxon, and Jutish provinces was a reality, and not just a later rationalization made by Bede, is suggested by the emergence of different dialects and of distinctive features in the dress of elite women in the three areas.[32] Both these factors suggest that the more wealthy or powerful people within the three districts recognized some form of common identity and were habitually associating together, for instance, in the type of public assemblies attested from many Germanic areas where important ceremonies could be held and judicial and other decisions were made.[33] Women's dress can be considered as a type of German *tracht* that could be worn on these and other special occasions in which the differences in costume, seen in variations in the form and positioning of brooches and other fastenings, might indicate regional or family origins.[34]

The exact nature of the political organization in southern and eastern England c.500 is unclear. Burials imply stratification within society,[35] but even the richest fall short of the distinctive "princely burials" found from the late sixth and seventh centuries when kingdoms were coming into existence. The homelands of the Germanic settlers are not known to have had kings in the fifth and sixth centuries either. In the eighth century, the Old Saxons of Germany were a loose confederation of provinces each with its own leading families, and it may be that we should envisage some similar form of organization in the Anglian, Saxon, and Jutish areas of Britain c.500.[36] The increasingly elaborate burials in the sixth century of the leading families represented in the major cemeteries have been seen as indicative of an insecure society in which dominant positions in localities were contested. Such contests could be compatible with an earlier organization along the lines of the Old Saxon model.

Although the archaeological evidence from southern and eastern England appears predominantly "Germanic" in form, most commentators agree that there must have been significant survival of the original British inhabitants, though there is less agreement on the precise circumstances and level at which this occurred. Archaeologists on the whole prefer to argue for substantial assimilation of Anglo-Saxon and British populations, and some are prepared to suggest that the majority of people buried in Anglo-Saxon-type cemeteries are the descendants of British who have adopted Germanic dress and other customs.[37] Historians on the whole are less sanguine about the idea of peaceful acculturation, and more inclined to posit British survival as slaves or dependent peasantry, and that assimilation may have been achieved by the killing of British men and the sexual appropriation of their women. But once again regional differences should be expected. The Anglian areas are more demonstrably Germanic in their material culture than the Saxon, and in the latter there are more signs of possible British integration at a higher level, including the claim that the founder of the West Saxon house was Cerdic, whose name is derived from British Caraticos. Bernicia, the most northerly of the Anglian provinces, has produced relatively little of the Germanic type of material found further south and may still have been in British hands c.500. In the sixth century it may have been subject to the type of elite takeover postulated for Dyfed.

Ethnic Identity

In the tenth century, Regino of Prüm explained that "different peoples differ between themselves in descent, manners, language and laws."[38] Early medieval writers were conscious that there were differences of this type between the various peoples of the British Isles. Bede equated peoples with the languages that they spoke, while Gildas believed that the British who had lived under Roman rule differed in fundamental ways from their Irish, Pictish, and Saxon enemies, who also differed from one another. According to him, the Scots and the Picts "were to some extent different in their customs, but they were in perfect accord in their greed for bloodshed: and they were readier to cover their villainous faces with hair than their private parts and neighbouring regions with clothes."[39] Archaeological evidence confirms that the different peoples of Britain did dress differently, and there is wider evidence from medieval Europe for variation in hairstyles and facial hair as ethnic markers. It was not only when early medieval people opened their mouths that their origins became apparent for their whole appearance would have signaled this already. Dress and outward appearance reinforced group identity; they conveyed this information to outsiders, but would also have been of great value in helping individuals with the same background to identify one another, for instance, on a battlefield. Matters of appearance would have also distinguished different social groups within a people's territory: freemen from slaves and dependent peasants; nobleman from ordinary freemen. Individuals probably carried multiple identities. They might not only be a Pict or a Scot, but were also a member of a particular family, social group, and region. The varied terminology through which an individual could be described in early medieval Irish sources could convey all these things.[40] Such information may also have been encoded in other ways through such things as Anglo-Saxon female dress and burial ritual.

In the period around 500 new peoples were being formed within Britain and this involved the creation of new identities to support them, a process known as ethnogenesis. The Pictish symbols are seemingly an example of the creation of new forms to support a new identity; the development of different dress-sets for women in the main Anglo-Saxon regions was another. A properly constituted early medieval people, as Regino of Prüm says, was believed to have a common descent, and this belief was encapsulated in the origin legend that, at its most basic in Britain and Ireland, described boatloads of new people arriving under the leadership of the founder of a dynasty at some suitably distant period.

But if new identities for whole people could be formed in this apparently conscious way, did it mean that an individual could recalibrate his identity and move from one people to another? Such questions of individual identity are significant for the vexed question of whether large numbers of British in eastern England had adopted a Germanic identity by 500. The identity received in childhood could be remarkably tenacious. Although Patrick spent a significant part of his adult life in Ireland, first as a slave for six years and then as a missionary and bishop, he never relinquished his identity as a British nobleman nor, like Gildas, his awareness of a gulf between the British and their Celtic neighbors. Key issues must have been the strength of the incentive to change and the willingness of the host people to accept it. Occasional references from Bede and other authors to "British" peasants in seventh-century contexts in areas that had apparently been under Anglo-Saxon influence for some time suggest that the process of assimilation might sometimes take longer than is commonly believed, but in the long term it evidently did occur.

Conclusion

The period around 500 has commonly been designated the "Dark Ages," both because of the shortage of written sources and because of what was perceived as a decline from the heights of Roman civilization. New archaeological evidence and approaches to the material are shedding increasing light on the period, and, though it was undoubtedly a time of much violence and uncertainty for the population, there was not the complete rupture with the past that has sometimes been assumed. Through the still foggy picture we can discern that by 500 the groupings of people that were to dominate the history of succeeding centuries were already in place.

Notes

1   Colgrave and Mynors (eds.), *Bede's Ecclesiastical History*, iii. 6.
2   Hood (ed. and trans.), *St. Patrick*.
3   Lapidge and Dumville (eds.), *Gildas: New Approaches*; Winterbottom (ed.), *Gildas*.
4   Higham, *King Arthur*.
5   Southern, "The army in late Roman Britain," pp. 404–5.
6   Breeze, *Roman Scotland*.
7   Faulkener, *Decline and Fall*; Millett, *Romanization*.
8   Wood, "The final phase," pp. 432–4; Woolf, "The Britons," pp. 345–55.
9   Winterbottom (ed.), *Gildas*, p. 26.
10   Raftery, *Pagan Celtic Ireland*.

11   Charles-Edwards, *Early Christian Ireland*, pp. 202–14.
12   Ibid., pp. 8–67; Ó Cróinín, "Ireland, 400–800."
13   Charles-Edwards, *Early Christian Ireland*, pp. 158–72.
14   Campbell, "Were the Scots Irish?"
15   Woolf, "Early historic Scotland."
16   Wainwright (ed.), *Problem of the Picts.*
17   Broun, "The seven kingdoms."
18   Woolf, "Dún Nechtáin."
19   Anderson and Anderson (eds.), *Adomnán's Life of Columba*, ii. 42.
20   Foster, *Picts, Gaels and Scots.*
21   Forsyth, "Some thoughts on Pictish symbols."
22   Southern, "The army in late Roman Britain," p. 405.
23   Winterbottom (ed.), *Gildas*, chs. 28–36, pp. 29–36 and 99–105.
24   Dark, *Britain*, pp. 105–92; Davies, *Wales in the Early Middle Ages*, pp. 90–102.
25   Dark, *Britain*, pp. 193–211.
26   Wood, "The final phase," pp. 434–5.
27   Faulkener, *Decline and Fall.*
28   Henig and Lindley (eds.), *Alban and St. Albans*; Williamson, *Origins of Hertfordshire.*
29   Woolf, "The Britons," pp. 361–8.
30   Hamerow, "The earliest Anglo-Saxon kingdoms"; Hines, "The becoming of the English."
31   Wood, *The Merovingian North Sea.*
32   Bibre, "North Sea language contacts"; Hines, "The becoming of the English."
33   Pantos and Semple (eds.), *Assembly Places.*
34   Rogers, *Cloth and Clothing*; see also Yorke, "Anglo-Saxon gentes and regna."
35   Stoodley, *The Spindle and the Spear.*
36   Green and Siegmund (eds.), *Continental Saxons.*
37   Higham, *Rome*; Lucy, *Anglo-Saxon Way of Death.*
38   Reynolds, *Kingdoms and Communities*, p. 257.
39   Winterbottom (ed.), *Gildas*, ch. 19, pp. 23 and 97.
40   Charles-Edwards, *Early Christian Ireland*, pp. 68–123.

Further Reading

Articles on all aspects of Roman Britain and its legacy can be found in the sister volume to this one, *A Companion to Roman Britain*, edited by Todd, which includes a very useful overview of late and immediate post-Roman sources for Britain by Wood. Major discussions of the problems in interpretation of the key texts for the fifth and sixth centuries are to be found in *Gildas: New Approaches*, edited by Lapidge and Dumville, and in the latter's *Saint Patrick AD 43–1993*. Esmonde Cleary, in *The Ending of Roman Britain*, and Dark, in *Britain and the End of the Roman Empire*, provide good surveys of archaeological and other evidence for the end of Roman Britain and the post-Roman period. An excellent review of the evidence for the Anglo-Saxon settlement is provided by Hamerow in *The New Cambridge Medieval History*, vol. 1. Higham (*Rome, Britain and the Anglo*-Saxons) and Lucy (*The Anglo-Saxon Way of Death*) also provide useful reviews of the archaeological evidence, albeit favoring "minimalist" interpretations, while Stoodley (*The Spindle and the Spear*) and Rogers (*Cloth and Clothing in Early Anglo-Saxon England*) can be recommended for their respective treatments of burials and the evidence for women's dress-sets. Articles by Hines ("The becoming of the English") and Bibre ("North Sea language contacts") explain the significance of the evidence for the development of different Old English dialects within Britain. Charles-Edwards, *Early Christian*

Ireland, is invaluable for many aspects of the early history of Ireland, and Ó Cróinín ("Ireland, 400–800") provides an outline of the main historical developments (insofar as these can be reconstructed). A traditional view of Scotland's early history will be found in the survey volume by Duncan, *Scotland: The Making of the Kingdom*, with Foster (*Picts, Gaels and Scots*) and Woolf ("Early historic Scotland to 761") providing a guide to new interpretations. Davies, *Wales in the Early Middle Ages*, is the major work to consult for that province, and her chapter in *The New Cambridge Medieval History*, vol. 1, gives a very useful overview of the Celtic kingdoms. James, *Britain in the First Millennium*, is an up-to-date introduction to the history of the whole of Britain (and includes some consideration of Ireland as well), and the collected essays *After Rome*, edited by Charles-Edwards, give a broader thematic review of developments in post-Roman Britain and Ireland.

Bibliography

Anderson, A. O. and Anderson, M. O. (eds.), *Adomnán's Life of Columba*, 2nd edn. (Oxford, 1991).

Bibre, P., "North Sea language contacts in the early middle ages: English and Norse," in T. R. Liszka and L. Walker (eds.), *The North Sea World in the Middle Ages* (Dublin, 2001), pp. 88–107.

Breeze, D., *Roman Scotland: Frontier Country* (London, 1996).

Broun, D., "The seven kingdoms in *De situ Albanie*: a record of Pictish political geography or imaginary map of ancient Alba?," in E. J. Cowan and R. A. McDonald (eds.), *Alba: Celtic Scotland in the Middle Ages* (East Linton, 2000), pp. 24–42.

Campbell, E., "Were the Scots Irish?," *Antiquity*, 75 (2001), 285–92.

Charles-Edwards, T. M. (ed.), *After Rome* (Oxford, 2003).

Charles-Edwards, T. M., *Early Christian Ireland* (Cambridge, 2000).

Colgrave, B. and Mynors, R. A. B. (eds.), *Bede's Ecclesiastical History of the English People* (Oxford, 1969).

Dark, K., *Britain and the End of the Roman Empire* (Stroud, 2000).

Davies, W., "The Celtic kingdoms," in P. Fouracre (ed.), *The New Cambridge Medieval History*, vol. 1: *c.500–c.700* (Cambridge, 2005), pp. 232–62.

Davies, W., *Wales in the Early Middle Ages* (Leicester, 1982).

Dumville, D. N., *Saint Patrick AD 493–1993* (Woodbridge, 1993).

Duncan, A. A. M., *Scotland: The Making of the Kingdom* (Edinburgh, 1975).

Esmonde Cleary, S., *The Ending of Roman Britain* (London, 1989).

Faulkener, N., *The Decline and Fall of Roman Britain* (Stroud, 2000).

Forsyth, K., "Some thoughts on Pictish symbols as a formal writing system," in D. Henry (ed.), *The Worm, the Germ and the Thorn: Pictish and Related Studies Presented to Isabel Henderson* (Balgavies, 1997), pp. 85–98.

Foster, S., *Picts, Gaels and Scots: Early Historic Scotland* (London, 1996).

Green, D. H. and Siegmund, F. (eds.), *The Continental Saxons from the Migration Period to the Tenth Century: An Ethnographic Perspective* (Woodbridge, 2003).

Hamerow, H., "The earliest Anglo-Saxon kingdoms," in P. Fouracre (ed.), *The New Cambridge Medieval History*, vol. 1: *c.500–c.700* (Cambridge, 2005), pp. 263–90.

Henig, M. and Lindley, P. (eds.), *Alban and St. Albans: Roman and Medieval Architecture, Art and Archaeology* (London, 2001).

Higham, N., *King Arthur: Myth-making and History* (London, 2002).

Higham, N., *Rome, Britain and the Anglo-Saxons* (London, 1992).

Hines, J., "The becoming of the English: identity, material culture and language in early Anglo-Saxon England," *Anglo-Saxon Studies in Archaeology and History*, 7 (1994), 49–59.

Hood, A. B. E. (ed. and trans.), *St. Patrick: His Writings and Muirchu's Life* (Chichester, 1978).

James, E., *Britain in the First Millennium* (London, 2001).

Lapidge, M. and Dumville, D. N. (eds.), *Gildas: New Approaches* (Woodbridge, 1984).

Lucy, S., *The Anglo-Saxon Way of Death: Burial Rites in Early England* (Stroud, 2000).

Millett, M., *The Romanization of Britain: An Essay in Archaeological Interpretation* (Cambridge, 1990).

Ó Cróinín, D., "Ireland, 400–800," in D. Ó Cróinín (ed.), *A New History of Ireland*, vol. 1: *Prehistoric and Early Ireland* (Oxford, 2005), pp. 182–234.

Pantos, A. and Semple, S. (eds.), *Assembly Places and Practices in Medieval Europe* (Dublin, 2004).

Raftery, B., *Pagan Celtic Ireland: The Enigma of the Irish Iron Age* (London, 1994).

Reynolds, S., *Kingdoms and Communities in Western Europe, 900–1300* (Oxford, 1984).

Rogers, P., *Cloth and Clothing in Early Anglo-Saxon England* (York, 2007).

Southern, P., "The army in late Roman Britain," in M. Todd (ed.), *A Companion to Roman Britain* (Oxford, 2004), pp. 393–408.

Stoodley, N., *The Spindle and the Spear: A Critical Enquiry into the Construction and Meaning of Gender in the Early Anglo-Saxon Inhumation Burial Rite* (Oxford, 1999).

Todd, M. (ed.), *A Companion to Roman Britain* (Oxford, 2004).

Wainwright, F. T. (ed.), *The Problem of the Picts* (Perth, 1955).

Williamson, T., *The Origins of Hertfordshire* (Manchester, 2000).

Winterbottom, M. (ed. and trans.), *Gildas: The Ruin of Britain and Other Documents* (Chichester, 1978).

Wood, I. N., "The final phase," in M. Todd (ed.), *A Companion to Roman Britain* (Oxford, 2004), pp. 428–42.

Wood, I. N., *The Merovingian North Sea* (Alingsås, 1983).

Woolf, A., "The Britons: from Romans to Barbarians," in H.-W. Goetz, J. Jarnut, and W. Pohl (eds.), *Regna and Gentes: The Relationship between Late Antique and Early Medieval Peoples and Kingdoms in the Transformation of the Roman World* (Leiden, 2003), pp. 344–80.

Woolf, A., "Dún Nechtáin, Fortriu and the geography of the Picts," *Scottish Historical Review*, 85 (2006), 182–201.

Woolf, A., "Early historic Scotland to 761," in R. Oram (ed.), *The Shorter History of Scotland* (Edinburgh, forthcoming).

Yorke, B. "Anglo-Saxon gentes and regna," in H.-W. Goetz, J. Jarnut, and W. Pohl (eds.), *Regna and Gentes: The Relationship between Late Antique and Early Medieval Peoples and Kingdoms in the Transformation of the Roman World* (Leiden, 2003), pp. 381–408.

CHAPTER FIVE

Economy

HOWARD B. CLARKE

Economic life relates essentially to the production and distribution of goods and services of all kinds. In a temperate climatic zone, the most important goods are food, clothing, and shelter, all of which are essential for the creation and maintenance of human life. So much is obvious; what is not so obvious, however, is how these basic activities were conducted in the earliest medieval centuries. There are simply too many unknowns and imponderables. Standard aspects of economic history, such as the volume of agrarian and industrial production or the quantity of coin being issued and the velocity of its circulation, are completely beyond our reach and will always remain so. Population levels and movements can only be guessed at. The economic impact of the decline and collapse of the western Roman Empire cannot be measured scientifically. Decline for some may have presented opportunities to others. Among the imponderables is the question of whether the spread of Christianity, with its liturgical emphasis on the elevation of bread and wine, contributed in any way to enhance their prestige as desirable consumables. Another imponderable is the possible effects of climatic cooling, as indicated by the advance of Alpine glaciers between the early fifth and the mid-eighth century: how far did greater coldness and dampness affect crop production in this North Atlantic archipelago? In the face of these and similar difficulties, it is hardly surprising that scholars tend to disagree with one another. This is abundantly clear from published post-lecture discussions at a symposium held in 1994.[1] Almost everything is impressionistic. A short chapter of this kind can do no more than offer a selection of facts, ideas, and opinions. There will be no definitive answers.

"How vain the effort must be to seek to reconstruct the agrarian world of early England from twenty sentences, often ambiguous, in the early laws!" James Campbell's *cri de cœur*, uttered (in German) 30 years ago, expresses a very English viewpoint. No part of the island of Britain possesses, even in outline, a written basis for the economic history of this period. Most of the entries in the Welsh annals (*Annales Cambriae*) are retrospective, whilst of their English counterpart it has been said that "the annalistic framework of the [*Anglo-Saxon*] *Chronicle* can only be regarded as a snare and delusion."[2] The latter's chief value for present purposes is to pinpoint key battles fought between native Britons and Anglo-Saxons, the results of which were economic as well as cultural and political. One of the more decisive occurred at Dyrham in the Cotswolds in 577, when the West Saxons appear to have made a dramatic push into British territory. Gildas's letter chastising a number of British princes a generation earlier can be interpreted only with difficulty, despite David Dumville's brave attempt to put chronological manners on this notoriously wayward author.[3] Bede, of course, is the supreme contemporary English historian of the later part of this period and provides us with a few economic insights. Saints' *Lives* are somewhat akin to "keyhole" archaeology, offering minute amounts of tantalizing detail. The Irish annals, though impressively full compared to the *Anglo-Saxon Chronicle*, are markedly synthetic down to the 730s. Yet it is Ireland that has a superlative, if scarcely appreciated, documentary treasure house for the seventh and eighth centuries: a collection of about 50 law texts containing an astonishing amount of contemporary detail about the agrarian world of that country. Here we can penetrate such refinements as trespassing by honeybees and the relative value of cats that would both purr and catch mice.[4]

A rare linkage between a narrative source and an archaeological discovery relates to a battle fought between King Æthelfrith of the Northumbrians and a British force near Chester (Roman *Deva*) in 616. At Herronbridge, south of the city, a mass grave of males without grave-goods and often with head wounds has been interpreted as the final resting place of the Northumbrian dead. Unlike the documentary record, archaeology is an expanding source of information, some of it truly spectacular. Indeed, one might enquire whether major sites such as Dinas Powys in Wales, Dunadd in Scotland, Lagore in Ireland, or Sutton Hoo in England distort our perception of the past. These, in turn, have more recent competitors: the Derrynavlan ecclesiastical treasure found (by metal detecting) in an obscure bog in Co. Tipperary, or an "Iona of the east" at Portmahomack north-east of Inverness, or another presumed royal, or at least princely, burial at Prittlewell near Southend-on-Sea. The economic implications of all such sites are important, but presumably not typical of their times. This point has been made most dramatically by the excavation of another cemetery about 5 miles from Prittlewell: the cremation burials at Rayleigh, some in decorated funerary urns, were accompanied by almost no weapons, the fragments of iron and a scatter of beads suggesting a low-status agricultural community of poor Germanic immigrants. Hundreds of cemeteries have been examined, but far fewer settlements and only two of the latter on a large scale, namely Mucking (Essex) and West Heslerton (North Yorkshire). The obvious danger is that partial excavation leads inevitably to partial understanding. Again, however, Ireland comes to the rescue in terms of landscape features and place-names, making it possible to estimate the range of magnitude of the number of settlements and even the number of inhabitants toward the end of the period c.450–750.

Regions and Sub-regions

Present-day political divisions of Britain and Ireland are of little relevance to the economic history of the early Middle Ages. There was no such thing as the Anglo-Saxon economy or the British economy or the Irish economy. The biggest economies were regional ones, many of these varying with changing geopolitical realities. And for most people living at that time, "the economy" (classical Latin *oeconomia*, "management of household affairs") was far more localized than that. We have, therefore, to adjust our focus to regional and sub-regional components of Britain and of Ireland, bearing always in mind that the baseline is the landscape and the seascape of a natural world that exerted enormous economic power on everyone, everywhere and continuously. Environmental factors such as soil quality, temperature variations, humidity, and the seasonal distribution of rainfall were all crucial. Medieval chroniclers, like modern commentators, were inclined to note extreme climatic events; these things mattered and were understood to be matters of concern. They mattered to one outstanding modern scholar, Cyril Fox, who brought together a body of ideas, formulated earlier, in a book first published in 1932. The book ends with a list of 25 "propositions" relating to distinctions between highland and lowland Britain (see map 6).[5] The tenth in this series identified an approximate dividing line running from Teesmouth to Torquay and coinciding roughly with a geological marker, the Paleozoic outcrop. The twenty-first is that soil character is the main controlling factor in the lowland distribution of population, elevation in the highland one. One outstanding medieval scholar, Bede, lived near the boundary of the two zones. Referring to Britain as "an island of the ocean," he began his *Ecclesiastical History* by listing economic resources; he clearly had lowland Britain in mind for the most part (*HE*, i. 1).

Fox's fifteenth proposition is that Britain is influenced by Ireland, particularly in its highland zone. Can the neighboring island be said to have a "personality?" The answer to this question is in the affirmative, even though (unsurprisingly, some might say) that personality is entirely different on the level of generalization at which the Fox thesis operates. The highlands of Ireland tend to be distributed in a broken chain around the perimeter, while much of the lowland is relatively unproductive bog-land. Indeed, the center of the island contains over 8,000 square miles of raised bogs, fens, and lakes, all impeding natural drainage. In prehistoric and early historic times, this terrain was crisscrossed with oak plank trackways: one near a monastic site at Lemonaghan (Co. Offaly) has been dated dendrochronologically to 684. In general, the early historic landscape was highly fragmented between mountains, woodlands, and bog-lands, hence the multiplicity of petty kingdoms. A common place-name element is *máigh*, "plain," the best known of which is Máigh Eo, "plain of the yew trees," giving rise to the anglicized village and county name Mayo. A few miles to the north-east is Kiltimagh, "wood of the plain," while Co. Londonderry has both Maghera, "plain" and, only a short distance away, Magherafelt, "plain of Fíolta." Thus, the plains of Ireland are small and scattered; there is no lowland zone in the British (English) sense. In broad terms, however, the historical geographer Anthony Orme has drawn a useful working distinction between the better-endowed south-eastern parts of the island and the physically harsher north and west.[6] I shall refer to this as the "Orme line." The advantaged zone lay opposite the island of Britain, opening up prospects of trading across the Irish Sea. Unlike so many modern scholars based in Britain, Bede was admirably conscious of the largest island to the west, remarking amongst other things on its milder and healthier climate (*HE*, i. 1).

Concepts promoted by scholars such as Fox and Orme have a certain economic validity. It will be seen, for example, that cattle constituted a relatively more important component of the primary economy of highland Britain and of Ireland, in the latter case especially north-west of the Orme line. Part of Fox's eleventh proposition is that

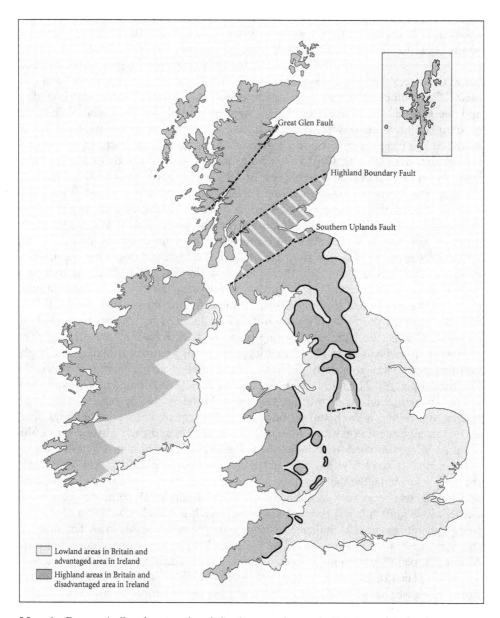

Great Glen Fault

Highland Boundary Fault

Southern Uplands Fault

Lowland areas in Britain and
advantaged area in Ireland

Highland areas in Britain and
disadvantaged area in Ireland

Map 6   Economically advantaged and disadvantaged areas in Britain and Ireland

there are pockets of lowland (intermont and coastal) in Britain's highland zone where cultures of lowland origin may establish themselves. A notable example is the central lowlands of Scotland. In the early Middle Ages, kingdoms and sub-kingdoms were economic units as well as political ones, in terms of tributary flows toward ruling and other elite families. A brief survey of a representative selection of such units now follows, starting with the (over-)kingdom of Leinster situated in the advantaged zone of Ireland. Leinster provides a good example of political stabilization between the fifth and the early eighth century. In St. Patrick's lifetime the kingdom extended northward to the River Boyne. Subsequent Uí Néill expansion southward pushed the boundary to the River Liffey and its tributary the Rye Water, the contraction of the over-kingship leaving dynastic segments stranded on the wrong side of the old frontier. At the same time, the over-kingship came to be monopolized by three segments of the Uí Dúnlainge confederation, based at Mullaghmast, Naas (both in Co. Kildare) and Newcastle Lyons (Co. Dublin). All of these lay on or near a long-distance routeway, the Slige Dála ("highway of the assemblies") linking the Shannon estuary with Dublin Bay. Across the Curragh from this routeway was the kingdom's most prestigious monastery, Kildare, where, according to Cogitosus' *Life of Brigid* (c.650, ch. 32), kings kept their treasure. The landscape and economic resources of the kingdom were extremely varied in practice, despite the location of most of its territory on the favorable side of the Orme line.

The kingdom of Rheged, astride the modern Anglo-Scottish border, illustrates the irrelevance of present-day political divisions in this early medieval context. Like the Pictish power centers focused either side of the Mounth or Grampian massif, on the Moray Firth and the Firth of Tay, Rheged was an estuarine political entity with a seaward outlook on the Solway Firth (all three being recognized later by vikings as *fjǫrðar*, "fjords"). Its original power center may have been at post-Roman Carlisle (*Luguvalium*), the nexus of a still partly intact road network.[7] The Tyne–Irthin gap, however, was a source of danger from aggressive Angles settling in Bernicia to the east, threatening tributary payments to members of the house of Rheged. The easternmost portion of the kingdom, around Catterick, appears to have been lost c.600, while the marriage of Oswiu, king of Bernicia (641–70), to a great-granddaughter of the first known king of Rheged, Urien, may have been intended to increase Anglian pressure on its British neighbor.[8] At any rate, Carlisle had become an Anglian stronghold by 685, its royal reeve taking pride in the Roman remains. The kingdom may have been reduced progressively to Galloway, the tribal district of the Novantae and a sub-region of the original loose confederation. Its last power centers may have been Dunragit ("stronghold of Rheged") at the head of Luce Bay and the kingdom's main monastic site, Whithorn. References in the *Annals of Ulster* to British warriors operating in Ireland in the period 682–709, it has been suggested, relate to dismembered war-bands of the house of Urien.[9] Whithorn itself was taken over by the Northumbrians c.730 and at least partially remodeled along English lines as a colonial church.[10]

If Rheged was a contracting kingdom in this period, collapsing by stages as a failed state, increasing amounts of tributary income would have flowed eastward to the heartland of Bernicia. In that regard the Northumbrian cultural renaissance had a favorable economic background. The royal stronghold at Bamburgh, which is called an *urbs*, "walled town," and a *civitas*, "city," by Bede (*HE*, iii. 6, 12, 16), typified the hillfort culture of highland Britain, standing as it did at the interface of the two zones. Bernicia's part partner and part rival in the Northumbrian over-kingship was Deira to the south, focused on the Derwent valley but also controlling the former Roman administrative center at York (*Eboracum*). Recent archaeological excavation and analysis suggest that Anglian migration into this region was gradual, fragmented, and relatively peaceful, pagan burials being concentrated east of the Derwent.[11] Like Bernicia, Deira expanded westward into British territory, absorbing the kingdom of Elmet in 617. Thereafter, greater centrality was accorded to York, although the consecration of Paulinus as archbishop in 625 did not prevent the establishment of Bernician episcopal rivals based at Lindisfarne (from 635) and at Hexham (from 678). This accords with the view that, in the early Middle Ages, ethnicity was "fluid and ambiguous; not determined solely by biological descent and blood relations, but intimately involved with relations of power, politics and loyalty."[12] Economic life was equally diversified. West Heslerton was divided into distinctive zones for housing, craftworking, and agricultural processing; building types were highly differentiated between post-hole constructed dwellings and sunken-featured storage buildings (*Grubenhäuser*).[13] Further south, toward the Humber estuary, a completely different, so-called "productive site" has been investigated at South Newbald; one interpretation is that it was operating as a market or fair from c.740 onward.[14]

Southern parts of lowland Britain are relatively better endowed with written records for the period under review and the charter evidence in particular gives us a different perspective on economic life. One example is the (under-)kingdom of the Hwicce in the English west midlands, a political entity whose boundaries are believed to have coincided with those of the diocese of Worcester established in 680. Both were defined by a series of natural features: the lower Wye, the Malvern Hills, Wyre Forest, the Forest of Arden, the Cotswold Hills, and the Bristol Avon. The economic focus comprised the valleys of the Severn and the Warwickshire Avon, with Gloucester (*Glevum*) as the most strategically located power center. British place-names are common, reflecting the continuance of native rulership into the last quarter of the sixth century. A prominent feature of settlements in the principal river valleys, long since cleared of much of their standing timber, is linkages to woodland outliers some distance away.[15] Woodland supplied not only timber, but also pannage for swine: an Evesham Abbey charter with an authentic basis refers to the right to mast from an island in the Severn at Ombersley sufficient for a herd of swine (S 54). Similarly, a Worcester charter links land at Shottery, near Stratford-upon-Avon, with three house-holders (*cassati*) at Nuthurst in the Forest of Arden (S 64). For the latter part of the period, charters introduce us to the widespread foundation of minster churches serving local districts. Between 701 and 709 Evesham itself was established in a great bend of the Warwickshire Avon on the initiative of the third bishop of the Hwicce, Ecgwine. The core of the estate on both sides of the river comprised 50 "hides" (measures) of land, a common endowment for early minster churches, while the substantial woodland outlier at Ombersley ("Ambr's wood or clearing") was assessed at a further 15 hides.

Fox's sixth proposition relates to relative proximity to Mediterranean civilization. In the context of early medieval Britain and Ireland, the prize has to be awarded to the kingdom of Kent. Physiographically, the terrain can be thought of as a peninsula defined by the Thames estuary, the Straits of Dover, the English Channel, Romney Marsh, the Weald, and the River Medway. Culturally, the land of the Cantiaci, focused chiefly on Canterbury (*Durovernum*), became an extension of Francia, the land of another Germanic people settling amongst a Gallo-Roman population. Richly furnished graves from the sixth century rarely lack Frankish imports in the recognizable forms of weapons, brooches, buckles, and vessels made of bronze and of glass. The first gold coins date from the early seventh century, following on from the Augustinian mission from Rome, while the laws of King Wihtred promulgated during the rye harvest (*Rugern*) of 695 refer to suspect foreigners encountered off the beaten track (*Laws*, ch. 28). The earliest extant original Anglo-Saxon charter, issued by Wihtred's uncle Hlothhere in 679, mentions actual economic resources in terms of fields, pastures, marshes, small woods, fenland, and fisheries (S 8). It reminds us that, for all early medieval peoples, the environment was the embodiment of past activity and a set of "affordances"; economic power rested on resources that were spatially and socially uneven in their local and regional distribution.[16] A model employing the concept of ecologically determined human decision-making has produced the following sequence for Kent: primary settlement on the best land by migrant groups in the fifth and sixth centuries, with kinship bonds as the main social tie; secondary settlement along routeways and an intensification of surplus production in the seventh century; and tertiary settlement with a degree of monetization in the eighth and ninth centuries.[17]

The Post-Roman Imprint

The central message of the previous section is that, between the mid-fifth and the mid-eighth centuries, there was an impressive number of regional, sub-regional, and indeed even more localized economies. A similar patterning is required when we come to consider the question of the post-Roman imprint on Britain and on Ireland. The principal divisions are clear enough: the civil zone of Roman Britain, broadly corresponding to the lowlands; the frontier or military zone broadly corresponding to the highlands south of the Antonine Wall; and, lastly, the rest of Scotland together with the whole of Ireland. Within each of these there were numerous variations: for example, the striking concentrations of Roman villas in the general vicinity of Cirencester (*Corinium*) and in south-eastern Wales focused on Caerwent (*Venta Silurum*). Few villa sites were demonstrably occupied after 400. One reason for this is that generations of "Romanists" (antiquarians and archaeologists with an exclusive interest in Roman remains) systematically destroyed the post-Roman stratigraphy in a combination of enthusiasm and ignorance. More recent investigations, as at Frocester (Gloucestershire), sometimes tell a different story. Here the main building was burnt down in the fifth century and a new three-bay structure was erected nearby, while the front corridor of the villa itself was converted into a longhouse. The fate of Roman towns has been much discussed. The general view is that they all ceased to function as genuine urban centers, the exceptions indicating continuing occupation of at least part of the site. One example is St. Albans (*Verulamium*), which appears to have survived in a British enclave in the Chiltern Hills district down to the middle of the fifth century. The best known such site is Wroxeter (*Viriconium*), not far from the Welsh border, where parts of the public baths complex were used, perhaps as a market and craftworking facility, until their deliberate abandonment in the seventh century.

Accepting the Eden valley and the adjacent Cumbrian coastal plain as an isolated part of lowland Britain, the only Roman town to have been established in the high-land zone was Carmarthen (*Moridunum Demetarum*) in Dyfed, a late, small, and peripheral place in the Roman scheme of things. Eighteen miles further west, at Llandisillio, a distant echo of classical Italy survives in the form of an inscription: "[Of] Clutorix son of Paulinus Marinus from Latium."[18] This and similar remnants remind us that part of the post-Roman imprint in highland Britain comprised two vernacular languages, British and Latin. At Dinas Powys, near Cardiff, imported *mortaria* were being used to grind fruit and vegetables in the Roman manner, while on the basis of the so-called Llandaff charters it has been suggested that blocks of land may have been donated by local rulers employing a Roman unit of measure-ment.[19] Whichever part of post-Roman Britain he came from, St. Patrick's back-ground was solidly Romano-British, as the son of a man called Calpurnius and the grandson of Potitus, and whose Latinity was far better than he modestly averred. Early in the sixth century, Gildas, it has been argued, was educated in a late Roman school in preparation for a secular administrative career, implying that some form of Roman government subsisted in his part of Britain.[20] He refers to threats to Hadrian's Wall, to its abandonment and that of the towns (*civitates*) in his own day (*De Excidio Britanniae*, ch. 19). At the fort called *Vindolanda* on the great wall, in the courtyard of the former commander's quarters (*praetorium*), a small rectangular building with a semicircular apse at its west end has been tentatively interpreted as a "church," reminiscent of the positioning of St. Cybi's church inside the Roman fort at Holyhead (Anglesey).

There can be little doubt, therefore, that the Roman economy of Britain declined to the point of collapse in the fifth and sixth centuries. The principal economic residue was probably the extensive road network, including fording points across rivers that legionary forces had once used. Ireland inherited none of this, but did evolve at some stage a set of five named long-distance routeways, four of which terminated at Dublin Bay and the fifth, from Connacht, at the Boyne estuary. The "logic" of such a pattern was clearly to facilitate travel and transport to and from the neighboring island. The 50-mile break in Ireland's serrated fringe between the mountains of the Cooley Peninsula and the Dublin Mountains is precisely the area with the greatest concen-tration of authentic Roman finds, suggestive of limited trading across the Irish Sea followed by actual Romanization in the late fourth and fifth centuries.[21] One aspect of Romanization was the beginning of Christianization, with the result that Pope Celestine I dispatched a Gaulish missionary, Palladius, as the bishop of Irish believers as early as 431. Another was the development and extensive use of the Latin-based ogham alphabet in southern Ireland in a Christianizing context. Yet another was the compilation of manuals for the teaching of Latin grammar to people who did not speak the language. Around the same time (c.600), monastic scholars began to rec-oncile pagan, biblical, and historical works into a conceptualization of the celestial city.[22] Half a century later, the monk whose real name was Toimtenach was able to describe, under the Latin nom de plume Cogitosus, the chief monastery of Leinster as a *civitas*, "city," with *suburbana*, "suburbs," in the sense of service lands inhabited by monastic tenants.[23] Accordingly, the Romanization of Ireland was a remarkable and unique post-Roman achievement.

Some Economic Mechanisms

Thus far, emphasis has been placed on economic diversity arising from physiographic, climatic, locational, and cultural factors, but there existed also a number of more universal economic constants and variables. We may begin with the truly daunting question of population levels and movements. It is a commonplace circumstance that the demographic history of medieval Europe can never aspire to anything more satisfactory than estimates, or even mere guesses. The general impression is that the seventh century came at the end of a prolonged downward phase in population, slow late Roman decline having been speeded up in the 540s owing to the start of a plague pandemic. Mark Baillie has suggested in addition that bombardment of the Earth by cometary debris may have been a contributory factor to economic depression in the period 540–90,[24] and Gildas refers to a "dreadful and notorious" famine at some time in the past (*De Excidio Britanniae*, ch. 20). A second major outbreak of plague – pneumonic as well as bubonic – commenced in 664 in both Britain and Ireland, ceasing c.687.[25] Thereafter, recovery may have been fairly rapid and, for the post-plague period centered on the eighth century, Ireland provides a basis for some sort of general population estimate. That basis is grounded in the landscape, place-names, and early Ordnance Survey maps, together with limited archaeological excavation, in the shape of over 45,000 ringforts (earthen raths and stone cashels).[26] Dendrochronological and radio-carbon dating suggest that most of these were constructed and occupied in the seventh to ninth centuries.[27] The ringfort was the dominant settlement form for the great majority of lords and farmers. A generous, if purely arbitrary, multiplier allowing for dependent relatives and servile personnel yields a crude base figure of 450,000. Alongside the ringforts there were several hundred lake dwellings (crannogs) and ecclesiastical sites, with the result that a minimum of half a million people is a reasonable estimate (allowing for the fact that some ringforts were built after the eighth century). For what it is worth, a comparable *average* density of population would produce a figure of just under 1.4 million for the island of Britain.

In addition to diseases (besides plague) and famine, enforced and voluntary migration were other factors governing the level of human population in any particular region or district. As we know from our own experience, groups of people and single individuals migrate for a great variety of reasons, including adverse circumstances at home and actual or perceived economic opportunities abroad. The breakdown of Roman control may have enabled Irish migrants, principally from the southern provinces of Leinster and Munster, to settle in Dyfed and the Lleyn Peninsula in Wales during the first half of the fifth century. On the other hand, serious doubt has been cast on the traditional view that migrants from north-eastern Ireland began c.500 to occupy land in south-western Scotland, leading to the formation of a new political entity, Dalriada.[28] Even so, one reflex of this possibly long-standing cultural association was the settlement of Colum Cille (Columba) and his companions on Iona in 563. Germanic migration into lowland Britain is no longer seen as an inexorable *Drang nach Westen*, "push toward the west." The movement of Anglian, Jutish, and Saxon settlers is now believed to have been random and sporadic, and not to have involved large numbers. The Romano-Britons stayed put, for the most part, and most of the occupants of "Anglo-Saxon" cemeteries, including most of the womenfolk, may have been of British stock. The dialects of Germanic spoken by the immigrants had a wide range of words relating to freedom and servitude, for males and for females as well as for the young. One such term is *wealh*, "foreigner," implying that Britons were enslaved in significant numbers by the newcomers.[29] Almost anyone might be enslaved, like the captured thegn (Latin *miles*) Imma, sold in 679 to a Frisian dealer in London (Bede, *HE*, iv. 22). In Ireland, with its economic emphasis on dairy farming, female slavery was so common that such a woman could be treated as a unit of currency (*cumal*). At the same time, legal provisions for manumission start to appear at an early date, as in King Wihtred's code issued in 695 (*Laws*, ch. 8).

As St. Patrick expressed concern and disapproval to the fifth-century strongman Coroticus, so did Gildas in the following century address himself to five *tyranni*, "warlords." Warlordism is a typical outcome when relatively effective statehood breaks down, as we have witnessed in our own time in Somalia, some West African states, and even Yugoslavia. In the interests of self-preservation, warlords surround themselves with armed militias and, in order to maintain those forces, exact tribute from subject groups and peoples with an appropriate degree of ruthlessness. Warlordism may also characterize societies affected by the destabilizing availability of wealth and the trappings of status from neighboring empires or similarly economically developed areas, as recent work on the Germanic neighbors of Rome or the Scandinavians on the fringes of eighth-century Europe has stressed. In the fifth and sixth centuries, Britain and Ireland were controlled largely by warlords, who only slowly acquired the attributes of kingship. The succession stakes were usually uncertain, which may explain why at least one East Anglian king was buried, at Sutton Hoo, with his own regalia. Accordingly, tribute-taking was a fundamental economic mechanism in the early Middle Ages. One authentic charter of this period, from the Hwiccian kingdom in 693, employs the term *tributarii*, "tribute-payers" (S 53), which, like similar words of continental origin, implies that land was settled by subject farmers who were liable to pay tribute when required. The most basic form of tribute was food: an Irish text called the "Last Testament of Morand" refers to tribute in terms of animals and crops, corn, mast, fruit, and fish. In Germanic territories, the basis for the collection of tribute became the hide (Old English *híd* or *híwisc*) or its equivalents. By the seventh century, the English had inherited a particular view of the hide as a quantity of land able to support the family of a "free" man and capable of being worked by a single plough-team – Bede's *terra n familiarum*, "land of so many households" (for example, *HE*, v. 19). Earlier in Bede's lifetime, the West Saxon king, Ine, had defined in law the food rent expected from 10 hides of land: 10 vats of honey, 300 loaves, 42 measures of ale, 2 cows or 10 wethers, 10 geese, 20 hens, 10 cheeses, a measure of butter, 5 salmon, 20 pounds of fodder, and 100 eels (*Laws*, ch. 70.1). Tribute-taking within and between political units was oppressive.

The economic counterpoint of tribute-taking was gift-giving. Whereas the former was well-nigh universal in its application, the latter was far more selective. The universalization of tribute-taking is most comprehensively demonstrated in a controversial English document known as the Tribal Hidage. Here whole population groups are assessed in multiples of one hundred and one thousand hides. Many of the smaller groups are concentrated in Mercia, and the document in its original form has often been associated with that kingdom, perhaps in the late seventh century. A case has been made, however, for placing it in the period of Northumbrian dominance in the time of King Edwin as ruler of both Bernicia and Deira (616–33).[30] Political dominance was necessarily underpinned by military might, and gift-giving was itself at least partly dependent on pillaging the wealth of subject groups in order to buy the loyalty of warriors in an age when economic productivity was so low. Some gift-giving was very basic, hence the literal meaning of Old English *hláford*, "provider of bread" and thus "lord." Gift-giving could be voluntary, or relatively so, as in the case of so many marriages: even today, a father or other male relative "gives" the bride away. Grants of land to monasteries were one aspect of gift-giving, establishing reciprocity between God and Man. Adomnán refers to the laying out of gifts of food in the monastic courtyard at Coleraine (Co. Londonderry) for benediction by a keenly discerning Columba (*Life of Columba*, i. 50). Hospitality to kinfolk and to strangers constituted another aspect, carefully nuanced in Ireland insofar as cuts of meat corresponded to social rank. In a world whose value system was typified by alliances, blood-prices (*wergilds*), fosterage of children, and political exiles, "necessary generosity" was the essence of economic reciprocity.[31]

Varieties of Economic Life

Broad ecologically determined parameters, the regionalized basis of the production and distribution of goods and services, the highly differentiated post-Roman imprint, and universally observed social necessities and niceties together constitute a complex backdrop to the economic life of Britain and Ireland in the period c.450–750. This may be examined under the classic subdivisions: primary (food and drink), secondary (clothing and other artifacts), and tertiary (exchanges conducted through barter and trade). We may start with by far the best-documented aspect – the rural economy of Ireland. The law texts cannot be localized accurately (the small number of place-names would include the Boyne valley and the Co. Tipperary area), but collectively they describe in minute detail an essentially mixed farming system to which the small plains on both sides of the Orme line would have been ideally suited. The textual weight of this written evidence moves from livestock farming, especially cattle, to tillage (cereals and other crops) and finally to hunting and gathering (including fishing). Cattle were clearly of central importance, the milk cow being a standard unit of value used for legal fines and tributary payments. The normal word for a freeman farming independently, *bóaire*, is etymologically derived from *bó*, "cow." At the same time, we are given a great deal of information about cereals: the eighth-century text *Bretha Déin Chécht* lists seven types of grain in order of value, starting with bread-wheat and ending with oats. Plowing was carried out using a team of up to six oxen, and the texts distinguish clearly between the infield of intensively cultivated ground and the outfield. One of the most important sources, *Bretha Comaithchesa*, refers to field boundaries comprising wooden fences, stone walls, and ditch-and-bank arrangements. Much of this has been confirmed archaeologically: for example, the classic wetland site at Coolure Demesne (Co. Westmeath) has produced an oak palisade dendrochronologically dated to c.402, and the earliest fish-traps found in the River Shannon date also from the fifth century.

The main social divisions in early historic Ireland were kings and nobles, free commoners, dependent commoners, and slaves.[32] Much the same was probably true of highland parts of Britain, characterized also by mixed farming but with a bias toward animal husbandry. Thus, a Welsh text known as the "Preface on Penance" implies that milk products featured large in the monastic diet.[33] Typical food-renders in Wales were ale, bread, meat, and honey – the latter used chiefly for making mead – while middens at high-status Dinas Powys yielded, in addition, evidence of the consumption of poultry, shellfish, salmon, sea trout, and vegetables. In some parts of that mountainous country there may have been extended settlements from the coastlands (*bro*) to upland pastures (*blaenau*), suggestive of the practice of transhumance. Pictish symbol stones concentrated in eastern Scotland illustrate a universal aristocratic, ritualized, food-gathering activity – the hunting of wild animals, a reminder that the fauna of the forests included wolves and foxes, three species of deer, boars and goats, martens and wild-cats, badgers and beavers, stoats and weasels, hares and squirrels, and all manner of other creatures. One of the chapters in Adomnán's *Life of Columba* (ii. 37) tells us about a quite different technique suited to a poor layman, for whom the saint provided a sharpened stake for capturing animals as large as a stag. Bede estimated the agrarian landscape of Iona at 5 hides, in addition to which, of course, there were the fruits of mainland rivers and the sea (*HE*, iii. 4). One of the monks who came over from Ireland is described as a gardener (*Life of Columba*, i. 18): accordingly, careful nurturing of slender economic resources could sustain a modest standard of living.

For much of the period here under review, the rural economy of lowland Britain was probably not so very different. The pattern of settlement ranged from single farmsteads to small farm clusters and to still relatively rare larger agglomerations. Fairly typical of early Germanic settlement may have been Lechlade in the upper Thames valley, comprising three post-hole constructed dwellings inside linear boundary ditches and six *Grubenhäuser* for storage and other purposes. One calculation is that field crops would have supplied about one-third of the necessary calories, the remainder coming from gardening, food-gathering, fishing, hunting, and animal husbandry.[34] Life was nevertheless precarious at times, as in Sussex in the 670s when starving men are said to have jumped off cliffs in mass-suicide groups (Bede, *HE*, iv. 13). Gradually, however, a major change occurred, beginning around this time. Initially, bishops and then kings and aristocratic laymen founded minster churches and in significant numbers by the first third of the eighth century. The upshot was the spread of multiple estates containing at least one substantial nucleated settlement: for example, a 60-hide unit centered on Farnham (Surrey), with its fields, woods, meadows, pastures, fisheries, rivers, and springs, was donated by King Cædwalla of Wessex c.686 (S 235). Archaeologists have begun to identify "villages" that may have started life in this period, as at Sedgeford (Norfolk) where a cemetery containing several hundred inhumation burials without grave-goods was found. As in remote Iona, but in much more favorable terrain, religious communities were busy developing ways to create and to utilize the wealth that stemmed from higher economic productivity. The proliferation of minsters may have been the catalyst behind the so-called "Middle Saxon shift" of settlement in lowland Britain, when former and often unimpressive farm clusters were replaced on new sites by church-based villages, or at least proto-villages.

Countless archaeological sites have produced evidence of craftworking in entirely rural contexts. Most artifacts are finished items made of relatively durable materials such as bone, metal (including coins), and pottery. Sites such as Irish crannogs, with good preservative qualities, can yield wooden artifacts. Least well preserved, of course, are items of clothing other than those made of leather. The latter was used for a wide variety of goods, some of them worn (belts, straps, and shoes), others carried (scabbards, sheaths, and shields) and yet others of general or specialized utility (containers, horse harness, ropes, skin boats, and tents). A few excavations have resulted in archaeobotanical samples of flax, a plant that was probably introduced to Ireland from Roman Britain.[35] There are no means of knowing how common linen garments were, but the likelihood is that sheep's wool was the main provider of fiber for clothing throughout the archipelago. Weights for vertical looms are tell-tale signs in houses and workshops. Other archaeological indicators of artisanal activities are crucibles for small-scale metalworking and residual slag. A high proportion of the secondary economy was probably conducted by non-specialists – men, women, and adolescents turning their hand to an extensive range of inherited skills, including the construction of houses and other farm buildings. Some craftworkers, on the other hand, can be presumed to have been specialists and quite possibly itinerant, such as those who carved monumental inscriptions in southern Ireland, parts of Wales, and Pictland north and south of the Mounth. In lowland Britain toward the end of this period, the foundation of numerous minster churches is likely to have given a major boost to stone masonry, carpentry, iron- and copper-working, weaving, leatherworking, and the manufacture of parchment and vellum. One of the revelations of the large-scale excavation at West Heslerton has been the identification of a craftworking/industrial zone within the settlement. Some Irish crannogs, too, were specializing economically: Bofeenan (Co. Mayo) was apparently devoted to the processing of iron ore.

Division of labor and craft specialization have been keys to economic progress across the centuries. One particular division of labor is often ignored or minimized – that between males and females. The contribution of women and of adolescent girls was universal, not only in the obvious spheres of child-bearing and rearing, food preparation and hearth minding, but also in spinning and weaving inside the home or in ancillary buildings, in all aspects of dairying, and in physically demanding tasks such as corn reaping, flax beating, and water carrying. To cite one specific body of evidence, the Irish law text *Cáin Lánamna* and its glosses accord flax-related entitlements to a divorcee.[36] More generally, was not the Germanic-speaking ideal *húsbonda*, "householder" (hence "husband") not normally expected to have a subservient *wífmann*, "weaving person," "woman" (hence "wife"), who between them provided that other essential of human existence *mete*, "food"? A recently recognized, if still controversial, archaeological context for craft specialization is the so-called "productive site." These have been identified by metal detecting and have added considerably to the number of known Anglo-Saxon settlements, even if they tend to confirm the existing pattern.[37] Flixborough (Humberside), for instance, was a carefully laid-out, high-status settlement with a great deal of industrial activity, including textile manufacture, linked to commercial transactions evidenced by imported pottery and 29 silver pennies (*sceattas*) of the early to mid-eighth century.[38] An alternative context for craft specialization was the proto-urban and urban one. A fairly clear-cut case is Ipswich ware, pottery which began to be traded widely inside the kingdom of the

East Angles from the middle of the seventh century, but less commonly outside. The coarse wares made in *Hamwic* (early Southampton) are found mainly in its immediate hinterland. Trading settlements such as these coexisted with minster churches in lowland Britain and with major cult settlements in Ireland and less frequently in highland Britain. These, too, attracted men and perhaps women with specialist artisanal skills. By the eighth century, even relatively remote Portmahomack was an important industrial center, its workshops producing a variety of liturgical objects as well as cross-slabs, fine leather, and possibly vellum.[39]

The tertiary sector of the economy of this period was everywhere limited by the availability of surplus produce and products for barter or for coin-based exchanges to acquire imported goods. Yet ecclesiastical and secular elites yearned for prestigious luxuries, for personal use or for gift-giving, and succeeded in acquiring a modicum of them. Sixth-century links with Mediterranean Europe were associated with Byzantine interest in north-western Europe.[40] Finds of imported pottery are distributed unevenly in south-western Britain and in southern Ireland, with a relatively substantial number at one particular site, Tintagel (Cornwall). Such a pattern has given rise to debates about whether only a few ships were engaged, say in search of tin, followed by local redistribution around the western sea lanes. From the late sixth century onward, more regular traffic with parts of western Gaul appears to have developed. For this, there is a scattering of documentary clues, such as the well-known attempt to deport Columbanus back to Ireland from the port of Nantes in 610, but ultimately in terms of volume of traffic we have to resort to archaeological discoveries, especially of the ceramic type known as E-ware. A primary route of importation has been proposed, starting with the Scilly Isles and proceeding northward via Ireland, the Isle of Man, and Galloway to the high-status power center at Dunadd in Dalriada.[41]

In this irregular and limited exchange network, a few ports entirely lacking in infrastructure functioned at least intermittently, examples being Dalkey Island off Dublin Bay and Meols at the tip of the Wirral Peninsula. Inland fairs, also occurring intermittently, existed at prestigious locations in Ireland: the probable site of the *óenach Macha*, "fair of Macha" (a goddess) still survives today as an elongated public green called The Mall on the eastern side of the hilltop at Armagh. Irregular and small-scale exchange sites have been identified archaeologically in lowland Britain, though they hardly feature in a literature dominated by the *wíc* emporia. A coastal find-spot at Bantham (Devon) has been interpreted as a traders' beach party gathering, with numerous objects datable to the late fifth and early sixth centuries, including 570 pieces of Mediterranean pottery. Well inland at Lake End, near Dorney (Buckinghamshire), a large, short-lived site with 130 pits dating to the mid-eighth century – containing local and a little imported pottery, numerous knives, some bone combs, and mysterious padlocks – is seen as evidence of a trading venue for a transient population.

The phenomenon of the *wíc*, from Latin *vicus*, is a post-Roman imitation of classical productive and trading settlements located just outside civilian and military centers: thus *Eboracum* becomes *Eoforwic*, *Londinium* becomes *Lundenwic* (with variants in both cases). The heyday of these trading settlements coincided with that of the low-value silver penny, the so-called *sceatta*, from c.675 to c.760, which in turn may have been stimulated by a desire to exchange goods in an orderly manner with Frankish and Frisian merchants. There was a pronounced tendency for each kingdom to have one major trading settlement of this kind, precocious Kent having three of them: Fordwich, Sandwich, and Sarre. This may have led to the unjustified assumption that kings founded such places rather than regulating them once they had come into existence. Regulate them they certainly did, as various provisions in early law codes demonstrate: kings of Kent are known from the laws of Hlothhere and Eadric to have had a *wíc-geréfa*, "port reeve," based in London c.680 (*Laws*, ch. 16). By the first half of the eighth century, a number of ecclesiastics and religious communities had been granted remission of toll on ships that they owned, trading mainly out of London. Even the upcountry bishop of Worcester had achieved this privilege for his two ships by the early 740s (S 98).

Conclusion

The foregoing is merely a brief summary of a subject of enormous complexity and indeed fascination. Though much less of a "dark age" than it once seemed to be, there is still a great deal of economic darkness around. The problems relate less to how little we know and more to how we know what we know; in other words, they are interpretative, methodological, and terminological. As Patrick Sims-Williams observed a generation ago, "The fact is that the academic mind is so flexible that it can reconcile almost anything about almost anything else."[42] One all-pervading temptation is to confuse change in the post-Roman centuries with decline, as articulated in particular by Gildas. Despite the general dearth of statistically valid information, at least one category of evidence is now sufficiently comprehensive for credible calculations to be made, namely, burial practices. In pagan culture, the dead were an important group of consumers, whereas in England a more economical mode of burial became fashionable in the half-century between 670 and 720. Apart from the occasional knife, non-perishable grave-goods were no longer being deposited with the dead from the 720s onward.[43] The economic implications of such a shift must have been significant, even if now unquantifiable. They may be one important factor behind the shifts clearly seen across these centuries. By the first half of the eighth century, there are many signs of the widespread economic take-off that had begun in the previous century, as Georges Duby posited with characteristic insight.[44] The earliest datable watermills, for example, have been found consistently to belong to this period. The most powerful indicator of economic growth is the astonishing number of monasteries established in Ireland and, to a far lesser extent, in Scotland and in Wales, paralleled by England's minster churches. All of these were centers of consumption and production to a degree that cannot now be measured. We do, however, have a broad hint: gaudy dress and decoration, and the showy use of gold, were behind demands for ecclesiastical reform at the synod of *Clofesho* in 747.[45]

What more might we wish to know? In the primary sector, a clearer understanding of the relation between the late Roman villa economy and the early Germanic one is required. At the other end of the period under review, more work needs to be done on the whole question of a possible transition from early farm clusters to nucleated settlements. For the seventh and eighth centuries, the superior Irish material, both documentary and archaeological, should be exploited more fully so that we may reinterpret some of the inferior British evidence. In the secondary sector, we might enquire further about the role of itinerant craftworkers and their impact on the apparent distribution of artifacts. Can we also estimate the influence of changing fashions? One methodological improvement would be to devise agreed symbols, calibrated to reflect appropriately the size of any given sample, for distribution maps; at present, there are far too many presentational variations to make comparisons trustworthy. In the tertiary sector, one wonders who were the traders – professional merchants or the servants of kings and churchmen? What caused the emergence of a more market-driven economy in south-eastern Britain from the late sixth century onward, after a long period when political and social forces seem to have been the main determinants, and long remained so in the rest of Britain and in Ireland? We might also wish that, in broad syntheses of the economic history of Europe, the Atlantic Archipelago should receive adequate treatment. In the most recent work of this kind – enormous and, in many ways, enormously impressive though it is – Ireland and highland Britain are virtually ignored and the Anglo-Saxons make only an occasional appearance.[46] Perhaps the subject will have attained academic maturity when it becomes possible to write a book on standards of living starting earlier than Christopher Dyer's c.850.[47] In the meantime, the safest conclusion may be – to borrow a motif from novelist Stella Gibbons – that the great majority of men, women, and children lived a life of rustic frugality on a cold comfort farm with the distinct possibility of finding something nasty in the woodshed.

Notes

1   Hines (ed.), *Anglo-Saxons*, passim.
2   Sims-Williams, "The settlement of England," p. 39.
3   D. Dumville in Lapidge and Dumville (eds.), *Gildas*, pp. 83–4.
4   Kelly, *Early Irish Farming*, pp. 111–12, 122, 145–6.
5   Fox, *Personality of Britain*, pp. 86–8.
6   Orme, *Ireland*, p. 2.
7   Phythian-Adams, *Land of the Cumbrians*, pp. 50, 56.
8   Smyth, *Warlords and Holy Men*, p. 23.
9   Ibid., pp. 25–6.
10 Blair, *Church in Anglo-Saxon Society*, pp. 30, 152, 187, 200, 202.
11 P. Rahtz in Geake and Kenny (eds.), *Early Deira*, p. 5.
12 S. G. Lucy in ibid., p. 12.
13 D. Powlesland in ibid., pp. 19–26.
14 K. Leahy in ibid., pp. 51–82.
15 W. J. Ford in Sawyer (ed.), *Medieval Settlement*, pp. 280–2.
16 Brookes, *Economics and Social Change*, pp. 3, 13.
17 Ibid., pp. 176, 180.
18 Blair, *Church in Anglo-Saxon Society*, p. 17.
19 Alcock, *Dinas Powys*, pp. 42, 134–5; Davies, *Wales in the Early Middle Ages*, p. 42.
20 M. Lapidge in Lapidge and Dumville (eds.), *Gildas*, pp. 47–9.
21 Laing, "The romanization of Ireland," pp. 268–75.
22 Doherty, "The monastic town," p. 47.
23 Ibid., pp. 59–62.
24 Baillie, "AD 450 event."
25 Maddicott, "Plague in seventh-century England," pp. 11–14, 22.
26 Stout, *Irish Ringfort*, p. 53.

27 Ibid., pp. 24–31.
28 Campbell, "Were the Scots Irish?"
29 Pelteret, *Slavery*, p. 43.
30 N. J. Higham in Geake and Kenny (eds.), *Early Deira*, pp. 46–7.
31 Duby, *Early Growth*, pp. 50–6.
32 Gerriets, "Economy and society," p. 47.
33 Davies, *Wales in the Early Middle Ages*, p. 35.
34 Duby, *Early Growth*, p. 23.
35 Kelly, *Early Irish Farming*, p. 269.
36 Ibid., pp. 269–70.
37 Ulmschneider, "Settlement, economy, and the 'productive' site," pp. 59–62.
38 Ibid., pp. 58, 63, 67.
39 Carver, "An Iona of the east," pp. 16–19.
40 Wooding, *Communication and Commerce*, pp. 5, 41–54.
41 Ibid., pp. 98–102.
42 Sims-Williams, "The settlement of England," pp. 28–9.
43 Blair, *Church in Anglo-Saxon Society*, p. 240.
44 Duby, *Early Growth*, pp. 5–72.
45 Blair, *Church in Anglo-Saxon Society*, p. 113.
46 McCormick, *Origins of the European Economy*, passim.
47 Dyer, *Making a Living in the Middle Ages*.

Further Reading

There is no single book dealing solely with the economy of Britain and Ireland in this period; indeed, the probability is that no one has ever attempted to compose such a work. There are, however, many books with some or even a great deal of economic history embedded in them. The emphasis often varies by discipline, but genuinely interdisciplinary approaches can be found. As has been stressed above, the most appropriate unit of study is the region or sub-region, examples of which are cited in the references. For England as a whole, the best general survey is C. J. Arnold, *An Archaeology of the Early Anglo-Saxon Kingdoms*, while J. Hines (ed.), *The Anglo-Saxons from the Migration Period to the Eighth Century* contains lively and thought-provoking commentary. The superlative source for the primary sector is F. Kelly, *Early Irish Farming*. In addition, the three principal settlement forms in early historic Ireland – raths, cashels, and crannogs – are revealed expertly in M. Stout, *The Irish Ringfort* and A. O'Sullivan, *The Archaeology of Lake Settlement in Ireland*. Useful insights on Scotland are to be found in A. P. Smyth's *Warlords and Holy Men*, which can now be supplemented by the conference-based collection edited by A. Woolf, *Landscape and Environment in Dark Age Scotland*. For Wales, the indispensable work remains W. Davies, *Wales in the Early Middle Ages*, updated somewhat in the relevant section of C. J. Arnold and J. L. Davies, *Roman and Early Medieval Wales*. The tertiary economic sector is best approached in J. M. Wooding, *Communication and Commerce* for the western sea lanes, and in the volume edited by T. Pestell and K. Ulmschneider, *Markets in Early Medieval Europe* for North Sea and cross-Channel trading.

Bibliography

Alcock, L., *Dinas Powys: An Iron Age, Dark Age and Early Medieval Settlement in Glamorgan* (Cardiff, 1963).
Arnold, C. J., *An Archaeology of the Early Anglo-Saxon Kingdoms*, 2nd edn. (London, 1997).

Arnold, C. J. and Davies, J. L., *Roman and Early Medieval Wales* (Stroud, 2000).

Baillie, M. G. L., "The AD 540 event," *Current Archaeology*, 15 (2001), 266–9.

Blair, J., *The Church in Anglo-Saxon Society* (Oxford, 2005).

Brookes, S., *Economics and Social Change in Anglo-Saxon Kent AD 400–900: Landscapes, Communities and Exchange* (Oxford, 2007).

Campbell, E., "Were the Scots Irish?," *Antiquity*, 75 (2001), 285–92.

Carver, M., "An Iona of the east: the early-medieval monastery at Portmahomack, Tarbat Ness," *Medieval Archaeology*, 48 (2004), 1–30.

Davies, W., *Wales in the Early Middle Ages* (Leicester, 1982).

Doherty, C., "Exchange and trade in early medieval Ireland," *Journal of the Royal Society of Antiquaries of Ireland*, 110 (1980), 67–90.

Doherty, C., "The monastic town in early medieval Ireland," in H. B. Clarke and A. Simms (eds.), *The Comparative History of Urban Origins in Non-Roman Europe: Ireland, Wales, Denmark, Germany, Poland and Russia from the Ninth to the Thirteenth Century* (Oxford, 1985), part 1, pp. 45–75.

Duby, G., *The Early Growth of the European Economy: Warriors and Peasants from the Seventh to the Twelfth Century*, trans. H. B. Clarke (London, 1974).

Dyer, C., *Making a Living in the Middle Ages: The People of Britain 850–1250* (London, 2002).

Fox, C., *The Personality of Britain: Its Influence on Inhabitant and Invader in Prehistoric and Early Historic Times*, 4th edn. (Cardiff, 1943).

Geake, H. and Kenny, J. (eds.), *Early Deira: Archaeological Studies of the East Riding in the Fourth to Ninth Centuries AD* (Oxford, 2000).

Gelling, M., *The West Midlands in the Early Middle Ages* (Leicester, 1992).

Gerriets, M., "Economy and society: clientship according to the Irish laws," *Cambridge Medieval Celtic Studies*, 6 (1983), 43–61.

Griffiths, D., Philpott, R. A., and Egan, G., *Meols, the Archaeology of the North Wirral Coast: Discoveries and Observations in the 19th and 20th Centuries, with a Catalogue of Collections* (Oxford, 2007).

Hamerow, H. F., "Settlement mobility and the 'Middle Saxon shift': rural settlements and settlement patterns in Anglo-Saxon England," *Anglo-Saxon England*, 20 (1991), 1–17.

Hines, J. (ed.), *The Anglo-Saxons from the Migration Period to the Eighth Century: An Ethnographic Perspective* (Woodbridge, 1997).

Hodges, R., *The Anglo-Saxon Achievement: Archaeology and the Beginnings of English Society* (London, 1989).

Hooke, D., *The Anglo-Saxon Landscape: The Kingdom of the Hwicce* (Manchester, 1985).

Kelly, F., *Early Irish Farming: A Study Based Mainly on the Law-texts of the Seventh and Eighth Centuries AD* (Dublin, 1997).

Kelly, S., "Trading privileges from eighth-century England," *Early Medieval Europe*, 1 (1992), 3–28.

Laing, L., "The romanization of Ireland in the fifth century," *Peritia*, 4 (1985), 261–78.

Lapidge, M. and Dumville, D. N. (eds.), *Gildas: New Approaches* (Woodbridge, 1984).

Lucy, S., *The Anglo-Saxon Way of Death: Burial Rites in Early England* (Stroud, 2000).

McCormick, M., *Origins of the European Economy: Communications and Commerce, AD 300–900* (Cambridge, 2001).

Maddicott, J., "Plague in seventh-century England," *Past & Present*, 156 (1997), 7–54.

Orme, A. R., *Ireland*. The World's Landscapes series, 4 (London, 1970).

O'Sullivan, A., *The Archaeology of Lake Settlement in Ireland* (Dublin, 1998).

Pelteret, D. A. E., *Slavery in Early Mediaeval England: From the Reign of Alfred until the Twelfth Century*. Studies in Anglo-Saxon History, 7 (Woodbridge, 1995).

Pestell, T. and Ulmschneider, K. (eds.), *Markets in Early Medieval Europe: Trading and "Productive" Sites, 650–850* (Macclesfield, 2003).

Phythian-Adams, C., *Land of the Cumbrians: A Study in British Provincial Origins AD 400–1120* (Aldershot, 1996).

Proudfoot, V. B., "The economy of the Irish rath," *Medieval Archaeology*, 5 (1961), 94–122.

Sawyer, P. H. (ed.), *Medieval Settlement: Continuity and Change* (London, 1976).

Sims-Williams, P., "The settlement of England in Bede and the *Chronicle*," *Anglo-Saxon England*, 12 (1983), 1–41.

Smyth, A. P., *Celtic Leinster: Towards an Historical Geography of Early Irish Civilization AD 500–1600* (Blackrock, Co. Dublin, 1982).

Smyth, A. P., *Warlords and Holy Men: Scotland AD 80–1000* (London, 1984).

Stout, M., *The Irish Ringfort* (Dublin, 1997).

Ulmschneider, K., "Settlement, economy and the 'productive' site: Middle Anglo-Saxon Lincolnshire, AD 650–780," *Medieval Archaeology*, 44 (2000), 53–79.

Wooding, J. M., *Communication and Commerce along the Western Sealanes AD 400–800* (Oxford, 1996).

Woolf, A. (ed.), *Landscape and Environment in Dark Age Scotland* (St. Andrews, 2006).

CHAPTER SIX

Kings and Kingship

BARBARA YORKE

Origins and Sources

By 600, we can confidently say that kingship was the predominant political system amongst all the peoples of Britain and Ireland, even though there may have been certain peripheral areas where royal authority had relatively little impact. The institution of kingship had developed at different dates amongst the main peoples of the study area. The origins of Irish kingship lie in the prehistoric past and cannot easily be identified; we can at least say that the institution was well established there by 550. In the areas that had been under direct Roman rule, kingdoms had emerged during the disturbed period following the break with Roman authority in c.410. Gildas indicates that some of the British kings of the west whom he addresses were at least second-generation rulers by the time that he was writing, probably in the first half of the sixth century (see chapter 4). Within the eastern areas of Britain in which a Germanic identity came to predominate, kingdoms seem to have been a fairly recent development by 600, and some dynasties may only have established themselves in the early years of the seventh century. The origins of kingship among the Picts cannot be dated with precision. Pictish kings may be a post-Roman development like their British counterparts, though it is also possible that interaction with the Roman Empire had stimulated their development at an earlier point. At least one Pictish kingdom was in existence before the end of the sixth century when King Bruide was visited by St. Columba (d.597).

The degree of survival of sources means that it is far easier to study kingship among the Irish and Anglo-Saxons than among the British and Picts. For the Irish and Anglo-Saxon kings, a range of sources exists from the seventh century onward of which genealogies, king-lists, law codes, and various forms of narrative source are the most useful, with the additional bonus for the Anglo-Saxons of the survival of charters recording royal donations of land. After the time of Gildas, sources for British kings are sparse until the ninth century and much has to depend on a projection back from later sources, some of which do seem to preserve material such as charters from an earlier period, though there are problems in knowing how much this material may have been modified when it was adapted for later use. The Picts are even worse served by written records, and apart from the survival of versions of a king-list, have to be studied through references to them in sources produced by the Irish or Anglo-Saxons, though it has been argued that later administrative records from the Scottish kingdom may throw some light on Pictish arrangements. There are, however, depictions of members of the Pictish elite on some of the surviving carved stones.

It has been argued in the past that there were major basic differences between the long-established kingship systems of the Irish and the more recently established kingships of the peoples of Britain. In this interpretation, an ancient sacral Indo-European form of kingship amongst the Irish was contrasted with a new warrior kingship, exemplified above all by that of the Anglo-Saxons.[1] However, most authorities now recognize that differences have been too starkly drawn and that the presentation of an Irish king as a "priestly vegetable," who had important symbolic roles but few active duties, depended on too ready an acceptance that the idealization of kingship in Irish law codes was an accurate reflection of reality.[2] As we shall see, military power was the basis of authority and one of the chief producers of income for all early medieval rulers in the Atlantic Archipelago, though there were other factors that have to be taken into account which meant that royal authority operated in varied ways amongst the different peoples.

Kingdoms and Sub-kingdoms

It is no easy matter to identify the number of kingdoms at any given time in the British Isles and Ireland in the period before 800. No contemporary sources list them in their entirety, and numbers were not stable. Nor can one be certain that an individual defined as a king in one culture would be so termed in another, something that may be very relevant to what has often been seen as a major contrast between many small kingdoms in Ireland and fewer, larger ones in mainland Britain. The situation is clearest for the Anglo-Saxons. Thirteen Anglo-Saxon provinces of varying size are recorded as having had royal houses in the seventh century: Bernicia, Deira, Mercia, East Angles, Middle Angles, Lindsey, Magonsaetan, Hwicce, East Saxons, Kent, West Saxons, South Saxons, and Wight. The historical trend was for the kingdoms of Northumbria (Bernicia and Deira combined), Mercia, and Wessex to become predominant. A major explanation for their success was probably their geographical locations which enabled them to expand in several different directions at the expense of British and Anglo-Saxon neighbors. By 750, only these three kingdoms plus Kent, the East Angles, the East Saxons, the South Saxons, and the Hwicce were ruled by their own royal houses, and of the latter group only the royal house of the East Angles continued into the ninth century.

Records are less precise for other areas of Britain. Gildas writing in c.550 referred to five rulers of major kingdoms in Wales and the south-west, but did not name their provinces. Three can be identified with kingdoms which appear as major players in written sources of the seventh and eighth centuries, namely Dumnonia, Dyfed, and Gwynedd. It can be suspected that Powys was another of the early kingdoms, but the identity of the fifth remains uncertain. Charters excerpted in the twelfth-century *Book of Llandaff* seem to indicate several smaller kingdoms in the south-east of Wales and adjoining areas of England, including Gwent and Ergyng, but in the course of the seventh century they were absorbed into a larger kingdom called Glywysing. By the eighth century, there is evidence for further kingdoms including Rhos (mid-north), Meirionydd and Ceredigion (center west coast), Builth and Brycheiniog (east, south of center), and some of these may have had an older origin.[3] There were probably three large British kingdoms in the north, Dumbarton/Strathclyde, Rheged, and Gododdin, though there also seem to have been some smaller kingdoms such as Elmet (western Yorkshire). The exact nature of arrangements among the Picts is also hard to reconstruct with any certainty. The surviving Pictish king-list could suggest the existence of one large Pictish kingdom, though it is perhaps more likely that the list preserves either the names of Pictish overkings or the rulers of the most powerful kingdom, that of Fortriu. Occasional references in narrative sources suggest that there were other Pictish kingdoms, though the reference in later sources to seven ancient Pictish provinces should be treated with care.[4]

Ireland has traditionally been seen as contrasting with the situation in mainland Britain by having large numbers of very small kingdoms. The lowest of the three ranks of kingship that are recognized in the Irish law codes was that of the *rí* (*rex*) who exercised authority over a *túath* (people). Some perceived differences between British and Irish kingship were possibly more terminologically apparent than real. In mainland Britain, units that were comparable in size to the Irish *túatha* were significant elements within kingdoms and essential to their administration. Best recorded are the *regiones* of southern England which appear in charters, narrative accounts, and an enigmatic document known as the *Tribal Hidage*. The latter lists a series of population groups with assessments in hides, the unit of land (nominally the area that would support a family) on which royal demands were levied. Smaller *regiones* might be assessed at 300 hides and the larger at 1,200 or occasionally more. The laws of King Ine of Wessex (688–725) provide a definition of the food rent that a king could demand from 10 hides and that was probably delivered to the royal vill from which the *regio* was administered. Northumbrian sources depict its early kings making circuits of the kingdom and staying at royal vills where it can be presumed their food rents were consumed.[5] The evidence from the Anglo-Saxon kingdoms seems to resemble later evidence from Wales and Scotland for similar subdivisions in the form, respectively, of *commotes* and *fermtouns* from which itinerant kings could extract food rents.[6] It is therefore tempting to suggest that such systems of royal provision also operated in Wales and Scotland in the early Middle Ages, though such a deduction cannot be proved conclusively.

The second tier of kings referred to in Irish laws, the *ruiri* or "overking," would appear to have controlled an area containing several *túatha* and so more closely commensurate with the territories of those called "kings" on the British mainland. However, the basis of power appears to have been different, though it is possible that different types of source provide idealized models that did not work in quite such different ways in practice. Whereas an Anglo-Saxon king, at least by the eighth century, seems to have supervised his *regiones* through royal officials and his levies were based on assessments made on land, the Irish *ruiri* functioned as the overlord of client kings who had independent rights over their own small kingdoms and with whom arrangements might have to be renegotiated on the death of either party.[7] Lordship in Ireland, unlike the situation in England and Wales, was founded not on land, but on cattle which were supplied by the lord to his clients in return for established obligations.[8] The Irish system of kingship seems likely to have had its roots in a prehistoric past that had been unaffected by Roman conquest which in Britain had imposed a system of taxes based on landed assessment upon native arrangements. However, the contrast is not absolute because of the importance in all areas of Britain and Ireland of relationships between individuals sealed by exchange of gifts and by the ubiquity of overlordship.

Overlordship

Overlordship may be briefly defined as a relationship in which a subordinate king recognized the authority of a more powerful ruler. In return for the latter's protection and patronage, the subordinate king would have to pay tribute, serve in the overking's army, and, especially in the Celtic-speaking areas, provide him with hospitality. Exact details would have varied between regions, but such relations of dependence were a basic feature of kingship in early medieval Britain and Ireland, and most rulers would have been either the overlords of other kings or obliged to recognize the overlordship of another. Complex tiers of overlordship could exist, and these are often seen to be particularly characteristic of Ireland with its large number of kings and shifting confederations of dominant dynasties. For instance, the area surrounding Strangford Loch in Ulster was divided between four subkingdoms which together constituted the kingdom of the Dál Fiatach whose dynasty was dominant over the rest. The kingdom of Dál Fiatach itself was a constituent part of the overkingdom of the Ulaid, control of which was contested with the other most powerful kingdoms in the confederation which also had their own subordinate rulers.[9] Other major confederations of this type in existence in the seventh and eighth centuries included those of Leinster and Munster.[10] Within Britain, tiers of overlordship can be found as well. The dominant Pictish kings of Fortriu were probably overlords, at least for part of the period, of rulers of other Pictish provinces. On occasion, they were overlords of other peoples in northern Britain, but at other times they had to recognize the overlordship of stronger dynasties from outside Pictland.

As the Pictish example suggests, major overlordships within Britain could transcend ethnic boundaries. The great Bernician/Northumbrian kings of the seventh century – Oswald (634–42), Oswiu (642–70), and Ecgfrith (670–85) – seem to have exercised an overlordship not only over the southern English, who had their own overlordship system from the late sixth century that is often referred to by historians (probably wrongly) as the "bretwaldaship," but also over the Picts, the British, and the Dalriadic kingdom in Argyll. By the second quarter of the eighth century, matters seem to have been arranged rather differently with the Pictish king Onuist (729–61) dominating all the kingdoms of the northern half of Britain and Æthelbald of Mercia (716–57) those of the south; the two may well have cooperated together in a form of joint overlordship.[11] The Scottish Dál Riata were also enmeshed in broader Irish systems of overlordship and, in addition to being part of the kingdom of the Dál Riata in north-east Antrim, would sometimes have had to recognize the authority of the dominant power of northern Ireland which in the latter part of the seventh century was the Cénel Conaill. The interaction of the great overlords of the British Isles brought the secular leaders of its different peoples into close contact and must have stimulated a sharing of ideas and culture between them, something that is represented by the circulation of elite items between the different provinces and the emergence of a distinctive insular style of elite decoration.[12]

A powerful king might have different types of relationship with subordinate rulers. The dominant power in southern Britain in the seventh and eighth centuries was Mercia. A distinction can be drawn in degree of subordination between an inner zone of provinces adjacent to the Mercian homelands and others that were on the periphery.[13] The rulers of the inner-zone provinces, such as those of the Hwicce and the Magonsaetan, were either members of the royal house or regarded as subordinate, and were eventually replaced by ealdormen who lacked independent royal status and were appointed by the Mercian kings. However, Anglo-Saxon and Welsh kingdoms of the outer zone, such as Powys or the East Angles, were only intermittently subordinate to Mercia, and Mercian kings had relatively little influence on their internal affairs.

Overlords could demand certain basic rights from their subject kings of which the most important seem to have been payment of tribute and military service. When Penda of Mercia's overlordship was challenged by Oswiu of Northumbria at the battle of the river *Winwaed* in 655, the former was able to muster a large army that contained contingents from his subject Anglo-Saxon and Welsh kingdoms. Bede informs us that "an incalculable and incredible store of royal treasures and gifts" was the price of peace.[14] Penda would have been expected to have rewarded those subordinate rulers who had fought with him by giving them a share in the treasure he had won. Such giving of gifts to reinforce power was part of the language of overlordship throughout Britain and Ireland. "The Book of Rights" gives a stylized view of the type of gifts that underkings could expect from their Dál Fiatach overlords, including horses with their harness, bracelets, cloaks, and ships. An overlord's authority might be increased through intermarriage or such actions as assisting a candidate to the throne. Such actions might also open up the way for an eventual takeover of the province which needed both superior physical force and, to achieve lasting effect, the establishment of a relationship with leading families and churches within the province.

Military Power

As accounts of the battles of the *Winwaed* and *Nechtansmere* – fought between the Northumbrian Ecgfrith and the Pictish Bruide in 685 – indicate, the power of the greater kings and overlords of the early medieval British Isles was founded on their military competence. All early medieval rulers needed to be military leaders, which is one reason why the rulership of minors and women was extremely rare. The formation of kingdoms in post-Roman Britain was founded on the ability of their leaders to exploit the Roman failure to maintain the borders of Britain and the seas around it. Whether events in Britain stimulated new developments in Ireland is hard to say, but the rise in power of Cénel Conaill and the Eóganachta in much the same period at the expense of previously dominant dynasties seems to have been achieved through military successes.[15]

One of the major functions of kings was to organize the defense of their people and to negotiate on their behalf with other rulers; failure to carry out either role satisfactorily might mean that their province would be indiscriminately ravaged and some of the population taken away as slaves. The ability of the more powerful kings to campaign over large distances, and to solve the logistical problems involved is extremely impressive, even though we are seldom given a clear insight into how they achieved their successes. Ships and horses, aided by the existence of Roman roads in Britain, would have been essential for rapid mobility and to enable such feats as the Northumbrian raid on Ireland in 684 and their ill-fated penetration into remote areas of Scotland the following year. In coastal areas of Ireland, the number of men and ships the subordinate king had to supply to his overking might be part of the agreement between them, and obligations to provide manned ships laid on households are recorded from Scottish Dalriada.[16]

There were probably basic similarities between the weaponry and methods of warfare of all the early medieval peoples of Britain, though also some distinctive features by which the different peoples were distinguished. A carved Pictish stone in the churchyard at Aberlemno (Angus) has been interpreted as depicting an engagement between Northumbrians and Picts.[17] Both sides are shown fighting on horseback and on foot, and are equipped with swords, spears, shields, and helmets, but there are subtle distinctions in the armor and weaponry of the two sides. The Picts and the Britons also differed from the Anglo-Saxons in their use of hilltop fortifications. The Anglo-Saxons generally employed open battle to decide disputes over power, but for early medieval Scotland there are references to sieges, and defeated kings were as likely to be killed by burning or drowning as by death on the battlefield which was the fate of many of their Anglo-Saxon counterparts.[18]

Early medieval armies would have contained contingents raised in different ways. Noblemen and subordinate kings would arrive with their own entourages and armies to fight. Obligations of loyalty or submission and expectations of reward were the factors that kings had to look to in order to keep their armies together. The contingents in which they would have had most trust, and which would have formed the core of their fighting forces, were the household troops that were in constant attendance upon them, often referred to as the king's *comitatus* in Anglo-Saxon contexts. The Anglo-Saxon *comitatus* consisted of some seasoned warriors, but a significant element were the young men aged between about 14 and 25 who sought to establish their reputations and win sufficient rewards to enable them to set up their own households and join the ranks of the nobility who would be summoned to join the kings on major campaigns. The shared values of the early medieval warrior culture made it possible for men from one ethnic grouping to take service in another. For instance, a number of exiled Northumbrian nobles and princes seem to have taken refuge and fought for the Dál Riata of Argyll,[19] while a controversial new interpretation of *Y Gododdin* claims that Anglo-Saxons fought on behalf of one of the warring British sides.[20] British and Pictish kings may have recruited Irish warriors, and such individuals may explain the existence of ogham stones and other evidence of an Irish presence in these provinces (see chapter 4).

Vernacular poems, such as *Beowulf* and *Y Gododdin*, express the heroic way in which kings and their entourages no doubt liked to be presented, but not everyone in early medieval Britain and Ireland saw them in the same light. Gildas and various Irish churchmen were extremely critical of the general behavior of the military companions with which kings surrounded themselves, portrayed by Gildas, in his habitual plain-speaking style, as "bloody, proud and murderous men, adulterers and enemies of God."[21] Anglo-Saxon writers are generally more circumspect, or at least represent a somewhat different perspective, even likening, on one occasion, the ties between a bishop and his clergy to the bond of the *comitatus* with its lord.[22] However, we do get glimpses in the Anglo-Saxon narrative sources of bored young aristocrats, including the future St. Guthlac, practicing their raiding skills within their home territories if there was no official campaigning to keep them occupied.[23] Unfortunate peasants may not have found much difference between a home or a foreign army riding through their crops.

War was necessary to produce the treasure that followers expected as a reward, and there was a danger of a vicious circle developing in which a large band of warriors was needed for success in battle, but successive battles were also needed to keep them paid and occupied. Early medieval kings also seem to have retained craftsmen and utilized diplomatic and other contacts to import precious goods and rare and unusual items. The need of kings to procure adequate supplies to reward those in their service may have stimulated the development of specialized Anglo-Saxon trading centers known as *wics* under royal protection and of coinage to aid foreign transactions. But in Anglo-Saxon England from the late seventh century, the reward increasingly desired at the end of a period of military service was bookland; that is, a grant of land – recorded in a charter or *boc* – with rights of free alienation on the same terms as grants to the newly founded Anglo-Saxon churches. Churchmen were exempt from military service, and it appears that some of the noblemen who had been granted bookland considered that they should be exempt as well, though it eventually became established in the eighth century that those who owned land had to provide men for the royal army in proportion to the size of their estates, the beginning of an important shift in the way in which armies were raised.[24]

Dynasties and Royal Succession

Among those to whom kings would look for support in their military endeavors were their own relatives; for, like other members of early medieval societies, kings were part of wider kin-groups whose members had complex obligations toward one another. These kin-groups were cognatic – that is, they were made up of relatives from both the father's and the mother's side – but when it came to establishing royal status and throneworthiness it was the agnatic or paternal descent that was all-important. In both Ireland and England, rival segments of the royal house, descended from different ancestors, competed for power. This gave rise to fluctuating succession patterns in which sometimes a powerful segment would dominate for several generations with the throne passing between close relations, while at others it oscillated between rival royal kin-groups, sometimes by agreement, but probably more often through dispute, with the result that successive kings might be only distantly related to one another.[25] A king who was successful in defeating other rulers in Ireland might aim to replace them with his own relatives, thus giving rise to a rapid proliferation, visible in the genealogical record, of new royal lines with a common ancestor. It was also the case in Ireland that a retrospective "fictive" kinship might be established whereby subject kings who had no genuine blood relationship to their overking were nevertheless claimed to be descended from a common ancestor to cement the new bonds between them. The rise of Cenél nEógain in the north of Ireland in the eighth century seems to have been underpinned by the creation of a fictional early history that united them and provinces they had recently conquered as northern Uí Néill descended from the mythical Niall of the Nine Hostages.[26] In the seventh century in Anglo-Saxon England, joint kingships had been common in which several rulers, often brothers but sometimes distant cousins, shared power as can be seen among the Hwicce of the West Midlands and the East Saxons. But by 750 single kingships had become the norm in those Anglo-Saxon kingdoms that were still in existence.

The succession practices of the Picts have often been viewed as quite different from those of the Irish, British, or Anglo-Saxons because of evidence that appears to suggest that they practiced succession through the maternal rather than the paternal line.[27] Bede states that it was the custom in his day "in all cases of doubt" that kings should be elected "from the female royal line rather than the male."[28] There do seem to be several examples of Pictish kings who appear to have had Pictish mothers, but foreign fathers, including Talorcan (653–7), son of King Eanfrith of Bernicia, Bruide (672–93), son of King Beli of Dumbarton, and the brothers Bruide (c.697–706) and Nechtan (706–24 and 728–9) whose father may have been a member of the Cenél Comgaill of the Dál Riata.[29] On the other hand, as in other areas of Britain, the kings are identified by patronymics; that is, by their paternal rather than maternal descent.[30] It is an undoubted peculiarity of the Pictish king-list that none of the kings in it had a father who was also a king of the Picts, though several instances of fraternal succession are known. Competition between rival lines for a Pictish overkingship, complicated by rival alliances with royal houses of the neighboring peoples of the north, may provide an explanation for the observable patterns. But one should not ignore the fact that, as Bede indicates, claims through a female of the royal house could sometimes be important. In other areas of Britain there were circumstances in which it could be a significant factor, in spite of the general preference for agnatic claims. The union of Bernicia and Deira was aided by Bernician princes marrying Deiran princesses, thus giving their offspring descent from both royal houses; while in the early ninth century in Wales, Merfyn (c.825–44), who took over the kingship of Gwynedd, was related to its previous rulers only through his mother and extended his power to neighboring Powys by marrying the sister of its king.[31] What appear to be very distant kin succeeding one another in Irish king-lists may on occasion be men who were, in fact, more closely related if kinship created by marriage is taken into account. A collection of genealogies of royal women from Leinster may suggest the importance attached to such alliances and to cognatic as well as agnatic descent.[32]

Royal women should not be left out of the equation when we seek to understand the operation of royal power in the early Middle Ages, even if there are relatively few references to them in British and Irish sources. The deaths of some significant queens are referred to in Irish annals,[33] but it is only in Anglo-Saxon narrative sources that there is detailed evidence for queens and other royal kinswomen taking an active role in the affairs of the kingdoms and promoting the interest of their families. For example, in Stephen's early eighth-century *Life* of Bishop Wilfrid of Northumbria (664–709), the queen is depicted going on a royal circuit, sometimes with the king and sometimes on her own. She and other female members of the royal house intervene to support or to oppose Wilfrid, and a prominent abbess from the royal house is shown playing a major role in deciding which princes will succeed to the throne. There is even one example of an Anglo-Saxon queen being included in a regnal list, namely Queen Seaxburh of Wessex, who seems to have ruled for about a year in 673–4. The active role of Anglo-Saxon royal women is also reflected in Old English poetry. In the poem *Beowulf* there is a significant role for queens in the court ceremonial surrounding the *comitatus*.[34] One looks in vain for comparable figures in works such as *Y Gododdin* of the British heroic tradition, though powerful queens are part of the mythic, prehistoric past in early Irish narrative literature. Pictish carved stones do occasionally depict women, and some of them are shown in comparable ways to men as, for example, in a hunting scene from Hilton of Cadboll (Highland) or a depiction of a woman wearing a large penannular brooch from Wester Denoon (Angus).

Kings' Duties within their Kingdoms: Law and Religion

Kings not only protected their people from external threats, but from internal anarchy as well. It was obviously in a king's interest to keep his kingdom quiescent as it enabled royal dues to be collected and inhibited challenges to his position, but it also seems to have been a general expectation that kings would guarantee the enforcement of law, though there were major differences between the extent of the involvement of Anglo-Saxon kings and that of their Celtic counterparts. Some 77 tracts on law survive from Ireland from the seventh and eighth centuries compared to a rather more modest four Old English law codes. Surviving versions of Welsh law only date from after 1200, and although they may preserve some earlier arrangements, it is evident that they also reflect the later evolution of law; no relevant texts survive to illuminate Pictish practice.[35] The Irish law tracts were produced by a professional class of jurists with whom the main responsibility for the interpretation of the law lay, and, as the large number of surviving texts suggests, they developed their own flourishing literary tradition. Later evidence suggests the existence of similar law professionals in Wales and Scotland, but there is no equivalent body in Anglo-Saxon England, and it would appear that they represent a distinctive Celtic practice with its roots in the prehistoric past. However, Anglo-Saxon law also drew upon established practice and, as in other areas of early medieval Europe, the maintenance of local law and order in early medieval Britain was the responsibility of local communities. The aim was to prevent the escalation of feud by bringing parties in dispute into settlement with the aid of recognized tariffs for specific crimes that might be graded according to status and by holding the kindred responsible for the good behavior of its members. Irish kings could issue proclamations of new law (*cánai*) in specific circumstances and presided over cases, but did not promulgate law or act as its final arbitrators in the same way as their Anglo-Saxon counterparts. Anglo-Saxon kings could apparently use their role as guarantors of law to extend the role of royal authority within society and to use their own officials to intervene in law enforcement, though the sources give at best only a partial insight into the workings of local courts.

How far was there also a well-entrenched belief in the societies of early medieval Britain that kings were essential in other ways for ensuring the welfare of their people through their ability to intervene with supernatural powers? As we have seen, belief in the sacral significance of kings has been an integral part of the traditional interpretation of early Irish kingship.[36] The topic is a difficult one to study as all relevant texts were perforce produced after the conversion to Christianity so all allusions to

Irish and Anglo-Saxon paganism come through a Christian filter and elements referred to may have been selected or adapted to be compatible with the new religion. Nevertheless, there are elements that jar with normal Christian concepts and may give an insight into older attitudes. The seventh-century Irish tract *De Duodecim abusivis saeculi* ("Concerning the Twelve Abuses of the World"), for instance, while drawing extensively on the work of Isidore of Seville, also refers to ideas of the king's responsibility for the weather and the state of the crops that seem to derive from an older belief system. Anglo-Saxon kings and at least some of the Irish claimed descent from pagan gods, and, although these were interpreted in the Christian era as heroes rather than divinities, it is hard to credit that if, for instance, a belief did not already exist before conversion to Christianity in Woden as the progenitor of some Anglo-Saxon royal lines that it would have been necessary to invent it. However, the religious role of pre-Christian kings should not be exaggerated because other religious specialists existed. Druids were, like the jurists, members of the highly respected professional classes of Ireland who would have had the major role in organizing religion and royal functions within it. Some religious role for Irish kings at the major public assemblies or fairs (the *óenach*) seems likely, though evidence from later sources for elaborate inauguration rites in which the king symbolically "married" his kingdom are now treated with greater skepticism than in the past. Although priests are not generally considered an integral part of Germanic pagan religion, Bede does refer to them as an element of Anglo-Saxon practice and associated them with royal entourages, but there is also some evidence of a role for kings in public rituals such as the taking of auguries.

The interest of the Irish and Anglo-Saxon kings in demonstrating connections with gods and ancient heroes needs to be interpreted in the context of establishing the charisma of kingship, and can be seen as part of the strategy by which kings sought to outpace rivals or strengthen their hold on new territories. Visible prehistoric sites might be pressed into service and given a new mythical history. The Uí Néill linked themselves with Tara after they had taken it from the Laigin of Leinster, and it was used to support their claim to be kings of all Ireland.[37] From the time when Christianity became the religion of the Roman Empire in the reign of Constantine it was, in turn, utilized to underpin temporal power. The emperor became God's representative on earth whose reign paralleled that of Christ as king of heaven and it became the duty of good Christians to obey their ruler. Such concepts could be adapted to the successor states of post-Roman Europe. A letter of advice from Bishop Daniel of Winchester, who had first-hand experience of converting West Saxons to Christianity, to the novice missionary Boniface, suggests that pagan Germans were more likely to be impressed by the association of Christianity with the wealth and success of the Roman Empire than with details of its theology (though it would be a mistake for modern commentators not to take into account the attractions of Christianity as a religion). The conversion of kings was essential for the success of the missions to the Irish and Anglo-Saxons. Only they could safeguard the position of churchmen by giving them legal protection and land, but the previous religious roles of kings may have been a significant factor as well. Royal conversion was a gradual process; even if one king was converted, it did not necessarily follow that his successor would also be a Christian. In some Anglo-Saxon kingdoms there was a period of 40–60 years during which some members of the royal house became

Christian while others remained pagan which may have been the result of a deliberate decision to keep the two religions in tandem. Bede records (no doubt with many glosses of his own) the conversion of the Anglo-Saxon royal houses in some detail, but we unfortunately lack a similar narrative of how Irish kings were persuaded to adopt the new religion. Retrospective accounts of how individual kings were won over when Christian missionaries produced more powerful magic than their druids are of little historical value.[38]

Bede was keen to emphasize that when it came to ecclesiastical matters the role of kings was to act on the instructions of leading churchmen, but it is apparent from his narrative that many kings were far from being passive consumers and instead were the ones taking the initiative in the new religion.[39] The royal houses which converted most speedily to Christianity were ones in which a king had spent a period in exile in a Christian country, namely Northumbria whose rulers Oswald and Oswiu had been in exile in Scottish Dalriada, and the kingdom of the East Angles whose king, Sigebert (accession c.630), had been in exile in Francia. These rulers took the initiative in inviting missionaries to come into their kingdoms and in directing their work, sometimes using their influence as overlords to introduce missionaries into subject kingdoms. King Oswiu was also responsible for promoting his brother Oswald as a saint and for taking the final decision at the synod of Whitby in 664 to adopt the current practices of Rome for the celebration of Easter. King Nechtan of the Picts is said to have made a similar decision over the calculation of Easter for his own people in 717.[40]

The situation in Ireland may have been differently nuanced as one of the reasons for the success of Christianity there was that it managed to align itself with the professional classes who traditionally had responsibility for such factors as the operation of law and religion. But like their Anglo-Saxon (and probably British and Pictish) counterparts, Irish kings founded religious houses that were closely associated with their dynastic rule. In the segmented Irish royal houses some branches became religious specialists, or defeated minor kings might take this option for their dynasties. St. Columba, the founder of Iona, was of the royal house of Cenél Conaill in northern Ireland, as was his biographer and the eighth abbot of Iona, Adomnán.[41] In Anglo-Saxon royal families, it was generally the women rather than the men who went into the church, leading to a proliferation of very influential royal nunneries.[42] Some equivalents can be found in Ireland, notably Kildare where the abbesses were drawn from the ruling families of Leinster, but major nunneries do not seem to have been as prevalent as in the Anglo-Saxon kingdoms, perhaps reflecting the differences in roles for royal women discussed previously.[43]

There was thus a tendency for the church to underpin existing patterns of power and for the message of Christianity to be diluted as it adapted itself to early medieval societies. But Christianity also had the potential to introduce major changes, and be a conduit for concepts and skills from the late Roman world. Many of those educated in the church could not but be aware that their societies did not live up to Christian ideals and that secular powers were not only the worst offenders, but also a major channel through which new attitudes could be imposed. Some, like Gildas in the sixth century and Boniface in the eighth, played the role of Old Testament prophets and hoped to hector their rulers into submission, but kings could also be made to see that using their authority to improve Christian standards was a way of extending their power over their subjects. One of the best examples of cooperation between churchmen and kings to improve contemporary society is the "Law of the Innocents" adopted at Birr in Ireland in 697 which aimed to protect non-combatants from the effects of war and reduce violence against women.[44] Its initiator was Adomnán, abbot of Iona, and its chief guarantor was his Cénel Conaill kinsman, Loingsech, the king of Tara. The *cain Adomnáin*, as it is also known, is an excellent example of an attempt to protect the weakest in society in accordance with Christian teaching, while under-lining to its other signatories from Ireland and northern Britain (including a Pictish king and bishop) the supremacy of the Cenél Conaill in both secular and religious spheres.

Conclusion

The period c.550–c.750 saw major changes in kingship as larger kingdoms expanded at the expense of smaller, though the pace of change was different in Britain and Ireland because of the large number of small Irish kingdoms. Although subject to different traditions, the needs and ethos of military power were similar in the different kingdoms of the British Isles whose rulers were brought into contact with each other through overlordship and movement between the royal courts because of marriage or exile. Christianity introduced new shared values and had a potential, which was not fully realized by 750, to develop the scope of the office of king and provide rulers with a greater sense of moral responsibility. The need to be acceptable to kindred, nobility, and military companions also provided some brake on the otherwise wide scope for royal bad behavior.

Notes

1   Binchy, *Celtic and Anglo-Saxon Kingship*; Byrne, *Irish Kings and High-kings.*
2   Wormald, "Celtic and Anglo-Saxon kingship."
3   Davies, "The Celtic kingdoms," pp. 251–5.
4   Anderson, *Kings and Kingship*, pp. 139–45.
5   Yorke, *Kings and Kingdoms*, pp. 162–7.
6   Davies, *Wales in the Early Middle Ages*, pp. 42–7; Grant, "The construction of the early Scottish state," pp. 51–5.
7   Charles-Edwards, "Early medieval kingships."
8   Charles-Edwards, *Early Irish and Welsh Kinship*, pp. 460–1.
9   McErlean et al., *Strangford Lough*, pp. 57–63.
10 Ó Cróinín, "Ireland, 400–800."
11 Charles-Edwards, " 'The Continuation of Bede.' "
12 Alcock, *Kings and Warriors.*
13 Charles-Edwards, "Wales and Mercia"; Yorke, *Kings and Kingdoms*, pp. 100–27.
14 Colgrave and Mynors (eds.), *Bede's Ecclesiastical History*, iii. 24.
15 Charles-Edwards, *Early Christian Ireland*, pp. 441–68; Lacey, *Cénel Conaill.*
16 Bannerman, *History of Dalriada*, pp. 27–156.
17 Alcock, *Kings and Warriors*, pp. 172–5.
18 Ibid., pp. 177–200; Halsall, *Warfare and Society*, passim.
19 Moisl, "The Bernician royal dynasty."
20 Koch, *Gododdin.*

21 Winterbottom (ed.), *Gildas*, ch. 27, pp. 29 and 99.
22 Lapidge and Herren (trans.), *Aldhelm*, pp. 150–1, 168–70.
23 Colgrave (ed.), *Felix's Life of Saint Guthlac*, chs. 16–19.
24 Brooks, "The development of military obligations."
25 Ó Corráin, "Irish regnal succession"; Yorke, *Kings and Kingdoms*, pp. 167–72.
26 Charles-Edwards, *Early Christian Ireland*, pp. 441–68; Lacey, *Cénel Conaill*, pp. 187–97, 320–4.
27 Anderson, *Kings and Kingship*, pp. 165–201.
28 Colgrave and Mynors (eds.), *Bede's Ecclesiastical History*, i. 1.
29 Clancy, "Philosopher king."
30 Woolf, "Pictish matriliny reconsidered."
31 Ibid.
32 Smyth, *Warlords and Holy Men*, pp. 67–8.
33 Davies, "Celtic women."
34 Enright, *Lady with a Mead Cup*.
35 Charles-Edwards, *Early Irish and Welsh Kinship*, pp. 3–19; Stacey, "Texts and society," pp. 226–30.
36 Wormald, "Celtic and Anglo-Saxon kingship."
37 Charles-Edwards, *Early Christian Ireland*, pp. 469–83.
38 Ibid., pp. 182–240.
39 Higham, *Convert Kings*; Yorke, *Kings and Kingdoms*.
40 Clancy, "Philosopher king."
41 Herbert, *Iona, Kells and Derry*, pp. 9–35, 47–56; Sharpe (trans.), *Adomnán of Iona: Life of St. Columba*.
42 Yorke, *Nunneries*, pp. 17–46.
43 Davies, "Celtic women."
44 O'Loughlin, *Adomnán at Birr*.

Further Reading

There is no one book that looks at kingship throughout Britain and Ireland during this period. The article on "Celtic kingship in the early middle ages" by Wendy Davies is a very useful comparative essay for the different Celtic areas (plus Brittany), and *The Origins of Anglo-Saxon Kingdoms*, edited by Steven Bassett (Leicester, 1989) is broader in scope than its title might suggest and has papers viewing the Anglo-Saxon kingdoms in a wider insular and continental perspective. Major classic works of survey for Scotland and Ireland are Anderson, *Kings and Kingship in Early Scotland* and Byrne, *Irish Kings and High-kings*. Both set out the available evidence in considerable detail, but need to be read alongside more recent revisionist works such as those by Charles-Edwards and Ó Corráin for Ireland or Sharpe and Woolf for Scotland. The study of kingship in early medieval Scotland is particularly lively at the moment, with differing views on many key aspects such as the question of matrilineal succession among the Picts. Wendy Davies's *Wales in the Early Middle Ages* provides a good account of problematic evidence, and in my *Kings and Kingdoms of Early Anglo-Saxon England* I have endeavored to provide an account of the major kingdoms and some general observations on the nature of Anglo-Saxon kingship. Other overviews of early Anglo-Saxon kingship have been provided by David Kirby, *The Earliest English Kings*, and in several works by Nicholas Higham, including his *Convert Kings*, which provides a detailed study of the politics of conversion. It is desirable that the kingship of the British Isles is viewed in a broader European context and J. M. Wallace-Hadrill's, *Early Germanic Kingship* is a key work that does this for the Anglo-Saxon kingdoms (see also chapter 9 of this volume). Guy Halsall's *Warfare and Society* places the evidence for Britain and Ireland of this important royal activity in a broader perspective. Leslie Alcock's *Kings and Warriors* provides a good review of the archaeological evidence for warfare and courtly life from northern Britain and seeks to reconcile it with written evidence.

Bibliography

Alcock, L., *Kings and Warriors, Craftsmen and Priests* (Edinburgh, 2003).

Anderson, M. O., *Kings and Kingship in Early Scotland* (Edinburgh, 1980).

Bannerman, J., *Studies in the History of Dalriada* (Edinburgh, 1974).

Bassett, S. (ed.), *The Origins of Anglo-Saxon Kingdoms* (Leicester, 1989).

Binchy, D. A., *Celtic and Anglo-Saxon Kingship* (Oxford, 1970).

Brooks, N., "The development of military obligations in eighth- and ninth-century England," in P. Clemoes and K. Hughes (eds.), *England before the Conquest: Studies in Primary Sources Presented to Dorothy Whitelock* (Cambridge, 1971), pp. 69–84.

Byrne, F. J., *Irish Kings and High-kings* (London, 1973).

Charles-Edwards, T. M., "'The Continuation of Bede,' ca.750: High-kings, kings of Tara and 'Bretwaldas',", in A. P. Smyth (ed.), *Seanchas: Studies in Medieval Irish Archaeology, History and Literature in Honour of Francis J. Byrne* (Dublin, 2000), pp. 137–45.

Charles-Edwards, T. M., *Early Christian Ireland* (Cambridge, 2000).

Charles-Edwards, T. M., *Early Irish and Welsh Kinship* (Oxford, 1993).

Charles-Edwards, T. M., "Early medieval kingships in the British Isles," in S. Bassett (ed.), *The Origins of Anglo-Saxon Kingdoms* (Leicester, 1989), pp. 28–39.

Charles-Edwards, T. M., "Wales and Mercia, 613–918," in M. Brown and C. Farr (eds.), *Mercia: An Anglo-Saxon Kingdom in Europe* (London, 2001), pp. 89–105.

Clancy, T., "Philosopher king: Nechtan mac-Der-Ilei," *Scottish Historical Review*, 83 (2004), 125–49.

Colgrave, B. (ed.), *Felix's Life of Saint Guthlac* (Cambridge, 1956).

Colgrave, B. and Mynors, R. A. B. (eds.), *Bede's Ecclesiastical History of the English People* (Oxford, 1969).

Davies, W., "The Celtic kingdoms," in P. Fouracre (ed.), *The New Cambridge Medieval History*, vol. 1: *c.500–c.700* (Cambridge, 2005), pp. 232–62.

Davies, W., "Celtic kingships in the early Middle Ages," in A. J. Duggan (ed.), *Kings and Kingship in Medieval Europe* (London, 1993), pp. 101–24.

Davies, W., "Celtic women in the early Middle Ages," in A. Cameron and A. Kuhrt (eds.), *Images of Women in Antiquity*, rev. edn. (London, 1993), pp. 145–66.

Davies, W., *Wales in the Early Middle Ages* (Leicester, 1982).

Enright, M. J., *Lady with a Mead Cup: Ritual, Prophecy and Lordship in the European Warband from La Tène to the Viking Age* (Dublin, 1996).

Grant, A., "The construction of the early Scottish state," in J. R. Maddicott and D. M. Palliser (eds.), *The Medieval State: Essays Presented to James Campbell* (London, 2000), pp. 47–71.

Halsall, G., *Warfare and Society in the Barbarian West, 450–900* (London, 2003).

Herbert, M., *Iona, Kells and Derry: The History and Hagiography of the Monastic Familia of Columba* (Dublin, 1996).

Higham, N., *The Convert Kings: Power and Religious Affiliation in Early Anglo-Saxon England* (Manchester, 1997).

Kirby, D., *The Earliest English Kings* (London, 1991).

Koch, J. T., *The Gododdin of Aneirin: Text and Context from Dark Age North Britain* (Cardiff, 1977).

Lacey, B., *Cénel Conaill and the Donegal Kingdoms AD 500–800* (Dublin, 2006).

Lane, A. and Campbell, E., *Dunadd: An Early Dalriadic Capital* (Oxford, 2002).

Lapidge, M. and Herren, M. (trans.), *Aldhelm: The Prose Works* (Cambridge, 1979).

McErlean, T., McConkey, R., and Forsythe, W., *Strangford Lough: An Archaeological Survey of the Maritime Cultural Landscape* (Belfast, 2002).

Moisl, H., "The Bernician royal dynasty and the Irish in the seventh century," *Peritia*, 2 (1983), 103–26.

Ó Corráin, D., "Irish regnal succession: a reappraisal," *Studia Hibernica*, 11 (1971), 7–39.

Ó Corráin, D., "Nationality and kingship in pre-Norman Ireland," in T. W. Moody (ed.), *Nationality and the Pursuit of National Independence* (Belfast, 1978), pp. 1–35.

Ó Cróinín, D., "Ireland, 400–800," in D. Ó Cróinín (ed.), *A New History of Ireland*, vol. 1: *Prehistoric and Early Ireland* (Oxford, 2005), pp. 182–234.

O'Loughlin, T. (ed.), *Adomnán at Birr, AD 697: Essays in Commemoration of the Law of the Innocents* (Dublin, 2001).

Sharpe, R. (trans.), *Adomnán of Iona: Life of St. Columba* (Harmondsworth, 1995).

Sharpe, R., "The thriving of Dalriada," in S. Taylor (ed.), *Kings, Clerics and Chronicles in Scotland, 500–1297* (Dublin, 2000), pp. 47–61.

Sims-Williams, P., *Religion and Literature in Western England: 600–800* (Cambridge, 1990).

Smyth, A. P., *Warlords and Holy Men: Scotland AD 80–1000* (London, 1984).

Stacey, R. C., "Texts and society," in T. M. Charles-Edwards (eds.), *After Rome* (Oxford, 2003), pp. 221–57.

Wallace-Hadrill, J. M., *Early Germanic Kingship in England and on the Continent* (Oxford, 1971).

Winterbottom, M. (ed.), *Gildas: The Ruin of Britain and Other Documents* (Chichester, 1978).

Woolf, A., "Dún Nechtáin, Fortriu and the geography of the Picts," *Scottish Historical Review*, 85 (2006), 182–201.

Woolf, A., "Pictish matriliny reconsidered," *Innes Review*, 49 (1998), 147–67.

Woolf, A., "The Verturian hegemony: a mirror in the north," in M. Brown and C. Farr (eds.), *Mercia: An Anglo-Saxon Kingdom in Europe* (London, 2001), pp. 106–11.

Wormald, P., "Celtic and Anglo-Saxon kingship: some further thoughts," in P. Szarmach (ed.), *Sources of Anglo-Saxon Culture* (Kalamazoo 1986), pp. 151–83.

Yorke, B., *The Conversion of Britain: Religion, Politics and Society in Britain, c.600–800* (Harlow, 2006).

Yorke, B., *Kings and Kingdoms of Early Anglo-Saxon England* (London, 1990).

Yorke, B., *Nunneries and the Anglo-Saxon Royal Houses* (London, 2003).

CHAPTER SEVEN

Communities and Kinship

DAVID E. THORNTON

The purpose of this chapter is to examine the local communities that existed in Britain and Ireland during the sub- and post-Roman periods. What was the nature of these communities? Should they be seen as population groups or territories? What were their internal dynamics and what were the personal networks that determined how their individual members interacted with one another? And how were such interactions, especially disputes, regulated by society? It is not an easy task to answer such questions for this particularly "dark" period: our extant historical documents are few and far between, and those that have survived are invariably later in date and not always reliable when dealing with the fifth to eighth centuries. Furthermore, most of these sources are concerned primarily with the important kingdoms and their rulers, and have little to say about the lives of their more ordinary inhabitants.

The fifth and sixth centuries represent a period of significant change and transition following the end of centralized Roman administration in the West. Writing probably in the mid-sixth century, the cleric Gildas referred to the Britons as "*ciues*," meaning possibly "countrymen" but also "citizens," and he described the British leader (*dux*) Ambrosius Aurelianus as being of the Roman people, "*gens*."[1] Like others living in post-Roman western Europe, Gildas clearly saw himself and his fellow Britons as continuing *Romanitas* in some way. However, it is also clear that Roman culture had effectively disappeared in most areas. Gildas himself stated: "the *ciuitates* of our land are not populated even now as they once were; right to the present day, they are deserted, in ruins and unkempt."[2] In fact, archaeological investigation has demonstrated that while many Romano-British towns were indeed still occupied by the late fifth and early sixth centuries, the nature of this occupation had changed significantly from what it had been two centuries earlier. These post-Roman communities were effectively squatting on the remains of their Roman predecessors, living "a sub-Iron Age lifestyle,"[3] little different from that of the Anglo-Saxon settlers.

Even in Ireland, which was never conquered by the Romans, the fifth and sixth centuries would seem to have witnessed significant socioeconomic and political changes reflected in the spread of new forms of settlement, notably the ringfort and crannog, which also had reflexes in parts of western Britain.[4] This same period in

Ireland witnessed the decline of the so-called "archaic" population groups mentioned on ogham inscriptions from the fourth to the sixth centuries as well as enumerated in later lists of *aithech-túatha* (lit. "rent-paying peoples").[5] Some of those peoples, such as the Corcu Duibne and the Osraige (or at least their ruling lineages), survived as independent kingdoms into the historical period, but most were probably reduced in status or even wiped out as political entities by the rise of new dynasties, most significantly the Uí Néill, during the course of the seventh century. An interesting feature of these early Irish population groups, it has been argued, is that they were not named after a biological ancestor (like Uí Néill, "Descendants of Niall") but after pagan divinities, whereas others took their names from animals (Artraige, "the bear-people") or colors (Ciarraige and Dubraige, both meaning "the black people"). The precise significance of these names is impossible to determine with any certainty, and the nature of these archaic peoples remains obscure. Similar obscurity pertains for England: occasional references in charters and narrative sources such as Bede, as well as unique documents such as the *Tribal Hidage*, must be supplemented by the evidence of archaeology, onomastics, and a degree of guesswork. The *Tribal Hidage*, which in its original form was probably compiled in the late seventh century, is a tax or tribute list of the various "peoples" then under the hegemony of the greater Mercia created by King Penda and assessed in "hides" (see below).[6] The extant list includes kingdoms, both large and small, such as the East Angles (assessed at 30,000 hides) and the *Cantware* (men of Kent, 15,000 hides), as well as far more obscure peoples such as the *Arosæte* (600 hides), who lived near the river Arrow (Warwickshire), and the *Hicce* (300 hides), whose name perhaps survives in modern Hitchin (Hertfordshire).

There are various ways of understanding these early local communities in Britain and Ireland. Some scholars have seen them primarily as "population groups," "folk areas," or "tribes," emphasizing therefore that it was the constituent "people" who gave a community its identity. Thus, the Old Irish word *túath* – like the Welsh cognate *tud* – literally means "people," though it is normally rendered as "petty kingdom" by historians, and while the precise meaning of the Old English (OE) suffix *-ingas* is debated (see below), it clearly referred to a group of people in some way. Similarly, it would seem that the OE word *scír* ("shire") meant a share or division, perhaps of people,[7] but later came to have a more territorial meaning. However, the exact nature of these population groups is more difficult to determine. As an example, we can examine the so-called *-ingas* names, mentioned above. Many modern English place-names, especially in the south and south-east of England, seem to have been formed by combining a personal name with the plural suffix *-ingas*: for example, Hastings (*Hæstingas*), Reading (*Rēadingas*), and so forth. The basic meaning of such names is "sons or descendants of X," and so earlier scholars regarded such place-names as evidence of the initial Anglo-Saxon settlements, perhaps by small, mobile family units. However, J. McN. Dodgson and others have shown that since the distribution of *-ingas* names does not correspond to that of early pagan cemeteries, they rather represent a later stage of colonization or secondary settlement away from the initial settlements, perhaps in the sixth (or early seventh) century.[8] The suffix may still have designated the descendants of a common ancestor, whether real or imagined, but alternative translations include "followers or dependents of X" (where X would be a "founder" rather than biological ancestor), suggesting a rather more complex form of social organization than that of a familial band of immigrants.

An alternative approach has been to see these early population groups in terms of spheres of jurisdiction or lordship, rather than simply groups of people. For example, the early English *scīr*, which should not be compared with the later county-shires but rather with the "small shires" characteristic of later medieval northern England and lowland Scotland (Hallamshire, Hexhamshire, and so on),[9] would seem to have designated an area under the jurisdiction of a *scīrman*, perhaps to be translated as "ealdorman." Thus, the laws of King Ine of the West Saxons (see below) state: "If anyone goes away from his lord without permission, or steals into another *scīr*, and is discovered there, he is to return to where he was before and pay 60 shillings to his lord." The same document also refers to a person seeking "justice in the presence of any *scīrman* or other judge."[10] The northern "shires" may have originated in seventh-century Northumbria, perhaps continuing earlier Romano-British patterns which were more effectively replaced further south.[11] Similarly, one early Irish law tract states that "a *túath* is not a *túath* without a scholar, without a church, without a poet, without a king to extend contracts and treaties to [other] *túatha*," and another states that every *rí túaithe* ("king of a túath") should have a *brithem* ("judge").[12] Again, the *túath* is defined in terms of those who exercised power over it, especially the king, rather than its constituent people or kindred groups.

However, these population or jurisdiction areas certainly had, or at least came to acquire, a territorial aspect as well. Bede and other Latin sources refer to larger examples of such units as *regiones*, "regions," and many later administrative units would seem to have derived from these older folk-areas. Thus, it has been argued that the *Woccingas* ("the people of Wocca") in what is now Surrey formed the basis of the later hundreds of Chertsey and Woking, in which their name is still preserved.[13] Some *regiones* were subdivided into smaller units which formed the basis of later parishes, perhaps in a similar way to the way in which the Hwicce (an early "kingdom" in the west Midlands) formed the basis of the diocese of Worcester.[14] The Hwicce are an interesting case in point, since it has been argued that their territory – itself an amalgamation of smaller peoples – was, in turn, based on an earlier Romano-British unit, and such continuity of Roman and even Iron Age territories has been postulated for other cases, though this is difficult to prove with any certainty. These territories, however delineated, served as the basis for a largely self-sufficient agrarian community, probably practicing transhumance, with a main, well-cultivated core and less-developed woodland and pasture. By c.700, the territory probably had one or more "central places" which served as an administrative focus and which, in many instances in England, became royal vills. Here, we are reminded of the so-called "multiple estate model" regarded as characteristic of the early medieval Celtic economy in Britain, but with an influence on English territorial organization as well.[15] Indeed, it has been argued that *-ingas* names may represent estates, with the *-ingas* place as the main settlement and those based on *-ingetūn* and *-ingaham*, such as Sneinton and Nottingham (both Nottinghamshire), as associated or attached settlements of the estate.[16]

Ethnicity, Kinship, and Status

Documents dating from the seventh and eighth centuries begin to give some indication of the nature of local communities. From these sources, it may be suggested that an individual's position in a community and his or her interaction with other members of the community were determined by a number of often interrelated factors: ethnicity, kinship, social status, and ties of lordship. Of these, the first is perhaps the most difficult to study: anthropological and historical research have shown that "ethnicity" is a very slippery concept, often based more on *perceived* identity than on biological or linguistic realities. For Britain, the old scenario, based on narrative sources such as the *Anglo-Saxon Chronicle*, of the mass migration of Germanic invaders, slaughtering the native population and pushing the surviving Romano-Britons westward, has long since been discarded. Today, historians and archaeologists talk more in terms of assimilation and intermarriage between the two ethnic groups. This would help explain more fully why the West Saxon kingdom at the end of the seventh century clearly contained a sufficient number of native British men and women for the laws of King Ine to include regulations concerning "Welshmen" (*Wilisc, Wyliscne mon*), though they were explicitly given a lower status than their English counterparts.[17] Interpretation of archaeological evidence may also support this view of early "English" communities as ethnically mixed, though with members who were at least perceived to be of Romano-British ancestry being at a distinct socioeconomic disadvantage.[18] Indeed, recent analysis of DNA from what are now England and Wales, indicating significant genetic variation between the two areas, has been interpreted as arising not necessarily from a mass migration from the continent into England but rather from an "apartheid-like" social organization: the deliberate limiting of intermarriage between the immigrant Germanic minority and the socially and economically disadvantaged native British majority could have resulted in differential reproductive successes on the part of the two groups which, over a number of generations, would lead to the expansion of the Germanic genetic variants at the expense of the "Celtic" DNA.[19] Evidence from other parts of Britain may indicate a similar picture of checkered assimilation. The Irish settlers who penetrated into various parts of south Wales, and other parts of western Britain, during the fifth and sixth centuries, clearly did so in sufficient numbers to leave a not-insignificant impression on the archaeological and onomastic records.[20] Individuals who were commemorated in bilingual Irish ogham and Latin inscriptions were clearly socio-economically and politically important local figures, leaders of, in many cases, culturally mixed communities. In south Wales, the Welsh side of the equation was eventually to dominate the process of assimilation, whereas in western Scotland the opposite appears to have prevailed.

Kinship, or ties of blood relationship, represented perhaps the most fundamental social network for most people, whether commoners or kings, in early medieval Britain and Ireland. One's family were one's best friends. Indeed, the Old English word *freond*, now "friend," could also mean "kinsman," and similarly Old Irish *fine*, "kindred, kinsman," was cognate with OE *wine* ("friend") and could indicate a supporter or friend. Kinship was primarily agnatic and patrilineal: that is, the most important family ties for practical purposes were traced through one's father and other direct male ancestors, and the most important kin were largely men who shared a common male ancestor. Cognatic and bilateral kindred could be important in certain circumstances, but it was one's agnates who counted for most.

Historians and anthropologists often distinguish between close kinsmen, especially the nuclear family, and more distant relatives of various degrees. The most basic kinship unit was undoubtedly the nuclear family, comprising a man, his wife (or wives), and children. In Anglo-Saxon England, the most fundamental land unit was the "hide" (OE *hīd*) which Bede describes as *terra unius familiae* ("the land of one family"), but originally – like its cognate *hīwisc* – it may have referred to the nuclear family or household itself.[21] The nuclear family was both patriarchal and patrilineal in character: the father, as head of the household, was the main authority, and most of his rights, including land, would have passed to his sons. Indeed, in Ireland, the *mac béoathar* or "son of a living father" had very little legal independence from his father, even if he had reached the age of majority, to the extent that "he controls neither foot nor hand."[22] Marriage was in many ways an economic transaction between families. Early English laws refer to a man buying or purchasing a wife and, in certain circumstances, the "bride price" could be paid back. The Celts seem to have categorized marriages according to the level of input of the two sets of kinsmen, including the contribution of property to the new household. Furthermore, in Ireland, and perhaps in Scotland and Wales, polygyny was recognized by law. The church opposed this practice and also sought to control the closeness of kinship between husband and wife. The children of a nuclear family would normally have been the offspring of the man and his wife, though various kinds of artificial kinship were recognized. In Ireland and probably Wales, fosterage involved the temporary movement of a child aged between 7 and 14 to another household, and in England spiritual kinship between godfather and godson was regarded on an equal footing with that of a lord and his "man."

Beyond the nuclear family, the significance of more distant kin seems to have varied to some extent. For England, historians have debated whether cousins and other kinsmen acted together as corporate "descent groups" or lineages, as was certainly the case among the Celtic-speaking peoples.[23] In Ireland, before c.700, the most important kin-group was the *derbfhine* ("true or certain kindred"), which comprised a man's living male relatives descended from his great-grandfather. In addition to this four-generation agnatic lineage, the Irish laws refer to other groups, such as the *íarfhine* or "after kindred" descended from a great-great-grandfather, and even the *indfhine* or "end kindred" descended from a great-great-great-grandfather, but for most practical purposes it was the *derbfhine* which counted. By the early eighth century, it appears that a narrower group of three generations, the *gelfhine* ("white or bright kindred"), had come to replace the *derbfhine* as the most fundamental lineage.

Kinship was an important mechanism for regulating various aspects of society and economy. Kinsmen were integrally involved in the settlement of disputes, and especially the blood-feud (discussed in more detail below), both on the side of the offender as well as that of the victim. In early Ireland, land and farming were largely organized by the kin, and the *derbfhine* functioned as a "joint-farming cooperative."[24] The *fintiu* ("kin-land") was jointly owned by the *derbfhine*, with each member having an equal share, and these men undertook collective plowing and pasturing, according to certain contracts. *Fintiu* was inherited "partibly," that is divided, among the kinsmen, and could not be alienated outside the *derbfhine* without the permission of the whole kin-group. It seems that much of the earliest Anglo-Saxon land had also been kin-land and was similarly inalienable and inherited partibly. However, the development of *bocland* ("book-land") in the seventh century allowed the perpetual alienation of land to the recently established church recorded in a charter (*boc*), and must have been designed to prevent the claims of later kinsmen. Kin-land could be carefully delimited in order to prevent anyone from outside the kindred using it. It has been suggested that the location of early (even pagan) Anglo-Saxon burials on or near the boundaries of later parishes may indicate that they functioned as boundary markers for early estates, though this has been debated by scholars.[25] However, the evidence from the Celtic-speaking areas seems more convincing: an early Irish law tract on claiming hereditary right to kin-land states that land boundaries could be marked by a *fert* (grave-mound) or *fertae* (a collection of mounds or of burials in one mound), and ogham inscriptions, which date from the fourth to sixth centuries and occur mostly in Cos. Kerry, Cork, and Waterford, have been seen as early boundary markers as well as graves.[26] Similar arguments have been put forward for so-called "early inscribed stones" from Wales as well as other parts of western Britain, dating from the fifth to seventh centuries.[27] The occurrence of patronymics on these early and ogham-inscribed stones may accordingly have indicated a claim to the bounded land by the kinsmen of the interred individual. Thus, it would appear that the connection between land and kinship continued after death.

In addition to ethnic and kinship ties, a person's position in society was also affected by his or her legal status or rank. Although documentary sources often give the impression that later social distinctions also prevailed in the early post-Roman period, it seems that this was not the case. Archaeological evidence for the Anglo-Saxon settlers in Britain, in the form of cemeteries and buildings, suggests that in the fifth and early sixth centuries, the earliest English society was hierarchically relatively "flat." During the sixth century, richer grave-goods indicate an emerging socioeconomic divide, which becomes even more marked in the seventh century. Status was partly hereditary and partly based on wealth, and as such it was by no means fixed: as an eighth-century Irish law tract on status from Munster, *Uraicecht Becc* ("Small Primer"), states, "the freeman goes into the seat of the unfree, and the unfree into the seat of the free." Beyond this fundamental distinction between being "free" and "unfree," our sources refer to kings, nobles, and commoners as different types of freemen. The early Irish law tracts (see below) were especially hierarchical and describe different "grades" of king, noble, and commoner respectively, as well as of "poet" (*fili*) and cleric. In both the Germanic and Celtic systems, status was indicated in terms of calculable "value": the higher one's status, the higher one's value. In England, *wergild* (or *wergeld*), meaning "man-price" or "man-money," was the compensation to be paid for a victim of a homicide to their kinsmen (see below), and was normally calculated in shillings, though the value of a shilling could vary between kingdoms and over time. In Ireland, value was represented in terms of one's honor-price (*log n-enech*, lit. "value of the face"), which – given the lack of a monetary system – was calculated in terms of various units of livestock or precious metal, especially the *sét* ("chattel," worth one heifer) and *cumal* (lit. "female slave," worth ten cows in many texts), both of which varied in precise value. Status was not simply a matter of individual pride and snobbery, but also had practical implications for one's role in society: the value of a person as an oath-helper or a witness in law suits, for example, might depend on their status (see below).

The most fundamental status was that of the male, free peasant, who was head of a household. In England, this was the *ceorl* ("churl," but it could also mean "husband"): it seems likely that originally the *ceorl* was a freeman who held one hide (*hīd*) of land – about 120 acres – but this definition was breaking down by the seventh century.[28] It is often stated that the equivalent of the *ceorl* in Ireland was the *bóaire* (lit. "cow-freeman"), defined in terms of certain property qualifications, such as the possession of 14 *cumals*, though the laws do describe different grades of *bóaire* and the richest *bóaire* would certainly have surpassed the Anglo-Saxon *ceorl* in terms of wealth. The laws also describe other grades of freeman, including the *ócaire* ("young-freeman") who, being poorer than the *bóaire*, was unable to maintain a household, and the *fer midboth* ("man of middle huts") who was a freeman past the age of fosterage (14 years) but who had not yet attained majority (21 years) and therefore had not inherited property. At the bottom of the social hierarchy were the unfree: hereditary slaves who were tied to their lord's land. Gildas states that the early Anglo-Saxons enslaved defeated Britons,[29] but by the seventh century we have evidence of English slaves too. As the passage from *Uraicecht Becc* quoted above indicates, though hereditary, slavery was by no means a fixed status, and the church was active in freeing slaves. According to Bede (*HE*, iv. 13), Bishop Wilfrid of York freed or "manumitted" 250 slaves on his estate at Selsey (Sussex); and laws of King Wihtred of Kent (see below) required manumission to take place in a church (*EHD*, I, 397 [9]). There were also those whose status was to some extent semi-free, and whose fortunes could go either way over time. The Irish laws describe various kinds of tenant – such as the *fuidir* and the *bothach* – who were relatively poor and were therefore obliged to work for a lord in return for land but were not tied to the land as such. The different grades of *fuidir* depended upon the amount of land held. However, over a number of generations, a family could descend to the status of *senchléithe* or household slave. Similarly, the *læt* of early seventh-century Kent was perhaps a freedman whose family would achieve full freedom after a number of generations.

Whereas the commoner status appears to have depended primarily on wealth, that of nobility was at least in part based on lord and client relationships. The early Anglo-Saxon nobleman, variously termed the *gesith* ("companion") and *gesithcund* ("gesith-born"), was essentially the king's "companion." As such, he owed his royal lord military service and could be penalized severely for failing to do so. Bede and other early Anglo-Saxon sources refer to nobles who would follow their king into exile or even make the ultimate sacrifice and die defending him in battle. The Irish noble or *aire* (lit. "freeman") was defined, not by his connection to the king, but rather by the number of clients that he had. Thus, the highest grade of noble, the *aire forgaill* ("*aire* of superior testimony") should have 20 free-clients and the same number of base-clients, while the *aire ardd* ("high *aire*") should have ten of each. This Irish system of clientship (*célsine*) formed a further social network, and can be compared with the various kinds of so-called "feudal" relations characteristic of early and high medieval Europe: the lord (*flaith*) would give a "fief" (*rath*), usually of cattle, to his client (*céle*) in return for certain food-rents and services, depending on the type of clientship. Thus, the free-client (*soer-chéle*), who was a nobleman or perhaps a freeman, paid a fixed annual interest for the "free-fief" for seven years, after which time it could become his property, and performed homage and personal service, especially attendance on his lord. On the other hand, the base-client (*doer-chéle* or *giallnae*) paid his lord food-rent and interest on the "fief," and also owed hospitality and manual services of various sorts. Whereas free-clientship could be terminated by the client with no penalty, base-clientship was rather more difficult to leave without the lord's permission. The latter was the typical form of clientship for a non-noble freeman and, despite the title, did not indicate some kind of servile status.

Law and Law-making: Dispute, Feud, and Settlement

By the seventh and eighth centuries, an individual's position in a community was determined by ethnicity, kinship ties, and status. Our best evidence for how these definitions worked out in practice is legal. For the period before c.750, most of our direct evidence of law comes from two Anglo-Saxon kingdoms (Kent and Wessex) and from Ireland. The extant Welsh laws were written down in the twelfth and thirteenth centuries and, while at least some provisions probably can be shown to derive from early medieval practices, much of it is late and, in some cases, has been influenced by English law. Similarly, no very early laws survive from what is now Scotland, though it may be assumed that the inhabitants of the Gaelic kingdom of Dalriada followed laws not entirely dissimilar to their cousins in Ireland. All surviving early English law (not here including ecclesiastical legislation) is in the vernacular, and was, at least in appearance, royal legislation. The earliest texts, dating from the seventh century, are all attributed in the extant manuscripts to kings: Æthelberht, king of Kent (probably written c.602–3); Hlothhere and Eadric, also kings of Kent (c.685); Ine, king of the West Saxons (688–92); and Wihtred of Kent (695; *EHD*, I, 391–407). Furthermore, Bede states how Æthelberht established for his people, "with the advice of his councilors, judicial decrees after the examples of the Romans."[30] However, it has been argued that royal involvement in these so-called law codes increased over time. In terms of linguistic style and arrangement, Æthelberht's "code," in particular, seems more like traditional Kentish customs (*ælþeaw*) presented in a written – rather than oral – medium, rather than straightforward royal legislation. (It is the new, *literary* mode that therefore is "after the examples of the Romans" as Bede mentions.) Hlothhere and Eadric explicitly state that they have added *domas* ("judgments, decisions") to the laws that their forefathers had made, and Ine speaks (in the first person) of establishing true law (*æw*) and true "royal judgments" (*cyne-domas*). The irregular and repetitive structure of Ine's code certainly has the appearance of a series of decisions responding to specific problems as they arose. Royal involvement in judicial process is indicated in the law of Æthelberht by the payment of fines (*wite*) to the king as well as compensation (*bot*) to the victim or his kinsmen. These seventh-century laws therefore appear to trace a shift from customary law recorded in writing to royal law made and enacted in writing.[31]

The development of medieval native Irish law, sometimes called "Brehon Law," is a rather different matter.[32] The surviving legal manuscripts are relatively late, dating mostly from the fifteenth and sixteenth centuries. However, it is believed that most of the texts contained therein were first written down, in Old Irish, originally between the early/mid-seventh and mid-eighth centuries. Then, in the ninth century, Irish jurists began glossing and adding commentaries to these texts, and continued to do so until the sixteenth century. In addition, the tracts themselves quote fragments of *fénechas* – that is, aphorisms and verse texts on customs – which are older, perhaps dating from the very earliest Christian period, and which had probably been transmitted orally. It is not always an easy task to separate the various strata that accumulated during a period of almost a thousand years. The texts themselves take the form of "tracts," which seem effectively to have been school-books or instruction manuals for aspiring professional judges. As such, they represent an attempt to describe existing legal tradition, and do not constitute royal legislation (*rechtge*): there is some evidence that kings could legislate under special circumstances, such as defeat in battle or at times of plague, but this was not written down, following Roman legal tradition as copied in England and on the continent. Many legal texts appear to have formed part of collections, such as *Senchas Mar* ("The Great Tradition") put together in the north of Ireland during the second quarter of the eighth century, and *Bretha Nemed* ("Judgments of Privileged [or Sacred] Persons"), which were compiled in Munster around the same time using tracts that had been transmitted or composed at different law schools. Other texts, such as the text of status *Críth Gablach* ("Branched Purchase"), from shortly after c.700, survive as independent tracts. The compilation of the collections may have been partly inspired by the *Collectio canonum Hibernensis*, a collection of ecclesiastical law based on biblical and conciliar material but touching also on secular customs, put together in the early eighth century. Indeed, scholars now generally agree that Christianity and canon law had a direct and major influence on the native legal tradition, though the result was different from what was happening elsewhere in Europe, again because of the lack of influence of Roman law. It is worth emphasizing that whereas the seventh-century Anglo-Saxon laws were associated with particular kingdoms, early Irish law was generally regarded as valid for the whole of Ireland, even though individual tracts had been originally composed at specific law schools.

While Irish native law was not legislated law, in the sense of emanating from or backed by some central authority, and so could not be "reformed" as such by means of subsequent law-making in the same way as Anglo-Saxon, it could undergo changes reflecting developments in social structure and practices. Indeed, the nature of the extant Irish tracts, referring to earlier *fénechas* and incorporating later glosses and commentaries, means that such changes can sometimes be detected. For example, from *Críth Gablach* we can determine that by the beginning of the eighth century, physical injury was to be compensated for by means of payment according to status. Originally, it seems that the offender had been required to provide his victim with "sick maintenance" (*folog n-othrusa*), perhaps in his own house, and to support the victim's retinue, until the victim had recovered, but this was subsequently changed, first to the provision of food, a doctor, and nurse at the victim's house, and finally to the payment of compensation.[33]

Indeed, most of the pre-viking laws from Britain and Ireland were "tort law": concerned with specifying the compensation due to a victim or his or her kinsmen to be paid by the offender and/or their kinsmen. As the example above shows, this could take the form of repairing any damage caused, but far more often it involved some kind of compensatory payment. The amount of compensation would depend partly on the nature of the offence, whether to the victim's person or property, and also on the status of the individuals involved, but could also depend on where the offence was committed. In Æthelberht's law, offences range from hair-pulling, for which the compensation was a mere 50 *sceattas*, to the killing of a man, for which

the ordinary *wergild* was 100 shillings. The purpose of the payment was to compen-
sate the victim or his kinsmen for any loss or damages incurred as a result of the
offence and thus put an end to any dispute which may otherwise have arisen.

The most infamous form of dispute was undoubtedly the feud or blood-feud. This
was common in both continental and insular Europe, and had been described by the
first-century Roman author Tacitus in his *Germania*. The feud can be defined as a
conflict or series of conflicts between individuals or groups of individuals – usually
kindred groups – resolved either through private vengeance or by means of the
payment of compensation for the initial offence, which in many cases was a homicide.
The killing of the slayer by the kinsmen of the victim should not necessarily be
regarded as being symptomatic of a lawless society, though the payment of compensation was presumably a more socially acceptable means of resolution. There are few
surviving records of real-life disputes, including feuds, before c.750, and those few
that do survive were invariably recorded by, and served the interests of, the church.[34]
Therefore, much of our knowledge of dispute settlement for this period derives from
provisions described in the laws.

The Old English word *wergild* ("man-price") is commonly used today for the
system of compensatory payments due for the injury or killing of a person found in
most Germanic and Celtic societies in the early medieval period. The *wergild* was
determined primarily by the status of the victim and was paid, in the case of homicide,
to the kinsmen, who could include members of both the maternal as well as paternal
agnatic lineage. For example, the laws of Hlothhere and Eadric give the *wergild* of
a freeman at 100 shillings (compare Æthelberht above) and that of a nobleman at
300 shillings. Ine's laws appear to give a much higher *wergild* for equivalent ranks,
though this may have been because of the lower value of coinage in Wessex. As stated
above, Ine also devotes some space to offenses involving Welshmen whose *wergild*
was usually lower than that of an equivalent Englishman. In Irish law, compensation
for a killing was of two kinds. First, there was a *wergild* payment called *éraic* (sometimes *cró*) which was fixed at seven *cumals* for all freemen – noble or commoner – and
was paid to the victim's *derbfhine*; on the other hand, there was the *lóg n-enech*
(honor-price) which was paid both to the victim's agnatic and his cognatic kinsmen
and was determined by the status of the kinsman: presumably because it was the kin
who had "lost face" by the offence. Similarly, later Welsh law also made a distinction
between *galanas*, which means both the feud and the *wergild* payment, and *sarhaed*
(or *sarhad*), which refers both to an injury involving an "insult" and the compensation paid for the insult, determined by status. It would seem that, as a general rule,
close kinsmen – the nuclear family – were entitled to a higher proportion of a *wergild*
than more distant relatives. Thus, Æthelberht's laws refer to the payment of 20 shillings "at the open grave" (that is, soon after the death of the victim) and then the
whole *wergild* within 40 days: this 20 shillings may correspond to the *healsfang*
("grasp of the hand") which was an initial payment made to close kinsmen who were
presumably most acutely aggrieved by the loss of the victim and, accordingly, most
likely to seek revenge (*EHD*, I, 392 [22]).

As well as the kin of the victim, those of the slayer were involved in the feud and
were liable to pay compensation, unless they repudiated him. Thus, according to
Æthelberht, if the slayer "departs from the land," his kinsmen should pay half of the
victim's *wergild*. Furthermore, the feud could also involve ties of lordship as well as

kinship. In Anglo-Saxon law, the master was liable for a homicide committed by his servant or slave, and the "saga" *Cynewulf and Cyneheard*, entered in the *Anglo-Saxon Chronicle sub anno* 755, describes a feud involving a series of killings in which some of the participants explicitly state "no kinsman was dearer to them than their lord" (*EHD*, I, 176). Feuds which cross over the boundaries between kingdoms were also covered in the laws. For Ireland, *Críth Gablach* describes how a posse of five armed men could be led by the *aire échta* ("nobleman of slaughter") into a neighboring *túath* to take revenge for an offence.[35]

According to both Anglo-Saxon and Irish laws, not all killings were necessarily grounds for pursuing a feud: there were certain "justifiable" killings which could not legitimately be avenged. For example, the late seventh-century fragmentary Irish tract *Córus Fine* ("Legal Ordering of the Kindred") states that killings in revenge for a man of one's *derbfhine*, for a foster-child of the kindred, for a man adopted into the kindred, or for a "sister's son" were all justifiable.[36] Elsewhere, it is stated: "It is lawful to kill in battle, or to kill a thief caught in the act of stealing. An unransomed captive [*cimbid*] may be killed by the individual or kin whom he has wronged, and a violator of the law [*fer coilles cáin*] may be killed by anybody."[37] In England, according to the laws of Ine, the killing of a thief would appear to have fallen into this category, and these laws also emphasize that the guilt of the slayer must be proved before the feud could be pursued. Æthelberht's earlier statement that "if one servant kills another *without cause*, he is to pay the full value" may imply that killing "with cause" would be treated differently (*EHD*, I, 395 [86]).

It is perhaps not surprising that the violence of the feud, and society in general, attracted the concern of the church. The *Penitential* of Bishop Theodore of Canterbury stipulates that if anyone kills a man in revenge for a kinsman, he should do penance for the homicide, though the period of penance could be reduced if he were willing to pay the required compensation.[38] Clearly, Theodore did not regard killing in revenge for a kinsman as a justifiable act. During the late seventh and eighth centuries, many Irish monasteries issued so-called *cána* (sing. *cáin*, "regulation" or "tax"), usually in the name of a saint, including the *Cáin Adomnáin* (AD 697), known in Latin as *Lex innocentium*: Adomnán's law sought to stop violence against "innocents," namely women, children, and clerics, and was prepared to employ penance, amputations, and even death, as well as compensation payments, in order to do so.[39] On the other hand, whereas the growing involvement of Anglo-Saxon royal legislation on the feud was previously regarded as an attempt to limit the feud and the apparent lawlessness, it is more common now to see this as an attempt to assume control of its mechanics and the ensuing profits, for example, via "fines" (OE *wite*). Indeed, the fact that later kings still legislated about the feud indicates that it continued to be an important element in society (see chapter 27).

The non-violent resolution of a blood-feud or any other kind of dispute required the willingness of the offender to come to a settlement with the victim and his or her kinsmen, and to pay the relevant compensation. Indeed, since the kinsmen of the offender were themselves involved in the dispute, it was in their interests to come to a settlement. As pointed out above, according to Æthelberht's laws, a slayer's kinsmen were responsible for paying half of the *wergild*, if the slayer "departs from the land" (*EHD*, I, 392 [23]). The laws therefore contained various methods and procedures aimed at bringing the relevant parties, notably the alleged offender, to a settlement. One of the most elementary means of self-help described in Irish law was that of *athgabál* or distraint: in its most primitive form, this involved the immediate seizure of the offender's chattels or property by the injured party as a way of compelling him to settle the dispute.[40] The property could then be held for a specified period or "stay" after which, if no settlement had been reached, it was forfeit. Later on, the injured party was required to give advance warning of intention to distrain the offender: here, the intended effect was the same – to enforce a settlement – but the means was less immediate and, no doubt, less contentious. Similarly, the laws of Ine would appear to prohibit an injured party from performing distraint (*wracu*, lit. "vengeance") "before he asks for justice for himself," presumably implying that it was permitted once the offender had failed to do him justice. An alternative way of enforcing a settlement was that of surety; that is, a person who was responsible for ensuring the correct actions of another. The eighth-century Irish tract entitled *Berrad Airechta* ("Shaving of the Court"), which incorporates earlier material, refers to three kinds of surety as the means of guaranteeing agreements and contracts: the *naidm* (earlier *macc*) or "binding surety" who "bound a contract" by pledges and was therefore responsible for enforcing it; the *ráth* ("paying-surety") who had agreed to pay a debt using his own property should the offender fail to do so; and also the *aitire* ("hostage-surety," lit. "go-between") who could be effectively imprisoned by the injured party in the case of a broken contract.[41] Later Welsh law also provided for a surety (*mach*) whose function corresponded to that of the Old Irish *naidm*.

If methods such as distraint and the use of sureties failed to achieve a settlement, the parties could resort to independent judgment by a judge or court. Even, in the relative anarchy of the mid-sixth century, Gildas stated that Britain had judges (*iudices*), though he added, perhaps for rhetorical effect, that they were wicked (*impius*).[42] The Kentish laws of Hlothhere and Eadric state that an injured party or plaintiff could bring a charge against an offender at "an assembly or meeting" (*mæðel oþþe þing*) and that the offender should give surety and should do the plaintiff "such right/rectification as the judges of the people of Kent shall prescribe for them" (*EHD*, I, 395 [8–10]). Such assemblies would appear to have been local public gatherings, involving legal experts who determined the final judgment and – like the later hundred-courts that replaced them – were held on or near boundaries, roads or rivers, or at places marked by stones or trees. In Ireland, a case could be brought before a judge (usually singular) or *brithem*, either at a similar public assembly (*airecht*, "court") or privately at the judge's house. Such lawsuits could involve the use of witnesses, preferably independent eye-witnesses to a contract, and also compurgators or "oath-helpers," who would support the oaths and pleadings given by the disputing parties but whose value as such depended on their respective status.

Conclusion

The communities that existed in Britain and Ireland following the disappearance of Roman administration were a product both of earlier forms of social organization and of new dynamics. The political, economic, and demographic changes of the post-Roman period were played out on the smaller stage as well as on a larger, more well-documented level. Groups of people, the basic element in any society, coalesced into larger groups and into territories occupied by these groups. People became kingdoms. The dynamics of these local communities were organized by means of interrelated networks, based on ethnicity, kinship, status, and lordship. These networks helped define an individual's position in society and formed the basis of how that society regulated itself. Thus, the settlement of disputes between individuals recognized the importance of kinship ties and status as the means of facilitating settlements and ensuring social cohesion within the community as a whole.

Notes

1. Winterbottom (ed.), *Gildas*, pp. 17, 24, 28, 90, 95, 98.
2. Ibid., pp. 28, 98.
3. Blair, *Anglo-Saxon Oxfordshire*, p. 3.
4. Edwards, *Archaeology of Early Medieval Ireland*, pp. 15–19, 35–7.
5. Charles-Edwards, *Early Irish and Welsh Kinship*, pp. 147–65; MacNeill, "Early Irish population-groups."
6. Davies and Vierck, "The contexts"; Dumville, "The Tribal Hidage"; Gelling, *The West Midlands*, pp. 79–85.
7. Cameron, *English Place Names*, p. 51.
8. Dodgson, "The significance"; Gelling, *Signposts to the Past*, pp. 106–21; Kuurman, "An examination."
9. Barrow, *Kingdom of the Scots*, pp. 7–68.
10. Whitelock (ed.), *English Historical Documents* (*EHD*), I, 400 (8), 403 (39).
11. Joliffe, "Northumbrian institutions."
12. Binchy (ed.), *Corpus Iuris Hibernici*, p. 1123.
13. Blair, *Early Medieval Surrey*, pp. 13–14. For the "hundred," see chapter 27 of this volume.
14. Hooke, *The Anglo-Saxon Landscape*; Sims-Williams, *Religion and Literature*, pp. 29–39.
15. See, e.g., Jones, "Early territorial organization" and "Post-Roman Wales."
16. Stafford, *The East Midlands*, p. 30.
17. *EHD*, I, 401 (23.3, 24.2), 402 (32), 405 (54.2), 407 (74); Grimmer, "Britons in early Wessex."
18. Härke, "'Warrior graves?'"
19. Thomas et al., "Evidence for an apartheid-like social structure"; Weale et al., "Y-chromosome evidence."
20. Richards, "The Irish settlement."
21. Charles-Edwards, "Kinship, status and the origins of the hide."
22. Charles-Edwards, *Early Irish and Welsh Kinship*, pp. 36–7.
23. Lancaster, "Kinship in Anglo-Saxon society – I."
24. Ó Corráin, "Ireland c.800," p. 553.
25. Bonney, "Early boundaries and estates"; Goodier, "The formation of boundaries."
26. Charles-Edwards, "Boundaries in Irish law."
27. Edwards, "Early-medieval inscribed stones"; Handley, "The early medieval inscriptions."
28. Charles-Edwards, "Kinship, status and the origins of the hide."
29. Winterbottom (ed.), *Gildas*, pp. 27, 98.
30. Sherley-Price and Latham (eds.), *Bede*, ii. 5.

31 Wormald, *"Exempla Romanorum"*; *"Inter cetera bona"*; *Making of English Law*, pp. 92–101.
32 Charles-Edwards, "Early Irish law"; Kelly, *Guide to Early Irish Law*.
33 Binchy, "Sick-maintenance in Irish law."
34 For example, Sharpe, "Dispute settlement," pp. 174–7; Wormald "A handlist," p. 259.
35 Binchy, *Críth Gablach*, pp. 70–2.
36 Charles-Edwards, *Early Irish and Welsh Kinship*, p. 505.
37 Kelly, *Guide to Early Irish Law*, pp. 128–9.
38 Whitelock, *The Beginnings*, p. 42.
39 Meyer (ed.), *Cáin Adamnáin*.
40 Binchy, "Distraint in Irish law."
41 Sharpe, "Dispute settlement," p. 183.
42 Winterbottom (ed.), *Gildas*, pp. 29, 99.

Further Reading

For two useful introductions to early medieval insular law, see Fergus Kelly's *A Guide to Early Irish Law*, and the late Patrick Wormald's *The Making of English Law*; for studies of law in practice, see the various papers collected in *The Settlement of Disputes in Early Medieval Europe*, edited by Wendy Davies and Paul Fouracre. Law and society for the Celtic-speaking peoples are comprehensively covered in Thomas Charles-Edwards, *Early Irish and Welsh Kinship*. Margaret Gelling's *Signposts to the Past* remains a useful introduction to early English society through place-names.

Bibliography

Barrow, G. W. S., *The Kingdom of the Scots: Government, Church and Society from the Eleventh to the Fourteenth Century*, 2nd edn. (Edinburgh, 2003).
Binchy, D. A. (ed.), *Corpus Iuris Hibernici*, 6 vols (Dublin, 1978).
Binchy, D. A., *Críth Gablach* (Dublin, 1941).
Binchy, D. A., "Distraint in Irish law," *Celtica*, 10 (1973), 22–71.
Binchy, D. A., "Sick-maintenance in Irish law," *Ériu*, 12 (1938), 78–134.
Blair, J., *Anglo-Saxon Oxfordshire* (Stroud, 1994).
Blair, J., *Early Medieval Surrey: Landholding, Church and Settlement before 1300* (Stroud, 1991).
Bonney, D., "Early boundaries and estates in southern England," in P. H. Sawyer (ed.), *Medieval Settlement: Continuity and Change* (London, 1976), pp. 72–82.
Cameron, K., *English Place Names* (London, 1996).
Charles-Edwards, T. M., "Boundaries in Irish law," in P. H. Sawyer (ed.), *Medieval Settlement: Continuity and Change* (London, 1976), pp. 83–7.
Charles-Edwards, T. M. "Early Irish law," in D. Ó Cróinín (ed.), *A New History of Ireland*, vol. 1: *Prehistoric and Early Ireland* (Oxford, 2005), pp. 331–70.
Charles-Edwards, T. M., *Early Irish and Welsh Kinship* (Oxford, 1993).
Charles-Edwards, T. M., "Kinship, status and the origins of the hide," *Past & Present*, 56 (1972), 3–33.
Davies, W. and Fouracre, P. (eds.), *The Settlement of Disputes in Early Medieval Europe* (Cambridge, 1986).
Davies, W. and Vierck, H., "The contexts of Tribal Hidage: social aggregates and settlement patterns," *Frühmittelalterliche Studien*, 8 (1974), 223–93.

Dodgson, J. McN., "The significance of the distribution of the English place-names in -*ingas*, -*nga*- in south east England," *Medieval Archaeology*, 10 (1967 for 1966), 1–29.

Dumville, D., "The Tribal Hidage: an introduction to its texts and their history," in S. Bassett (ed.), *The Origins of Anglo-Saxon Kingdoms* (Leicester, 1989), pp. 225–30.

Edwards, N., *The Archaeology of Early Medieval Ireland* (London, 1990).

Edwards, N., "Early-medieval inscribed stones and stone sculptures in Wales: context and function," *Medieval Archaeology*, 45 (2001), 15–39.

Gelling, M., *Signposts to the Past: Place-names and the History of England* (London, 1978).

Gelling, M., *The West Midlands in the Early Middle Ages* (Leicester, 1992).

Goodier, A., "The formation of boundaries in Anglo-Saxon England: a statistical study," *Medieval Archaeology*, 28 (1984), 1–21.

Grimmer, M., "Britons in early Wessex: the evidence of the law code of Ine," in N. Higham (ed.), *Britons in Anglo-Saxon England* (Woodbridge, 2007), pp. 102–14.

Handley, M., "The early medieval inscriptions of western Britain: function and sociology," in J. Hill and M. Swan (eds.), *The Community, the Family and the Saint: Patterns and Power in Early Medieval Europe* (Turnhout, 1998), pp. 339–61.

Härke, H., "'Warrior graves?' The background of the Anglo-Saxon weapon burial rite," *Past & Present*, 126 (1990), 22–43.

Hooke, D., *The Anglo-Saxon Landscape: The Kingdom of the Hwicce* (Manchester, 1985).

Joliffe, J. E. A., "Northumbrian institutions," *English Historical Review*, 41: 161 (1926), 1–42.

Jones, G. R. J., "Early territorial organization in Gwynedd and Elmet," *Northern History*, 10 (1975), 3–27.

Jones, G. R. J., "Post-Roman Wales," in H. P. R. Finberg (ed.), *The Agrarian History of England and Wales*, vol. 1, part 2: AD *43–1042* (Cambridge, 1972), pp. 283–382.

Kelly, F., *A Guide to Early Irish Law* (Dublin, 1988).

Kuurman, J. "An examination of the -ingas, -inga, place-names in the East Midlands," *English Place-Name Society Journal*, 7 (1975 for 1974), 11–44.

Lancaster, L., "Kinship in Anglo-Saxon society – I," *British Journal of Sociology*, 9 (1958), 230–50.

MacNeill, E., "Early Irish population-groups: their nomenclature, classification and chronology," *Proceedings of the Royal Irish Academy*, 29C (1911), 59–114.

Meyer, K. (ed. and trans.), *Cáin Adamnáin: An Old-Irish Treatise on the Law of Adamnan* (Oxford, 1905).

Ó Corráin, D., "Ireland c.800: aspects of society," in D. Ó Cróinín (ed.), *A New History of Ireland*, vol. 1: *Prehistoric and Early Ireland* (Oxford, 2005), pp. 549–608.

Richards, M., "The Irish settlement in Wales," *Journal of the Royal Society of Antiquaries of Ireland*, 90 (1960), 133–62.

Sharpe, R., "Dispute settlement in medieval Ireland: a preliminary inquiry," in W. Davies and P. Fouracre (eds.), *The Settlement of Disputes in Early Medieval Europe* (Cambridge, 1986), pp. 169–89.

Sherley-Price, L. and Latham, R. E. (ed. and trans.), *Bede: A History of the English Church and People* (Harmondsworth, 1968).

Sims-Williams, P., *Religion and Literature in Western England: 600–800* (Cambridge, 1990).

Stafford, P., *The East Midlands in the Early Middle Ages* (Leicester, 1985).

Thomas, M. G., Stumpf, M. P. H. and Härke, H., "Evidence for an apartheid-like social structure in early Anglo-Saxon England," *Proceedings of the Royal Society of London*, series B, 273 (2006), 2651–7.

Weale, M. E., Weiss, D. A., Jager, R. F., et al., "Y-chromosome evidence for Anglo-Saxon mass migration," *Molecular Biology and Evolution*, 19 (2002), 1008–21.

Whitelock, D., *The Beginnings of English Society (The Anglo-Saxon Period)* (Harmondsworth, 1952).

Whitelock, D. (ed. and trans.), *English Historical Documents*, vol. I: *c.500–1042*, 2nd edn. (London, 1979).

Winterbottom, M. (ed. and trans.), *Gildas: The Ruin of Britain and Other Documents* (Chichester, 1978).

Wormald, P., "*Exempla Romanorum*: the earliest English legislation in context," in A. Ellegård and G. Åkerström-Hougen (eds.), *Rome and the North* (Jonsered, 1996), pp. 15–27.

Wormald, P., "A handlist of Anglo-Saxon lawsuits," *Anglo-Saxon England*, 17 (1988), 247–81.

Wormald, P., "*Inter cetera bona . . . genti suae*: law-making and peace-keeping in the earliest English kingdoms," *Settimane di studio del centro italiano di studi sull'alto medioevo*, 42: 2 (1995), 963–96.

Wormald, P., *The Making of English Law: King Alfred to the Twelfth Century*, vol. I: *Legislation and its Limits* (Oxford, 1999).

CHAPTER EIGHT

Social Structure

THOMAS M. CHARLES-EDWARDS

The route adopted here to an understanding of early social structures in Ireland and Britain is from the individual to the collective. The starting-point is personal identity; this will lead to a consideration of the stages of an individual's life – the life-cycle – and then to class and status. After that, we shall turn to a personal relationship crucial for status, that between a lord and his follower (for kinship, see chapter 7).

Names and Personal Identity

"I was free according to the flesh, born to a decurion father. For I have sold my noble rank – I do not blush nor do I regret it – for the good of others; and so I am a slave in Christ to a foreign people." Thus Patrick wrote to the soldiers of Coroticus, a British king; and in his *Confession* he traced his descent: his father was a deacon, Calpurnius, and his grandfather a priest, Potitus.[1] It was on his grandfather's estate, which he locates close to a certain *vicus*, that Patrick was captured by Irish raiders and led off into slavery – a slavery from which he escaped back to Britain, only to return to Ireland to preach Christianity and so, as an alien, forfeit the status he had in Britain. Although it seems very probable that Patrick's life lay entirely within the fifth century, and that his activity in Ireland lay in the middle or second half of that century, he took it for granted that even the slave-raiding soldiers of Coroticus would understand Roman ranks. In the fifth century, therefore, some Britons still thought in terms familiar across the Latin-speaking part of the empire. Patrick identified himself by name, by his curial rank, by descent from two office-holders in the church, and by the location of his grandfather's lands, and so, by implication, by the city-territory in which he was born. He claimed respect not just in virtue of what he was in Ireland – a bishop – but in virtue of what he had been in Britain, born into the local gentry of a British *civitas*.

In Britain after the fifth century such assurance over old social landmarks would hardly have been possible. Yet Patrick was not unique, even in the slight historical sources that remain for the fifth and sixth centuries. An inscription at Penmachno in Caernarvonshire commemorates Cantiori, a citizen of Gwynedd and a cousin of

Maglus the magistrate.[2] The names are Celtic but the political framework appears Roman, just as the language is a British Romance, comparable with Gallo-Romance, the forerunner of French. The norm in the post-Roman inscriptions of western Britain and Ireland was, however, to identify someone merely by name and "son of X" (very occasionally "daughter of X"): name and paternity were enough to situate an individual. The royal genealogies in the *Anglo-Saxon Chronicle* are constructed from just such simple identifications as X son of Y: "Ine Cenreding, Cenred Ceolwalding" (Ine son of Cenred, Cenred son of Ceolwald).[3]

One can see the reason from the role of paternity within society: it gave a man his kindred, and to a lesser extent it did the same for a woman; it probably gave them their status; and it might give a man his occupation (early Irish poets were usually the descendants of poets, just as kings were the descendants of kings). Those unfortunates who lacked an acknowledged father were likely to be of very low rank. The son of a woman who had been given to his father in marriage was normally secure in his identity; not so the Irish "son of a bush," or the Welsh "son of bush and brake"; that is, a son conceived in a secret liaison carried on outside the domestic sphere: he might be lucky and be acknowledged by his father, but he might end up as a mere dependant of his maternal kinsmen.[4] In Ireland and Wales, therefore, the issue was not the legitimacy of the parents' union but the paternity of the child.

For such well-known persons as Ine or Columba, name and paternity were enough, but for the stranger more might be required. A young man named Fintan son of Tailchán wished to become a pilgrim on Iona – and so to leave his native Ireland for Britain. He arrived shortly after Columba's death in 597, when his successor, Baíthéne was briefly abbot:

> At that time his name was not known here so that, when he arrived, he was received as a stranger and guest . . . he was given a seat and asked by Baíthéne, who still did not know who he was, about his *gens* and province, his name, his manner of life and for what reason he had undertaken the effort of the journey.[5]

As was the custom throughout Irish society, Fintan, the guest and also the inferior in age and rank, had to identify himself. The extent of the information required brings into the open what, in other cases, was too well known to need stating. Fintan was not just the son of Tailchán but was a member of what Adomnán called a *gens*, a group that could be seen as a kindred but was apparently different from the normal variety. He was a celibate and a student of scripture, who wished to become a monk on Iona. This full-scale self-identification thus required a brief narrative giving the salient elements of his life and also placing him precisely within Irish society.

Even first names might tell one quite a lot about a person: English, Irish, and Welsh names normally revealed gender and ethnicity. They might also be varied to suit the context of utterance: the Englishman Trumwine was consecrated in 681 as bishop for those Picts who were under the rule of Ecgfrith, king of Northumbria. His name is of a standard type, a compound of two English words, in this case "army-friend"; in the Lindisfarne *Life of St. Cuthbert*, however, the same man is named Tumma, and this is a familiar version of the same name, similar to our Tom alongside Thomas.[6] The Franks used grand two-stem names, such as Trumhere, for their kings, whereas others seem most often to have had short forms like Tumma; the English made no such distinction, so that Penda and Peada (both short forms) coexisted with

Wulfhere and Æthelred (both long forms) among the Mercian kings of the seventh century. Yet there was a difference between the two forms, as indicated by an East Saxon king of the early seventh century, whom Bede calls Saberht, "Sea-Bright," but he states explicitly that his sons used to call him by the shortened and more familiar version of his name, Saba (*HE*, ii. 5).

Names could be attached to particular dynasties. Kings of Gwynedd in the seventh century had names with *cad*, "battle, army," as the first element, a fashion that, unusually, affected the West Saxon dynasty (Cædwalla). Whereas the East Saxon dynasty favored names beginning with "S," the Kentish dynasty had a fondness for two-stem forms that began with a vowel, and thus also alliterated: Wihtred, who died in 725, was Wihtred Ecgbryhting, Ecgbryht Earcenbryhting, Earcenbryht Eadbalding, Eadbald Æthelbryhting (*Anglo-Saxon Chronicle*, s.a. 694). To give a son a name associated with a dynasty did not, in itself, constitute a claim to royal status, but it was consistent with a claim based on descent, and it might also indicate other claims: the first element of Wihtred's name suggests a connection with the Isle of Wight, an independent kingdom when Wihtred was born; according to Bede, Wight and Kent were both Jutish settlements (*HE*, i. 15). Names could suggest a link with a mother's family: the Bernician kings Oswald and Oswiu both had names with the first element "Os" meaning "god"; this alliterated with their father's name Æthelfrith, but it may have derived from the Deiran dynasty to which their mother Acha belonged, since that contained such names as Osred and Oswine. Áedán mac Gabráin, the great warrior king of Dál Riata, proclaimed his ambitions in the names of his sons: most unusually for an Irish king, they included a British name, Artúr (Arthur), and what may be a name borrowed from the Old English word for "king," *cyning* (Conaing). The norm, only broken very occasionally, was to stick to the names favored by one's own nation, and variations from the norm were therefore significant.

Names, however, could be changed or added to mark a change of identity in the church: Wynfrith, the West Saxon missionary to Germany, took the Roman name Boniface. The new name signified an enhanced allegiance and role. British churchmen often had biblical names, such as Asser, Samson, or David; in some cases, these were apparently names given after birth and were used by the laity; Columba, the Latin for "dove," was hardly, however, the original name of the founder of Iona.[7] Not all ecclesiastical names, however, signified a turning away from native forms. Among the Irish and the Britons, monks often took a peculiar form of pet-name that also prefixed the possessive pronouns meaning "My" or "Thy": Fintan son of Tailchán became the founder and abbot of Taghmon in Co. Wexford – that is, Tech Munnu, "The House of Munnu," his pet-name being Munnu (from Mo Fhinnu "My Finnu," Finnu itself being a pet-form of Fintan); one of the great saints of South Wales was Teilo (*T'eiliau*, "Your Eiliau"), or, in his longer form, Eiludd (*Eliud*). This fashion, characteristic only of the sixth and early seventh centuries, must have derived from a conscious attempt to give monastic communities the affectionate idiom of speech proper to close family relationships.[8]

Life-cycles and Sexual Identity

Among the Franks, a woman had an especially high *wergild* in her child-bearing years; males, on the other hand, were protected by a triple *wergild* in their boyhood.[9] That is, if someone killed a woman or a boy of the age in question, the slayer and his kindred had to pay three times the normal *wergild* to make peace with the kinsmen of the slain. A similar phenomenon has been detected in early English furnished burials: those of women in the child-bearing years appear to be relatively rich.[10] Such burial-goods, it should be added, were strongly gendered, characterized by adornments for the women and weapons for the men. Among the Irish, there was supposed to be special protection for children up to the age of seven, so that the physical security of a commoner's child was as highly valued as that of a king's child.[11] People were valued not just for rank or wealth but for their current role in society: in these instances it seems that a concern for recruiting future adults was uppermost.

Distinctions of age played a major role in the societies of Britain and Ireland: a person would move from one period of his or her life into another, and these periods were recognized as distinct. Scholars distinguished "the ages of man," but similar distinctions were there in the ordinary vernaculars. There might also be "rites of passage" between one stage and another. Moreover, these periods in a life-cycle and the associated rites of passage became increasingly different for males and females as they grew older. They were also occasionally an object of concern for a social reformer: Adomnán, abbot of Iona, sponsored a law in 697 for Ireland, and for the Irish and Pictish kingdoms of north Britain.[12] His concern was to protect non-combatants from violence. His assumption was that clerics and monks had freely chosen non-combatant status, but that women and also boys up to the age at which they made their first armed expedition were, by reason of sex or age, non-combatants. The aim of his law was to use enhanced penalties and modes of enforcement to strengthen the protection of such non-combatants from violence inflicted on them. The presuppositions of this law reveal important features of society, but its limitations are also significant: slaves, too, were not expected to carry arms and yet they were not included among the protected non-combatants.

Adomnán's assumption, therefore, was that the trained ability to use violence was characteristic of the free male and that the time when he participated in his first expedition was a turning-point in his life. For the female, however, the major turning-points were matters of sex rather than of violence: this emerges in the very way a female was described, for generic terms for "woman" were also used in a more limited sense for "woman" as opposed to "maiden"; in this context, "woman" meant "female who had experienced sexual intercourse" as opposed to "female who remained a virgin": Irish *ben* as opposed to *ingen*; Welsh *gwraig* as opposed to *morwyn*; English *wif* or *wifmon* as opposed to *mægþ* or *mægþmon*. Moreover, a common Irish word for a "maiden" also meant "daughter" and "girl" – a complex of meanings connected age, family relationship, and sexuality. Other contrasts and their ambiguities were similarly significant: Irish *caillech* meant "female spouse," "nun," and "older woman," but its literal meaning was "veiled woman." For women, treatment of hair might be significant: the Irish maiden wore her hair long, so that, when she acknowledged passing from the status of virgin to that of a woman, she put her hair up and began using a veil. Hence *trillsech*, "wearing long tresses," also meant "maiden":[13] as opposed to *caillech*, "veiled person," in the sense of "spouse."[14] Æthelberht's laws contain a rule prescribing the payment due from a "free woman with long hair who misconducts herself": here long hair was probably a mark of status rather than of marital condition.[15] All three societies – Irish, British, and English – expected a girl to be first betrothed to a man and only later given to him, probably at a marriage feast. In early English law and in later Welsh law, it was normally part of the contract made at the betrothal that the girl was a virgin.[16] The English "morning-gift" or Welsh *cowyll*, given to the bride by the bridegroom the morning after their union was consummated, could thus be understood as a gift in exchange for her gift of her virginity. The virginity of the bride may also have been expected in Irish first marriages, at least as an ideal, but it was not a standard requirement of the law; and, in any case, divorce and remarriage, as well as polygyny, were, for the Irish secular lawyer, entirely acceptable.[17] All this makes it clear that for a female her sexual role had a significance paralleled for the male only by the taking of arms or the inheritance of land. As the woman's sexuality was of much greater concern than the sexual behavior of a man, so it was more tightly controlled.

For English men, the best textual evidence about their standard life-cycle is, unsurprisingly, for the nobility and for Northumbria (Bede, *HE*, iv. 22/20). A story told by Bede about a Northumbrian noble called Imma is informative both in this respect and in other ways also. Imma fought on the Northumbrian side against the Mercians at the Battle of the Trent in 679, a battle in which the Northumbrians were defeated and the joint-king Ælfwine was killed. The battle was part of a sequence of violent episodes between Mercia and Northumbria in the middle years of the seventh century. The way that Bede tells the story of the battle and its aftermath shows that war could be regarded as a feud between kings and their retinues: the Mercians, though victorious, were persuaded by Archbishop Theodore, acting as neutral peace-maker, to pay a *wergild* for Ælfwine to his brother, King Ecgfrith, and so avoid the continuation of bloodshed (*HE*, iv. 21/19).

Imma was a young man who was a member of Ælfwine's *militia*, and, as such, he is described as a *miles*, "soldier." Yet, these terms, *miles* and *militia*, meant something more for Bede than just "soldier" and "military service"; *militia* was used for the retinue of noble warriors, *milites*, that accompanied a king or queen. Elsewhere in Bede, Lilla was a *minister*, namely a thegn, but he was also a *miles* among other *milites*. In the later Old English translation of Bede's *Ecclesiastical History*, both *miles* and *minister regis* in this passage were translated by *cyninges thegn*, king's thegn, a term of both service and noble status (*HE*, ii. 9). Imma was left for dead on the battlefield, but recovered sufficiently by the following day to bind up his wounds and seek help. He was then found and taken prisoner by Mercians, who brought him to their lord, a *gesith*, "companion," of the Mercian king, Æthelred. The *gesith* interrogated Imma as to who and what he was; Imma, however, "was afraid to admit that he was a *miles*; instead he replied that he was a peasant and a poor man and was married; and he declared that he and others of similar condition had come on this expedition to bring supplies to the *milites*." Initially, the Mercian *gesith* believed Imma and arranged for medical care. Later, however, he noticed "from his appearance and the way he carried himself and his conversation that he was not of the poor common people, as he had said, but from the nobles."[18] He summoned Imma and inquired closely into his origins, promising not to do him any harm provided he admitted honestly to his identity. Imma admitted that he was a king's thegn, to which the *gesith* replied, "And I, for my part, have realized from each of your replies that you were not a peasant and now you deserve to die, for all my brothers and kinsmen were slain in that battle; yet I shall not kill you, lest I should violate my promise." However, he did the next best thing and sold him into slavery in London to a Frisian trader.

If one could grasp all the presuppositions that lie behind the story of Imma, one would have come a long way toward understanding early Anglo-Saxon society. Unfortunately, the very richness of the information means that there is not always enough other evidence to corroborate its details, and interpretations have accordingly differed.[19] An approach may be made via what Bede wrote in his *History of the Abbots* about the early life of Benedict Biscop, founder of Wearmouth and Jarrow, who died in 689, and what he wrote about the exile of Oswald and his brothers during the reign of Edwin as king of Northumbria (616–33). Biscop was born into a noble lineage. As a young man, Biscop was a king's thegn, serving Oswiu, king of Northumbria (642–70). When he reached the age of about 25, at which point he was going to receive as a gift from the king "an estate of land appropriate to his rank," he decided to give up a secular career for a religious life.[20] What this decision entailed was rejecting an "earthly *militia*, together with a corruptible gift" that accompanied such service, and also marriage and children. We may understand this as a package: the gift of land matching noble status was the gift that rewarded *militia*; and receiving land would have facilitated marriage. Elsewhere it seems that men who had followed the other path, of secular *militia*, and had received the gift of land associated with it, were then known in Northumbria as *gesithas* or, in Latin, *comites*, "companions," although the significance of the term may well have been different in other kingdoms.[21] This is somewhat paradoxical, since the point at which such a noble passed from being a king's thegn to being a *gesith* was also a shift from regular service in the king's household to life outside that household, on an estate (see, for example, Bede, *HE*, v. 4).

When Edwin became king of Northumbria in 616, he drove into exile the sons of his rival and predecessor, Æthelfrith, who had just been killed in battle. This was an episode in a feud between two royal dynasties, those of Bernicia and Deira, the components of what was to become Northumbria; the feud was to lead to the extinction of the Deiran dynasty in 651 and so enable the two kingdoms to acquire, as Northumbria, a unity that would endure. The sons of Æthelfrith, Eanfrith, Oswald, and Oswiu, went into exile among the Irish and the Picts "with a great youth of nobles" (Bede, *HE*, iii. 1, trans. Colgrave). What "youth" meant in this context was the younger element in a royal retinue, those who had not yet come to that point of decision reached by Biscop at about the age of 25. As *militia* might mean "military service" but often meant "noble military retinue," so "youth," *iuuentus*, also meant that portion of the retinue that was young. The reason why a large "youth" of nobles went into exile with the sons of Æthelfrith is explained by Bede's account of Biscop: they had not yet received the grant of land and had not married; they were thus free to go into exile, hoping that their lords would regain their kingdom and shower favor on those who had shared their exile. Young nobles at this stage of their lives were far more mobile than at others: for this reason, a generous and well-liked king could attract thegns from other kingdoms, as we are told Oswine of Deira did during his reign, 644–51 (Bede, *HE*, iii.14). We can also pinpoint the English term corresponding to Bede's *iuuentus*, "youth," and it was precisely the Old English form of Modern English "youth," namely *geoguð*, a term that contrasted with *duguð*, the body of older nobles attached to a king. The term *thegn* also had the element of young age in its background: in origin "child," it came to mean "servant" through the association of youth and household service; the other element, namely noble status, was acquired because such household service in a royal household was part of the life-cycle of a noble.

With these other pieces of evidence to help, we can return to the story of Imma. When he claimed that he was a poor married peasant who had come on the expedition not to fight but merely to bring supplies, he was putting as much distance as possible between himself and what he really was, a king's thegn. As a king's thegn, he was of noble rank, very probably unmarried, and by occupation a soldier as well as a household servant of his king, Ælfwine. Unfortunately, Imma's anxiety to disguise his identity as much as possible not only, perhaps, made detection more likely but also made it difficult for historians to answer one crucial question about Bede's story: why did Imma become liable to the feud? When the Mercian *gesith* discovered Imma's true identity, he declared that, by rights, he should avenge his brothers and kinsmen – who had been killed in the same Battle of Trent in which Imma was desperately wounded – and, therefore, should kill his Northumbrian captive. Because Imma uttered such an extensive list of lies – that he was poor, married, a peasant, and had not come to fight – it is impossible for us to be sure which of these characteristics was sufficient to make him safe from vengeance in the feud. No doubt they might all help, but we cannot say whether they were all essential.

Two lies, however, seem more important than the others: that he had not come to fight and that he was a poor peasant as opposed to a noble and a king's thegn. One may suspect that both of these were, in conjunction, crucial. The preceding chapter in Bede's *History* showed that the death of King Ælfwine in the Battle of the Trent was treated as part of a feud, a killing that drove on an enmity. Imma, however, was Ælfwine's thegn, and it is reasonable to suppose that he was involved in the feuds of his lord. Yet it may well be the case that if, by chance, he had not fought in the battle, he would not have been liable to vengeance. At all events, the story gives us, in passing, three precious pieces of information quite apart from Imma's liability to the feud as a king's thegn: first, feud was emphatically not just a matter between two kindreds; and thus attempts to control the feud were not, as such, efforts to reduce the power of the kindred; secondly, there was no divide between private feud and public war, for war also was feud; and, thirdly, a man might be recognized as a noble from a range of characteristics including the way he looked, the way he behaved, and the way he spoke. That Imma was Northumbrian and his captor a Mercian did not prevent his status from being transparent.

In seventh-century Northumbria there seems to have been an established noble male life-cycle. First, there was the critical point at which a boy sought entry into a royal household, a moment best captured in the *Life* of St. Wilfrid, in its account of the day when the young lad, in his fourteenth year, appeared at court.[22] He had already made connections through his service of royal *gesithas* entertained in his father's hall. In order to appear before royalty he had to choose the best approach: his links were better with the queen, Eanfled, than with the king, Oswiu. He also had to look good: he had to have horses and clothes for himself and his servants in which he and they could properly appear before a king or queen. The author of the *Life* was careful to note that he was a handsome youth. If all this was successful, the teenager was admitted to court and spent some years as a king's thegn – until, if we may generalize from Biscop's case, his mid-twenties. At that point, if his service in the royal household had been appreciated, he was likely to receive a grant of land for life (not in perpetuity) and was expected to marry and settle down with his own household on his own estate.[23] It should be clear that this life-cycle had the potential to allow the king to control his nobility and to impose a particular pattern of noble behavior. Not only was the period from the teens into the mid-twenties one in which an individual's character and culture were still in formation, but the king had great rewards to give or withhold: admission to his household in the first place, and then the gift that ended the period of thegnhood. This is likely to have been one way in which English culture was imposed on the British nobles still recorded in Wessex in Ine's late seventh-century laws;[24] and it will almost certainly have been a way in which Christianity took hold of a kingdom. If the missionary could convert the king, the missionary together with the king could convert his household;[25] and once the king's household was converted, so also was the up-and-coming generation of the nobility; and they, in turn, could, once they became *gesithas*, make their halls centers of the new faith.

If one asks whether there was a similar instrument of social control in the rest of Britain and Ireland, the answer is very uncertain. It is possible that this noble life-cycle also existed in other English kingdoms; and it is also true that, in the much later Welsh laws, from the twelfth and thirteenth centuries, there was a similar pattern of admission to a royal military retinue, the "house-host," an admission that appears to have been standard for the elite; and such service in the house-host was followed by inheritance of land.[26] One may make a guess from this, and suppose that long coexistence and rivalry between English and British kingdoms had led to a growing resemblance between their forms of social organization, at least at the level of the elite. Some color may be given to this supposition by the notorious fact that such forms of praise as "he earned his mead" were uttered both of the member of a British king's warband and his English counterpart: mead was an aristocratic drink appropriate to a royally munificent way of life; and to partake of it created a debt of honor that was discharged on the battlefield.[27] Yet it is not clear that the British king had so much land to give to aspiring young nobles; indeed, it is quite likely, given the long-term military weakness of the Britons, that he did not. Irish kings had royal retinues, but, as we shall see, nobility was sustained by being able to give cattle to one's own clients rather than by access to a royal household and royal favor. The English noble life-cycle may be part of the secret of English military and political success.

What was characteristic of social relationships between kings and their noble subjects among the Irish and the Britons was fosterage. This took somewhat different forms depending on whether the person fostered was the child of someone superior or inferior in rank and power to the fosterer.[28] It is clear for the Irish and probable for the Britons that children of very high rank were expected to have more than one set of foster-parents, so that some, at least, would be of lower status than the children they fostered.[29] Irish fosterage was a contractual relationship between the natural and the foster-parents, but although the relationships were governed by law, they also engendered multiple alliances, between foster-parents and foster-children, between different foster-children of the one set of foster-parents, between natural children and foster-children, and between the natural parents and the foster-parents.

Fosterage, therefore, was an important means by which rulers (and others) could bind families to themselves and to their children. The same capacity to create alliances can be seen in early English spiritual kinship, *godsibbræden*, "God-kinship," that is, relationships based on baptismal sponsorship and sponsorship at confirmation.[30] Here, too, the alliances were not just between god-parent and god-child, but between natural parents and god-parents, between different god-children of the one god-parent, and between natural children and god-children. God-parental relationships existed among the Irish and the Britons but never attained the same significance as they did among the English, probably because fosterage was the dominant form of constructed kinship.

Status and Class

The most elaborate distinctions of status were to be found among the Irish: an early eighth-century Irish lawyer cited social equality as characteristic of a primitive age before Irish law restored order.[31] There were numerous gradations of rank in the laws, but the main ones recognized by all contemporaries were between nobles, freemen, the "half-free," and slaves. They need, however, to be understood alongside distinctions of class – that is, arising from different relationships of property to pro-duction.[32] Here, there were two fundamental differences: between those who had at least a share in a plow-team and those who did not; and between those who had land but not capital and those who had both. Early Irish lawyers, it may be noted, were aware of the distinction between the three standard factors of production: land, labor, and capital. They used what amounts to this conceptual framework in assessing what shares of their property went to the husband and the wife (or their heirs) when they parted company, by death or by divorce.[33] Much the most important form of capital consisted of livestock – normal farming was mixed, with arable alongside dairying and rearing livestock for meat consumption – but the property relationships to land and livestock were different.[34] Nobles were lords who had a surplus of livestock beyond the needs of their own farms, and who therefore granted livestock to ordinary freemen; the latter had land by inheritance but lacked sufficient livestock to farm it adequately; they, therefore, needed to accept such grants and thereby become "render-payers," clients, to their lords. In exchange for granting livestock, the lord received fixed annual food-renders, hospitality, and personal service, such as help with the harvest. The relationship of noble to mere freeman was thus a relationship of class as well as status, since it was based on ownership of capital.

Livestock, however, is a form of capital that reproduces itself; moreover, the lord's grant of livestock to his client began by being merely a grant of use but on the lord's death it became a grant of ownership.[35] The potential was there for the client to become independent of his lord's heirs. This sometimes happened, but the norm was for the heirs of clients to be clients and the heirs of lords to be lords. A mechanism must have existed, therefore, to ensure that across the generations, on the whole, clients remained clients. The annual renders and hospitality must have been of such a value that they normally reduced the client's stock over time; and this seems to have been the assumption, since a client often took a second and even a third lord, presumably to keep his stock at a level to enable him to farm well.[36] All this signifies that the relationship between lord and client was based on a cycle by which the original grant of livestock was gradually, year by year, returned to the lord in renders and hospitality.

The distinction between the free and the unfree or half-free was also one of class as well as status. Once a freeman was an adult and was farming on his own, he was expected to have a share in a plow-team; a prosperous freeman or a noble would have an entire plow-team. In economic terms, this was the central requirement: the plow agriculture characteristic of Eurasia and North Africa since the prehistoric period, as opposed to the hoe-agriculture characteristic of sub-Saharan Africa, implied that the most fundamental distinction was going to be between those who had a share in a plow-team and those who did not.[37] A similar distinction was still present in the England of *Domesday Book*, where slaves were sometimes listed with demesne plows indicating that both slave and plow belonged to the lord, whereas *villani* were listed with their own plows; sometimes, however, the lord's plows were listed first, then the *villani* and their plows, and then slaves along with the stock and without any plows.[38] The one mode of description emphasized the link with the lord's plow-teams, the other the status of the slave as a mere chattel.

Irish society was largely untroubled by invasion in this period and untouched by external settlement; it is thus a complete contrast with Britain, where early Anglo-Saxon society was one of conquerors and colonists and the society of the Britons one organized for frequent war ever since the early fifth century. It is likely that the economic resources devoted to war were considerably less in Ireland than in Britain.[39] As for the English, the evidence of furnished burials indicates a shift from an early period of relatively small distinctions of displayed wealth to a later period, from the late sixth century, of greater social distance between the elite and the majority of the population – or, rather, that portion of the population that used the burial rite in which grave-goods were deposited.[40] There was also a greater readiness, also from the late sixth century, to look to the Roman world rather than to Germania for models of material culture.[41] Quite what such changes indicate is by no means clear, since there is no simple equation between burial rites, on the one hand, and social status, wealth, ethnicity, or religion on the other.[42] With these cautionary provisos, however, it may be worth setting out a speculative theory to take account of this cemetery evidence as well as some textual evidence from a later date. The latter comprises two items: first, the seventh- and eighth-century texts, notably Bede's *Ecclesiastical History*, show that the English had a concept of the land appropriate for a family, namely a "hide," a unit sometimes equivalent to a plowland;[43] and, secondly, the tendency for Anglo-Saxon royal lineages to become established in the sixth century rather than the fifth. For example, the East Anglian dynasty was known as the Wuffingas, the descendants of a Wuffa, who was the grandfather of Rædwald, the king whose support placed Edwin on the throne of Northumbria and who died about 625 (Bede, *HE*, ii. 15). Yet East Anglia was very probably one of the earliest areas controlled by the Anglo-Saxons.

The theory begins with the proposition that, in the context of a conquering and colonizing society – namely, that of the establishment of Anglo-Saxon settlements in England and their expansion westward and northward – there was a strong interest in offering highly favorable terms to new Germanic immigrants. A major element in these terms was the hide, namely a general expectation that the land appropriate for a free immigrant family would be roughly a full plowland. (The family in question was the nuclear family of parents and children, not the "extended family" or kindred.) In other words, the Germanic immigrant was being offered landed resources comparable with the wealthiest type of Irish freeman. In terms of plow agriculture, this was an obvious level at which to pitch a favorable colonial settlement: only the highly prosperous peasant had an entire plow-team. Competition among Anglo-Saxon settlements and their leaders, whether implicit or explicit, to attract such immigrants meant that no area of English settlement could afford to offer much less; and hence the situation arose by the seventh and eighth centuries when the hide was a general unit throughout those parts of Britain under English rule. At this stage of the settlement, the imperative among the colonizers was to offer not just relative prosperity but relative equality; in other words, there may have been leaders with considerable power, but they needed to emphasize their unity with their followers as a conquering and settling people. Hence, for them, the burial rite presented a rough equality and a Germanic identity.

After the middle years of the sixth century, however, a decisive shift occurred in favor of the English and against the Britons. This was the period that succeeded the 44 years of relative stability mentioned by Gildas;[44] it was a period of territorial expansion for the English and also of the foundation of several new kingdoms. Even for areas of old settlement, such as East Anglia, conditions were very different: they no longer had a boundary with the Britons; any expansion would have to be at the expense of English neighbors.[45] They no longer had such a need for new immigrants to establish their settlements at the expense of the Britons; and, at the same time, their kings were now competing against other English kings. This may have been the period when English kings established a control of their nobilities based around the royal household and a standard noble life-cycle, a period when the normal companions of kings ceased to be *gesithas*, "companions," and became king's thegns, now with connotations of service and inequality.

Some hides survived as independent farms, but most were replaced in a new change that was probably beginning before the end of the eighth century but was not complete for several centuries and, indeed, never embraced the whole of England.[46] In the settlement period, Anglo-Saxon immigrants were quite distinct from the native Britons. As late as the end of the seventh century, Ine distinguished between Britons and English very much as the Salic law (no later than the early sixth century) had distinguished between Franks and other Germanic barbarians, on the one hand, and Gallo-Romans on the other; and as Ine called the Britons *Wealas*, so the Franks called the Gallo-Romans *Walas*.[47] A common terminology and legal treatment stretched across the Channel. Given the Frankish evidence, it is very likely that some such treatment of the ethnic divide between English and British populations went back to the fifth century. Even at the end of the seventh century, moreover, British elements within the population of Wessex were probably to be found in distinct areas; this is indicated by the presence of British noblemen alongside British peasants, and it is also exemplified by the British inscriptions at Wareham in Dorset, well within Wessex, which have been dated to c.700.[48] By the time of Alfred, however, these pockets of British population in the heart of Wessex appear to have disappeared, just as, in Gaul, there emerged by the end of the seventh century a geographical and political divide between a Francia in the North and a Romania in the south. Only some of those now regarded as English will have been the heirs of the fifth-century settlement;

others will have been former Britons who had adopted the English language and ethnic identity. No longer, therefore, will the hide have distinguished free Germanic immigrants from Britons and from the unfree and half-free. Many hides are also likely to have been fragmented by the processes of partible inheritance. The eighth century appears to have been a period of increasing population, after the era of successive plagues, and it is also a period when expansion of English settlement into formerly British territory had slowed down very considerably.[49] All this made it more difficult to sustain in reality the old link between the status of a free English householder, a *ceorl*, and the hide. Moreover, the end of our period is likely to have seen the first emergence, especially in the Midlands, of a common-field agriculture that was associated with standard peasant holdings of only a quarter of a hide at best, namely a yardland, and with villages less likely to shift and more likely to be attached to a church.[50] The eighth century also saw the beginning of the process by which the royal household ceased to be quite so central in the noble life-cycle. The change by which inherited bookland began to be a mark of noble status meant that royal control over land was weakened. The young noble could expect to inherit bookland from his father: he was less dependent on royal favor given as a reward for service as a king's thegn. By the tenth century, the old two-stage career – first, king's thegn, then *gesith* – would be obsolete.[51]

This theory, then, posits three stages of social development: first, a colonial phase associated with the hide and the preservation among the settlers (not the Britons) of a rough social equality; the second phase was of the establishment, hand in hand, of a new kingship and a new aristocracy, both based on building the royal household into the framework of an aristocratic life-cycle; and the third phase was of ethnic assimilation of the British population remaining within English kingdoms, of the general though not universal obsolescence of the hide, and of the beginnings of a new order, especially in Mercia, namely common-field agriculture and the nucleated village.

No such pattern can be detected in areas that remained British, except to some extent for the role of the royal household. What is characteristic, at least of those Britons who lived in what would become Wales, was that their cultural institutions resembled those of the Irish, while their ordinary lay institutions were often closer to those of the English. By "lay," I here mean more than non-ecclesiastical: the church in the sense of the ecclesiastical hierarchy was one privileged order among others. The Irish sometimes distinguished "the people of craft" from "the farming people."[52] By "lay," I mean the farming people as opposed to the various hierarchies of skill – in the artistic use of words, in the worship of God, and in learning. The Irish poets had a set of seven ranks, with three sub-grades, modeled on the seven grades of the church; and, indeed, the seven grades themselves may well have originated in Ireland though they spread widely on the continent.[53] Part of the energy of early Irish culture is likely to derive from emulation and competition between these different learned orders.

Lordship, Estates, and Food-renders

We have already seen that the relationship between an Irish lord and his client was normally based upon livestock rather than upon land. In Wales and in England, however, it was based on land. Yet in all three societies, food-renders were the standard form of transfer by which those who cultivated the land handed over part of their surplus to their lords. In Ireland, all this was part of a contractual arrangement renewed with each generation; in Britain, it was inherited from one generation to the next; and, yet, the structure of the food-render among the Britons can be quite closely compared with its structure in Ireland. A standard food-render in all three societies delivered three kinds of agricultural produce: bread, an accompaniment to bread, and drink. Since the normal form of drink was ale, made from malted barley, two of the three constituents derived from the arable side of the farm, while the accompaniment came mainly from livestock. What constituted the accompaniment – in Latin sometimes called a *companaticum* or *companagium*, namely what went with bread, *panis* – depended on the season of the year: in the summer, dairy products were more important; in winter, meat.

What is characteristic of British food-renders in the early Middle Ages, as opposed to their English counterparts, is the priority of drink. Land was often defined as "the land of so many *modii*" (measures of ale); and what is meant is that, first, it delivered that amount of ale in the annual food-render, and, secondly, the amount of the other components, the bread and the *companaticum*, was fixed in relationship to the amount of ale. Hence, to say that a given piece of land was "land of three *modii*" was to specify by implication the entire annual food-render. Moreover, the priority of the ale element can be shown to be a long-standing aspect of Irish as well as of British food-renders by a paradoxical aspect of the terminology that they both share: the term for the accompaniment (which in Latin is seen as accompanying the bread) literally means "what goes with drink." Only because drink had the priority implicit in such phrases as "land of three *modii* (of ale)" would it make sense to call the accompaniment an accompaniment to the drink rather than to the bread.

Food-renders could be given a particular significance beyond that of a mere transfer of produce. An example is the Irish freeman who, in his family, was the first to grant livestock to clients: his father had been a mere render-paying commoner, but the son, through becoming a lord of clients, had aspirations to nobility. The rule, however, was that noble status followed lordship only in the third generation. The son, therefore, was still a commoner even though he was a lord; and because he was a commoner he was not entitled to ale in his render "for a render-payer is not entitled to ale until he be a lord," namely a lord by inheritance.[54]

The lordships of the Irish and Welsh, in spite of their different relationships to land and livestock, were united in the way they worked through food-renders rather than money rents or labor dues. For money, the Irish and Welsh used weights of silver or cattle (for high values, also female slaves); they did not use coins.[55] The Irish client only owed relatively slight labor dues, help with the harvest and with building his lord's ringfort. The Welsh peasant seems not to have owed much labor apart from building his lord's hall. The same cannot be said of English lordship. Here one should distinguish between what is sometimes called extensive and intensive lordship: extensive lordship also worked largely through food-renders and so resembled Irish and Welsh lordship; intensive lordship exacted much heavier labor dues, the forerunner of the week-work characteristic of the villein in the central Middle Ages. Intensive lordship has been associated with what was later called "inland," extensive lordship with "warland." On the inland, lords had land which, through paid servants or slaves or the labor dues of tenants, they farmed themselves.[56] On the inland, also, were classes of tenant whose conditions of tenure were associated with such intensive lordship.

Much of the detail in the contrast between inland and warland has to be worked out from later sources, and it is correspondingly uncertain what were the origin and date of this twofold approach to lordship. The evidence is best for old ecclesiastical estates, but that is true across the board and it does not prove that intensive lordship was peculiar to them. Slavery was a source of labor that could be used intensively: not only was slavery later associated with special forms of labor, notably plowing, but those freed from slavery often remained more closely subject to their former owners than were ordinary free tenants.[57] Slavery could be a penalty for an offence, and it was a heritable status, but the main source was captives in war; hence, it would not be surprising if the English, relatively successful in war, also had the servile manpower to pursue an intensive agriculture.

Conclusion

Certain things marked out Irish and British from Anglo-Saxon social institutions: the role of professional learned men, such as poets and judges, and the importance of agnatic lineages and fosterage. Those Englishmen who went to Ireland in the seventh century would have found many things familiar, but they would have had no doubt that, in terms of social arrangements, as in other ways, they were in a foreign land.

Notes

1 Howlett, *Book of Letters*, p. 30.
2 Nash-Williams, *Early Christian Monuments*, no. 103, dated to the beginning of the sixth century by Tedeschi, *Congeries Lapidum*, i. 212–14.
3 *Anglo-Saxon Chronicle, s.a.* 688, in *EHD*, I, no. 1.
4 Jenkins and Owen (eds.), *Welsh Law of Women*, pp. 32–3; Kelly, *Guide to Early Irish Law*, pp. 102–3.
5 Sharpe (trans.), *Adomnán*, i. 2, pp. 113–14. I have modified Sharpe's translation slightly for my own purposes.
6 Colgrave, *Two Lives*: Anon. Life, i. 3 (Tumma) = Bede's Life, c. 1 (Trumwine).
7 Sharpe, "The naming of Bishop Ithamar."
8 Russell, "Patterns of hypocorism," pp. 242–6.
9 Eckhardt (ed.), *Pactus legis Salicae*, xli. 16; Rivers (trans.), *Laws of the Salian and Ripuarian Franks*, p. 88.
10 Arnold, "Wealth and social structure"; Speake, *Saxon Bed Burial*, pp. 124–6.
11 *Díre* Tract, § 23 (and the ninth-century gloss in C), in Thurneysen, "Irisches recht," 22.
12 Meyer (ed.), *Cáin Adamnáin*; trans. Ní Dhonnchadha, "The Law of Adomnán."
13 Binchy (ed.), *Corpus iuris Hibernici*, iv. 1242. 16; also Binchy, "Sick maintenance in Irish law," 87–8.
14 Ní Dhonnchadha, "Caillech and other terms for veiled women," pp. 74–80.
15 Æthelberht, c. 73 (*friwif locbore*), in *EHD*, I, no. 29.
16 Compare the Welsh *twyllforwyn*, "false maiden," in Jenkins (trans.), *Law of Hywel Dda*, p. 49, with Æthelberht, c. 77.
17 *Tochmarc Emire*, § 26, in Van Hamel (ed.), *Compert Con Culainn*, p. 31. On Irish marriage, see Jaski, "Marriage laws in Ireland"; Ó Corráin, "Women in early Irish society" and "Marriage in early Ireland."

18 The terms used by Bede were *vultus, habitus,* and *sermones: habitus* might include clothing, but is translated *gebære,* "behavior, deportment," in the Old English Bede.
19 Alcock, *Economy, Society and Warfare,* p. 263; Brooks, "The development of military obligations," p. 74, n. 1; John, *Orbis Britanniae,* pp. 136–7.
20 Bede, *Historia abbatum,* c. 1, ed. Plummer, *Baedae opera historica,* i. 364–5.
21 Thacker, "Some terms for noblemen," pp. 207–9.
22 Colgrave (ed.), *Life of Bishop Wilfrid,* c. 1.
23 Campbell, "The sale of land"; Charles-Edwards, "The distinction between land and moveable wealth"; John, "Folkland reconsidered," and *Land Tenure in Early England,* pp. 24–63; Wormald, *Bede and the Conversion of England,* pp. 19–23.
24 Ine 24. 2, in *EHD,* I, no. 32.
25 As illustrated by Bede, *HE,* iii. 3 (trans. Colgrave): "the king himself was an interpreter of the heavenly word to his leaders and thegns."
26 Charles-Edwards, *Early Irish and Welsh Kinship,* pp. 175–6; Jenkins, *Law of Hywel Dda,* p. 131.
27 Jarman (trans.), *Aneirin,* xliii; *The Battle of Finnsburh,* lines 37–40, in Klaeber (ed.), *Beowulf,* p. 247.
28 Parkes, "Celtic fosterage" and "Fostering fealty."
29 Charles-Edwards, *Early Irish and Welsh Kinship,* pp. 78–82.
30 Lynch, *Christianizing Kinship.*
31 Binchy (ed.), *Corpus iuris Hibernici,* ii. 348. 10–11; Thurneysen (ed.), "Aus dem irischen Recht IV," 175–6, 179.
32 Charles-Edwards, "*Críth Gablach* and the law of status."
33 *Cáin Lánamna,* § 10, ed. and trans. Thurneysen, p. 28; trans. Ó Corráin, p. 24.
34 Kelly, *Early Irish Farming,* pp. 398–403.
35 Charles-Edwards, *Early Irish and Welsh Kinship,* pp. 344, 357–9
36 Thurneysen, "Irisches recht," p. 25, § 26.
37 Bloch, *French Rural History,* pp. 193–6; Goody, *Production and Reproduction,* pp. 35, 106–8.
38 Circuits I and III placed the slaves with the stock; II, IV and Cheshire and Shropshire in V placed them with the demesne: Roffe, *Decoding Domesday,* pp. 227–8.
39 Before the Viking Age, mail shirts seem to have been virtually unknown in Ireland: Charles-Edwards, "Irish warfare before 1100," p. 27.
40 Härke, "Warrior graves?" and "Early Anglo-Saxon social structure."
41 Geake, *Use of Grave-goods,* pp. 123–4, 129–36.
42 Halsall, *Early Medieval Cemeteries,* pp. 65–8.
43 Charles-Edwards, "Kinship, status and the origins of the hide," 14–15; Faith, *English Peasantry,* pp. 128–40.
44 Winterbottom (ed.), *Gildas,* § 26, pp. 28, 98–9.
45 Scull, "Archaeology, early Anglo-Saxon society," 75–6.
46 Faith, *English Peasantry,* pp. 137–40.
47 Eckhardt (ed.), *Pactus legis Salicae,* § 41. 9–10; Rivers (trans.), *Laws of the Salian and Ripuarian Franks,* p. 157; and Ine, 23.3, 24.2, 32, in *EHD,* I, no. 32.
48 Ine, 24.2; Royal Commission, *An Inventory . . . Dorset,* ii, *South East,* Part 2, pp. 310–12 and Plates 165 and 166; Yorke, *Wessex,* pp. 69–72.
49 Maddicott, "Plague" and "Prosperity and power."
50 Faith, *English Peasantry,* pp. 143–7; Hamerow, *Early Medieval Settlements,* pp. 104–24; Thirsk, "The common fields."
51 Loyn, "Gesiths and thegns"; Thacker, "Some terms for noblemen."
52 Irish *áes dána* versus *áes trebtha*: Charles-Edwards, *Early Christian Ireland,* p. 68.
53 Breatnach (ed.), *Uraicecht na Ríar,* pp. 81–9; Reynolds, "'At sixes and sevens.'"

54 Binchy (ed.), *Crith Gablach*, § 19, lines 254–5.
55 Charles-Edwards, "The seven bishop-houses," 253–5; Emanuel (ed.), *Latin Texts of the Welsh Laws*, e.g. p. 113; Kelly, *Early Irish Farming*, pp. 587–95.
56 Faith, *English Peasantry*, chs. 2–3.
57 Pelteret, *Slavery in Early Medieval England*, pp. 194–202; Postan, *Famulus*, pp. 5–14.

Further Reading

Blair, J., *Early Medieval Surrey: Landholding, Church and Settlement before 1300* (Stroud, 1991).
Davies, W., *Wales in the Early Middle Ages* (Leicester, 1982).
Edwards, N., *The Archaeology of Early Medieval Ireland* (London, 1990).
Hines, J. (ed.), *The Anglo-Saxons from the Migration Period to the Eighth Century: An Ethnographic Perspective* (Woodbridge, 1997).
Jones, G. R. J., "Post-Roman Wales," in H. P. R. Finberg (ed.), *The Agrarian History of England and Wales*, vol. 1, part 2: *AD 43–1042* (Cambridge, 1972), pp. 283–382.
Ó Corráin, D., "Ireland c.800: aspects of society," in D. Ó Cróinín (ed.), *A New History of Ireland*, vol. 1: *Prehistoric and Early Ireland* (Oxford, 2005), pp. 549–608.

Bibliography

Alcock, L., *Economy, Society and Warfare among the Britons and Saxons* (Cardiff, 1987).
Arnold, C. J., "Wealth and social structure: a matter of life and death," in P. Rahtz, T. Dickinson, and L. Watts (eds.), *Anglo-Saxon Cemeteries 1979*, British Archaeological Reports, British series, 82 (Oxford, 1980), pp. 81–142.
Bede, *Historia abbatum*, ed. C. Plummer, *Baedae opera historica*, 2 vols. (Oxford, 1896), i. 364–87.
Bede, *Historia ecclesiastica gentis Anglorum*, trans. B. Colgrave, revised R. Collins and J. McClure, *Bede: The Ecclesiastical History of the English People*, Oxford World's Classics (Oxford, 1994).
Binchy, D. A. (ed.), *Corpus iuris Hibernici*, 6 vols (Dublin, 1978).
Binchy, D. A. (ed.), *Crith Gablach* (Dublin, 1941).
Binchy, D. A., "Sick-maintenance in Irish law," *Ériu* 12 (1938), 78–134.
Bloch, M., *French Rural History: An Essay on its Basic Characteristics* (London, 1966).
Breatnach, L. (ed. and trans.), *Uraicecht na Ríar: The Poetic Grades in Early Irish Law* (Dublin, 1987).
Brooks, N., "The development of military obligations in eighth- and ninth-century England," in P. Clemoes and K. Hughes (eds.), *England before the Conquest: Studies in Primary Sources Presented to Dorothy Whitelock* (Cambridge, 1971), pp. 69–84.
Campbell, J., "The sale of land and the economics of power in early England: problems and possibilities," *The Haskins Society Journal: Studies in Medieval History*, 1 (1989), 23–37.
Chadwick, H. M., *Studies on Anglo-Saxon Institutions* (Cambridge, 1905).
Charles-Edwards, T. M., "Anglo-Saxon kinship revisited," in J. Hines (ed.), *The Anglo-Saxons from the Migration Period to the Eighth Century* (Woodbridge, 1997), pp. 171–204.
Charles-Edwards, T. M., "*Crith Gablach* and the law of status," *Peritia*, 5 (1986), 53–73.
Charles-Edwards, T. M., "The distinction between land and moveable wealth in Anglo-Saxon England," in P. H. Sawyer (ed.), *Medieval Settlement: Continuity and Change* (London: Arnold, 1976), pp. 180–7.

Charles-Edwards, T. M., *Early Christian Ireland* (Cambridge, 2000).

Charles-Edwards, T. M., *Early Irish and Welsh Kinship* (Oxford, 1993).

Charles-Edwards, T. M., "Irish warfare before 1100," in T. Bartlett and K. Jeffreys (eds.), *A Military History of Ireland* (Cambridge, 1996), pp. 26–51.

Charles-Edwards, T. M., "Kinship, status and the origins of the hide," *Past & Present*, 56 (1972), 3–33.

Charles-Edwards, T. M., "The seven bishop-houses of Dyfed," *Bulletin of the Board of Celtic Studies*, 24 (1970–2), 247–62.

Colgrave, B. (ed. and trans.), *The Life of Bishop Wilfrid by Eddius Stephanus* (Cambridge, 1927).

Colgrave, B. (ed. and trans.), *Two Lives of Saint Cuthbert* (Cambridge, 1940).

Davies, W., *An Early Welsh Microcosm* (London, 1978).

Eckhardt, K. A. (ed.), *Pactus legis Salicae, MGH*, Legum Sectio I, iv. 1 (Hanover, 1962).

Emanuel, H. D. (ed.), *The Latin Texts of the Welsh Laws* (Cardiff, 1967).

Faith, R., *The English Peasantry and the Growth of Lordship* (London, 1997).

Geake, H., *The Use of Grave-goods in Conversion-period England, c.600–c.850*, British Archaeological Reports, British series, 261 (Oxford, 1997).

Gelling, M., *The West Midlands in the Early Middle Ages* (Leicester, 1992).

Goody, J., *Production and Reproduction: A Comparative Study of the Domestic Domain* (Cambridge, 1976).

Halsall, G., *Early Medieval Cemeteries: An Introduction to Burial Archaeology in the Post-Roman West* (Glasgow, 1995).

Hamerow, H., *Early Medieval Settlements: The Archaeology of Rural Communities in North-West Europe, 400–900* (Oxford, 2002).

Härke, H., "Early Anglo-Saxon social structure," in J. Hines (ed.), *The Anglo-Saxons from the Migration Period to the Eighth Century* (Woodbridge, 1997), pp. 125–60.

Härke, H., "'Warrior graves?' The background of the Anglo-Saxon weapon burial rite," *Past & Present*, 126 (1990), 22–43.

Howlett, D., *The Book of Letters of Saint Patrick the Bishop* (Blackrock, Co. Dublin, 1994).

Jarman, A. O. H. (ed. and trans.), *Aneirin: The Gododdin* (Llandysul, 1988).

Jaski, B., *Early Irish Kingship and Succession* (Dublin, 2000).

Jaski, B., "Marriage laws in Ireland and on the continent in the early Middle Ages," in C. Meek and K. Simms (eds.), *The Fragility of her Sex? Medieval Irish Women in their European Context* (Blackrock, Co. Dublin, 1996), pp. 16–42.

Jenkins, D. (trans.), *The Law of Hywel Dda: Law Texts from Medieval Wales* (Llandysul, 1986).

Jenkins, D. and Owen, M. E. (eds.), *The Welsh Law of Women: Studies Presented to Professor Daniel A. Binchy on his Eightieth Birthday* (Cardiff, 1980).

John, E., "Folkland reconsidered," in E. John, *Orbis Britanniae and Other Studies* (Leicester, 1966), pp. 64–127.

John, E., *Land Tenure in Early England: A Discussion of Some Problems* (Leicester, 1960, repr. 1964).

John, E., *Orbis Britanniae and Other Studies* (Leicester, 1966).

Kelly, F., *Early Irish Farming: A Study Based Mainly on the Law-texts of the Seventh and Eighth Centuries AD* (Dublin, 1997).

Kelly, F., *A Guide to Early Irish Law* (Dublin, 1988).

Klaeber, Fr. (ed.), *Beowulf and the Fight at Finnsburg*, 3rd edn. (Boston, 1950).

Loyn, H. R., "Gesiths and thegns in Anglo-Saxon England from the seventh to the tenth century," *English Historical Review*, 70: 277 (1955), 529–49.

Lynch, J. H., *Christianizing Kinship: Ritual Sponsorship in Anglo-Saxon England* (Ithaca, NY, 1998).

Maddicott, J., "Plague in seventh-century England," *Past & Present*, 156 (1997), 7–54.

Maddicott, J., "Prosperity and power in the age of Bede and Beowulf," *Proceedings of the British Academy*, 117 (2002), 49–71.

Meek, C. E. and Simms, M. K. (eds.), *"The Fragility of her Sex"? Medieval Irish Women in their European Context* (Blackrock, Co. Dublin, 1996).

Meyer, K. (ed. and trans.), *Cáin Adamnáin*, Anecdota Oxoniensia, 12 (Oxford, 1905).

Nash-Williams, V. E., *The Early Christian Monuments of Wales* (Cardiff, 1950).

Ní Dhonnchadha, M., "Caillech and other terms for veiled women in medieval Irish texts," *Éigse*, 28 (1994–5), 71–96.

Ní Dhonnchadha, M., "The Law of Adomnán: a translation," in T. O'Loughlin (ed.), *Adomnán at Birr, AD 697* (Dublin, 2001), pp. 53–68.

Ó Corráin, D. (trans.), *"Cáin Lánamna,"* in A. Bourke et al. (eds.), *The Field-Day Anthology of Irish Writing*, vol. 4: *Irish Women's Writing and Traditions* (Cork, 2002), pp. 22–6.

Ó Corráin, D., "Marriage in early Ireland," in A. Cosgrove (ed.), *Marriage in Ireland* (Dún Laoghaire, 1985), pp. 5–24.

Ó Corráin, D., "Women in early Irish society," in M. Mac Curtain and D. Ó Corráin (eds.), *Women in Irish Society: The Historical Dimension* (Dublin, 1978), pp. 1–13.

Parkes, P., "Celtic fosterage," *Comparative Studies in Society and History*, 48: 2 (2006), 359–94.

Parkes, P., "Fostering fealty: a comparative study of tributary allegiances of adoptive kinship," *Comparative Studies in Society and History*, 45: 4 (2003), 741–82.

Pelteret, D. A. E., *Slavery in Early Medieval England: From the Reign of Alfred until the Twelfth Century*. Studies in Anglo-Saxon History, 7 (Woodbridge, 1995).

Postan, M. M., *The Famulus: The Estate Labourer in the Twelfth and Thirteenth Centuries*, *Economic History Review*, suppl. 2 (Cambridge, 1954).

Reynolds, R. E., "'At sixes and sevens' – and eights and nines: the sacred mathematics of sacred orders in the early Middle Ages," in *Clerics in the Early Middle Ages: Hierarchy and Image* (Aldershot, 1999).

Rivers, T. J. (trans.), *The Laws of the Salian and Ripuarian Franks* (New York, 1986).

Roffe, D., *Decoding Domesday* (Woodbridge, 2007).

Royal Commission on Historical Monuments, *An Inventory of the Historical Monuments in the County of Dorset*, vol. 2: *South-East*, part 2 (London, 1970).

Russell, P., "Patterns of hypocorism in early Irish hagiography," in J. Carey, M. Herbert, and P. Ó Riain (eds.), *Studies in Irish Hagiography: Saints and Scholars* (Dublin, 2001), pp. 237–49.

Scull, C., "Archaeology, early Anglo-Saxon society, and the origins of Anglo-Saxon kingdoms," *Anglo-Saxon Studies in Archaeology and History*, 6 (1993), 65–82.

Sharpe, R. (trans.), *Adomnán of Iona: Life of St. Columba* (Harmondsworth, 1995).

Sharpe, R., "The naming of Bishop Ithamar," *English Historical Review*, 117 (2002), 889–94.

Speake, G., *A Saxon Bed Burial on Swallowcliffe Down*, English Heritage Archaeological Reports, 10 (London, 1989).

Stafford, P., *The East Midlands in the Early Middle Ages* (Leicester, 1985).

Tedeschi, C., *Congeries Lapidum: Iscrizioni Britanniche dei Secoli V–VII* (Pisa, 2005).

Thacker, A. T., "Some terms for noblemen in Anglo-Saxon England, c.650–900," in D. Brown, J. Campbell, and S. C. Hawkes (eds.), *Anglo-Saxon Studies in Archaeology and History*, 2, British Archaeological Reports, British series, 92 (Oxford, 1981), pp. 201–36.

Thirsk, J., "The common fields," *Past & Present*, 29 (1964), 3–25.

Thurneysen, R., "Aus dem irischen Recht I," *Zeitschrift für celtische Philologie*, 14 (1923), 335–94; "Aus dem irischen Recht II," *Zeitschrift für celtische Philologie*, 15 (1924), 238–76; "Aus dem irischen Recht IV," *Zeitschrift für celtische Philologie*, 16 (1927), 167–230.

Thurneysen, R. (ed. and trans.), *Cáin Lánamna*, in R. Thurneysen et al., *Studies in Early Irish Law* (Dublin, 1936), pp. 1–75.

Thurneysen, R., "Irisches recht," *Abhandlungen der Preussischen Akademie der Wissenschaften*, Phil.-Hist. Klasse, no. 2 (Berlin, 1931).

Van Hamel, A. G. (ed.), *Compert Con Culainn and Other Stories* (Dublin, 1933).

Whitelock, D. (ed. and trans.), *English Historical Documents*, vol. I: *c.500–1042*, 2nd edn. (London, 1979).

Winterbottom, M. (ed. and trans.), *Gildas: The Ruin of Britain and Other Documents* (Chichester, 1978).

Wormald, P., *Bede and the Conversion of England: The Charter Evidence*, Jarrow Lecture 1984 (Jarrow, n.d.); reprinted in P. Wormald, *The Times of Bede: Studies in Early English Christian Society and its Historian* (Oxford, 2006).

Yorke, B., *Wessex in the Early Middle Ages* (London, 1995).

CHAPTER NINE

Britain, Ireland, and Europe, c.500–c.750

PAUL FOURACRE

Britain and Ireland may be geographically on the periphery of Europe, but whatever cultural and historical change has affected the mainland of Europe has always spread to them. The theme of this chapter is the changes sweeping across Europe in the period c.500–c.750 and it considers how the various parts of Britain and Ireland responded to them. But it is also about how and what Britain and Ireland contributed to the development of European culture as a whole in the early Middle Ages, for people from both were active in spreading their ideas and practices abroad. The term "Europe" itself is an ancient one, but one not much used by the Romans for whom it was of little significance when their empire stretched from the Atlantic to the Euphrates and down into Africa. In the post-Roman period, the term began to make a comeback, but now it was attached to a sense of Christian community and it was mostly used in association with the Franks, a people that had come to dominate north-west Europe. In fact, the Frankish leader Charlemagne (ruled 768–814) would be styled "father of Europe" and be crowned "Roman Emperor" in the year 800. Relations between the Franks and Britain must be an important part of the following discussion, for Frankish influence upon parts of Britain was strong indeed. But it is also the case that, by the end of our period, Frankish culture had received a significant input from both the Irish and the Anglo-Saxons, and it was through this Frankish medium that the insular peoples had an impact upon the wider European scene. Let us begin with what is now often referred to as the "transformation of the Roman world."

Britain, Ireland, and the Transformation of the Roman World

The "transformation of the Roman world" is a concept that is now generally preferred to the old view that the Roman Empire declined and then "fell." Historians are more comfortable with a notion of "transformation" than with one of "fall" because it allows for a more subtle understanding of change in the late Roman and early medieval periods. The "Roman world" is also a more useful concept than the "Roman Empire," for it includes those regions in the penumbra of the empire that sometimes felt the effects of the demise of Roman rule no less dramatically than provinces within it. The Atlantic Archipelago, like the area that would become Germany, or the Danube area, was one of those regions that straddled the old Roman borders.

It is important to look for such basic similarities between continental and insular regions, for all too often Britain and Ireland have been seen as the odd ones out in the post-Roman history of Europe. It is instructive, for example, to note parallels between the formation of Anglo-Saxon culture in eastern England and the establishment of Slav cultures in the Balkans and in central and eastern Europe. In both cases, we see the development of an ethnic identity based on shared language and a common, fairly simple, material culture. For both, the context was the decline of Roman military power and the destabilization of communities caused by population movement or invasions. Similar conditions thus produced comparable changes: the evolution of ranked societies which enjoyed military dominance but which lacked more sophisticated structures of power. What we suspect for England – that many people became "Anglo-Saxons" by learning the English language and adopting Anglo-Saxon dress and styles of housing[1] – is confirmed for the Slavs, both from archaeological evidence and from narratives that speak of large numbers of prisoners from the Balkans losing their identity and in effect becoming Slavs.[2]

All the peoples of Britain and Ireland to some extent recognized their common European and Roman cultural heritage, however much each of them might emphasize their unique origins or special history. Pictish decoration, for instance, owes far more to later Roman imperial form than once thought,[3] whilst Welsh kings traced themselves back to Magnus Maximus, a Roman military leader.[4] The Irish in the sixth century began to adopt the traditions of the Latin charter, emphatically a Roman legal device.[5] The fashion for gold-foil medallions known as *bracteates*, common across northern Europe at the beginning of our period, seems at first sight to reveal a quite different cultural world, but even here images of the god Woden, of birdmen, and of other strange creatures turn out to have roots in the imagery of late Roman imperial coins and medals.[6] Early poetry, royal genealogies, and fashions in pottery decoration, dress, and jewelry all provide evidence that peoples on both sides of the North Sea felt that they were part of the same community of "barbarians" who had risen to power after the decline of Rome. Eighth-century Anglo-Saxon writers would revive the classical term *Germani* (Germans) to refer to this community. It signaled that these peoples had the same geographical origins in north-west Europe, that they were speakers of the same language, and that they were "brothers," for the term *germanus* also means "full blood-brother."

In the fifth and sixth centuries, Britain was, like the rest of Europe, subject to population movement, widespread warfare, and the dislocation of fiscal structures and interregional networks of trade. New ruling elites come into view, and with them new kingdoms. How similar the experience of Britain was to that of other areas of the "Roman world" is a question that has sharply divided modern historians, but, as has already been suggested, the answer depends on which area is chosen for comparison. What kind of source material is available also affects our impression of change. According to cemetery archaeology, north-east Gaul, for instance, was in the sixth century home to communities living in a ranked society comparable to communities detected in cemeteries in eastern England.[7] The letters, saints' *Lives*, and legal materials from southern Gaul, on the other hand, reveal a still urbanized society that retained the essential hierarchical structures of the Roman world.[8] It is, above all, extended narrative writing in Latin that can lift the horizon beyond the local and convey a sense of large-scale power and widespread community.[9] With the exception of Gildas's *On the Ruin of Britain*,[10] this kind of writing is lacking for Britain in the period before Bede.

In Britain and Ireland, as in the Danube region, and also north-east Gaul, the disappearance of Roman government and military power brought "Romanized" and less (or non-) "Romanized" peoples together in the formation of new political entities. In these regions, we can therefore speak of a process of "state-formation," in contrast to areas such as Italy, Spain, and Gaul (the north-east apart) which retained far more of a Roman infrastructure. Here there were ready-formed states with striking continuities in institutions, personnel, law, and language. Nevertheless, even in those regions in which Roman culture had been severely weakened, there were contacts with the Latin south which would facilitate its revival. Evidence for these kinds of links with the Mediterranean is clear for the sixth century. *The Life of John the Almsgiver*, an early seventh-century text from the eastern Mediterranean, tells of a ship sailing from Alexandria in Egypt to Britain with a cargo of corn and returning with tin and gold.[11] Tintagel on the north Cornish coast, Dinas Powys in Wales, Whithorn and Dumbarton in Scotland, and Garranes and Clogher in Ireland were all important or even princely coastal settlements in the sixth century and have produced the remains of jars, bowls, and *amphorae*, the all-purpose vessels in which Mediterranean goods were transported.[12] The point here is that wherever and whenever wealth was concentrated in Britain and Ireland, it was possible to acquire high-status goods from the south. People were aware that such commodities could be obtained, and to possess them was a highly desirable way of demonstrating wealth and status. But we should also note that the evidence of imports from the south dwindles to next to nothing in the early seventh century. This may partly be due to the decline of whatever powers had concentrated wealth in places like Tintagel, and partly it follows the decline of Mediterranean trade in general.[13] In this respect, Britain and Ireland conformed to change across Europe, sharing in what appears to have been a widespread downturn in economic activity. Recession followed the dislocation of the ancient fiscal economy and was probably accompanied by a drop in population. We have no statistics with which to demonstrate demographic decline, nor do all historians accept that populations did indeed fall in the post-Roman period, but the evidence of shrinking towns and deserted fields is striking if ultimately inconclusive.[14] References to plague from the 540s onward may provide a clue as to why populations should have continued to fall, and plague would cross the English Channel and the Irish Sea, the movement of the disease itself being an indication of continuing links with the continent.[15]

The Spread of the Christian Church

The growth of Christianity was another development that affected Britain and Ireland as well as the continent. Christianity came from Rome and was manifest in later Roman Britain. In the post-Roman period, an organized church seems to have disappeared from sight in the lowland east, but in western Britain it continued to grow, bolstered by continental influence. Monasticism, for instance, apparently came to

Britain from Gaul. Inscribed memorial stones, widely found in western Britain, often bear formulae (such as "here lies") that reflect Gallic use.[16] Bede would later tell how the church at Whithorn was dedicated to St. Martin, premier saint of Gaul (*HE*, iii. 4). As we have noted, the site at Whithorn shows evidence of trading contacts with the Mediterranean, which might explain why it was a Christian center at such an early date. Ninian, a Briton trained in Rome and the founder of Whithorn in the early fifth century, was said to have evangelized the southern Picts. By the time Gildas was writing in the second quarter of the sixth century, Christianity was the norm amongst the Britons. Ireland was converted to Christianity over the fifth and sixth centuries, with help both from the continent and from Britain. A bishop, Palladius, was said to have been sent by Pope Celestine to Ireland in 431, perhaps to organize a nascent Christian community there. More famous is Patrick, a missionary from western (probably north-western) Britain who was active in the later fifth century.

Because it is relatively well documented, the spread of Christianity and the growth of the church allow us to see in some detail how ideas and institutions that came to Britain and Ireland from mainland Europe were shaped by local conditions and how insular forms and practices then influenced the way in which Christian culture developed on the continent. Coming from the Mediterranean, the language of Christianity in the West was Latin. The organization of the church was based on towns, and its administrative structure mirrored that of late Roman government: it had a cellular structure in which the bishop's diocese was usually coterminous with the *civitas*, the city-based unit of local government. The bishop was a figure of authority with widespread rights of jurisdiction, and bishops were in practice (though not necessarily in theory) figures of high social as well as religious status. Monasteries, another Mediterranean import (via Gaul), were centers of spiritual excellence, but were subject to the bishop's authority.

Transplanted into areas in which there were virtually no towns and no *civitas* structure, and into societies in which power and influence were exercised through families and followers rather than through office, we find a church in which the authority of the bishop became less clear cut and in which monasticism became more prominent. This is especially true of Ireland, in which each "tribe" (*túath*) had its own bishop, meaning that there were over a hundred dioceses in Ireland. Bishops, in consequence, were lesser figures than on the continent, and monasteries organized around leading family groups were relatively more powerful.[17] At the same time, monasteries retained their spiritual prestige and Irish monks, some of whom practiced a rather visible asceticism, acquired a reputation for exceptional holiness. As we shall see in more detail later, when, at the end of the sixth century and in the seventh century, Irish holy men traveled extensively on the continent (such travel being a form of ascetic devotion), their version of monasticism proved to be highly attractive. It appealed in particular to the Frankish elite who were keen to put their family resources at the disposal of the monks, but were wary of allowing local bishops to have authority over "their" monasteries. As a result, we see a wave of monastic foundations in Francia inspired by the Irish. The new monasteries were mostly built in the countryside and had a degree of immunity from the local bishop. This development would have a profound effect on Frankish culture.

Christianity spread amongst the Anglo-Saxons in the east of Britain only from the end of the sixth century onward. Bede's superlative account of the conversion of the

English lays great stress on the mission sent from Rome in 597, but his narrative also relates that Irish and Frankish missionaries were involved, and he inadvertently reveals that there was a British contribution too (*HE*, iv. 13). The Anglo-Saxons lagged behind the other peoples of Britain in converting to Christianity. Conversion is associated with the development of kingship, and the latter took place amongst the Anglo-Saxons only over the course of the sixth century. In the later sixth century, just prior to conversion in England, there are hints that the cult of the god Woden was being promoted by rulers of the newly emergent kingdoms. Woden certainly became a favored progenitor in the genealogies of several royal dynasties. The Germanic pantheon was apparently narrowing down to privilege this one god, perhaps as the first step in a move toward monotheism, and possibly as a reflection of the increasing pre-eminence of earthly rulers. There are even indications from Kent that the kings were grouping their lands to support the cult in a way that prefigured the later concentration of estates in the hands of the church.[18] It is striking to note that an increasing emphasis on Woden can also be detected amongst the continental Saxons, and amongst the Scandinavians who backed Woden's equivalent, Odin, in the same way.[19] Rulers on both sides of the North Sea were, it seems, attempting to control access to the supernatural as a way of consolidating their earthly power. The phenomenon reminds us that these peoples shared a great deal in cultural terms, and as suggested earlier in this chapter, when various Anglo-Saxons kings sought to bolster the legitimacy of their power, they emphasized their ancient continental or Scandinavian origins, and they imitated continental and Scandinavian forms of dress, ornament, and burial.[20] For example, the burial mounds of the Wuffinga kings of East Anglia at the famous site of Sutton Hoo seem to imitate the royal burials of Uppsala in Sweden. What the treasure from Sutton Hoo also shows us is the influence of the Franks on these rulers.

Britain, Ireland, and the Franks

The Franks originated in the lower Rhine area. In the first half of the sixth century, they extended their domination over Gaul, at the same time acquiring hegemony over most of what is now Germany. The term "Francia" would subsequently refer to their Germano-Gallic empire. The reach of their power was so extensive that Francia formed a kind of cultural bridge between the Mediterranean and North Sea zones. The Franks were also periodically active in northern Italy and in northern Spain, and it has been argued that southern Britain fell under their sway in the sixth century.[21] The argument that the Franks did have some control over the peoples across the English Channel rests on circumstantial evidence, but material evidence for some sort of Frankish presence in England comes from Kentish graves. After a mid- to late fifth-century phase in which graves included artifacts from Jutland that may have been brought to England by early settlers, Kentish graves contain many objects, especially jewelry, of Frankish provenance.[22] Such graves were often those of females of high social status, which might suggest intermarriage between the elites on both sides of the Channel. One Frankish bride we do know about is Bertha, wife of Æthelberht, king of Kent. Although Bertha was a princess, that is, a member of the Merovingian family from whom the Franks drew their kings, she was, as we might say, "minor royalty." The provision of a bride of lesser status to a king is supposedly an indication that the king was regarded as a subordinate client of the Frankish rulers. Finally, the earliest English law code, which is from Kent and issued by King Æthelberht, has *wergilds* (legal values set on a man's life) closely related to those seen in the Frankish *Lex Salica*.[23] Had Frankish law at one time been in use in Kent?

Together, these snippets of information allow us to see that there was indeed strong Frankish influence in southern England, but there is no hard evidence that the Franks actually ruled there. Had they done so, surely there would have been some explicit reference to their presence. Nevertheless, the fact that Æthelberht in 597 received missionaries from Rome rather than from Francia might suggest that he feared closer involvement with the Franks. If so, he would have been right to be concerned, for later Frankish history shows that conversion by the Franks usually meant becoming subject to Frankish ecclesiastical control, and the Franks tended to use their church as an arm of government. A bishop and an abbot from south-east England did in fact attend an important church council held in Paris in 614, which might mean that Æthelberht initially failed to prevent the Franks having some sort of jurisdiction over the fledgling Anglo-Saxon church.

The rise of the Franks coincided with the decline in long-distance trade between Britain and Ireland and the Mediterranean. At the end of the sixth century, however, we see an increase in trading activity with the near continent. The reasons for this revival are complex. They include the development of ship types, population movement, and climatic change.[24] But Irish immigration into – or at least political control of – south-west Scotland, British migration to Armorica (Brittany), the emergence of Anglo-Saxon kingdoms in eastern and southern England, and, above all, the consolidation of Frankish power in what is now Belgium, all played a part in providing the produce, carriers, markets, and protection necessary for trade. Evidence for the trade is to be found in a series of coastal emporia which stretched from the Channel coast to the Baltic.[25] These emporia, known to scholars as *wics*, contain rich archaeological evidence. They are first found at the beginning of the seventh century and most were in operation until roughly the mid-ninth century. *Wics* were, in effect, new ports in which wealth or produce from the hinterland was exchanged for those commodities that elites desired in order to display their power and high status.[26] Integral to their rise were new ventures in the minting of coins, first in imitation of Frankish gold coins, and then silver coins particularly associated with trade between the peoples on both sides of the North Sea.

A sure sign that trade had become more common and less exotic is the appearance of incidental references to it in narrative sources, and the production of charters and laws directly concerned with trade and traders. These we find from the late seventh century onward.[27] What is clear from the early charters and rather later laws is that rights and privileges associated with trade, notably tolls, pre-emption, and the provision of hospitality for merchants, are common to both sides of the Channel, and in fact basically similar to those found in Byzantine law.[28] One can point to common origins for these rights and privileges in the later Roman Empire, but it seems more likely that they were reintroduced into Britain via the Franks than that they were survivals from the Roman period. That they should be maintained in conformity with Byzantine practices has been taken to indicate that the Franks deliberately adhered to what were in effect international conventions because of their continuing trading contacts with the eastern Mediterranean. In any case, the use of these conventions shows that, in terms of trade, Britain was anything but isolated.

Ireland, England, and the Continent

Irish holy men followed in the wake of the traders. One man in particular was celebrated in Francia. This was the Leinster man, Columbanus, who appeared in Burgundy around the year 590. His fame was enshrined in one highly influential text, the *Life of Columbanus*, which was composed by the monk Jonas of Bobbio in the 640s.[29] The *Life* would subsequently exercise a powerful influence on religious culture in Francia. Columbanus set up a monastery at Luxeuil in Burgundy which came to be perceived as a model institution. He subsequently "converted" several leading Frankish families to his vision of the religious life. The families which had had contact with Columbanus, and those influenced by Luxeuil, then began to found new monasteries on their lands. These monasteries copied Luxeuil in seeking privileges that would limit the influence of the local bishop. The idea that monastic institutions should have freedom from bishops, and also have immunity from secular dues (i.e. freedom from taxation and a degree of jurisdiction over their lands), soon became prevalent and the principle was backed by the Merovingian rulers of Francia.[30] The ramifications of Columbanus' work in Francia were thus arguably great. The Frankish elite would now put themselves firmly behind this new form of monasticism, and it would spread into the lands from which they drew their resources; that is, into the countryside and away from the more Romanized south. Although this form of monasticism has often been described as "Iro-Fankish,"[31] it is actually hard to see what was specifically Irish about it, apart from a greater emphasis on private penance. There was a Columbanian monastic rule, but the Franks at this date took what they wanted from a variety of rules, what they termed the *regula mixta*. There were, moreover, different groups of Irish on the continent, and these were not connected with, or maybe even aware of, each other.[32]

At about the time that Jonas was composing the *Life of Columbanus*, another group of Irish arrived on the continent. These three brothers, Fursey, Foillan, and Ultan, came from Ulster but had spent several years in East Anglia prior to their move to Francia, probably as refugees from the attacks of the Mercian king, Penda. Their movements show how, around the middle of the seventh century, there were three-way contacts between Ireland, Francia, and England. A key figure here was Erchinoald who was "mayor of the palace" to the kings of Neustria and Burgundy and with whom these Irish holy men first made contact. Erchinoald was the most powerful non-royal leader in Francia, and his period of office lasted from 642 to 658. Erchinoald's relations with England continue those first begun with Bertha's marriage to Æthelberht, king of Kent, in the later sixth century. Bertha's descendant moved to Northumbria but remained in contact with the Franks. Æthelberht's (but maybe not Bertha's) son, Eadbald, married yet another Frank, Emma, who was probably Erchinoald's daughter: their son and granddaughter bore names related to his. Other Franks came to England, including Agilbert, who became a bishop amongst the West Saxons. Bede tells us that Agilbert had studied in Ireland for several years before coming to England in 646 (*HE*, iii. 7). The similarity of names on both sides of the Channel ("Agilbert," for example, is the Frankish form of "Æthelberht") suggests that these contacts were long-standing, and close enough for family ties to be formed across a group wider than that of the royal families.

Erchinoald not only took in Fursey, he also acquired an Anglo-Saxon female called Balthild who was said to be a slave. But since Erchinoald then provided her as a bride for his king (Clovis II), she may have been of high status, possibly a royal princess captured in warfare. As she came to Francia about the same time as Fursey, it may be that she too was from East Anglia and another victim of Penda's attack.[33] When Clovis II died in 657, Balthild became regent for her sons and ruled forcefully until forced from power in 664. In a remarkable find near Norwich in 1998 part of a gold seal ring was uncovered. It bears the legend "Baldehildis," and it might have been hers, conceivably sent to her homeland in East Anglia after she had risen to promi-nence in Francia. Balthild founded the monastery of Chelles, into which she was forcibly retired in 664 when she fell from power, and after her death in 680 she was proclaimed a saint. It is quite puzzling that Bede never mentions Balthild, although he knew of her husband Clovis. Moreover, he tells us that at this time "many" went to Francia to enter monasteries as there were few of them in England (*HE*, iii. 8). Girls in particular joined monasteries, Chelles amongst them. The emigrants included the daughter and step-daughter of Anna, king of the East Angles, both of whom became abbesses of the convent of Faremoutiers. Another abbess of Faremoutiers was Earcongota, daughter of another of Anna's daughters, Seaxburg, and of Earconberht, king of Kent. The "Earcon" element of these names probably signified their descent from Erchinoald via Emma. That these Anglo-Saxon women became abbesses in Francia suggests that their high status was recognized there, evidence that Franco-Anglo-Saxon family contacts remained strong. This might explain why they went to Francia rather than to Ireland, where there were actually plenty of female monastic establishments.[34] Certainly, many males went to Ireland to enter the reli-gious life there, as Agilbert had done. Nor do any Irish women seem to have joined the exodus of Irish to Britain and the continent. Travel to and from Ireland for reli-gious reasons was apparently a male preserve.

Exile, as well as religious devotion, played a part in these movements between Francia, England, and Ireland. This would seem to be the case with the Fursey group, for instance, and also with Agilbert who promptly returned to Francia when Balthild fell from power. Most remarkable of all was the removal to Ireland of the young Frankish prince Dagobert II in about the year 656. What happened to Dagobert next we learn only from an English source, Stephen of Ripon's *Life of St. Wilfrid*, com-posed shortly after Wilfrid's death in 709.[35] According to the *Life*, in about 676 the Franks sought Dagobert out in Ireland. Wilfrid equipped him as a king and sent him back to Francia, where he ruled until 679 when he was assassinated. Ireland, this curious story suggests, was firmly within the orbit of international politics. And according to his *Life*, albeit a highly partisan source, the English bishop Wilfrid was an important player in those politics.

From the middle of the seventh century, contacts with Rome began to play a bigger role in Francia and also in Britain and Ireland. The English, in particular, had enormous regard for the papacy. A stream of British, Irish, and English scholars and pilgrims, Wilfrid included, made their way to Rome, invariably via Francia, and by the eighth century so numerous were the English in Rome that we hear that the city had an English quarter. Two West Saxon kings abdicated and ended their days in

Rome. The Roman mission to England, on the other hand, had perhaps been less of a force in converting the English than Bede maintained. The last of the Romans, Archbishop Honorius, died in 653. Pope Vitalian eventually in 668 appointed the monk Theodore of Tarsus archbishop of Canterbury. Theodore was one of many refugees who had moved to Italy when the Arabs conquered Syria. He was joined by Hadrian, an African who would become abbot of St. Peter's (St. Augustine's) at Canterbury. According to Bede, Theodore and Hadrian traveled through Francia, staying with Agilbert, who had become bishop of Paris. The "mayor of the palace" Ebroin (Erchinoald's successor) then refused to let Hadrian cross to England because he feared that he was on a secret mission from the emperor to the kings of Britain (Bede, *HE*, iv. 1). This means the Byzantine emperor, and the story gains some credibility if we remember that the Byzantines were very active in Italy at this point. The emperor, Constans II, had moved his court to Italy in 662. He would be murdered in September 668, but not before Theodore and Hadrian had traveled to Francia. We have no record of a response outside Italy to Constans' dramatic move, except perhaps this indication that the Franks were alarmed. Paul the Deacon, an Italian who composed a *History of the Lombards* in the 790s, related in a single passage Constans' death, the warfare that followed, and Theodore and Hadrian's departure for England, but made no causal connections. He also added that Theodore and Hadrian went on to enrich the English church with healthy doctrines and that Theodore introduced a tariffed system of penance.[36] There is no evidence that Paul the Deacon was drawing on Bede's work here; nor were Theodore and Hadrian mentioned in the section on Vitalian in the set of papal biographies known as the *Book of the Popes*.[37] The latter was one of Paul the Deacon's main sources. He would thus seem to have had separate sources of information on Britain, and he was certainly interested in Britain to an extent that confirms the impression that Irish, Britons, and Anglo-Saxons had become familiar figures in Italy. Paul, in fact, commented on the large number and variety of English of both sexes coming to Rome, and he coined the term "Anglo-Saxons" (*Anglisaxones*) for them, noting that their dress was like that of his own people, the Lombards.[38] As for political contacts, he tells us that in 671 the Lombard prince, Pectarit, was about to cross the Channel en route to a refuge in Britain when he heard that it was safe to return to Italy.[39] He also says that, in about 688, the Lombard king, Cunipert, took an Anglo-Saxon wife, Hermelinda.[40] For this information we have no corroboration. If true, it would suggest that links between the Anglo-Saxons and Lombards were indeed close.

Once installed in Canterbury, Theodore reorganized the English church and strengthened the hand of the archbishop. The latter office took somewhat different forms throughout the Christian world, and Theodore seems to have drawn on his experience of the eastern Mediterranean where archbishops had rather stronger authority than in Italy and Francia.[41] In order to strengthen his position, he also promoted the cult of Pope Gregory the Great who had sent the original missionaries in 597.[42] Bede drew on Canterbury sources, and this is one reason why he too made Gregory the inspirational figure behind the conversion of the English. The result was that the English would acquire a unique sense of religious debt to Rome, hence the increasing volume of traffic between England and Italy. It has often been remarked that it was the English who brought the papacy out of the shadow of Roman politics and into contact with the wider church. This is an exaggeration, for there had always been contacts between Frankish rulers and bishops and the papacy, but it is true that the popes had more influence in England than in any other region beyond the Alps. English missionaries on the continent would carry this respect for papal authority with them.

English Missionaries on the Continent

Bede tells us that it was a certain Bishop Egbert who first conceived of missionary work amongst the "Germans" in the 680s whilst living as a monk in Ireland (*HE*, v. 9), although the *Life of Wilfrid* says that on the second of his three journeys to Rome, thus in 679, Wilfrid landed in Frisia and attempted in vain to convert the Frisians before moving on.[43] It seems clear that the idea of foreign mission owed much to the Irish example, but that the drive to convert "Germans" came from the specifically Anglo-Saxon sense of kinship with them. Willibrord, the first English missionary to survive and make headway abroad, arrived in Frisia in 690 and made straight for Pippin, "mayor of the palace" of Austrasia, who became his protector.[44] Earlier, as we have seen, the focus had been on those Neustrian Franks in the lands between the Channel coast and Paris who had had close relations with southern England and East Anglia. Now contact swung to the north and east, to the lands between the Meuse and Rhine where the Pippinid family had their lands. Mercian domination of the south and east of England from the 670s onward may partly account for the end of these close cross-Channel relations, but it is also the case that the old Neustrian families, such as that of Erchinoald, lost their pre-eminence as power in Francia shifted east to Austrasia and the Pippinids. This shift is in turn connected with the rising importance of Frisia and the need of the Franks to protect themselves from the Frisians, along with their desire to benefit from the wealth coming into Frisia from the trading center of Dorestad. The Pippinds controlled the rivers that flowed directly into such Frisian trade centers. Conversion, along with warfare, and also marriage were all employed in the struggle to subdue the Frisians.

Willibrord did not actually penetrate very far into Frisia, but he did, with Pippin's help, set up a bishopric in Utrecht, and founded the monastery of Echternach on the family lands of Plectrude, Pippin's wife. He traveled to Rome in 696 to be consecrated archbishop of the Frisians. He remained in the Frisian borderlands until his death in 739, and became a figure of great veneration. Many other Anglo-Saxons followed him to the continent, chief amongst them Boniface who came from Devon. He arrived in 718, traveled to Rome in 719, and then joined Willibrord before moving south to the mid-Rhine area where he made Hesse and Thuringia his field of mission. Like Willibrord, Boniface enjoyed Pippinid protection and aided them in consolidating their power. And, like Willibrord, he went to Rome to be consecrated archbishop, eventually becoming archbishop of Mainz. He also founded the monastery of Fulda in Hesse. So many English men, and women, followed Boniface to Fulda and to other monasteries newly established east of the Rhine that we can detect their particular style of writing in a host of manuscripts.[45] Boniface helped the Pippinids, led now by the redoubtable Charles Martel and his sons Pippin and Carloman, by extending the Frankish church eastward and by leading a reform of the church west of the Rhine and in Bavaria.[46] The promotion of reform not only enabled the Pippinids to reinforce their control over the church, it was also a source of considerable spiritual prestige. The Pippinids would draw heavily on this prestige to justify their rise to power, and when they became kings as the Carolingians, their government would be articulated around a rhetoric of reform or "correction."

We are fortunate in having a collection of Boniface's correspondence. From his own pen, we can see the extent to which he thought of himself as serving the papacy. Eventually Boniface resigned his see, in order that his chosen successor Lull, another Anglo-Saxon, might take over, and then he headed north where he was killed by Frisians in 754. Dead, Boniface was perhaps even more use to the Carolingians (as the Pippinids would be known after they had become kings) than he had been when alive. As a missionary martyr, his fame continued to grow. The Carolingians seized the throne in 751, and writers then began to weave Boniface into a narrative that celebrated, explained, and justified their rise from mayors to kings. It was an account that had the papacy sanction their coup d'état, and had Boniface anoint the new king, Pippin.[47] Traditionally, historians accepted all this at face value, and gave Boniface the credit for, as it were, putting the papacy and the Carolingians in touch with each other. We can now unpick this narrative construction, and doubt that Boniface was even present when Pippin was raised to throne.[48] Nor, as suggested earlier, did the papacy really need Boniface to put them in touch with the Franks: they had been begging the Franks for help against the Lombards since the time of Charles Martel. But the writing about Boniface was very successful. It constructed him as the greatest of the missionary heroes. But he was also the last of them. Thereafter, the Anglo-Saxons would be valued on the continent more for their scholarship than for their preaching of the faith. Their learning was particularly valuable to the Carolingian regime, for it was used to express a notion of religious order that expanded the moral remit of the king. This was a notion that suited an ambitious regime that was rising in power but was still careful to legitimate its actions.

That Anglo-Saxons, and Irish, should come to be seen as exceptionally learned and the bearers of a special holy wisdom is a mark of how rapidly these peoples had absorbed Christian learning. Important, too, was the notion of "correction" that we have already met. In its most general sense, "correction" meant adhering, or returning, to a way of life that was in accordance with scripture and with the law of the church. Rulers and subjects would prosper only if that way of life was scrupulously observed. It is in Ireland that we first see these ideas in a late seventh-century text, *On the Twelve Abuses of the World*, by an author referred to as Pseudo-Cyprian. Kings, it argued, should be aware of how much the good fortune of their subjects and their lands depended upon their correct behavior.[49] Already in 772 we see an Anglo-Saxon monk, Cathwulf, communicating these ideas to Charlemagne,[50] but it was through Charlemagne's Anglo-Saxon advisor, Alcuin (d.804), that they came to be more widely disseminated and became, in fact, a cornerstone of the Carolingian sense of order. It can be argued that this conception of the just ruler represents a first step in post-Roman political thought, and that it is no accident that it should come from a people who had not had experience of Roman rule.

Christianization and Social Change

Christianization did not just provide rulers with the vocabulary of moral justification, it was also part and parcel of a lengthy process of social change which provided the resources for the building of larger-scale political units. Comparison between what happened in Britain and on the continent here is especially useful. In northern and eastern Francia, we see that Christianization brought an end to the use of large communal cemeteries in which all members of a community had been buried. In their place, we find the formation of smaller burial grounds around churches, with the more prominent members of the community separated from the rest by being buried inside the church. This change followed shifts in settlement patterns in which peasant dwellings were now grouped around a hall (or *sala*).[51] What we appear to be seeing is the emergence of a society in which lords drew directly on the labor of peasants; that is, a society with a much stronger sense of hierarchy. Place-names began to have a personal element as settlements were named after lords; that is, the community was seen to "belong" to the lord.[52] The whole process has often been referred to as "manorialization." Careful work on Toxandria (the lower Meuse valley) has matched the charters from Willibrord's monastery of Echternach with settlement archaeology and can demonstrate how the monastery organized its newly acquired lands around the lords' halls in this way.[53] It was these lords, with their tightening control over the surplus produced in the countryside, who were the bedrock of any successful regime.

We see a similar process in England, in which the introduction of charters stabilized the landholding of the church and of its clients and was followed by the emergence of larger political units. Hesse, the land that stretched east from the Rhine along the River Maine, and which was Boniface's field of action, seems most like England in this respect. In both regions, as monasteries were established, lords quickly seized upon the charter as means of strengthening their hold over land and as an aid to passing on their lands to their children. Hesse was in the hands at least six different "peoples" when Boniface arrived.[54] By the time of his death, these peoples had been absorbed into the wider group of Franks, and the only trace of them to survive would be in the occasional area name. The document known as the *Tribal Hidage* may show a similar process in late seventh or eighth century England, though on a larger scale. It reveals the names of several groups which later were apparently absorbed into the larger kingdoms and then lost their identity.[55] The coincidence of the introduction of charters, the spread of religious organization, and the absorption of smaller into larger political units in the two regions suggests that the process of Christianization took place at similar stages of development, and hints at the possible dynamics between these processes.

The introduction of charters is a fitting point at which to end this survey. Charters are documents that have their origin in late Roman property law. They record, affirm, and, in some cases, give legal backing to all manner of transactions, but they are above all deeds of conveyance. Charters survive in increasing numbers from the seventh century onward,[56] and in the various regions that we see them it is fair to assume that property relations, and thus social structure, were broadly similar. Charters, as we have just seen, appeared in the wake of Christianization, which was itself an indicator of greater social and political stability. Charters thus show us that by the mid-eighth century large areas of Christian Europe held and disposed of property in much the same ways. Again, however, we meet insular variations on a common theme. Wales apparently developed its own form of charters based on the later Roman tradition. Ireland began to develop a charter tradition in the sixth century, but this seems then to have died out.[57] For Scotland, no charters survive from this period. The latter two areas were those in which Roman influence was most peripheral. The English charter tradition is a hybrid one. It shows influence from Rome in that some early charters have phrases similar to those found in one of Gregory the Great's charters. It also reveals Frankish influence, especially in the charters of one Earkonwald, bishop of London, whose name suggests that he was yet another descendant of Erchinoald.[58] English charters also show Welsh influence in the form of lengthy boundary clauses.

But these local variations are less impressive than the similarities between charters right across Europe. They show us a post-Roman consolidation of religious organization, of the way in which land was held and managed, and of the social hierarchy that managed the land. Of course, regional variation would remain, and each region would have its own history. The fact that the peoples of Britain and Ireland had played an important part in the development of common European cultural features would not preclude a turn to more insular ways, or at least a lessening of ties with the continent, as seems to be the case with Ireland in the ninth century. But it is also true that that identity as Europeans, as Catholic Christians, and as inheritors of Rome, which had grown up amongst all the peoples of Europe in the post-Roman centuries, would prove indelible.

Notes

1   Higham, *Rome, Britain and the Anglo-Saxons*, pp. 225–36.
2   Barford, *Early Slavs*, p. 58; Kobylinski, "The Slavs," pp. 524–36.
3   Archibald et al., "Heirs of Rome," pp. 226–30.
4   Dumville, "Sub-Roman Britain."
5   Davies, "The Latin charter tradition."
6   Behr, "The origins of kingship," pp. 31–9; Bente, "Firebed of the serpent," pp. 196–8.
7   Halsall, *Settlement and Social Organization*, pp. 251–62.
8   Wickham, *Framing the Early Middle Ages*, pp. 155–78.
9   Goffart, *Narrators of Barbarian History*.
10   Winterbottom (ed.), *Gildas*.
11   Festugière (ed.), *Leontius of Naples*.
12   Lebecq, "The northern seas," p. 642.
13   Loseby, "The Mediterranean economy;" Wickham, *Framing the Early Middle Ages*, pp. 708–20.
14   Samson, "Populous dark-age towns."
15   Maddicot, "Plague in seventh-century England"; Sarris, "The Justinianic plague."
16   James, *Britain in the First Millennium*, p. 104.
17   Stancliffe, "Religion and society in Ireland," pp. 402–7.
18   Behr, "The origins of kingship," pp. 39–52.
19   Hedeager, "Scandinavia," pp. 508–14.
20   Hines, "The Scandinavian character of Anglian England."
21   Wood, *Merovingian North Sea*.
22   Behr, "The origins of kingship"; Drewett et al., *South-East*, pp. 257–8.
23   See *EHD*, I, 357–9 for laws of Æthelberht; Eckhardt (ed.), *Pactus legis Salicae*.
24   Lebecq, "The northern seas," pp. 645–6.
25   Ibid., pp. 646–50.
26   Hodges and Hobley (eds.), *Rebirth of Towns in the West*.

27 For example, in the laws of Hlothhere, *EHD*, I, 360–1.
28 Middleton, "Early medieval port customs."
29 Krusch (ed.), *Jonas: Vita Columbani.*
30 Fouracre, "Eternal light and earthly needs," pp. 53–60.
31 Prinz, *Frühes Mönchtum*, pp. 450–500.
32 Wood, *Merovingian Kingdoms*, pp. 184–97.
33 Fouracre and Gerberding, *Late Merovingian France*, pp. 99–102.
34 Bittel, *Isle of the Saints*, p. 233.
35 Colgrave (ed.), *Life of Bishop Wilfrid.*
36 Bethmann and Waitz (eds.), *Paul the Deacon: History of the Lombards*, v. 30.
37 Duchesne (ed.), *Liber Pontificalis.*
38 Bethmann and Waitz (eds.), *Paul the Deacon: History of the Lombards*, vi. 37; iv. 22.
39 Ibid., v. 32.
40 Ibid., v. 37.
41 Thacker, "Gallic or Greek?"
42 Thacker, "Memorializing Gregory the Great."
43 Colgrave (ed.), *Life of Bishop Wilfrid*, pp. 26–7.
44 Angenendt, "Willibrord im Dienst der Karolinger."
45 McKitterick, "Anglo-Saxon missionaries in Germany."
46 Fouracre, *Age of Charles Martel*, pp. 130–4.
47 Scholz (trans.), *Royal Frankish Annals, s.aa.* 749, 750.
48 McKitterick, *History and Memory*, pp. 133–55.
49 Hellmann (ed.), "Pseudo-Cyprian"; Meens, "Politics, mirrors of princes and the Bible."
50 Story, "Cathwulf, kingship and the royal abbey of St. Denis."
51 Loveluck, "Rural settlement hierarchy," pp. 230–42; Theuws, "Landed property and manorial organization."
52 Prinz, "Frühes Mönchtum in Südwestdeutschland," p. 42.
53 Theuws, "Landed property and manorial organization."
54 Emerton (trans.), *Letters of Saint Boniface*, no. 33.
55 Hill (ed.), "Tribal Hidage."
56 See Sawyer, *Anglo-Saxon Charters.*
57 Davies, "The Latin charter-tradition."
58 Wormald, *Bede and the Conversion of England.*

Further Reading

P. Fouracre, "Forgetting and remembering Dagobert II: the English connection," in P. Fouracre and D. Ganz (eds.), *Frankland: The Franks and the World of Early Medieval Europe* (Manchester, 2008), pp. 70–89, goes into the later seventh-century relationship between Britain, Ireland, and the continent in more detail. H. Hamerow, *Early Medieval Settlements: The Archaeology of Rural Communities in North-West Europe, 400–900* (Oxford, 2002) provides a range of settlement models that show both basic similarities and regional differences across northern Europe. W. Levison, *England and the Continent in the Eighth Century* (Oxford, 1946) is regarded as the classic work on this subject. The analysis of the politics is now dated, but Levison's commentaries on the sources remain excellent. A. Lohaus, *Die Merowinger und England* (Munich, 1974) is the only work dedicated to Merovingian/British relations, but it says very little about the seventh century. M. McCormick, *Origins of the European Economy: Communications and Commerce, AD 300–900* (Cambridge, 2001) is an impressive survey of known trading contacts, but it is not really about the economy as a whole. J. M. H. Smith, *Europe after Rome: A New Cultural History of Europe 500–1000* (Oxford, 2005) provides a new and insightful account of how European culture developed which includes the insular regions. J. Story, *Carolingian Connections: Anglo-Saxon England and Carolingian Francia c.750–870* (Aldershot, 2003) is essential for the later history of relations. I. N. Wood, "The European Science Foundation's programme on the transformation of the Roman world and the emergence of early medieval Europe," *Early Medieval Europe* 6: 2 (1997), 217–27, is the starting-point for the discussion of "transformation." For more specialized reading, readers are advised to consult the relevant chapter bibliographies in P. Fouracre (ed.), *New Cambridge Medieval History*, vol. 1 (Cambridge, 2005).

Bibliography

Anderson, A. O. and Anderson, M. O. (eds.), *Adomnán's Life of Columba*, 2nd edn. (Oxford, 1991).

Angenendt, A., "Willibrord im Dienst der Karolinger," *Annales der historisches Vereins für den Niederrhien inbesondere das alte Erzbistum Köln*, 175 (1973), 63–113.

Archibald, M., Brown, M., and Webster, L., "Heirs of Rome: the shaping of Britain 400–900," in L. Webster, and M. Brown (eds.), *The Transformation of the Roman World, AD 400–900* (London, 1997), pp. 208–48.

Barford, P. M., *The Early Slavs: Culture and Society in Early Medieval Eastern Europe* (London, 2001).

Behr, C., "The origins of kingship in early medieval Kent," *Early Medieval Europe*, 9: 1 (2000), 25–52.

Bente, M., "The firebed of the serpent: myth and religion in the migration period mirrored through some golden objects," in L. Webster, and M. Brown (eds.), *The Transformation of the Roman World, AD 400–900* (London, 1997), pp. 194–206.

Bethmann, L. and Waitz, G. (eds.), *Paul the Deacon: History of the Lombards*, in *Historia Langobardorum, MGH, SRL* (Hanover, 1878), pp. 7–217.

Bittel, L., *Isle of the Saints: Monastic Settlement and Christian Community in Early Ireland* (Ithaca, 1993).

Colgrave, B. (ed. and trans.), *The Life of Bishop Wilfrid by Eddius Stephanus* (Cambridge, 1927; repr. New York, 1985).

Davies, W., "Adding insult to injury: power, property and immunities in early medieval Wales," in W. Davies and P. Fouracre (eds.), *Property and Power in the Early Middle Ages* (Cambridge, 1995) pp. 137–64.

Davies, W, "The Latin charter-tradition in western Britain, Brittany and Ireland in the early medieval period," in D. Whitelock, R. McKitterick, and D. Dumville (eds.), *Ireland in Early Medieval Europe: Studies in Memory of Kathleen Hughes* (Cambridge, 1982), pp. 258–80.

Drewett, P., Rudling, D., and Gardiner, M., *The South-East to AD 1000* (London, 1988).

Duchesne, L. (ed.), *Liber Pontificalis* [*Book of the Popes*], 2 vols. Bibliothèque des Écoles Françaises d'Athènes et de Rome, series 2, 3 (Rome, 1886–92).

Dumville, D., "Sub-Roman Britain: history and legend," *History*, 62 (1977), 173–92.

Eckhardt, K. A. (ed.), *Pactus legis Salicae*, in *MGH*, Legum Sectio I. iv (ii) (Hanover, 1962).

Emerton, E. (trans.), *The Letters of Saint Boniface* (New York, 1976).

Festugière, A. J. (ed and French trans.), *Leontius of Naples: Vie de Syméon le fou et vie de Jean de Chypre* [*Life of John the Almsgiver*] (Paris, 1974).

Fouracre, P., *The Age of Charles Martel* (Harmondsworth, 2000).

Fouracre, P., "Eternal light and earthly needs: practical aspects of the development of Frankish immunities," in W. Davies and P. Fouracre (eds.), *Property and Power in the Early Middle Ages* (Cambridge, 1995), pp. 53–81.

Fouracre, P. and Gerberding, R., *Late Merovingian France: History and Hagiography 640–720* (Manchester, 1996).

Goffart, W., *The Narrators of Barbarian History (AD 550–800)* (Princeton, NJ, 1986).

Halsall, G., *Settlement and Social Organization: The Merovingian Region of Metz* (Cambridge, 1995).

Hedeager, L., "Scandinavia," in P. Fouracre (ed.), *New Cambridge Medieval History*, vol. 1 (Cambridge, 2005), pp. 496–523.

Hellmann, S. (ed.), "Pseudo-Cyprian," *De XII Abusivis saeculi* [*On the Twelve Abuses of the World*]. Texte und Untersuchungen zur Geschichte der altchristliche Literatur, 34 (1909), pp. 1–61.

Higham, N., *Rome, Britain and the Anglo-Saxons* (London, 1992).

Hill, D. (ed.), "Tribal Hidage," in *An Atlas of Anglo-Saxon England* (Oxford, 1981) pp. 76–7.

Hines, J., "The Scandinavian character of Anglian England: an update," in M. Carver (ed.), *The Age of Sutton Hoo: The Seventh Century in North Western Europe* (Woodbridge, 1992), pp. 317–29.

Hodges, R. and Hobley, B. (eds.), *The Rebirth of Towns in the West AD 700–1050*. CBA Report 68 (London, 1988).

James, E., *Britain in the First Millennium* (London, 2001).

Kobylinski, Z., "The Slavs," in P. Fouracre (ed.), *New Cambridge Medieval History*, vol. 1 (Cambridge, 2005), pp. 524–44.

Krusch, B. (ed.), *Jonas: Vita Columbani*, in *MGH, SRM*, vol. 4 (Hanover, 1902), pp. 64–108.

Lebecq, S., "The northern seas (fifth to eighth centuries)," in P. Fouracre (ed.), *New Cambridge Medieval History*, vol. 1 (Cambridge, 2005), pp. 639–59.

Loseby, S., "The Mediterranean economy," in P. Fouracre (ed.), *New Cambridge Medieval History*, vol. 1 (Cambridge, 2005), pp. 605–38.

Loveluck, C., "Rural settlement hierarchy in the age of Charlemagne," in J. Story (ed.), *Charlemagne: Empire and Society* (Manchester, 2005), pp. 230–58.

McKitterick, R., "Anglo-Saxon missionaries in Germany: reflections on the manuscript evidence," *Transactions of the Cambridge Bibliographical Society*, 9 (1989), 291–329.

McKitterick, R., *History and Memory in the Carolingian World* (Cambridge, 2004).

Maddicott, J., "Plague in seventh-century England," *Past & Present*, 156 (1997), 7–54.

Meens, R., "Politics, mirrors of princes and the Bible: sins, kings and the well-being of the realm," *Early Medieval Europe*, 7: 3 (1998), 343–57.

Middleton, N., "Early medieval port customs, tolls and controls and foreign trade," *Early Medieval Europe*, 13: 4 (2005), 313–58.

Prinz, F., *Frühes Mönchtum im Frankenreich* (Munich, 1965).

Prinz, F., "Frühes Mönchtum in Südwestdeutschland und die Anfänge der Reichenau," in A. Borst (ed.), *Mönchtum, Episkopat und Adel zur Gründungszeit des Klosters Reichenau*. Vorträge und Forschungen 20 (Sigmaringen, 1974), pp. 37–76.

Samson, R., "Populous dark-age towns: the Finleyesque approach," *Journal of European Archaeology*, 2 (1994), 97–129.

Sarris, P., "The Justinianic plague: origins and effects," *Continuity and Change*, 17: 2 (2002), 169–82.

Sawyer, P., *Anglo-Saxon Charters: An Annotated List and Bibliography* (London, 1968).

Scholz, B. (trans.), *Royal Frankish Annals*, in *Carolingian Chronicles* (Ann Arbor, 1972), pp. 37–125.

Sherley-Price, L. and Latham, R. E. (ed. and trans.), *Bede: A History of the English Church and People*, with new introduction and notes by D. H. Farmer (Harmondsworth, 1990).

Stancliffe, C., "Religion and society in Ireland," in P. Fouracre (ed.), *New Cambridge Medieval History*, vol. 1 (Cambridge, 2005), pp. 397–425.

Story, J., "Cathwulf, kingship and the royal abbey of St. Denis," *Speculum*, 74 (1999), 1–24.

Thacker, A., "Gallic or Greek? Archbishops in England from Theodore to Ecgberht," in P. Fouracre and D. Ganz (eds.), *Frankland: The Franks and the World of Early Medieval Europe* (Manchester, 2008), pp. 44–69.

Thacker, A., "Memorializing Gregory the Great: the original transmission of a papal cult in the seventh and early eighth centuries," *Early Medieval Europe*, 7: 1 (1998), 59–84.

Theuws, F., "Landed property and manorial organization in Northern Austrasia: some considerations and a case study," in N. Roymans and F. Theuws (eds.), *Images of the Past: Studies on Ancient Societies in Northwestern Europe* (Amsterdam, 1991), pp. 299–407.

Whitelock, D. (ed. and trans.), *English Historical Documents*, vol. I: *c.500–1042*, 2nd edn. (London, 1979).

Wickham, C., *Framing the Early Middle Ages: Europe and the Mediterranean, 400–800* (Oxford, 2005).

Winterbottom, M. (ed. and trans.), *Gildas: The Ruin of Britain and Other Documents* (Chichester, 1978).

Wood, I. N., *The Merovingian Kingdoms 450–751* (Harlow, 1994).

Wood, I. N., *The Merovingian North Sea.* (Alingsås, 1983).

Wormald, P., *Bede and the Conversion of England: The Charter Evidence.* Jarrow Lecture 1984 (Jarrow, n.d.); reprinted in P. Wormald, *The Times of Bede: Studies in Early English Christian Society and its Historian* (Oxford, 2006).

Chapter Ten

Conversions to Christianity

Huw Pryce

In 597, a group of Italian monks led by Augustine, sent from Rome by Pope Gregory the Great, arrived in Kent. Their task was to convert the pagan Anglo-Saxons to Christianity. In the same year, an Irish abbot called Columba (Columcille) died in the monastery he had founded on the small island of Iona, over 500 miles away in the Inner Hebrides. Like Augustine, he was a monk with a commitment to missionary work. However, in important respects these two individuals represented two different strands in the spread of Christianity in Britain and Ireland. Columba was the heir to a Christian tradition whose roots lay in late Roman Britain and which had been transmitted to Ireland mainly by British churchmen; indeed, his own monastic teacher may well have been a Briton. Augustine, on the other hand, embodied a new wave of Roman influence originating in Rome itself. For Bede, writing in the early eighth century, the arrival of the Roman missionaries marked the beginning of a divinely ordained narrative: the transformation of the English into a Christian people. Viewed from a broader British and Irish perspective, however, the mission to Kent was but the latest phase in a process of religious change that had begun in late antiquity.

Historiographical Approaches

The contrasts between the traditions to which Columba and Augustine belonged have formed a major theme in interpretations of the religious history of this period. At its most stark, those contrasts have been viewed in terms of two rival institutions: the Celtic church and the Roman church. However, the notion of a Celtic church, common to all the Celtic countries and completely separate from the Roman church, has convincingly been discredited in recent decades.[1] At the same time, scholars have drawn more nuanced comparisons between the Irish and Anglo-Saxon churches that highlight connections and similarities as well as differences. This has been particularly true of church organization, with regard to the respective roles and relative importance of bishops and monasteries as sources of authority and pastoral care to the laity. Fruitful comparisons have also been drawn between different phases and contexts of missionary endeavor. Nevertheless, the potential for a comparative and integrative approach encompassing Britain and Ireland is far from exhausted. Much work has, quite legitimately, focused on the development of Christianity in particular countries, following the lead of two seminal books – namely, Kathleen Hughes's *The Church in Early Irish Society* (1966) and Henry Mayr-Harting's *The Coming of Christianity to Early Anglo-Saxon England* (1972) – that have helped to set the agenda for further research in recent decades. True, these books, together with subsequent studies of particular aspects of the early ecclesiastical history of the Celtic countries and Anglo-Saxon kingdoms, take pains to place the developments they consider in a wider insular and also continental context. However, attempts to examine the process of Christianization as a whole across Britain and Ireland have been confined to necessarily brief overviews within the broader frameworks of either general histories of those islands in the early Middle Ages or surveys of Christianization in medieval Europe more generally.

A second key historiographical theme is the development of more complex understandings of the nature of religion and hence of what was meant by conversion to Christianity. For one thing, there has been a shift in focus from the aims of missionaries to the values and expectations of those whom they sought to convert. The shift has been linked to the adoption of a more critical view of conversion narratives, notably Bede's influential *Ecclesiastical History of the English People* (731), which has concentrated attention on their purpose and thereby highlighted gaps and distortions in their accounts of missions. This, in turn, has encouraged a search for new perspectives informed not only by a wider range of sources, including a growing body of archaeological evidence, but also, more importantly, by comparisons with better evidenced missions in the medieval and modern worlds. Thus, for example, historians have become more aware of the problems inherent in assuming that paganism and Christianity were essentially equivalents – that is, two sides of a common coin called "religion" – and hence readier to try to assess how pagans understood conversion. Admittedly, this assumption appears to be supported by conversion narratives, but there is a strong case for interpreting these sources' descriptions of paganism as literary constructs created by Christian authors in antithesis to what they perceived to be the only true religion.

To talk of "true religion" raises a further issue that has bedeviled discussions of conversion and, indeed, of ecclesiastical history more generally: how does one define Christianity and therefore assess its impact on society? Broadly speaking, the more rigorous the definition, the more difficult it is to describe a society as Christian. Thus, some historians have gone so far as to question how far medieval Europe was Christianized at all, positing a radical gulf between an official ecclesiastical culture and a "folkloric" culture among the mass of the population.[2] If true, this would imply that attempts at conversion in the early Middle Ages were largely ineffective. Indeed, it has been argued that the faith was fatally compromised by "Germanization," namely an accommodation with the values and customs of pre-Christian society.[3] Yet such interpretations have been criticized for measuring Christianity against too rigid a yardstick, and most recent historians of early medieval conversions have accepted that Christianity was highly flexible and that its precise character varied according to the social and cultural complexion of the societies that professed it. Accordingly, they have tried to investigate what the faith meant to people at the time rather than assess how far it conformed with a supposedly universal and eternal norm. Of course, given the patchy and incomplete nature of the surviving evidence, such an investigation is far from straightforward in relation to early medieval Britain and Ireland. This is particularly true of two related issues. First, the lack of contemporary accounts by individuals of their adoption of Christianity effectively precludes the study of conversion in the strict sense of interior religious change: the best we can usually do is draw inferences from reports of individual or collective behavior or from archaeological evidence, especially from cemeteries. Similar problems confront attempts, second, to make sense of the coexistence of the new faith with aspects of pre-Christian culture.

We shall return to these points in the following discussion, which considers how and why the peoples of Britain and Ireland adopted Christianity in the period between Patrick's mission to the Irish in the fifth century and the official acceptance of the new religion by the last remaining pagan Anglo-Saxon kingdoms toward the end of the seventh. The emphasis will therefore be on conversion, used here as a convenient shorthand for the initial stages, extending from the first introduction of Christianity to its final displacement of public pagan cult, of a longer and deeper process of Christianization. This emphasis means that attention will first be given to the British and Irish before moving on to look in greater depth at the Anglo-Saxons, whose conversion was both later and better attested than that of their Celtic-speaking neighbors.

The British Church

In his *De Excidio Britanniae* ("The Ruin of Britain"), composed c.540 or perhaps a little earlier, the monk Gildas condemned not only various British secular rulers but also their bishops and priests. His testimony, together with that of inscribed memorial stones, shows that the church was well established by the sixth century among the British of the western parts of Britain that had not succumbed to Anglo-Saxon conquest. Recent scholarship has made a powerful case for regarding this church as the direct successor of late Romano-British Christianity, and this background provides an essential starting-point for any consideration of the conversion of the peoples of Britain and Ireland.

True, earlier generations of scholars denied a direct link with the church in Roman Britain: for them, the world revealed by Gildas was a creation of the post-Roman period that resulted from the arrival, through maritime contacts, of Christian influences from Gaul and the Mediterranean.[4] This view depended on two main assumptions: that late Roman Christianity in Britain was too weak to survive the end of imperial control at the beginning of the fifth century, followed by Anglo-Saxon settlement, and that both imported pottery and the formulae on memorial stones from the fifth and sixth centuries revealed new contacts between western Britain and the European continent. However, the pottery is found mostly on what are now identified as high-status secular, not ecclesiastical, sites (Tintagel is the prime example), and therefore the extent to which it attests to new Christian influences is unclear. More importantly, the Gaulish provenance of the formulae is by no means certain: they could equally well derive from epigraphic traditions in Roman Britain itself.[5] Moreover, there are strong grounds for supposing that Romano-British Christianity weathered the end of Roman rule and the Anglo-Saxon *adventus* and shared in some of the same developments as the Gaulish church of the fifth century, notably the development of the cults of martyred saints: Gildas refers to Julius and Aaron (probably at Caerleon) and Alban at St. Albans, whose tomb was visited about a century earlier by Bishop Germanus of Auxerre on his visit to Britain to combat the Pelagian heresy in 429. That visit, together with the career of St. Patrick (discussed below), show that an ecclesiastical hierarchy under bishops survived in Britain, and a church organization is also evidenced in the inscribed stones. Admittedly, the Anglo-Saxon conquests meant that that church became increasingly confined to western regions of Britain. Yet its demise in the areas of the island taken over by the Anglo-Saxons was less sudden and complete than has often been supposed. Taken together, scraps of evidence, such as the continued veneration of the tomb of St. Alban at St. Albans, the discovery c.600 of the cult of an unknown British saint called Sixtus by Augustine of Canterbury, and the acquisition by Ripon in the mid-670s of "holy places" abandoned by British clergy who had fled from the Northumbrians, suggest that pockets of Romano-British Christianity survived in areas dominated by pagan Anglo-Saxons, whose conquests, to judge by archaeological evidence, took longer and were more piecemeal than was once thought.

Nevertheless, the future of the Romano-British church lay in the west, in a world without villas and towns. Since these areas, extending from Galloway to Cornwall, had been largely untouched by Christianity in the Roman period, this implies a process of conversion in the fifth and early sixth centuries. Our ignorance of the precise chronology and nature of this process does not diminish its significance: the spread of Christianity in post-Roman western Britain and its displacement of Celtic and Roman cults marked an important religious change that in turn provided, as we shall see shortly, a prerequisite for the evangelization of Ireland. As far as Gildas was concerned, conversion had already been achieved by the time he wrote his *De Excidio*: for all his condemnation of the secular and ecclesiastical elites, nowhere does he accuse his British compatriots of paganism. Indeed, by his day the church was very much part of the establishment in the British kingdoms, to the extent that clergy purchased priestly office from secular rulers. In addition, as in Gaul from the fourth century, monasticism was developing. To judge by Gildas's writings, this included a puritanical, self-righteous strand alongside more wealthy and comfortable communities, and a similar picture of variety emerges from the *Life* of St. Samson, a British monk from south Wales who ended up as bishop of Dol in Brittany in the sixth century.[6]

The Conversion of Ireland

Ireland had never been conquered by the Roman Empire, where Christianity was the official religion for much of the fourth century. Nevertheless, by the early fifth century, Christianity had gained a foothold there – presumably as a result of contacts with Britain – for in 431 Palladius was ordained by Pope Celestine and "sent, as their first bishop, to the Irish who believe in Christ."[7] The immediate context for his appointment may have been the pope's fear that Pelagian heretics, recently defeated in Britain by Germanus of Auxerre (in 429), might take refuge in Ireland. Admittedly, though Palladius' first task was to provide ministry to an existing Christian community and preserve its orthodoxy, the papacy also seems to have envisaged that he would assume a missionary role beyond that community. Likewise, over 150 years later, Columbanus clearly saw Palladius in missionary terms when he wrote to Pope Boniface that the Irish had received their faith from the successors of the apostles Peter and Paul.[8] Yet, even if the new bishop sought to convert pagans in Ireland, perhaps with the assistance of three other bishops – Auxilius, Secundinus, and Iserninus – attested in sources from the late seventh century, his impact was probably confined to Leinster in the south-east of the island, the region with which those sources associate both Palladius and the three other bishops.

If Columbanus (d.615) regarded Palladius as the apostle of the Irish, authorized by Rome, this was no longer the view propounded by Irish churchmen from the late seventh century onward. For them, that honor fell to a Briton called Patrick. Contemporary evidence for Patrick consists of two short works he wrote: *The Letter to the Soldiers of Coroticus* and the *Confession*. The former was a response to a raid by Coroticus, a British leader, perhaps king of Strathclyde, together with Irishmen and Picts, who had attacked a group of converts just baptized by Patrick, killing some and taking the rest into captivity: the letter sought to secure their release. The *Confession*, written at some point after he had been ordained a bishop, is an attempt to justify his mission in Ireland to the ecclesiastical authorities in Britain, to whom he had become suspect after a friend had revealed to them a sin committed in his youth, and provides valuable evidence for Patrick's life and approach to missionary work. Modern scholarship has sought to recover the historical figure revealed by these texts from the picture provided by later hagiographical sources, beginning with the works of Muirchú and Tírechán in the late seventh century that sought to establish his credentials as a "national" apostle associated with the church of Armagh, which claimed him as its founder.[9] True, much remains controversial, not least the precise period in the fifth century when Patrick was active: both of his writings are conspicuously lacking in dates, and retrospective dates for his death supplied by later Irish annals are contradictory and colored by later ecclesiastical politics. Yet the writings have rightly attracted close attention, as they provide unique, first-hand accounts by a missionary from this period: by contrast, nearly all we know of the missions to the Anglo-Saxons derives from third parties, especially Bede in his *Ecclesiastical History*, written long after the events he describes.

Patrick belonged to a noble, Christian family from a Romano-British *civitas*; indeed, his father had been a deacon, his grandfather a priest. However, he states that he only became a believer after being enslaved as a young man in Ireland, and his mission to the Irish was very much an individual affair, inspired directly by the gospels, rather than one that was officially sponsored by the Romano-British church. As recent work has shown, his commitment to biblical authority is inscribed in his Latin style, which was modeled on that of the Bible, in a deliberate rejection of the literary conventions inculcated by a traditional Roman education in grammar and rhetoric that were followed by most other Christian authors of the fourth and fifth centuries.[10] He saw his particular task as taking Christianity "even to remote parts, where no one lived any further,"[11] namely to the shores of the Atlantic, including Mayo, and thus to a very different part of Ireland from Leinster where Palladius had been active. As an outsider in Ireland, his position as a missionary was clearly precarious: at one point he was imprisoned, and his practice of giving gifts to pagan kings and their sons and also to judges was designed to facilitate his access to those in power as well as freedom of movement. He succeeded in converting the sons and daughters of kings and also encouraged monastic vocations, including among wealthy women – that is, the adoption of ascetic and celibate living by individuals rather than the cenobitic (i.e. community) monasticism promoted by St. Benedict and others from the sixth century.

From the mid-sixth century, monastic communities began to be founded in Ireland too. As with the British church castigated by Gildas, their emergence suggests that the age of conversion was essentially over. The central role they came to play in the organization of the Irish church is discussed in chapter 11 of this volume. However, they also contributed significantly to the further spread of Christianity in Britain, among both the Picts and the Anglo-Saxons. This was particularly true of Iona, founded in 563 by Columba, a member of the powerful northern Irish royal dynasty of the Uí Néill. Columba is an early example of the Irish practice of *peregrinatio*, a form of self-imposed exile or pilgrimage in which the monk left his kin and his country behind him in order to serve Christ more effectively. Patrick had done something similar by abandoning the security of his status in Britain and becoming a missionary exile among the pagan Irish. Columba and other Irish monks, most notably his younger contemporary Columbanus, likewise saw pastoral work, including conversion, as part of their remit. Thus Columba preached to Bruide, king of the Picts, at his fort near Loch Ness, and Iona played an important part in the making of Pictish Christianity, though other influences also contributed to this process in the sixth and seventh centuries.[12] (For instance, while Bede's claim that Ninian, a British bishop of Whithorn in Galloway, had already converted the southern Picts at a much earlier period has met with understandable skepticism, it has recently been suggested that Ninian's name may have resulted from a scribal error for Uinniau or St. Finnian, and that this sixth-century British churchman – who was active in Ireland and a teacher of Columba – served as a bishop at Whithorn. If correct, this would be consistent with other evidence, including saints' cults, that points to a British role in the evangelization of the southern Picts in particular.)[13] Most famously, for 30 years in the middle of the seventh century (635–64), monks from Iona and their disciples undertook missionary work in Northumbria and other Anglo-Saxon kingdoms that marked a decisive turning point in the conversion of the English.

The Conversion of the English

Much more is known of the conversion of the English than of any of the other peoples of Britain and Ireland. This is mainly due to Bede, whose *Ecclesiastical History of the English People* set out to chart the development of the church in the various Anglo-Saxon kingdoms within the firm chronological framework of the Christian era devised in Rome by the monk Dionysius Exiguus in 525. Though, with the benefit of hindsight, Bede knew that Christianity had displaced paganism as the official religion throughout these kingdoms, he shows that the process suffered reverses and was not completed for 90 years. The earliest phase consisted of the Roman mission sent by Gregory the Great which led to the conversion of Kent under its powerful king Æthelberht (d.616) and also, temporarily, the kingdoms of the East Saxons and East Angles which were subject to his overlordship. Although the pagan reaction in Kent under Æthelberht's son and successor Eadbald was short-lived, it lasted considerably longer in the other two south-eastern kingdoms. True, the Roman missionaries gained a significant advance with Paulinus' baptism of King Edwin of Northumbria in 627. However, the Northumbrian mission was cut short by the death of Edwin at the hands of Penda of Mercia and the British king Cadwallon, probably of Gwynedd, in 633, and it took a new missionary effort, led by the monks of Iona at the invitation of Edwin's eventual successor King Oswald (634–42), to secure the conversion of the north and spread the new faith into other kingdoms subject to Northumbrian overlordship. The decisive shift from paganism to Christianity therefore occurred under Oswald and his brother Oswiu (642–70). The conversion of the Gewisse or West Saxons and the East Angles was undertaken by the Italian Birinus and Burgundian Felix respectively, but Oswald was also involved, notably as the sponsor of King Cynegils of Wessex at his baptism at Dorchester on Thames in 635. From c.653 onward, under Oswiu, it was Ionan monks or their disciples who restored Christianity to the East Saxons and also spread it to the Middle Angles and – after the death in 655 of its pagan ruler Penda – Mercia. By the time the 30-year dominance of Iona was ended by Oswiu's rejection of its Easter dating for that of the Roman church at the synod of Whitby in 664, only Sussex and the Isle of Wight remained pagan; the former kingdom was converted in the 670s and 680s, the latter in the wake of conquest by Cædwalla of Wessex in 686.

Modern discussions of the conversion of the English have focused heavily on Bede's testimony. Both his aims and the sources at his disposal have come under close scrutiny in recent decades, with important consequences for the interpretation of the narrative he provides.[14] Thus, his urgent concern to promote ecclesiastical reform, exemplified most vividly in the letter he wrote to Bishop Ecgberht of York in 734, but already evident in his biblical commentaries, led to a tendency to emphasize the virtues of the seventh-century past – represented, for example, by the Ionan missionary Aidan (d.651) – as a Golden Age in the church's pastoral mission. While his skill in constructing a narrative from very disparate sources, both written and oral, has rightly been stressed, so too have the resulting unevenness and gaps in his coverage. For example, the British, for whom Bede felt strong antipathy (largely because some of them still refused to accept the Roman Easter in the early eighth century), may well have played a significantly greater role in the process of conversion than he either realized or cared to admit.[15] In particular, his accusation that the British failed to preach to the pagan English was very probably misleading, as his silence on missions to the Anglo-Saxon peoples of the west midlands has led several scholars to suggest that this area was converted by British clergy.[16] Likewise, Bede may have underestimated the degree of involvement by the Frankish bishops and rulers in Augustine's mission to Kent.[17]

Paradoxically, then, advances in the understanding of Bede, while further enhancing his reputation as a scholar, have also encouraged a more critical approach to his account of the making of Anglo-Saxon Christianity and thereby opened up the subject to other perspectives. Accordingly, there has been a greater appreciation of the need to try to situate the different phases of conversion in a broader context through using a wider range of sources. In addition to exploring further the ways in which connections with both Celtic and continental neighbors helped to shape the course of conversion, historians have increasingly favored a comparative approach.

Thus, closer attention has been given to the adoption of Christianity in other periods and places: not only among other Germanic peoples in early medieval Europe, but also in early modern Mesoamerica, nineteenth-century Africa, and twentieth-century Polynesia. This has been accompanied by an openness to the interpretations of social anthropologists who have studied some of the modern examples.[18] One important result of this approach has been a shift in emphasis away from the missionary role of the churchmen who occupy center stage in Bede's narrative of conversion toward the expectations and motives of the elites which adopted Christianity. Linked to this shift has been a greater readiness to explore why, and how far, the royal families and aristocracies of the Anglo-Saxon kingdoms abandoned paganism. Moreover, while Bede explained conversion essentially in terms of religious conviction, as elites were persuaded of the truth of Christianity in accordance with the workings of divine providence, recent historiography has tended to stress how his *Ecclesiastical History* highlights the importance of cultural and especially political factors.

In attempting to assess what the Anglo-Saxons were converted from, scholars have relied on three main types of evidence: place-names, written sources, and, increasingly, archaeology. The light these shed on Anglo-Saxon paganism is very limited, and it is debatable how far they may be supplemented by comparisons with Christian accounts of paganism among the continental Germanic peoples in the early Middle Ages, let alone Tacitus' description of Germanic paganism in the first century AD or later medieval Scandinavian sources. Nevertheless, what Anglo-Saxon evidence there is allows some valuable conclusions. The fewer than 50 place-names referring to paganism fall into two main groups, which do not overlap.[19] One contains an element denoting a pagan place of worship (for example, Harrow, Middlesex, is derived from *hearg*, meaning "heathen temple," "sacred grove," or "idol"); the other, the name of a pagan god or goddess, such as Woden in Wednesbury, Staffordshire, Thunor in Thundersley, Essex, and Tiw in Tysoe, Warwickshire. The latter group shows that the Anglo-Saxons worshiped at least some of the same gods as other Germanic peoples on the continent, as described not only by Tacitus but also by the account of St. Boniface's destruction of the oak of Jupiter (meaning Thor or Thunor) at Geismar in Saxony in the eighth century. This picture of Germanic polytheism is amplified by Bede in his work on chronology, *De Temporum ratione*, whose brief references to the pagan calendar include the assertions that March had been called *Rhedmonath*, "after the goddess Rheda," and April *Eosturmonath*, after the goddess Eostre or Eastre.[20]

Despite its retrospective and strongly ecclesiastical perspective, Bede's *Ecclesiastical History* has generally been viewed as providing some reliable glimpses of pagan practice. In particular, it reveals the existence of a pagan priesthood, linked to, yet distinct from, kings, as exemplified most vividly by the account of Coifi, the chief priest whose deliberate desecration of the temple at Goodmanham is presented as a decisive stage in the conversion of the court of King Edwin of Northumbria. The account implies that such priests expected, and possibly depended on, royal patronage: Coifi complained that, despite his assiduous devotion to the pagan gods, Edwin had rewarded other followers more generously (Bede, *HE*, ii. 13). Although the precise relationship of pagan priests to early Anglo-Saxon kings remains elusive for lack of evidence, two comparisons may indicate that the latter enjoyed a leading role in religious matters.

First, early medieval sources suggest that, among the Germanic peoples east of the Rhine, the maintenance of heathen cults depended, not on priests, but on kings or other secular leaders.[21] This would be consistent, second, with the priority given by missionaries to converting the Anglo-Saxon royal courts and the lack of evidence for a separate order of powerful religious specialists similar to the druids of pre-Christian Irish society.

The references in Bede both to the temple at Goodmanham, containing idols, and to that of King Rædwald of the East Angles, with its altars to several gods (including Christ), are striking, for they stand in contrast to the absence of temples among the early medieval pagan Germanic peoples east of the Rhine. Indeed, some of the English place-name evidence is consistent with a picture of open-air devotion that brings to mind Tacitus' assertion that the Germanic peoples refused to confine their gods under a roof but worshiped them in groves. John Blair has suggested that Bede's references to temples may indicate a fairly recent change in pagan practice among the Anglo-Saxons that was influenced by Romano-British temples and perhaps also by Christian churches; moreover, the change was quite possibly the latest stage in a lengthy process of assimilating native and Roman traditions of ritual practice in Britain.[22] While this interpretation is necessarily speculative, it has the merit of challenging the assumption that Anglo-Saxon paganism was static or unresponsive to wider religious changes. Detailed descriptions of the forms of worship at temples or other cult sites are lacking, but Gregory the Great, Bede, and other sources assume that they included sacrifices of animals.

Though archaeology has yet to elucidate the form of pagan temples and shrines, it is playing an increasingly important role in our understanding of the conversion period. Recent archaeological scholarship has sought to break away from the traditional historical framework provided by the written evidence, especially Bede, and develop its own agendas drawing on a range of theoretical debates.[23] Of late, research on the fifth- to seventh-century furnished cremation and inhumation cemeteries of eastern England, usually regarded as pagan, has tended to concentrate on issues of ethnicity in the fifth and sixth centuries and increasingly complex social organization in the seventh.[24] The problem of recognition of changing beliefs has played a less significant role. Nevertheless, some artifacts, such as cremation urns with runic decoration, grave-goods, notably the warrior identified as Woden with a horned helmet and spears on the buckle-plate from Finglesham (Kent), and animal sacrifice, have been regarded as indicative of pagan symbolism.[25] Furthermore, the construction of richly furnished elite barrow graves, particularly in the early seventh century, exemplified by the Sutton Hoo mound 1 ship burial, has been seen as a political act symbolic "of pagan autonomy in confrontation, even defiance, of the predatory attentions of Christianity."[26] Equally, during the seventh century the presence of Christian artifacts in graves – for example, the sheet gold crosses at Prittlewell (Essex)[27] – is indicative of the spreading influence of Christianity, even if the beliefs of those buried with them are unclear. Moreover, that influence is strongly implied by cemeteries of the seventh and early eighth centuries which have a greater number of graves with few or no artifacts, and it is in this period also that findless churchyard burial has its origins.

Much recent scholarship has interpreted the Anglo-Saxons' conversion from paganism to Christianity in predominantly political terms.[28] At its starkest, the adoption of the new faith was more a matter of compulsion than conviction. To begin with, it is very likely that the peasant dependents of kings and nobles had to follow the religious preferences of their superiors. A major reason why the conversion of royal courts was so crucial was precisely because these contained not only kings and their relatives but also aristocratic followers who, once they had ceased active service in the king's warband, would retire to manage their estates: missionaries worked with the grain of existing structures of authority. Some rulers, too, were given little choice: thanks to his hegemony in southern England, Æthelberht was able to compel the kings of the East Saxons and East Angles to become Christians, and the Northumbrian overlords likewise used political subjection to impose religious con- formity; while the Isle of Wight was converted at the point of the sword by Cædwalla of Wessex, even though he himself was still not baptized. Yet compulsion could backfire: witness the pagan reactions in Essex and East Anglia after Æthelberht's death or the refusal of the aristocracy in Sussex to follow their king's example and convert, quite possibly because his conversion was associated with the overlordship of Wulfhere of Mercia.

At the level of royal houses and aristocracies, then, effective conversion required more than force. Indeed, it has frequently been emphasized that there were positive political advantages for kings to embrace Christianity. One crucial question that his- torians assessing those advantages have had to address is the extent to which conver- sion undermined the sacral dimension of royal authority. True, as already mentioned, the precise role of kings in the organization and practice of Anglo-Saxon paganism is uncertain. At the very least, though, the claims in genealogies composed from the eighth century onward that most Anglo-Saxon dynasties were descended from Woden implies that rulers were believed to be of divine descent which in turn helped to legitimate their authority. To acknowledge that Woden had been a mere mortal, as the Christian clergy who wrote down the genealogies insisted, threatened to deprive royalty of its sacral aura. Recent scholarship has addressed this issue by emphasizing two points. The first, illustrated by Bede's accounts of pagan revivals within particular dynasties, is that the acceptance of Christianity was a complex and gradual process rather than an instantaneous, all-encompassing event. Second, the adoption of the new faith eventually provided royal families with new sources of sacrality that more than compensated for those they had lost through their abandonment of the pre- Christian religion.

Bede shows that, in most royal houses, the initial conversion of a king was followed by a reversion to paganism led by one or more of his successors. Rather than simply following Bede's example and characterizing such setbacks to Christianization as "apostasy," several scholars have sought to explain the phenomenon as a kind of insurance policy whereby only some members of a dynasty were baptized along with the king so as to ensure that its break with paganism was not irreversible. For one thing, this would maximize the dynasty's prospects of maintaining power by ensuring the availability of a pagan candidate for kingship should the aristocracy of the kingdom refuse to accept the new religion. More generally, a selective attitude toward initial conversion allowed a royal family to keep open its channels of com- munication with the pre-Christian deities who might still retain some power for either good or ill.[29]

As Barbara Yorke has persuasively argued, the conversion of the Anglo-Saxon royal houses was a two-stage process.[30] In the first, transitional phase, Christianity coexisted with continued adherence to paganism by significant sections of a kingdom's elite: this adherence varied from the toleration of pagan worship by Christian kings to the accession of kings who were themselves practicing pagans. The initial acceptance of Christianity belonged to a wider context of cultural assimilation, reflected in the importation and imitation of artifacts from the late Roman and Byzantine worlds, often via Frankish courts. This was particularly true of Æthelberht of Kent, whose kingdom had close trading links with the Merovingian kingdoms and who was himself married to a Christian Frankish princess, Bertha. Admittedly, the king may have been reluctant to accept conversion from Frankish bishops in case this implied or facilitated political domination by their rulers; but his decision to request missionaries from the pope was no doubt driven to a significant degree by a desire to emulate the Christian kingship of his Frankish neighbors, while at the same time ensuring that this would be linked directly to the cradle of the Christian world in Rome.[31] He may even have welcomed the opportunity presented by the mission of stressing the Roman character of his kingdom and thereby creating a new common English identity that could be shared by both the Anglo-Saxon elite and the population of Romano-British descent.[32] Moreover, popes were at pains to emphasize the political and material benefits of conversion: Gregory the Great assured Æthelberht that he would win the same renown as Constantine the Great if he followed the emperor's example by spreading the new faith among "your subject princes and peoples," while Boniface V stressed to Edwin of Northumbria that all kingship derived from God; both letters were accompanied by gifts (Bede, *HE*, i. 32; ii. 10). The association of Christianity with the Mediterranean and Frankish worlds, as well as the biblical and Roman imperial models it provided of rulership legitimated by a single all-powerful deity, go a long way toward explaining its attraction to Anglo-Saxon kings.

At the same time, as already mentioned, early converts such as Æthelberht, brought up in a polytheistic tradition, may have been ready to accept Christianity because they understood it rather differently from the missionaries who baptized them, especially with respect to its exclusive claims to truth. During the transitional period of coexistence between paganism and Christianity, the church had to learn how to accommodate the new faith to the expectations of the host society. Thus, to cite the most famous example, in July 601 Gregory the Great, who a month earlier had urged King Æthelberht to destroy pagan shrines, ordered Mellitus, leader of the second Roman mission to Kent, to take a more gradualist approach: "the temples of the idols . . . should on no account be destroyed," but should rather be rededicated as churches, and the sacrifices of oxen to demons held there converted into "devout feasting" on saints' days (Bede, *HE*, i. 30). Irrespective of the extent to which these precise instructions were followed, the attitude they embodied must have helped to make the new religion more acceptable, and hence to facilitate the second phase of conversion, in which Christianity became the only religion practiced and permitted by the royal dynasties. In several cases, this final abandonment of paganism on the part of a royal family was marked by a dramatic gesture of commitment to Christianity, as kings "opted out" (in Clare Stancliffe's memorable phrase) by resigning their office to become monks: Sigibert of the East Angles (630/1), Centwine of the West Saxons

(685), Saebbi of the East Saxons (shortly before his death in 694), and Æthelred of Mercia (704) are all cases in point.[33]

By advertising their Christian credentials so publicly, these monk-kings arguably exemplified a desire on the part of royal families to take an active role in the leadership of the new religion and perhaps also to establish claims to sanctity – two miracles concerning the death and burial of Saebbi were recorded by the community of Barking to which he retired (Bede, *HE*, iv. 11). The same is certainly true of the attempts by Oswiu of Northumbria and his daughters, initially with little ecclesiastical support, to promote the cults of Edwin and Oswald, both of whom had been killed by pagans and thus could be seen as martyrs. Oswiu may have sought to adapt pre-Christian traditions of sacral kingship: the possession of a royal saint could be seen as compensating a dynasty for the loss of its divine descent from Woden. However, while individual ecclesiastics and monasteries welcomed retiring kings or fostered royal cults, on the whole the church seems to have disapproved of royal attempts to appropriate spiritual power. None of the kings who voluntarily resigned to become monks were imitated by any of their successors, and Oswald was exceptional in the degree to which his cult received ecclesiastical support, especially from Wilfrid and also from Bede, who portrayed him as an exemplary king in his *Ecclesiastical History*. Yet the notion of royal sacrality was not abandoned altogether: rather, it was transferred primarily to princesses and widowed queens who established double monasteries, mainly in the late seventh and early eighth centuries. These houses are discussed further in chapter 11 of this volume, but they merit attention here as a further instance of the attempts by dynasties to retain a sacral dimension in the second and final phase of conversion, not least because several of their female founders, such as Hild of Whitby, came to be venerated as saints.

Conclusion

Attempts to ensure that acceptance of Christianity did not undermine the sacrality of royal families are but one illustration of the way in which the new religion was adapted to existing assumptions and practices rather than marking a clean break with the pre-Christian past. To interpret such adaptation as fundamentally compromising a supposedly authentic or pure Christianity that missionaries sought to impart would be an oversimplification, however. For one thing, definitions of Christianity have in reality always been contested among its believers and varied between different periods and societies. Rather than participate in debates about "which versions of Christianity might be more 'real' than others," the historian's task is to investigate "the self-definitions of Christians in the past and their shifting parameters."[34] Thus, while the faith of early Kentish converts may have fallen short of the standards of reform-minded medieval churchmen, not to speak of protestant reformers or post-Tridentine Catholics, it is important to remember that Gregory the Great rejoiced at the news of their baptism. True, it took decades for the new faith to change certain long-established social practices: a comparison of the laws of Æthelberht with those of Wihtred (695) suggest that it was not until the late seventh century that Kentish kings sought to enforce ecclesiastical norms of marriage, while it was only from the eighth century onward that the Anglo-Saxon (and likewise the British and Irish) laity were commonly buried in churchyards.

However, the evolving character of Christianity's impact does not necessarily point to the continuing strength of paganism. Indeed, identifying the distinctively pagan components of pre-Christian Anglo-Saxon culture – and the same applies to the Celtic-speaking peoples of Britain and Ireland – is far from straightforward. To quote Patrick Wormald, among some historians of conversion

> there is an underlying assumption that the set of values abandoned for the Faith were as comprehensive and coherent as is Christianity itself, and these values are given the generic label of "paganism." As a result, we describe as survivals of "paganism" what may not have been very much to do with heathen cult at all, and what are often only indications that society had failed to remake itself completely.[35]

Of course, aspects of pagan cult did continue alongside Christianity, ranging in extent from a transitional period of syncretism in some cases to sacrifices and other practices in what seem to have been domestic contexts, to judge by the laws of Wihtred of Kent and the *Penitential* of Theodore. Nevertheless, however much the Anglo-Saxons remained attached to their ancestral myths or to practices deriving from a natural religion focused on the agrarian calendar, conversion to Christianity through baptism marked a fundamental change. Above all, paganism lost its status and power as an official religion supported by kings. Although the nature and extent of its organization are uncertain, its institutional coherence and identity must have atrophied as its priests were made redundant and royal and aristocratic elites no longer gave it public endorsement through participating in its rituals. Instead, those elites invested in a new ecclesiastical infrastructure designed to ensure that the initial impetus of conversion was followed up by a continuing and deepening process of Christianization. The resources transferred to this infrastructure were almost certainly far greater than those bestowed on pagan cult sites, and its impact was pervasive, affecting not only career opportunities and religious practices but also landholding strategies and culture. That culture included the recording of pre-Christian traditions which illustrate how, in important respects, Anglo-Saxon society – and the same is even truer of Ireland, where native traditions were preserved and elaborated by the quasi-professional learned order of poets and seers known as *filid* – remained, to borrow Peter Brown's description of the world of the early medieval Christian laity, "deeply profane."[36] Yet the clergy who wrote down those traditions had no doubts that the pagan gods belonged to the past.

Acknowledgment

I am very grateful to Nancy Edwards for commenting on this chapter and for help with the archaeological evidence.

Notes

1   For example, Davies, "The myth of the Celtic church."
2   For critical assessments of these views, see, e.g., Smith, "Oral and written"; Van Engen, "The Christian middle ages."
3   Russell, *Germanization of Early Medieval Christianity.*

4   See, e.g., Frend, "*Ecclesia Brittanica*," and critique in Sharpe, "Martyrs and local saints," pp. 85–102.

5   Handley, "The origins of Christian commemoration"; Thomas, *Tintagel*.

6   Sharpe, "Gildas as a father of the church," pp. 196–9.

7   Charles-Edwards, *Early Christian Ireland*, p. 205, citing *Chronicle of Prosper of Aquitaine*.

8   Walker (ed.), *Sancti Columbani opera*, pp. 38–9.

9   Binchy, "Patrick and his biographers"; Charles-Edwards, *Early Christian Ireland*, ch. 5; Doherty, "The cult of St. Patrick"; Sharpe, "St. Patrick."

10 Charles-Edwards, *Early Christian Ireland*, pp. 230–3.

11 Ibid., p. 215, citing *Confessio*, c. 51.

12 Yorke, *Conversion of Britain*, pp. 128–33.

13 Clancy, "The real St. Ninian."

14 Campbell, *Essays in Anglo-Saxon History*, chs. 1–4; Goffart, *Narrators of Barbarian History*, ch. 4; Kirby, *Bede's Historia ecclesiastica* and "Bede's native sources"; Thacker, "Bede's ideal of reform."

15 Charles-Edwards, "Bede, the Irish and the Britons"; Murray, "Bede and the unchosen race."

16 Bassett, "Church and diocese"; Sims-Williams, *Religion and Literature*, pp. 78–83.

17 Wood, "The mission of Augustine."

18 See, e.g., Blair, *Church in Anglo-Saxon Society*, pp. 169–70, 178–9; Higham, *Convert Kings*, ch. 1; Mayr-Harting, *Two Conversions*; Sanmark, *Power and Conversion*.

19 Wilson, *Anglo-Saxon Paganism*, ch. 1.

20 Ibid., pp. 35–6.

21 Wood, "Pagan religions," pp. 257–9.

22 Blair, "Anglo-Saxon pagan shrines."

23 Lucy, *Anglo-Saxon Way of Death*; Lucy and Reynolds (eds.), *Burial*.

24 Hills, *Origins of the English*.

25 Wilson, *Anglo-Saxon Paganism*, ch. 4.

26 Carver, "Reflections," p. 140.

27 Anon., *Prittlewell Prince*.

28 See, e.g., Higham, *Convert Kings*; Stancliffe, "Oswald"; Tyler, "Reluctant kings."

29 Angenendt, "The conversion of the Anglo-Saxons," pp. 749–54; Yorke, "The reception of Christianity"; cf. Tyler, "Reluctant kings," 157–60.

30 Yorke, "The adaptation of the Anglo-Saxon royal courts."

31 Cf. Wallace-Hadrill, *Early Germanic Kingship*, ch. 2; Wood, "The mission of Augustine," esp. p. 8.

32 Brooks, "Canterbury."

33 Stancliffe, "Kings who opted out."

34 De Jong, "Religion," p. 132.

35 Wormald, "Bede, *Beowulf* and the conversion," p. 66.

36 See Brown, *Rise of Western Christendom*, pp. 100–2, 299–320 (quotation at p. 320); Blair, *Church in Anglo-Saxon Society*, pp. 166–79.

Further Reading

For useful overviews covering Britain and Ireland, see the relevant parts of R. A. Fletcher, *The Conversion of Europe: From Paganism to Christianity 371–1386 AD* (London, 1997); T. M. Charles-Edwards, "Conversion to Christianity," in idem (ed.), *After Rome* (Oxford, 2003), pp. 103–39; and Yorke, *The Conversion of Britain*, ch. 2. British Christianity is best approached through C. Stancliffe, "The British church and the mission of Augustine," in R. Gameson (ed.), *St. Augustine and the Conversion of England* (Stroud, 1999), pp. 107–51, and Sharpe, "Martyrs and local saints." An authoritative account of the conversion of Ireland is provided in Charles-Edwards, *Early Christian Ireland*, ch. 5; see also D. N. Dumville, *Saint Patrick AD 493–1993* (Woodbridge, 1993), and C. E. Stancliffe, "Kings and conversion: some comparisons between the Roman mission to England and Patrick's to Ireland," *Frühmittelalterliche Studien*, 14 (1980), pp. 59–94. Mayr-Harting's *The Coming of Christianity to Anglo-Saxon England* (3rd edn, 1991) remains fundamental for the conversion of the Anglo-Saxons. The same is true of J. Campbell, "The first century of Christianity in England," reprinted in his *Essays in Anglo-Saxon History*, ch. 3, and idem, "Observations on the conversion of England," reprinted in the same collection, ch. 4. Blair, *The Church in Anglo-Saxon Society*, esp. ch. 1, provides an excellent reappraisal of the subject that draws extensively on both archaeological and written evidence. For stimulating attempts to assess the impact of Christianity from the perspective of the Anglo-Saxon elites, see Wormald, "Bede, *Beowulf* and the conversion of the Anglo-Saxon aristocracy" and Yorke, "The reception of Christianity."

Bibliography

Abrams, L., "Kings and bishops in the conversion of the Anglo-Saxon and Scandinavian kingdoms," in J. Brohed (ed.), *Church and People in Britain and Scandinavia* (Lund, 1996), pp. 15–28.

Angenendt, A., "The conversion of the Anglo-Saxons considered against the background of the early medieval mission," *Settimane de studio del centro italiano di studi sull'alto medioevo*, 32 (Spoleto, 1986), pp. 747–92.

Anon., *The Prittlewell Prince: The Discovery of a Rich Anglo-Saxon Burial in Essex* (London, 2004).

Bassett, S., "Church and diocese in the west midlands: the transition from British to Anglo-Saxon control," in J. Blair and R. Sharpe (eds.), *Pastoral Care before the Parish* (Leicester, 1992), pp. 13–40.

Binchy, D. A., "Patrick and his biographers: ancient and modern," *Studia Hibernica*, 2 (1962), 7–173.

Blair, J., "Anglo-Saxon pagan shrines and their prototypes," *Anglo-Saxon Studies in Archaeology and History*, 8 (1995), 1–28.

Blair, J., *The Church in Anglo-Saxon Society* (Oxford, 2005).

Blair, J. and Sharpe, R. (eds.), *Pastoral Care before the Parish* (Leicester, 1992).

Brooks, N., "Canterbury, Rome and the construction of English identity," in J. M. H. Smith (ed.), *Early Medieval Rome and the Christian West: Essays in Honour of Donald A. Bullough* (Leiden, 2000), pp. 221–46.

Brooks, N., *The Early History of the Church of Canterbury* (Leicester, 1984).

Brown, P., *The Rise of Western Christendom: Triumph and Diversity AD 200–1000* (Oxford, 1996).

Campbell, J., *Essays in Anglo-Saxon History* (London, 1986).

Carver, M., "Reflections on the meanings of monumental barrows in Anglo-Saxon England," in S. Lucy and A. Reynolds (eds.), *Burial in Early Medieval England and Wales* (London, 2002), pp. 132–43.

Charles-Edwards, T. M., "Bede, the Irish and the Britons," *Celtica*, 15 (1983), 42–52.

Charles-Edwards, T. M., *Early Christian Ireland* (Cambridge, 2000).

Charles-Edwards, T. M., "The social background to Irish *peregrinatio*," *Celtica*, 11 (1976), 43–59.

Clancy, T. O., "The real St. Ninian," *Innes Review*, 52 (2001), 1–28.

Davies, W., "The myth of the Celtic church," in N. Edwards and A. Lane (eds.), *The Early Church in Wales and the West* (Oxford, 1992), pp. 12–21.

de Jong, M., "Religion," in R. McKitterick (ed.), *The Early Middle Ages: Europe 400–1000* (Oxford, 2001), pp. 131–64.

Doherty, C., "The cult of St. Patrick and the politics of Armagh in the seventh century," in J.-M. Picard (ed.), *Ireland and Northern France AD 600–850* (Dublin, 1991), pp. 53–94.

Edwards, N. and Lane, A. (eds.), *The Early Church in Wales and the West* (Oxford, 1992).

Frend, W. H. C., "*Ecclesia Britannica*: prelude or dead end?," *Journal of Ecclesiastical History*, 30 (1979), 129–44.

Gameson, R. (ed.), *St. Augustine and the Conversion of England* (Stroud, 1999).

Goffart, W., *The Narrators of Barbarian History (AD 550–800)* (Princeton, NJ, 1988).

Handley, M. A., "The origins of Christian commemoration in late antique Britain," *Early Medieval Europe*, 10 (2001), 177–99.

Herbert, M., *Iona, Kells, and Derry: The History and Hagiography of the Monastic Familia of Columba* (Oxford, 1988).

Higham, N., *The Convert Kings: Power and Religious Affiliation in Early Anglo-Saxon England* (Manchester, 1997).

Hills, C., *Origins of the English* (London, 2003).

Howlett, D. R. (ed. and trans.), *The Book of Letters of Saint Patrick the Bishop* (Blackrock, 1994).

Hughes, K., *The Church in Early Irish Society* (London, 1966).

Kirby, D. P., *Bede's Historia ecclesiastica gentis Anglorum: Its Contemporary Setting* (Jarrow, 1992).

Kirby, D. P., "Bede's native sources for the *Historia ecclesiastica*," *Bulletin of the John Rylands Library*, 48 (1965–8), 341–71.

Lapidge, M. and Dumville, D. N. (eds.), *Gildas: New Approaches* (Woodbridge, 1984).

Loyn, H. R., "The conversion of the English to Christianity: some comments on the Celtic contribution," in R. R. Davies et al. (eds.), *Welsh Society and Nationhood: Historical Essays Presented to Glanmor Williams* (Cardiff, 1984), pp. 5–18.

Lucy, S., *The Anglo-Saxon Way of Death: Burial Rites in Early England* (Stroud, 2000).

Lucy, S. and Reynolds, A. (eds.), *Burial in Early Medieval England and Wales*. Society for Medieval Archaeology Monograph Series, 17 (London, 2002).

McClure, J. and Collins, R. (trans.), *Bede's Ecclesiastical History of the English People* (Oxford, 1994).

Mayr-Harting, H., *The Coming of Christianity to Early Anglo-Saxon England* (London, 1972).

Mayr-Harting, H., "St. Wilfrid in Sussex," in M. J. Kitch (ed.), *Studies in Sussex Church History* (London, 1981), pp. 1–17.

Mayr-Harting, H., *Two Conversions to Christianity: The Bulgarians and the Anglo-Saxons*. Stenton Lecture (Reading, 1994).

Murray, A., "Bede and the unchosen race," in H. Pryce and J. Watts (eds.), *Power and Identity in the Middle Ages: Essays in Memory of Rees Davies* (Oxford, 2007), pp. 52–67.

Nash-Williams, V. E., *The Early Christian Monuments of Wales* (Cardiff, 1950).

Ó Cróinín, D., *Early Medieval Ireland 400–1200* (Harlow, 1995), ch. 1.

Russell, J. C., *The Germanization of Early Medieval Christianity: A Sociohistorical Approach to Religious Transformation* (New York, 1994).

Sanmark, A., *Power and Conversion: A Comparative Study of Christianization in Scandinavia* (Uppsala, 2004).

Sharpe, R. (trans.), *Adomnán of Iona: Life of St. Columba* (Harmondsworth, 1995).

Sharpe, R., "Gildas as a father of the church," in M. Lapidge and D. Dumville (eds.), *Gildas: New Approaches* (Woodbridge, 1984), pp. 193–205.

Sharpe, R., "Martyrs and local saints in late antique Britain," in A. Thacker and R. Sharpe (eds.), *Local Saints and Local Churches in the Early Medieval West* (Oxford, 2002), pp. 75–154.

Sharpe, R., "St. Patrick and the see of Armagh," *Cambridge Medieval Celtic Studies*, 4 (1982), pp. 33–59.

Sims-Williams, P., *Religion and Literature in Western England: 600–800* (Cambridge, 1990).

Smith, J. M. H., "Oral and written: saints, miracles, and relics in Brittany, c.850–1250," *Speculum*, 65 (1990), 309–43.

Stancliffe, C., "Kings who opted out," in P. Wormald, D. Bullough, and R. Collins (eds.), *Ideal and Reality in Frankish and Anglo-Saxon Society* (Oxford, 1983), pp. 154–76.

Stancliffe, C., "Oswald, 'most holy and most victorious king of the Northumbrians,'" in C. Stancliffe and E. Cambridge (eds.), *Oswald: Northumbrian King to European Saint* (Stamford, 1995), pp. 33–83.

Stancliffe, C. and Cambridge, E. (eds.), *Oswald: Northumbrian King to European Saint* (Stamford, 1995).

Thacker, A., "Bede's ideal of reform," in P. Wormald, D. Bullough, and R. Collins (eds.), *Ideal and Reality in Frankish and Anglo-Saxon Society* (Oxford, 1983), pp. 130–53.

Thomas, C., *Christianity in Roman Britain to AD 500* (London, 1981).

Thomas, C., *Tintagel: Arthur and Archaeology* (London, 1993).

Tyler, D., "Reluctant kings and Christian conversion in seventh-century England," *History*, 92 (2007), 144–61.

Van Engen, J., "The Christian middle ages as an historiographical problem," *American Historical Review*, 91 (1986), 519–52.

Walker, G. S. M. (ed.), *Sancti Columbani opera*. Scriptores Latini Hiberniae, 2 (Dublin, 1970).

Wallace-Hadrill, J. M., *Early Germanic Kingship in England and on the Continent* (Oxford, 1971).

Wilson, D., *Anglo-Saxon Paganism* (London, 1992).

Winterbottom, M. (ed. and trans.), *Gildas: The Ruin of Britain and Other Documents* (Chichester, 1978).

Wood, I., "The mission of Augustine of Canterbury to the English," *Speculum*, 69 (1994), 1–17.

Wood, I., *The Missionary Life: Saints and the Evangelisation of Europe, 400–1050* (Harlow, 2001).

Wood, I., "Pagan religions and superstitions east of the Rhine from the fifth to the ninth century," in G. Ausenda (ed.), *After Empire: Towards an Ethnology of Europe's Barbarians* (Woodbridge, 1995), pp. 253–79.

Wormald, P., "Bede, *Beowulf* and the conversion of the Anglo-Saxon aristocracy," in R. T. Farrell (ed.), *Bede and Anglo-Saxon England*. British Archaeological Reports 46 (Oxford, 1978), pp. 32–95.

Wormald, P., Bullough, D., and Collins, R. (eds.), *Ideal and Reality in Frankish and Anglo-Saxon Society* (Oxford, 1983).

Yorke, B., "The adaptation of the Anglo-Saxon royal courts to Christianity," in M. Carver (ed.), *The Cross Goes North: Processes of Conversion in Northern Europe AD 300–1300* (York, 2003), pp. 243–57.

Yorke, B., *The Conversion of Britain: Religion, Politics and Society in Britain c.600–800* (Harlow, 2006).

Yorke, B., "The reception of Christianity at the Anglo-Saxon royal courts," in Gameson, R. (ed.), *St. Augustine and the Conversion of England* (Stroud, 1999), pp. 152–73.

CHAPTER ELEVEN

Church Organization and Pastoral Care

THOMAS PICKLES

In 796, Alcuin – an Anglo-Saxon churchman working at the court of Charlemagne – wrote to Charlemagne's treasurer, Meginfried, setting out his views on conversion, preaching, and pastoral care.[1] Alcuin argued that faith must be voluntary, rather than a matter for compulsion; people must be drawn into faith. Preachers should carefully calibrate their teaching to the needs of their audience, first teaching the faith, then the sacraments of baptism, and finally the gospels. If any of these three were overlooked, he warned, the hearer would not be able to obtain salvation.

Alcuin's letter recognizes two different levels of conversion: outward acceptance and genuine faith. Modern social theorists often distinguish three strands: adoption (sometimes called official conversion or nominal conversion), Christianization, and spiritual conversion. Definitions of these three strands vary from author to author. Adoption will be defined here as the outward acceptance of Christianity: Huw Pryce (in chapter 10) has already discussed the missions that brought kingdoms in each part of the British Isles to this point. Christianization will be understood as enthusiastic investment in Christian culture and institutions. Spiritual conversion will signify the inward transformation of belief systems at an individual level. Whereas chapter 10 concentrated on missions, this chapter will focus on the building of an ecclesiastical framework across the British Isles. Reviewing that process takes us to the heart of these issues: the social utility of Christianity encouraged investment in Christian institutions; this process of Christianization determined the scale, strengths, and weaknesses of the ecclesiastical framework; the resulting framework is the best indication we have of whether there was a sufficient level of preaching and pastoral care to bring people to spiritual conversion.

Christianization

Investment in Christian culture offered some obvious advantages to kings across the British Isles that need little elaboration: new Christian models of royal authority; association with Rome; association with the Frankish kings; a network of local institutions staffed with bishops, clergy, and monks, offering opportunities for royal patronage outside the military sphere; and access to technologies such as literacy and building in stone (see chapters 6, 9, and 10).

Two features of pre-Christian political power in England indicate that Anglo-Saxon leaders were ready to exploit the material advantages of Christianity. The first is the apparent connection between royal power and pre-Christian cult. Bede suggests that in pre-Christian Northumbria there was a close association between the king and a hierarchical priesthood set apart from lay society, and describes a permanent shrine that functioned as a carefully controlled sacred space (*HE*, ii. 13). Excavations at Yeavering in Northumberland have revealed that prehistoric ring ditches – one containing a possible pre-Christian shrine – were used to define the layout of a sixth- to early seventh-century royal center.[2] Kings could use religious communities to augment royal authority in a similar but more permanent and profitable way. Bede claimed that before 664 the religious community at Lindisfarne in Northumbria did not generate extra wealth to construct buildings for kings to stay in or to provide them with elaborate meals, which might imply that others operated as royal hostels (*HE*, iii. 26).

A second and related feature of pre-Christian political power in England is the monumentalization of burial: for example, the ship burial at Sutton Hoo, Suffolk and the chamber burial at Prittlewell, Essex.[3] During the late sixth and early seventh centuries, a few individuals were given spectacular burials, emphasizing their wealth, military power, capacity for hospitality, and connections with powerful external cultures. While we cannot be certain, these burials are likely to represent the most powerful political figures. Martin Carver has argued that these burials represent a robust statement of pre-Christian belief in the face of Christian expansion.[4] John Blair has preferred to see them as an attempt to emulate Christian burial in churches and religious communities in an effort to stabilize political power.[5] Either way, it seems that just prior to conversion, Anglo-Saxon rulers were seeking to reinforce their position through the construction of monuments. Again, religious communities could do this in a more permanent and prestigious way. Sutton Hoo shares strong topographical similarities with the religious community and royal cult center at Whitby, North Yorkshire: both stand on raised ground overlooking a major estuary. At Whitby, Oswiu, king of the Bernicians and Deirans, founded a community that sought to bind together the royal lines of Bernicia and Deira: it was placed under the leadership of Hild, who was the niece of Edwin, king of the Deirans; Oswiu's wife Eanflæd and daughter Ælfflæd became nuns there, and later abbesses of the community; and it received the remains of Edwin, king of the Deirans, and of Oswiu himself (*HE*, iii. 24).

Investment in Christian institutions held parallel attractions for elites across the British Isles. Before conversion to Christianity, military ability seems to have been the primary route to a position of authority. Christianity offered two new routes. Life as a monk or hermit could bring ascetic authority – a special wisdom acquired by individuals through extreme feats of fasting, endurance, and contemplation. Ordination as a priest or bishop could bring the institutional authority of the church. Some individuals could embody both of these at once. Adomnán's *Life of Columba* and Bede's *Life of Cuthbert* reveal Columba and Cuthbert combining feats of asceticism and miracles of prophecy and healing with their institutional authority as a priest and a bishop.[6] While women generally could not acquire authority through military prowess and were prohibited from ordination to the priesthood, they were capable of equaling their male counterparts in feats of asceticism – hence the proliferation of highly influential abbesses and female saints across the British Isles in this period, such as Brigit of Kildare and Hild of Whitby.[7] Elites could use this new ascetic and institutional authority to gain profound influence at a local and national level. Belief that the ascetic virtues of an individual could transform them into miracle workers prompted people to seek them out for assistance. Cogitosus could plausibly claim that Brigit of Kildare had saved a pregnant woman from birth pangs, opened the eyes of a blind man, facilitated harvesting during a rainstorm, and intervened to prevent a man from making a girl his sex slave.[8] Stephen of Ripon's *Life of Wilfrid* describes at length the way in which Wilfrid extended his influence as a bishop and an abbot across several kingdoms and engaged in disputes with the kings of Northumbria.[9]

Elite converts to the religious life expressed their newfound group identity through the distinctive material culture associated with the new religion. Bishop Conleth of Kildare apparently received special foreign vestments to wear during services, only for Saint Brigit – in an exceptional act – to give them away to the poor; fortunately, a miracle provided a replacement.[10] Benedict Biscop and Wilfrid, two Anglo-Saxon churchmen, undertook pilgrimages abroad, collecting books and pictures and returning with masons and glaziers to construct religious buildings according to continental techniques.[11] Indeed, those elites who entered the church might be compared with the intellectual aristocracy of nineteenth-century England – a group who used their learning, their rejection of some contemporary mores, and their investment in a distinctive intellectual culture to carve out a new social niche from which to reform and transform society.[12]

Investment in religious communities, in particular, was prompted by their political and social utility.[13] First and foremost, of course, there were spiritual benefits: provision for the perpetual commemoration of the founder through prayer, sometimes including the veneration of the founder or first abbot as a saint, along with access to regular preaching and pastoral care. Often constructed of stone, with jeweled fixtures and fittings, they were a clear statement of the wealth and status of their patron in the local landscape. As centers that produced surpluses and imported specialist goods for the domestic and liturgical demands of the community, they regularly became centers of trade and exchange. Because they had a responsibility to care for the poor and infirm, they were also useful social institutions and could increase the reputation of the founder amongst the surrounding lay population. Cogitosus provides an elaborate description of the community at Kildare, which he called a city on account of the buildings and the large number of people in regular attendance for all these reasons.[14]

Religious communities also paralleled and reinforced existing forms of social organization. Early medieval societies within the British Isles were governed by notions of kinship and lordship based on the concepts of the household and the extended kin-group (see chapter 7). Religious communities were conceived as religious households and their members as spiritual kin-groups. Old Irish *muinter* and Old English *hired* were terms used to describe both secular households and religious communities. Bede could say of Benedict Biscop, "He refused to bring forth children in the flesh, being predestined by Christ to raise up for Him sons nurtured in spiritual doctrine who would live forever in the world to come."[15] Columba's activities in Ireland and Dalriada were probably underpinned by the support of his wider kindred, lay and ecclesiastical.[16] Benedict Biscop, abbot of Wearmouth-Jarrow, appointed his cousin Eostorwine as his successor; Eostorwine's successor was Ceolfrith, and Ceolfrith had been trained in the religious community of his own brother Cynefrith at Gilling; Cynefrith resigned Gilling to their cousin Tunberht.[17]

Finally, as permanent institutions, religious communities required permanent endowments, either portions of family land or grants of royal land: they could therefore be used as an important asset in elite inheritance strategies. Sources from Ireland and England offer some insight into the relationship between elite power and ecclesiastical property; unfortunately, the sources from Wales and Scotland are not as forthcoming. Irish sources suggest that religious communities were often founded on inherited property by a whole kin-group. Members of a four generation kin-group – known as the *derbfine* – agreed to set aside a portion of their land permanently for the foundation of a community that would remain under the control of its members; it would thereby reinforce the kin-group identity, providing for its members a route to institutional authority, along with a permanent source of pastoral care and social support.[18] Conversely, Anglo-Saxon sources suggest that religious communities were often founded on acquired property and remained the property of an individual bishop or abbot. Royal diplomas or charters from England purport to record grants of land by the king for the foundation of religious communities, but they may have formalized a range of circumstances.[19] Such diplomas are known in Old English as a *boc*, "book," and the land granted as *bocland*, "bookland." To judge from the diplomas, bookland had special rights.[20] First, it was granted in perpetuity, perhaps because some royal grants were made only for the recipient's lifetime or period in office. Second, it was granted to an individual with full freedom to exploit, alienate, and bequeath it to a person of their choice, perhaps because other personal property was usually subject to partible inheritance, being split between all a person's heirs. Bede also seems to suggest that bookland was free from royal dues and services.[21] Apparently, then, Anglo-Saxon elites could found a religious community and thereby acquire a grant of personal property which was permanent, protected from partible inheritance, and free from royal services. Having reviewed some of the factors underlying Christianization – investment in Christian culture and institutions – it is time to consider the institutions that were created.

Bishops, Sees, and Dioceses

After the conversion of Rome to Christianity, the existing secular administration of the Roman Empire served as the basic structure for the building of Christian institutions. Within each diocese and province, a hierarchy of bishops was responsible for the running of the church: the patriarch or archbishop, the metropolitan, and the bishop. Patriarchs or archbishops generally had responsibility for a whole diocese, such as the imperial diocese of late Roman Britain. Metropolitans were an intermediary level between archbishops and bishops, with responsibility for consecrating other bishops and calling provincial ecclesiastical councils. Bishops were established in the *civitates*, major urban centers with their surrounding subject territories. In the *civitas*, the bishop constructed a cathedral served by a religious community composed of clergy. Then he worked within the surrounding territory through two types of church: first, by building baptismal churches (Italian *plebes* or *pievi* and Gallic *vici*), governed by a *rector* (ruler) and staffed by a small community of clergy; second, by gradually extending control over the private churches with clergy that had been founded at aristocratic villas. Bishops were, of course, vital to the provision of pastoral care and remained so: they were the only people qualified to ordain clergy to the level of deacon and priest and to consecrate churches and chrism for performing baptism. Ordinary clergy were not permitted to preach; those elevated to the level of deacon or priest were responsible for preaching and for the administration of the sacraments to the laity.

In areas where Roman institutions survived the disintegration of the empire in the fifth and sixth centuries, this system proved relatively powerful, efficient, and enduring – places like Italy, Spain, and Gaul. Yet where Roman institutions collapsed, or had never been established, episcopal organization had to be constructed within very different social and political systems – places like northern France, Brittany, and Germany, and Wales, Ireland, Scotland, and England. To begin with, the building blocks of political organization on which dioceses were based were not administrative units of regular sizes, but instead kingdoms of varying extent.

Wales and the south-western and western counties of England are the areas in which British post-Roman political organization survived longest. Here, if anywhere, we might expect to find episcopal structures close to the Roman model. Gildas's *Ruin of Britain*, written in the sixth century, assumed that there was a network of bishops, priests, and deacons in these areas, even if he did not approve of their behavior.[22] Inscribed stones dating from the fifth to the seventh century seem to confirm his assumption.[23] Indeed, it seems likely that former Romano-British city-territories served by a single bishop developed into kingdoms served by a number of bishops. Sometime before 705, Aldhelm, abbot of Malmesbury, wrote a letter to Geraint, king of Dumnonia and his bishops, which also mentions the bishops of Dyfed.[24] Dumnonia, in what is now Devon, and Dyfed, in Wales, were former Romano-British *civitates* – city-territories – that had become kingdoms with a plurality of bishops. Yet bishops and their sees are rarely mentioned in the surviving Welsh sources. During the ninth century, there are passing references to bishops at Bangor, St. David's, Llandeilo Fawr, and at one further unnamed site; it is also possible that there were further bishops at Glasbury and Dewstow before these were subsumed within the later see of Llandaff.[25] Archbishops or metropolitans are even harder to identify. Bede's account of the meetings between the Roman missionary Augustine and the Britons seems to reveal an episcopal hierarchy: a smaller synod of a single kingdom (*provincia*) attended by a plurality of bishops and scholars, along with a second larger synod of seven bishops and other scholars (*HE*, ii. 2). Elfoddw of Gwynedd (d.809) and Nobis of St. David's (d.873) are both called "archbishop" in contemporary sources: this could mean that they were acting as metropolitans, but it has also been interpreted as a mark of personal distinction rather than an institutional position.[26]

Missionaries from Wales were partly responsible for the conversion of Ireland, and Irish evidence reveals a very similar picture. Ireland was split into a large number of small kingdoms known as *túatha* (see chapters 6 and 7). Prescriptive sources from Ireland like the eighth-century *Rule of St. Patrick* assume that each *túath* had a chief bishop responsible for ordaining clergy, consecrating churches, and baptizing children.[27] Each *túath* was also expected to have its own synod or council, consisting not only of bishops but also of the heads of major religious communities and the most learned scholars and scribes from those communities.[28] Irish annals record the obituaries of a comparatively large number of bishops, which seems to support these prescriptions.[29] Put together, this implies a formidable network of chief bishops overseeing the work of lesser bishops and clergy. During the seventh and eighth centuries in Ireland, there were competing attempts to assert the authority of one see and its bishops over the rest. After the synod of Whitby in 664, where the Northumbrian King Oswiu abandoned Irish Easter dates in favor of Roman Easter dates, Bishop Wilfrid of York apparently claimed authority over the northern half of Ireland. Probably in reaction to this, the sees of Kildare and Armagh promoted their own claims to primacy within Ireland.[30]

Again, Irish missionaries worked in Scotland, so we might expect to find comparable episcopal structures to those in Wales and Ireland. However, the Scottish evidence is extremely fragmentary, and conclusions must remain tentative. Ptolemy identified five northern British sub-kingdoms: the *Novantae, Damnonii, Venicones, Votadini*, and *Selgovae*. One possibility is that these kingdoms formed the basis for a network of episcopal sees focused on Carlisle, Whithorn, Glasgow, Abercorn, Old Melrose, Abernethy, Paisley, Edinburgh, Hoddam, and Peebles.[31] Subsequent entries in the early Scottish annals and chronicles reveal passing glimpses of bishops at Iona, Whithorn, Abercorn, Kingarth, Abernethy, Rosemarkie, and Dunkeld, presumably working within the early kingdoms of what is now Scotland.[32] Tuathal, abbot of Dunkeld (d.864), was described in the annals as chief bishop of Fortriu (central Scotland), but, like the examples from Wales, it is unclear whether this reflects metropolitan status or was a mark of personal distinction.[33] Metropolitan bishops were only formally established in Scotland in the fifteenth century.

Whereas in Wales, Ireland, and Scotland the establishment of an episcopal network has to be pieced together from chance references and prescriptive sources, in England Bede's *Ecclesiastical History* gives us a comparatively detailed narrative account. When Gregory the Great sent missionaries to England in 597, he intended the construction of a Roman episcopal system based on his knowledge of former Roman administration in Britain: two metropolitan bishops, one at London and another at York, each with 12 bishops under his direction. However, this plan was not realized. A metropolitan see was established not at London but instead at Canterbury, the most important center in the kingdom of Kent where the missionaries landed. A further metropolitan see was established at York, but quickly abandoned; the see was restored in the 660s by Bishop Wilfrid, and finally became an archbishopric in 735. Further sees were gradually constructed in the emerging Anglo-Saxon kingdoms, yet this was a slow and difficult process. By 668, there were seven dioceses, only four of which were occupied and only two of the bishops had been correctly consecrated. Between 668 and 690, Archbishop Theodore successfully raised the number to 13 or 14 sees, and by 740 his successors had added a further three or four to raise the number to 16, 17, or 18. Nevertheless, this fell some way short of Gregory's proposal for 24 sees: the kingdoms of Kent, East Anglia, and Essex were perhaps adequately provided for, but the kingdoms of Wessex, Mercia, and Northumbria were not. During the seventh and eighth centuries, there is good evidence that episcopal councils were held on an annual basis, often including kings, bishops, and the abbots of important religious communities.[34]

Part of the problem with Anglo-Saxon dioceses was that kingdoms had expanded at a rapid rate and some dioceses were therefore very large. Subdividing those dioceses could then prove difficult because individual bishops might resist diminution of their authority. Witness Wilfrid of Ripon's tenure of the see of York in the later seventh century, recorded in Stephen of Ripon's *Life of Wilfrid*: three times he was exiled by the Northumbrian kings and his see was divided, but he repeatedly took his case to Rome in order to re-establish control.

Just as the absence of Roman imperial administrative structures in the British Isles meant that dioceses were based on kingdoms, so the absence of urban centers meant that episcopal sees were generally established as, or within, non-urban religious communities. Asser, in his late ninth-century *Life of King Alfred*, describes St. David's as an episcopal center and *monasterium*; charters in the Lichfield gospels say the same of Llandeilo Fawr.[35] Irish legal texts prescribe principles about the heads of religious communities (Latin *princeps*, Old Irish *airchennach*), assuming that some of these were bishops and that bishops worked from the chief church of each *túath* with its corresponding religious community.[36] Early Scottish sees were established in religious communities like Iona and Whithorn. Anglo-Saxon sees were sometimes established at former Roman towns, within important standing remains, like those at Canterbury, Dorchester, Leicester, Lichfield, Lincoln, London, Winchester, and York. Yet, perhaps with the exception of Canterbury, these were probably not functioning urban settlements. Religious communities were constructed to serve these sees, and alongside them other sees were placed in existing religious communities at Hexham, Ripon (briefly), Lindisfarne, and Selsey.

While on the continent cathedral communities tended to be communities of clergy, across the British Isles the constitution of these communities probably varied from place to place. At Canterbury, there seems to have been a community of clergy at Christ Church serving the cathedral, and at York there may have been a community of clergy serving St. Peter's.[37] Yet sometimes monks and the clergy serving the see may have lived side by side – consider Bede's description of Lindisfarne.[38] Even where this was not the case, communities of monks often played an important role in training bishops. Several Anglo-Saxon sees seem to have had an associated community of monks from which bishops were elected: St. Augustine's at Canterbury, Lindisfarne for Lindisfarne/Hexham, and Whitby for York.[39]

Beyond their cathedrals and cathedral communities, bishops needed to establish a network of local churches for which they could consecrate and supervise clergy administering pastoral care. However, it is difficult for any region to get a clear sense of the number, distribution, and organization of churches under episcopal control. Charters preserved in the archive of the eleventh-century see at Llandaff in Wales apparently record the foundation of a large number of local churches in south-east Wales from the sixth century onward: 36 religious communities (*monasteria*) and 38 churches (*ecclesiae*).[40] Evidence from Ireland suggests an even denser network of local churches: Tírechán's account of the mission of St. Patrick reveals a tiered hierarchy and dense distribution of churches in the seventh century.[41] Yet, in both Wales and Ireland, important questions remain unanswered. All churches with clergy were under episcopal authority in theory, but how many were in practice? How many churches under episcopal authority were considered the property of the see, of the individual bishop, or of other individuals answerable to the bishop? Were these patterns representative of other areas of Wales and Ireland? After all, the south-east regions of Wales covered by the Llandaff material are the regions with the most fertile lowlands, which might have been able to sustain an unusually dense network of churches.

Turning to England, the evidence has been interpreted in two different ways. Bede's *Ecclesiastical History* is our principal source for the period up to c.731. During the initial phases of missionary activity, up to c.660, Bede records the foundation of a number of churches that might be considered episcopal churches, equivalent to the Italian *plebes* and Gallic *vici*. Paulinus worked with the Northumbrian kings to found *basilicae* or *oratoria* alongside royal centers (*villae regales*) at York, *Cambodunum*, in the *regio Loidis* (near Leeds, West Yorkshire), and somewhere near Catterick, North Yorkshire (*HE*, ii. 14). Aidan and Cedd, he tells us, constructed churches (*ecclesiae*) throughout the districts around Lindisfarne and in Essex (*HE*, iii. 3, 22). Two of Bede's miracle stories also refer to possible private churches: Bishop John of Beverley performed miracles while visiting two aristocrats to consecrate churches on their estates (*HE*, v. 4–5). Some parish churches that preserve fragments of sculpture dating from the period between the seventh and ninth centuries might represent the location of other churches like these, though they could alternatively have been subsidiary sites attached to religious communities. Eric Cambridge and David Rollason have argued that this is sufficient evidence to show that episcopal and private churches did exist at an early date in England.[42]

Conversely, Bede also seems to reveal the difficulties of getting such episcopal churches constructed: Paulinus baptized in the River Swale, he says, "because oratories or baptisteries could not be built in that first stage of the nascent Church there."[43] Indeed, after c.660, Bede no longer uses these terms – *basilica, oratorium*, or *ecclesia* – referring instead to *monasteria* (religious communities). Individual bishops certainly founded some of these communities: Bishop Wilfrid was an enthusiastic founder of religious communities.[44] Yet such communities were probably not always considered the property of the see to be used by subsequent bishops, but often the property of the individual bishop, to be alienated as he saw fit. Although Bede records the two miracles of John of Beverley that may relate to private aristocratic churches, this evidence is slight and ambiguous: it remains possible that these were churches founded on estates held from the religious community at Beverley and that they would have been served by the community. Miracle accounts, charters, and laws only begin to mention such private aristocratic churches in the late ninth and tenth centuries. John Blair has therefore proposed that episcopal and private churches were limited to an early phase of missionary activity and not significant thereafter.[45]

All areas therefore reveal a network of bishops and dioceses. Wales and Ireland seem to have had a dense distribution of bishops; evidence for Scotland is fragmentary, but in England it is clear that there were many fewer bishops. Yet because there is ambiguous evidence for the scale and organization of episcopal and private churches, it is hard to judge the practical power of bishops and their efficiency in controlling and administering pastoral care. Conversely, it is clear that a large number of religious communities were founded and that they remained extremely influential institutions in the local landscape. An alternative approach has therefore been to consider the foundation and organization of religious communities and their role in pastoral provision, whether under episcopal direction or as a result of independent initiative.

Religious Communities

Religious communities were useful spiritual, political, and social assets as we saw above: for that reason, a large number were founded in Wales, Ireland, Scotland, and England. Within Wales, contemporary sources mention around 35 pre-Conquest religious communities; the Llandaff charters add a further 36; places identified as a *podum*, "monastery," place-names containing the element *llan*, "enclosure," and early inscribed stones, suggest the location of others. Individual communities are often difficult to date, but a large proportion of these will belong to the period between the sixth and ninth centuries. Over half of the communities mentioned in the Llandaff charters are recorded as existing in the seventh and eighth centuries.[46] Early legal and hagiographical texts from Ireland also suggest an impressive network of early religious communities, as we have seen above. Written sources and surviving stone sculpture from Scotland imply a similarly enthusiastic pattern of early foundation.[47] Finally, in England, putting the surviving charters alongside the testimony of Bede reveals a boom in the foundation of religious communities between c.680 and c.720 in particular.[48]

Not only were many communities founded, but also many types of community. Yet contemporary terms like *monasterium* could be applied to almost any type of community, suggesting that there was no clear distinction in the minds of contemporaries between communities with different constitutions. Communities could be ruled by a bishop, a monk-abbot, a priest-abbot, or an abbess. They might be composed mainly of monks – individuals who had taken a public vow to live apart from society, generally in chastity, with no personal possessions, and according to a formal rule that governed their behavior and activities. Bede's *History of the Abbots* on his community at Wearmouth-Jarrow, and Adomnán's *Life of Columba* on Iona provide the clearest evidence for this type of community. Some monks would also be ordained as deacons or priests, allowing them to preach and administer the sacraments to their brothers in the community and (perhaps) to those outside. Yet some communities probably contained only clergy: in this case, they could have had no personal possessions and lived according to a rule like monks, as the clergy at Canterbury and York seem to have done; or they could have retained personal property, lived in separate houses but in close proximity, and remained married. Some double houses existed, where monks or clergy lived side by side with nuns, such as Kildare in Ireland, or Barking, Coldingham, and Whitby in England.[49] Finally, there were communities consisting only of nuns.

Along with variation in composition, there was similar variation in organization. A key point to remember is that there was no normative rule governing life in religious communities as there would be in later centuries. Instead, it was common for individual abbots or abbesses to investigate the rules followed at a number of other religious communities, before devising their own. Bede's *History of the Abbots*, c. 11 tells us that Benedict Biscop took the best of what he found from the rules at some 17 religious communities that he visited. Religious communities were clearly multi-focal settlements.[50] Often, there was more than one principal church. Monks, nuns, and priests will sometimes have lived and eaten communally in a dormitory and refectory. Alternatively, some or all of them might have lived in individual cells. Clergy not living by a rule could have lived in private houses and remained married, even if these were in close proximity. Adomnán's *Life of Columba* and Bede's descriptions of communities in his *Life of Cuthbert* and in his *Ecclesiastical History* reveal a range of other buildings, including oratories, retreat houses, novice houses, scriptoria, workshops, and hospitals. Activities would have varied along a spectrum from prayer, meditation, and manual labor, to writing, sculpting, and metalwork, to pastoral work in the surrounding countryside.[51] Sizes would have ranged from single figures to perhaps hundreds, although claims for the latter may have included those who worked lands owned by a community.[52]

While it is tempting to think of religious communities as single institutions, the early communities of the British Isles were also sometimes part of larger federations.[53] Individual communities might establish daughter-houses: the community at Whitby, North Yorkshire founded a daughter-house 13 miles away at Hackness (*HE*, iv. 23). Such cases might mean that the abbot of one house had authority over another; thus, the abbot of Iona could appoint the head of the communities at Hinba and at Mag Lunge on Tiree.[54] Some of the estates of a community might be provided with a church and considered small communities – see the example of the Whitby estate of *Osingadun* discussed below. Flourishing communities might become predatory, acquiring influence over other communities. The late seventh-century Irish author Tírechán describes for us the predatory behavior of the community at Clonmacnoise, which exerted influence over communities within other *túatha* and placed upon them obligations of tribute and hospitality.[55]

Religious communities were therefore numerous and influential local institutions across the British Isles. Theoretically, then, they could have provided a framework for the provision of pastoral care. Contemporary evidence for the role of religious communities in pastoral care is provided by the prescriptions in ecclesiastical canons and the didactic ideals set out in early hagiographical and historical texts. Irish texts such as the *Rule of St. Patrick*, the *Córus Béscnai*, and the *Hibernensis* reveal that each *túath* was expected to have a senior religious community with responsibility for pastoral care within the *túath* – a public obligation to the whole *túath* and a particular obligation to the *manaig*, a term meaning both the members of the community and the tenants of its lands.[56] English texts are less explicit, but revealing in their assumptions and in the ideals they present. The *Penitential* of Theodore (ii. vi. 7) prescribes that anyone who moves a monastery must leave behind "a priest for the offices of the church" at the old site.[57] Bede's descriptions of Cuthbert as a monk, priest, and prior at Melrose in his *Life of Cuthbert* (c. 9) and his description of Lindisfarne in the *Ecclesiastical History* (iii. 26) depict members of religious communities – including ordained monks – undertaking pastoral tours in the surrounding countryside. Just as in Ireland, it seems that there was a blurred line between members of the community and those who worked the community's lands and that communities felt a special pastoral responsibility toward their tenants. Bede's *Life of Cuthbert* (c. 34) depicts Cuthbert traveling to an estate owned by the religious community at Whitby, North Yorkshire called *Osingadun*: Whitby is referred to as the larger *monasterium*, implying that the estate at *Osingadun* could be considered a smaller *monasterium*, the workers are referred to as brothers (*fratres*), and Cuthbert was visiting in order to dedicate a church. Quite apart from these formal responsibilities, it is also likely that the work of holy men and women like St. Brigit and the political and social functions of religious communities discussed under "Christianization" above often tied them into local societies.

Alongside this early written evidence from Ireland and England, there is later evidence from all regions that known early religious communities were often also mother-churches serving large mother-parishes in the twelfth and thirteenth centuries. Tenth-, eleventh-, and twelfth-century sources seem to reveal that these mother-churches were the backbone of an earlier pastoral system. Welsh law books contrast mother-churches of the highest rank with an abbot, a community (often known by the Old Welsh term *clas*), and priests with smaller churches and chapels; written agreements record the arrangements made between these communities and their daughter-churches for the provision of pastoral care in the twelfth century.[58] Like earlier Irish texts, the *Indarba Mochuda* and a text known as *The Ancient Territory of Fermoy* from the eleventh and twelfth centuries assume that each *túath* had a chief church with a community of clergy overseeing the churches of its *fairche* (mother-parish).[59] English laws from the tenth century state that any church founded within the area of jurisdiction of an old religious community must pay a portion of the dues it receives for pastoral care to that community.[60] Such late evidence is often interpreted as a reflection of a much earlier pastoral framework in which religious communities provided large territories with pastoral care before private churches were established within those territories, causing their fragmentation.

Ultimately, then, it seems clear that religious communities were expected to play an important part in the provision of pastoral care. Where the problem lies is in the potential gulf between this widespread expectation and the diversity of composition, between the theory and the reality. Prescriptive sources assert the primacy of bishops over pastoral care, but how many communities were they able to found or bring under their control? If there was diversity of composition, how many communities had a sufficient number of clergy or ordained monks to undertake such work effectively? Even if they did, how many lived up to the expectations set out in our prescriptive and didactic sources? Although Bede promoted the pastoral role of monks, how many monks responded to his call?

Conclusion

Enthusiastic investment in Christian institutions across the British Isles occurred partly because Christian ideology and institutions paralleled existing social conventions and offered new opportunities for kings and elites. To review that investment is to review the development from adoption to Christianization and to consider whether there was a framework for spiritual conversion through regular preaching and pastoral care. Yet, if it is possible to reconstruct the basic framework of institutions that existed, it is harder to assess the relative power of particular officials or institutions or the quality of religious observances and pastoral care. Such assessments depend very largely on the methodological approach that is taken to the surviving sources, which are mostly prescriptive or didactic.

Bishops compiled and issued prescriptive sources like the canons of ecclesiastical councils and penitentials (books prescribing penance to be performed for sins), which tend to assert the primacy of bishops in ecclesiastical organization. Yet such sources are open to the criticism that they often reveal what *should* be happening, not what *was* happening. Didactic monastic sources like Bede's *Life of Cuthbert* and *Ecclesiastical History* tend to promote the role of monks as bishops and preachers working from religious communities, while at the same time providing stinging critiques of communities that did not live up to the author's standards. Yet these works are setting out ideals to be imitated or avoided rather than giving disinterested accounts of what happened. Such problems of interpretation are common across the British Isles, but are most clear in the vigorous debate over pastoral care in Anglo-Saxon England.[61]

Bede's *Ecclesiastical History* and his *Letter to Ecgberht* can be considered as exemplifying this issue. The *Ecclesiastical History* seems to present a picture of a vibrant and effective church in England in the seventh century, charting the work of missionary monks to convert the Anglo-Saxon kingdoms. Conversely, the *Letter to Ecgberht* of 734 constituted a stinging critique of the effectiveness of ecclesiastical organization in early eighth-century England. Bede attacked the deplorable state of episcopal structures: there were too few bishops and those in episcopal office had too great a penchant for the excesses of the lay elite. Alongside this, many laymen had been acquiring land under the pretext of founding religious communities when really they were interested in the special benefits accorded to such land. His solution to this situation was the consecration of more bishops, along with the expropriation of such religious communities to provide centers in which new episcopal sees might be established.

Of course, a range of approaches can be taken to Bede's works. Each work could be viewed as no more than an example of a distinct genre of writing designed to fulfill Bede's responsibility as a teacher: that is, whatever the conditions on the ground, he may have felt an obligation to set out such ideals and warnings. From this perspective, his works may offer a limited insight into the actual authority and quality of particular officials or institutions. Alternatively, the *Ecclesiastical History* could be argued to present his picture of an ideal church in the past, in antithesis to realities on the ground in the present; then his letter might be thought to reflect his true feelings about the contemporary church. On this reading, ecclesiastical structures would be considered fundamentally flawed. Yet a third approach might be to emphasize that Bede's letter reveals the enthusiasm with which the Anglo-Saxon elite invested in Christian culture and blended it with their own social mores. If so, the features of the church that he laments might not be seen as flaws but as adaptations. Adaptations might be considered to have eroded the distinction between episcopal institutions and religious communities; they might also be considered to have facilitated rather than undermined further efforts to provide preaching and pastoral care, helping ecclesiastics relate to contemporary lay society.

Bede's solution to these perceived deficiencies also points to the potential for change within the structures outlined above, which must be factored into our assessments. Religious communities had to work hard to maintain their size and sustain sources of patronage; they could easily shrink, disappear, or come under the influence of outside lordship. The composition of a community could completely transform over time: Bede recalls that one community on the banks of the River Tyne had formerly housed monks but was by his time a community of nuns (*Life of Cuthbert*, c. 3). During the eighth and ninth centuries, there seems to have been widespread episcopal and royal appropriation of religious communities in Anglo-Saxon England.[62] Such appropriation may have been peculiarly necessary in England as a result of the particularly enthusiastic investment in such communities by kings and elites, but it was certainly not unique to England. Within individual communities, or indeed groups of communities, there could be movements to reform and adhere to a particular understanding of the religious life. Consider the development of the *Céli Dé* movement that spread across Ireland from the late eighth century and seems to have reached Scotland and perhaps Wales: it promoted an extreme form of asceticism and self-denial among monks within religious communities and attempted to codify and regulate the wider responsibilities of the community.[63] Finally, from the late eighth century onward, communities across the British Isles also had to contend with Scandinavian raiding. A text called the *History of Saint Cuthbert*, composed in the tenth or eleventh century, provides a striking glimpse into the problems such raids posed for religious communities: the death of some members, the displacement of others, the loss of land and moveable wealth.[64] Cuthbert's community managed to maintain possession of his relics, so that they were able to acquire new patrons and the restoration of their lands; many other communities were probably not so fortunate.

Notes

1   Alcuin, *Letter to Meginfried*, in Loyn and Percival (eds.), *Reign of Charlemagne*, no. 34, pp. 123–6.
2   Hope-Taylor, *Yeavering*.
3   Anon., *Prittlewell Prince*; Carver, *Sutton Hoo*.
4   Carver, "Why that? Why there? Why then?"
5   Blair, *Church in Anglo-Saxon Society*, pp. 51–7.
6   Anderson and Anderson (eds.), *Adomnán: Life of Columba*; Colgrave (ed.), *Two Lives of Saint Cuthbert*.
7   Connolly and Picard (trans.), "Cogitosus: *Life of St. Brigit*"; Bede, *HE*, iv. 23 on Hild.
8   See Connolly and Picard (trans.), "Cogitosus: *Life of St. Brigit*," iv. 1–2; v. 1–3; ix. 1–2; xi. 1–3; xxv. 1–6.
9   Colgrave (ed.), *Life of Bishop Wilfrid*.
10 Connolly and Picard (trans.), "Cogitosus: *Life of St. Brigit*," xxviii. 1–4.
11 Bede, *History of the Abbots*, cc. 2–6, in Webb (trans.), *Age of Bede*; Colgrave (ed.), *Life of Bishop Wilfrid*, cc. 3–5, 17, 22.
12 Whyte, "The intellectual aristocracy revisited."
13 Wood, *Proprietary Church*, pp. 118–21.
14 Connolly and Picard (trans.), "Cogitosus: *Life of St. Brigit*," xxxii. 8–10.
15 Bede, *History of the Abbots*, c. 1, in Webb (trans.), *Age of Bede*.
16 Herbert, *Iona, Kells, and Derry*, pp. 31–5, 310.
17 Bede, *History of the Abbots*, c. 8, and Anon., *Life of Ceolfrith*, c. 2, both in Webb (trans.), *Age of Bede*.
18 Charles–Edwards, *Early Christian Ireland*, pp. 84–96; Wood, *Proprietary Church*, pp. 140–7.
19 Blair, *Church in Anglo-Saxon Society*, pp. 87–91.

20 Wormald, *Bede and the Conversion of England*.
21 Bede, *Letter to Ecgberht*, 351, in Collins and McClure (trans.), *Bede: Ecclesiastical History*.
22 Winterbottom (ed.), *Gildas: The Ruin of Britain*.
23 Pryce, "Pastoral care in early medieval Wales," pp. 47–8.
24 Aldhelm, *Letter to Geraint*, in Lapidge and Herren (trans.), *Aldhem: The Prose Works*, pp. 155, 158.
25 Davies, *Wales in the Early Middle Ages*, pp. 158–60.
26 Asser, *Life of Alfred*, c. 79, in Keynes and Lapidge (trans.), *Alfred the Great; Welsh Annals*, 809, in Morris (trans.), *Nennius: British History and the Welsh Annals*, pp. 44–9; see also Davies, *Wales in the Early Middle Ages*, pp. 160–1.
27 O'Keeffe (ed.), "The rule of St. Patrick," c. 1.
28 Charles-Edwards, *Early Christian Ireland*, pp. 276–81.
29 Ibid., pp. 259–64; see also Charles-Edwards (trans.), *Chronicle of Ireland*.
30 Charles-Edwards, *Early Christian Ireland*, pp. 416–40.
31 Thomas, "The evidence from North Britain" and *Early Christian Archaeology of North Britain*, pp. 16–18.
32 Donaldson, "Bishops' sees before the reign of David I."
33 Ibid., pp. 12–17.
34 Cubitt, *Anglo-Saxon Church Councils*, pp. 17–60.
35 Davies, *Wales in the Early Middle Ages*, pp. 149–50.
36 Charles-Edwards, "The pastoral role of the church," p. 67; Sharpe, "Churches and communities in early medieval Ireland," pp. 105–9.
37 Brooks, *Early History of the Church of Canterbury*, pp. 87–91; Rollason, *Sources for York History*, pp. 153–5.
38 Bede, *Life of Cuthbert*, c. 16, in Colgrave, *Two Lives of Saint Cuthbert*.
39 Cubitt, "Wilfrid's 'usurping bishops.'"
40 Davies, *Wales in the Early Middle Ages*, pp. 143–5.
41 Tírechán, *Collectanea*, in Bieler (ed.), *The Patrician Texts*; Sharpe, "Churches and communities," pp. 86–9.
42 Cambridge and Rollason, "Debate: the pastoral organisation of the Anglo-Saxon church," 88–93.
43 Bede, *HE*, ii. 14 (trans. Collins and McClure).
44 Colgrave (ed.), *Life of Bishop Wilfrid*, cc. 8, 14–15, 17, 21–2, 41, 64.
45 Blair, *Church in Anglo-Saxon Society*, pp. 65–73, 118–21.
46 Davies, *Wales in the Early Middle Ages*, pp. 143–8.
47 Macquarrie, "Early Christian religious houses in Scotland."
48 Blair, *Church in Anglo-Saxon Society*, pp. 84–91.
49 Connolly and Picard (trans.), Cogitosus, *Life of St. Brigit*, pref., 6; Bede, *HE*, iv. 6–10, iv. 23–5 on Barking, Coldingham, and Whitby.
50 See Blair, *Church in Anglo-Saxon Society*, pp. 182–227; Herity, *Studies in the Layout, Buildings and Art in Stone*.
51 Foot, *Monastic Life in Anglo-Saxon England*, pp. 186–250.
52 Blair, *Church in Anglo-Saxon Society*, pp. 212–14; Charles-Edwards, "The pastoral role of the church," p. 67; Davies, *Wales in the Early Middle Ages*, p. 150.
53 Foot, *Monastic Life in Anglo-Saxon England*, pp. 251–82.
54 Herbert, *Iona, Kells, and Derry*, pp. 31–5.
55 Charles-Edwards, *Early Christian Ireland*, pp. 256–7.
56 Ibid., pp. 118–19.
57 *Penitential of Theodore*, in McNeill and Gamer (trans.), *Medieval Handbooks of Penance*, pp. 179–215.

58   Pryce, "Pastoral care in early medieval Wales," pp. 55–7.
59   Sharpe, "Churches and communities in early medieval Ireland," pp. 95–8; see *Indarba Mochuda*, in Plummer (ed.), *Bethada Náem nÉrenn*, I: 300–11; II: 293–302; O'Keeffe, "The ancient territory of Fermoy."
60   Blair, *Church in Anglo-Saxon Society*, pp. 440–51.
61   Blair, "Debate: ecclesiastical organisation"; Cambridge and Rollason, "Debate: the pastoral organisation of the Anglo-Saxon Church," 87–104.
62   Blair, *Church in Anglo-Saxon Society*, pp. 108–17, 121–34.
63   Clancy, "Iona, Scotland and the *Céli Dé*," pp. 111–20; Hughes, *Church in Early Irish Society*, pp. 173–93.
64   Anon., *History of Saint Cuthbert*, in Johnson South, *Historia de Sancto Cuthberto*.

Further Reading

Accessible translations of major sources include: McClure and Collins, *Bede: The Ecclesiastical History of the English People*; McNeill and Gamer, *Medieval Handbooks of Penance*; Sharpe, *Adomnán: Life of Columba*; Webb, *The Age of Bede*; and Winterbottom, *Gildas: The Ruin of Britain and Other Works*. Until recently, the historiography of the church in the British Isles was dominated by the notion of the "Celtic church" contrasted with England: see Davies, "The myth of the Celtic church," for why this is no longer acceptable.

Ecclesiastical structures in each region are summarized in the following overviews. Wales: Davies, *Wales in the Early Middle Ages*, ch. 6; Stancliffe, "The British church and the mission of Augustine." Ireland: C. Etchingham, *Church Organisation in Ireland, AD 650 to 1000* (Maynooth, 1999); Charles-Edwards, *Early Christian Ireland*, pp. 117–123, chs. 6 and 10. Scotland: I. B. Cowan, "The development of the parochial system," in I. B. Cowan, *The Medieval Church in Scotland*, ed. J. Kirk (Edinburgh, 1995), no. 1; Donaldson, "Bishops' sees before the reign of David I"; and Macquarrie, "Early Christian religious houses in Scotland." England: Blair, *The Church in Anglo-Saxon Society*, chs. 1–3; Cubitt, *Anglo-Saxon Church Councils, c.650–c.850*; Foot, *Monastic Life in Anglo-Saxon England, c.600–900*; and S. Foot, *Veiled Women*, 2 vols. (Aldershot, 2000).

For studies of pastoral care and the cult of saints across the British Isles, see Blair and Sharpe (eds.), *Pastoral Care before the Parish*, and Thacker and Sharpe (eds.), *Local Saints and Local Churches in the Early Medieval West*. For debate over pastoral care in early Anglo-Saxon England, see Cambridge and Rollason, "Debate: the pastoral organisation of the Anglo-Saxon church," followed by Blair, "Debate: ecclesiastical organisation and pastoral care in Anglo-Saxon England." For studies of the nature and layout of monastic sites, see Herity, *Studies in the Layout, Buildings and Art in Stone of Early Irish Monasteries*; J. Blair, "Minster churches in the landscape," in D. Hooke (ed.), *Anglo-Saxon Settlements* (Oxford, 1988), pp. 35–58; "Anglo-Saxon minsters: a topographical review," in J. Blair and R. Sharpe (eds.), *Pastoral Care before the Parish* (Leicester, 1992), pp. 226–66; and *The Church in Anglo-Saxon Society*, ch. 4; and R. Cramp, *Wearmouth and Jarrow Monastic Sites*, 2 vols. (Swindon, 2005).

Bibliography

Anderson, A. O. and Anderson, M. O. (eds.), *Adomnán's Life of Columba*, 2nd edn. (Oxford, 1991).

Anon., *The Prittlewell Prince: The Discovery of a Rich Anglo-Saxon Burial in Essex* (London, 2004).

Bieler, L. (ed. and trans.), *The Patrician Texts in the Book of Armagh*, Scriptores Latini Hiberniae 10 (Dublin, 1979).

Blair, J., *The Church in Anglo-Saxon Society* (Oxford, 2005).

Blair, J., "Debate: ecclesiastical organisation and pastoral care in Anglo-Saxon England," *Early Medieval Europe*, 4: 2 (1995), 193–212.

Blair, J. and Sharpe, R. (eds.), *Pastoral Care before the Parish* (Leicester, 1992).

Brooks, N., *The Early History of the Church of Canterbury* (Leicester, 1984).

Cambridge, E. and Rollason, D., "Debate: the pastoral organisation of the Anglo-Saxon Church: a review of the 'minster hypothesis,'" *Early Medieval Europe*, 4: 1 (1995), 87–104.

Carver, M., *Sutton Hoo: A Seventh-century Princely Burial Ground and its Context* (London, 2005).

Carver, M., "Why that? Why there? Why then? The politics of early medieval monumentality," in H. Hamerow and A. MacGregor (eds.), *Image and Power in the Archaeology of Early Medieval Britain* (Oxford, 2001), pp. 1–22.

Charles-Edwards, T. M. (ed. and trans.), *The Chronicle of Ireland*, 2 vols. Translated Texts for Historians, 44 (Liverpool, 2006).

Charles-Edwards, T. M., *Early Christian Ireland* (Cambridge, 2000).

Charles-Edwards, T. M., "The pastoral role of the church in the early Irish laws," in J. Blair and R. Sharpe (eds.), *Pastoral Care before the Parish* (Leicester, 1992), pp. 63–80.

Clancy, T. O., "Iona, Scotland and the *Céli Dé*," in B. E. Crawford (ed.), *Scotland in Dark Age Britain* (St. Andrews, 1996), pp. 111–20.

Colgrave, B. (ed. and trans.), *The Life of Bishop Wilfrid by Eddius Stephanus* (Cambridge, 1927; repr. New York, 1985).

Colgrave, B. (ed. and trans.), *Two Lives of Saint Cuthbert* (Cambridge, 1940).

Collins, R. and McClure, J. (trans.), *Bede: The Ecclesiastical History of the English People* (Oxford, 1994).

Connolly, S. and Picard, J.-M. (trans.), "Cogitosus, *Life of St. Brigit*," *Journal of the Royal Society of Antiquaries of Ireland*, 117 (1987), 11–27.

Cubitt, C., *Anglo-Saxon Church Councils c.650–c.850* (London, 1995).

Cubitt, C., "Wilfrid's 'usurping bishops': episcopal elections in Anglo-Saxon England c.600–800," *Northern History*, 25 (1989), 18–39.

Davies, W., "The myth of the Celtic church," in N. Edwards and A. Lane (eds.), *The Early Church in Wales and the West* (Oxford, 1992), pp. 12–21.

Davies, W., *Wales in the Early Middle Ages* (Leicester, 1982).

Donaldson, G., "Bishops' sees before the reign of David I," in G. Donaldson, *Scottish Church History* (Edinburgh, 1985), no. 2.

Foot, S., *Monastic Life in Anglo-Saxon England, c.600–900* (Cambridge, 2006).

Herbert, M., *Iona, Kells, and Derry: The History and Hagiography of the Monastic Familia of Columba* (Oxford, 1988; repr. Dublin, 1996).

Herity, M., *Studies in the Layout, Buildings and Art in Stone of Early Irish Monasteries* (London, 1995).

Hope-Taylor, B., *Yeavering: An Anglo-British Centre of Early Northumbria* (London, 1977).

Hughes, K., *The Church in Early Irish Society* (London, 1966).

Johnson South, T. (trans.), *Historia de Sancto Cuthberto: A History of Saint Cuthbert and a Record of his Patrimony* (Woodbridge, 2002).

Keynes, S. and Lapidge, M. (trans.), *Alfred the Great: Asser's Life of King Alfred and Other Contemporary Sources* (Harmondsworth, 1983).

Lapidge, M. and Herren, M. (trans.), *Aldhelm: The Prose Works* (Cambridge, 1979).

Loyn, H. and Percival, J. (eds. and trans.), *The Reign of Charlemagne* (London, 1975).

McNeill, J. T. and Gamer, H. M. (trans.), *Medieval Handbooks of Penance* (New York, 1938).

Macquarrie, A., "Early Christian religious communities in Scotland: foundation and function," in J. Blair and R. Sharpe (eds.), *Pastoral Care before the Parish* (Leicester, 1992), pp. 110–33.

Morris, J. (trans.), *Nennius: British History and the Welsh Annals* (London, 1980).

O'Keeffe, J. G. (ed. and trans.), "The ancient territory of Fermoy," *Ériu*, 10 (1926–8), 170–89.

O'Keeffe, J. G. (ed. and trans.), "The rule of St. Patrick," *Ériu*, 1 (1904), 216–24.

Plummer, C. (ed. and trans.), *Bethada Náem nÉrenn*, 2 vols. (Oxford, 1922).

Pryce, H., "Pastoral care in early medieval Wales," in J. Blair and R. Sharpe (eds.), *Pastoral Care before the Parish* (Leicester, 1992), pp. 41–62.

Rollason, D. W., Gore, D., and Fellows-Jensen, G., *Sources for York History to AD 1100* (York, 1998).

Sharpe, R., "Churches and communities in early medieval Ireland: towards a pastoral model," in J. Blair and R. Sharpe (eds.), *Pastoral Care before the Parish* (Leicester, 1992), pp. 81–109.

Sharpe, R., "Some problems concerning the organisation of the church in early medieval Ireland," *Peritia*, 3 (1984), 230–70.

Stancliffe, C., "The British church and the mission of Augustine," in R. Gameson (ed.), *St. Augustine and the Conversion of England* (Stroud, 1999), pp. 107–51.

Thacker, A., and Sharpe, R. (eds.), *Local Saints and Local Churches in the Early Medieval West* (Oxford, 2002).

Thomas, A. C., *The Early Christian Archaeology of North Britain* (London, 1971).

Thomas, A. C., "The evidence from North Britain," in M. W. Barley and R. P. C. Hanson (eds.), *Christianity in Britain, 300–700* (Leicester, 1968), pp. 93–121.

Webb, J. F. (trans.), *The Age of Bede*, rev. edn. by D. H. Farmer (Harmondsworth, 1983).

Whyte, W., "The intellectual aristocracy revisited," *Journal of Victorian Culture*, 10: 1 (2005), 15–45.

Winterbottom, M. (ed. and trans.), *Gildas: The Ruin of Britain and Other Documents* (Chichester, 1978).

Wood, S., *The Proprietary Church in the Medieval West* (Oxford, 2006).

Wormald, P., *Bede and the Conversion of England: The Charter Evidence*, Jarrow Lecture 1984 (Jarrow, n.d.); reprinted in P. Wormald, *The Times of Bede: Studies in Early English Christian Society and its Historian* (Oxford, 2006).

CHAPTER TWELVE

Latin Learning and Christian Art

MARTIN J. RYAN

The spread of Christianity and its attendant institutions throughout the Atlantic Archipelago changed fundamentally the nature of society and culture. However, as previous chapters have made clear, conversion to Christianity did not mean isolated cultures first coming into contact with a wider world after prolonged insularity. Rather, Christianity brought with it new modes of expression and new ways to see the world and the place and status of the various peoples of Britain and Ireland within it. The artistic and intellectual culture that developed over the course of the sixth to eighth centuries – insular culture – should be seen as a response to this new stimulus, distinctive in form but nevertheless making a claim to share in a wider Christian world. Even those areas where Christianity had survived the passing of Roman Britain were affected by the conversion of their neighbors. Missionaries brought claims for the universal authority of the church of Rome, and meetings such as the synod of Whitby challenged the orthodoxy and legitimacy of existing traditions.

Christianity also provided common languages – Latin and, to a lesser extent, Greek – that facilitated intellectual and cultural exchange. Anglo-Saxon scholars flocked to Ireland, Irish scholars debated with an African-born abbot and a Syrian-educated archbishop at Canterbury, and a shipwrecked Frankish bishop edified the monks of Iona with tales of his travels in the Holy Lands. This period likewise saw the growth of what became the dominant form of religious life in the Atlantic Archipelago: monasticism. For all the notions of monasteries as retreats from the world and the prominent anti-intellectual strain of early monasticism, monasteries in Britain and Ireland became centers of innovation in material and cultural production and integral parts of networks of international trade and exchange.

This chapter is concerned with two aspects of this material and cultural production: the cultivation of Latin learning and the visual arts in a Christian context. The former was essential for the performance of the liturgy and the sacraments; and the understanding and interpretation of the Bible, exegesis, was the ultimate goal of Christian learning. The latter, despite Old Testament injunctions against graven images and the antipathy of early Christian communities, likewise became central to Christian worship. At a basic level, the visual impact of art underlined the value of Christianity to societies in which status was advertised and affirmed through the conspicuous display of wealth. Art could also be used to outline Biblical events, to explain tenets of the Christian faith, or to provide moral or spiritual exemplars; the notion of pictures as books for the unlearned was widespread in the Middle Ages. Nor was this instructional element restricted only to the unlearned. Bede, for example, used illustrations from late antique manuscripts as guides to the interpretation of complex scriptural passages.[1]

There was more to art, however, than straightforward didacticism, particularly in the clerical and monastic setting where most of what is discussed in this chapter was produced and consumed. Christian writers on asceticism had inherited from the classical past the idea of the mind as being in constant movement. For the fifth-century writer Cassian, the mind was like a mill wheel: while the waters are flowing, it is impossible to stop the wheels from turning, just as it is impossible to stop the mind from wandering, but it is up to the miller to decide whether to grind wheat or weeds. What was required of the Christian was the constant occupation of the mind, the constant reading and meditation on Holy Scripture and other sacred writings, the grain of choice. This meditation was not, however, about clearing the mind or simply understanding the text that was being read. The text was used as a trigger for a series of associations and ideas, the starting-point for a mental journey.

Such processes were not confined to texts. Images and decoration could act as the starting-point for this process of creative and inventive recollection. Vine-scroll ornamentation could bring to mind a series of ideas about, for example, Christ as the true vine, the relationship between Him and the members of the church, or the eucharistic sacrifice. This decoration was not symbolic, in the sense that it stood for one particular thing, so much as an entry point or route through a particular way of thinking. In the same way, although pictures could have an illustrative function, they were polysemic and multi-layered and subject to the same meditative readings as texts. Christian art in the early Middle Ages was much like St. Augustine's description of the Bible: "lowly for the beginner but, on further reading, of mountainous difficulty and enveloped in mysteries."[2]

A chapter of this length can only hint at the riches of the learning and artworks produced in Britain and Ireland in this period. The aim is to offer a sample of the material and suggest ways in which it has been approached and understood by scholars. It begins with a discussion of Latin learning and education in the Atlantic Archipelago, with the evidence forcing a predominantly Irish and Anglo-Saxon focus. It then moves on to explore the influences and impulses operating on insular Christian art in this period, using the richly decorated gospel-books produced in Britain and Ireland as the key examples.

Education and Learning

"And this? Aldhelm of Malmesbury. Listen to this page: 'Primitus pantorum procerum poematorum pio potissimum paternoque presertim privilegio panegiricum poemataque passim prosatori sub polo promulgates . . .' . . . The words all begin with the same letter!"

"The men of my islands are all a bit mad," William said proudly.[3]

Such was the reaction of Adso, narrator of the medieval murder mystery *The Name of the Rose*, when confronted with Aldhelm's letter to the otherwise unknown Heahfrith. It was a steep learning curve for Adso: he had just been read a poem from the *Hisperica famina* and had not understood a word. Adso's surprise and confusion and his mentor William's pride in the eccentricity of it all are both common responses to the distinctive styles of Latin that developed in the Atlantic Archipelago over the course of the early Middle Ages. Writers such as the West-Saxon Aldhelm (c.640–709) and the anonymous seventh-century Hiberno-Latin "Faminators," as they have been named, have been frequently criticized for the obscure language they employed and their work has often been dismissed as childish and self-indulgent. Yet, however one judges such works, they are based upon considerable learning, and the texts produced in Britain and Ireland in this period would be widely copied and studied throughout the Middle Ages. Indeed, in many ways, the Atlantic Archipelago was the intellectual powerhouse of western Europe at this date.

Such attainments are all the more remarkable given that insular scholars had to learn Latin from scratch in the classroom or monastic cell. The works that had served the schoolrooms of the Roman world presumed the students, as native speakers, already had knowledge of the basics of the language and these works also made frequent reference to pagan writers and subject matters whose place in the Christian classroom was often disputed. It is not surprising, then, that some of the earliest surviving works of Irish or Anglo-Saxon scholarship are the basic textbooks that would aid the teaching of the rudiments of Latin. For example, the late sixth- or early seventh-century grammatical treatise the *Ars Asporii* presented a detailed, though by no means systematic, discussion of the basics of Latin grammar, expanding the *Ars minor* of the fourth-century Roman grammarian Donatus and supplying Christian examples instead of pagan ones.[4] The precise origins of this work have been disputed but a case can be made for Ireland and it was certainly circulating there by the early seventh century at the latest.[5] Over the course of the seventh and eighth centuries, insular scholars, particularly Anglo-Saxons, were to develop more systematic grammars with a focus on Latin accidence.

Though many of the features of the writings of the seventh and eighth centuries have been seen as distinctively and idiosyncratically insular, some of their roots lie in the late- and sub-Roman periods and wider traditions of Latin writing. The writings of the Romano-Britain Pelagius (fl.390–418) demonstrate considerable skill and intelligence and are evidence of the continuing high standards of education even in the period of economic stagnation that presaged the ending of Roman Britain. Though condemned as heretical, his writings would continue to be popular amongst British and Irish writers throughout the early Middle Ages. A generation later, the writings of Faustus and Fastidius show that sub-Roman Britain was still able to produce highly educated and capable writers. Even by the end of the fifth century, Patrick, though his own education had been severely curtailed, could write of those "who have successfully imbibed both law and Holy Scripture alike and have never changed their language [presumably Latin] from infancy but rather have always been bringing it nearer to perfection."[6] Nor was Patrick's own Latin necessarily as unskilled as he made out or as later commentators have sometimes assumed.

The little information about learning in sub-Roman Britain that can be gleaned from Patrick can be supplemented by the evidence of Gildas, probably born within a generation of Patrick's death. Though later traditions would ascribe to Gildas a monastic upbringing, the evidence from his writings suggests that he was educated in something closely resembling the traditional Roman manner of the civic schools: basic instruction in reading and writing from a *magister*, before moving on to studies under a *grammaticus* where the education would be grounded in the classics of Latin literature and then, if the student was sufficiently capable (and Gildas was), to a *rhetor* where the skills of public speaking and forensic debate would be learnt.[7] There is also the possibility that Gildas spent time in a monastic environment. Certainly, he is cited by the Irishman Columbanus (mid-sixth century to 615) as an expert on monastic discipline, and his writings suggest support for, or affinity with, the nascent monastic movement in Britain. He stands, therefore, on a cusp between the secular education of the Roman past and the ecclesiastical, and principally monastic, education of the early Middle Ages.

Gildas's writing style is difficult to summarize; he employed, amongst other things, intricate word order, alliteration, rhyme, and word-play.[8] For a long time, scholars placed Gildas in a context that looked forward: his writing style was seen as the beginnings of a tradition that would lead to such works as the *Hisperica famina* and to such authors as Aldhelm or Adomnán of Iona. The prose style of Columbanus, for example, demonstrates a clear debt to Gildas, and, as Winterbottom has argued, "in Columbanus . . . we see the first step of a series of steps that were to develop the vocabulary of Gildas into the bizarrerie of the *Hisperica Famina*."[9] Despite such parallels, scholars have increasingly stressed Gildas's debt to wider late antique and classical traditions and moved him closer to the mainstream of continental writers.[10]

Some at least of Gildas's contemporaries received the same standard of education, and not only clerics. Gildas describes King Maelgwn of Gwynedd as having been taught by a *magister elegans*, presumably a *rhetor*.[11] Yet, after Gildas, there is almost complete silence from the British kingdoms, not helped by the near-total absence of manuscripts from those regions in this period. The Latin inscriptions, predominantly memorials to the dead, still produced in the northern and western parts of Britain in the sixth and seventh centuries show the continuation of some level of Latin literacy and in some cases more. A late seventh-century inscription from Llanllyr in Ceredigion, for example, has been interpreted as showing a familiarity with the *Etymologiae* of Isidore of Seville (d.636) and a preference for the same kind of obscure and showy vocabulary that characterizes the *Hisperica famina*.[12] Other sources of evidence for Wales include the prayer copied into the late eighth-or early ninth-century Mercian manuscript known as the *Royal Prayer Book* and attributed to a Welshman, Moucan. It is a complex, allegorical piece that looks to the deuterocanonical *Prayer of Manasseh* as well as contemporary continental penitential prayers, suggesting continuing contact with wider European developments, as well as between Welsh learning and English Mercia.[13] On the other hand, the few surviving ninth-century Welsh manuscripts have been interpreted as suggesting Welsh learning to have been conservative and archaic: the evidence is probably too fragmentary for any definitive judgment.[14]

Evidence from elsewhere in Britain, outside the Anglo-Saxon kingdoms, is equally, if not more, scanty. The scarcity of Pictish sources has already been noted in this volume and the testimony of neighboring peoples adds little to the picture. Bede described the eighth-century Pictish King Nechtan as making "assiduous study of ecclesiastical writings" when deciding to adopt the Roman reckoning of Easter, and

Ceolfrith's response to Nechtan's request for more detailed information has been described as "presupposing mature ecclesiastical literacy."[15] Such an interpretation is surely correct, but it is difficult to go much beyond this, though material culture may help round out the picture. The situation is much the same for the kingdoms of the south-west. Aldhelm's letter to Geraint of Dumnonia on the Easter question suggests that there were in Devon "wily student[s] of books and clever interpreter[s] of scripture" (though Aldhelm does not mean this to be complimentary) but, again, it is difficult to take this description much further.[16]

By contrast, in Ireland, the late sixth and seventh centuries marked the beginnings of a Golden Age of Latin scholarship, a period of intense intellectual activity and innovation. Part of the explanation for the flourishing of Latin learning in Ireland lies in the importation of new or previously unavailable works from the continent in the context of a thriving, if controversy-riven, Irish church. Books on grammar produced in Ireland in the seventh century show a familiarity with a range of grammars produced in the late antique period and, unlike the earlier *Ars Asporii*, these seventh-century grammars show little hostility toward secular or pagan subject matter.[17] The works of Isidore of Seville seem to have been particularly popular and influential in Ireland, and Isidore's encyclopedic *Etymologiae* was known and copied in Ireland within a decade or so of his death.[18] Spain was likewise the source of an important collection of computistical material that reached Ireland in the 630s and introduced a new scientific sophistication into Irish studies of the computus, the methodology used to calculate the date of Easter.[19] Alongside this, however, must be set the various controversies that beset the Irish church in the seventh century (most famously, though not exclusively, the Paschal Controversy). Proponents and apologists for the different factions sought to buttress their positions through intense scholarly activity and intellectual endeavor. As Ó Corráin notes, "because of their [the controversies] intensity and because of the sheer energy and research devoted to their solution, they forced churchmen to give deep thought to themselves and their institutions . . . It led directly to a rapid – one might say urgent – cultivation of higher learning."[20]

Alongside the considerable achievements in computistics must be placed the extensive exegetical output. Whilst some Irish exegetes are known by name, such as Laidcend (d.661), author of an epitome of Gregory the Great's monumental *Moralia in Iob* and part of an erudite and productive scholarly circle based in the southern midlands of Ireland,[21] much of the material survives only in anonymous or pseudonymous later copies. Sometimes, Irish origins can be posited in part because of punning or concealed references to Irish people or places in the text. For the most part, however, scholars have relied on Irish symptoms, clusters of particular features and sources not in themselves unique to Irish texts but diagnostic when occurring together or in high frequency, to identify such works.[22] The seventh century also witnessed significant developments in Latin poetry in Ireland. In particular, the Irish pioneered a rhythmic octosyllabic verse form, which included frequent alliteration and rhyming and probably owed much to vernacular traditions.[23]

Amongst the most (in)famous of the material from an Irish cultural milieu is the set of related texts known as the *Hisperica famina*, probably the work of foreign scholars, perhaps Anglo-Saxons, living and studying in Ireland in the seventh century. The only complete version begins with a verbal battle between two speakers, then follows a description of the daily routine of a group of scholars, before it ends with a series of brief descriptions of natural phenomena and everyday objects. Although the texts have relatively simple syntax, they employ obscure vocabulary, using Greek-derived words, Semitic-Latin hybrids, and frequent synonyms (ensuring always to avoid the simplest word).[24] The probable influence of Columbanus and Gildas on the Faminators has already been noted, but the *Hisperica famina* are also further evidence of the influence of the writings of Isidore in Ireland, his *Etymologiae* supplying some of the vocabulary and his *Synonyma* likewise providing vocabulary and suggesting something of the style that the Faminators adopted.[25] The purpose of the *Hisperica famina* remains a matter of some dispute, though they seem to be a parody of the schoolroom colloquies that were the basis of much elementary education, employing complex and self-consciously erudite vocabulary in place of the simple language of the colloquies.

Whatever their sources and however they are interpreted, the *Hisperica famina* are witness to the considerable appeal of Ireland as a place of study and the delight taken in the opportunities offered by Latin learning. Likewise, Bede provides numerous examples of Anglo-Saxons traveling to Ireland to study in the seventh century, describing how the Irish "gave them their daily food, and also provided them with books to read and with instruction, without asking for any payment."[26] Yet, if the scholarly attractions of Ireland were to persist over the seventh and eighth centuries, Anglo-Saxon England was nevertheless developing its own learned culture that would (sometimes self-consciously) rival that of Ireland. Aldhelm's letter, cited earlier, was designed to demonstrate to Heahfrith, recently returned from studying in Ireland, the superiority of learning in England, and the complex style and recherché vocabulary Aldhelm adopted in the letter read like a conscious attempt to "out-Irish" the Irish.[27]

As Aldhelm's letter made clear, learning and biblical studies in Anglo-Saxon England were transformed by the arrival from Rome (but ultimately from Tarsus and North Africa respectively) of Theodore and Hadrian in 669–70 and their foundation of a school at Canterbury. Theodore was the new papal-appointed archbishop, and Hadrian, sent as his companion, would become the abbot of the monastery of St. Peter and St. Paul. They both spoke Greek and Latin, and Bede notes that even in his day there survived students from the school who knew these two languages like their native tongues. The curriculum of the school included such topics as Roman law, metrics, computistics, and astronomy, and it was attended by students from as far afield as Ireland.[28]

For a long time, little material was thought to survive from the school of Canterbury, but over the past few decades a significant corpus of work has been identified, including biblical commentaries and translations and adaptations of Greek works.[29] The biblical commentaries in particular give some indication of the enthusiasm and wonder that Theodore and Hadrian must have inspired in their students. Not only could they offer personal insight into places mentioned in the Bible and other Christian writings and explain the complexities of, for example, Hebrew weights and measures and the flora of the Holy Lands, they could draw on a familiarity with Patristic literature, principally Greek, that must have been unparalleled in western Europe.[30]

The influence of the school at Canterbury is seen most clearly in the writings of Aldhelm of Malmesbury. His early education was at the hands of an Irishman, perhaps the Maíldub who gave his name to Malmesbury, but it is evident from Aldhelm's own writings that it was the brief periods of time that he spent at Canterbury that transformed his writings. His distinctive prose style with its obscure and outré vocabulary and long, intricate sentences has certain affinities with Gildas, but Aldhelm was probably inspired by the same late antique continental models that influenced the Briton rather than depending directly on Gildas himself.[31] Aldhelm's prose style was not only to inspire his own students, but was also to prove influential to Latin authors across the whole of the Anglo-Saxon period, particularly practitioners of the "hermeneutic" style (i.e. "glossary-derived," a reference to the obscure vocabulary employed) in the tenth century and later. Equally influential on later writers was Aldhelm's poetry. Aldhelm had mastered whilst at Canterbury quantitative Latin verse (i.e. based on the length of syllables), a considerable achievement for a non-native Latin speaker, and his metrical techniques were imitated, almost slavishly, by later Anglo-Saxon writers such as the missionary Boniface (d.754). Aldhelm also developed his own rhythmic octosyllabic verse form, perhaps influenced by Irish models, which was to be imitated and extended by his pupil Æthilwald.[32]

Around the time that the school at Canterbury was transforming learning in the south, a similarly fruitful period was beginning in Northumbria. The most famous product of this period was Bede (c.672–735), but the considerable hagiographical output from the time, such as Stephen's *Vita Wilfridi* (c.710–20) or the anonymous *Vita Gregorii* (c.700), shows that he was not an isolated figure but part of a wider scholarly renaissance. Although it is Bede's historical and hagiographical works that have attracted most scholarly attention, they formed only a fraction of his output, which ranged across grammar, cosmography, exegesis, computistics, poetry, and metrics. Bede saw his own role as that of teacher and educator, and it was this peda-gogic focus that drove his scholarship. His grammatical treatises were designed for the monastic classroom and, despite consisting predominantly of extracts from earlier writers, they show an intelligent and creative mind at work, carefully selecting and shaping the source material.[33] Bede's longer work on chronology and the computus, *De Temporum ratione*, was also produced in response to the needs of his students who had apparently found his earlier, shorter work, *De Temporibus*, too compressed. The majority of Bede's scholarly output was, however, commentaries on various books of the Bible. Some, such as his commentary on the Canticle of Habbakuk, were clearly aimed at the beginner, whilst others, including groundbreaking work on the books of Ezra and Nehemiah, presupposed a more learned audience.

Bede was able to benefit from the considerable library established by the abbots of Wearmouth-Jarrow, in particular its founder, Benedict Biscop, whose numerous book-buying trips to the continent were chronicled by Bede in his *Historia abbatum*. Bede was not unaware of the scholarly advantages this provided, and a number of his biblical commentaries were specifically designed not just to explore and explain the Bible but to make available a range of opinions from the writings of earlier authors that might be unavailable to less wealthy and less well-provided institutions. Outside Wearmouth-Jarrow, Bede's influence was felt particularly on the school at York, probably founded by Bishop Ecgberht, a pupil and correspondent of Bede, and York's most famous alumnus, Alcuin (740–804), was by his own admission indebted to Bede's scholarship.[34]

The work of scholars over the past generation has placed Latin learning within the Atlantic Archipelago firmly within wider developments transforming the Roman world – and, in some respects, has placed them at the forefront of such developments. Although it was distinctive and drew on local traditions and, perhaps, vernacular culture, insular Latin learning was in no way "insular" and instead seemed to delight in the opportunities offered by the shared culture of the Christian world. This matrix can be seen also in the greatest works of visual art produced in this period, the decorated gospel-books, and it is to those that this chapter will now turn.

The Decorated Gospel-books and Insular Christian Art

You will make out intricacies, so delicate and so subtle, so full of knots and links, with colours so fresh and vivid, that you might say that all this was the work of an angel, and not of a man.[35]

Writing in the twelfth century, Gerald of Wales provided one of the best-known descriptions of the richly decorated gospel-books produced by insular artists and scribes in the early Middle Ages. The intricately decorated initials that open the gospels; the display scripts marking lections and chapter divisions; the full pages of patterns, decorations, and, sometimes, crosses known as "carpet pages"; the borders and infill formed of plain and zoomorphic interlace; the evangelist portraits and other illustrations – all raise the text to the status of icon whilst at the same time threatening to overwhelm the words themselves. The gospel-books emphasize the value placed on the written word, the Bible in particular, in insular society and the wealth and resources of the institutions that produced them. The *Lindisfarne Gospels* (c.710–20), for example, would have required the skins of over a hundred cattle and taken their illustrator-scribe at least two years to complete and would have been only one of many books produced on Lindisfarne at that time. The gospel-books are also amongst the most eloquent witnesses to the flowering of artistic culture promoted by the spread of Christianity through the Atlantic Archipelago and draw on decorative schemes and motifs first developed in metalworking, stone-carving and other media. They demonstrate the coming together of Celtic, Germanic, and Mediterranean traditions to produce a distinctively insular art form.

The gospel-books are also further testimony to the considerable artistic and technological skills cultivated in monasteries and religious institutions. Archaeological excavations have revealed evidence for a range of craft activities such as metalworking, glassmaking, and weaving taking place at religious sites, and written sources such as Æthelwulf's *De Abbatibus*, a ninth-century poem about a dependent house of Lindisfarne, highlight the skill and prestige of such craftsmen.[36] Liturgical vessels, such as the intricately decorated silver paten found at Derrynaflan, Tipperary, or book-bindings, such as the bejeweled gold and silver cover made for the *Lindisfarne Gospels*, or the more simple tooled-leather binding of the gospel of John buried with Cuthbert, were obvious vehicles for such skills, but there were other sometimes less edifying ones. Bede records how the nuns of Coldingham spent their time "weaving elaborate garments with which to adorn themselves as if they were brides" and the gold threads found during excavations of the nunnery at Barking may be evidence of just such activities.[37] On the other hand, a poem by Cuthbert, the eighth-century bishop of Hereford, describes how he completed a number of cross-cloths made with gold and silver thread begun by his predecessor and equally rich tapestries and vestments are recorded elsewhere, so perhaps the nuns of Barking should not be so quickly condemned.[38]

Though reflecting local tastes, traditions, and needs, the gospel-books belong, like education and learning, firmly within wider European developments, and many aspects of their decoration can be traced back to earlier Christian examples. The carpet pages that often stand at the start of the gospels and other key passages might be traced back to decorations in Coptic manuscripts such as the ankh-cross surrounded by birds and foliate decoration in the fifth-century *Glazier Codex*. A more recent suggestion is that the carpet pages may have been inspired by the carpets or prayer mats known to have been used in the Roman liturgy.[39] Other features, such as the use of decorated initials and display letters to mark sections of text, likewise derive from earlier late antique and early medieval developments. Yet, wherever such ideas ultimately came from, the insular artists and scribes made them their own and expanded them considerably with a decorative repertoire derived from their pre-existing artistic traditions. The simple carpet page of the *Glazier Codex* becomes transformed into the labyrinthine pages of the gospel-books, with interlace, interlocking spirals, and step- and fret-patterns. Similarly, the enlarged letters of late antique manuscripts become near-full page initials, with forms so contorted by decoration and stylization that some have doubted whether they were ever intended to be legible.

Individual works make clear the complex range of influences operating on these insular styles. The earliest of the decorated gospel-books to survive nearly intact is the *Book of Durrow*; almost everything about it has been the subject of considerable debate and the location and date of its production still remain uncertain, though most commentators favor a house of the Columban federation (perhaps Iona itself) and a date in the late seventh century. *Durrow* represents a stage in the continuing process of the fusing of the intricate trumpet spirals, triskeles (a device comprising three interlocked spirals), and peltae (a semi-circular shield-shaped device) of the Celtic La Tène style with the interlace and step-patterns found throughout the Mediterranean world and the zoomorphic interlace associated particularly with Germanic metalwork. This so-called "Hiberno-Saxon" style was first essayed on high-status metalwork, such as the bird-headed brooches produced at the Dalriadan center of Dunadd, Argyll in the seventh century, and later translated to manuscripts where it would, arguably, reach its creative zenith.[40]

A number of specific parallels or inspirations for the decorative schemes of *Durrow* have also been suggested. The richly furnished burials at Sutton Hoo, Suffolk have often been invoked. The shoulder clasps where cells of cloisonné garnet and millefiori glass are surrounded by borders of gold and garnet animal interlace, for example, have been seen to resemble the layout of some of the *Durrow* carpet pages, and the double-armed cross carpet page that opens the manuscript is inset with checkerboard squares that appear to imitate millefiori.[41] Though the apparent parallels between *Durrow* and Sutton Hoo have long been noted, similar decorative features can be found on metalwork from an Irish context, such as the glass studs mimicking cloisonné enamel on the paten from the Derrynaflan hoard or the checkerboard and step-patterns of the Moylough belt shrine, suggesting that inspiration for the *Durrow* artist need not have come only (or at all) from Anglo-Saxon craftsmanship.[42]

Perhaps the most interesting debt in *Durrow* is to stone-carving, seen clearly in a number of the evangelist symbol-portraits that precede each of the gospels. The calf symbol of Luke closely resembles the more naturalistic forms of animal carvings on Pictish stones; the arrangement and shape of legs, for example, is very similar to that of the boar on the stone at Clune Farm, Dores, and a number of the Burghead bulls. The lion symbol similarly resembles Pictish carvings such as the Ardross wolf and the Dore boar, particularly in the use of scrollwork to pick out the limbs and torso. Given the elusiveness of the Picts and their culture, these inspirations are of considerable significance and place the Picts firmly within the framework of the development of insular art in this period.

Borrowing may also have worked in the opposite direction. Cross-marked stones, sometimes featuring inscriptions, are found throughout the Atlantic Archipelago in this period. Indeed, their very ubiquity and relative simplicity makes saying anything definitive about their dating, origin, or purpose difficult.[43] Numerous types of crosses were employed on these stones and a number of them closely resemble those on the carpet pages of the decorated gospel-books. Some, such as a number of the stones from Hartlepool or Clonmacnoise, enclose the cross within a plain or decorated rectangular border further enhancing the impression of a simplified carpet page in stone.

The most closely contextualized of the gospel-books are the *Lindisfarne Gospels*, written and illustrated, according to their tenth-century colophon (i.e., the note added at the end of the manuscript), by Eadfrith, bishop of Lindisfarne from 698 to 721, in honor of Cuthbert. This is likely to have been carried out as part of wider initiatives surrounding the promotion of the cult of Cuthbert, including commissioning of hagiography and the translation of physical remains, beginning at the end of the seventh century and continuing into the first few decades of the eighth. The creation of the *Gospels* was also an act of personal devotion on the part of their illustrator-scribe and, given the physical exertion involved ("three fingers hold the pen but the whole body labors" was a common complaint of scribes), the preparation of the *Gospels* was likewise an act of bodily endurance and solitary worship and contemplation that might have rivaled the asceticism of Cuthbert.[44]

Like the *Book of Durrow*, the *Lindisfarne Gospels* employ a range of decorative devices and the spirals, triskeles, interlace, and step and fret patterns of *Durrow* can all be paralleled in the *Gospels*. The *Lindisfarne Gospels* did, however, introduce a range of significant innovations. The palette of the *Gospels* is more extensive than that used in earlier decorated gospels, where yellow, green, and red pigments predominate, perhaps reflecting the influence of Mediterranean manuscripts on the *Lindisfarne Gospels*, and other experimental techniques such as lead-point underdrawings were also employed by the artist.[45] The types of decoration and illustration were likewise innovative. The evangelist portraits present them as human scribes accompanied by their respective symbols, the first time such a scheme was employed in an insular gospel-book and, again, probably reflecting the influence of late antique Mediterranean manuscripts.[46] Additionally, zoomorphic interlace, used only infrequently in earlier gospel-books, dominates the decoration of the *Lindisfarne Gospels*. The zoomorphic interlace of the *Gospels*, moreover, is formed of recognizable animals, in particular long-necked and long-beaked swan- or goose-like birds, while earlier interlace tends to consist of apparently non-specific quadrupeds. Such experimentation was perhaps facilitated by existing expertise in the Lindisfarne scriptorium; the late seventh-century *Durham* and *Echternach Gospels* may both have been produced on Lindisfarne.[47]

The influence of the *Lindisfarne Gospels* can be seen on a number of later gospel-books. The *Lichfield Gospels*, whose provenance is unknown but which were at Llandeilo Fawr in Carmarthenshire by the early ninth century, contain similar zoomorphic interlace on their only surviving carpet page and it is possible that the artist had seen the *Lindisfarne Gospels* at first hand.[48] The decoration of the *Lindisfarne Gospels* is also mirrored by a number of pieces of Irish metalwork, notably the Tara brooch where interlaced animals and triskeles with zoomorphic terminals reminiscent of the *Gospels* decorate the back. These stylistic similarities have led to the coining of the term Tara-Lindisfarne style to describe such decoration, though, as Ryan has argued, direct influence of the *Gospels* on the brooch or vice versa is unlikely and both instead "represent autonomous expressions of a common tradition."[49]

As already suggested, some of the innovations of the *Lindisfarne Gospels* show the renewed influence of late antique and Mediterranean traditions on insular art. The conduit for these ideas is likely to have been a number of monastic centers in Northumbria, particularly those associated with Wilfrid and Benedict Biscop, which sought to emphasize their especial ties and allegiance with Rome and the Mediterranean world. These Romanizing ideals found their expression in material culture, both the importation of manuscripts and artworks and the creation of new works emulating Roman and Mediterranean models. Wilfrid, for example, commissioned a gospel-book, no longer extant, written in gold ink on purpled pages, a design that imitated Italian and Byzantine manuscripts. Likewise, the single-volume Bible now known as the *Codex Amiatinus*, produced at Wearmouth-Jarrow in the early eighth century, shows such a debt to late antique Italian exemplars, both in terms of the script employed and the decorative techniques and illustrations, that it was only in the nineteenth century that its Anglo-Saxon provenance was recognized. Architecture could also serve as an expression of *Romanitas*. When constructing Wearmouth, Benedict employed Frankish masons "to build him a stone church in the Roman style he had always loved so much" and, whilst his biographer does not explicitly connect building in stone with his Romanizing agenda, Wilfrid's churches were similarly constructed and Hexham was said to have been without parallel north of the Alps.[50]

Yet no simple antithesis should be made between insular and Romanizing centers. The ties between Wearmouth-Jarrow and Lindisfarne, for example, are well known and were extensive. The *Lindisfarne Gospels* drew on a textual source that contributed to *Codex Amiatinus* and the portrait of Matthew in the *Gospels* derives in parts either from the portrait of Ezra in the *Codex* or the original model for it. Nor, as recent research has shown, was the *Codex* necessarily a slavish imitation of its exemplars.[51] The *Gospels* and the *Codex* both represent vigorous and self-assured responses to a wider Christian world, celebrating the synthesis of cultural forms and religious traditions that characterized the Christianity of Britain and Ireland. Particular centers might foreground specific aspects of their cultural inheritance in some artworks, but this should not suggest a lack of openness to stylistic diversity and variety.

What the Romanizing centers of Northumbria did introduce were new techniques and decorative schemes that could be added to the melting pot of insular art. One such technique was relief carving in stone, used initially on architectural sculpture before being employed on free-standing monuments. Although introduced by foreign masons, relief carving was soon used to produce sculpture indebted to existing insular designs. A fragment of a wall panel from Jarrow features borders of simple and zoomorphic interlace reminiscent of the decorated gospel-books, whilst the porch at Wearmouth features a simplified zoomorphic interlace of two intertwined serpents.[52] The Romanizing monasteries are also likely centers for the introduction of vine-scroll ornament into Anglo-Saxon England, probably drawing inspiration ultimately from Mediterranean and Near Eastern models.

These techniques and designs came together in a new monument type: the free-standing, relief-carved cross, of which the earliest Anglo-Saxon examples date from the first half of the eighth century. The most famous of these is that at Ruthwell on the Solway Firth, perhaps dating from 740–60. It features an ambitious iconographic and decorative program with panels of figural sculpture and vine-scroll with Latin and runic tituli. The cross signals the triumph of recent developments in the Roman liturgy and the centrality of Christ's sacrifice. The sculptural program also alludes to distinctive features of the liturgy on Iona, a reminder and celebration of the twin sources of Northumbrian Christianity. Designed primarily for a monastic audience and reflecting the concerns and patterns of their lives, the cross nevertheless had relevance to the wider Christian community and stresses the universal participation of the faithful in the sacraments of the church.[53]

The influence of the Romanizing monasteries of Northumbria was also felt further north. Nechtan of the Picts requested masons from Wearmouth-Jarrow to construct him a stone church as the physical symbol of his rapprochement with Roman Christianity. These Northumbrian masons may also have introduced a new artistic form into Pictland: the relief-carved cross-slab. Such monuments first appeared in Northumbria in the late seventh and early eighth centuries, perhaps evolving from the simpler cross-marked stones and slabs.[54] The Pictish relief cross-slabs were more highly decorated than these Northumbrian examples, often with borders of interlace and geometric patterns and sometimes Latin inscriptions alongside the more familiar Pictish symbols. As numerous scholars have noted, they resemble nothing so much as folios in stone, with their layout, ornamentation, and even script clearly indebted to the decorated gospel-books.[55] Recent work has, however, challenged the exclusive link to the Wearmouth-Jarrow delegation and placed the Pictish cross-slabs in the context of longer-term cultural contacts between Pictland, Iona, and Northumbria.[56]

Conclusion

Great works continued to be produced over the course of the next century. The *Book of Kells*, the most ambitious of the decorated gospel-books, was produced, probably on Iona, in the late eighth or early ninth century and its complex and polysemous illustrations are only beginning to be unraveled by scholars. Likewise, in southern England, a new style of illuminated manuscript developed, the Tiberius group, more Romanizing in its appearance than the Northumbrian manuscripts but nevertheless featuring the spirals and interlace of the decorated gospel-books, another variation on the synthesizing theme of insular art. New sculptural styles similarly emerged. The Anglian school of sculpture, associated particularly with Mercia, fused the vegetal and figural elements of late antique carvings with interlace, geometric patterns, and other components from existing insular traditions. Pictish craftsmen in the late eighth century fused similar elements to produce the St. Andrews Sarcophagus, possibly the single most accomplished sculpture produced in Britain and Ireland in the early Middle Ages. Great minds, such as Alcuin or the Irishman Johannes Scotus Eriugena, likewise continued to be produced. Yet the particular religious cultures and institutions that fostered the flowering of learning and artistic culture in Britain and Ireland did not survive long into the ninth century. Francia and the Carolingian court instead became the intellectual and cultural center of Christian Europe. Such pre-eminence, however, was attained by building on the achievements of scholars such as Bede and Aldhelm and the countless anonymous insulars artists and craftsmen whose works had become one more part of the shared culture of Latin Christianity.

Notes

1 Henderson, *Bede and the Visual Arts*, p. 7.
2 Chadwick (trans.), *Saint Augustine: Confessions*, p. 40.
3 Eco, *Name of the Rose*, p. 311.
4 Law, *Grammar and Grammarians*, pp. 75–6.
5 Ó Cróinín, *Early Medieval Ireland*, pp. 175–6.
6 Hood (ed.), *St. Patrick*, p. 42.
7 Lapidge, "Gildas's education," pp. 40–7.
8 Wright, "Gildas's prose style," p. 115.
9 Winterbottom, "Columbanus and Gildas," 316.
10 Kerlouégan, *De Excidio*, pp. 471–2.
11 Winterbottom (ed.), *Gildas: The Ruin of Britain*, p. 104
12 Handley, "The origins of Christian commemoration," 196, n.146.
13 Sims-Williams, *Religion and Literature*, pp. 320–2.
14 Lapidge, "Latin learning."
15 Colgrave and Mynors (eds.), *Bede's Ecclesiastical History*, p. 533; Forsyth, "Literacy in Pictland," p. 42.
16 Lapidge and Herren (trans.), *Aldhelm: The Prose Works*, p. 159.
17 Ó Cróinín, *Early Medieval Ireland*, pp. 184–6.
18 Hillgarth, "Ireland and Spain," 7–10.
19 Ó Cróinín, "Irish provenance," 230–1.
20 Ó Corráin, "The historical and cultural background of the Book of Kells," p. 17.
21 Ó Cróinín, "Hiberno-Latin literature," pp. 378–9.
22 Ó Cróinín, "Bischoff's Wendepunkte."
23 Orchard, *Poetic Art of Aldhelm*, pp. 29–60.
24 Herren, *Hisperica famina*, pp. 44–9.
25 Ibid., pp. 17–22.
26 Colgrave and Mynors (eds.), *Bede's Ecclesiastical History*, p. 313.

27 Lapidge and Herren (trans.), *Aldhelm: The Prose Works*, pp. 145–6.
28 Herren, "Scholarly contacts," 30–5.
29 Lapidge and Bischoff, *Biblical Commentaries*, pp. 1–3.
30 Ibid., pp. 190–266.
31 Winterbottom, "Aldhelm's prose style."
32 Orchard, *Poetic Art of Aldhelm.*
33 Franklin, "The date of composition."
34 Allott, *Alcuin of York*, p. 40.
35 Henderson, *From Durrow to Kells*, p. 195.
36 Dodwell, *Anglo-Saxon Art*, pp. 50–1; Hinton, *Gold and Gilt*, pp. 47–9.
37 Colgrave and Mynors (eds.), *Bede's Ecclesiastical History*, p. 427; Webster and Backhouse, *Making of England*, pp. 88–9.
38 Sims-Williams, *Religion and Literature*, p. 340.
39 Brown, *Lindisfarne Gospels*, p. 319.
40 Campbell and Lane, "Celtic and Germanic interaction."
41 Backhouse, *Lindisfarne Gospels*, pp. 74–5; Henderson, *From Durrow to Kells*, p. 132.
42 Netzer, "The *Book of Durrow*," pp. 322–5; Ryan, "The Derrynaflan hoard," 1000.
43 Henderson and Henderson, *Art of the Picts*, pp. 159–61.
44 Brown, *Lindisfarne Gospels*, pp. 396–8.
45 Ibid., pp. 216–20, 275–91.
46 Ibid., pp. 349–53; Henderson, *From Durrow to Kells*, pp. 119–20.
47 Brown, *Palaeographer's View*, p. 105; though see Netzer, "Willibrord's scriptorium."
48 Backhouse, *Lindisfarne Gospels*, p. 66.
49 Ryan, "Some aspects of sequence and style," p. 66.
50 Colgrave (ed.), *Life of Bishop Wilfrid*, p. 47; Webb (trans.), *Age of Bede*, p. 191.
51 Chazelle, "Ceolfrid's gift," 149–52.
52 Cramp, *Early Northumbrian Sculpture*, p. 3.
53 Ó Carragáin, *Ritual and the Rood.*
54 Cramp, *Corpus of Anglo-Saxon Stone Sculpture*, p. 7.
55 Carver, "An Iona of the east," 14–16.
56 Henderson and Henderson, *Art of the Picts*, p. 176.

Further Reading

Learning and education in the sub-Roman period can be usefully approached through the various essays in *Gildas: New Approaches*, edited by M. Lapidge and D. Dumville (Woodbridge, 1984) and what little survives from Wales is surveyed by Lapidge, "Latin learning in Dark Age Wales." For Latin learning in Ireland, Ó Cróinín's *Early Medieval Ireland* and "Hiberno-Latin literature" provide the best introductions. The Anglo-Saxon evidence is particularly well served, and the first essay in Lapidge, *Anglo-Latin Literature* offers the ideal introduction. Orchard, *The Poetic Art of Aldhelm*, is a technical but readable discussion, and for Bede the best guide remains Brown, *Bede the Venerable*. There is no single-volume guide that covers the whole spectrum of insular art in this period. Nees, *Early Medieval Art* sets insular art within its wider contexts; Alexander, *Insular Manuscripts*, provides descriptions of the decorated gospel-books and related manuscripts; whilst Henderson, *From Durrow to Kells* provides an illustrated discussion of the corpus. Brown, *Lindisfarne Gospels*, is an authoritative and detailed guide to both the *Gospels* themselves and their place in wider Christian traditions. There are also important articles on a range of subjects in *The Age of Migrating Ideas: Early Medieval Art in Northern Britain and Ireland*, edited by R. M. Spearman and J. Higgitt (Edinburgh, 1993), and *From the Isles of the North: Early Medieval Art in Ireland and Britain*, edited by C. Bourke (Belfast, 1995).

Bibliography

Alexander, J. G., *Insular Manuscripts, Sixth to Ninth Century* (London, 1978).

Allott, S., *Alcuin of York* (York, 1974).

Backhouse, J., *The Lindisfarne Gospels* (Oxford, 1981).

Brown, G. H., *Bede the Venerable* (Boston, MA, 1987).

Brown, J., *A Palaeographer's View* (London, 1993).

Brown, M., *The Lindisfarne Gospels: Society, Spirituality and the Scribe* (London, 2003).

Campbell, E. and Lane, A., "Celtic and Germanic interaction in Dalriada: the seventh-century metalworking site at Dunadd," in R. M. Spearman and J. Higgitt (eds.), *The Age of Migrating Ideas: Early Medieval Art in Northern Britain and Ireland* (Edinburgh, 1993), pp. 52–63.

Carver, M., "An Iona of the east: the early-medieval monastery at Portmahomack, Tarbat Ness," *Medieval Archaeology*, 48 (2004), 1–30.

Chadwick, H. (trans.), *Saint Augustine: Confessions* (Oxford, 1991).

Chazelle, C., "Ceolfrid's gift to St. Peter: the first quire of the *Codex Amiatinus* and the evidence for its Roman destination," *Early Medieval Europe*, 12 (2003), 129–58.

Colgrave, B. (ed. and trans.), *The Life of Bishop Wilfrid by Eddius Stephanus* (Cambridge, 1927; repr. New York, 1985).

Colgrave, B. and Mynors, R. A. B. (eds.), *Bede's Ecclesiastical History of the English People* (Oxford, 1969).

Cramp, R., *Corpus of Anglo-Saxon Stone Sculpture*, vol. 1: *County Durham and Northumberland* (Oxford, 1984).

Cramp, R., *Early Northumbrian Sculpture*, Jarrow Lecture 1965 (Jarrow, n.d.).

Dodwell, C. R., *Anglo-Saxon Art: A New Perspective* (Manchester, 1982).

Eco, U., *The Name of the Rose*, trans. W. Weaver (London, 1984).

Forsyth, K., "Literacy in Pictland," in H. Pryce (ed.), *Literacy in Medieval Celtic Societies* (Cambridge, 1998), pp. 39–61.

Franklin, C. V., "The date of composition of Bede's *De Schematibus et Tropis* and *De Arte Metrica*," *Revue Bénédictine*, 110 (2000), 199–203.

Handley, M. A., "The origins of Christian commemoration in late antique Britain," *Early Medieval Europe*, 10 (2001), 177–99.

Henderson, G., *Bede and Visual Arts*, Jarrow Lecture 1980 (Jarrow, n.d.).

Henderson, G., *From Durrow to Kells: The Insular Gospel-books 650–800* (London, 1987).

Henderson, G. and Henderson, I., *The Art of the Picts: Sculpture and Metalwork in Early Medieval Scotland* (London, 2004).

Herren, M., *Hisperica famina I: The A-Text* (Toronto, 1974).

Herren, M., "Scholarly contacts between the Irish and the southern English in the seventh century," *Peritia*, 12 (1998), 24–53.

Hillgarth, J. N., "Ireland and Spain in the seventh century," *Peritia*, 3 (1984), 1–16.

Hinton, D. A., *Gold and Gilt, Pots and Pins: Possessions and Peoples in Medieval Britain* (Oxford, 2005).

Hood, A. B. E. (ed. and trans.), *St. Patrick: His Writings and Muirchu's Life* (Chichester, 1978).

Kerlouégan, F., *Le De Excidio Britanniae de Gildas: les destinées de la culture latine dans L'Ile de Bretagne au vie siècle* (Paris, 1987).

Lapidge, M., *Anglo-Latin Literature 600–899* (London, 1996).

Lapidge, M., "Gildas's education and the Latin culture of sub-Roman Britain," in M. Lapidge and D. Dumville (eds.), *Gildas: New Approaches* (Woodbridge, 1984), pp. 27–50.

Lapidge, M., "Latin learning in Dark Age Wales: some prolegomena," in D. E. Evans et al. (eds.), *Proceedings of the Seventh International Congress of Celtic Studies* (Oxford, 1985), pp. 91–107.

Lapidge, M. and Bischoff, B., *Biblical Commentaries from the Canterbury School of Theodore and Hadrian* (Cambridge, 1994).

Lapidge, M. and Herren, M. (trans.), *Aldhelm: The Prose Works* (Cambridge, 1979).

Law, V., *Grammar and Grammarians in the Early Middle Ages* (London, 1997).

Nees, L., *Early Medieval Art* (Oxford, 2002).

Netzer, N., "The *Book of Durrow*: the Northumbrian connection," in J. Hawkes and S. Mills (eds.), *Northumbria's Golden Age* (Stroud, 1999), pp. 315–26.

Netzer, N., "Willibrord's scriptorium at Echternach and its relationship to Ireland and Lindisfarne," in G. Bonner et al. (eds.), *St. Cuthbert, his Cult, and his Community to AD 1200* (Woodbridge, 1989), pp. 203–12.

Ó Carragáin, E., *Ritual and the Rood: Liturgical Images and the Old English Poems of the Dream of the Rood Tradition* (London, 2005).

Ó Corráin, D., "The historical and cultural background of the Book of Kells," in F. O'Mahony (ed.), *The Book of Kells* (Dublin, 1994), pp. 1–31.

Ó Cróinín, D., "Bischoff's Wendepunkte fifty years on," *Revue Bénédictine*, 110 (2000), 204–37.

Ó Cróinín, D., *Early Medieval Ireland, 400–1200* (Harlow, 1995).

Ó Cróinín, D., "Hiberno-Latin literature to 1169," in D. Ó Cróinín (ed.), *A New History of Ireland 1: Prehistoric and Early Ireland* (Oxford, 2005), pp. 371–404.

Ó Cróinín, D., "The Irish provenance of Bede's computus," *Peritia*, 5 (1983), 229–47.

Orchard, A., *The Poetic Art of Aldhelm* (Cambridge, 1994).

Ryan, M., "The Derrynaflan hoard and early Irish art," *Speculum*, 72 (1997), 995–1017.

Ryan, M., "Some aspects of sequence and style in the metalwork of eighth- and ninth-century Ireland," in M. Ryan (ed.), *Ireland and Insular Art AD 500–1200* (Dublin, 1987), pp. 66–74.

Sims-Williams, P., *Religion and Literature in Western England: 600–800* (Cambridge, 1990).

Webb, J. F. (trans.), *The Age of Bede*, rev. edn. by D. H. Farmer (Harmondsworth, 1998).

Webster, L. and Backhouse, J., *The Making of England: Anglo-Saxon Art and Culture AD 600–900* (London, 1991).

Winterbottom, M., "Aldhelm's prose style and its origins," *Anglo-Saxon England*, 6 (1977), 39–76.

Winterbottom, M., "Columbanus and Gildas," *Vigiliae Christianae*, 30 (1976), 310–17.

Winterbottom, M. (ed. and trans.), *Gildas: The Ruin of Britain and Other Documents* (Chichester, 1978).

Wright, N., "Gildas's prose style and its origin," in M. Lapidge and D. Dumville (eds.), *Gildas: New Approaches* (Woodbridge, 1984), pp. 107–28.

PART III

Britain and Ireland in the Long Ninth Century, c.750–c.900

CHAPTER THIRTEEN

Viking Raids and Conquest

DAWN HADLEY

Viking raids on the coastal regions of Britain and Ireland are first recorded in the last decade of the eighth century, and in due course over-wintering of viking armies, conquest, and permanent settlement occurred. There have been numerous studies detailing the chronology of events, yet many aspects of the Scandinavian impact remain obscure or simply irrecoverable. In part, this is because the written record is uneven in its coverage, while toponymic and other linguistic evidence and archaeological data are rarely capable of producing the precise dating desirable for historical accounts of events. This chapter considers the viking raids and first phases of conquest in their broadest context, considering the impact that the raiders had as they moved between the regions that normally form the units of historical investigation. As recent studies have suggested, such a perspective is a means by which we can begin to fill in some of the gaps in the written record, allowing us to come closer to understanding the intentions of the raiders, and also to some extent correcting for the inevitable national historiographical obsessions that determine the regional accounts of viking activity.[1]

The use of the term "vikings" by historians is problematic, often conveying a sense of commonality of identity and interests that the written record refutes. Its etymology is obscure – it may derive from the name of the Oslo Fjord, the Viken, or may more generally have meant "men of the fjords" – but it clearly came to mean "pirates" or "raiders," although it was only one of a range of terms (including "heathens," "Danes," and "Northmen") used by contemporaries to describe the Scandinavian raiders who plagued parts of western Europe from the late eighth century.[2] This and the following chapter will use the term "viking" only when referring to a raiding group, and in other contexts the more general term "Scandinavians" will be used. The leaders of the various viking armies have scarcely been accorded political sophistication, yet this appears mistaken given the extent of the geographical regions across which several of their leaders can be shown to have operated, alongside evidence for their broad-ranging economic contacts and their swift adaptation to western European modes of kingship. This chapter considers the Scandinavian impact purely from its ninth-century perspective, in order to avoid the teleological dangers of

the long-term impact of Scandinavian conquest and settlement coloring our understanding of earlier events.

The Beginnings of Scandinavian Activity in Britain and Ireland

One of the most well-known, and oft-cited, entries in the *Anglo-Saxon Chronicle*
appears under the year 793, where it is recorded that "dire portents," including
whirlwinds, lightning, and the sight of fiery dragons in the air, preceded "the ravages
of heathen men" on the church at Lindisfarne, an island off the Northumbrian coast
(*EHD*, I, 181). This is widely regarded as the opening salvo in the viking raids on
Britain. This part of the *Chronicle* was, it should be noted, written in its surviving
form at least a century after the events it records, but the assault on the island community is corroborated in contemporary letters written by a Northumbrian scholar
at the Carolingian court, Alcuin, who wrote of the church of St. Cuthbert being
"spattered with the blood of the priests of God, despoiled of all its ornaments" (*EHD*,
I, 843). Chroniclers elsewhere also begin to record raids on the British coast in the
790s. For example, the *Annals of Ulster*, which survive in later medieval manuscripts
but which are thought to convey reliable information from the Viking Age, record
raids on *Rechru* (probably Rathlin Island, off the coast of Antrim), and possibly on
Skye (Inner Hebrides) in 795, both islands which were the locations of religious
communities, while *Inis Pátraic* (probably St. Patrick's island, off the coast of Dublin)
was raided in 798 and the shrine of St. Do-Chonna was broken into and tribute of
cattle taken.[3] The monastery on Iona (Inner Hebrides) was possibly raided in 794,
and certainly in 802, and it was subject to another attack in 806, when 68 of its
brethren were killed.[4]

Terrifying, and occasionally fatal, as these raids undoubtedly were, there is little
to suggest that any of these religious communities were completely destroyed, a
deduction supported by the repeated attacks on St. Columba's monastery at Iona.
Nonetheless, the foundation of a new monastery of St. Columba at Kells (Co.
Meath), which commenced in 807, was probably a response to the attacks on the
island community, and the resignation upon its completion in 814 of the abbot of
Iona, Cellach, has been interpreted as an indication that he retired to Kells.[5] It is
possible that at roughly this time the remains of St. Columba were transferred to
Dunkeld (Perthshire), which is where they were said to be in a list of saints' resting-
places probably initially created in the late ninth century.[6] Indeed, the insecurity felt
at Iona by the mid-ninth century may be reflected in a note in the *Annals of Ulster*
that in 865 the abbot of Iona died not on the island but "in the territory of the
Picts."[7] The apparent disruption to the network of ecclesiastical communities in
northern Britain in the later eighth and early ninth centuries was not necessarily
because of viking destruction, but the turbulent circumstances must have threatened
the support networks of many communities. It has also been argued that it may have
been more difficult to encourage into the monastic way of life members of the wealthy
families that had previously typically supported and staffed such communities. In
contrast, however, David Dumville has argued that it may have been precisely this
local support that enabled many religious communities to survive.[8] Indeed, for all
the difficulties faced at Iona, there is evidence for continuity of ecclesiastical life there,
if in attenuated form, in the continuing tradition of stone sculpture production.[9]

What was the context for these late eighth-century raids on religious communities? Alcuin indicates that the appearance of Scandinavians on Lindisfarne in 793 was entirely unexpected when he states that "never before has such terror appeared in Britain as we have now suffered from a pagan race, nor was it thought that such an inroad from the sea could be made" (*EHD*, I, 843). However, it is, perhaps, unlikely that this attack represents the first foray of the Scandinavians westward, and it has been argued recently that the intensity and geographical range of raids c.800 would be more readily explicable if the raiders already had bases in northern Britain.[10] The lack of corroborating written evidence is not fatal to such an argument, since northern Britain is generally beyond the scope of the surviving historical records. Given that the earliest raiders appear to have been principally from northern Scandinavia, it is entirely plausible that they should have focused their initial attentions on northern Britain, and, for what it is worth, the later medieval sagas record a tradition of the Scottish isles serving as bases for raiding.[11] It is unlikely that there was a dense or even permanent level of Scandinavian settlement in northern Britain in the eighth century, and the overwhelming impact of Scandinavians on language and toponymy, of the northern isles in particular, undoubtedly derives from a later date.[12] Nonetheless, there is a little archaeological evidence to support the argument for Scandinavian presence in the northern isles prior to the attack on Lindisfarne. Björn Myhre has, for example, highlighted the presence in Norwegian graves of a number of eighth-century artifacts from Britain, and has also argued that Scandinavian grave-goods in some burials in the northern isles may date to the eighth century, although the latter claim is widely disputed.[13] Nonetheless, radio-carbon dating of settlement sites and pollen analysis of agricultural activity in Iceland and the Faroes are beginning to add credence to the argument that the Scandinavians were on the move some time before the raid on Lindisfarne.[14] Indeed, in his correspondence with the king of Northumbria, Alcuin implies that the Scandinavians were not unfamiliar to the Northumbrians before 793: "Look at the hairstyle, how you have wished to imitate the pagans in your beards and hair. Does not the terror now threaten of those whose hairstyle you wished to have?"[15] While not as frequently cited as his aforementioned expression of shock at the attack, this suggestion of prior exposure to the Scandinavians appears increasingly significant in the wake of emerging archaeological evidence for Scandinavian movement across the North Sea in the eighth century.

Although direct evidence of Scandinavian activity in northern Britain in the eighth century is not extensive, it is, nevertheless, apparent that Scandinavia was not isolated from contemporary western European developments. In the eighth century, a series of trading centers, or *emporia*, emerged more or less simultaneously around the shores of the Baltic and the North Sea, creating a trading network that, it has been argued, introduced the Scandinavians to the riches of western markets, and which eventually spilled over into piracy.[16] Myhre has even argued that late eighth-century raids on religious communities were not simply intended to acquire the movable wealth housed there, but may have been ideologically driven by fear of Christianity and the political regimes with which it was associated, in particular Charlemagne's expansionist kingdom.[17] This bold hypothesis is not universally accepted and requires further investigation, for which archaeological evidence will be crucial, but the causes of the viking raids must certainly be sought within a broader European context.

Our evidence is insufficient to deduce that the various raids were initially part of a coordinated plan; this seems unlikely given the apparently fragmented nature of eighth-century political organization in Scandinavia.[18] Nonetheless, to ignore the broader context underestimates the Scandinavian capacity for strategic responses to changing circumstances, a trait that was, as we shall see, to pose a considerable threat to the political organization of many parts of Britain and Ireland in the ninth century. Equally, in seeking an earlier context for the raids at the turn of the ninth century, we must not underplay the shockwaves that they surely sent around western Europe.

The Intensification of Raiding

Irish sources provide the most detailed insight into viking activity in the early decades of the ninth century, and it seems reasonable to infer that Ireland was more frequently raided than England at this time. Whether the comparatively undocumented regions of northern Britain escaped so lightly is not, however, as certain, and may be deemed unlikely given the aforementioned probability of the northern isles serving as a point of departure for viking raids; the poorly documented northern parts of Northumbria may also have been vulnerable in this period. According to the *Annals of Ulster*, large numbers of women were taken captive following an attack on Howth (Co. Dublin) in 821, the monastery at Bangor (Co. Down) was raided in 823 and again in 824 when the oratory of St. Comgall was destroyed and the saint's relics were scattered, while in the same year the abbot of the monastic site of Sceilig Mhichíl (Co. Kerry) was kidnapped, subsequently dying of hunger and thirst (*AU*, pp. 277, 281). Events in northern Britain are less well documented, but the intensity of viking activity is suggested by the Irish monk Dicuil, writing in Francia c.825, who states that islands two days' sailing from the north of Britain, the Shetlands or possibly the Faroes, had by then been abandoned by the Irish hermit monks who occupied them in summer months "because of Norse pirates."[19] Furthermore, the *Annals of Ulster* record that in 825 a monk of Iona, Blathmac, was killed by a group of raiders in an event that came to widespread attention, being recorded within a decade or so in a panegyric by Walafrid Strabo, abbot of the monastery of Reichenau on Lake Constance (Germany).[20] Although the chronicles give an impression of "hit-and-run" raids on religious communities, it should be noted that they scarcely trouble themselves with secular communities, which may also have suffered at this time, and one is left wondering where the raiders went in between their documented attacks; the taking of hostages and cattle surely implies that they remained in the vicinity.

It has been suggested that in the 830s and 840s the raiders may have increasingly focused on Britain and Ireland, having met more organized resistance in Francia than hitherto.[21] Viking armies ravaged Sheppey (off the north-east coast of Kent) in 835, and appeared in the Bristol Channel the following year. In 840, there were assaults on *Hamwic* (Southampton, Hampshire) and Portland (Dorset), and raids on Lindsey, East Anglia, and Kent in the following year, while the Northumbrians were heavily defeated in 844 (*EHD*, I, 186–7). In 851, the *Anglo-Saxon Chronicle* implies that the intentions of the raiders had changed when it records that "for the first time, heathen men stayed through the winter on Thanet" (*EHD*, I, 188). Such a development made the prospect of incessant raiding more likely, rather than it merely being a seasonal threat. From the 830s, the raiders in Ireland began to make forays further inland, including raids on Derry, Clondalkin (near Dublin), and the monastery of Lismore (Co. Waterford) in 833, and Glendalough (Co. Wicklow) and Slane (Co. Meath) on the Boyne the following year (*AU*, pp. 289, 291). In 836, "they carried off many prisoners and killed many and took many captives" in Brega (Co. Meath), and there was "a most cruel devastation of all the lands of Connacht [western Ireland] by the pagans" (*AU*, p. 295). Northern Britain was apparently experiencing similar developments, since the *Annals of Ulster* record that in 839 the "pagans" defeated "the men of Fortriu" in the central part of the Pictish territory in eastern Scotland, and this may suggest that, despite the silence of the written record, by this time other parts of the mainland of Scotland had been raided, and perhaps occupied.[22]

In 840, a group of raiders over-wintered on Lough Neagh in the north of Ireland, and in 841 the *Annals of Ulster* record the establishment of naval bases (*longphoirt*) at Linn Dúachaill (identified as Annagassan, Co. Louth) and Dublin, while the presence of viking armies is noted over the following years at Lough Ree (on the River Shannon in the midlands of Ireland), Cork, Dunrally (Co. Laois), Youghal (Co. Cork), and Clondalkin (*AU*, pp. 299–305). These locations were used as bases from which to raid over wide areas, and Dáibhí Ó Cróinín has observed that this development "has all the appearance of a coordinated plan by the Vikings to establish permanent bases."[23] It is, thus, particularly unfortunate that we have, as yet, little archaeological evidence for the *longphoirt*. It is, nonetheless, suggestive that the locations of these viking bases were seemingly informed not only by the need for accessible harbors but also by the local political geography, as many are near the borders between kingdoms (see p. 200).[24] They are also notably clustered on the eastern side of Ireland, implying a role in securing Scandinavian Irish Sea interests.

These developments led to a contemporary perception that by the 840s Ireland had been swamped by the raiders. For example, the *Annals of St.-Bertin* record in the entry for 847 that "The Irish, who had been attacked by the Northmen for a number of years, were made into regular tribute-payers. The Northmen also got control of the islands all around Ireland, and stayed there without encountering any resistance from anyone."[25] The precise details of this statement are debatable, but it is certain that the Scandinavian impact on Britain and Ireland was transformed in the 830s and 840s from raids on vulnerable coastal locations to more intensive campaigns ever-further inland. Increasing numbers of hostages began to be taken at this time, which held out the promise of economic gain through subsequent sale or ransom. The raiders seem to have had a skill for attacking suitably strategic targets, such as royal estates and the churches housing the relics of prominent saints, and they often attacked on feast days and festivals, suggesting good local intelligence and an understanding of the traditions of their victims.[26] The written sources do not directly illuminate the intentions of the raiders, and the relations between raiding groups is uncertain, yet the intensity of activity and the establishment of bases at roughly the same time in various regions of Britain and Ireland suggest that, even if this development was not part of a single coordinated plan, conquest and colonization were now intended in those regions.

The raiders did not, however, go unopposed, and it is important to place the apparent Scandinavian ambitions in the context of native efforts to defeat them. In 845, the king of Tara, Niall Caille, routed raiders in Donegal, the king of Osraige,

Cerball mac Dúngaile, reputedly killed 1,200 following a raid on Agnonn in 847, and in the following year several major victories are recorded, including the slaying of 700 at Forach by the new king of Tara, Maél Sechnaill (*AU*, pp. 303, 307). This change of fortunes came to the attention of the annalists at St.-Bertin, who recorded that "the Irish attacked the Northmen, won a victory with the aid of our Lord Jesus Christ, and drove them out of their land."[27] Victories against raiding armies are recorded elsewhere: for example, in 851 a West Saxon army "inflicted the greatest slaughter that we ever heard of until this present day" on a viking army that had entered the Thames and put the Mercian army to flight (*EHD*, I, 188). Shortly afterwards, the Scandinavian involvement in Wales first enters the written record. In 852, the *Brut y Tywysogion*, surviving in later medieval manuscripts but evidently based on earlier chronicles, records that Cyngen of Powys was slain by pagans, and raids on Anglesey are noted three years later. From this time, the indigenous response seems to have been coordinated by the king of Gwynedd, Rhodri Mawr "the Great" (844–78).[28] His virtues are extolled in a panegyric written by the Irish scholar Sedulius Scottus in Liège (Belgium). Another poem from Liège records a victory over the raiders, possibly a reference to Rhodri's defeat of a force led by Horm in 856, also mentioned in the *Annals of Ulster*.[29]

Concurrent with these native successes there are indications that the Scandinavians repeatedly found allies among local rulers, demonstrating the limitations of the authority exercised by those greater kings who coordinated native resistance. For example, in 838 a force from Cornwall combined with a viking army to oppose the West Saxon army, although they were resoundingly defeated at Hingston Down (Cornwall), and in 842 the *Annals of Ulster* state that the abbot of Linn Dúachaill "was fatally wounded and burned by heathens and Irish" (*EHD*, I, 187; *AU*, p. 301). Raghnall Ó Floinn has pointed out that shortly before this a *longphort* had been constructed at Linn Dúachaill on the boundary between the kingdoms of Conaille and Cíannachta, implying that the location of this fortification was informed by the local political geography and perhaps also knowledge of existing rivalries in the region.[30] The *Dub-Gaill* ("black foreigners") who arrived in Ireland in 849 were seemingly rivals to the pre-existing raiders, and they subsequently attacked the *longphoirt* at Dublin and Linn Dúachaill, encouraged, some historians have argued, by Irish allies.[31] A group described in the *Annals of Ulster* as *Gall-Gaedhil* ("foreign Gaels") supported Maél Sechnaill against viking raiders in 856, and while it is debatable who they were, and whether the Gaelic elements were of the Irish or Scottish variety, it is now thought most likely that they were Irish-speakers of Scandinavian descent (*AU*, p. 315). The name suggests integration and probably also marriage between the raiders and the local population, and it is subsequently perpetuated in the name of Galloway, although the *Gall-Gaedhil* need not have had a specific territorial association in the mid-ninth century.[32] Alliances between viking raiders and local rulers were probably sometimes sealed by marriage, and Ó Floinn has suggested that the two Irish kings in the early 850s with the Norse name Bróðir probably had mothers of Scandinavian stock.[33] By the mid-ninth century, the raiders may have been perceived as yet another complicating factor in the complex political map of Britain and Ireland, but the events of the following decades revealed that the raiders attempted to do more than merely meddle in and profit from inter-necine disputes.

The Origins of Political Conquest

The political conquest of parts of Britain and Ireland by Scandinavians began to take shape in the 850s and 860s, and it can plausibly be argued that it was the product of a conscious effort on the part of at least some of the raiders. In 853, the *Annals of Ulster* record the arrival in Ireland of Amlaíb (Óláfr), adding that "the foreigners of Ireland [*Gaill Erenn*] submitted to him, and he took a tribute from the Irish" (*AU*, p. 313). Amlaíb is described as "son of the king of Lochlann," and although it has been suggested that this referred to a district of Norway, it is currently thought more plausibly to refer to a Scandinavian colony in the western isles of Scotland.[34] In 859, Amlaíb joined forces with one Imar (Old Norse Ivarr) and the Irish king of Osraige, Cerball mac Dúngal, to raid the southern territory of the Uí Néill. In this, we can probably see the influence of internecine disputes, and, indeed, Cerball subsequently secured greater autonomy for Osraige under the overlordship of Meath at a meeting with Maél Sechnaill.[35] Similarly, in 862 an army from the northern Uí Néill was led by Áed Mac Néill into Meath in conjunction with "the kings of the foreigners," probably in response to an earlier raid into their territory by the southern Uí Néill under Maél Sechnaill (*AU*, p. 319). In the following year, after plundering ancient tumuli at Knowth, Dowth, and Brug na Bóinne, Amlaíb, Ivarr, and a third viking leader called Auisle were joined in an attack on the lands of Flann son of Conaing by the king of Meath, Lorcan (*AU*, p. 319).

The attentions of Amlaíb, Ivarr, and Auisle subsequently turned eastward to western Scotland and northern England. The reasons for this are debatable. It has, on the one hand, been argued that it was the result of failure to secure the territories they sought in Ireland. Alternatively, some have suggested that this turn of events was prompted by rivalries amongst different viking groups.[36] Another relevant factor may have been that Danish interest in England began to grow in the 860s, after an army known to the *Anglo-Saxon Chronicle* as "the great army" (*micel here*) landed in East Anglia in 865 and subsequently took advantage of internal warfare in Northumbria to capture York (see below p. 203; *EHD*, I, 191). This may help to explain the besieging of Dumbarton Rock, the stronghold of the Strathclyde Britons, for four months in 870 by Amlaíb and Ivarr. Sometimes regarded as a strange and isolated diversion for the Scandinavian leaders in Ireland, it has in contrast been argued that the siege makes more sense if it is seen as an attempt to facilitate control of a territory stretching from Dublin through western Scotland into northern England and York.[37] Indeed, in 866 Amlaíb and Auisle had led an army into "Fortriu" and "plundered the entire Pictish country," assisted by "the foreigners" in both Ireland and Scotland, suggesting that the Scandinavians in Ireland were already looking eastward, and perhaps also indicating some commonality of interest between the raiders in the two regions (*AU*, p. 321). The most direct route between Dublin and York can scarcely be said to be via Strathclyde, yet at this time there emerge traces of contact – and, also, rivalries – between the raiders in northern England and Ireland. For example, after Amlaíb and Ivarr returned to Dublin with "a great prey of Angles and Britons and Picts," the leader of that part of the "great army" active in Northumbria, Halfdan, subsequently led a force into Strathclyde and Galloway (*AU*, p. 327; *EHD*, I, 194). Halfdan disappears from the historical record in England after this time, but he may be the Alband who, according to the *Annals of Ulster*,

killed the son of Amlaíb "king of the Norsemen" in 875, and who was himself killed
in 877 in a battle between "the fair heathens and the dark heathens" at Loch Cuan
(Co. Down).[38] If this identification is sound, then it strengthens the argument that
Scandinavian ambitions were widely focused across a large swathe of northern Britain
and Ireland, although how realistic was any ambition to control such a territory is
another matter.

In this respect it is most unfortunate that the career of Ivarr cannot easily be disentangled from the conflicting accounts of the sagas and other later sources, since
there emerges from these texts the possibility that he was also one of the leaders of
the great army in England. Both the *Anglo-Saxon Chronicle* in its entry for 878 and
Æthelweard's late tenth-century version of the *Chronicle* indicate that one of the
leaders of the great army was called Iguuar/Ivar, while the late tenth-century *Life of
St. Edmund* states that Ivar was the leader of the army that killed King Edmund of
East Anglia in 869. It has been speculated that the Iguuar/Ivar of the great army
was the same man as the Imar (Ivarr) of the *Annals of Ulster*, and that both may also
be equated with the Ivar *beinlauss* ("boneless," an epithet giving rise to much improb-
able speculation) of *Ragnar Lothbrok's Saga*.[39] These sources are of increasing degrees
of unreliability, and no historical argument for the ninth century can be based on
saga evidence. Nonetheless, the reputation of Imar/Ivarr as a ruler with aspirations
to rule over a wide area was certainly recognized by contemporaries. When the *Annals
of Ulster* recorded his death in 873, it was claimed that Ivarr was "king of the Norse
of all Ireland and Britain" (*AU*, p. 329).

There is a striking similarity between the claims made of Ivarr and those made of
various indigenous leaders in the later ninth century. It is difficult to assess the impact
on Irish politics of the new viking threat posed from the 850s, but it may not be a
coincidence that this period witnessed the emergence of an Irish king, Maél Sechnaill
(845–62), king of Mide, head of Clann Cholmáin of the southern Uí Néill, with
pretensions to extend his authority at the expense of other Irish kings. The various
Irish annals contain numerous accounts of his attacks on his contemporaries. For
example, after Cinaed, son of Conaing, king of Cíannachta rebelled in 850, joining
with vikings to plunder territories and churches, he was "cruelly drowned in a pool"
by Maél Sechnaill. The latter was also not averse to taking hostages among his fellow
Irish, such as when he raided Munster in 858 (*AU*, pp. 310–11, 317). Maél Sechnaill's
reputation was such that when he died in 862 the *Annals of Ulster* described him as
the "king of all Ireland" (*AU*, p. 319). A stone cross at Kinnitty (Co. Offaly), apparently created not long after his death, exhorts the viewer to pray for Maél Sechnaill
"king of Ireland," with his status being reinforced by what is debatably an image of
Samuel calling David to the kingship.[40] These claims to have been king of Ireland
can scarcely be because he held any such political office, but because his authority,
built on military success, extended over other peoples and kings.

More generally, the late ninth century witnessed the emergence of rulers who were
described during their career as being kings of wide territories, including Rhodri
Mawr of Gwynedd, the only ninth-century Welsh king to be accorded the epithet
"the Great," and Alfred "the Great" of Wessex (871–99), said by the *Anglo-Saxon
Chronicle* upon his death in 899 to have been "king over the whole *Angelcynn* except
for that part which was under Danish rule."[41] The position of such kings rested
on military success against other peoples, seizure of land, and being able to accrue

followers through force of reputation and the rewards their military success enabled them to offer. The overkingships that emerged were inherently unstable, liable to collapse upon the death of individual rulers, and despite the reputations that may have attached to Maél Sechnaill, Alfred or Rhodri Mawr, or Imar/Ivarr for that matter, it was to be some considerable time before unified kingdoms of Irish, English, or Welsh emerged.[42] If the circumstances of the viking raids encouraged the emergence of native rulers who were capable of taking advantage of the failings of their contemporaries to extend their realms, it seems also to have prompted Scandinavian rulers to extend the horizons of their political ambitions. That native kings did not, apparently, respond to the threat in a pan-British/Irish alliance may be a reflection of the unrealistic quality of Scandinavian ambitions, and, at least as plausibly, their own incapacity to conduct their kingship on such a scale.

These considerations throw into sharp relief the claims that have been made about the origin of the Scottish kingdom over the course of the ninth century. This has frequently been assigned to the activities of the king of the Dál Riata, Cinaed mac Ailpín (c.840–58), who in the 840s apparently succeeded in undermining the Pictish overkingdom, which had previously been weakened by viking raids.[43] The mac Ailpín dynasty continued with an almost unbroken series of successions from the time of Cinaed, and later chroniclers, including the compiler of what is essentially a regnal list known to modern scholars as the *Chronicle of the Kings of Alba*, saw in this succession the origins of the lineage of the kings of the Scots.[44] Modern historians, admittedly constrained by the very limited nature of the reliable written record, incline toward Cinaed being perhaps as ambitious to extend his authority as other notable mid- to late ninth-century kings, but not necessarily any more successful in establishing a territorial basis for his ambitions, and it is debatable whether his successors recorded in the aforementioned regnal list had equal claims to the kingdoms of both Dál Riata and Pictland.[45] Although the political fate of many parts of what is now Scotland, including Strathclyde, Galloway, and Argyll, are thoroughly obscure for much of the ninth century, the decisive period in the creation of a kingdom of the Scots is now thought to lie in the tenth century; Domnall mac Constantín (889–900) is the first king to be described as "king of Alba" and the Picts essentially disappear from the historical record at this time.[46]

Conquest and the Establishment of Territorial Rule

The 860s witnessed viking raiders becoming increasingly involved in the political organization of the kingdoms of Northumbria, Mercia, and East Anglia. In 867, the great army went to York, which was at that time witnessing a struggle between two rival claimants for the throne, Osbert and Ælla. It is possible that the army was taking advantage of divisions among the Northumbrians, if not actually encouraged by one party or other (*EHD*, I, 191). Indeed, the army was subsequently responsible for appointing a local man, Ecgberht, as king, and he clearly forged a relationship with the archbishop of York, Wulfhere, as they fled together from York in 872. The latter returned to his see upon the emergence of a new Northumbrian king, Ricsige, whose background is obscure, but who may similarly have owed his position to collaboration with the great army.[47] In 869, the great army defeated the East Anglians, and their king, Edmund, was killed (*EHD*, I, 192). East Anglia was ruled subsequently by two kings, Æthelred and Oswald, known only from their coinage, but there are hints that they were Scandinavian appointees. Some of their coins were minted by King Edmund's moneyers, but they also display the characteristics of coins minted under Scandinavian rule, including blundered inscriptions, and they are notably modeled on Frankish coinage of the early 860s, with which the great army may have been familiar before it came to England.[48]

The great army also established a certain Ceolwulf as king of Mercia after over-wintering at Repton (Derbyshire), the site of a prestigious Mercian royal monastery and mausoleum, in 873–4 (*EHD*, I, 194). Although the *Anglo-Saxon Chronicle* dismisses him as "a foolish king's thegn," the Mercian bishops and at least some of the leading Mercian nobles were prepared to attend his councils and to witness his charters. Given this, and irrespective of the damning assessment of the *Chronicle*, in a text notably written in Wessex, it is possible that Ceolwulf was a member of a rival branch of Mercian royalty to that of the previous incumbent, Burgred, perhaps descended from earlier Mercian kings, Coenwulf (796–821) and Ceolwulf I (821–3).[49] The great army had apparently, once again, involved itself in an internecine dispute. Excavation and field survey at Repton have identified a ditched enclosure dating to the later ninth century, which incorporated the church into its course, while furnished burials appear to date to the same period and may have been for members of the great army.[50] The disarticulated remains of over 260 individuals found within a former mausoleum have also been associated with the events of 873–4, although the general lack of wound trauma suggests that they were not the murdered monastic community or the battle dead of that winter. Radio-carbon dates ranging from the seventh to the late ninth century indicate that the deposit includes the dead of earlier generations, although the presence of silver pennies of the early 870s suggests that all or part of the deposit was brought together in the wake of the great army's over-wintering.[51] An early eighteenth-century antiquarian account of a central burial amidst the deposit was not confirmed by recent excavation, but the excavators, Martin Biddle and Birthe Kjølbye-Biddle, have, nonetheless, suggested that this putative central burial may have been of Iguuar/Ivar/Imar (see above, p. 202). They note that Ivar *beinlausi* is said by saga tradition to have died and been buried in England, according to some sources in a mound.[52] Irrespective of this very speculative identification, the archaeology at Repton reveals the great army drawing on the power of the past and of existing regal traditions to underpin claims to authority; the political impact of the army establishing a base and burial place at a famed Mercian royal monastery should not be underestimated.[53] There are indications from the archaeological record that such a strategy was employed elsewhere: for example, burials accompanied by Scandinavian-type swords have been excavated close to churches at Kildale and Wensley (Yorkshire) and Santon Downham (Norfolk).[54]

Given its geographical position, it is not unlikely that north Wales was within the purview of the Irish viking armies in the second half of the ninth century, but the written evidence is slim. Rhodri Mawr, king of Gwynedd, who had extended his realm to incorporate the kingdoms of Powys (855) and Seisyllwg (872), fled to Ireland in 877 following a viking raid on Anglesey. The *Annals of Ulster* and the *Annales Cambriae*, apparently compiled from the eighth century at the episcopal community of St. David's (Pembrokeshire), both state that in the next year Rhodri was killed by the Saxons, and it has been argued that he was trying to regain his kingdom when defeated by the army of Mercia, which at this time was ruled by the Scandinavian appointee, Ceolwulf.[55] In 902, the *Annals of Ulster* record that the Scandinavians in Dublin were driven out, and later Irish and Welsh chronicles suggest that, led by a certain Ingimund (or Ogmundr in the Welsh annals), they attempted to settle in Wales, perhaps on Anglesey, and subsequently acquired land from Æthelflæd of Mercia near Chester. These accounts are problematic (some of the details are recorded only in the late medieval *Fragmentary Annals of Ireland* and the identification of Ingimund with Ogmundr is debatable) but at the very least they record a tradition of the movements of viking parties between Ireland, north Wales, and north-western England at the turn of the tenth century.[56] Finally, perhaps the most notable development in late ninth-century Welsh political life was the commonality of interest that emerged in the face of successive viking attacks between Welsh rulers and the kings of Wessex, which lasted to the early eleventh century.[57]

Securing Political Control

In consolidating their authority in England, successive Scandinavian rulers swiftly adapted to local styles of kingship. The community of St. Cuthbert, which had left Lindisfarne in 875, was responsible for appointing as leader of a viking army a certain Guthred. He swore allegiance to the community at a site associated with a former Northumbrian king, and was subsequently buried at York Minster.[58] Guthrum, one of the leaders of the great army, was defeated in battle against the West Saxons in 878, and subsequently accepted baptism, in a protracted ceremony described in some detail in Asser's *Life of King Alfred*. King Alfred stood as Guthrum's godfather, and Guthrum took the baptismal name of Æthelstan (*EHD*, I, 196, 200). He occupied East Anglia in 880, and at some point over the next decade was party to a peace treaty with Alfred. While this ostensibly legislated with respect to trade, compensation for unlawful death, and the movement of people between the two areas of jurisdiction, this treaty also, as Paul Kershaw has recently argued, facilitated the integration of the Scandinavian settlers into English society and saw Guthrum presenting himself in the guise of a western European king, for whom written legislation was commonplace. Guthrum appears to have been using his alliance with Alfred as a means to legitimize his rule, but, as Kershaw points out, Alfred was simultaneously using the opportunity to speak on behalf of the *Angelcynn*, which served as another means of strengthening his claims over other polities.[59]

Guthrum swiftly adapted to territorial kingship and its trappings, including the minting of coins, with some of his issues imitating contemporary coins of King Alfred. These coins often display poor literacy and are lighter than Alfred's coins, and it has long been thought that they were simply crude and inferior copies, but Mark Blackburn has recently argued that they were deliberately and consistently minted at a lighter weight, which was the traditional Anglo-Saxon standard prior to Alfred's reform of the coinage c.880. Thus, this imitative coinage reveals that Guthrum's reign was partly forged in the style of Alfred but was also shaped by local East Anglian traditions. Guthrum also minted coins in his baptismal name, Æthelstan, demonstrating a continued commitment to Christianity in this manifestation of his kingship.[60] There is no direct evidence for the ecclesiastical history of East Anglia from 880 onward, but given Guthrum's apparent commitment, if only political, to Christianity, and the issuing from the 890s of an even more overtly Christian coinage by his unknown successor(s) commemorating the murdered St. Edmund, it is not unreasonable to anticipate that churches in this region were no longer regarded simply as sources of plunder.[61]

The adoption of overt Christian symbolism and evidence for continental influences in the early issues of Scandinavian kings can be paralleled at York c.900. Coins minted in the names of two otherwise unknown Scandinavian kings, Siefrid and Cnut (c.895–905), bore liturgical inscriptions and incorporated a diverse array of crosses into the designs. Carolingian influence on this sophisticated and diverse coinage can also be discerned, including the use of a *Karolus* monogram on the coins of Cnut.[62] Mark Blackburn has argued that this coinage would have conveyed a number of contemporary messages, including the independence of York from Wessex, Mercia, and also other areas of Scandinavian control, and the royal status, administrative ability, and importance of Christianity to these Scandinavian kings, who were apparently "not only militarily powerful, but also politically and diplomatically astute, and who came to recognize the political benefits the church could offer to a newly established kingdom."[63]

In other parts of Britain and Ireland, in contrast, coinage was not minted prior to the Scandinavian conquests, and emerged only in the late tenth or early eleventh centuries. In such regions, the Scandinavian influence on the economy is rather to be detected in hoards of metalwork, including imported coins, jewelry, ingots, and hack-silver. In Ireland, silver hoards are concentrated in the regions in which alliances between the raiders and the Irish are most frequently recorded, and accordingly John Sheehan has suggested that these alliances, the mechanisms of which are otherwise unknown, were secured by gift-giving and tribute. Recent research indicates that the mainly tenth-century coin hoards are typically found at ecclesiastical sites, while the earlier coinless hoards more commonly occur at centers of secular power, such as crannogs or hillforts. Under Scandinavian influence, imported coins were melted down to create silver jewelry, in particular various types of arm-rings, which, given their broadly uniform weight, appear to have served as a means of storing and circulating silver in a barter economy, while also acting as symbols of status for secular rulers.[64]

Discussion

Reliable written sources for the ninth century illuminate Scandinavian interaction with indigenous authorities only in Ireland and England. From these, a common practice can be detected in Ireland of allying with indigenous rulers and would-be rulers from the 830s. More organized resistance and rivalries between different raiding groups may have been decisive factors in the transfer of Scandinavian efforts from Ireland to England in the later ninth century. Yet, despite Scandinavian domination of the Irish Sea zone during the course of the ninth century, any ambitions for unified Scandinavian political control across the Irish Sea zone had temporarily failed by the early tenth century, and following their expulsion from Dublin in 902, the Scandinavians may have appeared a spent force in Ireland. By the end of the ninth century, the major political successes achieved by the Scandinavians lay in England, where three of its four kingdoms were ruled, first, by Scandinavian appointees and then directly by

Scandinavian kings. Yet, by 900, much of Mercia was again under English control, in the form of Ealdorman Æthelred and his wife, Æthelflæd, daughter of King Alfred, although the mechanisms by which this occurred are undocumented.

The second half of the ninth century witnessed the emergence of indigenous kings who were militarily successful against the raiders, demonstrated political sophistication in dealing with their enemies, and an ability to exploit the weaknesses and occasional demise of contemporary rulers, and several of these came to be regarded at the time, and by later generations, as the agents of national unity. This is nowhere more apparent than in English historiography. Yet, few of their achievements were secure upon the deaths of any of these kings, including Alfred. Admittedly, from the perspective of the later tenth century, the incorporation of Mercia into Wessex looks assured. The ever-increasing influence of Wessex over its neighbor can be traced back into the earlier ninth century: King Ecgberht was recognized by the *Anglo-Saxon Chronicle* as a *Bretwalda* in 829, having conquered the kingdom of the Mercians, and there were Mercian requests for West Saxon help in dealing with the Welsh in 853 and a viking army at Nottingham in 868. In the ninth century, the West Saxons also subsumed Cornwall, and it is easy to regard the creation of an English kingdom under West Saxon aegis as inevitable.[65] Yet, this is largely a story told at the time, and subsequently, from the West Saxon standpoint. At the turn of the tenth century, following the death of King Alfred, his son, Edward the Elder, was challenged by his cousin, Æthelwold. Having seized royal residences in Wessex, Æthelwold was received by the viking army in Northumbria, which "accepted him as king," and a year or so later he garnered support in Essex and subsequently raided westward into Mercian territory. His army was eventually defeated by the army of Edward the Elder, and Æthelwold died in the ensuing battle alongside "Brihtsige, son of the *atheling* ["throneworthy"] Beornoth," who, to judge from the form of his name and the title his father was accorded, appears to have been a descendant of one of the royal houses of Mercia (*EHD*, I, 207). If Edward rather than Æthelwold had died in this battle, the redrawing of the political division between Mercia and Wessex must have been a possibility, as the price to be exacted for the support offered by Brihtsige.

The emergence of a unified English kingdom was neither inevitable nor necessarily desirable outside Wessex at the turn of the tenth century.[66] The events following the death of King Alfred serve as a reminder of the fragility of the overkingships that were emerging in the later ninth century. The reasons why Wessex alone of the Anglo-Saxon kingdoms survived Scandinavian domination are difficult to judge, and that "alone" overestimates the defeat of Mercia. Good fortune in battle at a decisive time in the 870s was doubtless a factor, but so too must have been Alfred's political negotiation with Guthrum, who swiftly adapted to the demands of kingship, although the broader threat was by no means over as Wessex continued to be harried by viking armies, and, as aforementioned events suggest, the longer-term West Saxon dominance was far from inevitable c.900.

Surveys of the Scandinavians in Britain and Ireland tend to identify contrasts in their impact on various regions, arguably because they generally assess the long-term outcomes of Scandinavian activity. When one focuses more specifically on the ninth century, then a marked similarity of activity can be detected. From the late eighth century, each generation witnessed conquest and some settlement, with attention moving, in turn, from the northern isles, through the western isles and into Ireland by the middle of the ninth century, and then on to mainland Scotland, north Wales, and England in the last quarter of the century. Yet by the turn of the tenth century, only the Scottish isles and parts of northern and eastern England had experienced any lasting conquest, and it is apparent at that point that Scandinavian capacity to realize their ambitions had varied quite significantly, in no small part as a result of the nature of indigenous responses.[67]

Notes

1   Dumville, "The Vikings in the British Isles."
2   Sawyer, *Kings and Vikings*, pp. 79–80.
3   *AU*, pp. 251–3; Downham, "An imaginary raid on Skye in 795?"
4   *AU*, p. 263; Crawford, *Scandinavian Scotland*, pp. 39–40.
5   Dumville, *Churches of North Britain*, p. 19.
6   Rollason, "Lists of saints' resting-places," pp. 61–8.
7   *AU*, p. 321; Dumville, *Churches of North Britain*, p. 20.
8   Dumville, *Churches of North Britain*, pp. 17–18.
9   Jennings, "Iona and the Vikings."
10   Dumville, "The Vikings in the British Isles," p. 210.
11   Crawford, *Scandinavian Scotland*, p. 41.
12   Ibid., pp. 40–2; Dumville, "The Vikings in the British Isles," p. 210.
13   Myhre, "The archaeology of the early Viking Age," pp. 7–8; "The beginning of the Viking Age."
14   Myhre, "The archaeology of the early Viking Age," pp. 7–8.
15   *EHD*, I, 844; Myhre, "The beginning of the Viking Age," p. 188.
16   Callmer, "Urbanisation in Scandinavia."
17   Myhre, "The archaeology of the early Viking Age," p. 27; "The beginning of the Viking Age," pp. 196–8.
18   Hedeager, "Kingdoms, ethnicity and material culture"; Morris, "Raiders, traders and settlers," p. 74.
19   Tierney, *Diculi*, pp. 72–7.
20   *AU*, p. 283; Crawford, *Scandinavian Scotland*, pp. 44–5.
21   Ó Cróinín, *Early Medieval Ireland*, pp. 244–5.
22   *AU*, p. 299; Crawford, *Scandinavian Scotland*, p. 49.
23   Ó Cróinín, *Early Medieval Ireland*, p. 238.
24   Ó Floinn, "The archaeology of the early Viking Age," pp. 161–2.
25   Nelson (trans.), *Annals of St.-Bertin*, p. 65.
26   Smyth, "The effect of Scandinavian raiders," pp. 7, 16–17, 21.
27   Nelson (trans.), *Annals of St.-Bertin*, p. 66.
28   Davies, *Wales in the Early Middle Ages*, pp. 200–1; Jones, *Brut y Tywysogion*, p. 4.
29   *AU*, p. 315; Ó Cróinín, *Early Medieval Ireland*, p. 248.
30   Ó Floinn, "The archaeology of the early Viking Age," p. 162.
31   *AU*, pp. 849–51; Ó Cróinín, *Early Medieval Ireland*, pp. 250–1.
32   Crawford, *Scandinavian Scotland*, p. 47; Dumville, *Churches of North Britain*, pp. 26–7.
33   Ó Floinn, "The archaeology of the early Viking Age," p. 163.
34   Crawford, *Scandinavian Scotland*, pp. 41, 49–50.
35   *AU*, pp. 317–19; Ó Cróinín, *Early Medieval Ireland*, p. 251.
36   Dumville, "The Vikings in the British Isles," p. 225; Ó Cróinín, *Early Medieval Ireland*, p. 244.

37 *AU*, p. 327; Crawford, *Scandinavian Scotland*, pp. 50–1; Ó Cróinín, *Early Medieval Ireland*, pp. 252–3.
38 *AU*, pp. 331–3; Ó Cróinín, *Early Medieval Ireland*, p. 254.
39 Biddle and Kjølbye-Biddle, "Repton," pp. 81–3; Smyth, *Scandinavian York and Dublin*, pp. 16–20.
40 Ó Corráin, "Ireland, Wales, Man and the Hebrides," p. 95.
41 *EHD*, I, 208; Davies, *Wales in the Early Middle Ages*, p. 106; Stafford, "Kings, kingships and kingdoms," pp. 14–15.
42 Stafford, "Kings, kingships and kingdoms," pp. 11–22.
43 Crawford, *Scandinavian Scotland*, pp. 48–51; Foster, *Picts, Gaels and Scots*, pp. 111–12.
44 Dumville, "Chronicle of the Kings of Alba."
45 Dumville, *Churches of North Britain*, pp. 34–6; Foster, *Picts, Gaels and Scots*, pp. 111–12.
46 *AU*, p. 351; Dumville, *Churches of North Britain*, pp. 34–6, and "The Vikings in the British Isles," pp. 216–17.
47 Rollason, *Sources for York History*, p. 63.
48 Blackburn, "Currency under the Vikings."
49 Hadley, *The Vikings in England*, p. 12.
50 Biddle and Kjølbye-Biddle, "Repton," pp. 57–9, 60–5.
51 Ibid., pp. 68–9.
52 Ibid., pp. 67–74, 81–4.
53 Richards, "Boundaries and cult centres," pp. 99–101.
54 Richards, "The case of the missing Vikings," pp. 160–1.
55 Dumville, "The Vikings in the British Isles," p. 220.
56 Griffiths, "The north-west frontier," pp. 179–81.
57 Dumville, "The Vikings in the British Isles," p. 220.
58 Rollason, "The wanderings of St. Cuthbert."
59 Kershaw, "The Alfred–Guthrum treaty," pp. 51–2, 58.
60 Blackburn, "Expansion and control," pp. 127–8, 136.
61 Hadley, *The Vikings in England*, pp. 29–37.
62 Blackburn, "The coinage of Scandinavian York," pp. 327–9, 330–1.
63 Ibid., p. 332.
64 Sheehan, "Early Viking-Age silver hoards."
65 *EHD*, I, 186, 188; Dumville, "The Vikings in the British Isles," p. 214.
66 Campbell et al., *The Anglo-Saxons*, p. 157.
67 Dumville, "The Vikings in the British Isles," pp. 222–30.

Further Reading

Few studies have surveyed the impact of viking raiding across the whole of Britain and Ireland. Exceptions include H. R. Loyn, *The Vikings in Britain* (London, 1977), and, more recently, C. Downham, *Viking Kings of Britain and Ireland: The Dynasty of Ívarr to AD 1014* (Edinburgh, 2007). The discrepancies in evidence and the historiographical perspectives of scholars studying particular regions of Britain and Ireland are reviewed in Dumville, "The Vikings in the British Isles." Study of the impact of viking raids and the initial stages of political conquest has largely been the preserve of historians: for example, Crawford, *Scandinavian Scotland*, and Ó Cróinín, *Early Medieval Ireland*, ch. 9. However, recent studies have highlighted the important insights that emerge from the study of archaeological and material culture evidence. H. B. Clarke, M. Ní Mhaonaigh, and R. Ó Floinn (eds.), *Ireland and Scandinavia in the Early Viking Age*

(Dublin, 1998) contains papers by J. Sheehan and J. Graham-Campbell on silver hoards and E. O'Brien on burials; J. Graham-Campbell, R. A. Hall, J. Jesch, and D. N. Parsons (eds.), *Vikings and the Danelaw: Select Papers from the Proceedings of the Thirteenth Viking Congress* (Oxford, 2001) includes studies of burials by J. D. Richards, and by M. Biddle and B. Kjølbye-Biddle, and a paper on the coinage of the southern Danelaw by M. A. S. Blackburn, who has discussed the coinage of other regions of England in "The coinage of Scandinavian York" and "Currency under the Vikings." The viking impact on England is traced through an interdisciplinary approach in my *The Vikings in England*, ch. 2.

Bibliography

Biddle, M. and Kjølbye-Biddle, B., "Repton and the 'great heathen army,' 873–4," in J. Graham-Campbell, R. A. Hall, J. Jesch, and D. N. Parsons, (eds.), *Vikings and the Danelaw: Select Papers from the Proceedings of the Thirteenth Viking Congress* (Oxford, 2001), pp. 45–96.

Blackburn, M. A. S., "The coinage of Scandinavian York," in R. A. Hall (ed.), *Aspects of Anglo-Scandinavian York* (York, 2004), pp. 325–49.

Blackburn, M. A. S., "Currency under the Vikings. Part 1: Guthrum and the earliest Danelaw coinages," *British Numismatic Journal*, 75 (2005), 18–43.

Blackburn, M. A. S., "Expansion and control: aspects of Anglo-Scandinavian minting south of the Humber," in J. Graham-Campbell, R. A. Hall, J. Jesch, and D. N. Parsons, (eds.), *Vikings and the Danelaw: Select Papers from the Proceedings of the Thirteenth Viking Congress* (Oxford, 2001), pp. 125–42.

Callmer, J., "Urbanisation in Scandinavia and the Baltic region c. AD 700–1100: trading places, centres and early urban sites," in B. Ambrosiani and H. Clarke (eds.), *Developments around the Baltic and the North Sea* (Stockholm, 1994), pp. 50–90.

Campbell, J., John, E., and Wormald, P., *The Anglo-Saxons* (Oxford, 1982).

Crawford, B. E., *Scandinavian Scotland* (Leicester, 1987).

Davies, W., *Wales in the Early Middle Ages* (Leicester, 1982).

Downham, C., "An imaginary raid on Skye in 795?," *Scottish Gaelic Studies*, 20 (2000), 192–6.

Dumville, D. N., "The Chronicle of the Kings of Alba," in S. Taylor (ed.), *Kings, Clerics and Chronicles in Scotland, 500–1297: Essays in Honour of Marjorie Ogilvie Anderson on the Occasion of her Ninetieth Birthday* (Dublin, 2000), pp. 73–86.

Dumville, D. N., *The Churches of North Britain in the First Viking Age* (Whithorn, 1997).

Dumville, D. N., "The Vikings in the British Isles," in J. Jesch (ed.), *The Scandinavians from the Vendel Period to the Tenth Century: An Ethnographic Perspective* (Woodbridge, 2001), pp. 209–40.

Foster, S., *Picts, Gaels and Scots: Early Historic Scotland* (London, 1996).

Griffiths, D., "The north-west frontier," in N. Higham and D. Hill (eds.), *Edward the Elder 899–924* (Manchester, 2001), pp. 167–87.

Hadley, D. M., *The Vikings in England: Settlement, Society and Culture* (Manchester, 2006).

Hedeager, L., "Kingdoms, ethnicity and material culture: Denmark in a European perspective," in M. Carver (ed.), *The Age of Sutton Hoo* (Woodbridge, 1992), pp. 279–300.

Jennings, A., "Iona and the Vikings: survival and continuity," *Northern Studies*, 33 (1998), 37–54.

Jones, T., *Brut y Tywysogion* (Cardiff, 1952).

Kershaw, P., "The Alfred–Guthrum treaty: scripting accommodation and interaction in Viking-Age England," in D. M. Hadley and J. D. Richards (eds.), *Cultures in Contact: Scandinavian Settlement in England in the Ninth and Tenth Centuries* (Turnhout, 2000), pp. 43–64.

Mac Airt, S. and Mac Niocaill, G. (eds. and trans.), *The Annals of Ulster (to AD 1131)*. Part 1: *Text and Translation* (Dublin, 1983).

Morris, C. D., "Raiders, traders and settlers: the early Viking Age in Scotland," in H. B. Clarke, M. Ní Mhaonaigh, and R. Ó Floinn (eds.), *Ireland and Scandinavia in the Early Viking Age* (Dublin, 1998), pp. 73–103.

Myhre, B., "The archaeology of the early Viking Age in Norway," in H. B. Clarke, M. Ní Mhaonaigh, and R. Ó Floinn (eds.), *Ireland and Scandinavia in the Early Viking Age* (Dublin, 1998), pp. 3–36.

Myhre, B., "The beginning of the Viking Age: some current archaeological problems," in A. Faulkes and R. Perkins (eds.), *Viking Revaluations: Viking Society Centenary Symposium* (London, 1993), pp. 182–204.

Nelson, J. L. (trans.), *The Annals of St.-Bertin* (Manchester, 1991).

Ó Corráin, D., "Ireland, Wales, Man and the Hebrides," in P. H. Sawyer (ed.), *The Oxford Illustrated History of the Vikings* (Oxford, 1997), pp. 83–109.

Ó Cróinín, D., *Early Medieval Ireland 400–1200* (Harlow, 1995).

Ó Floinn, R., "The archaeology of the early Viking Age in Ireland," in H. B. Clarke, M. Ní Mhaonaigh, and R. Ó Floinn (eds.), *Ireland and Scandinavia in the Early Viking Age* (Dublin, 1998), pp. 131–65.

Richards, J. D., "Boundaries and cult centres: Viking burial in Derbyshire," in J. Graham-Campbell, R. A. Hall, J. Jesch, and D. N. Parsons (eds.), *Vikings and the Danelaw: Select Papers from the Proceedings of the Thirteenth Viking Congress* (Oxford, 2001), pp. 97–104.

Richards, J. D., "The case of the missing Vikings: Scandinavian burial in the Danelaw," in S. Lucy and A. Reynolds (eds.), *Burial in Early Medieval England and Wales* (London, 2002), pp. 156–70.

Rollason, D. W., "Lists of saints' resting-places in Anglo-Saxon England," *Anglo-Saxon England*, 7 (1978), 61–93.

Rollason, D. W., Gore, D., and Fellows-Jensen, G., *Sources for York History to AD 1100* (York, 1998).

Rollason, D. W., "The wanderings of St. Cuthbert," in D. W. Rollason (ed.), *Cuthbert: Saint and Patron* (Durham, 1987), pp. 45–59.

Sawyer, P. H., *Kings and Vikings: Scandinavia and Europe AD 700–1100* (London, 1982).

Sheehan, J., "Early Viking-Age silver hoards from Ireland and their Scandinavian elements," in H. B. Clarke, M. Ní Mhaonaigh, and R. Ó Floinn (eds.), *Ireland and Scandinavia in the Early Viking Age* (Dublin, 1998), pp. 166–202.

Smyth, A. P., "The effect of Scandinavian raiders on the English and Irish churches: a preliminary reassessment," in B. Smith (ed.), *Britain and Ireland, 900–1300: Insular Responses to Medieval European Change* (Cambridge, 1999), pp. 1–38.

Smyth, A. P., *Scandinavian York and Dublin: The History and Archaeology of Two Related Viking Kingdoms*, 2 vols. (Dublin, 1975–9).

Stafford, P., "Kings, kingships and kingdoms," in W. Davies (ed.), *From the Vikings to the Normans 800–1100* (Oxford, 2003), pp. 11–39.

Tierney, J. J., *Diculi: Liber de mensura orbis terrae* (Dublin, 1967).

Whitelock, D. (ed. and trans.), *English Historical Documents*, vol. I: *c.500–1042*, 2nd edn. (London, 1979).

CHAPTER FOURTEEN

Scandinavian Settlement

DAWN HADLEY

In the ninth century, Scandinavian raiding and political conquest was followed by settlement in many regions of Britain and Ireland. Assessment of the scale, chronology, precise locations, and impact of this settlement has, however, proved a difficult task. The diverse sources of evidence available often appear to convey contradictory impressions, with the Scandinavian influence typically being unevenly expressed in differing contexts. For example, in contrast to its focus, often very detailed, on raids, battles, and treaties, the written record rarely provides any information on settlement. Meanwhile, archaeological evidence cannot always be closely dated, and it is difficult to distinguish between evidence for settlement, on the one hand, and the dissemination of Scandinavian influence among the indigenous population through the processes of trade or social emulation, on the other. It is, furthermore, problematic that the Scandinavian impact on language and names, extensive in some regions, is typically recorded in sources that long post-date the period of settlement. Interpretation of this diverse array of evidence has also been shaped considerably by the contrasting historiographical trends among researchers focusing on particular regions of Britain and Ireland.[1] Broader debates among early medievalists about the construction of ethnic, and other social, identities have begun to have an impact on the study of the Scandinavian settlement, although the influence of this broader scholarship has been unevenly felt.[2] This chapter discusses each region of Britain and Ireland in turn and explores the differing evidence and interpretative frameworks for Scandinavian settlement.

England

The *Anglo-Saxon Chronicle* reveals that the phase of political interference and conquest outlined in chapter 13 was followed by division of land and settlement in Northumbria, Mercia, and East Anglia between 876 and 880 (*EHD*, I, 195–6). Identification of the main regions of Scandinavian settlement has largely rested on the density of Scandinavian place-names in northern and eastern England, but there has been considerable debate about what this distribution reveals about the nature of that settlement.[3] For example, in the 1960s, Kenneth Cameron used place-name evidence to chart the chronology of Scandinavian settlement. He suggested that place-names formed with a Scandinavian first element and the English naming element -*tun* ("farmstead, settlement") represented the earliest phases of Scandinavian settlement, given that they are common in areas of prime agricultural land, while place-names formed with the Scandinavian naming elements -*by* ("farmstead, settlement") and -*thorp* ("secondary/outlying settlement") were typically located in upland and wolds regions and represented later colonization.[4] In contrast, Peter Sawyer subsequently argued that the absence of Scandinavian place-names from regions recovered early in the tenth century by English lords suggests that the proliferation of Scandinavian place-names occurred later, probably in the context of estate fragmentation.[5] Such attempts to establish settlement chronologies have, however, occasionally been called into question by archaeological evidence demonstrating earlier occupation of some sites once thought from their Scandinavian place-names to have been newly founded in the wake of settlement.[6]

Scandinavian place-names were first recorded, in most cases, at least two centuries after settlement commenced, often not until *Domesday Book* in 1086, and it is now accepted that not all Scandinavian place-names were necessarily coined in the first phases of settlement in the late ninth century.[7] Conversely, it is also now recognized that not all new names for places coined by Scandinavian settlers invariably survive into the written record; for example, in regions in which English land-ownership persisted, or was quickly restored, such new coinages are unlikely to have been recorded.[8] Place-name evidence has periodically been used to identify the ethnic identity of occupants of particular regions: for example, the place-names of north-western England have been deemed to reveal that Scandinavian settlers came principally from Norway, but settlers from other parts of Scandinavia, and Scandinavians who had previously settled in other parts of Britain, such as the Isle of Man, have also been detected.[9] However, other studies have regarded as dubious such attempts to identify the ethnic make-up of particular regions, let alone perceptions of ethnic self-consciousness.[10] Nonetheless, it is clear that some Scandinavian place-names were created in the context of contact between the settlers and members of local society, given the combination of English and Scandinavian elements to form place-names, the substitution of cognate Scandinavian names for pre-existing English names, and the presence of both Scandinavian and English place-names within the same estate.[11] However, the chronology and nature of the interaction between Scandinavian settlers and the local population is unclear from the onomastic evidence alone.[12]

Most recently, and in contrast to the growing skepticism about using place-name evidence to trace the chronology or nature of Scandinavian settlement, David Parsons and Lesley Abrams have argued that many of the typically Scandinavian place-names (especially those formed with the characteristic -*by* ending, which were overwhelmingly formed with Old Norse rather than Old English first elements) were coined in an entirely Scandinavian-speaking context, probably in the late ninth century. The implication of their argument is that these names emerged before processes of integration and acculturation had commenced.[13] Reacting to recent studies that have sought to underplay the significance of the scale of the place-name evidence, they also insist that these names indicate "Scandinavian settlers beyond a small military élite," a conclusion supported by the large numbers of Scandinavian field-names and the diverse range of personal names introduced into England by the settlers.[14]

The linguistic impact of the Scandinavian settlement on Old English was, indeed, extensive, although this is most apparent in Middle English (i.e. much later) written sources, which record many thousands of Scandinavian loan words, and reflect the Scandinavian impact even on matters of grammar.[15] The scale of the linguistic influence cannot convincingly be attributed to the effects of a small-scale elite conquest, but it is difficult to refine assessment of the scale of the settlement since there is not a predictable relationship between settlement and linguistic change.[16] A more productive line of research has recently been pursued by Matthew Townend, who has investigated the linguistic context of Anglo-Scandinavian social and political interaction, including, for example, the baptism of Guthrum at the behest of King Alfred and their subsequent forging of a treaty (see p. 205). He argues for the "adequate mutual intelligibility" of speakers of Old English and Old Norse, a conclusion based on, for example, the substitution by Norse speakers of cognate sounds and words in Old English place-names suggesting that the newcomers understood the names they encountered. The lack of references to interpreters, which *do* occur in other early medieval examples of linguistic contact, offers supporting evidence for the mutual comprehension of the Scandinavians and English when speaking in their own languages.[17]

Townend has also argued that the English and Scandinavians not only remained separate speech communities but that this linguistic divide broadly supports "the reality of the English/Danish distinction in Viking Age England." In this, he concurs with the argument long ago developed by Sir Frank Stenton that differences of social organization, economy, and law, as well as of language, "point to the reality of the difference between Danes and English," which Stenton saw as persisting into the tenth century and beyond.[18] This deduction does not, however, fit very well with the evidence for the apparently rapid Scandinavian adoption and adaptation of many aspects of English culture, including coinage (see chapter 13) and monumental stone sculpture.[19] Of course, such evidence does not itself preclude the possibility that Scandinavian settlers and their descendants continued to perceive themselves as a separate ethnic community, but it does indicate that the means of displaying that identity were frequently assimilated to Anglo-Saxon forms of material culture. There was, thus, a blurring of the distinctiveness of Scandinavian and English forms of cultural self-expression. Moreover, while there were undoubtedly separate speech communities in the late ninth century, inter-marriage between the settlers and the local population must have played an important part in the acculturation process, and this prompts consideration of what language(s) the offspring of such unions might have spoken. The predominant local language must have played a part in determining the language of mixed marriages, although the probable role of mothers in educating their children may have been as, or more, important.[20] Indeed, children may have played an important role as arbiters of cultural interaction and linguistic brokers.

Rural settlements demonstrating Scandinavian influence have proved notoriously elusive in the archaeological record. The upland farmsteads of Simy Folds (Co. Durham), Bryant's Gill (Cumbria), and Gauber High Pasture, Ribblehead (Yorkshire) are routinely cited in textbooks as examples of Scandinavian settlement, yet none has produced any diagnostically Scandinavian material culture, and radio-carbon dating now suggests that Simy Folds was founded long before Scandinavian settlement is likely to have commenced in this region.[21] Julian Richards has recently reviewed the criteria commonly used by archaeologists to identify Scandinavian rural settlements, including the introduction of new building forms and evidence for settlement disruption, and he has argued that few can securely be associated with Scandinavian occupation. Even the appearance of Scandinavian-style artifacts is not clear-cut evidence of Scandinavian settlement given the myriad ways in which they might have reached the site and their occurrence alongside indigenous material culture.[22] Richards also argued that the introduction into England of bow-sided buildings, which are characteristic of some tenth-century Danish settlements, is sometimes indicative of Scandinavian settlement, but the wide date ranges, locations, construction methods, and sizes of these buildings undermine confidence in this form of architecture as a reliable indicator of Scandinavian settlement.[23] Moreover, in several places in which Scandinavian settlement certainly occurred, such as York, there is conversely no evidence for the introduction of bow-sided buildings.[24] In any case, in Scandinavia, square and rectangular buildings are sometimes found, meaning that the settlers did not all arrive with a tradition of constructing exclusively bow-shaped houses.[25]

In response to the difficulty of identifying Scandinavian settlers in the archaeology of rural settlement in England, Julian Richards has suggested that we can no longer continue to ask whether particular rural settlements were ever occupied by Scandinavians, but rather we should explore the influence that Scandinavian settlement had on expressions of identity visible in material culture.[26] For example, at the high-status pre-viking settlement at Wharram Percy (Yorkshire) continuity of occupation into the ninth and tenth centuries witnessed the appearance of Scandinavian influences on elite material culture, including a decorated sword hilt-guard, a belt-slide and strap-end decorated in the Scandinavian Borre style, and Norwegian hone-stones.[27] It is impossible to state confidently that the lord who utilized this material culture was of Scandinavian descent, rather than an Anglo-Saxon lord who had chosen to adopt Scandinavian styles of lordly insignia, but it is apparent that lordship at this site was now expressed with reference to the new Scandinavian influence in local society.[28] Other recent studies of rural settlement have highlighted such processes as estate fragmentation and the emergence of a stratum of locally based "manorial" lords as important factors in settlement (re-)organization in the ninth century and later, and these processes were not confined to areas of Scandinavian settlement.[29] Thus, the arrival of Scandinavian settlers must have had a major impact on parts of the rural landscape of northern and eastern England, but that impact was undoubtedly mediated by a range of factors including the nature of lordship and of estate organization.

There was a notable expansion of urban life in eastern England from the later ninth century, but while this evidently occurred during the period of Scandinavian political control, the precise contribution of the Scandinavians remains elusive.[30] For example, significant economic reorganization seems to have occurred at York in the generation around 900. At roughly the same time that Scandinavian kings began to sponsor large issues of coins (see p. 206), the Coppergate manufacturing site was reorganized into regular tenements, which together must have been intended to encourage trade.[31] However, whether the impetus for these initiatives lay with the Scandinavian kings of York or, alternatively, with the archbishops of York, is unclear.[32] The developments in the York townscape are not specifically Scandinavian, and can be paralleled in the same period at, for example, Winchester, while the buildings excavated at Coppergate are of a type common to the trading centers of north-west Europe, and are not specific to a Scandinavian milieu.[33] We know little about how the late ninth-century Scandinavian kings of York conducted themselves, although their coinage reveals that they adapted and modified an indigenous component of royal authority and that they undoubtedly did so with the support of the archbishop (see p. 206). It is, thus, not implausible that the combined efforts of Scandinavian kings and the secular and ecclesiastical elite of York encouraged the economic developments identifiable in the archaeological record.

Pottery production in eastern England was transformed in the second half of the ninth century. It became increasingly restricted to urban contexts, such as Lincoln, Stamford (Lincolnshire), and Thetford (Norfolk), and the fast wheel was reintroduced for the first time since the Roman period. The styles and forms of some of the pottery indicate continental influence, and the continental potters, and indeed moneyers (see p. 204), operating in later ninth-century eastern English towns may have been deliberately introduced by the Scandinavian conquerors. At the very least, their presence reflects the wide-ranging continental contacts that the Scandinavians had in the later ninth century.[34] Yet, in few regions of Scandinavia was pottery made or even used in the ninth century, and it is striking that the influence of the settlers should be detectable in the development of an industry that has no Scandinavian counterpart. Both the Scandinavian settlers and the indigenous population, with a tradition of hand-made pottery, were faced with a new product. Moreover, since the vessels used in preparing, serving, and eating food were rarely merely functional, inhabitants of eastern England were also faced with a new cultural medium, and one that both groups speedily adopted, given the absence of importation of steatite vessels on any notable scale or of continuity of production of hand-made wares in many regions. This provides further evidence for the processes of acculturation, this time at the household and family level.[35] Finally, Leigh Symonds has recently analyzed patterns of pottery distribution and use in Lincolnshire, demonstrating that Lindsey (northern Lincolnshire) is dominated by wares from Lincoln and Torksey, while Stamford wares are largely found south of the River Witham, in the districts of Kesteven and Holland. The different pottery traditions are mirrored by the different sculptural traditions of Lindsey and south Lincolnshire in the tenth century, and Symonds concludes that regional identities were possibly expressed not only by the elite but also by wider society through their trading contacts and consumption of regionally distinctive patterns of pottery.[36] What role Scandinavian settlement played in such patterns must remain at least an open question.

In recent years, liaison between museum curators and metal-detector users has resulted in the recovery and recording of large amounts of metalwork demonstrating Scandinavian influence, much of which comes from the eastern counties from Yorkshire down to East Anglia. Some of this metalwork is purely Scandinavian, including trefoil brooches, small quadrangular openwork brooches, convex disc-brooches, and miniature Thor's hammers.[37] However, the majority of the metalwork recovered combines Scandinavian forms and styles with indigenous counterparts: for example, many disc-brooches with a characteristically flat Anglo-Saxon profile incorporate Scandinavian-style decoration.[38] Experimentation in the production of jewelry and dress accessories is also evident in the transfer to disc-brooches of designs typically found in Scandinavia on pendants, while designs found on some strap-ends are paralleled in Scandinavia mainly on disc-brooches.[39] Thus, it is thought likely that the manufacture of such artifacts occurred in the context of settlement and interaction with the Anglo-Saxon population, resulting in the modification of traditional Scandinavian forms of jewelry and dress accessories.[40] Gabor Thomas has argued that the lack of typically Scandinavian artifacts may reflect an avoidance of obviously "foreign" accessories. Thus, in this medium of small, personal objects, albeit seemingly mass-produced, there seems to have been no obvious signaling of an overtly Scandinavian identity; rather, it betrays cultural assimilation.[41] It is striking that artistic experimentation seems to have been most commonly expressed on female dress accessories, disc-brooches in particular, and the possibility that intermarriage was an important component of acculturation suggests itself.[42] The social interactions of the majority of society are not documented, but it is certainly the case that among the elite intermarriage was an important component of political alliances in the tenth century: for example, the sister of King Æthelstan of Wessex married King Sihtric of York following negotiations between the two rulers at Tamworth (Warwickshire) in 926 (*EHD*, I, 218).

Intriguingly, in Lincolnshire much of this metalwork has been recovered from districts in which Scandinavian place-names formed with the characteristic -*by* ending are common, which, as we have seen, were apparently formed in purely or overwhelmingly Norse settlement contexts.[43] As yet, there is insufficiently close dating of the metalwork, not least because of its recovery by metal-detectorists rather than during excavation, but an issue for future research will be to determine whether the contrasting impressions of onomastic and material culture evidence are to be explained by chronology or by the differing dynamics of the acculturation processes in diverse contexts.

Scandinavian burials have been identified in England at around only 30 sites, largely on the basis of practices no longer common among the Anglo-Saxons, namely cremation and inhumation with grave-goods.[44] While we have become increasingly cautious about assigning ethnic identity on the basis of burial rite, the supposition that many of the more extensively furnished burials of the decades around 900 are those of Scandinavians has recently begun to be confirmed scientifically. Stable isotope analysis, involving chemical analysis of teeth and bones, can reveal differences in the consumption in infancy of drinking water, which is itself geographically sensitive, and this, in turn, can reveal the region in which an individual spent their earliest years. Isotopic signatures indicative of origins in Scandinavia have been identified in recent analyses of elaborate burials at both Repton (Derbyshire) and Adwick-le-Street (Yorkshire).[45] In the context of the extensive Scandinavian linguistic influence, the small number of obviously Scandinavian burials has long been regarded as anomalous. Although there are undoubtedly new discoveries to be made – recent additions to the long-standing corpus of burials have, indeed, been excavated at Cumwhitton (Cumbria) and Adwick-le-Street – the fact that large numbers of burials of ninth- and tenth-century date continue to be regularly excavated, but those of overtly Scandinavian-type emerge but rarely, suggests that elaborate funerary display was a short-lived phenomenon among the Scandinavian settlers in England.[46]

The ways in which newly settled communities bury and commemorate their dead are rarely merely conservative reflections of practices in their homelands, and can be part of contemporary political strategies. For example, the late ninth-century cemetery at Heath Wood, Ingleby (Derbyshire), with its combination of cremation, mound burial in a visible hillside location, and sacrifice of animals and weapons, has been interpreted as a display of "instability and insecurity of some sort . . . a statement of religious, political and military affiliation in unfamiliar and inhospitable surroundings."[47] Here, it seems, the settlers were behaving in a self-consciously "Scandinavian" manner and expressing an overt commitment to paganism, as a statement of their appropriation of Mercian territory.[48] Such funerary displays, which arguably looked back consciously to the Scandinavian homelands, were, however, not the norm. Many of the burials identified as those of Scandinavians, largely on the basis of the presence of grave-goods, are to be found within pre-existing cemeteries, sometimes adjacent to churches, probably an indication of the practice of drawing on the power of the past to underpin authority over newly settled territory. The early tenth century witnessed the emergence of innovative forms of stone funerary sculptures, which drew ultimately on Anglo-Saxon practices of monumentation.[49] They take us beyond the remit of this chapter, but it is, nonetheless, important to note that these sculptures combine Christian imagery and traditional English styles with Scandinavian artistic influences and even sometimes incorporate scenes from Norse mythology. Sculptures came to be found at a wider variety of churches than in the eighth and ninth centuries, which suggests the influence of secular patrons, as does the more frequent depiction of secular imagery, including warriors.[50] Stone sculptures were scarcely known at this time in Scandinavia, beyond the island of Gotland, and thus the sculptures in England also represent the Scandinavians adopting and influencing an unfamiliar form of funerary display as part of the processes of acculturation.[51]

Those burials in England that appear to be of Scandinavians are mainly those of adult men, and they contain items strongly associated with early medieval masculinity and lordship, in particular weapons. Examples from a generation or so either side of 900 include burials accompanied by weapons (at Repton, Heath Wood, Hesket in the Forest in Cumbria, Kildale and Wensley, both in Yorkshire), equestrian equipment (such as the spurs and horse-bit at Hesket in the Forest and the spurs and possible bridle at Cumwhitton) and perhaps even horses on occasion (as at Reading, Berkshire), and also items associated with agriculture (such as the sickles at Hesket in the Forest and Wensley) or trade (such as a set of balances from a grave at Kildale).[52] It therefore appears that expressions of Scandinavian identity in a funerary context were constructed with an emphasis on masculine display, and it was by this means that claims to land and status were conveyed. If the corpus of Scandinavian burials is representative, then there seems to have been less investment in the graves of Scandinavian women, and they thus remain largely archaeologically indistinguishable from indigenous burials.[53] The overwhelmingly masculine display in the funerary record of the settlers in England is striking, and, in this respect, it contrasts with the situation elsewhere in Britain and Ireland (see below). Further indications that deliberate choices were made about burial display include the apparent absence of certain characteristically Scandinavian funerary practices, such as boat burial, and the inclusion of grave-goods of non-Scandinavian manufacture, such as Carolingian belt fittings and Anglo-Saxon swords and coins.[54] In the same way that Scandinavian rulers in England minted coins with a mixture of Anglo-Saxon and Carolingian influences as part of the material expression of their kingship (see chapter 13), the contents of Scandinavian burials suggest that they were created by communities practicing more than mere cultural conservatism: they were, rather, responding creatively to the circumstances of conquest and the need to underpin their authority over newly occupied territories.

Scotland

It has been suggested (see p. 197) that Scandinavian settlement in the northern isles of Scotland commenced in the eighth century before the first recorded viking raids on the British coast, although the evidence is largely circumstantial and it is not thought that extensive settlement occurred until after the mid-ninth century. The later Scandinavian sagas, poems, and histories (mainly of the twelfth to fourteenth centuries) have much to say about this subsequent Scandinavian colonization of parts of mainland Scotland and its isles, especially about the creation of the earldom of Orkney under Norwegian royal influence allegedly some time in the later ninth century, but the detail of these sources cannot be regarded as trustworthy. The *Annals of Ulster* and the *Anglo-Saxon Chronicle* occasionally inform us of events in Scotland, but do not elucidate the processes of settlement.[55] Accordingly, it is to the extensive archaeological and onomastic evidence that we must turn to explore the nature of the Scandinavian settlement. Burials reflecting Scandinavian influence are far more numerous in Scotland than in England, as are rural settlements, not least because the stone buildings of the northern and western isles are archaeologically much more visible than the timber structures more typical of England.[56] Scandinavian place-names are ubiquitous in Orkney, Shetland, and Caithness, and it was in these regions that the Norse dialect known as Norn was widely spoken into the later Middle Ages and beyond. Norse place-names are also common in the western isles.[57] It has aptly been observed in a recent review by James Barrett that "Viking-Age Scotland must provide one of the clearest examples of population movement into previously occupied territory known to archaeology."[58]

Although the place-name, linguistic, and archaeological evidence revealing Scandinavian influence suggests extensive Scandinavian settlement in the northern and western isles, nonetheless radically different interpretations of the nature, scale, and chronology of the settlement have been generated. For example, a generation ago, F. T. Wainwright wrote of a mass migration, in which the Scandinavians "arrived in numbers sufficient to overwhelm the earlier inhabitants politically, socially, cultur-ally and linguistically," while others have proposed that the indigenous population was expelled or even exterminated.[59] It is, above all, the linguistic impact of the Scandinavian settlers that has prompted suggestions that the indigenous population was overwhelmed, and unlike in England there are few linguistic indications of interaction between the settlers and the local population. Exceptions include some place-names from the western isles that incorporate both Gaelic and Scandinavian naming elements.[60] An attempt to draw deductions about interaction between the Norse and the indigenous populations on the basis of place-names on the isle of Lewis (Hebrides), where settlement names are typically Norse while landscape fea-tures are more commonly of Gaelic origin, led Magne Oftedal to conclude that the moors and hills of Lewis became "the domain of a subjugated Celtic-speaking class whose tasks were to attend to the shielings, the sheep and the peat-bogs."[61] However, interpretation of the place-names of the western isles is complicated by the revival of Gaelic from the thirteenth century, and it is not even certain which of the Celtic languages was spoken in these islands prior to Scandinavian settlement.[62] Place-names incorporating the Norse word for priest (*papar*; for example, Papa Stronsay and Papa Westray in Orkney) have been interpreted as evidence of the presence of ecclesiastical communities encountered by the Scandinavians. However, most such names are first recorded in later medieval sources, and even if they were contemporary in origin with the earliest Scandinavian encounters with religious communities few of the places with *papar* names have unequivocal evidence of ecclesiastical activity prior to the tenth century, although several, including Papa Stronsay and Papil (on West Burra, Shetland), do possess pre-viking sculptures.[63]

It tends to be archaeologists who emphasize the continuing influence of the indigenous population on the society and culture of the Scottish isles through the ninth century and beyond.[64] Attention has been drawn, for example, to the fact that what appear to be characteristically Scandinavian rectangular and bow-sided buildings, which contrast with the indigenous circular and cellular forms, are often found at pre-existing settlements, such as Buckquoy (Orkney) and Jarlshof (Shetland). Furthermore, at Jarlshof, local construction techniques were employed in at least one rectangular building, while at Buckquoy one of the rectangular buildings had a curved gable end, suggesting that it had incorporated part of an earlier house into its structure.[65] Interaction with the local community is also indicated by the presence of indigenous, as well as Scandinavian, material culture at settlements characterized by the appearance of rectangular and bow-sided buildings, including Buckquoy and Pool on Sanday (Orkney).[66] In particular, reliance on the local community is strongly suggested by the use of locally manufactured pottery at sites such as The Udal on North Uist (Hebrides), given that the settlers did not arrive with a tradition of pottery production.[67] The apparently straightforward association of the Scandinavian settlers with new building forms has also been weakened by more recent identification of such forms in pre-Norse settlements. Examples include roughly rectangular pre-Norse buildings at Skaill (Deerness, Orkney) and at the Wag of Forse (Caithness), and a rectangular courtyard area at Pool "more in keeping with Norse architectural styles than with expected native traditions."[68] At the latter, it has also been revealed that a pre-Norse round-house survived into the eleventh century.[69] Given that it is rarely possible to date building phases precisely, it is possible that many other circular buildings of ostensibly indigenous type survived into the ninth century and beyond. In sum, new building forms were once accepted as an index of Scandinavian settlement, but it is now recognized that they occur alongside indigenous material culture and are, thus, a less secure marker of ethnic identity.

Burials betraying Scandinavian influences, in the form of elaborate assemblages of grave-goods, are much more numerous in Scotland than in England. They include many more female and juvenile burials, and there is also more evidence for such distinctively Scandinavian practices as burial in ships and in ship-shaped settings of stones. Such burials have been excavated at Clibberswick on Unst (Shetland), Pierowall on Westray (Orkney), Càrn a'Bharraich on Oronsay, and Kiloran Bay on Colonsay (both in the Hebrides), and Reay in Caithness, and they appear to span the period from the mid-ninth to the mid-tenth century.[70] The greater visibility of Scandinavian burials in Scotland than England reflects a more overt and long-lived display of Scandinavian identity expressed through the burials of all members of the community. However, this need not simply be because of a greater scale of Scandinavian settlement in the northern and western isles, although that was probably a factor. Rather, it perhaps also indicates how extensive was the Scandinavian replacement of indigenous authority, and reflects a slower adaptation to indigenous modes of funerary display than in England. Rivalry between Scandinavian settlers in Scotland may also have been manifest in elaborate burial ritual.

Yet the distinctiveness of the Scandinavian influence on burials is only part of the picture. Although many sites have produced only two or three furnished burials, the apparently small-scale nature of such cemeteries may be misleading as there are often hints, in the form of disarticulated human remains and scatters of artifacts, that there were other burials in the vicinity, and in some cases they pre-date the Scandinavian burials. For example, at Westness on Rousay (Orkney) elaborate burials, including boat burials, were inserted into a cemetery of unfurnished cist burials, which have been radio-carbon dated to the seventh to ninth century.[71] In such contexts, the Scandinavians appear to have been adopting aspects of the funerary landscape of the local population, and we can surmise that this may have been a means by which they established their position. Intermarriage was probably another. This is suggested mainly by later written sources, including the sagas, but there is tantalizing burial and material culture evidence to support this late tradition.[72]

First, the presence of "Celtic" artifacts alongside those of Scandinavian manufacture in female graves in Scotland, including the bronze ladle and discs in a grave at Ballinaby (Islay) and ringed-pin in a grave at Càrn a'Bharraich, may reflect Scandinavian men having married women from Britain and Ireland.[73] At the very least, it reveals that it is mainly in female graves that insular links are expressed. Second, intriguing new research using stable isotope evidence from skeletal remains to identify aspects of diet has revealed that, despite their maritime setting, the inhabitants of the northern isles only began to consume a marine diet in the Viking Age, and among Scandinavian-type burials it is males that reveal signs of marine consumption. Female marine protein consumption is evident only later in unfurnished, and presumably Christian, cemeteries.[74] The scale of this research is too limited to have produced conclusive results, and factors relating to social status may also be relevant, but it hints at the possibility that at least some of the males in furnished graves were from a different cultural milieu than the females in such graves, and may provide further evidence of intermarriage with British women. Finally, a small number of inscriptions are suggestive of intermarriage. A silver and gold Irish-type brooch found at Hunterston (Ayrshire) bears a runic inscription stating that "Melbrigda owns [this] brooch," which indicates that an item of indigenous manufacture had at some point come into Scandinavian ownership, yet intriguingly Melbrigda is a Celtic personal name. A sculpture from the island of Bressay (Shetland), thought to be of ninth- or tenth-century date, incorporates an ogham inscription that appears to include the Norse word for daughter alongside what are thought to be a series of Pictish personal names.[75] None of this evidence confirms intermarriage, but it does offer some intriguing potential insights into processes of acculturation that are undocumented, or only appear in late sources.

We may doubt that there is any straightforward connection between material culture and ethnic identity, yet the visibility of Scandinavian influence in Scotland, even if it sometimes reflects the adoption of Scandinavian styles by the indigenous population, suggests that this region experienced the greatest level of Scandinavian settlement in Britain. There also appear to have been considerably fewer opportunities or imperatives for Scandinavians to acculturate and adopt and adapt indigenous styles of elite material culture and expressions of lordship, especially in the funerary context, than occurred elsewhere. Yet, the archaeological evidence also suggests a variety of possible scenarios for interaction between the settlers and the locals. Even in the same regions, expressions of identity might vary between differing contexts: for example, indigenous material culture is found at many settlement sites, but it is rare in burials.[76] This probably reflects the contrast between material culture used in everyday contexts, and that selected more consciously for the purposes of social display, and expression of a more overtly Scandinavian ethnic signature, in the context of funerary rites. This contrast serves as a reminder that distributions of material culture are not invariably passive reflections of ethnic identity, but that they may be manipulated in specific circumstances as part of the process of constructing ethnic and other social identities.

Wales

Written sources do not illuminate Scandinavian settlement in Wales. Nonetheless, it can be inferred from the smattering of Scandinavian place-names, mostly in coastal locations, although it is thought that some of these, especially in Pembrokeshire, may have been introduced in the wake of Norman expansion in the late eleventh century.[77] There are very few burials, metalwork hoards, or sculptured stones betraying Scandinavian influence in Wales, and those that are known – such as sparsely furnished burials at Talacre (Flintshire) and Benllech (Anglesey), a hoard of silver arm-rings from Red Wharf Bay (Anglesey), and sculptures with elements of Scandinavian influence at Whitford (Flintshire) and Penmom (Anglesey) – largely date to the tenth century.[78] Recently, however, excavations at Llanbedrgoch on Anglesey, at the heart of the kingdom of Gwynedd, have provided new insight into the ninth-century Scandinavian impact on Wales. The excavations revealed an enclosed settlement, perhaps an estate center, dating from as early as the seventh century, which in the ninth century developed as a trading post and manufacturing center. The strengthening of the defenses in the latter part of the ninth century may have been at royal instigation, and it broadly coincides with the reign of Rhodri Mawr (844–78). The presence of Scandinavian material culture at the site – including a copper-alloy belt buckle decorated in the Scandinavian Borre style and hack-silver, including fragments of arm-rings – cannot, however, be used to demonstrate a Scandinavian takeover, not the least because such artifacts occur alongside items of indigenous manufacture. Moreover, it is difficult to interpret the mixture of material culture when, as here and as opposed to Scotland, the site is such an isolated one. It can, however, be determined that the site came increasingly into an Irish-Sea milieu, given the similarity of its material culture with that found elsewhere around the coast of Ireland and the western seaboard of mainland Britain.[79]

Ireland

The written evidence has much to reveal about viking raids and interaction with Irish kings, but has little to say about settlement. There are few place-names of Scandinavian origin, or Irish place-names that had been Scandinavianized in some way, suggesting limited settlement, and it may be suggestive that these names tend to be restricted to the coastal areas. Archaeological evidence for Scandinavian rural settlement in Ireland is also thin, and essentially limited to hoards of metalwork (see p. 206), and, accordingly, Scandinavian settlement in Ireland has long been regarded as an essentially urban phenomenon. Over the past two decades, interpretation has shifted in the wake of increasing numbers of urban excavations, especially in Dublin. Where once urban settlements were regarded as trading outposts mainly engaged in long-distance exchange, they are now recognized as fully functioning urban settlements, with manufacturing and trading activities, and reliant on the rural hinterland for their resources. This has led John Bradley to deduce that, despite the lack of diagnostically Scandinavian material culture in the countryside, there must have been Scandinavian settlement around the nascent towns otherwise they would have been vulnerable to being cut off from the resources of their hinterlands.[80] Much of the archaeological evidence, such as buildings and traded goods revealed during the extensive excavations in Dublin at Fishamble Street and Wood Quay to the south of the River Liffey, dates to the tenth century, and comparatively little is known of the nature of ninth-century urbanism.[81] Nonetheless, the amount of silver brought into circulation by the Scandinavians in Ireland in the ninth century indicates considerable trading activity prior to the development of the tenth-century towns, and may reveal that the *longphoirt* served not only as military strongholds but also as economic centers.[82]

Few burials that betray Scandinavian influences have been excavated in Ireland, and most are seemingly isolated in eastern coastal locations.[83] One exception is the cluster of burials accompanied by weapons and, to a lesser extent, jewelry of Scandinavian type dating to the ninth century at Kilmainham and Islandbridge on the west side of Dublin. At both sites, furnished burials were inserted into pre-existing Christian cemeteries, characterized by west–east aligned, unaccompanied cist burials, one of which, at Kilmainham, is believed to have been associated with the monastery of St. Maignenn founded in the seventh century.[84] There has been debate about whether these cemeteries indicate the location of the *longphort* at Dublin, which would place it around 2 km upstream from the tenth-century town revealed during the excavations at Wood Quay and Fishamble Street. More recently, however, excavations at Temple Bar West, at the confluence of the rivers Liffey and Poddle, have uncovered traces of ninth-century buildings, prompting speculation that the *longphort* was located in this area. This has been reinforced by the discovery of ninth-century burials accompanied by Scandinavian-type artifacts at Ship Street Great and South Great George Street on the opposite banks of the River Poddle, in an area with early Christian communities.[85] Furthermore, in recent years it has become clearer that the long-held belief that the Scandinavians initiated urban centers may not be wholly accurate. Many of the towns that emerged in the later ninth and tenth centuries, many with origins as a *longphort*, were at ecclesiastical centers where trade and manufacture had previously been conducted.[86]

Isle of Man

Given its location, it is most unlikely that the Isle of Man avoided viking interest in the ninth century, but the direct evidence we have for this is limited. As in Scotland, the emergence of new building styles has been identified as the result of Scandinavian settlement. The most well-known example is from the Braaid where circular, rectangular, and bow-sided buildings have been identified, and there are a number of sites, such as Cronk ny Merriu, where rectangular buildings were constructed within Iron Age promontory forts.[87] However, none of the sites excavated thus far is closely datable or has associated finds of particularly Scandinavian type, while the chronological relationships between the three distinctive buildings at the Braaid is uncertain.[88] There are a number of striking burials from the island that betray Scandinavian influence, including the boat burials at Balladoole and Knock y Doonee. However, it is currently thought that they date to the tenth century, as do most of the hoards of silver jewelry and coins that were Scandinavian introductions and the distinctive sculpture with its amalgamation of Scandinavian mythology and Christian imagery.[89] When evidence for the Scandinavian impact on Man first emerges in the tenth century, it is apparent that a significant shift in its orientation has occurred. Man was British-speaking prior to the Viking Age, and there were political connections with Wales in the early Middle Ages, but by the tenth century the island was a Gaelic-speaking polity, with connections to the western isles, revealed in the similarity of silver jewelry in hoards from the two regions.[90] On present evidence, the extent to which this transition in the context of Manx society had occurred during the course of the ninth century is, however, uncertain.

Conclusion

The differing levels of Scandinavian and indigenous influence discernible in the linguistic and archaeological record of Britain and Ireland must relate not only to the scale of Scandinavian settlement, but also to the political status of the settlers vis-à-vis the newcomers and to pre-existing political rivalries. In England, the Scandinavians quickly adopted Anglo-Saxon styles of kingship, which included acceptance of baptism, engagement in written diplomacy, and the minting of coins (see chapter 13), and they assumed the political apparatus of three of the four existing English kingdoms. They evidently drew on the power of the church as a means of legitimizing their authority, a practice that extended to the burial strategies of some of the settlers. This political dimension seems to have had broader ramifications, as it is notable that innovative forms of material culture, including jewelry and pottery, were produced in the context of Anglo-Scandinavian interaction, and distinctive Scandinavian styles are relatively rare. In contrast, in Scotland, the Scandinavian imprint is far more visible. The political instability of ninth-century Scotland, albeit shadowy in the reliable written sources, appears to have limited the possibilities or impetus for Scandinavian adoption of indigenous forms of lordship, especially in a funerary context. Aside from the longer-lived tradition of burial with grave-goods, it is notable that Scandinavian influence on stone sculptures was minimal and mainly dates to the period from the later tenth century onward.[91] The disappearance of the Pictish language and almost total absence of Pictish place-names in the northern isles and Outer Hebrides, while largely the result of extensive Scandinavian settlement, may, in part, have been influenced by a shift to speaking Gaelic in the former Pictish kingdom. This arguably removed an important incentive to maintaining the Pictish linguistic heritage among the indigenous population.[92] Indeed, the disappearance of traditional Pictish imagery on picture stones during the ninth century, to be replaced by increasingly overt Christian imagery, has been identified as a means by which the dynasty of the Dál Riata descended from Cinaed mac Ailpín expressed its political ascendancy.[93] Thus, language shifts may have been related to local political factors in addition to the sheer weight of numbers of settlers.

In Ireland, Scandinavian settlement was seemingly largely restricted to urban locations, although not necessarily exclusively so as the hoards demonstrate. Older argument that the settlers were the founders of towns in Ireland has been superseded by a recognition of the influence of pre-existing centers of trade and manufacture on the locations of Scandinavian trading places. The reorientation of political and trading links of the Isle of Man and Wales with other parts of Britain and Ireland can be faintly discerned, but it is only in the tenth century and later that the details of this can be elucidated, and it is unsafe to assume too much about ninth-century developments from this later evidence.

What remains elusive is how the ninth-century inhabitants of those regions settled by Scandinavians perceived of themselves. Neither material culture nor language can reliably be equated to ethnic identity. Nonetheless, simply because ethnic identities could be malleable, it does not necessarily follow that feelings of "Scandinavianness" were quickly or invariably cast aside. In a deduction that applies equally well to other regions of Scandinavian settlement, James Barrett recently argued that the apparently conflicting evidence from Scotland implies "both large scale Norse migration *and* the co-existence of indigenous and immigrant groups in terms of material culture, biology, language and – by implication – possibly self-conscious ethnicity as well."[94] Yet, as we strive to make sense of our diverse sources, and in the light of the seemingly contradictory impressions that sometimes emerge from our scrutiny of this evidence, it is important that we do not assume that the Scandinavian settlers had a common identity, or that they and their descendants were invariably bound together by innate ethnic affiliations. "Scandinavianness" was apparently inter-cut with other identities, such as age, gender, profession, and political affiliation, caveats which apply equally to the indigenous peoples alongside whom they settled.

Notes

1 Dumville, "The Vikings in the British Isles."
2 Barrett, "Beyond war or peace"; Hadley, "Viking and native."
3 Abrams and Parsons, "Place-names."
4 Cameron, "The Grimston-hybrids," "Place-names in thorp," and *Scandinavian Settlement*.
5 Sawyer, *Kings and Vikings*, p. 103.
6 Richards, *Viking-Age England*, p. 47.
7 Fellows-Jensen, *Scandinavian Settlement Names*, pp. 269–372.
8 Townend, *Language and History*, p. 188.
9 Fellows-Jensen, "Scandinavian place-names," pp. 31–42.
10 Higham, "Viking-Age settlement," pp. 299–303.
11 Townend, *Language and History*, pp. 43–68.
12 Sawyer, *Kings and Vikings*, pp. 102–3.
13 Abrams and Parsons, "Place-names," pp. 394–403.
14 Ibid.
15 Kastovsky, "Semantics and vocabulary," pp. 332–6.
16 Barnes, "Norse in the British Isles," p. 81.

17 Townend, *Language and History*, pp. 43–179.
18 Ibid., pp. 2–3.
19 Bailey, *England's Earliest Sculptors*, pp. 77–94.
20 Hadley, *Vikings in England*, pp. 98–9.
21 Coggins, "Simy Folds: twenty years on"; King, "Post-Roman upland architecture"; Richards, "Identifying Anglo-Scandinavian settlements," pp. 298–9.
22 Richards, "Identifying Anglo-Scandinavian settlements," pp. 299–302.
23 Ibid., pp. 301–2.
24 Ibid.
25 Batey, "Aspects of rural settlement," p. 89.
26 Richards, "Identifying Anglo-Scandinavian settlements," pp. 302–3.
27 Richards, "Finding the Vikings," pp. 274–5.
28 Ibid., p. 276.
29 Higham, "Viking-Age settlement," pp. 307–8.
30 Hall, "The Five Boroughs."
31 Hall, "Afterword," p. 499.
32 Rollason, *Northumbria*, pp. 223–4, 230.
33 Richards, *Viking-Age England*, pp. 62–7.
34 Hinton, *Archaeology, Economy and Society*, pp. 82–7; Kilmurry, *Pottery Industry of Stamford*, pp. 176–95.
35 Hadley, *Vikings in England*, pp. 178–9.
36 Symonds, "Territories in transition," pp. 30–3.
37 Leahy and Paterson, "New light on the Viking presence," pp. 192–5; Thomas, "Anglo-Scandinavian metalwork," pp. 241–2.
38 Leahy and Paterson, "New light on the Viking presence," pp. 196–7.
39 Ibid., pp. 195–6.
40 Ibid., p. 193; Margeson, *Vikings in Norfolk*, pp. 15–18.
41 Thomas, "Anglo-Scandinavian metalwork," p. 252.
42 Hadley, *Vikings in England*, p. 127; Leahy and Paterson, "New light on the Viking presence," pp. 193–7.
43 Leahy and Paterson, "New light on the Viking presence," pp. 183–9, 198–9.
44 Richards, *Viking-Age England*, pp. 142–58.
45 Budd et al., "Investigating population movement," pp. 137–8; Speed and Walton Rogers, "A burial of a Viking woman."
46 Hadley, *Vikings in England*, pp. 246–50.
47 Richards et al., "Heath Wood, Ingleby," p. 66.
48 Richards, "Boundaries and cult centres," pp. 101–2.
49 Griffiths, "Settlement and acculturation," pp. 127, 131–8.
50 Bailey, *England's Earliest Sculptors*, pp. 76–94.
51 Ibid., p.76; Hadley, *Vikings in England*, pp. 258–60.
52 Hadley, *Vikings in England*, pp. 257–60.
53 Ibid., pp. 243–4.
54 Edwards, *Vikings in North-West England*, pp. 9, 16–17.
55 Crawford, *Scandinavian Scotland*, pp. 51–8.
56 Graham-Campbell and Batey, *Vikings in Scotland*, pp. 113–78.
57 Crawford, *Scandinavian Scotland*, pp. 37–41.
58 Barrett, "Beyond war or peace," p. 207.
59 Wainwright, *Northern Isles*, pp. 125–6; see also Crawford, "War or peace."
60 Crawford, *Scandinavian Scotland*, pp. 96–8.
61 Oftedal, "The Isle of Lewis," p. 187.
62 Crawford, *Scandinavian Scotland*, pp. 96–7.

63 Barrett, "Christian and pagan practice."
64 Barrett, "Beyond war or peace," p. 208; Sharples and Parker Pearson, "Norse settlement in the Outer Hebrides."
65 Graham-Campbell and Batey, *Vikings in Scotland*, pp. 155–67.
66 Ibid., pp. 163, 173.
67 Ibid., pp. 173–4.
68 Ibid., pp. 169, 171.
69 Ibid., p. 173.
70 Ibid., pp. 113–54.
71 Ibid., pp. 113–42.
72 Crawford, *Scandinavian Scotland*, pp. 47–8, 60, 64–8.
73 Graham-Campbell and Batey, *Vikings in Scotland*, pp. 116–18, 123–4.
74 Barrett and Richards, "Identity, gender, religion and economy."
75 Graham-Campbell and Batey, *Vikings in Scotland*, p. 43.
76 Barrett, "Beyond war or peace," p. 214.
77 Redknap, "Viking-Age settlement in Wales," pp. 139–40, 143.
78 Redknap, *Vikings in Wales*, pp. 18, 88–98.
79 Redknap, "Viking-Age settlement in Wales," pp. 147–69.
80 Bradley, "The interpretation of Scandinavian settlement."
81 Wallace, "The origins of Dublin."
82 Sheehan, "Early Viking-Age silver hoards."
83 Ó Floinn, "The archaeology of the early Viking Age," pp. 131–48.
84 O'Brien, "The location and context of Viking burials."
85 Hall, *Exploring the World of the Vikings*, pp. 87–8, 122–3.
86 Clarke, "The topographical development," pp. 61–3, 68–9.
87 Cubbon, "The archaeology of the vikings," p. 18; Gelling, "A Norse homestead."
88 Richards, "Identifying Anglo-Scandinavian settlements," pp. 298–9.
89 Cubbon, "The archaeology of the vikings," pp. 16–18; Graham-Campbell, "Viking Age silver hoards"; Margeson, "On the iconography of the Manx crosses."
90 Dumville, "The Vikings in the British Isles," p. 218; Graham-Campbell, "Viking Age silver hoards."
91 Graham-Campbell and Batey, *Vikings in Scotland*, pp. 248–52.
92 Barrett, "Beyond war or peace," p. 216.
93 Driscoll, "The relationship between history and archaeology," pp. 185–6.
94 Ibid., p. 215.

Further Reading

There is no volume exploring the Scandinavian settlements across the whole of Britain and Ireland, but many volumes explore the diverse array of evidence from particular regions. On England, see D. M. Hadley and J. D. Richards (eds.), *Cultures in Contact: Scandinavian Settlement in England in the Ninth and Tenth Centuries* (Turnhout, 2000) and J. Graham-Campbell, R. A. Hall, J. Jesch, and D. N. Parsons (eds.), *Vikings and the Danelaw: Select Papers from the Proceedings of the Thirteenth Viking Congress* (Oxford, 2001). The most recent work of synthesis is my *Vikings in England*. A recent edited collection on the vikings in Ireland is H. B. Clarke, M. Ní Mhaonaigh, and R. Ó Floinn (eds.), *Ireland and Scandinavia in the Early Viking Age* (Dublin, 1998). Various contributions to J. Hines, A. Lane, and M. Redknap (eds.), *Land, Sea and Home* (Leeds, 2004), especially the paper by J. H. Barrett, provide the most recent discussions of the vikings in Scotland, and there are also papers on the Scandinavian influence on rural settlements in England and on the recent excavations at

Llanbedrgoch in Wales (by M. Redknap). This volume also includes an extended review of the study of Scandinavian place-names in England and of the historical debates to which they have contributed (by L. Abrams and D. N. Parsons). A detailed discussion of the archaeological evidence for Scotland appears in Graham-Campbell and Batey, *Vikings in Scotland*. A valuable review of the vikings in Man appeared after this chapter was completed, and will now be the essential introduction to this subject: D. M. Wilson, *Vikings in the Isle of Man* (Aarhus, 2008).

Bibliography

Abrams, L. and Parsons, D. N., "Place-names and the history of Scandinavian settlement in England," in J. Hines, A. Lane, and M. Redknap (eds.), *Land, Sea and Home*. Proceedings of a Conference on Viking-period Settlement, Cardiff, July 2001 (Leeds, 2004), pp. 379–431.

Bailey, R. N., *England's Earliest Sculptors* (Toronto, 1997).

Barnes, M., "Norse in the British Isles," in A. Faulkes and R. Perkins (eds.), *Viking Revaluations: Viking Society Centenary Symposium* (London, 1993), pp. 65–84.

Barrett, J. H., "Beyond war or peace: the study of culture contact in Viking-Age Scotland," in J. Hines, A. Lane, and M. Redknap (eds.), *Land, Sea and Home*. Proceedings of a Conference on Viking-period Settlement, Cardiff, July 2001 (Leeds, 2004), pp. 207–18.

Barrett, J. H., "Christian and pagan practice during the conversion of Viking Age Orkney and Shetland," in M. Carver (ed.), *The Cross Goes North* (Woodbridge, 2002), pp. 207–26.

Barrett, J. H. and Richards, M. P., "Identity, gender, religion and economy: new isotope and radiocarbon evidence for marine resource intensification in early historic Orkney, Scotland, UK," *European Journal of Archaeology*, 7: 3 (2004), 249–71.

Batey, C., "Aspects of rural settlement in northern Britain," in D. Hooke and S. Burnell (eds.), *Landscape and Settlement in Britain AD 400–1066* (Exeter, 1995), pp. 69–94.

Bradley, J., "The interpretation of Scandinavian settlement in Ireland," in J. Bradley (ed.), *Settlement and Society in Medieval Ireland* (Dublin, 1988), pp. 49–78.

Budd, P., Millard, A., Chenery, C., Lucy, S., and Roberts, C., "Investigating population movement by stable isotope analysis: a report from Britain," *Antiquity*, 78 (2004), 127–41.

Cameron, K., *Scandinavian Settlement in the Territory of the Five Boroughs: The Place-name Evidence* (Nottingham, 1965).

Cameron, K., "Scandinavian settlement in the territory of the five boroughs: the place-name evidence, part II: place-names in thorp," *Mediaeval Scandinavia*, 3 (1970), 35–49.

Cameron, K., "Scandinavian settlement in the territory of the five boroughs: the place-name evidence, part III: the Grimston-hybrids," in P. Clemoes and K. Hughes (eds.), *England before the Conquest* (Cambridge, 1971), pp. 147–63.

Clarke, H. B., "The topographical development of early medieval Dublin," in H. B. Clarke (ed.), *Medieval Dublin: The Making of a Metropolis* (Blackrock, 1990), pp. 52–69.

Coggins, D., "Simy Folds: twenty years on," in J. Hines, A. Lane, and M. Redknap (eds.), *Land, Sea and Home*. Proceedings of a Conference on Viking-period Settlement, Cardiff, July 2001 (Leeds, 2004), pp. 325–34.

Crawford, B. E., *Scandinavian Scotland* (Leicester, 1987).

Crawford, I. A., "War or peace: Viking colonisation in the northern and western isles of Scotland reviewed," in H. Bekker-Nielsen (ed.), *The Eighth Viking Congress* (Odense, 1981), pp. 259–69.

Cubbon, M., "The archaeology of the Vikings in the Isle of Man," in C. Fell, P. Foote, J. Graham-Campbell, and R. Thomson (eds.), *The Viking Age in the Isle of Man* (London, 1983), pp. 13–26.

Driscoll, S., "The relationship between history and archaeology: artefacts, documents and power," in S. Driscoll and S. Nieke (eds.), *Power and Politics in Early Medieval Britain and Ireland* (Edinburgh, 1988), pp. 162–87.

Dumville, D. N., "The Vikings in the British Isles," in J. Jesch (ed.), *The Scandinavians from the Vendel Period to the Tenth Century: An Ethnographic Perspective* (Woodbridge, 2001), pp. 209–40.

Edwards, B. J. N., *Vikings in North-West England* (Lancaster, 1998).

Fellows-Jensen, G., "Scandinavian place-names of the Irish Sea province," in J. Graham-Campbell (ed.), *Viking Treasure from the North-West: The Cuerdale Hoard in its Context* (Liverpool, 1992), pp. 31–42.

Fellows-Jensen, G., *Scandinavian Settlement Names in the East Midlands* (Copenhagen, 1978).

Gelling, P., "A Norse homestead near Doarlish Cashen, Kirk Patrick, Isle of Man," *Medieval Archaeology*, 14 (1970), 74–82.

Graham-Campbell, J., "Viking Age silver hoards from Man," in C. Fell, P. Foote, J. Graham-Campbell, and R. Thomson (eds.), *The Viking Age in the Isle of Man* (London, 1983), pp. 53–80.

Graham-Campbell, J. and Batey, C., *Vikings in Scotland: An Archaeological Survey* (Edinburgh, 1998).

Griffiths, D., "Settlement and acculturation in the Irish Sea region," in J. Hines, A. Lane, and M. Redknap (eds.), *Land, Sea and Home*. Proceedings of a Conference on Viking-period Settlement, Cardiff, July 2001 (Leeds, 2004), pp. 125–38.

Hadley, D. M., "Viking and native: re-thinking identity in the Danelaw," *Early Medieval Europe*, 11: 1 (2002), 45–70.

Hadley, D. M., *The Vikings in England: Settlement, Society and Culture* (Manchester, 2006).

Hall, R. A., "Afterword," in R. A. Hall (ed.), *Aspects of Anglo-Scandinavian York* (York, 2004), pp. 498–502.

Hall, R. A., *Exploring the World of the Vikings* (London, 2007).

Hall, R. A., "The Five Boroughs of the Danelaw: a review of present knowledge," *Anglo-Saxon England*, 18 (1989), 149–206.

Higham, N., "Viking-Age settlement in the north-western countryside: lifting the veil?," in J. Hines, A. Lane, and M. Redknap (eds.), *Land, Sea and Home*. Proceedings of a Conference on Viking-period Settlement, Cardiff, July 2001 (Leeds, 2004), pp. 297–311.

Hinton, D., *Archaeology, Economy and Society: England from the Fifth to the Fifteenth Century* (London, 1990).

Kastovsky, D., "Semantics and vocabulary," in R. Hogg (ed.), *The Cambridge History of the English Language*, vol. 1 (Cambridge, 1992), pp. 290–408.

Kilmurry, K., *The Pottery Industry of Stamford* (Oxford, 1980).

King, A., "Post-Roman upland architecture in the Craven dales and the dating evidence," in J. Hines, A. Lane, and M. Redknap (eds.), *Land, Sea and Home*. Proceedings of a Conference on Viking-period Settlement, Cardiff, July 2001 (Leeds, 2004), pp. 335–44.

Leahy, K. and Paterson, C., "New light on the Viking presence in Lincolnshire: the artefactual evidence," in J. Graham-Campbell, R. A. Hall, J. Jesch, and D. N. Parsons (eds.), *Vikings and the Danelaw: Select Papers from the Proceedings of the Thirteenth Viking Congress* (Oxford, 2001), pp. 181–202.

Margeson, S., "On the iconography of the Manx crosses," in C. Fell, P. Foote, J. Graham-Campbell, and R. Thomson (eds.), *The Viking Age in the Isle of Man* (London, 1983), pp. 95–106.

Margeson, S., *The Vikings in Norfolk* (Norwich, 1997).

O'Brien, E., "The location and context of Viking burials," in H. B. Clarke, M. Ní Mhaonaigh, and R. Ó Floinn (eds.), *Ireland and Scandinavia in the Early Viking Age* (Dublin, 1998), pp. 201–18.

Ó Floinn, R., "The archaeology of the early Viking Age in Ireland," in H. B. Clarke, M. Ní Mhaonaigh, and R. Ó Floinn (eds.), *Ireland and Scandinavia in the Early Viking Age* (Dublin, 1998), pp. 131–65.

Oftedal, M., "Names of lakes on the Isle of Lewis in the Outer Hebrides," in H. Bekker-Nielsen (ed.), *The Eighth Viking Congress* (Odense, 1981), pp. 183–7.

Redknap, M., "Viking-Age settlement in Wales," in J. Hines, A. Lane, and M. Redknap (eds.), *Land, Sea and Home*. Proceedings of a Conference on Viking-period Settlement, Cardiff, July 2001 (Leeds, 2004), pp. 139–75.

Redknap, M., *Vikings in Wales: An Archaeological Quest* (Cardiff, 2000).

Richards, J. D., "Boundaries and cult centres: Viking burial in Derbyshire," in J. Graham-Campbell, R. A. Hall, J. Jesch, and D. N. Parsons (eds.), *Vikings and the Danelaw: Select Papers from the Proceedings of the Thirteenth Viking Congress* (Oxford, 2001), pp. 97–104.

Richards, J. D., "Finding the Vikings: the hunt for Scandinavian rural settlement in the northern Danelaw," in J. Graham-Campbell, R. A. Hall, J. Jesch, and D. N. Parsons (eds.), *Vikings and the Danelaw: Select Papers from the Proceedings of the Thirteenth Viking Congress* (Oxford, 2001), pp. 268–77.

Richards, J. D., "Identifying Anglo-Scandinavian settlements," in D. M. Hadley and J. D. Richards (eds.), *Cultures in Contact: Scandinavian Settlement in England in the Ninth and Tenth Centuries* (Turnhout, 2000), pp. 295–309.

Richards, J. D., *Viking-Age England*, 2nd edn (Stroud, 2000).

Richards, J. D., Beswick, P., Bond, J., McKinley, J., Rowland, S., and Worley, F., "Excavations at the Viking barrow cemetery at Heath Wood, Ingleby, Derbyshire," *Antiquaries Journal*, 84 (2004), 23–116.

Rollason, D. W., *Northumbria 500–1100: Creation and Destruction of a Kingdom* (Cambridge, 2003).

Sawyer, P. H., *Kings and Vikings: Scandinavia and Europe AD 700–1100* (London, 1982).

Sharples, N. and Parker Pearson, M., "Norse settlement in the Outer Hebrides," *Norwegian Archaeological Review*, 32 (1999), 41–62.

Sheehan, J., "Early Viking-Age silver hoards from Ireland and their Scandinavian elements," in H. B. Clarke, M. Ní Mhaonaigh, and R. Ó Floinn (eds.), *Ireland and Scandinavia in the Early Viking Age* (Dublin, 1998), pp. 166–202.

Speed, G. and Walton Rogers, P., "A burial of a Viking woman at Adwick-le-Street, South Yorkshire," *Medieval Archaeology*, 48 (2004), 51–90.

Symonds, L., "Territories in transition: the construction of boundaries in Anglo-Scandinavian Lincolnshire," in D. Griffiths, S. Semple, and A. Reynolds (eds.), *Boundaries in Medieval Britain* (Oxford, 2003), pp. 28–37.

Thomas, G., "Anglo-Scandinavian metalwork from the Danelaw: exploring social and cultural interaction," in D. M. Hadley and J. D. Richards (eds.), *Cultures in Contact: Scandinavian Settlement in England in the Ninth and Tenth Centuries* (Turnhout, 2000), pp. 237–55.

Townend, M., *Language and History in Viking Age England: Linguistic Relations between Speakers of Old Norse and Old English* (Turnhout, 2002).

Wainwright, F. T., *The Northern Isles* (Edinburgh, 1962).

Wallace, P., "The origins of Dublin," in H. B. Clarke (ed.), *Medieval Dublin: The Making of a Metropolis* (Blackrock, 1990), pp. 70–97.

Whitelock, D. (ed. and trans.), *English Historical Documents*, vol. I: *c.500–1042*, 2nd edn. (London, 1979).

CHAPTER FIFTEEN

Britain, Ireland, and Europe, c.750–c.900

JANET L. NELSON

Contacts in Contexts

By the ninth century, western Europe was held together by many ties. Those best documented in the contemporary sources are ecclesiastical: the Christianity that bound so much of the zone was a religion of the book, and literacy, libraries, and archive-keeping were mostly in the hands of churchmen. *Peregrinatio pro Christo*, self-exile for Christ, was a devotional practice characteristic of Ireland, perhaps a spiritualized form of the political exile, or enslavement, inflicted in the struggles between the hundred or so kingdoms in the region, but well-acclimatized in Anglo-Saxon England.[1] Mostly men, but including some women, *peregrini* carried religious books and tokens in their travel bags and ideas in their heads, and they found hospitality at monasteries and convents, royal courts, aristocratic halls, and, last but not least, Rome where St. Peter's heir, the pope, resided. A Northumbrian princess, Æthelthryth, going north from Rome in 782 (the York scholar Alcuin was probably in her retinue on the outward journey in 780), stopped at Lucca in Tuscany to buy for the huge sum of 700 gold *solidi* (her retinue must have included some hefty guards) a church she presumably intended for use as a hostel by less well-off and therefore vulnerable Anglo-Saxon women pilgrims.[2] The exceptionally full Lucca archives also reveal a Welsh pilgrim passing through the city in 786 (he got involved in a legal dispute there).[3] *Peregrinatio* thus provided *transmission*, while cultural homogeneity across most of Europe enabled *reception*. This chapter, then, is about *connections*, across the sea-ways and isles of the East Atlantic Archipelago (the late Tim Reuter's apt term) and beyond to the continent.

The Irish were not alone in taking the Old Testament seriously, but their peregrinatory habits enabled them to promote among the Franks some literal applications of the law of Moses, such as the payment of tithe (a tenth of one's income) and a sense of identification as a New Israel.[4] Something of an Irish speciality were elaborate penitentials, specifying penances to be imposed by priests for specific sins. By the late eighth century, these books had been diffused widely in Anglo-Saxon England and on the continent.[5] The status of the pope as chief priest, authorizer of mission, remitter of sins, and granter of privilege was also firmly established, thanks not least to insular teachers. True, sociologically speaking, the western church at this time was a loose confederation of churches rather than a centralized institution: there were many gaps in the structure for Irish *peregrini* to fill. Particular religious communities and individuals were bound by reciprocal gift-giving; and religious identities, loyalties, and obligations were imagined as ties of kinship, patronage, and lordship. Members of such communities, who thought of themselves as *familiae*, "households," associated themselves with other *familiae*, as brothers and sisters, bound to pray for each other.[6] Nevertheless, all this coexisted with an increasingly widespread sense of overarching papal authority. As more communities and individuals sought papal blessing and legal protection, people from the East Atlantic Archipelago following well-beaten tracks to Rome necessarily traveled via Francia.

Other reasons enhanced Francia's connective and attractive power around the year 800. When the monks of St.-Riquier, not far from the mouth of the river Somme in Picardy, commissioned an Anglo-Saxon scholar to update the *Life* of their founding saint, they supplied the information, plausible if not true, that Richarius, a Frankish noble, back in the 620s, had felt called "to travel across the sea to preach to the inhabitants of *Saxonia* or *Britannia*."[7] "Across the sea" was a reality for men habituated not just to gazing out soulfully across the *baie de Somme* but to seeing off and welcoming ashore crews, voyagers, pilgrims, and cargoes. Also c.800, the brethren of Jumièges, near the mouth of the Seine, recalled their seventh-century founder Philibert: "he had a lot of money, thanks to the patronage of kings and the generosity of the faithful . . . he was able to send his monks across the sea with boats full of merchandise."[8] In the 830s, the monks of St.-Wandrille, near Rouen, celebrated their closeness to the River Seine, "famous for its sea-borne traffic, and outstandingly rich in fish"; their former abbot, Gervold (788–807?), must have been often absent doing his other job as "collector of taxes and tolls in various ports and cities, but especially in Quentovic," and "in consequence very strong bonds of friendship existed between him and the most mighty king of the Angles or Mercians, Offa."[9] By now, the trading place of Quentovic, at the mouth of the River Canche, was long established, and half a dozen monasteries, including the three just mentioned, had their own warehouses there.[10] Coinage had oiled this trade, and in the reign of Charlemagne (768–814), silver pennies of good quality were being issued from 40 different mints (some working intermittently).[11] Movement of men, goods, books, and ideas was not new in the long ninth century, then, and certainly not one-way. But the reconstructed and recharged Frankish empire, with the court of Charlemagne pounding at its center, got the flow running at new volume and with new intensity, and brought Britain, for the first time since Rome's fall, and Ireland for the first time ever, into close and frequent contact with continental Europe.[12] Charlemagne promoted what scholars nowadays call the Carolingian Renaissance: at once a *correction* of law and morals, public and private, a major church reform with enhanced links to the papacy, and a revival of high culture.

Charlemagne's ancestors had drawn scholars and holy men into their ambit, but never on the scale that the new wealth of empire allowed. Irishmen and Anglo-Saxons, equipped with pure Latin learned from scratch rather than the spoken twang of evolving Romance languages, were among those who frequented Charlemagne's court. Their learned traditions in biblical commentary fitted them well to train the elite of a New Israel, as the Franks now defined themselves. On the receiving end of rough jokes about excessive conviviality (the earliest instance of the pun *scottus*,

"Irishman"/*sottus*, "drunk," dates from this period), the Irish offered "wisdom for sale" in a market-place of ideas. Charlemagne himself was eager to learn; his family and court followed him to school. Religious and scholarly contacts were supported by diplomatic and political ones. Irish kings, impressed by Charlemagne's generous gifts, wrote deferential letters of thanks.[13] Charlemagne's death was noted, with appreciative comment, in the contemporary *Annals of Ulster* (813, pp. 268–9). But the scholars stayed and their influence worked through the long ninth century.

Three of the immigrants from the archipelago deserve special mention. Alcuin, a Northumbrian cleric who was master of the cathedral school at York, was in Lombardy on his way home from Rome in 781 when he met Charlemagne traveling in the opposite direction, and was headhunted. For some years, he was busy at court teaching grammar, rhetoric, and dialectic: basic skills for public men but, for some, intellectual tools for further forays into philosophy and theology, in both fields laying foundations for post-ninth-century scholarship. Alcuin's later years were spent producing a revised edition of the Latin Bible, and promoting distinctively insular devotional practices of penance and prayer.[14] Alcuin's students, several of them Anglo-Saxons, diffused his teachings throughout the Carolingian world. Two of the best-known scholars of mid-ninth-century Francia were Irishmen. Sedulius Scottus celebrated in florid verse the victories of his patron, Bishop Hartgar of Liège, over the Northmen. He prayed from a bilingual psalter in Latin and Greek. His *Commonplace Book*, an eclectic collection of extracts from classical and patristic, Frankish, Italian, and, of course, Irish texts, provided Sedulius with a store of guidance for a clutch of Carolingian kings and aristocrats. His *Christian Rulers*, probably written for Charlemagne's grandson, King Charles the Bald of West Francia (840–77), taught the personal and public responsibilities of kingship.[15] John Scottus, first documented in Charles's entourage in 845, translated the works of the Greek theologian Pseudo-Dionysius, and presented them to the king. John's own theological writings were startlingly original. He wrote poetry in Greek as well as in Latin. He drew unexpected parallels: "just as poetry uses imaginary fables to make moral interpretations that rouse human minds, so theology uses inventions of the imagination to adapt Scripture to the mind's capacities."[16] Like Charlemagne, Charles made attempts to teach his courtiers, inspired by these scholarly advisers. Without the Irishmen, the Carolingian Renaissance would have been a lot less interesting; without Alcuin, it would have been inconceivable.

Letters are uniquely valuable historical sources because of their immediacy. They offer information, written *without hindsight*, about authors, recipients, contexts, concerns. Letters are, above all, communications, written and sent to create and maintain relationships and often, beyond them, networks.[17] Focusing in the rest of this chapter on a series of letters, I intend to put modern readers in contact with some ninth-century people.

Alcuin and Charlemagne's Letter to Offa, 796

In April 796, Charlemagne "wrote" – that is, he got his Anglo-Saxon adviser Alcuin to draft – a letter to King Offa of Mercia.[18] Charlemagne had not yet heard of the killing of the Northumbrian king on April 18. He got the news after the letter was written, but before it was "posted," that is, sent with a messenger, who also carried

another letter to Offa from Alcuin himself, which reported Charlemagne's abandonment, in light of the news, of part of the plans declared in the first letter.[19] Modern
English historians have interpreted this letter with a lot of hindsight as "the first
commercial treaty in English history" and the expression of a relationship between
"equals."[20]

Alcuin's role as adviser to Charlemagne, and his status vis-à-vis Offa, become clear
in the second, supplementary, letter, in which Alcuin contacted Offa directly, in his
own right. He said he could moderate and deflect Charlemagne's wrath. This claim
recalls a similar one in 793, in a personal letter written to the monastic community
of Lindisfarne, after Alcuin received the news that they had been raided by vikings,
and some of their "boys" (noble children offered as future monks) had been carried
off into captivity. Alcuin comforted the abbot and brethren: in his final section, he
promised to go to Charlemagne and "be of whatever help he could concerning the
captive boys and in any other matters of concern to you."[21] Reading between the
lines, we can infer that Alcuin believed that he could prod Charlemagne into
negotiating with the *pagani* for the boys' ransom. A northern world opens: one
in which a Northumbrian was familiar with Danish ships and ways, and with the
bay of Lindisfarne as a fine anchorage. Alcuin could help his prayer-brothers by
activating his Frankish connection, and the king of the Franks had contacts with
the Danes, maybe with their king who could put pressure on war-bands among
his people, or with the war-bands' leader(s). Charlemagne could have been willing
to pay the ransoms himself. Alcuin was a link-man, a self-appointed emissary, between
Northumbrians and Franks, just as, a few years earlier, on the road back north
from Rome, he had first met Charlemagne at Parma in Italy.[22] On highways as well
as sea-ways, significant encounters occurred.

Charlemagne's letter to Offa reveals further contacts. Its greetings clause starts,
according to the rules of letter-writing, with the superior, here Charlemagne "by the
grace of God king of the Franks and Lombards and patrician of the Romans,"
addressing the inferior, here Offa "king of the Mercians." The letter's first part makes
it clear that there have been previous contacts between them. It refers to "the old
pact" and the value of love (*caritas*) as the foundation of a treaty (*foedus*). It is diplomatically polite. Then, without losing its smooth tone, it gets down to brass tacks.
Charlemagne would be happy to offer the customary care and hospitality to pilgrims
with personal baggage passing en route for Rome. But he had unfortunately had
recent experience of "pilgrims" fraudulently involved in business (*negotiandum*) for
the sake of profit, and these people must pay tolls. Real *negotiatores* would receive
protection, "according to the ancient custom of business," provided, as usual, that
"ours" receive similar protection. The Latin terms here warn against assuming that
we know who these *negotiatores* were and just what their business was.

The next section deals with "the priest Odberht," who, now back from Rome,
"keeps assuring us that he wishes to exile himself for religious reasons [*peregrinare*],
and does not wish to accuse you [Offa]." Charlemagne reminded Offa that Odberht,
with other exiles (*exules*), had "come in fear of death, seeking the wings of our
protection," and Charlemagne had sent them to Rome, where, at a hearing before
the pope and the archbishop of Canterbury – a hearing before which the exiles had
bound themselves by oath to appear, "as you [Offa] have informed us" – their case
would be heard and judged. "What could be wiser than that papal censure should

settle a case where some others' judgement is discordant?" Key to understanding this coded message is the realization that the Franks' "Odberht" is the Kentish King Eadberht, ousted from his kingdom by Mercian pressure, and forced to become a cleric, hence made ineligible for kingship. What was at stake here, and reflected in the uncertainty over the meaning of "exile," was nothing less than power over the ancient kingdom of Kent. Eadberht feared for his life and, like other exiles, hoped for protection against the Mercians both from Charlemagne and from the pope. The price of survival, though, was self-exile: that is, self-exclusion from the throne by accepting the clerical tonsure. Religious forms and symbols were pressed into service to justify a *coup d'état*.

Charlemagne now responds directly to a request from Offa: "concerning the black stones that you want sent to you, let a messenger come [to us] who can discuss what sort you want. Then, wherever [such stones] can be found, we shall freely order them to be given and we shall give orders for assistance in their transport. But just as you must indicate your desire concerning the length of the stones, so our men have a request to make concerning the length of the cloaks, namely, that you should give orders that they should be such as used to reach us in the old times." Recent archaeological opinion has hardened around the meaning of the "black-stones": not, as used to be thought, round quern stones made of Rhineland lava, but building stones, or, given the concern for length, columns.[23] These might have been *spolia*, reused bits of ancient masonry, but in this case they are more likely to have been chunks of stone, new-quarried at a site where they could be worked and polished to look very like marble. Just such stones were being extracted at this very time, and near the Meuse, not far from Aachen. An example of the kind of item that could have been supplied to Offa is the large slab produced to Charlemagne's order for the inscribing of Pope Hadrian I's epitaph, which Alcuin composed and is still to be seen at St. Peter's in Rome.[24] As for the cloaks, they were in the nature of regularized gifts. They may have been transported across the sea by professional carriers, Frisian seamen, as they were in the version of this story reported decades later.[25] Here the king complains frankly: "What's the use of these little bits of cloth? . . . When I'm riding, I can't protect myself with them against wind and rain. When I have to answer a call of nature, I suffer because my legs are frozen!" In both cases, stones and cloaks, the *negotiatores* who effected the transfer of goods were the agents of either rulers or institutional producers. They were not traders in a free market, as in a modern economy.

The letter ends with gifts of other kinds. Charlemagne gives a "blessing" (*bene-dictio*) to each episcopal see of the kingdom of Æthelred and "your," that is, Offa's, kingdom of Mercia. In practice, this meant gifts to all the bishops of Southumbria and Northumbria. These were, in a sense, one-way gifts since Charlemagne was sole giver in a material sense; yet there was a return gift in the form of episcopal prayers for the soul of the lately deceased Pope Hadrian, "to show our faith and love," and hence further return in the sense affirmed by St. Augustine: "to intercede for a good man profits him who does it." Offa, too, was to ensure that prayers were offered "for us [Charlemagne] and for our faithful men, and for the whole Christian people." The living Charlemagne, as well as the dead Hadrian, were to be joint bene-ficiaries of divine help, solicited through the prayers of minster-men. Charlemagne's capacity to mobilize intercession, hence his symbolic authority, extended throughout

England. Then, underscoring the point, "from the treasury of human wealth" the two metropolitans were to receive individual gifts, while Offa himself got a sword-belt, a Hunnish sword, and two lengths of silk – spoils, these, of the fabled Hunnish, or Avar, treasure captured by the Franks only shortly before this letter was dispatched. Charlemagne had planned that the Northumbrian king, too, would be a co-beneficiary of his largesse.

This is where the "postscript" second letter countermanded the first. At the very moment "when, O woe, the gifts and the letters were already in the envoys' hands," the news reached Charlemagne, through envoys returning from Ireland to Francia evidently via Northumbria, that the Northumbrian king had been killed "by the faithlessness of his own people." Charlemagne immediately retracted his gifts to Northumbrian bishops and metropolitan, and "so much enraged was he against that people whom he called faithless, wicked, slayers of their own lords, and considered worse than the heathen," that it would be all Alcuin could do, he told Offa, to prevent actual reprisals.[26]

Charlemagne, far away though he was, and without formal rule over any English kingdom, knew how the withholding of gifts could punish the Northumbrians' infidelity to their king. Charlemagne's wrath and its consequences conveyed more powerfully, and presently, than any learned treatise the message that fidelity to king and lord was the royal road to divine blessing. Offa, his archbishop and bishops, by contrast, would receive shelter beneath the wings of Charlemagne, and the prayers of Mercian monks would benefit the soul of Pope Hadrian, at whose death Charlemagne had wept. Such religious concerns lay behind the original gifts and requests. Veiled imperial designs, if any, took second place.

Evidence of reinforced connections thereafter is precise. Charlemagne gave Alcuin the abbacy of Ferrières, not far from Orléans, in the province of Sens, together with its dependent but distant small monastery of St.-Josse on the hill above the port of Quentovic, hence well placed to maintain, and profit from, Anglo-Saxon contacts.[27] When the archbishop of Canterbury made the Channel crossing in 801 en route for Rome, Alcuin arranged for him to stay at St.-Josse, and sent a horse and saddle to be ready for his onward journey.[28] Alcuin's successor as abbot was Sigulf, one of his Anglo-Saxon students.[29] Alcuin wrote, perhaps in 796, to the new abbot of Monkwearmouth-Jarrow, recalling that his own name had been added by the abbot's predecessors to the monastery's *Book of Life*, and asking that this benefit be renewed.[30] In the 840s, the names of Abbot Sigulf, and of Charlemagne and his chamberlain Meginfrith, Alcuin's friend, were entered in an updated version of the same book.[31] Such commemoration was the nearest thing to a sure road to heaven.

Lupus of Ferrières, Charles the Bald, Æthelwulf, and Judith

Lupus was a Frankish scholar trained by former students of Alcuin. A protégé of Charles the Bald, Lupus in 840 became abbot of Ferrières. He was perhaps the man who saw to the entering of the names of Sigulf, Charlemagne, and Meginfrith in Monkwearmouth's *Book*. Like Alcuin, he wrote many letters, and was proud enough of them to have a collection made. Unlike Alcuin's letters, Lupus's were modeled stylistically on Cicero's, representing a more classical strand of third-generation Carolingian Renaissance output. In four of these letters we can follow up Anglo-Saxon connections.[32] All four were probably written at about the same moment in

852. The timing resulted from a conjuncture of fortunate circumstances for Lupus. In earlier days of civil war, St.-Josse had been granted out by Charles the Bald as a benefice to a Frankish magnate who otherwise might have sided with the Emperor Lothar against Charles. Lupus' increasingly frantic requests for St.-Josse's return had fallen on deaf ears. The community of Ferrières, wrote Lupus in 846, was "suffering an incredible lack of clothing, vegetables and fish."[33] Now, in 852, in Francia, "the grace of peace had returned" with the agreement between the three sons of Louis the Pious, Carolingian fellow-kings. This meant that the influence of the Emperor Lothar on the kingdom of his younger brother Charles was now benign, and St.-Josse could be returned to Lupus. In all four of the 852 letters written to recipients in England, Lupus flaunts the proud title of abbot of St.-Josse.

By now, Lupus had other reasons to feel a sense of relief. From the early 830s, the attacks of Northmen along the northern coasts had become the almost annual events recorded in contemporary annals, and pressure had continued intense in the 840s on Francia and on the archipelago where the Anglo-Saxons were beaten, the Irish were "made into regular tribute-payers," and "Northmen got control of the islands all around Ireland."[34] In 848, though, an Irish victory was noted in the *Annals of St.-Bertin* with some elation: "The Irish attacked the Northmen and drove them out of their land. Consequently, the king of the Irish sent envoys bearing gifts to Charles [the Bald] to make a friendship-treaty and alliance with him; the Irish king also sought permission to travel through Charles's kingdom on a pilgrimage to Rome."[35] These reports combine old and new. Pilgrimage to Rome, as ever, entailed contact with Francia. These mentions of Ireland or the Irish, the only ones in these Frankish annals, signal the annalist's sense, mid-century, of shared vulnerability to vikings and shared interest in effective responses. Following victory, the Irish king's idea of pilgrimage to Rome perhaps reflected a new confidence in the value of Frankish alliance as well as papal prayers; but the Welsh King Cynan's actual pilgrimage in 854 followed defeat and meant political as well as religious withdrawal, for Cynan died at Rome.[36] Viking defeat in Ireland may have been followed by renewed attacks on north Wales from 852. Already displacement effects had been felt in southern England. "Heathen men" were defeated in Devon and in Kent in 850, and in 851, when King Æthelwulf of Wessex with his son Æthelbald and the West Saxon levies "fought . . . at *Acleah* [in Surrey] and there made the greatest slaughter of a heathen host that we have heard tell of up to this present day, and there won the victory" (*Anglo-Saxon Chronicle*, 851).

This is the event referred to by Lupus when he addresses Æthelwulf as "king to be exalted with great praises to the praise and glory of God," a salutation immediately explained in the reference to news of the victory gained, "thanks to divinely-conferred strength, over the enemies of Christ," and the assurance that "we are praying that Almighty God will make you unbeatable against all the enemies of the Christian name."[37] Lupus continues, embracing geographical and social distance, that "a great space divides my smallness from your excellence." This is why he wants his deference to be better known to the king, the more so because he has learned about his zeal for divine worship from "Felix, your chancellor." Lupus asserts his readiness to obey whatever of the king's commands he can. Meanwhile, to provide an incentive to the king's God-pleasing action, Lupus gets in first with a request of his own. Ferrières' church needs to be roofed with lead, and the king can help. "We are interceding for you [even] without having received largesse from you, and we shall be still more

prompt to do that if we receive the gift which will bring benefit to both our souls."
Lupus ends with a little prayer, conventional yet apt: "May Almighty God make you
and your posterity rulers of your land for a very long time, for the spreading and preserving of his Faith, and in due course make you inheritors of eternal blessedness."

The next letter, to Felix, is a follow-up, surely sent in the same diplomatic bag. It
turns out that Felix is known to Lupus, who addresses him, exceptionally, as *dilectis-
simus amicus*, most beloved friend. Lupus continues, "some years have passed since
we met each other at the convent of Faremoutiers, and since then no opportunity
has arisen for us to speak closely [*familiariter*]. But since our mutual love has not
grown cold, I pray that my request to your laudable Æthelwulf will achieve the
desired outcome thanks to your diligence. Recalling to mind your spoken words
about his generosity, I am writing a letter to request him to deign to grant us some
lead to prolong the life of the roof-beams of the Ferrières church and to augment
his good works . . . and if I get what I ask for, thanks to God's mercy and your efforts,
ask that you will again concern yourself to ensure that the benefit of his munificence
is transported to the town [called] Market."[38]

The letter presupposes, or affects, the familiarity of friends who had met, perhaps
only once, at Faremoutiers, where Charles the Bald's aunt, Rhuothild, was abbess
(840–52). This was a place with strong Anglo-Saxon connections dating from the
seventh century (see chapter 9) and evidently still live in the 840s. Lupus had stayed
at Faremoutiers on August 6 en route for an assembly on August 8, plausibly identified as that of Verdun in 843.[39] If this dating is right, and this was indeed the occasion
of the meeting between Lupus and Felix, one of King Æthelwulf's counselors was in
Francia meeting one of Charles the Bald's counselors just two days before the assembly where the division of the Carolingian Empire was agreed. That conjuncture would
suggest, at the very least, that the West Saxon court was taking a very close interest
in developments in Francia.

Lupus' final request presupposes Felix's familiarity with the state-fixed port, *stapulae*, of Quentovic. The very term conveyed royal control. Here, under the watchful
eye of Charles the Bald's *praefectus* Grippo, documented a decade or so after Lupus's
letter but perhaps already in post in 852, traders from across the Channel met and
dealt with Frankish agents and moneyers. Like his predecessor Gervold, Grippo was
in a position to undertake ambassadorial business on the king's behalf; indeed, that
was an essential part of his job. A miracle-story reports Grippo saved from drowning
while en route home from a diplomatic mission to the king of the English.[40]

Lupus' two remaining letters to Anglo-Saxons were to churchmen at York. "To
Archbishop Wigmund of York and all who serve the Lord under him," Lupus, writing
for himself and for the community of Ferrières, sounded the note of *amicitia*, friendship.[41] "All through the recent hard times, the association initiated by our predecessors brought forth as signs of love [*caritas*] only prayers." The prayer-brotherhood
had persisted, then. "But now, with the grace of peace opening up, and the cell of
St.-Josse returned [to me], which are the reasons why we are writing this letter,"
Lupus said it was time to emulate the predecessors and to call the York community
back to recovering and demonstrating its *amicitia*. Prayers, public and private, were
the most important demonstration of all: "we beg you to be our remembrancers."
Had the prayer-brotherhood persisted, then? "But we must also strive to be of mutual
benefit . . ." To Abbot Ealdsige of the York minster community, Lupus likewise

issued a call to "renew the old treaty [*foedus renovare*] between our two churches." That meant prayers for each other, and exchange of letters. "And so that you may be the first to follow what I am promising, I am asking you urgently to send me the following books . . ." Lupus then presented a little list of biblical commentaries by Jerome and "your Bede" (a flattering touch), and Quintilian's 12-book work on oratory. "Please send these by the most reliable messengers to the cell of St.-Josse, where they will be copied by Lantramn whom you know well, and returned to you as soon as possible." This last bit reveals something important about St.-Josse, namely, that it had a scriptorium; further, that the scribe Lantramn, whose name is Frankish, had already been in touch with Abbot Ealdsige, had perhaps visited York. But the alternative possibility, that Ealdsige had visited Francia, perhaps en route for Rome, would reveal something equally important about York at a period when so little is known of it. The thought of its library aroused the "greed" of Lupus, and had evoked contacts before 852. Not long after this, Lupus wrote to Pope Benedict III (855–8) to request copies of the same books he had sought from York. This could mean that York no longer had them, and, stretching the point, that the wonderful York library was a thing of the past.[42] It might mean that Lupus's scholarship was so thorough that he wanted to compare manuscripts to find the best text.[43] A third possibility is that Lupus' epistolary charm had cut insufficient ice with Ealdsige's community, and that these canny Yorkshiremen had used delaying tactics, or even declined to lend. Lupus' letter collection shows no sign that he ever followed up the contacts reopened in the four letters. He had first-hand knowledge of the risks of lending books.

Lupus' letters, like Alcuin's, in revealing so much about one brief time-period, seem to contrast strongly with other sources for ninth-century contacts between England and Francia. Nevertheless, the mid-century is, as it happens, floodlit by a battery of sources that are both diverse and from both sides of the Channel. For the reign of Æthelwulf, the *Anglo-Saxon Chronicle* becomes fuller than before and it is complemented by the *Life of Alfred* by the Welsh priest Asser. For Francia, the very rich *Annals of St.-Bertin* is supplemented by other annals. There is the evidence of liturgy, laws, and charters. And, as ever, there are letters, papal, royal, and other.[44] As in the 840s, so in the 850s, viking activities are a constant contextual factor.[45] Increasing evidence of Anglo-Saxon/Frankish contacts has been considered symptomatic of a pair of joint responses to the vikings: a sense of common threat and a desire for concerted defense. There is something in this. Still, viking groups were so diverse, their impacts so varied, and conflicts between Christians were so common, that homogenization should be avoided. One fundamental point remains: for northern Europeans, contacts with Rome were perforce via Francia. The pull of Rome, stronger than ever in the mid-ninth century, is the main factor that explains Æthelwulf's decisions, first, to send his son Alfred to the pope in 853 to receive some kind of royal consecration; second, to journey to Rome himself, taking Alfred with him, in 855.

At the time, the first of those journeys could have seemed hardly more than a marginal insurance policy for a small boy with several older brothers in a highly competitive dynastic situation. Only retrospectively, after Alfred's unexpected succession, did 853 become significant. Far more important at the time seemed the second journey, Æthelwulf's. It, too, was intended to settle dynastic tensions. Before leaving his kingdom, the king divided it between the two elder of his four surviving sons. Was the king quitting his fatherland definitively? I think his intention was to return with such enhanced prestige as to be much better able to face down filial resentments. Taking with him both of his two younger sons, Æthelwulf, aged perhaps 45, en route through Francia in 855, stopped at the Carolingian court and became betrothed to King Charles the Bald's daughter Judith. Both sides stood to make political gains in terms of seeing off rival kin; and both may well have hoped for more success in seeing off vikings. Æthelwulf arrived at Rome with lavish gifts, including distinctively Saxon votive bowls, and large amounts of cash for immediate distribution that impressed clergy, nobles, and lesser folk.[46] Æthelwulf stayed in Rome for almost a year, presumably hoping the home front would have stabilized. Returning via Francia, Æthelwulf duly celebrated his Carolingian marriage with pomp and splendor, on October 9, 856, in a combined wedding-cum-queenly-consecration service composed by Archbishop Hincmar of Rheims himself.[47] Meanwhile, though, the king's eldest surviving son, Æthelbald, had rebelled with considerable West Saxon support, and demanded "the more princely part" (i.e. the core regions) of Wessex.[48] In the end, Æthelwulf and Judith were received back, and an agreement was reached that the kingdom should be divided between father and eldest son (the second son apparently accepted demotion). Two years later, Æthelwulf died. Judith promptly married Æthelbald, her stepson. If there was ecclesiastical criticism, it barely surfaced in the sources. The desire, perhaps on both sides, to prolong the cross-Channel alliance may have been decisive. But Æthelbald died in 860. Judith sold up her property in England and went back to her natal home.

Whatever her father may have thought, Judith had no intention of remaining a widow, or entering religious life. In 861, she eloped with a royal vassal, Baldwin, future count of Flanders.[49] This third marriage proved fruitful. The Flemish connection, refortified by a second marriage, between Judith's son Baldwin II and Alfred's youngest daughter, perhaps in 893, had long-term consequences not just in terms of dynastic memory – Ælfthryth's West Saxon lineage was preserved in the names of her Flemish descendants in the early tenth century, Adolf (Æthelwulf), Egbert (Ecgberht), Ealswide (Eahlswith), and her own name Elstrude (Ælfthryth) – but of strategic and economic ties.[50] In the shorter run, though, Judith's legacy may have been more direct and personal. It was very probably at the courts of her successive West Saxon husbands that her little step-son was brought up. Thus, for Alfred, as a boy and adolescent, the effects of his early childhood exposure to Carolingian cultural influence were heftily reinforced.

Archbishop Fulk of Rheims and King Alfred

From the 860s, new patterns occur in viking appearances in the sources. Broadly, when Frankish writers praise the defensive efforts of kings and aristocrats, vikings have gone "across the sea"; and the same is true, but with the move in the opposite direction, when Anglo-Saxons defend themselves successfully. Within the archipelago, similar contrasts and consequentials are visible, as when Irish victories mean more woe for the Welsh. There is no denying the vikings' great, and at the same time varied, impact. Nevertheless, on the whole, as the *Anglo-Saxon Chronicle* author noted under the year 896, "the *here* [i.e. the viking army] had not altogether utterly crushed the English people [*Angelcyn*]." Authors in Ireland, or elsewhere in the British Isles, or on the continent, had they taken a large view, might have said something similar. The once-fashionable historians' judgment that the vikings, and to a lesser extent Saracens and Magyars, put paid to the Carolingian experiment in Roman-imperial resuscitation, and set European progress into reverse until feudalism kicked in c.1000, has been subjected to thorough revision in recent years. The long ninth century has re-emerged, bloodied but unbowed, as an age of creativity with long-term effects.[51] It remains to explain, not so much this historiographical volte-face, but the real-life capacity of Britain, Ireland, and mainland Europe to withstand what threatened their shared culture. The answer, in brief, is that culture's capacity to include, accommodate, and connect. The final section of this chapter will use the evidence of two contemporary letters to suggest how.

Archbishop Fulk of Rheims wrote to Alfred of Wessex in 886 in the shadow of the vikings. So severe had their impact been during the past eight years, he told Pope Stephen V (885–91) probably also in 886, that "it seems there can be no free movement for anyone beyond [their] fortifications [*castella*]."[52] Fulk had received a letter from Alfred reviewing his effective defense of his kingdom against the vikings, and duly responded with praise for how well the king had "safeguarded peace with warlike weapons and divine support." But this put him in mind of an even more compelling royal duty: "to defend the ecclesiastical order with spiritual weapons." Alfred had rehearsed the constraints under which he had been laboring: "irruptions and attacks of pagans, passage of time, neglect of bishops, ignorance of subjects." The king had requested that Fulk should send Grimbald, monk and scholar, to help him. That put Fulk in mind of an historical parallel: "Just as God sent Remigius [bishop and patron saint of the church of Rheims] to the Franks of old, so too the English are now seeking a man from Remigius." Fulk then recalled another model: "St. Augustine, the first bishop of your people, sent to you by your apostle St. Gregory," who had done so well in applying Gregory's gradualist missionary tactics in England. Nevertheless, the present time now demanded new measures, and new men, or rather "spiritual watchdogs, able to bark out mighty growls on their master's behalf . . . and hence keep far hence the savage wolves of the impure spirits who threaten and devour our souls." Fulk was now sending the man Alfred requested: indeed, his letter was Grimbald's letter of introduction to the king. Fulk clearly expected that Alfred would give Grimbald the episcopal office he needed to promote pastoral care effectively.

This letter's tone has sounded "arrogant and patronising" to a modern English historian, but that does not seem to have been Alfred's reaction (Dorothy Whitelock, *EHD*, I, 883). On the contrary, this letter, as letters so often do, belongs in a chain, in which each draws strength from and links into others. Fulk explicitly echoes Alfred. He also sees himself as obliged to help Alfred, seeing his own church and Alfred's as sharing similar pasts, and facing similar problems in the present. Fulk meant it when he said that sending Grimbald, a colleague on whom he relied, was a sacrifice, but it was one he had to make, for Grimbald was a figure "nurtured by the Universal Church," in which (Fulk continued) "the members are mutually careful, one for another, and if one member rejoices, all rejoice, or if one suffers, all members suffer." This citation from St. Paul's First Epistle to the Corinthians sums up the spirit of apostolic cooperation that informs Fulk's letter. It was a spirit that spoke to the pastoral agenda of the long ninth century.

Alfred himself responded to it, among other stimuli, in the Introduction to his *Laws*, where he picked up Fulk's theme of collaborative conciliar action "through the flaming fire of the Holy Spirit."[53] Fulk's words also underlie the prefatory letter to Alfred's translation of Pope Gregory's *Pastoral Care*. This is often seen in exclusively English terms; and, of course, the churches of England are its primary concern. Yet, in seeking to provide for the restoration and care of those churches, seen not just as buildings but as groups of people, Alfred draws not only on other peoples' exemplary action in the case of Hebrews, Greeks, Romans, but also on the collaboration of the four men from whom he has "learnt" the "shepherd-book," namely, the Mercian Plegmund "my archbishop," the Welshman Asser "my bishop," the West Frank Grimbald "my mass-priest," and the continental Saxon John (also) "my mass-priest."[54] Patrick Wormald saw "good reason to suspect a connection" between Hincmar of Rheims' legal thinking and Alfred's, with Fulk as a "bridge."[55] Alfred's target audience consisted of bishops. In this letter to bishops, engaging them in his pastoral project, Alfred wanted every man-jack of them to become a bridge.

More often than showing men seeking power over one another, which no doubt they frequently were, letters reveal men in collaboration and in a shared desire to communicate with, to exchange with, to persuade and negotiate with, each other, across space, time, and death. I did not set out in this chapter to demonstrate that power and hierarchy have their limits in human relations, or that the early medieval world, if only because of its technological limitations, fostered a good deal of imaginative sociability that was horizontal, as it were, rather than vertical. Yet something like those connective aspects of Britain, Ireland, and Europe in the long ninth century have emerged rather strongly.

I end with a voyage and an arrival, reported in the *Anglo-Saxon Chronicle* under 891:

> And three Irishmen came to King Alfred in a boat without any oars, from Ireland, whence they had stolen away because they wished for love of God to be on pilgrimage, they care not where. The boat in which they travelled was made of two and a half hides, and they took with them enough food for seven days. And after seven days they came to land in Cornwall, and went immediately to King Alfred. Their names were as follows: Dubslaine and Macbethu and Maelinmum. And Swifne, the best teacher among the Scots [from Ireland] died.[56]

These three men in a boat exemplify many of the connections discussed in this chapter. *Peregrinatio pro Christo* is a sufficient explanation for the Irishmen's decision to "steal away" to Rome, even Jerusalem.[57] Perhaps they were also in flight from cruel vikings?[58] More positively, they do look as if they were attracted to the court of King Alfred, whither they "immediately" went. Some of their compatriots were already in semi-permanent residence there.[59] Perhaps it was an Irishman, late or early recruited, who suggested to Alfred that in translating the Psalms of David, and endowing each psalm with a short "interpretation," he employ, among other guides, the Greek Psalter-Commentary of Theodore of Mopsuestia (c.350–428), in Latin translation, transmitted to the early medieval west largely by Irish scholars.[60] Alfred, familiar with other commentary traditions, found Theodore's "realistic approach" congenial, presumably because it involved explaining difficult psalm texts in historical terms. For instance, in interpreting Psalm 13, Alfred noted that King David "lamented that there was so little loyalty in his days, and so little wisdom in the world; and so does each righteous man who sings it now, he sings it about his own times, and so did Christ about the Jews and so did King Ezekias [Hezekiah] about the . . . Assyrians."[61] Alfred's comment is explicitly and unabashedly self-referential, but at the same time it invokes and invites similar reactions on the part of contemporaries, thinking, like him, "about their own times." Perhaps the Irishmen in their boat without oars who got to the court of Alfred also got to Alfred's heart and who knows how many other hearts of "righteous singers now"? Some five hundred years later, Alfred's Psalter, with the king's Old English translations and interpretations of the first 50 psalms, in a copy made probably at Canterbury soon after the Norman Conquest of England, was in the possession of Jean Duc de Berry, who gave it to his favorite church foundation at Bourges, whence it came to the royal library in 1752, and remained after the Revolution in the Bibliothèque Nationale in Paris. One voyage, one cultural transmission, led to another . . . and another. Transmissions can seem fortuitous, or, as insurance lawyers say, acts of God. Connections are something else: they need to be explained by human action and human reception, past and present.

Notes

1   Charles-Edwards, "The social background"; Davies, "Celtic kingships"; Palmer, "Saxon or European?"
2   Wood, *Proprietary Church*, pp. 64, 775 n.146.
3   Ibid., p. 56.
4   Garrison, "The Franks"; Kottje, *Studien zum Einfluß*; Story, *Carolingian Connections*, pp. 85–6.
5   Hamilton, *The Practice of Penance*, pp. 3–7.
6   De Jong, "Carolingian monasticism," pp. 647–51; Schmid, *Gebetsgedenken*, pp. 532–97.
7   Krusch (ed.), *Vita Richarii, auctore Alcuino*, c. 8, p. 393.
8   Levison (ed.), *Vita Filiberti*, c. 23, p. 596.
9   Lohier and Laporte (eds.), *Gesta sanctorum partum*, i, 5, pp. 6–7; xii, 1, 2, pp. 84–5, 87–8.
10 Lebecq, "The role of monasteries"; Nelson, "England and the continent, II," 17–21.
11 Coupland, "The coinage of Charlemagne."
12 Smith, *Europe after Rome*, pp. 268–77.
13 Holder-Egger (ed.), *Einhard: Vita Karoli* c. 16; trans. in Dutton, *Charlemagne's Courtier*.
14 Bullough, *Carolingian Renewal*, pp. 161–240.
15 Staubach, *Rex christianus*, pp. 149–87.
16 Godman, *Poetry*, p. 59.
17 Constable, *Letters*; Garrison, " 'Send more socks.' "
18 Dümmler (ed.), *Alcuin: Epistolae* [hereafter Alcuin, *Ep.*] 100, pp. 144–6; Bullough, *Alcuin*, pp. 35 n.77, 85 n.207, 100, and "What has Ingeld to do with Lindisfarne?," 116 n.78.
19 Alcuin, *Ep.* 101, pp. 146–8.
20 Stenton, *Anglo-Saxon England*, p. 221; Wormald, "The age of Offa and Alcuin," p. 101.
21 Alcuin, *Ep.* 20, p. 58.

22 Arndt (ed.), *Vita Alcuini*, c. 9, p. 190.

23 Peacock, "Charlemagne's black stones."

24 Story et al., "Charlemagne's black marble."

25 Haefele (ed.), *Notker: Gesta Karoli*, I, 34, pp. 47–8; trans. in Thorpe, *Two Lives of Charlemagne.*

26 Alcuin, *Ep.* 101, p. 147.

27 Marshall (ed.), *Lupus of Ferrières: Epistulae* [hereafter Lupus, *Ep.*] 11, 29, pp. 20, 36.; also ed. (with different numbering) with French trans. in Levillain, *Loup de Ferrières*; relevant items trans. in *EHD*.

28 Alcuin, *Ep.* 230, pp. 374–5.

29 Lupus, *Ep.* 29, p. 36.

30 Alcuin, *Ep.* 24, p. 65.

31 Stevenson (ed.), *Liber Vitae ecclesiae Dunelmensis*, pp. 2, 7.

32 Lupus, Epp. 13, 14, 61, 62, pp. 21–3, 67–8, trans. *EHD*, I, nos. 215–218; Stafford, "Charles the Bald," p. 140.

33 Lupus, Ep. 45, p. 58.

34 *Annals of St.-Bertin*, 834–6, 839, 841–4, 847: see Grat et al. (eds.); Nelson (trans.).

35 Ibid., 848.

36 Davies, *Wales in the Early Middle Ages*, pp. 106, 116, 183; Williams (ed.), *Annales Cambriae*, 854.

37 Lupus, *Ep.* 13, pp. 21–2.

38 Lupus, *Ep.* 14, p. 22, in the edition of Levillain, *Ep.* 85, ii, pp. 72–3 n.4, suggesting that the date of the meeting of Lupus and Felix was 839.

39 Lupus, *Ep.* 105, p. 102, in the edition of Levillain, *Ep.* 28, i, p. 130–3 n.3.

40 Stafford, "Charles the Bald," p. 142; Nelson, "England and the continent, II," 21–2.

41 Lupus, *Ep.* 62, p. 68.

42 Lupus *Ep.* 103, p. 101; see also Lapidge, "Latin learning," p. 427.

43 Story, *Carolingian Connections*, p. 243.

44 Nelson, "Æthelwulf" and "The Franks and the English."

45 Davies, "Alfred's contemporaries," pp. 333–6.

46 *Vita Benedicti*, III, c. 34 in Duchesne (ed.), *Liber Pontificalis*; relevant items trans. in Davis, *Book of the Popes.*

47 Nelson, *Rulers*, ch. 15, pp. 304–8.

48 Stevenson (ed.), *Asser's Life of King Alfred*, c. 12; Keynes and Lapidge (trans.), *Alfred the Great.*

49 Reynolds, "Carolingian elopements."

50 Nelson, "England and the continent, II"; see also chapter 22 of this volume.

51 Nelson, "England and the continent, I."

52 Stratmann (ed.), *Flodoard: Historia*, IV, 1, p. 365; Nelson, "... *sicut olim* ...," pp. 140–1.

53 Keynes and Lapidge (trans.), *Alfred the Great*, pp. 163–4, cf. 184.

54 Ibid., pp. 125–6.

55 Wormald, *Making of English Law*, pp. 425–6.

56 *Anglo-Saxon Chronicle* 891, trans. Whitelock, pp. 200–1; trans. Garmonsway, p. 82.

57 Campbell (ed.), *Chronicle of Æthelweard*, p. 48.

58 Dumville, *Three Men in a Boat*, pp. 55–62.

59 Stevenson (ed.), *Asser's Life of King Alfred*, c. 76.

60 O'Neill (ed.), *King Alfred's Prose Translation*, pp. 37–44; Pratt, *Political Thought of King Alfred*, pp. 242–63, and "The writings of Alfred the Great," pp. 179–80.

61 Godden, "The player-king," p. 137; O'Neill (ed.), *King Alfred's Prose Translation*, pp. 187–8.

Further Reading

Matthew Innes, *An Introduction to Early Medieval Western Europe, 300–900: The Sword, the Plough, and the Book* (London, 2007), provides chronological depth and an excellent account of the general social, economic, and cultural context of the contacts discussed in this chapter. Julia M. H. Smith, *Europe after Rome: A New Cultural History 500–1000* (Oxford, 2005), is path-breaking cultural history, with a particularly interesting chapter on "Rome and the Peoples of Europe" that does justice to Ireland as well as England. R. McKitterick (ed.), *The Short Oxford History of Europe: The Early Middle Ages* (Oxford, 2001), has especially helpful chapters on economy (J.-P. Devroey) and religion (M. de Jong), and a wide-ranging account of contacts between Europe and the wider world (J. Shepard), as well as McKitterick's own highly informative chapters on Carolingian culture and politics. Ninth-century economic and political change is discussed in chapters 1 and 2 of my own *Charles the Bald* (London, 1992). Various contributors consider the varied impacts of vikings in P. H. Sawyer (ed.), *The Oxford Illustrated History of the Vikings* (Oxford, 1997), while Sawyer himself supplies a judicious introduction. Joanna Story gives a thorough conspectus of Anglo-Saxon contacts with the Franks in the eighth and ninth centuries in *Carolingian Connections*, while she assembles excellent, up-to-date contributions on most of the significant aspects of Charlemagne's reign in her edited volume on *Charlemagne: Empire and Society*.

Bibliography

Arndt, W. (ed.), *Vita Alcuini, MGH SS* XV.1 (Hanover, 1887), pp. 182–97.

Bately, J. (ed.), *The Anglo-Saxon Chronicle: A Collaborative Edition*, vol. 3: *MS A* (Cambridge, 1986).

Bullough, D. A., *Alcuin: Reputation and Achievement* (Leiden, 2004).

Bullough, D. A., *Carolingian Renewal: Sources and Heritage* (Manchester, 1991).

Bullough, D. A., "What has Ingeld to do with Lindisfarne?," *Anglo-Saxon England*, 22 (1993), 93–125.

Campbell, A. (ed.), *The Chronicle of Æthelweard* (London, 1962).

Charles-Edwards, T. M., "The social background to Irish *peregrinatio*," *Celtica*, 11 (1976), 43–59.

Constable, G., *Letters and Letter-Collections*. Typologie des sources fasc. 17 (Turnhout, 1976).

Constable, G., *Monastic Tithes: From their Origins to the Twelfth Century* (Cambridge, 1964).

Coupland, S., "The coinage of Charlemagne," in J. Story (ed.), *Charlemagne: Empire and Society* (Manchester, 2005), pp. 211–29.

Davies, W., "Alfred's contemporaries: Irish, Welsh, Scots and Breton," in T. Reuter (ed.), *Alfred the Great* (Aldershot, 2003), pp. 323–37.

Davies, W., "Celtic kingships in the early middle ages," in A. J. Duggan (ed.), *Kings and Kingship in Medieval Europe* (London, 1993), pp. 101–24.

Davies, W., *Wales in the Early Middle Ages* (Leicester, 1982).

Davis, R., *The Book of the Popes*, III: *The Ninth-century Popes* (Liverpool, 1995).

de Jong, M. "Carolingian monasticism: the power of prayer," in R. McKitterick (ed.), *New Cambridge Medieval History*, vol. II (Cambridge, 1995), pp. 622–53.

Duchesne, L. (ed.), *Liber Pontificalis*, 2 vols (Rome, 1886, 1892).

Dümmler, E. (ed.), *Alcuin: Epistolae, MGH Epp.* IV (Berlin, 1895).

Dumville, D. N., *Three Men in a Boat*. Inaugural Lecture in the University of Cambridge (Cambridge, 1997).

Dutton, P. E. (trans.), *Charlemagne's Courtier: The Complete Einhard* (Peterborough, Ont., 1998).

Garmonsway, G. N. (trans.), *The Anglo-Saxon Chronicle* (London, 1972).

Garrison, M., "The Franks as the New Israel? Education for an identity from Pippin to Charlemagne," in Y. Hen and M. Innes (eds.), *The Uses of the Past in the Early Middle Ages* (Cambridge, 2000), pp. 114–61.

Garrison, M., "'Send more socks': on mentality and the preservation context of early medieval letters," in M. Mostert (ed.), *Approaches to Medieval Communication* (Turnhout, 1999), pp. 69–99.

Godden, M., "The player-king: identification and self-representation in King Alfred's writings," in T. Reuter (ed.), *Alfred the Great* (Aldershot, 2003), pp. 137–50.

Godman, P., *Poetry of the Carolingian Renaissance* (London, 1985).

Grat, F., Vielliard, J., and Clémencet, S. (eds.), *Annales Bertiniani, Annales de Saint-Bertin* (Paris, 1964).

Grierson, P. "Commerce in the Dark Ages," *Transactions of the Royal Historical Society*, 5th series, 9 (1959), 123–40, at 128, reprinted in P. Grierson, *Dark Age Numismatics* (Aldershot, 1981), ch. 2.

Haefele, H. F. (ed.), *Notker: Gesta Karoli, MGH SRG* 12 (Berlin, 1959). Thorpe, L. (trans.), *Two Lives of Charlemagne* (Harmondsworth, 1969).

Hamilton, S., *The Practice of Penance, 900–1050* (Woodbridge, 2001).

Holder-Egger, O. (ed.), *Einhard: Vita Karoli, MGH SRG* 25 (Hanover, 1911).

Keynes, S. and Lapidge, M. (trans.), *Alfred the Great: Asser's Life of King Alfred and Other Contemporary Sources* (Harmondsworth, 1983).

Kottje, R., *Studien zum Einfluß des Alten Testaments auf Recht und Liturgie des frühen Mittelalters* (Bonn, 1964).

Krusch, B. (ed.), *Vita Richarii, auctore Alcuino, MGH SRM* 4 (Hanover, 1902), pp. 389–401.

Lapidge, M., "Latin learning in ninth-century England," in M. Lapidge, *Anglo-Latin Literature 600–899* (London, 1996), pp. 409–54.

Lebecq, S., "The role of monasteries in the Frankish world," in I. Hansen and C. Wickham (eds.), *The Long Eighth Century* (Leiden, 2001), pp. 121–48.

Levillain, L. (Fr. trans.), *Loup de Ferrières: Correspondance*, 2 vols (Paris, 1927, 1935).

Levison, W. (ed.), *Vita Filiberti, MGH SRM* 5 (Hanover, 1910), pp. 568–606.

Lohier, F. and Laporte, J. (eds), *Gesta sanctorum patrum fontanellensis coenobii* [*Deeds of the Abbots of St.-Wandrille*] (Paris, 1936).

Mac Airt, S. and Mac Niocaill, G. (eds. and trans.), *The Annals of Ulster (to AD 1131)*. Part I: *Text and Translation* (Dublin, 1983).

Marshall, P. K. (ed.), *Lupus of Ferrières: Epistulae* (Leipzig, 1984).

Nelson, J. L., "Æthelwulf," in *Oxford Dictionary of National Bibliography* (Oxford, 2003), vol. I, pp. 438–41.

Nelson, J. L., "Alfred's continental contemporaries," in T. Reuter (ed.), *Alfred the Great* (Aldershot, 2003), pp. 293–310.

Nelson, J. L. (trans.), *The Annals of St.-Bertin* (Manchester, 1991).

Nelson, J. L., "Early medieval rites of queen-making," in J. L. Nelson, *Rulers and Ruling Families in Early Medieval Europe* (Aldershot, 1999), ch. 15.

Nelson, J. L., "England and the continent in the ninth century, I: ends and beginnings," *Transactions of the Royal Historical Society*, 6th series, 12 (2002), 1–21.

Nelson, J. L., "England and the continent in the ninth century, II: Vikings and others," *Transactions of the Royal Historical Society*, 6th series, 13 (2003), 1–28.

Nelson, J. L., "The Franks and the English in the ninth century reconsidered," in P. E. Szarmach and J. T. Rosenthal (eds.), *The Preservation and Transmission of Anglo-Saxon*

Culture (Kalamazoo MI, 1997), pp. 141–58; reprinted in J. L. Nelson, *Rulers and Ruling Families in Early Medieval Europe* (Aldershot, 1999), ch. 6.

Nelson, J. L., *Rulers and Ruling Families in Early Medieval Europe* (Aldershot, 1999).

Nelson, J. L., "'... *sicut olim gens Francorum ... nunc gens Anglorum*': Fulk's letter to Alfred revisited," in J. Roberts and J. L. Nelson (eds.), *Alfred the Wise: Studies in Honour of Janet Bately* (Woodbridge, 1997), pp. 135–44; reprinted J. L. Nelson, *Rulers and Ruling Families in Early Medieval Europe* (Aldershot, 1999), ch. 7.

O'Neill, P. P. (ed.), *King Alfred's Prose Translation of the First Fifty Psalms* (Cambridge MA, 2001).

Palmer, J., "Saxon or European? Interpreting and reinterpreting St. Boniface," *History Compass*, 4: 5 (2006), 852–69.

Peacock, D., "Charlemagne's black stones: the re-use of Roman columns in early medieval Europe," *Antiquity*, 71 (1997), 709–15.

Pratt, D., *The Political Thought of King Alfred the Great* (Cambridge, 2007).

Pratt, D., "Problems of authorship and audience in the writings of Alfred the Great," in P. Wormald and J. L. Nelson (eds.), *Lay Intellectuals in the Carolingian World* (Cambridge, 2007), pp. 160–91.

Reynolds, S., "Carolingian elopements as a sidelight on counts and vassals," in B. Nagy and M. Sebök (eds.), *The Man of Many Devices, who Wandered Full Many Ways: Festschrift in Honour of János M. Bak* (Budapest, 1999), pp. 340–6.

Schmid, K., *Gebetsgedenken und adliges Selbstverständnis im Mittelalter. Ausgewählte Beiträge* (Sigmaringen, 1983), pp. 532–97.

Sheehy, M., "The *Collectio canonum Hibernensis*: a Celtic phenomenon," in H. Löwe (ed.), *Die Iren und Europa* (Stuttgart, 1982), vol. 1, pp. 525–35.

Smith, J. M. H., *Europe after Rome: A New Cultural History 500–1000* (Oxford, 2005).

Stafford, P., "Charles the Bald, Judith and England," in M. T. Gibson and J. L. Nelson (eds.), *Charles the Bald: Court and Kingdom*, 2nd edn. (Aldershot, 1990), pp. 139–53.

Staubach, N., *Rex christianus: Hofkultur und Herrschaftspropaganda im Reich Karls des Kahlen*, Teil II (Cologne, 1993).

Stenton, F. M., *Anglo-Saxon England*, 3rd edn (Oxford, 1971).

Stevenson, J. (ed.), *Liber Vitae ecclesiae Dunelmensis* (London, 1841).

Stevenson, W. H. (ed.), *Asser's Life of King Alfred* (Oxford, 1904).

Story, J., *Carolingian Connections: Anglo-Saxon England and Carolingian Francia c.750–870* (Aldershot, 2003).

Story, J., *Charlemagne: Empire and Society* (Manchester, 2005).

Story, J., Bunbury, J., Felici, A. C., et al. "Charlemagne's black marble: the origin of the epitaph of Pope Hadrian I," *Papers of the British School at Rome*, 73 (2005), 157–90.

Stratmann, M. (ed.), *Flodoard: Historia Remensis ecclesiae, MGH SS* 36 (Hanover, 1998).

Whitelock, D. (trans.), *The Anglo-Saxon Chronicle*, in *English Historical Documents*, vol. I, 2nd edn (London, 1979).

Whitelock, D. (ed. and trans.), *English Historical Documents*, vol. I: *c.500–1042*, 2nd edn. (London, 1979).

Whitelock, D., Brett, M., and Brooke, C. N. L. (eds.), *Councils and Synods*, 2 vols (Oxford, 1981), I, no. 4, pp. 8–10.

Williams, J. (ed.), *Annales Cambriae* (London, 1860).

Wood, S., *The Proprietary Church in the Medieval West* (Oxford, 2006).

Wormald, P., "The age of Offa and Alcuin," in J. Campbell (ed.), *The Anglo-Saxons* (London, 1982), pp. 101–28.

Wormald, P., *The Making of English Law: King Alfred to the Twelfth Century*, vol. 1: *Legislation and its Limits* (Oxford, 1999).

PART IV

Britain and Ireland, c.900–c.1100

CHAPTER SIXTEEN

Scotland

ALEX WOOLF

The Emergence of the Scottish Kingdom

The high point of the career of the West Saxon king Edward the Elder was recorded in the *Anglo-Saxon Chronicle* under the year 920: after he had built and manned a *burh*, or fortification, at Bakewell in the Peak District, he was chosen "as father and lord by the king of Scots and all the Scottish nation, and by Rægnald and the sons of Eadwulf and all that then dwelt in Northumbria, either English or Danish or Northmen or others, and also by the king of the Strathclyde Welsh and all the Strathclyde Welsh."[1] As well as being the first episode to indicate that West Saxon ambitions extended beyond Southumbria, this is also the first record to indicate that the dominant people in northern Britain were now the Scots rather than the Picts. Prior to this, all references to *Scottas* in the common stock of the *Anglo-Saxon Chronicle* had referred to Irish men, and Bede had used the equivalent Latin term *Scotti* to indicate either the inhabitants of Ireland or of the relatively small territory of Dál Riata, corresponding roughly to modern Argyll. The Picts had last appeared in the *Anglo-Saxon Chronicle* in an entry for the year 875 which described Healfdene's expedition into northern Britain following the breaking up of the Great Army at Repton.[2]

Healfdene's expedition against the Picts appears to be corroborated by both the Irish chronicles and the annotated king-list known variously as the *Chronicle of the Kings of Alba* or the *Older Scottish Chronicle*.[3] The latter text claims that the Danes occupied Pictavia for a year and seems to imply – the Latin is somewhat corrupt at this point – that the death of Constantín king of the Picts, recorded by the Irish chronicles under 876, was a result of this invasion. In a number of the surviving king-lists, this Constantín is described as the last king of the Picts, but the Irish chronicles, in noting the killing of his brother Aed in 878, describe him too as *rex Pictorum* ("king of the Picts"). The death of these two brothers in rapid succession, the one at the hands of the Danes and the other slain by his "friends" (*socii*), seems, to the chroniclers at least, to have heralded the fall of the Pictish kingdom, and a confused period follows in which the Irish chronicles are silent and the native king-lists disagree: the *Chronicle of the Kings of Alba* describes a period of rule by a son of the British king of Dumbarton and the later lists notice an apparent dynastic outsider, Giric son of Dúngal.[4] After the death of Aed, no further chronicle entries mention the Picts.

Any simple narrative that seeks, however, to replace the Picts with the Scots in this period must deal with the apparent paradox that the *Scotta Cyning*, who met with Edward of Wessex in 920, Constantín, appears to have been the son of Aed, last king of the Picts, and his predecessor, Domnall, noted in the king-lists and Irish chronicles, was the son of Aed's brother, Constantín. By the early eleventh century, Gaelic historians – and it is unclear whether they were working in Ireland or Scotland – sought to explain this by making the apical figure of the dynasty, Constantín and Aed's father, Cinaed son of Alpín, a *Scotus* from Dál Riata. Cinaed, however, who had died in 858, was described by contemporary annalists simply as *rex Pictorum* ("king of the Picts") and there was, in his lifetime, no hint that he was of Gaelic origin.[5] By the middle of the twelfth century, the disappearance of the Picts had been identified as an historiographical problem by Henry of Huntingdon.[6] By the end of that century, at the latest, stories had arisen of Cinaed's genocide against the Picts, stories that have persisted in the popular literature. For once, perhaps, Henry of Huntingdon's contemporary and acquaintance, Geoffrey of Monmouth, may have been closer to the truth when, in setting on one side the subject of Pictish history, he writes, "it is not my purpose to describe Pictish history, nor, indeed, that of the Scots, who trace their descent from them, and from the Irish too."[7]

The Scottish kingdom that Edward and his descendants encountered in the course of the tenth century drew its dynasty and its territorial extent from the historic Pictish kingdom, but its linguistic and literary culture seems to have been rapidly converging with that of Ireland. Whether the English perception of these northerners as *Scottas*, "Gaels," derives entirely from linguistic association or whether it was constrained by other factors, less apparent to modern scholars, is open to debate. In the Irish chronicles, the Gaelic label "Alba" seems to have been applied to the kingdom from 900 onward, but there is some literary evidence that suggests that in the vernacular the term was already in use at least as early as the 870s and perhaps much earlier. The change in annalistic usage from *rex Pictorum* to *rí Alban* ("king of Alba") may simply be one of many correlates of the linguistic switch from Latin to the vernacular that characterizes the chronicles of this period.[8]

The Problems of the Sources

The central problem of all Scottish history before the middle of the twelfth century is the absence of native sources. For the tenth and eleventh centuries, the problem is particularly acute as few of the surviving sources we use were composed anywhere near Scotland. The one exception to this is the text already alluded to under the name the *Chronicle of the Kings of Alba* (*CKA*), generally known in the past as the *Older Scottish Chronicle*.[9] This text covers the period from the kingship of Cinaed son of Alpín (d.858) to the early years of that of Cinaed son of Máel Coluim (d.995). It is not, however, a straightforward chronicle. At its core, there seems to lie a regnal list composed c.950. At least two phases of extension subsequently took place, bringing the coverage up to the 970s. To the basic king-list, additional notices of events, dated either by regnal years or by vaguer phrases such as "in his time" or "after a short while," have been added. In the period up to about 950, the strong focus of these additional notices on the middle Tay basin, together with one or two specific references, suggests that the material was put together at Dunkeld.[10] By the time of Cinaed son of Máel Coluim's reign, the geographical focus may have moved a little further east. The text is, however, more complex than that. It survives only in a fourteenth-century copy of a recension produced around 1200. Linguistic considerations strongly suggest that, while much of the annalistic material added to the original regnal list may date to the tenth century, a significant proportion may have been introduced in the course of producing the late twelfth- or early thirteenth-century recension.[11] Corruptions in the Latin, which often render the sense ambiguous, merely add to the complications. Without *CKA* (as it is known) we would be lost: with it, however, we are scarcely on firm ground.

The Irish chronicles, which have been the mainstay of Scottish historians up to the tenth century, continue to record the death of kings and some events, but are generally less interested in northern British affairs, presumably, in part at least, because the monasteries of the Columban federation no longer looked to Iona for leadership. English chronicles, on the other hand, contain more notices of Scottish rulers but generally only when they come into conflict with the West Saxons, for both dynasties spent much of the tenth and eleventh centuries engaged in the partition of the Northumbrian kingdom. The effect of these biases – *CKA* giving us local events in Perthshire and the English chronicles focusing on events south of the Forth – means that most of Scotland is, in this period, effectively without history. We can locate almost no events north of the Mounth (the eastern arm of the central Highlands, which reaches the coast just south of Aberdeen) or in the Western Isles or indeed the south-west (Ayrshire, Dumfries, and Galloway). We have no administrative documents from the tenth century and only a handful of land grants of apparently eleventh-century date surviving in twelfth-century or later copies.[12]

Constantín son of Aed

Historians increasingly view the reign of Constantín son of Aed (900–943) as perhaps the most significant in the history of the early Scottish kingdom. He was the first of his dynasty to be noted in the *Anglo-Saxon Chronicle*, and his perceived importance may in part simply reflect the role he played in English history, but the length of his reign, remarkable for any age, but truly astonishing for this era, must have contributed to the stable development of the kingdom. His father had been slain some 22 years before he came into the kingship, and he himself survived a retirement of some nine years after his abdication in 943, putting him in his mid-seventies, at the youngest, when he died. At the start of his reign, the kingdom was facing an assault by viking forces which had slain his cousin Domnall at Dunottar (Kincardineshire).[13] In his third year, we are told, Dunkeld "and all Alba" were plundered by the heathens. In 904, he reversed the kingdom's fortunes by defeating the Northmen in Strathearn (Perthshire), slaying their leader Ímar grandson of Ímar (Old Norse Ivarr; perhaps one of the refugees driven from Dublin by Cerball mac Muirecáin in 902).[14] The *Annals of Ulster*'s account of this battle ascribes the victory to the men of Fortriu, thus underlining the Pictish core to Constantín's regime. Some two years later,

Constantín seems to have cemented his domination of the north in a ceremony at Scone (the earliest record of this place which was to become the inauguration site of kings). *CKA* tells us that King Constantín and Bishop Cellach took oaths, on the Hill of Belief next to the royal *civitas* of Scone, swearing to uphold the laws and rights of the church and the gospels. The word *civitas* is usually used by Gaelic Latinists to denote a monastic center, but it is just possible that a secular site is intended. There is also a clause in the sentence, *pariter cum Scottis*, which might mean "along with the Scots" or, more likely, "after the fashion of the Scots." Unfortunately, this is precisely one of those long and convoluted sentences with which *CKA* abounds and which might or might not contain significant interpolation, so it is unclear whether it is the ecclesiastical customs, the manner of the oath-taking, or the presence of a wider convocation of *Scotti* that is being referred to.[15] The precise nature and function of this ceremony will probably always elude us, but it is, nonetheless, reminiscent of the exchange of oaths between the West Saxon King Ecgberht and Ceolnoth, archbishop of Canterbury, at the Council of Kingston in 838.[16] Kingston, like Scone, was to become the royal inauguration site for the dynasty and, also like Scone, lay at the tidal reach of the great arterial river of the kingdom (the Thames and Tay, respectively). The function of the Council of Kingston seems to have been the recognition by Ceolnoth and his fellow southern bishops that the Mercian hegemony had – in their view – finally come to an end and that, in their perception, Ecgberht and his heirs were to be their secular partners in future. It is tempting to read similar significance into the Council of Scone in 906. Indeed, it may mark the end of a period in which Constantín struggled to consolidate his succession against both internal and external rivals. It is probably not coincidence that Bishop Cellach heads the list of bishops of St. Andrews available to Walter Bower, abbot of Inchcolm, in the fifteenth century.[17] The fact that episcopal succession, as viewed from the later Middle Ages, began in this generation may underlie the view, whether real or constructed, that a significant transformation was taking place at this time.

Nothing further can be said of Constantín or his kingdom for another 12 years. Then, in 918, both the Irish chronicles and *CKA* record a battle between himself and Rægnald grandson of Ivarr (Middle Irish Ragnall ua Ímair; presumably, though not certainly, a grandson of Ivarr the Boneless). The *Annals of Ulster* locate this battle on the banks of the Tyne "among the northern Saxons," whilst *CKA* places it at *Tine More*, possibly the "Great Tyne" (in Northumberland, as opposed to the much smaller East Lothian river of the same name).[18] This battle is certainly the battle of Corbridge mentioned in the tenth- or eleventh-century Cuthbertine text *Historia de Sancto Cuthberto* which, while recounting the career of one Elfred Brihtwulfing, who had been granted lands in return for service by the Church of St. Cuthbert, states:

> These he performed faithfully until king Rægnald came with a great multitude of ships and occupied the territory of Ealdred son of Eadwulf, who was a friend of King Edward, just as his father Eadwulf had been a favourite of King Alfred. Ealdred, having been driven off, went therefore to Scotia, seeking aid from king Constantín, and brought him into battle against Rægnald at Corbridge. In this battle, I know not what sin being the cause, the pagan king vanquished Constantín, routed the Scots, put Elfred the faithful man of St. Cuthbert to flight and killed all the English nobles save Ealdred and his brother Uhtred.[19]

The structure of the *Historia de Sancto Cuthberto* follows the histories of individual estates claimed by the church. Because of this, the battle of Corbridge features in two separate sections of the narrative, which encouraged F. T. Wainwright to postulate two separate battles.[20] This is unnecessary.

The *Historia*'s protestation of the friendship between Ealdred son of Eadwulf and Edward the Elder looks like a retrospective claim, as Ealdred's choice of refuge, *Scotia* rather than Southumbria, indicates. The accounts of the battle suggest something of a stalemate, or at best a pyrrhic victory for Rægnald, and Edward's intervention in the north, with which this chapter opened, would seem to have been precipitated by the need for an "honest broker" in the very uncertain aftermath. Thus, the long history of Anglo-Scottish relations began with the most northerly English looking to the Scots for support and the dominant power in the south taking exception to this state of affairs.[21]

The death of Ealdred son of Eadwulf was perhaps one of the factors that provoked renewed conflict between Constantín and the West Saxons in 934, if he is, as seems likely, the "Adulf m'Etulfe king [sic] of the North Saxons" whose death is recorded in the seventeenth-century translation of the *Annals of Clonmacnoise*.[22] Whatever the cause, a number of English sources mention an invasion of Scotland by King Æthelstan in this year. The fullest account appears in the set of northern annals preserved within the twelfth-century Durham compilation, *Historia Regum Anglorum*:

> 934. King Æthelstan, going towards *Scotia* with a great army, came to the tomb of St. Cuthbert, commended himself and his expedition to his protection, and conferred on him many and diverse gifts befitting a king, as well as estates, and consigned to the torments of eternal fire anyone who should take any of these from him. He then subdued his enemies, laid waste *Scotia* as far as Dunottar and the mountains of Fortriu with a land force, and ravaged with a naval force as far as Caithness.[23]

A charter issued by Æthelstan at Nottingham, on June 7, on his way north, contains one of the longest lists of witnesses of any Anglo-Saxon charter, probably giving an indication of the extent of the army he led to Scotland. The list includes three Welsh kings, Hywel, Morgan, and Idwal, 18 bishops (including the two English metropolitans), and 13 *duces* or local rulers, six of whom bore Danish names.

The cliff-top stronghold of Dunottar, a dozen miles south of Aberdeen, had appeared as a royal center regularly in the records since the 680s. It is one of the most impressive early medieval sites in Britain, closely resembling the better known Tintagel in Cornwall (though now topped with a seventeenth-century castle). Here Constantín was brought to bay. By September 12, Æthelstan was back in the south, at Buckingham. The charter he issued on this occasion was witnessed by Constantín *sub-regulus*, amongst others (S 426). Clearly, the Scots king had been forced into submission. Although Constantín appears to have been allowed home for Christmas, he was compelled to return to Æthelstan's heartland in the course of the following year for a plenary court held at the ancient Roman capital of Cirencester. Here Constantín was joined in his submission by Owain, king of Strathclyde.

Both Owain and Constantín had met with Æthelstan previously, in July 927, but on that occasion the meeting had taken place on the border between Strathclyde and Northumbria, on the river Eamont, near Penrith (Cumberland).[24] On that occasion, while Æthelstan may have claimed some superiority, the location makes it clear that this was essentially a royal convention in which collaboration against the pagan threat, rather than imperial aspirations, topped the agenda. The event at Cirencester in 935 was more emphatically imperial and the northern kings were being reduced to the subordinate condition that the Welsh had experienced for some years. It seems, however, that Owain and Constantín were not comfortable with Æthelstan's vision.

By 935, Constantín must have been in his late fifties or perhaps even his sixties, and would have been becoming increasingly aware that his own sons and those of his predecessor, Domnall, were now grown men. If he was to maintain his position at home, he could not afford to appear weak. In 937, in alliance with the pagan ruler Óláfr Guthfrithsson, who had recently demonstrated his domination of the Irish midlands, Constantín, possibly accompanied by Owain of Strathclyde, invaded Æthelstan's *imperium*. Although in many ways one of the best attested early medieval campaigns (the *Anglo-Saxon Chronicle* contains a 73-line poem describing it),[25] we are remarkably ill informed as to detail. The site of the final battle, in which Constantín's son was slain and Æthelstan won a pyrrhic victory, remains unidentified, despite several different place-names appearing in the sources: *Brunanburh, Dún Brunde, Weondun*.[26] There is no consensus among modern historians as to whether Óláfr or Constantín was the senior partner in the alliance. Óláfr clearly wished to reclaim the kingship of Northumbria, which his uncles Rægnald and Sihtric had held (918–27) and doubtless Constantín hoped to create a buffer zone between himself and Æthelstan's kingdom. In the end, the campaign appears to have ended in something of a stalemate. Óláfr and Constantín returned to their homes licking their wounds, but Æthelstan's *imperium* seems to have receded. After the English king's death, in October 939, Óláfr was able to return to Northumbria and acceded to the kingship without resistance. The *Brunanburh* campaign is the last recorded event of Constantín's reign. By the end of 943 he had abdicated (whether willingly or not is unknown) and entered the monastic community at St. Andrews (Fife), where he resided for the last nine years of his life.[27]

The Alternating Kingship in the Later Tenth Century

Despite having left one son dead on the field of battle, Constantín was survived by at least one other. Nonetheless, it was not one of his own sons who succeeded him in the kingship but Máel Coluim, the son of his predecessor Domnall, who had been slain by vikings in 900. Máel Coluim must have been in his forties or fifties by the time of his accession and had, presumably, been waiting in the wings throughout the previous reign. His succession makes explicit the pattern that had been emerging since the 870s in the dynasty descended from Cinaed son of Alpín. Constantín son of Cinaed had been succeeded by his brother Aed and subsequently his son, Domnall, had been succeeded by Aed's son Constantín. For the rest of the century, indeed until 1005, this alternation of the kingship between the descendants of the sons of Cinaed was regularly observed, although increasing rivalry between the two branches became steadily more apparent, and we cannot be certain that this alternation was ever entirely amicable. This structure of dynastic succession almost certainly provided the prime motivation for the fetishistic treatment of Cinaed son of Alpín, the common agnatic ancestor of the two lines, in the historiography of the dynasty.

Precisely how the alternation of the kingship was managed is unclear. It is hard to imagine, for example, why Constantín son of Aed had not managed to secure the succession of one of his sons in 943, following such a long and apparently dynamic reign. Such a regular alternation brings to mind the arrangement arrived at between the Cenél nEógain and Clann Cholmáin segments of the Uí Néill dynasty in Ireland, which allowed them to monopolize the kingship of Tara between the eighth and the tenth centuries. In the Irish case, each segment had secure and quite separate power bases in the north and the midlands respectively. Each king of Tara had usually ruled his own "fifth" of Ireland for many years before succeeding to the overkingship. The apparent distance between the two segments (whose apical figure would seem to have lived in the early fifth century), which one might have expected would militate against any genuine sense of shared interest, was, to some extent, ameliorated by the frequent, almost systematic, intermarriage between them and particularly by the common practice for the new king of Tara to marry his predecessor's widow. Thus Flann Sinna, a Clann Cholmáin king of Tara (879–916), was both son-in-law and stepson to his Cenél nEógain predecessor, Aed Findlaith (862–79), just as his own successor, Niall Glúndub (916–19), Aed's son, was his son-in-law and stepson.[28] Such practices almost certainly helped to create a situation in which a proportion of the royal household remained in place despite the dynastic distance between each king and his successor.

Unfortunately, our information about the Scottish kingdom at this point is far too meager to allow a comparable analysis. We know the identity of a queen for the first time only in the mid-eleventh century (see below), and know nothing for certain about the territorial or landed background of the different branches of the family. In the eleventh century, when the segment descended from Aed son of Cinaed disappears from our sources, another, non-Alpinid, kin-group, Clann Ruaidrí, attempted to assert its right to the kingship. Clann Ruaidrí seem to have been based in the region of Moray, and it is possible that they inherited their claim from the family of Aed. This must remain simply a hypothesis but, since in Pictish times the fundamental divisions of the kingdom lay north and south of the Mounth, a later rivalry between those based around the Moray Firth and those located on the Middle Tay might reflect direct continuity throughout our period, suggesting, perhaps, that the two Alpinid branches had established separate power bases on either side of the Mounth.[29]

Máel Coluim reigned for 11 years (943–54). He led one military expedition into Moray against an otherwise unidentified Cellach (indicating that his own power base lay south of the Mounth) and also raided Northumbria c.950.[30] Unfortunately, we cannot be certain whether his attack on Northumbria was directed against the West Saxon dynasty or one of the Hiberno-Norse or Anglo-Danish claimants, since the chronology is not sufficiently refined. In 944, Æthelstan's half-brother and successor, Edmund, had expelled the Hiberno-Norse dynasty from Northumbria, and the following year he followed up this success with a ravaging of Strathclyde. The *Anglo-Saxon Chronicle* concludes the account of this campaign with the information that Edmund *let* Strathclyde "to Máel Coluim, king of the Scots, on condition that he should be his co-worker on both land and sea."[31] The precise meaning of this phrase and of the Old English word *let* is open to interpretation. Strathclyde, the last remaining British-speaking kingdom in the North, is usually thought to have recognized

Scottish overlordship for much of this period, although it may also, at times, have been under the sway of the Hiberno-Norse. Edmund's expedition may have been an attempt to extend West Saxon hegemony at the expense of the Scots or, alternatively, it may have been a combined, Anglo-Scottish operation against Hiberno-Norse influence in the region. Strathclyde certainly maintained its own kings into the eleventh century, so Máel Coluim's tenure must have been either short-lived or simply as overlord. If the events of 945 betoken generally good relations between Máel Coluim and the West Saxons, then the Northumbrian expedition of 950 may have been directed against either Óláfr Cúarán or Eiríkr Haraldsson, each of whom at some point around this time managed to detach Northumbria from the West Saxon *imperium*.[32]

Máel Coluim, *CKA* tells us, was killed by local men at Fetteresso, just inland from Dunottar. No motive is indicated in our sources, so we are left to speculate as to whether this action resulted from local resistance to royal power or from dynastic factionalism. He was succeeded by Constantín's son who is known by the name Ildulb (954–62). This seems to be a Gaelic rendering of the Germanic name Hildulf, which has led to speculation that he was of Norse descent on his mother's side. Hildulf, however, is not attested in any of the insular Norse ruling dynasties and might as easily be a Frankish name.[33] *CKA* claims that Edinburgh came into Scottish hands in his reign – it had been Northumbrian to this point – and, although the text is corrupt, seems to say that he was slain by vikings in Buchan in the far north-east. Later king-lists appear to place his death at Inver Cullen (Banffshire) just outside the bounds of late medieval Buchan. It is in the reign of his successor, Dub son of Máel Coluim (962–6), that we first see explicit evidence that the two branches of the Alpinid dynasty had come into conflict, for Ildulb's son Cuilén seems to have contested Dub's kingship, and eventually ousted him. Cuilén continued to reign alone until 971. Cuilén himself was slain by the Britons along with his brother Eochaid.[34] According to one Irish chronicle, he was burned in a house, and the later king-lists say that this was done on account of a woman.[35] Possibly Cuilén had been exercising his right to hospitality from a subjugated Strathclyde and had overstepped the bounds of acceptable behavior.

After Cuilén's death, *CKA* claims that Dub's brother Cinaed son of Máel Coluim (971–95) succeeded directly to the kingship, but the Irish chronicles note the killing of a further son of Ildulb, Amlaíb, in 977, giving him the royal title (*AU* 977.4). This is the first disagreement in the information gleaned from the Scottish and Irish sources since the death of Domnall in 900 and may suggest that Cinaed's kingship was challenged in its early years and that this challenge was ignored by the compilers of *CKA*. It should be noted, however, that *CKA* seems to have ceased to be maintained at some point, perhaps quite early, in the 970s and Amlaíb's career may simply have post-dated its terminus. "Amlaíb" is the Gaelic form of the Norse name Óláfr and its appearance in the Scots royal dynasty occurs at about the same time that Gaelic names began to appear in the Hiberno-Norse dynasties.[36] Whether they result from intermarriage or wider trends in cultural convergence, the appearance of personal names migrating from their traditional ethnic and linguistic environments may reflect the conversion of the Hiberno-Norse, which seems to have occurred in the mid-tenth century, but in part they simply bear witness to the nativization of the insular vikings.[37] While we cannot trace the precise link between Ildulb's family and any particular Norse group, Amlaíb's name serves to remind us that the Scottish kingdom was surrounded on three sides by polities of Scandinavian origin. We are, however, unable to say much at all about these polities, or, indeed, even how many there were. None of our narratives for this period notices events in the Scottish islands, Galloway, or the northern mainland, and later accounts, principally *Orkneyinga saga*, cannot be relied upon for much before the end of the eleventh century. Archaeological and onomastic evidence allows us to make general assumptions about the degree of Norse settlement in these areas, but as such the poor chronological definition of this material allows numerous interpretations to be drawn and no consensus has yet emerged.[38]

Cinaed son of Máel Coluim is the last king to be covered in the surviving text of *CKA*, which breaks off part way through his reign. It tells us that his first act was a ravaging of part of *Britannia*, presumably Strathclyde, perhaps as a punitive response to the killing of Cuilén. There follows an account of the Scots plundering of *Saxonia* which may or may not have been conceived as part of the same expedition since the places mentioned seem to be in or adjacent to Cumberland. In a subsequent raid, we are told that he carried off the son of the king of the Saxons.[39] It is hard to know who is meant since it is unlikely that any West Saxon *ætheling* would have been in harm's way in this period (Edgar had died in 975 leaving only minors and Æthelred's sons would only have been infants when Cinaed himself died). Commentators have seen this as a final instance of Gaelic chroniclers applying the term "king" to the rulers of Bamburgh, in which case this "son of the king of the Saxons" would most likely be a child of Eadwulf or Waltheof who are identified as earls by the eleventh- and twelfth-century Durham texts.[40]

Despite the explicitly aggressive language of the chronicle, Hudson has suggested that this last passage may, in fact, relate to a hostage exchange as part of the prelimi- naries for Cinaed's famous trip to Chester in 973.[41] In that year, the West Saxon ruler Edgar underwent an imperial consecration at Bath. With its thermal springs, extensive Roman ruins, and Old English name of *Acemannesceaster*, this location was probably redolent of Aachen with all its associations with the Frankish revival of empire. He followed this ceremony with a naval expedition circumnavigating Wales and ending up in Chester. At Chester, Edgar was met by six other insular kings who performed some kind of ceremony of submission, which may have included a sym- bolic rowing of Edgar on the Dee whilst he sat at the helm as *gubernator* – "steers- man."[42] Although strictly contemporary sources do not name the kings who attended Edgar at Chester, and twelfth-century writers seem to have been speculating, the most likely line-up would have included the Welsh kings of Gwynedd, Deheubarth, Morgannwg, and Gwent, together with Dyfnwal of Strathclyde and Cinaed of Scotland. Some of the twelfth-century writers also included Maccus son of Harold, who had recently made his appearance, in predatory fashion, on the coast of Wales and Ireland, but it is perhaps more likely that it was his presence that encouraged Edgar to focus his display of might in the Irish Sea zone.[43]

With the ending of the *Chronicle of the Kings of Alba*, the light goes out in Scotland, and for a generation we are confined to obits and the occasional battle notice in Irish chronicles for contemporary references and to king-lists or far later sources for a native perspective. The *Annals of Ulster* recount that Cinaed son of Máel Coluim was slain deceitfully in 995 but give no further details (*AU* 995.1).

The king-lists recount that Cinaed was slain through the treachery of a woman, Finele, daughter of the *mormaer* of the Angus, at Fettercairn in the Mearns, not far from where his father had been slain, also by local treachery.

Cinaed was succeeded by Cuilén's son Constantín (995–7), the strict alternation between the two lines once more being observed. This Constantín is the first ruler of the kingdom for whom a full pedigree survives, and thus it is only from his time that we can be sure that the Alpinid house claimed that their progenitor, Cinaed son of Alpín, was descended in the male line from the ancient kings of Dál Riata. As it stands, the genealogy presents some chronological difficulties:

> *Constantín* [997] *son of Cuilén* [971] *son of Ildulb* [962] *son of Constantín* [952] *son of Aed* [878] *son of Cinaed* [858] *son of Alpín son of Eochaid son of Aed Find* [778] *son of Eochaid* [697] *son of Domangart* [673] *son of Domnall Brecc* [642] *son of Eochaid Buide* [629] *son of Aedán* [608] *son of Gabrán* [558] *son of Domangart* [534] *son of Fergus son of Erc* . . . [and then back for about another 30 generations].[44]

The dates provided here are drawn from largely contemporary annalistic obits, and from these it can be seen that there is a major disjuncture between Aed mac Echdach (d.778) and his supposed father Eochaid mac Domangairt (d.697). This does not prove conclusively that the descent of the royal house from the Cenél nGabráin rulers of Dál Riata was a fabrication, but it must throw some doubt upon the connection. Early medieval dynasties were not above tampering with their pedigrees from time to time.[45] What we can say is that, despite the apparent Pictish character of the dynasty in the later ninth century, by the 990s they wished to be regarded as Gaels.[46]

Constantín's short reign ended with his killing in battle by a dynastic rival. Later king-lists say that this happened after a reign of 18 months at *Rathinveramon*, probably at the mouth of the Almond river which joins the Tay opposite Scone. He was succeeded by Cinaed son of Dub. This once more reflected the strict alternation of the kingship, as presented in our sources, but was to be the last example of this. After the death of Constantín we hear no more of the descendants of Aed son of Cinaed son of Alpín. The reign of Cinaed son of Dub (997–1005) is as opaque as that of his predecessor. The *Annals of Ulster* simply record his killing in a civil battle (*AU* 1005.5). Later king-lists locate his death at Monzievaird near Crieff in upper Strathearn (Perthshire). His killer is named as Máel Coluim son of Cinaed, his first cousin in the male line.

The Fall of the House of Alpín

The history of the kingdom of Scots in the later tenth century can be fairly characterized as a catalogue of men with strange names killing each other. Along the way, however, other elements can be drawn out. First, as we have seen, the clear identification of an Irish Gaelic origin for the kingdom had emerged by the end of the tenth century, though its authenticity is unverifiable. Second, although they have played little part in the narrative provided by our sources to date there have been occasional references, since 938, to a category of non-royal regional ruler. The death of a *mormaer* of Angus was noted in *CKA* in the year following *Brunanburh*, and a *satrap* of Atholl was killed during the conflict between Dub and Cuilén (c.965).[47] Three Scottish *mormair* are also mentioned fighting in Ireland in 975 (*AT* 975). From these brief notices, we might infer that the internal organization of the Scottish kingdom, as it appears clearly for the first time in the twelfth century, had already emerged or was in the process of emerging.

By the twelfth century, most, though not all, of the core territory of the kingdom north of the Forth was divided into provinces, each governed by a *mormaer* (usually described using the Latin term *comes*). These *mormair* seem to have been drawn from local families, but it is not clear that direct father-to-son succession was the norm. The precise number of *mormair* in the early period is unclear – a *topos* becomes apparent, from c.1100, of there being seven *comites* who acted as "peers of the realm," but it is hard to be precise as to which provinces they ruled (if, indeed, they were more than a notion). Provinces to which we have clear evidence of *mormair* being attached before the mid-twelfth century included Angus, Atholl, Marr, Buchan, Moray, Fife, and Strathearn, but there is some suggestion that Gowrie, the Mearns, and Ross may have possessed such officers and, by 1200, Menteith and Lennox also have *mormair*. Gowrie is certainly described as a *comitatus* by Máel Coluim IV (1153–65), but it may have always been in the hands of the king, as it was in his time. The *mormair* do not appear to have been particularly wealthy as individuals and seem to have derived much of their status from their office. Their main functions seem to have been to lead the army of the province in wartime and to prosecute royal justice. Although the provinces are often discussed as if they were extensive territories, and the *mormair* the equivalent of the great earls of eleventh-century England, the provinces were probably only as populous as the average Welsh *cantref* and considerably less so than an English shire. The extent to which we can project this twelfth- and thirteenth-century information about the office of *mormaer* back into our period is unclear, just as it is unclear whether the institution itself had its origins in a Gaelic or Pictish past. For the tenth and eleventh centuries, we know only that some named people bore the title *mormaer* and that they were associated in some way with provincial government.

During the reign of Máel Coluim son of Cinaed we begin to get a clear sense of internal division within the kingdom. For much of his reign, Máel Coluim's legitimacy seems to have been challenged by the family, Clann Ruaidrí, which provided Moray with its *mormair*. Two members of this family, Findláech son of Ruaidrí (d.1020) and his nephew Máel Coluim son of Máel Brigte (d.1029), are styled *rí Alban*, "king of Scotland," in their obits in Irish chronicles (*AU* 1020.2; *AT* 1029), although Findláech is simply styled "Mormaer of Moray" in the *Annals of Tigernach*. It seems likely that for much, perhaps all, of his reign, Máel Coluim son of Cinaed was what Irish writers would call a "king with opposition," and it is perhaps significant that he was the first Alpinid not to respect the alternation of the kingship. It may be that, although they did not claim agnatic descent from Aed son of Cinaed, Clann Ruaidrí in some way represented the interest group that had backed that branch of the royal dynasty.[48] Whatever their claim to the kingship, it seems to have re-awakened the ancient division of the kingdom, north and south of the Mounth, that stretched back to Pictish times. The failure of either side to put an end to this division, and the possible acceptance of it, at least at times, may perhaps be put down to the threat that lingered over the whole archipelago at this time – that posed by Cnut, who had become king of England in 1016 and king of Denmark in 1019. It may well have been to Cnut's advantage to encourage the division that we find in Scotland in this period as well as the inter-regnum that affected Ireland now.[49]

Whatever the case, neither of the Scottish dynasties seems to have been able to maintain internal order. Findláech was killed by the sons of his brother Máel Brigte, and Boite son of Cinaed (a brother or cousin of Máel Coluim) married a daughter to Gilla Comgáin son of Máel Brigte (d.1032), his own grandson being killed by Máel Coluim son of Cinaed in 1033 (*AU* 1033.7). Internecine strife seems to have riven the kingdom in this era. The inevitable result was that when Máel Coluim son of Cinaed finally died in 1034, he was not succeeded by a son and, as far as we know, the Alpinid dynasty was at an end. South of the Mounth, Donnchad, son of abbot Crínán of Dunkeld by Máel Coluim's daughter Bethoc, was elected to the kingship. This was the first succession through the female line since the obscure and possibly fictional reign of Eochaid son of Rhun in the 870s.

Donnchad's legitimacy was clearly in doubt, and an attempt to enhance his reputation with an attack on Durham, in 1039, ended in disaster.[50] Returning to Scotland, he attempted to confront the Moravian leader, Macbethad son of Findláech, but at Pitgaveny near Forres (Morayshire), he was slain in battle and Macbethad took the kingship and finally reunified the kingdom. The conflict between Donnchad and Macbethad, Shakespeare's Duncan and Macbeth, was the final act in a crisis that dated back to the first decade of the century.

Macbethad and Máel Coluim III

Macbethad held the kingdom together for 17 years despite attempts to unseat him by Donnchad's father, abbot Crínán (*AU* 1045.6), and an English invasion led by Earl Siward in 1054.[51] For at least part of his reign he seems to have enforced Scottish control on Strathclyde, for the only lasting achievement of Siward's invasion appears to have been to return a Strathclyde dynast to power under English protection.[52] Macbethad may have been secure enough in his kingship to make a pilgrimage to Rome in 1050, or at least to have alms scattered there on his behalf.[53] In doing this, he was following a fashion amongst insular kings of the time. Cnut had attended Conrad II's imperial coronation in Rome in 1027, but Sihtric of Dublin and the northern Uí Néill king Flaithbertach had gone there on pilgrimage in 1028 and 1030 respectively.[54] Other Gaelic kings would follow later in the century.

In 1057, Macbethad's reign ended when he was slain at Lumphanan (Aberdeenshire) by Máel Coluim, the son of Donnchad. Máel Coluim, however, did not reap the immediate benefit of this act for Macbethad's stepson Lulach, the son of his cousin Gilla Comgáin, succeeded to the kingship. It is not clear whether Lulach was Macbethad's designated heir (*tanáiste*) or whether he himself had been an exile (his father had, after all, been one of Findláech's killers). His reign, however, was short-lived and he was slain, *per dolum*, "through treachery," by Máel Coluim within a few months.

The reign of Máel Coluim III, known universally since the fourteenth century, but almost certainly in error, as Malcolm Canmore,[55] marks the great turning point in Scottish history. From his time onward, the affairs of the kingdom become increasingly easy to discern. This is partly due to his ceaseless conflict with successive English regimes and the brinksmanship he exercised in knowing when to submit and when to take advantage of England's adversity, and partly from the not-unconnected flight to his court of many refugees from William the Conqueror's England, including Máel Coluim's wife, Saint Margaret.

Máel Coluim submitted to Edward the Confessor at the earliest opportunity in 1058 and, at the same time, became the sworn brother of Earl Tostig, who ruled Northumbria in Edward's name. When Tostig, however, was on his journey to Rome, Máel Coluim felt no compunction in raiding Northumbria savagely. At some point in the 1060s, he seems to have finally subsumed Strathclyde into the Scottish kingdom, and the protection he offered to Earl Gospatric in the 1070s, when he had fallen out with William, helped finally to secure the steadily increasing hegemony that the Scots had achieved over Northumbria north of the Tweed. At the same time, when William invaded in 1072, Máel Coluim was willing to become his man at a ceremony at Abernethy, one of the great churches of the Pictish kingdom. In 1079, Máel Coluim was once more raiding northern England but, once again, was ready to submit when William's son Robert Curthose and Edgar Ætheling (Máel Coluim's brother-in-law) led an army to Falkirk in 1080. In 1091, Edgar having returned from his adventures in Apulia and William II being in France, Máel Coluim, this time accompanied by his brother-in-law, invaded once again. William and his brother Robert returned from Normandy and compelled submission. On this occasion, William II insisted that submission should not take place on the border but that Máel Coluim should visit him in the south, just as he had visited Edward in 1058 and as Constantín had visited Æthelstan in 935.[56] On his return home, in 1093, Máel Coluim, apparently enraged by his treatment, set out with an army once again. At Alnwick, possibly under safe conduct, he and his eldest son by Margaret, Edward, were slain by Robert Mowbray, Earl of Northumberland.

The End of an Era

When news of Máel Coluim and Edward's death reached the Scottish court, Margaret allegedly died of grief and the king's brother, Domnall Bán, was elected to succeed him. William Rufus was not happy with this state of affairs, and in 1094 he sent one of his household knights, Máel Coluim's oldest son, Donnchad (who had been handed over as a hostage at Abernethy 21 years earlier), into Scotland at the head of an army. The Anglo-Norman era in Scottish history had arrived.

Notes

1 Bately, *ASC* MS A, *s.a.* 920.
2 Bately, *ASC* MS A. *s.a.* 875.
3 Charles-Edwards (ed.), *Chronicle of Ireland*, pp. 325–6; Hudson, "Scottish Chronicle," 153–4. For the various king-lists, see Anderson, *Kings and Kingship*.
4 Hudson, "Scottish Chronicle."
5 Broun, "Alba."
6 Greenaway (ed.), *Henry Archdeacon of Huntingdon*, I. 8, 24–5.
7 Thorpe (ed.), *Geoffrey of Monmouth*, IV. 17, 123–4.

8 Broun, "Alba."

9 Hudson, "Scottish Chronicle."

10 Broun, "The birth of Scottish history" and "Dunkeld."

11 Dumville, "The Chronicle of the Kings of Alba."

12 All printed, but without translation, in Lawrie, *Early Scottish Charters.*

13 Hudson, "Scottish Chronicle," 155.

14 *AU* 904.4; Hudson, "Scottish Chronicle," 155.

15 Hudson, "Scottish Chronicle," 150, 156; Charles-Edwards, *The Early Medieval Gaelic Lawyer*, pp. 60–1.

16 Brooks, *Early History of the Church of Canterbury*, pp. 146–7.

17 Watt, *Ecclesia Scoticana*, p. 77.

18 *AU* 918.4; Hudson, "Scottish Chronicle," 157 (where Hudson explains *more* as a loan word from Old English meaning "hills").

19 Johnson South, (ed.), *Historia de Sancto Cuthberto*, §22.

20 Wainwright, "The battles at Corbridge." For a more detailed discussion of these problems, see Woolf, *From Pictland to Alba.*

21 Davidson, "The (non)submission of 920."

22 Murphy (ed.), *The Annals of Clonmacnoise*, s.a. 928 (*recte* 934).

23 Translated in Whitelock, *EHD*, no. 3.

24 Cubbin, *ASC* MS D, s.a. 927.

25 Campbell, *The Battle of Brunanburh.*

26 For the most recent contributions to the debate, see Cavill et al., "Revisiting *Dingesmere*," and Halloran, "The Brunanburh campaign." The definitive discussion remains Campbell, *The Battle of Brunanburh.*

27 Hudson, "Scottish Chronicle," 157.

28 Connon, "*Bánshenchas* and the Uí Néill queens"; Woolf, "View from the west."

29 Woolf, "The 'Moray question'" and "Dún Nechtáin."

30 Hudson, "Scottish Chronicle," 158.

31 Bately, *ASC*, MS A, s.a. 945.

32 Sawyer, "The last Scandinavian kings of York."

33 Woolf, *From Pictland to Alba*, pp. 192–3.

34 Hudson, "Scottish Chronicle," 160.

35 Hennessey (ed.), *Chronicum Scotorum*, s.a. 969 (*recte* 971); see also Anderson, *Kings and Kingship.*

36 Woolf, "Amlaíb Cúarán."

37 Abrams, "The conversion of the Scandinavians."

38 For a recent attempt, see Barrett, "Culture contact"; see also chapter 14.

39 Hudson, "Scottish Chronicle," 161.

40 For example, Duncan, *Scotland*; Hudson, "Scottish Chronicle"; Smyth, *Warlords and Holy Men.*

41 Hudson, "Scottish Chronicle," 161 n.78.

42 Thornton, "Edgar"; Williams, "An outing on the Dee."

43 Woolf, *From Pictland to Alba.*

44 This pedigree is printed in full in its original form by John Bannerman in *Studies in the History of Dalriada*, pp. 65–6.

45 Thornton, *Kings, Chronologies and Genealogies.*

46 Broun, "Alba."

47 Hudson, "Scottish Chronicle," 157, 159.

48 Woolf, "The 'Moray Question.'"

49 Hudson, "Cnut and the Scottish kings"; Woolf, *From Pictland to Alba.*

50 Rollason (ed.), *Symeon of Durham: Libellus de Exordio*, iii. 9, 169.

51 Cubbin, *ASC* MS D, *s.a.* 1054.
52 Duncan, *Kingship of the Scots*, pp. 34–41.
53 Marianus Scottus, *s.a.*1050, cited in Anderson, *Early Sources*, I. 588.
54 Woolf, *From Pictland to Alba*, p. 259.
55 Duncan, *Kingship of the Scots*, pp. 51–2.
56 All these events are recounted in the *Anglo-Saxon Chronicle* with color filled in by the twelfth-century chroniclers.

Further Reading

For many years, the standard reference work on early Scottish history has been Duncan's *Scotland: The Making of the Kingdom*. Though still an excellent introduction, it has been superseded in detail in many places largely due to the revolution in our understanding of, and critical awareness with regard to, medieval Celtic sources that took place in the late 1970s and early 1980s. For an approach looking back on the period from the relatively better attested twelfth and thirteenth centuries, G. W. S. Barrow's *The Kingdom of the Scots: Government, Church and Society from the Eleventh to the Fourteenth Century* (2nd edn., Edinburgh, 2003) remains a classic. Barrow's methodology is to separate the new from the old in Anglo-Norman Scotland and thus to reconstruct the character of the earlier kingdom. This methodology provides much food for thought, but is beset with problems. My own *From Pictland to Alba* is the most recent synthesis of the period c.780–1070, and Dauvit Broun's *Scottish Independence and the Idea of Britain: From the Picts to Alexander III* (Edinburgh, 2007) explores the core detail of the medieval historiography. This work, and others by Broun, are essential for understanding the multiple layers of texts such as the *Chronicle of the Kings of Alba* and the king-lists. These texts are most accessible in Marjorie Anderson's *Kings and Kingship*, which remains the key collection. Benjamin Hudson has contributed many fine articles in the field, although his monograph, *Kings of Celtic Scotland* (Westport, CT, 1994), relies a little too heavily on late literary sources for its interpretation of some of the thornier issues. Some of the literary texts are made available in modern English translation in Thomas Clancy's *The Triumph Tree: Scotland's Earliest Poetry AD 550–1350* (Edinburgh, 1998). Of fundamental importance is Alan Anderson's magnum opus *Early Sources of Scottish History AD 500–1286*, which, together with his *Scottish Annals from English Chroniclers, AD 500 to 1286* (Edinburgh, 1908; Stamford, 1991), provide translations of almost every piece of primary evidence. While some of Anderson's interpretations are inevitably dated, the very existence of this compendium speeds up all research in the field. The value of much later narratives, deriving from the fourteenth and fifteenth centuries, for understanding our period remains one of the most contentious issues in early Scottish history, and to a great extent represents a generational divide in the scholarship, with those educated since the 1980s largely rejecting them. Specific issues that excite debate include the importance of Cinaed mac Ailpín, and the related topic of the disappearance of the Picts, the date and manner of the absorption of Strathclyde into the Scottish kingdom, and the extent to which Scottish "state-hood" was "precocious" when compared to other Celtic-speaking areas. As well as a generational divide, there is also something of a division between scholars working within Scotland, who engage in regular debate at small conferences and through seminar series, and those beyond the national frontier whose access to debate and discussion is largely confined to published materials. This has led to the phenomenon that much heated debate remains invisible and publications by scholars based in Scotland often represent a negotiated consensus, whilst those by outsiders tend to excite more controversy. The small number of scholars working in the field and the fact that most debate occurs orally make it harder to present these debates bibliographically.

Bibliography

Abrams, L. J., "The conversion of the Scandinavians of Dublin," *Anglo-Norman Studies*, 20 (1998), 1–29.

Anderson, A. O. (ed.), *Early Sources of Scottish History, AD 500–1286*, 2 vols. (Edinburgh, 1922; Stamford, 1990).

Anderson, M. O., *Kings and Kingship in Early Scotland* (Edinburgh, 1973).

Bannerman, J., *Studies in the History of Dalriada* (Edinburgh, 1974).

Barrett, J., "Culture contact in Viking Age Scotland," in J. H. Barrett (ed.), *Contact, Continuity and Collapse: The Norse Colonization of the North Atlantic* (Turnhout, 2003), pp. 73–111.

Bately, J. (ed.), *The Anglo-Saxon Chronicle: A Collaborative Edition*, vol. 3: *MS A* (Cambridge, 1986).

Brooks, N., *The Early History of the Church of Canterbury* (Leicester, 1984).

Broun, D., "Alba: Pictish homeland or Irish offshoot?" in P. O'Neill (ed.), *Exile and Homecoming: Papers from the Fifth Australian Conference of Celtic Studies* (Sydney, 2005), pp. 234–75.

Broun, D., "The birth of Scottish History," *Scottish Historical Review*, 76 (1997), 4–22.

Broun, D., "Dunkeld and the origin of Scottish Identity," *The Innes Review*, 48 (1997), 112–24.

Campbell, A. (ed.), *The Battle of Brunanburh* (London, 1938).

Cavill, P., Harding, S., and Jesch, J. "Revisiting *Dingesmere*," *Journal of the English Place-name Society*, 36 (2004), 25–38.

Charles-Edwards, T. M. (ed. and trans.), *The Chronicle of Ireland*, 2 vols. Translated Texts for Historians, 44 (Liverpool, 2006).

Charles-Edwards, T. M., *The Early Medieval Gaelic Lawyer* (Cambridge, 1999).

Connon, A., "The *Bánshenchas* and the Uí Néill queens of Tara," in A. P. Smyth (ed.), *Seanchas: Studies in Early and Medieval Irish Archaeology, History and Literature in Honour of Francis J. Byrne* (Dublin, 2000), pp. 98–108.

Cubbin, G. P. (ed.), *The Anglo-Saxon Chronicle: A Collaborative Edition*, 6, MS D (Cambridge, 1996).

Davidson, M. R., "The (non)submission of the northern kings in 920," in N. J. Higham and D. H. Hill (eds.), *Edward the Elder 899–924* (London, 2001), pp. 200–11.

Dumville, D. N., "The Chronicle of the Kings of Alba," in S. Taylor (ed.), *Kings, Clerics and Chronicles in Scotland, 500–1297: Essays in Honour of Marjorie Ogilvie Anderson on the Occasion of her Ninetieth Birthday* (Dublin, 2000), pp. 73–86.

Duncan, A. A. M., *The Kingship of the Scots, 842–1292: Succession and Independence* (Edinburgh, 2002).

Duncan, A. A. M., *Scotland: The Making of the Kingdom* (Edinburgh, 1975).

Greenaway, D. (ed. and trans.), *Henry Archdeacon of Huntingdon: Historia Anglorum* (Oxford, 1996).

Halloran, K., "The Brunanburh campaign: a reappraisal," *Scottish Historical Review*, 84 (2005), 133–48.

Hennessy, W. M. (ed. and trans.), *Chronicum Scotorum: A Chronicle of Irish Affairs from Earliest Times to 1135* (London, 1866).

Hudson, B. T., "Cnut and the Scottish kings," *English Historical Review*, 107 (1992), 350–60.

Hudson, B. T. (ed. and trans.), "The Scottish Chronicle," *Scottish Historical Review*, 77 (1998), 129–61.

Johnson South, T. (ed.), *Historia de Sancto Cuthberto: A History of Saint Cuthbert and a Record of his Patrimony* (Woodbridge, 2002).

Lawrie, A. C. (ed.), *Early Scottish Charters prior to 1153* (Glasgow, 1905).

Mac Airt, S. and Mac Niocaill, G. (eds. and trans.), *The Annals of Ulster (to AD 1131)*, Part I: *Text and Translation* (Dublin, 1983).

Murphy, D. (ed.), *The Annals of Clonmacnoise* (Dublin 1896; Felinfach 1993).

Rollason, D. (ed. and trans.), *Symeon of Durham: Libellus de Exordio atque Procursu istius hoc est Dunhelmensis Ecclesie* (Oxford, 2000).

Sawyer, P. H., *Anglo-Saxon Charters: An Annotated List and Bibliography* (London, 1968).

Sawyer, P. H., "The last Scandinavian kings of York," *Northern History*, 31 (1995), 39–44.

Smyth, A. P., *Warlords and Holy Men: Scotland AD 80–1000* (London, 1984).

Stokes, W. (ed. and trans.), *The Annals of Tigernach* (reprinted from *Revue Celtique*, 1895–7; repr. Felinfach, 1993).

Thornton, D. E., "Edgar and the eight kings, AD 973," *Early Medieval Europe*, 10 (2001), 49–80.

Thornton, D. E., *Kings, Chronologies and Genealogies: Studies in the Political History of Early Medieval Ireland and Wales* (Oxford, 2003).

Thorpe, L. (ed. and trans.), *Geoffrey of Monmouth: The History of the Kings of Britain* (Harmondsworth, 1966).

Wainwright, F. T., "The battles at Corbridge," *Saga-Book of the Viking Society*, 13 (1950), 156–73; reprinted in H. P. R. Finberg (ed.), *Scandinavian England: Collected Papers by F. T. Wainwright* (Chichester, 1975), pp. 163–80.

Watt, D. E. R., *Ecclesia Scoticana: Series Episcoporum Ecclesiae Catholicae Occidentalis, Series VI, Britannia, Scotia et Hibernia, Scandinavia*, vol. 1 (Stuttgart, 1991).

Whitelock, D. (ed. and trans.), *English Historical Documents*, vol. I: *AD 500–1042*, 2nd edn. (London, 1979).

Williams, A., "An outing on the Dee: King Edgar at Chester, AD 973," *Medieval Scandinavia*, 14 (2004), 229–44.

Woolf, A., "Amlaíb Cúarán and the Gael, 941–981," in S. Duffy (ed.), *Medieval Dublin III* (Dublin, 2002), pp. 34–42.

Woolf, A., "Dún Nechtáin, Fortriu and the geography of the Picts," *Scottish Historical Review*, 85 (2006), 182–201.

Woolf, A., *From Pictland to Alba 789 to 1070* (Edinburgh, 2007).

Woolf, A., "The 'Moray question' and the kingship of Alba in the tenth and eleventh centuries," *Scottish Historical Review*, 79 (2000), 145–64.

Woolf, A., "View from the west: an Irish perspective on West Saxon dynastic practice," in N. J. Higham and D. H. Hill (ed.), *Edward the Elder, 899–924* (London, 2001), pp. 89–101.

CHAPTER SEVENTEEN

Ireland, c.900–c.1000

EDEL BHREATHNACH

In 1005, Brian Bórama (d.1014), the most powerful king in Ireland at the time, visited the primatial city of Armagh and deposited 20 ounces of gold there. On that occasion, Brian presided over an entry made by his secretary Máel Suthain into the ninth-century manuscript, the *Book of Armagh*:[1]

> Saint Patrick, when going to heaven, ordered that the whole fruit of his labour, as well as of baptism and of causes of alms, should be paid to the apostolic city which in Irish is named Ardd Macha. So I have found in the books of the Irish. I, namely, Calvius Perennis [Latin translation of Máel Suthain], have written in the sight of Brian, emperor of the Irish [*Imperator Scotorum*], and what I have written he has confirmed for all the kings of Cashel.

Historians have regarded the use of the title *Imperator Scotorum* as reminiscent of the honorific title, *Imperator Romanorum*, used by the Ottonian royal house and as an indication that the Irish king "knew the value of an outward look."[2] Use of such a title placed Brian above all his peers. It also confirmed the alliance between Brian and Armagh, Ireland's primatial church, and declared Brian's provincial kingship of Cashel as pre-eminent.

The entry in the *Book of Armagh* epitomizes how Ireland had changed in the tenth century. Brian had emerged from relatively obscure origins in the south-west and, following his brother Mathgamain's death in 976, had become king of Cashel. He and his brother had countered and exploited the vikings of their own region and further afield in Dublin. He had challenged the midland and northern dynasties of the Uí Néill, who had claimed rightful possession of the notional kingship of Ireland since the late seventh century. Brian's tumultuous career began in the tenth century, a century during which many radical changes occurred in Ireland.[3]

The focus of scholars in relation to tenth-century Ireland has tended to be on the wars of provincial kings and their aspirations to be recognized as the most important king in Ireland. Analysis of the century is dominated by the careers of Brian Bórama and of his rival, the southern Uí Néill king Máel Sechnaill mac Domnaill (d.1022). Views on tenth-century Irish politics have been percolated through later pseudo-historical narratives which describe the careers of three tenth-century kings, Brian Bórama, Cellachán Chaisil (d.954, king of Munster), and Muirchertach mac Néill (d.943, king of the northern Uí Néill). These narratives date to the twelfth century and were composed by propagandists to bolster the authority of these kings' descendants.[4] They portray tenth-century Irish kings in a typical early medieval mode as heroic Christian kings vying with one another to rid the island of the accursed vikings and to restore peace to its people. This was simplification of a period that involved far more than a mighty struggle between native and foreigner. In church matters, historians have concentrated on the fortunes of the most important churches, especially Armagh and Clonmacnoise. Topics covered have included relations with major dynasties, the secularization of these churches, and their amassing of estates, as well as an effort to understand the respective roles of different church officials. Unlike the church in Anglo-Saxon England and Carolingian Europe, the Irish church seems not to have been subject to a Benedictine reform movement, although by the early eleventh century continental influence began to be felt in the Irish church, especially through the establishment of the new diocese of Dublin.[5] A consequence of the extensive excavations in Dublin since the 1960s has been the concentration on the question of urbanization in Ireland and the trade networks of the Irish Sea zone. Recent discoveries in Dublin and in Waterford have begun to clarify the development of Scandinavian urban centers from small communities to fully fledged defended ports and trading towns,[6] the establishment of Scandinavian dynasties in Ireland, and the careers of individual Scandinavian kings and also the participation of these dynasties and kings in the politics of the Irish Sea and Britain.[7] In recent decades, mainly due to the seminal work of Charles Doherty, the nature of settlement patterns other than Scandinavian towns have been studied, concentrating on the extent to which large monastic settlements, such as Armagh and Clonmacnoise, constituted "monastic towns."[8]

Since there is a tendency in the analysis of early medieval Ireland to provide general surveys from the fifth to the twelfth centuries and not to focus on any one period, many issues relating to tenth-century Ireland need considerable work. There is a need to reassess the nature of kingship in Ireland during this period: this requires an examination of the power structures that prevailed in the country, the extent of royal authority and administration, the planning of military campaigns, and, insofar as sources only reflect the concerns of royalty and ecclesiastics, how society was ordered or changed during the tenth century. The role of women in tenth-century society has been particularly neglected even though annalistic and genealogical sources, as well as an important corpus of material on royal women compiled in the twelfth century, provides much vital information on queens and marriage alliances.[9] Analysis of Ireland's economy in the tenth century and a view of settlement patterns outside the Scandinavian towns and monasteries require an interdisciplinary approach that integrates archaeological and historical evidence. The following chapter attempts to concentrate specifically on one century to gain a clearer view of developments in that society.

The Kingdoms of Ireland: National and Regional Identities

The kingdom, as defined by Susan Reynolds, was the ideal type of political unit; the king, the ideal type of ruler: the kingdom was not merely a territory which happened to be ruled by a king, it comprised and corresponded to a "people" (*gens, natio, populus*) which was assumed to be a natural, inherited community of tradition, custom, law, and descent.[10] In Ireland, the terms *gens, natio, plebs, populus* were known, and they were paralleled by numerous native terms that identified the complex layers of kindred, community, and kingdoms that constituted the *natio* of the Irish.[11] As an island that did not encounter any major influx of people from prehistory to the vikings, Ireland was homogeneous culturally and linguistically. Differences between people and kingdoms were expressed for an elite stratum in society by an influential learned class mainly in the form of genealogies. Tenth-century Ireland, like contemporary Britain and Europe, had the kingdom as its core secular unit.

Early Irish law distinguished between the legal status of a hierarchy of kings: *rí túaithe*, "the king of a small kingdom," *rí túatha*, "the king of a number of small kingdoms," *rí cóicid*, "a provincial king" or *rí ruirech*, "a king of kings," and *ruiri*, "a great king."[12] This legal definition is, as in the nature of legal codes, a simplification of both the definition of the hierarchy of kings and the definition of kingdoms. Nevertheless, it reflects accurately that kingdoms were defined either by geographical units or by relationships between kings. Although often by necessity defined by existing geophysical features, the borders of Irish kingdoms appear to have been fluid. By the tenth century, however, the impression is gained from the sources that these borders had become fixed and that one would have been aware of crossing from one major kingdom to another, if not of crossing into a smaller kingdom.

The smallest kingdom, the *túath*, was the approximate equivalent of the Anglo-Saxon hundred or modern Irish townland.[13] By the tenth century, its king rarely registers in the sources. References to the next level of king, who is the *rí túatha*, "the king of a number of small kingdoms," are plentiful and these references attest to a complexity not reflected in the laws. Kings are designated by their titles as either ruling over a people or a territory: in the *Annals of Ulster*, for example, 40 kings are rulers of a people, while 25 are rulers of a territory or a place. In both instances, the extent of the kingdom varies greatly and this is reflected in the number of entries for the rulers of different kingdoms. The smaller the kingdom, the fewer the references and often they only occur as a result of dealings with greater kings. For example, references to the kings of Osraige (the name of a population group) are relatively plentiful (*AU* 928, 933, 975, 996) as theirs was a pivotal border kingdom between the provinces of Leinster and Munster whose kings needed to be brought to heel by ambitious provincial kings. At the other end of the scale is the reference to the king of the Corcu Thrí (a people in Co. Sligo): in 994 (*AU*) Fogartach son of Diarmait, king of Corcu Thrí, is killed by neighboring people the Gailenga of Corann. As to territorially defined kingdoms, they ranged from the very important east midland kingdom of Brega (*AU* 903, 925, 966, 976), where the ancient royal site of Tara was located, to the small kingdom of Tuirbe (on the coast in north Co. Dublin). In 903 (*AU*) Aindiaraid son of Máelmuire, king of Tuirbe, died. No more is heard of that kingdom, presumably because, by the late tenth century, it had been subsumed into the newly created Scandinavian kingdom of Dublin.

The next level of king, the *rí cóicid*, "king of a province," or *rí ruirech*, "king of kings," was an overking. When tackling definitions of the provincial kingships as they existed in this period, one is again faced with various titles, some originating from the learned classes, others more politically real. Theoretically, the provincial kingships consisted of the overkingships of Leinster (east), Mumu (Munster, south), Connacht (west), Mide (midlands), and Ulaid (north). Each kingship, with the exception of Leinster, had an alternative title named after its ancient capital: Mumu/Caisel (Cashel, Co. Tipperary), Connacht/Cruachu (Rathcroghan, Co. Roscommon), Mide/Uisnech (Usnagh, Co. Westmeath), and Ulaid/Emain (Navan Fort, Co. Armagh). While both sets of titles survived to the tenth century, usage was more complicated, especially with regard to northern overkings. The kingdom of the Ulaid had long since been reduced to a lesser kingdom by the dominant dynasties of the northern Uí Néill and, therefore, the title "king of the Ulaid" no longer referred to a northern provincial kingship. Instead, whichever king of the two main branches of the northern Uí Néill was dominant, the king of Cenél Conaill or Cenél nEógain, was understood to be the provincial king of the north. The writ of provincial kings was not confined to their own provinces, and, as the tenth century progressed, a pattern that was already evident from the late seventh century onward took firm root; that is, a small group of powerful kings vying with one another for overlordship over large swathes of the island. Since much depended on the success of an individual king, not all provincial kings were players: in the tenth century, the rivalry was between the kings of Munster, Mide, and the north.

The use of the title *Imperator Scotorum* by Brian Bórama expressed the long-standing notion, propounded by the learned classes in Ireland and aspired to by Irish kings, that there was a supreme kingship of the island. Traditionally, this notion had been associated with the kingship of Tara, a prehistoric ceremonial site in modern Co. Meath.[14] The political significance of the kingship of Tara – that of an exceptional kingship which proclaimed a king more powerful than all others in Ireland – is evident from very early sources dating to at least the seventh century. In the late seventh century, midland and northern kings of the Uí Néill dynasty sought to monopolize the kingship of Tara, and with few exceptions succeeded in doing so until the tenth century. Any inroad into their monopoly was made by a few exceptional kings of Munster, such as the ninth-century king Feidlimid mac Crimthainn. In reality, however, the title "king of Tara" was normally accorded to a king whose authority extended over the provincial kings of Connacht, Leinster, Mide, and the north. Authority over Munster was less attainable. By the tenth century, the prestige of the title, although revered in literature, was replaced by the title *rí Érenn*, "king of Ireland," a title that had been coined in the late seventh century and one that could easily be translated as *Imperator Scotorum*.

Use of the titles "king of Ireland" and "king of Tara" in tenth-century annalistic entries, while potentially instructive, can also be difficult as it is necessary to be constantly mindful that, in later revisions of sources, a title can often be subject to a retrospective perspective grounded in later political realities and aspirations. Furthermore, it is essential to emphasize always that the kingships of Ireland and Tara were not hereditary – a king did not automatically succeed to these kingships – and that for the most part the perception that a king achieved this supreme status comes to us from third parties, mainly the learned men who compiled the sources. The truth of an individual's achievement can only be gleaned from assessment of his reign. The rarely used title, *ardrí Érenn*, "the high-king of Ireland," is accorded the northern king Domnall úa Néill (d.980). His long reign, which began in the 960s, was under constant pressure from various quarters: in the north-west from Cenél Conaill, in the midlands and east from Clann Cholmáin and the vikings of Dublin. Despite some

spectacular defeats, such as the battle of Cell Móna (Kilmona, Co. Westmeath) in
970 at the hands of Domnall son of Congalach mac Maíle Mithig and Amlaíb Cúarán,
king of Dublin, there were periods during his reign when Domnall acted as the most
senior king in Ireland.[15] The climax of Domnall's career was between 963 and 968
when he defeated a combination of the Leinstermen and Dublin vikings. For the last
decade of his career, he was considerably weakened and eclipsed by rising stars such
as Máel Sechnaill son of Domnall, and when he died in Armagh in 980, he could
hardly have been considered *ardrí Érenn*, "high-king of Ireland."

Another important tenth-century king, Flann Sinna (d.916), who belonged to the
midland Uí Néill dynasty of Clann Cholmáin ("the descendants of Colmán"), is
styled *rí Temrach* in the *Annals of Ulster* and *rí Uisnig*, "king of Uisnech," in the
twelfth-century codex, the *Book of Leinster*.[16] Whereas the title "king of Tara" reflects
the annalistic view of him as holding supreme authority at some stage in his career,
the title "king of Uisnech" was a title designated to the provincial kings of Mide and
specifically to the king of the Clann Cholmáin dynasty. Flann did not immediately
succeed his powerful father, Máel Sechnaill (d.862), as king of Ireland, only as king
of their dynasty Clann Cholmáin. Regnal lists state that Áed Findliath (d.879) of the
northern dynasty of Cenél nEógain assumed the supreme kingship on Máel Sechnaill's
death. The alternation of the kingship of Ireland between Clann Cholmáin and Cenél
nEógain for two hundred years between 734 and 944 is a phenomenon apparent
from regnal king-lists of the period. Flann Sinna began to gain recognition as the
king of Ireland before the death of his father-in-law, Áed Findliath, in 879. In the
first decade of his reign, Flann defeated north-eastern dynasties and raided Armagh
in 882. The vikings were both allies and a menace: they helped Flann in his campaign
in the north-east, yet in 888 they defeated him. The most successful period of Flann's
reign was the brief period between 905 and 908. In 905, he went to the south-eastern
kingdom of Osraige, and in 906 he led an expedition from Osraige into Munster as
far as Limerick. The climax of his career was in 908 when he and his allies defeated
the king of Munster, Cormac mac Cuilennáin at the battle of Belach Mugna in south
Leinster. Yet, in the same year, his rivals for the kingship of Tara, Niall Glúndub and
Domnall sons of Áed Findliath, led a raid into the heart of his own midlands kingdom
and burned one of its ceremonial centers, Tlachtga (Hill of Ward, Co. Meath). Any
assessment of his career suggests that Flann can only have been regarded as king of
Ireland – that is, the most powerful king on the island – between 905 and 908, suggesting that titles can only be an indicator of a king's position given the constant
shifting political situation.

Succession and Rule

The issue of succession to the different types of kingship has been a thorny question
in the historiography of early medieval Ireland.[17] This debate has mainly concentrated
on the laws of succession and on the degree within a kin-group eligible to succeed
to a kingship. Succession within a kin-group was complicated at provincial kingship
level by politics. The provincial kingship of Munster in the tenth century is a case in
point. Since the sixth century, this kingship was held by different branches of a people
who called themselves Eóganachta, claiming descent from a prehistoric ancestor,
Eógan Már, but whose original relationship with one another is obscure. Between
the sixth and tenth centuries, with few exceptions, the kingship of Munster was held

by 30 kings from six branches of the Eóganachta dynasties, and whereas a father and son often held the kingship, it rarely happened in direct succession. The kingship transferred from one dynasty to another, a pattern replicated throughout other dynasties in Ireland. Succession normally depended on the might or weakness of individual kings and on their relationships with client kings within Munster and with powerful dynasties elsewhere, particularly in the midlands and the north.

At the beginning of the tenth century, the Eóganachta grasp on the kingship of Munster was in crisis. This may be the reason that the kingship was held by the king-bishop Cormac mac Cuilennáin (d.908). Although apparently from among the Eóganachta, Cormac's origins are obscure. His ecclesiastical affiliation as a bishop is no clearer. His kingship is characteristic of a certain type of kingship that emerged in Munster, and no where else in Ireland, between the late eighth and mid-tenth centuries whereby senior clerics assumed the kingship of Munster. Most of them were abbots of Emly (Co. Tipperary), the royal church of the Eóganachta. While an argument might be made that these clerics assumed the kingship of Munster in times of crisis – and their reigns could be regarded as a type of interregnum – it would also appear from the secular laws that the higher echelons in Munster articulated their province's secular and ecclesiastical authority somewhat differently from other provinces. The three leading individuals in Munster were the *ollam uas rígaib rí Muman*, "a master of kings [is] the king of Munster," *ollam uasalesguib*, "a noble master bishop," and *ollam mórchathrach*, "a master of a great monastery."[18] That two of these offices, king and bishop or king and abbot, could be held by one individual may not have been so unusual given that they were regarded as constituent parts of the one privileged social order in Munster.

Cormac's death at the battle of Belach Mugna in 908 caused difficulties in the succession to the kingship of Munster among the Eóganachta dynasties. There was a brief revival of Eóganachta fortunes when Cellachán Caisil son of Búadachán (d.954) of the Eóganacht Chaisil became king of Munster. Cellachán, whose career is the subject of the twelfth-century biography *Caithréim Chellacháin Chaisil* – a work likely to be his dynasty's response to the triumphal biography of Brian Bórama, *Cogadh Gáedhel re Gallaibh* – was modestly successful in his own province, although he had to submit to Donnchad son of Flann Sinna (d.944), the then claimant to the kingship of Ireland. It is during Cellachán Caisil's reign that the family of Brian Bórama began to rise to power in earnest.[19] They were not Eóganachta but were of the In Déis Tuaiscirt, "the vassal people of the north" (later known as Dál Cais, "the people of Cas," their reputed eponymous ancestor), whose kingdom had extended across the River Shannon from east Co. Limerick northward into Co. Clare. In 944, Cellachán Caisil defeated Cennétig son of Lorcán, Brian Bórama's father, who clearly felt confident enough to challenge Cellachán. Cennétig's death notice in the *Annals of Inisfallen* in 951 describes him as *rígdamna Cassil*, "worthy of the kingship of Cashel [Munster]." It was Cennétig's sons, Mathgamain (d.976) and Brian, however, who fulfilled their father's ambitions, and it is by examining their careers and that of Brian Bórama's arch-rival, Máel Sechnaill son of Domnall (d.1022), Flann Sinna's great-grandson, that the practice of royal power and governance in tenth-century Ireland can be best assessed.

For a king of a sub-kingdom of Munster and not of the Eóganachta such as Mathgamain to become king of Munster, he had to pursue a military strategy that built up his reputation as one worthy to take hold of the provincial kingship. The

Irish annals are replete with references to raids, hostings, battles, and murders of kings and ecclesiastics and are sometimes taken to reflect a state of anarchy. However, Mathgamain's (and Brian's) career demonstrates that, far from being so, these references offer an insight into a well-developed military strategy. Mathgamain's initial campaign targeted important settlements on the River Shannon, such as Clonmacnoise and the viking settlement of Limerick. His control of these places did not just mean that he controlled the Shannon and its fleets, he also controlled places that were economically and politically vital. In 959 (*AFM*), he attacked Clonmacnoise, a major monastery strategically located on the Shannon on the borders of Connacht, Mide, and Munster; it was the site of a bridge across the river, very wealthy, and, therefore, a place where supplies of corn were readily available.

In 972, according to the *Annals of Inisfallen*, Mathgamain, in collaboration with his Eóganacht rival for the kingship of Munster, Máel Muad son of Bran and other nobles of Munster, imposed three laws (*cánai*) by which Norse mercenaries (*suaittrech*) were banished, foreigners were expelled from Limerick, and the fortress was burned. Considering that Mathgamain was killed four years later by Murchad son of Bran, this coordinated action involving a number of tenth-century Irish kings was unusual. The use of the term *cáin* is noteworthy: in the *Annals of Inisfallen* prior to the eleventh century, this term is associated with ecclesiastical laws, which even though they had an effect on secular society were nonetheless imposed by kings acting with or at the behest of leading clerics.[20] A further example of Mathgamain son of Cennétig acting in the role of king as arbitrator and judge is suggested by his intervention in ecclesiastical affairs in 973 (*AI*) when he arbitrated between the abbots of Armagh and Emly concerning the right of Armagh to collect revenues in Munster. He settled the dispute through the enactment of an agreement in Armagh's favor. As Mathgamain's loyalty to Emly, the chief church of the Eóganachta, was probably not particularly strong, he presumably seized the opportunity to ally himself to Armagh, the most important church in Ireland. It was an act that signified that, as king of Munster, he was then thinking beyond the confines of his own province. However, Mathgamain's ambitions were not realized as he was killed in 976 by Máel Muad son of Bran. Mathgamain had established the recently successful Dál Cais dynasty's right to hold the provincial kingship of Munster, and his brother Brian took no time in avenging his death and in killing his rival Máel Muad. This happened in 978 at the battle of Belach Lechta (a pass in the Ballyhoura Mountains in Co. Cork).

Brian Bórama's career from king of Munster to *Imperator Scotorum* may be assessed not as a narrative of victories and defeats, but by understanding the strategy he adopted in attempting to be recognized as the most powerful king in Ireland. His strategy of bringing an army into other kingdoms and attempting to acquire hostages from their kings is a template for how a small number of powerful provincial kings operated from the tenth to the twelfth centuries, all with the objective of being recognized as obtaining supreme authority over their peers. To do so, Brian had to secure his own province. In 977, for example, he dealt with the vikings of Limerick who had established a base on the monastic island of Scattery in the Shannon estuary.

For any Munster king to seek national recognition, as Cormac mac Cuilennáin had found to his cost, he had to take the hostages of, and assert his power over, the buffer-kingdom of Osraige (located between Munster and Leinster) and from there deal with Leinster. In 983, Brian took the hostages of Osraige and Leinster. The kingdom of Connacht was always a power to be reckoned with and to acquire its hostages was no easy task. Kings of Connacht could be power-brokers between potential kings of Ireland and their power increased from the tenth century onward so that by the twelfth century they themselves were contenders for the position. In 983, Brian brought a fleet into Connacht but his forces did not fare well there. The use of ships for warfare was a new departure in Ireland in the tenth century and this, of course, was due to the vikings who Brian Bórama, like other Irish kings, soon realized were as much of use as they were an enemy. In 984, for example, Brian made a significant alliance with the Haraldssons of Waterford: "a great naval expedition by the sons of Aralt to Port Láirge [Waterford], and they and the sons of Cennétig exchanged hostages there as a guarantee of both together providing a hosting to attack Dublin" (*AI*). By contemplating an attack on Dublin, Brian was directly challenging Máel Sechnaill whose control of Dublin at the time was strengthened by his half-brother's position as its king. From now on, he had to engage with his rival Máel Sechnaill. A standard strategy for a king in such a situation was to raid the heartland of his rival's kingdom – as Máel Sechnaill had done to Brian in 982. He had dramatically struck at the heart of Dál Cais territory when he felled the sacred tree at Mag Adar, the inauguration site of Dál Cais. In 988, Brian brought another fleet up the Shannon and plundered Mide, Máel Sechnaill's kingdom, as far as Uisnech, its ancient royal capital. Máel Sechnaill responded in 990 by attacking north Munster, while in 992 he had greater success than Brian in Connacht. Between 992 and 997 both kings sought to gain the upper hand, but in 997 they decided to reach an accommodation in dividing Ireland's rule between them. They acted in consort in the following year and in doing so took the hostages of Connacht, Leinster, and the vikings in 998. The agreement faltered in the following years mainly because Brian was too ambitious and not willing to be a joint-ruler of Ireland. He set his sights on Dublin, defeating its king Sitric son of Amlaíb and his allies the Leinstermen in the battle of Glenn Máma in 999,[21] and on Tara, still the symbolic, mythical capital of Ireland. His effort to reach Tara in 1000 was thwarted by Máel Sechnaill with the assistance of the Dublin vikings and the Leinstermen. While Máel Sechnaill had managed to profane the sacred tree of Mag Adar in 982, Brian's attempt to enter the *ferann ríg*, "royal demesne," of Tara did not succeed.

Apart from pursuing military campaigns, Irish kings exerted other means of control, including deep involvement in church affairs. Brian took the hostages of the main monasteries of Munster, Lismore, Cork, and Emly in 987 (*AI*) as a guarantee of the banishment of thieves (*foglaide*) and lawless people (*áessa escána*) from their precincts and thus bringing them into the ambit of his power. In 990, he involved himself in ransoming the lector (*fer léiginn*) of Ros Ailithir (Rosscarbery, Co. Cork) from the vikings, implying that he was willing to bargain with them for the safe return of a member of his province's ecclesiastical elite. Of course, the Dál Cais and Brian's descendants, the Uí Briain, influenced, as many Irish kings did, appointments to key churches in Munster.[22] In 990, the abbacy of Emly was assumed by Brian's brother, Marcán (d.1010), who also held the abbacies of Inis Cealtra (Co. Clare) and of Terryglass (Co. Tipperary), both monasteries located on the Shannon. Mathgamain and Brian's fostering of an allegiance to Armagh – probably to the detriment of Emly's coffers – has already been noted.

Kings of the north regularly offered tribute to the primatial church: in 947, the Cenél nEógain gave the full measure of the *Finnfaídech Pátraic*, "bell of St. Patrick," of pure silver to Armagh. In 993, Dub dá Leithe, abbot of Armagh, the same successor of Patrick with whom Mathgamain had reached an accommodation in 973, went on a visitation of the kingdom of Cenél nEógain where he conferred the grade of king (*grád ríg*) on the youthful king Áed son of Domnall (d.1004) in the presence of Patrick's community (*sámud Pátraic*). References to religious ordination of early Irish kings are rare. In Áed's case, it has been suggested that the intervention of the abbot of Armagh was an attempt to secure his kingship after a period of instability, perhaps a northern version of Munster's king-abbots and the king-bishop Cormac mac Cuilennáin.[23] Kings did not always please the successor of Patrick. Máel Sechnaill fell foul of the interests of Armagh when in 986 (*Chronicon Scotorum*) he took the shrine of Patrick from Áth Firdiad (Ardee, Co. Louth) to Áth Sige (Assey near Tara, Co. Meath). It would appear that he and the abbot of Patrick, Dub dá Leithe again, were on opposite sides of a dispute between two local kings and that as a result Máel Sechnaill effectively profaned the shrine. When they came to terms, Dub dá Leithe exacted a heavy penalty from Máel Sechnaill. This incident is a dramatic instance of the workings of power in tenth-century Ireland in which two of the most powerful men on the island came into conflict and, as often was the case, Dub dá Leithe, abbot of Armagh was the victor.

As in any society, great kings did not act alone. There existed around them their kin-group and other social groups which sustained their rule or, in many instances, frustrated it. Society was a network of complex relationships involving blood relations, ties by marriage and maternal connections, and political alliances. This section of the chapter attempts to identify members of the nobility in tenth-century Ireland and, in doing so, also to explain the role women played in that social group. Annalistic references to queens and royal women are fairly sparse. The only ecclesiastical office recorded is that of the abbesses of Kildare (*AU* 916, 979; *AI* 964), all of whom appear to have belonged to a people known as the Fothairt whose secular power had long since declined but who held on to this important office by their genealogical association with St. Brigit, founder of Kildare. With regard to lay women, most of the annalistic entries record the obits of the daughters of important kings: in 928, Muirgel, variously described as sister or daughter of Flann Sinna, died in Clonmacnoise while Flann's daughter, Gormflaith died in penitence in 948. Three queens are mentioned in the *Annals of Ulster*: Lígach, queen of Brega (923), Der bhFáil, queen of Tara (931), and Flann daughter of Donnchad, queen of Ailech (940). The paucity of information concerning women is compensated for by two sources: a king-list known as *Baile in Scáil*, originally composed in the ninth century but refashioned in the eleventh century[24] and the *Banshenchas*, "Lore of Women," a comprehensive list of the mothers of the kings of Tara and other provincial kings and their offspring.[25]

The complexity of royal marriages and relationships, which must have influenced so much of the polity of tenth-century Ireland, is clear in both sources. For example, Flann Sinna's mother was Lann daughter of Dúngaile, king of Osraige, who had originally been married to Áed Findliath, the northern king who was Flann's predecessor as king of Ireland. Lann's brother Cerball mac Muirecáin, king of Osraige had had pretensions to the provincial kingship of Leinster but these were checked by Flann Sinna's father, Máel Sechnaill I. Her nephew Cellach was killed at the battle of Belach Mugna in 908, an ally of the king of Munster Cormac mac Cuilennáin. Her sisters were married to Scandinavian kings of Dublin. Flann Sinna had three wives: Máel Muire daughter of the king of Alba (who had already been married to Áed Findliath), Eithne daughter of Áed Findliath (who had been married to Flannacán king of Brega), and Gormflaith daughter of Flann son of Conaing, also king of Brega (whose mother was Áed Findliath's sister). If these somewhat incestuous relationships make any sense, they do so in a political context: women ensured the close and necessary family connections between the northern and midland dynasties of the Uí Néill. However, this type of familial web was not confined to the Uí Néill. Another daughter of Flann Sinna, Gormflaith, is presented to us in the literature as a genuine historic queen, a scheming queen, and a sovereignty goddess. One of the attributes of mythical sovereignty goddesses, who represented fertility and the well-being of the kingdom, was that they were serially married to kings of a particular kingdom. Hence the most famous of them, Eithne and Medb, were the consorts of numerous mythical and heroic kings of Tara. Gormflaith is said to have married Cormac mac Cuilennáin (although this alliance is doubtful as Cormac's celibacy is celebrated), Cerball son of Muirecáin, king of Leinster (d.909), and Niall Glúndub, king of Tara (d.919). Whereas the early tenth-century Gormflaith's alliances are intriguing, those of a second Gormflaith, daughter of Murchad son of Finn, king of Leinster (d.972) are equally notable.

The relationship between Brian Bórama and Máel Sechnaill and Sitric son of Amlaíb Cúarán, king of Dublin and Máel Mórda son of Murchad is complicated greatly by this later Gormflaith. She is associated with Amlaíb to whom she bore Sitric, with Máel Sechnaill and Brian, becoming one of his four wives. She was the mother of Donnchad (d.1064) who succeeded his father to the kingship of Munster. All Brian's alliances involving women seem to have been politically inspired and offer another insight into the course of his career and his political strategies.[26] His first wife was daughter of the king of Uí Fhiachrach Aidne, a kingdom located in southern Connacht bordering on Munster; Gormflaith belonged to the Leinster dynasty and may have been taken as a wife when Brian was extending his influence in the east; his third wife was the daughter of a king of Uí Áeda Odba, a kingdom that, although small, was almost halfway between Dublin and Tara and, therefore, very strategically located; his fourth wife was the daughter of the king of Connacht, again part of a political strategy, namely, the need for Brian to have good relations with the king of Connacht. Brian had three known daughters: one married into the Eóganacht dynasty that had killed her uncle Mathgamain; a second married the northern king Flaithbertach ua Néill; and a third married Sitric, king of Dublin, son of Gormflaith, Brian's second wife.

The Vikings

Like a play within a play, the vikings were highly active in Ireland throughout the tenth century with competing dynasties in Dublin, Limerick, and Waterford. Their internal disputes often involved Irish kings as allies or enemies and they became absorbed in Irish politics to the extent that, from 940 to 981, Amlaíb (Óláfr) Cúarán, king of Dublin, spent a number of decades – when not attempting to seize the kingship of York – extending Dublin's power. The vikings became necessary to Irish kings who realized the military advantages of their fleets and also the economic trading network to which they belonged. The tenth century heralded the first phase of the planned urbanization of Dublin, and, in 997, having until then depended on Anglo-Saxon and Scandinavian coinage, Sitric son of Amlaíb struck the first Dublin coin.[27]

In 902, the annals report that the vikings were expelled from Dublin, and whatever the general population of the settlement – which may not have been that big – it was abandoned for 12 years by its ruling elite. When they returned in 914, their energies were spent securing and expanding their settlements in Dublin, Limerick, and Waterford, warring among themselves, and becoming involved in Irish politics. It has been suggested recently that tenth-century Dublin, Limerick, and Waterford were ruled by different dynasties descended from a viking king Ívarr (d.873), who was active in Ireland and Britain in the 850s and 860s.[28] The Dublin vikings concentrated their efforts to extend their sphere of influence on Leinster, the midlands, and the north, thus bringing them immediately into conflict with the northern king of Tara, Niall Glúndub whom they defeated and killed near Dublin in 919. The Limerick vikings used their naval power to control the Shannon and to wage war in Munster, Connacht, and the midlands. Waterford was allied to Dublin and assumed the role of checking Limerick's power in Munster. The rivalry between Dublin and Limerick, which ultimately involved a power struggle as to which one would be the dominant naval power and Scandinavian trading center in Ireland, was fought until the late 930s when the Limerick vikings lost the battle.

At this stage, the ever-present attraction to the kings of Dublin – that of control of York and the north of England – intervened. Amlaíb son of Gothfrith, king of Dublin appears to have been among those defeated at the battle of *Brunanburh* in 937. In 939–40, he was joined by his cousin Amlaíb son of Sitric (Amlaíb Cúarán) who succeeded him as king of York. With the reign of Amlaíb Cúarán, the Scandinavians in Ireland entered a new phase. While maintaining a very keen interest in the wealthier kingdom of York – he spent two periods there (941–5 and 946–53) – Amlaíb Cúarán integrated more effectively than previous Scandinavian kings into the ecclesiastical and political polity of Ireland. Amlaíb's strategy is best illustrated by his relations with Congalach mac Maíle Mithig and his ambition to control his kingdom of Brega. Amlaíb and Congalach had a relationship of convenience. In its initial phase, Amlaíb was Congalach's ally in the latter's conflict with his rival, the northern pretender for the kingship of Ireland, Rúaidrí ua Canannáin (d.950). It was not particularly successful and ended with Congalach looting Dublin with Bróen son of Máel Mórda, king of Leinster in 944. Blacair, Amlaíb's replacement while he was in York, responded by intensifying a campaign in Brega and looting the main churches of Brega, including Kells and Slane. On his return, Amlaíb avenged the destruction of Dublin when, in alliance with the Leinstermen, Congalach's erstwhile allies, he defeated and killed him in 956. For more than a decade following that victory, Amlaíb was the strongest king in the east midlands and effectively operated as an Irish king. He protected his expanded kingdom of Dublin mainly from the Leinstermen, involved himself in the political factions of north Leinster, and, with the assistance of Domnall son of Congalach, defeated the king of Ireland, Domnall ua Néill in 980. That his integration was not just political but cultural is evidenced by his marriages and his patronage of the Columban *familia* and of Irish poets. He married the famous Gormflaith, daughter of the king of Leinster – mother of his son and future king of Dublin, Sitric – and also a daughter of his ally, Domnall son of Congalach. Whether he converted to Christianity in Dublin or in York, his affiliations toward existing Columban foundations in Brega, and possible patronage of new foundations in Brega and Dublin, suggest strongly that he was the first viking king of Dublin to espouse Christianity fully. This is further reflected in his decision to go to Iona in 981 where he died.[29]

While Amlaíb maintained Dublin's dominance for some years, including a decisive victory over the Leinstermen in 978, the rise of Máel Sechnaill, from the mid-970s onward, increasingly threatened his position. The armies of Dublin and Mide met at Tara in 980 where Máel Sechnaill defeated the forces of Dublin and the Isles and where Ragnall son of Amlaíb was killed. Fortuitously for Máel Sechnaill, his other rival as king of Ireland, Domnall ua Néill, died in Armagh in the same year. He followed up his victory against the vikings by attacking Dublin and releasing Domnall Cláen, king of Leinster, who was being held as a hostage there. An irony of the relationship between Amlaíb and Máel Sechnaill was that both of the king of Mide's wives had been part of the Dublin king's life: Gormflaith had been his wife and Máel Muire was Amlaíb's daughter.

Archaeological evidence demonstrates that in the tenth century Dublin slowly progressed from a riverine base to an urban center. In Howard Clarke's assessment:

> By that date [989 when Máel Sechnaill purportedly levied a gold tax on the householders of Dublin] the archaeology of Dublin confirms that an informal, yet recognizably urban streetscape existed. The foreigners of Áth Cliath [Dublin] were assumed to be wealthy and organized, and were treated as such. At the same time they were slowly becoming less foreign.[30]

The Scandinavians in Ireland participated in two economies. Their military and trading interests expanded from the Irish Sea eastward to Britain and, as evident from Amlaíb Cúarán's career, were focused on the kingship of York.[31] Within Ireland, one of the primary indicators of the economic relations between the Scandinavians and the Irish are Viking Age hoards.[32] Provenanced coinless hoards, most of which date to the late ninth and early tenth centuries, are from Munster, Ulster, and the midlands with a particular concentration in the western regions of the kingdom of Mide. Of the provenanced mixed and coin hoards, which date mainly to the tenth century, three-quarters were found in northern Leinster. Neither category occurs in Connacht. Hoards were deposited in rural secular, urban, and ecclesiastical sites: silver ornaments predominate in hoards from secular sites, while coins and small ingots are found in urban and ecclesiastical sites. Clearly, viking silver was an important component in the Irish economy, and control of such a resource would have been important for kings like Máel Sechnaill. Similarly, the Irish landscape changed as the Scandinavians settled in the tenth century. Not only were their encampments (*longphoirt*) evident and the main urban settlements developing, it has been argued by Doherty that, as elsewhere, their military presence may have caused the militarization of Irish society and a fundamental change in the administration of authority and the ordering of society which in effect was in line with much that was happening elsewhere in England and western Europe.[33]

The Church

In her assessment of the church in Ireland in the tenth century, Kathleen Hughes noted that there was a decrease in annalistic entries regarding minor churches and that major churches were emerging into an increasingly dominant position and building up overlordships.[34] This issue is nowhere more striking than in relation to the abbacy of Armagh. By the tenth century, Armagh was the primary church in Ireland with an extensive settlement and estates populated both by lay and clergy. It was administered by a hierarchy of ecclesiastical officials many of whom inherited their positions and was patronized by kings of every province. It was a center of learning both native and Latin. Its abbot could impose Patrick's law – in reality a tribute on churches and kingdoms – throughout the country. In effect, he was regarded as another provincial king and, when particularly powerful, competed with the king of Ireland. He operated different writs. He had his own ecclesiastical settlement which was large and always vulnerable to attack. Beyond Armagh itself, the abbot had an ecclesiastical writ which, as seen previously in relation to his accommodation with Mathgamain, his extraction of a penalty from Máel Sechnaill, and his anointing of the king of Cenél nEógain, could extend over the whole island. Indeed, in the tenth century, a number of the abbots of Armagh were the most powerful men in Ireland. Possibly as a result of viking activity in the Irish Sea zone and in Scotland, two of them became the successors of Patrick and Columba, thus controlling a sizable number of major monasteries and their client churches.[35] Máel Brigte mac Tornáin (d.927), who held both offices, probably erected one of the high crosses at Kells which is inscribed as the cross of Patrick and Columba.[36] A second double headship of the communities of Patrick and Columba occurred when the distinguished successor of Patrick, Dub dá Leithe, who had assumed office in 965, was recorded in the *Annals of Ulster* in 989 to have taken on the headship of the *familia* of Columba with the consent of the men of Ireland and Scotland.[37] Dub dá Leithe was a significant figure in the history of Armagh: he was the first hereditary abbot belonging to the Uí Sinaig family who ruled Armagh to the twelfth century.[38] As seen from the events in 986 when he clashed with Máel Sechnaill, he was deeply involved in local secular politics, especially if it impinged on the kingdoms of Conaille, north Brega, and the Airgialla. Many of the abbots of Armagh belonged to dynasties of the kingdom of Airgialla, including the Uí Sinaig, and they effectively controlled that kingdom and surrounding kingdoms in the manner of an overking. Hence we find the *máer*, "steward," of Patrick collecting Armagh's revenues from Sliab Fuait (mountain range in Co. Armagh) south to the river Boyne. The steward was often second only to the abbot as in the case of Muiredach son of Domnall (d.924), "deputy abbot" (*tánaise abbad*) of Armagh, who was also abbot of Monasterboice (Co. Louth), chief steward of the southern Uí Néill, and *cenn adcomairc fer mBreg*, "chief counsellor [in a juridical sense] of the men of Brega."

The office of *máer* of Armagh draws attention to ecclesiastical offices other than that of abbot in the tenth-century Irish church. Of the six who held the abbacy of Armagh, two were bishops, both eminent: Iosep (d.936) was abbot, bishop, *sapiens*, and *ancorita*, while Cathasach mac Duilgen (d.957) was *suí espoc Goídel*, "learned bishop of the Irish." The annals record an array of bishops in tenth-century Ireland. Some, as might be expected, were in larger monasteries (Armagh, Clonmacnoise,

Clonard, Kildare, Bangor, Emly, Cork, and Lismore). A very small number resided in lesser churches (Trim 931), and since such churches were normally affiliated to greater churches, these bishops were probably providing for the spiritual needs of part of a greater *paruchia*. An interesting phenomenon is the appearance in the tenth century of bishops with wider remits, either territorial (Leth Cuinn, Laigen, Tuadmuman) or relating to a particular people (Síl Áeda Sláine, Uí Néill, Cenél nEógain, Túath Luigne). They do not suggest the existence of an evolving diocesan structure – especially as they were not permanent bishoprics – but probably reflect what was happening in secular governance, namely, the tendency toward centralization and investing power in overkings.

The economic and political importance of Irish monasteries is apparent from the numerous raids on them in the tenth century both by Irish and vikings. Armagh, Clonmacnoise, and Kildare were targeted by the vikings in the first half of the century as sources of wealth, especially slaves. Monasteries and churches were subject to politically inspired raids from all sides. In 951, in his war with Congalach mac Maíle Mithig, Gothfrith son of Sitric, king of Dublin attacked the client churches of Kells and Armagh in the kingdom of Brega, while in 970 the kings of the north, including Domnall ua Néill, attacked the client churches of Armagh in the kingdom of Conaille. Yet great monasteries profited from the patronage of great kings in the tenth century, and the physical evidence of this can be seen in highly decorated crosses such as Muiredach's cross at Monasterboice and the cross of Patrick and Columba at Kells. Medieval patrons sought certain returns for their patronage – the *ius patronus* – which included an expectation of an easier path to heaven and, more importantly, certain rights in the elections to abbatial, episcopal, and sacerdotal office. Flann Sinna's expectations as patron of Clonmacnoise must have been considerable. The annals record that he and Abbot Colmán Conaillech caused the *damliag*, "stone church," of Clonmacnoise to be constructed in 909, a year after his victory against Cormac mac Cuilennáin at Belach Mugna. This *damliag* is the largest surviving pre-Romanesque church in Ireland.[39] Flann also intended to remind all who visited Clonmacnoise of his power and his patronage by causing the magnificent Cross of the Scriptures to be erected, carefully aligned in front of the west doorway of the *damliag*. The now badly damaged inscription on the cross bears testament to so much of what happened in tenth-century Ireland: "A prayer for King Flann, son of Máel Sechnaill, a prayer for the king of Ireland, for Colmán, who made this cross for King Flann."[40] Here the relationship between king and abbot is confirmed, as is a king's view of himself as ruler of the whole island.

Conclusion

In popular and scholarly literature, the tenth century in Ireland has been blighted by a fiction that was originally concocted about it in the twelfth century by the descendants of its powerful kings and in particular the Uí Briain, descendants of Brian Bórama. In some respects, it is a century that lost out to the dramatic events of the eleventh and twelfth centuries in Ireland. Yet when these same events are analyzed, it can be fairly stated that the seeds were sown in the tenth century. Power became invested in a small number of provincial kingships. The notion of a kingship of the whole island edged toward reality. The development of urban trading centers created a new wealth which Irish kings sought to control and also opened the island to new influences that ultimately brought reform to Irish kingship and the Irish church. Although diverging in many respects from the situation elsewhere in the tenth century, Ireland's experience was not completely different, and at the heart of that experience was the beginning of the reordering of society. A more detailed and fresh examination of the topics dealt with in this chapter might elucidate more comprehensively how that came about.

Notes

1   Gwynn, "Brian in Armagh (1005)," p. ciii.
2   Ní Mhaonaigh, *Brian Boru*, p. 30.
3   Doherty, "The Vikings in Ireland."
4   Ó Corráin, "Caithréim Cheallacháin Chaisil"; Ní Maonaigh, *Brian Boru*, pp. 66–79.
5   Ó Floinn, "The foundation relics."
6   Clarke, "Proto-towns and towns."
7   Downham, *Viking Kings of Britain and Ireland*.
8   Doherty, "The monastic town in early medieval Ireland."
9   Connon, "The *Bánshenchas*."
10 Reynolds, *Kingdoms and Communities*, p. 250.
11 Charles-Edwards, *Early Irish and Welsh Kinship*, pp. 545–60 (glossary).
12 Kelly, *A Guide to Early Irish Law*, pp. 16–17.
13 Doherty, "The Vikings in Ireland," pp. 324–30.
14 Bhreathnach (ed.), *The Kingship and Landscape of Tara*.
15 Jaski, "Vikings and the kingship of Tara," 339–46.
16 Best et al. (eds.), *The Book of Leinster*, p. 198 (LL 42b).
17 Jaski, *Early Irish Kingship*.
18 Ibid., p. 100.
19 Ní Mhaonaigh, *Brian Boru*, pp. 21–8.
20 Charles-Edwards, *The Early Mediaeval Gaelic Lawyer*.
21 Mac Shamhráin, "The battle of Glenn Máma."
22 Ó Corráin, "Dál Cais: church and dynasty."
23 Jaski, *Early Irish Kingship*, pp. 60–1.
24 Murray (ed.), *Baile in Scáil*.
25 Dobbs, "The Ban-shenchus."
26 Ní Mhaonaigh, *Brian Boru*, pp. 30–3
27 Clarke, "Proto-towns and towns," pp. 361–2.
28 Downham, *Viking Kings of Britain and Ireland*.
29 Bhreathnach, "Columban churches"; Doherty, "The Vikings in Ireland," pp. 296–305.
30 Clarke, "Proto-towns and towns," p. 362
31 Smyth, *Scandinavian York and Dublin*.
32 Sheehan, "Early Viking-Age silver hoards," pp. 172–3.
33 Doherty, "The Vikings in Ireland," pp. 326–7.
34 Hughes, "The Irish church, 800–c.1050," pp. 646–7.
35 Herbert, *Iona, Kells, and Derry*, pp. 78–9.
36 Stalley, "The tower cross at Kells."
37 Herbert, *Iona, Kells, and Derry*, pp. 83–5.
38 Ó Fiaich, "The church of Armagh."
39 Manning, "Clonmacnoise cathedral," pp. 71–7.
40 Ó Murchadha, "Rubbings taken of the inscriptions."

Further Reading

Any work that deals specifically with tenth-century Ireland has been referred to in the endnotes. Further reference is made to the events outlined in this chapter in survey volumes of early Ireland, including D. Ó Corráin, *Ireland before the Normans* (Dublin, 1972), D. Ó Cróinín, *Early Medieval Ireland 400–1200* (London, 1995), and D. Ó Cróinín (ed.) *A New History of Ireland 1: Prehistoric and Early Ireland* (Oxford, 2005). There are various articles that provide more detail. They include Ó Corráin, "Dál Cais"; J. Ryan, "Brian Boruma, king of Ireland," in E. Rynne (ed.), *North Munster Studies: Essays in Commemoration of Monsignor Michael Moloney* (Limerick, 1967), pp. 355–74; and A. Woolf, "Amlaíb Cúarán and the Gael, 941–981," in S. Duffy (ed.) *Medieval Dublin III* (Dublin, 2002), pp. 34–42.

Bibliography

Best, R. I., Bergin, O., and O'Brien, M. A. (eds.), *The Book of Leinster formerly Lebar na Núachongbála*, vol. 1 (Dublin, 1954).

Bhreathnach, E., "Columban churches in Brega and Leinster: relations with the Norse and the Anglo-Normans," *Journal of the Royal Society of Antiquaries of Ireland*, 129 (1999), 5–18.

Bhreathnach, E. (ed.), *The Kingship and Landscape of Tara* (Dublin, 2005).

Bugge, A. (ed. and trans.), *Caithréim Cellacháin Caisil: The Victorious Career of Cellachan at Cashel or the Wars between the Irishmen and the Norsemen in the Middle of the Tenth Century* (Christiana, 1905).

Charles-Edwards, T. M., *Early Irish and Welsh Kinship* (Oxford, 1993).

Charles-Edwards, T. M., *The Early Mediaeval Gaelic Lawyer* (Cambridge, 1999).

Clarke, H., "Proto-towns and towns in Ireland and Britain in the ninth and tenth centuries," in H. B. Clarke, M. Ní Mhaonaigh, and R. Ó Floinn (eds.), *Ireland and Scandinavia in the Early Viking Age* (Dublin, 1998), pp. 331–80.

Connon, A., "The *Bánshenchas* and the Uí Néill queens of Tara," in A. P. Smyth (ed.), *Seanchas: Studies in Early and Medieval Irish Archaeology, History and Literature in Honour of Francis J. Byrne* (Dublin, 2000), pp. 98–108.

Dobbs, M. E., "The Ban-shenchus," *Revue Celtique*, 47 (1930), 282–339; 48 (1931), 163–233; 49 (1932), 437–89.

Doherty, C., "The monastic town in early medieval Ireland," in H. B. Clarke and A. Simms (eds.), *The Comparative History of Urban Origins in Non-Roman Europe: Ireland, Wales, Denmark, Germany, Poland and Russia from the Ninth to the Thirteenth Century* (Oxford, 1985), part 1, pp. 45–75.

Doherty, C., "The Vikings in Ireland: a review," in H. B. Clarke, M. Ní Mhaonaigh, and R. Ó Floinn (eds.), *Ireland and Scandinavia in the Early Viking age* (Dublin, 1998), pp. 288–330.

Downham, C., *Viking Kings of Britain and Ireland: The Dynasty of Ívarr to AD 1014* (Dunedin, 2007).

Gwynn, A., "Brian in Armagh (1005)," *Seanchas Ardmhacha*, 9 (1978), 35–50.

Hennessy, W. M. (ed. and trans.), *Chronicum Scotorum: A Chronicle of Irish Affairs, from the Earliest Times to AD 1135; with a Supplement, containing the Events from 1141 to 1150*. Rolls series 46. (London, 1866).

Herbert, M., *Iona, Kells, and Derry: The History and Hagiography of the Monastic Familia of Columba* (Oxford, 1988).

Hogan, E. (ed.) *Móirtimchell Éirenn uile dorigne Muirchertach mac Néill* (Dublin, 1901).

Hughes, K., "The Irish church, 800–c.1050," in D. Ó Cróinín (ed.), *A New History of Ireland*, vol. 1 (Oxford, 2005), pp. 635–55.

Jaski, B., *Early Irish Kingship and Succession* (Dublin, 2000).

Jaski, B., "Vikings and the kingship of Tara," *Peritia*, 9 (1995), 310–53.

Kelly, F., *A Guide to Early Irish Law* (Dublin, 1988).

Mac Airt, S. (ed.), *The Annals of Inisfallen* (Dublin, 1944; reprinted 1977).

Mac Airt, S. and Mac Niocaill, G. (eds. and trans.), *The Annals of Ulster (to AD 1131)*, Part I: *Text and Translation* (Dublin, 1983).

Mac Shamhráin, A., "The battle of Glenn Máma, Dublin and the high-kingship of Ireland: a millennial commemoration," in S. Duffy (ed.), *Medieval Dublin II* (Dublin, 2001), pp. 53–64.

Manning, C., "Clonmacnoise cathedral," in H. King (ed.), *Clonmacnoise Studies*, vol. 1 (Dublin, 1998), pp. 57–86.

Murphy, D. (ed. and trans.), *The Annals of Clonmacnoise being Annals of Ireland from the Earliest Period to AD 1408, translated into English AD 1627 by Conell Mageoghagan* (Dublin, 1896; reprinted Felinfach, 1993).

Murray, K. (ed.), *Baile in Scáil. "The Phantom's Frenzy."* Irish Texts Society 58 (Dublin, 2004).

Ní Mhaonaigh, M., *Brian Boru: Ireland's Greatest King* (Stroud, 2007).

Ó Corráin, D., "Caithréim Cheallacháin Chaisil: history or propaganda?," *Ériu*, 25 (1974), 1–69.

Ó Corráin, D., "Dál Cais: church and dynasty," *Ériu*, 24 (1973), 52–73.

Ó Fiaich, T., "The church of Armagh under lay control," *Seanchas Ardmhacha*, 5 (1969), 75–127.

Ó Floinn, R., "The foundation relics of Christ Church cathedral and the origins of the diocese of Dublin," in S, Duffy (ed.), *Medieval Dublin VII* (Dublin, 2006), pp. 89–102.

Ó Murchadha, D., "Rubbings taken of the inscriptions on the Cross of the Scriptures, Clonmacnois," *Journal of the Royal Society of Antiquaries of Ireland*, 110 (1980), 47–51.

O'Donovan, J. (ed. and trans.), 1851 *Annála Rioghachta Éireann: Annals of the Kingdom of Ireland by the Four Masters from the Earliest Period to the Year 1616*, 7 vols. (Dublin, 1851; 3rd edn., 1990).

Reynolds, S., *Kingdoms and Communities in Western Europe 900–1300*, 2nd edn. (Oxford, 1997).

Sheehan, J., "Early Viking-Age silver hoards from Ireland and their Scandinavian elements," in H. B. Clarke, M. Ní Mhaonaigh, and R. Ó Floinn (eds.), *Ireland and Scandinavia in the Early Viking Age* (Dublin, 1998), pp. 166–202.

Smyth, A. P., *Scandinavian York and Dublin: The History and Archaeology of Two Related Viking Kingdoms*, 2 vols. (Dublin, 1975–9).

Stalley, R., "The tower cross at Kells," in C. E. Karkov, R. T. Farrell, and M. Ryan (eds.), *The Insular Tradition* (New York, 1997), pp. 115–41.

Stokes, W. (ed. and trans.), *The Annals of Tigernach* (reprinted from *Revue Celtique*, 1895–7; repr. Felinfach, 1993).

Todd, J. H. (ed.) *Cogadh Gaedhil re Gallaibh: The War of the Gaedhil with the Gaill or the Invasions of Ireland by the Danes and Other Norsemen* (London, 1867).

CHAPTER EIGHTEEN

Ireland, c.1000–c.1100

SEÁN DUFFY

For historians, one of the most basic challenges in terms of organizing principles is posed by periodization: where should I begin and end, and – often more testing – at what junctures should I divide my narrative so that it is presented in sensible and comprehensible modules? Despite its omnipresence in the titles of books, chapters, and essays, the hard-and-fast calendric century is rarely a sound choice of internal structural device for a work of history (hence the allure of "the long century"). Oddly enough, though, eleventh-century Ireland proves an exception in this regard. It is, in fact – and I am conscious that this is a conventional platitude – a century of special interest, one that played host to events and developments that were without precedent in Ireland and that never recurred, and yet a century that has been subjected to far more callous disregard than some of its relatively less "eventful" precursors or successors.

One reason for this is that it has – historiographically speaking – fallen between two stools. Historians of early medieval Ireland, seeking to conclude their narratives on a high note, have traditionally done so after recounting the death of the famous high-king Brian Bórama (Boru) at the battle of Clontarf in 1014. On the other hand, historians of later medieval Ireland generally choose to begin proceedings with the English invasion of the 1160s. Eleventh- and early twelfth-century Ireland has, therefore, often assumed the character of a snappy epilogue or a lengthy prologue.[1] This is all the more regrettable because the eleventh century witnessed a spectacular transformation in the Irish body politic, which occurred just as the new century and the new millennium dawned.

The Eleventh-century Transformation

On December 30, 999, Brian Bórama, from a Munster dynasty formerly of no great distinction, defeated the combined armies of Leinster and of the Norse of Dublin in the decisive battle of Glenn Máma.[2] On New Year's Eve, Brian's forces converged on Dublin, and on New Year's Day 1000 the viking settlement was comprehensively sacked, its king forced to flee, and the king of Leinster deposed. The events are of consequence because they marked a turning-point in Brian's long struggle to force his great opponent, Máel Sechnaill mac Domnaill (d.1022), to recognize Brian as his superior, and by 1002 this remarkable ambition had been realized.[3]

Máel Sechnaill was overking of the Uí Néill, the southern branch of which dominated the Irish midlands from the Shannon to the Irish Sea, the northern Uí Néill ruling from modern Donegal to the River Bann. For half a millennium or more, the Uí Néill had held exclusive rights to the almost mystical "kingship of Tara"; over the course of time, and certainly during the ninth and tenth centuries, an equation came to be made between possession of this arcane trophy and exclusive entitlement to claim the kingship of all Ireland. This meant that, although there were at any one time a half-dozen or more provincial rulers powerful enough to make a bid for national supremacy, the force of tradition and Uí Néill propaganda combined to deny them the honor.[4]

Hence the significance of Brian Bórama's achievement: he flouted this convention; he energetically punctured the pretensions of the Uí Néill, exposing the make-believe of the emperor's clothes, and demonstrating that one did not have to be a descendant of the eponymous Niall to put forward a claim to the high-kingship. Instead, the Uí Néill would have to fight it out with all comers if they were to (re)claim the high-kingship; and such a claim could be put forward by anyone sufficiently determined and dominant to pull it off – as England's Henry II at least implicitly was to do in 1171.

But as often happens during the messy business of regime change, it took some time for contemporary partisans to see the writing on the wall. Thus, when Brian fell at Clontarf in 1014, Máel Sechnaill of the Uí Néill was re-insinuated by his propagandists into the old high-kingship. It was only at the latter's death in 1022 that the *ancien régime* was also pronounced dead, and a long "interregnum" instituted. Of course, Ireland was not kingless after 1022; rather, it was the verdict of the men of letters that none of the competing candidates for the high-kingship from among the ranks of the province-kings was a worthy incumbent. These included Brian Bórama's most senior surviving warrior son, Donnchad (d.1064). From his position as king of Munster, Donnchad spent four decades trying in vain for the kind of national supremacy his father had attained. If he failed to make the grade, it was no fault of Brian's: the latter, come what may, fundamentally altered the ground rules of Irish politics at the very start of the eleventh century – by undermining the Uí Néill monopoly so that the high-kingship of Ireland was now up for grabs – and this remained the case for a century and a half thereafter, until play was abandoned soon after the English invasion.

Clontarf in Irish Tradition

Of course, Brian Bórama is best remembered now for something else, for an event that remains one of the most celebrated – iconic is the obligatory description these days – in Irish history: the high-king's death in his hour of victory at Clontarf in 1014,[5] thereby ending what, for instance, Edmund Curtis called (echoing the existing consensus) "the Norse tyranny."[6] This perception of the battle of Clontarf as representing a watershed in Irish history is of long standing. It owes its origin in part to propaganda sources like *Cogadh Gáedhel re Gallaibh* ("The War of the Irish with the Foreigners"), compiled almost a century after Brian's death, which certainly enhanced the image of Brian as Ireland's archetypal shield and protector – although we cannot say how widely such texts circulated, and more surely went into the making of the myth than that alone. One of the most valuable compilations of medieval Irish annals is that found in Trinity College Dublin MS 1293, popularly known as the *Annals of Loch Cé*. The text has been transcribed from multiple sources and its family tree is a complex one but, as with most Irish annal collections, it is nonetheless remarkably faithful to its source texts. At some point in its construction, however, a compiler did exercise one extraordinary piece of editorial intervention. It is more than likely that the *literati* behind the Loch Cé compilation had access to early medieval material, but the manuscript only begins with the year AD 1014. Although it has substantial lacunae and is defective at the end, MS 1293 is not acephalous: it is a book that intentionally begins at 1014, and the reason for so doing is undoubtedly because that was the year of the battle of Clontarf.

The account of the battle, more than 1,200 words in length, is anything but annalistic in tone and more the stuff of romance, but what concerns us here is not its derivation or form but rather the fact that even in the Middle Ages the year 1014 ranked as a key historical milestone. Some compilers of Irish annals, in seeking to begin at the "beginning," used the device of grafting the national origin myth onto a biblical chronology, thus taking their story back to the Flood. Others – the majority – who were either clerics themselves or utilized vestigial scraps from long-extinct ecclesiastical scriptoria, were content to begin Ireland's story with *the* great landmark, its conversion to Christianity in the fifth century. That those who put together the Loch Cé annals thought of the battle of Clontarf in not dissimilar terms – the end of one epoch and the beginning of something very new – is surely significant. It is evident that the compiler viewed Clontarf as not only a highlight of Irish history, but, for all intents and purposes, Brian Bórama's victory over his enemies in the battle was seen as possibly the single most glorious achievement by any of his nation.

And it is an attraction that has remained compelling for Irish nationalist historians, and their audience, through the ages. Thus Brian has been, for generations of Irish people, the hero-figure who led his people to victory over their would-be conquerors, and secured their freedom from foreign oppression:[7] the proof – if proof were needed – is that, of the 50 or so "high-kings" deemed to have reigned from the dawn of Irish history until the institution was smothered in the early aftermath of the English invasion, Brian Bórama is undoubtedly (however depressingly) the only one who commands general recognition today.

Debunking the "Myth" of Clontarf

This perception enjoyed (and, in popular conviction, enjoys) remarkable longevity. It was as recent as the 1960s that misgivings began to emerge about the naïveté of the established depiction of the all-conquering, viking-vanquishing Brian. It lasted as long as it did partly because of the chasm of investigation that, as already noted, had afflicted the 1014–1169 period of Ireland's history. In part, too, it lasted because of the solace that the image had brought: in the past, the Irish had thought of 1014 in the way that many of their modern counterparts think of 1916. And, just as, in the aftermath of the doomed Easter Rising it was possible to see, in the bloody execution of its leaders, lives sacrificed in the cause of Ireland – what one historian called "the triumph of failure"[8] – so, because the battle of Clontarf took place on Good

Friday, it was heavy with similar overtones of Christian martyrdom, in the form of King Brian's death in his hour of victory over the heathen Norse.

But just as the late 1960s saw modern revisionists engage in a very public interrogation of the motivation behind the Easter Rising and its justification, a quieter process of questioning was already underway aimed at exposing the "myth" of Brian Bórama's expulsion of the vikings. It is not that Irish historians were hitherto unaware of the fallacy of this belief, but rather that they tended to preach their new heresies to the converted readers of academic journals and the like.[9] If there was an element of complacent resignation here – when the legend becomes fact, print the legend – one should in fairness point out that opportunities for the wider broadcast of the fruits of new historical research were limited in Ireland, all the more so for prospective debunkers of national myths, certainly before the 1960s. One of the first trenchant euhemerizing assaults on Brian came from Donnchadh Ó Corráin in his groundbreaking *Ireland before the Normans* (1972). Here, having emphatically delivered the verdict – upon which many, if not all, were now agreed – that Brian Bórama did not banish the vikings from Ireland, he addressed himself to the obvious next question: so what then was the battle of Clontarf about? The answer was equally emphatic:

> The battle of Clontarf was not a struggle between the Irish and the Norse for the sovereignty of Ireland; neither was it a great national victory which broke the power of the Norse forever (long before Clontarf the Norse had become a minor political force in Irish affairs). In fact Clontarf was part of the *internal* struggle for sovereignty and was essentially the revolt of the Leinstermen against the dominance of Brian, a revolt in which their Norse allies played an important but secondary role.[10]

This was not (as Professor Ó Corráin would be the first to concede) an entirely new rationalization,[11] but, put in such cogent terms, in such an important work, by so prominent a scholar, the impact has been formidable. Few now, beyond the ranks of the purveyors of popular fiction, perpetuate the portrayal of Brian, eliminator of the viking scourge – even if, in place of naïve certainty, many of us now have instead only a confused picture of petty provincial enmities being played out at Clontarf, and a vague curiosity as to what all the fuss was about.

This latter point is far from trivial. *Of course* it is correct that the vikings who began to attack Ireland, like Britain, in the closing years of the eighth century, and who had constructed some stable settlements there, including Dublin, by the middle of the ninth, were not "banished" forever from Ireland when defeated in the battle of Clontarf. And *of course* it is the case that the descendants of the Scandinavians who founded Dublin, and the other "Ostman" towns, continued to inhabit them and to govern them – at least internally, if at times subordinately – long after 1014. But there must surely have been something about the events of Good Friday 1014 that cannot be explained away as the resolution of a quarrel between the king of Munster and insubordinate Leinster and Dublin rebels. Such an interpretation, after all, offers no basis for viewing Clontarf as a victory – and no one doubts that Clontarf *was* a victory – for Brian Bórama, since he forfeited his very life in the engagement. The danger is therefore that in "talking down" the significance of Clontarf – albeit in a laudable attempt to expose an illusion – we have thrown the baby out with the bathwater. The fact is that the only way in which Clontarf could be considered a victory for Brian is if he gave his life confronting an enemy a great deal more menacing than the kings of Leinster and Dublin: in this way, the high-king's followers could reluctantly accept his loss as the price that had to be paid for what he had averted on that fateful day.

Clontarf's External Aspect

Thus, the portrayal of Clontarf as part of an "*internal* struggle" for power in Ireland cannot be valid, and is something of an indictment of the insularity of Irish historiography. It is strange how little regard is paid to the temporal context of the encounter. The devastating viking raids on England in 1006–7 and 1009–12 culminated in the invasion by the king of Denmark himself, Swegn Forkbeard, in the summer of 1013: by the end of the year, as we know, England had been conquered, Swegn had been acknowledged king, and the ousted Æthelred II was in exile in Normandy by the early days of 1014. Swegn then died, on February 3, whereupon the Danes chose his younger son Cnut as king of England, but the English sent for Æthelred, who returned during Lent (March 10–April 25) and banished Cnut. The battle of Clontarf took place on Good Friday, April 23. It is perhaps unlikely that those who gathered for the battle knew of Æthelred's restoration, but presumably they had heard of Swegn's death and the attempt to have Cnut succeed him. In other words, the largely viking force that invaded Ireland in April 1014 did so in quite the most extraordinary circumstances: they may have been the Danes' allies or enemies, or neither, but it is hardly credible to deny any link between their objective in Ireland and that of the Danish fleet in England. This is the backdrop against which Clontarf must be viewed, an international dimension that, on closer inspection, proves to be a set component of eleventh-century Irish politics in general.

The invasion commander at Clontarf was the earl of Orkney, Sigurd Hlödvisson, who, according to *Njals saga*, agreed to participate only after Sitric Silkbeard of Dublin promised the kingship of Ireland if Brian was slain. Sigurd's mother is stated in *Orkneyinga saga* to have been the daughter of the king of Osraige, the buffer state between Brian's kingdom of Munster and that of his restive Leinster subordinates. Also, Sigurd married a daughter of Máel Coluim II (1005–34) of Scotland, whose own mother, according to the *Prophecy of Berchán*, was a noblewoman from one of the Leinster dynasties based just south of Dublin.[12] When it comes to identifying these Irish women and dating possible alliances underlying the marriage vows, there is no such thing as safe ground, and it is futile to venture beyond saying that a powerful man whose mother is of aristocratic Irish blood is liable to have had ambitions there. Sigurd seems to fit into this category, and, if his father-in-law Máel Coluim II also had an Irish mother, the latter may have harbored similar aspirations.

Máel Coluim became king of Scots in 1005. In the same year, Brian took the remarkable step (given his Munster background) of confirming the ecclesiastical supremacy of Armagh, the great northern church that had long acted as a center of religion and learning for the people of both Ireland and Scotland. This may not be coincidental, if we are to attribute any significance to the famous contemporary record of Brian's visit to the primatial church, inscribed on folio 16*b* of the *Book of Armagh*, wherein the high-king is given the rather ambiguous and possibly loaded title *Imperator Scotorum*.[13] In this regard it may be worth noting that, while modern writers have generally tended to view Máel Coluim as the "rightful" king, eleventh-century Armagh annalists repeatedly bestow the title "king of Scotland" on the contemporary rulers of Moray, deadly rivals of Máel Coluim's family for the kingship: this can presumably be interpreted as Armagh's mark of favor toward the house of Moray, and a not-so-subtle expression of reservation regarding the legitimacy of Máel Coluim's claim.[14] It is surely therefore of interest that one of the leaders of Brian's army to die alongside him at Clontarf was the *mormaer* of Mar in Aberdeenshire. What he was doing there we do not know, and perhaps it is rash to hypothesize some link with Brian as *Imperator Scotorum*, but we can probably assume that, if he was willing to lose his life fighting on Brian's side, he was no friend of Earl Sigurd or of his father-in-law, King Máel Coluim. In any event, whatever brought the ruler of the Deeside lordship of Mar to stand shoulder to shoulder with the Shannonside warlord, Brian Bórama, his presence at the battle surely situates Clontarf on a standing higher than that of an internal Irish squabble.

Ireland's Maritime Frontier

Accordingly, we cannot afford to be blind to the broad landscape against which the events at Clontarf were played out. Irish annalists, for instance, puff up but do not dream up the titles they bestow on their dead kings. So when Brian is accorded in his obit, among his lesser titles, that of "king of the Welsh," it constitutes evidence of interests there, although it would be a challenge at this remove to say anything definite about it. Irish involvement in Wales was both of a quotidian nature and of the greatest magnitude throughout the entire eleventh century.[15] An Irishman briefly became king of Deheubarth (south Wales) in 1022. Eleven years later the Irish slew his Welsh successor in Deheubarth. We cannot state who the killers were but geographical proximity would suggest Leinstermen or Munstermen. The Leinster dynasty most likely to have been involved in transmarine activity at that point is the southern lineage of Uí Chennselaig,[16] led by Diarmait mac Máel na mBó who, at his death in 1072, was (like Brian, and only Brian) also described by an Irish annalist as "king of the Welsh"; what is more, the Welsh annals, which have nothing particularly nice to say about Brian in their detailed account of the battle of Clontarf, have by comparison an unusually glowing obituary notice of the Leinster king.

We can presumably, therefore, take it that there is some basis to the extravagant designation of "king of the Welsh" applied in Irish sources to Diarmait mac Máel na mBó. It is notable that when Cynan ab Iago, the would-be ruler of Gwynedd (north Wales), fled across the Irish Sea in or after 1039, he married into the dynasty of Sitric Silkbeard of Dublin, and the product of that marriage was his famous son Gruffudd ap Cynan (d.1137) who was later to establish stable rule for his family in north Wales.[17] It is perfectly conceivable that the Irish annals labeled Diarmait mac Máel na mBó "king of the Welsh" for no greater reason than that he had accepted the submission of Cynan ab Iago and had championed his cause with a view to securing the restoration of his dynastic line in Gwynedd; and we can envisage King Diarmait providing Cynan with sanctuary in Ireland and military resources for coup attempts across the Irish Sea.

Diarmait mac Máel na mBó certainly had a track record in this kind of patronage. When they were in exile in Ireland in the winter of 1051–2, it was the Leinster king who played host to two of the sons of Earl Godwine of Wessex, Leofwine and Harold, and, following the latter's death at Hastings, at least two of his sons in turn fled to Ireland, Diarmait again providing a fleet in 1068, which they used in an unsuccessful assault on Bristol and the harrying of Devon and Somerset, and in a repeat attempt to recover ground in the west country in 1069 – which met with such resistance that it was all Harold's sons could do to make it back in one piece to Leinster, never to be heard of again.[18] That the Godwinesons' relationship with King Diarmait was similar to that which he seems to have had with the family of Cynan ab Iago of Gwynedd – what might traditionally have been viewed as the bond between a lord and his clients – is suggested by an event that occurred in 1068. The province of Munster had recently obtained a worthy successor to Brian Bórama in the person of his grandson, Toirdelbach Ua Briain (d.1086). Although a protégé of Diarmait mac Máel na mBó, Toirdelbach's gratitude was short-lived, and in 1068 he led an expedition into Leinster to assert pre-eminence over his erstwhile patron,[19] obtaining as a trophy from Diarmait what the Irish annals call "the standard of the king of the English": the most likely provenance of this treasured artifact is surely that it was the battle-standard borne by Harold at Hastings, and bestowed by his sons on Diarmait mac Máel na mBó, presumably as some kind of acknowledgment of his overlordship, after they had found refuge in Ireland under his protection.

Dublin: The Key to Success

It was most probably direct domination of the Hiberno-Scandinavian settlement at Wexford that first maneuvered Diarmait mac Máel na mBó's long-ailing dynasty into a position of prominence and power throughout the south-eastern quadrant of Ireland. But Diarmait's great leap forward, what propelled him to national importance and gave him a recognition factor in England and Wales, was the fact that in 1052 he succeeded in adding Dublin and its hinterland *Fine Gall* ("the territory of the foreigners") to his personal domain.[20] Its import lies in the fact that Diarmait expelled the Hiberno-Scandinavian king of Dublin and appropriated the kingship of Dublin to himself (instead of the undemanding assertion of authority with which Brian and others had been content, whereby Dublin's ruler merely submitted and handed over hostages and booty, but remained or soon reappeared as king).

And several consequences flowed from King Diarmait's action. First, for all intents and purposes, in 1052 Dublin was transformed from a viking beachhead on Leinster soil into being the capital of that province. Second, boosted by its acquisition, Diarmait mac Máel na mBó and his south Leinster dynasty of Uí Chennselaig were able, after three centuries in the wilderness, to displace their north Leinster counterparts as overkings of all Leinster.[21] Third (in light of the precedent it set, as we shall see), he then proceeded to bestow Dublin on his favored son, Murchad, who ruled from Dublin under his father's remote direction.[22] And, fourth, in exploiting the maritime gateway that Dublin provided, Murchad invaded the Isle of Man in 1061 and exacted tribute from its inhabitants, thereby extending the Leinster dynasty's lordship to encompass this transmarine satellite, no doubt emulating longstanding viking practice.[23] Murchad died as king of "the foreigners" in 1070, and when his father followed him to the grave two years later, the annalists recognized him as king of Dublin and of *Innse Gall*, the Gaelic term for the Hebrides and Man: apparently, control of Dublin provided a key with the potential to unlock access to specific overseas territory.

It was control of Dublin after 1052 that provided Diarmait with access to the resources to take the war to his rival province-kings beyond Leinster's borders and stake a claim to being king of all Ireland. Like Brian Bórama, he was not of Uí Néill stock, but since Brian had exposed the irrelevance of such a prerequisite, Diarmait was now to take full advantage of this new era of equal opportunities. By the time of his death in 1072, he had become the most successful Irish king since Brian. He was king of Leinster and of the viking bases at Wexford and Dublin and, having obtained submissions from neighboring Osraige and Munster, was ruler of Leth Moga, the southern half of Ireland. Unfortunately for the Leinstermen's hopes of elevating themselves to a position of paramountcy throughout Ireland, while attempting an offensive into the northern half (Leth Cuinn) by gaining overlordship of the southern Uí Néill kingdom of Mide (Meath), Diarmait met his end there in the battle of Odba in 1072.

The Career Path to Kingship

It is because of his achievements in this inter-provincial game of snakes-and-ladders that Diarmait mac Máel na mBó was described in an (admittedly slightly retrospective) obit as *rí hÉrend co fressabra*, "king of Ireland with opposition."[24] This is a term coined after the Uí Néill ascendancy had crumbled, intended to provide a dispassionate depiction – insofar as that could be expected from retained mandarins – of the new style of province-king who bid for, while rarely achieving, unopposed mastery over the whole island.

It should come as no surprise, therefore, that King Diarmait's competitors and successors looked to his policies and his methods, and sought to replicate them, in order to follow in his footsteps. It is surely of no small significance that no sooner had Diarmait met his end at Odba in 1072 than – as *Le Roi est mort, vive le Roi!* – Toirdelbach Ua Briain marched his armies on Dublin and accepted the offer of its kingship from the Ostmen: the very fact of doing so seems to have secured him a place in posterity as the second *rí hÉrend co fressabra*, "king of Ireland with opposition." And, just as Diarmait had appointed his son Murchad to rule the city and its territory under him, by 1075 the annals confirm that Toirdelbach had followed suit, and his son and successor Muirchertach (d.1119) is recorded as having taken over the kingship of Dublin: he was in effect serving an apprenticeship which, in time, would qualify him to succeed as the third *rí hÉrend co fressabra*.[25]

While Muirchertach ruled and probably resided in Dublin, there seems little doubt that Toirdelbach appointed another son, Diarmait (d.1115), to govern the viking-founded town of Waterford, and that he himself had one of his royal residences in Limerick, the third of the great urban achievements of the vikings in Ireland. Thus, as the last quarter of the eleventh century began, there must have seemed every reason to suppose that Toirdelbach's family – the Uí Briain, the descendants of Brian Bórama – would prove successful in the latter's object of attaining durable rule over Ireland. But in light of the traditional depiction of Brian as having driven the vikings out of Ireland, it is striking that his grandson was now the champion of the towns, these Trojan horses inherited from the Viking Age, making them quintessentially his own for the purpose of familial and dynastic aggrandizement. As F. J. Byrne perceptively noted,[26] at the height of the Viking Age the Uí Néill had been resilient

enough to thwart the emergence of permanent viking bases in the northern half of
Ireland, while their southern counterparts had had to tolerate what they could not
force out. But by the eleventh century, those footholds were flourishing towns, the
greatest concentrations of wealth on the island, and the southern kings prospered
through transaction with them, as the Uí Néill, bemoaning perhaps their short-
sighted inhospitality, saw their former vigor wither for lack of resources and their
ancient primacy scorned.

The Uí Briain and Canterbury

As with Diarmait mac Máel na mBó before them, the domestic elevation of the Uí
Briain consequent on their command of the towns seems to have conferred an immediate international profile: it was to Toirdelbach's court, the annals tell us, that a
delegation of Jews repaired in 1079, presumably (if vainly) seeking leave to set up
shop (*AI s.a.* 1079). With the profile, came responsibilities. When the clergy and
people of Dublin came together in 1074 to elect as their bishop Gilla Pátraic, an
Irish monk schooled under Wulfstan at Worcester, Archbishop Lanfranc consecrated
him, sending him back to Dublin with a letter for its Ostman leader and another for
its overlord, Toirdelbach Ua Briain.[27] It is a letter of praise for this peace-loving and
just ruler (as Gilla Pátraic had described him to Lanfranc), but also an exhortation
to Toirdelbach to convene an assembly of clerics for the purposes of prohibiting by
edict the many abuses in Ireland of which Lanfranc had heard reports (primarily in
the area of marriage customs).[28]

It was long held that this appeal fell on deaf ears and that it was not until the
latter part of the reign of Toirdelbach's son, Muirchertach Ua Briain, that the issue
of spiritual and structural reform of the Irish church got underway – indeed, this
process is almost invariably referred to as "the twelfth-century reform" of the church,
and the council held under Muirchertach's auspices at Cashel in 1101 is perennially
cited as its official unveiling. In fact, however, it appears that Toirdelbach presided
over a synod held in Dublin in 1080, attended by the most senior cleric in the
country, the successor of St. Patrick at Armagh, and the leading churchmen of
Munster, if not of other provinces.[29] When their deliberations led to a difference of
opinion, they dispatched a letter to Lanfranc at Christmas 1080 asking him to clarify
the issues concerned, as he duly did in a letter that, if it arrived while the synod was
still in session, indicates that the latter must surely have continued into 1081.

Furthermore, in 1085 Toirdelbach again presided over an assembly of the bishops
of Ireland, and the clergy and people of Dublin, which elected another Irishman,
Donngus Ua hAingliu, a monk under Lanfranc at Canterbury, to replace the late
Gilla Pátraic, and he too was consecrated by the English primate.[30] Following
Donngus's death, his nephew Samuel, a monk at St. Albans, was consecrated by
Archbishop Anselm in 1096, having been chosen in an assembly by the Dubliners
with the assent of Toirdelbach's son Muirchertach, and later that year another
Ostman town, Waterford, got its first bishop when Muirchertach and his brother
Diarmait presided over an assembly of senior clerics and laymen, which chose Máel
Ísu Ua hAinmire, an Irish monk trained at Winchester, and sent him too for formal
consecration at the hands of the archbishop of Canterbury.[31] Only when Limerick,
the third great viking-built town – and now the Uí Briain's capital – got a bishop in

the person of the celebrated Gille (Gilbert) was the Canterbury link broken. (He was elected some time after the great council of Cashel in 1101 and before c.1107 when the first of his surviving letters was penned.)[32]

Thus, it would appear that for the last quarter of the eleventh century, the Uí Briain made no objection to the involvement of Canterbury in the Irish church (over which Lanfranc, in particular, was vigorous in asserting a primacy that had no historical precedent).[33] On the face of it, it appears odd that a dynasty seeking sovereign authority throughout all Ireland in matters secular would allow and indeed promote the ecclesiastical encroachment of Canterbury. Perhaps it is the case that this was tolerated while relations with the Conqueror and Rufus were on an even keel, and that the political crises at the outset of Henry I's reign, in which (as we shall see) Muirchertach Ua Briain was implicated, upset the balance and made recourse to Canterbury unworkable. Or perhaps the absence of a resident archbishop of Canterbury during Anselm's exile from April 1103 to August 1106 explains the particular circumstances that denied Gille of Limerick the possibility of a Canterbury consecration, and it may well have occasioned second thoughts as to the advisability of reliance on an external superior.

But the most likely explanation is that the Uí Briain had stomached Canterbury's pretensions only for as long as it suited them; in other words, while Ireland's de facto ecclesiastical capital, Armagh, lay within the compass of the former high-kings, the Uí Néill. However, if a solution could be found whereby an acknowledgment of Armagh's primacy carried no political implications – did not smack of deference to the Uí Néill – then Canterbury could be put aside. And that solution presented itself in 1101. The site of the 1101 council was Cashel, the ancient capital of Munster, and the highlight of the gathering was Muirchertach's bestowal of the Rock of Cashel in perpetuity on the Irish church.[34] Two years later, he visited Armagh in person and laid an offering of gold on the altar, as his great-grandfather Brian had done almost exactly a century earlier in 1005. Here was the ground being laid for Muirchertach's solution, as was formally enacted at the council of Ráith Bressail in 1111.[35] This established the territorial diocesan structure that has survived in large part ever since: there would be two ecclesiastical provinces (later increased to four), that of Cashel for the southern half and Armagh for the northern, but with the latter having the primacy. And, possibly taking advantage of the vacancy at Canterbury following Anselm's death in 1109, Canterbury's claims to superior status or to any jurisdiction over the affairs of the Irish church would be repudiated.[36]

Supranational Aspirations

The delicate diplomacy required of the Uí Briain in their dealings with the English primate was, of course, a consequence of their domination of the towns. This domination also encouraged supranational aspirations.[37] It is worthy of note that in 1073, within a year of Toirdelbach claiming lordship over Dublin, two Uí Briain met violent deaths in Man, almost certainly in the act of asserting a claim to it arising from Dublin's acquisition.[38] Similarly, when his son Muirchertach took charge of Dublin in 1075, he became patron of the exiled heirs of Iago of Gwynedd, and the *Historia* composed in honor of the latter's grandson, Gruffudd ap Cynan, chronicles a long alliance between the two.[39] It commenced in the very year that Muirchertach took control of Dublin, when he supplied Gruffudd with the city-state's fleet in response to the first of the Welshman's regular pleas for such assistance to establish himself in Gwynedd.[40] As already noted, another of Toirdelbach's sons, Diarmait Ua Briain, had control of Waterford, and the *Historia Gruffud vab Kenan* gives Diarmait's naval aid much of the credit for the success of Gruffudd ap Cynan and Rhys ap Tewdwr of Deheubarth (south Wales) at the battle of Mynydd Carn in the following year, which secured both men in their respective kingships.

After 1066, partisan entanglements in Wales led Irish kings directly to encounters with Normans, and specifically with an Anglo-Norman court alert to Ireland's role in offering asylum and assistance to insular enemies. William the Conqueror's expedition to St. David's in 1081 may be viewed in such a context, as may perhaps that mysterious eulogy in the "Peterborough" *Anglo-Saxon Chronicle* that maintains that, had he lived but another couple of years beyond 1087, William would have won Ireland by astuteness without the use of weapons.[41] The observation may be baseless, but it is just conceivable that there is something to it. In the autumn of 1085, William, alerted to an imminent invasion of England by Cnut IV of Denmark in alliance with the count of Flanders, returned from Normandy to England,[42] and it was amid this crisis that the *Domesday* survey was commissioned.[43] Although the invasion was postponed in 1085, it was expected in the following year, and it may be partly against that background that William exacted the "oath of Salisbury" from his tenants-in-chief and their major tenants on August 1, 1086.[44] We do not know whether William was aware at that point of the assassination of Cnut in Odense on July 10, or of the death of Toirdelbach Ua Briain four days later at Kincora near Limerick, but no doubt such good news travels fast. Be that as it may, William was forced to cross the Channel soon afterward to counter raids by Philip I, and was himself dead within a year. If, therefore, we are to ascribe any credence to the Peterborough chronicler's curious remark about the Conqueror and Ireland, perhaps he is echoing some rumor of Norman aspirations to fill the vacancy in Ireland's high-kingship following Toirdelbach's death.

Recent intervention by the Uí Briain in the affairs of Wales must have been a bone of contention, and there may have been an undiscriminating antipathy to the Irish generally for suspected favoritism to the conquered English. But it must also have been known at William's court that, if past performance was anything to go by, forces from Ireland were likely to lend their backing to Scandinavian ambitions in England, as had been made manifest on numerous occasions within living memory. Ben Hudson has surely amassed enough crumbs of evidence to convince most skeptics of Cnut the Great's influence, if not power, in towns such as Dublin, and perhaps even Sitric Silkbeard's espousal of the Anglo-Danish regime.[45] In 1058, the Dublin fleet had augmented forces drawn from the Orkneys and Hebrides in support of the western expedition of Magnus son of Harald Hardrada, which an Irish annalist at least believed was intent on the conquest of England.[46] When Harald Hardrada himself invaded England in 1066, Adam of Bremen thought there was an Irish king in his army.[47] And, bearing in mind that two of Harold Godwineson's sons and his daughter Gytha had fled to Sweden after Hastings, it may not be a coincidence that the Danish invasion of England in 1069, in which the future Cnut IV participated, overlapped with the last attempt (as noted above) by two more of Harold's sons to effect a restoration in England – which saw them bring from Ireland a fleet of 60 ships acquired from Diarmait Mac Máel na mBó.[48] Cnut commanded the Swedish armada of 200 ships that struck at York in 1075. This was the year in which Muirchertach Ua Briain took the kingship of Dublin, banishing overseas its Hiberno-Scandinavian ruler, who "died beyond the sea, having assembled a great fleet [to come] to Ireland."[49] Perhaps the annalist believed that the Swedish fleet bound for England would also provide succor to Dublin's exiled Ostman ruler.

The Reign of Muirchertach Ua Briain

The demise of Toirdelbach Ua Briain in 1086 did not halt the progress of his dynasty, although the ensuing succession contest between his sons unquestionably sowed the seeds of later, and predictable, destabilization among the Uí Briain.[50] From this dispute, by the late 1080s, Muirchertach Ua Briain emerged the victor and was happy to follow the now time-honored blueprint: control of Dublin was essential, and at some unknown date he became the third consecutive *rí hÉrend co fressabra*, high-king "with opposition," to appoint his heir to the position of king of the city-state.[51] Dublin in turn, we have seen, opened up possibilities in the Isles, and by the mid-1090s members of the Uí Briain were again not only active on the Isle of Man (where Olaf, a son of Muirchertach's late brother Tadc, met a violent end in 1096), but, according to the *Manx Chronicle*, when the king of the Isles died leaving only a minor, the nobles of the Isles sent to Muirchertach requesting a regent until their own royal heir came of age, and he responded, we are told, by offering them the services of another of Tadc's sons, Domnall.[52] Like much in this early portion of the chronicle, this sounds rather far-fetched, but we have confirmatory evidence from the Irish annals (admittedly from a good deal later, in 1111) that this Domnall did indeed take possession of the kingship of the Isles at that point.

Irish expansionism in the region may have been one concern that prompted Harald Hardrada's grandson, King Magnus III Barelegs of Norway, to make at least two western expeditions at the turn of the century,[53] although it is quite conceivable that he was just the latest (and, for all intents and purposes, the last) in a long succession of Scandinavian royal figures with territorial ambitions elastic enough to embrace any and all parts of the archipelago. The Irish certainly got off lightly on Magnus's first expedition in 1098, where the targets of his energy were the Western Isles, Man, and Britain's western littoral from Galloway to Gwynedd. Almost all sources, on the other hand, are agreed that the primary or at least initial objective of Magnus' 1102 campaign was Ireland, and the Irish annals indicate a successful occupation of Dublin from his Manx base. War with Muirchertach Ua Briain looked inevitable, and perhaps it was at this juncture that the latter commissioned the superb piece of history-cum-romance-cum-propaganda known as *Cogadh Gáedhel re Gallaibh* ("The War of the Irish with the Foreigners") already referred to, which is ostensibly an account of Brian's struggle against the vikings, barely concealing the fact that its real hero is Muirchertach, a later member of Brian's lineage facing a similar threat in a later age. Also, Dublin's impressive city walls have been dated archaeologically to c.1100, quite possibly by directive of Muirchertach in the face of that same threat.

As it transpired, both kings seem to have recognized that more was to be achieved by joining forces than locking horns. A truce gave time to hammer out an agreement which saw the Norwegian king's son, the future King Sigurd Jerusalem-farer, married off to a daughter of Ua Briain. King Magnus evidently envisaged a cadet western kingdom ruled by this younger son under the protection of an Irish father-in-law of distinguished pedigree. For Muirchertach, who had striven without success through-out his adult life (like his forefathers back to and including Brian) to wring submission from the recalcitrant rulers of Ireland's far north, the services of dedicated Norwegian and insular allies stationed to his enemy's flank and rear must have evoked the prospect of ultimate victory. That was not to be. The ignominious demise of the great Magnus Barelegs, slain in a petty ambush on the shores of Ulster in the summer of 1103, all but ended Norway's western dream. And when Muirchertach's family lost their grip on Dublin, soon after he himself fell gravely ill in 1114, the Uí Briain too had to bid farewell to 40 years of intervention in the north Irish Sea region – in truth, it was always a bit of a long shot for a dynasty rooted in Ireland's south-west.

Close Encounters of a New Kind

Involvement in southern Britain somehow seems much more plausible. When we read that Muirchertach's brother Diarmait brought the Waterford fleet across St. George's Channel to help secure Rhys ap Tewdwr in the kingship of Deheubarth, it seems entirely credible.[54] When we read that Rhys was driven into exile in Ireland some years later in 1088, but returned within the year and effected a restoration with Irish aid, it can be believed; as can the statement that when Rhys was killed in battle in 1093 by the Normans, then making heavy inroads into south Wales, his young son Rhys was brought for safety to Ireland – evidently the ruling line of Deheubarth had Irish allies. But to be told that this young boy, Rhys ap Gruffudd ap Tewdwr, remained in his Irish exile for the next 20 years, only returning to Wales as a grown man, and that he nevertheless was greeted with acclaim by his compatriots and in due course managed to secure at least the substance of his ancestral patrimony – this seems like the stuff of legend. And yet it appears to be true, with all the implications it has in terms of, for instance, cross-channel lines of communication, language use, cultural diversities, Welsh attitudes to Ireland and the Irish, and so forth. Of course, the life story of Rhys's now elderly contemporary in Gwynedd, Gruffudd ap Cynan, was far from dissimilar, except that this latter Welsh king was actually born in Ireland, and apparently never set foot in his homeland until adulthood – here, too, is food aplenty for thought.

Hardly less credible, were it not amply corroborated, is Orderic Vitalis's well-known tale of Arnulf de Montgomery, lord of Pembroke, one of the Normans who, in the last decade of the eleventh century, had annexed so much of south Wales: when Henry I ascended the throne in 1100, Arnulf's family were to the fore in rebelling, and when that rebellion began to falter there was nothing for it but to look west and to make contact with the greatest of the Irish, Muirchertach Ua Briain. These contacts led to another of Muirchertach's daughters being given in marriage, this time to Arnulf de Montgomery, who obtained with her substantial naval assistance against King Henry, but it was of little avail. Forced to flee to Ireland, Orderic Vitalis has Arnulf sending Norman troops into battle against his father-in-law's enemies and hoping to succeed to Ua Briain's kingdom in right of his new wife, but beating a hasty retreat when his treacherous hosts turned against him. The latter piece of anti-Irish bias does not stand up to scrutiny: that much is clear from the fact that Muirchertach later sent a letter of thanks to Anselm for his intercession with King Henry on his son-in-law's behalf. William of Malmesbury may be closer to the mark when he says that it was only when Henry I instituted a trade embargo between England and Ireland that a rapid cooling occurred in Ua Briain's ardor for intrigue.[55] Whatever the precise course of events, and whatever the driving force behind it all, the Montgomery alliance of 1102 allows us to sneak a glimpse at what was by any reckoning a world of strange associations and remarkable possibilities.

Conclusion

Precisely one hundred years links the events of 1102 with those that saw an upstart Irish dynast named Brian Bórama call the bluff of the straw kings who had postured unchallenged since time immemorial, and grasp the high-kingship for himself. The Uí Néill had depended for their ascendancy on the force of tradition and the persuasiveness of their propaganda. Brian and his successors fought their way up, and fought to stay up. And for a century after Clontarf all but one of Ireland's would-be kings were men of Brian's own blood – his son, grandson, and great-grandson, respectively. But a century in power can make even an upstart forget. In time, he may feel the impulse to convince others, as he has convinced himself, of his *right* to rule. And so it was that *Cogadh Gáedhel re Gallaibh* made its appearance in the latter stages of Muirchertach Ua Briain's reign, propaganda commissioned to persuade the world of his dynasty's royal birthright by reason of their assumed role in saving the Gael from the viking Gall.

Is the *Cogadh* an exercise in celebration or the product of desperation? It is difficult to know, but, whatever the case may be, it was probably already too late. Muirchertach himself had rubbed shoulders – his daughter had shared a marriage-bed – with a new type of Gall, a Norman. When, later in the twelfth century, these new foreigners decided to take a gamble and follow in the vikings' footsteps to Ireland, they faced an every-man-for-himself polity. For, in circumstances where it was thought a suitable goal for a man to *aim* to become *rí hÉrend co fressabra* ("king of Ireland with opposition"), there was no possibility of concerted resistance from the Irish. That was the legacy of the eleventh century.

Notes

1   Byrne, *Irish Kings and High-kings*, p. 269.
2   Mac Shamhráin, "The battle of Glenn Máma."
3   Ní Mhaonaigh, *Brian Boru*.
4   Binchy "The fair of Tailtiu"; Byrne, *Rise of the Uí Néill*, and *Irish Kings and High-kings*, pp. 7–69, pp. 254–74; Jaski, *Early Irish Kingship*.
5   Ó Corráin, "Brian Boru"; Ryan, "The battle of Clontarf."
6   Curtis, *History of Ireland*, ch. 2.
7   Ní Mhaonaigh, "*Cogad Gáedel re Gallaib*"; Todd (ed.), *Cogadh*.
8   Dudley-Edwards, *Patrick Pearse*.
9   Ryan, "The battle of Clontarf" and "Brian Boruma."
10 Ó Corráin, *Ireland before the Normans*, p. 130 (emphasis added).
11 Ryan, "The battle of Clontarf," p. 43.
12 Hudson, *Prophecy of Berchan*.
13 Gwynn, "Brian in Armagh"; Mac Shamhráin, "Brian Bóruma, Armagh and the High-kingship."
14 Duffy, "Ireland and Scotland, 1014–1169."

15 Duffy, "Ostmen, Irish and Welsh" and "The 1169 invasion."
16 Ó Corráin, "The Uí Chennselaig."
17 Evans (ed.), *Historia Gruffud*; Maund (ed.), *Gruffudd ap Cynan*; Russell (ed.), *Vita Griffini*.
18 Hudson, "The family of Harold Godwinson."
19 Duffy, "'The western world's tower.'"
20 Byrne, *Irish Kings and High-kings*, p. 271.
21 Ó Corráin, "The Uí Chennselaig."
22 Duffy, "Irishmen and Islesmen."
23 Duffy, "The royal dynasties of Dublin and the Isles."
24 Best (ed.), *The Book of Leinster*, 1, p. 98.
25 Candon, "Muirchertach Ua Briain"; Duffy, "'The western world's tower.'"
26 Byrne, *Irish Kings and High-kings*, p. 268.
27 Holland, "Dublin and the reform" and "The synod of Dublin."
28 Clover and Gibson (eds.), *The Letters of Lanfranc*, nos 9, 10.
29 Holland, "The synod of Dublin."
30 Bethell, "English monks and Irish reform"; Gwynn, *The Irish Church*.
31 Richter (ed.), *Canterbury Professions*.
32 Fleming, *Gille of Limerick*.
33 Brett, "Canterbury's perspective."
34 Holland, "Cashel, synod of (1101)."
35 Holland, "Ráith Bressail, synod of."
36 Flanagan, *Irish Society*, ch. 1.
37 Candon, "Muirchertach Ua Briain."
38 Duffy, "Irishmen and Islesmen," 109.
39 Evans (ed.), *Historia Gruffud*, passim.
40 Duffy, "Ostmen, Irish and Welsh."
41 Hudson, "William the Conqueror and Ireland."
42 Maddicott, "Responses to the threat of invasion."
43 Higham, "The Domesday survey."
44 Holt, "1086."
45 Hudson, "Cnut and Viking Dublin" and "Cnut and the Scottish kings."
46 Etchingham, "North Wales, Ireland and the Isles."
47 Waitz (ed.), *Adam of Bremen: Gesta Hammaburgensis Ecclesiae*, iii, 51.
48 Hudson, "The family of Harold Godwinson."
49 Duffy, "Irishmen and Islesmen," 102.
50 Ryan, "The O'Briens in Munster."
51 Duffy, "Irishmen and Islesmen."
52 Broderick (ed.), *Cronica Regum Mannie*, fol. 33v.
53 Power, "Magnus Barelegs' expeditions" and "Meeting in Norway."
54 Duffy, "The 1169 invasion."
55 Chandler, "The last of the Montgomerys"; Curtis, "Murchertach O'Brien"; Thompson, "Note de recherche."

Further Reading

There is no full-scale study of eleventh-century Ireland, but the standard political narrative is Ó Corráin, *Ireland before the Normans*, ch. 4, to which may now be added chapters by F. J. Byrne and M. T. Flanagan in D. Ó Cróinín (ed.), *A New History of Ireland*, vol. 1: *Prehistoric and Early Ireland* (Oxford, 2005). Byrne, *Irish Kings and High-kings*, remains essential, and his opening contribution to A. Cosgrove (ed.), *A New History of Ireland*, vol. 2: *Medieval Ireland 1169–1534* (Oxford, 2005) is a minor masterpiece. Kingship is the subject of a lengthy monograph by Jaski (*Early Irish Kingship and Succession*), but Ó Corráin's "Nationality and kingship in pre-Norman Ireland" is unsurpassed. For individual reigns, Ní Mhaonaigh's *Brian Boru* is brilliant on the literary sources in particular, less insightful on the political context, where Mac Shamhráin, "Brian Bóruma, Armagh and the high-kingship" sheds much light, and even the dated essays by Ryan ("The battle of Clontarf," "Brian Boruma," and "The O'Briens in Munster") still have something to offer. There are traditional biographical studies of Diarmait mac Máel na mBó and Muirchertach Ua Briain by Ó Corráin ("The career of Diarmait") and Duffy ("The western world's tower"), respectively, while Muirchertach's ambition is impressively captured in a pioneering paper by Candon ("Muirchertach Ua Briain").

For eleventh-century Ireland in a broader context, several essays by Hudson (see Bibliography) splendidly assemble from a vast array of sources the possible Irish associations of Cnut, the Godwinesons, and the Conqueror. For studies of Dublin and its transmarine connections, and of Hiberno-Scottish and Hiberno-Welsh relations in the period, see my articles in the Bibliography, and Etchingham ("North Wales, Ireland and the Isles") has greatly advanced study of what he calls the "insular Viking zone." Magnus Barelegs' western involvement is a subject that Power has made her own (see "Magnus Barelegs' expeditions to the west" and "Meeting in Norway"). Flanagan, *Irish Society*, also has a wealth of information. For the church, and church reform in particular, the many essays by Gwynn are fundamental, though beginning to show their age, and a deeper understanding of the sociopolitical context of the contemporary Irish church makes Mac Shamhráin, *Church and Polity* very valuable. Flanagan, *Irish Society*, ch. 1, is excellent on Ireland and Canterbury, but must now be read in conjunction with Holland.

Bibliography

Best, R. I., Bergin, O., and O'Brien, M. A. (eds.), *The Book of Leinster formerly Lebar na Núachongbála*, vol. 1 (Dublin, 1954).

Bethell, D., "English monks and Irish reform in the eleventh and twelfth centuries," in T. D. Williams (ed.), *Historical Studies*, 8 (Dublin, 1971), pp. 111–35.

Binchy, D. A. "The fair of Tailtiu and the feast of Tara," *Ériu*, 18 (1958), 113–38.

Bracken, D. and Ó Riain-Raedel, D. (eds.), *Ireland and Europe in the Twelfth Century: Reform and Renewal* (Dublin, 2006).

Brett, M., "Canterbury's perspective on church reform and Ireland, 1070–1115," in D. Bracken and D. Ó Riain-Raedel (eds.), *Ireland and Europe in the Twelfth Century: Reform and Renewal* (Dublin, 2006), pp. 13–35.

Broderick, G. (ed. and trans.), *Cronica Regum Mannie & Insularum: Chronicle of the Kings of Man and the Isles, BL Cotton Julius A.vii* (Douglas, Isle of Man, 1979).

Byrne, F. J., "Historical note on Cnogba (Knowth)," in G. Eogan, "Excavations at Knowth, Co. Meath," *Proceedings of the Royal Irish Academy*, 66 C (1968), 383–400.

Byrne, F. J., *Irish Kings and High-kings* (London, 1973).

Byrne, F. J., *The Rise of the Uí Néill and the High-kingship of Ireland* (Dublin [1970]).

Candon, A., "Muirchertach Ua Briain, politics and naval activity in the Irish Sea, 1075–1119," in G. Mac Niocaill and P. F. Wallace (eds.), *Keimelia* (Galway, 1988), pp. 397–415.

Chandler, V., "The last of the Montgomerys: Roger the Poitevin and Arnulf," *Historical Research*, 62 (1989), 1–14.

Clover, H. and Gibson, M. (eds.), *The Letters of Lanfranc, Archbishop of Canterbury* (Oxford, 1979).

Curtis, E., *A History of Ireland* (London, 1936).

Curtis, E., *A History of Medieval Ireland from 1086 to 1513*, 2nd edn. (London, 1938).

Curtis, E., "Murchertach O'Brien, high king of Ireland, and his Norman son-in-law, Arnulf de Montgomery, c.1100," *Journal of the Royal Society of Antiquaries of Ireland*, 6th series, 11 (1921), 116–24.

Dudley-Edwards, R., *Patrick Pearse: The Triumph of Failure* (London, 1977).

Duffy, S., "The 1169 invasion as a turning-point in Irish–Welsh relations," in B. Smith (ed.), *Britain and Ireland 900–1300: Insular Responses to Medieval European Change* (Cambridge, 1999), pp. 98–113.

Duffy, S., "Ireland and Scotland, 1014–1169: contacts and caveats" in A. P. Smyth (ed.), *Seanchas: Essays presented to Francis J. Byrne* (Dublin, 2000), pp. 346–56.

Duffy, S., "Irishmen and Islesmen in the Kingdoms of Dublin and Man, 1052–1171," *Ériu*, 43 (1992), 93–133.

Duffy, S., "Ostmen, Irish and Welsh in the eleventh century," *Peritia*, 9 (1996), 378–96.

Duffy, S., "The royal dynasties of Dublin and the Isles in the eleventh century," in S Duffy (ed.), *Medieval Dublin VII* (Dublin, 2006), pp. 51–65.

Duffy, S., "'The western world's tower of honour and dignity': the career of Muirchertach Ua Briain in context," in D. Bracken and D. Ó Riain-Raedel (eds.), *Ireland and Europe in the Twelfth Century: Reform and Renewal* (Dublin, 2006), pp. 56–73.

Etchingham, C., "North Wales, Ireland and the Isles: the insular Viking zone," *Peritia*, 15 (2001), 145–87.

Evans, D. S. (ed.), *Historia Gruffud vab Kenan / Gyda rhagymadrodd a nodiadau gan* (Cardiff, 1977).

Evans, D. S. (ed. and trans.), *A Mediaeval Prince of Wales: The Life of Gruffudd ap Cynan* (Felinfach, 1990).

Flanagan, M. T., *Irish Society, Anglo-Norman Settlers, Angevin Kingship* (Oxford, 1989).

Fleming, J., *Gille of Limerick (c.1070–1145): Architect of a Medieval Church* (Dublin, 2001).

Gwynn, A., "Brian in Armagh (1005)," *Seanchas Ardmhacha*, 9 (1978), 35–50.

Gwynn, A., "Ireland and Rome in the twelfth century," *Irish Ecclesiastical Record*, 57: 3 (1941), 213–32.

Gwynn, A., *The Irish Church in the Eleventh and Twelfth Centuries*, ed. G. O'Brien (Dublin, 1992).

Higham, N. J., "The Domesday survey: context and purpose," *History*, 78 (1993), 7–21.

Holland, M., "Cashel, synod of (1101)," in S. Duffy (ed.), *Medieval Ireland: An Encyclopedia* (New York, 2005), pp. 65–6.

Holland, M., "Dublin and the reform of the Irish church in the eleventh and twelfth centuries," *Peritia*, 14 (2000), 111–60.

Holland, M., "Ráith Bressail, synod of," in S. Duffy (ed.), *Medieval Ireland: An Encyclopedia* (New York, 2005), pp. 397–8.

Holland, M., "The synod of Dublin in 1080," in S. Duffy (ed.), *Medieval Dublin III* (Dublin, 2002), pp. 81–94.

Holt, J. C., "1086," in *Domesday Studies. Papers Read at the Novocentenary Conference of the Royal Historical Society and the Institute of British Geographers, Winchester, 1986* (Woodbridge, 1987), pp. 41–64.

Hudson, B., "Cnut and Viking Dublin" and "Cnut and the Scottish kings," reprinted in B. Hudson, *Irish Sea Studies 900–1200* (Dublin, 2006), chs. 2 and 3.

Hudson, B., "The family of Harold Godwinson and the Irish Sea province," *Journal of the Royal Society of Antiquaries of Ireland*, 109 (1979) 92–100; reprinted in B. Hudson, *Irish Sea Studies 900–1200* (Dublin, 2006), ch. 6.

Hudson, B., *Prophecy of Berchan: Irish and Scottish High-kings of the Early Middle Ages* (Westport, CT, 1996).

Hudson, B., "William the Conqueror and Ireland," *Irish Historical Studies*, 29 (1994), 145–58.

Jaski, B., *Early Irish Kingship and Succession* (Dublin, 2000).

Mac Airt, S. (ed.), *The Annals of Inisfallen* (Dublin, 1951).

Mac Shamhráin, A., "The battle of Glenn Máma, Dublin, and the high-kingship of Ireland: a millennial commemoration," in S. Duffy (ed.), *Medieval Dublin II* (Dublin, 2002), pp. 53–64.

Mac Shamhráin, A., "Brian Bóruma, Armagh and the high-kingship," *Seanchas Ardmhacha*, 20: 2 (2005), 1–21.

Mac Shamhráin, A. *Church and Polity in Pre-Norman Ireland: The Case of Glendalough* (Maynooth, 1996).

Maddicott, J. R., "Responses to the threat of invasion, 1085," *English Historical Review*, 122, no. 498 (2007), 986–97.

Maund, K. L. (ed.), *Gruffudd ap Cynan: A Collaborative Biography* (Woodbridge, 1996).

Ní Mhaonaigh, M., *Brian Boru: Ireland's Greatest King* (Stroud, 2007).

Ní Mhaonaigh, M., "*Cogad Gáedel re Gallaib*: some dating considerations," *Peritia*, 9 (1995), 354–77.

Ó Corráin, D., "Brian Boru and the battle of Clontarf," in L. de Paor (ed.), *Milestones in Irish History* (Cork, 1986), pp. 31–40.

Ó Corráin, D., "The career of Diarmait mac Máel na mBó, king of Leinster," *Journal of the Old Wexford Society*, 3 (1971), 27–35; 4 (1972–3), 17–24.

Ó Corráin, D., *Ireland before the Normans* (Dublin, 1972).

Ó Corráin, D., "Nationality and kingship in pre-Norman Ireland," in T. W. Moody (ed.), *Nationality and the Pursuit of National Independence* (Belfast, 1978), pp. 1–35.

Ó Corráin, D., "The Uí Chennselaig kingship of Leinster, 1072–1126," *Journal of the Old Wexford Society*, 5 (1974), 26–31; 6 (1977), 45–54; 7 (1978), 46–9.

Ó Riain, P., "The shrine of the Stowe missal, redated," *Proceedings of the Royal Irish Academy*, section C, 91 (1991), 285–95.

Power, R., "Magnus Barelegs' expeditions to the west," *Scottish Historical Review*, 66 (1986), 107–32.

Power, R., "Meeting in Norway: Norse-Gaelic relations in the kingdom of Man and the Isles, 1090–1270," *Saga-book: Viking Society for Northern Research*, 29 (2005), 5–66.

Richter, M. (ed.), *Canterbury Professions, with Palaeographical Notes by T. J. Brown*. Canterbury and York Society, 67 (Torquay, 1973).

Russell, P. (ed.), *Vita Griffini Filii Conani: The Medieval Latin Life of Gruffudd ap Cynan* (Cardiff, 2005).

Ryan, J., "The battle of Clontarf," *Journal of the Royal Society of Antiquaries of Ireland*, 68 (1938), 1–50.

Ryan, J., "Brian Boruma, king of Ireland," in E. Rynne (ed.), *North Munster Studies: Essays in Commemoration of Monsignor Michael Moloney* (Limerick, 1967), pp. 355–74.

Ryan, J., "The O'Briens in Munster after Clontarf," *North Munster Antiquarian Journal*, 2 (1941), 141–52; 3 (1942), 1–52.

Thompson, K., "Note de recherche: Arnoul de Montgommery," *Annales de Normandie*, 45 (1995), 49–53.

Todd, J. H. (ed.), *Cogadh Gaedhil re Gallaibh: The War of the Gaedhil with the Gaill, or the Invasions of Ireland by the Danes and Other Norsemen* (London, 1867).

Waitz, G. (ed.), *Adam of Bremen: Gesta Hammaburgensis Ecclesiae Pontificum*, MGH SS, 2nd edn. (Hanover, 1876).

CHAPTER NINETEEN

Northumbria

WILLIAM M. AIRD

Until recently, the historiography of Northumbria in the tenth and eleventh centuries has been dominated by the theme of the political unification or "making" of the kingdom of England. The underlying idea is that England's pre-existing "national" unity was already in place, waiting to be rediscovered and given political expression by that national icon Alfred the Great and his immediate successors in the tenth century. Alfred's West Saxon dynasty "re-conquered" or unified England by their efforts and, in so doing, stole a march on other European countries by giving the kingdom a political unity through which to express its enduring national identity.[1]

The idea of reuniting the disparate branches of an ethnic group through a war of liberation is common in the historiographies of nation-states. The idea of *re*-conquest, rather than conquest, allows aggression to be justified. For medieval theologians, the concept of the *iustum bellum* or "just war" underlies many accounts of conquest in the period. The West Saxon conquest of "England" has been portrayed as just such a *re*-conquest, a war of liberation, bringing under the political rule of one dynasty an ethnically coherent people. In accounts of the process, "West Saxon" identity expands by degrees to become "English" identity. The West Saxon/"English" kings thus restored, rather than created, the kingdom of the English, the only legitimate political expression of ethnic unity.[2]

This interpretation of the trajectory of England's history in the tenth and eleventh centuries has obscured the importance of other elements in the historical development of the nation-state. Regional narratives give place to an overarching national story. However, there has been renewed interest in the older sociopolitical and cultural regions of Britain, perhaps drawing impetus from the contemporary movement toward political devolution.[3] In the specific case of Northumbria, the "national narrative" has also influenced the characterizations of key elements in the region's early history. The contribution of Scandinavian settlers has generally been viewed negatively by those for whom the period is characterized by the liberation narrative of West Saxon triumph (see chapter 13). Thus, modern interpreters of the history of the region have found it hard to accept that Northumbrians found it more advantageous to accept Scandinavian lordship rather than making common cause with fellow "Englishmen" under the leadership of their "natural" allies, the kings of Wessex. For historians operating with the assumptions of this narrative structure, the Scandinavian presence in Northumbria is described with something of the fascinated horror expressed by medieval writers reporting the first "viking" attacks at the end of the eighth century.[4]

Similarly, and especially with reference to the most northerly parts of Northumbria, the influence of another emerging kingdom has been underplayed and negatively characterized. Medieval – and some modern – writers referred to the Scots in terms not too dissimilar to the language used to characterize the Scandinavians, as barbarian hordes, enemies of God who deserved destruction. The kingdom of the Scots began to coalesce in the tenth and eleventh centuries, and the territorial ambitions of its rulers extended south across the Forth and into Bernicia.[5]

This chapter moves away from the still influential West Saxon "master-narrative" and toward a reconstruction that questions the assumption that Northumbria was predestined to be included in the kingdom of England. Scots and Scandinavians are seen as net contributors to the history of Northumbria, agents of change and not merely obstacles to an inevitable – and wholly desirable – incorporation of the region into the kingdom of England. The terms historians have employed in describing the north of England have also tended to conceal significant divisions within the region itself. Although a convenient term, "Northumbria" consisted of several areas, each of which should be examined. The inhabitants of southern or "Deiran Northumbria," consisting largely of the later county of Yorkshire, experienced the period differently from those who lived to the north of the River Tees in Bernicia, or from those who lived west of the Pennines.[6] Finally, the "narrative of competition," which so often characterizes – and characterized – historical writing about early medieval England, might be interrogated. In subscribing to the view of the rise of Wessex/England, it is often all too easy to write off other regions as in decline, as relics of a once glorious past giving place to those more suited to realizing the "national" destiny. Although politically fragmented and influenced by Scandinavian and Scot, Northumbria still had a significant historical contribution to make in the tenth and eleventh centuries.

Before the eleventh century, sources are scarce for Northumbria. There are no surviving charters from the pre-viking period, although texts transmitted by the community of St. Cuthbert in the eleventh century seem to contain earlier documents. Similarly, there are no Northumbrian law codes before the early eleventh century when two texts attributed to Archbishop Wulfstan of York appeared: *Norðleoda laga* ("The Law of the North People") and (less likely to have been Wulfstan's) "The Law of the Northumbrian Priests."[7] West of the Pennines, the sources are even rarer; there is only one pre-Norman document: "Gospatric's writ." Historians describing conditions here have to rely on working back from later materials in the hope of uncovering the earlier history and institutions of the region.[8] There are, however, contemporary sources produced in Northumbria that represent an alternative to the West Saxon kings' "house history," the *Anglo-Saxon Chronicle*, originally designed to promote the political aspirations of Alfred and his successors. In particular, two ecclesiastical institutions, which survived the successive upheavals of the tenth and eleventh centuries, produced historical tracts partly as a way of coping with these changes. There was even a "Northern Recension" of the *Anglo-Saxon Chronicle*, offering a Northumbrian voice in the West Saxon house history. Series of northern annals were preserved in later texts such as *Historia regum Anglorum* ("History of the Kings of the English"), attributed to Symeon of Durham, and in the work of Roger of Wendover.[9] The sources emanating from the archiepiscopal see of York and the community of St. Cuthbert provide a "Northumbrian" perspective on the tenth and eleventh centuries.[10] These ecclesiastical institutions were located in two of the constituent regions of the early kingdom of Northumbria – that is, York in Deira, and the Church of St. Cuthbert in Bernicia – but both had more widespread interests. The historical experience of these two regions differed during these two centuries. For example, the Scots were a more immediate concern for the community of St. Cuthbert, whereas the archbishops of York's interests were not only heavily entwined with those of the Scandinavian settlers of the ninth and tenth centuries, but also increasingly affected by the policies of the West Saxon kings. In addition, the region was part of a "northern world" much longer than was the case for southern England, which established links with the nearer continent much earlier.

Northumbria in the Tenth Century

There has been a growing historical skepticism about the conclusions to be drawn from the evidence associated with the Scandinavians in Northumbria from the ninth to the eleventh centuries. For example, place-name analysis, once seen as a secure guide to the extent of Scandinavian settlement, has been called into question.[11] The extent and nature of the Scandinavian settlement has thus been re-examined and, for some, the presence of Scandinavian kings at York in the later ninth and first half of the tenth century no longer marks a definitive crisis for the survival of native Northumbrian institutions. There is evidence to suggest that the Scandinavian settlement enhanced, rather than diminished, the power and prestige of these institutions. For example, drawing analogies with similar configurations in the German empire of the same era, a persuasive case has been made for characterizing the archbishops of York as "prince-bishops" wielding political as well as ecclesiastical power.[12]

The fact that there is evidence for the existence of archbishops and their clerical communities at York during the Scandinavian period suggests a pragmatic tolerance of Christianity.[13] Indeed, the Church of St. Peter prospered in this period. Archbishop Wulfstan I (931–56) played a significant role in the politics of Northumbria and demonstrated an ambivalent attitude to the West Saxon kings in their dealings with the region.[14] He was ready to make use of the Scandinavian element in his see and was instrumental in the reception of the Scandinavian king Óláf Guthfrithson in 939, operating alongside him in struggles against Edmund and Eadred of Wessex.[15] York was a flourishing urban center in this period, and its role as an *emporium* provided a positive point of contact between native and settler. Economic success enabled its rulers to exercise political influence north of the Humber.[16] It was not in the interests of the Scandinavians to disrupt the commercial activities of the city of York, and the success of Viking Age York might be seen as the result of a flourishing partnership between immigrants and natives. Evidence for intermarriage between Northumbrians and Scandinavians only seems surprising if we employ rigid definitions of ethnicity in our reconstruction of the past (see chapter 14).

Scandinavian kings of York may have been employed by the archbishops as mercenaries, defenders of the region against the encroachments of other external enemies, including the West Saxon kings.[17] Regional interests took precedence over any idea that York and its hinterland properly "belonged" to an overarching kingdom of the English. The support of pagan Scandinavian kings by Christian ecclesiastical communities questions the assumption of hostility between the two. In the absence of native Northumbrian rulers, the prince-bishops in charge of the churches of York and St. Cuthbert, together with their Scandinavian allies, were stepping into the political vacuum left by the waning power of the royal houses of Bernicia and Deira. Churchmen also needed kings, for the conceptual hierarchy at the center of their worldview was founded on the presence of kings and they envisaged themselves as priestly advisers ensuring political order in the world.

Thus, there were alliances between archbishops of York and Scandinavian kings, with, for example, Archbishop Wulfstan I supporting the reinstatement of Eric Bloodaxe at York in 952.[18] Further north, the ecclesiastical community of St. Cuthbert benefited in the long term from its dealings with the Scandinavians.[19] The community was originally based on Holy Island (Lindisfarne), near the Bernician royal centers of Yeavering and Bamburgh. According to the *Historia de Sancto Cuthberto* ("The History about St. Cuthbert"), in 875 the community began seven years of wandering about Northumbria, before settling at Chester-le-Street (County Durham).[20] The *Historia*, written in the eleventh century but drawing on earlier materials, presents a dramatic view of the viking incursions in the region. The coffin containing the incorrupt body of Cuthbert was wheeled around Northumbria by a band of refugees with the pagans who had driven them from Lindisfarne snapping at their heels. This account obscured another reality, where the community of St. Cuthbert visited ecclesiastical sites over which it asserted proprietary claims.[21]

Just as the Church of York entered alliances with the Scandinavians in Deira, the community of St. Cuthbert established a similar relationship with Scandinavian leaders. The *Historia de Sancto Cuthberto* recounts the inauguration of a Scandinavian king under the auspices of the saint. In gratitude, this king, Guthred, granted the community all the land between the rivers Tyne and Wear, this becoming the core of the "liberty of St. Cuthbert."[22] By the eleventh century, the *Historia* gave the West Saxon King Alfred, and his successors, key roles in the protection of the Church of St. Cuthbert, reflecting the community's desire to be associated with the successful dynasty, but not to the exclusion of other possible benefactors.[23]

The community of St. Cuthbert retained its landed interests north of the Tyne in the region dominated by the house of Bamburgh. Scandinavian settlement seems to have been concentrated south of the Tees, so the extent of the contact that the rulers of Bamburgh, the successors of the kings of Bernicia, had with the Scandinavians was confined largely to dealing with military incursions. To counteract these attacks by the York vikings, the rulers of Bamburgh allied with those closest at hand and able to provide military support, namely the Scots.[24] Ealdred of Bamburgh, for example, was driven into Scotland by Rægnald in 914, where he enlisted the aid of Causantin (Constantín) II (900–43; see chapter 16). Ealdred and Causantin were assisted by Elfred *Brihtwulfing*, an adherent of the Church of St. Cuthbert. These allies were defeated by Rægnald at Corbridge in 918 and the Scandinavian attempted to settle his own men on Cuthbertine lands.[25]

St. Cuthbert acquired a great number of estates during the tenth century and many of these belonged to other ecclesiastical institutions, which had fared less well against the Scandinavians. The lands of the Church of Hexham were almost certainly absorbed in this way. By the end of the century, the Church of St. Cuthbert was laying claim to estates in a region extending from Lothian in the north to Yorkshire in the south, and from Carlisle in the west to Durham in the east. Despite the Scandinavians and attacks from the increasingly confident Scots, the bishops and community of St. Cuthbert, with their extensive landholdings and their ability to raise and mobilize troops, emerged as key players in Northumbrian politics, alongside the archbishops of York and the rulers of Bamburgh. Anyone wishing to extend his lordship into the region had to reach an accommodation with these groups.[26]

The West Saxon Kings and Northumbria

Following Alfred's containment of the Scandinavians in the ninth century, his successors began to encroach on Scandinavian areas in the following century (see chapter 20). It was understandable that the emerging West Saxon monarchy should attempt to neutralize the threat represented by the Northumbrians. In the history of the Old English state, Northumbria appears as a refuge for opponents of Wessex. As early as 894, a West Saxon envoy had appeared at York and, shortly afterward, Alfred's nephew, the *ætheling* Æthelwold, sought allies there against Edward the Elder and in so doing anticipated Northumbria's later role as a potential recruiting ground for opposition against southern kings.[27]

In the first half of the tenth century, West Saxon kings began to make their presence felt in Northumbria. In 909, Edward the Elder "ravaged" the region over five weeks.[28] In 927, Æthelstan (924–39) captured York itself and razed its fortifications.[29] Seven years later, he granted Amounderness in the north-west to the Church of St. Peter in York (S 407). Similar grants were made to the Church of St. Cuthbert, presumably to win recognition of West Saxon claims to overlordship: several liturgical manuscripts, ecclesiastical vestments and vessels, bells, gold and silver drinking horns, banners, a lance, and golden armlets. The estate of Bishop Wearmouth with its dependent settlements was also confirmed to St. Cuthbert. Whether the king had any effective power over the estates in question is another matter, but Æthelstan and the clerics serving St. Cuthbert were mutually reinforcing each other's claims to authority.[30] Æthelstan was also credited with confirming the right of sanctuary to the Church of St. Cuthbert.[31]

Æthelstan's example was followed by his brother Edmund (939–46) who, during a campaign against the Scots, visited the Church of St. Cuthbert and "knelt before his tomb, poured out prayers and commended himself and his men to God and the holy confessor."[32] In the histories of the Church of St. Cuthbert, there was a close association between their patron and the kings of Wessex. Whether this was of lasting help is another matter given that the center of West Saxon power lay so far south. For the Northumbrians, especially those in Bernicia, a more immediate problem was presented by the growth of the power of the kings of Scotland.

The economic structure of Northumbria would have seemed unfamiliar to the southern kings used to the intensively farmed heartlands of Wessex and Mercia. Much of the economy of Northumbria beyond the agricultural plains of the east coast (for example, the Vale of York) was based on pastoralism, making use of the extensive upland landscapes of the Pennines and Cheviots. Apart from York, Chester, and perhaps Carlisle, there were no large towns and certainly none of the urban development associated with Alfred's dynasty.[33] The far north was a country of cattle and sheep, rendering customary dues to estate centers.[34] In these circumstances, it is no wonder that the West Saxon kings targeted centers of wealth and political power, particularly York and its mint, for particular attention: they simply did not have the manpower to impose their presence across Northumbria.

The Kings of Scots and Northumbria in the Tenth Century

At the beginning of the tenth century, the kings of *Alba* ruled a diverse collection of peoples (see chapter 16). Although their heartland lay north of the rivers Forth and Clyde, they had ambitions to extend their lordship south into Cumbria in the west and Northumbria in the east. The extension of political control over these disparate ethnic communities helped create Scottish identity. The diverse ethnic character of the kingdom of the Scots meant that the Anglian roots of Bernicia, or the British origins of Strathclyde–Cumbria, were no obstacle to their incorporation. Only if "Englishness," however we might define it, is seen in rigidly irredentist terms does the prospect of the incorporation of Northumbria into an enlarged Scottish kingdom seem implausible.[35]

During the tenth century, the kings of *Alba* began to intervene more often in Northumbria. After the Scandinavian settlement of Deira at the end of the ninth century, Bernicia was under the lordship of the rulers of Bamburgh. Taking advantage of the problems caused by the Scandinavian kings of York and the absence from the region for long periods of the West Saxons, the Scots made inroads into Northumbria, forcing Alfred's successors to recognize their claims there. For example, around 950, Máel Coluim (Malcolm) I plundered as far as the Tees, seizing many people and cattle.[36] War as slaving raid was to characterize Scots incursions into Northumbria well into the twelfth century.

When the sources mention the Scots kings in connection with their West Saxon counterparts in the tenth century, they are usually one of several parties agreeing to recognize the lordship of the southern ruler. For example, in 920, according to the *Anglo-Saxon Chronicle* (A), "the king of the Scots and all the nation of the Scots chose him [Edward the Elder] as father and lord; and [so also did] Rægnald and Eadwulf's sons and all those who live in Northumbria, both English and Danish and Norwegians and others; and also the king of the Strathclyde Britons and all the Strathclyde Britons."[37] This southern source emphasizes, and probably exaggerates, the power of the West Saxons, but the entry does demonstrate the diversity of contending powers in the region.[38] Similar exaggeration in the entry for 934 claimed that Æthelstan attacked and subdued Scotland. The Scots and their Norse allies retaliated but were defeated at *Brunanburh* in 937. Æthelstan's successor, Edmund, "brought all Northumbria into his domain," driving out the Scandinavians Óláf Sihtricson and Rægnald Guthfrithson in 944, and the following year he "raided across all the land of Cumbria and ceded it to Malcolm, king of Scots, on the condition that he would be his co-operator both on sea and on land."[39] Again, it is doubtful that Edmund really had the power to dispose of such large territories in the north of England. These entries perhaps represent the acknowledgment of West Saxon lordship, rather than the reality of a more immediate political domination. Another version of the same annal, preserved in the thirteenth century by Roger of Wendover, adds that Edmund, in addition to despoiling Cumbria, blinded the two sons of its king, Dunmail and gave the kingdom to Máel Coluim to hold from him for the defense of northern England.[40] This entry may indicate that Máel Coluim already held the more northerly British kingdom of Strathclyde and that Edmund ravaged what became English Cumbria. In effect, the West Saxon could do nothing about Scots' possession of the region and was again asserting his claims to lordship in an attempt to stabilize relations in the region.

During Eadred's reign, Máel Coluim raided as far as the Tees, taking advantage of the readmission of the Scandinavian Óláf to York in 949–50. The steady southerly progress of Scots lordship in Bernicia was recognized in the mid-970s. After an imperial coronation ceremony at Bath in 973, Edgar demonstrated his lordship in an elaborate ritual conducted at Chester. There, eight "under-kings," who probably included Cinaed (Kenneth) II, king of Scots, Máel Coluim, king of the Cumbrians, and Maccus, king "of many islands," took the oars of a boat steered by Edgar himself and rowed their lord along the River Dee.[41] The symbolism of the ship of state with Edgar at its helm needs little elaboration.[42] The Durham *Historia regum Anglorum* describes Edgar as dividing the Northumbrian ealdormanry into a southern part and a northern one, extending from the Tees to *Myreforth*, possibly the mud-flats between the mouth of the River Esk and the Solway Firth.[43] The *Historia regum* also states that Edgar gave Lothian to Cinaed and sent him home with great honor. This suggests that the Scots may have already been in possession of northern Bernicia and Edgar was recognizing a fait accompli. There is debate over the date of the acquisition of Lothian by the Scots. In particular, the failure of the *Anglo-Saxon Chronicle* to mention it, together with the assertion by northern sources that Lothian was given in 1018, has raised doubts.[44] Whatever arrangements Cinaed made with Edgar, the Scots continued to view Northumbria as a legitimate target, as when in 980 a northern "ship-army" raided as far south as Cheshire.[45]

Northumbria in the Eleventh Century

Many of the themes that characterized the 900s also shaped Northumbria's history in the eleventh century. Renewed Scandinavian attacks during Æthelred II's reign limited the direct intervention of West Saxon kings in the region.[46] In Archbishop Wulfstan II *Lupus* ("The Wolf," d.1023), however, Æthelred II found an ally. During the later tenth century, the West Saxon kings realized that appointing their own men to the archbishopric of York enabled them to exercise political influence far beyond that which could be imposed militarily. Thus, after the deposition and subsequent death of Archbishop Wulfstan I in the early 950s, a series of southern appointees held York. To prevent these placemen from "going native," they were often allowed to retain or acquire ecclesiastical office and other property in Southumbria. For example, Archbishop Oscytel (957–71) retained the see of Dorchester, and Oswald (970/1–92) and Wulfstan II held Worcester as well as York. The link with Worcester persisted into the eleventh century.[47]

Archbishop Wulfstan II's Danish background may have given him an insight into northern mentalities, but he provided legal texts for his West Saxon lord and his apocalyptic *Sermo Lupi ad Anglos* ("Sermon of the Wolf to the English") suggests that he was not sympathetic to the idea of renewed Scandinavian attacks.[48] After several generations of settlement and cultural interaction in Northumbria, it was not certain that those of Scandinavian descent would necessarily welcome further incursions by other Scandinavians. After Cnut's conquest, Wulfstan worked hard to reconcile "English" and Danes, and this culminated in the issuing of legal codes for the Danish king at Winchester in 1020 or 1021. The policy implemented at York may have been successful, but beyond the Tees, West Saxon influence was more tenuous. Links were established with the Church of St. Cuthbert, but, by and large, the ruling house of Bamburgh lay beyond the West Saxon orbit. It is likely that the West Saxon "appointments" made here were, in fact, retrospective, and claims to influence in the region possibly empty. Gradually, however, even those north of the Tyne began to turn south for allies against the Scots.

The *De Obsessione Dunelmi et de probitate Uchtredi comitis, et de comitibus qui ei successerunt* ("Concerning the Siege of Durham and the Probity of Earl Uchtred and the Earls who Succeeded Him") is an anonymous work probably written by a member of the Church of St. Cuthbert between 1070 and 1100.[49] It deals with the descent of certain estates belonging to that church, but also includes information on the rulers of Northumbria in the early eleventh century.[50] The *De Obsessione* describes a siege of Durham by the Scots probably in 1006. It outlines the relationship between Earl Uchtred and King Æthelred II as well as his association with the Church of St. Cuthbert. It was with his assistance that the community relocated to Durham from Chester-le-Street in 995. Durham's naturally defensive site made it a more secure location, and Uchtred recruited men from the area between the rivers Coquet and Tees to clear the peninsula surrounded by the River Wear upon which the Church of St. Cuthbert was re-established.[51]

During the siege, Uchtred organized the defense of Durham as his father, the elderly Earl Waltheof, refused to leave Bamburgh. As a reward for his efforts, Æthelred II granted him Waltheof's title in addition to the earldom of York. Despite the evidence presented by the *De Obsessione*, it is unlikely that the West Saxon kings were able to impose their will definitively on Northumbria, especially beyond the Tees, before the succession of Cnut.

Æthelred's reign ended with the invasion of Swegn and the accession of his son Cnut of Denmark in 1016.[52] Briefly, Uchtred and Northumbria had provided Æthelred's son Edmund Ironside with the resources to resist the Danes, but, with his death (November 30, 1016), Cnut was secure in England. Cnut (1016–35) followed the example of his tenth-century West Saxon predecessors by visiting Northumbria in order to establish his lordship.

The Scots' threat continued and, as well as the siege of Durham in 1006, the Scots under Máel Coluim II, in alliance with Owen, king of Strathclyde, defeated the Northumbrians at Carham-on-Tweed in 1018.[53] The battle was associated with the concession of Lothian to the king of Scots by Earl Uchtred's successor Eadulf, but this was probably a formal recognition of Scots' possession of Lothian since the 970s, although it is possible that Earl Uchtred had been making successful inroads there before his death.[54]

To deter further incursions, Cnut invaded Scotland in 1027, forcing Máel Coluim II and two other kings, Mælbætha and Iehmarc, to submit to him.[55] Cnut also appointed Eric of Hlathir (1016–23 × 1033) as earl of Northumbria, although his jurisdiction probably excluded the liberty of St. Cuthbert and the lands of Bamburgh. Eric was followed by the Scandinavian, Siward (1023 × 1033–55), who extended control north of the Tyne by marrying into the house of Bamburgh and establishing relationships with the two most important ecclesiastical institutions in Northumbria.[56] According to the *Historia de Sancto Cuthberto*, Cnut granted the community Staindrop (County Durham) and its dependencies, as well as Brompton in Yorkshire. These grants are associated with a barefoot pilgrimage that Cnut made to Cuthbert's shrine from Garmondsway, a distance of 5 miles or thereabouts.[57] The pious nature of the visit recalls those of the Cnut's West Saxon predecessors and is in keeping with his desire to present himself as a thoroughly Christian king. Given the recent paganism of elements of the Danish army, Cnut's extravagant piety was as much a political statement as a religious one.[58] Similarly, Cnut developed a close relationship with the archbishop of York. His father, Swegn, had been buried in the Minster in 1014, before his remains were repatriated in the mid-1020s.[59] Archbishop Wulfstan II (1002–23) seems to have ensured that the city remained loyal to Cnut.[60]

During Cnut's reign there may have been an attempt to introduce monastic reform to the Church of St. Cuthbert. Archbishop Wulfstan II may have attempted to introduce clerical reform at York, as his "Sermon to the English" and "The Canons of Edgar" suggest.[61] Reform has often been associated with the political aspirations of southern kings. During the episcopate of Edmund (1020–42), monks were brought to Durham from the abbey of Peterborough, just one example of a series of links between the reformed Fenland houses and the north of England,[62] and part of an attempt by Cnut to exert more control over the Church of St. Cuthbert.[63] The constitution of the ecclesiastical corporation at Durham proved resistant to reform, and it was not until 1083 that the Benedictine rule was fully introduced and a cathedral priory established.[64]

Despite these attempts to forge stronger links, Northumbria, especially north of the Tees, was still largely beyond the reach of southern royal government. Judging by *Domesday Book*, the West Saxon and Danish kings still held relatively little land in the north of England. They managed to bring Yorkshire and a small part of Cumbria into the royal taxation system of the geld, hence the appearance of these areas in *Domesday*. At some point, presumably during the eleventh century, the administrative divisions familiar south of the Humber were introduced into Yorkshire. The county was "shired" and divided into three "*ridings*" (*trithings* = third parts). These divisions were, in their turn, made up of *wapentakes* (for example, "Skyrack wapentake," "Staincross wapentake"), seen as the northern version of the hundred.[65] The Scandinavian origins of the terms *wapentake* and *riding* suggest that the Danes retained some influence in the region, although it is difficult to demonstrate that this is a legacy of the tenth century, rather than of the eleventh.[66] Despite these innovations, earlier administrative divisions, the small "northern shires" ("sokes" or "multiple estates"), are still referred to.[67] Other areas of the north, such as south Lancashire, were subsumed in the *Domesday* entry for Cheshire, and north Lancashire and those parts of Cumbria that remained free of Scots' lordship appeared in the Yorkshire folios. There are hints that royal officials may also have been active in eleventh-century Yorkshire before the settlement of the Normans, but the evidence is far from conclusive.[68]

After the brief reigns of Harold Harefoot (d.1040) and Harthacnut (d.1042), the West Saxon royal dynasty was restored to England in the person of Edward the Confessor (1043–66). Although in his early years Edward attempted to impose his own will, it became clear that the Godwine family dominated affairs.[69] One by one, they acquired the major earldoms of England and, in 1055, Tostig became earl of Northumbria. Tostig based his regime in York, but attempted to extend his influence into Bernicia. His position was difficult as he had few "natural" supporters in either of the regions of Northumbria, and there are suggestions that his regime had to overcome opposition in the Church of St. Cuthbert.[70] According to a miracle story preserved at Durham, one of Tostig's men was struck down when he attempted to force an entry to the church in order to arrest a fugitive.[71]

Opposition to Tostig's rule coalesced in 1065, and the earl was driven out of Northumbria. In addition to attempting to levy heavy taxes and impose West Saxon law rather than the *Laws of Cnut* – which recognized northern custom and represented the "good old law" of happier times – on the Northumbrians, Tostig executed prominent members of the local nobility.[72] The rebels attacked the earl's residence at York and marched south announcing that Morkar, the brother of Earl Edwin of Mercia, was their new ruler. It is possible that the rebels chose an "outsider" in order to bring the separate regions together, but Morkar's family had well-established connections with Northumbria.[73] The community of St. Cuthbert may have encouraged the rebellion by exhuming the relics of King Oswine of Deira, a seventh-century martyr.[74] So, on the eve of the Norman invasion of the kingdom of England, Northumbria asserted its independence in a way that was to have a significant impact on the unfolding of the events of 1066.[75]

The Norman Conquest and Northumbria

The invasion of England by William the Conqueror and his allies in the autumn of 1066 presented a familiar set of problems for those living north of the Humber. As with the Danish conquest of 1016, the Northumbrians were faced with an outside power whose ambitions were to extend effective rule as far as possible. The combined forces of Bernician and Deiran Northumbria had driven out Tostig Godwineson and installed Morkar as earl. It is to be doubted whether Morkar's authority ran north of the River Tees, and there is evidence of the continuing importance of members of the house of Bamburgh there. According to the *Historia regum*, Morkar "handed over the 'earldom' [*comitatus*] beyond the Tyne" to Osulf, son of Earl Eadulf;[76] this was more likely the formal recognition of already existing authority rather than appointment.

For the Northumbrians, the crucial battles of 1066 were those fought near York at Fulford Gate and Stamford Bridge. Earl Tostig, driven out of the kingdom by his brother Harold, returned to make a bid for power after the accession of Harold in January 1066. Beginning with raids on the south coast in April, Tostig's fleet moved north to attack Lindsey. An army, including "Northumbrians" and led by Earls Edwin and Morkar, drove Tostig north to the mouth of the River Tyne where he joined the fleet of Harald Hardrada, king of Norway (1015–66) , who was pursuing a claim of his own to England, based on his kinship with the Danish kings.[77] On September 20, 1066, the combined forces of King Harald and Tostig defeated Earls Edwin and Morkar, and, a few days later, York surrendered.[78] In the south, King Harold Godwineson, awaiting the arrival of William of Normandy, was forced to ride north to deal with the Norwegian threat. The armies met at Stamford Bridge, east of York on September 25, 1066. Harold defeated and killed his brother and Harald Hardrada. Events in Northumbria had a bearing on Harold's defense of his kingdom against the Normans, and it might be argued that his victory outside York both exhausted and exhilarated Harold and his men. The hard-fought battle and the march south exhausted Harold's men before the confrontation with Duke William, and the exhilaration of victory in Northumbria probably encouraged him to offer battle, when containing the Norman threat may have been the more prudent strategy.[79]

William the Conqueror's coronation at Westminster on Christmas Day, 1066, did not automatically bring him the submission of Northumbria. In his dealings with the region and its centers of power, the new king employed methods recognizable as those of his predecessors. In the years immediately following Hastings, William attempted to rule through Northumbrians. It might be argued that he had little choice but to do so, given the call on his resources in the West Saxon heartlands. In 1067, Earl Morkar of Northumbria was arrested, and his earldom was granted to Copsi, who had served as Tostig's lieutenant. It seems that Copsi was appointed to the earldom north of the River Tyne, for he targeted Osulf of Bamburgh, forcing him into the woods and mountains. At the ancient comital center of Newburn-on-Tyne, Osulf trapped and killed Copsi.[80] Later that year, Osulf himself was killed and the earldom was purchased by his kinsman, Gospatric, a man connected by marriage to both the earls of Bamburgh and southern kings, and perhaps, like Copsi, a member of Tostig's entourage.[81]

As Norman settlement pushed further north, royal administrators appeared at York and Durham. In 1068, Gospatric and a group of English nobles, including the West Saxon claimant to the throne, Edgar the Ætheling, fled north to Scotland. There, Edgar's sister Margaret married Máel Coluim III, thereby giving the Scots king a further legitimate excuse to assert claims to include the southern regions of Bernician Northumbria within his sphere of influence.[82] In January 1069, Robert Cumin, sent north by the Conqueror to secure the earldom after Gospatric's desertion, was murdered, along with his troops at Durham. Whether the community of St. Cuthbert was a party to the slaughter is unclear, but the earl's death heralded a general rising in Northumbria. The Northumbrians, supported by a Danish fleet, attacked York, whose Norman garrison set fire to the city. The flames spread to York Minster, destroying the archiepiscopal archive.[83]

The Conqueror's reaction to this resistance to his lordship in Northumbria was a winter campaign of such ferocity that it was singled out by medieval historians as an atrocity. William's troops plundered and destroyed to such an extent that famine was induced and with it a great mortality.[84] The so-called "harrying of the north" left an indelible impression on the English-born, Norman monk Orderic Vitalis, writing some 75 years after the event: "My narrative has frequently had occasion to praise William, but for this act which condemned the innocent and the guilty alike to die by slow starvation I cannot commend him."[85]

The devastation induced Bishop Æthelwine and the community of St. Cuthbert to abandon Durham for the comparative safety of Lindisfarne.[86] Despite Gospatric's involvement in the attack on York, William I accepted his surrender and allowed him to retain his earldom. It was not until 1072, when the Conqueror led an expedition into Scotland, that he deposed Gospatric. The earl fled north, where his family secured Dunbar from Máel Coluim III. As his successor, William appointed another earl with close connections to the Northumbrian nobility. Despite his involvement in the rebellions of 1068–70, Waltheof was pardoned by the king and, presumably in an attempt to secure his loyalty, he married the Conqueror's niece, Judith.

King William's relationship with the Church of St. Cuthbert provides an interesting commentary on the difficulties the Normans experienced in extending their rule beyond Yorkshire. After Bishop Æthelwine fled his see in 1071, the king appointed a Lotharingian cleric, Walcher, as bishop, echoing his predecessor Cnut's attempt to influence affairs beyond the Tees by installing Bishop Edmund in the 1020s. Walcher attempted to reform the cathedral chapter by introducing a rule for canons.[87] On his return from an expedition to Scotland, in 1072, the Conqueror visited Durham. Two accounts of his visit survive, each presenting a different view of the king's relationship with the saint. Symeon of Durham, writing in the early twelfth century, suggested that the Conqueror threatened violence on the elders of the community of St. Cuthbert if they could not prove that the saint's incorrupt body was present.[88] An earlier account, however, tells us that the king approached the shrine reverently, heard the story of the saint's life, and, as a consequence, made gifts to the church.[89] This earlier account seems more in keeping with the policies of the Conqueror's predecessors: it was in the king's interests to win allies for the new bishop, rather than alienate the locals with threats of violence.

In 1075, after the arrest and subsequent execution of Earl Waltheof, the Conqueror abandoned his policy of ruling through members of the native nobility.[90] The earldom of Northumbria, here meaning the Bernician lands between the Tyne and the Tweed, was entrusted to Bishop Walcher. The bishop managed to rule until 1080, when he and members of his household were murdered at Gateshead on the River Tyne. The immediate context of the bishop's death was an invasion of the region by Máel Coluim III of Scotland. Walcher's regime necessarily relied on cooperation with members of the Northumbrian aristocracy, and the late Earl Waltheof's uncle, Ligulf, protested at the bishop's ineffectiveness in the face of the Scots' attack. Local rivalries also added to the volatility of the situation, and Ligulf's family was murdered by Bishop Walcher's kinsman, Gilbert. The bishop protested his innocence of the crime and agreed to meet the Northumbrians at Gateshead, where Walcher and his men were murdered by members of the house of Bamburgh.[91] The incident demonstrated that it was virtually impossible to ensure the survival of a regime loyal to the Norman monarchy in the region without widespread settlement of French landholders.

Bishop Walcher's death led to another punitive expedition to Northumbria but also to the appointment of a successor. Bishop William of Saint-Calais, a monk and former abbot of Saint-Vincent, Le Mans, had proved himself an able administrator in Maine, a county the Normans found difficult to control. One of the key problems for Bishop William was the deep-rooted power of the families of the north-east. In 1083, he managed to sever, at a stroke, their controlling interests in the cult of St. Cuthbert. He reformed the community of St. Cuthbert, insisting that its members accepted Benedictine monasticism or leave the church. The bishop was assisted in his task by the fact that, at the beginning of the 1070s, there had been something of a monastic revival in Northumbria.[92]

Symeon of Durham described how three monks, inspired by reading Bede's *Historia ecclesiastica*, set out for Northumbria to visit the shrines of the saints described by the venerable doctor. Led by Aldwine, prior of the abbey of Winchcombe in the Vale of Evesham, they made their way north to York and then on to the Tyne. With Bishop Walcher's aid, the monks established themselves at *Munecaceastre* ("Monkchester") and then at Jarrow, Bede's former home. The whole account of Aldwine and his companions, the re-establishment of Benedictine monasticism in Northumbria, and the reformation of the community of St. Cuthbert in 1083, has the characteristics of the foundation narratives that often accompanied the establishment of monastic communities in this period. When Bishop William introduced the *Rule of St. Benedict* to the community of St. Cuthbert in 1083, he relied on Aldwine as his first prior.

There has been some debate as to how far the reformation in 1083 was a violent one. Given the precarious nature of Norman rule in Bernician Northumbria, the violent removal of members of the community of St. Cuthbert would seem imprudent. Accepting the *Rule of St. Benedict* would regularize the status of the monks and force them to choose between their wives and families and their service at the saint's shrine. The lack of explicit accounts of violence suggests that this more subtle reforming approach was adopted.

The key point, however, is that a monastic reformation of the Church of St. Cuthbert had taken place largely under the direction of southern-appointed bishops and with a significant contribution by English monks connected with the diocese of Worcester. Once again, ecclesiastical personnel brought Northumbria into closer relationship with the south. However, the key to an even more complete integration of the region into the kingdom of England was the settlement of French families in Northumbria. In Yorkshire, this process began in the aftermath of the "harrying of the north." French lords were established on compact lordships which gave them a greater measure of military security and economic viability.[93] The process of settlement moved north during the final decades of the eleventh century, but it was not until well into the reign of Henry I (1100–35) that Bernician Northumbria saw the establishment of French lordships in Northumberland and soon afterward across the Anglo-Scottish frontier.[94]

As Norman power was extended into Northumbria, the kings of Scots also advanced claims to lordship. Máel Coluim III's five attacks were as much about demonstrating his right to intervene in the affairs of Northumbria as they were plundering expeditions. The community of St. Cuthbert recognized the reality of the situation and was careful to establish links with the kings of the Scots. This was as much out of self-interest as self-preservation: the Church of St. Cuthbert claimed estates in Lothian as far north as the River Forth and on either bank of the River Tweed, the frontier between Scots and English Northumbria.[95] In 1093, Máel Coluim III and his English wife, Margaret, attended the foundation of Bishop William's new cathedral church at Durham, when an agreement (*conventio*) was drawn up by which the monks of Durham granted the Scots royal couple the privileges of confraternity, a share in the spiritual benefits on membership of the Church of St. Cuthbert. Their names were entered in the *Liber vitae* ("The Book of Life") and their obituaries were commemorated.[96]

Conclusion

As the home of Bede, the kingdom of Northumbria was arguably the birthplace of the idea of English identity. Yet, as the history of the region in the tenth and eleventh centuries demonstrates, it was here that notions of "English" identity and the "natural" political unity of all the English were challenged. Historical models that portray the West Saxon conquests of the tenth century as "*re*-conquest" or "unification" are liable to undervalue the continuing distinctiveness of the lands between the Humber and the Forth. Similarly, a history of Northumbria in this period should recognize the influence and ambitions of the emerging kingdom of the Scots as much as that of the West Saxon kings and their Danish and Norman successors.

Long after 1100, the Anglo-Scottish border remained a permeable frontier. Lords of French extraction settled on estates in both Scotland and England, creating political dilemmas for their descendants which reached into the later Middle Ages. Similarly, the Church of St. Cuthbert maintained claims to estates in Lothian throughout the medieval period. Pilgrims from Scotland made their way to Durham and to the other shrines of the north-east of England in search of communion with the ancient Northumbrian saints, whose beneficence was not confined solely to the inhabitants of England. In other words, it is difficult to understand the historical development of Northumbria in the tenth and eleventh centuries if one starts with the idea that the region always was, and was always going to be, "English."

Notes

1   Foot, "Historiography."
2   Stenton, *Anglo-Saxon England*; cf. John, "The West Saxon conquest" and Stafford, "Kings, kingships and kingdoms"; see also chapter 20 of this volume.
3   See, e.g., Aird, "Copsi"; Hadley, *Northern Danelaw*; Phythian-Adams, *Land of the Cumbrians*.
4   Wormald, "Viking studies."
5   Duncan, *Kingship of the Scots*; see also chapter 16 of this volume.
6   For convenient maps of these areas, see Hill, *Atlas of Anglo-Saxon England*.
7   Rollason, *Northumbria*, p. 12; cf. *EHD*, I, 432–3, 434–9; Wormald, *Making of English Law*, p. 208.
8   Phythian-Adams, *Land of the Cumbrians*, pp. 18, 174–81; cf. Kirby, "Strathclyde and Cumbria."
9   Rollason, *Northumbria*, pp. 15–19.
10 Gransden, *Historical Writing*, pp. 114–23; Hart, *Early Charters*; Rollason, *Northumbria and Symeon*.
11 See, e.g., Hadley, "In search of the Vikings" and "Viking and native"; see also chapter 14 of this volume.
12 Rollason, *Northumbria*, p. 229.
13 Abrams, "The conversion."
14 Whitelock, "The dealings of the kings."
15 Hart, "Wulfstan"; cf. Keynes, "Wulfstan I."
16 Graham-Campbell, "Review article"; Hall, *Viking Age York*; Hinton, "The large towns," pp. 226–8.
17 Coupland, "From poachers to gamekeepers."
18 Rollason, *Northumbria*, p. 265.
19 Aird, *St. Cuthbert and the Normans*, pp. 34–44.
20 Johnson South, *Historia de Sancto Cuthberto*, §20, at pp. 58–9; Rollason, "The wanderings."
21 Rollason, "The wanderings."
22 Craster, "The patrimony"; Johnson South, *Historia de Sancto Cuthberto*, §13, at pp. 52–3.
23 Simpson, "The Alfred/St. Cuthbert episode."
24 Davidson, "The (non)submission."
25 Rollason, *Northumbria*, p. 274.
26 Aird, *St. Cuthbert and the Normans*, pp. 9–59.
27 Swanton, *Anglo-Saxon Chronicle*, A, *s.aa.* 900, 903, 904; cf. Campbell, *Chronicle of Æthelweard*, p. 51.
28 Abrams, "Edward the Elder's Danelaw"; Swanton, *Anglo-Saxon Chronicle*, A, *s.a.* 909.

29 Rollason, *Northumbria*, p. 217; Swanton, *Anglo-Saxon Chronicle*, E, *s.a.* 927.

30 Johnson South, *Historia de Sancto Cuthberto*, §§26–7, at pp. 64–7 and 108–10.

31 Hall, "The sanctuary of St. Cuthbert"; Rollason, *Northumbria*, pp. 272–3.

32 Johnson South, *Historia de Sancto Cuthberto*, §28, at pp. 66–7 and 110–11.

33 Kermode, "Northern towns."

34 Hadley, *Northern Danelaw.*

35 Duncan, *Kingship of the Scots*, p. 5.

36 Ibid., p. 24.

37 Anderson, *Scottish Annals*, p. 65.

38 Davidson, "The (non)submission."

39 Swanton, *Anglo-Saxon Chronicle*, A, *s.aa.* 944, 945.

40 Duncan, *Kingship of the Scots*, p. 23 and n.53.

41 Williams, "An outing on the Dee."

42 Darlington and McGurk, *Chronicle of John*, *s.a.* 973.

43 Duncan, *Kingship of the Scots*, p. 24.

44 Ibid., p. 25.

45 Whitelock, *EHD*, *ASC*, C, *s.a.* 980.

46 Forte et al., *Viking Empires*, pp. 184–216.

47 Whitelock, "The dealings of the kings"; see also chapter 20 of this volume.

48 *Sermo Lupi*, in *EHD*, I, 854–9.

49 Morris, *Marriage and Murder.*

50 Meehan, "The siege of Durham"; Morris, *Marriage and Murder*; Rollason et al., *Sources for York History*, pp. 24–5.

51 Aird, *St. Cuthbert and the Normans*, pp. 46–7.

52 Lawson, *Cnut.*

53 *Historia regum*, *s.a.* 1018, in Arnold, *Symeonis monachi*, II; cf. Duncan, *The Kingship of the Scots*, p. 28 and n.3. On Owen of Strathclyde, see Duncan, *The Kingship of the Scots*, p. 29 and n.6.

54 Meehan, "The siege of Durham."

55 Duncan, *Kingship of the Scots*, pp. 29–30; Hudson, "Cnut and the Scottish kings."

56 Aird, "Siward."

57 Rollason (ed.), *Symeon*, pp. 166–7.

58 Lawson, "Cnut."

59 Rollason et al., *Sources for York History*, p. 174.

60 Whitelock, "Archbishop Wulfstan."

61 Wormald, "Wulfstan."

62 Stafford, *East Midlands*, pp. 133–4, and *Unification and Conquest*, p. 124.

63 Rollason, *Northumbria*, p. 272.

64 Aird, *St. Cuthbert and the Normans*, pp. 107–8, 111–12, and 122–3.

65 Williams and Martin, *Domesday Book*, ff.315, f.316v.

66 Palliser, "Yorkshire Domesday."

67 Hall, "Pre-Conquest estates."

68 Rollason, *Northumbria*, pp. 270 and n.19.

69 Barlow, *Edward the Confessor* and *The Godwins*; Mason, *House of Godwine.*

70 Aird, *St. Cuthbert and the Normans*, pp. 54–9.

71 Arnold, *Symeonis monachi*, I, pp. 243–5; cf. Rollason (ed.), *Symeon*, pp. 176–7.

72 Aird, *St. Cuthbert and the Normans*, p. 57.

73 Sawyer (ed.), *Charters of Burton Abbey*, xliii–xliv; cf. Kapelle, *Norman Conquest of the North*, pp. 100–1.

74 Kapelle, *Norman Conquest of the North*, p. 98; cf. Aird, *St. Cuthbert and the Normans*, pp. 57–8.

75 Wilkinson, "Northumbrian separatism."

76   Arnold, *Symeonis monachi*, II, p. 198.
77   Krag, "Harald Hardrada."
78   Swanton, *Anglo-Saxon Chronicle*, CDE, *s.a.* 1066.
79   Bradbury, *Battle of Hastings*; Lawson, *Battle of Hastings*.
80   Aird, "Copsi."
81   Aird, "Osulf."
82   *Historia regum*, *s.a.* 1068, in Arnold, *Symeonis monachi*, II, p. 186.
83   Aird, *St. Cuthbert and the Normans*, pp. 70–5.
84   Palliser, "Domesday Book."
85   Chibnall, *Ecclesiastical History of Orderic Vitalis*, pp. 232–3.
86   *Historia regum*, *s.a.* 1069, in Arnold, *Symeonis monachi*, II, p. 189.
87   Leyser, "Walcher."
88   Rollason (ed.), *Symeon*, pp. 196–7.
89   *Cronica Monasterii Dunelmensis*, in Craster, "Red Book," 528.
90   Lewis, "Waltheof."
91   Aird, *St. Cuthbert and the Normans*, p. 97.
92   Ibid., pp. 131–6.
93   Aird, *St. Cuthbert and the Normans*, pp. 184–226; Dalton, *Conquest, Anarchy and Lordship*.
94   Barrow, *Anglo-Norman Era*.
95   Aird, *St. Cuthbert and the Normans*, pp. 227–67.
96   Barrow, "Scots in the Durham Liber Vitae," pp. 109–16.

Further Reading

There are two general studies of Northumbria: Higham's *The Kingdom of Northumbria* and Rollason's *Northumbria, 500–1100*. The northern sources for the history of Northumbria in the tenth and eleventh centuries are found in Hart, *Early Charters*; Johnson South (ed.), *Historia de Sancto Cuthberto*; Rollason et al., *Sources for York History*; and Rollason (ed.), *Symeon of Durham*. For the social and economic structure of the region, see Hadley, *The Northern Danelaw*. Recent developments in the study of the Scandinavian impact on Northumbria are well represented in two collections of essays: J. Graham-Campbell, R. A. Hall, J. Jesch, and D. N. Parsons (eds.), *Vikings and the Danelaw: Select Papers from the Proceedings of the Thirteenth Viking Congress* (Oxford, 2001) and D. M. Hadley and J. D. Richards (eds.), *Cultures in Contact: Scandinavian Settlement in England in the Ninth and Tenth Centuries* (Turnhout, 2000). For the early medieval history of Cumbria, see Phythian-Adams, *Land of the Cumbrians*. For the impact of the Norman Conquest, see Kapelle, *The Norman Conquest of the North*; Aird, *St. Cuthbert and the Normans*; and Dalton, *Conquest, Anarchy and Lordship*. Finally, for biographies of the major individuals mentioned, the reader is referred to the *Oxford Dictionary of National Biography*.

Bibliography

Abrams, L., "The conversion of the Danelaw," in J. Graham-Campbell, R. A. Hall, J. Jesch, and D. N. Parsons (eds.), *Vikings and the Danelaw: Select Papers from the Proceedings of the Thirteenth Viking Congress* (Oxford, 2001), pp. 31–44.

Abrams, L., "Edward the Elder's Danelaw," in N. J. Higham and D. H. Hill (eds.), *Edward the Elder 899–924* (London, 2001), pp. 128–43.

Aird, W. M., "Copsi, earl of Northumbria (d.1067)," *Oxford Dictionary of National Biography* (Oxford, 2004).

Aird, W. M., "Northern England or southern Scotland? The Anglo-Scottish border in the eleventh and twelfth centuries and the problem of perspective," in J. C. Appleby and P. Dalton (eds.), *Government, Religion and Society in Northern England, 1000–1700* (Stroud, 1997), pp. 27–39.

Aird, W. M., "Osulf, earl of Bamburgh (d.1067)," *Oxford Dictionary of National Biography* (Oxford, 2004).

Aird, W. M., *St. Cuthbert and the Normans: The Church of Durham, 1071–1153* (Woodbridge, 1998).

Aird, W. M., "Siward, earl of Northumbria (d.1055)," *Oxford Dictionary of National Biography* (Oxford, 2004).

Anderson, A. O., *Scottish Annals from English Chroniclers, AD 500 to 1286* (London, 1908; corrected edn., Stamford, 1991).

Arnold, T. (ed.), *Symeonis monachi opera omnia*, 2 vols. (London, 1882–5).

Barlow, F., *Edward the Confessor* (London, 1970).

Barlow, F., *The Godwins* (London, 2002).

Barrow, G. W. S., *The Anglo-Norman Era in Scottish History* (Oxford, 1980).

Barrow, G. W. S., "Scots in the Durham Liber Vitae," in D. Rollason, A. J. Piper, M. Harvey, and L. Rollason (eds.), *The Durham Liber Vitae and its Context* (Woodbridge, 2004), pp. 109–16.

Bradbury, J., *The Battle of Hastings* (Stroud, 1998).

Campbell, A. (ed.), *The Chronicle of Æthelweard* (London, 1962).

Chibnall, M. (ed.), *The Ecclesiastical History of Orderic Vitalis, Volume II, Books III and IV* (Oxford, 1969).

Coupland, S., "From poachers to gamekeepers: Scandinavian warlords and Carolingian kings," *Early Medieval Europe*, 7 (1998), 85–114.

Craster, H. H. E., "The patrimony of St. Cuthbert," *English Historical Review*, 69 (1954), 5–19.

Craster, H. H. E., "The Red Book of Durham," *English Historical Review*, 40 (1925), 504–35.

Dalton, P., *Conquest, Anarchy and Lordship: Yorkshire, 1066–1154* (Cambridge, 1994).

Darlington, R. R. and McGurk, P. (eds.), *The Chronicle of John of Worcester*, vol. II: *The Annals from 450 to 1066* (Oxford, 1995).

Davidson, M. R., "The (non)submission of the northern kings in 920," in N. J. Higham and D. H. Hills (eds.), *Edward the Elder 899–924* (London, 2001), pp. 200–11.

Davis, R. H. C., "Alfred the Great: propaganda and truth," *History*, 55 (1971), 169–82, reprinted in R. H. C. Davis, *From Alfred the Great to Stephen* (London, 1991), pp. 33–46.

Duncan, A. A. M., *The Kingship of the Scots, 842–1292: Succession and Independence* (Edinburgh, 2002).

Fernández-Armesto, F., "The survival of a notion of *Reconquista* in late tenth- and eleventh-century León," in T. Reuter (ed.), *Warriors and Churchmen in the High Middle Ages: Essays Presented to Karl Leyser* (London, 1992), pp. 123–43.

Fletcher, R. A., *Bloodfeud: Murder and Revenge in Anglo-Saxon England* (London, 2002).

Foot, S., "The historiography of the Anglo-Saxon 'nation-state,'" in L. Scales and O. Zimmer (eds.), *Power and the Nation in European History* (Cambridge, 2005), pp. 125–42.

Forte, A., Oram, R., and Pedersen, F., *Viking Empires* (Oxford, 2005).

Graham-Campbell, J., "Review article: the archaeology of Anglian and Anglo-Scandinavian York," *Early Medieval Europe*, 5: 1 (1996), 71–82.

Gransden, A., *Historical Writing in England, c.550 to c.1307* (London, 1974).

Hadley, D. M., "In search of the Vikings: the problems and the possibilities of interdisciplinary approaches," in J. Graham-Campbell, R. A. Hall, J. Jesch, and D. N. Parsons (ed.), *Vikings and the Danelaw: Select Papers from the Proceedings of the Thirteenth Viking Congress* (Oxford, 2001), pp. 13–30.

Hadley, D. M., *The Northern Danelaw: Its Social Structure, c.800–1100* (London, 2000).

Hadley, D. M., "Viking and native: re-thinking identity in the Danelaw," *Early Medieval Europe*, 11: 1 (2002), 45–70.

Hadley, D. M., *The Vikings in England: Settlement, Society and Culture* (Manchester, 2006).

Hall, D., (1989), "The sanctuary of St. Cuthbert," in G. Bonner, D. Rollason, and C. Strancliffe (eds.), *St. Cuthbert, his Cult and Community to AD 1200* (Woodbridge, 1989), pp. 425–36.

Hall, K. M., "Pre-Conquest estates in Yorkshire," in H. E. J. Le Patourel, M. H. Long, and M. F. Pickles (eds.), *Yorkshire Boundaries* (Leeds, 1993), pp. 25–38.

Hall, R. A., *Viking Age York* (London, 1994).

Hart, C., *The Early Charters of Northern England and the North Midlands* (Leicester, 1975).

Hart, C. (2004), "Wulfstan (d.955/6)," *Oxford Dictionary of National Biography* (Oxford, 2004).

Higham, N. J., *A Frontier Landscape: The North West in the Middle Ages* (Macclesfield, 2004).

Higham, N. J., *The Kingdom of Northumbria, AD 350–1100* (Stroud, 1993).

Hill, D., *An Atlas of Anglo-Saxon England* (Oxford, 1981).

Hinton, D. A., "The large towns 600–1300," in D. M. Palliser (ed.), *The Cambridge Urban History of Britain*, vol. I: *600–1540* (Cambridge, 2000), pp. 217–43.

Hudson, B. T., "Cnut and the Scottish kings," *English Historical Review*, 107 (1992), 350–60.

John, E., "The West Saxon conquest of England," in E. John, *Reassessing Anglo-Saxon England* (Manchester, 1996), pp. 83–98.

Johnson South, T. (ed.), *Historia de Sancto Cuthberto: A History of Saint Cuthbert and a Record of his Patrimony* (Woodbridge, 2002).

Kapelle, W. E., *The Norman Conquest of the North: The Region and its Transformation, 1000–1135* (London, 1979).

Kermode, J. (2000), "Northern towns," in D. M. Palliser (ed.), *The Cambridge Urban History of Britain: Volume I, 600–1540* (Cambridge, 2000), pp. 657–79.

Keynes, S., "Wulfstan I, archbishop of York (931–56)," in M. Lapidge, J. Blair, S. Keynes, and D. Scragg (eds.), *The Blackwell Encyclopaedia of Anglo-Saxon England* (Oxford, 1999), pp. 492–93.

Kirby, D. P., "Strathclyde and Cumbria: a survey of historical development to 1092," *Transactions of the Cumberland and Westmorland Antiquarian and Archaeological Society*, 62, n.s. (1962), 77–94.

Krag, C., "Harald Hardrada (1015–1066)," *Oxford Dictionary of National Biography* (Oxford, 2004).

Lawson, M. K., *The Battle of Hastings, 1066* (Stroud, 2002).

Lawson, M. K., "Cnut (d.1035)," *Oxford Dictionary of National Biography* (Oxford, 2004).

Lawson, M. K., *Cnut: The Danes in England in the Early Eleventh Century* (London, 1993).

Lewis, C. P., "Waltheof, earl of Northumbria (c.1050–1076)," *Oxford Dictionary of National Biography* (Oxford, 2004).

Leyser, H., "Walcher, earl of Northumbria (d.1080)," *Oxford Dictionary of National Biography* (Oxford, 2004).

Mason, E., *The House of Godwine: The History of a Dynasty* (London, 2004).

Meehan, B., "The siege of Durham, the battle of Carham and the cession of Lothian," *Scottish Historical Review*, 55 (1976), 1–19.

Morris, C. J. (1992), *Marriage and Murder in Eleventh-century Northumbria: A Study of "De Obsessione Dunelmi,"* University of York, Borthwick Paper, no. 82 (York, 1992).

Palliser, D. M., *The Cambridge Urban History of Britain: Volume I, 600–1540* (Cambridge, 2000).

Palliser, D. M., "Domesday Book and the 'harrying of the north,'" *Northern History*, 29 (1993), 1–23.

Palliser, D. M., "An introduction to the Yorkshire Domesday," in *Great Domesday Book: County Edition: Yorkshire*, 2 vols. (London, 1992).

Phythian-Adams, C., *Land of the Cumbrians: A Study in British Provincial Origins*, AD 400–1120 (Aldershot, 1996).

Rollason, D. W., *Northumbria, 500–1100: Creation and Destruction of a Kingdom* (Cambridge, 2003).

Rollason, D. W. (ed.), *Symeon of Durham: Libellus de Exordio atque procursu istius, hoc est Dunhelmensis ecclesie* [*Tract on the Origins and Progress of this the Church of Durham*] (Oxford, 2000).

Rollason, D. W., "The wanderings of St. Cuthbert," in D. W. Rollason (ed.), *Cuthbert: Saint and Patron* (Durham, 1987), pp. 45–59.

Rollason, D. W., Gore, D. and Fellows-Jensen, G., *Sources for York History to* AD *1100* (York, 1998).

Sawyer, P. H. (ed.), *Charters of Burton Abbey* (Oxford, 1979).

Simpson, L., "The Alfred/St. Cuthbert episode in the *Historia de Sancto Cuthberto*: its significance for mid-tenth century history," in G. Bonner, D. Rollason, and C. Stancliffe (eds.), *St. Cuthbert, his Cult and Community to* AD *1200* (Woodbridge, 1989), pp. 397–412.

Stafford, P., *The East Midlands in the Early Middle Ages* (Leicester, 1985).

Stafford, P., "Kings, kingships and kingdoms," in W. Davies (ed.), *From the Vikings to the Normans 800–1100* (Oxford, 2003), pp. 11–39.

Stafford, P., *Unification and Conquest: A Political and Social History of England in the Tenth and Eleventh Centuries* (London, 1989).

Stenton, F. M., *Anglo-Saxon England*, 3rd edn. (Oxford, 1971).

Swanton, M. J. (ed.), *The Anglo-Saxon Chronicle* (London, 1996).

Whitelock, D., "Archbishop Wulfstan, homilist and statesman," in R. W. Southern (ed.), *Essays in Medieval History* (London, 1968), pp. 42–60.

Whitelock, D., "The dealings of the kings of England with Northumbria in the tenth and eleventh centuries," in P. Clemoes (ed.), *The Anglo-Saxons: Studies in Some Aspects of their History and Presented to Bruce Dickens* (London, 1959), pp. 70–88; reprinted in D. Whitelock, *History, Law and Literature in 10th–11th Century England* (London, 1981), no. 3.

Whitelock, D. (ed. and trans.), *English Historical Documents*, vol. I: *c.500–1042* (London, 1955).

Whitelock, D. (ed.), *Sermo Lupi ad Anglos* (London, 1939); translated in D. Whitelock (ed.), *English Historical Documents* (London, 1955), vol. I, no. 240, pp. 854–9.

Wilkinson, B., "Northumbrian separatism in 1065–66," *Bulletin of the John Rylands Library*, 23 (1939), 504–26.

Williams, A., "An outing on the Dee: King Edgar at Chester, AD 973," *Medieval Scandinavia*, 14 (2004), 229–44.

Williams, A. and Martin, G. H. (eds.), *Domesday Book: A Complete Translation* (Harmondsworth, 2002).

Winchester, A. J. L., *Landscape and Society in Medieval Cumbria* (Edinburgh, 1987).

Woolf, A., *From Pictland to Alba 789–1070* (Edinburgh, 2007).

Wormald, P., *The Making of English Law: King Alfred to the Twelfth Century*, vol. I: *Legislation and its Limits* (Oxford, 1999).

Wormald, P., "Viking studies: whence and wither," in R. T. Farrell (ed.), *The Vikings* (Chichester, 1982), pp. 128–53.

Wormald, P., "Wulfstan, archbishop of York and homilist (d.1023)," *Oxford Dictionary of National Biography* (Oxford, 2004).

CHAPTER TWENTY

Southumbria

CHARLES INSLEY

The purpose of this chapter is to outline the broad narrative of the creation of the English state in the tenth and eleventh centuries and the crucial shift in the balance of power in the British Isles that this represented, and to explore some of the key related themes – ideological, ecclesiastical, dynastic, and economic – that were part of the process of the making of England.

The Making of England

Much of the historiography of the past century has dwelt on the theme of "the making of England": however, in the past 20 years, historians have sought to redress the balance of emphasis.[1] The English kingdom of the tenth century was not the product of inevitable historical forces, but of the political skill, ruthlessness, and aggression of its tenth-century kings and, above all, dynastic chance. Nevertheless, the process by which the Anglo-Saxon kingdoms and territories south of the Humber were welded into one kingdom in the tenth century is still central to our understanding of early medieval British history. The tenth and eleventh centuries saw the emergence in Southumbrian England of a state that had the potential to dominate the rest of the British Isles in a way that no single kingdom had done before. Although England came to dominate the Atlantic Archipelago during the twelfth and thirteenth centuries,[2] the beginnings of this process lay in the tenth century and the claims to pan-British overlordship that were a key part of the political program of kings such as Æthelstan (924–39) and Edgar (957/9–75).

The viking attacks and settlements of the later ninth century permanently changed the political and economic landscape of the southern English kingdoms.[3] Last man standing was the kingdom of Wessex which had, earlier in the ninth century, absorbed the kingdom of Kent. Despite several concerted viking attempts to subdue Wessex, it had emerged from the last decade of the ninth century largely intact. This was a product of a number of factors, not least a relatively stable internal dynamic, unlike Northumbria and Mercia; but, most of all, it was the political and military skill of its kings – Alfred the Great above all – that allowed Wessex to survive.

In the south and east of Britain, the new political landscape wrought by the vikings was increasingly dominated by Alfred's successors in Wessex who, in the first 40 years of the tenth century, created a new political unit, the kingdom of England, stretching from Cornwall to south Yorkshire. Alongside the creation of this new kingdom, its rulers, above all Æthelstan and, to a lesser extent, Edgar, developed a rhetoric of imperial rule over all of Britain and the beginnings of the English political and economic dominance over Britain, if not Ireland. Only hindsight, of course, tells us that the hegemony established, at least in part, by Edward (899–924), Æthelstan, and Edgar in the tenth century would endure; from a tenth-century perspective, such long-term domination of Britain was by no means inevitable, and it can be argued, for instance, that what had once been the kingdom of Northumbria was not securely part of the English kingdom until at least the twelfth century, if not much later (see chapter 19). Nevertheless, we can detect a subtle, but permanent shift in the balance of political and economic power between the north and west and the south and east of the Atlantic Archipelago. This shift was underpinned by the growing economic power of the new English kingdom and the extent to which that economy was controlled by, and harnessed to, the English state.

Despite this, the English kingdom and the embryonic hegemony established by its kings were undoubtedly fragile. The level of overlordship wielded by Æthelstan during the 930s over the rest of Britain was perhaps not attained again by an English king until Edward I.[4] Subsequent kings also articulated elaborate claims to overlordship in their charters, but only Edgar went some way toward realizing them (see chapter 19). Nor were the internal dynamics of the English kingdom as stable as its great wealth and sophisticated administration might suggest. Although historians often focus on Alfred's military and strategic defeat of the vikings, or the intellectual underpinnings of that victory, arguably Alfred's greatest achievement had been to confine the succession to the kingdom of Wessex to members of his own immediate family, ruthlessly excluding collaterals, such as his nephew Æthelwold.[5] This triumph of family over wider kin should not be underrated as an achievement, since it flew in the face of political and social custom across northern Europe. Every English king between 899 and 1014 was a descendant of Alfred in the male line. Nevertheless, this in no way means that successions between these dates were harmonious affairs. Most of the successions that followed the death of Alfred were contested, or involved the division of the kingdom between two heirs, often half-brothers. Even if the succession was contained within one family, it was a family where second and third marriages were common and dynastic tension was never far from the surface.[6]

The conquest of England by the Danish kings Swegn Forkbeard (1014) and Cnut (1016–35) in the first two decades of the eleventh century also proved that the English kingdom, for all its wealth and sophistication, was vulnerable to a renewed and arguably much more systematic viking attack, the ultimate aim of which became conquest of the entire kingdom. Contemporaries and subsequent writers blamed the king, Æthelred II "the Unready," but recent historians have, to some extent, exonerated the king from sole responsibility for the calamities of 1013–16, looking instead at the structural limitations of English royal government in the face of a sustained viking assault from the 990s and the tensions this caused, which in turn stretched political consensus within the kingdom of England to breaking point and beyond.[7] Whereas the period up to the 950s had been dominated by military campaigns, from the 950s through to the 990s, the English kingdom had faced little in the way of major external threats. It is likely that a senior figure such as Ealdorman Byrhtnoth, the hero/victim of the battle of Maldon in August 991, would have gained little military experience in his long career as an ealdorman (956–91), certainly in comparison to men of the previous two generations, for whom war was a more or less constant companion.[8]

The Danish conquest of England between 1014 and 1017 was more traumatic than most historians would credit.[9] Much scholarship over the past 50 or more years has rightly stressed the administrative and economic strength of the English kingdom: its small size meant that it could be ruled effectively, even repressively, by its kings. This administrative and economic power, though, was underpinned by ideological strength.[10] The military failings of Æthelred's kingship and the accession of Cnut in 1016 permanently tarnished this image and fractured the sense of political and ideological cohesion that had driven the English kingdom in the tenth century. In practical terms, this meant that the shared consensus within the political elite about what the English kingdom was, and what being English meant, was gone and with it automatic attachment to Alfred's family. This consensus was not reconstructed, even after the succession of one of Æthelred's sons in 1042, Edward the Confessor – and we should remember that the backers of Harald Harefoot (1036–40) had engineered the murder of another son of Æthelred, Alfred the Atheling, in 1036 (ASC, C, s.a. 1036). While the English kingdom of the mid-eleventh century appeared outwardly strong and stable, the lack of ideological consensus among the political elite, or any strong attachment to Edward's dynasty, made the kingdom vulnerable in the event of a disputed or unclear succession.[11]

When it comes to the events of 1066, attention naturally focuses on the two main protagonists, Harold Godwineson and William of Normandy, the Conqueror.[12] What should not be forgotten, though, is that 1066 was in essence a succession dispute, albeit a complicated one. In 1066 and the years immediately preceding it, there were six or seven individuals who may have felt themselves to have some sort of claim to the English throne, only two of whom were descendants of Æthelred II. If we deal in counterfactual history for a moment, had the events leading up to the Norman Conquest happened a century earlier, it seems very likely that Edgar the Atheling, a great-grandson of Æthelred II and the one "legitimate" claimant, despite his youth in 1066, would have succeeded without any problem. Other tenth-century kings, notably Eadwig, Edward the Martyr, and Æthelred himself had all succeeded to the throne at a young age. However, in 1066, the young Edgar was not even in the running.

The conquest of 1066 and the settlement of a new Norman and French elite in England in the decade afterward, coupled with the large-scale displacement of the native political elite, constituted a seismic change.[13] Despite these wholesale tenurial changes, however, the English kingdom that William I (1066–87) passed on to his son William II (1087–1100) was in many respects still an Anglo-Saxon kingdom.[14] Its administrative and economic structures had changed relatively little since 1066, and if the Norman kings brought a new level of political skill and ruthlessness to the job, they did so in a framework of ideas and ideologies of kingship established in the tenth century.

Kingship, Ideology, and Identity

England was as much an ideological construction as it was political or military. West Saxon battlefield prowess was crucial in the process and was celebrated as such, but it was underpinned by a framework of ideology that aimed to create loyalty not just to an English kingdom, but the family of Alfred as the divinely ordained kings of the English.

In large part, the ideology of the kings of England was little different from that of other early medieval kings across Europe and based extensively on the Old Testament view of kings as judges and warriors.[15] This view of kingship and, indeed, lordship, stressed the king's responsibilities as protector of his people, arbitrator in their disputes, and leader in war, in return for which kings received a variety of dues and renders, such as the obligations to build and repair bridges and fortifications that we see detailed in charters from the late eighth century on.[16]

However, rule in an early medieval society was a fragile thing: most kingdoms, including England, lacked the mechanisms of a coercive, centralized state. Southern England's small size and relative lack of difficult terrain, compared to the continental empires of Charlemagne or Otto I ("the Great"), meant that it could be ruled effectively through the institutions that did exist, such as the basic units of local government and justice, the hundreds or wapentakes (the Scandinavian equivalent of the hundred in eastern England) and the shires, along with their courts. Alongside the shire and hundred system, English kings could collect tax and organize their populations for war, as well as controlling the coin used for trade. Nevertheless, these structures could not just be imposed from above; they depended on a high degree of consent and negotiation by and with the ruled. Kings could terrorize their subjects as a strategy for ruling: even in the eleventh century, the murder of the king's housecarls in 1041 while they were tax-collecting in Worcestershire provoked three days of violent ravaging of the county as retribution (*ASC*, C, 1041). Northumbria, where southern English rule was at its weakest and least effective, for both Old English and Norman kings, was also the part of the kingdom most frequently ravaged. Ravaging was not rule, however, but an alternative to it, and was usually carried out in default of more effective engagement with northern society.

For effective rule, English kings needed to engage with local elite society: it was these men, as ealdormen and earls, thegns, members of the shire and hundred courts, bishops and abbots, who mediated English royal power in the localities. Edward, Æthelstan, or Edgar might claim to be kings over all the Anglo-Saxons, or of *Engla Lond*, but they relied on their relationships with leading regional families to make those claims real in the midlands and eastern England during the tenth century. This relationship between king and subject, ruler and ruled, might be created through mechanisms of social organization, such as local justice or the structures of kinship; it might be through patronage and reward; but it was also through persuasion and propaganda. In their charters and law codes, English kings presented themselves to their aristocracies as the divinely ordained rulers of the English and all of Britain.[17] In this, the kings of England were largely successful. Their dynastic propaganda created a very close identity between the dynasty and the kingdom: the family of Alfred were portrayed as the natural God-given rulers of this new kingdom of England.

One of the reasons why so much English historiography has focused on the "pre-existing" unity of England was the impact of the eighth-century Northumbrian monk and scholar, Bede. For Alfred and his tenth-century successors, Bede's construction of an "English people" in the *Ecclesiastical History*, with a divinely ordained destiny as a new chosen people, in the image of the Old Testament Israelites, must have seemed ideal as a way of expressing their claims to lordship over the southern English.[18] Bede in no way equated political unification with the idea of a single English people; nevertheless, this is how it was used. Alfred had the *Ecclesiastical History* translated into English as one of the texts that formed the core of his political–dynastic agenda. When placed alongside the other Latin texts that Alfred had translated, this agenda fused the notion of fortitude and triumph against the pagans, the duties of Christian leaders, both lay and ecclesiastical, and the special status of the English people as the new Israelites.[19] This narrative of a divinely ordained, highly Christian pastoral kingship, forged in adversity, was a potent one during the tenth century.

This narrative was most forcefully pushed in the *Anglo-Saxon Chronicle*, originally compiled at or close to Alfred's court, but later produced in a number of southern English monastic houses in the tenth and eleventh centuries.[20] The main purpose of the *Chronicle*, in both its earliest Alfredian phase, when it was clearly and directly linked to the court, and its later phases, when links between its various versions and the court were more diffuse, was to construct a southern English narrative which placed Wessex and the story of its kings – in particular, the family of Alfred and his predecessors – at its heart. The later versions of the *Chronicle* could be highly critical of the crown – as the compiler of the annals for 978–1016 was – but the narrative never departed from the central theme of the divine backing of the kingdom of the English.

The dissemination of these ideas might be questioned: if the *Chronicle*, royal charters, and legislation were a form of propaganda, how did they reach their audience, most of whom were neither literate nor understood Latin? The *Chronicle*, like the legislation, was in the vernacular and contained the sort of narrative material that might have been read out at great meetings of the political nation, such as the royal councils held three times per year. It is harder to prove an audience for the charters, most of which during the tenth and eleventh centuries were in complex and highly rhetorical Latin. Nevertheless, the themes of dynastic commemoration, the Christian history of the world and the place of the English within it, were common themes in these charters and were perhaps echoes of the sorts of discussions and debates had within royal councils.[21]

This was an extremely powerful and effective narrative, building a sense of cohesion and consensus among the elite of the English kingdom around the royal family. For all that tenth-century politics were probably highly factional, the legitimacy of the dynasty and its claims to lordship over all of the southern English was never seriously questioned. Disputes between members of the royal family might be bitter, as they were in 957–9, or might even spill over into violence and murder, as they did in 975, but they all happened within the context of unquestioned West Saxon dynastic legitimacy.

The same was not true in the eleventh century. Powerful though this dynastic narrative was, it depended also on the military and political prestige of the southern English kings. The extremely close identity between the royal dynasty and the kingdom was badly – perhaps fatally – damaged by the failure of Æthelred II and the collapse of English rule in 1016. For a dynasty whose prestige rested on the idea that their successes were the result of divine favor, military defeat was disastrous because it shattered the image and consensus built in the tenth century. Cnut's court, a significant number of whom were Danish, had far less emotional investment in this tenth-century sense of English identity.

The current trend in assessing Cnut's conquest of England in 1016 is to stress the continuities of his reign with that of his English predecessors and the limited nature of its impact: in the words of Cnut's most recent biographer, Ken Lawson, "The Danish conquest is relatively forgotten today . . . because it was short-lived and without significant consequences."[22] This underplays the real trauma of Cnut's conquest, which was ideological, rather than tenurial.[23] The aristocratic elite that had dominated political life in England for much of the tenth century played a much less significant role after 1020.[24] The same families had monopolized political and ecclesiastical office for over 70 years from the 930s and, whatever their factional differences, identified themselves very closely with the dynasty of Alfred. The personnel of Cnut's court and those of his successors Harald Harefoot (1036–40), Harthacnut (1040–2), and Edward "the Confessor" (1042–66) were markedly different from that of their predecessors. The family of the late tenth-century ealdorman of part of Mercia, Leofwine, might survive and prosper after 1016, but they were an exception.[25] To a very large extent, the senior aristocracy of Cnut's court were "new" men, either Englishmen who had risen to the top of the political tree, such as the family of Earl Godwine, or Danish followers of Cnut, such as Earl Ranig of south-west Mercia, Earl Siward of Northumbria, or powerful thegns such as Tofig the Proud or Osgod Clapa.[26]

The political perspective of this elite was different; there was much less ingrained attachment to Alfred's dynasty, even after the succession of Edward "the Confessor," the last surviving son of Æthelred II in 1042. They did not depend on the legitimating narratives of divine ordination that had played such a key role in the tenth century. Indeed, for a significant part of Cnut's court, their identity rested on the fact that they had overturned that dynastic legitimacy. While it is true that historians can point to continuities in the style of Cnut's kingship, Cnut was also portrayed, in the Norse praise poetry addressed to him, as conqueror of the English and their kings.[27] In the tenth century, there had been one narrative of English history, one – West Saxon – view of the past which had subsumed and all but overwritten other narratives. In the eleventh century, though, there were competing narratives and competing identities: the consensus about what England was, its regnal solidarity, which was such a marked feature of the tenth century, was completely absent after 1020. If the narratives produced during the period 1020–66 (the *Encomium* of Queen Emma and the *Life* of King Edward the Confessor) are any indication, the court culture of the Anglo-Scandinavian kings was one heavily focused on display and competition and perhaps suggests a more polarized elite society.[28] This loss of consensus and identity lies behind the disastrous failure of the English kingdom to resolve issues of succession during the reign of Edward the Confessor, especially after it became clear, possibly as early as 1051, that his marriage to Edith, daughter of Earl Godwine, was unlikely to produce children. Edward's death in 1066 was ultimately so disastrous for the English kingdom because the lack of consensus and the fragmentation of English identity meant that there were so many possible kings after him.

Church and State

As in other early medieval states, the church was an integral part of the fabric of the emerging English kingdom in the tenth and eleventh centuries. The West Saxon kings of late ninth and tenth centuries, like their Carolingian predecessors and Ottonian contemporaries, had a considerable ecclesiastical presence at court, above all in the form of senior ecclesiastics among the king's closest advisers, men such as Ælfheah of Winchester and Oda of Canterbury in the 930s to 950s, Archbishops Dunstan of Canterbury and Oswald of York and Bishop Æthelwold of Winchester between the 960s and the 980s, and Archbishop Wulfstan of York in the first two decades of the eleventh century. English kings were well aware of the power of belief and Christianity; they belonged to a society in which "holiness and power fed on each other"[29] One of the most powerful images of an English king and English king-ship in this period is that of Edgar on folio 2 of the New Minster refoundation charter of c.966, now in the British Library, in which Edgar was pictured, almost prostrate, offering up the charter to Christ.[30] The king is flanked by Saints Mary and Peter, holding a cross and cross-key (symbols of judgment and salvation), while Christ, enthroned in majesty, is flanked by angels. A sumptuous piece of art, the frontispiece also illustrates the nature of tenth-century kingship. A couplet on the adjacent folio describes Edgar as prostrate, and this, coupled with the image of Edgar himself, stresses the humility and penitential aspect of kingship.[31] However, Edgar's kingship is also juxtaposed with the imperial kingship of Christ, thus exalting Edgar's own kingship. Very similar iconographic motifs are found in contemporary Ottonian art, which is not surprising, given both the dynastic and cultural contacts between the English court and the Ottonians since Æthelstan's reign, and the Ottonian emphasis on penitential kingship.[32] This brings us to the heart of the ideology of tenth-century English kingship, which was intensely Christian but also imperial. Another image of Edgar which reinforces the highly Christian nature of tenth- and eleventh-century English kingship can be seen in the copy of the *Regularis concordia*, the monastic rule instituted under Edgar's auspices in c.970, where the king, enthroned, is flanked by the greatest churchmen of the age, St. Dunstan, archbishop of Canterbury (959–88) and St. Æthelwold, bishop of Winchester (963–84).[33]

The tenth-century church also shaped some of the more practical aspects of English kingship. Senior ecclesiastics played a major role at meetings of the royal court in shaping royal policy, and kings such as Æthelstan, Edgar, Æthelred II, and Cnut relied heavily on them. In the eleventh century, from the reign of Cnut through and beyond the Norman Conquest, this reliance was increasingly coupled with royal service as chaplains as a route to preferment. In particular, senior ecclesiastics almost certainly had a role in royal legislation, which in the tenth century was primarily concerned with articulating statements about royal power, obligations, and lordship, often with heavy religious overtones. English kings made law because the Christian model of kingship, rooted in the Old Testament, was clear about the role of the king as judge and arbiter.[34] Archbishop Wulfstan II of York was perhaps the foremost exponent of this tradition of legislation, drafting legislation for both Æthelred and Cnut, as well as being the moving force behind the former's penitential ordinance of 1009, which promulgated a national penance as a way of addressing the national sin and moral decay that had in contemporary eyes clearly brought about the return of the vikings.[35] Wulfstan also produced one of the most important pieces of early medieval political thought in his so-called *Institutes of Polity*, a meditation on the duties and responsibilities of Christian lordship.[36]

One notable feature of the tenth-century English episcopate, compared to the eleventh century, was the high number of monks on the bishops' bench. As far as twelfth-century monastic writers were concerned – men such as William of Malmesbury, John of Worcester, Hugh Candidus at Peterborough, or the compiler of the *Abingdon Chronicle* – the tenth century was a Golden Age of monasticism and one that reached its apogee in the quasi-monastic kingship of Edgar. The question of "monasticism" and the "tenth-century reform" is a difficult one in examining the role played by the church in the creation of the English kingdom, since it is often viewed through the perspectives of the twelfth century. It is much less clear whether the church reform that spread from post-Carolingian Europe to England in the middle of the tenth century should be seen in exclusively monastic terms, or whether the hard-and-fast distinction between monk and secular clerk apparent in the twelfth century was so clear in the tenth.

The so-called "anti-monastic reaction," which followed the death of Edgar in 975, was nothing of the sort, being rather a complex factional clash which involved a number of issues, including royal succession and the impact of royal multiple marriages.[37] Tied up with this was the fraught relationship between the new Benedictine foundations or refoundations of Edgar's reign and the kin of their benefactors, who sought some measure of control over monastic property.[38] The significance of these new foundations in the tenth century was that they represented a further consolidation of royal presence in Mercia. These houses, such as Pershore, Worcester, Evesham, Peterborough, Thorney, and Ramsey, were strongly identified with the West Saxon dynasty. Although royal nunneries in Wessex, such as Shaftesbury and Wilton, may have functioned as centers of dynastic memory, these Mercian abbeys were also places where Alfred's dynasty was commemorated and prayed for. The foundation or refoundation of these houses was thus an integral part of the consolidation of the English kingdom and English royal power in the later tenth century.

Wessex, Mercia, and Northumbria

It is probably legitimate to speak of a political entity called England after c.920; until then, Mercia had remained an independent kingdom, despite the terminology of the (West Saxon) *Anglo-Saxon Chronicle*, which consistently referred to its ruler, Alfred's son-in-law Æthelred, as an "ealdorman," implying his subjection to the West Saxon kings. In the fragmentary remains of a Mercian chronicle, known as the *Mercian Register*, Æthelred was simply described as "Lord of the Mercians" without any reference to West Saxon overlordship. Historians have tended to contrast the experience of Wessex and Mercia during the late ninth and early tenth centuries. Mercia is seen as a kingdom in decline, unable to resolve the segmentary nature of its royal succession (that is, various "throneworthy" dynasties and branches of dynasties) and hence exceptionally vulnerable to the threat posed by the vikings, whereas Wessex is seen as the great success story of the Viking Age, with a stable succession and poised on the edge of "greatness" as the kernel of what would become England. While there are elements of truth in this analysis, it is too simplistic. The rebellion of Alfred's nephew Æthelwold against his cousin Edward in 902–3 indicates that the succession in Wessex was potentially less stable than it seemed; nor had the aristocracy entirely bought into Alfred's attempts to contain the succession within his own branch of the family. On the other hand, although Mercia had suffered greatly at the hands of the vikings, the western part of the kingdom was still a formidable proposition, with its own rulers capable of extensive military campaigns. During the reign in Wessex of his brother-in-law Edward, Æthelred and his wife, Æthelflæd, waged campaigns against their Scandinavian neighbors, built *burhs* (fortified towns) along the strategic frontier of the River Mersey, including Thelwall and Manchester, issued charters and minted coins in their own names, with no reference to Wessex at all. The assumption that Mercia was in some sort of limbo in this period, effectively subordinate to Wessex and waiting to be incorporated into "England," cannot be sustained.[39] Æthelred and Æthelflæd's actions, in particular the foundation of the New Minster, Gloucester, along with the increased attention given to Chester and Worcester, suggest that the two were busily attempting to reorient Mercia away from its former focus in the upper Trent valley.[40] Æthelred's death in 911 changed little, for his formidable wife carried on as sole ruler of Mercia until her death in 918 (*ASC*, A, *s.a.* 918). Only then did Mercia's independent existence come to an end.

Edward used the death of Æthelflæd as an opportunity to annex Mercia and end its independent existence. Æthelflæd and Æthelred's daughter, Ælfwynn, was swiftly "deprived of all authority," in the words of the *Mercian Register* (*s.a.* 919), and incarcerated. This seems to have been followed by some sort of West Saxon aristocratic colonization of Mercia, although the sources to illuminate this process are lacking.[41] Indeed, the silence and sparseness of the sources dealing with the midlands for the period 900–925 is unlikely to be mere accident, and probably represent a deliberate attempt to suppress Mercia's early tenth-century history. However, this absence of evidence, or the language of subordination used in the *Anglo-Saxon Chronicle*, should not obscure what was almost certainly a ruthless takeover by Edward and one which, for all the silence of our sources, may have been violent. Most of the aristocratic families associated with Mercia, the east midlands, and East Anglia later in the tenth century originated in Wessex, in particular the family of Ealdorman Ælfhere, who ruled Mercia in the 970s and 980s, and the family of Ealdorman Æthelstan "Half-king," who ruled much of eastern England from the 930s to the 950s.[42]

The one exception to this seems to be the family of Wulfric Spott (fl. c.980–c.1004), whose antecedents, in particular his mother Wulfrun, seem to have been Mercian. Wulfrun's family appear to have rapidly accommodated themselves to the new regime in Mercia. An indication of the importance of this family can be seen in the will of Wulfric.[43] The will shows Wulfric to have been the owner of some 80 estates in the midlands, the bulk of which were concentrated in the north midlands, in Staffordshire, and Derbyshire.[44] In particular, a number of these estates (Doncaster, Conisborough, Beighton, Mosborough, Wales, and Thorpe Salvin) were located along the Don Valley in south Yorkshire, on the southern edge of what was in the early tenth century a major frontier zone, that between Southumbria and Northumbria.[45] We should probably regard Wulfric's family as something like "marcher" lords, a powerful midlands family entrusted by Edward, or possibly Æthelflæd, with control of this strategic area.

The campaigns of Edward and his sister in eastern England and the north midlands brought all of Southumbria under Edward's control by 920, when the *Anglo-Saxon Chronicle* (an admittedly highly partial witness) described a meeting between Edward and the rulers of northern Britain at Bakewell (*ASC*, A, *s.a.* 920). Although Edward's control over Mercia after 918 came against a background of long-term collaboration and intermarriage between Wessex and Mercia stretching back into the ninth century, Mercia itself did not cease to exist on the death of its last native rulers between 911 and 918. Edward's son Æthelstan may have been fostered at the Mercian court, and it is likely that some of Æthelstan's supporters in 924, when, according to the *Mercian Register*, he was "chosen by the Mercians as king," saw themselves as much "Mercian" as "English."[46] It is even possible that Edward envisaged some form of partition on his death since he was succeeded briefly in Wessex by another son, Ælfweard (*ASC, s.a.* 924). Ælfweard was dead within weeks and so, by dynastic accident as much as design, Æthelstan became king of both Wessex and Mercia.

Æthelstan's background raises the issue of Mercian "separatism" in the tenth century. To an extent, this is a red herring: at no point following Edward's annexation of the kingdom after 918 did the Mercians seek genuine independence from Wessex. Only once, in 1016, were the two kings of a divided England (Cnut and Edmund "Ironside") not related, and these were exceptional circumstances. Nevertheless, in 924 and again in 957, the kingdom was divided along the border between Wessex and Mercia, while the sense in which Mercia still had some sort of residual regnal identity in the early eleventh century is underpinned by the *Anglo-Saxon Chronicle* entry for 1007, which described Eadric Streona's appointment as "ealdorman of all the kingdom of Mercia"; *ASC*, D, 1007.

A more meaningful question than that of Mercian "separatism" is that of the relationship between Mercia and dynastic strategies within the royal family. Æthelstan himself had been accepted as king in Mercia before being accepted in Wessex; indeed, despite being the son of Edward the Elder's first marriage to Ecgwynn, it seems likely that Edward intended his children by his second, consecrated (i.e. "official") marriage to Ælflæd to take precedence, with Æthelstan relegated to some sort of subordinate rulership in Mercia. This distinction in the way in which Mercia appears to have been treated raises an important question about its status, inasmuch as it may have been viewed as a convenient way to deal with collateral members of the royal family. Succession by brother dominated Southumbrian politics between 924 and 978, and it is possible that Edward the Elder viewed Mercia as a way of resolving the inevitable tensions between royal brothers. These tensions are hinted at in the witness lists of royal land grants, or charters, issued in this period, where royal brothers were given a degree of prominence, especially in the reigns of Edmund (939–46) and Eadwig (955–9).[47]

The relationship between Southumbria and Northumbria in this period was complex and continually evolving, and the process by which Northumbria became part of England was a long drawn-out and often violent one.[48] Hand in hand with military campaigns went attempts to harness the support of the major religious communities of the north. Nevertheless, for much of the period up to 955, the relationship between Southumbria and Northumbria was often violent and antagonistic. When southern kings did manage to exercise some sort of overlordship, such as Æthelstan between 927 and 934, or after his great victory at *Brunanburh* in 937, it proved to be ephemeral (*ASC*, C, 937). It is not even clear whether southern English kings in this period regarded Northumbria as part of the kingdom of the English. The royal styles (titles used to describe the king) of the charters of King Eadred (946–55) seem to suggest that Northumbria was explicitly not part of England: in one charter the king is described as "most glorious king of the English, governor of the Northumbrians and the Pagans [the vikings of York?] and Emperor of the Britons," implying that Northumbria was quite distinct from England (S 550).

During the later tenth century, Northumbria – or at least its southern part – was drawn more under southern English political control. The suppression of the Scandinavian kingdom of York and the death in battle of its last king, the dramatically named Erik Bloodaxe, in the early 950s, paved the way for greater southern control of southern Northumbria.[49] A key element of this seems to have been control of the archbishopric of York (see chapter 19).

Despite increasing southern control over the north, Northumbria remained largely peripheral to England, and English royal power was always exceptionally limited there, especially north of the Tees in what had been the ancient kingdom of Bernicia. Where we can recover or reconstruct the itineraries of English kings, usually from the places of issue of royal charters, it appears that they rarely visited the north, and when they did it was generally with an army in tow. Northerners rarely visited meetings of the royal court, although it should be said that charter witness lists are not an entirely reliable guide to everyone who was present. Nevertheless, the attendance of significant numbers of northern English at court was unusual. A revealing insight is offered by the charter that confirmed, after some wrangling, the will of the Essex thegn Æthelric of Bocking in the 990s, which refers to the council at Cookham, in Berkshire, where Æthelric's will was debated: "all the thegns gathered there from far and wide, both West Saxons and Mercians, Danes and English" (S 939). There is no mention of Northumbrians. In the final analysis, southern lordship over Northumbria was always limited and frequently problematic. The crisis of 1065, in which the Northumbrians rebelled against their earl, Tostig, was caused, in part, by northern rejection of Tostig's attempt to impose a greater level of lordship on the north, in particular taxation and West Saxon law.[50] William I found the north as intractable as his predecessors. Revolts in the north after 1066 were as much a rejection of rule from southern England as of the Normans. As late as 1085, William ravaged much of north-eastern England in anticipation of its invasion by the Danes (*ASC, s.a.* 1085). The north was no easier to rule from the south in 1087 than it had been a century earlier.

The Economy

Much of the discussion so far has been about the creation of a single, more or less unified English kingdom south of the River Humber during the tenth and eleventh centuries. This has been described largely in political and religious terms. However, linked to the creation of the English kingdom was the decisive shift in the economic center of gravity of the British Isles during this period toward the south-east. England in 1100 was a wealthier, more diverse, more monetized, and more productive economy than the Southumbrian kingdoms had been in 900.[51] More importantly, it was much wealthier, more monetized, and more productive in 1100 than its neighbors to the north and west at the same date, and was far more urbanized.[52] In other words, there had been developments in southern England not paralleled, or at least, not in the same way, elsewhere in the Atlantic Archipelago.

The question here is the extent to which the kings of England were passive but lucky onlookers of a process over which they had no control, or actively involved in driving these economic developments. In particular, three issues are worth pursuing: manorialization and the intensification of the agricultural economy; *burhs*, towns, and trade; and the coinage. The process by which the later medieval agricultural landscape of midland and southern England came into being during the ninth to the twelfth centuries – manorialization – is still imperfectly understood, and it is clear that it did not happen in a uniform way.[53] What seems clear is that it was a process of agricultural reorganization over which English kings had little direct control, except on their own estates. On a very basic level, what can be seen is a shift from large estates with scattered populations to a world of smaller, more intensively farmed estates with concentrated populations and an economy geared toward producing a much greater surplus.[54] What emerged by the twelfth and thirteenth centuries was a highly regional landscape in southern England: a belt of territory running from the Humber down through the east and west midlands to the south coast, characterized by nucleated settlements and relatively compact estates. To the east, in Lincolnshire, East Anglia, and Kent, the agricultural landscape retained a more dispersed pattern, with larger estates. To the west and the south-west, the geography also militated against the formation of compact estates and nucleated settlement.

What was driving these changes is unclear. Population change may have put more pressure on resources and hence the need for more intensive farming.[55] Alternatively, the process may have begun with an intensification of lordship by lay and ecclesiastical landlords in the ninth century, perhaps related to the emergence of a more stratified aristocracy during this period.[56] The archaeological and documentary record seem to support this view. Excavations of thegnly sites, such as Goltho, in Lincolnshire, or Raunds Furnell in Northamptonshire, show the building of new aisled halls in the later ninth and tenth centuries as these places became the centers of new estates.[57] The eleventh-century treatise on ranks and status known as *Gethyncho* also refers to this process, describing a thegn who had five hides of land – a relatively small estate – as possessing a hall, a bell-tower, and a gate; that is, some form of pallisaded enclosure (*EHD*, I, 468–71). This, then, was a process well under way during the tenth and eleventh centuries, and one that would not be complete until the late twelfth or early thirteenth century. Nevertheless, if the kings of England had little to do with manorialization as such, they were certainly its beneficiaries, in terms of a much richer agricultural economy which they could tax and which could service a growing, if still small, urban population.[58]

Two areas where English kings had a direct involvement were in the growth of towns in Southumbrian England and in their control of coinage. There were, of course, towns in early and mid-Anglo-Saxon England. However, they were relatively small in number and often functioned as largely political or ecclesiastical centers. There were also a number of trading towns – the *emporia* – such as *Hamwic*, under modern Southampton, *Lundenwic*, in the area around the Strand and Aldwych, and *Gyppeswic*, modern Ipswich.[59] However, unlike later towns, these settlements functioned largely as entrepôts for high-status trade and exchange, with virtually no local hinterland. This pattern was dislocated during the ninth century, partly, but not entirely, as a result of viking activity.[60] One of the West Saxon responses to the vikings during this period was to organize the fortification of key strategic locations, some of which, for instance Exeter, were existing towns, but some of which – Wallingford, for example – were not.[61] These places were fortified as a means of containing and limiting the possibility of viking incursions into the heart of Wessex. The main witness to this reorganization of defense is an early tenth-century document known as the *Burghal Hidage*, which lists the *burhs* and their defensive requirements.[62] Although a number of *burhs* flourished and later became towns, many did not and were clearly abandoned once the viking threat had receded.

What Alfred and his successors were *not* doing was initiating a policy of urbanization; their need was purely military. Nevertheless, the *burhs*, as well as those built or fortified later in the midlands by Æthelred and Æthelflæd, and those towns occupied by Scandinavian settlers in the north-east midlands, provided a means for tenth- and eleventh-century kings to consolidate their control over internal trade.[63] *Burhs* became the location for royal mints and for local administration and jurisdictions. Commercial activity over 20 shillings within *burhs* was subject to royal regulation; Æthelstan, Edgar, and Cnut all legislated to control burghal markets.[64] This in itself was nothing new: earlier lords who had controlled towns had sought to exploit commercial activity; the archbishops of Canterbury had levied tolls at Fordwich, effectively the port for Canterbury, since the eighth century. What was new in the tenth century was the relatively systematic way in which commercial activity was regulated and that it was done at the behest of the state.

Further royal involvement in trade can be seen in the intensification of royal control over the coinage, a process linked to the development of the *burhs*. Although earlier coinages had been minted in the name of the king – for instance, Offa's silver penny coinage in Mercia – control over it was limited.[65] Æthelstan's Grateley decrees stipulated that coin should be minted in *burhs*.[66] By locating mints in *burhs*, Æthelstan and his successors placed royal minting in spaces controlled by the king. Issues of coin in early tenth-century England still had regional characteristics, especially in the midlands, but the coin was of a consistent weight.

Significant change came with Edgar's 973 coin legislation which instituted much greater central control of dies and a cycle of recoinages, in which old coin was recalled, melted down, and reminted in a new issue.[67] This, like many other things in tenth-century England, was based on earlier Carolingian custom, in particular the *renovatio monetae*, instituted by the 864 Edict of Pîtres.[68] What Edgar achieved was a standard, kingdom-wide penny, bearing the king's head and the name of the moneyer. It seems likely that the main reason for monetary reform was to assist in the payment of tax, especially after the revival of Danish raids on England in the last decade of the tenth century. The need for large-scale regular tax to pay for mercenaries by the end of the first decade of the eleventh century seems to have led to a reduction in the weight of the penny, highlighting the ability of the crown to control the amount of silver bullion in circulation in response to economic circumstances.[69]

The increasing amount of coin in circulation during the tenth and eleventh centuries is likely to be indicative of more than just the demands of royal taxation. This is not to say that tenth- and eleventh-century England was a cash economy. The value of a sheep at 2d suggests that the silver penny was hardly small change, and that most of the population may have encountered pennies only rarely.[70] What can be said is that, by the end of the eleventh century, commercial activity within England was increasingly dominated by cash, while the growing role of towns as market centers for rural hinterlands was also drawing coin into the rural, agrarian economy.[71] It is perhaps also significant that what was probably a very lively property market in tenth- and eleventh-century England was expressed in cash terms.[72] English kings were not initiating economic growth or driving economic developments, but, through their control of coin and towns, they were certainly able to take advantage of growth and harness it to the state.

Conclusion

Although this chapter has specifically rejected traditional views of the "making" of England, the creation of a single southern English kingdom, which, by the end of the eleventh century, was extremely wealthy and effectively governed, was of huge significance for the rest of the Atlantic Archipelago. The claims of England's kings to a wider British hegemony were equally important. Ultimately, the tenth- and eleventh-century English kingdom lacked the capacity to mobilize the resources to enforce these claims, but it created a framework of pan-British ideology seized on by the Anglo-Norman and Angevin kings of England who, in the twelfth and thirteenth centuries, unleashed wars of conquest on their northern and western neighbors.

Despite England's wealth and effective government, it was also in some respects extremely fragile and, at its physical extremities, royal power was weak. English kings, both Anglo-Saxon and Norman, struggled with the difficult problems of ruling Northumbria from the south: in terms of effective political control, England did not extend much beyond the Humber. England's tenth-century kings and their ecclesiastical advisers had created a strong sense of dynastic and regnal identity to legitimize what was a process of conquest and annexation, but this dynastic cohesion was vulnerable. The succession disputes of the tenth century were less damaging than they might have been, a piece of luck largely due to the tendency for Alfred's descendants to die young. The conquest of the kingdom by Cnut was disastrous from this point of view, however effective Cnut was as king. In the final analysis, the regnal solidarity established by the tenth-century kings was only re-established after the Norman Conquest, when William I, William II, and Henry I, with a new and largely Norman political elite, but building on the traditions of their Anglo-Saxon predecessors, refashioned the monarchy as the focus for political solidarity and identity.

Notes

1   See chapter 1 of this volume for discussion of English historiography of this period.
2   Davies, *First English Empire* and "The state: the tyranny of a concept"; Frame, *Political Development of the British Isles.*
3   Brooks, "England in the ninth century"; Keynes, "The Vikings in England."
4   Davies, *First English Empire*, pp. 4–53; Wood, "The making of King Aethelstan's empire."
5   Keynes and Lapidge, *Alfred the Great*, pp. 173–8.
6   Stafford, "Political ideas."
7   Keynes, *Diplomas of King Æthelred*, pp. 154–231; Stafford, "The reign of Æthelred II".
8   Abels, "Byrhtnoth."
9   Fleming, *Kings and Lords in Conquest England*; Lawson, *Cnut*, p. 214.
10 Wormald, *"Engla Lond."*
11 Baxter, "The earls of Mercia"; Fleming, *Kings and Lords in Conquest England*, pp. 53–103.
12 Bates, "William I"; Fleming, "Harold II."
13 Crouch, *The Normans*, pp. 87–128; Golding, *Conquest and Colonisation*; Williams, *The English and the Norman Conquest.*
14 Campbell, "Observations" and "The significance of the Anglo-Norman state"; Warren, *Governance*, pp. 25–55.
15 Leyser, *Medieval Germany and its Neighbours*, pp. 73–104.

16 Brooks, "The development of military obligations."
17 Insley, "Where did all the charters go?," 111–20; Keynes, "Royal government and the written word"; Wormald, *Making of English Law*, and "The uses of literacy in Anglo-Saxon England."
18 Smyth, "The emergence of English identity"; Wormald, "*Engla Lond.*"
19 Keynes and Lapidge, *Alfred the Great*, pp. 28–35; Nelson, "The political ideas of Alfred of Wessex"; Whitelock, "The prose of Alfred's reign."
20 See chapter 3; *EHD*, I, 109–25; Lapidge et al., *Blackwell Encyclopedia*, pp. 35–6.
21 Insley, "Assemblies and charters" and "Where did all the charters go?"
22 Lawson, *Cnut*, p. 214.
23 Fleming, *Kings and Lords in Conquest England*, pp. 21–52; Mack, "Changing thegns"; Williams, "'Cockles amongst the Wheat.'"
24 Fleming, *Kings and Lords in Conquest England*, pp. 48–52.
25 Baxter, "The earls of Mercia."
26 Fleming, *Kings and Lords in Conquest England*, p. 47; Insley, "Where did all the charters go?," 122–4.
27 Townend, "Contextualizing the *Knútsdrápur*" and "Norse poets and English kings."
28 Fleming, "The new wealth"; Insley, "Where did all the charters go?," 123–6; Tyler, "'The eyes of the beholders.'"
29 Stafford, *Unification and Conquest*, p. 186.
30 S 745; British Library, Cotton Vespasian A. viii.
31 Deshman, *Benedictional*, pp. 195–6, and "*Christus rex*," 379–81, 399–401; Gameson, *The Role of Art*, pp. 6–7; Kharkov, *Ruler Portraits*, pp. 84–118.
32 Althoff, *Otto III*, pp. 132–40.
33 Kharkov, *Ruler Portraits*, pp. 93–9.
34 Wormald, *Making of English Law*, pp. 416–84.
35 Ibid., pp. 330–66; see also *EHD*, I, 928–34 for Wulfstan's indictment of contemporary English society, the famous "sermon of the Wolf."
36 Swanton, *Anglo-Saxon Prose*, pp. 87–201; For Wulfstan, see Wormald, "Wulfstan."
37 Stafford, *Unification and Conquest*, pp. 56–9, 188–91.
38 Ibid., pp. 188–91.
39 Costambeys, "Æthelflæd"; Stafford, "Political women," pp. 45–9.
40 Heighway, "Anglo-Saxon Gloucester" and "Gloucester and the New Minster."
41 See the fragmentary *Mercian Annals* incorporated into the B and C versions of the *Anglo-Saxon Chronicle* and collectively known as the *Mercian Register* (*EHD*, I, 110).
42 Hart, "Æthelstan Half-king"; Stafford, *Unification and Conquest*, p. 38; Williams, "Ælfhere."
43 S 1536; Sawyer, *Charters of Burton Abbey*, no. 29.
44 Ibid.
45 Sawyer, *Charters of Burton Abbey*, pp. xvi–xvii.
46 *Mercian Register*, s.a. 924 (*EHD*, I, 199); Foot, "Æthelstan."
47 Stafford, *Unification and Conquest*, p. 43.
48 For a full discussion of the relationship between Southumbria and Northumbria, see chapter 19.
49 Costambeys, "Erik Bloodaxe."
50 Aird, *St. Cuthbert and the Normans*, p. 57.
51 Griffiths, "Exchange, trade and urbanization," pp. 81–2.
52 Ibid., pp. 81–2, 86–104.
53 Fleming, "Lords and labour"; Stafford, *Unification and Conquest*, pp. 201–3.
54 Fleming, "Lords and labour," pp. 109–13.
55 Faith, *The English Peasantry*.
56 Aston, "The origins of the manor"; Fleming, "Lords and labour," pp. 109–10.

57   Beresford, "Goltho Manor."
58   Griffiths, "Exchange, trade and urbanization," pp. 97–9.
59   Hinton, "The large towns."
60   Griffiths, "Exchange, trade and urbanization," pp. 82–4.
61   *ASC*, A, *s.a.* 877, describes Exeter as having a fortress.
62   Biddle and Hill, "Late Saxon planned towns"; Brooks, "The administrative background"; Hill, "Gazetteer."
63   Griffiths, "Exchange, trade and urbanization," pp. 95–6; Stafford, *Unification and Conquest*, pp. 212–14.
64   Griffiths, "Exchange, trade and urbanization," p. 97.
65   Ibid, p. 79.
66   *EHD* I, 384 (II Æthelstan, ch. 14).
67   *EHD* I, 258; Dolley and Metcalf, "The reform"; see Stewart, "Coinage and recoinage" for a critique of Dolley's scheme; see also Stafford, *Unification and Conquest*, pp. 141–2.
68   Nelson, *Charles the Bald*, pp. 30–1, 33, 207–9.
69   Blackburn, "Æthelred's coinage."
70   Stafford, *Unification and Conquest*, p. 214.
71   Ibid.
72   Campbell, "The sale of land."

Further Reading

There is an enormous amount of literature dealing with England in the tenth and eleventh centuries. Probably still the best and most accessible introduction to the period, along with the rest of Anglo-Saxon England, is Campbell et al. (eds.), *The Anglo-Saxons*. The best account of the politics of the period is Stafford, *Unification and Conquest*. There is a considerable amount of primary source material available, in both print and online media: the translations and extracts collected in the first two volumes of *EHD* are still perhaps the easiest introduction to the corpus. Most of the major primary sources can be found there, although not necessarily in their entirety. For royal law, the work of the late Patrick Wormald, *The Making of English Law*, is indispensable. For charters, Keynes, *The Diplomas of King Æthelred* is still the benchmark for modern discussions of charters. It also contains one of the best accounts of the politics of the troubled reign of Æthelred II. The Norman Conquest also, inevitably, is extremely well covered. A good, accessible general introduction is provided by Golding, *Conquest and Colonisation*. D. Bates, *William the Conqueror* (London, 1989) is the best modern account of William's reign. Williams, *The English and the Norman Conquest* is an important book which explores the experience of the English aristocracy after 1066. Economic history of the period has attracted less attention from the historian. Two important works are R. Hodges, *The Anglo-Saxon Achievement: Archaeology and the Beginnings of English Society* (London, 1989) and C. Dyer, *Making a Living in the Middle Ages: The People of Britain 850–1520* (London, 2002). For biographies of the major lay and ecclesiastical figures of the period, the reader is directed to the *Oxford Dictionary of National Biography* (Oxford, 2004).

Bibliography

Abels, R., "Byrhtnoth, magnate and soldier (d. 991)," *Oxford Dictionary of National Biography* (Oxford, 2004).
Aird, W. M., *St. Cuthbert and the Normans: The Church of Durham, 1071–1153* (Woodbridge, 1998).
Althoff, G., *Otto III* (Darmstadt, 1996), trans. P. G. Jestice (Philadelphia, 2003).
Aston, T. H., "The origins of the manor in England," in T. H. Aston (ed.), *Social Relations and Ideas: Essays in Honour of R. H. Hilton* (Leicester, 1983), pp. 1–43.

Bates, D., "William I, king of England and duke of Normandy (1027/8–1087)," *Oxford Dictionary of National Biography* (Oxford, 2004).

Baxter, S., "The earls of Mercia and their commended men in the mid-eleventh century," *Anglo-Norman Studies*, 23 (2001), 23–46.

Beresford, G., "Goltho Manor, Lincs.: the buildings and their surrounding defences," *Anglo-Normans Studies*, 4 (1981), 13–36.

Biddle, M. and Hill, D., "Late Saxon planned towns," *Antiquaries Journal*, 51 (1971), 70–85.

Blackburn, M. A. S., "Æthelred's coinage and the payment of tribute," in D. Scragg (ed.), *The Battle of Maldon, AD 991* (Oxford, 1991), pp. 156–99.

Brooks, N., "The administrative background to the Burghal Hidage," in D. Hill and A. R. Rumble (eds.), *The Defence of Wessex: The Burghal Hidage and Anglo-Saxon Fortifications* (Manchester, 1996), pp. 128–50.

Brooks, N., "England in the ninth century: the crucible of defeat," *Transactions of the Royal Historical Society*, 5th series, 29 (1979), 1–20.

Brooks, N., "The development of military obligations in eighth- and ninth-century England," in P. Clemoes and K. Hughes (eds.), *England before the Conquest: Studies in Primary Sources Presented to Dorothy Whitelock* (Cambridge, 1971), pp. 69–84.

Campbell, J., "Observations on English government from the tenth to the twelfth century," *Transactions of the Royal Historical Society*, 5th series, 25 (1975), 39–54, reprinted in J. Campbell, *Essays in Anglo-Saxon History* (London, 1986), pp. 155–70.

Campbell, J., "The sale of land and the economics of power in early England: problems and possibilities," *The Haskins Society Journal: Studies in Medieval History*, 1 (1989), 23–37.

Campbell, J., "The significance of the Anglo-Norman state in the administrative history of Western Europe," in J. Campbell, *Essays in Anglo-Saxon History* (London, 1986), pp. 171–90.

Campbell, J., "Some agents and agencies of the late Anglo-Saxon state," in J. C. Holt (ed.), *Domesday Studies* (Woodbridge, 1987), pp. 201–18.

Campbell, J., John, E., and Wormald, P., *The Anglo-Saxons* (London, 1982).

Costambeys, M., "Æthelflæd, ruler of the Mercians (d. 918)," *Oxford Dictionary of National Biography* (Oxford, 2004).

Costambeys, M., "Erik Bloodaxe, Viking leader and King of Northumbria (d. 954)," *Oxford Dictionary of National Biography* (Oxford, 2004).

Crouch, D., *The Normans: The History of a Dynasty* (London, 2002).

Davies, R. R., *Conquest, Coexistence and Change: Wales 1063–1415* (Oxford, 1987).

Davies, R. R., *The First English Empire: Power and Identities in the British Isles 1093–1343* (Oxford, 2000).

Davies, R. R., "The state: the tyranny of a concept?," *Journal of Historical Sociology*, 15 (2002), 71.

Davies, W. (ed.), *From the Vikings to the Normans* (Oxford, 2003).

Deshman, R., *The Benedictional of Æthelwold* (Princeton, NJ, 1995).

Deshman, R., "*Christus Rex et Magi Reges*: kingship and Christology in Ottonian and Anglo-Saxon art," *Frühmittelalterliche Studien*, 10 (1976), 367–405.

Dolley, R. H. M. and Metcalf, D. M., "The reform of the English coinage under Eadgar," in R. H. M. Dolley (ed.), *Anglo-Saxon Coins: Studies Presented to F. M. Stenton* (London, 1961), pp. 136–68.

Faith, R., *The English Peasantry and the Growth of Lordship* (London, 1997).

Fleming, R., "Harold II, king of England (1022/3?–1066)," *Oxford Dictionary of National Biography* (Oxford, 2004).

Fleming, R., *Kings and Lords in Conquest England* (Cambridge, 1991).

Fleming, R., "Lords and labour," in W. Davies (ed.), *From the Vikings to the Normans* (Oxford, 2003), pp. 107–37.

Fleming, R., "The new wealth, the new rich and the new political style in late Anglo-Saxon England," *Anglo-Norman Studies*, 23 (2001), 1–22.

Foot, S., "Æthelstan, king of England (893/4–939)," *Oxford Dictionary of National Biography* (Oxford, 2004).

Frame, R., *The Political Development of the British Isles, 1100–1400* (Oxford, 1995).

Gameson, R., *The Role of Art in the Late Anglo-Saxon Church* (Oxford, 1995).

Golding, B., *Conquest and Colonisation: The Normans in Britain, 1066–1100* (Basingstoke, 1994).

Griffiths, D., "Exchange, trade and urbanization," in W. Davies (ed.), *From the Vikings to the Normans* (Oxford, 2003), pp. 73–104.

Hart, C. R., "Æthelstan Half-king (fl. 932–56)," *Oxford Dictionary of National Biography* (Oxford, 2004).

Heighway, M., "Anglo-Saxon Gloucester to AD 1000," in M. L. Faull (ed.), *Studies in Late Anglo-Saxon Settlement* (London, 1984), pp. 35–53.

Heighway, M., "Gloucester and the New Minster of St. Oswald," in D. Hill and N. J. Higham (eds.), *Edward the Elder* (Manchester, 2001), pp. 102–11.

Hill, D. (ed.), *Ethelred the Unready*, British Archaeological Reports, British series 59 (Oxford, 1978).

Hill, D., "Gazetteer of Burghal Hidage sites," in D. Hill and A. R. Rumble (eds.), *The Defence of Wessex: The Burghal Hidage and Anglo-Saxon Fortifications* (Manchester, 1996), pp. 189–231.

Hinton, D. A., "The large towns 600–1300," in D. M. Palliser (ed.), *The Cambridge Urban History of Britain* I: *600–1540* (Cambridge, 2000), pp. 217–43.

Insley, C., "Assemblies and charters in late Anglo-Saxon England," in P. S. Barnwell and M. Mostert (eds.), *Political Assemblies in the Earlier Middle Ages* (Turnhout, 2003), pp. 47–60.

Insley, C., "Politics, conflict and kinship in early eleventh-century Mercia," *Midlands History*, 25 (2000), 28–42.

Insley, C., "Where did all the charters go? Anglo-Saxon charters and the new politics of the eleventh century," *Anglo-Norman Studies*, 24 (2002), 109–27.

Keynes, S., "Æthelred, king of England (c.966x8–1016)," *Oxford Dictionary of National Biography* (Oxford, 2004).

Keynes, S., *The Diplomas of King Æthelred "the Unready" 978–1016: A Study in their Use as Historical Evidence* (Cambridge, 1980).

Keynes, S., "Royal government and the written word in late Anglo-Saxon England," in R. McKitterick (ed.), *The Uses of Literacy in Early Medieval Europe* (Cambridge, 1990), pp. 226–57.

Keynes, S., "The Vikings in England," in P. H. Sawyer (ed.), *The Oxford Illustrated History of the Vikings* (Oxford, 1997), pp. 44–82.

Keynes, S. and Lapidge, M. (trans.), *Alfred the Great: Asser's Life of King Alfred and Other Contemporary Sources* (Harmondsworth, 1983).

Kharkov, C. E., *The Ruler Portraits of Anglo-Saxon England* (Woodbridge, 2004).

Lapidge, M., Blair, W. J., Keynes, S. D., and Scragg, D. (eds.), *The Blackwell Encyclopaedia of Anglo-Saxon England* (Oxford, 1999).

Lawson, M. K., *Cnut: The Danes in England in the Early Eleventh Century* (London, 1993).

Leyser, K. J., *Medieval Germany and its Neighbours 900–1250* (London, 1982).

Loyn, H. R., "The hundred in England," in H. R. Loyn, *Society and Peoples: Studies in the History of England and Wales, c.600–1200* (Westfield, 1992), pp. 113–34.

Mack, K., "Changing thegns: Cnut's conquest and the English aristocracy," *Albion*, 16 (1984), 375–87.

Nelson, J. L., *Charles the Bald* (London, 1992).

Nelson, J. L., "The political ideas of Alfred of Wessex," in A. J. Duggan (ed.), *Kings and Kingship in Medieval Europe* (London, 1993), pp. 125–58.

Sawyer, P. H., *Anglo-Saxon Charters: An Annotated List and Bibliography* (London, 1968).

Sawyer, P. H. (ed.), *Charters of Burton Abbey*, Anglo-Saxon Charters II (Oxford, 1979).

Smyth, A. P., "The emergence of English Identity, 700–1000," in A. P. Smyth (ed.), *Medieval Europeans: Studies in Ethnic Identity and National Perspectives in Medieval Europe* (Basingstoke, 1998), pp. 24–52.

Stafford, P., "Political ideas in late tenth-century England: charters as evidence," in P. Stafford, J. L. Nelson, and J. Martindale (eds.), *Law, Laity and Solidarities: Essays in Honour of Susan Reynolds* (Manchester, 2001), pp. 68–82.

Stafford, P., "Political women in Mercia, eighth to early tenth centuries," in M. Brown and C. Farr (eds.), *Mercia: An Anglo-Saxon Kingdom in Europe* (London, 2001), pp. 35–49.

Stafford, P., "The reign of Æthelred II: a study in the limitations on royal policy and action," in D. Hill (ed.), *Ethelred the Unready*, British Archaeological Reports, British series 59 (Oxford, 1978), pp. 15–46.

Stafford, P., *Unification and Conquest: A Political and Social History of England in the Tenth and Eleventh Centuries* (London, 1989).

Stewart, I., "Coinage and recoinage after Edgar's reform," in K. Jonsson (ed.), *Studies in Late Anglo-Saxon Coinage in Memory of Bror Emil Hildebrand*, Numismatiska Meddelanden, 35 (1990), pp. 455–85.

Swanton, M. J., *Anglo-Saxon Prose*, 2nd edn. (London, 1993).

Townend, M., "Contextualizing the *Knútsdrápur*: Skaldic praise-poetry at the court of Cnut," *Anglo-Saxon England*, 30 (2001), 145–79.

Townend, M., "Norse poets and English kings: Skaldic performance in Anglo-Saxon England," *Offa*, 58 (2001), 269–75.

Tyler, E. M., "'The eyes of the beholders were dazzled': treasure and artifice in the *Encomium Emmae Reginae*," *Early Medieval Europe*, 8: 2 (1998), 247–70.

Warren, W. L., *The Governance of Anglo-Norman and Angevin England, 1066–1272* (London, 1987).

Whitelock, D. (ed. and trans.), *English Historical Documents*, vol. I: *c.500–1042*, 2nd edn. (London, 1979).

Whitelock, D., "The prose of Alfred's reign," in E. G. Stanley (ed.), *Continuations and Beginnings* (Oxford, 1966), pp. 67–103.

Williams, A., "Ælfhere (d. 983)," *Oxford Dictionary of National Biography* (Oxford, 2004).

Williams, A., "'Cockles amongst the wheat': Danes and English in the western midlands in the first half of the eleventh century," *Midland History*, 11 (1986), 1–22.

Williams, A., *The English and the Norman Conquest* (Woodbridge, 1995).

Wood, M., "The making of King Aethelstan's empire: an English Charlemagne," in P. Wormald, D. Bullough, and R. Collins (eds.), *Ideal and Reality in Frankish and Anglo-Saxon Society: Studies Presented to J. M. Wallace-Hadrill* (Oxford, 1983), pp. 251–72.

Wormald, P., "Æthelred the lawmaker," in D. Hill (ed.), *Ethelred the Unready*, British Archaeological Reports, British series 59 (Oxford, 1978), pp. 47–80.

Wormald, P., "*Engla Lond*: the making of an allegiance," *Journal of Historical Sociology*, 7 (1994), 1–24.

Wormald, P., "The making of England," *History Today* (February 1995), 26–32.

Wormald, P., *The Making of English Law: King Alfred to the Twelfth Century*, vol. I: *Legislation and its Limits* (Oxford, 1999).

Wormald, P., "The uses of literacy in Anglo-Saxon England and its neighbours," *Transactions of the Royal Historical Society*, 5th series, 27 (1977), 95–114.

Wormald, P., "Wulfstan, archbishop of York and homilist (d.1023)," *Oxford Dictionary of National Biography* (Oxford, 2004).

CHAPTER TWENTY-ONE

Wales and West Britain

JOHN REUBEN DAVIES

Background

By the tenth century, the Britons and the English had long since come to define themselves as peoples in opposition to each other. These peoples, as Bede so clearly explained, could be identified by their language (*HE*, i. 1). The linguistically diverse western Britain of the early sixth century, where British, Irish, and Latin were spoken, had homogenized into a culturally – but not territorially – coherent zone containing speakers of British alone. Across the Channel, meanwhile, quite a different process had occurred. At the beginning of the eighth century, two linguistically different population groups, one speaking the West Germanic Frankish language, the other a dialect of spoken vulgar Latin, were nonetheless both accepted as Franks. In this way, the defining characteristics of nationality became non-linguistic in continental Europe, but linguistic in Britain: in other words, the distinction was not territorial but cultural. Yet, as we shall see, by the tenth century, any sense of cultural solidarity among the Britons of Cornwall, Wales, and the north had little, if any, bearing on political decision-making and development.

The Britons of Wales and Cornwall, from at least as early as the sixth century, were governed by kings who ruled over territorial kingdoms. In the south-western peninsula, the west British kingdom of Dumnonia had fallen under West Saxon control and ceased to exist around the beginning of the ninth century, to the extent that, by the tenth century, nearly all the place-names were English rather than British. The kingdom of Cornwall, on the other hand, remained as an independent British territory in the face of pressure from Wessex, cut off from fellow Brittonic-speakers in Wales and Brittany by the sea and the West Saxons. The four principal Welsh kingdoms, meanwhile, roughly inhabited the four corners of Wales: Gwynedd in the north-west, Powys in the north-east, Glywysing in the south-east, and Dyfed in the south-west. In the central belt we also know of Ceredigion on the west coast, and Brycheiniog to its east. During the ninth century, Powys was absorbed into Gwynedd; Ceredigion came under the control of Gwynedd's rulers too, but was later taken into the possession of Dyfed. In this way, the lesser kingdoms lost their political identities, but they held on to their character as distinct territories.

Important in these Welsh political adjustments was the dynastic change that occurred in ninth-century Gwynedd. In 825, Merfyn "Frych" ap Gwriad (d.844) became the first of a new royal line in Gwynedd, and his son, Rhodri "Mawr" (d.878), as king of Gwynedd, added Ceredigion and Powys to the territories under his rule. In time, by a combination of inheritance, marriage alliance, and conquest, Rhodri's sons and their descendants took control of all the territories of the north and south, with the exception of Glywysing.[1] So it was that the kingships of Gwynedd and Dyfed came to dominate Wales, and were held by branches of the same north-Welsh dynasty, ultimately descended from Merfyn Frych and his son Rhodri Mawr. Down to the Edwardian conquest of 1282–3 the rulers of north and south Wales traced their descent from Rhodri; and as late as the fifteenth century, the court poet of Owain Glyn Dŵr (d.1415) claimed this lineage for his master.[2]

The advent of Merfyn Frych and his line coincided with a period in which the Welsh territories were enduring repeated invasions from Mercia. During the eighth century, the Mercian kings had started to make assaults on the Welsh, their forces reaching deep into the south-west. This kind of aggression is mentioned in the annalistic sources 18 times before 1039, and was so far successful that large areas of north Wales came into Mercian hands during the ninth century, probably as far as the River Conwy.[3]

The Cornish kingdom was also suffering sustained attacks during the ninth century, but from its neighbors, the West Saxons.[4] We may infer that overlordship, at least, had been exercised over the Cornish since the early to mid-ninth century, for Kenstec became the first Cornish bishop to make profession of obedience to Canterbury in 833 × 870; and at this time the bishop of Sherborne had been charged to make an annual visitation of Cornwall to root out the errors of the Cornish church.[5] In fact, it was probably during the reign of Ecgberht that Cornwall came under West Saxon control. We find no further conflicts between the Cornish and the West Saxons after Ecgberht's reign until the time of King Æthelstan, but in the meantime, King Alfred was disposing of Cornish lands in his will as though they were part of his kingdom.[6]

Among the Britons of Wales, the *Anglo-Saxon Chronicle* speaks of north Welsh subjection to the Mercian king, Burgred (d.?874), in 853, following a joint Mercian and West Saxon campaign.[7] In 878, further conflict with the "Saxons" resulted in Rhodri's death by strangling.[8] To the extent that the reality of a politically united Anglo-Saxon kingdom developed in the last decades of the ninth century, so West Saxon overlordship in relation to the Welsh kings becomes more explicit and visible in the sources. King Alfred's lordship or *dominium* was accepted by the southern Welsh kings as a means of protection against the aggressive policy of Rhodri Mawr's son and successor in Gwynedd, Anarawd (878–916). When Anarawd's relations with his Scandinavian raiding partners broke down, he too sought Alfred's protection, and promised obedience to the West Saxon king on the same terms as Æthelred of the Mercians had.[9] Ultimately, during the first half of the tenth century, we can see the relationship between the king of the English and the Welsh kings becoming explicitly one of king and under-kings.

Britons and Anglo-Saxons in the Tenth Century

By the tenth century, then, the kings of Wessex and England were accustomed to obtaining submission from British kings in a relationship of overlordship which, among the Welsh at least, entailed reciprocal responsibilities of service and protection. Soon after the Mercians submitted to Edward the Elder at Tamworth in 918, Hywel

"Dda" (d.950) and Clydog (d.920), sons of Cadell ap Rhodri Mawr (d.910), rulers respectively of Dyfed and Ceredigion, and Idwal "Foel" ab Anarawd (d.942), king of Gwynedd, submitted to the West Saxon king at the same place (*ASC*, A, *s.a.* 922). When King Æthelstan (924–39) came into possession of Northumbria in 927, Hywel Dda and Owain ap Hywel (the latter of Gwent, d. c.930) were the representatives of the Welsh who met the English king at Eamont Bridge, near Penrith, to "establish peace with pledge and oaths" (*ASC*, D, *s.a.* 926). William of Malmesbury claimed that Æthelstan required an annual tribute from the Welsh kings, with substantial payments of gold, silver, cattle, and hunting animals;[10] the mid-tenth-century author of the Welsh prophetic poem *Armes Prydein Fawr* considered the tribute rendered to the English kings a heavy burden.[11] From the year after the meeting at Eamont Bridge, down to 956, West Saxon royal charters were regularly witnessed by Welsh rulers styled as *subreguli*, "little under-kings." Present at the West Saxon royal court on these occasions were Hywel Dda of Dyfed (later of Gwynedd too), and afterward his son Owain, Idwal Foel ab Anarawd of Gwynedd, Morgan "Hen" ab Owain of Glywysing (c.930–74), and Tewdwr ab Elise of Brycheiniog (d. after 973).[12]

Meanwhile, as the Welsh kings were formalizing their relationship with the English king, the West Britons were decisively subdued by English military pressure. About 927, King Æthelstan led an expedition against the Britons of Cornwall; during the campaign, Æthelstan refortified the city of Exeter and expelled its British inhabitants.[13] He may have had the help of the Welsh in this task, for Hywel Dda and Idwal Foel were present at Exeter with Æthelstan on Easter day, April 16, 927 (S 400). Æthelstan's quashing of this apparent British uprising meant that the Cornish were to be confined behind the boundary of the River Tamar from then on. To emphasize this final settlement of ethno-political divisions, a new bishopric was created specifically for the Cornish. Although Cornwall now became politically a part of the new English kingdom, and took on Anglo-Saxon administrative features, most notably the hundred system, the indigenous Brittonic culture was not subsumed.[14] The Cornish language continued to be spoken by a majority of the population, and Brittonic place-names predominate.

Back among the Welsh, at the opening of the tenth century, a marriage alliance had helped to lever Hywel Dda (Rhodri Mawr's grandson) into the kingship of Dyfed on the death of his father-in-law. Having in this way begun his career in the south, Hywel gradually expanded his dominion. In 942, the same year that King Edmund re-conquered Mercia, the king of Gwynedd, Idwal Foel, was slain by King Edmund's forces. The result was that Hywel (Idwal's cousin) annexed the kingdom of Gwynedd and so achieved control of most of Wales. About this time, Brycheiniog lost its distinct political identity, and was subsumed into the southern Welsh political entity known as Deheubarth – literally the "south part." Only Glywysing in the south-east remained independent of Hywel's rule. But Hywel Dda's near pan-Welsh hegemony lasted just eight years, until his death in 950.

The phenomenon of Hywel Dda's kingship may be seen as a symptom of what Wendy Davies has argued was a new type of rulership in Wales: overkingship. Davies has doubted that overkings existed in Wales (unlike England) before the tenth and eleventh centuries.[15] From Hywel Dda's reign, however, kings with weak personal associations with the territories they claimed to rule were aspiring to a wider dominance over neighboring rulers and becoming alienated from the roots of royal power. Their expansionist ambitions, moreover, had no basis of administrative machinery on which to build a secure and enduring regime. In the south-east, however, the ruler's connection with his territory continued to be firm; indeed, it had become eponymous. For, from the time of Morgan ab Owain (Morgan Hen, c.930–74), the kingdom that had previously been known as Glywysing came to be called Morgannwg, or Gwlad Forgan – Glamorgan – the *gwlad* ("country" or "kingdom") of Morgan.

These two kings, Hywel Dda and Morgan Hen, were the most frequent Welsh visitors at the court of their overlord, the king of the English. Hywel's subscription always took precedence over other Welsh kings in the 22 surviving English royal charters that he witnessed. This precedence and relationship with the English king had a price. Hywel, Morgan, and other Welsh rulers contributed resources and military capability to the English.[16] Military cooperation with the English king against Strathclyde – and perhaps the West Britons too – showed a certain acceptance of the politics of reality; the actions of these rulers did not demonstrate an ideology of solidarity among the Brittonic-speaking peoples. We need not be surprised; for we find the English fighting for the Welsh in Wales, too, on numerous occasions.[17] While the contemporary clerical author of *Armes Prydein Fawr* was certainly anti-English, he was not necessarily a British nationalist; for him, his enemy's enemy was his friend. He well embodied the notion that any sense of "Celtic" solidarity represented more a shared sense of having been oppressed and threatened by the "English" than any appeal to racial or cultural affinity.[18]

Hywel's death in 950 led to warfare and conflict between the next generations of the line of Merfyn and Rhodri. The Gwynedd kingship returned by battle to the descendants of Anarawd: Iago and Idwal ab Idwal Foel. Yet, by 988, Hywel's grandson had again achieved hegemony comparable to that of his grandfather. Maredudd ab Owain ap Hywel Dda, "the most famous king of the Welsh" (according to the Welsh chroniclers), ruled Gwynedd and other parts of north Wales from 986, and from 988 until his death in 999 held power in Deheubarth.[19]

Wales in the Eleventh Century

In the opening years of the eleventh century, English aggression against the Welsh continued to emanate from the Mercian dynasty, now governed as an earldom rather than a kingdom. As the century progressed, the question of how a Welsh ruler could contend with an increasingly powerful and aggressive neighbor with ample resources was becoming more pressing.

For J. E. Lloyd, the eleventh century was a period in which outsiders (those who did not belong to the line of Merfyn Frych and Rhodri Mawr) secured power in Wales. But Kari Maund has had reservations about this view, and argued that the direct line was surprisingly resilient; the outsiders were often linked with it "by kinship and alliance," sometimes through the female line. Conflict could therefore be not so much between rival dynasties as between cousins, however distant.[20] The point may be well made in relation to the most significant Welsh figure of the eleventh century, Gruffudd ap Llywelyn ap Seisyll (d.1063), conventionally seen as an intruder into the kingship of Gwynedd.[21] Although Gruffudd's father, Llywelyn ap Seisyll, was essentially an outsider, he was nevertheless linked through the female line and by marriage to the line of Merfyn and Rhodri.[22] Llywelyn's rule in Gwynedd, together with his marriage into and defense of the Deheubarth line, provided his son, Gruffudd, with sufficient claim to bid for power in the north and the south, even though he was not of direct descent from the main Gwynedd line. By 1039, Gruffudd was established as ruler of the re-emergent eastern kingdom, Powys; in that year, too, he claimed the kingship of Gwynedd.

In the south, Rhydderch ab Iestyn had been the head of a rising dynasty, which he had brought to prominence in the south-east.[23] In 1023, Rhydderch had broken the direct hereditary succession to the major kingdom of Deheubarth and established himself as ruler of south Wales. He was killed in 1033, and Deheubarth reverted to the old dynasty under Hywel ab Edwin (d.1044) and his brother, Maredudd (d.1035).[24] Rhydderch ap Iestyn's sons, however, remained active in south-east Wales, and Gruffudd ap Rhydderch (d. c.1055) ruled Morgannwg for more than 20 years.[25] But Gruffudd ap Rhydderch was eventually slain in battle by Gruffudd ap Llywelyn ap Seisyll in 1055.[26] That death made way for the total conquest of the south by the other Gruffudd, who now became the first, and only, Welsh king to rule the whole of Wales – including the south-east.

Gruffudd ap Llywelyn ap Seisyll spent most of his reign campaigning to establish and maintain his own position. We should not therefore think of his rule as in any sense administratively developed. His principal preoccupation was the English. After successful campaigns in and around Hereford, Gruffudd accepted by a formal oath that he would be a faithful under-king, apparently content with English recognition of his territorial gains. Gruffudd had already made an alliance with the Mercians, and this alliance was strengthened by a marriage between Gruffudd and Edith, daughter of Earl Ælfgar. But Ælfgar's death in the late summer of 1062 heralded the opportunity for aggression by Harold, earl of Wessex. In the late summer of 1063, Harold and his brother Tostig advanced on Gruffudd by land and sea in an invincible pincer movement; Gruffudd retreated inland, but was killed by his personal retinue, and his head delivered to Edward the Confessor.[27] Gwynedd and Powys were given to his half-brothers, Bleddyn and Rhiwallon, and in the south the old dynasty of Deheubarth was restored. On the death of Gruffudd ap Llywelyn, the Welsh annalists described him as the "head and shield and defender of the Britons."[28] For the Anglo-Saxon chronicler, he was "king over all the Welsh."[29] His defeat and death were to have far-reaching consequences.

First, the fall of Gruffudd ap Llywelyn had a deep impact on Welsh relations with their neighbors. During Gruffudd's ascendancy, the Scandinavian and Irish threat had been limited. In the early years of the eleventh century, Irish-based vikings had terrorized the coastal lowlands of north and south Wales; they were also willing to sell their services to any Welsh exile or pretender who was prepared to pay for them. Once Gruffudd was overthrown, Welsh political exiles, such as Gruffudd ap Cynan of Gwynedd, and Rhys ap Tewdwr of Deheubarth, began to recruit support from the Irish and from the Scandinavians of Dublin. Viking attacks on the Welsh coastline were soon resumed.

To the east, the consequences of Gruffudd's downfall were even more far-reaching. Gruffudd's rule had changed the relationship of Welsh kings with their English counterparts and overlords. The initiative had moved to the Welsh side, with Gruffudd penetrating deep into English territory, taking in English settlements from the Dee estuary in the north to the Severn estuary in the south, wreaking destruction as he advanced. Gruffudd's court in the north-east was at the former Mercian *burh* of

Rhuddlan, and he collected renders from former English manors. In the sout-east, he had re-established Welsh control on the borderlands of Gwent and in the disputed frontier zone of Archenfield (the early medieval Welsh kingdom of Ergyng). So Gruffudd had not only imposed some manner of unity across the Welsh kingdoms, he had also extended boundaries into English territory and curbed the English advance.

Gruffudd's hegemony, like the hegemonies of the overkings who had gone before him – Hywel Dda, Maredudd ab Owain, Rhydderch ab Iestyn and his son Gruffudd – had not been founded on any institutional base. Instead, he had relied on military might and personal dependence. So his death left a potential vacuum of authority and power. Harold's victory provided an opportunity for English overlordship in Wales to be reasserted. Gruffudd ap Llywelyn's successors in the north, Bleddyn and Rhiwallon ap Cynfyn, gave hostages to King Edward, swore oaths of loyalty and obedience to him, and agreed to pay tribute (few, if any, historians have doubted the *Anglo-Saxon Chronicle* in this account).[30]

Bleddyn ap Cynfyn (d.1075) represented again the direct line of Merfyn and Rhodri, but his hold on his newly acquired territories was contested by Gruffudd ap Llywelyn's sons who had to be slain in battle (along with his own brother, Rhiwallon) before the chronicler could report, in 1069, that "Bleddyn ap Cynfyn held Gwynedd and Powys."[31] Bleddyn, however, was no mere puppet of Edward the Confessor or Harold. During Edward's reign, he engaged in destructive raids on settlements in English territory, and later took part in Anglo-Saxon revolts against the new Norman regime.[32]

The Coming of the Normans

When Harold, as king of the English, was killed at Hastings in 1066, Normans soon moved into his Welsh lands. Three border earldoms were established by the Conqueror: Chester, under Hugh d'Avranches (d.1101), Shrewsbury, under Roger de Montgomery (d.1094), and Hereford, under William fitz Osbern (d.1071). Lowland Gwent and Glamorgan were firmly in the hands of Norman magnates by the 1080s, and remained so from then on, with native "kings" holding on to some form of royal status and control in the uplands.[33]

In north Wales, Bleddyn ap Cynfyn became the target of Robert of Rhuddlan's aggression, but Bleddyn's rule was to be ended not by a Norman, but by the king of Deheubarth in 1075. *Brut y Tywysogion*, as with Gruffudd ap Llywelyn before him, claimed for Bleddyn "the whole kingdom of the Britons," but this probably means the whole of north Wales, Gwynedd and Powys.[34] Native rule was maintained in Gwynedd after Bleddyn's demise, and by 1081 the renowned Gruffudd ap Cynan (d.1137) had disposed of Bleddyn's successor; but just as he was establishing control in the region, he was lured into captivity by Hugh d'Avranches, earl of Chester, and Robert, Hugh's cousin, the lord of Rhuddlan.[35] By 1086, Robert was in control of the kingdom of Gwynedd, paying the Conqueror an annual rent of £40 for the "whole of North Wales."[36] Robert held Gwynedd until his death at Welsh hands in 1093, and the Norman grip was finally loosened in 1098 after the intervention of Magnus Bareleg, king of Norway, who happened to be passing on his way to the Hebrides and Man.[37] The following year, Gruffudd ap Cynan was in possession of Anglesey, and a long process of attrition against the Normans in north Wales began.

The native Welsh kings in the south had submitted quickly. In 1081, King William went in person to St. Davids to receive – perhaps demand – the submission of Rhys ap Tewdwr, king of Deheubarth (a great-grandfather of Gerald of Wales).[38] While there, William must have met the celebrated Bishop Sulien, "the most learned of the Britons";[39] and we need not dismiss the chronicler's gloss that there was an element of pilgrimage in the Conqueror's journey to the heart of St. David's *cultus*, the home of his shrine.[40] But Rhys's rule was soon bearing the usual scars of Welsh inter-dynastic strife; he had been expelled from his kingdom by the sons of Bleddyn; he had returned and killed them; he had then to contend with another pretender to his kingdom. In 1093, viewing this instability in Dyfed as an opportunity, the Normans of Brycheiniog invaded Rhys's territories and killed him. "And then fell the kingdom of the Britons," wrote a Welsh chronicler.[41] John of Worcester concurred, as he wrote that this was the day from which "kings ceased to bear rule in Wales";[42] for, from that point to the end of the century, the great kingdoms of Wales, Gwynedd and Deheubarth, whose rulers alone could claim the title "king of the Britons," were devoid of a native ruler. In characteristically emotive language, J. E. Lloyd declared that Rhys's death "opened the flood-gates of Norman rapacity in South Wales";[43] but his judgment is borne out by *Planctus Ricemarch*, "Rhygyfarch's Lament," a bitter comment by the son of Bishop Sulien on the viciousness and destructiveness of the Norman campaigns.[44]

Church and Kingdom

By the end of the eleventh century, Wales was divided ecclesiastically into three bishoprics corresponding to the major political divisions. From the see of Bangor, the kingdom of Gwynedd received its ecclesiastical administration. At Mynyw (*Menevia*) sat the bishops or archbishops of St. Davids, their remit stretching across Deheubarth. In the south-east, the kingdom of Morgannwg had a bishopric based at Llandaf. The re-emergent Powys, however, was in want of a bishopric; by the end of the eleventh century, it was a wasteland, with no ecclesiastical center or administration; the church chroniclers could not even put a name to it. Only in 1141 was the see of St. Asaph to be established, within sight of the Anglo-Norman *caput* at Rhuddlan.

Two centuries earlier, at the beginning of our period, there had been several other bishoprics in operation. At Llandeilo Fawr – the "Great Church of Teilo" – Teilo's bishop must have had responsibility for the region of Ystrad Tywi, but the days of this bishopric were already numbered. By the end of the ninth century, Teilo's bishops were likely subject to the authority of the archbishop of St. Davids; by the 1020s, the bishopric had gone, and Ystrad Tywi was for a time in the hands of the bishop of Glamorgan. In 1023, the king of Morgannwg, Rhydderch ab Iestyn, had extended his rule across the whole of Deheubarth, and Bishop Joseph had taken this opportunity to expand his diocese. Bishop Joseph died at Rome in 1045, apparently gaining papal sanction for his new jurisdiction. To the east, the bishops of "Glamorgan" had taken over the bishopric of Ergyng, a Welsh border-kingdom known in English as Archenfield. The bishops of St. Davids, meanwhile, had taken over Brycheiniog's bishopric, based at Glasbury; and the bishopric of Ceredigion, based at St. Padarn's great church, Llanbadarn Fawr, also fell into abeyance as St. Davids extended its authority in line with that of the kings of Deheubarth.[45]

This kind of close interface of the political and the ecclesiastical may be seen from the earliest period of Welsh church history, and by the beginning of our period we have good evidence for the close relationship between kings, bishoprics, and the cult of saints. By the ninth century – and no doubt earlier – Welsh royal dynasties were associating themselves with particular saints. The best known and most explicit example is the linking of the dynasty of Powys with St. Germanus in *Historia Brittonum* and on the Pillar of Elise. The royal dynasty of Glywysing, in the person of Hywel ap Rhys, was associated with the cult of St. Illtud in the last quarter of the ninth century. In the late eleventh century, the *Lives* of the Welsh saints continued the idea of association of royal dynasty and saint. The dynasty of Ceredigion was linked to St. David by Rhygyfarch in his *Life* of St. David, and Lifris has St. Cadog as a founding member of the dynasty of Gwynllwg and Glywysing in his *Life* of that saint. In the twelfth century, St. Dyfrig becomes the grandson of a king of Ergyng, and perhaps most significantly, the *Life* of St. Padarn associates St. David with Rheinwg (Dyfed), St. Teilo with Morgannwg, and St. Padarn with Seisyllwg (Ceredigion and Ystrad Tywi).

On a different plane, we might look to this association of saint and dynasty to explain the distribution of certain types of toponym. The most common type of place-name in Wales, as any visitor to the country quickly notices, begins with the word *llan*, and usually has the name of a saint suffixed. *Llan* means "church" or "ecclesiastical enclosure," and so the place-name Llanddewi, for example, means "the church of Dewi" (St. David). A notable feature of these place-names is that certain ones are repeated in what appear to be significant patterns of distribution. As we have already seen, after the rise of the Second Dynasty of Gwynedd in the middle of the ninth century, certain kings exercised a wide hegemony. The political circumstances appear to have been favorable for the propagation of patterns of the "*llan* + saint" type of place-name. So, the distribution of the place-name Llanddewi coincides with the overkingdom of Deheubarth; Rhodri Mawr's hegemony across Powys and Ceredigion similarly provides a context in which the toponym Llanbadarn (*Llan* + Padarn) could have come to spread out of Ceredigion and into the southerly part of Powys. If the *llan* was the ecclesiastical center of the great estate, or *maenor* (see below), then we might therefore suppose that the suffix of a dynastic saint was often either an indication of direct royal control, or ecclesiastical proprietorship by the relevant episcopal church. A similar kind of process appears to have been at work in Cornwall too, where names in *lan* originally referred to a sacred ecclesiastical enclosure, but were later extended to designate the estate on which the church was situated.[46]

But all this only hints at the connection between kings, kingdoms, and the organization of the church. The idea of bishoprics being coterminous with kingdoms first becomes clearly visible in 809 when the A-text of *Annales Cambriae* records the death of Elfoddw, "*archiepiscopus Guenedote regionis*" ("the archbishop of the Venedotian kingdom [i.e. Gwynedd]"). The association of episcopal jurisdiction with kingdom is thus explicit and unequivocal. Then there is the well-known Welsh law tract on the "seven bishop-houses of Dyfed," which appears to show that in Dyfed each petty kingdom – the later *cantrefi* – had its own bishop. In the *Anglo-Saxon Chronicle*, Cyfeiliog, "bishop of Ergyng," was captured by vikings in 914. Finally, the B-text of *Annales Cambriae* records the death of a bishop of Morgannwg in 1025. In fact, it was the very principle – and presumption – of the coterminous nature of episcopal and secular rule that was the beginning and end of Llandaf's claims concerning its diocesan boundaries in the early twelfth century.[47] And so the churchmen of Llandaf explicitly promoted the theory that bishoprics went with king-doms. In the *Life* of St. Euddogwy from the *Book of Llandaf*, the river Tywi is said to have been the dividing line between two bishoprics and two kingdoms, namely Llandaf and Morgannwg, and St. Davids and Deheubarth.

From the point at which the bishoprics of Wales come dimly into view in the early Middle Ages, until the time when their boundaries and organization become finally settled in the twelfth century, the sources point to a structure of episcopal organiza-tion and jurisdiction that is closely tied up with the fates of kings and kingdoms. This might not be startling news, but there have been those who see no correlation between bishoprics and kingdoms. The reduction in the number of bishops in Wales between the seventh century and the twelfth, from possibly dozens to four, was a direct reflection of political developments – the consolidation of kingdoms and the expanding remit of kingly overlordship.

The history of ecclesiastical and political development similarly inform each other in Cornwall during our period too. We have already noted that after Ecgberht's victory over the Britons of Cornwall in the ninth century, the Cornish bishop, Kenstec, had been obliged to acknowledge the archbishop of Canterbury as his canonical superior; and that at this time the bishop of Sherborne had been charged to make an annual visitation of Cornwall and root out the errors of the Cornish church. By the reign of Alfred, however, it was plain that the vast diocese of Sherborne would have to be divided. As a first stage, Alfred gave Asser – who had come from being the bishop of St. Davids in Dyfed – the monastery of Exeter and the whole *paruchia* belonging to it in Devon and Cornwall; that is, jurisdiction over all its dependent lands and all its rights.[48] Asser was probably an auxiliary bishop to the bishop of Sherborne; Alfred may have placed him in Exeter because, as a Welshman, he would have been particularly suited to look after the interests of the native element in the population of the south-west. Afterward, as bishop of Sherborne, Asser himself presided over the enormous south-western diocese. Upon his death in 909, however, the diocese of Sherborne was divided into three: Dorset was adminis-tered from Sherborne; Somerset was made into a new bishopric with its see at Wells; and Devon and Cornwall were given a see at Crediton.[49]

Æthelstan finally founded a see for Cornwall based, apparently, at St. Germans, although there may have been an episcopal church at Padstow too.[50] A bishop with a British name, Conan (?926–37×955), was appointed, but Conan was apparently a suffragan or auxiliary to the bishop of Crediton, who retained ultimate jurisdiction in the undivided bishopric.[51] By 994, Æthelred the Unready had given Bishop Ealdred a charter establishing a see in Cornwall at St. Germans with full diocesan jurisdiction (S 880), but this was short-lived. Bishop Lyfing (1027–46) persuaded Cnut to let him hold Cornwall together with Crediton.[52] Finally, in 1050, the sees were united and moved to Exeter, thus ending any concession to a separate Cornish ecclesiastical identity.[53] As we saw in Wales, then, so in Cornwall: ecclesiastical orga-nization, with its modifications, transformations, and revolutions, was molded by, and was a representation of, the political landscape in which it sat.

Economy and Political Development

What we know of Welsh economy before the twelfth century points to a more-or-less exclusive pattern of agrarian subsistence. The dominant characteristic was agricultural production for distribution, and the land was worked in large estates by a politically and economically dependent population. We can point with a degree of certainty to the existence of these large estates in the south from at least the late eighth century, for the terminology associated with them was established by about 800, when the extent of the estate of Myddyn-fych was briefly recorded in the gospel book of St. Teilo's church at Llandeilo Fawr.[54] A marginal note records the *nobilitas* (status) and *mensura* (measure) of *mainaur med diminih*, that is, *maenor Myddyfnych* (modern Myddyn-fych). A *maenor* was a large estate – in the case of Myddyn-fych, measuring several miles across – with its administrative center at a *llys* or court, and its religious center at a *llan* or church. The basic working unit was the *tref*, a small settlement, and these *trefi* were the component elements of the *maenor*. The *maenor* at Myddyn-fych is comparable to the "multiple" or "great" estates found in England, and the tendency there and in Wales for boundaries to run along natural features has led to the supposition that such estates had very early origins. Control of a *maenor*, whether by king, churchman, or lay lord, brought with it the receipt of regular rents and renders – beer, bread, meat, honey – once or twice a year.[55] Responsibility for the collection of the expected render lay with the *maer* or reeve, whose office is certainly attested by the tenth century. The existence of the *maer* tells of the centrality of the provision of render to the landlord of the estate, and gives the *maenor* the character of a small unit of government. Control of a *maenor*, that is, of the profits from the management of land, was thus a basic level of lordship; and so the exercise of power can be seen to have extended from a fundamental level of rule associated with control, in the first instance, of a defined unit of land and labor.

By the twelfth century, the Welsh law tracts present a systematized picture of the *maenor* (or *maenol* in north Wales). In Gwynedd, the scheme described four *trefi* per *maenol*; 12 *maenolau* plus two extra *trefi* per *commote* (i.e. 50 *trefi*), with two commotes in a *cantref* (literally "a hundred *trefi*"), neatly making a hundred *trefi* in a *cantref*. We should not, however, be tempted to project this highly schematized model backward, for it suggests an institutional and administrative stability and uniformity that was not evident for most of the early Middle Ages. Wendy Davies asked the pertinent question whether both land usage and political organization can have been so static and unchanging in a period of considerable political change, and climatic and demographic alteration.[56] Indeed, Davies has seen, in the south-east at least, a trend toward fragmentation of larger estates into smaller, independent *trefi*, from the ninth century onward, even if they may still have been grouped for fiscal purposes. This need not, however, indicate some kind of descent into chaos; rather, it seems to represent the alienation and distribution of land among elite followers of the greater landlords. Although the Welsh sources for this period are troublesome, the more certain West Saxon evidence provides a corroborative parallel. By contrast with the English situation, however, Welsh lords failed to secure control of the labor of agricultural workers on their estates, as English thegns did; nor do we see the planned villages, common fields, or gentrified residences of late Anglo-Saxon society.

Wales also lacked the urbanized settlements that had grown up in England by the late tenth century. The only town was the English *burh* at Rhuddlan, which intermittently came under the control of the kings of Gwynedd. Small-scale, dispersed landholding was militating against the widespread production of agricultural surplus, whereas in England, the intensification of agricultural exploitation combined with the development of a cash economy had led to demand for traders and regulated markets. We might also look to the fragmented political structures, small populations, large land areas, and poor overland communications as factors in the inhibited urban development of Wales. This absence of towns meant the absence of commercial centers, a developed economy, and mercantile classes. In turn, the lack of an urban class was no doubt a significant factor in the political immaturity and incoherence of Welsh governance; for it was the development of such urban professional and mercantile classes that marked political progress elsewhere. By the middle of the eleventh century, English towns had evolved a corporate solidarity and administrative separation from the countryside which displayed a level of political sophistication simply unthinkable among the Welsh, and which led to trade and contact with the most developed towns of northern Europe.

The Welsh economy nevertheless did have at least a certain degree of diversity. In the heartlands of tenth-century Gwynedd (as Dawn Hadley also mentions in chapter 14), a small trading and manufacturing settlement at Llanbedrgoch on Anglesey had links with Francia, England, and the Scandinavians of Ireland. Gwynedd at least – and no doubt the other maritime territories – was part of an Irish Sea trading network.[57] We might also consider the economic implications of the annual tribute that William of Malmesbury claimed was owed yearly by the Welsh kings to Æthelstan. Although we may not be sure that this tribute was ever paid, it is some indication that the Welsh could be expected to muster 20 lb of gold, 300 lb of silver, and 25,000 cattle.[58] While we have no written evidence of mining, we know that there was gold in the River Mawddach (Meirionydd/Ardudwy) and at Dolaucothi (Llanwrda, Carmarthenshire); and, in 1188, Gerald of Wales saw silver-mining going on between St. Asaph and Basingwerk.[59] The minting of coinage, however, was not a development to reach Welsh territories until the Normans came. The single extant penny bearing the name of King Hywel was the product of an English mint at Chester, and there is little indication that coins were used as currency in the usual sense. The implication of the hoards of mostly English coins found in Wales is that, having been acquired elsewhere, they were used by weight.[60] In the reign of William the Conqueror – possibly a little later – mints were founded at Cardiff, St. Davids, and Rhuddlan: we may infer that they were founded to provide coinage to pay the royal tribute, and at Cardiff and Rhuddlan, the garrisons too.[61]

Conclusion

With the clarity of hindsight, which is the privilege of historians, we may view the tenth and eleventh centuries as the age in which the destiny of the British peoples of Wales and West Britain was set for the rest of the medieval period. The Britons of Cornwall were subsumed into the ever-expanding West Saxon kingdom, and confined west of the Tamar, to be governed according to West Saxon practice, both politically and ecclesiastically. But whereas the West Saxon domination of Cornwall might seem late by comparison with the Anglo-Saxon settlement of the rest of England, should we not think it significant that it happened at all? The process did not begin until the seventh or even the eighth century, and was hardly part of the same course of Anglo-Saxon settlement that had happened further east in the fifth, sixth, and early seventh centuries. Complete military conquest did not come about until the tenth century, and cultural assimilation was a different matter again. Should we therefore regard the successful West Saxon conquest of Cornwall in the tenth century as any more inevitable than a Mercian conquest of the Welsh, or a Northumbrian conquest of Strathclyde? It is the very West Saxon nature of the emergent Anglo-Saxon kingdom that is at the heart of the matter: the Cornish had always been on the border with Wessex, whereas the Welsh were not. However aggrieved the mid-tenth-century Dimetian author of *Armes Prydein Fawr* felt toward the English "shit-shovelers" (*kechmyn*) as he composed his poetic political prophecy, it was not until the coming of the Normans that the Welsh of Wales would be subject to truly successful campaigns of colonization. Then Rhygyfarch of Llanbadarn Fawr would have good cause to lament.

Before the advent of the Normans, then, the Welsh kings had maintained the territorial and administrative integrity of their kingdoms in relation to the English (if not always in relation to each other); this was at the price of military cooperation, and the rendering of tribute and submission through much of the tenth century. The Welsh had also been preserved from large-scale Scandinavian invasion. What is more, the Welsh kingdoms survived alongside the creation of a single southern-English kingdom, which Charles Insley reminds us was extremely wealthy and well governed by the end of the eleventh century (see chapter 20). But while it is interesting to know why the West Saxon dynasty was so successful in uniting the Anglo-Saxon kingdoms, the matter of the "failure" of the Welsh to establish a pan-Welsh polity is perhaps one for modern nationalist politicians, and not for historians. The West Saxon achievement was that of a dynasty, not of a people: the unitary English kingdom was a political triumph, not a national destiny. The kind of process that led to the unification of the Anglo-Saxon kingdoms had already happened in Wales by the end of the ninth century, producing the consolidated kingdoms of Gwynedd, Dyfed, and Glywysing, where powerful kings had taken over the rule of smaller kings, depriving them of their royal status. The process which produced brief periods of hegemony in the tenth and eleventh centuries was the development of overkingship, where greater kings ruled over lesser kings, and over territories that retained their political identity.

So, we should rather notice that until the last decade of the eleventh century, in the Welsh territories, British kings ruled British peoples without interruption of alien conquest (that is, by a non-Welsh people). The political units over which these kings ruled, moreover, retained their integrity to a large extent; for although great kings exercised hegemony from time to time over the kingdoms of the north and the south, the principal divisions of north Wales (Gwynedd) and south Wales (Deheubarth), which had solidified during the tenth century, endured. The heartlands of the most powerful of those kingdoms, Gwynedd and Dyfed, survived (with notable interruptions) under quasi-independent native Welsh rule until the Edwardian conquest in the last decades of the thirteenth century.

Amid the vicissitudes of political success and disaster, moreover, the British people were still able to make their own important contribution to the cultural history of Britain – this, the era of *Pedair Cainc y Mabinogi* (still selling well in paperback today). Nor should we forget that the great monastic revival of the tenth century was fueled in England by the products of Welsh and Cornish scriptoria.[62] Welsh writers in Latin, moreover, rank highly among the ecclesiastical authors of our period in Britain; indeed, it is from the ranks of British churchmen of the tenth and eleventh centuries that we encounter some of the more intriguing figures of Britain's medieval ecclesiastical history, among them, Bishops Asser and Sulien of St. Davids, Rhygyfarch and Ieuan of Llanbadarn Fawr (both sons of Bishop Sulien), and Lifris of Llancarfan. By the end of our period, however, the pattern of domination by the English crown and its magnates was already set, and it was the churchmen who were the first to recognize and accept this fact. While the native rulers of Wales struggled to maintain their independence after the coming of the Normans, their ecclesiastical counterparts saw almost at once where the future lay, and consequently prospered as they integrated into the province of Canterbury, taking a full role in the life of the Anglo-Norman kingdom and the universal church, yet establishing at the same time the core of a definite and enduring cultural identity and coherence in their writings.[63]

Notes

1 Dumville, "The 'six sons' of Rhodri Mawr."
2 Johnston (ed.), *Gwaith Iolo Goch.*
3 *AC* A, *s.aa.* 778, 784, 796, 877, 881, 943, 951; *AC* B, C, *s.aa.* 816, 818, 822, 983, 992, 1012; *ByT* (Pen 20), *s.aa.* 849, 965 (= 967), 1033 (= 1035), 1037 (= 1039); *ASC* B, C, *s.a.* 916.
4 *ASC* A, E, *s.a.* 815; *ASC* A, E, *s.a.* 825; S 273; *ASC* A, E, *s.a.* 838; *ASC* A, E, *s.a.* 838; *AC* A, *s.a.* 875.
5 Richter (ed.), *Canterbury Professions*, p. 24, no. 27; S 1451a, edited in Conner, *Anglo-Saxon Exeter*, pp. 221–5.
6 "the land at Stratton in Triggshire," King Alfred's will, in Keynes and Lapidge (trans.), *Alfred the Great*, p. 175.
7 *ASC* A, *s.a.* 853; E, *s.a.* 852.
8 *AC* A, *s.a.* 877; *AU*, *s.a.* 878.1.
9 Asser, *De rebus gestis Ælfredi*, § 80, in Keynes and Lapidge (eds.), *Alfred the Great*, p. 96; Pratt, *Political Thought*, pp. 107–11.
10 Mynors et al. (eds.), *William of Malmesbury, Gesta regum Anglorum*, ii. 134; I, pp. 214–17.
11 Isaac, *Armes Prydein Fawr*, lines 21–2, 72, 78, 84, 86, 123.
12 Hywel Dda: S 400, 407, 413, 416, 417, 418a, 420, 425, 427, 433, 434, 435, 436, 520, 544, 550, 552a, 1792; Owain ap Hywel Dda: S 566; Idwal Foel: S 400, 407, 413, 416, 417, 418a, 425, 434, 435, 436, 1792; Morgan Hen: S 407, 413, 417, 418a, 425, 434, 435, 436, 544, 550, 552a, 566, 633, 1792; Tewdwr ab Elise: S 425.
13 Mynors et al. (eds.), *William of Malmesbury, Gesta regum Anglorum*, ii. 134; I, p. 217.
14 Thomas, "Settlement history."
15 Davies, *Patterns of Power*, pp. 83–90.
16 *ASC* A, *s.a.* 894; Coxe (ed.), *Rogeri de Wendover*, I, 398.
17 *ByT* (Pen 20) *s.aa.* 893 (= 895), 977 (= 978), 979 (= 980), 991 (= 992); *ASC* C, *s.aa.* 1046, 1055, 1065.
18 Ward-Perkins, "Why did the Anglo-Saxons not become more British?," 531.
19 Thornton, "Maredudd ab Owain."
20 Lloyd, *History of* Wales; Maund, *Ireland, Wales, and England*, esp. pp. 207–9.
21 Maund, *Ireland, Wales, and England*, pp. 64–8.
22 For Llywelyn's lineage, see Maund, *Ireland, Wales, and England*, pp. 59–62; for his career, see Davies, "Gruffydd."
23 Maund, *Ireland, Wales, and Enland*, pp. 20–2, 108.
24 Ibid., pp. 22–5.
25 Ibid., pp. 25–7.

26 Ibid., pp. 25–6, for the date of his death.
27 *AU*, *s.a.* 1039.1; *ByT* (Pen 20), *s.a.* 1061 (= 1063); *ByT* (RB), *s.a.* 1060 (= 1063).
28 *ByT* (Pen 20), *s.a.* 1061 (= 1063); *ByT* (RB), *s.a.* 1060 (= 1063).
29 "se wæs kyning ofer eall Weal cyn," *ASC* D, *s.a.* 1063.
30 *ASC* D, *s.a.* 1063.
31 *ByT* (RB), *s.a.* 1069.
32 Maund, *Ireland, Wales, and England*, pp. 68–76.
33 Crouch, "The slow death of kingship in Glamorgan."
34 *ByT* (Pen 20), *s.a.* 1073 (= 1075); *ByT* (RB), *s.a.* 1075.
35 Maund, *Ireland, Wales, and England*, pp. 82–90.
36 *Domesday Book*, Cheshire, fol. 269r.
37 *ByS*, *s.a.* 1096 (= 1098); *ByT* (Pen 20), *s.a.* 1096 (= 1098); *ByT* (RB), *s.a.* 1094 (= 1098).
38 Maund, *Ireland, Wales, and England*, pp. 33–8.
39 *ByT* (RB), *s.a.* 1091.
40 *AC* B, *s.a.* 1082 (= 1081); *ByT* (Pen 20), *s.a.* 1079 (= 1081); *ByT* (RB), *s.a.* 1081; Cowley, "The relics of St. David."
41 *ByT* (RB), *s.a.* 1093.
42 McGurk (ed.), *Chronicle of John of Worcester*, *s.a.* 1093.
43 Lloyd, *History of Wales*, II, 398.
44 Lapidge, "The Welsh Latin poetry," 88–92.
45 Davies, *Book of Llandaf*, pp. 9–18, and "The archbishopric of St. Davids."
46 For all this, see Davies, "The saints of south Wales"; Olson, *Early Monasteries*; Padel, "Local saints."
47 Davies, *Book of Llandaf*, pp. 32–45, 63–75.
48 Asser, *De rebus gestis Ælfredi*, § 81, in Keynes and Lapidge (eds.), *Alfred the Great*, p. 97, also pp. 49–50.
49 Winterbottom and Thomson (eds.), *William of Malmesbury, Gesta pontificum Anglorum*, ii. 75, 80; I, pp. 249, 281.
50 Ibid., ii. 96; I, p. 319; S 880, charter of Æthelred II granting privileges to the bishop of Cornwall, "*pro amore . . . sancti confessoris Germani necnon et beati eximii Petroci.*"
51 Finberg, "Sherborne," pp. 118–19.
52 Winterbottom and Thomson (eds.), *William of Malmesbury, Gesta pontificum Anglorum*, ii. 94; I, p. 315; Mynors et al. (eds.), *William of Malmesbury, Gesta regum Anglorum*, i. 100; I, p. 147.
53 Winterbottom and Thomson (eds.), *William of Malmesbury, Gesta pontificum Anglorum*, ii. 94; I, p. 315.
54 Davies, *Wales in the Early Middle Ages*, pp. 43–6; Jenkins and Owen, "The Welsh marginalia"; Jones, "Multiple estates" and "Post-Roman Wales."
55 Davies, *Early Welsh Microcosm*, pp. 44–9, and *Wales in the Early Middle Ages*, p. 46.
56 Davies, *Wales in the Early Middle Ages*, p. 46.
57 Redknap, *Vikings in Wales*, pp. 147–69.
58 Mynors et al. (eds.), *William of Malmesbury, Gesta regum Anglorum*, ii. 134; I, pp. 214–17.
59 Edmondson, "Mining," p. 92; Thorpe (trans.), *Gerald of Wales: The Journey through Wales*, II. 10, p. 196.
60 Davies, *Wales in the Early Middle Ages*, p. 54.
61 Boon, *Welsh Hoards*, p. 40.
62 Dumville, *English Caroline Script*; *Liturgy and the Ecclesiastical History*; and *Wessex and England*.
63 Davies, *Book of Llandaf*, and "Aspects of church reform."

Further Reading

The standard narrative was set by Lloyd's *History of Wales*, which, though dated, is still worth reading. Wendy Davies's *Wales in the Early Middle Ages* replaces Lloyd for the pre-Norman period, providing a clearer sense of chronological development, and dealing with social, economic, ecclesiastical, and cultural history. More controversial is her *Early Welsh Microcosm*, which uses the difficult evidence of the "Llandaf charters" to trace political, economic, and social change in the south-east; her *Patterns of Power* is invigorating and original. The only other survey of note is Maund, *The Welsh Kings*; her *Ireland, Wales, and England* is dense, but important for the eleventh century. A good book on Cornwall is lacking, but one could start with Hoskins, *The Westward Expansion of Wessex*. The work of H. P. R. Finberg is fundamental, and his article on Sherborne is the fullest account of the history of bishops in Cornwall. Darby and Finn's *Domesday Geography of South-west England* is essential reading for an idea of settlement and economy in eleventh-century Cornwall. The work of Olson and Padel is of the highest importance for other aspects of the ecclesiastical history of Cornwall. Much may be gleaned, too, from Conner's *Anglo-Saxon Exeter*. For the ecclesiastical history of Wales, a good full-length survey is still to be written, but one may look at the relevant chapters of Wendy Davies's *Wales in the Early Middle Ages*, as well as Edwards and Lane's *The Early Church in Wales and the West*, H. Pryce's "Pastoral care," and my own "The saints of south Wales." My *Book of Llandaf and the Norman Church in Wales* has much of relevance for an understanding of the pre-Norman period.

Bibliography

Boon, G. C., *Welsh Hoards 1979–1981: The Coinage of Cnut in Wales, the Coinage of the Empress Maud, the Earliest Portrait Esterlings* (Cardiff, 1986).

Breeze, A., "*Armes Prydein*, Hywel Dda, and the reign of Edmund of Wessex," *Études Celtiques*, 33 (1997), 209–22.

Charles-Edwards, T. M., "The seven bishop-houses of Dyfed," *Bulletin of the Board of Celtic Studies*, 24 (1970–2), 247–62.

Colgrave, B. and Mynors, R. A. B. (eds.), *Bede's Ecclesiastical History of the English People* (Oxford, 1969; rev. imp., 1991).

Conner, P. W., *Anglo-Saxon Exeter: A Tenth-century Cultural History* (Woodbridge, 1993).

Cowley, F., "The relics of St. David: the historical evidence," in J. W. Evans and J. M. Wooding (eds.), *St. David of Wales: Cult, Church and Nation* (Woodbridge, 2007), pp. 274–81.

Coxe, H. O. (ed.), *Rogeri de Wendover Chronica, sive Flores historiarum*, 5 vols. (London, 1841–4).

Crouch, D., "The slow death of kingship in Glamorgan, 1067–1158," *Morgannwg*, 29 (1985), 20–41.

Darby, H. C. and Finn, R. W. (eds.), *The Domesday Geography of South-west England* (Cambridge, 1967).

Darlington, R. R. and McGurk, P. (eds.), *The Chronicle of John of Worcester*, vol. II: *The Annals from 450 to 1066* (Oxford, 1995).

Davies, J. R., "The archbishopric of St. Davids and the bishops of *Clas Cynidr*," in J. W. Evans and J. M. Wooding (eds.), *St. David of Wales: Cult, Church and Nation* (Woodbridge, 2007), pp. 296–304.

Davies, J. R., "Aspects of church reform in Wales, c.1093–c.1223," *Anglo-Norman Studies*, 30 (2008), 85–99.

Davies, J. R., *The Book of Llandaf and the Norman Church in Wales* (Woodbridge, 2003).

Davies, J. R., "The saints of south Wales and the Welsh church," in A. T. Thacker and R. Sharpe (eds.), *Local Saints and Local Churches in the Early Medieval West* (Oxford, 2002), pp. 361–95.

Davies, M., "Gruffydd ap Llywelyn, king of Wales," *Welsh History Review*, 21 (2002–3), 207–48.

Davies, R. R., *Conquest, Coexistence, and Change: Wales 1063–1415* (Oxford, 1987).

Davies, S., *Welsh Military Institutions, c.633–1283* (Cardiff, 2003).

Davies, W., *An Early Welsh Microcosm: Studies in the Llandaff Charters* (London, 1978).

Davies, W., *Patterns of Power in Early Wales* (Oxford, 1990).

Davies, W., *Wales in the Early Middle Ages* (Leicester, 1982).

Dumville, D. N., *English Caroline Script and Monastic History: Studies in Benedictinism, AD 950–1030* (Woodbridge, 1993).

Dumville, D. N., *Liturgy and the Ecclesiastical History of Late Anglo-Saxon England* (Woodbridge, 1992).

Dumville, D. N., "The 'six' sons of Rhodri Mawr: a problem in Asser's *Life of King Alfred*," *Cambridge Medieval Celtic Studies*, 4 (1983), 5–18.

Dumville, D. N., *Wessex and England from Alfred to Edgar* (Woodbridge, 1992).

Dumville, D. N. and Keynes, S. D. (eds.), *The Anglo-Saxon Chronicle: A Collaborative Edition*, 23 vols. (Cambridge, 1983–).

Dyer, C., *Making a Living in the Middle Ages: The People of Britain 850–1250* (London, 2002).

Edmondson, J. C., "Mining in the later Roman Empire and beyond: continuity or disruption?," *Journal of Roman Studies*, 79 (1989), 84–102.

Edwards, N. and Lane, A. (eds.), *The Early Church in Wales and the West* (Oxford, 1992).

Evans, J. W. and Wooding, J. M. (eds.), *St. David of Wales: Cult, Church and Nation* (Woodbridge, 2007).

Finberg, H. P. R., *The Early Charters of Devon and Cornwall*, 2nd edn. (Leicester, 1963).

Finberg, H. P. R., "Sherborne, Glastonbury, and the expansion of Wessex," *Transactions of the Royal Historical Society*, 5th series, 3 (1953), 101–24.

Fulton, H., "Tenth-century Wales and *Armes Prydein*," *Transactions of the Honourable Society of Cymmrodorion*, new series, 7 (2001), 5–18.

Ganz, J. (trans.), *The Mabinogion* (Harmondsworth, 1976).

Halliday, F. E., *A History of Cornwall* (London, 1959).

Hoskins, W. G., *The Westward Expansion of Wessex* (Leicester, 1960).

Isaac, G. R., "*Armes Prydein Fawr* and St. David," in J. W. Evans and J. M. Wooding (eds.), *St. David of Wales: Cult, Church and Nation* (Woodbridge, 2007), pp. 161–81.

Jenkins, D. and Owen, M. E., "The Welsh marginalia in the Lichfield Gospels, part 1," *Cambridge Medieval Celtic Studies*, 5 (1983), 37–66.

Johnston, D. R. (ed.), *Gwaith Iolo Goch* (Cardiff, 1988).

Jones, G. R. J., "Multiple estates and early settlement," in P. H. Sawyer (ed.), *English Medieval Settlement* (London, 1979), pp. 9–34.

Jones, G. R. J., "Post-Roman Wales," in H. P. R. Finberg (ed.), *The Agrarian History of England and Wales*, vol. 1, part 2: *AD 43–1042* (Cambridge, 1972), pp. 283–382.

Jones, T. (ed.), *Brenhinedd y Saesson, or The Kings of the Saxons* (Cardiff, 1971).

Jones, T. (trans.), *Brut y Tywysogion or the Chronicle of the Princes, Peniarth MS 20 Version* (Cardiff, 1952).

Jones, T. (ed.), *Brut y Tywysogion or the Chronicle of the Princes, Red Book of Hergest Version*, 2nd edn. (Cardiff, 1973).

Keynes, S. D. and Lapidge, M. (trans.), *Alfred the Great: Asser's Life of King Alfred and Other Contemporary Sources* (Harmondsworth, 1983).

Kirby, D. P., "Hywel Dda: anglophil?," *Welsh History Review*, 8 (1976–7), 1–13.

Lapidge, M., "The Welsh Latin poetry of Sulien's family," *Studia Celtica*, 8/9 (1973–4), 68–106.

Lloyd, J. E., *A History of Wales from the Earliest Times to the Edwardian Conquest*, 3rd edn., 2 vols. (London, 1939).

Loyn, H. R., "Welsh and English in the tenth century: the context of the Athelstan charters," *Welsh History Review*, 10 (1980–1), 283–301.

Mac Airt, S. and Mac Niocaill, G. (eds. and trans.), *The Annals of Ulster (to AD 1131)*, Part I: *Text and Translation* (Dublin, 1983).

McGurk, P. (ed.) *The Chronicle of John of Worcester*, vol. III: *The Annals from 1067 to 1140 with the Gloucester Interpolations and the Continuation to 1141* (Oxford, 1998).

Maund, K. L., *Ireland, Wales, and England in the Eleventh Century* (Woodbridge, 1991).

Maund, K. L., *The Welsh Kings: The Medieval Rulers of Wales* (Stroud, 2000).

Moore, D., *The Welsh Wars of Independence c.410–c.1415* (Stroud, 2005).

Morris, J. (gen. ed.), *Domesday Book*, 35 vols in 39 (Chichester, 1975–86; 3 index vols, 1992).

Mynors, R. A. B. et al. (eds.), *William of Malmesbury, Gesta regum Anglorum: The History of the English Kings*, 2 vols. (Oxford, 1998–9).

Olson, L., *Early Monasteries in Cornwall* (Woodbridge, 1989).

Olson, L. and Padel, O. J., "A tenth-century list of Cornish parochial saints," *Cambridge Medieval Celtic Studies*, 12 (1986), 33–71.

Padel, O. J., "Local saints and place-names in Cornwall," in A. T. Thacker and R. Sharpe (eds.), *Local Saints and Local Churches in the Early Medieval West* (Oxford, 2002), pp. 303–60.

Padel, O. J., "Two new pre-Conquest charters for Cornwall," *Cornish Studies*, 6 (1978), 20–7.

Phillimore, E., "The *Annales Cambriæ* and Old-Welsh genealogies from *Harleian MS 3859*," *Y Cymmrodor*, 9 (1888), 141–83.

Pratt, D., *The Political Thought of King Alfred the Great* (Cambridge, 2007).

Pryce, H., "British or Welsh? National identity in twelfth-century Wales," *English Historical Review*, 116 (2001), 775–801.

Pryce, H., "Pastoral care in early medieval Wales," in J. Blair and R. Sharpe (eds.), *Pastoral Care before the Parish* (Leicester, 1992), pp. 41–62.

Redknap, M., *Vikings in Wales: An Archaeological Quest* (Cardiff, 2000).

Richter, M. (ed.), *Canterbury Professions* (Torquay, 1973).

Sawyer, P. H., *Anglo-Saxon Charters: An Annotated List and Bibliography* (London, 1968).

Sharpe, R. and Davies, J. R. (eds. and trans.), "Rhygyfarch's *Life* of St. David," in J. W. Evans and J. M. Wooding (eds.), *St. David of Wales: Cult, Church and Nation* (Woodbridge, 2007), pp. 107–55.

Thacker, A. T. and Sharpe, R. (eds.), *Local Saints and Local Churches in the Early Medieval West* (Oxford, 2002).

Thomas, A. C., "Settlement history in early Cornwall I: the antiquity of the hundreds," *Cornish Archaeology*, 3 (1964), 70–9.

Thornton, D. E., "Maredudd ab Owain (d.999): the most famous king of the Welsh," *Welsh History Review*, 18 (1996–7), 567–91.

Thorpe, L. (trans.), *Gerald of Wales: The Journey through Wales and the Description of Wales* (Harmondsworth, 1978).

Ward-Perkins, B., "Why did the Anglo-Saxons not become more British?," *English Historical Review*, 115 (2000), 513–33.

Williams (ab Ithel), J. (ed.), *Annales Cambriae*. Rolls Series, 20 (London, 1860).

Winterbottom, M. and Thomson, R. M. (eds.), *William of Malmesbury, Gesta pontificum Anglorum: The History of the English Bishops*, 2 vols. (Oxford, 2007).

CHAPTER TWENTY-TWO

Britain, Ireland, and Europe, c.900–c.1100

SIMON MACLEAN

In the year 990, Sigeric, the new archbishop of Canterbury, left England to collect the pallium, the mark of his office, from the pope. Crossing the Channel to Flanders, he embarked on an epic journey covering some 1,150 miles and lasting 11 weeks, averaging about 14.5 miles a day between 79 staging points.[1] Sigeric's recorded itinerary is a unique example of its kind for this period of Anglo-Saxon history, but it points implicitly to the existence of an infrastructure that must have supported countless similar journeys as northern Europeans made the long pilgrimage to Rome. That a churchman from Kent could set out secure in the knowledge that he would be able to find hospitality in places as distant and different as Laon, Lausanne, and Lucca tacitly illustrates the extensive networks of contact, friendship, and commerce that criss-crossed the continent and supported the wide-ranging activities of Europe's social and political elites. The elites of Britain and Ireland, as symbolized by Sigeric, were thoroughly embedded in this wider world. They looked south instinctively: for many archbishops of Canterbury, the Alps and the Rhine were probably more recognizable landmarks than the Pennines or the Tweed.

Regular cross-Channel contact was not a new phenomenon but rested on centuries of familiarity that – even for those parts of Europe that had not been part of the Roman Empire – helped to distribute a shared mental geography and sociology that complemented more local expressions of identity. Yet their very ubiquity is what makes continental connections difficult for the historian to study. Because they did not exist as distinct categories of thought or action, it did not occur to contemporaries to write about "foreign policy" or "relations with Europe." Our sources, consequently, are fragmentary and often tantalizingly allusive. Sigeric's excepted, the travels of merchants, pilgrims, and nobles can only be glimpsed fleetingly rather than followed in detail. The written sources are also unevenly distributed: we have a reasonable amount of information about contacts between the continent and Southumbria, but drastically less about those involving Northumbria, Scotland, and Ireland, and virtually nothing concerning Wales. We should hesitate before interpreting from this pattern a direct correlation between weight of evidence and volume of traffic, since it also reflects respective rates of text production and survival more generally. For similar reasons, we have to be careful about reading the survival of more evidence for cross-Channel contact from the eleventh century than the tenth as a straightforward indicator of increasing activity. Although it cannot hope to take account of all the existing evidence, this chapter will attempt to make sense of how insular elites responded and contributed to the major political, economic, and ecclesiastical developments of tenth- and eleventh-century Europe.

The Age of Æthelstan

The first coherent narratives of what we might characterize as diplomatic activity in this period were written in the aftermath of the Norman Conquest of England in 1066, when apologists for the new regime constructed historical justifications by delineating a long series of cross-Channel agreements and promises whose logical outcome was alleged to be the legitimate kingship of Duke William. These histories began in the reigns of King Æthelred II of England and Duke Richard II of Normandy, whose alliance was symbolized by the former's marriage in 1002 to the latter's sister Emma. However, a more complete account of this sort of contact has to begin almost a century earlier with a remarkable series of marriages secured during the reigns of the English kings Edward the Elder (899–924) and his son Æthelstan (924–39).

The sequence began sometime between 893 and 899 with the wedding of Edward's sister – Alfred's daughter – Ælfthryth and Baldwin II, count of Flanders, which built on well-established existing connections between Wessex and Flanders. There followed several further betrothals between Edward's daughters and various northern European dynasts. First out of the blocks was Eadgifu, who around 919 married Charles III "the Straightforward" (or "the Simple"), the Carolingian king of west Francia (898–923/9). Then, in 926, the most powerful noble in the west Frankish kingdom, Hugh "the Great," asked for and received the hand of Eadgifu's sister, Eadhild. Finally, in 929 two more sisters, Edith and Edgiva, were dispatched at the request of Henry I, the Saxon king of east Francia (919–36), who wanted a choice of bride for his son and heir Otto.[2] Edith was the winner, and Edgiva was compensated with a slightly less prestigious husband in the shape of Louis, brother of King Rudolf II of Burgundy. By 930, Æthelstan had a half-sister in a position of influence at almost every major court in north-western Europe, giving him a presence by proxy on the continent that was inestimably greater than that enjoyed by any of his predecessors. The contrast with the immediate past is striking and can be explained in large part by the marriage policies of the ninth-century Carolingians, who betrothed their sons to noblewomen of indigenous elites and programmatically avoided unions between male heirs and foreign princesses. Although they sometimes allowed their daughters to become queens at foreign courts, one really has to go back to the sixth century to find a similar constellation of marriage alliances involving the Franks and their neighbors.

The political situation on the continent helps us understand this pattern. The disintegration of the Frankish Empire in 888 led to the appearance of several smaller kingdoms, none of whose rulers was a direct male-line adult descendant of the ruling Carolingian house. This, coupled with a diminished material base, meant that their power was not only compromised but also equal, so that none of them was able to assert lasting dominance over the others. The desire to improve their stock with royal blood of a more mature vintage was an integral part of these rulers' struggle to establish their families' dynastic futures. The royal house of Wessex was, by this time, considerably more antique than most of its continental counterparts: contemporary appreciation of its prestige is preserved in Hrotsvitha of Gandersheim's claim that Edith brought the charisma of sanctity to Otto's family thanks to her descent from the seventh-century saint-king Oswald.[3] A more specific context for the alliances of the 920s was created by the deposition in 923 of Charles the Straightforward (the last male-line Carolingian – he had been a minor in 888), after which his wife Eadgifu took their infant son Louis to Wessex for safe-keeping. It is almost certain that she played an important role in arranging the subsequent marriages, which may have been conditional on commitment to Louis's future succession – it is noticeable that Raoul, the king of west Francia (923–36) and so Louis's direct competitor, was the one major ruler excluded. Acquisition of an English wife thus enabled a man like Hugh the Great to boost his status not just through the prestige of the marriage itself, but also through the opportunity to position himself as the guarantor of the exiled king's rights.

Æthelstan's quasi-imperial pretensions, reflected in the increasingly inflated titulature of his charters, were perhaps shaped by a sense of himself as a European dynastic paterfamilias as well as by his ambitions to extend the power of Wessex through Britain. His notional superiority was also displayed in an avidly acquired relic collection whose highlights included the lance used to pierce Christ's side while he was on the cross and other items associated with the great Frankish emperor Charlemagne (768–814). From this, it has been inferred that Æthelstan consciously modeled himself on Charlemagne; from the fact that these resonant relics were sent to him by Hugh the Great, we could argue that this persona was also recognized by outsiders. The king's imperial posturing was not empty bluster since Anglo-Saxon attempts to interfere in continental politics subsequently enjoyed a certain amount of success. Upon hearing of Raoul's death in 936, Æthelstan was able to establish two exiles from his court as rulers in their ancestral homelands: Louis IV in west Francia and Alan "Twistedbeard" in Brittany.[4] In 939, he sent a fleet to support Louis against internal enemies (the first evidence for such direct intervention in continental affairs by an English king, and therefore remarkable despite its failure), and as late as 946 his brother and successor Edmund was still making his voice heard on behalf of the young Carolingian.[5] These strident interventions must have rested on a regular exchange of embassies: how else would Arnulf's people have been able to recognize Æthelstan's brother, drowned off Flanders in 933 and given an honorable funeral by the count (*EHD*, I, no. 26)?

The period of close contact defined by the marriages of Æthelstan's half-sisters did not last long, but these unions were remembered long after the deaths of the participants. A mid-tenth century genealogy intended to exalt the bloodline of Arnulf of Flanders carefully advertised the count's Anglo-Saxon connections alongside his ties to the Carolingian and Robertian houses.[6] At around the same time, Hrotsvitha identified Edith's Englishness as a key part of the story of the Ottonians' rise to greatness in Germany; and in the early eleventh century an author at the Saxon royal nunnery of Quedlinburg still thought it worth stressing that Otto I's queen had been "daughter of the king of the English."[7] These extended family ties remained important enough for the ealdorman Æthelweard to dedicate his Latin translation of a version of the *Anglo-Saxon Chronicle*, sometime between 978 and 988, to the Saxon abbess Mathilda, granddaughter of Otto and Edith, on the basis that they shared descent from the family of Alfred. In his prefatory letter, he recalled the marriage alliances of the 920s, though he admitted to not knowing all the details and hoped his cousin could enlighten him. Their correspondence, which may also lie behind a rare English notice in 982 on the deeds of Otto II and his nephew ("son of the aetheling Liudolf, son of Otto the Elder and King Edward's daughter"), was thus based on a general awareness of shared background that was apparently important enough for Æthelweard to imagine that an account of English history would be of interest to a distant cousin in Germany.[8] It was not just the families themselves who remembered the significance of the age of Æthelstan in cross-Channel relations. A text from the 970s dedicated to the archbishop of Cologne referred to the story of the embassies as "known to nearly all," while, west of the Rhine, the historian Richer was able to elaborate his sources' information about the careers of Eadgifu and Æthelstan with details that had either passed down through his family or were circulating in late tenth-century Rheims.[9] The marriage alliances of the earlier tenth century therefore helped to shape not only the family memories of Anglo-Saxon and continental ruling dynasties, but also to articulate the mental geography of northern European elites more generally.

The Age of Monastic Reform

Dynastic links also helped to grease the wheels of other types of elite contact. High politics in north-west Europe in the second half of the tenth century was heavily influenced by the discourse of Benedictine monastic reform. The architects of the reform presented themselves as wielders of new brooms, sweeping away corrupt practices and returning monastic lifestyles to a purer form based on a more authentic reading of the Benedictine Rule. In truth, the exaggerated rhetoric often masked fundamental continuities in the political and social functions of monastic communities, with reform sometimes invoked by lay patrons as a way of asserting their control over important foundations, another crucial resource in the competitive political world of post-Carolingian Europe. The nurseries of the reform were to be found at Gorze in Lotharingia, Ghent in Flanders, and Fleury in west Francia (which claimed to have the body of St. Benedict himself), all houses which were reformed in the 930s. The ideology of reform snaked out along the political networks of which these institutions were nodal points, and by the reign of King Edgar (957/9–75) at the latest had become prominent in England. That Wessex at least was fully integrated into these networks is confirmed by the travels of high-profile ecclesiastics like Oswald, later bishop of Worcester and archbishop of York, who was at Fleury during the late 950s, and Dunstan, future archbishop of Canterbury, who spent two years at St. Peter's in Ghent around the same time. Connections between the Southumbrian elite and the monasteries of Francia had their roots in the age of Æthelstan. Bishop Oda of Ramsbury (and later Canterbury) is known to have visited Fleury at some point, with the most likely date perhaps 936 when, according to Richer, he was among those charged with escorting Louis IV to Boulogne.[10] Oda, as well as being one of Æthelstan's closest confidants, also happened to be Oswald's uncle.

An older school of thought attributed the appearance of monastic reform in England directly to the continental sojourning of Dunstan and Oswald. Certainly, the *Regularis concordia*, the nearest thing we have to a reformers' mission statement, advertises their intention to improve "the rude English church" with "the seemly customs of the Gallic churches as well as those of Rome," and the two years spent by the continental reformer Abbo of Fleury at the East Anglian monastery of Ramsey (where he reportedly found that English food and beer made him fat) exemplifies the intensification of contacts between leading figures and institutions either side of the Channel in the late tenth century.[11] However, the enthusiasm of the reformers and their hagiographers for trashing the prior state of the English church in order to justify and glorify their own actions means that the continental-inspiration model, with its downbeat valuation of the indigenous past, has to be taken with a pinch of salt. The roots of the Edgarian reform were manifold and not all of its continental influences were contemporary, since some of the Frankish canon collections that informed English thinking derived from the Carolingian-sponsored reforms of the early ninth century. Nor was the traffic all one way: a large part of Fleury's tenth-century library, for instance, came from England. Links of this sort also predated Edgar. Both Edward the Elder and Æthelstan were apparently regarded as honorary lay brothers in the community of St. Samson at Dol in Brittany, while Bishop Cenwald of Worcester's visit to St. Gall (modern Switzerland) on its patron's feast day in 929 should probably be seen as the expression of a similar confraternity (*EHD*, I, no. 228). Associations between reform-minded rulers and churchmen on either side of the Channel were, in other words, already longstanding and complex by the time Dunstan and Oswald packed their bags and headed for the coast.

The circle of those involved in reform extended beyond Wessex, as shown by the remarkable *Life of St. Cathróe of Metz* written at Gorze during the 980s.[12] A Scottish teacher of some repute, Cathróe spent his early career at Dunkeld, Armagh, and Abernethy and enjoyed the favor of King Constantine II (900–43). His hagiographer describes his desire to go on pilgrimage, his long journey through southern Scotland and England, and his monastic adventures on the continent, where he made contact with major sponsors of reform, visited Fleury for instruction, and was placed in charge of abbeys at Waulsort and Metz. His journey can be dated to the early 940s, and his death (en route back from a visit to Otto I's second wife, the Empress Adelheid) to the early 970s. Cathróe's career unfolded partly along channels articulated by reform: he was escorted to the south coast by Archbishop Oda of Canterbury, whose connections with Fleury may have paved the way for his own subsequent visit (in fact, Oda is known to have traveled to Rome for the pallium in 941 – did he also accompany Cathróe across the sea?); and his later career was based on the contacts he made in reforming circles surrounding Adalbero, bishop of Metz.

Yet Cathróe's case also warns us against accepting our sources' presentation of all cross-Channel contact as enveloped within the culture of monasticism. His success depended above all on the worldly connections typical of the insular elite. The kings, bishops, and nobles whose patronage supported his pilgrimage (including Dyfnwal of Strathclyde, Erik of York, and Edmund of Wessex) are known more often than not to have been his relations and friends. These people helped him because of who he was rather than what he thought about the Benedictine Rule. Similarly, Edmund's taking-in of "unreformed" monks ejected from St.-Bertin by Arnulf of Flanders tells us more about the positive relationship between the two rulers than about their respective attitudes to monastic principles. Various unreformed Flemish abbots, meanwhile, asked successive archbishops of Canterbury to renew their friendship and patronage (which dated from the days of Fulk and Alfred), showing that associations formed by proximity and politics were not always superseded by the dictates of monastic fashion.[13] Reform did not completely define such contact: for Cathróe, as for the monastic communities of Flanders, political connections, family, and friendship remained important bridges across the Channel.

The reinforcing of ties between churchmen in this period could nevertheless be seen as having a homogenizing effect, with distinct insular forms of religious life coming under pressure to adapt to broader European models. That pressure is clearest in direct encounters between representatives of different traditions. Cathróe, for example, seems to have been absorbed seamlessly into the Frankish monastic world, at least in the view of his Lotharingian hagiographer. Indeed, the appropriation of Cathróe and his fellow-travelers as hero-saints of the continental reform fed into a growing Lotharingian fascination with Irish and Scottish monastic traditions in the tenth and eleventh centuries. Other travelers remained more conspicuous. A treatise *On the Condition of the Holy Church* composed at Laon in the 960s couches its discussion in the form of a debate between two fictional characters, one cast as a Frankish reformer, the other apparently as a Scottish or Irish churchman who, for all that he resided in Francia, retained rather different views on monastic matters.[14] This sort of cultural variety is still very much in evidence in the work of the northern Irish historian Marianus Scottus (1028–82), who served in prominent church positions in Cologne, Fulda, and Mainz. His chronicle was written in an ancient genre (universal history) that was more characteristic of the culture in which he died than the one into which he had been born – his was the first to be penned by an Irishman – yet its definitions of monastic life retain an Irish flavor. If such cultural differences lingered in the consciousnesses of people who had spent decades in the Frankish and German heartlands, it is hardly surprising that tenth-century monastic practices in Britain and Ireland were not completely transformed by continental influence.

The traffic of ideas and personnel occasioned by the reform period also coincided with the apparent Carolingianization of some aspects of Anglo-Saxon political discourse. The considerable cultural pressure exerted by the sheer size of the nearby Frankish world helped mold royal legislation from the reign of Alfred onward, culminating in the laws of Cnut in the early eleventh century. The similarities reside partly in the laws' general character, in particular their increasing emphasis on morality and sin, but there is also evidence for more direct borrowing: laws on oaths issued by Edward, Æthelstan, Edmund, and Cnut, for instance, echo Carolingian capitularies both conceptually and verbally.[15] Outside Italy, no tenth-century continental rulers are known to have issued written legislation of any substance, so Anglo-Saxon reverence for this material may derive less from its contemporary continental provenance than from its status as an emblem of a past age of Frankish imperial greatness.

Several Anglo-Saxon rulers of this period harbored quasi-imperial pretensions, and none more so than Edgar, whose second coronation at Bath in 973 was seemingly intended to confer on him a sort of notional emperorship. Bath's natural springs, reminiscent of Charlemagne's palace at Aachen, and extant Roman buildings suggest the occasion was staged with wider European historical models in mind. There may also have been a more immediate inspiration: Otto II's marriage and the coronation of his empress Theophanu had been celebrated at Rome with full imperial splendor a year earlier, when Oswald was probably in the city. The Christological depictions of rulership applied to Edgar and his queen Ælfthryth in texts like the *Regularis concordia* and the *Benedictional of Æthelwold* also echo Ottonian ideologies. We have to pause, however, before inferring direct German influence: the first iconographic expressions of these ideologies actually appeared in England before Germany. Meanwhile, the English coronation *ordo* used to solemnize Edgar's status had also been used to inaugurate the Frankish king Louis IV in 936. Such political ideas bubbled to the surface as the result of a complex cross-Channel dialogue rather than through the adoption of off-the-peg continental models of authority by the rulers of Wessex.

Anglo-Saxon enthusiasm for Frankish ideologies is, nonetheless, encapsulated well by Patrick Wormald's description of England's "ideological climate" as belonging to a "Carolingian zone."[16] The extent to which the elites of Scotland, Wales, and Ireland shared similar cultural assumptions is rendered opaque by the dearth and nature of the sources. Still, Cathróe's upbringing evidently did not leave him unprepared for the challenges of maneuvering his way through elite society in England, Francia, and Germany – his apparently seamless transitions are consistent with the broad similarities that historians have identified between Scottish and Ottonian kingship. The southern Welsh king Hywel Dda ("the Good") also belonged to the same political universe to judge by the Anglo-Saxon influence inferred by historians from his decision to issue written law. That wider currents might have reached Wales through an English filter is not surprising, but Hywel's visit to Rome in 928 shows that he also had first-hand experience of, and contacts within, the continental kingdoms of post-Carolingian Europe.[17]

In the end, however, it is less the programmatic statements of legislating rulers than the casualness of tenth-century sources' references to cross-Channel affairs that is most striking. Although he was by no means the first to do so, the artlessness with which an author such as Flodoard of Rheims used the term "transmarinus" when referring to the English kingdom suggests that he thought of it as analogous to the term "transrhenensis": to a denizen of Rheims in the mid-tenth century, the kings across the sea were no more exotic than those across the Rhine.[18] More often than not, observers did not even think that foreignness was worth mentioning. The developments of the tenth century did not lead to the absorption of elite society in Britain and Ireland into some sort of homogeneous European culture. Evidently, though, people of different cultural backgrounds were familiar enough with each other that difference was not a major issue in itself.

The Age of Cnut

The rule is proved by a glaring exception: when it came to the matter of armed Scandinavians, the authors of our sources were rarely so sanguine. Yet by 1016 England was ruled by Cnut, a Christian Dane. The irony of his status as poacher turned gamekeeper was not lost on contemporaries like the Saxon chronicler Thietmar of Merseburg: "Like the basilisk in the deserted wastes of Libya, a man who had previously joined his father in invading and thoroughly wasting the land of the Angles was now its sole defender."[19] The return of viking raids in 980, which escalated into more concerted attacks from 991, was organized in large part by two Scandinavian rulers, Óláf Tryggvason from Norway and Swegn Forkbeard from Denmark. After two decades of sustained aggression, Swegn forced Æthelred II into exile and gained recognition as king in 1013; by the end of 1016, Æthelred and Swegn were dead and Cnut, the latter's son, began establishing himself as sole ruler. Traditional explanations of these events blamed Æthelred's weakness, but the version of the *Anglo-Saxon Chronicle* on which this view is founded was written with hindsight and must be used with care. Developments in Denmark, where Swegn's father Harald Bluetooth (c.950–c.987) had accumulated unprecedented levels of power, were more important. Harald's authority is manifest in his ability to mobilize manpower and resources in major construction projects, including his dynastic mausoleum at Jelling, the massive circular camps known as the Trelleborgs, and the half-mile-long bridge at Ravning Enge. Yet these projects are also monuments to Harald's vulnerability. The Trelleborgs were constructed for defense more than attack and hint at the existence of internal enemies, perhaps inflamed by the king's decision to convert to Christianity or by dynastic in-fighting. The flow of Middle Eastern silver through Russia–Ukraine to the Baltic also started to dry up in the 960s, contributing to the abandonment of important trading-posts like Birka in Sweden and, consequently, to the Danes coming under increasing pressure from Germany. A combination of all these factors – drastic economic change, cultural pressure from Christian missionaries, and dynastic centralization and conflict – contributed to the renewal of raiding on England.

Cnut treated his kingdoms as separate units and even attempted to efface the negative connotations of his Scandinavian identity, performing extravagant acts of religious patronage to atone for the martyrdoms of King Edmund of East Anglia (d.869) and Archbishop Ælfheah of Canterbury (d.1012) and issuing a law code that self-consciously advertised his adherence to the kingdom's legal traditions. But sharing a king who was the head of a de facto North Sea empire meant that links between England and Scandinavia were inevitably reoriented to some extent, witnessed, for instance, by the role of English missionaries in the establishment of the early Scandinavian church. Cnut's entourage in England was evidently constituted in part by Norse speakers, to judge by skaldic poetry written in his praise, and Scandinavian earls held high office under him. But to juxtapose Cnut's Danishness with his Englishness is to obscure the more cosmopolitan aspects of his court, at which Flemish, French, and Latin were also spoken and read. Cnut's own mother was a Polish princess, a constant reminder of which he bore in his baptismal name – Lambert – which probably derived from her family. The king's political ambitions also played out on a broader European canvas. Famously, he participated with King Rudolf of Burgundy in the ceremonies for the imperial coronation of Conrad II at Rome in 1027.[20] His dealings with Conrad probably turned on issues surrounding the frontier between the Danish and German realms, such as the status of the bishopric of Schleswig, but the trip also gave him the opportunity to negotiate toll exemptions for pilgrims and merchants traveling through Burgundy and Italy. The obligations that Cnut's Danishness placed upon him thus created specific advantages for his English subjects.

Cnut's role as a bridge between these different worlds was created in part by his need to portray himself as a mainstream European ruler. His trip to Rome (the first by an English king since the ninth century) was not just about sorting out the detail of frontier diplomacy, it was also meant to advertise his adherence to a shared international model of rulership, authority, and tradition. This was a club to which Scandinavian rulers were newcomers; gifts from pope and emperor of "vessels of gold and silver and silk robes and very costly garments," about which he boasted in a letter to his English subjects, confirmed his membership (*EHD*, I, no. 49). The message was still being transmitted after his death: the *Encomium Emmae Reginae*, written c.1040 for his wife Emma at the court of their son Harthacnut, used Virgilian models to endow Cnut with an "imperial and civilized European identity."[21] Cnut's efforts to perform that identity were helped by the betrothal of his daughter Gunnhild to the emperor's son King Henry (III) in 1035 and their marriage a year later.[22] The union seems to have cemented relations between the two realms in ways that survived Cnut's death in 1035 and Gunnhild's in 1038: Henry sent ambassadors and gifts to the coronation of Edward the Confessor in 1042, and in 1049 Edward reciprocated by dispatching ships to assist an imperial campaign against Flanders.[23] Cnut's meeting with Rudolf also meant that he became a figure of note in Burgundy, where one contemporary writer acquired an otherwise inexplicable interest in Scottish politics.[24]

Cnut's use of his influence with such figures to broker a reduction of burdens on English and Danish pilgrims and traders reminds us that below the level of royal and elite contact, the background noise of mercantile activity must have constituted the greatest volume of cross-Channel contact. The law code known as IV Æthelred (c.1000) refers casually to the presence in London of traders from Rouen, Flanders, Ponthieu, Normandy, Huy, Liège, Nivelles, and the Empire buying and selling goods like fish, wine, pepper, and cloth.[25] Everyday items of Norwegian and Danish provenance have also been discovered in the Scandinavian-controlled towns of the north and east. In general, though, the sources are disproportionately revealing about non-consumable luxuries, whose status was more likely to attract comment in writing and preservation in archaeological contexts. Thus Ælfric's *Colloquy* describes a merchant carrying ivory, silk, and other luxuries, while of all the textiles uncovered by excavations at Coppergate in York, no less than 22 percent were silk. We cannot always be sure that such high-status commodities were bought rather than exchanged. While the identical dimensions of two silks found in York and Lincoln allow us to imagine that they originated among the wares of some traveling salesman, a story recalled by the Canterbury monk and historian Eadmer about a bishop of Benevento who received from Cnut's queen Emma a fabulous cope in exchange for some relics reminds us that there were alternative mechanisms for the transfer across Europe of high-status objects.[26]

Either way – and it was, of course, both ways – Byzantine silk and other surviving exotica were most likely not unloaded onto British soil from ships that had come directly from the Mediterranean or the Black Sea. As IV Æthelred implies, most overseas trade was probably relatively short-distance, with ports on the south and east coasts dealing regularly with their nearest counterparts in Francia and Scandinavia, respectively. This arrangement was formalized to some extent by rulers' granting of rights and properties at English ports to certain continental monasteries, including Fécamp in Normandy and St. Peter's at Ghent. We should probably think of these trade routes as constituting one of a series of overlapping commercial networks that in aggregate formed a kind of staggered global economy. This disjointed connectedness is why a shortage of silver in the Caliphate could, as we have seen, have a butterfly effect capable of altering economic activity in Sweden and provoking Scandinavian raiding on the coast of England. Attempts were made to control the flow of commerce by rulers like Queen Margaret of Scotland (d.1093) who, according to her biographer Turgot, introduced foreign traders peddling "precious wares which until then were unknown in Scotland."[27] However, queens, kings, and princes were not the prime movers in creating economic activity; rather, the profitability of ports, towns, and other centers of commerce usually predated, and attracted, their interest. Although it is difficult to evaluate and probably easy to overestimate the relative importance of overseas trade to the economies of the archipelago, the harmonization of continental coin standards with those of England during the eleventh century – Flanders c.1026, Cologne shortly thereafter, and Normandy c.1077 – leaves little doubt that cross-Channel trade was becoming increasingly profitable and regularized.

The Age of Papal Reform

Contacts with the papacy also took on a new character in the eleventh century. Although Cnut was the first English king in over a century to visit the holy city, Rome had always been a draw for insular rulers – like Hywel Dda – wishing to exalt themselves through the ostentatious humility of pilgrimage, while archbishops of Canterbury and, latterly, York were accustomed to visit the pope to acquire the pallium at the start of their tenures. In the eleventh century, royal pilgrimages to Rome seem to have increased in number: the annals record trips made by Irish rulers in 1028, 1042, 1051, and 1064, and in 1050, according to Marianus Scottus, the Scottish king Macbeth "scattered money like seed to the poor at Rome."[28] Developments in Rome itself help explain this trend. From the middle of the century, a series of reforming popes started to change the aspirations and character of the Holy See. The most celebrated is Gregory VII (1073–85), whose assertion of papal rights over, among other things, episcopal appointments, brought him into open conflict with the emperor Henry IV (1056–1105). However, Gregory's startling confidence was rooted in the reformist posturing of a series of earlier popes beginning with Leo IX (1049–54). Despite the fact that the papal reform culminated with a pope and an emperor shrieking at each other about which of them had the right to depose the other, its initial success and cachet were down to imperial patronage: Leo, an Alsatian, was an appointee and cousin of Henry III.

This drew the papacy into a network of family and alliance of which the English kings were already members: until Gunnhild's death, Harthacnut and Edward the Confessor had both been Henry's brothers-in-law. We have already seen that Edward sent help to Henry in 1049, so it is not surprising that English bishops are known to have been present at papal councils at Rome and Vercelli in 1050 (*ASC* 1049, 1050). Leo's most famous synod, held at Rheims in 1049, also attended by English bishops, was the first papal assembly convoked north of the Alps and received a glowing notice in the *Anglo-Saxon Chronicle*: the papacy was getting closer literally as well as figuratively. It also seems more than coincidental that Macbeth's trip to Rome took place in 1050. He may even have been present at Rheims, since Leo's biographer states that there was a delegation of "Scotti" in attendance.[29] Either way, Macbeth's pilgrimage in itself suggests that he too belonged, or wanted to belong, to this international network of kings and reformers.

Relations between its members were not stress-free, as shown by Leo's refusal of the pallium to Edward's next appointment to the see of Canterbury, Stigand. Moreover, despite the evident enthusiasm of rulers and bishops to be seen to be involved in these councils, and of popes to dictate to them in ecclesiastical matters, the impact of reformist ideologies on practices of church organization in Britain and Ireland before 1100 was probably minimal. Although the odor of papal authoritarianism hangs around Gregory VII's demands that Lanfranc, archbishop of Canterbury (1070–89), reform the lifestyles of the Irish, the prime mover may in fact have been the archbishop, who probably initiated the correspondence as part of an attempt to bolster his own authority over the Irish bishops.[30] Some aspects of English church reform after 1050 superficially reflect a desire to follow papal strictures; for example, the movement of episcopal sees from rural to urban sites such as Lincoln and Exeter. On the other hand, we might do better to ascribe this adoption of continental norms to the fact that many eleventh-century English bishops had continental educations: Duduc of Wells, for instance, was a Saxon and Ulf of Dorchester a Norman. There was also a considerable cohort of Lotharingian bishops, whose appearance in England is attributable to Cnut and thus predates the era of papal assertiveness. The cosmopolitan character of the mid-eleventh-century episcopate is illustrated by the career of Leofric, bishop of Exeter (1046–72). Perhaps Cornish by birth, his Lotharingian upbringing was reflected in his imposition of the Rule of St. Chrodegang (a monastic code from Metz) on the newly urbanized cathedral canons of Exeter, but he was also a major patron of Anglo-Saxon vernacular literature.

Still, the papacy's rising profile became increasingly hard to ignore, and its claims for Rome as a source of jurisdiction, rather than simply a place of holy pilgrimage, were heard with increasing frequency. Simultaneously, canon lawyers, such as Ivo of Chartres (d.1117), provided theoretical underpinning for the definition of a supranational ecclesiastical hierarchy. Such messages were clearly well established in the consciousness of men like William of St. Calais, bishop of Durham, who appealed to Rome after being denied the right to trial for treason before a tribunal of bishops in 1088 – the first known appeal of its kind by an English bishop for centuries (*EHD*, II, no. 84). To see this dispute as a manifestation of church/state tension would be anachronistic: Archbishop Lanfranc supported the king against the bishop, and the case was ultimately resolved without much reference to Rome. The significance of the post-1049 papacy for insular politics was not down to the popes' sudden acquisition of constitutional authority, but to the fact that the papacy's reforming profile and close links to the empire made it a credible external source of authority that kings as well as bishops could invoke in their attempts to legitimize local political maneuvers. When it suited the interests of rulers to appeal to papal authority, as it did in 1070 when William the Conqueror collaborated with Roman legates to depose the old guard among the English episcopate, they had no hesitation. For the popes, the opportunity to position themselves as arbiters enabled them to act out their fantasies of influence over kings and emperors, and incrementally to advance the notion, however theoretical, of formal supremacy.

The Age of the Normans

It is in this context that we should see Alexander II's approval of the Norman Conquest of England. William of Normandy's invasion of 1066 was essentially the final move in a complex dispute over the succession to the throne of an England already enmeshed in a web of continental connections. The problem was presented by Edward the Confessor's childlessness, which seems to have become an issue by the middle of the 1050s when envoys were sent to find Edward the Exile, the king's nephew, at the Hungarian court where he had ended up after fleeing his homeland in 1016. The Exile died soon after arriving in England and his son Edgar inherited his claim to the throne, though he seems not to have begun pressing it before 1066. A long jostle for position between the remaining principal claimants – Earl Harold Godwineson, Duke William of Normandy, and King Harald Hardrada of Norway – became a sprint for the finishing line as soon as Edward died in January 1066. Harold was the man on the spot and was able to have himself made king, claiming a deathbed bequest by Edward. Within a few months, he had to face his opponents in battle. Harald, who had no right to the throne by family and acted on a promise allegedly made to his predecessor by Harthacnut, was defeated at Stamford Bridge, near York, in late September. William's claim was altogether more complex. It rested ultimately (according to post-1066 sources) on a supposed promise made by Edward in 1051, and was enhanced by the assertion that Harold had sworn oaths of loyalty to the duke while campaigning with him in Brittany. Above all, William considered the justice of his claim proved by divine favor as expressed in the outcome of the battle of Hastings on October 14. Whatever Edward the Confessor's final intentions may have been, the fact that he had apparently offered the position of heir to at least two, if not three, people (Edward the Exile, Harold, and William) meant that conflict between them or their successors was all but inevitable. Given its context in the politics of royal succession, we must see the Conquest less as a modern-style territorial annexation than a result of the close dynastic ties that had been developing between England and its neighbors since the age of Æthelstan; and, in particular, of the increasing complexity of these ties in the early and mid-eleventh century, during which rulers belonging to three different families exercised and transmitted claims to legitimate royal power.

England's connections to Normandy were long-standing and intimate, but no more so than its ties with France, Germany, Flanders, or Scandinavia. The marriage in 1002 of Æthelred and Emma built on an alliance sealed between king and duke in 991 (*EHD*, I, no. 230), but cross-Channel links had a greater antiquity even than that. A contemporary poem about William Longsword (d.942), second leader of the Northmen following their settlement in Francia in 911, states that he had been born "overseas" to a pagan father and Christian mother, possibly indicating that he was of English origin.[31] Other sources add to the sense of connectedness. Writing for Duke Richard II sometime around 1020, Dudo of St. Quentin recorded a fanciful claim that England, and with it Scotland and Ireland, was subject to Normandy.[32] A distorted version of this claim could also lurk behind William of Jumièges's post-Conquest story that Duke Robert the Magnificent (1028–35) had attempted an invasion of England in 1033.[33] There was also a frequent exchange of political exiles between England and Normandy, among them Edward the Confessor. Apologists for the Conqueror retrospectively knitted this history of Anglo-Norman contacts into an elaborate narrative intended to undermine the legitimacy of other claimants and establish the idea that Duke William was the natural and inevitable successor to the Confessor.

We should not allow the persistence and coherence of that narrative to seduce us: William's claims to England were no better, indeed much weaker, than others', and the Normans' relationship with their northern neighbors was not as special as they made out. Ignoring the post-1066 polemics means, for example, that we can see Dudo's odd story and the alleged 1033 invasion as linked to Norman support for the royal claims of the exiled Edward the Confessor rather than early ducal aspirations to the English crown. We also have to be wary of assuming that Edward's Norman upbringing encouraged a powerful "Norman party" at the English court. The *Anglo-Saxon Chronicle* seemingly identifies such a faction by talking about groups of trouble-making "Frenchmen," but, significantly, only during the crises of 1051–2 and 1066. "Them and us" ethnic terminology spat out at times of open conflict tells us something about contemporary perceptions, but not necessarily about the nature of political factions under normal circumstances: ethnic difference was not invisible, but it was usually politically neutral. The kingdom was much more cosmopolitan than suggested by the English vs Normans conceptualization produced by the events of 1066 and passed into modern historiography. A significant minority of small landholders in late Anglo-Saxon England had French or Norman names, and it is probable that some of them were English by descent, suggesting a high degree of intermarriage. If the elite population of England had a heterogeneous character in the age of Edgar, this was all the more true after the Europeanizing reigns of Cnut and Edward.

Taking a longer view, then, we should look at the Norman Conquest less as an epochal moment up to which all previous history led than as the outcome of a succession crisis that was absolutely characteristic of eleventh-century politics and whose continental framework was inevitable given the long-established international connections of the dynasties involved. Still, an armed conquest is an armed conquest, and there is no doubt that the invasion radically altered social and political relations between groups inside Britain and Ireland. By the end of the century, few of the kingdom's leading landholders and none of its bishops were English (most were Norman). Arguably, even the landscape was Europeanized as castles and churches constructed according to imported architectural models began to spring up. The nature of cross-Channel relations was also altered, though exactly how has been a matter of some debate. Arguments that William's dominions should be viewed as constituting a Norman Empire have to be qualified: playing up the evidence for cross-Channel landholding, for example, can obscure the extent to which many aristocrats focused their interests in one or other of the territories involved. Generally speaking, governmental continuity was the order of the day in both Normandy and England, and Williams I and II spent relatively little of their time – no more than half – north of the Channel. In the relationship between its parts, the structure of William's "empire" was thus not radically different from that of Cnut.

Yet regardless of formal considerations, the fact that a single dynasty ruled two adjacent territories had major political implications, as illustrated by the 1075 rebellion against the king. The conspiracy was led by the last English earl Waltheof, Roger earl of Hereford, a Norman, and Ralph earl of East Anglia and lord of Gael in Brittany. The plot collapsed relatively quickly after the capture of Norwich castle, but two years later William was still pursuing Ralph in Brittany until the arrival of King Philip of France forced him to beat a hasty retreat (*ASC* E, 1076). The fact that some members of the Norman aristocracy played out their ambitions on a cross-Channel stage shows how political conflict with its roots in England could be internationalized in an instant and had the potential to drag in all manner of northern French counts and rulers. The mixed origins of the rebels confirm that even after 1066 the elite remained multicultural, and that ethnicity was not a simple determinant of allegiance.

Although the Normans did not immediately try to extend territorial control over Wales, Scotland, and Ireland, they were able to exert considerable pressure. Lanfranc's attempts to interfere in the Irish church have already been mentioned; we should also note that his successor, Anselm, tried to suspend the Welsh bishoprics of St. David's and Llandaff. These efforts may not have met with more than nominal success, but with the Normans' imposition of a Breton bishop on the see of Bangor in 1092 the aspirations of European ecclesiasts were parachuted directly into an area where they had previously had limited influence. Meanwhile, the chivalric mores of continental aristocratic culture, with its particular expectations about the conduct of war and the treatment of rebels and prisoners, seeped ever further north and west. Mediated through the influence of their larger neighbor, the non-English parts of the archipelago were thus confronted ever more directly by the norms of European elite behavior.

The infiltration of such norms also crept along networks of influence that bypassed the Anglo-Norman court. The same matrix of dynastic marriage, exile, and alliance that made the succession to Edward the Confessor so complex had a parallel impact north of the border by bringing to Scotland, as wife of King Máel Coluim III (1058–93), Margaret, daughter of Edward the Exile. English by descent, Hungarian/German by upbringing, and royal through and through, she is represented by her biographer as a cosmopolitanizer of court and kingdom: "it was at her instigation that the natives of Scotland purchased from these traders clothing of various colors, with ornaments to wear; so that from this period, through her suggestion, new costumes of different fashions were adopted, the elegance of which made the wearers appear like a new race of beings."[34] As part of her attempt to reform the Scottish church, she approached Lanfranc and acquired spiritual patronage and practical help from Canterbury – again, on her own initiative rather than at the behest of the Normans.[35]

The novelties attributed to Margaret by Turgot are, of course, exaggerated: we know that Norman knights, exiles from the crisis of 1051–2, were already present at the Scottish court in the reign of Macbeth. But the queen's position meant that her influence on future developments was altogether more permanent. In 1100, one of Margaret's daughters, Edith/Mathilda, was to marry King Henry I of England; and in 1102 another, Mary, married Count Eustace III of Boulogne. Marriage between the royal and comital houses of the west was not new in 1066 or 1002 or even in 919. However, it is arguable that the increasingly intricate web of dynastic ties that was beginning to enmesh the kingdoms of Britain and Ireland by c.1100 had its roots in the age of Æthelstan. Above all, it was the ever-shifting configuration of international dynastic politics that cemented the place of kingdoms like Scotland and England in the wider worlds of the European elite.

Conclusion

The diverse evidence for cross-Channel contact in this period resists easy categorization. By way of conclusion to our selective survey, it may be worth distinguishing contact from influence. Contact – people traveling to and from the continent – was so regular and ubiquitous that it often did not seem worthy of mention, and the likelihood is that the types and volume of traffic stayed more or less constant throughout our period. Influence – that is, the degree to which ecclesiastical and political norms transferred across the Channel in either direction – was surely more variable. We might wonder whether the apparently greater Europeanization of Britain in 1100 compared with 900 is a mirage created by the much greater survival rate of sources: we know from his letters about Lanfranc's attitude toward the papacy, but can only guess at Oda's or Sigeric's thoughts on the subject. However, the increase in the amount of sources could itself be interpreted as reflecting a progressive intensification of relations. Similarly, the prominence of southern England in our evidence may be more than a trick of the light, since the rising power of Wessex increasingly put it in a position to mediate continental cultural influences to its insular neighbors. In any case, there is little doubt that the major developments affecting European politics in the tenth and eleventh centuries (including the fall of the Carolingian Empire, the assertiveness of monastic and papal reform, and the rise of powerful dynasties in Denmark, Normandy, and elsewhere) had knock-on effects for the manner in which continental and insular dynasts interacted with each other. Although the Norman Conquest intensified such relationships more than any other single event, all these interactions helped form layers of memory and mental geography that shaped activity and firmly placed the elites of Britain and Ireland on a continental stage long before William advanced onto the field at Hastings. This process resulted from constant interchange, and the direction of influence should not be seen as exclusively south–north.

The fact that the elites of the archipelago increasingly shared similar concerns with their southern neighbors did not mean that national and local identities were gradually obliterated by a monolithic sense of belonging to Christendom or Europe. Such identities continued to coexist: the self-definition of a man like Lanfranc, born in Italy and trained in Normandy, as a "new Englishman" reflects the continued heterogeneity of the insular elite and its ability to accommodate outsiders.[36] Others, such as the Scots, Welsh, and Irish labeled as barbarians by their newly "civilized" Anglo-Norman neighbors, may have had their sense of difference sharpened rather than softened. Standing on the edge of the twelfth century, a more sobering conclusion is also possible: that the papal revival and the development of a supranational aristocratic culture were consummated in the new imperialism of the "Europeanized" elite, whose ultimate expression was the Crusades. Understandings between the powerful that emerged from the contacts, alliances, and interactions we have been considering were not necessarily benevolent and could catalyze aggression as well as comprehension. Whichever ending we prefer, there can be no doubt that the links forged between Britain, Ireland, and Europe by 1100 were deep, complex, and permanent.

Acknowledgment

For help in writing this chapter, I thank Rob Bartlett, David Ditchburn, Charlie Insley, Steve Marritt, and Alex Woolf.

Notes

1 Ortenberg, "Archbishop Sigeric's pilgrimage."
2 Campbell (ed.), *Chronicle of Æthelweard*, pp. 1–2; von Winterfield (ed.), "Hrotsvitha: *Gesta Ottonis*," pp. 207–8.
3 von Winterfield (ed.), "Hrotsvitha: *Gesta Ottonis*," p. 207.
4 Lauer (ed.), *Les annales de Flodoard, s.a.* 936.
5 Ibid., *s.a.a.* 939, 946.
6 Bethmann (ed.), *Witger: Genealogia*.
7 Giese (ed.), *Annales Quedlinburgenses, s.a.* 929.
8 ASC C, 982; Campbell (ed.), *Chronicle of Æthelweard*, pp. 1–2.
9 *EHD*, I, no. 24; Hoffmann (ed.), *Richer: Historiarum libri IIII*, II. 2, 3, 12, 16, 49.
10 Hoffmann (ed.), *Richer: Historiarum libri IIII*, II. 4.
11 Symons (ed.), *Regularis concordia*, c. 5.
12 Anderson, *Early Sources*, pp. 431–43.
13 *EHD*, I, no. 26; Stubbs, *Memorials of St. Dunstan*, pp. 380–95.
14 Löwe, "*Dialogus*."
15 Attenborough, *Laws*, pp. 121, 149, 153; Robertson, *Laws*, pp. 12, 185.
16 Wormald, *Making of English Law*, p. 124.
17 Dumville (ed.), *Annales Cambriae, s.a.* 928.
18 See, e.g., Lauer (ed.), *Les annales de Flodoard, s.a.* 936.
19 Warner (trans.), "Thietmar: *Chronicon*," 8. 7.
20 Bresslau (ed.), *Wipo: Gesta Chuonradi Imperatoris*, c. 16.
21 Tyler, "Talking about history," 362–3.
22 Bresslau (ed.), *Wipo: Gesta Chuonradi Imperatoris*, c. 35; Tschan (trans.), *Adam of Bremen: History*, II. 56.
23 ASC 1042, 1049; Barlow (ed.), *Vita Eadwardi Regis*, 1. 1.
24 France (ed.), *Rodulfus Glaber: Historiarum libri quinque*, II. 3.
25 Robertson, *Laws*, pp. 70–3.
26 Clarke and Ambrosiani, *Towns in the Viking Age*, pp. 96–7; Rule (ed.), *Eadmer: Historia novorum*, pp. 111–14.
27 Forbes-Leith (trans.), "Turgot, *Life of St. Margaret*," c. 14.
28 Anderson, *Early Sources*, p. 588; Waitz (ed.), *Marianus Scottus: Chronicon*, p. 558.
29 Robinson (trans.), *Life of Leo IX*, II. 4.
30 Clover and Gibson (eds.), *Letters of Lanfranc*, no. 8.
31 Van Houts, *Normans in Europe*, p. 41.
32 Christiansen (trans.), *Dudo: De Moribus*, c. 103.
33 Van Houts (ed.), *William of Jumièges*, VI. 9–10 (11).
34 Forbes-Leith (trans.), "Turgot, *Life of St. Margaret*," c. 14.
35 Clover and Gibson (eds.), *Letters of Lanfranc*, no. 50.
36 Ibid., no. 2.

Further Reading

Donald Bullough's oft-quoted aside, made in 1975, that "England and the Continent in the Tenth Century" was one of the major unwritten works of medieval history, still more or less holds true today, though V. Ortenberg, *The English Church and the Continent in the Tenth and Eleventh Centuries* (Oxford, 1992) is very useful. Several substantial article-length studies offer excellent routes into aspects of the topic, particularly those by Grierson ("The relations between England and Flanders") and Leyser ("The Ottonians and Wessex"), as well as the essays collected in J. Campbell, *Essays in Anglo-Saxon History* (London, 1986). Eleventh-century contacts have been covered much more thoroughly, thanks to interest in the Danish and Norman Conquests. Gillingham, "Britain, Ireland and the south," supplies the best entry point to this material, along with the first two chapters of D. Matthew, *Britain and the Continent 1000–1300* (London, 2005). The eleventh century can also be conveniently approached through the numerous existing studies of individual rulers, including: R. Lavelle, *Aethelred II, King of the English 978–1016* (Stroud, 2002); M. K. Lawson, *Cnut: The Danes in England in the Early Eleventh Century* (London, 1993); P. Stafford, *Queen Emma and Queen Edith: Queenship and Women's Power in Eleventh-century England* (Oxford, 1997); F. Barlow, *Edward the Confessor* (London, 1970); and D. Bates, *William the Conqueror* (London, 1989). P. Stafford, *Unification and Conquest: A Political and Social History of England in the Tenth and Eleventh Centuries* (London, 1989) offers insightful discussions of relations between England and all its neighbors across the whole period. The continental connections of Scotland and Wales have received little direct attention since the evidence is thin until the very end of our period. The essential discussion of Cathróe is D. N. Dumville, "St. Cathróe of Metz and the hagiography of exoticism," in J. Carey, M. Herbert, and Ó Riain (eds.), *Studies in Irish Hagiography: Saints and Scholars* (Dublin, 2001), pp. 172–88. Ireland has attracted more interest: see H. Löwe (ed.), *Die Iren und Europa im früheren Mittelalter* (Stuttgart, 1982).

Bibliography

Anderson, A. O., *Early Sources of Scottish History*, vol. I (Stamford, 1990; first pub. 1922).

Attenborough, F. L., *The Laws of the Earliest English Kings* (Cambridge, 1922).

Barlow, F. (ed.), *Vita Eadwardi Regis: The Life of King Edward who Rests at Winchester*, 2nd edn. (Oxford, 1992).

Bethmann, L. (ed.), *Witger: Genealogia*, MGH SS 9 (Hanover, 1851), pp. 302–4.

Bresslau, H. (ed.), *Wipo: Gesta Chuonradi Imperatoris*, in *Die Werke Wipos*, MGH SRG (Hanover, 1915).

Campbell, A. (ed.), *The Chronicle of Æthelweard* (London, 1962).

Christiansen, E. (trans.), *Dudo: De Moribus*, in *History of the Normans* (Woodbridge, 1998).

Clarke, H. and Ambrosiani, B., *Towns in the Viking Age*, 2nd edn. (Leicester, 1995).

Clover, H. and Gibson, M. (eds.), *The Letters of Lanfranc, Archbishop of Canterbury* (Oxford, 1979).

Deshman, R., "*Christus Rex et Magi Reges*: kingship and Christology in Ottonian and Anglo-Saxon art," *Frühmittelalterliche Studien*, 10 (1976), 367–405.

Douglas, D. C. and Greenaway, G. W. (eds.), *English Historical Documents*, vol. 2: *1042–1189* (London, 1981).

Dumville, D. N. (ed.), *Annales Cambriae* (Cambridge, 2002).

Forbes-Leith, W. (trans.), "Turgot, *Life of St. Margaret*," in M. Stouck (ed.), *Medieval Saints: A Reader* (Peterborough, Ont., 1999), pp. 273–94.

France, J. (ed.), *Rodulfus Glaber: Historiarum libri quinque* (Oxford, 1989).

Gardiner, M., "Shipping and trade between England and the continent during the eleventh century," *Anglo-Norman Studies*, 22 (1999), 71–93.

Giese, M. (ed.), *Annales Quedlinburgenses* (Hanover, 2004).

Gillingham, J., "Britain, Ireland and the south," in W. Davies (ed.), *From the Vikings to the Normans* (Oxford, 2003), pp. 203–32.

Grierson, P., "The relations between England and Flanders before the Norman Conquest," *Transactions of the Royal Historical Society*, 4th series, 23 (1941), 71–112.

Hare, M., "Cnut and Lotharingia: two notes," *Anglo Saxon England*, 29 (2000), 261–78.

Hoffmann, H. (ed.), *Richer: Historiarum libri IIII, MGH SS* 38 (Hanover, 2000).

Lauer, P. (ed.), *Les annales de Flodoard* (Paris, 1906).

Lewis, C. P., "The French in England before the Norman Conquest," *Anglo-Norman Studies*, 17 (1994), 123–44.

Leyser, K., "The Ottonians and Wessex," in K. Leyser, *Communications and Power in Medieval Europe*, vol. I (London, 1994), pp. 73–104.

Löwe, H., "*Dialogus de statu sanctae ecclesiae*: Das Werk eines Iren im Laon des 10. Jahrhunderts," *Deutsches Archiv*, 17 (1961), 12–90.

Ortenberg, V., "Archbishop Sigeric's pilgrimage to Rome in 990," *Anglo-Saxon England*, 19 (1990), 197–246.

Robertson, A. J., *The Laws of the Kings of England from Edmund to Henry I* (Cambridge, 1925).

Robinson, I. (trans.), *Life of Leo IX*, in *The Papal Reform of the Eleventh Century* (Manchester, 2004).

Rule, M. (ed.), *Eadmer: Historia novorum* (London, 1884).

Stubbs, W., *Memorials of St. Dunstan, Archbishop of Canterbury* (London, 1874).

Symons, T. (ed.), *Regularis concordia: The Monastic Agreement of the Monks and Nuns of the English Nation* (London, 1953).

Tschan, F. J. (trans.), *Adam of Bremen: History of the Archbishops of Hamburg-Bremen* (New York, 2002).

Tyler, E. M., "Talking about history in eleventh-century England: the *Encomium Emmae Reginae* and the court of Harthacnut," *Early Medieval Europe*, 13 (2005), 359–83.

Van Houts, E., *The Normans in Europe* (Manchester, 2000).

Van Houts, E. (ed.), *William of Jumièges: Gesta Normannorum Ducum* (Oxford, 1992–5).

von Winterfeld, P. (ed.), "Hrotsvitha of Gandersheim: *Gesta Ottonis*," in *Hrotsvithae Opera* (Berlin, 1902).

Waitz, G. (ed.), *Marianus Scottus: Chronicon, MGH SS* 5 (Hanover, 1844), pp. 481–568.

Warner, D. (trans.) "Thietmar of Merseburg: *Chronicon*," in *Ottonian Germany* (Manchester, 2001).

Whitelock, D. (ed. and trans.), *English Historical Documents*, vol. I: *c.500–1042*, 2nd edn. (London, 1979).

Wormald, P., *The Making of English Law: King Alfred to the Twelfth Century*, vol. I: *Legislation and its Limits* (Oxford, 1999).

CHAPTER TWENTY-THREE

The Institutional Church

CATHERINE CUBITT

"Bitter is the wind tonight
It tosses the ocean's white hair:
Tonight I fear not the fierce warriors of Norway
Coursing on the Irish Sea"[1]

These words, copied into a manuscript by an Irish monk, act as a poignant evocation of the impact of the viking raids upon the church in the British Isles. They conjure up a world not only of sudden violence and destruction, but also of monastic vulnerability, the disruption of the tranquil contemplative life. The viking attacks and settlement of the eighth and ninth centuries have been interpreted as a watershed in the history of the church in the British Isles. Indeed, viking raiding loomed so large in scholarship that it came to function as an explanatory device to account for the perceived change from a supposedly flourishing monastic church of the pre-Viking Age to the clerical and secularized church of the tenth and eleventh centuries. But such an explanation was neither sufficient nor satisfying: it begged questions about the intensity of the raids, their long-term impact, and whether other factors might be at work in the transformations of the ninth and tenth centuries.

The debate in scholarship of the Irish church has perhaps been the most thoroughgoing, asking whether the viking raids really differed from native attacks on religious houses, and questioning the extent of their impact on the fortunes of monasteries.[2] Modern scholarly consensus no longer sees viking raiding as fundamentally disruptive of the church, and therefore doubts that it was the agent of change, arguing instead for much greater continuity between the seventh and eighth and the ninth and tenth centuries.[3] The old picture of development from the early monastic church to an eighth-century episcopal one, which fell into decline and secularization thereafter, has been rejected by many scholars who would prefer to see elements of monasticism and episcopacy coexisting with secular and royal control at all periods of church life.[4]

The tenth and eleventh centuries are, however, still neglected areas in the historiography of the Irish church. Neither Hughes nor Ó Cróinín expends many pages on the later period by comparison with their treatment of the pre-Viking Age, and even Etchingham's admirable revisionist account of pastoral care stops at the year 1000.[5] Honorable exceptions to this include the fine study by Máire Herbert of the monasteries of St. Columba (Colum Cille), which traces their history continuously from their seventh-century inception to the twelfth century, and Christina Harrington's stimulating treatment of women in the church.[6]

The myth of a Golden Age of monasticism was also propagated for the early medieval Welsh church which also was thought to have declined through the impact of the viking raids and through secularization. Churches in Wales did indeed suffer disruption and depredation, with St. David's bearing repeated attacks, particularly in the mid-ninth century and the second half of the eleventh century. But St. David's survived as an influential ecclesiastical institution.[7] Powerful arguments have been put forward questioning the nature of the monastic life in Wales and arguing for greater continuity from the sixth to the eleventh centuries.[8]

Similar debates have taken place among historians of the English church concerning the ferocity and impact of the viking raids in the eighth and ninth centuries and the effect of their settlement in the Anglo-Saxon kingdoms. However, students of the church have tended to converge on the view that viking destruction of monasteries and political disruption led to a genuine decline in church life, with a real drop in learning and manuscript production in the ninth century.[9] This is in part a genuine reflection of the discontinuities in the church – the cessation of major monasteries and bishoprics and a measurable decline in manuscript numbers – but to invoke the vikings as a sufficient cause of so great a transformation is to overlook further questions: for example, why the West Saxon kings failed to revive sees in the east and north, and what happened to the estates of former monasteries.[10]

When monastic life did begin to revive in England in the mid-tenth century, this renewal was prompted by the influence of continental monastic reform and by an idealized image of early monasticism in England. The leaders of reform in England – Archbishop Dunstan of Canterbury, Bishop Æthelwold of Winchester, and Archbishop Oswald of Worcester–York – drew from the pages of Bede's *Ecclesiastical History* a powerful evocation of a church run by saintly religious leaders, chiefly monks and nuns, and consisting of Benedictine monasteries.[11] This deeply unhistorical picture is not unlike the view of the early Irish church propounded by modern historians before the revisionism of Ó Corráin and others, and is an important reminder of the enduring potency that myths of monastic perfection and of Golden Ages possess.

The tenth-century Benedictine reforms in England have dominated the pages of history textbooks, relegating the early tenth century and later eleventh century to the margins. Recently, the extent of the impact of Benedictine reform has been questioned by John Blair, who has stressed its limited geographical impact and its concentration in royal and court circles.[12] His skepticism about the influence of reform is a refreshing reminder of its limitations. But reform brought with it new ways of thinking about the church and its personnel, derived not only from contemporary continental movements but also from the rich pastoral and canonical literature of the Carolingian renaissance. This disseminated ideas concerning the separation of the lay and religious spheres, the distinction between monks and clergy, and enhanced the authority of bishops as both pastoral and political leaders. Ultimately, these ideas were to strike at deeply entrenched features of the early medieval church, such as hereditary control of churches and the right of clergy to marry. It was the muted impact of the Carolingian reforms upon the churches in Ireland, Wales, and Scotland that accentuated the differences between them and the Anglo-Saxon church, and left them appearing so deviant in the eyes of eleventh- and twelfth-century reformers.[13]

For the English church, the end of the period 900–1100 is framed by another invasion of Norsemen, the Norman Conquest of 1066. Like their Scandinavian ancestors, the Normans have been viewed as a transformative element in the English church, responsible for the introduction of much-needed reforms. The poster-boy for the inadequacies of the pre-Conquest English church has been Archbishop Stigand of Canterbury, the man who held simultaneously two of the wealthiest sees in England (Winchester and Canterbury), owed his elevation to the archbishopric to the expulsion of his predecessor, and obtained his pallium from a schismatic pope.[14] Yet, Stigand's ministry was controversial among his own peers and he was hardly a typical figure among the English episcopate. His contemporaries, Archbishop Ealdred of York and Bishop Wulfstan II, shared with Stigand a tendency to combine dioceses but were exemplary churchmen and monks, the former a revered statesman, who seems to have done much to mediate the effects of the Conquest for the English, and the other a man of great sanctity and a model of pastoral zeal.[15] Concentration upon the Conquest as the moment when up-to-date continental ideas and learning entered the country ignores both the long history of cultural cooperation between northern France, Normandy, Flanders, and England, which goes back beyond the tenth century, and the presence in eleventh-century England of Norman and Lotharingian clerics such as Giso of Wells and Leofric of Exeter.[16]

Dioceses and Bishops

Bishops were key figures in all the churches of Britain and Ireland in the tenth and eleventh centuries. However, their roles, powers, and spheres of authority may have differed greatly. To what extent were a bishop's powers limited by his territorial jurisdiction, his diocese? In England, episcopal authority had long been territorially based and circumscribed, coterminous with political authority with usually two or perhaps three bishops per kingdom in the eighth and ninth centuries. But the tenth and eleventh centuries saw some reorganization of sees and there are hints of territorial fluidity. An episcopal hierarchy and provincial structure had been fixed early in the Anglo-Saxon church, with two archdioceses and provinces. The superiority of the archbishop of Canterbury had been reinforced in the eighth and ninth centuries by consecration, but issues of supremacy between York and Canterbury did not emerge until after the Conquest.[17] Wales, Scotland, and Ireland lacked archdioceses and provincial structures. In England, bishops and their dioceses were fundamental to the church in terms not only of its territorial organization but also of the provision of leadership within and without the church. In the Ireland and Wales, bishops shared prominence with abbots of great communities, such as Armagh and Clonmacnoise in Ireland, where both abbacies and episcopal office in the tenth and eleventh centuries could be held by the laity. While the Church of Armagh in Ireland achieved a de facto pre-eminence, there was no formal metropolitan structure which seems also to have been true in Wales and Scotland.

There is some evidence for bishops holding authority in areas geographically separate from their main jurisdictional territories in Ireland and Scotland.[18] Tenth-century Ireland may have witnessed the increasing territorialization of episcopal authority. Where earlier references tended to associate bishops with individual churches rather than with territories, tenth- and eleventh-century annals do link bishops with demarcated regions. While these may be relatively small, they are always larger than a single *túath*. The term "suí-episcop" is used in a number of these annalistic references, and Etchingham argues that it appears to designate a superior bishop with authority over extensive domains. The churches associated with these bishops – Clones, Clonfert, Clonmacnoise, Cloyne, Downpatrick, Emly, Inishkeen, Kildare, and Scattery Island – are all, with the exception of Inishkeen, the sites of twelfth-century reformed bishops. However, the annals do not suggest a continuous history for these higher bishoprics: only one or two bishops are recorded for each church and Etchingham conjectures that their fortunes may have fluctuated, dependent on shifts in ecclesiastical and political power. Lesser bishops are also recorded in the annals, but again individual churches only feature sporadically so it is impossible to construct a continuous sequence of bishops for any one church. Armagh and Iona do have more bishops recorded for the tenth century than other churches. It seems likely, therefore, that Ireland in the tenth and eleventh centuries did possess numerous bishops with territorial jurisdiction, some very small scale but others claiming extensive jurisdictions but without a metropolitan hierarchy. The history of Irish bishoprics was probably not stable and fluctuated according to religious and political circumstances.[19]

In Scotland, the evidence for the presence of bishops is very scant and uncertain, but there were probably bishops at Glasgow, Muthill, Brechin, Dunblane, Dunkeld, and St. Andrews, churches probably also served by communities of Celi Dé.[20] It is likely that Wales was provided with a number of bishoprics but the evidence is very fragmentary and hard to reconstruct. A late ninth- or early tenth-century law tract may indicate that each of the seven *cantrefs* of Dyfed were provided with a bishop, but this interpretation is contested and some suggest that the "bishop houses" referred to were collegiate churches or monasteries subject to the control of the bishop of St. David's.[21] The difference in interpretation is a significant one since the provision of seven bishops within the see of St. David's would suggest plentiful provision, not unlike that supposed for Ireland. Wendy Davies, on the other hand, has argued for fewer bishops and "well-scattered." The see of St. David's in the south-west is reasonably securely attested with annalistic obits evidencing a continuous existence. There were probably also two sees in the south-east, at Llandeilo Fawr and perhaps at Welsh Bicknor and possibly another in the north at Bangor and perhaps also at Llanelwy.[22] These sees were territorially organized, although neither their bases nor their territories were fixed: the bishopric at Llandeilo Fawr seems to have been disbanded and eventually transferred to Llandaff in the late tenth or early eleventh century, and the same may have happened to the see at Bicknor. There are two references to archbishops: Asser describes his kinsman Nobis of St. David's in this way, and the word is also used in the annals for Elfoddw of Gwynedd (probably based at Bangor), but these uses do not designate a formal jurisdiction but probably a honorary title.[23]

The importance of cooperation between major ecclesiastical powers and secular authority in the early Middle Ages can be seen in relations between bishops and their territories and royal power. John Reuben Davies has argued that, in Wales, episcopal structures were influenced by secular overkingships and territories (see chapter 21). In England, the increasing dominance of the West Saxon kings led to a very close alliance between royal and ecclesiastical authority. Bishops were a kind of hinge between church and the king, central figures in royal government and the provision of spiritual counsel to the king. This early association between bishop and kingdom and parsimonious attitude to the provision of bishops continued to be influential in the very different political circumstances of the tenth and eleventh centuries when the kingdom of Wessex was gradually imposing its control on those areas that had fallen under Scandinavian occupation. These two factors, the rise of the West Saxon kings to overlordship over England and the impact of viking raids and settlement, had a profound effect on the history of dioceses that was most marked in the north and east of England. The instability caused by viking depredations in the ninth century resulted in the loss of many sees: those of Hexham, Leicester, and *Dommuc* (in East Anglia) disappeared and were never revived. Other bishoprics suffered major disruption with the bishops of Lindisfarne forced to flee their vulnerable island site and resettle first at Chester-le-Street in 883 and then in 995 at Durham.[24]

The tenth-century West Saxon kings did not seek to revive diocesan organization where it had lapsed, but rather sought to provide pastoral leadership in the north and east by bishops firmly based in areas under West Saxon control.[25] The former kingdom of Northumbria received ministry solely from the archbishop of York who, from 961 to 1062, was also bishop of Worcester. Likewise, East Anglia was served only by the see of Elmham; the see of Dorchester swallowed much of the midlands, including the former diocese of Leicester and ultimately that of Lindsey. In the course of the tenth century, a de facto hierarchy emerges among the Anglo-Saxon dioceses with Canterbury, Winchester, London, Worcester–York the most prestigious and politically important sees. The sees of Sherborne, Ramsbury, and Wells were less prominent, with the latter two being used at times as stepping-stone sees for able men on their way to more prestigious bishoprics. Rochester and Sussex were very much second- or third-rank affairs, with gaps in their episcopal lists and with considerable impoverishment at Selsey. The see of Cornwall seems for many years effectively to have been served by an assistant bishop without a properly endowed see until 994 when Æthelred the Unready was prevailed upon to grant a privilege safeguarding the position of Crediton and establishing it as a full see. Even then, its position was weak and in 1050 the see was transferred by Bishop Leofric to Exeter.

The history of the dioceses in England and their episcopal succession appears superficially very different from that of Wales, Scotland, and Ireland where the episcopal lists are fragmentary in the extreme and a clear hierarchy of sees is lacking. But it is possible to overestimate the stability and efficiency of the English sees, by comparison. Some territorial fluidity continued right up to the Conquest: in the 950s, it appears that the diocese of Selsey may have been briefly absorbed into that of Winchester, and in the eleventh century, bishops dismayed at the lack of resources of their sees were apt to hold more than one, Bishop Hermann combining Ramsbury with Sherborne in 1058, for example.[26] There are numerous gaps in episcopal lists which may hint at sees being held vacant and evidence for lesser bishops. It is likely that the larger sees were served by assistants; we know that episcopal ministry in the see of Canterbury was carried out at some points in the eleventh century by a "bishop" of St. Martin's Church, Canterbury. Nor should one separate too firmly the monastic and episcopal spheres in England. Monks were appointed to bishoprics, including outstanding appointments such as that of Dunstan, former abbot of Glastonbury, to Canterbury. In a number of cases, the newly elevated bishop held on to his monastic abbacy: the saintly reformer Archbishop Dunstan seems to have retained control of his foundation at Westminster for the duration of his lifetime.[27] Ealdred, bishop of Worcester delegated his diocesan functions to the monk Æthelwig of Evesham.[28]

The great size of many of the English dioceses does not seem to have been an issue at the Norman Conquest, an event that otherwise led to great changes in the English church. Stigand and a number of English bishops were deposed at a great council at Winchester in 1070. The remaining bishops included Wulfstan II of Worcester, the saintly monk and the last of a dying breed of Anglo-Saxon bishops, for William I's new appointments solely favored men of continental extraction, usually either monks or his own clergy. His continental episcopal appointments paralleled those to abbacies (discussed below). By 1087, the church was governed by outsiders, men whose training and careers were initially made outside England.[29]

The new episcopate brought changes: not all new, some had been anticipated before 1066. The archaic geography of English cathedral sees jarred upon the incomers and a number of sees were moved to more convenient locations, continuing a practice seen before the Conquest in the move of Ramsbury to Old Sarum and Crediton to Exeter. The huge diocese of Dorchester was preserved, but its cathedral shifted from the south-western extremity to Lincoln, a strategic move, placing its Norman bishop Remigius not only on major communication routes but also in a position to strengthen Norman power in a contentious border area. The building of a new cathedral was soon accompanied by a castle, a pattern found at other newly built cathedrals at Durham and Rochester.[30] New bishops wanted grand new cathedrals designed in new, fashionable, continental styles, and built to impress. These new cathedrals – at Lincoln, York, Rochester, and Winchester, for example – were architecturally innovative and constructed on a much larger scale than their Anglo-Saxon predecessors.[31]

Stigand's deposition left the way open for William to make a significant appointment to the important see of Canterbury, a man whom he could trust and who could take the English church in a new direction. His choice of Lanfranc, abbot of Bec, a monk of Italian extraction and one of the great scholars of his day, was inspired. Lanfranc's training as a monk did not prevent him from being an able administrator, determined to reform the pastoral life of his church. After the papal councils of the 1070s, he initiated a series of regular councils for the whole of the English church which introduced measures against simony and clerical marriage, partly in line with the new reformist thinking at Rome but partly moderating its zeal.[32]

Lanfranc's councils were not simply legislative assemblies, promulgating new pastoral initiatives, but represented his new conception of his authority and dignity as archbishop, bringing together the bishops of all England in subjection to his authority. His was a new vision of church structure and hierarchy, one which saw Canterbury as holding supreme authority within the kingdom of England and over the whole of Britain.[33] This authority was intimately linked in Lanfranc's mind with his pastoral responsibilities for the whole Christian community within Britain and Ireland. Although Lanfranc had to justify his claims by ancient custom (in practice ambiguous), his Anglo-Saxon predecessors had never felt the need to assert themselves in this way, perhaps because of the profoundly close relationship between kingship and ecclesiastical authority before the Conquest. Canterbury had held a position of highest respect within the Anglo-Saxon church, with its archbishops taking precedence at councils, but it had never tried to subordinate the archbishops of York to its authority. Indeed, in the tenth and eleventh centuries, occupants of the see had been at times eclipsed as royal servants and spiritual leaders by outstanding prelates at Winchester such as Æthelwold or Wulfstan and Ealdred at York. It was Wulfstan and Ealdred who provided continuity in religious authority at the conquests of Cnut and William, respectively, with Wulfstan continuing to draft legislation and Ealdred consecrating the new king in the place of Stigand. Nor had the archbishops of Canterbury tried to exercise spiritual authority over Ireland, Scotland, or Wales.

Lanfranc's bold claims met with resistance within England from the new archbishop of York, Thomas of Bayeux. Thomas refused to make a written profession of obedience and give an oath to Lanfranc before his consecration, and left Canterbury therefore without consecration. Although Lanfranc's determination to establish Canterbury's primacy was influential over future archbishops, with his successor Anselm taking up the cause again, he failed to achieve much, lacking sufficient royal and papal support. At the two English councils convened in 1072 to hear the case, Archbishop Thomas agreed only to promise personal obedience to Lanfranc, and not to his successors, and to attend Lanfranc's councils. Thomas outlived Lanfranc, dying in 1100, and therefore the issue of York's position with regard to Canterbury was shelved. Lanfranc was able to demand and obtain professions, but not oaths, from those bishops who had been consecrated by the pope or by another bishop.[34]

Lanfranc's aspirations for primacy over the bishops of Ireland, Wales, and Scotland also remained notional. He was able to consecrate Bishop Patrick of Dublin in London in 1074 but only because Patrick was probably seeking to strengthen his position as metropolitan within Ireland. In keeping with his view that his primacy was made necessary by his pastoral obligations, Lanfranc used the occasion to send two letters, to King Guthric of Dublin, and to the high king of Ireland, Toirdelbach of Munster, in which he condemned certain irregular practices on the part of the Irish, for example, simony, wrongful marriages, and irregular baptisms.[35] Martin Holland has argued that Lanfranc wished to promote Dublin as a metropolitan subordinate to Canterbury in parallel to York. These plans did not come to fruition despite the complaints of Archbishop Anselm concerning the absence of a hierarchy of bishops and dioceses in Ireland. Instead, Holland argues, the new king of Dublin, Muirchertach Ua Briain, sponsored a reform of the Irish church that side-stepped the authority of Canterbury. Muirchertach seems to have been responsible for two synods, at Cashel in 1101 and at Ráith Bressail in 1111. The synod of Ráith Bressail established two metropolitans for the Irish church and a number of suffragan sees. The proposed elevation of Dublin under Lanfranc had been a threat to the ancient status of Armagh, and Muirchertach was prudent in winning Armagh over by a lengthy visit there in 1103 and the bestowal of many gifts.[36]

In Scotland, where the archbishops of Bremen–Hamburg had some claim to jurisdiction, English religious authority was also asserted as a result of a request for consecration. Earl Paul of the Orkneys sent his candidate for the see there to Archbishop Thomas of York for consecration and Thomas was forced to refer the matter to Lanfranc because he lacked sufficient suffragans to perform the ceremony. Lanfranc allowed two of his suffragans to travel to York to assist Thomas. But Wales seems to have been outside Canterbury's claims.[37]

In Wales and Scotland, great changes in ecclesiastical and diocesan arrangements came in the wake of the Conquest. The marriage of the Scottish king Máel Coluim to the Anglo-Saxon princess Margaret inaugurated a period of very active royal intervention in the church, resulting in the creation of a systematic organization of sees by the twelfth century. These were created from existing bishoprics and secular administrative divisions. The four northern dioceses of Aberdeen, Moray, Ross, and Caithness seem to have been new creations of King David and they coincide with secular provincial boundaries. South of Mounth, there were three large dioceses at St. Andrews, Glasgow, and Dunkeld, with two smaller ones at Dunblane and Brechin. All these had outlying dependent churches which indicate that their position must have predated David's reforms.[38] The late eleventh and twelfth centuries in Wales also saw the territorialization of bishoprics with the creation of a new see at Bangor and the appointment in 1092 of a bishop at Bangor. Earlier diocesan arrangements had been fluid: in the tenth century, the church of Llandaff emerged as a powerful bishopric, absorbing other bishoprics and cults at Welsh Bicknor, Ergyng, Llancarfan, and Llandeilo Fawr. By the twelfth century, the idea of a territorially defined church had become sufficiently well established for turf wars to develop between the bishops of Llandaff and St. David's. The later eleventh and twelfth centuries saw a hardening of attitude to matters of episcopal authority with both the Welsh and Scottish churches anxious to avoid subordination to Canterbury. Ultimately, the Scottish church obtained papal protection to safeguard against Canterbury's imperialist ambitions. In Wales, the see of St. David's tried unsuccessfully to establish itself as the primatial see there.[39]

The Norman Conquest ushered in important changes, some due to the new regime but some the culmination of earlier developments. Archbishop Lanfranc, for example, was not the first bishop in the islands to pursue church reform, but episcopal initiatives have tended to be overlooked in the secondary literature which has focused instead upon monasteries and their communities.

Monasticism

The regulation of monastic life by the Carolingian reforms transformed the nature of monasticism in Europe. It elevated the Rule of St. Benedict as the single authoritative guide to how monks should live in community. At the same time, the life of the secular clergy who lived in community was also affected by reform demands for regulation and uniformity which resulted in the advocacy of the Rule of Chrodegang for such clerics. These measures, which were partly enacted through great episcopal councils held throughout the Empire in the early ninth century, attempted to create an orderly religious landscape in which communities of monks were clearly differentiated from those of regular clergy. Although not adopted in Britain until at least a century later, these reforms were deeply influential both on the contemporary situation and on the historiography of church life.

From the ninth to eleventh centuries, the monastic church in Britain and Ireland was suffering from the viking raids that targeted the wealth and vulnerability of monasteries in pursuit of plunder. In Wales and Ireland, monasteries suffered depredations but were able to recover. The exceptionally rich church of St. David's was raided eleven times, while other houses, such as Penmon in Angelsey, are only recorded as being attacked once. In 1089, the shrine of St. David's was stolen and stripped of its gold and silver.[40] Island and coastal communities were particularly vulnerable to attack: Iona was raided several times, first in 802 and then again in 806 when 68 members of the community were reported to have been killed. In 814/15 most of the community moved to a new monastery in inland Ireland at Kells, but some must have remained with the relics of St. Colum Cille since in 825 the abbot, Blathmac, was murdered by vikings attempting to carry off the reliquary.[41] Despite the ferocity of such raids, religious communities in Wales and Ireland proved resilient. The monastery of Kells, for example, rose to prominence in the ninth and tenth centuries, and became the head of the Columban federation of churches. Though repeatedly raided in the tenth century, when a viking attack recorded in 951 is said to have led to the loss of 3,000 men, and a great spoil of cattle, gold, and silver, such raids underline the importance of Kells as a center rather than indicating its terminal decline.[42] In England, the picture in the north-east is very different. Monastic life seemed to collapse. Although some communities, for example at Ripon, continued in existence, others, like Bede's great twin houses of Wearmouth and Jarrow, seem to have ceased entirely. At Lastingham, evidence of religious continuity is provided by tenth-century sculpture, including fragments of a cross. The community had probably become clerical rather than monastic and the church may have acted as a mother-church.[43] The bishops of Lindisfarne and their community were forced to flee their vulnerable island site to an inland refuge.

The question of assessing the impact of viking raids is complex. The evidence is usually scanty and difficult to interpret, and the task is not made easier by a tradition of viewing early medieval monasticism through the clear-cut definitions propagated by the Carolingian reforms. It is likely that communal religious life in early medieval Britain and Ireland consisted largely of houses of secular clergy, following a common liturgical routine and providing pastoral care to the local community, but not bound to the ascetic monastic life. Without the world-denying restrictions of monastic vows, members of religious communities were free to own property and to inherit. Clerical celibacy was not strictly enforced before the late eleventh and twelfth centuries with the result that many houses were probably the dynastic property of families responsible for the provision of pastoral clergy in them.[44] This was a ubiquitous pattern of the religious life. Donnchad Ó Corráin's description of clerical families in Ireland as "professional hereditary clergy, whose family and private property had become inextricably bound up with church property and church office" could be applied to both England and Wales.[45] Thomas Charles-Edwards has commented that, in Wales, "the normal *clas* church were hardly monastic . . . since the *claswyr* no longer had to take monastic vows such as celibacy, but formed a corporation, usually consisting of one or more kindreds in the possession of the church and its lands."[46] Charles-Edwards suggests that a stricter form of monasticism existed side by side with clerical communities in Wales, and Pryce has pointed to eleventh-century evidence for the existence of a distinct monastic vocation and for the existence of some stricter monastic communities.[47] Sharpe has suggested that, in Ireland, strict monasticism – in the sense of living according to a rule – may have disappeared entirely by the tenth century.[48]

The monastic federation of Armagh was pre-eminent amongst the Irish churches in the tenth and eleventh centuries and worked closely with the dominant secular dynasties, with the northern Uí Néill in the ninth and tenth centuries and subsequently with Brian Bórama when his kingship eclipsed that of the Uí Néill. This close cooperation reinforced the territorial authority of Armagh: at the end of the tenth century, the coarb of Armagh recognized Áed, son of Domnall as king of the Uí Néill and was able to make a full visitation – a tribute-taking itineration – of the north of Ireland. Armagh earned the right to make a circuit of Meath in the late tenth century, in compensation for the violation of the shrine of Patrick by its king, Maél Sechnaill II. The prerogative of making tribute-taking circuits of territories may only have been exercised irregularly but represented a significant and lucrative privilege.[49] When Brian Bórama visited Armagh in 1005, he recognized its rights on behalf of future kings of Cashel, an important concession duly recorded in the *Book of Armagh*.[50] The monasteries of Clonmacnoise and Kells were two of the greatest of the houses affiliated together as part of the *familia* of St. Colum Cille (also known as St. Columba). The head of these communities had been Iona, but the viking attacks of the ninth century, especially viking settlement in the Western Isles, had diminished contacts between Iona and Ireland, and between Iona and Scotland where a number of monasteries belonged to the *familia* of Colum Cille, chief among them Dunkeld. Iona remained a monastic settlement, despite frequent viking raiding, and is known in the tenth century to have been a place of pilgrimage; Amlaíb Cúarán, the Scandinavian king of Dublin, retired and died there in 981.[51]

In the course of the tenth century, Kells came to be the most prominent house of the federation. Some measure of its wealth and size can be seen in the account of the annals for 951 when it was attacked by Gothfrith and the Dublin Norse and became a temporary viking base. Over 3,000 men were said to have been taken captive, along with a great spoil of cattle, horses, gold, and silver. Monasteries within the federation included Derry, Drumcliff, and Durrow. On two occasions in the tenth century, the great monastic federations of Armagh and Kells were united under one comarb, or abbot.[52] The obit of Máel Brigte mac Tornáin in 927 records that he was comarb of both Patrick (Armagh) and of Colum Cille, and then in 989, according to the *Annals of Ulster*, Dub dá Leithe, comarb of St. Patrick became comarb of Colum Cille. However, this association between the two great monastic houses was short-lived, probably for political reasons. The rise of Brian Bórama and his alliance with Armagh may have prompted Máel Sechnaill to gain influence over the church of Kells, inaugurating an association between the Clann Cholmáin dynasty of the southern Uí Neill in the eleventh century.[53]

In the tenth and eleventh centuries, communities such as Clonmacnoise, Kells, and Armagh were powerhouses of economic and political power, religious centers that functioned as proto-towns and perhaps even as ecclesiastical states. Archaeological and topographical studies have revealed large enclosures, often with concentric rings of ditches, with multiple churches and considerable settlements. At Armagh, all the ecclesiastical sites were contained within an oval enclosure, measuring 250 meters north–south and 200 meters east–west, at the entrance to which, just before the cathedral, stood a great high cross. The street pattern shows that there was a massive oval outer enclosure, 480 meters north–south and not less than 360 meters east–west. The inner sanctuary contained the ceremonial center, a place of great religious and political significance, while within the outer enclosure there must have stood housing for the lay inhabitants and industrial and craft-working activity. Many monasteries acquired a market: at Clonmacnoise, this took place outside the ceremonial center and was marked by a cross. In 1179, a hundred houses at Clonmacnoise were destroyed by a fire, evidence of the populous nature of these centers, which commanded not only suburban farms beyond the enclosure but also more widely scattered estates and thus formed redistributive centers.[54] Monasteries were major centers of population in a rural landscape.

In the tenth and eleventh centuries, Irish monasteries were under dynastic control with the office of abbot or vice-abbot combined with lay positions, including that of king.[55] The monastery of Kildare, the community of St. Brigid and the most important economic center in Leinster, was dominated by the Uí Dúnchada dynasty until its political eclipse in the mid-tenth century. The last abbot – Muiredach mac Fáeláin

– was killed in 967 by Amlaíb Cúarán of Dublin and by his own nephew.[56] Office at Armagh from 965 until 1134 was dominated by the Uí Sínaich, supported by the politically dominant dynasty of the Cenél nEógain whose king, Domnall (956–80), retired to the monastery there to die. Ten monastic bishops at Armagh are recorded from 965 to 1134 and, in every case where genealogical links are known, they also seem to stem from the Uí Sínaich.[57] The secular responsibilities and privileges of monasteries, including economic and jurisdictional prerogatives, were exercised by laymen, monastic managers, known as *erenaghs*. The involvement of the great Irish monasteries in battles, their dominance by family succession, and the holding of multiple offices by one person has suggested a picture of a church in decline, over-whelmed by secular interactions. On the one hand, Irish monasteries in this period contrast with those on the continent and in England in the later tenth century when Benedictine reform was being imposed on many communities. However, such reform was aimed not only at the lax lifestyle of the brothers but also at secular and family influence; religious communities outside Ireland were also powerfully involved in the secular world. Carolingian monasteries had been important economic centers and major organs of royal control: the position of lay abbot had developed in the ninth century to provide for the management of the church's wealth and secular involve-ments and to enable kings to reward their followers using monastic resources. Moreover, Tomás Ó Fiaich has pointed to the number of able abbots appointed to Armagh in the tenth and eleventh centuries, notably Dub dá Leithe (965–98) who defended and extended the rights of Armagh and became leader of the Columban federation and enhanced Armagh's reputation for learning in the same period and its place as a retreat for prominent laymen.[58]

Viking attacks were only one factor amongst many in the changes in monastic life from the eighth to the tenth centuries. In areas under West Saxon domination, many monasteries passed with their endowment into the hands of the West Saxon kings who siphoned their landed estates to enrich royal coffers. The monastery at Abingdon long preserved traditions of its appropriation and abuse as a possession of the West Saxon kings, particularly of Alfred the Great.[59] But perhaps the great majority simply became minor collegial churches, retained by the local aristocracy and staffed by a small number of clergy and serving the laity in their neighborhood. This seems to have been the fate of the once prestigious monastery of St. Æthelthryth at Ely whose history records that in the tenth century it was served by a small community of clerks.[60]

In England, understanding of the tenth-century church is hampered by the propa-ganda of the monastic reform movement that came to prominence in the second half of the tenth century. This was influenced by contemporary continental reforms which sought to restore the purity of monastic life in accordance with strict Benedictine principles and was fueled not only by sojourns at continental reform centers, particu-larly the monastery at Fleury which possessed the relics of Benedict himself, but also by texts from the ninth-century Carolingian reforms. The reform was led by three bishops, Dunstan, archbishop of Canterbury (d.988), Æthelwold, bishop of Win-chester (d.984), and Oswald, bishop of Worcester and archbishop of York (d.992). Their vision of the English church was shaped by their unhistorical view of a past Golden Age of Benedictine monasticism which they endeavored to recreate. Communities of secular clergy, often living with wives and families, represented a corrupt deviation from the correct norm, the celibate life of a Benedictine monk. They sought to cleanse the English church and to restore its purity by establishing new communities of Benedictine monks and by returning former monastic sites and lands to religious use. Thus, Bishop Æthelwold refounded the monastery of Ely and expelled the clergy from the cathedral community, Old Minster, Winchester. Replacing secular clergy with monks in the service of an episcopal cathedral was justified in Æthelwold's eyes by Bede's description of the very early communities at Christ Church, Canterbury and at Lindisfarne. However, it represented a very unusual step since cathedral chapters were generally served by clergy, whether under a rule like that of Chrodegang, a continental creation, or not. It was to be an influential move, later implemented, for example, at Canterbury and then after the Conquest at Durham and elsewhere.[61]

This extension of strict Benedictine monasticism into cathedral communities reflected the wider concern of this episcopally led reform movement for pastoral care and particularly for the sacred status of the eucharist. In the course of the eighth and ninth centuries, the mass came to occupy the most central place in religious devotion and to be considered so sacred that there were fears concerning pollution in relation to it. This attitude can be found in the writings of Bede but became particularly prominent in the Carolingian reforms. Anxiety about the sacrality of the sacrament centered on the sexual activities of its celebrants and communicants. Sexual continence was required from both: from the laity in the immediate period before the mass, but for the priesthood this came to be a total ban. Thus celibacy was required from the higher clergy, and virgin priests were seen as the most appropriate celebrants. These ideas had two further effects on the nature of monasticism: child oblation came to be particularly valued as a means of guaranteeing the purity of the priesthood within monasteries, and the role of women in religious life came be correspondingly devalued. Since women could not celebrate the mass, although their prayers might be a useful contribution to the economy of salvation, women's monasticism was distinctly less significant. This was reflected in the comparative insignificance of nunneries in the Benedictine reforms. Very few new houses were founded,[62] though the female houses of Wilton, Shaftesbury, and Nunnaminster remained spiritually, politically, and culturally important, particularly for the West Saxon aristocracy. They acted as repositories and educational establishments for royal and aristocratic women, particularly for widows and excess daughters.[63] In the case of Ireland, Christina Harrington has argued that, while the Irish did engage with continental teaching and began to manifest concerns about contact between male and female religious and sexuality, women's houses and spiritual life continued to flourish. For example, St. Brigid's community of Kildare, headed by both abbot and abbess, remained religiously and politically important. Its offices had been dominated by members of two Leinster dynasties, the Uí Dúnlainge and the Fothairt. Harrington argues that Kildare functioned as the head of women's monasteries in Ireland and that its abbess was accorded the status of a bishop to reflect this authority. Other female communities also flourished throughout the tenth and eleventh centuries, and female saints were considered as powerful as male: when the hated Norman invader, Strongbow, died after raiding the monastery of Kildare, the annals attributed his death to the intervention of Brigid herself.[64] In England, the new emphasis on virginity as a crucial ingredient in the monastic life and as a guarantee of ritual purity lent fresh prominence to the cult of the Virgin Mary to whom many of the new monasteries were dedicated. Abingdon, Ramsey, and Worcester were dedicated to her and endowed with fresh estates.[65]

The great foundations of the Benedictine reform became some of the wealthiest houses in England, even after the Conquest. This reflects not only royal generosity but also the active participation of the nobility. St. Oswald's foundation at Ramsey, for example, was endowed by Æthelwine, ealdorman of East Anglia. The success of these foundations entailed a fairly substantial transference of landed wealth into the church's hands, which could not have been achieved without committed royal support.[66] The role of King Edgar was crucial to the success of the movement, not so much for the generosity of his endowments but for underwriting the whole movement. At a great council in Winchester, Edgar promulgated a set of regulations for monastic life, a monastic customary known as the *Regularis concordia*. This, drafted by Dunstan, Æthelwold, and their continental associates, provided guidelines for the daily routine of the monastery, supplementing the Benedictine Rule and adding detailed rulings concerning liturgical life.[67] It represents a uniquely English compilation, but drew extensively upon continental works. In one respect, English practice exceeded their Frankish models: Edgar imposed this document upon all monasteries where, in the Carolingian realms, no one monastic customary was enforced. Tenth-century reform in England was deeply entwined with royal control: the *Regularis concordia* specified frequent prayers for king and country and placed all monasteries under the lordship of the king, while convents were subject to the queen.[68]

It is the presence of a powerful monarchy whose authority was profoundly imbued with sacrality that marks out the late Saxon church and monasticism from that of the Celtic areas. Edgar's power underwrote monastic reform: on his death, ealdormen and more lowly thegns took the opportunity to claw back lands and properties made over to the Benedictine reformers. The monastery at Ely had, for example, been able, under the direction of Bishop Æthelwold, to acquire extensive properties in East Anglia and had repossessed the Isle of Ely, its original seventh-century holding. With Edgar out of the way, many local lords brought claims of coercion and cheating against the community and were able to regain property or renegotiate its price. Ely's endowments ranged across Cambridgeshire, Suffolk, Hertfordshire, and Norfolk, and included mother-churches like Dereham in Norfolk and many local churches. It had been granted extensive jurisdictional privileges. In some ways, Ely was like the major Irish monasteries, an ecclesiastical state with lucrative fiscal and jurisdictional privileges.[69] But where houses like Clonmacnoise and Kells were controlled by royal and aristocratic dynasties, Ely represented an outpost of West Saxon monarchical power: it held its powers by royal delegation, it acted as host to the royal court, and mediated West Saxon authority in Anglo-Scandinavian East Anglia. It could act as a tool of royal control but, at the Conquest, its identification with Anglo-Saxon kingship was such that its island fastness in the difficult territory of the Fens allowed it to act as a bastion of anti-Norman resistance. For this, it was punished severely with a great fine and the loss of many estates.[70]

While Ely acted as an extension of West Saxon control in the east of England, the north was neglected. The most northerly of reformed houses was the aristocratic foundation at Burton-on-Trent. Although in the eleventh century, Archbishops Ælfric and Ealdred of York were generous patrons of the church at Beverley, where their seventh-century predecessor in the see of York was culted, no Benedictine communities were founded.[71] With its scarce provision of bishops and the absence of reformed monasteries, Northumbria perhaps more resembled the Scottish territories than the south of England, although it was subject to West Saxon control. Its special inheritance of prestigious monastic sites – for example, at Wearmouth, Jarrow, and

Whitby – did not attract the attention or generosity of kings or religious until after the Conquest. In 1073–4, a small community was established at Jarrow by a colony from the south under the leadership of Aldwine, prior of Winchcombe. Under the inspiration of Bede's *History*, small communities were founded at Tynemouth, Wearmouth, and Whitby, and the movement expanded into Scotland and the borders with refoundations at Coldingham and Melrose under royal patronage.[72]

The events of 1066 brought huge changes for monasticism in Britain. Since monasteries were key players not only in the religious and cultural life of the country but also in the political, it was inevitable that William the Conqueror would ensure that the major monasteries of the Old English kingdom were in safe hands, and by 1087 almost all were governed by abbots of Norman or continental extraction. Between 1066 and 1135 over 60 new abbots were appointed from foreign stock. The new Norman land-owning aristocracy had gained landed wealth that could be used to ensure the safe passage of their souls and those of their families. But many of these great men preferred to endow monasteries back home in Normandy rather than invest in the recently annexed England. Land and churches in England were granted to Norman communities. Further, when new foundations were established in England, they were commonly subordinated to continental monasteries. In the reign of the Conqueror, it has been estimated that of some 34 new foundations in England, 18 were subject to continental communities and 16 were either independent or subordinate to English houses. But after William's death, this picture gradually changed. Many of the great houses of Anglo-Saxon England continued to flourish: St. Augustine's Canterbury, for example, received many grants in the 20 years after the Conquest. As the eleventh century wore on, other monasteries came back into fashion, particularly if they were governed by politically adept abbots such as Faricius at Abingdon and Baldwin at Bury. The new aristocracy not only gave to the church but also took away land and estates: many houses such as the cathedral of Worcester suffered under the new regime.[73]

The Welsh church was particularly vulnerable to Norman asset-stripping. Many of the estates of Llandaff and St. David's, for example, fell into lay hands and were only regained after strenuous appeals to pope and archbishop. Rees Davies has described the "massive disendowment" of the Welsh church between 1080 and 1130. Abbeys and monasteries in Normandy and England grew fat and prosperous from this transfer of land and churches. St. Peter's, Gloucester was granted properties formerly belonging to Llancarfan and Llanbadarn Fawr. Within five years of the battle of Hastings, William FitzOsbern granted the tithes of all his lands between Wye and Usk to his two monasteries, Lire and Cormeilles, situated in Normandy. This siphoning off of Welsh resources was a means of strengthening Norman control of Wales, a fact underlined by the fact that all of the 19 new monasteries founded there lay within the shadow of Norman castles.[74]

In Scotland, the impetus to catch up with English and continental developments came through royal patronage. Margaret and her husband, Máel Coluim, not only attempted to regularize the diocesan organization of the church but also to found Benedictine communities, most notably at Dunfermline, a foundation closely associated with the royal house. Later, in the reign of their son, David, the influence of the new reformed continental monasticism came to be felt with foundations belonging to the Turonensian order.[75] The new monasticism of orders like the Cistercians was not felt in England until the twelfth century, but in the eleventh century, Norman patrons introduced the influence of Cluny, with the founding of the first Cluniac house in 1077 by William I of Warenne at Lewes. By 1154, roughly 30 Cluniac houses or dependencies had been founded in England, from large houses like Bermondsey to small cells. The popularity of the Cluniac order probably reflected its influence in Normandy where William of Volpiano had been prominent in initiating reform in accordance with Cluniac principles.[76]

The eleventh century ended with great changes taking place across the church in Britain and Ireland as the Normans introduced new monastic orders and new structures in England and as their influence and the effects of the Conquest extended to Ireland, Scotland, and Wales. But these transformations built upon existing ecclesiastical developments, whether the poorly recorded dioceses of Scotland, Wales, and Ireland or the strength of the monastic order in England.

Notes

1   Hughes, *Church in Early Irish Society*, p. 201.
2   For a useful review, see Abrams, "The conversion of the Scandinavians," pp. 1–5.
3   Ó Corráin, *Ireland before the Normans*, pp. 80–9.
4   Ó Corráin, "The early Irish churches," pp. 327–41.
5   Etchingham, *Church Organisation*; Hughes, *Church in Early Irish Society*; Ó Croinin, *A New History of Ireland*.
6   Harrington, *Women in a Celtic Church*; Herbert, *Iona, Kells, and Derry*.
7   Davies, *Wales in the Early Middle Ages*, pp. 116–18; Pryce, "Ecclesiastical wealth," pp. 23–7.
8   Pryce, "Pastoral care," pp. 49–51. See also Davies, *Wales in the Early Middle Ages*, pp. 149–58.
9   Blair, *Church in Anglo-Saxon Society*, pp. 291–2; Dumville, "Ecclesiastical lands," pp. 29–36.
10 Barrow, "Survival and mutation"; Cubitt, *Sin and Society*; Dumville, "Ecclesiastical lands"; Fleming, "Monastic lands."
11 Wormald, "Æthelwold and his continental counterparts," pp. 38–9.
12 Blair, *Church in Anglo-Saxon Society*, pp. 349–94.
13 See Pryce, "Pastoral care," p. 55. For responses to continental ideas in Ireland, see Harrington, *Women in a Celtic Church*, pp. 191–2.
14 Barlow, *English Church*, pp. 77–81; Smith, "Archbishop Stigand," pp. 199–206, 215–18.
15 For Wulfstan II, see Barrow and Brooks (eds.), *Bishop Wulfstan*; and Mason, *St. Wulfstan*; for Ealdred, see Barlow, *English Church*, pp. 86–95; and see the entries in the *Oxford Dictionary of National Biography*.
16 Keynes, "Giso, bishop of Wells."
17 Brooks, *Early History*, pp. 164–7, 224.
18 Etchingham, *Church Organisation*, p. 459.
19 Ibid., pp. 173–94.
20 Macquarrie, "Early Christian religious communities," pp. 110–33.
21 Charles–Edwards, "The seven bishop–houses," supported by Davies above, but contested by Pryce, "Pastoral care," p. 52, and Davies, *Wales in the Early Middle Ages*, p. 160.
22 Davies, *Wales in the Early Middle Ages*, pp. 158–60.
23 Ibid., p. 160, and Davies, *Early Welsh Microcosm*, pp. 146–59.
24 Barrow, "Survival and mutation," pp. 156–61.
25 These episcopal fluctuations can be traced in Pryde et al. (eds.), *Handbook of British Chronology*, pp. 209–24; see also Barlow, *English Church*, pp. 162–83; Barrow, "Survival and mutation," pp. 155–76; and Cubitt, *Sin and Society*.

26 Kelly (ed.), *Charters of Selsey*, pp. lxviii–lxxii.
27 Keynes, "Wulfsige," pp. 56–9.
28 Barlow, *English Church*, pp. 96–115, 162–83, 208–231; Darlington, "Æthelwig," pp. 3–4.
29 Loyn, "William's bishops," pp. 223–35.
30 Bates, *Bishop Remigius*; Loyn, *English Church*, pp. 74–5.
31 Fernie, *Architecture of Norman England*, pp. 108–9, 115–24.
32 Cowdrey, *Lanfranc*, pp. 120–8; Gibson, *Lanfranc*, pp. 116–61.
33 Cowdrey, *Lanfranc*, pp. 120–5; Gibson, *Lanfranc*, pp. 116–31.
34 Cowdrey, *Lanfranc*, pp. 87–103; Gibson, *Lanfranc*, p. 116.
35 Cowdrey, *Lanfranc*, pp. 144–6; Gibson, *Lanfranc*, p. 124.
36 Holland, "Dublin and the reform of the Irish Church."
37 Cowdrey, *Lanfranc*, pp. 147–8.
38 Ash, "The diocese of St. Andrews," pp. 105–26; Barrow, *Kingdom of the Scots*, pp. 66–7, and *Kingship and Unity*, pp. 61–83.
39 Davies, *Conquest, Coexistence and Change*, pp. 190–1.
40 Pryce, "Ecclesiastical wealth," pp. 25–6.
41 Herbert, *Iona, Kells, and Derry*, pp. 68–77; Hughes, *Church in Early Irish Society*, p. 198.
42 Herbert, *Iona, Kells, and Derry*, pp. 78–87; Ó Corráin, *Ireland before the Normans*, pp. 80–9.
43 Hadley, *Northern Danelaw*, p. 262.
44 Blair, *Church in Anglo-Saxon Society*, pp. 341–54.
45 Ó Corráin, *Ireland before the Normans*, p. 84.
46 Charles–Edwards, "The seven bishop–houses," p. 256.
47 Pryce, "Pastoral care," pp. 50–1.
48 Sharpe, "Churches and communities."
49 Hughes, *Church in Early Irish Society*, pp. 217–18; Ó Fiaich, "The church of Armagh," pp. 82–122.
50 Gwynn, "Brian in Armagh," pp. 41–3; Hughes, *Church in Early Irish Society*, pp. 217–18.
51 Bhreathnach, "Columban churches," pp. 5–18; Herbert, *Iona, Kells, and Derry*, pp. 78–9.
52 Herbert, *Iona, Kells, and Derry*, pp. 78–86.
53 Ibid., pp. 78–97.
54 Doherty, "The monastic town"; Graham, "Early medieval Ireland," pp. 22–37; Swan, "Monastic proto–towns," p. 84.
55 Hughes, *Church in Early Irish Society*, pp. 222–3.
56 Doherty, "The monastic town," p. 63.
57 Ó Fiaich, "The church of Armagh," pp. 84–95, 102–3.
58 Ibid., pp. 105–15.
59 Fleming, "Monastic lands."
60 Fairweather (trans.), *Liber Eliensis*, pp. 76–82; Keynes, "Ely Abbey 672–1109," pp. 1–32.
61 Wormald, "Æthelwold and his continental counterparts," pp. 13–42.
62 Cubitt, "Virginity and misogyny," pp. 1–32.
63 Stafford, "Queens, nunneries."
64 Harrington, *Women in a Celtic Church*, pp. 191–225.
65 Cubitt, "The tenth-century Benedictine reform," and "Virginity and misogyny."
66 Knowles, *Monastic Order*, pp. 31–56.
67 Cubitt, "The tenth–century Benedictine reform," pp. 79–80; Symons, "*Regularis concordia*: history and derivation."

68   Cubitt, "The tenth–century Benedictine reform," pp. 77–94; Wormald, "Æthelwold and his continental counterparts," pp. 13–42.
69   Keynes, "Ely Abbey 672–1109," pp. 1–32.
70   Ibid.
71   Barlow, *English Church*, pp. 89–90.
72   Loyn, *English Church*, p. 81.
73   Cownie, "The Normans as patrons"; Golding, "Coming of the Cluniacs."
74   Davies, *Conquest, Coexistence and Change*, pp. 172–210.
75   Barrow, *Kingdom of the Scots*, pp. 61–83, and *Kingship and Unity*, pp. 165–211.
76   Golding, "Coming of the Cluniacs."

Further Reading

The institutional history of the English church to 1100 is well served, not least by John Blair's *The Church in Anglo-Saxon Society*, a comprehensive study which sheds new light through its prioritization of the material evidence for the church. A more traditional textual approach is taken by Frank Barlow in his two volumes, *The English Church 1000–1066* and *The English Church, 1066–1154* (London, 1979); see also the handy short book by Loyn, *The English Church 950–1154*. For the Celtic areas, the following general histories have much to offer: Barrow, *Kingship and Unity: Scotland 1000–1306* and his *The Kingdom of the Scots*; R. R. Davies, *Conquest, Coexistence and Change*; Wendy Davies, *Wales in the Early Middle Ages*; D. Ó Corráin, *Ireland before the Normans*; and Kathleen Hughes, *The Church in Early Irish Society*. These can be updated by Nancy Edwards and Alan Lane (eds.), *The Early Church in Wales and the West* (Oxford, 1992) and Colmán Etchingham, *Church Organisation in Ireland AD 650 to 1000*. Máire Herbert's *Iona, Kells, and Derry* is an exemplary study of the Columban affiliation and its hagiography, and Christina Harrington's *Women in a Celtic Church* is a highly accessible study which usefully discusses women's spirituality in the context of the wider development of the Irish church. For the Conquest and its effects, see H. E. J. Cowdrey's *Lanfranc* and the survey by Brian Golding, *Conquest and Colonisation: The Normans in Britain, 1066–1100* (Basingstoke, 1994). *The Oxford Dictionary of National Biography*, edited H. C. G. Matthew, 60 vols. (Oxford, 2004), is an extremely useful and up-to-date resource for biographies of individuals.

Bibliography

Abrams, L. J., "The conversion of the Scandinavians of Dublin," *Anglo-Norman Studies*, 20 (1998), 1–29.
Ash, M., "The diocese of St. Andrews under its 'Norman' bishops," *Scottish Historical Review*, 55 (1976), 105–26.
Barlow, F., *The English Church 1000–1066* (London, 1979).
Barrow, G. W. S., *The Kingdom of the Scots: Government, Church and Society from the Eleventh to the Fourteenth Century* (London, 1973).
Barrow, G. W. S., *Kingship and Unity: Scotland 1000–1306* (London, 1981).
Barrow, J., "Survival and mutation: ecclesiastical institutions in the Danelaw in the ninth and tenth centuries," in D. M. Hadley and J. D. Richards (eds.), *Cultures in Contact: Scandinavian Settlement in England in the Ninth and Tenth Centuries* (Turnhout, 2000), pp. 155–76.
Barrow, J. and Brooks, N. (eds.), *Bishop Wulfstan and his World* (Aldershot, 2005).
Bates, D., *Bishop Remigius of Lincoln 1067–1092* (Lincoln, 1992).
Bhreathnach, E., "Columban churches in Brega and Leinster: relations with the Norse and the Anglo-Normans," *Journal of the Royal Society of Antiquaries of Ireland*, 129 (1999), 5–18.

Blair, J., *The Church in Anglo-Saxon Society* (Oxford, 2005).

Blair, J. and Sharpe, R. (eds.), *Pastoral Care before the Parish* (Leicester, 1992).

Brooks, N., *The Early History of the Church of Canterbury* (Leicester, 1984).

Charles-Edwards, T. M., "The seven bishop-houses of Dyfed," *Bulletin of the Board of Celtic Studies*, 24 (1970–2), 247–62.

Clarke, H. B. and Simms, A. (eds.), *The Comparative History of Urban Origins in Non-Roman Europe: Ireland, Wales, Denmark, Germany, Poland, and Russia from the Ninth to the Thirteenth Century*, British Archaeological Reports, International Series 255, 2 vols. (Oxford, 1985).

Cowdrey, H. E. J., *Lanfranc: Scholar, Monk and Archbishop* (Oxford, 2003).

Cownie, E., "The Normans as patrons of English religious houses, 1066–1135," *Anglo-Norman Studies*, 18 (1996), 47–62.

Cubitt, C., *Sin and Society in Tenth- and Eleventh-century England* (forthcoming).

Cubitt, C., "The tenth-century Benedictine reform in England," *Early Medieval Europe*, 6 (1997), 77–94.

Cubitt, C., "Virginity and misogyny in tenth- and eleventh-century England," *Gender and History*, 12 (2000), 1–32.

Darlington, R. R., "Æthelwig, abbot of Evesham," *English Historical Review*, 48 (1933), 1–22.

Davies, R. R., *Conquest, Coexistence and Change: Wales 1063–1415* (Oxford, 1987).

Davies, W., *An Early Welsh Microcosm: Studies in the Llandaff Charters* (London, 1978).

Davies, W., *Wales in the Early Middle Ages* (Leicester, 1982).

Doherty, C., "The monastic town in early medieval Ireland," in H. B. Clarke and A. Simms (eds.), *The Comparative History of Urban Origins in Non-Roman Europe: Ireland, Wales, Denmark, Germany, Poland, and Russia from the Ninth to the Thirteenth Century* (Oxford, 1985), 1, pp. 45–75.

Dumville, D. N., "Ecclesiastical lands and the defence of Wessex in the first Viking-Age," in D. N. Dumville (ed.), *Wessex and England from Alfred to Edgar* (Woodbridge, 1992), pp. 29–54.

Edwards, N. and Lane, A. (eds.), *The Early Church in Wales and the West* (Oxford, 1992).

Etchingham, C., *Church Organisation in Ireland AD 650 to 1000* (Maynooth, 1999).

Etchingham, C., "Pastoral provision in the first millennium: a two-tier service?," in E. FitzPatrick and R. Gillespie (eds.), *The Parish in Medieval and Early Modern Ireland: Community, Territory and Building* (Dublin, 2006), pp. 79–90.

Fairweather, J. (trans.), *Liber Eliensis: A History of the Isle of Ely from the Seventh Century to the Twelfth* (Woodbridge, 2005).

Fernie, E. C., *The Architecture of Norman England* (Oxford, 2000).

Fleming, R., "Monastic lands and England's defence in the Viking Age," *English Historical Review*, 100 (1985), 247–65.

Gibson, M., *Lanfranc of Bec* (Oxford, 1978).

Golding, B., "The coming of the Cluniacs," *Anglo-Norman Studies*, 3 (1980), 65–77.

Graham, B. J., "Early medieval Ireland: settlement as an indicator of economic and social transformation, c.500–1199 AD," in B. J. Graham and L. J. Proudfoot (eds.), *An Historical Geography of Ireland* (London, 1993), pp. 19–57.

Gwynn, A., "Brian in Armagh (1005)," *Seanchas Ardmhacha*, 9 (1978), 35–50.

Hadley, D. M., *The Northern Danelaw: Its Social Structure, c.800–1100* (London, 2000).

Harrington, C., *Women in a Celtic Church: Ireland 450–1150* (Oxford, 2002).

Herbert, M., *Iona, Kells, and Derry: The History and Hagiography of the Monastic Familia of Columba* (Oxford, 1988).

Holland, M., "Dublin and the reform of the Irish church in the eleventh and twelfth centuries," *Peritia*, 14 (2000), 111–60.

Hudson, B. T., "Kings and church in early Scotland," *Scottish Historical Review*, 73 (1994), 145–70.

Hughes, K., *The Church in Early Irish Society* (London, 1966).

Kelly, S. E. (ed.), *Charters of Selsey* (Oxford, 1998).

Keynes, S., "Ely Abbey 672–1109," in P. Meadows and N. Ramsay (eds.), *A History of Ely Cathedral* (Woodbridge, 2003), pp. 3–58.

Keynes, S., "Giso, bishop of Wells (1061–88)," *Anglo-Norman Studies*, 19 (1997), 203–71.

Keynes, S., "Wulfsige, monk of Glastonbury, abbot of Westminster (900[sic]–3), and bishop of Sherborne, (c.993–1002)," in K. Barker, D. A. Hinton, and A. Hunt (eds.), *St. Wulfsige and Sherborne* (Oxford, 2005), pp. 53–94.

Knowles, D., *The Monastic Order in England* (Cambridge, 1966).

Loyn, H. R., *The English Church 950–1154* (Harlow, 2000).

Loyn, H. R., "William's bishops: some further thoughts," *Anglo-Norman Studies*, 10 (1988), 222–35.

Macquarrie, A., "Early Christian religious communities in Scotland: foundation and function," in J. Blair and R. Sharpe (eds.), *Pastoral Care before the Parish* (Leicester, 1992), pp. 110–33.

Mason, E., *St. Wulfstan of Worcester c.1008–1095* (Oxford, 1990).

Ó Corráin, D., "The early Irish churches: some aspects of organisation," in D. Ó Corráin (ed.), *Irish Antiquity: Essays and Studies Presented to Professor M. J. O'Kelly* (Dublin, 1981), pp. 327–41.

Ó Corráin, D., *Ireland before the Normans* (Dublin, 1972).

Ó Cróinín, D., *A New History of Ireland*, vol. 1: *Prehistoric and Early Ireland* (Oxford, 2005).

Ó Fiaich, T., "The church of Armagh under lay control," *Seanchas Ardmhacha*, 5 (1969), 75–127.

Olson, L., *Early Monasteries in Cornwall* (Woodbridge, 1989).

Pryce, H., "Ecclesiastical wealth in early medieval Wales," in N. Edwards and A. Lane (eds.), *The Early Church in Wales and the West* (Oxford, 1992), pp. 22–32.

Pryce, H., "Pastoral care in early medieval Wales," in J. Blair and R. Sharpe (eds.), *Pastoral Care before the Parish* (Leicester, 1992), pp. 41–62.

Pryde, E. B., Greenway, D. E., Porter S., and Roy, I. (eds.), *Handbook of British Chronology* (London, 1986).

Sharpe, R., "Churches and communities in early medieval Ireland: towards a pastoral model," in J. Blair and R. Sharpe (eds.), *Pastoral Care before the Parish* (Leicester, 1992), pp. 81–109.

Smith, M. F., "Archbishop Stigand and the eye of the needle," *Anglo-Norman Studies*, 16 (1994), 199–218.

Stafford, P., "Queens, nunneries and reforming churchmen: gender, religious status and reform in tenth- and eleventh-century England," *Past and Present*, 163 (1999), 3–35.

Swan, L., "Monastic proto-towns in early medieval Ireland: the evidence of aerial photography, plan analysis and survey," in H. B. Clarke and A. Simms (eds.), *The Comparative History of Urban Origins in Non-Roman Europe: Ireland, Wales, Denmark, Germany, Poland, and Russia from the Ninth to the Thirteenth Century* (Oxford, 1985), 1, pp. 77–102.

Symons, T., "*Regularis concordia*: history and derivation," in D. Parsons (ed.), *Tenth-century Studies: Essays in Commemoration of the Millennium of the Council of Winchester and Regularis concordia* (Chichester, 1975), pp. 37–59, 214–17.

Winterbottom, M. and Thomson, R. M. (eds.), *William of Malmesbury, Saints' Lives: Lives of SS Wulfstan, Dunstan, Patrick, Benignus and Indract* (Oxford, 2002).

Wormald, P., "Æthelwold and his continental counterparts: contact, comparison and contrast," in B. Yorke (ed.), *Bishop Æthelwold: His Career and Influence* (Woodbridge, 1988), pp. 13–42.

CHAPTER TWENTY-FOUR

Pastoral Care and Religious Belief

CATHERINE CUBITT

In 1992, Richard Sharpe concluded an account of pastoral care in the early Irish church with the claim that the evidence he had examined "bore witness to what was one of the most comprehensive pastoral organizations in northern Europe."[1] This bold statement reflected a major shift in the scholarship of the early medieval church in Britain and Ireland, from a concentration upon monasticism to a concern with other aspects of church life, in particular the church's ministry to the laity. His contribution formed part of a collection of essays, *Pastoral Care before the Parish*, which brought together studies of pastoral ministry in Ireland, Wales, Scotland, and England before the formation of the parochial network. The volume was important because it achieved a dialogue between students of the church across the national boundaries of these islands, transcending issues of terminology and the uneven distribution of the evidence, and attempted to reconstruct the mechanisms of pastoral care on the ground. As a collection of essays, it highlighted the importance of the contribution of topographical, onomastic, and archaeological evidence to the study of pastoral care, disciplines that can step in not only to deepen understanding of the local church but also to suggest networks and systems where textual sources fail. It was this combination of different types of evidence that enabled Sharpe to posit a dense distribution of local churches in Ireland before the year 900.

The combination of archaeological, toponymic, and textual evidence in the study of pastoral care has been highly significant in enabling scholars to begin to reconstruct the pastoral systems of the early church. In his contribution to *Pastoral Care before the Parish*, Pryce quotes Wendy Davies's view that "we hear virtually nothing of any provision for regular ministry to the people . . . until the twelfth century."[2] While acknowledging the difficulty and scarcity of the evidence, Pryce himself is able to make a strong case for pastoral ministry in Wales from the sixth to the eleventh century by looking to new evidence; for example, that of burial practice and topography. Scrutiny of later medieval patterns can be used to identify mother-churches, which could be detected, for example, in the diocese of St. Asaph and in Dyfed.

The so-called "minster-model" of pastoral care emerged as the volume's winner. This postulates that before the formation of the local church and the parochial system, the laity received the religious ministry from mother-churches, collegiate foundations with responsibility for the cure of souls in large territories, providing a sort of team ministry. This had long been put forward as the model of pastoral care in the early English church and its transferal to other regions was facilitated by the recognition that monastic life throughout Britain and Ireland in the early Middle Ages was probably dominated by mixed communities or houses of regular clergy rather than by Benedictine monasticism or by a strictly contemplative lifestyle, isolated from the pastoral ministry.

The current popularity among scholars for a model of a system of pastoral care based on mother-churches is not without its problems. The "minster-model" tends to rely upon the assumption that pastoral needs were paramount and that a network of mother-churches was established to meet them. Some would question the extent to which the early medieval church was driven by pastoral issues. Etchingham has controversially argued that the pastoral ministry of the early Irish church was largely limited to the class of *manaig*, monastic tenants, and not intended for the populace at large,[3] while, for England, Rollason and Cambridge have also questioned the extent to which the English church before the tenth century was concerned to provide pastoral care to the lower levels in society.[4] Further, the ubiquity of the model tends to have a leveling effect on the development of the church, ironing out regional and chronological variation and overshadowing evidence for the existence of minor local churches before the tenth century. The latter are particularly well attested in early medieval Ireland and Cornwall. This may suggest a more diverse development for the pastoral church with mother- and minor-churches growing up at the same time and without a tidy hierarchical structure.

The "minster-model" sees religious communities as the primary source of pastoral care and puts forward an almost autonomous ministry on the part of mother-churches. The traditional role of the bishop in the dioceses, examining and ordaining clergy and making pastoral visitations of the laity tends to be relegated to the sidelines. Skepticism has been expressed concerning the ability of tenth- and eleventh-century bishops to regulate their dioceses before the institution of the rural archdeaconry in the later eleventh century.[5] But other recent scholarship has highlighted the role of bishops as pastoral leaders in England, and placed greater trust in the wealth of regulatory texts composed by or for bishops in the tenth and early eleventh centuries. While bishops and mother-churches coexisted – mother-churches were often important episcopal estates, providing pastoral bases for diocesan visitation, and some bishoprics were based in mother-churches as at, for example, Sherborne in Wessex – bishops provided services which the clergy of mother-churches could not. By the ninth century, it was customary for bishops in England at least to provide consecrated oil for use by priests in baptism and to anoint the sick.[6] An eighth-century Irish tract, the *Riagail Phátraic* describes the duty of the bishop in classic terms: "It falls on the souls of the men of Ireland owing to the testament of Patrick that each *túath* have a chief bishop for ordination of their clergy, for consecration of their churches, and to give spiritual guidance to lords and rulers of churches, for sanctifying and blessing their children after baptism . . ."[7]

In Wales, hagiography produced in the eleventh and twelfth centuries concerning earlier saints highlights the authority and pastoral role of the bishop.[8] The early twelfth-century life of the sixth-century saint, Padarn, describes how episcopal responsibilities were divided between the three great saints of south Wales, David, Teilo, and Padarn:

> the three southern kingdoms of the Britons succeeded under the three episcopacies of the three saints. The Kingdom of Seisyll, *Seisyllwg*, received the consecration of churches, and the imposition of ecclesiastical degrees, and confirmation of episcopal baptism, and the chrismal oil, and all episcopal duties from the episcopacy of saint Padarn. The kingdom of Rhain, *Rheiwg*, received these aforesaid rights from the episcopacy of Saint David. And the kingdom of Morgan, *Morgannwg*, received episcopal duties from Saint Eiludd, Teilo.[9]

This passage probably has no early authentic basis but represents a twelfth-century idealization. There are indicators, therefore, of the importance of episcopal ministry in this period but little to fill out the picture, particularly for Ireland, Scotland, and Wales. Even for Anglo-Saxon England, descriptions of bishops at work in their dioceses are rare. However, we are fortunate to possess in William of Malmesbury's *Life* of Wulfstan II of Worcester, an exceptionally rich and detailed account of episcopal ministry in the eleventh century.

Bishops and Pastoral Care

> Whenever Bishop Wulfstan II of Worcester visited his dioceses, he would never let the people go without a mass and a sermon, officiating frequently and with all care. He never indulged in food by day, until he had signed all the children, whatever their number, who were brought to him from all around. This was what he always did, from dawn to dusk, and not only in the winter but in the heat of the summer too. Often, in a single day, as careful witnesses prove, he confirmed two, often three or more thousand . . . even in old age. It was a matter for general wonder that, when eight priests carrying the chrism in turn gave in to fatigue, he kept going without tiring.[10]

Wulfstan II is portrayed as tirelessly on the move, spending long days preaching and anointing with oil the children brought to him for confirmation. Bishops alone were able to carry out the higher sacramental rituals of the consecration of priests and churches and of confirming baptized children. Preaching, although not an episcopal prerogative at this period, was a significant responsibility for the bishop, the means by which he must teach correct and essential doctrine and denounce outstanding abuses. Wulfstan's authority and power as a preacher is very much a key theme of his biography, and the importance to the saint of preaching is supported by the existence of a number of manuscripts of vernacular sermons copied at Worcester during his episcopate.[11] The bishop's appearance in the locality could also provide the occasion for the resolution of long-running problems. Wulfstan is described as giving spiritual advice and as being a compassionate confessor. Early eleventh-century sources urge local priests to refer unrepentant sinners to their bishops. William describes how the usually gentle Wulfstan did not hesitate to reprimand outstanding sinners, threatening the recalcitrant with divine punishment.[12] Wulfstan must have exercised his episcopal powers of excommunication and public penance upon those who refused to submit to pastoral correction. While the usual administration of confession and penance was performed by priests, certain major sins required a more serious form of expurgation which involved the sinner in temporary expulsion from the community of the church and the suspension of normal secular functions, such as sword-wearing and marital obligations. This form of penance, public penance, was administered through rituals of expulsion, reconciliation, and readmission before the assembled church and could only be performed by the bishop. Sinners who refused all invitations to penance could be excommunicated by the bishop, expelled from the Christian community, and banned from all social congress until they were reconciled.[13]

Pastoral Care in the Localities

Bishop Wulfstan II's biography shows a man always on the move; it is no wonder that, as his biographer commented, he was forced to take a break once a year.[14] In his perambulation of his diocese, Wulfstan II can be observed usually stopping over at one of his episcopal vills, estates owned by the bishop, normally offering a hall, church, and provisions. Many of these in the Worcester diocese were ancient ecclesiastical foundations, formerly independent monasteries which the see had gained possession of in earlier centuries.[15] These were minster churches that had borne the prime responsibility for pastoral care. Their hold on pastoral provision and its revenues was becoming eroded by the new thegnly churches that were being founded all over England in the tenth and eleventh centuries. Laws decreed by King Edgar attempted to regulate this situation by reserving the tithes and certain church dues to the old minster churches, while allowing the thegn who owned a church with a graveyard to divert a third of his tithe to it. A church without a graveyard was not entitled to the tithe, but the thegn must provide for the priest from the remaining nine-tenths of his revenue. This ruling, drawing upon Carolingian law, attempted to impose a degree of order on the rapidly changing pastoral landscape. Some degree of regulation upon the growth of the local church was presumably imposed by the need for episcopal consecration of both the newly founded church and the priests who provided the local ministry.[16] Wulfstan II was both a keen consecrator of new churches and zealous in encouraging their foundation, both on his episcopal property and on the land of others.[17] The tenth and early eleventh centuries saw a wealth of ecclesiastical legislation and guidance compiled by two leading church figures, Ælfric, abbot of Eynsham, the homilist, and Archbishop Wulfstan, a response to the burgeoning of the local church and the growth of the local clergy.

Clerical standards must have varied considerably between establishments and regions. Wulfstan II himself restored the church at Westbury, a former ancient minster, providing it with monks governed by his close associate and eventual biographer, Coleman, and with books. He also apparently reacted with displeasure when, visiting another episcopal estate, he discovered the liturgical equipment of its church soiled and in disrepair.[18] An early eleventh-century list of liturgical equipment belonging to Sherburn-in-Elmet gives an indication of the type of equipment such a church might have possessed: two gospels books, various liturgical books including a missal, lectionaries, and hymn books, as well as one chalice and a paten, two mass vestments, three chasubles, and altar equipment.[19] But small, local churches may have been very differently equipped, and their learning and religious knowledge must have appeared rustic and rudimentary to the learned monks of the great Benedictine houses such as Ælfric himself who remembered with disdain and indignation the ignorant misinterpretation of scripture by his own teacher, a country priest.[20] Local priests were subject not only to their diocesan bishops but also to their thegnly proprietors, who may have been less scrupulous about poor equipment or clerical misdemeanors such as marriage or drunkenness.[21]

Pastoral care in towns, especially cathedral cities, must also have presented a varied scene. Winchester, for example, the premier city of the West Saxon kingdom, was provided with a magnificent cathedral newly built in the late tenth century and served by a newly reformed Benedictine community, a second strict Benedictine monastery, also of great wealth, an ancient royal convent, and a number proprietary churches.[22] While most town-dwellers in the city must have resorted to their local church for mass, the sacraments, and for preaching, they were also able to attend the dramatic performance of the liturgical rituals for great feasts like Easter and Christmas and witness the numerous miracles worked by the holy relics belonging to the cathedral, which attracted countless pilgrims.[23] While the city of York lacked the magnificent monasteries of Winchester, it was also served by an ancient cathedral staffed there by secular clergy, and by a number of ancient and more recent urban churches. One such was founded and dedicated to St. Olaf by the Anglo-Scandinavian Earl Siward who was buried there in 1055.[24] Earlier in the tenth century, wealthy Anglo-Scandinavian citizens had clearly prized their association with the cathedral and had sought to be buried in its churchyard in graves marked by elaborately carved stone covers.[25]

Archbishop Wulfstan of York and Ælfric composed between them an influential corpus of vernacular homilies. Ælfric's great achievement was the production of two series of homilies to be read in alternation over a cycle of two years, providing sound and clear teaching for each Sunday and feast day. Their works represent a peak of pastoral endeavors, but they rest upon a much older tradition of vernacular preaching and teaching, manifest, for example, in other and earlier collections of sermons translated from Latin into English in the tenth century. The use of the vernacular to ensure that key religious texts were accessible to those unlearned in Latin, whether clergy or laity, was a very ancient tradition in England, reaching back to the eighth century and earlier. Old English versions of the Lord's Prayer, the Creed, and of penitential prayers and texts for use in confession survive and these translations were made in the second half of the tenth century and perhaps earlier. They provide an indication of the pastoral aims and activities of earlier tenth-century churchmen.[26]

The great flowering of the vernacular and the production of ecclesiastical law of the English church c.1000 demonstrates the vitality of the pre-Conquest church. Historians, however, have contrasted the strength of the pre-Conquest Norman church, with its efflorescence of church councils, with the scant English evidence for effective church legislation and oversight within the diocese. Archbishop Lanfranc inaugurated a series of primatial and general councils, asserting his authority as head of the whole English church and marking out the new order where king and archbishop worked closely together but religious and secular law were distinct. These councils were inaugurated in 1070 with two that met at Winchester and Windsor under the presidency of papal legates. In the following decade and a half, a total of six councils was convened by Lanfranc. These were a powerful tool for imposing the new order: "unsatisfactory" English bishops and abbots were deposed and cathedral sees moved to more prestigious locations. The administration of pastoral care was high on the agenda, with rulings on baptism and marriage. Simony was forbidden and clerical celibacy enjoined, though Lanfranc's rulings on clerical marriage were milder than both the strictures of the earlier Anglo-Saxon church and of Gregorian reform, forbidding priests who lived in colleges and communities to have wives but permitting those priests who lived alone with their wives in villages or fortifications to continue. No new relationships were to be formed. The governance of the diocese was placed on a new footing with the introduction of regular convocation of diocesan synods and the establishment of rural archdeaconries to provide pastoral oversight at a more local level within the diocese. Evidence for archdeacons is slight before the Conquest, but the practice seems to have become widespread within 50 years of the Conquest. Lanfranc's initiatives regularized pastoral care within England and strengthened episcopal regulation of the diocese. However, at the same time, a divide was opening up between the higher and lower clergy as foreign bishops appointed their own, continental followers to archdeaconries who may not have spoken much English.[27]

Mother-churches and the Growth of the Local Church

What happened at the local level with regard to the cure of souls? How far was it possible to deliver the basic essentials of pastoral care to village and local communities? What structures and institutions existed to mediate between bishops and communities? In pre-Conquest England, the responsibility for preaching and the administration of the sacraments was borne by minster churches, communities of secular clergy who ministered to fairly sizable geographical areas by visitation and by providing services in the monastic church. This extremely influential model for the pastoral ministry in the early Middle Ages has been successfully applied to the church in Ireland, Wales, and Scotland, and with more modification or reservation to Cornwall. In Wales, a church like Llancarfan in the eleventh century seems to have housed an abbot, a teacher, and a priest as well as canons. Such churches have been termed *clas*, and their territories were probably coterminous with the secular administrative region of the *cantref*. In some cases, at St. Davids and Llandeilo Fawr, they may also have been the seats of a bishop.[28] Scotland presents a similar picture with sparse evidence pointing to mother-churches at, for example, Meigle, St. Vigeans, Abernethy, Lochleven, Govan, and Deer. For the latter, we are fortunate in possessing an illustrated gospel book made in Scotland in the late eighth or ninth century with later annotations, including some Gaelic notes about benefactions. From these, we can see that the community at Deer also possessed dependent churches and chapels.[29] Scottish place-names may also provide some clues to early mother-churches: Thomas Clancy has suggested that the Gaelic place-name element *annaid* may in some places refer to a superior church, responsible for pastoral provision. He argues that these possessed a number of attributes, the relics of a patron saint, responsibility for subordinate churches, and the right to take dues. In some cases, these churches became parish churches in the parochial organization of the twelfth and thirteenth centuries. Although he is cautious about the universal applicability of this model, case studies from the West Highlands and from Moray and Perthshire supply corroborative evidence. He concludes that the early medieval Scottish church may have possessed an extensive local pastoral organization, based on mother-churches served by small communities.[30]

Richard Sharpe proposed for Ireland a network not only of mother-churches but also of small, local churches. He argued cogently from the evidence of legal and hagiographical texts from the seventh, eighth, and ninth centuries, and from place-names, for the existence of a pastoral organization consisting of mother-churches serving peoples and communities, with many small churches served by a single priest within localities. These mother-churches included episcopal bases and hereditary churches held by the laity. The great monasteries, such as Clonmacnoise and Durrow, also laid claim to ownership of mother-churches. Although the evidence grows scant, Sharpe suggests that mother-churches continued to provide pastoral care through the tenth and eleventh centuries, training clergy and providing pastors for minor churches. These mother-churches often provided the basis for the establishment of a parish church system from the twelfth century, although at the most local level it is possible that there was some shrinkage of the pastoral network with small churches falling into disuse.[31] Sharpe sets out an agenda for research, in part stressing the need for topographical and archaeological exploration of the local church. Recent assessments of early stone churches have both supported Sharpe's arguments concerning the density of local churches and nuanced them, suggesting diversity of function and regional variation. Ó Carragáin has pointed out that not all early churches were contemporary, some may have fallen out of use, and that in areas where the number of local churches seems to have exceeded the pastoral needs of the local population, some churches may have served other functions.[32]

Mother-churches have been identified at a dozen or so sites in Cornwall, such as St. Buryan and Padstow. These early, large collegiate churches in Cornwall were probably absorbed into the English minster system as Wessex extended its control into Cornwall. However, Cornish ecclesiastical topography is characterized rather by its myriad tiny parishes, many of ancient origin and bearing the name of an otherwise unknown local saint, which suggest that minster churches did not dominate the pastoral landscape, but that the scattered farmsteads of Cornwall may have been more often served by local churches.[33] A similar pattern has been detected in Wales where local place-names and dedications also suggest the presence of many small, local churches, and also in Ireland where the major monasteries may have functioned as secular communities with pastoral care but where, as we have seen, archaeological and place-name evidence indicates a proliferation of minor churches.[34]

The presence of so many ancient and minor churches in these regions is a marked contrast with scholarly interpretations of the English church where the local church is considered to be a creation of the tenth and eleventh centuries. Minster churches held ecclesiastical rights over wide territories. These great lands were broken up in the course of the tenth century and parceled out amongst the nobility, creating a class of minor thegns holding estates of smaller size. The minster churches retained residual but important rights over their former territories – for example, the right to take ancient church dues and to provide the holy oil used in liturgical rituals – but the sacramental ministry was now largely provided by small churches recently founded on their estates by the local landholder. The foundation of such churches became a mark of thegnly status: an eleventh-century tract described a church as one of a number of assets required by a man to achieve the rank of thegn. On a less legalistic level, these new proprietary churches represented an investment of capital on the part of their founders and owners who also needed to provide liturgical vessels and books.

The priest himself was maintained by church dues and offerings, although the land-owner was allowed a considerable cut of these so that a church could prove a valuable economic asset as well as a social one.[35] The local prestige of church ownership or at least patronage can be seen very clearly in the proud inscription put up at Kirkdale in Yorkshire, dating to the mid-eleventh century: "Orm Gamalson bought St. Gregory's minster when it was completely broken and fallen, and he had it newly built from the ground for Christ and St. Gregory in the days of Edward the king and in the days of Tostig the earl."[36]

Elsewhere in the Danelaw, thegnly investment in churches can be detected in the funerary monuments that they commissioned, grave-markers in the form of long slabs decorated with coarse interlace patterns, monuments known as "hogbacks" which resemble small houses, and standing crosses, now, alas, often fragmentary. These sculptural remains date from the early tenth century and are inscribed with a variety of designs. A number bear images of warriors, standing holding their weapons, or sitting on their high seats; others also display not only Christian imagery such as crucifixion scenes but also scenes from Scandinavian myth. The cross shaft from Gosforth, for example, juxtaposes a crucifixion scene with episodes from the story of Ragnarok, the Norse story of the end of the world. These seem at times to have been deliberately selected to provide an analogy to the doctrines represented by the Christian scenes.[37] These considered juxtapositions hint at ways in which the Christian faith may have been taught to the Scandinavian incomers, new ways of thinking designed to render comprehensible and attractive the doctrines of the local church.

The Conversion of the Vikings

These Anglo-Scandinavian carvings speak suggestively of interactions between the English church and the viking incomers. While there is much controversy and uncer-tainty about whether Scandinavian settlement in the Danelaw consisted of numerous peasant farmers or whether it represented an elite takeover of Anglo-Saxon estates, it is clear that the vikings were pagans for whom churches and monasteries through-out Britain and Ireland were initially attractive not for their spiritual benefits but rather for the opportunities they provided for looting. Assemblages found in Scandinavian graves of metalwork taken from shrines, book covers, and church para-phernalia are an indicator of the reality of the viking raids recorded in annals. However, in the course of the tenth century, these men and their descendants settled in England and silently abandoned their pagan practices and adopted Christian beliefs. Very little evidence of pagan burial for the vikings exists, and the settlers seem very quickly to have been interred in Christian cemeteries.

By what means they were persuaded to listen to Christian teaching, and to what extent the efforts of their teachers to instill Christian moral values were successful, are questions impossible to answer. It is likely that both the formal ministry of local priests and the informal pressures of intermarriage with the local communities com-bined to evangelize the incomers and their descendants. The ties of pagan religion may have been very firmly rooted in the homeland and not readily transportable. Cults firmly linked to place, for example to sacred trees and hallowed groves, and rituals focusing on the memory of ancestors would have lost their potency in a new country. The fact that tenth-century sculpture records the continuing currency of stories about Scandinavian gods and heroes need not undermine this view because these tales were carried in the minds of the settlers, unlike sacred places. The ability of the church to absorb these, and even harness them to reinforce Christian doctrine, shows some sophistication and acuity, and this adaptability on the part of the church in the Danelaw probably also contributed considerably to easing the path to Christianity. Moreover, religious rituals and beliefs are intimately embedded in social practices and structures; the Scandinavian settlers quickly integrated into local society. A story recorded by Byrhtferth in his *Life of St. Oswald* tells how the future archbishop of Canterbury, Oda, the son of a viking who was one of the viking settlers who had come to England in the ninth century with the great army of Ivarr and Ubbe, decided himself to convert to Christianity and entered the household of a noble Anglo-Saxon, receiving his religious education from the household priest. Oda's kinsman was Oswald, archbishop of York and monastic reformer: within less than a hundred years, his family had gone from pagan elite to pillars of the Anglo-Saxon ecclesiastical establishment.[38] As this suggests, social mechanisms such as fosterage may have played an important part in the conversion of the elite.

It is impossible to say when the Scandinavian settlers in Ireland were converted; conjectures range from the mid-ninth to the early eleventh century. Bhreathnach has suggested that the Columban churches may have played a part, noting a relationship between Amlaíb Cúarán (Óláfr Sihtricson) and the Columban churches of Skreen, Moone, and Swords and his eventual retirement and death at Iona in 981. Amlaíb was baptized in England, sponsored by King Edmund in 943, during his first reign as king of York, before his return to Dublin in 945. The two Scandinavian kingdoms of York and Dublin were very closely linked, and it is possible that because of the English tradition of imposing Christian baptism upon viking leaders who allied or submitted to the Anglo-Saxon kings, English influence may have played a part in the conversion of the Scandinavian rulers of Dublin.[39]

The Church and Lay Piety

The processes of conversion must have resulted in a two-way traffic between the two belief systems with the result that Christian ideas and rituals were also changed. But it was a quite remarkable achievement, carried out in regions, particularly the north and east of England, where episcopal oversight was apparently minimal and the normal power-houses of early medieval religion, large, wealthy monasteries, were absent. Little of the apparatus of the post-Carolingian reform church is visible: a clear ecclesiastical hierarchy crowned by active bishops busy enforcing the strictures of canon law and ensuring the provision of orthodox teaching. But the absence of textual evidence for an active and interventionist church does not mean that religious life was completely lacking; pastoral care took place but is well nigh invisible in the historical record. This situation can be paralleled in Scotland and Wales where only fragmentary evidence survives for the church. It is clear from, for example, the move to ecclesiastical burial sites in Wales in the course of the ninth century that Christian teaching was reaching the laity. Sculptural evidence from both Scotland and Wales, where motifs such as figures on horseback and hunting scenes betoken a rapprochement between secular values and Christian ones, suggests successful penetration by the church of lay society.[40] The *Book of Deer* uniquely preserves records of donations by local aristocrats to the monastery, indicating again lay commitment.[41]

It is impossible to probe the limits or depth of Christianization in these areas because of the want of evidence, but we should not doubt the impact of the church's teaching. Rituals, moral practices, and beliefs may nonetheless have varied: Archbishop Lanfranc's letters to the Irish complained about abhorrent Irish marriage practices, consanguinity, serial polygamy, and even wife swapping. The behavior of bishops and priests was also castigated: incorrect infant baptism and consecrations of bishops, sale of holy orders and the ordination of bishops to villages and small towns. Lanfranc advocated that church councils be held to remedy such abuses. Lanfranc's criticisms echo those of Pope Gregory VII and reflect eleventh-century reform thinking; his strictures endeavor to kickstart reform in the Irish church and to end its isolation from continental currents of thought and practice.

Marriage and sexual morality lay at the fulcrum of the church's relations with the laity. Christian teaching on these issues lay at the hard edge of acculturation to its ideals. Marriage was a potent tool in social exchanges and the church's teaching on sex was particularly repressive. Intercourse was only sanctioned within marriage for the sake of procreation, and even then strictly regulated and limited with regard to when it could be done.[42] Even King Edgar, whose commitment to monastic reform and christocentric kingship was exemplary, enjoyed numerous liaisons, not all of which were sanctioned by marriage.[43] Edgar's piety was no cynical power ploy and should not be undermined by his reputation as a lover. Ælfric, enjoining the periods of abstinence from sex in one of his sermons, directly addressed his audience, saying that he knew that this teaching was hard for them to follow.

However, help was at hand. The church had a highly developed system of penance which could be invoked to save the sinner from the consequences of sexual and other sins. Listed amongst Ælfric's collection of books necessary to the priestly ministry was a penitential, a handbook laying down a tariff of penances appropriate to individual sins. Priests were not supposed to follow these slavishly but rather to use confession as an occasion for teaching and spiritual guidance. It is hard to know how often the laity made use of penance and confession. Ælfric seems to have expected them to make confession at least once a year as part of their Lenten preparation for Easter.[44] Further, some examples survive from tenth- and eleventh-century England showing that major crimes, such as the killing of a close relative, were atoned for by pilgrimages.[45] The Welsh dossier of charters, the *Book of Llandaff*, attests a number of instances where bishops imposed penance on laymen for major crimes, such as murder or the violation of a church.[46] William of Malmesbury tells a story of how Bishop Wulfstan II of Worcester was importuned by a woman for sexual favors. He had responded to her approaches to him in church under the mistaken impression that she wanted to make her confession.[47]

A story from twelfth or thirteenth-century Ireland gives important insights into penitential teaching – and its working – there. A woman pestered a young monk for sex so that he eventually gave way, making an assignation with her in a walled garden. However, when she arrived, she found that it was full of people, nobles, and royals and even her own husband. When she expressed her horror and reproached her partner for wishing to take his pleasure so publicly, the monk pointed to the heavenly host, which had also taken up ringside seats, and asked her why she thought it more shameful to sin in the sight of earthly men than before Christ and the saints. The effect was immediate and she repented of her sin. This story illustrates how the church could use the ignominy of shame, an important aspect of lay culture, to reinforce Christian teaching and the practice of penance.[48] The penances assigned usually consisted of fasting on bread and water, other types of self-denial, and the giving of alms. Almsgiving, both as part of a formal penance and as a virtuous religious practice in its own right, was the most common form of lay piety. It is widely advocated in Anglo-Saxon sermons, and is manifest in the many grants of property to the church and in lay wills which frequently mention bequests of alms.

When thinking about religion, the minds of the laity naturally turned to death and the fate of the soul in the afterlife. Evidence for lay piety tends to cluster around preparation for death. Guild regulations from tenth- and eleventh-century England show groups of laymen coming together to make financial provision for burial and collective commemoration. The records of the monastery of Ely preserve the desire of one layman, a middling thegn, to be buried at Ely where his friends were buried and to travel to the monastery to visit the grave of a friend.[49] Monasteries were regarded as spiritual beacons, as islands of divine proximity and spiritual purity. Burial in a monastic cemetery, close to the saints, could help the passage of the soul in the afterlife. Some laymen renounced the secular life and spent their last days in monasteries under monastic vows, as Óláfr Sihtricson did.

The strength of lay piety in early medieval Britain and Ireland should not be underestimated: the evidence for extensive lay investment in the church is strong. But questions of belief are harder to probe. The available sources derive from the church and paint a normative picture of lay piety. In practice, lay religious beliefs must have been very mixed. Some indication of the intertwining of Christian beliefs with elements derived from lay culture can be seen in the charms used to ward off and cure disease and agricultural disaster which mix together liturgical formulae with beliefs in elves and other supernatural beings.[50] For the laity, religion was probably less a matter of correct doctrine than a much-needed support and solace in the face of the brutal realities of life. Belief in the support of the saints and their ability to intervene beneficially in everyday life was important. Cults could be controlled and promoted by the church, but it is also likely that they were part of local community life. The cult of the murdered royal saint, Kenelm, was promoted at the reformed community of Winchcombe, but the passion of the saint suggested that local cult sites in the neighborhood, including a sacred well, were important features. His story – his murder at the instigation of his wicked stepsister – taps into folklore and oral traditions suggesting some currency among the laity.[51]

Saints Cults

Here begins the *Secgan* concerning God's saints who first rested in England. St. Alban, martyr, who rests near St. Albans near the river which is called *Waerlam*. Then Colum Cille rests in that place which is called Dunkeld, near the river which is called the *Tua*. Then St. Cuthbert rests in that place which men call Durham . . .[52]

So begins *The Resting Places of English Saints*, a fascinating guide to the saints and their cults in the late Saxon period. This composite document has a core probably dating from the ninth century and was extensively revised in the early eleventh; it records 89 saints, chiefly of English origin. Many of these are names well known from

Bede's *History* and other works, but a number, especially those added late, are of saints whose cults are ill recorded and which centered on relatively minor churches. The compilation as a whole paints a picture of a saintly topography dominated by monasteries and where many of the cults may have possessed a largely local following. The list is preserved in three eleventh-century manuscripts where it may have been included as part of a nationalizing agenda that emphasized the network of saints throughout the kingdom.[53]

The revisions to the earlier lists of saints embedded in the collection indicate the ways in which the local landscape of sanctity in England had been changing in the course of the ninth and tenth centuries. A crucial factor here is the increasing urbanization of Anglo-Saxon England. Towns were becoming flourishing economic centers with industry and commerce, centers of population attracting traders and others visitors. Cults situated in such hubs naturally benefited from this vitality, as the various accounts of the cult of Swithun at Winchester amply demonstrate.[54] Miracles recorded frequently involve local townspeople – merchants, moneyers, craftsmen, and royal officials – as well as those visiting the city. Swithun was an obscure ninth-century bishop of Winchester whose cult was established in the late tenth century by Bishop Æthelwold who enshrined the saint in a splendid reliquary in the cathedral. Swithun's miraculous powers attracted the needy from all over the south of England and beyond: from Hampshire, Bedfordshire, the Isle of Wight, London, and Rochester, for example, as well as from the continent. Those benefiting from his healing included slaves and peasants as well as aristocrats and the rich. The success of Swithun's relics in accomplishing so many miracles would have acted as a great money-spinner for the cathedral, attracting gifts and grants. In fact, the cult proved so successful that the cathedral brethren became fed up with having to get up in the night in order to offer thanks to the saint for another nocturnal healing![55]

The cult of Swithun typifies many aspects of reform interest in saints: the quest for the relics of long-dead English saints, their ceremonial translation, and their utilization to support both the ideology and the practice of reform by enlisting a team of heavenly patrons in addition to the support provided by the earthly king, Edgar. Similarly, at Ely, the ancient cult of St. Æthelthryth was charged with renewed vitality, particularly because, as a celebrated virgin, she could act as an icon of virginity for monks. Swithun and Æthelthryth were culted at their original churches; elsewhere, the relics of earlier Anglo-Saxon saints were transported from their original resting-places – sometimes over great distances – to new shrines in Benedictine communities. Relics of Wilfrid at Ripon were removed to Canterbury in the tenth century, and those of other northern saints seem to have found their way to Glastonbury. Monastic reform had the effect of centralizing saints' cults to areas closer to the West Saxon heartlands, moving them to their own places of power. The earlier pattern of local cults, with saints' bodies and relics remaining in their original place of burial, was disrupted by the movement of their relics to new churches and by the new dominance of major cults like those of Swithun or Æthelthryth.[56] In tenth-century England, saints' cults were enmeshed with the power structures of church and state: they supported the agenda of reformed monasticism by promoting the power of virgin saints and of saintly bishops like Swithun. The monastic reform movement was closely linked to royal authority, particularly that of Edgar. The royal house of Wessex also had its own reserves of sanctity to draw upon in the form of saintly kings, most notably in the eleventh century, Edward the Martyr, the assassinated brother of Æthelred the Unready whose cult was promoted by the royal nunnery of Shaftesbury and subsequently supported by royal law.[57]

The promotion of saints' cults in tenth- and eleventh-century England looks different from that of Ireland, Wales, Scotland, and Cornwall. Here, the pattern evidenced by place-names and church dedications seems much more localized. Cornwall, for example, boasts roughly a hundred saints who appear to have been culted only in one or two places and are known only by their name: the place-names Ventoninny, St. Anthony in Meneage, and St. Anthony in Roseland preserve the name of an otherwise unknown saint, St. Antoninus. Many cults are unique apparently to one place. These individuals may have been founders of a small monastery or local holy men or women whose memory remained potent.[58] Sometimes, however, church dedications or place-names incorporating a saint's name could be a mark of federations of churches, such as the case of St. Teilo in south Wales.[59] Here, as in England, saints' cults were intricately bound up with church structures. The strength of dynastic control upon the church in Ireland is also reflected in saints' cults with, for example, the production of genealogies of saints, the diffusion of cults by ecclesiastical families, and the dynastic custodianship of saints' relics.

Devotion to the saints not only focused upon the body or corporeal remains of the saint, but also upon objects and places associated with him or her. The tomb of the saint could provide a potent site for lay pilgrimage and for prayers. At Winchester, Swithun was moved from his humble grave outside the cathedral to a magnificent shrine at the high altar, an event celebrated by great public ceremony and feast.[60] In Wales, saints were allowed to rest in their original graves, undisturbed; the grave itself formed the focus for devotions, either in the church itself or in the churchyard where a special chapel might be built. These saints might be holy figures from the distant past; for example, at Llansadwrn (Angelsey), a early inscribed stone in the graveyard commemorates the holy couple, Saturninus and his wife. The Welsh name, Sadwrn, combined in the place-name with the element *llan*, is a later form of the Roman name, Saturninus. Unlike the Irish or English, the Welsh appeared to prefer not to move the bodies of their saints.[61] Evidence suggests that in Cornwall, too, saints remained buried in their churches and formed the focus for devotion.[62] In England, it was customary to publicize a cult by translating the body to a more impressive and accessible shrine.

While the cults of local saints appears to have been a shared characteristic of the churches in Cornwall, Ireland, Wales, and Scotland, attitudes to the translation and disarticulation of saintly bodies varied between these regions. Neither in Wales nor England was it usual to dismember bodies to provide relics of parts of saints' bodies, although this seems to have happened in Ireland. Such relics were, however, reverenced in England as King Æthelstan's relic collection shows (see chapter 22). Wales, Ireland, and Scotland manifest a strong reverence for another type of relic, secondary relics, objects associated with the saint, which is not an important aspect of cults in England.[63] Some wealthy laity possessed their own shrines and relics, and in the course of the late tenth and eleventh centuries a notable devotion of the cult of the cross developed in England. Both laity and religious made great gifts of life-size crucifixes bearing the figure of Christ and of statues of other saints. The monastery of Waltham Abbey in Essex possessed a miracle-working stone crucifix and was patronized by Harold Godwineson and other members of the Anglo-Scandinavian aristocracy who gave it sumptuous gifts.[64]

It is a great loss for the historian than no such statues have survived, but for Ireland, Wales, and Scotland we are fortunate to possess a good many shrines and relics. In the course of the ninth century, the staff and the bell of the saint came to be revered as particularly powerful. Miracle stories record, for example, how the ninth-century king, Feidlimid son of Crimthainn, was punished in a dream by St. Ciaran for plundering his monastery of Clonmacnoise. The saint stabbed the king in the stomach with his staff with the result that the king eventually died. Only four crozier relics are known from Scotland, but some 50 survive from Ireland. A greater number of bells survive, approximately 75 from Ireland, 19 from Scotland, and seven from Wales, no doubt because of their greater durability. Croziers, bells, and other secondary relics, such as books or items of the saint's clothing, continued to be reverenced until late in the Middle Ages. Examples from Kilmichael Glassary, Argyll and Guthrie, Angus were enshrined in the twelfth and fourteenth centuries respectively. Often they came to be held by hereditary lay custodians in whose families they remained for generations. The Bachall Mor of Molaug (great staff) is kept by the Livingstone family on the island of Lismore in Argyll. Such relics could be processed around the locality on the saint's feast and other occasions and could be used for oath-swearing and dispute settlement. In the twelfth century, Gerald of Wales remarked: "the common people, and the clergy, too not only in Ireland and Scotland, but also in Wales, have such a reverence for portable bells, staffs crooked at the top and encased in gold, silver or bronze, and similar relics of the saints, that they are more afraid of swearing oaths upon them and then breaking their word than they are upon the Gospels."[65]

It is possible to trace long continuities in the cult of saints in Cornwall, Wales, and Ireland. In the late eleventh and early twelfth centuries, Welsh communities participated in the revival of Latin hagiography which took place also in England. There, the lives of St. David and of Cadog were composed in the late eleventh century and a dossier of saints' lives was compiled at the burgeoning see of Llandaff to buttress its claims to privileges and territories.[66] In England, the saints of the Anglo-Saxons continued to act as powerful guardians of their communities, with new Latin lives penned for St. Æthelthryth of Ely and Dunstan of Canterbury. A number of English saints whose cults seem never previously to have been the subject of a written hagiography were freshly written up. The new Norman and continental heads of English communities were not slow to call upon their ancient patrons to protect their houses from despoliation and to give the potency of saintly charisma to their churches. Holy men of the recent past and present were venerated and their saintly status affirmed by the production of a written hagiography: lives were produced for Wulfstan II of Worcester, Archbishop Anselm of Canterbury and his associate Gundulf of Rochester, and for King Edward the Confessor, for example.[67]

The strong evidence from the churches of England, Scotland, Wales, and Ireland for flourishing saints' cults, popular with both the lay elite and the ordinary people, is a testament to the pastoral work of the church in other areas. The laity and church interacted in many ways – through the sacraments, intercession, and penances. The evidence for the mechanisms for pastoral care is not always plentiful, but the widespread appeal of the saints, whose power could intervene in this world and in ensuring salvation in the next, indicates the extent to which the church had penetrated society.

Notes

1   Sharpe, "Churches and communities," p. 109.
2   Davies, *Wales in the Early Middle Ages*, p. 184; Pryce, "Pastoral care," p. 41.
3   Etchingham, "Pastoral provision."
4   Cambridge and Rollason, "Pastoral organization."
5   Blair, *Church in Anglo-Saxon Society*, pp. 495–7.
6   Jones, "The chrism mass."
7   Quoted by Clancy, "Annat in Scotland," p. 94.
8   Davies, *Early Welsh Microcosm*, pp. 146–7.
9   Wade-Evans (ed.), *Vitae sanctorum Britanniae et genealogiae*, pp. 266–7. For the dating of this life, see Davies, *Wales in the Early Middle Ages*, p. 208 and the *Oxford Dictionary of National Biography* 21078.
10 Winterbottom and Thomson (eds.), "William of Malmesbury, *Vita Wulfstani*," c. 14, pp. 86–7; on Wulfstan, see Mason, *St. Wulfstan*, and the collection of essays edited by Barrow and Brooks, *Bishop Wulfstan and his World*.
11 Gameson, "St. Wulfstan."
12 Winterbottom and Thomson (eds.), "William of Malmesbury, *Vita Wulfstani*," cc. 15–17, pp. 89–97.
13 Hamilton, *Practice of Penance*, and "Rites for public penance."
14 Winterbottom and Thomson (eds.), "William of Malmesbury, *Vita Wuflstani*," c. 10, pp. 120–1.
15 See, for example, ibid.; Mason, *St. Wulfstan*, pp. 168–9.
16 Blair, *Church in Anglo-Saxon Society*, pp. 368–95; Cubitt, *Sin and Society*.
17 Winterbottom and Thomson (eds.), "William of Malmesbury, *Vita Wulfstani*," cc. 15, 17, pp. 89–90, 95–7.
18 Ibid., c. 18, pp. 97–9.
19 Barker (ed.), *York Gospels*, pp. 96–7.
20 Wilcox (ed.), *Ælfric's Prefaces*, p. 7.
21 Wood, *Proprietary Church*, pp. 519, 30.
22 Biddle (ed.), *Winchester*, pp. 306–22, 329–30.
23 Barrow, "Churches," pp. 130–9; Rosser, "The cure of souls."
24 Townend, "Knútr," 268–73.
25 Stocker, "Monuments and merchants."
26 Fulk and Cain, *History*, pp. 70–86.
27 Cowdrey, *Lanfranc*, pp. 120–43.
28 Pryce, "Pastoral care," pp. 54–5.
29 Macquarrie, "Early Christian religious houses."
30 Clancy, "Annat in Scotland."
31 Sharpe, "Churches and communities."
32 Ó Carragáin, "Church buildings and pastoral care," esp. pp. 97, 110–11.
33 Padel, "Local saints," pp. 303–16.
34 Davies, "The myth of the Celtic church," pp. 19–21.
35 Blair, *Church in Anglo-Saxon Society*, pp. 368–425; Wood, *Proprietary Church*, pp. 519–75.
36 Townend, *Scandinavian Culture*, p. 1.
37 Bailey, *Viking Age Sculpture*, pp. 101–42; Stocker and Everson, "Five towns funerals," pp. 223–41.
38 Abrams, "The conversion of the Danelaw"; Raine (ed.), *Byrhtferth: Vita Oswaldi*, pp. 404–5.
39 Abrams, "Conversion of the Scandinavians," 24–7; Breathnach, "Columban churches," pp. 5–18.

40   Pryce, "Pastoral care," pp. 45–6.
41   Macquarrie, "Early Christian religious houses," pp. 130–1.
42   Payer, *Sex and the Penitentials.*
43   Yorke, "Sisters under the skin?," 95–117.
44   Cubitt, *Sin and Society.*
45   Ibid.
46   Davies, *Early Welsh Microcosm*, pp. 133, 185–7, nos. 249b, 257, 259, 263, 264b.
47   Winterbottom and Thomson (eds.), "William of Malmesbury, *Vita Wulfstani*," pp. 30–3.
48   Harrington, *Women in a Celtic Church*, pp. 239–41.
49   Cubitt, *Sin and Society*; Fairweather (trans.), *Liber Eliensis*, pp. 110–11.
50   Hall, *Elves in Anglo-Saxon England*; Jolly, *Popular Religion*, pp. 96–131.
51   Cubitt, "Folklore and historiography" and "Sites and sanctity."
52   Liebermann (ed.), *Die Heiligen Englands*, p. 9.
53   Rollason, "Lists of saints' resting-places."
54   Rollason, *Saints and Relics*, pp. 182–8.
55   Lapidge (ed.), *Cult of St. Swithun*, pp. 217–551, 598–601; Rollason, *Saints and Relics*, pp. 181–95.
56   Rollason, "The shrines of saints."
57   Ridyard, *Royal Saints.*
58   Padel, "Local saints."
59   Davies, "The saints of south Wales."
60   Lapidge (ed.), *Cult of St. Swithun*, pp. 16–18.
61   Edwards, "Celtic saints," pp. 227–43.
62   Padel, "Local saints," pp. 341–7.
63   Edwards, "Celtic saints," pp. 244–65.
64   Raw, *Anglo-Saxon Crucifixion Iconography*, pp. 40–2.
65   Edwards, "Celtic saints," pp. 244–65, quotation from Gerald of Wales, at p. 252.
66   Davies, *Book of Llandaf.*
67   Ridyard, "'Condigna veneration.'"

Further Reading

A number of essay collections pursue issues of pastoral care and lay religion across national divides in an important and helpful fashion. John Blair and Richard Sharpe (eds.), *Pastoral Care before the Parish* is fundamental. Another collection of essays, *Pastoral Care in Late Anglo-Saxon England*, edited by Francesca Tinti (Woodbridge, 2005), extends to the tenth and eleventh centuries. Valuable essays on the Welsh and Cornish churches can be found in Nancy Edwards and Alan Lane (eds.), *The Early Church in Wales and the West* (Oxford, 1992). *The Parish in Medieval and Early Modern Ireland*, edited by Elizabeth FitzPatrick and Raymond Gillespie, tackles the issue of parishes over many centuries; the essays are up to date with helpful summaries of current debate and set Irish problems in the context of broader historiography. Colmán Etchingham's *Church Organisation in Ireland AD 650 to 1000* is an important study with a valuable review of historiography in its opening sections. John Blair's *The Church in Anglo-Saxon Society* is important for its treatment of lay piety and saints' cults. These are also well served by David Rollason's general study, *Saints and Relics in Anglo-Saxon England*. John Reuben Davies, *The Book of Llandaf and the Norman Church in Wales* is an important study of the eleventh-century Welsh church and hagiography. Another first-rate collaborative volume, Alan Thacker and Richard Sharpe (eds.), *Local Saints and Local Churches in the Early Medieval West*, puts together essays for England and the Celtic world to explore the significance of local cults; it is invaluable for a comparative view.

Bibliography

Abrams, L. J., "The conversion of the Danelaw," in J. Graham-Campbell, R. Hall, J. Jesch, and D. N. Parsons (eds.), *Vikings and the Danelaw: Select Papers from the Proceedings of the Thirteenth Viking Congress, Nottingham and York, August 21–30, 1997* (Oxford, 2001), pp. 31–44.

Abrams, L. J., "The conversion of the Scandinavians of Dublin," *Anglo-Norman Studies*, 20 (1998), 1–29.

Bailey, R., *Viking Age Sculpture in Northern England* (London, 1980).

Barker, N. (ed.), *The York Gospels* (Lewes, 1986).

Barrow, J., "Churches, education and literacy in towns 600–1100," in D. M. Palliser (ed.), *The Cambridge Urban History of Britain*, vol. 1 (Cambridge, 2000), pp. 127–52.

Barrow, J. and Brooks, N. (eds.), *Bishop Wulfstan and his World* (Aldershot, 2005).

Bhreathnach, E., "Columban churches in Brega and Leinster: relations with the Norse and the Anglo-Normans," *Journal of the Royal Society of Antiquaries of Ireland*, 129 (1999), 5–18.

Biddle, M. (ed.), *Winchester in the Early Middle Ages* (Oxford, 1976).

Blair, J., *The Church in Anglo-Saxon Society* (Oxford, 2005).

Blair, J. and Sharpe, R. (eds.), *Pastoral Care before the Parish* (Leicester, 1992).

Cambridge, E. and Rollason, D., "The pastoral organization of the Anglo-Saxon church: a review of the 'minster hypothesis,'" *Early Medieval Europe*, 4 (1995), 87–104.

Charles-Edwards, T. M., "The seven bishop-houses of Dyfed," *Bulletin of the Board of Celtic Studies*, 24 (1970–2), 247–62.

Clancy, T. O., "Annat in Scotland and the origins of the parish," *Innes Review*, 46 (1995), 91–115.

Cowdrey, H. E. J., *Lanfranc: Scholar, Monk and Archbishop* (Oxford, 2003).

Cubitt, C., "Folklore and historiography: oral stories and the writing of Anglo-Saxon history," in E. Tyler and R. Balzaretti (eds.), *Narrative and History in the Early Middle Ages* (Turnhout, 2006), pp. 189–223.

Cubitt, C., *Sin and Society in Tenth- and Eleventh-century England* (forthcoming).

Cubitt, C., "Sites and sanctity: revisiting the cults of murdered and martyred Anglo-Saxon royal saints," *Early Medieval Europe*, 9 (2000), 53–83.

Davies, J. R., *The Book of Llandaf and the Norman Church in Wales* (Woodbridge, 2003).

Davies, J. R., "The saints of south Wales and the Welsh church," in A. T. Thacker and R. Sharpe (eds.), *Local Saints and Local Churches in the Early Medieval West* (Oxford, 2002), pp. 361–95.

Davies, W., *An Early Welsh Microcosm: Studies in the Llandaff Charters* (London, 1978).

Davies, W., *The Llandaff Charters* (Aberystwyth, 1979).

Davies, W., "The myth of the Celtic church," in N. Edwards and A. Lane (eds.), *The Early Church in Wales and the West* (Oxford, 1992), pp. 12–21.

Edwards, N., "Celtic saints and early medieval archaeology," in A. T. Thacker and R. Sharpe (eds.), *Local Saints and Local Churches in the Early Medieval West* (Oxford, 2002), pp. 225–65.

Etchingham, C., *Church Organisation in Ireland AD 650 to 1000* (Maynooth, 1999).

Etchingham, C., "Pastoral provision in the first millennium: a two-tier service?," in E. FitzPatrick and R. Gillespie (eds.), *The Parish in Medieval and Early Modern Ireland: Community, Territory and Building* (Dublin, 2006), pp. 79–90.

Fairweather, J. (trans.), *Liber Eliensis: A History of the Isle of Ely from the Seventh Century to the Twelfth* (Woodbridge, 2005).

FitzPatrick, E. and Gillespie, R. (eds.), *The Parish in Medieval and Early Modern Ireland: Community, Territory and Building* (Dublin, 2006).

Fulk, R. D. and Cain, C. M., *A History of Old English Literature* (Oxford, 2003).

Gameson, R., "St. Wulfstan, the library of Worcester and the spirituality of the medieval book," in J. Barrow and N. Brooks (eds.), *Bishop Wulfstan and his World* (Aldershot, 2005), pp. 59–109.

Gittos, H. and Bradford Bedingfield, M. (eds.), *The Liturgy of the Late Anglo-Saxon Church* (London, 2005).

Hadley, D. M. and Richards, J. D. (eds.), *Cultures in Contact: Scandinavian Settlement in England in the Ninth and Tenth Centuries* (Turnhout, 2000).

Hall, A., *Elves in Anglo-Saxon England: Matters of Belief, Health, Gender and Identity* (Woodbridge, 2007).

Hamilton, S., *The Practice of Penance, 900–1050* (Woodbridge, 2001).

Hamilton, S., "Rites for public penance in late Saxon England," in H. Gittos and M. Bradford Bedingfield (eds.), *Liturgy of the Late Anglo-Saxon Church* (London, 2005), pp. 65–103.

Harrington, C., *Women in a Celtic Church: Ireland 450–1150* (Oxford, 2002).

Jolly, K. L., *Popular Religion in Late Saxon England* (Chapel Hill, NJ, 1996).

Jones, C. A., "The chrism mass in later Anglo-Saxon England," in H. Gittos and M. Bradford Bedingfield (eds.), *The Liturgy of the Late Anglo-Saxon Church* (London, 2005), pp. 105–42.

Lapidge, M. (ed.), *The Cult of St. Swithun* (Oxford, 2003).

Liebermann, F. (ed.), *Die Heiligen Englands: Angelsächsisch und Lateinisch* (Hannover, 1889).

Macquarrie, A., "Early Christian religious communities in Scotland: foundation and function," in J. Blair and R. Sharpe (eds.), *Pastoral Care before the Parish* (Leicester, 1992), pp. 110–33.

Mason, E., *St. Wulfstan of Worcester c.1008–1095* (Oxford, 1990).

Ó Carragáin, T., "Church buildings and pastoral care in early medieval Ireland," in E. FitzPatrick and R. Gillespie (eds.), *The Parish in Medieval and Early Modern Ireland: Community, Territory and Building* (Dublin, 2006), pp. 91–123.

Padel, O. J., "Local saints and place-names in Cornwall," in A. T. Thacker and R. Sharpe (eds.), *Local Saints and Local Churches in the Early Medieval West* (Oxford, 2002), pp. 303–60.

Payer, P., *Sex and the Penitentials: The Development of a Social Code, 550–1150* (Toronto, 1984).

Pryce, H., "Pastoral care in early medieval Wales," in J. Blair and R. Sharpe (eds.), *Pastoral Care before the Parish* (Leicester, 1992), pp. 41–62.

Raine, J. (ed.), *Byrhtferth: Vita Oswaldi*, in *Historians of the Church of York*, Rolls Series, 3 vols. (1879), I, pp. 399–475.

Raw, B., *Anglo-Saxon Crucifixion Iconography and the Art of the Monastic Revival* (Cambridge, 1990).

Ridyard, S. J., "'Condigna veneratio': post-Conquest attitudes to the saints of the Anglo-Saxons," *Anglo-Norman Studies*, 9 (1986), 179–201.

Ridyard, S. J., *The Royal Saints of Anglo-Saxon England: A Study of West Saxon and East Anglian Cults* (Cambridge, 1988).

Rollason, D. W., "Lists of saints' resting-places in Anglo-Saxon England," *Anglo-Saxon England*, 7 (1978), 61–93.

Rollason, D. W., *Saints and Relics in Anglo-Saxon England* (Oxford, 1989).

Rollason, D. W., "The shrines of saints in later Anglo-Saxon England: distribution and signficance," in L. A. S. Butler and R. K. Morris (eds.), *The Anglo-Saxon Church: Papers on History, Architecture, and Archaeology in Honour of Dr H. M. Taylor* (London, 1986), pp. 32–43.

Rosser, G., "The cure of souls in English towns before 1000," in J. Blair and R. Sharpe (eds.), *Pastoral Care before the Parish* (Leicester, 1992), pp. 266–84.

Sharpe, R., "Churches and communities in early medieval Ireland: towards a pastoral model," in J. Blair and R. Sharpe (eds.), *Pastoral Care before the Parish* (Leicester, 1992), pp. 81–109.

Stocker, D., "Monuments and merchants: irregularities in the distribution of stone sculpture in Lincolnshire and Yorkshire in the tenth century," in D. M. Hadley and J. D. Richards (eds.), *Cultures in Contact: Scandinavian Settlement in England in the Ninth and Tenth Centuries* (Turnhout, 2000), pp. 179–212.

Stocker, D. and Everson, P., "Five towns funerals: decoding diversity in Danelaw stone sculpture," in J. Graham-Campbell, R. Hall, J. Jesch, and Parsons, D. N. (eds.), *Vikings and the Danelaw: Select Papers from the Proceedings of the Thirteenth Viking Congress* (Oxford, 2001), pp. 223–43.

Thacker, A. T. and Sharpe, R. (eds.), *Local Saints and Local Churches in the Early Medieval West* (Oxford, 2002).

Townend, M., "Knútr and the cult of St. Ólafr: poetry and patronage in eleventh-century Norway and England," *Viking and Medieval Scandinavia*, 1 (2005), 251–79.

Townend, M., *Scandinavian Culture in Eleventh-century Yorkshire*. Kirkdale Lecture (Kirkdale, 2007).

Wade-Evans, A. W. (ed.), *Vitae sanctorum Britanniae et genealogiae* (Cardiff, 1944).

Wilcox, J. (ed.), *Ælfric's Prefaces* (Durham, 1994).

Winterbottom, M. and Thomson, R. M. (eds.), "William of Malmesbury, *Vita Wulfstani*," in M. Winterbottom and R. M. Thompson (eds.), *William of Malmesbury, Saints' Lives: Lives of SS Wulfstan, Dunstan, Patrick, Benignus and Indract* (Oxford, 2002), pp. 8–155.

Wood, S., *The Proprietary Church in the Medieval West* (Oxford, 2006).

Yorke, B., "Sisters under the skin? Anglo-Saxon nunneries in southern England," *Reading Medieval Studies*, 15 (1989), 95–117.

CHAPTER TWENTY-FIVE

Nobility

JULIA CRICK

Historians of early medieval Britain and Ireland in general agree that the societies that they study were dominated by a ruling elite immediately distinguishable from the general population by occupation and demeanor. In recent historiography, the pre-Conquest English aristocracy has emerged as a dynamic force – politically dangerous, but complex, multi-layered, entrepreneurial, culturally sophisticated;[1] lords and aristocratic kin feature prominently in studies of the next best-documented area of the archipelago, Ireland, although as a grayer presence;[2] the aristocracy occupies a well-established place in the historiography of Wales, where much of the evidence is retrospective;[3] and of Scotland, a region largely bereft of contemporary records.[4] Yet, however deeply the terms "aristocratic" and "noble" have become embedded in the historiography of both islands, few historians have been prepared to venture beyond scrutiny of a particular region to generalization across the archipelago.[5] Looked at in the field, nobles, individually and collectively, performed multiple functions, as lords, agents, protectors, consumers, patrons, and, in some circumstances, men of letters.[6] To view the nobility comparatively, therefore, is to describe and analyze an abstraction.

There is plenty of evidence for something approximating to, or described as, a nobility across the British Isles. English, Irish, and Welsh law codes all indicate a fundamental social division.[7] Indeed, almost wherever written sources allow us to look in the centuries before 1100, we see traces of a royal penumbra: men and women distinguished by birth and by proximity to royal blood whose higher ranks constituted the medium for the exercise of power, both royal and divine, both in the king's presence and beyond. Individuals emerge with some distinctness: Odda, ealdorman (commander) of the western shires, cousin of kings, lord of Deerhurst (Gloucestershire) where his estate church still stands and where he was buried in 1053.[8] Beyond the narrow geographical and chronological reach of the English *Domesday Book* (1086), however, nobles, especially those below the topmost stratum, appear more generally as an undifferentiated blur. These are the people whose feasting, fighting, praying, and talking fill the written sources – the king can do none of these activities alone – and who were or must have been instrumental in extending his power beyond his presence, sometimes in kingdoms hundreds of miles across.[9] These are the people who must have exercised lordship in the locality, whether we can see them doing so or not. In these respects, not only England and, we imagine, Scotland and Wales, but also Ireland can be fitted into a wider model, as illustrating characteristics "of any medieval society dominated by a landed warrior aristocracy."[10] The question for us is the extent to which these local elites can be regarded as variants of a larger group and, if so, how this group should be characterized.

Historiography

To understand any ruling elite is simultaneously to negotiate fundamental problems about structures, resources, and politics. The pursuit of such questions in Britain and Ireland has often been routed down particular channels – royal power, clerical potency, political unification – and been driven by local concerns and achieved by the interrogation of relatively controlled sets of data. Historians of parts of continental Europe, notably Germany, have approached these questions differently.[11] The superior archival and legislative resources of the post-Carolingian territories have sustained important investigations of aristocratic networks in local and central politics and society; political solidarities structured not by blood or belief but by ties of association have emerged particularly clearly.[12] To what extent the insights thereby gained can and should be exported to the western edge of Europe remains to be seen.[13] Our sub-royal elite, whether we call them nobles or aristocrats, or something quite different, will not necessarily resemble the nobles on whom historians of the species have cut their teeth. Indeed, we can expect them to be different, from each other and from their counterparts on the continent.[14] But therein lies the problem. Ireland, in particular, is often taken as an exception to western European norms in this respect as in others, but such views need to be scrutinized very carefully.[15] First, descriptions of continental nobles bear striking resemblance to individuals identifiable in sources from Britain and Ireland.[16] Second, recent study shows that systems of creation and distribution of wealth in Ireland were less dissimilar to those of mainland Europe than was once held to be the case: in short, if a reasonably complex hierarchy was unsustainable in Ireland, the argument has yet to be articulated convincingly in print.[17] And, third, the conceptual framework upon which study of the medieval aristocracy has been constructed depends on circumstances unknown in Ireland and largely untraceable in Britain: the usurpation of public power by the magnate class of the late Empire.[18]

Comparison has been little assisted by historiographical tradition, until very recently at least. The terminology used to describe the elite of early England approximates quite closely to modern English usage: ruling families and their collaterals tend to be termed "royal" and only "aristocratic" once out of contention for kingship. Historians of Ireland and Wales, on the other hand, employ different terminology. Sometimes they follow their sources in describing the elite in economic and social rather than in political terms: as lords, rather than nobles, as men defined by their relationship with subordinates rather than their deference to superiors. In Irish historiography, the term "aristocratic" is routinely applied to ruling dynasties; royal denotes "kingly." Likewise, in writing about Wales, Wendy Davies can define as the aristocracy "those creating and contending for the kingships."[19] This usage, while at first disconcerting to English historians, has considerable merit. What is the difference between a discarded segment and a royal collateral? Frankish politics show as clearly as do Irish that political viability and access to royal power remained live issues for the upper aristocracy in the first millennium. The term "aristocratic" can also serve a further purpose: to denote the existence of a landholding class. In this sense, insular societies have been described as having nobles without being aristocratic, an important if paradoxical hypothesis.[20]

Historiographical divergence must also be understood as the product of historical processes (see chapter 2). In interpreting the sub-royal elite, the fulcrum of political and economic power in a kingdom, historians are compelled to expose their working assumptions about the nature of political and social authority more generally. English history-writing for four centuries has been preoccupied by the significance given to 1066 and the alleged changes it brought, including "feudalism," with its implications for the nobility, its antiquity and its rights. Latterly, the constitutional tendencies of English historiography have encouraged additional emphasis on the governmental responsibilities of English aristocracy. State formation and aristocratic power are seen as concomitants. Elsewhere, historians have been detained by different historiographical questions. This includes, for example, in Ireland a debate continuing as late as the 1990s about the tribal nature of Irish society, a state that would leave little room for a class of royal satellites and that has been challenged by a more "European" narrative of "feudalization," bringing Ireland into the huge debate over that latter term. These questions have been revived more recently by the suggestion that post-Roman Britain exhibited some of the "tribal" characteristics of Ireland before the emergence of a new elite in the Middle Saxon period.[21]

Despite differences of focus and terminology, historians of early medieval Britain and Ireland have pursued no less doggedly than their counterparts on the continent the dynamics that drove society and politics, investigating the circle of royal advisers, leading magnate families in the locality, the landed politics of the church.[22] In the absence of runs of records and, for Ireland, virtually no records of governmental action, insights have generally been derived from close contextual study.[23] Generalization exists – English and Irish (and later Welsh) law codes categorize social structures in a manner that is at once sweeping and minutely detailed – which historians have properly felt disinclined to take at face value. As sociologists predict, classification represents social reality very inadequately, serving to prop up and perpetuate the groups that create it.[24] But if so, the existence of such classification in itself commands attention: the power of defining admission and exclusion to these groups in the early Middle Ages rested with an elite whose privilege was, in some respects, exceptionally complete, extending not just to the consumption of agricultural surplus and the patronage of the materials and craft skills necessary for the creation of a superior material culture, but also to the production and conservation of knowledge in written and unwritten forms.[25]

Formidable methodological problems remain. Extant sources cluster in date of production or geographical range or both, leaving huge vacant spaces. Most Irish material obviously applicable to questions of social rank has been assigned an early date, from before the ninth century, and indeed bears close comparison with English sources of similar date and complexion (vernacular law codes, Latin hagiography, vernacular poetry). Enter the Viking Age, however, and English and Irish sources offer much less that is directly comparable: on both sides, vernacular annals and a few saints' lives, some identifiably tenth- and eleventh-century vernacular composition, but on the Irish side no datable legal material and almost no charters.[26] We risk perpetuating an archaizing vision of Ireland by comparing tenth-century English material with much earlier Irish prescription. On the other hand, traces of the workings of government, which accumulate for southern England after 850 (royal law codes, royal and aristocratic land grants, later writs, and *Domesday Book*), document a different order of activity, one that the elite managed and executed. The relative silence of Irish sources on such matters confounds Germanist historians attuned to following the trail of the self-documenting governments of the Carolingians, or the West Saxon ascendancy, but we should remember the exceptional nature of West Saxon rule. In Northumbria in the century before the Conquest, an English-speaking noble dynasty ruled a virtually independent polity governed differently from the south, sharing few of the characteristics of southern English society and none of its documentation (see chapter 19).

Change remains a central question, then, for students of Scotland and Wales grappling with non-contemporary evidence, for historians of England and Ireland working with the benefit of demonstrably early witnesses often preserved in later form. The critical problem is how to interpret the emergence of the relatively well-documented aristocracy of Southumbrian England: whether to pursue the elite elsewhere using much less tractable sources, silent or over-loquacious on the subject of privilege, or to posit that land-owning and therefore, by sociological definition at least, aristocratic societies will necessarily have dealt with practical affairs in writing. I will approach the subject in two ways: first, through a nobility defined – insofar as definition is possible – politically, and thus in relation to political change or systems; and, second, through a definition by economic and other aspects of status and thus in relation to economic change.

Recognition: Political Relationships

When insular writers had occasion to use Latin to describe the social elite of their own regions, they drew on a stock of terms in use on the European continent for much the same purpose.[27] Kings appear in public *cum optimatibus* "with the[ir] aristocrats" (literally, "with the best men"), in Ireland as in England, and the style occurs in Welsh laws neatly translating Welsh *uchelwr* ("nobleman").[28] Groups of *satellites* ("attendants") and *seniores* ("elders") presumably included nobles, although sometimes in England the circumstances indicate that the *seniores* gathered together were ecclesiastical as well as secular.[29] Other styles have administrative or military connotations. *Comes* and *dux* (literally, "companion" and "leader"), established terms of continental and Anglo-Saxon administrative history from the eighth century onward, find a small place in Irish sources although often as retrospective references.[30] Thus, the *Annals of Ulster* record the death of kings and "other leaders [*duces*] and nobles [*nobiles*]" at the battle of Cennfuait in 917. A lone Celtic-Latin charter commemorates a tenth-century Cornish *comes* Maenchi (S 1207). Meanwhile, English and Irish Latinists, as those on the continent, retrieved from classical, possibly biblical, antiquity, the term *satraps* ("provincial governor," originally of the Persian Empire; S 22, 884).

Common terminology can mislead, of course. Narrative sources deploy perhaps the most ambiguous description of all: *nobilis*. In continental sources, *nobilis* becomes a term of social rather than moral description only in the eighth century.[31] Both meanings are found in English sources in the early eighth century. Bede is clear about nobility of birth (*carnis origine nobilis, natu nobilis*), a quality that he associates with patrician origin in the case of Roman churchmen or, more usually, descent from a king. He sometimes contrasts innate nobility with its social opposite (*ignobilis, mediocres, de paupere uulgo*), and passes judgment on the conduct of the *nobilis*, declaring it to be noble, sub-noble (*ignobilis*), or more than noble (*nobilior*).[32] Often, though, Bede's nobles are high-ranking companions of the king, drawn from the same territory and those of others, who accompany him in war and peace.[33] Irish sources, too, make some play with the term *nobilis*. The *uir nobilis* of the Uí Néill, who gave his blind son to St. Colmán Elo, and Cormac, son of Diarmait, the *ui*[*r*] *nobil*[*is*] held captive by a wicked king and freed through St. Fintan's intervention, appear to be of kingly descent.[34] The Irish annals record the deaths of tenth- and eleventh-century kings "and other nobles," usually in battle.[35] In all these circumstances, *nobilis* means effectively someone of royal descent. Irish sources also make significant use of the term "the good" (Old Irish *maith*, "good"), which appears with frequency in the Irish annals (*Annals of Inisfallen, s.aa.* 919, 1045, 1088; *Annals of Ulster, s.aa.* 858, 1080, 1100, 1110), in Middle Irish romance, where it can apply to groups of Norse as well as Irish, in the *Táin Bó Cuailnge*, and is usually translated "noble." Indeed, the term appears to convey the same dual-faceted meaning as *nobilis*, superiority of character as well as birth. We are back with *optimates* and elders.

Who, then, were these best men, and what did they do? As the terminology suggests, across Europe rank was calibrated against the superior to whom proximity and obligation were owed. Administrative obligation merged with social duty. The elite served as royal representatives – provincial governors and leaders who wielded designated power – and also as royal intimates: as companions and attendants. From the moment our written sources begin, the relationship of king and subordinate is clearly marked, visible across English-speaking Britain, and disconcertingly fully formed: all sources – charters, hagiography, correspondence – conspire to give the same picture. The same notion lies behind the most readily identifiable English term for noble, "servant," the *minister* (Old English *thegn*), of royal government, whose numbers later admitted two grades, the uppermost tier including members of the royal household with governmental responsibility (S 706 [AD 962] *cubicularius*). Although relationships are articulated differently in Irish and Welsh sources, the generic resemblances are plain enough. Men (and indeed women) of status, whatever languages they spoke, never appear unaccompanied: their entourages reflect their social standing. English kings had military retinues; pre-Conquest lords were owed escort services,[36] and aristocrats, ecclesiastical and lay, had their own hierarchies of dependents, including *cnihtas* and thegns.[37] Likewise, the Welsh king was accompanied by an entourage of great complexity[38] and elite Welshmen traveled "with their own men," *cum suis*.[39] The standing of an Irish king was defined in law by his entourage, as seven times that of a noble, as many as 700 according to *Críth Gablach*, although only 60 *optimates* accompanied King Dimma on a mission to his son's foster-household according to the *Life* of St. Fintan of Taghmon.[40]

Clearly, some members of an entourage were expected to do more than provide military protection. Ó Corráin has emphasized the evidence for men of status defined by service to the king in the tenth and eleventh centuries: the *máer*, the *rechtaire*, and the more elevated *airri*.[41] These relatively early references lend substance to anecdotal or retrospective accounts. Early Latin hagiography records the presence of royal functionaries. St. Finan leads a deputation to the King of Cashel to request the alleviation of tax (*censum plebis*) and is refused by the king's *proconsul* (representative).[42] The *Life* of Ruadan tells how King Diarmait's royal agent (*prefectus regis*) and his *preco* (literally, "herald") traveled without the king into a territory under the king's control where the *preco* betrayed his master's trust by attacking the *castellum* ("fortified stronghold") of a local lord.[43] These are relatively rare glimpses of administrative machinery presupposed by the existence of complex political units. The social status of these men is not stated, but the Welsh laws, very retrospectively, describe an aristocratic courtly entourage of great complexity providing military and administrative support and the English evidence points in the same direction.[44] All this suggests that in Ireland, particularly after the Viking Age, and perhaps in Wales, although the evidence there is retrospective, service – and especially royal service – played a significant part in structuring the nobility.

Nobiles were advisers as well as enforcers. This can be seen not just in the higher echelons of English royal government in the centuries of Mercian and West Saxon rule but at a more basic level. English sources attach nobles to kingdoms or former kingdoms: the *sapientes* ("wise men") of the Gewisse and Mercians, or the *Myrcna witena* ("wise men of the Mercians"), who witnessed the disposal of an estate seized by forfeiture in 901.[45] Bede tells us about King Edwin with all the nobles *of his people*.[46] More than two centuries later, the chronicler Æthelweard wrote of the loss of nearly the entire nobility of Kent (*Cantiae nobilitatis*) in battle against the Danes in 902, under the leadership of their ealdormen, presumably a mustering tantamount to the shire, those militarily and politically active men gathered in peacetime presumably within the shire court.[47] Irish nobles, too, had collective responsibilities as references to the "royal assembly of the nobles of Ireland" in 858 indicate (*AU*, 858). When the fictional nobles of the Dál Cais muster at Cashel prior to a hosting, they feast and then deliberate in council before beginning hostilities.[48] As Patrick Wormald observed, "it is reasonable to wonder how much difference there was in practice between an *óenach* [Irish assembly] and a *witena-gemot* [English royal council]."[49]

Across the British Isles, different strata operated within the nobility, minor as well as major players of different sorts, including those of local as well as wider significance, and of different ages.[50] Older nobles will have had military entourages of their own. In *Críth Gablach*, the size of entourage constituted one of the more visible indications of status proper to higher social strata, from nobles to kings (the size of dwelling and treasure constituted others). The Old English translator of Bede's *History*, working in the late ninth century, interpreted the *domus* (household) of Blaecca, *prefectus* of Lincoln at the time of its conversion as a *duguth*, an entourage of older retainers. One thinks, too, of the *heorðweorod* (household companions) accompanying Ealdorman Byrhtnoth into battle at Maldon in Essex in 991, a complex household with a chamberlain (*burthegn*) and including his kinsmen.[51] The behavior of young nobles is logged in Irish hagiography, in the *Táin*, and by Bede.[52] In all cases, social complexity is assumed.

Nobles of service, defined and identified by service, were also nobles of blood, defined and set apart by birth: bardic families of twelfth-century Wales or the *filid* of Ireland enjoyed hereditary status.[53] James Campbell observed long ago that the terminology of regality and nobility could overlap: "It would have been possible in the eighth century [in England] for the same man to have been described by different writers and in different contexts as *rex*, *subregulus*, *princeps*, *dux*, *praefectus* and *comes*."[54] Such fluidity of terminology is likely to have been born out of political complexity: to an overlord, a king might be a *dux*, though still a king to his own people (for example, S 1184). Terminological slippage of this kind apparently occurred elsewhere. The Welsh annals avoid mention of kings for the tenth and eleventh centuries.[55] In Ireland, where political complexity proliferated, terminology did likewise and non-royal terms are used to describe rulers.[56] Ó Corráin noted that a middle-ranking king, *ruirig*, could be described as a lord, *tigerna*, and he attributed the downgrading this seemed to represent to the annexation of territory by major kings.[57] We find unexpected corroboration of this point of view in the corpus of early Irish saints' lives: where eighth-century writers had noted the presence of a king (*rex*) or queen (*regina*) in hagiographical texts, redactors from c.1200 onward routinely replaced the royal with aristocratic terminology *dux/comes*, or *ductrix/comitissa*. An Irishman working c.1200 saw early Ireland as a land not of kings but of *duces*.

The resulting sources must be very carefully interpreted for the history of kings and kingship as well as for that of nobility. While a restricted kind of fluidity may have continued for poetic purposes after the ninth century, beyond this date at least in England we have a clear sense of hierarchy at the apex of society, primarily because of the success of the West Saxon dynasty in excluding collateral claimants. More widely attested in the Irish polity in the period after 750 is a phenomenon apparently unknown in the English system: submerged lineage-segments removed from access to kingship but able to proliferate and reproduce themselves for generations, perhaps centuries.[58] In England, on the other hand, local aristocrats could weather changes of regime and outlive the royal dynasties that had patronized them for a short time, but for an ex-kingly dynasty deletion appears to have been irreversible: there are no identifiable instances of the political re-emergence of royal lines generations after the suppression of the ruling dynasty that legitimated them. The Irish dynasties which dug themselves in did so within the confines of the church where hereditary succession to office appears to have been commonplace. In England, despite family dominance, stability of succession was much less assured and monastic property in practice (although not necessarily in theory) less autonomous. Here we encounter a second marked difference. As has been widely noted, Irish succession worked on a strongly agnatic principle, property devolving down the male side. The Irish church legislated to exclude female heirs;[59] certainly historians acknowledge the polygynous or polygamous nature of Irish society. The focus on male inheritance may have worked to consolidate the inheritance. It will also have had profound consequences for social structure.[60]

From the seventh century, and probably much earlier, the pool of king-worthy English families declined. English royal dynasties were expelled, exterminated, or demoted as their kingdoms were absorbed by powerful neighbors, and in the ninth century, the process reached an abrupt conclusion. Four English kingdoms disappeared, and a single linear family managed to monopolize the throne in the surviving kingdom, Wessex. The higher prospects for English noble families vanished, at least south of the Humber. In the north, under Norse rule and later, aristocrats survived, prospered, and resisted, without aspiring to royal power in their own right. In the south, aristocrats hove into sight about whose origins we know little or nothing: take two mid-tenth-century midlands aristocrats, one Ælfsige Hunlafing, a thegn, presumably of Scandinavian extraction, and the staggeringly wealthy widow Æthelgifu, who owned land in London as well as in three shires, whose connections remain quite obscure. Their descendants, and those of every Southumbrian noble family, could no longer aspire to kingship as a scion of a noble family might have done two centuries earlier.[61] Two contemporary fictional calls to arms illustrate the difference: the Irish hero, Donnchad, exhorted to fight because of the kings in his ancestry "from whom the nobles branched off";[62] Ælfwine, at the battle of Maldon in 991, boasting of his noble lineage:

> that I am of a great family amongst the Mercians:
> my grandfather was called Ealhhelm,
> a wise and prosperous *ealdorman*.[63]

Nevertheless, even in tenth-century England, aristocratic power could be expressed in royal terms. Æthelweard, ealdorman of the Western Shires, traced his descent and, by extension, his legitimacy, to King Alfred.[64] Other ealdormen who represented the king's interest in the shire belonged to families affiliated to the royal dynasty by ties of blood or marriage: ealdormen like Sighelm and Ordgar, fathers-in-law of Edward the Elder and Edgar. After Cnut's conquest, ties between regality and nobility were reinvented when the new regime governed through a network of brothers, cousins, and relatives by marriage.[65]

In certain respects, then, the nobles of Britain and Ireland conform to a recognizable pattern. Insular and continental writers drew on a common Latin vocabulary to describe their nobilities; standard Irish and Welsh terms for noble perform the same elision between "noble" and "best" as Greek (*aristos*) and Latin (*optimas*). In Britain and Ireland, we see a nobility defined by blood and distinguished by service to the person of the king and sometimes to the kingdom more generally; conversely, even when nobles perform functions we might regard as governmental, as in tenth-century England, their ideological affiliation to the king is sometimes expressed in terms of blood. The main discontinuity observed here centers on king-worthiness. While nobility and regality remain closely linked constructs everywhere, in England, at least, a gulf is apparent by 750 which widened dramatically in the next century. Few nobles could aspire to be kings.

Social Distinction

The ruler's entourage must have conveyed complex messages about his authority – sub-kings present and absent, the number and caliber of his trusted lieutenants, the splendor of material culture on display and, for those who gained admission, the excellence of the entertainment on offer.[66] Feasting nobles not only belonged to the stock images of Irish, Welsh, and English poets; banquets provided the backdrop for political dramas in the tenth century no less than in the eighth when historical kings disgraced themselves or dropped dead at such occasions (Eadwig, Ceolred of Mercia). In recent years, historians and archaeologists have laid new stress on the adversity of material conditions in early medieval Ireland and England: the frequency of famine, the consequences of crop failure, the prevalence of disease and malnutrition.[67] Such reflections throw new light on the behavior of the elite: the enjoyment of plenty at the king's table, their hunting and superior diet, but also their appearance.[68] Irish law tracts associate superior nutrition with superior status.[69] The white teeth, clear skin, and white hands of the elite upon which Irish contemporaries remarked are status symbols: signs of good nutrition and freedom from manual labor.[70] The eleventh-century *Life* of Illtud tells how the saint's wife failed to recognize him after he turned to the church because "on her arrival, she saw a man engaged in digging, with his face and clothes all dirty, very different from the handsome soldier she used to behold."[71] In Irish sources, manual labor reduced the status of a noble.[72]

Clothing and jewelry conveyed implicit economic as well as aesthetic messages: setting aside agricultural land in the case of linen, but more particularly the harnessing of labor and craft skills (one thinks of the goldsmiths in the service of late Saxon aristocratic women).[73] When the tenth-century aristocratic Englishwoman Æthelgifu divided her property, her wealth was measured in land, stock, and moveable wealth, and she made careful provision for the division of her textiles.[74] Precisely these items conjured wealth and luxury in Irish poetry: the victors returning from the battle of Clontarf to Munster each with "enough to furnish his house with gold and silver, and cloth of color, and all kinds of property in like manner," or the villainous cook in the *Voyage of Máel Dúin* who admitted embezzling his church's resources "so that my house became full of counterpanes and pillows of raiment, both linen and gold, of every colour, and of brazen pails and of small brazen vessels, and of brooches of silver with pins of gold."[75]

Although the aspiration to participate in a higher material culture, and the sense of social distance and superiority that it brought, apparently extended across the British Isles, the means to realize it did so only very unequally, although the evidence here is treacherous. *Domesday Book* documents the existence of a cash-rich upper class in lowland England living off urban as well as rural profit.[76] In eleventh-century England, at least, mercantile activity provided one route of entry into the nobility.[77] The wealth of commercial Dublin must have sustained a prosperous elite on the east coast of Ireland, but we know very little about its composition. Indications of much earlier liquidity among the English petty elite come from incidental references in charters. In the 830s, a Kentish land-owner, Abba, had made provision in his will for his wife to use land to generate a sum ("2000" units unstated) from her brothers-in-law in order to make a pilgrimage (S 1482). A century later, one Wiohstan, otherwise obscure, financed a pilgrimage to Rome with his wife and son by cashing in his hereditary land with his local bishop, including land acquired by marriage and by purchase (S 1206). Just before the Conquest, a conjugal couple, Oswulf and Æthelgyth, used inherited land to make provision for their souls without being obviously of thegnly status: wealth without nobility, perhaps (S 1235).

In Ireland, outside the operation of bookland and largely beyond the reach of coin, relationships worked very differently, and although kings could afford pilgrimage, luxury, and church endowment, it is less clear how far such privileges extended down the social scale. The problem lies not in separating noble from non-noble, as in England, but noble from royal. In the England of *Domesday Book*, kings and nobles acted as lords, with tenants and dependents (free and unfree), private churches, and fortified residences. In Ireland, nobility and lordship likewise coalesced, and in early prescription non-kingly lords, as later English ones, were defined by association with free and unfree clients of both kinds, and appropriate residences, some fortified.[78] Multiple high-status fortified sites, both ringforts and crannogs, were occupied in Ireland at the time of the compilation of the early law codes, as on a lesser scale in Wales, although many were later abandoned.[79] Irish hagiographers refer to the lords of such places as kings, *duces*, or "rich men" (the *homo dives* or "potentate"), or even saints.[80] Thus, although the residence of an Irish or Welsh potentate looked physically different from that of an English lord, on both sides of the Irish Sea lordly dwellings housed a similar range of occupants: kings, nobles, and bishops.[81]

Conclusion

It has been claimed that one feature separating the Irish polity from those of France and England was the lack of a nobility capable of representing royal authority in the periphery;[82] nevertheless, individual nobles could and did represent kings in Ireland, just as continental and English nobles could and did bid for kingship. In Ireland, royal and aristocratic merge into often inseparable categories, but even in relatively well-documented lowland England, nobles do not always stand up to be counted: haze engulfs the lower end of the aristocracy where socially ascendant merchants or freemen may have come into possession of bookland but scarcely qualified as noble. Marked differences emerge between England and Ireland (and Wales): land tenure, the visibility of women, the size and spread of the nobility, patterns of residence, access to liquid and landed wealth and the willingness to manipulate it for social and spiritual purposes, the relationship to royal power. These are offset by prevailing similarities: the conviction of innate superiority, the presence of age bands and levels of service within the nobility, a focus on royal descent as the central defining mechanism for nobility, the importance of retinue, the capacity to muster and disperse, the maintenance of a clear line which individuals could cross when they had the means to do so but which was carefully guarded. In important respects, the Irish as well as the English elite fit a recognizable European pattern, but insular nobles also need to be taken on their own terms, as self-proclaimed nobles displaying regional variety, not as mutants of an ideal continental type.

More than 40 years ago, Donald Bullough noted that "one of the essential characteristics of early medieval institutional and social history is the always delicate balance between the delegation of royal authority (without which there could be no government of a unit bigger than a "hearth-troop") and the maintenance of royal control."[83] If historians are to focus on kingship, as Irish historians exhort each other to do, then the medium in which royal power functioned, however difficult the source base, becomes of critical importance. For historians of Ireland, nobles are constructed in two ways: they are aristocrats defined in relation to kings and also lords defined by clientage. If kingly power in Ireland functioned through sub-kings and discarded septs, what did lordly power entail? Historians of England have considered both nobility and lordship, but the strongly royal pull of their source material, the fact that law is so strongly shaped by royal interests, means that the natural vantage point for viewing Anglo-Saxon society is from above and not, as the Irish law codes suggest, from somewhere in the middle. We can detect the presence of middle-ranking nobles but their activities of clientage and lordship are crucial parts of their status, not much heralded in Latin sources other than *Domesday Book*, but recoverable in part.[84] This redoubles the need for additional studies of noble groups as well as individual careers.

The final observation concerns vernacular sources. The entertainment literature of the early British Isles contains messages for its elite audience familiar enough to wide modern audiences through the medium of translation but discredited as descriptions of social reality. Recent insights, many of them inspired by and documented using archaeology, into the economic and social circumstances affecting large proportions of the inhabitants of the British Isles lend new meaning to this material. In it, we find rehearsal of social values, inculcation of elite aspiration which, although perhaps set in the past, had messages for the present. Indeed, young nobles across Europe may have engaged in variants of similar occupations, rarely described so grittily again before the advent of written Old French. As the author of the *Táin* said of Cúchulainn, "His spirit was strong in him; he felt fit for a festival, or for marching or mating, or for an ale-house or the mightiest assembly in Ireland."[85]

Notes

1 Fleming, "Rural elites" and "The new wealth"; Gillingham, "Thegns and knights"; Keynes, "Crime and punishment" and "The Fonthill letter"; Wormald, "Æthelweard."

2 Charles-Edwards, "The context and uses of literacy" and *Early Irish and Welsh Kinship*, pp. 337–63; Kelly, *Guide to Early Irish Law*, pp. 26–8, and *Early Irish Farming*, pp. 363, 421–2; McLeod, "Interpreting early Irish law," part 1, 57–65; part 2, 41–56.

3 Charles-Edwards, *Early Irish and Welsh Kinship*, pp. 364–411; Davies, *Early Welsh Microcosm*, pp. 107–20, and *Patterns of Power*, pp. 9–31.

4 Alcock, "The activities of potentates."

5 For exceptions, see Davies, *Patterns of Power*; Fleming, "Lords and labour"; Sawyer, "The Vikings and Ireland," esp. p. 359; Wickham, *Framing the Early Middle Ages*, pp. 303–33; Wormald, "Celtic and Anglo-Saxon kingship," p. 166.

6 Charles-Edwards, "The context and uses of literacy"; Keynes, "The Fonthill letter" and "Royal government"; Wormald, "Æthelweard."

7 Bullough, "Anglo-Saxon institutions"; Charles-Edwards, "The context and uses of literacy," p. 71, and note 2 above.

8 Williams, *Land, Power and Politics*.

9 See Davies, "Celtic kingships"; Ó Corráin, *Ireland before the Normans*, pp. 30–1.

10 Davies, *Patterns of Power*, p. 89.

11 For surveys, see Airlie, "The aristocracy"; Fouracre, "The origins of the nobility in Francia"; Reuter, "The medieval nobility."

12 Althoff, *Family, Friends and Followers*; Innes, *State and Society*; Le Jan, *Famille et pouvoir*; MacLean, *Kingship and Politics*; Werner, *Naissance de la noblesse*.

13 On the problems, see Davies, *Patterns of Power*, pp. 1–4.

14 Wickham, "Problems of comparing," pp. 227–8, and *Problems in Doing Comparative History*.

15 Bullough, "Early medieval social groupings," p. 13; Fouracre, "Cultural conformity," 155.

16 As characterized by Airlie, "The aristocracy," p. 431; Innes, *State and Society*, p. 258.

17 On kinship structures, see Charles-Edwards, *Early Irish and Welsh Kinship*, esp. pp. 87, 477; Ó Corráin, "Nationality and kingship," pp. 32–5; on the economy, see Kelly, *Early Irish Farming*; Hall, "The documentary and pollen analytical records"; on wealth and complex lordship, see Fouracre, "The origins of the nobility in Francia," pp. 22–3; in Britain, Davies, *Patterns of Power*, p. 91.

18 Fouracre, "Cultural conformity"; Innes, *State and Society*, pp. 259–63. Exceptions might be found in Wales and northern Britain.

19 Davies, *Patterns of Power*, p. 34.

20 Wickham, *Framing the Early Middle Ages*, pp. 303–6, 358–64.

21 Ibid., ch. 6.

22 Brooks, *Early History*; Hart, "Athelstan"; Keynes, *The Diplomas*; Ó Corráin, "Dál Cais" and "The early Irish churches"; Ó Fiaich, "The church of Armagh"; Williams, *Land, Power and Politics*. On differences of approach, see Reuter, "The medieval nobility," p. 194.

23 Keynes, *The Diplomas*; Ó Corráin, "Dál Cais."

24 Weber, *On Charisma*, pp. 138, 179. On the Irish laws, see Charles-Edwards, *Early Irish and Welsh Kinship*, p. 4.

25 On the Irish *filid*, see Charles-Edwards, "The context and uses of literacy." On craft, see Mytum, *Origins of Early Christian Ireland*, pp. 210–51.

26 But see Charles-Edwards, "The context and uses of literacy"; Davies, "The Latin charter-tradition." For England, see Keynes, "England."

27 For continental terms, see Le Jan, *Famille et pouvoir*, p. 10; Nelson, "Nobility in the ninth century," pp. 47–51; Werner, *Naissance de la noblesse*, pp. 295–325. For Britain, see Davies, *Early Welsh Microcosm*, pp. 108–12, and *Patterns of Power*. For England, Thacker, "Some terms for noblemen"; Loyn, "Kings, gesiths and thegns." On Ireland, Ó Corráin, "Ireland, Scotland and Wales," pp. 44–5.

28 *Optimates*: Ó Corráin, "Ireland, Scotland and Wales," pp. 44–5 and *Vita S. Fintan*, cc. 24, 25 (Heist, *Vitae*, pp. 204–5). For England, see Colgrave, *Life of Bishop Wilfrid*, pp. 132–3, c. 60; Sawyer, *Anglo-Saxon Charters* (hereafter S) 114, 1438, 95, 192, 174. On *uchelwr*, Charles-Edwards, *Early Irish and Welsh Kinship*, p. 364.

29 *Satellites*: Colgrave, *Felix's Life*, c. 16; *seniores*: Davies, *Early Welsh Microcosm*, p. 108. For royal and archiepiscopal *sapientes*: S 169, 188, 293, 1436.

30 *Dux, comes*: see Thacker, "Some terms for noblemen," pp. 205–9. The first original charter dates from 736 (S 89).

31 Nelson, "Nobility in the ninth century," pp. 47–8.

32 On nobility of birth, see Colgrave and Mynors, *Bede's Ecclesiastical History* (*HE*), ii. 7; ii. 15; iii. 19; on contrast with the non–noble, see iii. 27; v. 7; on scales of nobility, see ii. 15; iv. 9.

33 Bede, *HE*, ii. 14; iii. 1; iii. 14; iii. 24.

34 *Vita S. Colmani* (Elo), c. 34: for other references to *nobiles* see cc. 7, 31; *Vita S. Fintani* (Clonenagh), c. 20 (Heist, *Vitae*, pp. 151, 212, 219–20).

35 *et alii nobiles*: *Annals of Ulster* (ed. Hennessey and MacCarthy, hereafter *AU*) *s.aa.* 909, 918, 1014, 1045.

36 Gillingham, "Thegns and knights," pp. 137–42.

37 See the leases of Oswald of Worcester S 1300–1375.

38 Charles-Edwards, "The heir-apparent," pp. 183–90.

39 See Brocmail: *Bede HE*, ii. 2; also Davies, *Early Welsh Microcosm*, pp. 105–6.

40 c. 24 (Heist, *Vitae*, pp. 204–5).

41 Ó Corráin, *Ireland before the Normans*, pp. 26–8. For the *máer*: *AU*, *s.aa.* 814, 888, 894, 922, 924, 929, 1104; *Annals of Inisfallen*, ed. Mac Airt (hereafter *AI*), *s.a.* 1095,

including the Scottish *mormaer* who fell at the battle of Clontarf (*AU, s.a* 1014), the *rechtaire* and the more elevated *airri* (*AI, s.aa.* 1031 and 962, 1032); also Dumville, "Latin and Irish," p. 326.

42 c. 26 (Heist, *Vitae*, p. 158).

43 Heist, *Vitae*, pp. 163–4.

44 Carr, "Teulu."

45 Keynes, "The control of Kent," pp. 115–18.

46 Colgrave and Mynors, *Bede's Ecclesiastical History*, ii. 14.

47 Campbell, *Chronicle of Æthelweard*, p. 52.

48 Bugge, *Caithréim*, cc. 26–8, p. 74.

49 Wormald, "Celtic and Anglo-Saxon kingship," p. 169.

50 Davies, *Early Welsh Microcosm*, p. 116; Gillingham, "Thegns and knights"; also, more generally, Davies, *Small Worlds*; Wickham, "Debate," p. 198.

51 *Battle of Maldon*, lines 24, 112–15, 121, 204, 224 (Scragg, "The Battle of Maldon," pp. 18–19, 22–3, 26–7).

52 On young nobles elsewhere, see Gillingham, "Thegns and knights"; Halsall, *Warfare and Society*; Innes, *State and Society*.

53 Charles-Edwards, "The context and uses of literacy."

54 Campbell, "Bede's *reges* and *principes*," p. 91.

55 Davies, *Patterns of Power*, pp. 11–12.

56 Dumville, "Latin and Irish," pp. 326–7; Ó Corráin, *Ireland before the Normans*, pp. 29–30.

57 Ó Corráin, *Ireland before the Normans*, pp. 29–31.

58 Ó Corráin, "Dál Cais," "The early Irish churches," p. 328, and *Ireland before the Normans*, pp. 39–42; Ó Fiaich, "The church of Armagh," pp. 81–2.

59 *Collectio canonum Hibernensis*, lib. XXXII, cc. 17–20, in Wasserschleben (ed.), *Die Irische Kanonensammlung*, pp. 115–16; McAll, "The normal paradigms," p. 19; Ó Corráin, "The early Irish churches," p. 333.

60 Nelson, "Nobility in the ninth century," pp. 46–7; on polygamous dynasties, see Ó Corráin, *Ireland before the Normans*, pp. 38–41; on polygyny, see Charles-Edwards, *Early Irish and Welsh Kinship*.

61 S 1497, S 566: compare Colgrave, *Felix's Life*, cc. 1–17.

62 Bugge, *Caithréim*, c. 50 (p. 88).

63 *ealdorman*, by this date, a royal official: *Battle of Maldon*, lines 216–19 (Scragg, "The Battle of Maldon," pp. 26–7).

64 Wormald, "Æthelweard"; compare Ordgar or Odda: Williams, *Land, Power and Politics*, pp. 3, 14.

65 Keynes, "Cnut's earls."

66 Campbell, "Bede's *reges* and *principes*," pp. 92–5; Simms, "Guesting and feasting."

67 Fleming, "Bones for historians" and "Lords and labour"; Ó Corráin, "Ireland"; Mytum, *Origins of Early Christian Ireland*, pp. 166–209.

68 Charles-Edwards, "Food, drink and clothing"; Fleming, "Lords and labour"; Gillingham, "Thegns and knights."

69 *Críth Gablach*, cc. 66–84 (in MacNeill, "Ancient Irish law," pp. 283–90).

70 White hands of chiefs: Todd (ed.), *Cogadh*, c. 92 (pp. 160–3).

71 *Vita S. Illtudi*, c. 16, in Doble and Evans (eds.), *Lives of the Welsh Saints*, p. 112.

72 Kelly, *Early Irish Farming*, p. 448.

73 On textiles, see Fleming, "Lords and labour," pp. 122–6. On goldsmiths, see Fell et al., *Women in Anglo-Saxon England*, p. 97.

74 S 1497. For Irish analogies, see Kinsella, *The Tain*, p. 54; Todd (ed.), *Cogadh*, c. 72, pp. 118–19.

75 Todd (ed.), *Cogadh*, c. 71 (pp. 118–19); Oskamp, *Voyage of Máel Dúin*, c. 33, p. 169.

76 Fleming, "Rural elites" and "The new wealth."

77 *Geþyncðo*, c. 6, in Liebermann, *Die Gesetze der Angelsachsen*, I, 456–69 (458–9), and *EHD*, I, no. 52.

78 See note 2 above; also *Críth Gablach*, cc. 107–38 (in MacNeill, "Ancient Irish law," pp. 296–309); Mytum, *Origins of Early Christian Ireland*, pp. 105–35.

79 Clinton, "Settlement patterns"; Mytum, *Origins of Early Christian Ireland*, p. 145.

80 *Vita S. Aidi* cc. 26, 48; *Vita S. Finani*, c. 19; *Vita S. Fintani* (Clonenagh), c. 20; *Vita S. Fintani* (Taghmon), c. 31 (Heist, *Vitae*, pp. 151–2, 156, 175–6, 181).

81 On England, Blair, "Hall and chamber"; see also Fleming, "Lords and labour," pp. 107–20; on Welsh lords, Davies, *Patterns of Power*.

82 MacLean, *Kingship and Politics*, p. 48.

83 Bullough, "Anglo-Saxon institutions," pp. 654–5.

84 On lordship, see Abels, *Lordship*; Faith, *The English Peasantry*; Fleming, "Lords and labour" and *Kings and Lords*; see also Baxter, *The Earls of Mercia*.

85 *The Táin*, trans. Kinsella, p. 146.

Further Reading

The largest and most established literature about the nobility concerns England, particularly in the eleventh century. The evidence of *Domesday Book* underpins two monographs: P. A. Clarke's *The English Nobility under Edward the Confessor* (Oxford, 1994) and Robin Fleming's *Kings and Lords*. Useful discussion is to be found in textbooks, like those of H. R. Loyn (*The Governance of Anglo-Saxon England, 500–1087* [London, 1984]) and Williams (*Kingship and Government*), but much important work lies in articles. Simon Keynes has examined the role of nobles, individually and collectively, in relation to royal power ("The control of Kent," "Crime and punishment"). For the workings of nobles in the provinces, largely in the eleventh century, see the work of Ann Williams and Cyril Hart. Robin Fleming has constructed a powerful case for the economic dynamism of the pre-Conquest elite ("Acquiring, flaunting and destroying silk," "The new wealth," and "Rural elites"). On lordship, see the monographs of Richard Abels (*Lordship*), Stephen Baxter (*The Earls of Mercia*), and Rosamond Faith (*The English Peasantry*); on the lesser nobility, see John Gillingham, "Thegns and knights." The Prosopography of Anglo-Saxon England database (http://www.pase.ac.uk/) and Simon Keynes, *An Atlas of Attestations in Anglo-Saxon Charters, c.670–1066* (Cambridge, 2002) provide essential data for future study. Outside the zone illuminated by the evidence of *Domesday Book* and charters, Wendy Davies has pioneered the study of the nobility (*Early Welsh Microcosm*, *Patterns of Power*). The evidence for stratification in the Irish law codes has been very widely discussed (by Charles-Edwards, Kelly, MacNeill, McLeod, and Mytum) and Ó Corráin has argued that the growing scale of political structures in the centuries before Anglo-Norman intervention presupposed governmental roles for sub-kingly nobles ("Ireland" and "Nationality and kingship"). The military and cultural activities of the sub-royal elite in Ireland have been analyzed by Thomas Charles-Edwards, "Irish warfare before 1100," in *A Military History of Ireland*, ed. T. Bartlett and K. Jeffery (Cambridge, 1996), pp. 26–51, and "The context and uses of literacy"; for the role of the church in perpetuating former kingly dynasties, see Ó Corráin, "Dál Cais" and "The early Irish churches," and Ó Fiaich, "The church of Armagh." As in Wales and Scotland, much discussion shades over the difference between kingly and non-kingly nobles (see the work of Alcock in Scotland and Davies in Wales). For rare attempts to view the nobility across the British Isles, see Wendy Davies, *Patterns of Power*, Chris Wickham, *Framing the Early Middle Ages*, and Robin Fleming, "Lords and labour."

Bibliography

Abels, R., *Lordship and Military Obligation in Anglo-Saxon England* (London, 1988).

Airlie, S., "The aristocracy," in R. McKitterick (ed.), *The New Cambridge Medieval History*, vol. II: *c.700–c.900* (Cambridge, 1995), pp. 431–50.

Alcock, L. "The activities of potentates in Celtic Britain, AD 500–800: a positivist approach," in S. T. Driscoll and M. R. Nieke (eds.), *Power and Politics in Early Medieval Britain and Ireland* (Edinburgh, 1988), pp. 22–46.

Alcock, L., "Message from the dark side of the moon: western and northern Britain in the age of Sutton Hoo," in M. Carver (ed.), *The Age of Sutton Hoo* (Woodbridge, 1992), pp. 205–15.

Althoff, G., *Family, Friends and Followers: Political and Social Bonds in Medieval Europe*, trans. C. Caroll (Cambridge, 2004).

Baxter, S., *The Earls of Mercia: Lordship and Power in Late Anglo-Saxon England* (Oxford, 2007).

Blair, J., "Hall and chamber: English domestic planning 1000–1250," in G. Meirion-Jones and M. Jones (eds.), *Manorial Domestic Buildings in England and Northern France* (London, 1993), pp. 1–21.

Brooks, N., *The Early History of the Church of Canterbury: Christ Church from 597 to 1066* (Leicester, 1984).

Bugge, A. (ed. and trans.), *Caithréim Cellacháin Caisil: The Victorious Career of Cellachan at Cashel or the Wars between the Irishmen and the Norsemen in the Middle of the Tenth Century* (Christiana, 1905).

Bullough, D. A., "Anglo-Saxon institutions and early English society," *Annali della fondazione italiana par la storia amministrativa*, 2 (1965), 647–59.

Bullough, D. A., "Early medieval social groupings: the terminology of kinship," *Past and Present*, 45 (1969), 3–18.

Campbell, A. (ed. and trans.), *The Chronicle of Æthelweard* (London, 1962).

Campbell, J., "Bede's *reges* and *principes*," in *Essays in Anglo-Saxon History* (London, 1986), pp. 85–98.

Carr, A. D., "Teulu and Penteulu," in T. M. Charles-Edwards (ed.), *The Welsh King and his Court* (Cardiff, 2000), pp. 63–81.

Charles-Edwards, T. M., "The context and uses of literacy in early Christian Ireland," in H. Pryce (ed.), *Literacy in Medieval Celtic Societies* (Cambridge, 1998), pp. 62–82.

Charles-Edwards, T. M., *Early Irish and Welsh Kinship* (Oxford, 1993).

Charles-Edwards, T. M., "Food, drink and clothing in the laws of court," in T. M. Charles-Edwards, M. E. Owen, and P. Russell (ed.), *The Welsh King and his Court* (Cardiff, 2000), pp. 319–37.

Charles-Edwards, T. M., "The heir-apparent in Irish and Welsh law," *Celtica*, 9 (1971), 180–90.

Clinton, M., "Settlement patterns in the early historical kingdom of Leinster (seventh to mid twelfth century)," in A. P. Smyth (ed.), *Seanchas: Studies in Early and Medieval Irish Archaeology, History and Literature in Honour of Francis J. Byrne* (Dublin, 1999), pp. 275–98.

Colgrave, B. (ed. and trans.), *Felix's Life of Saint Guthlac* (Cambridge, 1956).

Colgrave, B. (ed. and trans.), *The Life of Bishop Wilfrid by Eddius Stephanus* (Cambridge, 1927).

Colgrave, B. and Mynors, R. A. B. (ed. and trans.), *Bede's Ecclesiastical History of the English People* (Oxford, 1969).

Davies, W. "Celtic kingships in the early Middle Ages," in A. J. Duggan (ed.), *Kings and Kingship in Medieval Europe* (London, 1993), pp. 101–24.

Davies, W., *An Early Welsh Microcosm: Studies in the Llandaff Charters* (London, 1978).

Davies, W., "The Latin charter-tradition in western Britain, Brittany and Ireland in the early mediaeval period," in D. Whitelock, R. McKitterick, and D. Dumville (eds.), *Ireland in Early Mediaeval Europe: Studies in Memory of Kathleen Hughes* (Cambridge, 1982), pp. 258–80.

Davies, W., *Patterns of Power in Early Wales* (Oxford, 1990).

Davies, W., *Small Worlds: The Village Community in Early Medieval Brittany* (London, 1988).

Doble, G. H. and Evans, D. S (ed.), *Lives of the Welsh Saints* (Cardiff, 1971).

Dumville, D. N., "Latin and Irish in the *Annals of Ulster*, AD 431–1050," in D. Whitelock, R. McKitterick, and D. N. Dumville (eds.), *Ireland in Early Mediaeval Europe: Studies in Memory of Kathleen Hughes* (Cambridge, 1982), pp. 320–41.

Faith, R., *The English Peasantry and the Growth of Lordship* (London, 1997).

Fell, C., with Clark, C. and Williams, E., *Women in Anglo-Saxon England* (London, 1985).

Fleming, R., "Acquiring, flaunting and destroying silk in late Anglo-Saxon England," *Early Medieval Europe*, 15: 2 (2007), 127–58.

Fleming, R., "Bones for historians: putting the body back into biography," in D. Bates, J. Crick, and S. Hamilton (eds.), *Writing Medieval Biography: Essays in Honour of Frank Barlow* (Woodbridge, 2006), pp. 29–48.

Fleming, R., *Kings and Lords in Conquest England* (Cambridge, 1991).

Fleming, R., "Lords and labour," in W. Davies (ed.), *From the Vikings to the Normans* (Oxford, 2003), pp. 107–37.

Fleming, R., "The new wealth, the new rich and the new political style in late Anglo-Saxon England," *Anglo-Norman Studies*, 23 (2001), 1–22.

Fleming, R., "Rural elites and urban communities in late-Saxon England," *Past & Present*, 141 (1993), 3–37.

Fouracre, P., "Cultural conformity and social conservatism in early medieval Europe," *History Workshop* Journal, 33 (1992), 152–61.

Fouracre, P., "The origins of the nobility in Francia," in A. J. Duggan (ed.), *Nobles and Nobility in Medieval Europe: Concepts, Origins, Transformations* (Woodbridge, 2000), pp. 17–24.

Gillingham, J., "Thegns and knights in eleventh-century England: who was then the gentleman?," *Transactions of the Royal Historical Society*, 6th series, 5 (1995), 129–53.

Hall, V. A., "The documentary and pollen analytical records of the vegetational history of the Irish landscape AD 200–1650," *Peritia*, 14 (2000), 342–71.

Halsall, G., *Warfare and Society in the Barbarian West, 450–900* (London, 2003).

Hart, C. R., "Athelstan 'Half-king' and his family," *Anglo-Saxon England*, 2 (1973), 115–144.

Heist, W. W. (ed.), *Vitae sanctorum Hiberniae ex Codice olim Salmanticensi nunc Bruxellensi* (Brussels, 1965).

Hennessey, W. M. and MacCarthy, B. (ed. and trans.), *Annals of Ulster, Otherwise, Annals of Senat: A Chronicle of Irish Affairs from AD 431 to AD 1540*, 3 vols. (Dublin, 1887–1901).

Innes, M., *State and Society in the Early Middle Ages: The Middle Rhine Valley, 400–1000* (Cambridge, 2000).

Kelly, F., *Early Irish Farming: A Study Based Mainly on the Law-texts of the Seventh and Eighth Centuries* AD (Dublin, 1997).

Kelly, F., *A Guide to Early Irish Law* (Dublin, 1988).

Keynes, S., "Cnut's earls," in A. R. Rumble (ed.), *The Reign of Cnut: King of England, Denmark and Norway* (London, 1994), pp. 43–88.

Keynes, S., "The control of Kent in the ninth century," *Early Medieval Europe*, 2: 2 (1993), 111–31.

Keynes, S., "Crime and punishment in the reign of Æthelred the Unready," in I. Wood and N. Lund (eds.), *People and Places in Northern Europe 500–1600: Essays in Honour of Peter Hayes Sawyer* (Woodbridge, 1991), pp. 67–81.

Keynes, S., *The Diplomas of King Æthelred "the Unready" 978–1016: A Study in their Use as Historical Evidence* (Cambridge, 1980).

Keynes, S., "England, c.900–1016," in T. Reuter (ed.), *New Cambridge Medieval History*, vol. III: *c.900–c.1024* (Cambridge, 1999), pp. 456–84.

Keynes, S., "The Fonthill letter," in M. Korhammer (ed.), *Words, Texts and Manuscripts: Studies in Anglo-Saxon Culture Presented to Helmut Gneuss on the Occasion of his Sixty-fifth Birthday* (Cambridge, 1992), pp. 53–97.

Keynes, S., "Royal government and the written word in late Anglo-Saxon England," in R. McKitterick (ed.), *The Uses of Literacy in Early Medieval Europe* (Cambridge, 1990), pp. 226–57.

Kinsella, T. (trans.), *The Tain: Translated from the Irish Epic Tain Bo Cuailnge* (London, 1969).

Le Jan, R., *Famille et pouvoir dans le monde franc (viie–xe siècle): essai d'anthropologie sociale* (Paris, 1995).

Liebermann, F., *Die Gesetze der Angelsachsen* (Halle, 1903–16).

Loyn, H. R., "Kings, gesiths and thegns," in M. Carver (ed.), *The Age of Sutton Hoo* (Woodbridge, 1992), pp. 75–9.

Mac Airt, S. (ed. and trans.), *The Annals of Inisfallen* (Dublin, 1951).

McAll, C., "The normal paradigms of a woman's life in the Irish and Welsh law texts," in D. Jenkins and M. E. Owen (eds.), *The Welsh Law of Women: Studies Presented to Professor Daniel A. Binchy on his Eightieth Birthday, 3 June 1980* (Cardiff, 1980), pp. 7–22.

MacLean, S., *Kingship and Politics in the Late Ninth Century* (Cambridge, 2005).

McLeod, N., "Interpreting early Irish law: status and currency (part 1)," *Zeitschrift für Celtische Philologie*, 41 (1986), 46–65.

McLeod, N., "Interpreting early Irish law: status and currency (part 2)," *Zeitschrift für Celtische Philologie*, 42 (1987), 41–115.

MacNeill, E., "Ancient Irish law: the law of status or franchise," *Proceedings of the Royal Irish Academy*, 36 (1923), sec. C, 265–316.

Mytum, H., *The Origins of Early Christian Ireland* (London, 1992).

Nelson, J. L., "Nobility in the ninth century," in A. J. Duggan (ed.), *Nobles and Nobility in Medieval Europe: Concepts, Origins, Transformations* (Woodbridge, 2000), pp. 43–51.

Ó Corráin, D., "Dál Cais: church and dynasty," *Ériu*, 24 (1973), 52–73.

Ó Corráin, D., "The early Irish churches: some aspects of organisation," in D. Ó Corráin (ed.), *Irish Antiquity: Essays and Studies Presented to Professor M. J. O'Kelly* (Dublin, 1981), pp. 327–41.

Ó Corráin, D., *Ireland before the Normans* (Dublin, 1972).

Ó Corráin, D., "Ireland c.800: aspects of society," in D. Ó Cróinín (ed.), *A New History of Ireland*, vol. 1: *Prehistoric and Early Ireland* (Oxford, 2005), pp. 549–608.

Ó Corráin, D., "Ireland, Scotland and Wales, c.700 to the early eleventh century," in R. McKitterick (ed.), *The New Cambridge Medieval History*, vol. II: *c.700–c.900* (Cambridge, 1995), pp. 43–63.

Ó Corráin, D., "Nationality and kingship in pre-Norman Ireland," in T. W. Moody (ed.), *Nationality and the Pursuit of National Independence* (Belfast, 1978), pp. 1–35.

Ó Fiaich, T., "The church of Armagh under lay control," *Seanchas Ardmhacha*, 5 (1969), 75–127.

Oskamp, H. P. (ed. and trans.), *The Voyage of Máel Dúin: A Study in Early Irish Voyage Literature* (Groningen, 1970).

Reuter, T., "The medieval nobility in twentieth-century historiography," in M. Bentley (ed.), *Companion to Historiography* (London, 1997), pp. 177–202.

Reuter, T., "Nobles and others: the social and cultural expression of power relations in the Middle Ages," in A. J. Duggan (ed.), *Nobles and Nobility in Medieval Europe: Concepts, Origins, Transformations* (Woodbridge, 2000), pp. 85–98.

Sawyer, P. H., *Anglo-Saxon Charters: An Annotated List and Bibliography* (London, 1968).

Sawyer, P. H., "The Vikings and Ireland," in D. Whitelock, R. McKitterick, and D. Dumville (eds.), *Ireland in Early Mediaeval Europe: Studies in Memory of Kathleen Hughes* (Cambridge, 1982), pp. 345–61.

Scragg, D., "The Battle of Maldon," in D. Scragg (ed.), *The Battle of Maldon AD 991* (Oxford, 1991), pp. 1–36.

Simms, K., "Guesting and feasting in Gaelic Ireland," *Journal of the Royal Society of Antiquaries of Ireland*, 108 (1978), 67–100.

Thacker, A. T., "Some terms for noblemen in Anglo-Saxon England, c.650–900," in D. Brown, J. Campbell, and S. C. Hawkes (eds.), *Anglo-Saxon Studies in Archaeology and History*, 2, British Archaeological Reports, British series 92 (Oxford, 1981), pp. 201–36.

Todd, J. H. (ed. and trans.), *Cogadh Gaedhil re Gallaibh: The War of the Gaedhil with the Gaill, or the Invasions of Ireland by the Danes and Other Norsemen* (London, 1867).

Wasserschleben, H. (ed.), *Die Irische Kanonensammlung*, 2nd edn. (Leipzig, 1885).

Weber, M., *On Charisma and Institution Building: Selected Papers*, ed. and trans. S. N. Eisenstadt (London, 1968).

Werner, K. F., *Naissance de la noblesse: l'essor des élites politiques en* France, 2nd edn. (Paris, 1998).

Wickham, C., "Debate: 'The feudal revolution' IV," *Past & Present*, 155 (1997), 196–208.

Wickham, C., *Framing the Early Middle Ages: Europe and the Mediterranean, 400–800* (Oxford, 2005).

Wickham, C., "Problems of comparing rural societies in early medieval western Europe," *Transactions of the Royal Historical Society*, 6th series, 2 (1992), 221–46.

Wickham, C., *Problems in Doing Comparative History*. Reuter Lecture 2004 (Southampton, 2005).

Williams, A., *Kingship and Government in Pre-Conquest England c.500–1066* (Basingstoke, 1999).

Williams, A., *Land, Power and Politics: The Family and Career of Odda of Deerhurst*. Deerhurst Lecture 1996 (Deerhurst, 1997).

Wormald, P., "Æthelweard, d.998?," *Oxford Dictionary of National Biography* (Oxford, 2004), I, pp. 432–3.

Wormald, P., "Celtic and Anglo-Saxon kingship: some further thoughts," in P. E. Szarmach (ed.), *Sources of Anglo-Saxon Culture* (Kalamazoo, MI, 1986), pp. 151–83.

CHAPTER TWENTY-SIX

Settlement and Social Differentiation

SALLY CRAWFORD

Documentary sources from different parts of Britain suggest that social status could be signaled by settlement form. Irish texts suggest that different social ranks attracted a range of buildings and equipment commensurate with their status, and Old English documentary evidence shows that status could be precisely signaled through buildings. One Old English document, the *Geþyncðo*, stated that a *ceorl* who was sufficiently prosperous could attain the rights of a thegn if he possessed, as a minimum, "five hides of land, a bell and a *burh*-gate." This list of requirements was enlarged in a twelfth-century document from Rochester, which also demanded that a thegn should have "a church and a kitchen"; without these appurtenances, a man was not a thegn.[1]

Archaeological evidence from settlements at this period does more than merely corroborate the documentary sources. The archaeologically visible changes in settlement size, form, layout, and location, compared to the earlier period, are the physical signs of important changes in social organization and hierarchies, and have offered a complex picture of social change and the signaling of social status through material wealth. The archaeological evidence also shows that land use, economy, and society are intimately linked in this period. Although documentary and archaeological sources have given us a broad picture of society moving, at varying speeds and levels of intensity in different parts of Britain, toward the "feudal" society of the later medieval period, recent excavated evidence has emphasized that our current picture of early medieval society contains a raft of unresolved and evolving problems.

Ireland

Irish *crannog* (man-made island) and *rath* (walled settlements, also called ringfort) sites in Ireland were almost certainly elite sites, and their appearance from the seventh century indicates that Irish society was undergoing a process of change.[2] Elite leaders were declaring their status by the construction of these conspicuous sites, whose imposing structures were almost certainly for display and to mark boundaries rather than for defense. Environmental archaeology has also revealed a process of expansion in agriculture in this period in Ireland, linked to these social changes.[3]

Ringforts are found all across Ireland, but their distribution and spatial organization do not fall into any simple pattern. They occur singly, in pairs, and in clusters.

At Clogher (Co. Tyrone) and other important sites, ringforts cluster more densely, and this may support a theory that ringforts reflect the development of a more militarized society. This is not to suggest that ringforts were built for defensive purposes, but that they were a sign of a new development within elite society – the elite now needed centers for tribute, much of which would have arrived on the hoof, and consequently needed protection from cattle-rustling.[4] Finds of high-status metalworking and the importation of exotic artifacts at excavations at rath sites, such as Deer Park Farms (Co. Antrim) and Moynagh Lough (Co. Meath), confirm the impression that rath and crannogs were, if not central places, then places where wealth, power, and status were concentrated and displayed.[5]

Raths, however, come in a variety of sizes and forms, ranging from large, multivallate structures to smaller structures with a single ditch. Other, less archaeologically visible, structures include unenclosed settlements, some of which have been identified only through the survival of associated underground chambers, *souterrains*. It has long been assumed that the size, distribution, and layout of these various settlement structures reflected the wider social organization of Irish society, and it has been suggested that the location of these settlements and their relationship to each other can be interpreted as follows: the small ringfort of the *bóaire* (free farmer), and groups of even smaller ringforts belonging to the *ócaire* (farmer of lower rank), were clustered around the high-status ringforts. The social status of the family was indicated by the location of their ringfort, with the higher-status groups living toward the edge of the territories, surrounded by (and, to some extent, protected from cattle-rustling by) the lower-status dependent client groups, with the middle-ranking farmers distributed around the interior of the territory.[6] In early Irish society, land was crucial to the economic and social survival of a kin group. There is some documentary and place-name evidence to support the idea that unenclosed settlements may have been occupied by dependants of the ringforts; those who lived within and without the ringforts were all members of the same family group, so that there was no sharp distinction in status between ringfort inhabitants and people living around the ringforts, rather a gradation of status.[7] Craftsmen have left considerable evidence of their activity at the highest status sites, such as Garryduff (Co. Cork), Ballinderry (Co. Offaly), and Lagore (Co. Meath), and it has been suggested that craftsmen may have had their own social organization outside the normal kinship/client organization of early medieval Irish society.[8] Mapping the current evidence of settlements, monastic sites, and monuments with parishes indicates that the system in Ireland up to the ninth century may not have been so different from that in England, with multiple estates controlled by the elite, who were provided with renders by their tenants, both bond and free.[9]

Of the ringforts in Ireland that have been dated by radio-carbon and dendrochronology, the majority provide dates between AD 600 and 900.[10] While some ringforts may have continued in use beyond this date, it seems that the ninth century marks a decline in their use. It also marks a change in the focus of elite ecclesiastical patronage and display, characterized by a hiatus in the production of elaborate stonework and luxury manuscripts. At the same time, large quantities of metalwork were still being made (thistle brooches, for example) and imported.[11] This period also coincides with a decline in the building of mills, possibly linked to a decline in corn production, and perhaps a movement toward nucleation of settlement. There are good reasons to implicate the vikings in the social changes that the archaeological evidence implies.

Irish society did not disappear under the vikings – the vikings certainly did not take enough land for this – but the vikings and their entrepôt settlements offered a market for slaves. The decline in corn production, it has been suggested, was linked to a rise in the export of people as slaves and a concomitant fall in population and change in agricultural production and the relationships between lords and their clients. All this was an important factor in the rise of new, more powerful kings controlling larger kingdoms in the tenth, eleventh, and twelfth centuries, and with new centers of power, such as the monastery at Downpatrick and its associated promontory enclosure, strongly defended, of the eastern Ulster kings.[12]

Scotland

Documentary evidence relating to the structure of society in Scotland in this period is sketchy, but by the end of the period a picture of society and settlement emerges that is strikingly similar in several respects to that in Ireland. Perhaps from the middle of the sixth century, and certainly by the early eighth century, Pictish kings had political force and strong administrative capabilities.[13] The archaeological evidence shows a hierarchy of settlements, the most important of which were the fortified residences of the king and his nobles, for example at Dundurn (Perthshire) and Craig Clatchard (Fife). Hillforts, the highest status sites at the beginning of this period, are relatively well understood thanks to a ground-breaking campaign of excavations carried out in the 1970s and 1980s.[14] Documentary references to the hillfort at Dunadd (Argyll) show that it was in use in the early eighth century. Finds from the excavations at the site included E-ware amphorae and other ceramics, which demonstrate the presence of an elite with control of resources and prestige goods, and some access to long-distance networks.[15] The power and wealth of this elite is paralleled, and expressed, by the flourishing of Class II Pictish symbol stones.

Documentary sources from the twelfth century record that land in Scotland was divided into *thanages*, large, multiple estates managed for the king by a member of the nobility. The archaeological evidence suggests that this system of lordship, land-ownership, and obligation was in use at a much earlier date.[16] Later records indicate that thanages were divided into portions or "petts," and each pett was controlled by a tenant, almost certainly related to the noble, who owed dues to the lord.

Archaeological evidence suggests that the principal settlement of the noble was probably a ringfort or a farmstead marked out by ditches or walls to demonstrate status; for example, the possible timber hall and enclosure at Dalpatrick, near Strageath.[17] Toward the bottom of the social pile, and probably the most numerous class, were the dependant commoners, who probably lived in unenclosed settlements, their houses too ephemeral to leave a clear trace in the soil. It is possible that the scooped houses excavated from the unenclosed settlement of Easter Kinnear (Fife) might be an example of the houses of this group, and a building-type that might belong to rural, lower-class settlements is the so-called "Pitcarmick house," roughly rectilinear, stone-footed buildings varying in size from about 10 to 30 meters. They occur in clusters, or singly, and may be associated with large field systems. There is no evidence from Pictland of large villages: rather, it seems that people lived in small houses next to the field systems, or in small, unenclosed settlements, perhaps part of the estate's holdings.[18]

A further type of elite settlement form from Scotland must also be taken into account: the palisaded enclosure. Usually dated to the late Bronze Age and early Iron Age, recent radio-carbon dates have led to a review of the chronology of these sites, and suggest that this form of structure continued in use through the early medieval period. Their function is not clear, but their association with high-status sites in northern Britain, such as Yeavering (Northumberland), Sprouston (Roxburghshire), Doon Hill (Dunbar), and Kirk Hill, St. Abb's (Berwickshire), indicates that they may have had a role in controlling trade, or in high-status craft production.[19]

Northern Britain between the eighth and eleventh centuries has been characterized as "still fundamentally rural and occupied by kin-based societies," and it is true that, on one level, not much changed in Scotland from the beginning of the early medieval period to the end.[20] There were no urban centers, coinage was still not widely used or circulated, and most people still lived in scattered settlements or hamlets. However, the archaeological evidence does point to a reorganization of social display and living patterns toward the end of our period. High-status defended sites, such as Dundurn (Perthshire) and Dunadd (Argyll), became less important, and they appear to have been replaced by the undefended lowland sites such as Forteviot in Strathearn, Perthshire (although forts on coastal sites, such as Burghead, Inverness-shire and Green Castle, Portknockie, Banffshire, seem to have continued in use, perhaps as a defense against the vikings).[21] The supply of high-quality religious sculpture also came to an end, linked, perhaps, to a change in patterns of patronage, or at least reduced access by the church and the elite to resources available to them before. Alex Woolf, drawing parallels with evidence from Wales, suggests that this might have been linked to a secularization of monastic sites as resources were "redirected towards royal rather than religious projects," and, again, the vikings are implicated in this change, as kings appropriated land in their defense.[22]

Wales

The picture of social organization in early medieval Wales is relatively difficult to interpret. Up to the seventh century, settlement evidence for Wales consists mostly of defended or undefended high-status sites yielding the familiar evidence of elite presence: imported pottery, ornamental metalwork, and Germanic glass, all of which help to date a phase of use to the early medieval period at sites such as Dinas Powys (Glamorgan), Coygan Camp (Camarthenshire), Carew Castle (Pembrokeshire; all defended), and the undefended sites of Longbury Bank (Pembrokeshire), Kenfig and Twlc Point (Glamorgan), and Linney Burrows (Pembrokeshire).[23] After the seventh century, the evidence for these sort of high-status sites in Wales all but stops, though there is evidence from the documentary sources to show that some hillforts were still centers of some importance and activity. The annals record that Degannwy (Caernarfonshire) was burned in 812, and destroyed by the Anglo-Saxons in 822, for example, while Castle Hill, Tenby (Pembrokeshire) was mentioned as a royal settlement in a poem dating to the late ninth or early tenth century, but these sketchy references do no more than show that these sites saw some sporadic activity, and need not mean that the sites were continuously occupied.[24] Even occasional archaeological discoveries, such as a Hiberno-Norse bead fragment and two ninth-century radio-carbon dates from the site of Hen Gastell (Glamorgan), have not done much to change the overall impression that there was a change in the location of high-status sites in Wales in the eighth or perhaps the ninth century.[25]

Why should this shift have occurred? During the troubled period of viking incursions around Britain, conditions for sea travel may have become much more difficult and dangerous, and the routes for trade in luxury imports may have simply collapsed, which may explain the lack of these sorts of diagnostic goods at what used to be high-status sites. It may be that there was some sort of reorganization of society, similar to that which provoked the move away from hillforts in Scotland and Ireland at this period. At present, however, the current state of knowledge is too sketchy to do more than speculate: we are still almost totally ignorant about the location of high-status settlement sites in Wales between the eighth and eleventh centuries, and we know even less about other, lower-status settlement sites for the same period.[26]

Much of the very sketchy evidence for high-status settlement in Wales implies that some assimilation or emulation of neighboring or invading cultures and society was taking place at the highest levels of Welsh society. Llangorse (Breconshire), for example, is a crannog site, dated by dendrochronology to the late ninth and early tenth centuries, and mentioned in the *Anglo-Saxon Chronicle* and two Llandaff charters as the seat of the kings of Brycheiniog. The archaeological evidence suggests that it was a high-status site, but crannogs are typical of Irish elite society, and otherwise unknown in Wales. Were the kings of Brycheiniog demonstrating their Irish ancestry through their elite residences?[27] Viking influence in Wales has also been identified in the archaeological record. At Llanbedrgoch (Anglesey) a new kind of eighth- to tenth-century site for Wales has been recovered by archaeological excavation. Unlike previously known sites, this one was low-lying, fortified, and multifunctional. In the seventh century, there was a native Welsh settlement here, consisting of wooden houses, with a mixture of circular and rectangular ground plans, enclosed by a boundary ditch. The main activity of the settlement appears to have been farming. By the ninth century, the enclosure boundary had been turned into a solid dry-stone wall, around 2 meters wide, perhaps built to demonstrate power and status, but perhaps with a defensive purpose. Originally interpreted as a viking site, the archaeological evidence for Llanbedrgoch might also point to Scandinavian influence on a Welsh elite community.[28] The presence of an Anglo-Saxon elite is evident at places such as Rhuddlan, which excavation has proved beyond doubt to be the site of the Anglo-Saxon *burh* of *Cledmutha*, founded by Edward the Elder in AD 921.[29]

There is some archaeological evidence for native low-status settlements in Wales, consisting of oval wattle-and-daub huts, grouped together on unenclosed sites. At Trostrey Castle (Monmouthshire) some of the structures were datable by radio-carbon dating to our period. The oval huts had double walls and internal partitions, giving a hint that use of the internal spaces was organized and segregated.[30] Though not enough has been done on landscape studies in Wales, evidence from the classic site of Llanynys (Denbighshire) suggests that some nucleated settlement around a church began toward the end of this period in Wales in areas outside Anglo-Norman control.[31]

Anglo-Saxon England

In contrast to the loosely structured, undifferentiated, and unenclosed settlements of the earlier Anglo-Saxon period, settlements from middle and late Anglo-Saxon

England, such as Goltho (Lincolnshire), Faccombe Netherton (Hampshire), and Raunds Furnells (Northamptonshire), show a formal, planned layout with ditched enclosures, reflecting the architectural requirements of the thegnly class demanded by the documentary sources.[32] The change in settlement structure visible in Anglo-Saxon archaeology from the seventh century onward, characterized by more formal layout of sites, re-use of building plots, the increasing use of fences and boundary ditches, and the development of larger halls, all point to a significant shift in social organization from the seventh century onward. This shift is also reflected in the development of a range of types of site. Where the earlier Anglo-Saxon period was characterized by rural, shifting settlements, consisting of relatively small, timber-built, earth-fast halls and satellite sunken-featured buildings, the later Anglo-Saxon period saw the building of churches, monastic sites, *wic* proto-urban sites, manufacturing or "productive" sites, elite settlements, and royal sites used intermittently as arenas for public performances of ritual, ceremonial, economic, or judicial purposes. From the ninth century, defended *burhs* appeared and, with them, the beginning of an urban population.

The seventh century saw the emergence of an elite group in Anglo-Saxon England with access to exotic imports and control of resources and economies. The documentary evidence for the growth of kingship is supported by the archaeological evidence of rich, "princely" graves at Sutton Hoo (Suffolk), Taplow (Buckinghamshire), and Prittlewell (Essex). Though few settlements associated with this elite have been excavated, Yeavering in Northumbria remains the type site, with its aligned, earth-fast buildings, cemetery, and ritual structures such as the "amphitheater" and the large enclosure.

Later royal sites are perhaps less easy to identify, unless they are mentioned in documentary sources. The palace at Cheddar (Somerset), which was the meeting place of the witan, was mentioned as a royal estate in King Alfred's will. The earliest archaeology on the site pre-dates AD 930, and consists of five timber buildings arranged around a courtyard south of a substantial ditch. In the late tenth or early eleventh century, the site underwent a complete refurbishment. A new hall was built, as well as a new masonry chapel on the site of an earlier wooden hall. Just before the Norman Conquest, the chapel was rebuilt on a larger scale, while the main hall was reduced in size.

However, the archaeological evidence suggested that the site was in use periodically, like Yeavering, emphasizing the continued peripatetic nature of kingship. The first phase of the site's use included the burial of one human within the settlement, apparently with his hands tied behind his back at the time of death.[33] The documentary evidence indicates that the site was important, and this is reflected in the rebuilding and improvement on the site over the two centuries it was in use as a palace. The site was enclosed, but there was no evidence of large defensive structures: this was a high-status site, not a militarily threatened or threatening one. The single grave of a possible victim of execution hints at public displays of judicial power taking place here, though it should be noted that other possible execution victims have been found at other settlement sites of this period which have not been associated with royal residences.[34]

Without the documentary sources, could we be sure this was a royal site? The first phase of the site at Cowdery's Down (Hampshire) included a large structure that was attached to a fenced enclosure with another building inside it, and another enclosure and building sharing a party fence. The next phase had another building over this fence, showing single ownership, and another and larger structure in the second enclosure. This was remodeled into a single compound, with new buildings, in the third phase, during which the settlement as a whole was expanding, with even larger buildings.[35] The site has been interpreted as one always of high status but also showing increasing ostentation in its buildings. It is not on the same scale as Cheddar, but it shows strong control and ownership. Also from Hampshire is the site at Chalton, where there is a two-phase sequence of enclosures and buildings, but in this case with lesser buildings grouped round a square, as though signaling a "chief" with dependents and labor force.[36] Although the buildings are smaller than the largest at Cowdery's Down, it is Chalton that yielded a hanging-bowl escutcheon. In this context, Portchester in Hampshire is also of interest. The fort was owned by the bishop of Winchester in the early tenth century, which does not prove earlier possession, but could be an indicator that someone of more than average importance had an interest in, and may occasionally have visited, it. Ninth-century artifacts, notably coins including a gold one from Carolingia, metalwork, and glass, seem to suggest higher status than most settlements. By the eleventh century, it contained buildings such as an aisled timber hall and a stone-footed tower, and it is always quoted in association with the Old English text that cites the expectation that a thegn's residence would contain a *burh*-gate and a bell. Also with a probable bell tower, and perhaps a mill, too, is the small later Anglo-Saxon settlement at Springfield Lyons (Essex) with halls and a possible kitchen. But this settlement does not appear to have had an enclosure, unlike the well-known settlement at Goltho, (Lincolnshire) with its kitchen, bowers, and workshop. The distinction between "thegnly" and "royal" domestic architecture is relatively undifferentiated in late Anglo-Saxon England, in spite of the textual evidence for the growing power of kingship.

Documentary sources attest to the organization of land into multiple estates owned by royal or ecclesiastical proprietors before the tenth century, whose tenants contributed different specialist products, and who owed food or produce renders, which would be supplied to, and controlled by, administrative or estate centers. Multiple estates are more visible in place-name evidence than in the archaeology, but the variety of organized settlements visible in the archaeological record support the idea of agricultural and human resources being controlled and organized in a coherent way. In this context, the environmental evidence offers important insights into the management of agriculture at this time. Market Lavington is a case in point, not only for the difficulty of reading the ephemeral archaeological evidence for the status of a site, but also for the important contribution a study of the environmental evidence in conjunction with the settlement evidence can make. Market Lavington in Wiltshire was settled by the fifth century, as the early Anglo-Saxon inhumation cemetery there indicates, but evidence for the later period is scarce, particularly in terms of material culture, even though Market Lavington was a royal estate of 15 hides, in the possession of Queen Edith, at the time of *Domesday*. Environmental sampling of ditches dated to the later Anglo-Saxon period, though, indicated a change in agriculture in the later period with more diverse production, and on a far larger scale, than before, with evidence for vineyards from c. AD 900 onward. In addition, the presence of herring bones in the ditches speaks volumes about a complex trade from the coast to this inland site.[37]

Important rural middle/late Anglo-Saxon rural settlements have been excavated at Yarnton (Oxfordshire). The site at Yarnton illustrates a decisive change in settlement layout in the eighth century, with more ordered settlement divided into paddocks, a droveway, and buildings set out within enclosures. During the ninth century, a second hall was built within a new enclosure, and a small cemetery was present on the site. These changes are associated with environmental evidence for the intensification of arable farming, the resumption of hay cultivation, and the expansion of the area under cultivation to include heavier clay soils. Perhaps the change to a new settlement form and the evidence for intensification of farming reflect the need to provide grain, poultry, and perhaps other produce as renders to the nearby minster at Eynsham. Elsewhere in Anglo-Saxon England there is similar evidence for increasing specialization and intensification of agriculture.[38]

So-called "productive sites," increasingly recognized, especially through metal-detecting, appear to be a facet of this increasing control and intensification of production. These are sites where unusually high concentrations of artifacts for the region have been found: they are "productive" in the sense that they produce finds for metal-detectorists, rather than reflecting a specific function of the site in the Anglo-Saxon period.[39] There may have been many types of site which produce evidence that might lead to them being labeled "productive." One such place, at Lake End Road West, Dorney, Buckinghamshire, was quite different in character from settlements north of the Chilterns, or further upstream for that matter, consisting almost entirely of groups of large pits (over 120) apparently lacking any accompanying buildings. The content of the pits was not particularly distinctive, but there were hints of cess in some primary fills, succeeded by refuse deposits. In addition, however, imported Tating Ware, normally considered a luxury good and evidence for a high-status site, was also found here. Considering all of the evidence, the excavators posit the presence of some kind of seasonal market here.[40] Sites such as Dorney were trading places, rather than residences, which in turn raises questions about identifying sites such as Portchester and Chalton as "high status" on the basis of their associated material culture. Portchester may have had a market or trading function, rather than being an elite residence. By contrast, Goltho may have been a thegnly residence, but the material evidence from the site is distinctly lacking in imported or luxury goods.

The documentary evidence also indicates a later break-up of large estates into smaller estates in the tenth and eleventh centuries. Again, the viking incursions may be implicated in this change. The later Anglo-Saxon period saw the breakdown of multiple estates into smaller estates in some parts of Britain. Robin Fleming has argued that some of the changes seen in estate, agricultural, and settlement management for this period are a result of the kings appropriating lands formerly granted to the church as part of the defense against the vikings.[41] Chris Loveluck has argued for a similar phenomenon to explain changes at Flixborough, suggesting that the site's relative poverty in artifacts in the tenth century is related to the break-up of large estates under the influence of Anglo-Scandinavian military settlement, with its consequent disruption of estate networks and therefore a concomitant lessening of support for estates geared to intensive production.[42] It may be that the vikings were also implicated in the changes to social organization seen in the Irish and Scottish evidence.[43] Evidence from sites such as Cogges (Oxfordshire) or Raunds (Northamptonshire), with its classic manorial grouping of church, cemetery, and manor house, offers support for the idea that, in the tenth century, Anglo-Saxon England saw a process by which land was divided up into smaller manorial units with their villages.[44] At Market Lavington, the exact location of the later Anglo-Saxon settlement is not clear, though finds of a bronze strap-end, a bone comb, and a tenth-century book-clasp near the church suggest that the church here, too, may have provided a nucleus for what had become a village.

Differentiating between Religious and Secular Society

Discussions of early medieval society based on the documentary sources have tended to draw a clear distinction between secular and ecclesiastical society, but the archaeological evidence for this period suggests that secular society and its development were inextricably intertwined with the church.[45] One of the problems in identifying elite residences that are not mentioned in the surviving documentary sources is in deciding, on the basis of the artifactual evidence, whether the site under excavation is a religious site or a secular one. At the Anglo-Saxon site of Flixborough (Lincolnshire), for example, there are aligned buildings with archaeological evidence of writing, high-status artifacts, and human burial, as well as evidence for craft production, including metalworking. None of these features, singly or in combination, may be used to "prove" the presence of either a secular or an ecclesiastical site, as aligned buildings, burials, and craft production have been found on both. Styli, like those found at the site of Staunch Meadow, Brandon, in Norfolk, were once thought to demonstrate the presence of manuscript production, which in turn was thought to have been certain proof of an ecclesiastical site, but styli could equally be connected with the clerical staff associated with an elite or royal residence, who were employed to write charters, grants, and other texts for a secular lord.[46] The picture is complicated by the evidence that a high-status site might have evolved from a secular to an ecclesiastical site and back again. Flixborough may have begun as a secular settlement, but had become a monastic site by the mid-eighth century. The site then reverted to secular use by the end of the Anglo-Saxon period.[47]

Settlement structures and building layouts reflect, to some extent, the social structure and organization of the population using them, and the difficulty that archaeologists find in distinguishing elite secular from ecclesiastical sites might well be because they are trying to make a distinction where no distinction existed. Minster churches, for example, were endowed by the secular, as well as the ecclesiastical elite, and were often led by relatives of the patrons. They also served many of the same social functions as secular elite sites, being useful as administrative and judicial meeting places, providing accommodation for visiting royalty, being places for displaying the generosity of patrons, and for conspicuous gift-giving. Minsters and monasteries, as major landowners, and conspicuous consumers of high-status goods, were communal and economic centers, occupying a significant place within the wider secular framework.[48]

Not only did ecclesiastical sites mirror secular elite sites in their social functions, they also possessed many of the attributes that became associated with royal sites only at a much later, post-Conquest date, not only in Anglo-Saxon England, but in other parts of Britain too. Principal amongst these attributes was that monastic sites were more stable than palace sites, and were continuously, rather than seasonally, occupied. As such, they attracted trade, markets, craftspeople, and estate workers, and developed more complex layouts that many secular estate centers. Ancillary buildings were required for craft and domestic activities at both secular and ecclesiastical sites, and these ancillary buildings, found at monastic sites such as Whitby and Hartlepool, were vernacular buildings similar to any found at estate centers or royal vills, giving the archaeology of these sites a domestic, secular character. Planned sites, such as Wicken Bonhunt (Essex) and North Elmham (Norfolk), illustrate the degree of social control exerted by the elite, both secular and ecclesiastical, in later Anglo-Saxon society. It is also, in this context, hardly surprising that minsters became the core of larger settlements, including towns like Bampton (Oxfordshire) and Whithorn (Dumfries and Galloway), or planned *burhs* like Oxford, which incorporated the minster of St. Frideswide.[49]

The intimate relationship between secular and ecclesiastical society is exemplified by the connection between different sites in the Irish landscape. Typically, a royal site consisted of not just an elite dwelling, but a complex of dispersed but interconnected sites, each with a specific function which, taken together, formed a royal landscape. The necessary components of a royal center have been identified as royal ringfort, a prehistoric ritual center, and a monastic enclosure. Ecclesiastical enclosures, too, were made up of a variety of different sites performing different functions, not all of which were necessarily monastic: a monastic enclosure might include, as well as a church, a holy well, a children's burial ground, and a burial ground for the general population; the monastic enclosure was an extension of the royal site, and served as a "central place" for the ruling group, the *túath*, whose members controlled the monastery.[50] The complexity of many sites, in terms of layout, patterning, and phasing, can only be interpreted in the context of the evolving and intimate relationship between elite secular and religious society, which were clearly not separate, but were two aspects of a social continuum.

Urban Layouts and Living Conditions

Across Britain, where the population adopted an urban lifestyle, the development of urbanism proceeded with more or less success according to geography, natural resources, and political factors. The extent to which Scandinavian traders and settlers were a catalyst for the growth of urbanism in Britain is still a matter for debate. The impact of the Scandinavians in promoting and developing urban sites – where "urban," never particularly easy to define in an early medieval context, is taken to mean a dense, nucleated settlement where the majority of the population is devoted to trade, manufacturing, and administration – is perhaps most clearly seen in Ireland. Excavations at Dublin have shown a familiar pattern of typically Scandinavian urban settlement, which has everything in common with similar sites in England and in Scandinavia, and owes nothing to native Irish settlement patterns. Artifacts from the site also belong to the wider culture of the Scandinavian world, and again show very little signs of quotidian contact with the Irish hinterland. To a large extent, it would seem that Dublin was an isolated entrepôt looking toward the east, with little communication or interaction with the native hinterland except in terms of acquiring goods for trade, most notably slaves. Irish towns, run by and for Irish leaders, seem not to have developed. Beyond the boundaries of Dublin, the landscape and its population continued in a determinedly agrarian lifestyle. The town wall was culturally impermeable, though the presence of Scandinavians may have disrupted the consolidation of the power of the elite, since the occupation of crannog and rath sites seems to have declined after the ninth century, at the same time as the Scandinavians were creating their urban enclaves in Ireland.[51]

The picture in Scotland is much harder to assess, due in part to the poor quality of archaeological evidence for this period, but it is clear enough that, while the vikings certainly settled in Scotland, they did not establish any towns in this part of Britain. The archaeological evidence from Scotland as a whole reinforces a picture of a non-urban society, with small-scale settlement and craft activity as the norm.[52] Urbanization in Wales was also almost non-existent. The old Roman towns did continue as foci for religious activity, but did not continue to have any urban function, and the Anglo-Saxon attempts to establish a *burh* at Rhuddlan were unsuccessful. There is no evidence for towns in Wales until the Anglo-Norman period.[53]

Urbanization was most successful in Anglo-Saxon England. By 1066, it has been calculated that a tenth of the Anglo-Saxon population lived in towns, and excavations at Oxford, for example, have demonstrated that towns like this supported a dense population with a well-organized civic structure.[54] Excavations at the Royal Opera House site in London showed that, during the eighth century, there was a big expansion in industrial and economic activity, reflected in the increasing evidence for weaving, smithing, jewelry manufacture, and bone and antler working in many of the buildings. The houses, as well as providing evidence for intensive manufacturing, also included the trappings of elite status – glass vessels and imported pottery, as well as personal items. The growing prosperity of the people who lived in these houses is demonstrated by the volume of goods associated with the buildings and the lack of evidence for repair (implying that replacement of damaged goods was an easier option). The evidence points to a rising class of artisans and traders. If, as seems likely, these traders and craftspeople were supporting themselves entirely by trade and manufacture, then they would also have needed suppliers of other goods – butchers, bakers, and other essentials – and so what we have, at this site, is solid evidence for the beginnings of a genuinely urban way of life.[55]

The impact that urban life must have had on traditional Anglo-Saxon social structures is hard to evaluate, but both documentary and archaeological sources give clues to the profound changes that had taken place in a population to a greater or lesser extent removed from agricultural responsibility. The uniformity of the size and shape of plots for dwellings in towns as geographically separate as Dublin, York, and Oxford suggests a strongly structured, hierarchical society, with the paramount group controlling urban development, but with a relatively uniform, unstratified community of craftsmen, merchants, and traders who made up the bulk of the urban population.

Conclusion

The way in which a society works – the roles negotiated for or by individuals within society – is determined by a number of factors. It has been said that the study of society in early medieval Europe is a study of the way in which social relations were determined by the need of the elite to maintain control of agricultural production.[56] In all parts of Britain and Ireland, elite, royal, and ecclesiastical sites were intimately linked, to the point of being archaeologically inseparable. All parts of Britain and Ireland show strong signs of some central organizing authority, whose primary focus was the control of agricultural land and resources, including labor resources, and the control of trade and supply. At the same time, the fuller archaeological record in England and Ireland points to some change within the period, especially between the early and later centuries, with the eighth and ninth a particularly significant turning-point.

Notes

1 Whitelock, *English Historical Documents*, I, 468 (no. 51); "*7 gif ceorl geþeah, þaet he haefde v hida fullice agenes landes, bellan 7 burhgeat, setl 7 sundornote on cynges healle, þonne waes he þanon forð þegenrihtes wyrðe*" [and if a ceorl prospered, so that he owned fully five hides of his own land, bell and *burh*-gate, seat and special office in the king's hall, then he was from then onwards entitled to a thegn's rights].
2 Stout, *Irish Ringfort.*
3 Baillie, *Tree Ring Dating*, p. 192; Bell, "Environmental archaeology," p. 276.
4 Patterson, *Cattle, Lords and Clansmen*, pp. 52 and 100.
5 Edwards, *Archaeology of Early Medieval Ireland*, p. 33.
6 Stout, *Irish Ringfort*, p. 235.
7 Patterson, *Cattle, Lords and Clansmen*, pp. 102–3.
8 Ibid., p. 42. Nerys Patterson has suggested that, in south-west Ireland, control of craftsmen was a serious political issue.
9 Mallory and McNeill, *Archaeology of Ulster*, p. 224.
10 Stout, *Irish Ringfort*, p. 24.
11 Mallory and McNeill, *Archaeology of Ulster*, p. 228.
12 Ibid.
13 Driscoll, "The archaeology of state formation in Scotland," p. 88.
14 See especially the work of Leslie and Elizabeth Alcock, "Reconnaissance excavations."
15 Lane and Campbell, *Dunadd*, p. 253.
16 See Driscoll, "The archaeology of state formation," p. 88.
17 Ibid., p. 52.
18 Ibid., p. 107; Proudfoot et al., "The early historic period," p. 229.
19 Johnson and Rees, "Excavation at an early historic palisaded enclosure."
20 Woolf, *From Pictland to Alba*, p. 312.
21 Proudfoot et al., "The early historic period," p. 225.
22 Woolf, *From Pictland to Alba*, p. 313.
23 Edwards, *Landscape and Settlement*, p. 2.
24 Ibid.
25 Ibid., p. 3.
26 Ibid.
27 Ibid.
28 Redknap, *Vikings in Wales*, p. 69.
29 Edwards, *Landscape and Settlement*, p. 4.
30 Ibid.
31 Jones, "Post-Roman Wales."
32 Reynolds, *Later Anglo-Saxon England.*
33 Rahtz, *Saxon and Medieval Palaces at Cheddar.*
34 Reynolds, *Later Anglo-Saxon England.*
35 Millet, "Excavations at Cowdery's Down," pp. 193–7.
36 Ibid., pp. 247–9.
37 Williams and Newman, "Market Lavington," p. 180.
38 Hey, *Yarnton.*
39 Ulmschneider, "Settlement, economy and the 'productive' site."
40 Foreman et al., *Gathering the People.*

41 Fleming, "Monastic lands and England's defence."

42 Loveluck, *Rural Settlement*, p. 154.

43 Woolf, *From Pictland to Alba*, p. 318.

44 Blair, *Anglo-Saxon Oxfordshire*, p. 135.

45 See especially Blair, *The Church in Anglo-Saxon Society*, which is essential reading for this period.

46 Newman, "Exceptional finds, exceptional sites?"

47 Hines, "Religion: the limits of knowledge," p. 391; Loveluck, "Wealth, waste and conspicuous consumption"; Reynolds, *Later Anglo-Saxon England*, p. 111.

48 Blair, "Palaces or minsters?," p. 121.

49 Blair, *The Church in Anglo-Saxon* Society, pp. 287–90; Newman, "Exceptional finds, exceptional sites?," p. 102; Reynolds, *Later Anglo-Saxon England*, p. 140.

50 Patterson, *Cattle, Lords and Clansmen*, p. 101; Warner, "The archaeology of early historic Irish kingship."

51 Edwards, *Archaeology of Early Medieval Ireland*, pp. 90–3.

52 Proudfoot et al., "The early historic period," p. 239

53 Edwards, *Landscape and Settlement*, p. 8.

54 Reynolds, *Later Anglo-Saxon England*, p. 57.

55 Malcolm and Bowsher, *Middle Saxon London*, p. 102

56 Driscoll, "The archaeology of state formation in Scotland," p. 81.

Further Reading

For the archaeology of settlement, economy, and social structure in later Anglo-Saxon England, Wales, and Ireland, the key works are Andrew Reynolds, *Later Anglo-Saxon England*, and Nerys Patterson, *Cattle, Lords and Clansmen*. For the church in society, John Blair, *The Church in Anglo-Saxon Society*, is indispensable. For a discussion of social structure outside Anglo-Saxon England, Nancy Edwards, *The Archaeology of Early Medieval Ireland*, covers many of the topics, and her edited volume, *Landscape and Settlement in Medieval Wales*, provides information on social structure in Wales.

Bibliography

Alcock, L. and Alcock, E., "Reconnaissance excavations on early historic fortifications and other royal sites in Scotland 1974–84: A, excavations and other fieldwork at Forteviot, Perthshire, 1981; B, excavations at Urquhart Castle, Inverness-shire, 1983; C, excavations at Dunnottar, Kincardineshire, 1984," *Proceedings of the Society of Antiquaries of Scotland*, 122 (1992), 215–88.

Baillie, M. G. L., *Tree Ring Dating and Archaeology* (London, 1982).

Bell, M., "Environmental archaeology as an index of continuity and change in the medieval landscape," in M. Aston, D. Austin, and C. Dyer (eds.), *The Rural Settlements of Medieval England: Studies Dedicated to Maurice Beresford and John Hurst* (Oxford, 1989), pp. 269–86.

Blair, J., *Anglo-Saxon Oxfordshire* (Stroud, 1994).

Blair, J., *The Church in Anglo-Saxon Society* (Oxford, 2005).

Blair, J., "Palaces or minsters? Northampton and Cheddar reconsidered," in M. Lapidge (ed.), *Anglo-Saxon England*, 25 (Cambridge, 1996), pp. 97–122.

Driscoll, S., "The archaeology of state formation in Scotland," in W. S. Hanson and E. A. Slater (eds.), *Scottish Archaeology: New Perceptions* (Aberdeen, 1991), pp. 81–111.

Edwards, N., *The Archaeology of Early Medieval Ireland* (London, 1990).

Edwards, N. (ed.), *Landscape and Settlement in Medieval Wales* (Oxford, 1997).

Fleming, R., "Monastic lands and England's defence in the Viking Age," *English Historical Review*, 100 (1985), 247–65.

Foreman, S., Hiller, J., and Petts, D., *Gathering the People, Settling the Land* (Oxford, 2002).

Hey, G., *Yarnton: Saxon and Medieval Settlement and Landscape: Results of Excavations 1990–96* (Oxford, 2004).

Hines, J., "Religion: the limits of knowledge" in J. Hines (ed.), *The Anglo-Saxons: From the Migration Period to the Eighth Century* (Woodbridge, 1997), pp. 375–410.

Johnson, M. and Rees, A., "Excavation of an early historic palisaded enclosure at Titwood, Mearnskirk, East Renfrewshire," *Scottish Archaeological Journal*, 25: 2 (2003), 129–46.

Jones, G. R. J., "Post-Roman Wales," in H. P. R. Finberg (ed.), *The Agrarian History of England and Wales*, vol. 1, part 2: *AD 43–1042* (Cambridge, 1972), pp. 283–382.

Lane, A. and Campbell, E., *Dunadd: An Early Dalriadic Capital* (Oxford, 2000).

Loveluck, C., *Rural Settlement, Lifestyles and Social Change in the Later First Millennium AD: Anglo-Saxon Flixborough in its Wider Context* (Oxford, 2007).

Loveluck, C., "Wealth, waste and conspicuous consumption: Flixborough and its importance for middle and late Anglo-Saxon rural settlement studies," in H. Hamerow and A. MacGregor (eds.), *Image and Power in the Archaeology of Early Medieval Britain: Essays in Honour of Rosemary Cramp* (Oxford, 2001), pp. 79–130.

Malcolm, G. and Bowsher, D., *Middle Saxon London: Excavation at the Royal Opera House 1989–99* (London, 2003).

Mallory, J. P. and McNeill, T. E., *The Archaeology of Ulster: From Colonization to Plantation* (Belfast, 1991).

Millett, M., with James, S., "Excavations at Cowdery's Down, Basingstoke, Hampshire, 1978–81," *Archaeological Journal*, 140 (1983), 151–279.

Newman, J., "Exceptional finds, exceptional sites? Barham and Coddenham, Suffolk," in T. Pestell and K. Ulmschneider (eds.), *Markets in Early Medieval Europe: Trading and Productive Sites 650–850* (Oxford, 2003), pp. 97–109.

Patterson, N., *Cattle, Lords and Clansmen: The Social Structure of Early Ireland*, 2nd edn. (London, 1994).

Proudfoot, V., Ralston, I., and Armit, I., "The early historic period: an archaeological perspective," in K. J. Edwards and I. B. Ralston (eds.), *Scotland: Environment and Archaeology, 8000BC–AD1000* (Chichester, 1997), pp. 217–40.

Rahtz, P., *The Saxon and Medieval Palaces at Cheddar* (Oxford, 1979).

Redknap, M., *Vikings in Wales: An Archaeological Quest* (Cardiff, 2000).

Reynolds, A., *Later Anglo-Saxon England: Life and Landscape* (Stroud, 1999).

Stout, M., *The Irish Ringfort* (Dublin, 1997).

Ulmschneider, K., "Settlement, economy and the 'productive' site: Middle Anglo-Saxon Lincolnshire, AD 650–780," *Medieval Archaeology*, 44 (2000), 53–80.

Warner, R., "The archaeology of early historic Irish kingship," in S. T. Driscoll and M. R. Nieke (eds.), *Power and Politics in Early Medieval Britain and Ireland* (Edinburgh, 1988), pp. 47–68.

Whitelock, D. (ed. and trans.), *English Historical Documents*, vol. I: *c.500–1042*, 2nd edn. (London, 1979).

Williams, P. and Newman, R., "Market Lavington, Wiltshire, an Anglo-Saxon cemetery and settlement: excavations at Grove Farm, 1986–90," *Wessex Archaeology Report*, 19 (2006).

Woolf, A., *From Pictland to Alba 789–1070* (Edinburgh, 2007).

CHAPTER TWENTY-SEVEN

Localities

DAVID E. THORNTON

The Scandinavian incursions in Britain and Ireland from the late eighth to the tenth centuries mark a watershed in the history of these two islands. The demographic and political changes characteristic of this period had significant effects, both direct and indirect, from the upper echelons of Anglo-Saxon and Celtic societies down to the level of local communities. Beyond the obvious threat of the viking raids on many communities, the settlement of Norse-speaking peoples – notably in northern and eastern England, the Scottish Isles, and parts of Ireland – led to the emergence of new communities and new social and cultural structures. Furthermore, the conquest of the so-called Danelaw and Northumbria by the successors of Alfred the Great during the tenth century was accompanied by the imposition of new administrative patterns based on existing West Saxon models. The disappearance of the pre-viking "tribal units" and the development of a more centralized form of royal government affected the workings of local administration and justice.

Most communities in early medieval Britain and Ireland were and continued to be rural and agrarian in character, and consequently most people lived in small villages and estates. The high-status sites of the Celtic areas and the royal vills of England were the exception. From the ninth century onward, we see the gradual development of proto-urban and urban sites, notably in England, in the form of Alfredian and later boroughs, and in the Danelaw and the north, notably York. By the tenth century, there is evidence for the existence of borough courts, and in Ireland viking *longphoirt* were developing into proto-urban settlements, especially Dublin. Towns involved different social structures and different forms of organization.

The position of an individual within his or her community was in part determined by three interrelated factors: kinship, status, and, depending on location, ethnicity (see chapter 7). Local communities in early medieval Britain and Ireland were socially mixed, reflecting the social stratification of society at large. The role played by an individual within a community, and the ability to interact with others, were to a significant degree determined by his or her social status. Indeed, in later Welsh law, the value of a dog was partly a matter of its breed and age, but also depended upon the status of its owner, though a dog belonging to a *bilain* (literally "villein"), of whatever breed, was always valued at four pence.[1] A person's status was a matter of both kinship and economic standing. The most fundamental social distinction was between free and unfree, and there is evidence of slavery and the manumission of slaves.[2] Most early medieval societies divided freemen into king, noble, and peasant, though each of these broad divisions could in turn be subdivided. For example, the Irish laws from the seventh and eighth centuries describe a highly graded system of social hierarchy (see chapter 7), though how far this operated in practice and to what extent the system survived to the tenth and eleventh centuries are unclear.

In England, the main term for a non-noble freeman was *ceorl*, and from the eleventh century, we gain an insight into the different categories of peasant from *Domesday Book* and a document know as *Rectitudines singularum personarum*.[3] Clearly, there existed a kind of hierarchy: at the top was the *geneat* ("companion") or, in *Domesday Book*, the *radman*; below was the cottager, called *kotsetla*, *cottarius*, and *bordarius*; and at the bottom the *gebur* or *colibertus*, many of whom were probably freed slaves. The status of most of these appears to have depended largely on economic circumstances, and indeed the *Norðleoda Laga* ("The Law of the North People") provides that an individual could increase his *wergild*, and by implication his status, if he were to acquire sufficient land. This included the *ceorl* and his offspring who could increase his *wergild* to the level of a thegn "if he has five hides of land on which he discharges the king's dues" (*EHD*, I, 469–70). On the other hand, in lowland Scotland descent was equally important. Thus, the *Leges inter Brettos et Scottos* ("Laws among/between the Britons and Scots") state that "all those who are lower in kinship [*bassiores in parentela*] are rustics, and have the rights of a rustic."[4] Status was not simply a matter of social standing and snobbery, but had a direct and practical influence on many aspects of an individual's life and therefore on his or her involvement within the community. In the Danelaw, there existed the *lahslit* (from Old Norse "breach of the law") which was a fine paid by an offender according to his own status: the higher his status, the more he was required to pay.[5]

Despite the modern preference for ethno-political terms such as "Anglo-Saxon England," the polities of early medieval Britain and Ireland were certainly not comprised of mutually exclusive "ethnic" populations, and this applies equally to the local communities. Indeed, the Scandinavian settlements added a further component to the ethnic melting pot in many areas. In the tenth century, English kings were very conscious that they ruled, or at least claimed to rule, over a variety of peoples, and by the eleventh century their successors recognized three prevailing "laws": those of Wessex, Mercia, and the "Danelaw." Ethnic concerns would have been particularly important in communities that lay along the border between different demographic or political areas, and thus a number of legal texts, such as the *Dunsæte Ordinance* and the *Leges inter Brettos et Scottos*, survive which specifically deal with regulating the interaction of different "ethnic" groups (see pp. 451–2). However, even in other areas, we might expect ethnically mixed communities. While the occurrence of the word *wealh* in English laws of the tenth and eleventh centuries probably refers to a slave rather than indicating the presence of Welshmen in southern England, the large parts of Britain and Ireland that were occupied by Scandinavian settlers during this period must have resulted in many mixed localities (see chapter 14). Indeed, recent DNA studies suggest that, whereas Shetland and the Orkneys experienced heavy Norwegian settlement during this period, areas that are also traditionally seen as Scandinavian in character, such as the Hebrides, underwent less settlement and that was predominantly by Scandinavian men.[6] Elsewhere, the degree of intermarriage with the indigenous populations must have also been high. On the other hand, similar studies in Ireland would suggest that the so-called "Ostman" towns came to be occupied largely by native Irish.[7]

Individual rural and urban settlements were not isolated communities but were part of wider collective localities and networks, and thus integrated into the existing administrative structures. The kingdoms of the tenth and eleventh centuries comprised hierarchies of administrative units, concerned with larger and smaller areas, paralleled by a hierarchy of courts for the administration of justice. The evidence is more abundant for late Anglo-Saxon England than for the contemporary Celtic regions, though some comments can be ventured. For England, the late ninth and tenth centuries seem to have been a period of change and development. The largest administrative division of late Anglo-Saxon England was the "shire," serving as a unit of local government for legislative, financial, and military purposes, and in turn subdivided into hundreds. The Old English word *scīr* meant a share or division, perhaps of people, originating as such in the pre-Viking period and continuing to represent forms of lordship in northern England and southern Scotland.[8] However, the later shires were clearly territorial in character.[9] The English system of shires was well established by the time of the *Domesday* survey and was probably more or less fixed by the reign of Æthelred the Unready (978–1016). However, the origin of individual shires probably followed the reconquest of England by the successors of Alfred the Great during the tenth century. The shires of Wessex – Somerset, Dorset, Wiltshire, and Hampshire – may have originated as early as the late seventh or eighth centuries, and were certainly in existence by the time of Alfred. The absorption by Wessex during the eighth and ninth centuries of the Brittonic kingdom of Dumnonia in the south-west and of old Anglo-Saxon kingdoms in the south-east led to the creation of the newer shires of Cornwall and Devon, and Kent, Sussex, Essex, and Surrey, respectively. Finally, during the tenth century, Alfred's successors seem to have imposed this "West Saxon" model on the reconquered Scandinavian areas, though it has also been suggested that the Mercian shires may have been established relatively late, during the reign of Æthelred, perhaps under the direction of the king's son-in-law, ealdorman Eadric Streona (1007–17).[10]

The names and sizes of individual shires reflect this varied origin of the system as a whole. The West Saxon shires took their names from the royal estates from which they were administered: Somerton, Dorchester, Wilton, and "Hamton" (Southampton). The later midlands shires were also named after the relevant centers, such as Chester, Stafford, Winchcombe (for "Winchcombshire," which was abolished by Eadric Streona), Nottingham, and so forth. Other shires took their names from existing "tribal" or political divisions, such as Norfolk and Suffolk, Devon, and Essex. The size of shires as recorded in *Domesday Book* and the so-called *County Hidage* varied (for example, 4,800 hides for Wiltshire and only 500 for Staffordshire), but in the case of the Mercian shires, the fairly regular assessment at 12,000 or 24,000 hides probably reflects their late and artificial origin. The Northumbrian shires, especially Yorkshire, were significantly larger than their southern equivalents, and were accordingly divided for administrative purposes (see below).

During the reign of Alfred, the West Saxon shires had been under the administration of an ealdorman (with two for Kent), and it was the ealdorman (later earl) and local bishop who presided over the shire court (*scirgemot*) in the mid-tenth century. By the late tenth century, however, the main administrative duties within the shire seem to have passed to one of the king's reeves known as the shire-reeve (*scirgerefa*) or "sheriff." The position of the sheriff underlines the importance of the shire court as the main instrument of royal administration of the localities, but at heart the late Anglo-Saxon shire court remained a "folk court" rather than a royal court.[11] The shire court was to meet twice a year, around Easter and Michaelmas, though a law of Cnut adds that the court could meet more often if necessary. In theory, all freemen of the shire were expected to attend, but the court's main suitors, who declared the law, were probably of wealthy status. The fact that the shire court only met twice in a year meant that, for most Englishmen from the tenth until as late as the fourteenth century, the most important unit of local administration was rather the "hundred."[12]

The Old English word *hund-red* designated both a territorial division of the shire, in theory for taxation purposes assessed at 100 hides, and also a sphere of jurisdiction in the form of the hundred court. The model hundred is said to have comprised a royal vill, an assembly place, a minster, a market place, and a judicial execution cemetery.[13] As with the shire, the hundred in its developed form is thought to have originated in Wessex and to have been imposed by Alfred's successors during the following centuries. As a consequence, there was significant variation in the size of hundreds, especially those of Wessex. Hundreds usually took their names from the assembly place where the hundred court would meet – many being old meeting places, earlier than the tenth-century hundreds themselves – and contain references to prominent natural or man-made features such as trees, hillocks, river crossings, stones, and so forth, as well as boundaries. Examples include Mutlow (in Cambridgeshire and Sussex), meaning "moot or assembly hill"; Doddingtree (Worcestershire), "Dudda's tree"; and Ossulstone (Middlesex), "Oswulf's stone." Some such sites may also have had (pagan) religious significance, such as Thurstable in Essex, meaning "the pillar of Thunor."

The hundred was by far the most widespread administrative division of the shire in late Anglo-Saxon England, but it was not the only one. The Scandinavian conquests and settlements in the north and east resulted in the development of some new divisions. In the Danelaw and Yorkshire, the main unit was the wapentake (Old English *wæpentæc* from Old Norse *vápnatak*, "a taking of weapons"), which functioned more or less like the hundred. In the larger shires of Yorkshire and Lincolnshire, there were ridings (literally "thirding" from Old Norse *þriðjungr*), which were larger than hundreds and wapentakes and, like the latter, were probably Scandinavian in origin. On the other hand, the so-called lathes of Kent, and perhaps the rapes of Sussex, probably originated much earlier as post-Roman territorial units, but had been more or less superseded by hundreds by the time of the *Domesday* survey.

We can trace the development of the hundred from tenth- and early eleventh-century royal legislation, including the short tract known as the *Hundred Ordinance* which was probably drawn up in the mid-tenth century and contains the earliest known reference to the hundred court (*hundredgemot*) and its major officer, the "hundredman." The *Hundred Ordinance* specifies that the court should meet every four weeks, that each man should do justice (*riht*) to another, and that specific days should be assigned for hearing individual cases (*EHD*, I, 430). Similar provisions occur in the laws of Edward the Elder earlier in the tenth century (II Edward 8),[14] and, although the "hundred" is not specified by name in the latter, it is likely that at least an embryonic hundred can be traced here. The *Hundred Ordinance* is primarily concerned with theft of property and the pursuit and bringing to justice of a thief and those who might aid him. It provides for following a trail into another hundred, in which case the local hundredman was to be informed and was expected to join in. The

Ordinance also refers to the "tithingman" who was in charge of a "tithing" (*teoþing*). From an earlier law of Æthelstan, we see tithings as groups of ten men organized into local "peace-guilds" (*friþgeld*), ten of which would constitute a "hundred" (VI Æthelstan; *EHD*, I, 424–5). The importance of the hundred court was reinforced in subsequent legislation, notably that of Æthelred and Cnut. Indeed, one law of Cnut specifies that no one could appeal to the king for justice, unless he had already failed to obtain it in his own hundred. The hundred thus came to be the main court for most Englishmen of the eleventh century, and was concerned with a wide variety of matters, including criminal and civil actions, as well as property transfer and disputes, and some ecclesiastical issues. Given the financial benefits attendant upon justice, it is not surprising that by 1086 many hundreds and wapentakes were in private hands.

Administrative hierarchies not dissimilar to the late Anglo-Saxon shire and hundred/ wapentake pattern probably existed in other parts of the British Isles in the same period, though the sources from the Celtic-speaking areas are relatively meager in comparison to England. For Wales, for example, there is evidence of the *cantref* and *commote* as units of administration by the central Middle Ages, though how far they can be pushed back is not clear.[15] By the twelfth and thirteenth centuries, the basic unit was the *commote* (Welsh *cwmwd*, "neighborhood"). According to the somewhat idealized pattern in the much later law tracts, four *trefi* ("farmsteads, townships") comprised one *maenol* (large estate), and 50 *trefi* (that is, 12 *maenolau* plus two *trefi* reserved for the king's use) made up one *commote*. Furthermore, 2 *commotes* (100 *trefi*) made one *cantref*. The word *cantref* literally means "100 townships" (*cant* + *tref*) and is cognate with the Gaelic *cét treb*, "100 houses," which is found in early medieval Scottish Dál Riata. It is tempting to suggest some common form of socio-economic organization underlying these two related concepts. The "numerical" parallel between the Welsh *cantref* and the English hundred, as well as the Dalriadan *cét treb*, is interesting but generally the *cantrefi* were larger than the hundreds. Indeed, the *commote* was closer in size and function to the hundred. The center of the later medieval *commote* was the *maerdref* or royal township, which comprised the royal demesne plus a *llys* or court. The *llys* was the administrative and judicial center of the *commote*, as well as the focus for food render (*gwestfa*) and labor dues. The relationship between some English royal vills and hundreds offers an interesting parallel.[16]

Scattered evidence may support the view that the *cantref* existed in some Welsh kingdoms as an administrative and ecclesiastical division as early as the ninth century.[17] The names of most later medieval *cantrefi* and *commotes* combine a personal name with a territorial suffix, and it has been suggested that, as such, they represent a kind of place-name that had ceased to be coined by about 1100.[18] To what extent these pre-Conquest units were similar in organization and function to the later *cantrefi* and *commotes* is, of course, impossible to determine. Some of these names are attested in documents of the earlier period, but as minor kingdoms and sub-kingdoms, in some cases with their own dynasties. As in England, therefore, the absorption of small polities by larger kingdoms and their redefinition as administrative divisions would appear to account for some Welsh *cantrefi*. It has been suggested that, during the eleventh century, the *cantref* was gradually replaced by the *commote* as the basic unit of administration and justice in Wales. Indeed, we have reference to the "lost" *cantref* of Dunoding (probably an earlier minor kingdom) being "replaced" by the *commotes* of Eifionydd and Ardudwy.[19]

How were these communities and localities organized internally, and in what ways were the relations between individuals controlled? It is not easy to answer these questions in any detail, though some evidence is supplied by laws and accounts of lawsuits. For England, there is a notable gap between the four surviving law codes of the seventh century (see chapter 7) and the laws of Alfred the Great of Wessex from the end of the ninth century. Alfred seems to imply that Offa of Mercia was responsible for some laws, comparable to those of Ine and Æthelberht, but as they are no longer extant we cannot be certain of their content and character. From Alfred until Cnut, however, most English kings, with a few, minor exceptions, issued at least two law codes and some, such as Æthelred the Unready, issued a greater number which were very lengthy. In addition to such codes associated with kings, whether explicitly or otherwise, there are also a number of seemingly independent legal documents which contain laws directed at a specific problem or group. One example is the so-called *Dunsæte Ordinance* which seems to have regulated the interaction between the English and Welsh on either side of a river, probably the Wye in Archenfield, Herefordshire, during the early tenth century.[20] The surviving tenth- and eleventh-century English laws were mostly composed in Old English, though some survive only as Latin translations, especially in the twelfth-century compilation known as *Quadripartitus*, and they are usually less formal than the earlier codes. The historical interpretation of these later law codes is a somewhat difficult task since it is not entirely clear what the codes represent and why they were composed. On the one hand, they are royal legislation and as such may be interpreted as evidence of royal administration in action. Thus, historians have detected in these later codes the growing direct influence of royal government in areas traditionally within the scope of the customary law of local communities.[21] For example, crimes increasingly become injuries against society and not simply against the victim and his or her kindred: this trend may be detected in the payment of fines to the king for breach of his peace (*mund*) in addition to compensation to the kindred.[22] On the other hand, some scholars have argued otherwise.[23] For example, it may be significant that the provisions of law codes are never cited in any of the surviving early medieval English lawsuits. Accordingly, it could be argued that the law codes do not reflect the reality of late Anglo-Saxon society but are essentially ideological statements by monastic reformers, like Wulfstan archbishop of York and Worcester, who in many cases probably composed the codes on behalf of the kings whose names appear in the title. No doubt, each code should be treated individually, as a particular response to specific circumstances.

While there is certainly plenty of legal material surviving from late Anglo-Saxon England, the situation is less fruitful for the Celtic-speaking areas. In Ireland, the great period of redaction of the laws was the seventh and eighth centuries:[24] after c.800, no new laws were written down but instead the existing tracts were glossed and commentated on until the sixteenth century. Irish secular law was essentially oral tradition and, while it doubtless continued to develop and evolve, we have no surviving witnesses except the conservative and often enigmatic later glosses and commentaries. It is difficult, therefore, to be certain to what extent the provisions of the seventh- and eighth-century law tracts can be taken to describe Irish law in the tenth or eleventh centuries: doubtless some practices remained more or less constant but many would have changed over time, as we know from the laws themselves.

The situation for Wales is in some respects similar, in others inverse. There are no surviving law codes from the pre-Conquest period, but there are numerous legal texts in Welsh and Latin which are preserved in a series of great compilations from the twelfth and thirteenth centuries.[25] Like the Irish laws of the seventh and eighth centuries, these texts are not royal legislation as such, but the work of lawyers for lawyers. However, these law books begin with a prologue that attributes the collection and redaction of Welsh law to the tenth-century ruler Hywel Dda ("Howel the Good"), and consequently it is thus referred to as *Cyfraith Hywel*, the Law of Hywel. While this attribution has generally been rejected by historians and must be seen as an attempt in the twelfth century to give Welsh law a legitimacy and official authority it lacked,[26] this does not mean that the extant laws were composed *ab initio* in the post-Conquest period. It seems likely that medieval Welsh law, like its Irish cousin five centuries earlier, had been developing and changing long before it came to be written down and organized into thematic tractates by professional lawyers. For example, there are sufficient textual echoes of the early eighth-century Irish ecclesiastical legal compilation *Collectio canonum Hibernensis* to suggest that it had passed to Wales, perhaps directly from Ireland into Dyfed, and had been integrated into Welsh "law" sometime between c.750 and c.1050.[27] The relevant material then re-emerges in the twelfth-century texts, superficially no different from genuinely native Welsh law. Some provisions in medieval Welsh law make sense only in an earlier context and had apparently been transmitted orally before being written down by later jurists. Historians have also compared the extant Welsh laws with earlier documents, such as the *Dunsæte Ordinance* and the "customs" (*consuetudines*) in the Herefordshire part of *Domesday Book*, to detect evidence of pre-Conquest practices. The problem faced by the historian of medieval Wales is similar to that faced by his or her Irish colleague: whereas the latter must decide how much, if at all, the provisions of seventh-century legal tracts can be used to study later Irish law and society, the former must decide how far the twelfth- and thirteenth-century laws can be extrapolated backward. In both cases, arguments must be carefully hedged and remain provisional at best.

As for Wales, no substantial legal documents have been preserved from early medieval Scotland, though some provisions in the later medieval laws may date from the earlier period. One possible exception are the *Leges inter Brettos et Scottos* which survive in their earliest form as a French translation in a manuscript of the thirteenth century, but which are probably derived from an older but now lost Gaelic text, perhaps from the eleventh century.[28] The title as well as the mixture of Gaelic, English, and Brittonic terminology would suggest that these *Leges* originated in the Scottish lowlands, perhaps the old Brittonic kingdom of Strathclyde where they had a function similar to that of the *Dunsæte Ordinance*.

In addition to law texts, lawsuits and other accounts of disputes can reveal much about the workings of communities. Again, for Anglo-Saxon England there is a relatively large amount of material surviving, though nothing comparable to that from the continent for the same period. The Celtic areas preserve very few reliable accounts of disputes, and it is therefore unclear to what extent we might generalize from the handful of disputes from Ireland and Scotland dating c.1100.[29] The case for Wales is similar but is complicated by the charters and other deeds preserved in the so-called *Book of Llandaff*, which purport to describe numerous disputes and feuds in south-east Wales dating back to the sixth century, but the authenticity and reliability of which is hotly debated by historians.[30] It is unlikely that these charters, and a handful appended to the Latin *Life of St. Cadog*, describe genuine, historical conflicts, yet they may reflect the *kinds* of dispute that occurred in eleventh or twelfth-century Wales, and perhaps earlier too: a skilful forger would hardly fabricate narrations which would have seemed unrealistic or obviously fake to his contemporary audience. If we were to ignore this charter material, then there is only one genuine record of a dispute surviving from pre-Conquest Wales.[31]

Furthermore, the relatively more voluminous and reliable Anglo-Saxon material relates almost exclusively to disputes involving, and often settled in favor of, the church and has been preserved in documents copied by religious houses. It is not always clear therefore to what extent this material, like the Llandaff charters for Wales, is representative of the many disputes and lawsuits outside the ecclesiastical sphere that have not been preserved. For example, the majority of Anglo-Saxon cases are property disputes between a religious house or a member of the clergy and another party. The fact that the church was a major landholder and that the records of these disputes were preserved initially in ecclesiastical archives cannot be coincidental. A small minority of lawsuits dealt with other offences, including the theft of moveable property, murder, sexual offences, and one case of alleged witchcraft.[32] In contrast, most of the so-called narrations in the Llandaff charters do not describe property disputes, even though a land grant invariably constitutes an element in the resolution. Instead, we find a variety of other, repeated narrative frameworks. In some cases, for example, there is an argument between a layman and a member of the church of Llandaff which becomes violent and results in the death of the clergyman. Occasionally, violence occurs in the presence of the bishop. In other instances, a layman, usually a king, breaks a peace which he had previously made with another king over the altar and relics at Llandaff. Alternatively, there are a few examples where the sanctuary of the church of Llandaff is broken and violence ensues. In all cases, the bishop of Llandaff excommunicates the perpetrator who eventually shows penance and donates land to Llandaff as part of the resolution. Almost all of these narrations involve violent acts committed against or at Llandaff, and it is likely that the church's interest stems not simply from the fact of murder but that the victim was a member of the Llandaff community or the murder took place in the church. Furthermore, these disputes are resolved by the threat of eternal damnation and, while clearly demonstrating the ideological power of the church over wayward aristocrats and kings, these narrations do not indicate how disputes in early medieval Wales which lay outside ecclesiastical concerns were resolved. Narrative sources, such as the *Anglo-Saxon Chronicle* or the Irish annals also preserve accounts of disputes, though these often involve individuals of relatively high social status and political importance and so, as with the ecclesiastical charter material, may not be entirely representative.

The feud or blood-feud is a dispute between individuals or groups of individuals, often resulting from an initial homicide, which involves violence and further killing, or the threat thereof, as one possible means of resolution. For the tenth and eleventh centuries, the greater survival of primary sources means that there are many more recorded accounts of feuds. In most cases, a feud would focus on the kinsmen of the victim as well as those of the killer. The kinsmen in question could be immediate kin. For example, in the famous feud recorded in *De Obsessione Dunelmi*, Earl Uhtred, ruler of Bamburgh, having failed to fulfill a contract against his political rival Thurbrand Hold, was later killed by Thurbrand but avenged by his son Ealdred. Ealdred, in turn, was eventually killed by Thurbrand's son Carl, despite a period of reconciliation.[33] The Irish annals specify instances of revenge (Old Irish *dígal*) being exacted by sons or brothers of murder victims. In 1007, the king of the Ulaid ("Ulster") Dub Tuinne mac Eochada, nicknamed *in Torc* ("the Boar"), was killed by Muiredach mac Matudáin *i ndighail a athar*, "in revenge for his father," and the annals do indeed record the killing of Muiredach's father, Matudán mac Domnaill, by Dub Tuinne in the same year (*AU*, I, 436–9). In both of these cases, it was the killer who became the victim of the revenge killing. Alternatively, it is possible that a killer's kinsmen could be considered valid targets by those of the victim. In the *De Obsessione Dunelmi*, many years after the death of Earl Ealdred at the hands of Carl son of Thurbrand, Ealdred's grandson, Earl Waltheof, exacted revenge by arranging for the killing of all but one of Carl's sons and all his grandsons. Here the feud had skipped a generation, and it was the descendants of the killer who were attacked. Similarly, the Irish annals record that Matudán mac Domnaill was in the church of St. Brigit at Downpatrick when he was killled by Dub Tuinne mac Eochada, and the fact that Matudán had previously killed Dub Tuinne's uncle Máel Ruanaid mac Ardgair implies that he had sought sanctuary there against possible revenge attacks. The victim's kinsmen were not the only people who could pursue a feud: a lord was expected to do so, and an eleventh-century document known as the *Cambridge Thegns' Guild* states that if the killer of a guild member refuses to pay compensation, then all members should avenge him and bear the feud (*EHD*, I, 604).

The violent pursuit of a feud, as detailed in the examples above, represented one avenue for the victim's kinsmen. Alternatively, they could seek compensation from the killer and/or his kinsmen. Both have already been discussed (see chapter 7). The fuller sources of the tenth century, at least for England, often provide additional details, and in the process remind us of the continued vigor of this system. By the tenth century in England, the *wergild* was discharged by a series of distinct payments, each made 21 days apart, paid to the victim's kin and to other interested parties.[34] First, the *healsfang* was paid to the victim's immediate family, which appears to have comprised sons, brothers, and paternal uncles (Old English *fedran*; Latin *fratres patris*).[35] Then the *manbot*, or "compensation," was paid, in this case to the victim's lord rather than the kinsmen. Next, the *fihtwite* ("fine for fighting") was paid to the king due to breach of the peace, and, finally, the rest of the *wergild* in installments. Formal payments to the king and lord indicate that the mechanics of the feud was probably changing alongside late Anglo-Saxon society and administration. The payment of the *wergild* was bilateral; that is, it could fall on both the killer's paternal and also his maternal kin, but the former were obliged to pledge two-thirds of the amount due and were clearly more important.[36]

The Celtic sources, as discussed in chapter 7, distinguish between two kinds of compensation for murder: a basic *wergild* paid on account of the act of murder and an honor-price paid as a result of the insult caused by the murder to the "honor" of the victim's kin. The earlier Irish laws describe the *éraic* (*wergild*), sometimes called *cró* (literally "blood"). The Scottish *Leges inter Brettos et Scottos* also refer to a payment called *cro* which, however, was not fixed but depended on the status of the victim. In later Welsh law, the term *galanas* ("enmity") was used for both the feud and, more often, the ensuing compensation payment.[37] Here, the *galanas* was paid to both paternal and maternal kin, and the payment was divided by a relatively complex system of "thirding" among the killer and his immediate family (one-third) and then among his paternal and maternal kinsmen (two-thirds between them, though, as in England, the paternal kinsmen paid a larger portion). The occurrence of the cognate *galnes* in the *Leges* may imply that the origins of the later medieval Welsh *galanas* could be traced to the earlier period.

In addition to the basic *wergild* payment, both the Irish and Welsh laws refer to an additional payment due to the loss of honor on the part of the victim's kin. In Ireland, this was the *log n-enech* ("value of a face"), sometimes *díre*, which, unlike the *éraic*, was determined by the status of the victim's kinsmen, and was paid bilaterally to both agnatic and cognatic kin (see chapter 7). The *Leges inter Brettos et Scottos* mention a payment called *enach*, though it is not stated explicitly whether this was a compensation for loss of honor. The equivalent in Wales was the *sarhaed* ("insult") which referred both to an insult, or injury implying insult, and to the compensation for the insult. Like the Irish *log n-enech*, the *sarhaed* was determined by the status of the victim's kinsmen. The law books have varying accounts of how the *sarhaed* was to be paid: for example, in some it was paid together with the *galanas*, in another it was divided among the victim's wife (one-third) and his brothers, cousins, and second-cousins (two-thirds); whereas in one account, it was paid to the victim's nuclear family only and was paid before the *galanas*.

In addition to issuing laws concerning *wergild* and similar payments, early medieval kings could in theory attempt to regulate the occurrence of the feud. Thus, the ninth- and tenth-century Anglo-Saxon kings issued a series of laws relating directly to feuding and, while their provisions certainly sought to control the course of a feud, no ruler went so far as to forbid the feud outright.[38] The implication may be that the feud continued to be seen by society as an acceptable, though violent, means of disputing. The kings were, however, clearly concerned to limit the spread of violence by imposing certain rules about how and when a feud could be legitimately pursued, and by reducing the necessary involvement of kinsmen. The laws of Alfred the Great, for example, state that a man cannot attack an opponent who is at home "before he asks for justice for himself" (*EHD*, I, 415). Even when justice has not been done by less violent methods, the opponent is permitted to be "besieged" in his home unmolested for seven days and, should he then surrender himself, must remain unharmed for a further 30 days. A man unable to besiege his opponent should seek the support of the ealdorman and, failing that, of the king before resorting to violence. Alfred also stressed that a man may fight on behalf of his lord or kinsman, or if his opponent has committed certain sexual offences, without incurring a vendetta (Alfred 42.5–7; *EHD*, I, 415). Later on, Æthelstan regulated that kindred could expel particularly troublesome members (III Æthelstan 6),[39] which may have served to reduce the obligations of kinsmen during feuds. This was certainly the aim of King Edmund (939–46) in his code on blood-feud.

Edmund's code opens by stating the king's desire for peace and concord within his dominions, and describing his distress at "the illegal [*unrihtlican*] and manifold conflicts [*gefeoht*]" which were occurring (*EHD*, I, 428). These conflicts were presumably not simply blood-feuds (*fæhþe*), as the code proceeds to regulate feuding and does not declare them "illegal" as such. Edmund states that a killer must carry (*wege*) a feud himself or pay compensation within 12 months, with the help of his kinsmen (*freond*). However, his kindred are permitted to abandon him and refuse to pay compensation, as long as they no longer harbor him, and they cannot be attacked in revenge by the victim's kinsmen. As well as seeking thus to limit the outbreak and spread of a feud, this code, and the associated tract known as *Wer*,[40] also describe carefully the procedure for settling existing feuds, through mediation by the "leading men" (*witan*, probably not "council" in this context) with reference to the law (*folcriht*). It is interesting to note that the one certainly genuine Welsh dispute from the pre-Conquest period, preserved in the *Lichfield Gospels*, was resolved by the "goodmen" (*degion*).[41] This evidence highlights the role of local notables, rather than "professional" judges, in the settlement of disputes and feuds during this period.

The tenth and eleventh centuries marked a period of transition in the organization and administration of Britain and Ireland, and this was apparent in the nature of local communities, especially in the development of new administrative hierarchies and the growing reach of royal government in the localities. On the other hand, we should not ignore the degree of continuity that was characteristic of this period: despite the claims of royal charters and laws, the persistence of violent disputing, indeed its acceptance in many law codes, indicates that for many people in pre-Conquest Britain and Ireland, many aspects of everyday life remained relatively stable.

Notes

1 Fletcher, *Latin Redaction A of the Law of Hywel*, pp. 66–7.
2 Pelteret, *Slavery*.
3 Liebermann (ed.), *Die Gesetze*, I, 444–53.
4 Seebohm, *Tribal Custom in Anglo-Saxon Law*, pp. 307–18.
5 Stenton, *Anglo-Saxon England*, p. 507.
6 Bowden et al., "Excavating past population structures"; Goodacre et al., "Genetic evidence."
7 McEvoy et al., "The scale and nature of Viking settlement."
8 Barrow, *Kingdom of the Scots*, pp. 7–68.
9 Cameron, *English Place Names*, p. 51.
10 Taylor, "The origin of the Mercian shires."
11 Wormald, "Charters, law and the settlement of disputes," p. 162.
12 Gelling, *Signposts to the Past*, p. 209; Loyn, "The hundred in the tenth and early eleventh centuries."
13 Reynolds, *Later Anglo-Saxon England*, pp. 75–81.
14 Liebermann (ed.), *Die Gesetze*, I, 144–5.
15 Davies, *Conquest, Coexistence and Change*, pp. 20–3.
16 Sawyer, "The royal *tun*," pp. 281–5.
17 Charles-Edwards, "The seven bishop-houses of Dyfed."
18 Richards, "Early Welsh territorial suffixes."
19 Jones and Jones (trans.), *The Mabinogion*, p. 68.
20 Gelling, *West Midlands in the Early Middle Ages*, pp. 113–14; Thorpe, *Ancient Laws and Institutes of England*, pp. 352–7, 518–20.
21 For example, the late Patrick Wormald in his *The Making of English Law*.
22 Stafford, "King and kin," pp. 22–5.
23 Hyams, "Feud and the state in late Anglo-Saxon England."
24 Charles-Edwards, "Early Irish law"; Kelly, *Guide to Early Irish Law*.
25 Charles-Edwards, *The Welsh Laws*.
26 Pryce, "The prologues to the Welsh lawbooks."
27 Pryce, "Early Irish canons."
28 Loth, "Persistance des institutions"; Seebohm, *Tribal Custom in Anglo-Saxon Law*, pp. 307–18; Woolf, *From Pictland to Alba*, pp. 346–9.

29 Sharpe, "Dispute settlement in medieval Ireland."
30 Maund, "Fact and narrative fiction."
31 Jenkins and Owen, "The Welsh marginalia . . . part 2."
32 Wormald, "A handlist of Anglo-Saxon lawsuits."
33 Morris, *Marriage and Murder*, pp. 2–4, 20–2.
34 *EHD*, I, 429; Liebermann (ed.), *Die Gesetze*, I, 392–3 (*Wer* 4, 6).
35 Liebermann (ed.), *Die Gesetze*, I, 392–3 (*Wer* 5).
36 Ibid. (*Wer* 3).
37 Charles-Edwards, *Early Irish and Welsh Kinship*, pp. 181–200.
38 Hyams, "Feud and the state"; Wormald, "Giving God and king their due."
39 Liebermann (ed.), *Die Gesetze*, I, 170.
40 Liebermann (ed.), *Die Gesetze*, I, 392–5.
41 Evans and Rhys (ed.), *Liber Landavensis*, p. xliii; Jenkins and Owen, "The Welsh marginalia . . . part 2."

Further Reading

For discussion of early medieval law, see T. M. Charles-Edwards, *The Welsh Laws*, Fergus Kelly, *A Guide to Early Irish Law*, and Patrick Wormald, *The Making of English Law*; also, T. M. Charles-Edwards, *Early Irish and Welsh Kinship*. On disputes and the blood-feud, see the papers in Wendy Davies and Paul Fouracre (eds.), *The Settlement of Disputes in Early Medieval Europe* (Cambridge, 1986), and, more recently, Paul Hyams, *Rancor and Reconciliation in Medieval England: Wrong and its Redress from the Tenth to Thirteenth Centuries* (Ithaca, 2003).

Bibliography

Barrow, G. W. S., *The Kingdom of the Scots: Government, Church and Society from the Eleventh to the Fourteenth Century*, 2nd edn. (Edinburgh, 2003).

Bowden, G. R., Balaresque, P., King, T. E., et al., "Excavating past population structures by surname-based sampling: the genetic legacy of the Vikings in northwest England," *Molecular Biology and Evolution*, 25: 2 (2008), 301–9.

Cameron, K., *English Place Names* (London, 1996).

Charles-Edwards, T. M., "Early Irish law," in D. Ó Cróinín (ed.), *A New History of Ireland*, vol. 1: *Prehistoric and Early Ireland* (Oxford, 2005), pp. 331–70.

Charles-Edwards, T. M., *Early Irish and Welsh Kinship* (Oxford, 1993).

Charles-Edwards, T. M., "The seven bishop-houses of Dyfed," *Bulletin of the Board of Celtic Studies*, 24 (1970–2), 247–62.

Charles-Edwards, T. M., *The Welsh Laws* (Cardiff, 1989).

Cyril, H., *The Danelaw* (London, 1992).

Davies, R. R., *Conquest, Coexistence and Change: Wales 1063–1415* (Oxford, 1987).

Duncan, A. A. M., *Scotland: The Making of the Kingdom* (Edinburgh, 1975).

Evans, J. G. and Rhys, J. (eds.), *Liber Landavensis: The Text of the Book of Llan Dav* (Aberystwyth, 1979).

Fletcher, I. F., *Latin Redaction A of the Law of Hywel* (Aberystwyth, 1986).

Gelling, M., *Signposts to the Past: Place-names and the History of England* (London, 1978).

Gelling, M., *The West Midlands in the Early Middle Ages* (Leicester, 1992).

Goodacre, S., Helgason, A., Nicholson, J., et al., "Genetic evidence for a family-based Scandinavian settlement of Shetland and Orkney during the Viking periods," *Heredity*, 95 (2005), 129–35.

Hyams, P. R., "Feud and the state in late Anglo-Saxon England," *Journal of British Studies*, 40: 1 (2001), 1–43.

Jenkins, D. and Owen, M. E., "The Welsh marginalia in the Lichfield Gospels, part 2: the 'surexit' memorandum," *Cambridge Medieval Celtic Studies*, 7 (1984), 91–120.

Jones, G. and Jones, T. (trans.), *The Mabinogion* (London, 1974).

Kelly, F., *A Guide to Early Irish Law* (Dublin, 1988).

Liebermann, F. (ed.), *Die Gesetze der Angelsachsen*, 3 vols. (Halle, 1903–16).

Loth, J., "Persistance des institutions et de la langue des Brittons du Nord (ancien royaume de Stratclut), au 12e siècle," *Revue Celtique*, 47 (1930), 383–400.

Loyn, H. R., *The Governance of Anglo-Saxon England 500–1087* (London, 1984).

Loyn, H. R., "The hundred in the tenth and early eleventh centuries," in H. Hearder and H. R. Loyn (eds.), *British Government and Administration: Studies Presented to S. B. Chrimes* (Cardiff, 1974), pp. 1–15.

Mac Airt, S. and Mac Niocaill, G. (eds. and trans.), *The Annals of Ulster (to AD 1131)*, Part I: *Text and Translation* (Dublin, 1983).

McEvoy, B., Brady, C., Moore, L. T., et al., "The scale and nature of Viking settlement in Ireland from Y-chromosome admixture analysis," *European Journal of Human Genetics*, 14 (2006), 1288–94.

Maund, K. L., "Fact and narrative fiction in the Llandaff charters," *Studia Celtica*, 31 (1997), 173–93.

Morris, C. J., *Marriage and Murder in Eleventh-century Northumbria: A Study of "De Obsessione Dunelmi,"* University of York, Borthwick Paper, no. 82 (York, 1992).

Pelteret, D. A. E., *Slavery in Early Mediaeval England: From the Reign of Alfred until the Twelfth Century* (Woodbridge, 1995).

Pryce, H., "Early Irish canons and medieval Welsh law," *Peritia*, 5 (1986), 107–27.

Pryce, H., "The prologues to the Welsh lawbooks," *Bulletin of the Board of Celtic Studies*, 33 (1986), 151–87.

Reynolds, A., *Later Anglo-Saxon England: Life and Landscape* (Stroud, 1999).

Richards, M., "Early Welsh territorial suffixes," *Journal of the Royal Society of Anquities of Ireland*, 95 (1965), 205–12.

Sawyer, P. H., "The royal *tun* in pre-Conquest England," in P. Wormald, D. Bullough, and R. Collins (eds.), *Ideal and Reality in Frankish and Anglo-Saxon Society* (Oxford, 1983), pp. 273–99.

Seebohm, F., *Tribal Custom in Anglo-Saxon Law* (London, 1911).

Sharpe, R., "Dispute settlement in medieval Ireland: a preliminary inquiry," in W. Davies and P. Fouracre (eds.), *The Settlement of Disputes in Early Medieval Europe* (Cambridge, 1986), pp. 169–89.

Stafford, P., "King and kin, lord and community: England in the tenth and eleventh centuries," in P. Stafford (ed.), *Gender, Family and the Legitimation of Power: England from the Ninth to Early Twelfth Century* (Aldershot, 2006).

Stenton, F. M., *Anglo-Saxon England*, 3rd edn. (Oxford, 1971).

Taylor, C. S., "The origin of the Mercian shires," in H. R. P. Finberg (ed.), *Gloucestershire Studies* (Leicester, 1957), pp. 17–45.

Thorpe, B., *Ancient Laws and Institutes of England*, 2 vols. (London, 1840).

Whitelock, D. (ed. and trans.), *English Historical Documents*, vol. I: *c.500–1042*, 2nd edn. (London, 1979).

Woolf, A., *From Pictland to Alba 789–1070* (Edinburgh, 2007).

Wormald, P., "Charters, law and the settlement of disputes in Anglo-Saxon England," in W. Davies and P. Fouracre (eds.), *The Settlement of Disputes in Early Medieval Europe* (Cambridge, 1986), pp. 149–68.

Wormald, P., "Giving God and king their due: conflict and its resolution in the early English state," *Settimane di studio del centro italiano di studi sull'alto medioevo*, 44 (1997), 549–90.

Wormald, P., "A handlist of Anglo-Saxon lawsuits," *Anglo-Saxon England*, 17 (1988), 247–81.

Wormald, P., *The Making of English Law: King Alfred to the Twelfth Century, vol. I: Legislation and its Limits* (Oxford, 1999).

CHAPTER TWENTY-EIGHT

Queens and Queenship

PAULINE STAFFORD

In 1067, Margaret, great-niece of King Edward the Confessor, granddaughter and great-granddaughter, respectively, of the English kings, Edmund Ironside and Æthelred II, fled north to Scotland. She was accompanied by her brother, Edgar the Ætheling, a significant claimant on the English throne which had recently been taken by the Norman conqueror William. On her arrival in Scotland, she was married to Máel Coluim III, succeeding if not replacing his earlier wife, Ingibjorg. She and Máel Coluim went on to produce sons, who became kings of the Scots, whilst one of their daughters, Edith/Mathilda, married King Henry I, himself the son of the Norman William – a marriage which Henry eagerly sought and which involved Edith/Mathilda's consecration as queen. Margaret is the first wife of a king of the Scots about whom much can be known, and we are ostensibly very well informed about her, thanks to a *Life* produced for that same daughter by Margaret's own former chaplain, Turgot, a monk of Durham. The *Life* tells of Margaret bringing new manners to the Scottish court. It presents her as a concerned mother of her children, a mistress of Máel Coluim's household, and a church reformer – one who held her own in church councils. It gives a moving account of her death, only four days after the murders of her husband and son on a raid into Northumbria, though it does not tell us of the succession struggle that followed, between her husband's brother, Donald, and the son of his first wife, Donnchad.[1]

Margaret's life highlights many of the themes that historians involved in the study of early medieval royal women now see as significant: the importance of a marriage that transmitted blood claims on the English throne to her descendants if not her husband; her role as a mother; the complexity of a succession where claims were still open, and where the sons of different mothers struggled against each other. These are common elements of a politics that has been characterized as "family politics,"[2] a type of politics in which women could and did play roles, active as well as passive; roles that brought significant dangers as well as opportunities. Such family politics were enmeshed with those of the household or court, which functioned as the political center of the kingdom. "Public" and "private" were not, at this date, defined and separated in our modern sense.[3] Neither were "church" and "state," at least not as they came to be in later centuries, and the court was the legitimate forum for much ecclesiastical politics. Margaret's involvement in such questions is certainly not unique in broader early medieval context, though its nature, at least as presented in her *Life*, is remarkable. The sudden illumination provided by the *Life* underlines the source problems that beset this period in general, including questions of genre, in this case hagiography. Scarcity of sources is especially marked in the study of its women. The consecration of Margaret's daughter, however, is more specifically a result of developments in queenship occurring since the ninth century.

This chapter will focus on queens. It is almost exclusively concerned with queens in the sense of the sexual partners of kings. While sometimes it means the mother of the current ruler, it does not, for the most part, include regnant queens. The latter are women who ruled as kings in their own right; there were very few of them in the early Middle Ages. The general approach of this volume has been to incorporate discussion of women within thematic or chronological chapters. This chapter is unusual in its isolation of one group. The rationale for this difference is the upsurge of interest in this category of women in recent historiography, which merits specific attention. It is also designed to balance the dominant place occupied by kings and kingship in the volume as a whole. If there are questions about kingship, and its parallel or divergent development across Britain and Ireland, there are equally those about queenship – in some ways more intransigent.

In spite of recent interest, it will become apparent that the pattern of historiography differs between England, on the one hand, and the rest of Britain and Ireland, on the other. Far more attention has been paid to English queens than to those of Ireland, Wales, or Scotland. In part at least, these differences reflect the volume of sources available, though there are also important historiographical differences. A body of older work on Irish queens – from, for example, Thurneysen through the important studies by Proinsias Mac Cana to, most recently, Enright – is characterized by the approaches of a comparative philology, often utilizing insights from comparative religion, applied to literary sources.[4] The emphasis on queens as goddess figures in much Irish historiography is a result of this. As we shall see, important work is now beginning on Irish queens, though there is still considerable scope for study of the literary sources. That study may not so much reveal timeless, if not archaic, mythology, as the historical and changing conditions of royal women.

Sources

Beginning with Margaret's *Life* may have raised false hopes about the nature, if not quantity, of source material available. There are a number of *Lives* of queens marked out for sanctity,[5] but they are not common, and surviving ones from Britain and Ireland are rare at this date. Precious as it is, the *Life* is nonetheless a source to be used with care, since it is written within the conventions of hagiography. Among its complex functions, Margaret's *Life* may have provided, if not been designed to provide, a "Mirror of Princesses/Queens" for her daughter, analogous to the "Mirror of Princes/Kings," such as Asser's *Life of King Alfred*.[6] It is also a saint's life, and in this respect parallels that of Margaret's uncle, King Edward the Confessor, the *Life of King Edward who Rests at Westminster*, written only a generation or so earlier.[7] This latter text was also produced for a woman, in this case another queen, Edward's widow, Edith. It is one of two important texts commissioned by English queens in the eleventh century, the other being the so-called *Encomium Emmae Reginae* written for Queen Emma.[8] It may be no accident that these three texts were produced now, after what seems to have been a period of significant development in English queenship. It is also no accident that the latter two, at least, were produced in the context of a succession dispute.

Tenth- and eleventh-century England is relatively well served by sources for the study of queens. The aforementioned narrative works can be studied alongside much incidental reference in Latin and vernacular sources, and especially in conjunction with substantial charter material. Charters not only provide evidence of queens' lands and some details of patronage and other involvement in the politics of landholding, they also include witness lists. Queens, virtually alone among women, appear in the witness lists of English royal charters. Their appearances here have been used to chart their fluctuating political significance. In addition, there is a body of texts relevant to the inauguration of queens. By contrast, we know very little about Scottish royal women before Margaret, and what we do have is largely from Irish annals. Typically, these are notices of marriages, like that of Máel Muire, sister of Custantin son of Cinaed to Áed, king of the northern Uí Néill. Although such references appear "sparse" by some standards,[9] they are rich by comparison with the surprisingly few references to women, royal or other, in English annals.[10] Both Welsh and Irish annals provide some information about royal women, often in a genealogical context or with genealogical details which underscore their significance in marriage alliance and for the claims of their husbands and sons. One Irish text, *Banshenchas*, has an almost unique status as a text devoted to royal women, and it is beginning to receive the serious attention it deserves.[11] Once again, the text concentrates on women as wives, or especially as mothers – in this case of kings of Tara. It is clear that Irish annals, like the vernacular literary sources, have much still to offer for the study of queens.

Where references to women are so sparse, there is mileage to be gained in careful exploration of the few who are included, not only for empirical data, but for an understanding of the factors that have led to that inclusion.[12] New ways of reading the sources, often against the grain, have been important to advances in the history of early medieval women. A particular challenge as well as a mode of reading have recently emerged from the burgeoning field of gender studies. The roles and relations of men and women, it is argued, are of central social and psychological significance in all societies. As a result, female, if not male, figures can carry symbolic meanings, both in texts, and in the wider thought-world that produced those texts.

This might be considered most useful in the study of overtly literary or mythological texts. The legendary Irish queen Medb, for example, with her many husbands, should not be interpreted simply as a sign of early Irish promiscuity and certainly not necessarily as an indication of ruling queens. Rather, she symbolized the transfer of kingship through the metaphor of marriage. In the eleventh-century Irish tract *Baile in Scáil*, she bestowed the cup of sovereignty on successive kings. By this date, she did not choose her partners herself – as she seems to have done in possibly earlier versions of her story – but was instructed by the king-god Lug, a demotion which, as Máire Herbert has argued, is perhaps to be linked to the disputed emergence of the powerful tenth- and eleventh-century overkings in Ireland.[13] Political myth here, as always, responded to changing political situations. In the story of Medb, the metaphor for the transmission of kingship is of marriage, and Medb herself is a symbolic woman. But such symbolic women may appear in texts more conventionally categorized as historical. Thus, it could be argued, the reference to Margaret herself in the *Anglo-Saxon Chronicle* entry for 1067 needs to be read with the symbolic meanings of women in mind: she, King Harold's mother Gytha, and William's wife Mathilda all appear in the same entry, and represent to some extent the respective fates of English and Norman in the wake of 1066.[14] Some recent literary work has produced subtle readings questioning whether representations of queens tell us anything about queens or women, as opposed to the role of gender in the Anglo-Saxon cultural matrix.[15]

Such awareness can and will enrich our reading of sources. But these symbolic meanings were themselves deeply rooted in the social realities of the politics of marriage, blood claims, and succession. In the story of Medb, the metaphor for the transmission of kingship is marriage. Marriage was a sort of contract, and it may be this that makes it an appropriate parallel to the relationship between king and people. Medb may be a symbolic woman, but she is surely also a reminder of the significance of women and marriage in claims to rule, to which we shall return.

As so often in this volume, the divergent nature of the surviving sources makes comparisons difficult. In particular, the survival of a range of English documentation concerning landholding shows us queens, and other women, involved and active; the almost total absence of such documentation from elsewhere in Britain and Ireland may produce a false contrast. *Domesday Book* similarly provides an opportunity to reconstruct a queen's estate, household, and land-based influence in a detail virtually unparalleled in the western European Middle Ages, let alone in early medieval Wales, Scotland, or Ireland. It is thus salutary to remark that a common theme links much of the evidence, however fragmentary. It is often in the context of sources concerned with the politics of family, household, and inheritance that royal women appear; their appearance here, and elsewhere, is a reminder that far more of early medieval politics was about family, household, and inheritance than has sometimes been recognized.

Family Politics and Household

There were few women who ruled in their own right anywhere in early medieval Europe. Normally speaking, women were excluded from rule by their sex. Royal blood created a pool of candidates for kingship, but other norms affected choice within that pool. Male sex was a universally necessary qualification, even where claims might be transmitted by women. In early Ireland, there are clear statements of the general perception of women's incapacity, which extended to rule. So *vir* (man) comes from *virtus*, meaning strength – for "making war, working, defending, ruling and public speaking." Woman, *mulier*, is from *mollitia* meaning "fragility, weakness, lowliness and subjection."[16] Isidore of Seville is one source for these commonly held ideas. There are, however, rare cases of women ruling kingdoms. In Wessex, for example, in the seventh century, Queen Seaxburh appears to have ruled for one year. Her reign was noted in the regnal lists and in the later *Anglo-Saxon Chronicle* under the year 672. But, as here, such rule seems to have been as widows or queen-mother/regents; the *Chronicle* explicitly states that "In this year Cenwealh died, and his queen Seaxburh reigned one year after him." Seaxburh's rule has elements of regency during a contested period in West Saxon succession politics.[17]

The most famous example of a women ruling in any part of Britain or Ireland at this date is Æthelflæd, wife of the last ruler of Mercia. She took over from her husband on his death in the early tenth century and ruled Mercia for seven years. She is recorded as directing military campaigns, paralleling those of her brother, Edward the Elder, and that record comes from a chronicle or source that may have been produced at her court. At her death in 918, her daughter, Ælfwynn, was briefly accepted by some Mercians as their ruler.[18] These events have to be seen in the context of the very delicate political balance between Wessex and Mercia in the first half of the tenth century, which was secured by dynastic alliance. Æthelflæd was the sister of the West Saxon king, Edward the Elder, and both were children of Alfred. Fear of West Saxon domination may have been sufficient to produce acceptance of female rule in parts of Mercia in 918, but it is also likely that her rule represents the aspirations of the Mercian elite to power within the new polity of Wessex-cum-Mercia/Southumbria. It is also testimony to the significance of queenship in Mercia at this date (see below).

If women rarely ruled in their own right, they appear to have been able to transmit the all-important royal blood that carried claims, though the evidence is mostly indirect; that is, it consists of the importance of marriage to kings' daughters – or in some cases widows – in the transfer of the throne to men who were not sons of the previous king. Only in earlier Pictish kingship is there any suggestion of matriliny – the transmission of blood claims from male to male via the mother – though the realities of that have been much discussed. This alleged matriliny may differ more in degree than in kind from the legitimating functions of marriage to royal women elsewhere.[19] Marriage to a royal widow – who was often herself a king's daughter – seems to have been a key way in which Irish royal claims were cemented (see chapters 16 and 17). In Wales, where at least in the view of the (later) customary laws, women were excluded from inheritance, the daughters of kings appear to have transmitted claims to their husbands. Thus, Hywel Dda's rule in Dyfed involved marriage to Elen, daughter of Llywarch of Dyfed; the "intrusive" King Llywelyn of Gwynedd married Angharad, daughter of Maredudd, king of Gwynedd and Dyfed. The great Rhodri's wide rule was legitimized by, if not solely built on, his own marriage to Angharad, daughter of Meurig of Ceredigion, and on his female ancestry, via his mother Nest, daughter of Cadell of Powys and his grandmother who brought the blood of Gwynedd kings. If we begin from the idea of legitimating marriages and female royal blood, Welsh "intrusive" kings do not look all that different from Pictish matriliny. The historical "Lady Macbeth" was a woman of royal birth, married for the blood she brought.[20] It was thus no novel practice for the Scottish king Máel Coluim to take as his second wife, Margaret, the lineal descendant of the tenth-century English kings, after the Norman Conquest of England, thereby creating claims on the English throne for his male descendants. The Norman king, Henry I, was all too aware of the claims, and one way to neutralize them, when, soon after his accession, he took the daughter of Máel Coluim and Margaret as his wife. At periods of dynastic uncertainty, and also of struggle for the throne between dynasties, as in England after 1066, the blood brought by the mother could be particularly important. That may well have been a factor in elevating the status of queens (see below), here seen as heir-bearing consorts.

These functions of marriage, and of women, are just one indication of the importance of what has been called "family politics" at this date. The early Middle Ages was a period of intensely personal rule by kings, throughout these islands, and of hereditary transmission of that rule – though not necessarily directly from father to son. Succession to the throne was a central political question, which drew into itself other political issues and factions. The king's relationships with other family members, his sons but also the wider kin-group, were a crucial part of politics in the sense of the management of relationships critical to power. Relatives were potential claimants, or the potential progenitors of claimants, but also, as kin, potential allies. The general significance of family ties in early medieval society is underlined by the social practice of pro-parenthood, or fictive kinship. Fosterage or godparenthood was an important way of making or keeping allies. At royal as at other levels, the household was often the place where such fictive kinsfolk lived.

The royal household or court was in every sense a political place. This included its role in linking the king and his family outward. Surrounding the king, it took its place at the center of the kingdom. Alfred's idealized household was conceived as the place to which men journeyed from far and wide. The sons of nobles could be fostered – or held hostage – there. Alfred is described as loving such boys "as his own children."[21] A period of formative, personal development close to the king combined with strong notions of kinship ties and reciprocity to bind the ideal relationships that should result. The household was the place where royal power was displayed, where the gifts on which it relied were exchanged, where the relationships on which it depended were cemented.[22] Far more than the battlefield or the raiding party, the household was a sphere where women could play a role.

The king's wife – or mother – had, at least potentially, an important part in the royal household. The Welsh tractates give the queen a formalized position and duties there. These tractates are late, as we now have them, and may reflect later practice,[23] but eleventh-century Welsh praise poems refer to mistresses of households along with their lords. An early eleventh-century elegy for Aeddon, lord of Mynydd Bodefon, Anglesey, recalled the days when he and his wife Llyny ruled the household.[24] This is a noble not a royal household, but the *Mabinogi* give royal women a comparable role in court life. Margaret's idealized portrayal in her *Life* presents her in the midst of "the tumult of lawsuits . . . the manifold cares of rule," and multiplying "the ornaments of the royal hall" so that the royal table and house glittered with reflections of gold and silver.[25] Margaret's mid-eleventh-century English aunt-in-law, Queen Edith, is also portrayed in the *Life* of Edward at the heart of the court, and, like Margaret, as responsible for the suitable presentation of the king in this all-important context. Idealized portraits like these, however, too readily iron out differences. How simply can the Scottish royal household of c.1100, for example, be compared with the mid-eleventh-century English one of the half-Norman Edward, the latter in contact with Ottonian imperial practice? Future work certainly needs to consider more carefully the varieties of royal household, and whether and how this has an impact on the sphere and nature of the activity of queens.

The picture of Margaret amid the lawsuits and cares of rule need not, however, be entirely dismissed as hyperbole. English queens of the tenth and eleventh centuries were certainly involved in hearing legal cases; wills were declared to Queen Emma, and, after the Norman Conquest, William I's queen, Mathilda, sat in judgment in a case in Worcestershire.[26] The royal household's functions at the heart of the kingdom meant that if a woman sat at the king's side there – whether his wife or mother – she might well fulfill such roles. But again, such fragmentary sources need careful handling. Tenth- and eleventh-century England experienced, as we shall see, significant developments in queenship. It is thus dangerous to fill out fragmentary Welsh, Scottish, or Irish evidence with English detail – at least until that evidence has been thoroughly studied and contextualized. And we cannot assume that courts always and everywhere provided a sphere for female activity, let alone for the same type of activity.

One of the most striking elements in the portrait of Margaret is the role she is given in ecclesiastical affairs, including setting up and speaking at councils. In one of them, she took a leading part as a proponent of new "reformed" practices in the Scottish church "like another Helena."[27] Margaret's concern with ecclesiastical affairs has parallels throughout early medieval Europe. It derived from a royal household where, as in early medieval politics more generally, ecclesiastical and secular should not be sharply differentiated. It also drew on long-standing models of Christian queenship dating back, as this simile confirms, to Helena, mother of Constantine. But the extent of Margaret's role, as presented here, was remarkable. It is rooted in general patterns of early medieval politics, but it may have drawn inspiration from the alliances and interactions of English queens and churchmen, reforming or not, in the tenth and eleventh centuries, and to the advancing notions of queenship that they fostered.[28] It may also be contextually specific to a late eleventh-century world in which reformers such as Anselm, archbishop of Canterbury, worked closely with high-ranking women like Adela of Blois, daughter of William I and sister-in-law of Margaret's own daughter.[29]

But Margaret also recalls the queens and royal women of the conversion age in England, women like Æthelburh, the Kentish bride of King Edwin of Northumbria, or Osthryth, daughter of King Oswiu, who married a Mercian ruler. Such women played important parts in court-centered conversion and Christianization. But the foreignness of both in-marrying wife and religious practice readily combined to make them potential objects of suspicion and resentment in their new homes. Such women, like Margaret, were vulnerable, especially as widows. Æthelburh fled Northumbria after Edwin's death, and Osthryth was murdered by Mercian nobles.[30] Margaret's death, four days after that of her husband and eldest son, pre-empted such a fate. The family and court-centered politics of the early Middle Ages could be violent, and women had no automatic protection in them. Indeed, their status as women placed by marriage between families could leave them especially exposed.

Both the risks and the potential of women's place in familial politics is nowhere more obvious than in the whole area of succession. The deaths of Margaret's husband, Máel Coluim, and son unleashed a succession struggle between Máel Coluim's brother Donald and Donnchad, Máel Coluim's older son by his first wife, Ingibjorg. That struggle was both usual at this date, throughout Britain and Ireland, and foreseeable. Succession to the throne is at the heart of early medieval politics: anticipation of it, provision for it, and struggle to achieve it, whether before or after a king's death. Strict rules determining the heir to the throne were rare. Norms existed: claimants should be male, usually of royal blood, older family members were often preferred to younger. There were also strong arguments in favor of adult rulers, which meant that there was as much reason for fraternal (i.e. brother to brother) as vertical (i.e. father to son) succession. In some areas, especially parts of Ireland, practice and norms favored candidates who would alternate between different segments of a royal dynasty. But everywhere, these were norms and arguments, not strict rules of succession, and all contained room for maneuver. New situations could empower particular arguments whilst not overriding others. Arguments for division or joint rule, for example, were always possible since all (male at least) family members had some claims, sons of the previous ruler often strongest of all. The Norman Conquest of 1066, by joining England and Normandy, opened up the possibility of providing for two sons, and thus fostered the sort of dissension we see among the sons of William I. That same possibility had played a central role in English politics throughout the tenth and eleventh centuries, from the inception of the joint rule of Wessex and Mercia c.925, and fraternal rivalries surfaced bitterly in the 970s and 1030s. The Danish conquest of 1016 added a new ruling family to complicate English succession arguments.

It must be stressed that early medieval succession to the throne was neither an anarchic free for all, nor irrational. It is not obvious, for example, at a date when kings ruled in the fullest sense, that automatic father–son succession is a better system than practices that involve an element of choice among suitable candidates. The uncertainties of such practices, however, did ensure that the making of that choice was a central political question. This meant that it was also one that, because it produced arguments, alignments, and even factions, drew other political questions into itself. Succession was, however, centrally a question of inheritance, and thus a legitimately family affair. It stood at the heart of family politics, and women often stood there with it.

Marriage and women have been seen as playing a crucial part in managing, and contesting, Irish succession. Máire Herbert, for example, has suggested that, for the ninth and tenth centuries at least, marriage was a central mechanism in the alternating succession of the Uí Néill: "In the context of Irish regnal politics, marriage exchange of royal daughters evidently facilitated smooth alternation of power between the northern and southern Uí Néill, while taking of a predecessor's wife seems to indicate forced rather than consensual alternation."[31] The precise context here was Áed Findliath's aggressive reassertion of older alternating patterns when he took Máel Séchnaill's widow, whilst at Áed's death, Máel Séchnaill's son, Flann took Áed's widow, Máel Muire, daughter of the Scottish king, Cinaed. Máire Herbert both confirms the essentially political nature of royal marriage decisions at this date and alerts us to the need to look carefully at different marriage patterns. Marriage as a social practice is a rich and powerful matrix. The union of husband and wife contains potential elements of equality and partnership alongside subordination and domination. The giving and receiving of wives means that marriage partakes in all the complexity of gift-exchange. The new stage of the family that marriage begins has implications for inheritance and property transmission. The study of varying patterns and meanings of royal marriages still has much to offer. Those noted by Paul Fouracre, Jinty Nelson, and Simon MacLean between Britain and the continent (see chapters 9, 15, and 22) are clearly part of "international" or at least inter-kingdom relations, and need careful reading for changes and shifting balances in these. Irish ones involving, for example, the women of Osraige, discussed by Edel Bhreathnach (see chapter 17), flag the importance of Osraige as a kingdom between the territories of the northern and southern Uí Néill. The "noblewomen" married by tenth-century southern English kings would certainly repay more scrutiny, not least in the light of

Julia Crick's comments on the nature of nobility (see chapter 25). In some cases, at least, those "noblewomen" represented segments of the West Saxon ruling dynasty, in others of older Mercian royal lines.

It is more difficult to determine the impact of such politically important marriages on the women themselves. Máel Muire, wife successively of Flann and Áed, is one of the "sparse category" of royal women who have obits in the Irish annals. That prominence no doubt reflects a significance derived first from her birth and then from her importance as a royal widow. One can only speculate exactly what any of this meant for Máel Muire herself. The vulnerability of women like Æthelburh and Osthryth is a warning that the sort of relations between kings that led to marriages in the first place, could also place the brides in danger should those relations shift, or should other groups within a kingdom disapprove. Margaret died opportunely days after her husband and son; one can only wonder how far the stories of her death not only established her saintly piety, but also answered claims of a darker fate. But marriage could offer opportunities. It made a woman the wife of a king, and perhaps the mistress of his household. But it could also make her mother of sons who were possible future claimants on the throne. This gave her a potential place in the politics of succession, the maximum outcome of which could be regency.

Many kings at this date, throughout Britain and Ireland, were dedicated serial monogamists. Their wives may not always have been secure players in, let alone foci for, political groupings. The accession, or designation, of a son, however, made clear which royal wife was to be the king's mother. This was a unique position. The mother of a known and designated heir has the secure position that enhances her political significance, as appears from comparable situations in other cultures.[32] Some of the sources behind the Irish *Banshenchas* listed only those wives who became mothers of kings, perhaps influenced by the Old Testament Book of Kings. It is difficult to know what such recognition meant for these women, partly because it is unclear whether it is retrospective or represents a position acknowledged during their lifetimes. In late eighth-century Mercia, the situation is clearer. Offa of Mercia forefronted his wife Cynethryth as part of his attempt to designate their son.[33] But even where the identity of the next heir is more debatable, a very common situation at this date, mothers may still be of great significance as supporters of their sons, including when practice favored the succession of adult males. The most high-profile example of this is the career of Queen Emma in eleventh-century England, a central figure in the succession dispute of the later 1030s. In mid-tenth-century England, Eadgifu, third wife of Edward the Elder, played a dominant role in politics some 15 years and more after Edward's death, when her two sons, Edmund and Eadred ruled in turn. Her significance is attested by the fact that she was a prime target during the succession struggle that followed Eadred's death.[34]

Eadred suffered from apparently chronic illness, and Eadgifu's maximum role was a type of regency. Minorities, and other forms of "rule-in-the-king's absence," are known from this period. It may be significant that it is the kingdom of the English/ Southumbria that saw two regencies in the tenth century: first, in the case of the illness of the current king, Eadred; in the second, due to the minority of King Æthelred II. In both cases, women as mothers seem to have played a large role, especially so in the mid-tenth century. It was under Eadred, in particular, that Eadgifu's charter witnesses became so frequent as to suggest recognition of a very significant political role. In the eleventh century, Queen Emma was to parallel Eadgifu's significance, though this time as a result not of minority but of the rule of two kingdoms, and consequent absence of her Danish husband, King Cnut. In the same way, William I's wife, Mathilda, exercised powers of regency sometimes in England as well as in Normandy.[35]

As with marriage practices, we need to be aware how far the general structures of family and its politics operate within specific contexts. Female regency is a result of the role of mother and of her commitment to the inheritance of her own children: she is, quite simply, often the safest guardian of those children's future. But female regency pits respect for woman-as-mother against less-flattering notions of woman-as-incapable. And given that other adult candidates are almost always available and arguable in the early Middle Ages, the dangers of minority rule, or, in the case of Eadgifu and Eadred, probably the rule of a king incapacitated by illness, need never occur. The capacity to tolerate and survive "rule-in-the-king's absence" observable in tenth-century England may suggest the degree of commitment of the elites to the southern English kingdom and its unity and not merely to the person of the king. It is perhaps a sign of a political situation already setting that southern English kingdom apart. Yet, conversely, in the eleventh century, it was the needs of conquering kings like Cnut and William, ruling kingdoms but often with long periods of absence, that led them to such reliance on their wives – and arguably now it was *insecurity* vis-à-vis sections of their elites that was a major factor in the fore-fronting of women.

Situations requiring or allowing regency do not necessarily deliver its powers to women, in spite of what might be considered their obvious trustworthiness vis-à-vis other potential regents. There seem to have been other factors that helped to make female regency acceptable by the late tenth century in England. Eadgifu first came to prominence during the reign of an adult, able-bodied son, Edmund: the factors that produced her significance may have included her landed power in Kent. The situation is rather clearer by the end of that century. In the early 980s, Ælfthryth, widow of King Edgar, seems to have had some regency role during the minority of her son, Æthelred. In this case, she owed her position not merely to the recurring family situation, but to other developments in queenship. These no doubt included an unquantifiable tradition already established by Eadgifu. But her acceptability also owed something to the role that church reformers had given her during her husband's reign. An ideology of queenly power certainly developed in southern England in the tenth century to which eleventh-century queens were heirs.

Queenship, Office, and Consecration

Kingship is a formalized and specialized role, concerning whose conduct and duties there is a general and clear perception; that is, it is an office. There is little doubt about the existence of clear notions of kingship in Britain and Ireland by AD 800, if not long before. There is a wealth of commentary on kings, in which early Ireland is especially rich. The Irish definitions of good and bad kingship are contained in advice literature and encapsulated in the tract *De Duodecim abusivis saeculi* (Concerning the Twelve Abuses of the World). The latter was extremely influential in Carolingian and, later, in English kingship:[36] the coronation sermon preached by

Dunstan, archbishop of Canterbury, in the 970s was based on it. Christian Ireland was, as Paul Fouracre has suggested (see chapter 9), the source of the first non-Roman political thought. That thought centered on kings, and it was concerned with their role, and with the attributes of their office, or, as early medieval writers would have called it, with their "*ministerium.*" People knew what they expected of kings, though expectations could and did shift. There seem also to have been widespread notions of a kingship in some sense separable from – or perhaps additional to – the person of the king. In England by c.1000, and probably in eleventh-century Scotland, this was marked by a double payment in the event of the murder of a king: half "for the kingship/*cynedom.*"[37]

Inauguration rituals were one of the key points at which this special role of the king was made clear. Such inaugurations took place in Ireland, for example, at Tara and perhaps at the rock of Cashel. In the tenth-century saga of Conall Corc, taking possession of the rock of Cashel meant succession to the Munster kingship.[38] The best-attested rituals are the clerically managed ones that formed part of the inauguration of English kings, probably from the end of the eighth century, when consecration first appears in England as part of the making of a king. Consecration added powerful sacramental elements to king-making. The king's change of status was marked in ways that paralleled those of baptism and the making of priests, specifically in the ordination using holy oil; its solemnity was underlined, the king ruling "by the grace of God" made clear.[39] And, by the late tenth century in England, the king made a threefold promise to his people to protect the church, forbid robbery and all unrightness, and to enjoin justice and mercy. That consecration promise, or oath, was an explicit recognition of kingship's official nature and of the link between king and people. It should, however, be noted that the prayers of the ceremony refer specifically to the king's responsibility for the prosperity and fertility of his people, to his justice and protection. Such ideas belong in the same thought-world as the Irish material – Dunstan's sermon was preached at just such an English royal inauguration – and all owe much to Old Testament models of kingship. There is still room for debate about whether such consecration was also practiced in Ireland.[40] It is as well to remember that, with or without it, a strongly parallel notion of kingship had developed there before AD 800.

Turning to queenship, what we are seeking is thus a similarly clear and formalized role for the female consort of a definitively male ruler, a role some or all of which might also in some circumstances be filled by his mother or even other royal women.[41] There is much less in the way of advice or similar literature that gives us a sense of wider perceptions and expectations of queens. Queens are notably absent from the first tract of political thought to survive from early England, the so-called "Institutes of Polity, Civil and Ecclesiastical" produced by Archbishop Wulfstan II of York in the early eleventh century. That tract describes the duties of various office-holders and status groups as a blueprint for the ideal holy society: the queen's absence from it is especially noteworthy given the date, in the aftermath of what look like significant developments in English queenship (see below).

Yet there are recurring images of royal women in early literary and other sources that suggest at least one area of widely recognized activity, namely in the household. The "lady with the mead cup" in the poem *Beowulf*, and the comparable figures in the *Mabinogi*, signal an accepted role. Asser's *Life of King Alfred*, a ninth-century

"Mirror of Princes," has little on queens in the household. But it felt it necessary to explain their lowly position, which may not be typical even of ninth-century Wessex.[42] It is characteristic of the historiography that such female figures in Irish literature, like Medb in *Fled Bricrend* (Bricriu's Feast), are as likely to be interpreted as goddess and prophetess as explored for evidence of queenly activity or notions of queenship.[43] But Irish sources certainly employ the same imagery as their Welsh and English counterparts. It may be difficult to interpret the role of the historical Gormflaith in the murderous struggles around the Leinster succession. But the accounts of her utilize topoi of household activity and hospitality which suggest that this was seen as her natural environment.[44]

The queen/wife as converter of a pagan husband is another image invoked in conversion-age sources, at least in England.[45] This should arguably be included among the range of religious activities with political implications that recur in the lives of early medieval queens: the monastic holdings of Offa of Mercia's wife and daughters, the responsibilities of tenth-century southern English queens for nunneries, their patronage of religious houses, and Margaret's reforming councils. Converting wives have good biblical origins. The first datable works which functioned as "Mirrors of Queens" return to that same source. Ælfric's homily on Esther was probably written with an eye to the English queens of the reform period c.AD 1000.[46] Esther was a favorite figure for those addressing ninth-century Carolingian queens. Works like the Old English vernacular *Judith* are almost impossible to locate geographically or chronologically, though the most recent suggestion of a late ninth-/early tenth-century date fits the apogee of Mercian queenly power almost too neatly.[47] Cynewulf's *Elene* returns to the most famous historical Christian royal woman, Helena, mother of Constantine. Unfortunately, it is variously dated to the eighth, ninth, and now even later tenth century.[48] Helena certainly became a significant figure in Mercian queenly traditions. Cynethryth's coinage seems to draw its iconographic inspiration from hers; the timing of Æthelflæd of Mercia's first independent action after her husband's death to the feast of Helena's Invention (i.e. Finding) of the Cross does not look coincidental.[49] Helena, like Esther if not Judith, is a reminder that the activities of queens as well as kings were legitimized, and extended, by reference to the sources of Christian authority.

Recurring images, however, fall short of establishing a defined and accepted *ministerium* for queens. For that we might turn, as with kings, to inauguration. What made a queen? On one level, the answer is simple: marriage made a queen. All queens were or had been the wives of kings. The title given to English queens in the witness list of charters sometimes emphasizes it: *coniunx*/wife. Queenship is thus no more or less than the crown on the head of wife and mother, at most the formalization of their roles. Marriage, however, was far from simple in the early Middle Ages. It was made through a series of gifts and exchanges of greater or lesser formality. There were different types of quite acceptable sexual union defined by the mix of these elements. This in turn affected, though it did not entirely determine, how easily the union could be ended and left room for argument over inheritance. The arrival of Christian ideas of marriage added other arguments to interpreting the mix, if not other elements to it. "Queen" in seventh-century England may thus have meant "fully, legitimately – in a Christian sense – married wife of a king," marking out a woman who had undergone such a marriage.[50] In this sense, "queen" can mark out a particular wife in a context of serial monogamy, if not polygamy. It may both denote the fullness of a marriage, and thus the unassailable legitimacy and inheritance claims of its children, and create a more unique position for its holder on which other roles may be built. The Irish material would bear more scrutiny with such questions in mind.

Offa's wife, Cynethryth, was described in charters not only as "*regina*" (queen) but as "queen of the Mercians," even "by the grace of God." Cynethryth's elevation began with full Christian marriage, in the interests of her (future) son Ecgfrith. But her extended titles suggest that there was more to her position. They raise tantalizing questions about her relationship with the Mercians as a people – a relationship that appears to parallel that of her king/husband – and about her inauguration into such a position. In Cynethryth's case, consecration is very unlikely. But by the late tenth century in England, queens certainly were consecrated. By this date, queenship was becoming more clearly defined and visible.

The practice of consecrating queens had developed in ninth- and tenth-century Francia and England, though it may have owed something to the activity and prominence of ninth-century Mercian queens. The queenly consecration rite was not based on the marriage ceremony. As used in Francia and England at this date, it grew out of the king's rite, with an addition not from the marriage rite but from that for the making of an abbess, an undoubted female office.[51] Like her husband, the consecrated queen incarnated the prosperity and wealth of the kingdom, symbolized in her crown. The ring she received was not marital, but paralleled her husband's in the symbolism of protection of the people, in her case especially of their Christian faith against heretics. Some versions of the rite included the same ritual prostration as the king performed, symbolizing the annihilation or at least shedding of the old self to be remade. All included anointing, that crucial status-changing ritual that made a queen, like a king, "anew." This rite and symbolism neither replaced nor precluded ideas about her fertility or her role as a royal bedfellow. Debate surrounding the consecration of Ælfthryth in 973 shows how far these latter remained the primary functions of queens in some eyes. Yet the rites suggest that England had gone some way toward the very debatable notion of an office of queen, parallel in some respects to that of king.

As so often, the bias in the nature and survival of sources makes comparison very difficult. In England, the survival of *ordines* for queenly as well as kingly consecration enables us to see this formalization of the role of the king's wife. An *ordo* is a liturgical text, listing the prayers and, sometimes, the accompanying ceremonies that were involved in an ecclesiastical rite. No *ordines* for the making of Irish queens have survived. That does not mean there never were any. As in the case of kings, the lack of early Irish pontificals (i.e. bishops' books containing texts for the rituals and ceremonies in which a bishop might be involved, including possibly this one) means we cannot be certain whether ecclesiastical inauguration occurred, but has left no trace, or never happened. Later evidence for other aspects of the queenly role is tantalizing: a later Irish queen would have a recognized position, comparable to that of the Tánaiste or heir, endowed with specific lands and revenues.[52] There are some apparent parallels here with the sort of provision that we see for eleventh-century English queens in *Domesday Book*, and in the royal wills and other documents that precede it.[53] But, as in the elaborate provisions for queens in the Welsh laws of court, it is unwise simply to project this backward. And such provision need not have implied anything more than the normal family provision for wives.

Queenship in the sense of an office recognized and conferred by consecration may not have developed in Britain and Ireland outside England at this date. Developments in the role of queen occurred in dialogue with the politics of tenth- and eleventh-century Southumbria. As with developments in ninth- and tenth-century English kingly consecration, ecclesiastical influence, and the Carolingian "reform" of which this was a vehicle, were important. Elaboration of an iconography that paralleled the queen with Mary, queen of heaven, underlined the earthly counterpart's special position, though it also rewrote Mary in her image.[54] This iconography was developed under the auspices of reformers. Reformers were happy to enhance a queenly role in a reforming movement that itself enhanced royal power. All of this was part of the political and ideological offensive that extended and underpinned West Saxon hegemony. *Domesday Book* allows us to establish just how significant the landholding of the queen was by the mid-eleventh century, and how far it contributed to the wide geographical footprint of English royal power. The queen held, for example, concentrations of land in the strategically important north-east midlands and in the Welsh marches. Some of the resource base, including a separate household, that underpinned kingship seems to have supported English queens by this date. Her household did not, however, act as a rival powerbase to that of the king. Rather, it remained closely connected to that of the king, and both functioned as part of the mechanisms for control of the kingdom of the English.

The conquests, royal exiles, and complex dynastic succession questions of eleventh-century England may have entrenched both queenly consecration and the development of the queen's role and importance. Tenth-century Francia and ninth-century Mercia, two other times and places of rapid queenly development, offer important parallels here. Consecration was a very public way of affirming the status of a royal wife and mother, and, through that, the status of her husband and sons. When William of Normandy took the English crown, he was very careful to stage-manage the crowning and consecration of his wife Mathilda 18 months or so later. That anxiety is an indication that, once established, consecration was a practice not to be foregone, not least because of its potential implications for heirs born of a consecrated queen and thus for the constantly shifting parameters of the game of succession. William's actions underscore a century of development of English queenship. They are also specific to the insecurities of conquest and dynastic change.

It would, however, be wrong to conclude discussion of queenship on such an unambiguous note. Contradiction and ambiguity dog the history of queenship. On the one hand, the consecration of the queen paralleled that of the king, and points to the official nature of her position, yet, on the other, there were critical differences. In comparison with the king's rite, there was no enthronement, no sword of warrior rule, no rod of justice. But Mary, queen of heaven, is sometimes portrayed in England at this date with such a rod, Æthelflæd commanded armies, and Mathilda sat in judgment. The queen took no oath binding her and people. But Cynethryth was queen "of the Mercians," Æthelflæd explicitly their lady, and at least one eleventh-century English queen was associated with the English, Anglo-Saxon people and rule (*imperium*) over them. "The history of queenship is littered with 'buts'."[55] Its study is still in its infancy, and is ripe for vigorous pursuit. But it is a quest for the elusive, and, in comparison with kingship, that fact is telling in itself.

Notes

1 Huneycutt, *Matilda of Scotland*; Wall, "Queen Margaret of Scotland."
2 Nelson, "Kingship and royal government"; Stafford, "Sons and mothers," and *Queens, Concubines and Dowagers*.
3 McNamara and Wemple, "The power of women through the family"; Nelson, "The problematic in the private."
4 Enright, *Lady with a Mead Cup*; Mac Cana, "Aspects of the theme"; Thurneysen, "Göttin Medb?"
5 Folz, *Les Saintes reines*.
6 Huneycutt, "The idea of the perfect princess."
7 Barlow (ed.), *Vita Eadwardi Regis*.
8 Campbell (ed.), *Encomium Emmae Reginae*.
9 Herbert, "*Rí Éirenn, Rí Alban*", p. 68.
10 Stafford, "Reading women" and "The annals of Æthelflæd."
11 Connon, "The *Banshenchas*"; Ní Bhrolcháin, *An Banshenchas: The Lore of Women*.
12 Stafford, "Reading women" and "Succession and inheritance."
13 Herbert, "Goddess and king."
14 Stafford, "Chronicle D, 1067 and women."
15 Klein, *Ruling Women*.
16 Ní Dhonnchadna, "The *Lex Innocentium*," pp. 62–3.
17 Yorke, *Kings and Kingdoms*, pp. 142–8, and *Wessex*, pp. 79–84.
18 Stafford, "Political women in Mercia" and "The annals of Æthelflæd."
19 Bede, *HE*, i. 1; for most recent discussion, see Woolf, "Pictish matriliny."
20 Duncan, *Scotland*, p. 99.
21 Stevenson (ed.), *Asser's Life of King Alfred*, cc. 75 and 76.
22 Nelson, "Kingship and royal government."
23 Charles-Edwards, *The Welsh Laws*; Charles-Edwards et al., *The Welsh King and his Court*.
24 Jarman, *The Cynfeirdd*, p. 119.
25 Huneycutt, *Matilda of Scotland*, pp. 167–8.
26 *Domesday Book*, I, fo. 238v.
27 Huneycutt, *Matilda of Scotland*, p. 169.
28 Stafford, *Queen Emma and Queen Edith*.
29 LoPrete, *Adela of Blois*.
30 Bede, *HE*, ii. 20, and *Recapitulatio s.a.* 697.
31 Herbert, "*Rí Éirenn, Rí Alban*," p. 68.
32 Richards, "African kings."
33 Stafford, "Political women in Mercia."
34 Stafford, *Queen Emma and Queen Edith*, and *Unification and Conquest*.
35 Bates, "Origins of the justiciarship"; Stafford, *Queen Emma and Queen Edith*.
36 Moore, "La Monarchie Carolingienne."
37 *Norðleoda Laga/Wer*, *EHD*, I, 469; Thomson and Innes (eds.), *Law of the Bretts and Scots [Leges inter Brettos et Scotos]*.
38 Charles-Edwards, *Early Christian Ireland*, p. 475; Fitzpatrick, "Royal inauguration assembly," p. 83.
39 Nelson, "Inauguration rituals."
40 Enright, *Iona, Tara and Soissons*, is a maximalist argument.
41 Nelson, "Women at the court of Charlemagne."
42 Nelson, "The queen in ninth-century Wessex."

43 Enright, *Lady with a Mead Cup*, pp. 270–2.
44 Ó Cróinín, "Three weddings and a funeral."
45 Nelson, "Queens as converters of kings."
46 Clayton, "Ælfric's Esther."
47 Griffiths (ed.), *Judith*, pp. 44–7.
48 Klein, *Ruling Women*.
49 Gannon, *Iconography of Early Anglo-Saxon Coinage*, p. 40; Stafford, "Political women."
50 Stafford, "Political women."
51 Nelson, "Early medieval rites of queen-making."
52 Simms, *From Kings to Warlords*, p. 72.
53 Stafford, *Queen Emma and Queen Edith*.
54 Clayton, *The Cult of the Virgin Mary*.
55 Stafford, *Queen Emma and Queen Edith*, p. 179.

Further Reading

England is best served for studies of queens and queenship. My own *Queen Emma and Queen Edith* provides a view of developments during the tenth and eleventh centuries; see also my essay collection, *Gender, Family and the Legitimation of Power: England from the Ninth to Early Twelfth Century* (Aldershot, 2006). Stacy Klein's *Ruling Women* is a significant new treatment from the literary viewpoint. There is no up-to-date survey of work on Irish queens, but important specific studies by Connon, Herbert, Ní Bhrolchain, and Ó Cróinín are cited in the bibliography. The study of Scottish queens is largely confined to work on Margaret and her immediate antecedents: see Huneycutt's biography of her daughter, *Matilda of Scotland*, and Wall's article "Queen Margaret of Scotland." Duncan's *Scotland: The Making of the Kingdom* brings together much of the exiguous material on others. Welsh royal women still appear chiefly in relation to studies of kings which take marriage and its politics seriously; thus, for example, D. E. Thornton, "Maredudd ab Owain (d. 999): the most famous king of the Welsh," *Welsh History Review*, 18: 4 (1997), 567–91. *The Welsh King and his Court*, edited by Charles-Edwards et al., is largely concerned with the situation after 1100, but there are references to the earlier period and suggestive lines of approach throughout.

Bibliography

Barlow, F. (ed.), *Vita Eadwardi Regis: The Life of King Edward who Rests at Westminster*, 2nd edn. (Oxford, 1992).
Bates, D., "Origins of the justiciarship," *Anglo-Norman Studies*, 4 (1982), 1–12.
Campbell, A. (ed.), *Encomium Emmae Reginae*, with intro. by S. Keynes (Cambridge, 1998).
Charles-Edwards, T. M., *Early Christian Ireland* (Cambridge, 2000).
Charles-Edwards, T. M., *The Welsh Laws* (Cardiff, 1989).
Charles-Edwards, T. M., Owen, M. E., and Russell, P. (eds.), *The Welsh King and his Court* (Cardiff, 2000).
Clayton, M., "Ælfric's Esther: a speculum reginae?," in H. Conrad O'Briain, A. M. D'Arcy, and J. Scattergood (eds.), *Text and Gloss: Studies in Insular Language and Literature Presented to Joseph Donovan Pheifer* (Dublin, 1999), pp. 89–101.
Clayton, M., *The Cult of the Virgin Mary in Anglo-Saxon England* (Cambridge, 1990).
Connon, A., "The *Banshenchas* and the Uí Néill queens of Tara," in A. P. Smyth (ed.), *Seanchas: Studies in Early and Medieval Irish Archaeology, History and Literature in Honour of Francis J. Byrne* (Dublin, 2000), pp. 98–108.

Duggan, A. (ed.), *Queens and Queenship in Medieval Europe* (Woodbridge, 1997).

Duncan, A. A. M., *Scotland: The Making of the Kingdom* (Edinburgh, 1975).

Enright, M. J., *Iona, Tara and Soissons: The Origins of the Royal Anointing Ritual* (Berlin, 1985).

Enright, M. J., *Lady with a Mead Cup: Ritual, Prophecy and Lordship in the European Warband from La Tène to the Viking Age* (Dublin, 1996).

Fitzpatrick, E., "Royal inauguration assembly and the church in medieval Ireland," in P. S. Barnwell and M. Mostert (eds.), *Political Assemblies in the Earlier Middle Ages* (Turnhout, 2003), pp. 73–93.

Folz, R., *Les Saintes reines du moyen âge en occident, vie–xiiie siècles* (Brussels, 1992).

Gannon, A., *The Iconography of Early Anglo-Saxon Coinage: Sixth to Eighth Centuries* (Oxford, 2003).

Griffiths, M. (ed.), *Judith* (Exeter, 1997).

Herbert, M., "Goddess and king: the sacred marriage in early Ireland," in L. O. Fradenburg (ed.), *Women and Sovereignty* (*Cosmos*, vol. 7; Edinburgh, 1992), pp. 264–75.

Herbert, M., "*Rí Éirenn, Rí Alban*: kingship and identity in the ninth and tenth centuries," in S. Taylor (ed.), *Kings, Clerics and Chronicles in Scotland, 500–1297* (Dublin, 2000), pp. 62–72.

Huneycutt, L., "The idea of the perfect princess: the *Life of St. Margaret* in the reign of Mathilda II (1100–1118)," *Anglo-Norman Studies*, 12 (1990), 81–98.

Huneycutt, L., *Matilda of Scotland: A Study in Medieval Queenship* (Woodbridge, 2003).

Jarman, A. O. H., *The Cynfeirdd: Early Welsh Poets and Poetry* (Cardiff, 1981).

Klein, S. S., *Ruling Women: Queenship and Gender in Anglo-Saxon Literature* (Indiana, 2006).

LoPrete, K., *Adela of Blois: Countess and Lord* (Dublin, 2006).

Mac Cana, P., "Aspects of the theme of king and goddess in Irish literature," *Études Celtiques*, 7 (1955–6), 76–114 and 8 (1958), 59–68.

McNamara, J. A. and Wemple, S., "The power of women through the family in medieval Europe," in M. Hartmann and L. W. Banner (eds.), *Clio's Consciousness Raised: New Perspectives on the History of Women* (New York, 1974), pp. 103–18.

Moore, M. E., "La Monarchie Carolingienne et les anciens modèles Irlandais," *Annales, ESC*, 51: 2 (1996), 307–24.

Nelson, J. L., "Early medieval rites of queen-making and the shaping of medieval queenship," in A. Duggan (ed.), *Queens and Queenship in Medieval Europe* (Woodbridge, 1997), pp. 301–15.

Nelson, J. L., "Inauguration rituals," in P. H. Sawyer and I. Wood (eds.), *Early Medieval Kingship* (Leeds, 1977), pp. 50–71.

Nelson, J. L., "Kingship and royal government," in R. McKitterick (ed.), *The New Cambridge Medieval History*, vol. II: *c.700–900* (Cambridge, 1995), pp. 383–430.

Nelson, J. L., "The problematic in the private," *Social History*, 15 (1990), 355–64.

Nelson, J. L., "The queen in ninth-century Wessex," in S. Keynes and A. P. Smyth (eds.), *Anglo-Saxons: Studies Presented to Cyril Roy Hart* (Dublin, 2006), pp. 69–77.

Nelson, J. L., "Queens as converters of kings in the earlier Middle Ages," in C. La Rocca (ed.), *Agire da donna, modelli e pratiche di rappresentazione (secoli VI–X)* (Turnhout, 2007), pp. 95–107.

Nelson, J. L., "Women at the court of Charlemagne: a case of monstrous regiment?," in J. C. Parsons (ed.), *Medieval Queenship* (New York, 1993), pp. 43–61.

Ní Bhrolchain, M. (ed.), *An Banshenchas: The Lore of Women* (Dublin, 2001).

Ní Dhonnchadha, M., "The *Lex Innocentium*: Adomnán's law for women, clerics and youth, 697 AD," in M. O'Dowd and S. Wickert (eds.), *Chattel, Servant or Citizen: Women's Status in Church, State and Society* (Belfast, 1995), pp. 58–69.

Ó Cróinín, D., "Three weddings and a funeral: rewriting Irish political history in the tenth century," in A. P. Smyth (ed.), *Senchas: Studies in History Presented to Francis John Byrne* (Dublin, 2000), pp. 212–24.

Richards, A. L., "African kings and their royal relatives," *Journal of the Royal Anthropological Institute*, 91 (1961), 135–50.

Simms, K., *From Kings to Warlords: The Changing Political Structure of Gaelic Ireland in the Later Middle Ages* (Woodbridge, 1987).

Stafford, P., "'The annals of Æthelflæd': annals, history and politics in early tenth-century England," in J. Barrow and A. Wareham (eds.), *Myth, Rulership, Church and Charters: Essays in Honour of Nicholas Brooks* (Aldershot, 2008), pp. 101–16.

Stafford, P., "Chronicle D, 1067 and women: gendering conquest in eleventh-century England," in S. Keynes and A. P. Smyth (eds.), *Anglo-Saxons: Studies Presented to Cyril Roy Hart* (Dublin, 2006), pp. 208–23.

Stafford, P., "Political women in Mercia, eighth to early tenth centuries," in M. Brown and C. Farr (eds.), *Mercia: An Anglo-Saxon Kingdom in Europe* (London, 2001), pp. 35–49.

Stafford, P., *Queen Emma and Queen Edith: Queenship and Women's Power in Eleventh-century England* (Oxford, 1997).

Stafford, P., *Queens, Concubines and Dowagers: The King's Wife in the Early Middle Ages* (Athens, 1983, reprinted with new preface, 1998).

Stafford, P., "Reading women in annals: Eadburg, Cuthburg, Cwenburg and the Anglo-Saxon chronicles," in C. La Rocca (ed.), *Agire da donna, modelli e pratiche di rappresentazione (secoli VI–X)* (Turnhout, 2007), pp. 269–89.

Stafford, P., "Sons and mothers: family politics in the early Middle Ages," in D. Baker (ed.), *Medieval Women* (Oxford, 1978), pp. 79–100.

Stafford, P., "Succession and inheritance: a gendered perspective on Alfred's family history," in T. Reuter (ed.), *Alfred the Great* (Aldershot, 2003), pp. 251–64.

Stafford, P., *Unification and Conquest: A Political and Social History of England in the Tenth and Eleventh Centuries* (London, 1989).

Stevenson, W. H. (ed.), *Asser's Life of King Alfred* (Oxford, 1904, 1959).

Thomson, T. and Innes, C. I. (eds.), *Law of the Bretts and Scots*, in *The Acts of the Parliaments of Scotland, 1124–1423* (Edinburgh, 1844), pp. 663–5.

Thurneysen, R., "Göttin Medb?," *Zeitschrift für Celtische Philologie*, 8 (1929), 108–10.

Wall, V., "Queen Margaret of Scotland (1070–1093): burying the past, enshrining the future," in A. Duggan (ed.), *Queens and Queenship in Medieval Europe* (Woodbridge, 1997), pp. 27–38.

Woolf, A., "Pictish matriliny reconsidered," *Innes Review*, 49 (1998), 147–67.

Yorke, B., *Kings and Kingdoms of Early Anglo-Saxon England* (London, 1990).

Yorke, B., *Wessex in the Early Middle Ages* (London, 1995).

Bibliography

Abels, R., "Byrhtnoth, magnate and soldier (d.991)," *Oxford Dictionary of National Biography* (Oxford, 2004).

Abels, R., *Lordship and Military Obligation in Anglo-Saxon England* (London, 1988).

Abrams, L., "The conversion of the Danelaw," in J. Graham-Campbell, R. Hall, J. Jesch, and D. N. Parsons (eds.), *Vikings and the Danelaw: Select Papers from the Proceedings of the Thirteenth Viking Congress, Nottingham and York, August 21–30, 1997* (Oxford, 2001), pp. 31–44.

Abrams, L., "The conversion of the Scandinavians of Dublin," *Anglo-Norman Studies*, 20 (1998), 1–29.

Abrams, L., "Edward the Elder's Danelaw," in N. J. Higham and D. H. Hill (eds.), *Edward the Elder, 899–924* (London, 2001), pp. 128–43.

Abrams, L., "Kings and bishops in the conversion of the Anglo-Saxon and Scandinavian kingdoms," in J. Brohed (ed.), *Church and People in Britain and Scandinavia* (Lund, 1996), pp. 15–28.

Abrams, L. and Parsons, D. N., "Place-names and the history of Scandinavian settlement in England," in J. Hines, A. Lane, and M. Redknap (eds.), *Land, Sea and Home.* Proceedings of a Conference on Viking-period Settlement, Cardiff, July 2001 (Leeds, 2004), pp. 379–431.

Aird, W. M., "Copsi, earl of Northumbria (d.1067)," *Oxford Dictionary of National Biography* (Oxford, 2004).

Aird, W. M., "Northern England or southern Scotland? The Anglo-Scottish border in the eleventh and twelfth centuries and the problem of perspective," in J. C. Appleby and P. Dalton (eds.), *Government, Religion and Society in Northern England, 1000–1700* (Stroud, 1997), pp. 27–39.

Aird, W. M., "Osulf, earl of Bamburgh (d.1067)," *Oxford Dictionary of National Biography* (Oxford, 2004).

Aird, W. M., *St. Cuthbert and the Normans: The Church of Durham, 1071–1153* (Woodbridge, 1998).

Aird, W. M., "Siward, earl of Northumbria (*d.*1055)," *Oxford Dictionary of National Biography* (Oxford, 2004).

Airlie, S., "The aristocracy," in R. McKitterick (ed.), *The New Cambridge Medieval History*, vol. II: *c.700–c.900* (Cambridge, 1995), pp. 431–50.

Alcock, L. "The activities of potentates in Celtic Britain, AD 500–800: a positivist approach," in S. T. Driscoll and M. R. Nieke (eds.), *Power and Politics in Early Medieval Britain and Ireland* (Edinburgh, 1988), pp. 22–46.

Alcock, L., *Dinas Powys: An Iron Age, Dark Age and Early Medieval Settlement in Glamorgan* (Cardiff, 1963).

Alcock, L., *Economy, Society and Warfare among the Britons and Saxons* (Cardiff, 1987).

Alcock, L., *Kings and Warriors, Craftsmen and Priests* (Edinburgh, 2003).

Alcock, L., "Message from the dark side of the moon: western and northern Britain in the age of Sutton Hoo," in M. Carver (ed.), *The Age of Sutton Hoo* (Woodbridge, 1992), pp. 205–15.

Alcock, L. and Alcock, E., "Reconnaissance excavations on early historic fortifications and other royal sites in Scotland 1974–84: A, excavations and other fieldwork at Forteviot, Perthshire, 1981; B, excavations at Urquhart Castle, Inverness-shire, 1983; C, excavations at Dunnottar, Kincardineshire, 1984," *Proceedings of the Society of Antiquaries of Scotland*, 122 (1992), 215–88.

Alexander, J. G., *Insular Manuscripts, Sixth to Ninth Century* (London, 1978).

Allott, S., *Alcuin of York* (York, 1974).

Althoff, G., *Family, Friends and Followers: Political and Social Bonds in Medieval Europe*, trans. C. Caroll (Cambridge, 2004).

Althoff, G., *Otto III* (Darmstadt, 1996), trans. P. G. Jestice (Philadelphia, 2003).

Anderson, A. O. (ed.), *Early Sources of Scottish History, AD 500–1286*, 2 vols. (Edinburgh, 1922; Stamford, 1990).

Anderson, A. O., *Scottish Annals from English Chroniclers, AD 500 to 1286* (London, 1908; corrected edn., Stamford, 1991).

Anderson, A. O. and Anderson, M. O. (eds.), *Adomnán's Life of Columba*, 2nd edn. (Oxford, 1991).

Anderson, M. O., *Kings and Kingship in Early Scotland* (Edinburgh, 1973, rev edn. 1980).

Angenendt, A., "The conversion of the Anglo-Saxons considered against the background of the early medieval mission," *Settimane de studio del centro italiano di studi sull'alto medioevo*, 32 (Spoleto, 1986), pp. 747–92.

Angenendt, A., "Willibrord im Dienst der Karolinger," *Annales der historisches Vereins für den Niederrhien inbesondere das alte Erzbistum Köln*, 175 (1973), 63–113.

Anon., *The Prittlewell Prince: The Discovery of a Rich Anglo-Saxon Burial in Essex* (London, 2004).

Archibald, M., Brown, M., and Webster, L., "Heirs of Rome: the shaping of Britain 400–900," in L. Webster, and M. Brown (eds.), *The Transformation of the Roman World, AD 400–900* (London, 1997), pp. 208–48.

Arndt, W. (ed.), *Vita Alcuini, MGH SS* XV.1 (Hanover, 1887), pp. 182–97.

Arnold, C. J., *An Archaeology of the Early Anglo-Saxon Kingdoms*, 2nd edn. (London, 1997).

Arnold, C. J., "Wealth and social structure: a matter of life and death," in P. Rahtz, T. Dickinson, and L. Watts (eds.), *Anglo-Saxon Cemeteries 1979*, British Archaeological Reports, British series 82 (Oxford, 1980), pp. 81–142.

Arnold, C. J. and Davies, J. L., *Roman and Early Medieval Wales* (Stroud, 2000).

Arnold, T. (ed.), *Symeonis monachi opera omnia*, 2 vols. (London, 1882–5).

Ash, M., "The diocese of St. Andrews under its 'Norman' bishops," *Scottish Historical Review*, 55 (1976), 105–26.

Aston, T. H., "The origins of the manor in England," in T. H. Aston (ed.), *Social Relations and Ideas: Essays in Honour of R. H. Hilton* (Leicester, 1983), pp. 1–43.

Attenborough, F. L., *The Laws of the Earliest English Kings* (Cambridge, 1922).

Backhouse, J., *The Lindisfarne Gospels* (Oxford, 1981).

Bailey, R., *England's Earliest Sculptors* (Toronto, 1997).

Bailey, R., *Viking Age Sculpture in Northern England* (London, 1980).

Baillie, M. G. L., "The AD 540 event," *Current Archaeology*, 15 (June 2001), 266–9.

Baillie, M. G. L., *Tree Ring Dating and Archaeology* (London, 1982).

Bannerman, J., *Studies in the History of Dalriada* (Edinburgh, 1974).

Barford, P. M., *The Early Slavs: Culture and Society in Early Medieval Eastern Europe* (London, 2001).

Barker, N. (ed.), *The York Gospels* (Lewes, 1986).

Barlow, F., *Edward the Confessor* (London, 1970).

Barlow, F., *The English Church 1000–1066* (London, 1979).

Barlow, F., *The English Church, 1066–1154* (London, 1979).

Barlow, F., *The Godwins* (London, 2002).

Barlow, F. (ed.), *Vita Eadwardi Regis: The Life of King Edward who Rests at Winchester*, 2nd edn. (Oxford, 1992).

Barnes, M., "Norse in the British Isles," in A. Faulkes and R. Perkins (eds.), *Viking Revaluations: Viking Society Centenary Symposium* (London, 1993), pp. 65–84.

Barrett, J. H., "Beyond war or peace: the study of culture contact in Viking-Age Scotland," in J. Hines, A. Lane, and M. Redknap (eds.), *Land, Sea and Home*. Proceedings of a Conference on Viking-period Settlement, Cardiff, July 2001 (Leeds, 2004), pp. 207–18.

Barrett, J. H., "Christian and pagan practice during the conversion of Viking Age Orkney and Shetland," in M. Carver (ed.), *The Cross Goes North* (Woodbridge, 2002), pp. 207–26.

Barrett, J., "Culture contact in Viking Age Scotland," in J. H. Barrett (ed.), *Contact, Continuity and Collapse: The Norse Colonization of the North Atlantic* (Turnhout, 2003), pp. 73–111.

Barrett, J. H. and Richards, M. P., "Identity, gender, religion and economy: new isotope and radiocarbon evidence for marine resource intensification in early historic Orkney, Scotland, UK," *European Journal of Archaeology*, 7: 3 (2004), 249–71.

Barrow, G. W. S., *The Anglo-Norman Era in Scottish History* (Oxford, 1980).

Barrow, G. W. S., *The Kingdom of the Scots: Government, Church and Society from the Eleventh to the Fourteenth Century* (London, 1973; 2nd edn. Edinburgh, 2003).

Barrow, G. W. S., *Kingship and Unity: Scotland 1000–1306* (London, 1981).

Barrow, G. W. S., "Scots in the Durham Liber Vitae," in D. Rollason, A. J. Piper, M. Harvey, and L. Rollason (eds.), *The Durham Liber Vitae and its Context* (Woodbridge, 2004), pp. 109–16.

Barrow, J., "Churches, education and literacy in towns 600–1100," in D. M. Palliser (ed.), *The Cambridge Urban History of Britain*, vol. 1 (Cambridge, 2000), pp. 127–52.

Barrow, J., "Survival and mutation: ecclesiastical institutions in the Danelaw in the ninth and tenth centuries," in D. M. Hadley and J. D. Richards (eds.), *Cultures in Contact: Scandinavian Settlement in England in the Ninth and Tenth Centuries* (Turnhout, 2000), pp. 155–76.

Barrow, J. and Brooks, N. (eds.), *Bishop Wulfstan and his World* (Aldershot, 2005).

Bassett, S., "Church and diocese in the west midlands: the transition from British to Anglo-Saxon control," in J. Blair and R. Sharpe (eds.), *Pastoral Care before the Parish* (Leicester, 1992), pp. 13–40.

Bassett, S. (ed.), *The Origins of Anglo-Saxon Kingdoms* (Leicester, 1989).

Bately, J. (ed.), *The Anglo-Saxon Chronicle: A Collaborative Edition*, vol. 3: *MS A* (Cambridge, 1986).

Bates, D., *Bishop Remigius of Lincoln 1067–1092* (Lincoln, 1992).

Bates, D., "Origins of the justiciarship," *Anglo-Norman Studies*, 4 (1982), 1–12.

Bates, D., *William the Conqueror* (London, 1989).

Bates, D., "William I, king of England and duke of Normandy (1027/8–1087)," *Oxford Dictionary of National Biography* (Oxford, 2004).

Batey, C., "Aspects of rural settlement in northern Britain," in D. Hooke and S. Burnell (eds.), *Landscape and Settlement in Britain AD 400–1066* (Exeter, 1995), pp. 69–94.

Baxter, S., "The earls of Mercia and their commended men in the mid-eleventh century," *Anglo-Norman Studies*, 23 (2001), 23–46.

Baxter, S., *The Earls of Mercia: Lordship and Power in Late Anglo-Saxon England* (Oxford, 2007).

Bede, *Historia abbatum*, ed. C. Plummer, *Baedae opera historica*, 2 vols. (Oxford, 1896), i. 364–87.

Bede, *Historia ecclesiastica gentis Anglorum*, trans. B. Colgrave, revised R. Collins and J. McClure, *Bede: The Ecclesiastical History of the English People*, Oxford World's Classics (Oxford, 1994).

Beech, G. T., Bourin, M., and Chareille, P. (eds.), *Personal Names Studies of Medieval Europe: Social Identity and Familial Structures* (Kalamazoo, MI, 2002).

Behr, C., "The origins of kingship in early medieval Kent," *Early Medieval Europe*, 9: 1 (2000), 25–52.

Bell, M., "Environmental archaeology as an index of continuity and change in the medieval landscape," in M. Aston, D. Austin, and C. Dyer (eds.), *The Rural Settlements of Medieval England: Studies Dedicated to Maurice Beresford and John Hurst* (Oxford, 1989), pp. 269–86.

Bente, M., "The firebed of the serpent: myth and religion in the migration period mirrored through some golden objects," in L. Webster, and M. Brown (eds.), *The Transformation of the Roman World, AD 400–900* (London, 1997), pp. 194–206.

Beresford, G., "Goltho Manor, Lincs.: the buildings and their surrounding defences," *Anglo-Normans Studies*, 4 (1981), 13–36.

Best, R. I., Bergin, O., and O'Brien, M. A. (eds.), *The Book of Leinster formerly Lebar na Núachongbála*, vol. 1 (Dublin, 1954).

Bethell, D., "English monks and Irish reform in the eleventh and twelfth centuries," in T. D. Williams (ed.), *Historical Studies*, 8 (Dublin, 1971), pp. 111–35.

Bethmann, L. (ed.), *Witger: Genealogia, MGH SS* 9 (Hanover, 1851), pp. 302–4.

Bethmann, L. and Waitz, G. (eds.), *Paul the Deacon: History of the Lombards*, in *Historia Langobardorum, MGH SRL* (Hanover, 1878), pp. 7–217.

Bhreathnach, E., "Columban churches in Brega and Leinster: relations with the Norse and the Anglo-Normans," *Journal of the Royal Society of Antiquaries of Ireland*, 129 (1999), 5–18.

Bhreathnach, E. (ed.), *The Kingship and Landscape of Tara* (Dublin, 2005).

Bhreathnach, E., "Medieval Irish history at the end of the twentieth century: unfinished work," *Irish Historical Studies*, 32: 126 (2000), 260–71.

Bibre, P., "North Sea language contacts in the early middle ages: English and Norse," in T. R. Liszka and L. Walker (eds.), *The North Sea World in the Middle Ages* (Dublin, 2001), pp. 88–107.

Biddle, M. (ed.), *Winchester in the Early Middle Ages* (Oxford, 1976).

Biddle, M. and Hill, D., "Late Saxon planned towns," *Antiquaries Journal*, 51 (1971), 70–85.

Biddle, M. and Kjølbye-Biddle, B., "Repton and the 'great heathen army,' 873–4," in J. Graham-Campbell, R. A. Hall, J. Jesch, and D. N. Parsons, (eds.), *Vikings and the Danelaw: Select Papers from the Proceedings of the Thirteenth Viking Congress* (Oxford, 2001), pp. 45–96.

Bieler, L. (ed. and trans.), *The Patrician Texts in the Book of Armagh*, Scriptores Latini Hiberniae 10 (Dublin, 1979).

Binchy, D. A., *Celtic and Anglo-Saxon Kingship* (Oxford, 1970).

Binchy, D. A. (ed.), *Corpus iuris Hibernici*, 6 vols (Dublin, 1978).

Binchy, D. A. (ed.), *Críth Gablach* (Dublin, 1941).

Binchy, D. A., "Distraint in Irish law," *Celtica*, 10 (1973), 22–71.

Binchy, D. A. "The fair of Tailtiu and the feast of Tara," *Ériu*, 18 (1958), 113–38.

Binchy, D. A., "Irish history and Irish law: I and II," *Studia Hibernica*, 15 and 16 (1975 and 1976), 7–36 and 7–45.

Binchy, D. A., "Patrick and his biographers: ancient and modern," *Studia Hibernica*, 2 (1962), 7–173.

Binchy, D. A., "Sick-maintenance in Irish law," *Ériu*, 12 (1938), 78–134.

Bittel, L., *Isle of the Saints: Monastic Settlement and Christian Community in Early Ireland* (Ithaca, 1993).

Blackburn, M. A. S., "Æthelred's coinage and the payment of tribute," in D. Scragg (ed.), *The Battle of Maldon, AD 991* (Oxford, 1991), pp. 156–99.

Blackburn, M. A. S., "The coinage of Scandinavian York," in R. A. Hall (ed.), *Aspects of Anglo-Scandinavian York* (York, 2004), pp. 325–49.

Blackburn, M. A. S., "Currency under the Vikings. Part 1: Guthrum and the earliest Danelaw coinages," *British Numismatic Journal*, 75 (2005), 18–43.

Blackburn, M. A. S., "Expansion and control: aspects of Anglo-Scandinavian minting south of the Humber," in J. Graham-Campbell, R. A. Hall, J. Jesch, and D. N. Parsons, (eds.), *Vikings and the Danelaw: Select Papers from the Proceedings of the Thirteenth Viking Congress* (Oxford, 2001), pp. 125–42.

Blair, J., "Anglo-Saxon minsters: a topographical review," in J. Blair and R. Sharpe (eds.), *Pastoral Care before the Parish* (Leicester, 1992), pp. 226–66.

Blair, J., *Anglo-Saxon Oxfordshire* (Stroud, 1994).

Blair, J., "Anglo-Saxon pagan shrines and their prototypes," *Anglo-Saxon Studies in Archaeology and History*, 8 (1995), 1–28.

Blair, J., *The Church in Anglo-Saxon Society* (Oxford, 2005).

Blair, J., "Debate: ecclesiastical organisation and pastoral care in Anglo-Saxon England," *Early Medieval Europe*, 4: 2 (1995), 193–212.

Blair, J., *Early Medieval Surrey: Landholding, Church and Settlement before 1300* (Stroud, 1991).

Blair, J., "Hall and chamber: English domestic planning 1000–1250," in G. Meirion-Jones and M. Jones (eds.), *Manorial Domestic Buildings in England and Northern France* (London, 1993), pp. 1–21.

Blair, J., "Minster churches in the landscape," in D. Hooke (ed.), *Anglo-Saxon Settlements* (Oxford, 1988), pp. 35–58.

Blair, J., "Palaces or minsters? Northampton and Cheddar reconsidered," in M. Lapidge (ed.), *Anglo-Saxon England*, 25 (Cambridge, 1996), pp. 97–122.

Blair, J. and Sharpe, R. (eds.), *Pastoral Care before the Parish* (Leicester, 1992).

Bloch, M., *French Rural History: An Essay on its Basic Characteristics* (London, 1966).

Blom, I., Hagemann, K., and Hall, C. (eds.), *Gendered Nations: Nationalisms and Gender Order in the Long Nineteenth Century* (Oxford, 2000).

Bonney, D., "Early boundaries and estates in southern England," in P. H. Sawyer (ed.), *Medieval Settlement: Continuity and Change* (London, 1976), pp. 72–82.

Boon, G. C., *Welsh Hoards 1979–1981: The Coinage of Cnut in Wales, the Coinage of the Empress Maud, the Earliest Portrait Esterlings* (Cardiff, 1986).

Bourke, C. (ed.), *From the Isles of the North: Early Medieval Art in Ireland and Britain* (Belfast, 1995).

Bowden, G. R., Balaresque, P., King, T. E., et al., "Excavating past population structures by surname-based sampling: the genetic legacy of the Vikings in northwest England," *Molecular Biology and Evolution*, 25: 2 (2008), 301–9.

Bracken, D. and Ó Riain-Raedel, D. (eds.), *Ireland and Europe in the Twelfth Century: Reform and Renewal* (Dublin, 2006).

Bradbury, J., *The Battle of Hastings* (Stroud, 1998).

Bradley, J., "The interpretation of Scandinavian settlement in Ireland," in J. Bradley (ed.), *Settlement and Society in Medieval Ireland* (Dublin, 1988), pp. 49–78.

Breatnach, L., "Canon law and secular law in early Ireland: the significance of *Bretha Nemed*," *Peritia* 3 (1984), 439–59.

Breatnach, L., *A Companion to the Corpus Iuris Hibernici*. Early Irish Law Series 5 (Dublin, 2005).

Breatnach, L. (ed. and trans.), *Uraicecht na Ríar: The Poetic Grades in Early Irish Law* (Dublin, 1987).

Breeze, A., "*Armes Prydein*, Hywel Dda, and the reign of Edmund of Wessex," *Études Celtiques*, 33 (1997), 209–22.

Breeze, D., *Roman Scotland: Frontier Country* (London, 1996).

Bresslau, H. (ed.), *Wipo: Gesta Chuonradi Imperatoris*, in *Die Werke Wipos*, MGH SRG (Hanover, 1915).

Brett, M., "Canterbury's perspective on church reform and Ireland, 1070–1115," in D. Bracken and D. Ó Riain-Raedel (eds.), *Ireland and Europe in the Twelfth Century: Reform and Renewal* (Dublin, 2006), pp. 13–35.

Broderick, G. (ed. and trans.), *Cronica Regum Mannie & Insularum: Chronicle of the Kings of Man and the Isles, BL Cotton Julius A.vii* (Douglas, Isle of Man, 1979).

Brookes, S., *Economics and Social Change in Anglo-Saxon Kent AD 400–900: Landscapes, Communities and Exchange* (Oxford, 2007).

Brooks, N., "The administrative background to the Burghal Hidage," in D. Hill and A. R. Rumble (eds.), *The Defence of Wessex: The Burghal Hidage and Anglo-Saxon Fortifications* (Manchester, 1996), pp. 128–50.

Brooks, N., "Canterbury, Rome and the construction of English identity," in J. M. H. Smith (ed.), *Early Medieval Rome and the Christian West: Essays in Honour of Donald A. Bullough* (Leiden, 2000), pp. 221–46.

Brooks, N., "The development of military obligations in eighth- and ninth-century England," in P. Clemoes and K. Hughes (eds.), *England before the Conquest: Studies in Primary Sources Presented to Dorothy Whitelock* (Cambridge, 1971), pp. 69–84.

Brooks, N., *The Early History of the Church of Canterbury* (Leicester, 1984).

Brooks, N., "England in the ninth century: the crucible of defeat," *Transactions of the Royal Historical Society*, 5th series, 29 (1979), 1–20.

Broun, D., "Alba: Pictish homeland or Irish offshoot?" in P. O'Neill (ed.), *Exile and Homecoming: Papers from the Fifth Australian Conference of Celtic Studies* (Sydney, 2005), pp. 234–75.

Broun, D., "The birth of Scottish History," *Scottish Historical Review*, 76 (1997), 4–22.

Broun, D., *The Charters of Gaelic Scotland and Ireland in the Early and Central Middle Ages* (Cambridge, 1995).

Broun, D., "Dunkeld and the origin of Scottish Identity," *The Innes Review*, 48 (1997), 112–24.

Broun, D., *The Irish Identity of the Kingdom of the Scots* (Woodbridge, 1999).

Broun, D., *Scottish Independence and the Idea of Britain: From the Picts to Alexander III* (Edinburgh, 2007).

Broun, D., "The seven kingdoms in *De situ Albanie*: a record of Pictish political geography or imaginary map of ancient Alba?," in E. J. Cowan and R. A. McDonald (eds.), *Alba: Celtic Scotland in the Middle Ages* (East Linton, 2000), pp. 24–42.

Brown, G. H., *Bede the Venerable* (Boston, MA, 1987).

Brown, J., *A Palaeographer's View* (London, 1993).

Brown, M., *The Lindisfarne Gospels: Society, Spirituality and the Scribe* (London, 2003).

Brown, P., *The Rise of Western Christendom: Triumph and Diversity AD 200–1000* (Oxford, 1996).

Budd, P., Millard, A., Chenery, C., Lucy, S., and Roberts, C., "Investigating population move-
    ment by stable isotope analysis: a report from Britain," *Antiquity*, 78 (2004), 127–41.
Bugge, A. (ed. and trans.), *Caithréim Cellacháin Caisil: The Victorious Career of Cellachan at
    Cashel or the Wars between the Irishmen and the Norsemen in the Middle of the Tenth Century*
    (Christiana, 1905).
Bullough, D. A., *Alcuin: Reputation and Achievement* (Leiden, 2004).
Bullough, D. A., "Anglo-Saxon institutions and early English society," *Annali della fondazione
    italiana par la storia amministrativa*, 2 (1965), 647–59.
Bullough, D. A., *Carolingian Renewal: Sources and Heritage* (Manchester, 1991).
Bullough, D. A., "Early medieval social groupings: the terminology of kinship," *Past and
    Present*, 45 (1969), 3–18.
Bullough, D. A., "What has Ingeld to do with Lindisfarne?," *Anglo-Saxon England*, 22 (1993),
    93–125.
Burrow, J. W., *A Liberal Descent: Victorian Historians and the English Past* (Cambridge,
    1981).
Byrne, F. J., "Historical note on Cnogba (Knowth)," in G. Eogan, "Excavations at Knowth,
    Co. Meath," *Proceedings of the Royal Irish Academy*, 66 C (1968), 383–400.
Byrne, F. J., *Irish Kings and High-kings* (London, 1973).
Byrne, F. J., *The Rise of the Uí Néill and the High-kingship of Ireland* (Dublin [1970]).
Callmer, J., "Urbanisation in Scandinavia and the Baltic region c.AD 700–1100: trading places,
    centres and early urban sites," in B. Ambrosiani and H. Clarke (eds.), *Developments around
    the Baltic and the North Sea* (Stockholm, 1994), pp. 50–90.
Cambridge, E. and Rollason, D., "Debate: the pastoral organisation of the Anglo-Saxon
    Church: a review of the 'minster hypothesis,' " *Early Medieval Europe*, 4: 1 (1995), 87–104.
Cambridge, E. and Rollason, D., "The pastoral organization of the Anglo-Saxon church:
    a review of the 'minster hypothesis,' " *Early Medieval Europe*, 4 (1995), 87–104.
Cameron, K., *English Place Names* (London, 1996).
Cameron, K., *Scandinavian Settlement in the Territory of the Five Boroughs: The Place-name
    Evidence* (Nottingham, 1965).
Cameron, K., "Scandinavian settlement in the territory of the five boroughs: the place-name
    evidence, part II: place-names in thorp," *Mediaeval Scandinavia*, 3 (1970), 35–49.
Cameron, K., "Scandinavian settlement in the territory of the five boroughs: the place-name
    evidence, part III: the Grimston-hybrids," in P. Clemoes and K. Hughes (eds.), *England
    before the Conquest* (Cambridge, 1971), pp. 52–69.
Campbell, A. (ed.), *The Battle of Brunanburh* (London, 1938).
Campbell, A. (ed.), *The Chronicle of Æthelweard* (London, 1962).
Campbell, A. (ed.), *Encomium Emmae Reginae*, with intro. by S. Keynes (Cambridge,
    1998).
Campbell, E., "Were the Scots Irish?," *Antiquity*, 75 (2001), 285–92.
Campbell, E. and Lane, A., "Celtic and Germanic interaction in Dalriada: the seventh-century
    metalworking site at Dunadd," in R. M. Spearman and J. Higgitt (eds.), *The Age of
    Migrating Ideas: Early Medieval Art in Northern Britain and Ireland* (Edinburgh, 1993),
    pp. 52–63.
Campbell, J., "Bede's *reges* and *principes*," in *Essays in Anglo-Saxon History* (London, 1986),
    pp. 85–98.
Campbell, J., *Essays in Anglo-Saxon History* (London, 1986).
Campbell, J., "Observations on English government from the tenth to the twelfth century,"
    Transactions of the Royal Historical Society, 5th series, 25 (1975), 39–54, reprinted in
    J. Campbell, *Essays in Anglo-Saxon History* (London, 1986), pp. 155–70.
Campbell, J., "The sale of land and the economics of power in early England: problems and
    possibilities," *The Haskins Society Journal: Studies in Medieval History*, 1 (1989), 23–37.

Campbell, J., "The significance of the Anglo-Norman state in the administrative history of Western Europe," in J. Campbell, *Essays in Anglo-Saxon History* (London, 1986), pp. 171–90.

Campbell, J., "Some agents and agencies of the late Anglo-Saxon state," in J. C. Holt (ed.), *Domesday Studies* (Woodbridge, 1987), pp. 201–18.

Campbell, J., *Stubbs and the English State*, Stenton Lecture (Reading, 1989).

Campbell, J., "The united kingdom of England: the Anglo-Saxon achievement," in A. Grant and K. J. Stringer (eds.), *Uniting the Kingdom? The Making of British History* (London, 1995), pp. 30–47.

Campbell, J., John, E., and Wormald, P., *The Anglo-Saxons* (London, 1982).

Candon, A., "Muirchertach Ua Briain, politics and naval activity in the Irish Sea, 1075–1119," in G. Mac Niocaill and P. F. Wallace (eds.), *Keimelia* (Galway, 1988), pp. 397–415.

Carr, A. D., "Teulu and Penteulu," in T. M. Charles-Edwards (ed.), *The Welsh King and his Court* (Cardiff, 2000), pp. 63–81.

Carver, M., "An Iona of the east: the early-medieval monastery at Portmahomack, Tarbat Ness," *Medieval Archaeology*, 48 (2004), 1–30.

Carver, M., "Reflections on the meanings of monumental barrows in Anglo-Saxon England," in S. Lucy and A. Reynolds (eds.), *Burial in Early Medieval England and Wales* (London, 2002), pp. 132–43.

Carver, M., *Sutton Hoo: A Seventh-century Princely Burial Ground and its Context* (London, 2005).

Carver, M., "Why that? Why there? Why then? The politics of early medieval monumentality," in H. Hamerow and A. MacGregor (eds.), *Image and Power in the Archaeology of Early Medieval Britain* (Oxford, 2001), pp. 1–22.

Cavill, P., Harding, S., and Jesch, J. "Revisiting *Dingesmere*," *Journal of the English Place-name Society*, 36 (2004), 25–38.

Chadwick, H. (trans.), *Saint Augustine: Confessions* (Oxford, 1991).

Chadwick, H., *Studies on Anglo-Saxon Institutions* (Cambridge, 1905).

Chandler, V., "The last of the Montgomerys: Roger the Poitevin and Arnulf," *Historical Research*, 62 (1989), 1–14.

Chaplais, P., "The Anglo-Saxon chancery: from the diploma to the writ," *Journal of the Society of Archivists*, 3: 4 (1966), 160–76, reprinted in F. Ranger (ed.), *Prisca Munimenta*, (1973), pp. 43–62.

Chaplais, P., "The origin and authenticity of the royal Anglo-Saxon diploma," *Journal of the Society of Archivists*, 3: 2 (1965), 48–61; reprinted in F. Ranger (ed.), *Prisca Munimenta* (1973), pp. 28–42.

Chaplais, P., "Who introduced charters into England? The case for Augustine," *Journal of the Society of Archivists* 3: 10 (1969), 526–42; reprinted in F. Ranger (ed.), *Prisca Munimenta* (1973), pp. 88–107.

Charles-Edwards, T. M. (ed.), *After Rome* (Oxford, 2003).

Charles-Edwards, T. M., "Anglo-Saxon kinship revisited," in J. Hines (ed.), *The Anglo-Saxons from the Migration Period to the Eighth Century* (Woodbridge, 1997), pp. 171–204.

Charles-Edwards, T. M., "Bede, the Irish and the Britons," *Celtica*, 15 (1983), 42–52.

Charles-Edwards, T. M., "Boundaries in Irish law," in P. H. Sawyer (ed.), *Medieval Settlement: Continuity and Change* (London, 1976), pp. 83–7.

Charles-Edwards, T. M. (ed. and trans.), *The Chronicle of Ireland*, 2 vols. Translated Texts for Historians, 44 (Liverpool, 2006).

Charles-Edwards, T. M., "The context and uses of literacy in early Christian Ireland," in H. Pryce (ed.), *Literacy in Medieval Celtic Societies* (Cambridge, 1998), pp. 62–82.

Charles-Edwards, T. M., "'The Continuation of Bede,' ca.750: High-kings, kings of Tara and 'Bretwaldas'," in A. P. Smyth (ed.), *Seanchas: Studies in Medieval Irish Archaeology, History and Literature in Honour of Francis J. Byrne* (Dublin, 2000), pp. 137–45.

Charles-Edwards, T. M., "Conversion to Christianity," in T. M. Charles-Edwards (ed.), *After Rome* (Oxford, 2003), pp. 103–39.

Charles-Edwards, T. M., "*Críth Gablach* and the law of status," *Peritia*, 5 (1986), 53–73.

Charles-Edwards, T. M., "The distinction between land and moveable wealth in Anglo-Saxon England," in P. H. Sawyer (ed.), *Medieval Settlement: Continuity and Change* (London: Arnold, 1976), pp. 180–7.

Charles-Edwards, T. M., *Early Christian Ireland* (Cambridge, 2000).

Charles-Edwards, T. M. "Early Irish law," in D. Ó Cróinín (ed.), *A New History of Ireland*, vol. 1: *Prehistoric and Early Ireland* (Oxford, 2005), pp. 331–70.

Charles-Edwards, T. M., *Early Irish and Welsh Kinship* (Oxford, 1993).

Charles-Edwards, T. M., *The Early Medieval Gaelic Lawyer* (Cambridge, 1999).

Charles-Edwards, T. M., "Early medieval kingships in the British Isles," in S. Bassett (ed.), *The Origins of Anglo-Saxon Kingdoms* (Leicester, 1989), pp. 28–39.

Charles-Edwards, T. M., "Food, drink and clothing in the laws of court," in T. M. Charles-Edwards, M. E. Owen, and P. Russell (ed.), *The Welsh King and his Court* (Cardiff, 2000), pp. 319–37.

Charles-Edwards, T. M., "The heir-apparent in Irish and Welsh law," *Celtica*, 9 (1971), 180–90.

Charles-Edwards, T. M., "Irish warfare before 1100," in T. Bartlett and K. Jeffreys (eds.), *A Military History of Ireland* (Cambridge, 1996), pp. 26–51.

Charles-Edwards, T. M., "Kinship, status and the origins of the hide," *Past & Present*, 56 (1972), 3–33.

Charles-Edwards, T. M., "The lure of Celtic languages, 1850–1914," in M. Costambeys, A. Hamer, and M. Heale (eds.), *The Making of the Middle Ages* (Liverpool, 2007), pp. 15–35.

Charles-Edwards, T. M., "The pastoral role of the church in the early Irish laws," in J. Blair and R. Sharpe (eds.), *Pastoral Care before the Parish* (Leicester, 1992), pp. 63–80.

Charles-Edwards, T. M., "The seven bishop-houses of Dyfed," *Bulletin of the Board of Celtic Studies*, 24 (1970–2), 247–62.

Charles-Edwards, T. M., "The social background to Irish *peregrinatio*," *Celtica*, 11 (1976), 43–59.

Charles-Edwards, T. M., "Wales and Mercia, 613–918," in M. Brown and C. Farr (eds.), *Mercia: An Anglo-Saxon Kingdom in Europe* (London, 2001), pp. 89–105.

Charles-Edwards, T. M., *The Welsh Laws* (Cardiff, 1989).

Charles-Edwards, T. M., Owen, M. E., and Russell, P. (eds.), *The Welsh King and his Court* (Cardiff, 2000).

Chazelle, C., "Ceolfrid's gift to St. Peter: the first quire of the *Codex Amiatinus* and the evidence for its Roman destination," *Early Medieval Europe*, 12 (2003), 129–58.

Chibnall, M. (ed.), *The Ecclesiastical History of Orderic Vitalis, Volume II, Books III and IV* (Oxford, 1969).

Christiansen, E. (trans.), *Dudo: De Moribus*, in *History of the Normans* (Woodbridge, 1998).

Clanchy, M., *From Memory to Written Record, England 1066–1307*, 2nd edn. (Oxford, 1993).

Clancy, T. O., "Annat in Scotland and the origins of the parish," *Innes Review*, 46 (1995), 91–115.

Clancy, T. O., "Iona, Scotland and the *Céli Dé*," in B. E. Crawford (ed.), *Scotland in Dark Age Britain* (St. Andrews, 1996), pp. 111–20.

Clancy, T. O., "Philosopher king: Nechtan mac-Der-Ilei," *Scottish Historical Review*, 83 (2004), 125–49.

Clancy, T. O., "The real St. Ninian," *Innes Review*, 52 (2001), 1–28.

Clancy, T. O., *The Triumph Tree: Scotland's Earliest Poetry AD 550–1350* (Edinburgh, 1998).

Clark, C., *Words, Names and History: Selected Writings of Cecily Clark*, ed. P. Jackson (Cambridge, 1995).

Clarke, H. and Ambrosiani, B., *Towns in the Viking Age*, 2nd edn. (Leicester, 1995).

Clarke, H. B., "Proto-towns and towns in Ireland and Britain in the ninth and tenth centuries," in H. B. Clarke, M. Ní Mhaonaigh, and R. Ó Floinn (eds.), *Ireland and Scandinavia in the Early Viking Age* (Dublin, 1998), pp. 331–80.

Clarke, H. B., "The topographical development of early medieval Dublin," in H. B. Clarke (ed.), *Medieval Dublin: The Making of a Metropolis* (Blackrock, 1990), pp. 52–69.

Clarke, H. B. and Simms, A. (eds.), *The Comparative History of Urban Origins in Non-Roman Europe: Ireland, Wales, Denmark, Germany, Poland, and Russia from the Ninth to the Thirteenth Century*, British Archaeological Reports, International Series 255, 2 vols. (Oxford, 1985).

Clarke, H. B., Ní Mhaonaigh, M., and Ó Floinn, R. (eds.), *Ireland and Scandinavia in the Early Viking Age* (Dublin, 1998).

Clarke, P. A., *The English Nobility under Edward the Confessor* (Oxford, 1994).

Clayton, M., "Ælfric's Esther: a speculum reginae?," in H. Conrad O'Briain, A. M. D'Arcy, and J. Scattergood (eds.), *Text and Gloss: Studies in Insular Language and Literature Presented to Joseph Donovan Pheifer* (Dublin, 1999), pp. 89–101.

Clayton, M., *The Cult of the Virgin Mary in Anglo-Saxon England* (Cambridge, 1990).

Clinton, M., "Settlement patterns in the early historical kingdom of Leinster (seventh to mid twelfth century)," in A. P. Smyth (ed.), *Seanchas: Studies in Early and Medieval Irish Archaeology, History and Literature in Honour of Francis J. Byrne* (Dublin, 1999), pp. 275–98.

Clover, H. and Gibson, M. (eds.), *The Letters of Lanfranc, Archbishop of Canterbury* (Oxford, 1979).

Coggins, D., "Simy Folds: twenty years on," in J. Hines, A. Lane, and M. Redknap (eds.), *Land, Sea and Home*. Proceedings of a Conference on Viking-period Settlement, Cardiff, July 2001 (Leeds, 2004), pp. 325–34.

Colgrave, B. (ed. and trans.), *Felix's Life of Saint Guthlac* (Cambridge, 1956).

Colgrave, B. (ed. and trans.), *The Life of Bishop Wilfrid by Eddius Stephanus* (Cambridge, 1927; repr. New York, 1985).

Colgrave, B. (ed. and trans.), *Two Lives of Saint Cuthbert* (Cambridge, 1940).

Colgrave, B. and Mynors, R. A. B. (eds.), *Bede's Ecclesiastical History of the English People* (Oxford, 1969; rev. imp., 1991).

Collins, R. and McClure, J. (trans.), *Bede: The Ecclesiastical History of the English People* (Oxford, 1994).

Conner, P. W., *Anglo-Saxon Exeter: A Tenth-century Cultural History* (Woodbridge, 1993).

Connolly, S. and Picard, J.-M. (trans.), "Cogitosus, *Life of St. Brigit*," *Journal of the Royal Society of Antiquaries of Ireland*, 117 (1987), 11–27.

Connon, A., "The *Bánshenchas* and the Uí Néill queens of Tara," in A. P. Smyth (ed.), *Seanchas: Studies in Early and Medieval Irish Archaeology, History and Literature in Honour of Francis J. Byrne* (Dublin, 2000), pp. 98–108.

Constable, G., *Letters and Letter-Collections*. Typologie des sources fasc. 17 (Turnhout, 1976).

Constable, G., *Monastic Tithes: From their Origins to the Twelfth Century* (Cambridge, 1964).

Cosgrove, A. (ed.), *A New History of Ireland*, vol. 2: *Medieval Ireland 1169–1534* (Oxford, 2005).

Costambeys, M., "Æthelflæd, ruler of the Mercians (d.918)," *Oxford Dictionary of National Biography* (Oxford, 2004).

Costambeys, M., "Erik Bloodaxe, Viking leader and King of Northumbria (d.954)," *Oxford Dictionary of National Biography* (Oxford, 2004).

Coupland, S., "The coinage of Charlemagne," in J. Story (ed.), *Charlemagne: Empire and Society* (Manchester, 2005), pp. 211–29.

Coupland, S., "From poachers to gamekeepers: Scandinavian warlords and Carolingian kings," *Early Medieval Europe*, 7 (1998), 85–114.

Cowan, E. J., "The invention of Celtic Scotland," in E. J. Cowan and R. A. McDonald (eds.) *Alba: Celtic Scotland in the Middle Ages* (East Linton, 2000), pp. 1–23.

Cowan, I. B., "The development of the parochial system," in I. B. Cowan, *The Medieval Church in Scotland*, ed. J. Kirk (Edinburgh, 1995), no. 1.

Cowdrey, H. E. J., *Lanfranc: Scholar, Monk and Archbishop* (Oxford, 2003).

Cowley, F., "The relics of St. David: the historical evidence," in J. W. Evans and J. M. Wooding (eds.), *St. David of Wales: Cult, Church and Nation* (Woodbridge, 2007), pp. 274–81.

Cownie, E., "The Normans as patrons of English religious houses, 1066–1135," *Anglo-Norman Studies*, 18 (1996), 47–62.

Coxe, H. O. (ed.), *Rogeri de Wendover Chronica, sive Flores historiarum*, 5 vols. (London, 1841–4).

Cramp, R., *Corpus of Anglo-Saxon Stone Sculpture*, vol. 1: *County Durham and Northumberland* (Oxford, 1984).

Cramp, R., *Early Northumbrian Sculpture*, Jarrow Lecture 1965 (Jarrow, n.d.).

Cramp, R., *Wearmouth and Jarrow Monastic Sites*, 2 vols. (Swindon, 2005).

Craster, E., "The patrimony of St. Cuthbert," *English Historical Review*, 69 (1954), 5–19.

Craster, H. H. E., "The Red Book of Durham," *English Historical Review*, 40 (1925), 504–35.

Crawford, B. E., *Scandinavian Scotland* (Leicester, 1987).

Crawford, I. A., "War or peace: viking colonisation in the northern and western isles of Scotland reviewed," in H. Bekker-Nielsen (ed.), *The Eighth Viking Congress* (Odense, 1981), pp. 259–69.

Crouch, D., *The Normans: The History of a Dynasty* (London, 2002).

Crouch, D., "The slow death of kingship in Glamorgan, 1067–1158," *Morgannwg*, 29 (1985), 20–41.

Cubbin, G. P. (ed.), *The Anglo-Saxon Chronicle: A Collaborative Edition*, 6, MS D (Cambridge, 1996).

Cubbon, M., "The archaeology of the vikings in the Isle of Man," in C. Fell, P. Foote, J. Graham-Campbell, and R. Thomson (eds.), *The Viking Age in the Isle of Man* (London, 1983), pp. 13–26.

Cubitt, C., *Anglo-Saxon Church Councils c.650–c.850* (London, 1995).

Cubitt, C., "Folklore and historiography: oral stories and the writing of Anglo-Saxon history," in E. Tyler and R. Balzaretti (eds.), *Narrative and History in the Early Middle Ages* (Turnhout, 2006), pp. 189–223.

Cubitt, C., *Sin and Society in Tenth- and Eleventh-century England* (forthcoming).

Cubitt, C., "Sites and sanctity: revisiting the cults of murdered and martyred Anglo-Saxon royal saints," *Early Medieval Europe*, 9 (2000), 53–83.

Cubitt, C., "The tenth-century Benedictine reform in England," *Early Medieval Europe*, 6 (1997), 77–94.

Cubitt, C., "Virginity and misogyny in tenth- and eleventh-century England," *Gender and History*, 12 (2000), 1–32.

Cubitt, C., "Wilfrid's 'usurping bishops': episcopal elections in Anglo-Saxon England c.600–800," *Northern History*, 25 (1989), 18–39.

Curtis, E., *A History of Ireland* (London, 1936).

Curtis, E., *A History of Medieval Ireland from 1086 to 1513*, 2nd edn. (London, 1938).

Curtis, E., "Murchertach O'Brien, high king of Ireland, and his Norman son-in-law, Arnulf de Montgomery, c.1100," *Journal of the Royal Society of Antiquaries of Ireland*, 6th series, 11 (1921), 116–24.

Cyril, H., *The Danelaw* (London, 1992).

Dalton, P., *Conquest, Anarchy and Lordship: Yorkshire, 1066–1154* (Cambridge, 1994).

Darby, H. C. and Finn, R. W. (eds.), *The Domesday Geography of South-west England* (Cambridge, 1967).

Dark, K., *Britain and the End of the Roman Empire* (Stroud, 2000).

Darlington, R. R., "Æthelwig, abbot of Evesham," *English Historical Review*, 48 (1933), 1–22.

Darlington, R. R. and McGurk, P. (eds.), *The Chronicle of John of Worcester*, vol. II: *The Annals from 450 to 1066* (Oxford, 1995).

Davidson, M. R., "The (non)submission of the northern kings in 920," in N. J. Higham and D. H. Hill (eds.), *Edward the Elder 899–924* (London, 2001), pp. 200–11.

Davies, J. R., "The archbishopric of St. Davids and the bishops of *Clas Cynidr*," in J. W. Evans and J. M. Wooding (eds.), *St. David of Wales: Cult, Church and Nation* (Woodbridge, 2007), pp. 296–304.

Davies, J. R., "Aspects of church reform in Wales, c.1093–c.1223," *Anglo-Norman Studies*, 30 (2008), 85–99.

Davies, J. R., *The Book of Llandaf and the Norman Church in Wales* (Woodbridge, 2003).

Davies, J. R., "The saints of south Wales and the Welsh church," in A. T. Thacker and R. Sharpe (eds.), *Local Saints and Local Churches in the Early Medieval West* (Oxford, 2002), pp. 361–95.

Davies, M., "Gruffydd ap Llywelyn, king of Wales," *Welsh History Review*, 21 (2002–3), 207–48.

Davies, R. R., *Conquest, Coexistence and Change: Wales 1063–1415* (Oxford, 1987).

Davies, R. R., *The First English Empire: Power and Identities in the British Isles 1093–1343* (Oxford, 2000).

Davies, R. R., *The Matter of Britain and the Matter of England* (Oxford, 1996).

Davies, R. R., "The state: the tyranny of a concept?," *Journal of Historical Sociology*, 15 (2002), 71.

Davies, S., *Welsh Military Institutions, c.633–1283* (Cardiff, 2003).

Davies, W., "Adding insult to injury: power, property and immunities in early medieval Wales," in W. Davies and P. Fouracre (eds.), *Property and Power in the Early Middle Ages* (Cambridge, 1995) pp. 137–64.

Davies, W., "Alfred's contemporaries: Irish, Welsh, Scots and Breton," in T. Reuter (ed.), *Alfred the Great* (Aldershot, 2003), pp. 323–37.

Davies, W., "Braint Teilo," *Bulletin of the Board of Celtic Studies*, 26 (1976), 123–33.

Davies, W., "The Celtic kingdoms," in P. Fouracre (ed.), *The New Cambridge Medieval History*, vol. 1: *c.500–c.700* (Cambridge, 2005), pp. 232–62.

Davies, W., "Celtic kingships in the early Middle Ages," in A. J. Duggan (ed.), *Kings and Kingship in Medieval Europe* (London, 1993), pp. 101–24.

Davies, W., "Celtic women in the early Middle Ages," in A. Cameron and A. Kuhrt (eds.), *Images of Women in Antiquity*, rev. edn. (London, 1993), pp. 145–66.

Davies, W. "Charter-writing and its uses in early medieval Celtic societies," in H. Pryce (ed.), *Literacy in Medieval Celtic Societies* (Cambridge, 1998), pp. 99–112.

Davies, W., *An Early Welsh Microcosm: Studies in the Llandaff Charters* (London, 1978).

Davies, W. (ed.), *From the Vikings to the Normans* (Oxford, 2003).

Davies, W., "The Latin charter-tradition in western Britain, Brittany and Ireland in the early mediaeval period," in D. Whitelock, R. McKitterick, and D. Dumville (eds.), *Ireland in Early Mediaeval Europe: Studies in Memory of Kathleen Hughes* (Cambridge, 1982), pp. 258–80.

Davies, W., *The Llandaff Charters* (Aberystwyth, 1979).

Davies, W., "Looking backwards to the early medieval past: Wales and England, a contrast in approaches," *Welsh History Review*, 22 (2004), 197–221.

Davies, W., "The myth of the Celtic church," in N. Edwards and A. Lane (eds.), *The Early Church in Wales and the West* (Oxford, 1992), pp. 12–21.

Davies, W., *Patterns of Power in Early Wales* (Oxford, 1990).

Davies, W., *Small Worlds: The Village Community in Early Medieval Brittany* (London, 1988).

Davies, W., *Wales in the Early Middle Ages* (Leicester, 1982).

Davies, W. and Fouracre, P. (eds.), *The Settlement of Disputes in Early Medieval Europe* (Cambridge, 1986).

Davies, W. and Vierck, H., "The contexts of Tribal Hidage: social aggregates and settlement patterns," *Frühmittelalterliche Studien*, 8 (1974), 223–93.

Davis, R., *The Book of the Popes*, III: *The Ninth-century Popes* (Liverpool, 1995).

Davis, R. H. C., "Alfred the Great: propaganda and truth," *History*, 55 (1971), 169–82, reprinted in R. H. C. Davis, *From Alfred the Great to Stephen* (London, 1991), pp. 33–46.

de Jong, M. "Carolingian monasticism: the power of prayer," in R. McKitterick (ed.), *New Cambridge Medieval History*, vol. II (Cambridge, 1995), pp. 622–53.

de Jong, M., "Religion," in R. McKitterick (ed.), *The Early Middle Ages: Europe 400–1000* (Oxford, 2001), pp. 131–64.

de Jong, M. and Theuws, F (eds.), *Topographies of Power in the Early Middle Ages* (Leiden, 2001).

Deshman, R., *The Benedictional of Æthelwold* (Princeton, NJ, 1995).

Deshman, R., "*Christus Rex et Magi Reges*: kingship and Christology in Ottonian and Anglo-Saxon art," *Frühmittelalterliche Studien*, 10 (1976), 367–405.

Dobbs, M. E., "The Ban-shenchus," *Revue Celtique*, 47 (1930), 282–339; 48 (1931), 163–233; 49 (1932), 437–89.

Doble, G. H. and Evans, D. S (ed.), *Lives of the Welsh Saints* (Cardiff, 1971).

Dodgson, J. McN., "The significance of the distribution of the English place-names in -*ingas*, -*nga*- in south east England," *Medieval Archaeology*, 10 (1967 for 1966), 1–29.

Dodwell, C. R., *Anglo-Saxon Art: A New Perspective* (Manchester, 1982).

Doherty, C., "The cult of St. Patrick and the politics of Armagh in the seventh century," in J.-M. Picard (ed.), *Ireland and Northern France AD 600–850* (Dublin, 1991), pp. 53–94.

Doherty, C., "Exchange and trade in early medieval Ireland," *Journal of the Royal Society of Antiquaries of Ireland*, 110 (1980), 67–90.

Doherty, C., "The monastic town in early medieval Ireland," in H. B. Clarke and A. Simms (eds.), *The Comparative History of Urban Origins in Non-Roman Europe: Ireland, Wales, Denmark, Germany, Poland and Russia from the Ninth to the Thirteenth Century* (Oxford, 1985), part 1, pp. 45–75.

Doherty, C., "The Vikings in Ireland: a review," in H. B. Clarke, M. Ní Mhaonaigh, and R. Ó Floinn (eds.), *Ireland and Scandinavia in the Early Viking age* (Dublin, 1998), pp. 288–330.

Dolley, R. H. M. and Metcalf, D. M., "The reform of the English coinage under Eadgar," in R. H. M. Dolley (ed.), *Anglo-Saxon Coins: Studies Presented to F. M. Stenton* (London, 1961), pp. 136–68.

Donaldson, G., "Bishops' sees before the reign of David I," in G. Donaldson, *Scottish Church History* (Edinburgh, 1985), no. 2.

Donovan, M., Passmore, K., and Berger, S. (eds.), *Writing National Histories: Western Europe since 1800* (London, 1999 and 2005).

Douglas, D. C. and Greenaway, G. W. (eds.), *English Historical Documents*, vol. 2: *1042–1189* (London, 1981).

Downham, C., "An imaginary raid on Skye in 795?," *Scottish Gaelic Studies*, 20 (2000), 192–6.

Downham, C., *Viking Kings of Britain and Ireland: The Dynasty of Ívarr to AD 1014* (Edinburgh, 2007).

Drewett, P., Rudling, D., and Gardiner, M., *The South-East to AD 1000* (London, 1988).

Driscoll, S., "The archaeology of state formation in Scotland," in W. S. Hanson and E. A. Slater (eds.), *Scottish Archaeology: New Perceptions* (Aberdeen, 1991), pp. 81–111.

Driscoll, S., "The relationship between history and archaeology: artefacts, documents and power," in S. Driscoll and S. Nieke (eds.), *Power and Politics in Early Medieval Britain and Ireland* (Edinburgh, 1988), pp. 162–87.

Duby, G., *The Early Growth of the European Economy: Warriors and Peasants from the Seventh to the Twelfth Century*, trans. H. B. Clarke (London, 1974).

Duchesne, L. (ed.), *Liber Pontificalis [Book of the Popes]*, 2 vols. Bibliothèque des Écoles Françaises d'Athènes et de Rome, series 2, 3 (Rome, 1886–92).

Dudley-Edwards, R., *Patrick Pearse: The Triumph of Failure* (London, 1977).

Duffy, S., "The 1169 invasion as a turning-point in Irish–Welsh relations," in B. Smith (ed.), *Britain and Ireland 900–1300: Insular Responses to Medieval European Change* (Cambridge, 1999), pp. 98–113.

Duffy, S., "Ireland and Scotland, 1014–1169: contacts and caveats" in A. P. Smyth (ed.), *Seanchas: Essays presented to Francis J. Byrne* (Dublin, 2000), pp. 346–56.

Duffy, S., "Irishmen and Islesmen in the Kingdoms of Dublin and Man, 1052–1171," *Ériu*, 43 (1992), 93–133.

Duffy, S., "Ostmen, Irish and Welsh in the eleventh century," *Peritia*, 9 (1996), 378–96.

Duffy, S., "The royal dynasties of Dublin and the Isles in the eleventh century," in S. Duffy (ed.), *Medieval Dublin VII* (Dublin, 2006), pp. 51–65.

Duffy, S., " 'The western world's tower of honour and dignity': the career of Muirchertach Ua Briain in context," in D. Bracken and D. Ó Riain-Raedel (eds.), *Ireland and Europe in the Twelfth Century: Reform and Renewal* (Dublin, 2006), pp. 56–73.

Duggan, A. (ed.), *Queens and Queenship in Medieval Europe* (Woodbridge, 1997).

Dümmler, E. (ed.), *Alcuin: Epistolae, MGH Eppistolae* IV (Berlin, 1895).

Dumville, D. N. (ed.), *Annales Cambriae* (Cambridge, 2002).

Dumville, D. N., "The Chronicle of the Kings of Alba," in S. Taylor (ed.), *Kings, Clerics and Chronicles in Scotland, 500–1297: Essays in Honour of Marjorie Ogilvie Anderson on the Occasion of her Ninetieth Birthday* (Dublin, 2000), pp. 73–86.

Dumville, D. N., *The Churches of North Britain in the First Viking Age* (Whithorn, 1997).

Dumville, D. N., "Ecclesiastical lands and the defence of Wessex in the first Viking-Age," in D. Dumville (ed.), *Wessex and England from Alfred to Edgar* (Woodbridge, 1992), pp. 29–54.

Dumville, D. N., *English Caroline Script and Monastic History: Studies in Benedictinism, AD 950–1030* (Woodbridge, 1993).

Dumville, D. N., "Kingship, genealogies and regnal lists," in P. H. Sawyer and I. N. Wood (eds.), *Early Medieval Kingship* (Leeds, 1977), pp. 72–104.

Dumville, D. N., "Latin and Irish in the *Annals of Ulster*, AD 431–1050," in D. Whitelock, R. McKitterick, and D. N. Dumville (eds.), *Ireland in Early Mediaeval Europe: Studies in Memory of Kathleen Hughes* (Cambridge, 1982), pp. 320–41.

Dumville, D. N., *Liturgy and the Ecclesiastical History of Late Anglo-Saxon England* (Woodbridge, 1992).

Dumville, D. N., "St. Cathróe of Metz and the hagiography of exoticism," in J. Carey, M. Herbert, and P. Ó Riain (eds.), *Studies in Irish Hagiography: Saints and Scholars* (Dublin, 2001), pp. 172–88.

Dumville, D. N., *Saint Patrick AD 493–1993* (Woodbridge, 1993).

Dumville, D. N., "The 'six' sons of Rhodri Mawr: a problem in Asser's *Life of King Alfred*," *Cambridge Medieval Celtic Studies*, 4 (1983), 5–18.

Dumville, D. N., "Sub-Roman Britain: history and legend," *History*, 62 (1977), 173–92.

Dumville, D. N., *Three Men in a Boat*. Inaugural Lecture in the University of Cambridge (Cambridge, 1997).

Dumville, D., "The Tribal Hidage: an introduction to its texts and their history," in S. Bassett (ed.), *The Origins of Anglo-Saxon Kingdoms* (Leicester, 1989), pp. 225–30.

Dumville, D. N., "The Vikings in the British Isles," in J. Jesch (ed.), *The Scandinavians from the Vendel Period to the Tenth Century: An Ethnographic Perspective* (Woodbridge, 2001), pp. 209–40.

Dumville, D. N., *Wessex and England from Alfred to Edgar* (Woodbridge, 1992).

Dumville, D. N. and Keynes, S. D. (eds.), *The Anglo-Saxon Chronicle: A Collaborative Edition* (Cambridge, 1983–).

Duncan, A. A. M., *The Kingship of the Scots, 842–1292: Succession and Independence* (Edinburgh, 2002).

Duncan, A. A. M., *Scotland: The Making of the Kingdom* (Edinburgh, 1975).

Dutton, P. E. (trans.), *Charlemagne's Courtier: The Complete Einhard* (Peterborough, Ont., 1998).

Dyer, C., *Making a Living in the Middle Ages: The People of Britain 850–1250* (London, 2002).

Eckhardt, K. A. (ed.), *Pactus legis Salicae, MGH*, Legum Sectio I, iv. 1 (Hanover, 1962).

Eco, U., *The Name of the Rose*, trans. W. Weaver (London, 1984).

Edmondson, J. C., "Mining in the later Roman Empire and beyond: continuity or disruption?," *Journal of Roman Studies*, 79 (1989), 84–102.

Edwards, B. J. N., *Vikings in North-West England* (Lancaster, 1998).

Edwards, N., *The Archaeology of Early Medieval Ireland* (London, 1990).

Edwards, N., "Celtic saints and early medieval archaeology," in A. T. Thacker and R. Sharpe (eds.), *Local Saints and Local Churches in the Early Medieval West* (Oxford, 2002), pp. 225–65.

Edwards, N., "Early-medieval inscribed stones and stone sculptures in Wales: context and function," *Medieval Archaeology*, 45 (2001), 15–39.

Edwards, N. (ed.), *Landscape and Settlement in Medieval Wales* (Oxford, 1997).

Edwards, N. and Lane, A. (eds.), *The Early Church in Wales and the West* (Oxford, 1992).

Emanuel, H. D. (ed.), *The Latin Texts of the Welsh Laws* (Cardiff, 1967).

Emerton, E. (trans.), *The Letters of Saint Boniface* (New York, 1976).

Enright, M. J., *Iona, Tara and Soissons: The Origins of the Royal Anointing Ritual* (Berlin, 1985).

Enright, M. J., *Lady with a Mead Cup: Ritual, Prophecy and Lordship in the European Warband from La Tène to the Viking Age* (Dublin, 1996).

Esmonde Cleary, S., *The Ending of Roman Britain* (London, 1989).

Etchingham, C., *Church Organisation in Ireland, AD 650 to 1000* (Maynooth, 1999).

Etchingham, C., "Early medieval Irish history," in K. McCone and K. Simms (eds.), *Progress in Medieval Irish Studies* (Maynooth, 1996), pp. 123–53.

Etchingham, C., "North Wales, Ireland and the Isles: the insular Viking zone," *Peritia*, 15 (2001), 145–87.

Etchingham, C., "Pastoral provision in the first millennium: a two-tier service?," in E. FitzPatrick and R. Gillespie (eds.), *The Parish in Medieval and Early Modern Ireland: Community, Territory and Building* (Dublin, 2006), pp. 79–90.

Evans, D. S. (ed.), *Historia Gruffud vab Kenan / Gyda rhagymadrodd a nodiadau gan* (Cardiff, 1977).

Evans, D. S. (ed. and trans.), *A Mediaeval Prince of Wales: The Life of Gruffudd ap Cynan* (Felinfach, 1990).

Evans, J. G. and Rhys, J. (eds.), *Liber Landavensis: The Text of the Book of Llan Dav* (Aberystwyth, 1979).

Evans, J. W. and Wooding, J. M. (eds.), *St. David of Wales: Cult, Church and Nation* (Woodbridge, 2007).

Fairweather, J. (trans.), *Liber Eliensis: A History of the Isle of Ely from the Seventh Century to the Twelfth* (Woodbridge, 2005).

Faith, R., *The English Peasantry and the Growth of Lordship* (London, 1997).

Faulkener, N., *The Decline and Fall of Roman Britain* (Stroud, 2000).

Fell, C., with Clark, C. and Williams, E., *Women in Anglo-Saxon England* (London, 1985).

Fell, C., Foote, P., Graham-Campbell, J., and Thomson, R. (eds.), *The Viking Age in the Isle of Man* (London, 1983).

Fellows-Jensen, G., "Scandinavian place-names of the Irish Sea province," in J. Graham-Campbell (ed.), *Viking Treasure from the North-West: The Cuerdale Hoard in its Context* (Liverpool, 1992), pp. 31–42.

Fellows-Jensen, G., *Scandinavian Settlement Names in the East Midlands* (Copenhagen, 1978).

Fernández-Armesto, F., "The survival of a notion of *Reconquista* in late tenth- and eleventh-century León," in T. Reuter (ed.), *Warriors and Churchmen in the High Middle Ages: Essays Presented to Karl Leyser* (London, 1992), pp. 123–43.

Fernie, E. C., *The Architecture of Norman England* (Oxford, 2000).

Festugière, A. J. (ed and French trans.), *Leontius of Naples: Vie de Syméon le fou et vie de Jean de Chypre* [*Life of John the Almsgiver*] (Paris, 1974).

Finberg, H. P. R., *The Early Charters of Devon and Cornwall*, 2nd edn. (Leicester, 1963).

Finberg, H. P. R., "Sherborne, Glastonbury, and the expansion of Wessex," *Transactions of the Royal Historical Society*, 5th series, 3 (1953), 101–24.

Fitzpatrick, E., "Royal inauguration assembly and the church in medieval Ireland," in P. S. Barnwell and M. Mostert (eds.), *Political Assemblies in the Earlier Middle Ages* (Turnhout, 2003), pp. 73–93.

FitzPatrick, E. and Gillespie, R. (eds.), *The Parish in Medieval and Early Modern Ireland: Community, Territory and Building* (Dublin, 2006).

Flanagan, M. T., *Irish Royal Charters: Texts and Contexts* (Oxford, 2005).

Flanagan, M. T., *Irish Society, Anglo-Norman Settlers, Angevin Kingship* (Oxford, 1989).

Fleming, J., *Gille of Limerick (c.1070–1145): Architect of a Medieval Church* (Dublin, 2001).

Fleming, R., "Acquiring, flaunting and destroying silk in late Anglo-Saxon England," *Early Medieval Europe*, 15: 2 (2007), 127–58.

Fleming, R., "Bones for historians: putting the body back into biography," in D. Bates, J. Crick, and S. Hamilton (eds.), *Writing Medieval Biography: Essays in Honour of Frank Barlow* (Woodbridge, 2006), pp. 29–48.

Fleming, R., "Harold II, king of England (1022/3?–1066)," *Oxford Dictionary of National Biography* (Oxford, 2004).

Fleming, R., *Kings and Lords in Conquest England* (Cambridge, 1991).

Fleming, R., "Lords and labour," in W. Davies (ed.), *From the Vikings to the Normans* (Oxford, 2003), pp. 107–37.

Fleming, R., "Monastic lands and England's defence in the Viking Age," *English Historical Review*, 100 (1985), 247–65.

Fleming, R., "The new wealth, the new rich and the new political style in late Anglo-Saxon England," *Anglo-Norman Studies*, 23 (2001), 1–22.

Fleming, R., "Rural elites and urban communities in late-Saxon England," *Past & Present*, 141 (1993), 3–37.

Fletcher, I. F., *Latin Redaction A of the Law of Hywel* (Aberystwyth, 1986).

Fletcher, R. A., *Bloodfeud: Murder and Revenge in Anglo-Saxon England* (London, 2002).

Fletcher, R. A., *The Conversion of Europe: From Paganism to Christianity 371–1386 AD* (London, 1997).

Folz, R., *Les Saintes reines du moyen âge en occident, vie–xiiie siècles* (Brussels, 1992).

Foot, S., "Æthelstan, king of England (893/4–939)," *Oxford Dictionary of National Biography* (Oxford, 2004).

Foot, S., "The historiography of the Anglo-Saxon 'nation-state,'" in L. Scales and O. Zimmer (eds.), *Power and the Nation in European History* (Cambridge, 2005), pp. 125–42.

Foot, S., *Monastic Life in Anglo-Saxon England, c.600–900* (Cambridge, 2006).

Foot, S., *Veiled Women*, 2 vols. (Aldershot, 2000).

Forbes-Leith, W. (trans.), "Turgot, *Life of St. Margaret*," in M. Stouck (ed.), *Medieval Saints: A Reader* (Peterborough, Ont., 1999), pp. 273–94.

Foreman, S., Hiller, J., and Petts, D., *Gathering the People, Settling the Land* (Oxford, 2002).

Forsyth, K., "Literacy in Pictland," in H. Pryce (ed.), *Literacy in Medieval Celtic Societies* (Cambridge, 1998), pp. 39–61.

Forsyth, K., "Some thoughts on Pictish symbols as a formal writing system," in D. Henry (ed.), *The Worm, the Germ and the Thorn: Pictish and Related Studies Presented to Isabel Henderson* (Balgavies, 1997), pp. 85–98.

Forte, A., Oram, R., and Pedersen, F., *Viking Empires* (Oxford, 2005).

Foster, S., *Picts, Gaels and Scots: Early Historic Scotland* (London, 1996).

Fouracre, P., *The Age of Charles Martel* (Harmondsworth, 2000).

Fouracre, P., "Cultural conformity and social conservatism in early medieval Europe," *History Workshop* Journal, 33 (1992), 152–61.

Fouracre, P., "Eternal light and earthly needs: practical aspects of the development of Frankish immunities," in W. Davies and P. Fouracre (eds.), *Property and Power in the Early Middle Ages* (Cambridge, 1995), pp. 53–81.

Fouracre, P., "Forgetting and remembering Dagobert II: the English connection," in P. Fouracre and D. Ganz (eds.), *Frankland: The Franks and the World of Early Medieval Europe* (Manchester, 2008), pp. 70–89.

Fouracre, P. (ed.), *New Cambridge Medieval History*, vol. 1 (Cambridge, 2005).

Fouracre, P., "The origins of the nobility in Francia," in A. J. Duggan (ed.), *Nobles and Nobility in Medieval Europe: Concepts, Origins, Transformations* (Woodbridge, 2000), pp. 17–24.

Fouracre, P. and Gerberding, R., *Late Merovingian France: History and Hagiography 640–720* (Manchester, 1996).

Fox, C., *The Personality of Britain: Its Influence on Inhabitant and Invader in Prehistoric and Early Historic Times*, 4th edn. (Cardiff, 1943).

Frame, R., *The Political Development of the British Isles, 1100–1400* (Oxford, 1990).

France, J. (ed.), *Rodulfus Glaber: Historiarum libri quinque* (Oxford, 1989).

Franklin, C. V., "The date of composition of Bede's *De Schematibus et Tropis* and *De Arte Metrica*," *Revue Bénédictine*, 110 (2000), 199–203.

Frend, W. H. C., "*Ecclesia Britannica*: prelude or dead end?," *Journal of Ecclesiastical History*, 30 (1979), 129–44.

Fulk, R. D. and Cain, C. M., *A History of Old English Literature* (Oxford, 2003).

Fulton, H., "Tenth-century Wales and *Armes Prydein*," *Transactions of the Honourable Society of Cymmrodorion*, new series, 7 (2001), 5–18.

Gameson, R., *The Role of Art in the Late Anglo-Saxon Church* (Oxford, 1995).

Gameson, R. (ed.), *St. Augustine and the Conversion of England* (Stroud, 1999).

Gameson, R., "St. Wulfstan, the library of Worcester and the spirituality of the medieval book," in J. Barrow and N. Brooks (eds.), *Bishop Wulfstan and his World* (Aldershot, 2005), pp. 59–109.

Gannon, A., *The Iconography of Early Anglo-Saxon Coinage: Sixth to Eighth Centuries* (Oxford, 2003).

Ganz, J. (trans.), *The Mabinogion* (Harmondsworth, 1976).

Gardiner, M., "Shipping and trade between England and the continent during the eleventh century," *Anglo-Norman Studies*, 22 (1999), 71–93.

Garmonsway, G. N. (trans.), *The Anglo-Saxon Chronicle* (London, 1972).

Garrison, M., "The Franks as the New Israel? Education for an identity from Pippin to Charlemagne," in Y. Hen and M. Innes (eds.), *The Uses of the Past in the Early Middle Ages* (Cambridge, 2000), pp. 114–61.

Garrison, M., " 'Send more socks': on mentality and the preservation context of early medieval letters," in M. Mostert (ed.), *Approaches to Medieval Communication* (Turnhout, 1999), pp. 69–99.

Geake, H., *The Use of Grave-goods in Conversion-period England, c.600–c.850*, British Archaeological Reports, British series 261 (Oxford, 1997).

Geake, H. and Kenny, J. (eds.), *Early Deira: Archaeological Studies of the East Riding in the Fourth to Ninth Centuries AD* (Oxford, 2000).

Geary, P., *Women at the Beginning: Origin Myths from the Amazons to the Virgin Mary* (Princeton, NJ, 2006).

Gelling, M., *Signposts to the Past: Place-names and the History of England* (London, 1978).

Gelling, M., *The West Midlands in the Early Middle Ages* (Leicester, 1992).

Gelling, P., "A Norse homestead near Doarlish Cashen, Kirk Patrick, Isle of Man," *Medieval Archaeology*, 14 (1970), 74–82.

Gerriets, M., "Economy and society: clientship according to the Irish laws," *Cambridge Medieval Celtic Studies*, 6 (1983), 43–61.

Gibson, M., *Lanfranc of Bec* (Oxford, 1978).

Giese, M. (ed.), *Annales Quedlinburgenses* (Hanover, 2004).

Gillingham, J., "The beginnings of English imperialism," *Journal of Historical Sociology*, 5: 4 (1992), 392–409, reprinted in J. Gillingham, *The English in the Twelfth Century: Imperialism, National Identity and Political Values* (Woodbridge, 2000), pp. 3–18.

Gillingham, J., "Britain, Ireland and the south," in W. Davies (ed.), *From the Vikings to the Normans* (Oxford, 2003), pp. 203–32.

Gillingham, J., *The English in the Twelfth Century: Imperialism, National Identity and Political Values* (Woodbridge, 2000).

Gillingham, J., "Thegns and knights in eleventh-century England: who was then the gentleman?," *Transactions of the Royal Historical Society*, 6th series, 5 (1995), 129–53.

Gittos, H. and Bradford Bedingfield, M. (eds.), *The Liturgy of the Late Anglo-Saxon Church* (London, 2005).

Godden, M., "The player-king: identification and self-representation in King Alfred's writings," in T. Reuter (ed.), *Alfred the Great* (Aldershot, 2003), pp. 137–50.

Godman, P., *Poetry of the Carolingian Renaissance* (London, 1985).

Goffart, W., *The Narrators of Barbarian History (AD 550–800)* (Princeton, NJ, 1988).

Golding, B., "The coming of the Cluniacs," *Anglo-Norman Studies*, 3 (1980), 65–77.

Golding, B., *Conquest and Colonisation: The Normans in Britain, 1066–1100* (Basingstoke, 1994).

Goodacre, S., Helgason, A., Nicholson, J., et al., "Genetic evidence for a family-based Scandinavian settlement of Shetland and Orkney during the Viking periods," *Heredity*, 95 (2005), 129–35.

Goodier, A., "The formation of boundaries in Anglo-Saxon England: a statistical study," *Medieval Archaeology*, 28 (1984), 1–21.

Goody, J., *Production and Reproduction: A Comparative Study of the Domestic Domain* (Cambridge, 1976).

Graham, B. J., "Early medieval Ireland: settlement as an indicator of economic and social transformation, c.500–1199 AD," in B. J. Graham and L. J. Proudfoot (eds.), *An Historical Geography of Ireland* (London, 1993), pp. 19–57.

Graham-Campbell, J., "Review article: the archaeology of Anglian and Anglo-Scandinavian York," *Early Medieval Europe*, 5: 1 (1996), 71–82.

Graham-Campbell, J., "Viking Age silver hoards from Man," in C. Fell, P. Foote, J. Graham-Campbell, and R. Thomson (eds.), *The Viking Age in the Isle of Man* (London, 1983), pp. 53–80.

Graham-Campbell, J. and Batey, C., *Vikings in Scotland: An Archaeological Survey* (Edinburgh, 1998).

Graham-Campbell, J., Hall, R. A., Jesch, J., and Parsons, D. N. (eds.), *Vikings and the Danelaw: Select Papers from the Proceedings of the Thirteenth Viking Congress* (Oxford, 2001).

Gransden, A., *Historical Writing in England, c.550 to c.1307* (London, 1974).

Grant, A., "The construction of the early Scottish state," in J. R. Maddicott and D. M. Palliser (eds.), *The Medieval State: Essays Presented to James Campbell* (London, 2000), pp. 47–71.

Grat, F., Vielliard, J., and Clémencet, S. (eds.), *Annales Bertiniani, Annales de Saint-Bertin* (Paris, 1964).

Green, D. H. and Siegmund, F. (eds.), *The Continental Saxons from the Migration Period to the Tenth Century: An Ethnographic Perspective* (Woodbridge, 2003).

Greenaway, D. (ed. and trans.), *Henry Archdeacon of Huntingdon: Historia Anglorum* (Oxford, 1996).

Grierson, P. "Commerce in the Dark Ages," *Transactions of the Royal Historical Society*, 5th series, 9 (1959), 123–40, at 128, reprinted in P. Grierson, *Dark Age Numismatics* (Aldershot, 1981), ch. 2.

Grierson, P., "The relations between England and Flanders before the Norman Conquest," *Transactions of the Royal Historical Society*, 4th series, 23 (1941), 71–112.

Griffiths, D., "Exchange, trade and urbanization," in W. Davies (ed.), *From the Vikings to the Normans* (Oxford, 2003), pp. 73–104.

Griffiths, D., "The north-west frontier," in N. Higham and D. Hill (eds.), *Edward the Elder 899–924* (Manchester, 2001), pp. 167–87.

Griffiths, D., "Settlement and acculturation in the Irish Sea region," in J. Hines, A. Lane, and M. Redknap (eds.), *Land, Sea and Home*. Proceedings of a Conference on Viking-period Settlement, Cardiff, July 2001 (Leeds, 2004), pp. 125–38.

Griffiths, D., Philpott, R. A., and Egan, G., *Meols, the Archaeology of the North Wirral Coast: Discoveries and Observations in the 19th and 20th Centuries, with a Catalogue of Collections* (Oxford, 2007).

Griffiths, M. (ed.), *Judith* (Exeter, 1997).

Grimmer, M., "Britons in early Wessex: the evidence of the law code of Ine," in N. Higham (ed.), *Britons in Anglo-Saxon England* (Woodbridge, 2007), pp. 102–14.

Gwynn, A., "Brian in Armagh (1005)," *Seanchas Ardmhacha*, 9 (1978), 35–50.

Gwynn, A., "Ireland and Rome in the twelfth century," *Irish Ecclesiastical Record*, 57: 3 (1941), 213–32.

Gwynn, A., *The Irish Church in the Eleventh and Twelfth Centuries*, ed. G. O'Brien (Dublin, 1992).

Hadley, D. M., "In search of the Vikings: the problems and the possibilities of interdisciplinary approaches," in J. Graham-Campbell, R. A. Hall, J. Jesch, and D. N. Parsons (ed.), *Vikings and the Danelaw: Select Papers from the Proceedings of the Thirteenth Viking Congress, Nottingham and York, August 21–30, 1997.* (Oxford, 2001), pp. 13–30.

Hadley, D. M., *The Northern Danelaw: Its Social Structure, c.800–1100* (London, 2000).

Hadley, D. M., "Viking and native: re-thinking identity in the Danelaw," *Early Medieval Europe*, 11: 1 (2002), 45–70.

Hadley, D. M., *The Vikings in England: Settlement, Society and Culture* (Manchester, 2006).

Hadley, D. M. and Richards, J. D. (eds.), *Cultures in Contact: Scandinavian Settlement in England in the Ninth and Tenth Centuries* (Turnhout, 2000).

Haefele, H. F. (ed.), *Notker: Gesta Karoli, MGH SRG* 12 (Berlin, 1959). Thorpe, L. (trans.), *Two Lives of Charlemagne* (Harmondsworth, 1969).

Hall, A., *Elves in Anglo-Saxon England: Matters of Belief, Health, Gender and Identity* (Woodbridge, 2007).

Hall, D., (1989), "The sanctuary of St. Cuthbert," in G. Bonner, D. Rollason, and C. Stancliffe (eds.), *St. Cuthbert, his Cult and Community to AD 1200* (Woodbridge, 1989), pp. 425–36.

Hall, K. M., "Pre-Conquest estates in Yorkshire," in H. E. J. Le Patourel, M. H. Long, and M. F. Pickles (eds.), *Yorkshire Boundaries* (Leeds, 1993), pp. 25–38.

Hall, R. A., "Afterword," in R. A. Hall (ed.), *Aspects of Anglo-Scandinavian York* (York, 2004), pp. 498–502.

Hall, R. A., *Exploring the World of the Vikings* (London, 2007).

Hall, R. A., "The Five Boroughs of the Danelaw: a review of present knowledge," *Anglo-Saxon England*, 18 (1989), 149–206.

Hall, R. A., *Viking Age York* (London, 1994).

Hall, V. A., "The documentary and pollen analytical records of the vegetational history of the Irish landscape AD 200–1650," *Peritia*, 14 (2000), 342–71.

Halliday, F. E., *A History of Cornwall* (London, 1959).

Halloran, K., "The Brunanburh campaign: a reappraisal," *Scottish Historical Review*, 84 (2005), 133–48.

Halsall, G., *Early Medieval Cemeteries: An Introduction to Burial Archaeology in the Post-Roman West* (Glasgow, 1995).

Halsall, G. (ed.), *Humour, History and Politics in Late Antiquity and the Early Middle Ages* (Cambridge, 2002).

Halsall, G., *Settlement and Social Organization: The Merovingian Region of Metz* (Cambridge, 1995).

Halsall, G., *Warfare and Society in the Barbarian West, 450–900* (London, 2003).

Hamerow, H., "The earliest Anglo-Saxon kingdoms," in P. Fouracre (ed.), *The New Cambridge Medieval History*, vol. 1: *c.500–c.700* (Cambridge, 2005), pp. 263–90.

Hamerow, H., *Early Medieval Settlements: The Archaeology of Rural Communities in North-West Europe, 400–900* (Oxford, 2002).

Hamerow, H. F., "Settlement mobility and the 'Middle Saxon shift': rural settlements and settlement patterns in Anglo-Saxon England," *Anglo-Saxon England*, 20 (1991), 1–17.

Hamilton, S., *The Practice of Penance, 900–1050* (Woodbridge, 2001).

Hamilton, S., "Rites for public penance in late Saxon England," in H. Gittos and M. Bradford Bedingfield (eds.), *Liturgy of the Late Anglo-Saxon Church* (London, 2005), pp. 65–103.

Hammond, M. H., "Ethnicity and the writing of medieval Scottish history," *Scottish Historical Review*, 85: 1, no. 219 (2006), 1–27.

Handley, M., "The early medieval inscriptions of western Britain: function and sociology," in J. Hill and M. Swan (eds.), *The Community, the Family and the Saint: Patterns and Power in Early Medieval Europe* (Turnhout, 1998), pp. 339–61.

Handley, M. A., "The origins of Christian commemoration in late antique Britain," *Early Medieval Europe*, 10 (2001), 177–99.

Hare, M., "Cnut and Lotharingia: two notes," *Anglo Saxon England*, 29 (2000), 261–78.

Härke, H., "Early Anglo-Saxon social structure," in J. Hines (ed.), *The Anglo-Saxons from the Migration Period to the Eighth Century* (Woodbridge, 1997), pp. 125–60.

Härke, H., "'Warrior graves?' The background of the Anglo-Saxon weapon burial rite," *Past & Present*, 126 (1990), 22–43.

Harrington, C., *Women in a Celtic Church: Ireland 450–1150* (Oxford, 2002).

Hart, C. R., "Æthelstan Half-king (fl. 932–56)," *Oxford Dictionary of National Biography* (Oxford, 2004).

Hart, C. R., "Athelstan 'Half-king' and his family," *Anglo-Saxon England*, 2 (1973), 115–144.

Hart, C. R., *The Early Charters of Northern England and the North Midlands* (Leicester, 1975).

Hart, C. R. (2004), "Wulfstan (d.955/6)," *Oxford Dictionary of National Biography* (Oxford, 2004).

Hedeager, L., "Kingdoms, ethnicity and material culture: Denmark in a European perspective," in M. Carver (ed.), *The Age of Sutton Hoo* (Woodbridge, 1992), pp. 297–300.

Hedeager, L., "Scandinavia," in P. Fouracre (ed.), *New Cambridge Medieval History*, vol. I (Cambridge, 2005), pp. 496–523.

Heighway, M., "Anglo-Saxon Gloucester to AD 1000," in M. L. Faull (ed.), *Studies in Late Anglo-Saxon Settlement* (London, 1984), pp. 35–53.

Heighway, M., "Gloucester and the New Minster of St. Oswald," in D. Hill and N. J. Higham (eds.), *Edward the Elder* (Manchester, 2001), pp. 102–11.

Heist, W. W. (ed.), *Vitae sanctorum Hiberniae ex Codice olim Salmanticensi nunc Bruxellensi* (Brussels, 1965).

Hellmann, S. (ed.), "Pseudo-Cyprian," *De XII Abusivis saeculi [On the Twelve Abuses of the World]*. Texte und Untersuchungen zur Geschichte der altchristliche Literatur, 34 (1909), pp. 1–61.

Hen, Y. and Innes, M., *Uses of the Past in the Early Middle Ages* (Cambridge, 2000).

Henderson, G., *Bede and Visual Arts,* Jarrow Lecture 1980 (Jarrow, n.d.).

Henderson, G., *From Durrow to Kells: The Insular Gospel-books 650–800* (London, 1987).

Henderson, G. and Henderson, I., *The Art of the Picts: Sculpture and Metalwork in Early Medieval Scotland* (London, 2004).

Henig, M. and Lindley, P. (eds.), *Alban and St. Albans: Roman and Medieval Architecture, Art and Archaeology* (London, 2001).

Hennessy, W. M. (ed. and trans.), *Chronicum Scotorum: A Chronicle of Irish Affairs, from the Earliest Times to AD 1135; with a Supplement, containing the Events from 1141 to 1150*. Rolls series 46. (London, 1866).

Hennessey, W. M. and MacCarthy, B. (ed. and trans.), *Annals of Ulster, Otherwise, Annals of Senat: A Chronicle of Irish Affairs from AD 431 to AD 1540*, 3 vols. (Dublin, 1887–1901).

Herbert, M., "Goddess and king: the sacred marriage in early Ireland," in L. O. Fradenburg (ed.), *Women and Sovereignty* (*Cosmos*, vol. 7; Edinburgh, 1992), pp. 264–75.

Herbert, M., *Iona, Kells, and Derry: The History and Hagiography of the Monastic Familia of Columba* (Oxford, 1988; repr. Dublin, 1996).

Herbert, M., "*Rí Éirenn, Rí Alban*: kingship and identity in the ninth and tenth centuries," in S. Taylor (ed.), *Kings, Clerics and Chronicles in Scotland, 500–1297* (Dublin, 2000), pp. 62–72.

Herbert, M., "Sea-divided Gaels? Constructing relationships between Irish and Scots c.800–1169," in B. Smith (ed.), *Britain and Ireland 900–1300: Insular Responses to Medieval European Change* (Cambridge, 1999), pp. 87–97.

Herity, M., *Studies in the Layout, Buildings and Art in Stone of Early Irish Monasteries* (London, 1995).

Herren, M., *Hisperica Famina I: The A-Text* (Toronto, 1974).

Herren, M., "Scholarly contacts between the Irish and the southern English in the seventh century," *Peritia*, 12 (1998), 24–53.

Hey, G., *Yarnton: Saxon and Medieval Settlement and Landscape: Results of Excavations 1990–96* (Oxford, 2004).

Higham, N. J., *The Convert Kings: Power and Religious Affiliation in Early Anglo-Saxon England* (Manchester, 1997).

Higham, N. J., "The Domesday survey: context and purpose," *History*, 78 (1993), 7–21.

Higham, N. J., *A Frontier Landscape: The North West in the Middle Ages* (Macclesfield, 2004).

Higham, N. J., *King Arthur: Myth-making and History* (London, 2002).

Higham, N. J., *The Kingdom of Northumbria, AD 350–1100* (Stroud, 1993).

Higham, N. J., *Rome, Britain and the Anglo-Saxons* (London, 1992).

Higham, N. J., "Viking-Age settlement in the north-western countryside: lifting the veil?," in J. Hines, A. Lane, and M. Redknap (eds.), *Land, Sea and Home*. Proceedings of a Conference on Viking-period Settlement, Cardiff, July 2001 (Leeds, 2004), pp. 297–311.

Hill, D., *An Atlas of Anglo-Saxon England* (Oxford, 1981).

Hill, D. (ed.), *Ethelred the Unready*, British Archaeological Reports, British series 59 (Oxford, 1978).

Hill, D., "Gazetteer of Burghal Hidage sites," in D. Hill and A. R. Rumble (eds.), *The Defence of Wessex: The Burghal Hidage and Anglo-Saxon Fortifications* (Manchester, 1996), pp. 189–231.

Hill, D. (ed.), "Tribal Hidage," in *An Atlas of Anglo-Saxon England* (Oxford, 1981) pp. 76–7.

Hillgarth, J. N., "Ireland and Spain in the seventh century," *Peritia*, 3 (1984), 1–16.

Hills, C., *Origins of the English* (London, 2003).

Hines, J. (ed.), *The Anglo-Saxons from the Migration Period to the Eighth Century: An Ethnographic Perspective* (Woodbridge, 1997).

Hines, J., "The becoming of the English: identity, material culture and language in early Anglo-Saxon England," *Anglo-Saxon Studies in Archaeology and History*, 7 (1994), 49–59.

Hines, J., "Religion: the limits of knowledge" in J. Hines (ed.), *The Anglo-Saxons: From the Migration Period to the Eighth Century* (Woodbridge, 1997), pp. 375–410.

Hines, J., "The Scandinavian character of Anglian England: an update," in M. Carver (ed.), *The Age of Sutton Hoo: The Seventh Century in North Western Europe* (Woodbridge, 1992), pp. 317–29.

Hines, J., Lane, A., and Redknap, M. (eds.), *Land, Sea and Home* (Leeds, 2004).

Hinton, D., *Archaeology, Economy and Society: England from the Fifth to the Fifteenth Century* (London, 1990).

Hinton, D. A., *Gold and Gilt, Pots and Pins: Possessions and Peoples in Medieval Britain* (Oxford, 2005).

Hinton, D. A., "The large towns 600–1300," in D. M. Palliser (ed.), *The Cambridge Urban History of Britain*, vol. I: *600–1540* (Cambridge, 2000), pp. 217–43.

Hodges, R., *The Anglo-Saxon Achievement: Archaeology and the Beginnings of English Society* (London, 1989).

Hodges, R. and Hobley, B. (eds.), *The Rebirth of Towns in the West AD 700–1050*. CBA Report 68 (London, 1988).

Hoffmann, H. (ed.), *Richer: Historiarum libri IIII, MGH SS* 38 (Hanover, 2000).

Hogan, E. (ed.) *Móirtimchell Éirenn uile dorigne Muirchertach mac Néill* (Dublin, 1901).

Holder-Egger, O. (ed.), *Einhard: Vita Karoli, MGH SRG* 25 (Hanover, 1911).

Holland, M., "Cashel, synod of (1101)," in S. Duffy (ed.), *Medieval Ireland: An Encyclopedia* (New York, 2005), pp. 65–6.

Holland, M., "Dublin and the reform of the Irish church in the eleventh and twelfth centuries," *Peritia*, 14 (2000), 111–60.

Holland, M., "Ráith Bressail, synod of," in S. Duffy (ed.), *Medieval Ireland: An Encyclopedia* (New York, 2005), pp. 397–8.

Holland, M., "The synod of Dublin in 1080," in S. Duffy (ed.), *Medieval Dublin III* (Dublin, 2002), pp. 81–94.

Holt, J. C., "1086," in *Domesday Studies*. Papers Read at the Novocentenary Conference of the Royal Historical Society and the Institute of British Geographers, Winchester, 1986 (Woodbridge, 1987), pp. 41–64.

Hood, A. B. E. (ed. and trans.), *St. Patrick: His Writings and Muirchu's Life* (Chichester, 1978).

Hooke, D., *The Anglo-Saxon Landscape: The Kingdom of the Hwicce* (Manchester, 1985).

Hope-Taylor, B., *Yeavering: An Anglo-British Centre of Early Northumbria* (London, 1977).

Hoskins, W. G., *The Westward Expansion of Wessex* (Leicester, 1960).

Howlett, D. R. (ed. and trans.), *The Book of Letters of Saint Patrick the Bishop* (Blackrock, Co. Dublin, 1994).

Hudson, B. T., "Cnut and the Scottish kings," *English Historical Review*, 107 (1992), 350–60.

Hudson, B. T., "Cnut and Viking Dublin" and "Cnut and the Scottish kings," reprinted in B. Hudson, *Irish Sea Studies 900–1200* (Dublin, 2006), chs. 2 and 3.

Hudson, B. T., "The family of Harold Godwinson and the Irish Sea province," *Journal of the Royal Society of Antiquaries of Ireland*, 109 (1979) 92–100; reprinted in B. Hudson, *Irish Sea Studies 900–1200* (Dublin, 2006), ch. 6.

Hudson, B. T., *Kings of Celtic Scotland* (Westport, CT, 1994).

Hudson, B. T., "Kings and church in early Scotland," *Scottish Historical Review*, 73 (1994), 145–70.

Hudson, B. T., *Prophecy of Berchan: Irish and Scottish High-kings of the Early Middle Ages* (Westport, CT, 1996).

Hudson, B. T. (ed. and trans.), "The Scottish Chronicle," *Scottish Historical Review*, 77 (1998), 129–61.

Hudson, B. T., "William the Conqueror and Ireland," *Irish Historical Studies*, 29 (1994), 145–58.

Hughes, K., *The Church in Early Irish Society* (London, 1966).

Hughes, K., "The Irish church, 800–c.1050," in D. Ó Cróinín (ed.), *A New History of Ireland*, vol. 1 (Oxford, 2005), pp. 635–55.

Huneycutt, L., "The idea of the perfect princess: the *Life of St. Margaret* in the reign of Mathilda II (1100–1118)," *Anglo-Norman Studies*, 12 (1990), 81–98.

Huneycutt, L., *Matilda of Scotland: A Study in Medieval Queenship* (Woodbridge, 2003).

Hyams, P. R., "Feud and the state in late Anglo-Saxon England," *Journal of British Studies*, 40: 1 (2001), 1–43.

Hyams, P. R., *Rancor and Reconciliation in Medieval England: Wrong and its Redress from the Tenth to Thirteenth Centuries* (Ithaca, 2003).

Innes, M., *An Introduction to Early Medieval Western Europe, 300–900: The Sword, the Plough, and the Book* (London, 2007).

Innes, M., *State and Society in the Early Middle Ages: The Middle Rhine Valley, 400–1000* (Cambridge, 2000).

Insley, C., "Assemblies and charters in late Anglo-Saxon England," in P. S. Barnwell and M. Mostert (eds.), *Political Assemblies in the Earlier Middle Ages* (Turnhout, 2003), pp. 47–59.

Insley, C., "Politics, conflict and kinship in early eleventh-century Mercia," *Midlands History*, 25 (2000), 28–42.

Insley, C., "Where did all the charters go? Anglo-Saxon charters and the new politics of the eleventh century," *Anglo-Norman Studies*, 24 (2002), 109–27.

Isaac, G. R., "*Armes Prydein Fawr* and St. David," in J. W. Evans and J. M. Wooding (eds.), *St. David of Wales: Cult, Church and Nation* (Woodbridge, 2007), pp. 161–81.

Jackson, K. H., *The Gaelic Notes in the Book of Deer* (Cambridge, 1972).

James, E., *Britain in the First Millennium* (London, 2001).

Jarman, A. O. H. (ed. and trans.), *Aneirin: The Gododdin* (Llandysul, 1988).

Jarman, A. O. H., *The Cynfeirdd: Early Welsh Poets and Poetry* (Cardiff, 1981).

Jaski, B., *Early Irish Kingship and Succession* (Dublin, 2000).

Jaski, B., "Marriage laws in Ireland and on the continent in the early Middle Ages," in C. Meek and K. Simms (eds.), *The Fragility of her Sex? Medieval Irish Women in their European Context* (Blackrock, Co. Dublin, 1996), pp. 16–42.

Jaski, B., "Vikings and the kingship of Tara," *Peritia*, 9 (1995), 310–53.

Jenkins, D. (trans.), *The Law of Hywel Dda: Law Texts from Medieval Wales* (Llandysul, 1986).

Jenkins, D., and Owen, M. E. (eds.), *The Welsh Law of Women: Studies Presented to Professor Daniel A. Binchy on his Eightieth Birthday* (Cardiff, 1980).

Jenkins, D. and Owen, M. E., "The Welsh marginalia in the Lichfield Gospels, part 1" *Cambridge Medieval Celtic Studies*, 5 (1983), 37–66.

Jenkins, D. and Owen, M. E., "The Welsh marginalia in the Lichfield Gospels, part 2: the 'surexit' memorandum," *Cambridge Medieval Celtic Studies*, 7 (1984), 91–120.

Jennings, A., "Iona and the Vikings: survival and continuity," *Northern Studies*, 30 (1998), 37–54.

John, E., "Folkland reconsidered," in E. John, *Orbis Britanniae and Other Studies* (Leicester, 1966), pp. 64–127.

John, E., *Land Tenure in Early England: A Discussion of Some Problems* (Leicester, 1960, repr. 1964).

John, E., *Orbis Britanniae and Other Studies* (Leicester, 1966).

John, E., "The West Saxon conquest of England," in E. John, *Reassessing Anglo-Saxon England* (Manchester, 1996), pp. 83–98.

Johnson, M. and Rees, A., "Excavation of an early historic palisaded enclosure at Titwood, Mearnskirk, East Renfrewshire," *Scottish Archaeological Journal*, 25: 2 (2003), 129–46.

Johnson South, T. (ed.), *Historia de Sancto Cuthberto: A History of Saint Cuthbert and a Record of his Patrimony* (Woodbridge, 2002).

Johnston, D. R. (ed.), *Gwaith Iolo Goch* (Cardiff, 1988).

Johnston, E., "Early Irish history: the state of the art," *Irish Historical Studies*, 33: 131 (2003), 342–8.

Joliffe, J. E. A., "Northumbrian institutions," *English Historical Review*, 41: 161 (1926), 1–42.

Jolly, K. L., *Popular Religion in Late Saxon England* (Chapel Hill, NJ, 1996).

Jones, C. A., "The chrism mass in later Anglo-Saxon England," in H. Gittos and M. Bradford Bedingfield (eds.), *The Liturgy of the Late Anglo-Saxon Church* (London, 2005), pp. 105–42.

Jones, G. and Jones, T. (trans.), *The Mabinogion* (London, 1974).

Jones, G. R. J., "Early territorial organization in Gwynedd and Elmet," *Northern History*, 10 (1975), 3–27.

Jones, G. R. J., "Multiple estates and early settlement," in P. H. Sawyer (ed.), *English Medieval Settlement* (London, 1979), pp. 9–34.

Jones, G. R. J., "Post-Roman Wales," in H. P. R. Finberg (ed.), *The Agrarian History of England and Wales*, vol. 1, part 2: AD 43–1042 (Cambridge, 1972), pp. 283–382.

Jones, T. (ed.), *Brenhinedd y Saesson, or The Kings of the Saxons* (Cardiff, 1971).

Jones, T. (trans.), *Brut y Tywysogion or the Chronicle of the Princes, Peniarth MS 20 Version* (Cardiff, 1952).

Jones, T. (ed.), *Brut y Tywysogion or the Chronicle of the Princes, Red Book of Hergest Version*, 2nd edn. (Cardiff, 1973).

Kapelle, W. E., *The Norman Conquest of the North: The Region and its Transformation, 1000–1135* (London, 1979).

Kastovsky, D., "Semantics and vocabulary," in R. Hogg (ed.), *The Cambridge History of the English Language*, vol. 1 (Cambridge, 1992), pp. 290–408.

Kelly, F., *Early Irish Farming: A Study Based Mainly on the Law-texts of the Seventh and Eighth Centuries AD* (Dublin, 1997).

Kelly, F., *A Guide to Early Irish Law* (Dublin, 1988).

Kelly, S., "Trading privileges from eighth-century England," *Early Medieval Europe*, 1 (1992), 3–28.

Kelly, S. E. "Anglo-Saxon lay society and the written word," in R. McKitterick (ed.), *The Uses of Literacy in Early Mediaeval Europe* (Cambridge, 1990), pp. 36–62.

Kelly, S. E., *Charters of Abingdon Abbey*, part 1 (Oxford, 2000).

Kelly, S. E. (ed.), *Charters of Selsey* (Oxford, 1998).

Ker, N., *Catalogue of Manuscripts Containing Anglo-Saxon* (Oxford, 1957), plus "A supplement to *Catalogue of Manuscripts containing Anglo-Saxon*," *Anglo-Saxon England*, 5 (1976), 121–31.

Kerlouégan, F., *Le De excidio Britanniae de Gildas: les destinées de la culture latine dans L'Ile de Bretagne au vie siècle* (Paris, 1987).

Kermode, J. (2000), "Northern towns," in D. M. Palliser (ed.), *The Cambridge Urban History of Britain: Volume I, 600–1540* (Cambridge, 2000), pp. 657–79.

Kershaw, P., "The Alfred–Guthrum treaty: scripting accommodation and interaction in Viking-Age England," in D. M. Hadley and J. D. Richards (eds.), *Cultures in Contact: Scandinavian Settlement in England in the Ninth and Tenth Centuries* (Turnhout, 2000), pp. 43–64.

Keynes, S., "Æthelred, king of England (c.966x8–1016)," *Oxford Dictionary of National Biography* (Oxford, 2004).

Keynes, S., *An Atlas of Attestations in Anglo-Saxon Charters, c.670–1066* (Cambridge, 2002).

Keynes, S., "Cnut's earls," in A. R. Rumble (ed.), *The Reign of Cnut: King of England, Denmark and Norway* (London, 1994), pp. 43–88.

Keynes, S., "The control of Kent in the ninth century," *Early Medieval Europe*, 2: 2 (1993), 111–31.

Keynes, S., "Crime and punishment in the reign of Æthelred the Unready," in I. Wood and N. Lund (eds.), *People and Places in Northern Europe 500–1600: Essays in Honour of Peter Hayes Sawyer* (Woodbridge, 1991), pp. 67–81.

Keynes, S., *The Diplomas of King Æthelred "the Unready" 978–1016: A Study in their Use as Historical Evidence* (Cambridge, 1980).

Keynes, S., "Ely Abbey 672–1109," in P. Meadows and N. Ramsay (eds.), *A History of Ely Cathedral* (Woodbridge, 2003), pp. 3–58.

Keynes, S., "England, c.900–1016," in T. Reuter (ed.), *New Cambridge Medieval History*, vol. III: *c.900–c.1024* (Cambridge, 1999), pp. 456–84.

Keynes, S., "The Fonthill letter," in M. Korhammer (ed.), *Words, Texts and Manuscripts: Studies in Anglo-Saxon Culture Presented to Helmut Gneuss on the Occasion of his Sixty-fifth Birthday* (Cambridge, 1992), pp. 53–97.

Keynes, S., "Giso, bishop of Wells (1061–88)," *Anglo-Norman Studies*, 19 (1997), 203–71.

Keynes, S., "Royal government and the written word in late Anglo-Saxon England," in R. McKitterick (ed.), *The Uses of Literacy in Early Medieval Europe* (Cambridge, 1990), pp. 226–57.

Keynes, S., "The Vikings in England," in P. H. Sawyer (ed.), *The Oxford Illustrated History of the Vikings* (Oxford, 1997), pp. 44–82.

Keynes, S., "Wulfsige, monk of Glastonbury, abbot of Westminster (900[sic]–3), and bishop of Sherborne, (c.993–1002)," in K. Barker, D. A. Hinton, and A. Hunt (eds.), *St. Wulfsige and Sherborne* (Oxford, 2005), pp. 53–94.

Keynes, S., "Wulfstan I, archbishop of York (931–56)," in M. Lapidge, J. Blair, S. Keynes, and D. Scragg (eds.), *The Blackwell Encyclopaedia of Anglo-Saxon England* (Oxford, 1999), pp. 492–93.

Keynes, S. and Lapidge, M. (trans.), *Alfred the Great: Asser's Life of King Alfred and Other Contemporary Sources* (Harmondsworth, 1983).

Kharkov, C. E., *The Ruler Portraits of Anglo-Saxon England* (Woodbridge, 2004).

Kilmurry, K., *The Pottery Industry of Stamford* (Oxford, 1980).

King, A., "Post-Roman upland architecture in the Craven dales and the dating evidence," in J. Hines, A. Lane, and M. Redknap (eds.), *Land, Sea and Home*. Proceedings of a Conference on Viking-period Settlement, Cardiff, July 2001 (Leeds, 2004), pp. 335–44.

Kinsella, T. (trans.), *The Tain: Translated from the Irish Epic Tain Bo Cuailnge* (London, 1969).

Kirby, D. P., *Bede's Historia ecclesiastica gentis Anglorum: Its Contemporary Setting* (Jarrow, 1992).

Kirby, D. P., "Bede's native sources for the *Historia ecclesiastica*," *Bulletin of the John Rylands Library*, 48 (1965–8), 341–71.

Kirby, D. P., *The Earliest English Kings* (London, 1991).

Kirby, D. P., "Hywel Dda: anglophil?," *Welsh History Review*, 8 (1976–7), 1–13.

Kirby, D. P., "Strathclyde and Cumbria: a survey of historical development to 1092," *Transactions of the Cumberland and Westmorland Antiquarian and Archaeological Society*, 62, n.s. (1962), 77–94.

Klaeber, Fr. (ed.), *Beowulf and the Fight at Finnsburg*, 3rd edn. (Boston, 1950).

Klein, S. S., *Ruling Women: Queenship and Gender in Anglo-Saxon Literature* (Indiana, 2006).

Knowles, D., *The Monastic Order in England* (Cambridge, 1966).

Kobylinski, Z., "The Slavs," in P. Fouracre (ed.), *New Cambridge Medieval History*, vol. I (Cambridge, 2005), pp. 524–44.

Koch, J. T., *The Gododdin of Aneirin: Text and Context from Dark Age North Britain* (Cardiff, 1977).

Kottje, R., *Studien zum Einfluß des Alten Testaments auf Recht und Liturgie des frühen Mittelalters* (Bonn, 1964).

Krag, C., "Harald Hardrada (1015–1066)," *Oxford Dictionary of National Biography* (Oxford, 2004).

Krusch, B. (ed.), *Jonas: Vita Columbani, MGH, Scriptores Rerum Merovingicarum*, eds. B. Krusch and W. Levison, vol. 4 (Hanover, 1902), pp. 64–108.

Krusch, B. (ed.), *Vita Richarii, auctore Alcuino, MGH, Scriptores Rerum Merovingicarum*, eds. B. Krusch and W. Levison, vol. 4 (Hanover, 1902), pp. 389–401.

Kuurman, J. "An examination of the -ingas, -inga, place-names in the East Midlands," *English Place-Name Society Journal*, 7 (1975 for 1974), 11–44.

Lacey, B., *Cénel Conaill and the Donegal Kingdoms AD 500–800* (Dublin, 2006).

Laing, L., "The romanisation of Ireland in the fifth century," *Peritia*, 4 (1985), 261–78.

Lancaster, L., "Kinship in Anglo-Saxon society – I," *British Journal of Sociology*, 9 (1958), 230–50.

Lane, A. and Campbell, E., *Dunadd: An Early Dalriadic Capital* (Oxford, 2000).

Lapidge, M., *Anglo-Latin Literature 600–899* (London, 1996).

Lapidge, M., *Anglo-Latin Literature, 900–1066* (London, 1993).

Lapidge, M., *The Anglo-Saxon Library* (Oxford, 2006).

Lapidge, M. (ed.), *The Cult of St. Swithun* (Oxford, 2003).

Lapidge, M., "Gildas's education and the Latin culture of sub-Roman Britain," in M. Lapidge and D. Dumville (eds.), *Gildas: New Approaches* (Woodbridge, 1984), pp. 27–50.

Lapidge, M., "Latin learning in Dark Age Wales: some prolegomena," in D. E. Evans et al. (eds.), *Proceedings of the Seventh International Congress of Celtic Studies* (Oxford, 1985), pp. 91–107.

Lapidge, M., "Latin learning in ninth-century England," in M. Lapidge, *Anglo-Latin Literature 600–899* (London, 1996), pp. 409–54.

Lapidge, M., "The Welsh Latin poetry of Sulien's family," *Studia Celtica*, 8/9 (1973–4), 68–106.

Lapidge, M. and Bischoff, B., *Biblical Commentaries from the Canterbury School of Theodore and Hadrian* (Cambridge, 1994).

Lapidge, M. and Dumville, D. N. (eds.), *Gildas: New Approaches* (Woodbridge, 1984).

Lapidge, M. and Herren, M. (trans.), *Aldhelm: The Prose Works* (Cambridge, 1979).

Lapidge, M., Blair, W. J., Keynes, S. D., and Scragg, D. (eds.), *The Blackwell Encyclopaedia of Anglo-Saxon England* (Oxford, 1999).

Lauer, P. (ed.), *Les annales de Flodoard* (Paris, 1906).

Lavelle, R., *Aethelred II, King of the Engish 978–1016* (Stroud, 2002).

Law, V., *Grammar and Grammarians in the Early Middle Ages* (London, 1997).

Lawrie, A. C. (ed.), *Early Scottish Charters prior to 1153* (Glasgow, 1905).

Lawson, M. K., *The Battle of Hastings, 1066* (Stroud, 2002).

Lawson, M. K., "Cnut (d.1035)," *Oxford Dictionary of National Biography* (Oxford, 2004).

Lawson, M. K., *Cnut: The Danes in England in the Early Eleventh Century* (London, 1993).

Le Jan, R., *Famille et pouvoir dans le monde franc (viiᵉ–xᵉ siècle): essai d'anthropologie sociale* (Paris, 1995).

Leahy, K. and Paterson, C., "New light on the Viking presence in Lincolnshire: the artefactual evidence," in J. Graham-Campbell, R. A. Hall, J. Jesch, and D. N. Parsons (eds.), *Vikings and the Danelaw: Select Papers from the Proceedings of the Thirteenth Viking Congress* (Oxford, 2001), pp. 181–202.

Lebecq, S., "The northern seas (fifth to eighth centuries)," in P. Fouracre (ed.), *New Cambridge Medieval History*, vol. 1 (Cambridge, 2005), pp. 639–59.

Lebecq, S., "The role of monasteries in the Frankish world," in I. Hansen and C. Wickham (eds.), *The Long Eighth Century* (Leiden, 2001), pp. 121–48.

Levillain, L. (Fr. trans.) *Loup de Ferrières: Correspondance*, 2 vols (Paris, 1927, 1935).

Levison, W., *England and the Continent in the Eighth Century* (Oxford, 1946).

Levison, W. (ed.), *Vita Filiberti, MGH SRM 5* (Hanover, 1910), pp. 568–606.

Lewis, C. P., "The French in England before the Norman Conquest," *Anglo-Norman Studies*, 17 (1994), 123–44.

Lewis, C. P., "Waltheof, earl of Northumbria (c.1050–1076)," *Oxford Dictionary of National Biography* (Oxford, 2004).

Leyser, H., "Walcher, earl of Northumbria (d.1080)," *Oxford Dictionary of National Biography* (Oxford, 2004).

Leyser, K., "The Anglo-Saxons 'at home'," in D. Brown, J. Campbell, and S. C. Hawkes (eds.), *Anglo-Saxon Studies in Archaeology and History*, 2, *British Archaeological Reports*, British series 92 (Oxford, 1981), pp 237–42; reprinted in K. Leyser, *Communications and Power in Medieval Europe*: vol. I: *The Carolingian and Ottonian Centuries*, ed. T. Reuter (London, 1994), pp. 105–10.

Leyser, K., *Medieval Germany and its Neighbours 900–1250* (London, 1982).

Leyser, K., "The Ottonians and Wessex," in K. Leyser, *Communications and Power in Medieval Europe*, vol. I: *The Carolingian and Ottonian Centuries*, ed. T. Reuter (London, 1994), pp. 73–104.

Liebermann, F. (ed.), *Die Gesetze der Angelsaschen*, 3 vols. (Halle, 1903–16).

Liebermann, F. (ed.), *Die Heiligen Englands: Angelsächsisch und Lateinisch* (Hannover, 1889).

Lloyd, J. E., *A History of Wales from the Earliest Times to the Edwardian Conquest*, 3rd edn., 2 vols. (London, 1939).

Lohaus, A., *Die Merowinger und England* (Munich, 1974).

Lohier, F. and Laporte, J. (eds), *Gesta sanctorum patrum fontanellensis coenobii* [*Deeds of the Abbots of St.-Wandrille*] (Paris, 1936).

LoPrete, K., *Adela of Blois: Countess and Lord* (Dublin, 2006).

Loseby, S., "The Mediterranean economy," in P. Fouracre (ed.), *New Cambridge Medieval History*, vol. 1 (Cambridge, 2005), pp. 605–38.

Loth, J., "Persistance des institutions et de la langue des Brittons du Nord (ancien royaume de Stratclut), au 12e siècle," *Revue Celtique*, 47 (1930), 383–400.

Love, R. and Lapidge, M., "England and Wales (600–1550)," in G. Philippart (ed.), *Hagiographies: histoire internationale de la littérature hagiographique latine et vernaculaire, en Occident, des origines à 1500*, vol. 3 (Turnhout, 2001), pp. 203–325.

Loveluck, C., "Rural settlement hierarchy in the age of Charlemagne," in J. Story (ed.), *Charlemagne: Empire and Society* (Manchester, 2005), pp. 230–58.

Loveluck, C., *Rural Settlement, Lifestyles and Social Change in the Later First Millennium AD: Anglo-Saxon Flixborough in its Wider Context* (Oxford, 2007).

Loveluck, C., "Wealth, waste and conspicuous consumption: Flixborough and its importance for middle and late Anglo-Saxon rural settlement studies," in H. Hamerow and A. MacGregor (eds.), *Image and Power in the Archaeology of Early Medieval Britain: Essays in Honour of Rosemary Cramp* (Oxford, 2001), pp. 79–130.

Löwe, H., "*Dialogus de statu sanctae ecclesiae*: Das Werk eines Iren im Laon des 10. Jahrhunderts," *Deutsches Archiv*, 17 (1961), 12–90.

Löwe, H. (ed.), *Die Iren und Europa im früheren Mittelalter* (Stuttgart, 1982).

Loyn, H. R., "The conversion of the English to Christianity: some comments on the Celtic contribution," in R. R. Davies et al. (eds.), *Welsh Society and Nationhood: Historical Essays Presented to Glanmor Williams* (Cardiff, 1984), pp. 5–18.

Loyn, H. R., *The English Church 950–1154* (Harlow, 2000).

Loyn, H. R., "Gesiths and thegns in Anglo-Saxon England from the seventh to the tenth century," *English Historical Review*, 70: 277 (1955), 529–49.

Loyn, H. R., *The Governance of Anglo-Saxon England 500–1087* (London, 1984).

Loyn, H. R., "The hundred in England," in H. R. Loyn, *Society and Peoples: Studies in the History of England and Wales, c.600–1200* (Westfield, 1992), pp. 113–34.

Loyn, H. R., "The hundred in the tenth and early eleventh centuries," in H. Hearder and H. R. Loyn (eds.), *British Government and Administration: Studies Presented to S. B. Chrimes* (Cardiff, 1974), pp. 1–15.

Loyn, H. R., "Kings, gesiths and thegns," in M. Carver (ed.), *The Age of Sutton Hoo* (Woodbridge, 1992), pp. 75–9.

Loyn, H. R., *The Vikings in Britain* (London, 1977).

Loyn, H. R., "Welsh and English in the tenth century: the context of the Athelstan charters," *Welsh History Review*, 10 (1980–1), 283–301.

Loyn, H. R., "William's bishops: some further thoughts," *Anglo-Norman Studies*, 10 (1988), 222–35.

Loyn, H. R. and Percival, J. (eds. and trans.), *The Reign of Charlemagne* (London, 1975).

Lucy, S., *The Anglo-Saxon Way of Death: Burial Rites in Early England* (Stroud, 2000).

Lucy, S. and Reynolds, A. (eds.), *Burial in Early Medieval England and Wales*. Society for Medieval Archaeology Monograph Series, 17 (London, 2002).

Lynch, J. H., *Christianizing Kinship: Ritual Sponsorship in Anglo-Saxon England* (Ithaca, NY, 1998).

Mac Airt, S. (ed.), *The Annals of Inisfallen* (Dublin, 1944; reprinted 1951, 1977).

Mac Airt, S. and Mac Niocaill, G. (eds. and trans.), *The Annals of Ulster (to AD 1131)*, Part I: *Text and Translation* (Dublin, 1983).

Mac Cana, P., "Aspects of the theme of king and goddess in Irish literature," *Études Celtiques*, 7 (1955–6), 76–114 and 8 (1958), 59–68.

Mac Niocaill, G., *Notitiae as Leabhar Cheanannais, 1033–1161* (Dublin, 1961).

Mac Shamhráin, A., "The battle of Glenn Máma, Dublin and the high-kingship of Ireland: a millennial commemoration," in S. Duffy (ed.), *Medieval Dublin II* (Dublin, 2001), pp. 53–64.

Mac Shamhráin, A., "Brian Bóruma, Armagh and the high-kingship," *Seanchas Ardmhacha*, 20: 2 (2005), 1–21.

Mac Shamhráin, A. *Church and Polity in Pre-Norman Ireland: The Case of Glendalough* (Maynooth, 1996).

McAll, C., "The normal paradigms of a woman's life in the Irish and Welsh law texts," in D. Jenkins and M. E. Owen (eds.), *The Welsh Law of Women: Studies Presented to Professor Daniel A. Binchy on his Eightieth Birthday, 3 June 1980* (Cardiff, 1980), pp. 7–22.

McClure, J. and Collins, R. (trans.), *Bede's Ecclesiastical History of the English People* (Oxford, 1994).

McCone, K. and Simms, K., *Progress in Medieval Irish Studies* (Maynooth, 1996).

McCormick, M., *Origins of the European Economy: Communications and Commerce, AD 300–900* (Cambridge, 2001).

McErlean, T., McConkey, R., and Forsythe, W., *Strangford Lough: An Archaeological Survey of the Maritime Cultural Landscape* (Belfast, 2002).

McEvoy, B., Brady, C., Moore, L. T., et al., "The scale and nature of Viking settlement in Ireland from Y-chromosome admixture analysis," *European Journal of Human Genetics*, 14 (2006), 1288–94.

McGurk, P. (ed.) *The Chronicle of John of Worcester*, vol. III: *The Annals from 1067 to 1140 with the Gloucester Interpolations and the Continuation to 1141* (Oxford, 1998).

Mack, K., "Changing thegns: Cnut's conquest and the English aristocracy," *Albion*, 16 (1984), 375–87.

McKitterick, R., "Anglo-Saxon missionaries in Germany: reflections on the manuscript evidence," *Transactions of the Cambridge Bibliographical Society*, 9 (1989), 291–329.

McKitterick, R., *History and Memory in the Carolingian World* (Cambridge, 2004).

McKitterick, R. (ed.), *The Short Oxford History of Europe: The Early Middle Ages* (Oxford, 2001).

MacLean, S., *Kingship and Politics in the Late Ninth Century* (Cambridge, 2005).

McLeod, N., "Interpreting early Irish law: status and currency (part 1)," *Zeitschrift für Celtische Philologie*, 41 (1986), 46–65.

McLeod, N., "Interpreting early Irish law: status and currency (part 2)," *Zeitschrift für Celtische Philologie*, 42 (1987), 41–115.

McNamara, J. A. and Wemple, S., "The power of women through the family in medieval Europe," in M. Hartmann and L. W. Banner (eds.), *Clio's Consciousness Raised: New Perspectives on the History of Women* (New York, 1974), pp. 103–18.

MacNeill, E., "Ancient Irish law: the law of status or franchise," *Proceedings of the Royal Irish Academy*, 36 (1923), sec. C, 265–316.

MacNeill, E., *Celtic Ireland* (Dublin, 1921, reissued Dublin, 1981, with contribution by D. Ó Corráin).

MacNeill, E., "Early Irish population-groups: their nomenclature, classification and chronology," *Proceedings of the Royal Irish Academy*, 29C (1911), 59–114.

MacNeill, E., *Phases of Irish History* (Dublin, 1919).

McNeill, J. T. and Gamer, H. M. (trans.), *Medieval Handbooks of Penance* (New York, 1938).

Macquarrie, A., "Early Christian religious communities in Scotland: foundation and function," in J. Blair and R. Sharpe (eds.), *Pastoral Care before the Parish* (Leicester, 1992), pp. 110–33.

Maddicott, J., "Plague in seventh-century England," *Past & Present*, 156 (1997), 7–54.

Maddicott, J., "Prosperity and power in the age of Bede and Beowulf," *Proceedings of the British Academy*, 117 (2002), 49–71.

Maddicott, J. R., "Responses to the threat of invasion, 1085," *English Historical Review*, 122, no. 498 (2007), 986–97.

Malcolm, G. and Bowsher, D., *Middle Saxon London: Excavation at the Royal Opera House 1989–99* (London, 2003).

Mallory, J. P. and McNeill, T. E., *The Archaeology of Ulster: From Colonization to Plantation* (Belfast, 1991).

Manning, C., "Clonmacnoise cathedral," in H. King (ed.), *Clonmacnoise Studies*, vol. 1 (Dublin, 1998), pp. 57–86.

Margeson, S., "On the iconography of the Manx crosses," in C. Fell, P. Foote, J. Graham-Campbell, and R. Thomson (eds.), *The Viking Age in the Isle of Man* (London, 1983), pp. 95–106.

Margeson, S., *The Vikings in Norfolk* (Norwich, 1997).

Marshall, P. K. (ed.), *Lupus of Ferrières: Epistulae* (Leipzig, 1984).

Mason, E., *The House of Godwine: The History of a Dynasty* (London, 2004).

Mason, E., *St. Wulfstan of Worcester c.1008–1095* (Oxford, 1990).

Matthew, D., *Britain and the Continent 1000–1300* (London, 2005).

Maund, K. L., "Fact and narrative fiction in the Llandaff charters," *Studia Celtica*, 31 (1997), 173–93.

Maund, K. L. (ed.), *Gruffudd ap Cynan: A Collaborative Biography* (Woodbridge, 1996).

Maund, K. L., *Ireland, Wales, and England in the Eleventh Century* (Woodbridge, 1991).

Maund, K. L., *The Welsh Kings: The Medieval Rulers of Wales* (Stroud, 2000).

Mayr-Harting, H., *The Coming of Christianity to Early Anglo-Saxon England* (London, 1972; 3rd edn. 1991).

Mayr-Harting, H., *Two Conversions to Christianity: The Bulgarians and the Anglo-Saxons*. Stenton Lecture (Reading, 1994).

Mayr-Harting, H., "St. Wilfrid in Sussex," in M. J. Kitch (ed.), *Studies in Sussex Church History* (London, 1981), pp. 1–17.

Meehan, B., "The siege of Durham, the battle of Carham and the cession of Lothian," *Scottish Historical Review*, 55 (1976), 1–19.

Meek, C. E., and Simms, M. K. (eds.), *"The Fragility of her Sex"? Medieval Irish Women in their European Context* (Blackrock, Co. Dublin, 1996).

Meens, R., "Politics, mirrors of princes and the Bible: sins, kings and the well-being of the realm," *Early Medieval Europe*, 7: 3 (1998), 343–57.

Meyer, K. (ed. and trans.), *Cáin Adamnáin: An Old-Irish Treatise on the Law of Adamnan* (Oxford, 1905).

Middleton, N., "Early medieval port customs, tolls and controls and foreign trade," *Early Medieval Europe*, 13: 4 (2005), 313–58.

Millett, M., *The Romanization of Britain: An Essay in Archaeological Interpretation* (Cambridge, 1990).

Millett, M., with James, S., "Excavations at Cowdery's Down, Basingstoke, Hampshire, 1978–81," *Archaeological Journal*, 140 (1983), 151–279.

Moisl, H., "The Bernician royal dynasty and the Irish in the seventh century," *Peritia*, 2 (1983), 103–26.

Moore, D., *The Welsh Wars of Independence c.410–c.1415* (Stroud, 2005).

Moore, M. E., "La Monarchie Carolingienne et les anciens modèles Irlandais," *Annales, ESC*, 51: 2 (1996), 307–24.

Morris, C. D., "Raiders, traders and settlers: the early Viking Age in Scotland," in H. B. Clarke, M. Ní Mhaonaigh, and R. Ó Floinn (eds.), *Ireland and Scandinavia in the Early Viking Age* (Dublin, 1998), pp. 73–103.

Morris, C. J., *Marriage and Murder in Eleventh-century Northumbria: A Study of "De Obsessione Dunelmi,"* University of York, Borthwick Paper, no. 82 (York, 1992).

Morris, J. (gen. ed.), *Domesday Book*, 35 vols in 39 (Chichester, 1975–86; 3 index vols, 1992).

Morris, J. (trans.), *Nennius: British History and the Welsh Annals* (London, 1980).

Murphy, D. (ed. and trans.), *The Annals of Clonmacnoise being Annals of Ireland from the Earliest Period to AD 1408, translated into English AD 1627 by Conell Mageoghagan* (Dublin, 1896; reprinted Felinfach, 1993).

Murray, A., "Bede and the unchosen race," in H. Pryce and J. Watts (eds.), *Power and Identity in the Middle Ages: Essays in Memory of Rees Davies* (Oxford, 2007), pp. 52–67.

Murray, K. (ed.), *Baile in Scáil. "The Phantom's Frenzy."* Irish Texts Society 58 (Dublin, 2004).

Myhre, B., "The archaeology of the early Viking Age in Norway," in H. B. Clarke, M. Ní Mhaonaigh, and R. Ó Floinn (eds.), *Ireland and Scandinavia in the Early Viking Age* (Dublin, 1998), pp. 3–36.

Myhre, B., "The beginning of the Viking Age: some current archaeological problems," in A. Faulkes and R. Perkins (eds.), *Viking Revaluations: Viking Society Centenary Symposium* (London, 1993), pp. 182–204.

Mynors, R. A. B. et al. (eds.), *William of Malmesbury, Gesta regum Anglorum: The History of the English Kings*, 2 vols. (Oxford, 1998–9).

Mytum, H., *The Origins of Early Christian Ireland* (London, 1992).

Nash-Williams, V. E., *The Early Christian Monuments of Wales* (Cardiff, 1950).

Nees, L., *Early Medieval Art* (Oxford, 2002).

Nelson, J. L., "Æthelwulf," in *Oxford Dictionary of National Bibliography* (Oxford, 2003), vol. I, pp. 438–41.

Nelson, J. L., "Alfred's continental contemporaries," in T. Reuter (ed.), *Alfred the Great* (Aldershot, 2003), pp. 293–310.

Nelson, J. L. (trans.), *The Annals of St.-Bertin* (Manchester, 1991).

Nelson, J. L., *Charles the Bald* (London, 1992).

Nelson, J. L., "Early medieval rites of queen-making," in J. L. Nelson, *Rulers and Ruling Families in Early Medieval Europe* (Aldershot, 1999), ch. 15.

Nelson, J. L., "Early medieval rites of queen-making and the shaping of medieval queenship," in A. Duggan (ed.), *Queens and Queenship in Medieval Europe* (Woodbridge, 1997), pp. 301–15.

Nelson, J. L., "England and the continent in the ninth century, I: ends and beginnings," *Transactions of the Royal Historical Society*, 6th series, 12 (2002), 1–21.

Nelson, J. L., "England and the continent in the ninth century, II: Vikings and others," *Transactions of the Royal Historical Society*, 6th series, 13 (2003), 1–28.

Nelson, J. L., "The Franks and the English in the ninth century reconsidered," in P. E. Szarmach and J. T. Rosenthal (eds.), *The Preservation and Transmission of Anglo-Saxon Culture* (Kalamazoo MI, 1997), pp. 141–58; reprinted in J. L. Nelson, *Rulers and Ruling Families in Early Medieval Europe* (Aldershot, 1999), ch. 6.

Nelson, J. L., "Inauguration rituals," in P. H. Sawyer and I. Wood (eds.), *Early Medieval Kingship* (Leeds, 1977), pp. 50–71.

Nelson, J. L., "Kingship and royal government," in R. McKitterick (ed.), *The New Cambridge Medieval History*, vol. II: *c.700–900* (Cambridge, 1995), pp. 383–430.

Nelson, J. L., "Nobility in the ninth century," in A. J. Duggan (ed.), *Nobles and Nobility in Medieval Europe: Concepts, Origins, Transformations* (Woodbridge, 2000), pp. 43–51.

Nelson, J. L., "The political ideas of Alfred of Wessex," in A. J. Duggan (ed.), *Kings and Kingship in Medieval Europe* (London, 1993), pp. 125–58.

Nelson, J. L., *Politics and Ritual in Early Medieval Europe* (London, 1986).

Nelson, J. L., "The problematic in the private," *Social History*, 15 (1990), 355–64.

Nelson, J. L., "The queen in ninth-century Wessex," in S. Keynes and A. P. Smyth (eds.), *Anglo-Saxons: Studies Presented to Cyril Roy Hart* (Dublin, 2006), pp. 69–77.

Nelson, J. L., "Queens as converters of kings in the earlier Middle Ages," in C. La Rocca (ed.), *Agire da donna, modelli e pratiche di rappresentazione (secoli VI–X)* (Turnhout, 2007), pp. 95–107.

Nelson, J. L., *Rulers and Ruling Families in Early Medieval Europe* (Aldershot, 1999).

Nelson, J. L., "'. . . sicut olim gens Francorum . . . nunc gens Anglorum*": Fulk's letter to Alfred revisited," in J. Roberts and J. L. Nelson (eds.), *Alfred the Wise: Studies in Honour of Janet Bately* (Woodbridge, 1997), pp. 135–44; reprinted J. L. Nelson, *Rulers and Ruling Families in Early Medieval Europe* (Aldershot, 1999), ch. 7.

Nelson, J. L., "Women at the court of Charlemagne: a case of monstrous regiment?," in J. C. Parsons (ed.), *Medieval Queenship* (New York, 1993), pp. 43–61.

Netzer, N., "The *Book of Durrow*: the Northumbrian connection," in J. Hawkes and S. Mills (eds.), *Northumbria's Golden Age* (Stroud, 1999), pp. 315–26.

Netzer, N., "Willibrord's scriptorium at Echternach and its relationship to Ireland and Lindisfarne," in G. Bonner et al. (eds.), *St. Cuthbert, his Cult, and his Community to AD 1200* (Woodbridge, 1989), pp. 203–12.

Newman, J., "Exceptional finds, exceptional sites? Barham and Coddenham, Suffolk," in T. Pestell and K. Ulmschneider (eds.), *Markets in Early Medieval Europe: Trading and Productive Sites 650–850* (Oxford, 2003), pp. 97–109.

Ní Bhrolchain, M. (ed.), *An Banshenchas: The Lore of Women* (Dublin, 2001).

Ní Dhonnchadha, M., "Caillech and other terms for veiled women in medieval Irish texts," *Éigse*, 28 (1994–5), 71–96.

Ní Dhonnchadha, M., "The Law of Adomnán: a translation," in T. O'Loughlin (ed.), *Adomnán at Birr, AD 697* (Dublin, 2001), pp. 53–68.

Ní Dhonnchadha, M., "The *Lex Innocentium*: Adomnán's law for women, clerics and youth, 697 AD," in M. O'Dowd and S. Wickert (eds.), *Chattel, Servant or Citizen: Women's Status in Church, State and Society* (Belfast, 1995), pp. 58–69.

Ní Mhaonaigh, M., *Brian Boru: Ireland's Greatest King* (Stroud, 2007).

Ní Mhaonaigh, M., "*Cogad Gáedel re Gallaib*: some dating considerations," *Peritia*, 9 (1995), 354–77.

Ó Carragáin, E., *Ritual and the Rood: Liturgical Images and the Old English Poems of the Dream of the Rood Tradition* (London, 2005).

Ó Carragáin, T., "Church buildings and pastoral care in early medieval Ireland," in E. FitzPatrick and R. Gillespie (eds.), *The Parish in Medieval and Early Modern Ireland: Community, Territory and Building* (Dublin, 2006), pp. 91–123.

Ó Corráin, D., "Brian Boru and the battle of Clontarf," in L. de Paor (ed.), *Milestones in Irish History* (Cork, 1986), pp. 31–40.

Ó Corráin, D. (trans.), "*Cáin Lánamna*," in A. Bourke et al. (eds.), *The Field-Day Anthology of Irish Writing*, vol. 4: *Irish Women's Writing and Traditions* (Cork, 2002), pp. 22–6.

Ó Corráin, D., "Caithréim Cheallacháin Chaisil: history or propaganda?," *Ériu*, 25 (1974), 1–69.

Ó Corráin, D., "The career of Diarmait mac Máel na mBó, king of Leinster," *Journal of the Old Wexford Society*, 3 (1971), 27–35; 4 (1972–3), 17–24.

Ó Corráin, D., "Dál Cais: church and dynasty," *Ériu*, 24 (1973), 52–73.

Ó Corráin, D., "The early Irish churches: some aspects of organisation," in D. Ó Corráin (ed.), *Irish Antiquity: Essays and Studies Presented to Professor M. J. O'Kelly* (Dublin, 1981), pp. 327–41.

Ó Corráin, D., "The historical and cultural background of the Book of Kells," in F. O'Mahony (ed.), *The Book of Kells* (Dublin, 1994), pp. 1–31.

Ó Corráin, D., "Ireland c.800: aspects of society," in D. Ó Cróinín (ed.), *A New History of Ireland*, vol. 1: *Prehistoric and Early Ireland* (Oxford, 2005), pp. 549–608.

Ó Corráin, D., *Ireland before the Normans* (Dublin, 1972).

Ó Corráin, D., "Ireland, Scotland and Wales, c.700 to the early eleventh century," in R. McKitterick (ed.), *The New Cambridge Medieval History*, vol. II: *c.700–c.900* (Cambridge, 1995), pp. 43–63.

Ó Corráin, D., "Ireland, Wales, Man and the Hebrides," in P. H. Sawyer (ed.), *The Oxford Illustrated History of the Vikings* (Oxford, 1997), pp. 83–109.

Ó Corráin, D., "Irish regnal succession: a reappraisal," *Studia Hibernica*, 11 (1971), 7–39.

Ó Corráin, D., "Marriage in early Ireland," in A. Cosgrove (ed.), *Marriage in Ireland* (Dún Laoghaire, 1985), pp. 5–24.

Ó Corráin, D., "Nationality and kingship in pre-Norman Ireland," in T. W. Moody (ed.), *Nationality and the Pursuit of National Independence* (Belfast, 1978), pp. 1–35.

Ó Corráin, D., "The Uí Chennselaig kingship of Leinster, 1072–1126," *Journal of the Old Wexford Society*, 5 (1974), 26–31; 6 (1977), 45–54; 7 (1978), 46–9.

Ó Corráin, D., "Women in early Irish society," in M. Mac Curtain and D. Ó Corráin (eds.), *Women in Irish Society: The Historical Dimension* (Dublin, 1978), pp. 1–13.

Ó Cróinín, D., "Bischoff's Wendepunkte fifty years on," *Revue Bénédictine*, 110 (2000), 204–37.

Ó Cróinín, D., *Early Medieval Ireland 400–1200* (Harlow, 1995).

Ó Cróinín, D., "Hiberno-Latin literature to 1169," in D. Ó Cróinín (ed.), *A New History of Ireland 1: Prehistoric and Early Ireland* (Oxford, 2005), pp. 371–404.

Ó Cróinín, D., "Ireland, 400–800," in D. Ó Cróinín (ed.), *A New History of Ireland*, vol. 1: *Prehistoric and Early Ireland* (Oxford, 2005), pp. 182–234.

Ó Cróinín, D., "The Irish provenance of Bede's computus," *Peritia*, 5 (1983), 229–47.

Ó Cróinín, D. (ed.), *A New History of Ireland*, vol. 1: *Prehistoric and Early Ireland* (Oxford, 2005).

Ó Cróinín, D., "Three weddings and a funeral: rewriting Irish political history in the tenth century," in A. P. Smyth (ed.), *Senchas: Studies in History Presented to Francis John Byrne* (Dublin, 2000), pp. 212–24.

Ó Fiaich, T., "The church of Armagh under lay control," *Seanchas Ardmhacha*, 5 (1969), 75–127.

Ó Floinn, R., "The archaeology of the early Viking Age in Ireland," in H. B. Clarke, M. Ní Mhaonaigh, and R. Ó Floinn (eds.), *Ireland and Scandinavia in the Early Viking Age* (Dublin, 1998), pp. 131–65.

Ó Floinn, R., "The foundation relics of Christ Church cathedral and the origins of the diocese of Dublin," in S, Duffy (ed.), *Medieval Dublin VII* (Dublin, 2006), pp. 89–102.

Ó Murchadha, D., "Rubbings taken of the inscriptions on the Cross of the Scriptures, Clonmacnois," *Journal of the Royal Society of Antiquaries of Ireland*, 110 (1980), 47–51.

Ó Riain, P., "The shrine of the Stowe missal, redated," *Proceedings of the Royal Irish Academy*, section C, 91 (1991), 285–95.

O'Brien, E., "The location and context of Viking burials," in H. B. Clarke, M. Ní Mhaonaigh, and R. Ó Floinn (eds.), *Ireland and Scandinavia in the Early Viking Age* (Dublin, 1998), pp. 201–18.

O'Donovan, J. (ed. and trans.), *Annála Rioghachta Éireann: Annals of the Kingdom of Ireland by the Four Masters from the Earliest Period to the Year 1616*, 7 vols. (Dublin, 1851; 3rd edn., 1990).

O'Keeffe, J. G. (ed. and trans.), "The ancient territory of Fermoy," *Ériu*, 10 (1926–8), 170–89.

O'Keeffe, J. G. (ed. and trans.), "The rule of St. Patrick," *Ériu*, 1 (1904), 216–24.

O'Loughlin, T. (ed.), *Adomnán at Birr, AD 697: Essays in Commemoration of the Law of the Innocents* (Dublin, 2001).

Olson, L., *Early Monasteries in Cornwall* (Woodbridge, 1989).

Olson, L. and Padel, O. J., "A tenth-century list of Cornish parochial saints," *Cambridge Medieval Celtic Studies*, 12 (1986), 33–71.

O'Neill, P. P. (ed.), *King Alfred's Prose Translation of the First Fifty Psalms* (Cambridge MA, 2001).

Orchard, A., *The Poetic Art of Aldhelm* (Cambridge, 1994).

Orme, A. R., *Ireland*. The World's Landscapes series, no. 4 (London, 1970).

Orpen, G. H., *Ireland under the Normans 1169–1333* (Oxford, 1911, reissued with an introduction by S. Duffy, Dublin, 2005).

Ortenberg, V., "Archbishop Sigeric's pilgrimage to Rome in 990," *Anglo-Saxon England*, 19 (1990), 197–246.

Ortenberg, V., *The English Church and the Continent in the Tenth and Eleventh Centuries* (Oxford, 1992).

O'Sullivan, A., *The Archaeology of Lake Settlement in Ireland* (Dublin, 1998).

Oskamp, H. P. (ed. and trans.), *The Voyage of Máel Dúin: A Study in Early Irish Voyage Literature* (Groningen, 1970).

Padel, O. J., "Local saints and place-names in Cornwall," in A. T. Thacker and R. Sharpe (eds.), *Local Saints and Local Churches in the Early Medieval West* (Oxford, 2002), pp. 303–60.

Padel, O. J., "Two new pre-Conquest charters for Cornwall," *Cornish Studies*, 6 (1978), 20–7.

Palliser, D. M., *The Cambridge Urban History of Britain: Volume I, 600–1540* (Cambridge, 2000).

Palliser, D. M., "Domesday Book and the 'harrying of the north,'" *Northern History*, 29 (1993), 1–23.

Palliser, D. M., "An introduction to the Yorkshire Domesday," in *Great Domesday Book: County Edition: Yorkshire*, 2 vols. (London, 1992).

Palmer, J., "Saxon or European? Interpreting and reinterpreting St. Boniface," *History Compass*, 4: 5 (2006), 852–69.

Pantos, A. and Semple, S. (eds.), *Assembly Places and Practices in Medieval Europe* (Dublin, 2004).

Parkes, P., "Celtic fosterage," *Comparative Studies in Society and History*, 48: 2 (2006), 359–94.

Parkes, P., "Fostering fealty: a comparative study of tributary allegiances of adoptive kinship," *Comparative Studies in Society and History*, 45: 4 (2003), 741–82.

Patterson, N., *Cattle, Lords and Clansmen: The Social Structure of Early Ireland*, 2nd edn. (London, 1994).

Payer, P., *Sex and the Penitentials: The Development of a Social Code, 550–1150* (Toronto, 1984).

Peacock, D., "Charlemagne's black stones: the re-use of Roman columns in early medieval Europe," *Antiquity*, 71 (1997), 709–15.

Pelteret, D. A. E., *Slavery in Early Mediaeval England: From the Reign of Alfred until the Twelfth Century* (Woodbridge, 1995).

Pestell, T. and Ulmschneider, K. (eds.), *Markets in Early Medieval Europe: Trading and "Productive" Sites, 650–850* (Macclesfield, 2003).

Phillimore, E., "The *Annales Cambriæ* and Old-Welsh genealogies from *Harleian MS 3859*," *Y Cymmrodor*, 9 (1888), 141–83.

Phythian-Adams, C., *Land of the Cumbrians: A Study in British Provincial Origins, AD 400–1120* (Aldershot, 1996).

Plummer, C. (ed. and trans.), *Bethada Náem nÉrenn*, 2 vols. (Oxford, 1922).

Postan, M. M., *The Famulus: The Estate Labourer in the Twelfth and Thirteenth Centuries*, *Economic History Review*, suppl. 2 (Cambridge, 1954).

Power, R., "Magnus Barelegs' expeditions to the west," *Scottish Historical Review*, 66 (1986), 107–32.

Power, R., "Meeting in Norway: Norse-Gaelic relations in the kingdom of Man and the Isles, 1090–1270," *Saga-book: Viking Society for Northern Research*, 29 (2005), 5–66.

Pratt, D., *The Political Thought of King Alfred the Great* (Cambridge, 2007).

Pratt, D., "Problems of authorship and audience in the writings of Alfred the Great," in P. Wormald and J. L. Nelson (eds.), *Lay Intellectuals in the Carolingian World* (Cambridge, 2007), pp. 160–91.

Prinz, F., *Frühes Mönchtum im Frankenreich* (Munich, 1965).

Prinz, F., "Frühes Mönchtum in Südwestdeutschland und die Anfänge der Reichenau," in A. Borst (ed.), *Mönchtum, Episkopat und Adel zur Gründungszeit des Klosters Reichenau*. Vorträge und Forschungen 20 (Sigmaringen, 1974), pp. 37–76.

Proudfoot, V., "The economy of the Irish rath," *Medieval Archaeology*, 5 (1961), 94–122.

Proudfoot, V., Ralston, I., and Armit, I., "The early historic period: an archaeological perspective," in K. J. Edwards and I. B. Ralston (eds.), *Scotland: Environment and Archaeology, 8000BC–AD1000* (Chichester, 1997), pp. 217–40.

Pryce, H., "British or Welsh? National identity in twelfth-century Wales," *English Historical Review*, 116 (2001), 775–801.

Pryce, H., "Early Irish canons and medieval Welsh law," *Peritia*, 5 (1986), 107–27.

Pryce, H., "Ecclesiastical wealth in early medieval Wales," in N. Edwards and A. Lane (eds.), *The Early Church in Wales and the West* (Oxford, 1992), pp. 22–32.

Pryce, H., "Modern nationality and the medieval past: the Wales of John Edward Lloyd," in R. R. Davies and G. H. Jenkins (eds.), *From Medieval to Modern Wales: Historical Essays in Honour of K. O. Morgan and R. A. Griffiths* (Cardiff, 2004), pp. 14–29.

Pryce, H., "Pastoral care in early medieval Wales," in J. Blair and R. Sharpe (eds.), *Pastoral Care before the Parish* (Leicester, 1992), pp. 41–62.

Pryce, H., "The prologues to the Welsh lawbooks," *Bulletin of the Board of Celtic Studies*, 33 (1986), 151–87.

Pryde, E. B., Greenway, D. E., Porter S., and Roy, I. (eds.), *Handbook of British Chronology* (London, 1986).

Raftery, B., *Pagan Celtic Ireland: The Enigma of the Irish Iron Age* (London, 1994).

Rahtz, P., *The Saxon and Medieval Palaces at Cheddar* (Oxford, 1979).

Raine, J. (ed.), *Byrhtferth: Vita Oswaldi*, in *Historians of the Church of York*, Rolls Series, 3 vols. (1879), I, pp. 399–475.

Raw, B., *Anglo-Saxon Crucifixion Iconography and the Art of the Monastic Revival* (Cambridge, 1990).

Redknap, M., "Viking-Age settlement in Wales," in J. Hines, A. Lane, and M. Redknap (eds.), *Land, Sea and Home*. Proceedings of a Conference on Viking-period Settlement, Cardiff, July 2001 (Leeds, 2004), pp. 139–75.

Redknap, M., *Vikings in Wales: An Archaeological Quest* (Cardiff, 2000).

Reuter, T., "The making of England and Germany, 850–1050: points of comparison and difference," in A. P. Smyth (ed.), *Medieval Europeans: Studies in Ethnic Identity and National Perspectives in Medieval Europe* (Basingstoke, 1998), pp. 53–70.

Reuter, T., "The medieval nobility in twentieth-century historiography," in M. Bentley (ed.), *Companion to Historiography* (London, 1997), pp. 177–202.

Reuter, T., "Nobles and others: the social and cultural expression of power relations in the Middle Ages," in A. J. Duggan (ed.), *Nobles and Nobility in Medieval Europe: Concepts, Origins, Transformations* (Woodbridge, 2000), pp. 85–98.

Reynolds, A., *Later Anglo-Saxon England: Life and Landscape* (Stroud, 1999).

Reynolds, R. E., "'At sixes and sevens' – and eights and nines: the sacred mathematics of sacred orders in the early Middle Ages," in *Clerics in the Early Middle Ages: Hierarchy and Image* (Aldershot, 1999).

Reynolds, S., "Carolingian elopements as a sidelight on counts and vassals," in B. Nagy and M. Seb k (eds.), *The Man of Many Devices, who Wandered Full Many Ways: Festschrift in Honour of János M. Bak* (Budapest, 1999), pp. 340–6.

Reynolds, S., *Kingdoms and Communities in Western Europe 900–1300* (Oxford, 1984; 2nd edn., 1997).

Richards, A. L., "African kings and their royal relatives," *Journal of the Royal Anthropological Institute*, 91 (1961), 135–50.

Richards, J. D., "Boundaries and cult centres: Viking burial in Derbyshire," in J. Graham-Campbell, R. A. Hall, J. Jesch, and D. N. Parsons (eds.), *Vikings and the Danelaw: Select Papers from the Proceedings of the Thirteenth Viking Congress* (Oxford, 2001), pp. 97–104.

Richards, J. D., "The case of the missing Vikings: Scandinavian burial in the Danelaw," in S. Lucy and A. Reynolds (eds.), *Burial in Early Medieval England and Wales* (London, 2002), pp. 156–70.

Richards, J. D., "Finding the Vikings: the hunt for Scandinavian rural settlement in the northern Danelaw," in J. Graham-Campbell, R. A. Hall, J. Jesch, and D. N. Parsons (eds.), *Vikings and the Danelaw: Select Papers from the Proceedings of the Thirteenth Viking Congress* (Oxford, 2001), pp. 268–77.

Richards, J. D., "Identifying Anglo-Scandinavian settlements," in D. M. Hadley and J. D. Richards (eds.), *Cultures in Contact: Scandinavian Settlement in England in the Ninth and Tenth Centuries* (Turnhout, 2000), pp. 295–309.

Richards, J. D., *Viking-Age England*, 2nd edn (Stroud, 2000).

Richards, J. D., Beswick, P., Bond, J., McKinley, J., Rowland, S., and Worley, F., "Excavations at the Viking barrow cemetery at Heath Wood, Ingleby, Derbyshire," *Antiquaries Journal*, 84 (2004), 23–116.

Richards, M., "Early Welsh territorial suffixes," *Journal of the Royal Society of Anquities of Ireland*, 95 (1965), 205–12.

Richards, M., "The Irish settlement in Wales," *Journal of the Royal Society of Antiquaries of Ireland*, 90 (1960), 133–62.

Richter, M. (ed.), *Canterbury Professions* (Torquay, 1973).

Ridyard, S. J., "'Condigna veneratio': post-Conquest attitudes to the saints of the Anglo-Saxons," *Anglo-Norman Studies*, 9 (1986), 179–201.

Ridyard, S. J., *The Royal Saints of Anglo-Saxon England: A Study of West Saxon and East Anglian Cults* (Cambridge, 1988).

Rivers, T. J. (trans.), *The Laws of the Salian and Ripuarian Franks* (New York, 1986).

Robertson, A. J., *The Laws of the Kings of England from Edmund to Henry I* (Cambridge, 1925).

Robinson, I. (trans.), *Life of Leo IX*, in *The Papal Reform of the Eleventh Century* (Manchester, 2004).

Roffe, D., *Decoding Domesday* (Woodbridge, 2007).

Rogers, P., *Cloth and Clothing in Early Anglo-Saxon England* (York, 2007).

Rollason, D. W., "Lists of saints' resting-places in Anglo-Saxon England," *Anglo-Saxon England*, 7 (1978), 61–93.

Rollason, D. W., *Northumbria 500–1100: Creation and Destruction of a Kingdom* (Cambridge, 2003).

Rollason, D. W., *Saints and Relics in Anglo-Saxon England* (Oxford, 1989).

Rollason, D. W., "The shrines of saints in later Anglo-Saxon England: distribution and signfi-cance," in L. A. S. Butler and R. K. Morris (eds.), *The Anglo-Saxon Church: Papers on History, Architecture, and Archaeology in Honour of Dr H. M. Taylor* (London, 1986), pp. 32–43.

Rollason, D. W. (ed.), *Symeon of Durham: Libellus de exordio atque procursu istius, hoc est Dunhelmensis ecclesie [Tract on the Origins and Progress of this the Church of Durham]* (Oxford, 2000).

Rollason, D. W., "The wanderings of St. Cuthbert," in D. W. Rollason (ed.), *Cuthbert: Saint and Patron* (Durham, 1987), pp. 45–59.

Rollason, D. W., Gore, D., and Fellows-Jensen, G., *Sources for York History to AD 1100* (York, 1998).

Rosenwein, B. H. (ed.), *Anger's Past: Social Uses of an Emotion in the Middle Ages* (Cornell, 1998).

Rosenwein, B. H., *Emotional Communities in the Early Middle Ages* (Cornell, 2006).

Rosser, G., "The cure of souls in English towns before 1000," in J. Blair and R. Sharpe (eds.), *Pastoral Care before the Parish* (Leicester, 1992), pp. 266–84.

Royal Commission on Historical Monuments, *An Inventory of the Historical Monuments in the County of Dorset*, vol. 2: *South-East*, part 2 (London, 1970).

Rule, M. (ed.), *Eadmer: Historia novorum* (London, 1884).

Russell, J. C., *The Germanization of Early Medieval Christianity: A Sociohistorical Approach to Religious Transformation* (New York, 1994).

Russell, P., "Patterns of hypocorism in early Irish hagiography," in J. Carey, M. Herbert, and P. Ó Riain (eds.), *Studies in Irish Hagiography: Saints and Scholars* (Dublin, 2001), pp. 237–49.

Russell, P. (ed.), *Vita Griffini Filii Conani: The Medieval Latin Life of Gruffudd ap Cynan* (Cardiff, 2005).

Ryan, J., "The battle of Clontarf," *Journal of the Royal Society of Antiquaries of Ireland*, 68 (1938), 1–50.

Ryan, J., "Brian Boruma, king of Ireland," in E. Rynne (ed.), *North Munster Studies: Essays in Commemoration of Monsignor Michael Moloney* (Limerick, 1967), pp. 355–74.

Ryan, J., "The O'Briens in Munster after Clontarf," *North Munster Antiquarian Journal*, 2 (1941), 141–52; 3 (1942), 1–52.

Ryan, M., "The Derrynaflan hoard and early Irish art," *Speculum*, 72 (1997), 995–1017.

Ryan, M., "Some aspects of sequence and style in the metalwork of eighth- and ninth-century Ireland," in M. Ryan (ed.), *Ireland and Insular Art AD 500–1200* (Dublin, 1987), pp. 66–74.

Samson, R., "Populous dark-age towns: the Finleyesque approach," *Journal of European Archaeology*, 2 (1994), 97–129.

Sanmark, A., *Power and Conversion: A Comparative Study of Christianization in Scandinavia* (Uppsala, 2004).

Sarris, P., "The Justinianic plague: origins and effects," *Continuity and Change*, 17: 2 (2002), 169–82.

Sawyer, P. H., *Anglo-Saxon Charters: An Annotated List and Bibliography* (London, 1968).

Sawyer, P. H. (ed.), *Charters of Burton Abbey*, Anglo-Saxon Charters II (Oxford, 1979).

Sawyer, P. H., *Kings and Vikings: Scandinavia and Europe AD 700–1100* (London, 1982).

Sawyer, P. H., "The last Scandinavian kings of York," *Northern History*, 31 (1995), 39–44.

Sawyer, P. H. (ed.), *Medieval Settlement: Continuity and Change* (London, 1976).

Sawyer, P. H. (ed.), *The Oxford Illustrated History of the Vikings* (Oxford, 1997).

Sawyer, P. H., "The royal *tun* in pre-Conquest England," in P. Wormald, D. Bullough, and R. Collins (eds.), *Ideal and Reality in Frankish and Anglo-Saxon Society* (Oxford, 1983), pp. 273–99.

Sawyer, P. H., "The Vikings and Ireland," in D. Whitelock, R. McKitterick, and D. Dumville (eds.), *Ireland in Early Mediaeval Europe: Studies in Memory of Kathleen Hughes* (Cambridge, 1982), pp. 345–61.

Schmid, K., *Gebetsgedenken und adliges Selbstverständnis im Mittelalter. Ausgewählte Beiträge* (Sigmaringen, 1983), pp. 532–97.

Scholz, B. (trans.), *Royal Frankish Annals*, in *Carolingian Chronicles* (Ann Arbor, 1972), pp. 37–125.

Scottish Historical Review, "Writing Scotland's history: what have historians made of the nation's past?," 76 (1997), nos. 201–2.

Scragg, D., "The Battle of Maldon," in D. Scragg (ed.), *The Battle of Maldon AD 991* (Oxford, 1991), pp. 1–36.

Scull, C., "Archaeology, early Anglo-Saxon society, and the origins of Anglo-Saxon kingdoms," *Anglo-Saxon Studies in Archaeology and History*, 6 (1993), 65–82.

Seebohm, F., *Tribal Custom in Anglo-Saxon Law* (London, 1911).

Sharpe, R. (trans.), *Adomnán of Iona: Life of St. Columba* (Harmondsworth, 1995).

Sharpe, R., "Churches and communities in early medieval Ireland: towards a pastoral model," in J. Blair and R. Sharpe (eds.), *Pastoral Care before the Parish* (Leicester, 1992), pp. 81–109.

Sharpe, R., "Dispute settlement in medieval Ireland: a preliminary inquiry," in W. Davies and P. Fouracre (eds.), *The Settlement of Disputes in Early Medieval Europe* (Cambridge, 1986), pp. 169–89.

Sharpe, R., "Gildas as a father of the church," in M. Lapidge and D. Dumville (eds.), *Gildas: New Approaches* (Woodbridge, 1984), pp. 193–205.

Sharpe, R., "Martyrs and local saints in late antique Britain," in A. T. Thacker and R. Sharpe (eds.), *Local Saints and Local Churches in the Early Medieval West* (Oxford, 2002), pp. 75–154.

Sharpe, R., "The naming of Bishop Ithamar," *English Historical Review*, 117 (2002), 889–94.

Sharpe, R., "St. Patrick and the see of Armagh," *Cambridge Medieval Celtic Studies*, 4 (1982), pp. 33–59.

Sharpe, R., "Some problems concerning the organisation of the church in early medieval Ireland," *Peritia*, 3 (1984), 230–70.

Sharpe, R., "The thriving of Dalriada," in S. Taylor (ed.), *Kings, Clerics and Chronicles in Scotland, 500–1297* (Dublin, 2000), pp. 47–61.

Sharpe, R. and Davies, J. R. (eds. and trans.), "Rhygyfarch's *Life* of St. David," in J. W. Evans and J. M. Wooding (eds.), *St. David of Wales: Cult, Church and Nation* (Woodbridge, 2007), pp. 107–55.

Sheehan, J., "Early Viking-Age silver hoards from Ireland and their Scandinavian elements," in H. B. Clarke, M. Ní Mhaonaigh, and R. Ó Floinn (eds.), *Ireland and Scandinavia in the Early Viking Age* (Dublin, 1998), pp. 166–202.

Sheehy, M., "The *Collectio canonum Hibernensis*: a Celtic phenomenon," in H. Löwe (ed.), *Die Iren und Europa* (Stuttgart, 1982), 1, pp. 525–35.

Sherley-Price, L. and Latham, R. E. (ed. and trans.), *Bede: A History of the English Church and People* (Harmondsworth, 1968; with new intro. and notes by D. H. Farmer, 1990).

Simms, K., *From Kings to Warlords: The Changing Political Structure of Gaelic Ireland in the Later Middle Ages* (Woodbridge, 1987).

Simms, K., "Guesting and feasting in Gaelic Ireland," *Journal of the Royal Society of Antiquaries of Ireland*, 108 (1978), 67–100.

Simpson, L., "The Alfred/St. Cuthbert episode in the *Historia de Sancto Cuthberto*: its significance for mid-tenth century history," in G. Bonner, D. Rollason, and C. Stancliffe (eds.), *St. Cuthbert, his Cult and Community to AD 1200* (Woodbridge, 1989), pp. 397–412.

Sims-Williams, P., "Celtomania and Celtoscepticism," *Cambrian Medieval Celtic Studies*, 36 (1998), 1–35.

Sims-Williams, P., *Religion and Literature in Western England: 600–800* (Cambridge, 1990).

Sims-Williams, P., "The settlement of England in Bede and the *Chronicle*," *Anglo-Saxon England*, 12 (1983), 1–41.

Sims-Williams, P., "The visionary Celt: the construction of an ethnic preconception," *Cambrian Medieval Celtic Studies*, 11 (1986) 71–96.

Smith, J. M. H., *Europe after Rome: A New Cultural History 500–1000* (Oxford, 2005).

Smith, J. M. H., "Oral and written: saints, miracles, and relics in Brittany, c.850–1250," *Speculum*, 65 (1990), 309–43.

Smith, M. F., "Archbishop Stigand and the eye of the needle," *Anglo-Norman Studies*, 16 (1994), 199–218.

Smyth, A. P., *Celtic Leinster: Towards an Historical Geography of Early Irish Civilization AD 500–1600* (Blackrock, Co. Dublin, 1982).

Smyth, A. P., "The effect of Scandinavian raiders on the English and Irish churches: a preliminary reassessment," in B. Smith (ed.), *Britain and Ireland, 900–1300: Insular Responses to Medieval European Change* (Cambridge, 1999), pp. 1–38.

Smyth, A. P., "The emergence of English Identity, 700–1000," in A. P. Smyth (ed.), *Medieval Europeans: Studies in Ethnic Identity and National Perspectives in Medieval Europe* (Basingstoke, 1998), pp. 24–52.

Smyth, A. P., *Scandinavian York and Dublin: The History and Archaeology of Two Related Viking Kingdoms*, 2 vols (Dublin, 1975–9).

Smyth, A. P., *Warlords and Holy Men: Scotland AD 80–1000* (London, 1984).

Southern, P., "The army in late Roman Britain," in M. Todd (ed.), *A Companion to Roman Britain* (Oxford, 2004), pp. 393–408.

Speake, G., *A Saxon Bed Burial on Swallowcliffe Down*, English Heritage Archaeological Reports, 10 (London, 1989).

Spearman, R. M. and Higgitt, J. (eds.), *The Age of Migrating Ideas: Early Medieval Art in Northern Britain and Ireland* (Edinburgh, 1993).

Speed, G. and Walton Rogers, P., "A burial of a Viking woman at Adwick-le-Street, South Yorkshire," *Medieval Archaeology*, 48 (2004), 51–90.

Stacey, R. C., "Texts and society," in T. M. Charles-Edwards (eds.), *After Rome* (Oxford, 2003), pp. 221–57.

Stafford, P., "'The annals of Æthelflæd': annals, history and politics in early tenth-century England," in J. Barrow and A. Wareham (eds.), *Myth, Rulership, Church and Charters: Essays in Honour of Nicholas Brooks* (Aldershot, 2008), pp. 101–16.

Stafford, P., "Charles the Bald, Judith and England," in M. T. Gibson and J. L. Nelson (eds.), *Charles the Bald: Court and Kingdom*, 2nd edn. (Aldershot, 1990), pp. 139–53.

Stafford, P., "Chronicle D, 1067 and women: gendering conquest in eleventh-century England," in S. Keynes and A. P. Smyth (eds.), *Anglo-Saxons: Studies Presented to Cyril Roy Hart* (Dublin, 2006), pp. 208–23.

Stafford, P., *The East Midlands in the Early Middle Ages* (Leicester, 1985).

Stafford, P., *Gender, Family and the Legitimation of Power: England from the Ninth to Early Twelfth Century* (Aldershot, 2006).

Stafford, P., "Introduction," in M. Costambeys, A. Hamer, and M. Heale (eds.), *The Making of the Middle Ages* (Liverpool, 2007), pp. 1–14.

Stafford, P., "King and kin, lord and community: England in the tenth and eleventh centuries," in P. Stafford (ed.), *Gender, Family and the Legitimation of Power: England from the Ninth to Early Twelfth Century* (Aldershot, 2006).

Stafford, P., "Kings, kingships and kingdoms," in W. Davies (ed.), *From the Vikings to the Normans 800–1100* (Oxford, 2003), pp. 11–39.

Stafford, P., "The meanings of hair in the Anglo-Norman world: masculinity, reform, and national identity," in M. van Dijk and R. Nip (eds.), *Saints, Scholars, and Politicians: Gender as a Tool in Medieval Studies. Festschrift in Honour of Anneke Mulder-Bakker on the Occasion of her Sixty-fifth Birthday*, Medieval Church Studies, 15 (Turnhout, 2005), pp. 153–71.

Stafford, P., "Political ideas in late tenth-century England: charters as evidence," in P. Stafford, J. L. Nelson, and J. Martindale (eds.), *Law, Laity and Solidarities: Essays in Honour of Susan Reynolds* (Manchester, 2001), pp. 68–82.

Stafford, P., "Political women in Mercia, eighth to early tenth centuries," in M. Brown and C. Farr (eds.), *Mercia: An Anglo-Saxon Kingdom in Europe* (London, 2001), pp. 35–49.

Stafford, P., *Queen Emma and Queen Edith: Queenship and Women's Power in Eleventh-century England* (Oxford, 1997).

Stafford, P., *Queens, Concubines and Dowagers: The King's Wife in the Early Middle Ages* (Athens, 1983, reprinted with new preface, 1998).

Stafford, P., "Queens, nunneries and reforming churchmen: gender, religious status and reform in tenth- and eleventh-century England," *Past and Present*, 163 (1999), 3–35.

Stafford, P., "Reading women in annals: Eadburg, Cuthburg, Cwenburg and the Anglo-Saxon chronicles," in C. La Rocca (ed.), *Agire da donna, modelli e pratiche di rappresentazione (secoli VI–X)* (Turnhout, 2007), pp. 269–89.

Stafford, P., "The reign of Æthelred II: a study in the limitations on royal policy and action," in D. Hill (ed.), *Ethelred the Unready*, British Archaeological Reports, British series 59 (Oxford, 1978), pp. 15–46.

Stafford, P., "Sons and mothers: family politics in the early Middle Ages," in D. Baker (ed.), *Medieval Women* (Oxford, 1978), pp. 79–100.

Stafford, P., "Succession and inheritance: a gendered perspective on Alfred's family history," in T. Reuter (ed.), *Alfred the Great* (Aldershot, 2003), pp. 251–64.

Stafford, P., *Unification and Conquest: A Political and Social History of England in the Tenth and Eleventh Centuries* (London, 1989).

Stafford, P., "Women and the Norman Conquest," *Transactions of the Royal Historical Society*, 6th series, 4 (1994), 221–49.

Stalley, R., "The tower cross at Kells," in C. E. Karkov, R. T. Farrell, and M. Ryan (eds.), *The Insular Tradition* (New York, 1997), pp. 115–41.

Stancliffe, C., "The British church and the mission of Augustine," in R. Gameson (ed.), *St. Augustine and the Conversion of England* (Stroud, 1999), pp. 107–51.

Stancliffe, C., "Kings and conversion: some comparisons between the Roman mission to England and Patrick's to Ireland," *Frühmittelalterliche Studien*, 14 (1980), pp. 59–94.

Stancliffe, C., "Kings who opted out," in P. Wormald, D. Bullough, and R. Collins (eds.), *Ideal and Reality in Frankish and Anglo-Saxon Society* (Oxford, 1983), pp. 154–76.

Stancliffe, C., "Oswald, 'most holy and most victorious king of the Northumbrians,'" in C. Stancliffe and E. Cambridge (eds.), *Oswald: Northumbrian King to European Saint* (Stamford, 1995), pp. 33–83.

Stancliffe, C., "Religion and society in Ireland," in P. Fouracre (ed.), *New Cambridge Medieval History*, vol. 1 (Cambridge, 2005), pp. 397–425.

Stancliffe, C. and Cambridge, E. (eds.), *Oswald: Northumbrian King to European Saint* (Stamford, 1995).

Staubach, N., *Rex christianus: Hofkultur und Herrschaftspropaganda im Reich Karls des Kahlen*, Teil II (Cologne, 1993).

Stenton, F. M., *Anglo-Saxon England*, 3rd edn. (Oxford, 1971).

Stevenson, J. (ed.), *Liber Vitae ecclesiae Dunelmensis* (London, 1841).

Stevenson, W. H. (ed.), *Asser's Life of King Alfred* (Oxford, 1904, 1959).

Stewart, I., "Coinage and recoinage after Edgar's reform," in K. Jonsson (ed.), *Studies in Late Anglo-Saxon Coinage in Memory of Bror Emil Hildebrand, Numismatiska Meddelanden*, 35 (1990), pp. 455–85.

Stocker, D., "Monuments and merchants: irregularities in the distribution of stone sculpture in Lincolnshire and Yorkshire in the tenth century," in D. M. Hadley and J. D. Richards (eds.), *Cultures in Contact: Scandinavian Settlement in England in the Ninth and Tenth Centuries* (Turnhout, 2000), pp. 179–212.

Stocker, D. and Everson, P., "Five towns funerals: decoding diversity in Danelaw stone sculpture," in J. Graham-Campbell, R. Hall, J. Jesch, and Parsons, D. N. (eds.), *Vikings and the Danelaw: Select Papers from the Proceedings of the Thirteenth Viking Congress* (Oxford, 2001), pp. 223–43.

Stokes, W. (ed. and trans.), *The Annals of Tigernach* (reprinted from *Revue Celtique*, 1895–7; repr. Felinfach, 1993).

Stoodley, N., *The Spindle and the Spear: A Critical Enquiry into the Construction and Meaning of Gender in the Early Anglo-Saxon Inhumation Burial Rite* (Oxford, 1999).

Story, J., *Carolingian Connections: Anglo-Saxon England and Carolingian Francia c.750–870* (Aldershot, 2003).

Story, J., "Cathwulf, kingship and the royal abbey of St. Denis," *Speculum*, 74 (1999), 1–24.

Story, J., *Charlemagne: Empire and Society* (Manchester, 2005).

Story, J. et al. "Charlemagne's black marble: the origin of the epitaph of Pope Hadrian I," *Papers of the British School at Rome*, 73 (2005), 157–90.

Stout, M., *The Irish Ringfort* (Dublin, 1997).

Stratmann, M. (ed.), *Flodoard: Historia Remensis ecclesiae, MGH SS* 36 (Hanover, 1998).

Stubbs, W., *Memorials of St. Dunstan, Archbishop of Canterbury* (London, 1874).

Swan, L., "Monastic proto-towns in early medieval Ireland: the evidence of aerial photography, plan analysis and survey," in H. B. Clarke and A. Simms (eds.), *The Comparative History of Urban Origins in Non-Roman Europe: Ireland, Wales, Denmark, Germany, Poland, and Russia from the Ninth to the Thirteenth Century* (Oxford, 1985), 1, pp. 77–102.

Swanton, M. J. (ed.), *The Anglo-Saxon Chronicle* (London, 1996).

Swanton, M. J., *Anglo-Saxon Prose*, 2nd edn. (London, 1993).

Symonds, L., "Territories in transition: the construction of boundaries in Anglo-Scandinavian Lincolnshire," in D. Griffiths, S. Semple, and A. Reynolds (eds.), *Boundaries in Medieval Britain* (Oxford, 2003), pp. 28–37.

Symons, T., "*Regularis concordia*: history and derivation," in D. Parsons (ed.), *Tenth-century Studies: Essays in Commemoration of the Millennium of the Council of Winchester and Regularis concordia* (Chichester, 1975), pp. 37–59, 214–17.

Symons, T. (ed.), *Regularis concordia: The Monastic Agreement of the Monks and Nuns of the English Nation* (London, 1953).

Taylor, C. S., "The origin of the Mercian shires," in H. R. P. Finberg (ed.), *Gloucestershire Studies* (Leicester, 1957), pp. 17–45.

Tedeschi, C., *Congeries Lapidum: Iscrizioni Britanniche dei Secoli V–VII* (Pisa, 2005).

Thacker, A. T., "Bede's ideal of reform," in P. Wormald, D. Bullough, and R. Collins (eds.), *Ideal and Reality in Frankish and Anglo-Saxon Society* (Oxford, 1983), pp. 130–53.

Thacker, A. T., "Gallic or Greek? Archbishops in England from Theodore to Ecgbehrt," in P. Fouracre and D. Ganz (eds.), *Frankland: The Franks and the World of Early Medieval Europe* (Manchester, 2008), pp. 44–69.

Thacker, A. T., "Memorializing Gregory the Great: the original transmission of a papal cult in the seventh and early eighth centuries," *Early Medieval Europe*, 7: 1 (1998), 59–84.

Thacker, A. T., "Some terms for noblemen in Anglo-Saxon England, c.650–900," in D. Brown, J. Campbell, and S. C. Hawkes (eds.), *Anglo-Saxon Studies in Archaeology and History*, 2, British Archaeological Reports, British series 92 (Oxford, 1981), pp. 201–36.

Thacker, A. T. and Sharpe, R. (eds.), *Local Saints and Local Churches in the Early Medieval West* (Oxford, 2002).

Theuws, F., "Landed property and manorial organization in Northern Austrasia: some considerations and a case study," in N. Roymans and F. Theuws (eds.), *Images of the Past: Studies on Ancient Societies in Northwestern Europe* (Amsterdam, 1991), pp. 299–407.

Thirsk, J., "The common fields," *Past & Present*, 29 (1964), 3–25.

Thomas, A. C., *The Early Christian Archaeology of North Britain* (London, 1971).

Thomas, A. C., "The evidence from North Britain," in M. W. Barley and R. P. C. Hanson (eds.), *Christianity in Britain, 300–700* (Leicester, 1968), pp. 93–121.

Thomas, A. C., "Settlement history in early Cornwall I: the antiquity of the hundreds," *Cornish Archaeology*, 3 (1964), 70–9.

Thomas, C., *Christianity in Roman Britain to AD 500* (London, 1981).

Thomas, C., *Tintagel: Arthur and Archaeology* (London, 1993).

Thomas, G., "Anglo-Scandinavian metalwork from the Danelaw: exploring social and cultural interaction," in D. M. Hadley and J. D. Richards (eds.), *Cultures in Contact: Scandinavian Settlement in England in the Ninth and Tenth Centuries* (Turnhout, 2000), pp. 237–55.

Thomas, H. M., *The English and the Normans: Ethnic Hostility, Assimilation and Identity 1066–c.1220* (Oxford, 2003).

Thomas, M. G., Stumpf, M. P. H., and Härke, H., "Evidence for an apartheid-like social structure in early Anglo-Saxon England," *Proceedings of the Royal Society of London*, series B, 273 (2006), 2651–7.

Thompson, K., "Note de recherche: Arnoul de Montgommery," *Annales de Normandie*, 45 (1995), 49–53.

Thomson, T. and Innes, C. I. (eds.), *Law of the Bretts and Scots*, in *The Acts of the Parliaments of Scotland, 1124–1423* (Edinburgh, 1844), pp. 663–5.

Thornton, D. E., "Edgar and the eight kings, AD 973," *Early Medieval Europe*, 10 (2001), 49–80.

Thornton, D. E., *Kings, Chronologies and Genealogies: Studies in the Political History of Early Medieval Ireland and Wales*. Occasional Publications of the Oxford Unit for Prosopographical Research, 10 (Oxford, 2003).

Thornton, D. E., "Maredudd ab Owain (d.999): the most famous king of the Welsh," Welsh History Review, 18 (1996–7), 567–91.

Thorpe, B., *Ancient Laws and Institutes of England*, 2 vols. (London, 1840).

Thorpe, L. (ed. and trans.), *Geoffrey of Monmouth: The History of the Kings of Britain* (Harmondsworth, 1966).

Thorpe, L. (trans.), *Gerald of Wales: The Journey through Wales and the Description of Wales* (Harmondsworth, 1978).

Thurneysen, R., "Aus dem irischen Recht I," *Zeitschrift für celtische Philologie*, 14 (1923), 335–94; "Aus dem irischen Recht II," *Zeitschrift für celtische Philologie*, 15 (1924), 238–76; "Aus dem irischen Recht IV," *Zeitschrift für celtische Philologie*, 16 (1927), 167–230.

Thurneysen, R. (ed. and trans.), *Cáin Lánamna*, in R. Thurneysen et al., *Studies in Early Irish Law* (Dublin, 1936), pp. 1–75.

Thurneysen, R., "Göttin Medb?," *Zeitschrift für Celtische Philologie*, 8 (1929), 108–10.

Thurneysen, R., "Irisches recht," *Abhandlungen der Preussischen Akademie der Wissenschaften*, Phil.-Hist. Klasse, no. 2 (Berlin, 1931).

Tierney, J. J., *Dicuili: Liber de mensura orbis terrae* (Dublin, 1967).

Tinti, F. (ed.), *Pastoral Care in Late Anglo-Saxon England* (Woodbridge, 2005).

Todd, J. H. (ed. and trans.), *Cogadh Gaedhil re Gallaibh: The War of the Gaedhil with the Gaill, or the Invasions of Ireland by the Danes and Other Norsemen* (London, 1867).

Todd, M. (ed.), *A Companion to Roman Britain* (Oxford, 2004).

Townend, M., "Contextualizing the *Knútsdrápur*: Skaldic praise-poetry at the court of Cnut," *Anglo-Saxon England*, 30 (2001), 145–79.

Townend, M., "Knútr and the cult of St. Ólafr: poetry and patronage in eleventh-century Norway and England," *Viking and Medieval Scandinavia*, 1 (2005), 251–79.

Townend, M., *Language and History in Viking Age England: Linguistic Relations between Speakers of Old Norse and Old English* (Turnhout, 2002).

Townend, M., "Norse poets and English kings: Skaldic performance in Anglo-Saxon England," *Offa*, 58 (2001), 269–75.

Townend, M., *Scandinavian Culture in Eleventh-century Yorkshire*. Kirkdale Lecture (Kirkdale, 2007).

Tschan, F. J. (trans.), *Adam of Bremen: History of the Archbishops of Hamburg-Bremen* (New York, 2002).

Tyler, D., "Reluctant kings and Christian conversion in seventh-century England," *History*, 92 (2007), 144–61.

Tyler, E. M., "'The eyes of the beholders were dazzled': treasure and artifice in the *Encomium Emmae Reginae*," *Early Medieval Europe*, 8: 2 (1998), 247–70.

Tyler, E. M., "Talking about history in eleventh-century England: the *Encomium Emmae Reginae* and the court of Harthacnut," *Early Medieval Europe*, 13 (2005), 359–83.

Ulmschneider, K., "Settlement, economy and the 'productive' site: Middle Anglo-Saxon Lincolnshire, AD 650–780," *Medieval Archaeology*, 44 (2000), 53–80.

Van Engen, J., "The Christian Middle Ages as an historiographical problem," *American Historical Review*, 91 (1986), 519–52.

Van Hamel, A. G. (ed.), *Compert Con Culainn and Other Stories* (Dublin, 1933).

Van Houts, E., *The Normans in Europe* (Manchester, 2000).

Van Houts, E. (ed.), *William of Jumièges: Gesta Normannorum Ducum* (Oxford, 1992–5).

von Winterfeld, P. (ed.), "Hrotsvitha of Gandersheim: *Gesta Ottonis*," in *Hrotsvithae Opera* (Berlin, 1902).

Wade-Evans, A. W. (ed.), *Vitae sanctorum Britanniae et genealogiae* (Cardiff, 1944).

Wainwright, F. T., "The battles at Corbridge," *Saga-Book of the Viking Society*, 13 (1950), 156–73; reprinted in H. P. R. Finberg (ed.), *Scandinavian England: Collected Papers by F. T. Wainwright* (Chichester, 1975), pp. 163–80.

Wainwright, F. T., *The Northern Isles* (Edinburgh, 1962).

Wainwright, F. T. (ed.), *The Problem of the Picts* (Perth, 1955).

Waitz, G. (ed.), *Adam of Bremen: Gesta Hammaburgensis Ecclesiae Pontificum, MGH SS*, 2nd edn. (Hanover, 1876).

Waitz, G. (ed.), *Marianus Scottus: Chronicon, MGH SS* 5 (Hanover, 1844), pp. 481–568.

Walker, G. S. M. (ed.), *Sancti Columbani opera*. Scriptores Latini Hiberniae, 2 (Dublin, 1970).

Wall, V., "Queen Margaret of Scotland (1070–1093): burying the past, enshrining the future," in A. Duggan (ed.), *Queens and Queenship in Medieval Europe* (Woodbridge, 1997), pp. 27–38.

Wallace, P., "The origins of Dublin," in H. B. Clarke (ed.), *Medieval Dublin: The Making of a Metropolis* (Blackrock, 1990), pp. 70–97.

Wallace-Hadrill, J. M., *Early Germanic Kingship in England and on the Continent* (Oxford, 1971).

Ward-Perkins, B., "Why did the Anglo-Saxons not become more British?," *English Historical Review*, 115 (2000), 513–33.

Warner, D. (trans.) "Thietmar of Merseburg: *Chronicon*," in *Ottonian Germany* (Manchester, 2001).

Warner, R., "The archaeology of early historic Irish kingship," in S. T. Driscoll and M. R. Nieke (eds.), *Power and Politics in Early Medieval Britain and Ireland* (Edinburgh, 1988), pp. 47–68.

Warren, W. L., *The Governance of Anglo-Norman and Angevin England, 1066–1272* (London, 1987).

Wasserschleben, H. (ed.), *Die Irische Kanonensammlung*, 2nd edn. (Leipzig, 1885).

Watt, D. E. R., *Ecclesia Scoticana: Series Episcoporum Ecclesiae Catholicae Occidentalis, Series VI, Britannia, Scotia et Hibernia, Scandinavia*, vol. 1 (Stuttgart, 1991).

Weale, M. E., Weiss, D. A., Jager, R. F., et al., "Y-chromosome evidence for Anglo-Saxon mass migration," *Molecular Biology and Evolution*, 19 (2002), 1008–21.

Webb, J. F. (trans.), *The Age of Bede*, rev. edn. by D. H. Farmer (Harmondsworth, 1983; repr. 1998).

Weber, M., *On Charisma and Institution Building: Selected Papers*, ed. and trans. S. N. Eisenstadt (London, 1968).

Webster, L. and Backhouse, J., *The Making of England: Anglo-Saxon Art and Culture AD 600–900* (London, 1991).

Werner, K. F., *Naissance de la noblesse: l'essor des élites politiques en* France, 2nd edn. (Paris, 1998).

Whitelock, D. (trans.), *The Anglo-Saxon Chronicle*, in *English Historical Documents*, vol. I, 2nd edn. (London, 1979) and vol. II, 2nd edn. (London, 1981).

Whitelock, D., "Archbishop Wulfstan, homilist and statesman," in R. W. Southern (ed.), *Essays in Medieval History* (London, 1968), pp. 42–60.

Whitelock, D., *The Beginnings of English Society (The Anglo-Saxon Period)* (Harmondsworth, 1952).

Whitelock, D., "The dealings of the kings of England with Northumbria in the tenth and eleventh centuries," in P. Clemoes (ed.), *The Anglo-Saxons: Studies in Some Aspects of their History and Presented to Bruce Dickens* (London, 1959), pp. 70–88; reprinted in D. Whitelock, *History, Law and Literature in 10th–11th Century England* (London, 1981), no. 3.

Whitelock, D. (ed. and trans.), *English Historical Documents*, vol. I: *c.500–1042* (London, 1955; 2nd edn., 1979).

Whitelock, D., "The prose of Alfred's reign," in E. G. Stanley (ed.), *Continuations and Beginnings* (Oxford, 1966), pp. 67–103.

Whitelock, D. (ed.), *Sermo Lupi ad Anglos* (London, 1939); translated in D. Whitelock (ed.), *English Historical Documents* (London, 1955), vol. I, no. 240, pp. 854–9.

Whitelock, D., Brett, M., and Brooke, C. N. L. (eds.), *Councils and Synods*, 2 vols (Oxford, 1981), I, no. 4, pp. 8–10.

Whyte, W., "The intellectual aristocracy revisited," *Journal of Victorian Culture*, 10: 1 (2005), 15–45.

Wickham, C., "Debate: 'The feudal revolution' IV," *Past & Present*, 155 (1997), 196–208.

Wickham, C., *Framing the Early Middle Ages: Europe and the Mediterranean, 400–800* (Oxford, 2005).

Wickham, C., "Problems of comparing rural societies in early medieval western Europe," *Transactions of the Royal Historical Society*, 6th series, 2 (1992), 221–46.

Wickham, C., *Problems in Doing Comparative History*, Reuter Lecture 2004 (Southampton, 2005).

Wilcox, J. (ed.), *Ælfric's Prefaces* (Durham, 1994).

Wilkinson, B., "Northumbrian separatism in 1065–66," *Bulletin of the John Rylands Library*, 23 (1939), 504–26.

Williams, A., "Ælfhere (d.983)," *Oxford Dictionary of National Biography* (Oxford, 2004).

Williams, A., "'Cockles amongst the wheat': Danes and English in the western midlands in the first half of the eleventh century," *Midland History*, 11 (1986), 1–22.

Williams, A., *The English and the Norman Conquest* (Woodbridge, 1995).

Williams, A., *Kingship and Government in Pre-Conquest England c.500–1066* (Basingstoke, 1999).

Williams, A., *Land, Power and Politics: The Family and Career of Odda of Deerhurst*. Deerhurst Lecture 1996 (Deerhurst, 1997).

Williams, A., "An outing on the Dee: King Edgar at Chester, AD 973," *Medieval Scandinavia*, 14 (2004), 229–44.

Williams, A. and Martin, G. H. (eds.), *Domesday Book: A Complete Translation* (Harmondsworth, 2002).

Williams, J. (ed.), *Annales Cambriae*, Rolls Series 20 (London, 1860).

Williams, P. and Newman, R., "Market Lavington, Wiltshire, an Anglo-Saxon cemetery and settlement: excavations at Grove Farm, 1986–90," *Wessex Archaeology Report*, 19 (2006).

Williamson, T., *The Origins of Hertfordshire* (Manchester, 2000).

Wilson, D., *Anglo-Saxon Paganism* (London, 1992).

Wilson, D. M., *Vikings in the Isle of Man* (Aarhus, 2008).

Winchester, A. J. L., *Landscape and Society in Medieval Cumbria* (Edinburgh, 1987).

Winterbottom, M., "Aldhelm's prose style and its origins," *Anglo-Saxon England*, 6 (1977), 39–76.

Winterbottom, M., "Columbanus and Gildas," *Vigiliae Christianae*, 30 (1976), 310–17.

Winterbottom, M. (ed. and trans.), *Gildas: The Ruin of Britain and Other Documents* (Chichester, 1978).

Winterbottom, M. and Thomson, R. M. (eds.), *William of Malmesbury, Gesta pontificum Anglorum: The History of the English Bishops*, 2 vols. (Oxford, 2007).

Winterbottom, M. and Thomson, R. M. (eds.), *William of Malmesbury, Saints' Lives: Lives of SS Wulfstan, Dunstan, Patrick, Benignus and Indract* (Oxford, 2002).

Winterbottom, M. and Thomson, R. M. (ed.), "William of Malmesbury, *Vita Wulfstani*," in M. Winterbottom and R. M. Thompson (eds.), *William of Malmesbury, Saints' Lives: Lives of SS Wulfstan, Dunstan, Patrick, Benignus and Indract* (Oxford, 2002), pp. 8–155.

Wood, I. N., "The European Science Foundation's programme on the transformation of the Roman world and the emergence of early medieval Europe," *Early Medieval Europe* 6: 2 (1997), 217–27.

Wood, I. N., "The final phase," in M. Todd (ed.), *A Companion to Roman Britain* (Oxford, 2004), pp. 428–42.

Wood, I. N., *The Merovingian Kingdoms 450–751* (Harlow, 1994).

Wood, I. N., *The Merovingian North Sea* (Alingsås, 1983).

Wood, I., "The mission of Augustine of Canterbury to the English," *Speculum*, 69 (1994), 1–17.

Wood, I., *The Missionary Life: Saints and the Evangelisation of Europe, 400–1050* (Harlow, 2001).

Wood, I., "Pagan religions and superstitions east of the Rhine from the fifth to the ninth century," in G. Ausenda (ed.), *After Empire: Towards an Ethnology of Europe's Barbarians* (Woodbridge, 1995), pp. 253–79.

Wood, M., "The making of King Aethelstan's empire: an English Charlemagne," in P. Wormald, D. Bullough, and R. Collins (eds.), *Ideal and Reality in Frankish and Anglo-Saxon Society: Studies Presented to J. M. Wallace-Hadrill* (Oxford, 1983), pp. 251–72.

Wood, S., *The Proprietary Church in the Medieval West* (Oxford, 2006).

Wooding, J. M., *Communication and Commerce along the Western Sealanes AD 400–800* (Oxford, 1996).

Woolf, A., "Amlaíb Cúarán and the Gael, 941–981," in S. Duffy (ed.), *Medieval Dublin III* (Dublin, 2002), pp. 34–42.

Woolf, A., "The Britons: from Romans to Barbarians," in H.-W. Goetz, J. Jarnut, and W. Pohl (eds.), *Regna and Gentes: The Relationship between Late Antique and Early Medieval Peoples and Kingdoms in the Transformation of the Roman World* (Leiden, 2003), pp. 344–80.

Woolf, A., "Dún Nechtáin, Fortriu and the geography of the Picts," *Scottish Historical Review*, 85 (2006), 182–201.

Woolf, A., "Early historic Scotland to 761," in R. Oram (ed.), *The Shorter History of Scotland* (Edinburgh, forthcoming).

Woolf, A., *From Pictland to Alba 789–1070* (Edinburgh, 2007).

Woolf, A. (ed.), *Landscape and Environment in Dark Age Scotland* (St. Andrews, 2006).

Woolf, A., "The 'Moray question' and the kingship of Alba in the tenth and eleventh centuries," *Scottish Historical Review*, 79 (2000), 145–64.

Woolf, A., "Pictish matriliny reconsidered," *Innes Review*, 49 (1998), 147–67.

Woolf, A., "The Verturian hegemony: a mirror in the north," in M. Brown and C. Farr (eds.), *Mercia: An Anglo-Saxon Kingdom in Europe* (London, 2001), pp. 106–11.

Woolf, A., "View from the west: an Irish perspective on West Saxon dynastic practice," in N. J. Higham and D. H. Hill (ed.), *Edward the Elder, 899–924* (London, 2001), pp. 89–101.

Wormald, P., "Æthelred the lawmaker," in D. Hill (ed.), *Ethelred the Unready*, British Archaeological Reports, British series 59 (Oxford, 1978), pp. 47–80.

Wormald, P., "Æthelweard, d.998?," *Oxford Dictionary of National Biography* (Oxford, 2004), I, pp. 432–3.

Wormald, P., "Æthelwold and his continental counterparts: contact, comparison and contrast," in B. Yorke (ed.), *Bishop Æthelwold: His Career and Influence* (Woodbridge, 1988), pp. 13–42.

Wormald, P., "The age of Offa and Alcuin," in J. Campbell (ed.), *The Anglo-Saxons* (London, 1982), pp. 101–28.

Wormald, P., "Bede, *Beowulf* and the conversion of the Anglo-Saxon aristocracy," in R. T. Farrell (ed.), *Bede and Anglo-Saxon England*. British Archaeological Reports 46 (Oxford, 1978), pp. 32–95.

Wormald, P., *Bede and the Conversion of England: The Charter Evidence*, Jarrow Lecture 1984 (Jarrow, n.d.); reprinted in P. Wormald, *The Times of Bede: Studies in Early English Christian Society and its Historian* (Oxford, 2006).

Wormald, P., "Celtic and Anglo-Saxon kingship: some further thoughts," in P. E. Szarmach (ed.), *Sources of Anglo-Saxon Culture* (Kalamazoo, MI, 1986), pp. 151–83.

Wormald, P., "Charters, law and the settlement of disputes in Anglo-Saxon England," in W. Davies and P. Fouracre (eds.), *The Settlement of Disputes in Early Medieval Europe* (Cambridge, 1986), pp. 149–68.

Wormald, P., "*Engla Lond*: the making of an allegiance," *Journal of Historical Sociology*, 7 (1994), 1–24.

Wormald, P., "*Exempla Romanorum*: the earliest English legislation in context," in A. Ellegård and G. Åkerström-Hougen (eds.), *Rome and the North* (Jonsered, 1996), pp. 15–27.

Wormald, P., "Giving God and king their due: conflict and its resolution in the early English state," *Settimane di studio del centro italiano di studi sull'alto medioevo*, 44 (1997), 549–90.

Wormald, P., "A handlist of Anglo-Saxon lawsuits," *Anglo-Saxon England*, 17 (1988), 247–81.

Wormald, P., "*Inter cetera bona . . . genti suae*: law-making and peace-keeping in the earliest English kingdoms," *Settimane di studio del centro italiano di studi sull'alto medioevo*, 42: 2 (1995), 963–96.

Wormald, P., "The making of England," *History Today* (February 1995), 26–32.

Wormald, P., *The Making of English Law: King Alfred to the Twelfth Century*, vol. I: *Legislation and its Limits* (Oxford, 1999).

Wormald, P., "The uses of literacy in Anglo-Saxon England and its neighbours," *Transactions of the Royal Historical Society*, 5th series, 27 (1977), 95–114.

Wormald, P., "Viking studies: whence and wither," in R. T. Farrell (ed.), *The Vikings* (Chichester, 1982), pp. 128–53.

Wormald, P., "Wulfstan, archbishop of York and homilist (d.1023)," *Oxford Dictionary of National Biography* (Oxford, 2004).

Wormald, P., Bullough, D., and Collins, R. (eds.), *Ideal and Reality in Frankish and Anglo-Saxon Society* (Oxford, 1983).

Wright, N., "Gildas's prose style and its origin," in M. Lapidge and D. Dumville (eds.), *Gildas: New Approaches* (Woodbridge, 1984), pp. 107–28.

Yorke, B., "The adaptation of the Anglo-Saxon royal courts to Christianity," in M. Carver (ed.), *The Cross Goes North: Processes of Conversion in Northern Europe AD 300–1300* (York, 2003), pp. 243–57.

Yorke, B. "Anglo-Saxon gentes and regna," in H.-W. Goetz, J. Jarnut, and W. Pohl (eds.), *Regna and Gentes: The Relationship between Late Antique and Early Medieval Peoples and Kingdoms in the Transformation of the Roman World* (Leiden, 2003), pp. 381–408.

Yorke, B., *The Conversion of Britain: Religion, Politics and Society in Britain c.600–800* (Harlow, 2006).

Yorke, B., *Kings and Kingdoms of Early Anglo-Saxon England* (London, 1990).

Yorke, B., *Nunneries and the Anglo-Saxon Royal Houses* (London, 2003).

Yorke, B., "The reception of Christianity at the Anglo-Saxon royal courts," in Gameson, R. (ed.), *St. Augustine and the Conversion of England* (Stroud, 1999), pp. 152–73.

Yorke, B., "Sisters under the skin? Anglo-Saxon nunneries in southern England," *Reading Medieval Studies*, 15 (1989), 95–117.

Yorke, B., *Wessex in the Early Middle Ages* (London, 1995).

Index

Aachen (Nordrhein-Westfalen), 235, 259
Aaron, saint, 146
Abba, testator, 422
abbesses, 83, 276; making of, 471
Abbo, abbot of Fleury, 362
abbots, 168, 280–1
abdication, royal, 133, 153, 237, 256;
    see also exile(s)
Abercorn (W. Lothian), 165
Aberdeen, 382
Abernethy (Perthshire), 165, 263, 400
Abingdon (Berkshire), monastery, 32,
    386–7, 389
acculturation, 216–17
Acemannesceaster, see Bath
Acleah (Surrey), 237
Adalbero, bishop of Metz, 362
Adam of Bremen, 295
Adela of Blois, daughter of William I, 465
Adelheid, east Frankish queen and empress,
    362
administrative units, 77–9, 448–50;
    Anglo-Saxon, 50, 78, 448–9; British,
    77–8; Irish, 78; Pictish, 78; Romano-
    British, 42–3, 48–50; Scottish, 434;
    Welsh, 450; *see also* shire (*scīr*)
Adolf (Æthelwulf), count of Boulogne, 240
Adomnán, abbot of Iona, 67, 68, 86–7,
    108, 161, 168, 169, 180; *Cain
    Adomnáin* (Law of the Innocents), 87,
    101, 110; *Life of St. Columba*, 47
adoption, 101
Adwick-le-Street (Yorkshire), 217

Áed Findliath mac Néill (d.879), 201, 257,
    272, 276–7, 461, 466
Aed mac Echdach, king of Dál Riata
    (d.778), 260
Aed son of Cinaed, king of the Picts
    (d.878), 251–2, 256–7, 260
Áed son of Domnall (d.1004), 276, 384
Áedán mac Gabráin, king of Dál Riata
    (d.606), 109
Ælfflæd, abbess of Whitby, 161
Ælfgar, earl of Mercia, 345
Ælfheah, archbishop of Canterbury, 328,
    365
Ælfhere, ealdorman, 330
Ælfric, abbot of Eynsham, 398–9, 404, 470
Ælfric, archbishop of Canterbury, 388
Ælfsige Hunlafing, 421
Ælfthryth (Elstrude), daughter of Alfred,
    wife of Baldwin II of Flanders, 240, 359
Ælfthryth, queen, wife of Edgar, 364, 468,
    471
Ælfweard, king (d.924), 331
Ælfwine, Northumbrian joint-king, 111,
    113
Ælfwynn, daughter of Æthelflæd, Lady of
    the Mercians, 330, 463
Ælla, king of Northumbria (d.867), 203
Æthelbald, king of Mercia (d.716), 79
Æthelbald, West Saxon king (d.860), 237,
    240
Æthelberht, king of Kent (d.616), 130–1,
    132, 148, 152, 153; laws, 98–9, 100–1,
    131, 154, 451

Æthelburh, wife of Edwin of Northumbria, 465, 467

Æthelflæd, Lady of the Mercians (d.918), 205, 207, 330, 334, 463, 470, 472

Æthelfrith, king of Northumbrians, 58, 112

Æthelgifu, English noblewoman, 421–2

ætheling, 207, 259

Æthelred, king of East Angles, 204, 206

Æthelred, king of the Mercians (d.716), 109, 154; *gesith* of, 111, 113

Æthelred, king of Northumbria (d.796), 235–6

Æthelred, lord of the Mercians (d.911), 329–30, 334, 342

Æthelred II "the Unready," king of the English (d.1016), 259, 289, 309, 310, 323–4, 326–7, 349, 359, 365, 369, 380, 407, 448, 450, 459, 467–8

Æthelric of Bocking, thegn, 332

Æthelstan, king of the English (d.939), 217, 255, 307, 308, 322–3, 331, 334, 342, 343, 351, 359–63, 407, 450, 455

Æthelstan "Half King," ealdorman (d.956), 330

Æthelthryth, Northumbrian princess, 231

Æthelthryth, queen and saint, 386, 406, 408

Æthelweard, ealdorman and chronicler, 361, 421; *Chronicle*, 27, 202, 361, 419

Æthelwig, abbot of Evesham, 380

Æthelwine, bishop of Durham, 313

Æthelwine, ealdorman, 388

Æthelwold, nephew of King Alfred (d.902), 207, 307, 323

Æthelwold, saint, bishop of Winchester, 328, 329, 377, 381–2, 386–8, 406

Æthelwulf, author of *De Abbatibus*, 184

Æthelwulf, king of Wessex (d.858), 237–40

Æthilwald, pupil of Aldhelm, 183

Aetius, consul, 45

"ages of man," 110; *see also* life-cycle

Agilbert, bishop among West Saxons, 132, 133, 134

agnatic kinship, 82, 94, 455

Agnonn (Ireland), raid on, 200

agriculture, 438; common-field, 118, 350; hoe agriculture, 116; *see also* farming

Aidan, bishop of Lindisfarne, 149, 167

Aindiaraid, son of Máelmuire, king of Tuirbe (d.903), 270

Airgíalla, population group and kingdom, 280

aithech-túatha (rent-paying peoples), 92

Alan Twistedbeard, Breton count, 360

Alba, 4, 18, 251–2; "king of," 203

Alban, saint, 146, 405

Aland, *see* Halfdan

Alcuin, scholar from York, abbot of Tours, 136, 160, 184, 189, 196, 233–6

Aldhelm, abbot of Malmesbury, 164, 178, 179, 180, 181, 182, 183, 189

Aldwine, prior of Winchcombe, 314, 389

ale, and the food-render, 119

Alfred "the Great," king of West Saxons (d.899), 6, 202–3, 205, 207, 214, 239–43, 303, 306, 307, 322, 342, 349, 359, 361, 386, 421, 446, 448–9, 464; and *Anglo-Saxon Chronicle*, 24, 30, 304, 325–6; laws, 241, 451, 455; *Pastoral Care*, 241; Psalter, 242–3; *see also* Asser

Almond, river, 260

almsgiving, 405

Alnwick (Northumberland), 263

Alpinid dynasty, 257, 258, 260, 261, 262

Alps, 57, 358

Ambrosius Aurelianus, 42, 48

Amlaíb (Óláfr), son of Ildulb, king of Alba (?) (d.977), 258

Amlaíb (Óláfr), viking leader, 201–2

Amlaíb Cuarán (Óláfr Sihtricson), king of York, king of Dublin (d.981), 258, 272, 275, 277–9, 308, 385, 386, 403, 405

Amounderness (Lancashire), 307

amphorae, 128

Anarawd ap Rhodri, king in Wales (d.916), 342

Angelcynn, 4, 18, 202, 205, 241; "king of," 202

Angeln, 51

Angharad, daughter of Maredudd, 463

Angharad, daughter of Meurig of Ceredigion, 463

Angles/Angli, 4, 51, 61, 65

Anglesey, 200, 204–5

Anglo-Saxon Chronicle(s), 24, 27, 30, 94, 101 108, 195–6, 198, 201–2, 204, 212, 237, 239–42, 251, 253, 256, 257, 295, 304, 308, 309, 326, 330, 342, 346, 348, 453, 462

Anglo-Saxon(s), 4, 50–2, 58, 66, 72; *Anglisaxones*, 134

Anglo-Scottish border, 316

Angus, 260, 261

Annales Cambriae, 204, 348
annals/annalists, 23–4, 28–9, 30, 57, 58, 287, 290, 291, 296
annals, Northern, 304
Annals of Clonmacnoise, 24, 256
Annals of Inisfallen, 24, 274, 418
Annals of Loch Cé, 287
Annals of St.-Bertin, 199, 237, 239
Annals of Tigernach, 24
Annals of Ulster, 24, 61, 196, 198–202, 204–6, 233, 253, 254, 259, 260, 270, 272, 276, 280, 417–18, 454
anointing, 280; *see also* consecration
Anselm, archbishop of Canterbury, 294, 297, 371, 382, 408, 465
Antonine Wall, 43, 48, 63
Antoninus, saint, 407
Antrim, 46, 79
archbishop(s), 134, 163, 164, 378–9, 381
archdeacon(rie)s, 396, 400
Archenfield (Herefordshire), 346, 347, 451
architecture: building in stone, 187, 188, 401; cathedral, 381
Arculf, Frankish bishop, 177
Ardross (Rossshire), 186
Ardudwy (Gwynedd), 450
Argyll (Scotland), 46–7, 79, 203, 251
aristocrats, 233, 240; use of term aristocratic, 415–16; *see also* nobility
Armagh, 70, 147, 165, 268–9, 271–2, 274–6, 279–81, 289–90, 293–4, 378–9, 384–6
Armes Prydein Fawr, 343, 344, 352
armies, 44, 79–82
Armorica, 131
Arnulf I, Flemish count, 360, 362
Arosæte, 92
Arrow, river, 92
Ars Asporii, 179, 181
Arthur, king, 42
Artraige, population group, 92
Artúr (Arthur), son of Áedán mac Gabráin, 109
asceticism, 172, 178, 186; ascetic authority, 161; ascetic living, 148; and women 162, 148
assemblies, 51, 84–5, 102, 419, 424, 449
Asser, bishop of St. Davids, and Sherborne, 109, 242, 349, 353, 379; *Life of King Alfred*, 166, 205, 239, 460, 469–70
Áth Firdiad (Ardee, Co. Louth), 276

Áth Sige (Assey, Co. Tara), 27
Atholl (Perth and Kinross), 261
Augustine, saint, archbishop of Canterbury, 143, 149, 164, 241
Augustine, saint, bishop of Hippo, 178, 235
Auisle, viking leader, 201
Aurelius Caninus, 48
authority, 77, 84, 143, 152, 204, 218, 279, 307, 381, 421; ascetic and institutional, 161; papal, 368; and writing of the past, 17, 25; *see also* legitimation; power
Auxilius, bishop, 147
Avon, river (Bristol), 62
Avon, river (Warwickshire), 62

Bachall Mor of Molaug (great staff), 408
Baíthéne, abbot of Iona, 108
Bakewell (Derbyshire), meeting, 251, 308, 330; *see also* "submission" to southern English kings
Baldwin, abbot of Bury St. Edmunds, 389
Baldwin (I), count of Flanders, 240
Baldwin (II), count of Flanders, 240, 359
Balinderry (Co. Offaly), high-status site, 433
Balladoole (Isle of Man), 224
Ballinaby (Islay), 221
Balthild, Frankish queen, 133
Bamburgh (Northumberland), 61, 306, 307, 308, 310, 314; rulers, 255, 259
Bangor (Co. Down), 198, 281
Bangor (Gwynedd), see of, 164, 347, 379, 383
Banshenchas, 276, 461, 467
Bantham (Devon), 70
baptism, 160, 167, 205, 396, 399–400, 403; baptismal churches, 164
barbarians, image of Scots as, 304, 372; "Celtic," 13
Barking (Essex), 154, 168, 185
barter, 70
Basingwerk (Flintshire), 351
Bath (Somerset), 259, 309, 363
Battle of Maldon, 419, 421
Bede, Northumbrian monk and scholar, 5–6, 42, 58, 59, 61, 83, 85, 97–8, 111, 129, 132, 133, 151, 161, 162, 165, 167, 168, 169, 170, 172, 178, 180, 182, 183–4, 189, 239, 251, 314, 315, 341, 406, 418–19; *De Temporum ratione*, 150, 183; *Ecclesiastical History*, 45, 83, 86, 143, 144, 147, 148, 149, 154, 171, 314,

377, 387, 389; and England, 315, 325–6; on the hide, 66, 95, 116; and languages, 5–6, 41, 52, 341; letter to Bishop Ecgberht, 149

Bedfordshire, 406

bees, 58

Belach Lechta (Co. Cork), 274

Belach Mugna (Co. Kildare), 272–3, 276

Beli, king of Dumbarton, 83

bells, 408

Benedict, saint, 148; *see also* Benedictine monasticism

Benedict III, pope, 239

Benedict Biscop, founder and abbot of Wearmouth and Jarrow, 162, 163, 168, 183, 187; early life, 112, 114

Benedictine monasticism, 377, 386–8, 396, 398–9

Benedictine reform, 269, 314–15, 361–3, 377, 386–8, 404; *see also* monastic reform

Benedictional of Æthelwold, 364

Benllech (Anglesey), 222

Beowulf, 24, 81, 84, 249

Bermondsey (London), 390

Bernicia, 49, 52, 61, 62, 67, 77, 79, 83, 109, 112, 161, 304, 305, 306, 307, 308, 309, 311, 312, 313, 315

Berrad Airechta, Irish law tract, 102

Bertha, wife of Æthelberht of Kent, 130, 132, 153

Bethoc, daughter of Máel Coluim II, 262

Beverley (Yorkshire), 167, 388

Bible, 233, 243, 287; biblical Latin style, 147; commentaries, 182–3, 232, 239; *see also* book(s); Old Testament

Bicknor (Monmouthshire), 379, 383

Birdoswald (Cumberland), 44

Birinus, missionary, 149

Birka, 365

Birr, synod, 87

Bishop Wearmouth (Durham), 307

bishop(s), 129, 163–8, 235–6, 241–2, 280–1, 328–9, 377–83, 386, 388, 403–4, 406; behavior, 171; episcopal councils, 164–6, 171; episcopal hierarchy, 163–4; numbers and distribution, 164–6, 171; and pastoral care, 396–400; penance and penitentials, 171; responsibilities, 164, 397–8; *see also* archbishops; dioceses; prince-bishops; sees

Blathmac, monk of Iona, 198, 383

Bleddyn ap Cynfyn, king of Gwynedd and Powys (d.1075), 345, 346; sons, 347

blood-price, 67, 469; *see also* wergild

bóaire, 67, 97

boat(s), *see* ship(s)

Bofeenan (Co. Mayo), 69

Boite, son of Cinaed, 262

Boniface (Wynfrith), saint, missionary, archbishop, 85–6, 109, 135–6, 137, 150, 183; correspondence, 136

Boniface V, pope, 147, 153

Book of Armagh, 32, 268, 289, 385

Book of Deer, 31, 400, 403

Book of Durrow, 185–6

Book of Kells, 31, 32, 188–9

Book of Life, 236

Book of Llandaff, 31, 77, 349, 404, 452–3

Book of the Popes, 134

bookland/*bocland*, 82, 95–6, 118, 163, 422–3

book(s), 232, 239

bowl(s), 240

Boyne, river, 61, 64, 67

Braaid, the (Isle of Man), 223

bracteates, 127

Bracton, 33

Brechin (Angus), 379, 383

Brega (Co. Meath), 199, 270; plain, 5

Brehon Law, 98

Bremen-Hamburg, archbishops of, 382

Bressay (Shetland), 221

Bretha Nemed, Irish law tract, 99

bretwalda, 79, 207

Brian Bórama (Boru), king of Munster and Ireland (d.1014), 268–9, 271–5, 277, 281, 285–90, 291, 292, 294, 296–8, 384–5

Bridei, *see* Bruide

Brigit of Kildare, saint, 162, 170, 385, 387

Brihtsige, son of Beornoth, 207

Bristol, 291

Britain, 3, 63; lowland, 5, 28, 333; upland, 5, 28, 333; writing history of, 3–5

Britannia, 3–4, 43–4, 48–9, 232, 259

British/Brittonic language, 341; British Romance, 108; and culture, 341, 343, 344, 352

British/Britons/*Britones*, 4, 45, 48–50, 52–3, 58, 66, 94, 117–18, 341, 342, 343, 351–2; church, 145–6

Brittany, 360, 362, 369

Bróen, son of Máel Mórda, king of Leinster (fl.943–7), 278
Brompton (Yorkshire), 310
brooch, thistle, 433
Bruide, king of the Picts (d.584), 76, 148
Bruide, king of the Picts (d.693), 80, 83
Bruide, king of the Picts (d.706), 83
Brunanburh, battle, 256, 278, 308, 331
Brut y Tywysogion, 200, 346
Bryant's Gill (Cumbria), 214
Brycheiniog, 78, 341, 347, 436
Buchan (Aberdeenshire), 258, 261
Buckingham (Buckinghamshire), 255
Buckquoy (Orkney), 220
buildings, 62, 162, 215, 220, 224, 434, 437–8, 441; *see also* architecture
Builth, 78
Burghal Hidage, 333
Burghead (Moray), 48, 186
Burgred, king of the Mercians (d.874), 204, 342
burhs, 333–4, 436
burials, 51, 58, 71, 96, 151, 154, 197, 204, 405; in churchyards, 151, 399; execution, 437; furnished, 110, 116; monuments, 161, 402; Scandinavian, 217–24; *see also* cemeteries; grave-goods; graveyards
Burton-on-Trent (Staffordshire), 388
Bury St. Edmunds (Suffolk), 389
Byrhtferth, monk and scholar, 403
Byrhtnoth, ealdorman, 323, 419
Byzantium/Byzantine, 70, 131, 134, 187, 366

Cadell ap Rhodri Mawr, king of Seisyllwg and Dyfed (d.910), 343
Cadog, saint, 408; *Life*, 348
Cadwallon, British king (d.634), 149
Cædwalla, king of the West Saxons (d.689), 68, 149, 152
Caerleon (Monmouthshire), 146
Caerwent (Gwent), 63
cáin, 274
Cáin Adomnáin (Law of the Innocents), 87, 101, 110
Caithness (Scotland), 219, 255, 382
Caithréim Cheallacháin Chaisil, twelfth-century biography, 273
Calpurnius, St. Patrick's father, 64, 107
Cambodunum, 167
Cambridge Thegns' Guild, 454

Cambridgeshire, 388
Canon law, 30
"Canons of Edgar," 311
Canterbury (Kent), 63, 134, 243, 334, 389, 406; archbishops, 31, 234, 236, 334, 358, 378, 380; school, 182–3; see of, 165, 387; submission to, 342, 353; *see also* Anselm; archbishops; Dunstan; Lanfranc; Oda; Stigand; Theodore of Tarsus
Cantiaci, 62; *see also* Kent
Cantiori, citizen of Gwynedd, 107–8
cantref (Welsh administrative unit), 261, 350, 450
Cantware, 92; *see also* Kent
capital as a factor of production, 115
Cardiff, mint, 351
Carew Castle (Pembrokeshire), 435
Carham-on-Tweed (Northumberland), 310
Carl, son of Thurbrand Hold, 453–4
Carlisle (Cumberland), 61, 165, 306, 307
Carmarthen (Dyfed), 64
Cárn a'Bharraich (Oronsay, Hebrides), 220
Carolingian reform(s), 362, 377, 383–4, 386, 398, 403
Carolingian(s), rulers of Francia, 136; Carolingian Europe, 415–18, 423; models, 32–3, 363–4; Renaissance, 232, 233, 236, 241, 377
Cashel (Co. Tipperary), 268, 271, 273, 419; Rock of, 294, 469; synod (1101), 293–4, 382
cashels, 65
Cassian, John, monk and ascetic author, 178
Castle Hill, Tenby (Pembrokeshire), 435
Cathasach mac Duilgen (d.957), 280
cathedral communities, 166, 168, 386–7
Cathróe of Metz, 362–3
Cathwulf, monk, 136
cats, 58
Catterick (North Yorkshire), 61, 167
cattle, 59, 67, 78–9, 97, 307, 433
Causantín, *see* Constantín II
Ceallachán Chaisil, king of Munster (d.954), 269, 273
Cedd, bishop of the East Saxons, 167
Celestine I, pope, 64, 129, 146
Celi Dé, 172, 379
celibacy, clerical, 148, 384, 386–8, 400
Cell Móna (Kilmona, Co. Westmeath), 272

Cellach, abbot of Iona, 196
Cellach, bishop of Alba, 254
Cellach, ruler of Moray (?), 257
"Celtic," 11–12, 14–15, 16; alleged
  barbarism, 13; charters, 32; church, 15,
  16, 143, 174; identity, 344; kingship, 16
cemeteries, 44, 50–2, 58, 221; communal,
  137; see also burials; graveyards
Cenél Comgail, 83
Cenél Conaill, 46, 79–80, 86–7, 271
Cenél nEógain, 82–3, 257, 271–2, 276,
  386
Cenél nGabráin, 260
Cennétig, son of Lorcáin (d.951), 273
Centwine, king of the West Saxons
  (d.?685), 153
Cenwald, bishop of Worcester, 362
Ceolfrith, abbot of Wearmouth-Jarrow, 163,
  181
Ceolnoth, archbishop of Canterbury, 254
Ceolred, king of the Mercians (d.716), 422
Ceolwulf I, king of the Mercians (d. after
  823), 204
Ceolwulf II, king of the Mercians (d. after
  873/4), 204–5
ceorl, 96–7, 118
Cerball mac Dúngal, king of Osraige
  (d.888), 199–201
Cerball mac Muirecáin, king of Leinster
  (d.909), 253, 277
Cerdic, king of the West Saxons (d.534), 52
cereals, 67
Ceredigion: bishopric, 347; kingdom, 78,
  341, 342, 343, 348
chancery, royal, 32
Charlemagne, king of the Franks, then
  emperor (d.814), 126, 136, 160, 232,
  233–6, 325
Charles the Bald, king of the West Franks
  (d.877), 233, 236–8, 240
Charles Martel (d.741), 135, 136
Charles the Straightforward/Simple,
  Frankish king (d.929), 359–60
charms, 24, 405
charter(s), 17, 23, 26, 29, 30–3, 62, 63, 64,
  66, 76–8, 82, 96, 127, 131, 137–8, 163,
  239, 253, 255, 304, 326, 328, 331, 436,
  452–3, 461; see also witness lists
Cheddar (Somerset), 437
Chelles, monastery, 133
Chertsey (Surrey), 93

Cheshire, 309, 311
Chester (Cheshire), 58, 205, 259, 307, 309,
  330, 448; mint, 351
Chester-le-Street (County Durham), 306,
  310, 380
Cheviots, 307
child oblation, 234, 387
children, 109–10, 112
Chiltern Hills, 63
chrism, 164, 396–7, 401
Christ Church, Canterbury, 166
Christian symbolism, 202, 206, 224
Christian(s)/Christianity, 41, 85–7, 197,
  205–6, 221, 223, 231, 239; definitions,
  144, 154; late Roman, 145–6; and the
  royal household, 114
Christianization, 128–30, 136–7, 145,
  160–3; impact, 7, 57, 64, 85–7, 136–8,
  177–8; see also conversion
Chrodegang, Rule of, 383, 387
Chronicle of Ireland, 24
Chronicle of the Kings of Alba (also Older
  Scottish Chronicle), 203, 251–3, 254,
  258–9
chronicles/chroniclers, 23–4, 59; see also
  annals
church dues, 398, 401; see also tithes
church reform, 26, 31, 293, 329, 381, 459,
  465, 472; see also Carolingian reform;
  monastic reform; papacy; religious reform
church(es), 64, 82, 86; episcopal churches,
  166–7, 398; private, 164, 167, 414, 423;
  thegnly, 398, 401–2; see also local
  (churches); minster(s)/minster churches;
  mother-church
Cíannachta, kingdom, 200
Ciaran, saint, 408
Ciarraige (Kerry), 92
Cicero, Roman author, 236
Cinaed mac Ailpín, king of the (Dál Riata)
  Picts (d.858), 203, 225, 252, 256, 260,
  461, 466
Cinaed, son of Conaing, king of the
  Cíannachta (d.851), 202
Cinaed, son of Dub, king of Alba (d.1005),
  260
Cinaed, son of Mael Coluim, king of Alba
  (d.995), 252–3, 258–9, 309
Cirencester (Gloucestershire), 63, 255
Cistercian order, 389
cities, 64; see also civitas

civitas, 61, 64, 91, 107, 129, 147, 163–4, 254

Clann Cholmáin, 71–2, 257, 385

Clann Ruaidrí, 257, 261

clas, 170, 384, 400

class and status, 115–18

Cledmutha, Anglo-Saxon *burh*, 436

clergy, 163–4, 384, 396, 398, 400–2; communities, 166, 168, 384, 386–7, 396; responsibilities, 164; *see also* priests; religious communities

Clibberswick (Unst, Shetland), 220

client kings, 78–9, 273

clientage/clientship, 97, 115–16, 119, 423–4

climate, 57, 59

cloaks, 235

Clofesho (Leicestershire), 71

Clogher (Co. Tyrone), 128, 433

Clonard (Co. Meath), 281

Clondalkin (nr. Dublin), 199

Clones (Co. Monaghan), 379

Clonfert (Co. Galway), 379, 401, 408

Clonmacnoise (Co. Offaly), 169, 186, 269, 274, 276, 281, 378–9, 385, 388; cross, 281

Clontarf, battle, 285–90, 298, 422

clothing, 69, 237, 422; *see also* dress

Clovis II, king, 133

Cloyne (Co. Cork), 379

Clune Farm, Dores (Inverness), 186

Cluniac order, 390

Cluny (France), 390

Clyde, river, 308

Clydog ap Cadell, king of Ceredigion (d.920), 343

Cnut, king of Denmark and England (d.1035), 262, 289, 295, 309, 310, 311, 312, 313, 323–4, 326–7, 335, 349, 363–7, 370, 382, 421, 449–51, 468

Cnut, late ninth-century Scandinavian king, 206

Cnut IV, king of Denmark (d.1086), 295

coarse wares, 70

Codex Amiatinus, 187–8

Coenwulf, king of the Mercians (d.821), 204

Cogadh Gáedhel re Gallaibh, 273, 286, 296, 298

Cogges (Oxfordshire), 439

Cogitosus (Toimtenach), 61, 64, 162

cognatic kinship, 82, 94, 455

Coifi, priest, 150

coins/coinage, 49, 63, 70, 82, 131, 204–6, 213, 215, 218, 224, 278, 232, 325, 333–4, 351, 367; of queen Cynethryth, 470; Welsh, 351; *see also sceattas*; silver

Coldingham (Berwickshire), 168, 184, 389

Coleman, hagiographer, 398

Coleraine (Co. Londonderry), 67

Collectio canonum Hibernensis, 32–3, 99, 452

colloquies, 182

colonizing society, early Anglo-Saxon, 116

Columba (Colum Cille/Columcille), founder and abbot of Iona, saint, 65, 67, 76, 86, 108, 109, 143, 148, 161, 163, 376, 383, 385, 405

Columban federation, 253, 384–6

Columbanus, Irish monastic founder, 70, 132, 147, 148, 180, 182

Comgall, saint, 198

comitatus, 81–2, 84, 87

commemoration, 162, 236, 238, 315

commerce/merchants, 422–3; *see also* trade/traders

commote (*cwmwd*, Welsh administrative unit), 78, 350, 450

communication(s), 233, 242, 358; commercial, 234–5, 238

comparative history, 9, 23, 414–16

compensation, legal, 100–2, 454–5

compurgator, 102

computistics, 24, 180, 181, 182, 183

Conaille, kingdom, 200, 280–1

Conaing, son of Áedán mac Gabráin, 109

Conan, bishop in Cornwall, 349

confession, *see* penance/penitential(s)

Congalach mac Maíle Mithig (d.956), 278–9, 281

Conleth, bishop of Kildare, 162

Connacht, 64, 199, 270–1, 274–5

Conrad II, east Frankish king, emperor (d.1039), 262, 365

consecration: of kings, 239–40, 259, 276, 280, 363–4, 468–9, 472; of queens, 459, 471–2; *ordines*, 364, 471

Constantín, son of Cinaed, king of the Picts (d.876), 251, 256, 461

Constantín, son of Cuilén, king of Alba (d.997), 260

Constantín II, son of Áed, king of Alba (abd. 943, d.952), 252, 253–7, 306, 362

Constantine, king of Dumnonia
  (sixth century), 48
Constantine the Great, emperor (d.337), 153
conversion (to Christianity), 6, 41, 45, 53,
  128–30, 133–4, 143–55, 160; adoption,
  160; elite, 150, 161–3; nominal, 160;
  official royal, 84–7, 160–1; political,
  131, 151–2; and royal household, 114;
  Scandinavians, 205–6, 258, 279, 402–3;
  spiritual, 160; women, 465
Conwy, river, 342
Cooley Peninsula, 64
Coolure Demesne (Co. Westmeath), 67
Copsi, earl of Northumbria, 313
Coquet, river, 310
Corbridge, battle, 254, 306
Corcu Duibne, 92
Corcu Thrí, 270
Cork, 96, 199, 274–5, 281
Cormac mac Cuilennáin, king of Munster
  (d.909), 272–4, 277
Cormeilles (France), 389
Cornish language, 343
Cornwall, 44, 146, 401; bishops in, 349,
  380, 396; kingdom, 341, 343; *lan* names
  in, 348; saints and cults, 407; West Saxon
  control, 207, 342, 351–2
Coroticus, British king (fifth century), 66,
  107, 147
Córus Fine, Irish law tract, 101
"correction," 136, 232; *see also* Carolingian
  reform(s)
Cotswold Hills (Gloucestershire), 62
councils, 166, 381–2, 399–400; *see also*
  assemblies; synods
County Hidage, 448
courts, legal, 448–9
court(s), royal, 232, 238, 240, 242–3, 459,
  464–5; *see also* household
Cowdery's Down (Hampshire), 437
Coygan Camp (Camarthenshire), 435
craftworkers/craftworking, 69, 72, 184,
  433, 442
Craig Clatchard (Fife), 434
crannogs, 65, 69, 91, 206, 423, 432, 433,
  436
Crediton, see of, 349, 380
cremation, 216–17
Crínán, abbot of Dunkeld, 262
Crith Gablach, Irish law tract, 99, 101,
  418–19

Cronk ny Merriu (Isle of Man), 224
cross, free-standing, 188; *see also*
  Clonmacnoise; Gosforth; Kells; Kinnity;
  Monasterboice; Ruthwell; sculpture/
  stone-carving
Cruithne, sons of, 25
Crusades, 372
Cuilén, son of Ildulb, king of Alba (d.971),
  258–60, 261
Cumberland, 5, 259
Cumbria(ns), 5, 308, 309
Cumwhitton (Cumbria), 217
Cuneglasus, 48
Curragh, the, 61
Custantin, king of the Picts, *see* Constantín,
  son of Cinaed
Cuthbert, bishop of Hereford, 185
Cuthbert, bishop of Lindisfarne, saint, 161,
  169–70, 184, 306, 310–13; Church, 254;
  community, 172, 304–7, 312, 315–16;
  cult, 186; liberty of, 306, 310; Lindisfarne
  Life, 108; prince-bishops, 306; and
  reform, 311, 314–15; sanctuary, 307
Cyfeiliog, bishop of Ergyng, 348
Cyfraith Hywel, 452
Cymry, 4, 5
Cynan, king of Powys (d.855), 237
Cynan ab Iago (d.1060), 290–1
Cynefrith, abbot of Gilling, 163
Cynegils, king of the West Saxons (d.?642),
  149
Cynethryth, wife of Offa, 467, 470–2
Cynewulf, poet, 470
cyninges thegn, *see* king's thegn

Dagobert II, king of Austrasia (d.679),
  133
Dál Cais (In Déis Tuaiscirt), 273–5, 419
Dál Fiatach, 79, 80
Dál Riata/Dalriada, 42, 46–7, 65, 79, 81,
  83, 86, 98, 109, 163, 203, 225, 252,
  260, 450
Dalkey Island, 70
Damnonii, 165
Danelaw, 380–1, 402–3, 446–7
Daniel, bishop of Winchester, 85
Danube area, 127, 128
David, saint, 109, 397, 408; cult, 347; *Life*,
  348
David I, king of Scotland (d.1153), 383,
  389

De Duodecim abusivis saeculi ("On the Twelve Abuses of the World"), 85, 136, 468

De Obsessione Dunelmi ... ("Concerning the Siege of Durham ..."), 310, 453–4

deacon, 107, 147, 164

Dee, river, 259, 309

Deer (Aberdeenshire), 400; *see also* Book of Deer

Deer Park Farms (Co. Antrim), 433

Deheubarth, kingdom, 259, 295, 343, 344, 345, 347, 348, 349, 352; Irish involvement in, 290, 297

Deira, kingdom, 49, 62, 67, 77, 83, 161, 304, 305, 306, 308, 312

Der bhFáil, queen of Tara (d.931), 276

derbfhine, 95, 100, 163

Dereham (Norfolk), 388

Derry (Ireland), 199, 385

Derrynavlan/Derrynaflan (Co. Tipperary), 58, 184; hoard, 185

Derwent, river, 62

devolution, 303

Devon, 237, 291, 349, 448; *see also* Dumnonia

Dewstow (Monmouthshire), 164

dialectic, 233

Diarmait mac Máel na mBó, king of Leinster (d.1072), 290–3, 295

Diarmait Ua Briain (d.1115), 292, 293–4, 297

Dicuil, Irish monk, 198

diet, 221, 422; English, 362

Dinas Powys (South Glamorgan), 58, 64, 68, 128, 435

dioceses, 163–8, 378–83, 396–400; England, 62, 165–6, 379–81; Ireland, 164–5, 378–9, 382; and kingdoms 93, 163–8, 347–9, 378; origins, 163; Scotland, 165, 379, 382–3; Wales, 164, 347–9, 379, 383; *see also* sees

diplomas, 163; *see also* charter(s)

disease, 65; *see also* plague

disputes, 101–2, 452–6

distraint, 102

divorce, 111, 115

DNA, 94, 447

Doddingtree (Worcestershire), 449

dog, value of, 446

Dol (Brittany), 146

Dolaucothi (Llanwrda, Carmarthenshire), 351

Domesday Book, 26, 213, 295, 311, 414, 417, 423–4, 447–9, 452, 462; slaves in, 116

Dommuc (England), 380

Domnall Bán, king of Alba (deposed 1094 and 1097), 263

Domnall Cláen, son of Lorcán, king of Leinster (fl.978–84), 279

Domnall, son of Áed Findliath (d.915), 272

Domnall, son of Congalach mac Maíle Mithig (d.976), 272, 278

Domnall, son of Constantín, king of Alba (d.900), 203, 252, 253, 256

Domnall Ua Briain, son of Tadc, 296

Domnall ua Néill, king of Cenél nEógain and Ireland (d.980), 279, 281, 386

Donald, brother of Máel Coluim III, 459, 465

Donatus, Roman grammarian, 179

Donegal (Ireland), 199

Donnchad, son of Crínán, king of Alba (d.1040), 262

Donnchad, son of Flann Sinna, king of Mide (d.944), 273

Donnchad, son of Máel Coluim III, 263, 459, 465

Donngus Ua hAingliu, bishop of Dublin, 293

Doon Hill, Dunbar (East Lothian), 435

Dorchester (Dorset), 448

Dorchester on Thames (Oxfordshire), 50, 149, 166, 380–1

Dorestad, 135

Dorney (Buckinghamshire), 439

Dorset, 448

Downpatrick (Co. Down), 379, 454

dress, 50–3, 134, 184–5, 215–17; ecclesiastical, 71, 162, 184–5; *see also* clothing; fashion

Drumcliff (Scotland), 385

Dub dá Leithe, abbot of Armagh, 276, 280, 385–6

Dub, son of Máel Coluim, king of Alba (d.966), 258, 261

Dub Tuinne mac Eochada, king of Ulaid (d.1007), 454

Dublin, 3, 199–201, 204, 206, 223, 253, 262, 268–72, 275, 277–81, 285, 288,

289, 291–2, 293, 295, 296, 297, 345, 350, 382, 385, 403, 422, 441, 446; synods, 293
Dublin Bay, 64
Dublin Mountains, 64
Dubraige, 92
Dubslaine, Irish pilgrim, 242
Dudo of St.-Quentin, chronicler, 369–70
Duduc, bishop of Wells, 368
Dumbarton (Strathclyde), 48–9, 78, 128, 252; Dumbarton Rock, siege of, 201
Dumnonia, kingdom, 48, 77, 164, 341, 448
Dumnonii, northern, 49; *see also* Damnonii
Dunadd (Strathclyde/Argyll), 47, 58, 70, 185, 434, 435
Dunbar (East Lothian), 313
Dunblane (Perthshire), 379, 383
Dundurn (Perthshire), 434, 435
Dunfermline (Fife), 389
Dunkeld (Perthshire), 165, 196, 253, 379, 383, 385, 405
Dunoding (Gwynedd), 450
Dunottar, 253, 255, 258
Dunragit (Dumfries & Galloway), 61
Dunrally (Co. Laois), 199
Dunsæte Ordinance, 447, 451–2
Dunstan, archbishop of Canterbury, saint, 328, 361–2, 377, 380, 386, 388, 408, 469
Durham, 255, 262, 306, 310, 311, 312, 313, 316, 380–1, 387, 405; cathedral, 315
Durham Gospels, 187
Durrow (Co. Offaly), 385, 401
Dyfed, 65, 164, 395; bishop-houses, 348, 379; kingdom, 46, 48, 52, 77, 341, 342, 343, 347, 349, 352
Dyfnwal, king of Strathclyde (d.975), 259, 362
Dyfrig (*Dubricius*), saint, 348
Dyrham (Avon), 58

Eadbald, king of Kent (d.640), 132, 149
Eadberht, king of Kent (eighth century), 234–5
Eadfrith, bishop of Lindisfarne, 186
Eadgifu, west Frankish queen, 359–61
Eadgifu, wife of Edward the Elder, 467–8
Eadhild, wife of Hugh the Great, 359

Eadmer of Canterbury, chronicler, 366
Eadred, king of the English (d.955), 305, 309, 331, 467–8
Eadric, king of Kent (d.686), 71, 98, 100, 102
Eadric Streona, ealdorman of Mercia, 331, 448
Eadulf, lord of Bamburgh, 310
Eadwig, king of the English (d.959), 331, 422
Eadwulf of Bamburgh, 251, 254, 308; sons, 251
ealdormen, 80, 324, 419, 421, 448; *see also scīrman*
Ealdred, archbishop of York, 378, 380–2, 388
Ealdred, earl, 453–54
Ealdred, son of Eadwulf, lord of Bamburgh, 254–5, 306; "king of the North Saxons," 255
Ealdsige, abbot of York minster, 238–9
Ealswide (Eahlswith), daughter of Baldwin and Ælfthryth, 240
Eamont (Cumbria): bridge, 343; river, 255
Eanfled, Northumbrian queen, 113, 161
Eanfrith, king of Bernicia (d.634), 83
Earconbehrt, king of Kent (d.664), 133
Earcongota, daughter of Seaxburgh, 133
Earkonwald, bishop of London, 138
East Angles: dynasty of (Wuffingas), 116; kingdom, 70, 77, 80, 86, 92, 148, 149, 165, 198, 201, 203, 212, 216, 380, 388
East Saxons: dynasty, 109; kingdom, 77, 83, 148, 165
Easter, disputes over dating, 86, 149, 165, 181
Easter Rising (Dublin, 1916), 287
ecclesiastical sites, 196–9, 204, 206; and secular, 440–1
Ecgberht, archbishop of York, 183
Ecgberht, king in Northumbria (d.873), 203
Ecgberht, king of the West Saxons (d.839), 207, 254, 342, 349
Ecgfrith, king of the Northumbrians (d.685), 79, 108
Ecgfrith, son of king Offa (d.796), 471
Ecgwine, bishop of Hwicce, 62
Echternach, monastery, 135, 137
Echternach Gospels, 187

Eden, river, 64

Edgar, king of the English (d.975), 259, 309, 322–3, 328, 361–4, 387, 398, 404, 406, 421

Edgar the Ætheling, 263, 324, 313, 459

Edgiva/Eadgifu, English princess, 359

Edict of Pîtres (864), 334

Edinburgh, 49, 165, 258

Edith, queen, wife of Edward the Confessor, 327, 461, 464

Edith/Eadgyth, East Frankish queen, 359–61

Edith/Ealdgyth, daughter of Earl Ælfgar, 345

Edith/Mathilda, daughter of Margaret of Scotland and Máel Coluim III, English queen, 371, 459, 463

Edmund, bishop of Durham, 311, 313

Edmund, king of the East Angles (d.869), 202–4, 365; saint, 206, 365

Edmund, king of the English (d.946), 257, 305, 308, 331, 343, 360, 362–3, 403, 467–8; laws, 455

Edmund Ironside (d.1016), 310, 459

education, 233; Latin, 179–80, 182

Edward, son of Máel Coluim and Margaret, 263

Edward the Confessor, king of the English (d.1066), 263, 311, 327, 345, 346, 367–70, 402, 408, 459–60

Edward the Elder, king of the West Saxons and latterly of the Mercians (d.924), 207, 251–2, 254–5, 307, 308, 323, 330–1, 342, 359, 362–3, 421, 463; laws, 449

Edward the Exile, son of Edmund Ironside, 369

Edward the Martyr, king of the English (d.978), 324, 407

Edwin, earl of Mercia, 312

Edwin, king of Deira and Bernicia (Northumbria, d.633), 67, 112, 149, 153, 154, 161, 419, 465

Egbert (Ecgberht), archbishop of Trier, 240

Eifionydd (Gwynedd), 450

Eiludd, *alias* Teilo, 109

Eiríkr Haraldsson, 258

Eithne, daughter of Áed Findliath, 277

Eithne, goddess, 277

Elen, daughter of Llywarch of Dyfed, 463

Elene, 470

Elfoddw, (arch)bishop of Gwynedd, 164, 348

Elfred *Brihtwulfing*, 254, 306

Elise, Pillar of, 348

Elmet, kingdom, 49, 62, 78

Elmham (Norfolk), 380

Ely (Cambridgeshire), 386, 388, 405–6

Emly (Co. Tipperary), 273–5, 379

Emma, probable daughter of Erchinoald, 132, 133

Emma, queen, wife of Æthelred II and of Cnut, 327, 359, 366, 369, 461, 464, 467–8

emporia, 70, 131, 197, 305, 333; *see also* wics

Encomium Emmae Reginae, 327, 366, 461

Englalond, 4, 325

English invasion of Ireland, 285, 286, 287

entourage, 418–19; *see also* familia; household

environmental sampling, 438

envoy(s), *see* messenger(s)

Eochaid, son of Ildulb, 258

Eochaid, son of Rhun, 262

Eochaid mac Domangairt, king of Dál Riata (d.697), 260

Eóganachta, 46, 80, 272–4

Eostorwine, abbot of Wearmouth-Jarrow, 163

Eostre (Eastre), pagan goddess, 150

Eosturmonath (April), 150

Erchinoald, "mayor of the palace," 132–3, 138

Érenn, 4, 271; *see also* "king of Ireland"

Ergyng: bishopric, 347 383 (*see also* Cyfeiliog); dynasty, 348; kingdom, 77, 346

Eric/Erik Bloodaxe, king of York (d.954), 306, 332, 362

Eric of Hlathir, earl of Northumbria, 310

Esk, river, 309

Essex, 207, 448

Esther, 470

ethnic identity, 51–3, 127, 225, 303, 308, 341, 370; *see also* identities

ethnicity, 16, 34, 62, 94, 108–9, 305, 371, 447–8

ethnogenesis, 16, 53

Euddogwy (*Oudoceus*), saint: *Life* of (*Vita S. Oudocei*), 349

Eustace III, count of Boulogne, 371

Evesham (Worcestershire), 62, 329
e-ware, 70, 434
excommunication, 397
exegesis, 23–4, 27, 177, 181, 182, 183
Exeter (Devon), 333, 343; monastery, 349; see of, 349, 380–1
exile(s), 67, 133, 231, 234–5, 262, 360; see also peregrinatio

Faccombe Netherton (Hampshire), 437
fairche, see mother-parish
fairs, 70, 85
Falkirk, 263
familiae, 232
family politics, 459, 463–4, 466; see also marriage; succession
famine, 65, 422
Faremoutiers, convent, 133, 238
Faricius, abbot, 89
farming, 44, 67, 333; intensification, 439; Irish farming, 115, 118; pastoral, 307; see also manorialization
Farnham (Surrey), 68
Faroe Isles, 197–8
fashion, 127; see also dress
fasting, 405
feasting, 414, 421–2
Fécamp, 366
federates, 45, 50
Feidlimid mac Crimthainn, king of Munster (d.847), 271, 408
Felix, Burgundian missionary, 149
Felix, "chancellor" of West Saxon king, 237–8
Fenlands, 28
Fergus Mór, legendary king of Dál Riata, 46–7
fermtoun, 78
Ferrières, monastery, 236, 237
Fettercairn (Kincardineshire), 260
feud, 84, 100–2, 111, 112, 113, 453–6; war as, 111
feudalism, 9, 16, 241, 416
fidelity, 236, 243
fields, 67; see also agriculture
Fife, 261
filid, 11, 96, 155, 420
Findláech, son of Ruaidrí, king of Alba (?)(d.1020), 261–2
Fine Gall, 291
fine(s), 98, 101

Finglesham (Kent), 151
Finnian, saint, 148
Fintan, son of Tailchán (alias Munnu), 108, 109
Firth of Tay, 61
fish/fishing, 67, 232, 237
Flaithbertach ua Néill, king of Ailech (d.1036), 262, 277
Flanders, 240, 362–3, 378; count of, 295
Flann, queen of Ailech, 276
Flann Sinna mac Maíle Sechnaill, king of Ireland (d.916), 257, 272–3, 276–7, 466
flax, 69
fleets, 291, 294, 295, 297, 360
Fleury, monastery, 361–2, 386
Flixborough (Humberside/North Lincolnshire), 69, 439
Flodoard of Rheims, chronicler, 364
Fogartach, son of Diarmait, king of Corcu Thrí (d.994), 270
Foillan, Irish exile, 132
"folklore/folkloric," 24, 144
food, see diet
food gathering, 67
food rents, 66, 78, 97; food-renders 68, 115–16, 118–20, 450
Forach (Ireland), 200
Fordwich (Kent), 71, 334
Forest of Arden (Warwickshire), 62
forgery, 25–6
Forteviot, Strathearn, 435
Forth, river, 253, 304, 315
fortifications, 325, 330; see also burhs
Fortriu, 47, 78–9, 165, 199, 201, 253, 255
fosterage/fostering, 67, 101, 114–15, 120, 403, 464
Fothairt (population group/dynasty), 276, 387
Fragmentary Annals of Ireland, 205
Francia/Franks, 6, 30, 50–1, 63, 71, 86, 108, 109, 126, 129, 130–1, 133, 137, 149, 153, 232, 232–41, 341, 351; see also Carolingian(s); Merovingian rulers of Francia
Frankish (language), 341
free(man), 52, 67, 96–7, 116; and violence, 110
friend(s)/friendship, 94, 238
Frisian(s), 66, 71, 111, 135–6, 235
Frocester (Gloucestershire), 63
Fulford Gate (Yorkshire), battle, 312

Fulk, archbishop of Rheims, 241–2
Fursey, Irish exile, 132, 133

Gaelic, 12, 46, 252; names, 258
Gael(s), 12, 260
Gailenga, population group, 270
Gall, 12
Gall-Gaedhil, 200
Galloway, 61, 70, 146, 148, 296, 200, 203, 253
Garmondsway (Durham), 311
Garranes (Co. Cork), 128
Garryduff (Co. Cork), 433
Gateshead (Tyne and Wear), 314
Gauber High Pasture, Ribblehead (Yorkshire), 214
Gaul, 70, 145–6
Geismar (Saxony), 150
geld, 311
gender, 18, 110, 220–1; and division of labor, 69
genealogies, 17, 23, 26, 29, 30, 33, 76, 85, 108, 152, 260
geneat, 447
gens/gentes, 91, 108, 270
Geoffrey of Monmouth, chronicler, 252
Geraint, king of Dumnonia (d.710), 164, 181
Gerald of Wales (*Giraldus Cambrensis*), bishop-elect of St. David's, 184, 347, 408
Germanic language, 66, 69
Germans (*Germani*), 127, 135; "Germanization," 144;
Germanus, bishop of Auxerre, 49–50, 146
Germanus, saint, 348
Gervold, abbot of St.-Wandrille, 232, 238
gesith ("companion"), 97, 111, 112, 114, 117
Gethynctho, tract on status, 333, 401, 432
Gewisse, 419; see also West Saxons/Wessex
Ghent, 361, 366
gift(s)/gift-giving, 66, 67, 70, 79–80, 232, 235–8, 240, 466
Gildas, author of *On the Ruin of Britain*, 41–2, 45–7, 49, 50, 52–3, 58, 64, 65, 66, 71, 76–7, 81, 86, 91, 102, 117, 128, 164, 145–6, 148, 179–80, 182, 183
Gilla Comgáin, *mormaer* of Moray, 262
Gilla Pátraic, bishop of Dublin, 293
Gille (Gilbert), bishop of Limerick, 294
Gilling (Yorkshire), 163

Giric son of Dúngal, 252
Giso, bishop of Wells, 378
Glamorgan: bishops, 347, 348 (Morgannwg); lordship, 346; *see also* Morgannwg
Glanvill, author of legal treatise, 33
Glasbury (Powys), bishopric, 164, 347
Glasgow, 165, 379, 383
glassmaking, 184
Glastonbury (Somerset), 380, 406
Glazier Codex, 185
Glendalough (Co. Wicklow), 199
Glenn Máma (nr. Newcastle, Co. Dublin), battle, 275, 285
Gloucester, 62, 330, 389
Glywysing: dynasty, 348; kingdom, 78, 341, 342, 352
goddess, *see* Eithne; Eostre; Medb; Rheda
Gododdin, 48–9, 78, 84
godparenthood, 205, 464; *see also godsibbræden*
gods, pagan, 42, 85
godsibbræden, 115
Godwine, earl of Wessex, 327; family (Godwinesons), 291, 311; *see also* Harold II
Golden Ages, 6, 18, 25, 149, 377, 386
Goltho (Lincolnshire), 333, 437
Goodmanham (Yorkshire), 150, 151
goodmen, 456; "the good," 418
Gormflaith, daughter of Flann Sinna, 276–7
Gormflaith, daughter of Flann, son of Conaing, 277
Gormflaith, daughter of Murchad, son of Finn, 277, 470
Gorze, monastery, 361
Gosforth (Tyne and Wear), cross, 402
Gospatric, earl of Northumbria (d.1073 x 5), 263, 313
Gospatric's writ, 304
gospel-books, 32, 184–8; *see also* manuscripts
Gotland (Sweden), 218
Govan (Glasgow), 400
Gowrie (Perthshire), 261
grammar, 233; Latin, 179, 181, 183
Grately Decrees, 334
grave-goods, 96, 197, 204, 216, 220; *see also* burials
graveyards, 398; *see also* burials; cemeteries
Great Army, 201–4, 251

Greek(s), 233, 242; language, 182; *see also* Byzantium

Gregorian reform, *see* Gregory VII

Gregory I (the Great), pope, saint, 134, 138, 143, 148, 151, 153, 165, 181, 241

Gregory VII, pope, 367–8, 400, 404

Grimbald, monk of St.-Bertin, 241–2

Grippo, *praefectus* of Quentovic, 238

Gruffudd ap Cynan, ruler of Gwynedd (d.1137), 290, 294–5, 297, 345

Gruffudd ap Llywelyn ap Seisyll, king in Wales (d.1063), 344–6

Gruffudd ap Rhydderch, king of Morgannwg (d. c.1055), 345, 346

guild, 405, 450; *see also Cambridge Thegns' Guild*

Gundulf, bishop of Rochester, 408

Gunnhild, Cnut's daughter, 366–7

Guthlac, saint, 82

Guthred, viking leader and king, 205, 306

Guthric, king of Dublin, 382

Guthrie (Angus), 408

Guthrum (Æthelstan), viking leader and king of the East Angles (d.889/90), 205, 207, 214

Gwent, 77, 259; lordship, 346

Gwynedd: Irish involvement in, 294–5, 297; kingdom/kings, 48, 77, 109, 149, 164, 200, 222, 259, 290–1, 295, 296, 297, 341, 342, 343, 344, 345, 346, 347, 350, 351, 352; Second Dynasty of, *see* Merfyn "Frych" ap Gwriad

Gwynllwg dynasty, 348

Gytha, mother of Harold II, 462

Hackness (Yorkshire), 169

Hadrian, abbot of St. Peter and St. Paul Canterbury, 134, 177, 182

Hadrian I, pope, 235–6

Hadrian's Wall, 43–4, 48, 64

hagiography, 23, 30; evidence, 416–19, 423; *see also* saints' *Lives*

hair, 52; and identity, 110–11; pulling, 99

Halfdan/Healfdene, viking leader, 201–2, 251

half-free, 115

Hallamshire (Yorkshire), 93

Hampshire, 406, 448

Hamwic (Hampshire), 70, 198, 333

Harald Bluetooth, Danish king (d. c.987), 365

Harald Hardrada, king of Norway (d.1066), 295, 312, 369

Harald Harefoot, king of the English (d.1040), 311, 327

Harold II (Godwineson), earl of Wessex and king of the English (d.1066), 26, 290–1, 312, 324, 345, 346, 369, 408, 462; sons, daughter, 291, 295

Harrow (Middlesex), 150

"harrying of the North," 313

Hartgar, bishop of Liège, 233

Harthacnut, king of the English (d.1042), 311, 327, 366–7, 369

Hartlepool (Durham), 186

harvest, 115

Hastings, battle, 6, 291, 295, 313, 369, 389

Hastings (Sussex), 92

Heahfrith, correspondent of Aldhelm, 179, 182

Heath Wood, Ingleby (Derbyshire), viking cemetery, 217

Hebrides, 46, 291, 295, 296, 447

hegemony, 17, 130, 151, 263; *see also* overkingship/overlordship

Helena, mother of Emperor Constantine, 465, 470

Hen Gastell (Glamorgan), 435

Hengist and Horsa, 45

Henry I, east Frankish king (d.936), 359

Henry I, king of England (d.1135), 294, 297, 298, 315, 371, 459, 463

Henry II, king of England (d.1189), 286

Henry III, east Frankish king, emperor (d.1056), 366–7

Henry IV, east Frankish king, emperor (d.1105), 367

Henry of Huntingdon, chronicler, 252

Hereford, 345

Herefordshire, 452

Herman, bishop of Ramsbury, 380

hermeneutic, Latin style, 27, 183

heroic culture, 81

Herronbridge (Cheshire), 58

Hertfordshire, 388

Hesse, 137

Hexham (Northumberland), 62, 166, 187, 306, 380

Hexhamshire, 93

Hibernia, 4

Hiberno-Saxon style, 185

hide(s), 66, 92, 95, 97, 116–18, 448
high-kingship, Irish, 286–7, 289, 292, 294, 295–8; *see also* "king of Ireland"; Tara
Hild, abbess of Whitby, 154, 161, 162
hillforts, 43, 81; culture, 61–2; Scotland, 434; Wales, 435–6
Hincmar, archbishop of Rheims, 240, 242
Hingston Down (Cornwall), battle, 200
Hisperica Famina, 179, 180, 181–2
Historia Brittonum, 42, 46, 348
Historia Gruffud vab Kenan, 294–5
Historia Regum Anglorum, 255, 304, 309, 312
Historia de Sancto Cuthberto, 172, 254–5, 306, 310
historiography, 23, 28, 29; English, 12–14, 15, 31, 207, 415–16; Irish, 10–13, 15, 25, 34, 269, 285, 287–8, 415–16; Irish nationalist, 287, 289; Marxist, 12, 17; materialist, 12, 15; national, 10–15, 195, 303–4; nationalist, 6, 10–15, 16; Scottish, 8, 12–13, 25; and sources, 25, 28; Welsh, 10–13, 15
History of the Lombards, 134
Hitchin (Hertfordshire), 92
Hlothhere, king of Kent (d.685), 63, 71, 98, 100, 102
hoards, 206, 222, 279
Hoddam (Dumfries and Galloway), 165
Holy Island, *see* Lindisfarne
Holyhead (Gwynedd), 64
homilies, 23; *see also* preachers/preaching
Honorius, archbishop of Canterbury, 134
honor-price, 96, 454; debt, 114
Horm, 200
horse(s), 80–1, 236
hospitality, 67, 79, 258; and the Irish client, 115
hostages, 274–5, 291
hosting/military service/mustering, 418–19
household, 97, 162; royal, 459–60, 464, 469–70; servants, 418–19; service, 112–13; significance of entry into, 113–14; and succession, 257
Howth (Co. Dublin), 198
Hrotsvitha of Gandersheim, chronicler and dramatist, 360
Hugh Candidus, chronicler, 329
Hugh d'Avranches, earl of Chester, 346
Hugh the Great, Frankish count, 359–60
Humber, river, 5, 28, 62, 305, 312, 315

Hun(s), 236
Hundred Ordinance, 449–50
hundreds, 270, 343, 449–50
Hunterston (Ayrshire), 221
hunting, 67, 68, 84, 422
husband, 69, 97
Hwicce, 62, 66, 77, 80, 83, 93
Hywel "Dda" ap Cadell, king in Wales (d.950), 255, 342–3, 344, 346, 364, 367, 452, 463; coin of, 351
Hywel ab Edwin, king of Deheubarth (d.1044), 345
Hywel ap Rhys, king of Glywysing (ninth century), 348

Iago, king of Gwynedd (d.979), 294
Iceland, 197
identities, 4, 11–12, 14, 16, 17, 18, 25, 34, 212, 215–18, 220–2, 225, 325–7, 372; English, 303, 315–16; Germanic, 117; national, 303; personal, 107–9; racial, 11, 16; *see also* burial; dress; ethnic identity
ideology, 324–7
Idwal "Foel" ab Anarawd, king of Gwynedd (d.942), 255, 343
Iehmarc, king (?Echmarcach mac Ragnaill, Irish sea kingdom/Dublin, d. after 1061), 310
Ieuan ap Sulien of Llanbadarn Fawr, 353
Ildulb, son of Constantín, king of Alba (d.962), 258
Illtud, saint, 348
Ímar, grandson of Ímar (Ivarr), 253
Imma, Northumbrian thegn/noble, 66, 111–13
immigration, 116–17, 131; *see also* migration
Imperator Scotorum, 268, 271, 289–90
inauguration, 306; English, 469, 471; Irish, 469, 471; of queens, 470–1; rituals, 254, 469; *see also* consecration
Indo-European, 11–12, 77
Ine, king of the West Saxons (d. c.726), 66, 78, 108, 109; laws, 93, 98, 100, 102, 117 451
-ingas, 92
Ingibjorg, wife of Máel Coluim III, 459, 465
Ingimund (Ogmundr), viking leader, 205
inheritance, 420; *see also* succession
Inis Cealtra (Co. Clare), 275

Inis Pátraic (St. Patrick Island, Dublin), 196
Inishkeen (Co Monaghan), 379
"inland," 119–20; and slavery, 120
Innse Gall (Hebrides and Man), 291
inscriptions: Latin, 180; Roman, 43–4
Institutes of Polity, Civil and Ecclesiastical, 328, 469
insular art, 80, 184–89
insult (*sarhaed*), 100
intrusive kings, 344, 463
Inver Cullen (Banffshire), 258
Iolo Goch, court poet of Owain Glyn Dŵr (fl.1345–97), 342
Iona (Hebrides, Strathclyde), 68, 86, 143, 148, 149, 165, 166, 168, 169, 177, 185, 188, 196, 253, 279, 379, 383, 385, 403
Iosep, abbot and bishop of Armagh (d.936), 280
Ipswich/*Gyppeswic* (Suffolk), 69, 333
Irish chronicles, as sources for Scottish history, 251–2, 252–3, 258, 261
Irish Sea, 3, 5, 12, 59, 64, 206, 222, 259, 297; trading network, 351
Irthin, river, 61
Iserninus, bishop, 147
Isidore of Seville, 85, 180, 181, 182, 462
Isle of Man, 5, 70, 213, 223–4, 291, 294, 296
Isle of Wight, 51, 77, 109, 149, 152, 406
itineraries, royal, 332
iustum bellum (just war), 303
Ívarr (Imar, Ivar, Iguuar), viking king (d.873), 201–4, 278, 403
Ivo of Chartres, 368

Jarrow (Tyne and Wear), 188, 314, 384, 388–9; see also Monkwearmouth-Jarrow
Jean, duc de Berry, 243
Jerome, saint, 239
Jerusalem, 242
jewelry, 185, 187, 206, 216–17, 224, 422
Jews, 242–3, 293
John, abbot of Beverley/bishop of Hexham, 167
John, continental Saxon, adviser of Alfred, 242
John Scottus/Johannes Scotus Eriugena, Irish scholar, 189, 233
John of Worcester, chronicler, 329, 347
Joseph, bishop of Glamorgan, 347

judge(s), 93, 148, 456; *judices*, 50
Judith, 470
Judith, Carolingian princess, West Saxon queen, 240
Judith, niece of William the Conqueror, 313
Julius, saint, 146
Jumièges (Seine-Maritime), 232
Jupiter (Thor or Thunor), 150
Jutes, 51, 65

Kells (Co. Meath), 196, 278, 280–1, 383, 385, 388; crosses, 280
Kenelm, saint, 405
Kenstec, bishop of Cornwall, 342, 349
Kent, 45, 51, 62–3, 71, 77, 92, 98, 102, 109, 148, 165, 235, 237, 419, 448–9; Frankish links, 62–3, 130–1
Kerry, Co., 96
Kildale (Yorkshire), 204
Kildare, 61, 86, 165, 168, 276, 281, 379, 385, 387
Kilmichael Glassary (Argyll and Bute), 408
Kiloran Bay (Colonsay, Hebrides), 220
Kiltimagh (Co. Mayo), 59
Kincora (Co. Clare), 295
kindred, 82–3, 87, 95
"king of Ireland," 202, 271, 281, 286
king(s), 48, 76–88, 93, 232, 233, 237, 269–72, 418, 420, 434; killing of, 233–4, 236; king-bishop, 273; Old Testament, 243; ousting, 235; political strategies, 273–7; sixth-century royal lineages among the English, 116; and social control, 113–14, 118; see also warlords
king's thegn (*cyninges thegn, minister regis*), 111, 113
kin(ship), 82–3, 94–6, 419, 453–5; bilateral, 454–5; fictive 82–3; maternal, 454–5; paternal, 108, 454–5; spiritual, 162; study of, 11–12, 15–16, 33
"king with opposition," 261, 292–8
Kingarth (Argyll and Bute), 165
kingdoms, 5, 42, 59, 76–88, 93, 164–6, 269–70; Anglo–Saxon, 49, 51, 77, 79, 81–6; British, 48–9, 76; as economic units, 61–2; Irish, 46, 76, 78–80, 82–3, 86; Picts, 47, 76, 78–9, 81, 83; Welsh, 48, 77; see also "sea kingdom"
king-lists, 23, 26, 76–8, 83–4, 252, 258; see also regnal lists

kingship, 48, 66, 76–88, 130, 136, 161, 202–3, 233, 270–3, 325–6, 420, 423–4, 437, 468–9; access to, 415–16, 420–1; and charisma, 85; peripatetic, 437; royal landscape, 441; sacral, 77, 84, 152–4, 388

Kingston (-on-Thames, Surrey), Council of, 254

Kinnitty (Co. Offaly), stone cross, 202

Kirk Hill, St. Abb's (Berwickshire), 435

Kirkdale (Yorkshire), 402

Knock y Doonee (Isle of Man), 224

La Tène, 185

labor dues, 450

Lagore (Co. Meath), 58; high-status site, 433

Laidcend, Irish exegete, 181

Lake End (Buckinghamshire), 70

lan (Cornish place-name element), 348

Lancashire, 311

landscape 58, 59, 61, 65; royal 441

Lanfranc, archbishop of Canterbury, 293, 294, 368, 371–2, 381–3, 399–400, 404

language(s), 41–3, 46, 47, 50–3, 341; of Britain, 5–6, 64, 341; Celtic, 47, 219; at Cnut's court, 365; and (national) identity, 10–11, 12, 14, 28, 52; *see also* British; Cornish; Germanic; Latin/Latinity; linguistics; Romance; vernacular

Lantramn, scribe, 239

Lastingham (Yorkshire), 384

lathes, 449

Latin/Latinity, 64, 129, 147, 177, 232, 234, 242, 326, 341; hermeneutic style, 27, 183; and vernacular in chronicles, 252; *see also* education; grammar

law, 84, 93–102, 449–52; Brehon, 98–9; Carolingian and its influence, 232, 334, 363–4 (*see also* "correction"); customary, 33; "Good old law," 312; *Lex Salica* and Kentish law, 131; local administration, 84, 449–51; of Moses, 231; penitential, 328; royal, 31–3, 84, 98, 328, 363–4, 451, 455–6; texts and nature, 23, 29, 30, 33, 84, 98–9, 451–2; texts as sources, 57–8, 67, 416–17; tort, 99–100; and trade, 131, 334, 366; *see also* individual kings

Law of the Innocents, *see Cáin Adomnáin*

lawsuits, 451, 453; *see also* courts; disputes

lay/laity: belief, 405; lay/cleric, 27; lay as Irish "farming people," 118 ; and learning, 26–27, 30, 180–1; piety, 403–5

Le Mans, 314

lead, 237–8

learned professions, among the Irish, 120; *see also filid*

leather, 69

Lechlade (Gloucestershire), 68

Lectio divina, 178

Leeds (Yorkshire), 167

Leges in Brettos et Scottos, 447, 452, 454–5

legitimation, 14, 25–6, 33, 83, 85, 130, 152, 326–7, 470; *see also* authority

Leicester, 166, 380

Leinster, 45, 61, 64, 65, 79, 83, 85, 86, 147, 285, 289, 290, 291, 292, 385, 387; king, 285, 289, 291; kingship, 270–2, 276

Lemonaghan (Co. Offaly), 59

Lennox (East Dunbartonshire), 261

Leo IX, pope, 367–8

Leofric, bishop of Exeter, 368, 378, 380

Leofwine, ealdorman in Mercia, 327

Leofwine, son of Earl Godwine of Wessex, 290

Leth Cuinn (northern half of Ireland), 292

Leth Moga (southern half of Ireland), 292

letters, 233–42

Lewes (Sussex), 390

Lewis (Hebrides), 219

Lex Salica, 131

Liber vitae of Durham, 315

liberation, narrative, 303

libraries, 231, 239; Anglo–Saxon, 27; *see also* York

Lichfield (Staffordshire), 166

Lichfield Gospels, 31, 187, 456; *see also* St. Teilo

Liège (Belgium), 200

Life of Columbanus, 132

Life of Gregory, 183

Life of Illtud, 422

Life of John the Almsgiver, 128

Life of King Edward who Rests at Westminster, 327, 460, 464

Life of Margaret, 459–60

Life of Ruadan, 419

Life of St. Cadoc, 453

Life of St. Edmund, 202

Life of St. Fintan (Taghmon), 418

Life of Wilfrid, 133, 135
life-cycle, 81, 109–15, 419, 424; of English
  nobles, 111, 117, 118; *see also* widows
Liffey, river, 61, 223
Lifris of Llancarfan, 353; *Life of St. Cadog*
  (*Vita S. Cadoci*), 348
Lígach, queen of Brega (d.923), 276
Ligulf, Northumbria nobleman, 314
Limerick, 272–4, 277–8, 292, 295
Lincoln, 166, 216, 381
Lindisfarne (Northumberland), 62, 161,
  166, 167, 169, 184, 196, 205, 234, 306,
  313, 380, 384, 387
Lindisfarne Gospels, 184, 186–8
Lindsey (Lincolnshire), 77, 198, 216, 312,
  380
linguistics, and Scandinavian influence, 214,
  219
Linn Dúachaill (Annagassan, Co. Louth),
  199–200
Linney Burrows (Pembrokeshire), 435
Lire (France), 389
Lismore (Argyll), 408
Lismore (Co. Waterford), monastery, 199,
  275, 281
literacy, 26, 41, 180, 231
literature, 23–4, 424
liturgical material, 23–4, 30; equipment,
  398
liturgy, 185, 188, 239
Liudolf, brother of Otto I, 361
livestock, as capital, 115; *see also* cattle
Livingstone family, 408
llan (Welsh place-name element), 168, 348
Llanbadarn Fawr (Ceredigion), St. Padarn's
  church, 347, 348, 389
Llanbedrgoch (Anglesey), 222, 351, 436
Llancarfan (Vale of Glamorgan), 383, 389,
  400
Llandaf(f) (Cardiff), 64 164, 166, 167, 168,
  379, 389, 408, 452–3; *Book of*, 31, 77,
  349, 404, 452–3; charters, 436; see of,
  347, 348–9
Llanddewi (generic place-name), 348
Llandeilo Fawr (Carmarthenshire), 166,
  187, 400; bishops, 164, 347, 379, 383,
  400; church, 350; *see also* St. Teilo
Llandisillio (Dyfed), 64
Llanelwy (Denbighshire), *see* St. Asaph
  (Llanelwy)
Llangorse (Breconshire), 436

Llanllyr (Ceredigion), 180
Llansadwrn (Anglesey), 407
Lleyn Peninsula, 65
llys (Welsh "court"), 350
Llywelyn ap Seisyll, king of Gwynedd
  (d.1023), 344, 463
local church(es), 166–7, 395–6, 398–402
Loch Cuan (Co. Down), battle, 202
Loch Ness, 148
Lochleven (Scotland), 400
Loingsech, king of Tara (d.703), 87
Lombardy/Lombards, 233–4
London/*Lundenwic*, 66, 70, 71, 111, 165,
  166, 333, 380, 406, 421
Longbury Bank (Pembrokeshire), 435
longphort, 199–200, 223, 279, 446
Lorcan, king of Meath (d.864), 201
lord(s)/lordship, 67, 118–20, 137, 236,
  415, 423–4; agrarian, 333, 350;
  extensive and intensive, 119–20;
  and livestock, 118–19
Lothar, emperor (d.855), 237
Lothian, 306, 309, 310
Lough Neagh (Ireland), 199
Lough Ree (Ireland), 199
Louis IV, west Frankish king (d.954), 360,
  364
Louis the Pious, emperor (d.840), 237
loyalty, 236, 243
Lucca (Tuscany), 231
Luce Bay (Wigtownshire), 61
Lulach, son of Gilla Comgain, king of Alba
  (d.1058), 262
Lumphanan (Aberdeenshire), 262
Lupus, abbot of Ferrières, 236–9
Luxeuil, monastery, 132
Lyfing, bishop of Crediton, 349

Mabinogi/Pedair Cainc y Mabinogi
  (Mabinogion), 352, 464, 469
Macbethad, son of Findláech, king of Alba
  (d.1057), 262, 367–8; wife, 463
Macbethu, Irish pilgrim, 242
Maccus, son of Harold, King of Many
  Islands, 259, 309
Máel Brigte mac Tornáin (d.927), 280, 385
Máel Coluim, king of the Cumbrians, 309
Máel Coluim, son of Mael Brigte, king of
  Alba (?) (d.1029), 261–2
Máel Coluim I, son of Domnall, king of
  Alba (d.954), 256–7, 308, 309

Máel Coluim II, son of Cinaed, king of Alba (d.1034), 260–2, 289–90, 310

Máel Coluim III, son of Donnchad (Malcolm Canmore), king of Alba (d.1093), 262, 313, 314, 315, 371, 382, 389, 459, 463, 465

Máel Coluim IV, son of Henry, king of Alba (d.1165), 261

Máel Ísu Ua hAinmire, bishop of Waterford, 293

Máel Muad, son of Bran (d.978), 274

Máel Muire, sister of Constantín, son of Cinead, 277, 461, 466–7

Máel Ruanaid mac Ardgair, 454

Máel Sechnaill mac Domnaill, king of Tara (d.1022), 268, 272–3, 275–7, 279–81, 286, 384–5

Máel Sechnaill mac Maíle Ruanaid (d.862), 6, 202–3, 272

Máelbætha, king, 310

Maelgwn, king of Gwynedd (d. c.547), 180

Maelinmum, Irish pilgrim, 242

maenor/mainaur/maenol (Welsh "estate"), 348, 350

maer (Welsh "reeve"), 350

Máer, 280

Mag Adar, sacred tree, 275

Mag Lunge (Tiree), 169

Maghera (Co. Londonderry), 59

Magherafelt (Co. Londonderry), 59

Maglocunus, king of Gwynedd; 48; *see also* Maelgwn

Maglus the magistrate, cousin of Cantiori, 108

Magnus, son of Harald Hardrada, 295

Magnus "Barelegs," king of Norway (d.1103), 296–7, 346

Magnus Maximus, Roman military commander, 48

Magonsaetan, 77, 80

Magyars, 241

Maine, 314

Maldon, battle, 323–4, 419, 421

Malmesbury (Wiltshire), 164, 183

Malvern Hills, 62

Man, Isle of, 5, 70, 213, 223–4, 291, 294, 296

manaig, 169

Manchester (Lancashire), 330

manorialization, 137, 215, 333, 438–9; *see also* lord(s)/lordship

manumission, 66

manuscripts, 30, 135; Coptic, 185; decoration, 184, 185–7; evangelist portraits, 186, 187; gospel-books, 184–8; Hiberno-Saxon, 185; interlace, 184–7, 188; La Tène, 185; late antique 178, 185, 186–7; study of, 24; Tara–Lindisfarne, 187; Tiberius group 189; vine-scroll, 178, 188

Manx Chronicle, 296

Mar(r) (Aberdeenshire), *mormaer* of, 261, 290

Marcán mac Cennétig, abbot of Emly, 275

Maredudd ab Edwin, king of Deheubarth (d.1035), 345

Maredudd ab Owain ap Hywel Dda, king of Deheubarth, Gwynedd and Powys (d.999), 344, 346

Margaret, queen, wife of Máel Coluim III, saint, 263, 313, 315, 367, 371, 382, 389, 459–60, 462, 465, 470

Marianus Scottus, chronicler, 363, 367

market, 62, 63; *see also stapulae*

marriage, 80, 83, 154, 276–7, 359–61, 366, 470; alliance, 130–2, 276–7, 289, 343, 421, 459, 463; betrothal, 110–11; Christian teaching on, 404; clerical, 381, 400; customs, 293; as gift exchange, 466–7; intermarriage, 94, 221, 305, 370; and legitimation, 463; and making of queens 470; patterns, 359, 466; polygamy, 420, 467, 471; polygyny, 111, 420; serial monogamy, 467, 471; and succession 83, 257, 277, 466; symbolism, 461; and vulnerability of women, 467; *see also* morning gift

martyrdom, 288

martyred saints, 146; *see also* Edmund; Edward the Martyr

Mary: cult, 387; as queen of heaven, 472

Mary, daughter of Queen Margaret, 371

masculinity, 18, 218, 462; *see also* violence

mass, 387

Mathgamain mac Cennétig, king of Munster (d.976), 268, 273–7, 280

Mathilda, abbess of Essen, 361

Mathilda, wife of William I, 462, 464, 468, 472

matriliny, Pictish, 83, 463

Matudán mac Domnaill (king of Uliad), 454

Mawddach, river, 351
Mayo, 59, 147
mead, earning of, 114
Mearns, the, 260, 261
Meath, Ireland, 384
Medb, goddess/legendary Irish queen, 277, 461–2, 470
Mediterranean, 62, 70, 145
Medway, river, 62
Meginfried, treasurer of Charlemagne, 160
Meigle (Perthshire), 400
Mellitus, archbishop of Canterbury, 153
Melrose (Roxburghshire), 169, 389; Old Melrose, 165
memory, 178, 360–1
mensura (measure of land), 350
mentalities, 15, 28
Menteith (Perthshire), 261
Meols (Merseyside), 70
mercenaries, 305
Mercia/Mercians, 307; hegemony, 92, 254; kingdom, 66–7, 77, 79–80, 92, 165, 203, 206–7, 212, 233–6, 322, 342, 419; separatism, 331; shires, 448; tenth-century rule, 329–31, 463; and Wales, 342, 344–5
Mercian kings, forms of names, 108–9
Mercian Register, 330
Merfyn "Frych" ap Gwriad, king of Gwynedd (d.844), 83, 341, 342, 344; line of (Second Dynasty of Gwynedd), 341–2, 344, 346, 348
Merovingian rulers of Francia, 130, 132
Mersey, river 330
messenger(s), 233–6
metal detecting, 58, 69
metalwork/metalworking 49, 69, 184, 185–6, 216–17, 433
metropolitan, bishop, 163, 164, 165
Metz, 362
Meuse, river, 235
Middle Angles, 77, 149
Middle English, 214
Middle Saxon shift, 68
Mide, kingdom, 271, 279
migration, 42, 50–1, 65, 219
miles, as thegn, 111
militarization of Irish society, 279, 433
military service, 80–2
militia, 66, 111, 112
mills, 433, 438

mining, in Wales, 351
minority, royal, 467–8
minster model, *see* mother-church
minster(s)/minster churches, 62, 68, 69, 70, 71, 235, 238, 398, 400; as centers of settlement, 440; *see also* church(es); monasteries/monasticism; mother-churches
miracles, 161–2, 406
mission(s)/missionaries, 85, 135–6, 231, 241; *see also* conversion
Monasterboice (Co. Louth), 280–1; cross, 281
monasteries/monasticism, 71, 128–9, 137, 146, 148, 177, 184–5, 280–1, 376–8, 383–90, 395; and bishops, 132; as *civitas*, 64; double, 154; female, 148 (*see also* nunneries); layout, 385; raids on, 196, 281, 383–4 (*see also* vikings); Romanizing centers, 187–8; *see also* Benedictine monastcism; minster(s)/minster churches; religious communities
monastic reform, 31, 329, 361–4, 386–8; rhetoric, 361, 386; Welsh and Cornish contribution, 352
monastic rules, 132, 168, 384; *see also* Benedictine monasticism; *Regularis Concordia*
money/moneyers, 119, 204, 216, 232, 238, 240, 422; economy, 334; *see also* coins/coinage
monks, 234; definition, 168; ordination, 168; preaching, 168, 169; serving sees, 166
Monkwearmouth-Jarrow (Tyne and Wear) monastery, 163, 168, 236; *see also* Jarrow; Wearmouth
Mons Badonicus (Mount Badon), battle, 42, 48
Montgomery, Arnulf de, 297–8
Monynagh Lough (Co. Meath), 433
Monzievaird (Perthshire), 260
Moone (Kildare), 403
Moray, 257, 261, 290, 382, 400
Moray Firth, 61
Morgan "Hen" ab Owain, king of Glywysing (d.974), 255, 343, 344
Morgannwg, kingdom of, 259, 344, 345, 347, 349; *see also* Glamorgan
Morkar, earl of Northumbria, 312, 313
mormaer, 260–1, 290

morning gift, 111
mother-church, 170, 396–398, 400–2
motherhood, 459, 468
mother-parish, 170
Moucan, Welsh author, 180
Mount Badon (*Mons Badonicus*), battle, 42, 48
Mounth, the, 5, 61, 69, 253, 257
Moylough belt shrine, 186
Mucking (Essex), 58
Muirchertach mac Néill, king of northern Uí Néill (d.943), 269
Muirchertach Ua Briain, king of Ireland (d.1119), 292, 293–8, 382
Muirchú, *Life of Patrick*, 147
Muiredach mac Fáeláin, abbot of Kildare, 385
Muiredach mac Matudáin, king of Ulaid (d.1008), 454
Muiredach, son of Domnall, abbot of Monasterboice, 280–1
Muirgel, daughter of Flann Sinna, 276
Mullaghmast (Co. Kildare), 61
multiple estates, 68, 311, 350, 93, 433, 434, 438, 439
Munecaceastre (Monkchester), 314
Munster, 65, 46, 79, 96, 270–4, 277, 286, 289, 290–1, 292, 293, 422, 469; raid on, 202
Murchad, son of Diarmait mac Máel na mBó, king of Dublin (d.1070), 291–2
Muthill (Perthshire), 379
Mutlow (Cambridgeshire and Sussex), 449
Myddyn-fych, *Med Diminih* (Ammanford, Carmarthenshire), 350
Mynydd Carn, battle, 295
Mynyw (*Meneuia*), *see* St. Davids
Myreforth, 309
myths, 83, 85, 287; political, 461; *see also* Golden Ages; origins

Naas (Co. Kildare), 61
names, 8, 12, 34, 46, 221, 258; biblical, used by Britons, 109; and dynasties, 109; first names, 108–9; Frankish, 108; patronymics, 83, 96; and personal identity, 107–9; pet-forms, 108–9; two-stem forms, 108–9
Nantes, 70
narrative, 303, 304

natio/nation, 5, 10–15, 270; nation-state, 303
nationalism, 10–15, 34; *see also* historiography
Navan Fort (Emain Macha, Co. Armagh), 271
navies, 46, 47, 80–1, 278; *see also* fleets
Nechtan, king of the Picts (d.729), 83, 86, 180, 188
Nechtansmere, battle, 80
negotiatores, 234–5
Nest, daughter of Cadell of Powys, 463
New Israel, 231, 232
Newburn-on-Tyne (Tyne and Wear), 313
Newcastle Lyons (Co. Dublin), 61
Niall, eponym of Uí Néill, 286
Niall Caille, king of Tara, 199
Niall Glúndub, son of Áed Findliath (d.919), 257, 277
Ninian, founder of Whithorn, saint, 129, 148
Njals saga, 289
nobility, 47–8, 52, 68, 77, 81–2, 87, 96–7, 115–16, 119, 350, 401–2, 414–32, 447; royal control of noble life-cycle, 113–14; royal descent, 414, 418, 420–1, 423; settlement forms, 438; terminology, 417–18; wealth, 422, 432; *see also* aristocrats; clientage/clientship; *gesith*; *militia*; social divisions; status; *thegn*
Nobis, bishop of St. David's, 164, 379
non-combatants, protection of, 110
Norðleoda laga (Law of the North People), 304, 447
Norfolk, 388, 448
Norman Conquest, 6, 14, 335, 359, 369–72, 416; and the church, 378, 380–3, 389–90, 400; and historical writing, 13–14, 25; and royal succession, 466, 468, 472; and sources, 31
Normandy, 295, 369–72, 378, 389
Normans, 311, 312, 315
Norn, 219
Norse mythology, 218
Northmen, *see* vikings
Northumbria/Northumbrians, 6, 61, 67, 77–81, 83, 86, 161, 162, 165, 198, 201, 203, 207, 212, 231, 233–4, 236, 253, 255, 257–8, 263, 303–16, 343, 352; (administrative) divisions, 93, 311, 448; economy, 307; French settlement, 315;

Irish mission to, 148; kings, forms of names, 109; overlordship, 79; society, 417, 421; sources, 304; tenth-century rule, 322–3, 325, 331–2

Northumbrian Priests' Law, 304

Nottingham, 207, 255, 448

Novantae, 61, 165

nuclear family, 95, 117

nun, word for, 110

Nunnaminster (Hampshire), 387

nunneries, 86, 168, 329, 387; *see also* monasteries/monasticism

Nuthurst (Warwickshire), 62

oath-helper 102

oath-taking, royal, 254

Oda, archbishop of Canterbury, 328, 361–2, 372, 403

Odba (nr. Navan, Co. Meath), battle, 292

Odberht, *see* Eadberht

Odda of Deerhurst, 414

Offa, king of the Mercians (d.796), 232–6, 467, 470; coinage, 334; laws, 451

office, royal, 469; queenly, 469–72; *see also* kingship

ogham, 43, 46, 48, 64, 81, 91, 96, 221

Olaf Ua Briain, son of Tadc (d.1096), 296

Óláf Tryggvason, Norwegian king (d.999), 365

Óláfr Guthfrithsson, king of York, of Dublin (d.941), 256, 305, 309

Óláfr Sihtricson, *see* Amlaíb Cuarán

Old English, 14–15, 28–30, 214

Old Irish, 14–15, 28–30

Old Norse, 214; *see also* Norn

"Old North," 48

Old Sarum (Wiltshire), 381

Old Testament, 41, 86, 231, 243, 325, 328, 467, 469, 470

Ombersley (Worcestershire), 62

Onuist, king of the Picts (d.761), 79

Orderic Vitalis, chronicler, 297, 313

Ordgar, ealdorman of West Wessex, 421

ordination, 161

origins: dynastic, 256, 260; legends/myths, 14, 25, 41–2, 47, 53, 130, 287; periods of, 10, 12, 14–15, 25

Orkney(s), 47–8, 219–20, 289, 295, 447

Orkneyinga saga, 259, 289

Orléans, 236

Osbert, king of Northumbria (d.867), 203

Oscytel, archbishop of York, 309

Osgod Clapa, thegn, 327

Osingadun, 169–70

Osraige, kingdom, 92, 201, 270, 272, 274, 276, 289, 292, 466

Osred, king of the Northumbrians (d.716), 109

"*Ossulstone*" (Middlesex), 449

Osthryth, daughter of King Oswiu, Mercian queen, 465, 467

Ostman towns (Ireland), 288, 291, 292–3, 448

Osulf, son of Eadulf, lord of Bamburgh, 312, 313

Oswald, bishop of Worcester and archbishop of York, saint, 309, 328, 360, 361–2, 364, 377, 386, 403

Oswald, king of East Anglia, 204

Oswald, king of the Northumbrians (d.642), 79, 86, 109, 112, 149, 154

Oswine, king of Deira (d.651), 109, 112, 312

Oswiu, king of the Northumbrians (d.670), 61, 79–80, 86, 109, 112, 113, 149, 154, 161, 165, 465

Otto I, east Frankish king and emperor (d.973), 325, 359, 361–2

Otto II, east Frankish king and emperor (d.983), 361, 364

Outer Hebrides, 224

overkingship/overlordship, 46–7, 61–2, 78–80, 207, 255–6, 257–8, 270–1, 286, 323, 342–4, 346, 348, 352, 420

Owain, king of Strathclyde (d.937?), 255

Owain Glyn Dŵr (d.1415), 342

Owain ap Hywel, king of Deheubarth (d.988), 343

Owen, king of Strathclyde (d.1018), 310

Padarn, saint, 396–7; *Life*, 348; *see also* Llanbadarn Fawr

Padstow (Cornwall), 401; episcopal church, 349

pagans/paganism, 71, 85, 144, 147–8, 150–5, 218, 402–3; priesthood, 150–1; temples and shrines, 151, 153

pagi, 50

Paisley (Renfrewshire), 165

Paleozoic outcrop, 59; *see also* Britain, lowland and upland

palisaded enclosure (Scotland), 435

Palladius, bishop and missionary, 45, 64, 129, 146–7
pallium, 358, 367–8
Papa Stronsay (Orkney), 219–20
Papa Westray (Orkney), 219
papacy, 133, 136, 231, 232, 234–5, 237, 367–8; papal reform, 367–8
Papil (West Burra, Shetland), 220
parish church, *see* local church(es)
parishes, *see* mother-parish; *pievi*
Parma (Lombardy), 234
partible inheritance, 95, 118
paruchia, 281, 349
Paschal Controversy, *see* Easter
pastoral care, 148, 171, 395–405; *see* church(es); minster(s)/minster churches; religious communities
paternity and personal identity, 108
patriarch, ecclesiastical office, 163
patriarchal family, 95
Patrick, bishop of Dublin, 382
Patrick, saint, 41, 44–5, 53, 61, 64, 66, 145, 147, 148, 166, 179, 268, 276, 384–5; bell, 276; cross, 280, 281; Roman identity, 107; shrine, 276; successors, 276, 280
patrilineal descent, 95
patristic learning, 233; texts, 27
Paul, apostle and saint, 241
Paul, earl of the Orkneys, 382
Paul the Deacon, chronicler, 134
Paulinus, archbishop of York, 62, 149, 167
Peada, king of the Middle Angles and then Mercians (d.656), 108
peasant(ry), 52–3, 82, 96, 447; *see also* *bóaire*; *ceorl*; free(man); slave
pedigrees, 23, 26; *see also* genealogies
Peebles (Tweeddale), 165
Pelagius, Romano-British monk, 179; Pelagianism, 146
Pembroke, 297
Pembrokeshire, 222
penance/penitential(s), 30, 101, 132, 171, 231, 233, 397, 404–5
Penda, king of the Mercians (d.655), 80, 92, 108, 132, 133, 149
Penmachno (Conwy), inscription, 107–8
Penmon (Anglesey), 222, 383
Pennines, 304
"people of craft" (Irish category), 118
peoples, 447; *see also* *gens/gentes*

peregrinatio, 148, 231, 242; *see also* pilgrim(s)/pilgrimage
periodization, 6, 14, 285
Pershore (Worcestershire), 329
Perthshire, 400
Peterborough (Northamptonshire), 311, 329
pet-names, 108–9
Philibert, saint, 232
Philip I, west Frankish king (d.1108), 295, 371
philosophy, 233
Picardy, 232
Picts, 4, 41–3, 47–8, 76–7, 148, 251; divisions of kingdom, 261; Pictavia, 251; Pictland, 69, 203
Pierowall (Westray, Orkney), 220
pievi, 164
pilgrim(s)/pilgrimage, 162, 231, 234, 237, 242, 262, 362, 367, 422
pillaging, 67
Pippin, "mayor of the palace," 135
Pippinid family, 135
"Pitcarmick house" type, 434
Pitgaveny (Morayshire), 262
place-names, 46, 50–1, 58, 62, 65, 67, 150, 212–13, 219–20, 222, 305, 343
plague, 65, 128
plebes, 164
Plegmund, archbishop of Canterbury, 242
plowing, 67, 116, 120
Poddle, river, 223
podum (monastery), 168
poetry, *see* songs
political thought, 85, 136, 233, 364; Anglo–Saxon, 136; Carolingian, 136, 363–4, 468–9; Irish, 136, 468–9; Ottonian, 364
polity, 5
pollen analysis, 197
Pool (Sanday, Orkney), 220
pope, *see* papacy
population, 57, 65, 128, 333, 434; movement, 50, 219
population groups, 92
port(s), 70–1, 232, 236, 238
Portchester (Hampshire), 438
Portland (Dorset), 198
Portmahomack (Highland), 58, 70
port-reeve, 71
postmodernism, 16–17, 19, 28

Potitus, St. Patrick's grandfather, 64, 107
pottery, 49, 69, 70, 145, 216, 220, 224
power, 14, 17, 25–6, 31, 127; and authority, 17; military, 80–2; *see also* authority; hegemony; king(s); kingship
Powys, 77, 80, 83, 204, 341, 342, 345, 347; dynasty, 348
prayer, 233, 235, 237–8
Prayer of Manasseh, 180
preachers/preaching, 160, 397, 400; *see also* homilies
prehistoric ring ditches, 161
priests, 107, 147, 168–9, 397–9, 402; abbots, 168; pre-Christian, 85, 161; responsibilities, 164;
primacy, 165; of Canterbury, 293–4, 381–3
prince-bishops, 305–6
princesses, Anglo-Saxon, 154
Prittlewell (Essex), 58, 151, 161
production factors, 115
productive sites, 62, 69, 439
propaganda, 286, 296, 298; *see also* ideology
Prophecy of Berchán, 289
provinces, Scottish, 261
Psalter, 233, 242
Pseudo-Dionysius, theologian, 233
public/private distinction, 459

Quadripartitus, 451
Quedlinburg, 360
queen-mothers, 461, 462, 467
queens, 83–4, 86, 131, 133, 154, 276–9, 459–72; and conversion, 465, 470; and ecclesiastical politics, 465, 470; hearing lawsuits, 464; household, 472; lands, 462, 471–2; Mercian, 463, 467, 470–2; *see also* succession
queenship, 468–72; models, 465, 470, 472
Quentovic, 232, 236, 238
Quintilian, grammarian, 239

radio-carbon dating, 197, 204, 214, 221
Rædwald, king of the East Angles (d.616x627), 116, 151
Rægnæld (Rgnall na Ímarr), king of York (d.921), 254–5, 256, 306, 308
Raghnall, son of Amlaíb Cuarán (d.980), 279
Ragnar Lothbrok's Saga, 202
Ragnarok, 402
raiding, 43–7, 80–2

Ráith Bressail, synod, 294, 382
Ralph, earl of East Anglia, 371
Ramsbury (Wiltshire), 380–1
Ramsey (Cambridgeshire), monastery, 329, 362, 387
Ranig, earl, 327
ranked societies, 127; *see also* social divisions
ransom, 234
Raoul, west Frankish king (d.936), 360
rapes (local unit), 449
Rathcroghan (Cruachu, Co. Roscommon), 271
raths, 65, 432, 433
Raunds Furnell (Northamptonshire), 437, 439
ravaging, 307, 325, 332; *see also* "harrying of the North"
Rayleigh (Essex), 58
Reading (Berkshire), 92
Reay (Caithness), 220
Rechru (Rathlin Island, Antrim), 196
re-conquest, 303, 315
Rectitudines singularum personarum, 447
Red Wharf Bay (Anglesey), 222
Reformation, 13–15, 27
regency, 462, 467–8
Regino of Prüm, chronicler, 52–3
regio(nes), 78, 93
regions, 305
regnal lists, 252, 462
Regularis concordia, 328, 362, 364, 388
Reichenau (Germany), monastery, 198
relics, 360, 406–7
religious communities, 168–70, 232, 384, 396; buildings, 162, 169; clerical, 166, 384; constitutions, 168–9, 171–2; cult centers, 161, 162; double houses, 168; endowment, 163; episcopal centers, 166, 398; estates, 169–70, 385; federations, 169; and kinship, 162–3; and naming practice, 109; number and distribution, 168; pastoral care, 169–70, 384; political and social utility, 162; raiding of, 172; royal and episcopal appropriation, 172; royal hospitality, 161; size, 169; tenants, 64, 169–70; trade, 162; transformation, 172; *see also* minster(s)/minster churches; monasteries/monasticism; nunneries
religious reform, 71, 171, 172
Remigius, archbishop of Rheims, saint, 241
Remigius, bishop of Lincoln, 381

Renaissance, Northumbrian, 61, 183
"render-payers" (clients, *aithig*), 115
renovatio monetae, 334
rent-paying peoples, 92
Repton (Derbyshire), 204, 217, 251
Resting Places of English Saints, 196, 405
retinues, 417–18, 421
Rheda, pagan goddess, 150
Rhedmonath (March), 150
Rheged, 48–9, 61, 78
Rheims, 240, 367–8
rhetoric, 180, 233
Rhineland, 235
Rhiwallon ap Cynfyn, co-ruler of Gwynedd
  (d.1069), 345, 346
Rhodri "Mawr" ap Merfyn, king of
  Gwynedd (d.878), 6, 200, 202–4, 222,
  342, 344, 348, 463
Rhuddlan: *burh*, 345–6, 350; lordship, 346,
  347; mint, 351
Rhuothild, abbess of Faremoutiers, 238
Rhydderch ab Iestyn, king in south Wales
  (d.1033), 345, 346, 347
Rhygyfarch ap Sulien (*Ricemarch*, d.1099),
  353; *Life of St. David* (*Vita S. Dauid*),
  348; *Planctus*, 347, 352
Rhys ap Tewdwr, king of Deheubarth
  (d.1093), 295, 297, 345, 347
Rí hÉrend co fressabra, 292–8; *see also* "king
  with opposition"
Riagail Phátraic, on bishops, 396
Richard II, Norman duke (d.1027), 359,
  369
Richarius, monastic founder, saint, 232
Richer, chronicler, 361
Ricsige, king of the Northumbrians
  (fl.873–6), 203
ridings, 311, 449
ringforts, 65, 91, 423, 432–3
Ripon (Yorkshire), 146, 166, 406
rites of passage, 110
roads, 44, 61, 64, 81
Robert, lord of Rhuddlan, 346
Robert Cumin, earl of Northumbria, 313
Robert Curthose, son of William I, 263
Robert the Magnificent, Norman duke
  (d.1035), 369
Robert Mowbray, earl of Northumberland,
  263
Rochester (Kent), 381, 406
Roger, earl of Hereford, 371

Roger de Montgomery, earl of Shrewsbury
  (d.1094), 346
Roger of Wendover, chronicler, 304, 308
Roman Empire, 41, 57, 66, 85, 163, 415;
  in Britain, 41–4
Romance language(s), 232
Romanization, 6, 43–4, 64
Rome/Romans, 63, 130, 133, 134, 135,
  153, 160, 163, 166, 231–7, 239, 241–2,
  262, 358, 364–5, 367–8, 422
Romney Marsh (Kent), 62
Ros Ailithir (Rosscarbery, Co. Cork), 275
Rosemarkie (Highlands), 165
Ross (Scotland), 261, 382
Rouen, 232
Royal Prayer Book, 180
royal rule/government, 325, 415–19, 421,
  423; agents, 419–20; officials, Scottish
  (*see mormaer*); *see also* administrative
  units; nobility
Rúaidrí ua Canannáin (d.950), 278
Rudolf II, Burgundian king (d.937), 359
Rudolf III, Burgundian king (d.1032),
  365–6
runes, 43
Ruthwell (Solway Firth), 188; cross, 188
Rye Water, river, 61

sacraments, 160, 397–8; *see also* mass
sacrifice, animal, 151
Saebbi, king of the East Saxons (d. c.694),
  154
sagas, 30
St. Albans (Hertfordshire), 49, 63, 146,
  293, 405
St. Andrews (Fife), 254, 256, 379, 383;
  sarcophagus, 189
St. Anthony in Meneage (Cornwall), 407
St. Anthony in Roseland (Cornwall), 407
St. Asaph (Llanelwy), 351, 395; see of, 347,
  379
St. Augustine's, Canterbury (Kent), 166
St.-Bertin, 362
St. Buryan (Cornwall), 401
St. Davids (Pembrokeshire), 164, 166, 204,
  295, 347, 377, 379, 383, 389, 400;
  archbishops/bishops, 347, 349; mint,
  351; see of (Mynyw/*Meneuia*), 347
St. Do-Chonna, shrine, 196
St.-Gall, 32, 362
St. Germans (Cornwall), see of, 349

St.-Josse (St.-Judoc, Pas-de-Calais), monastery, 236–9
St. Maignenn, monastery, 223
St. Peter's (Rome), 235
St.-Riquier (Somme), monastery, 232
St.-Samson (Dol), 362
St. Teilo (Carmarthenshire), 347, 407; bishops, 347; gospel-book (also known as the *Lichfield Gospels*), 350
St. Vigeans (Angus), 400
St.-Vincent of Le Mans, abbey, 314
St.-Wandrille (Seine-Maritime), monastery, 232
saints, 161–2; royal, 86, 154, 360, 405, 406–7; study of, 11, 17
saints' cults, 348, 405–8; *see also* martyred saints; saints, royal
saints' *Lives*, 29, 30, 58, 348, 408, 459–60; study of, 28; *see also* hagiography
sala (hall), 137
Salisbury, oath of (1086), 295
Salzburg, 32
Samson, saint, 109, 146
Samuel Ua hAingliu, bishop of Dublin, 293
Sandwich (Kent), 71
Santon Down (Norfolk), 204
Saracens, 241
Sarre (Kent), 71
satrap, 417; *see also mormaer*
Saxonia, 232
Saxons/Saxony, 51
Scandinavians, 66, 447–8; Anglo–Saxon imitations of, 130; *see also* vikings
Scattery Island (Co. Clare), 379
sceattas, 69, 70
Sceilig Mhichil (Co. Kerry), 198
schools, 180, 233; curriculum, 182
Scilly Isles, 70
scīrman, 93
Scone (Perthshire), 253
Scotia, 255
Scotti, 4, 43, 251–2, 254; *scottus* (Irishman), 232–3, 242
scriptoria, 239, 287; in Cornwall and Wales, 352
sculpture/stone-carving, 167, 218, 224, 402–3, 435; Anglian School, 189; cross-marked stones, 186; cross–slabs 188; Pictish symbol stones, 43, 48, 53, 68, 77, 81, 84, 186, 224–5, 434; relief-carving, 188; stone, 202, 214, 218, 222

"sea kingdom," 5, 47; *see* also Irish Sea; Isle of Man
Seaxburgh, daughter of King Anna, 133
Seaxburh, West Saxon queen, 84, 462
Secundinus, bishop, 147
Sedgeford (Norfolk), 68
Sedulius Scottus, Irish scholar, 200, 233
sees, 163–8; movement of, 368, 381
Seine, river, 232
Seisyllwg, kingdom, 204, 348
Selgovae, 165
Selsey (Sussex), 97, 166, 380
Senchas Már, Irish law tract, 99
Sens, 236
Sermo Lupi ad Anglos ("Sermon of the Wolf to the English"), 309, 311
servitude, 66; *see also* slave; slavery
settlement, 212–25; nucleation in Ireland, 433; patterns, 137, 269; rural, 44, 49, 215, 219, 439; Scotland, 434; unenclosed, Ireland, 433; in Wales, 436 (*see also* village)
Severn, river, 5, 62
sexual morality, 404
Shaftesbury, nunnery, 329, 387
Shannon, river, 61, 67
Sheppey (Kent), 198
Sherborne, 380, 396; see of, 342, 349
Sherburn-in-Elmet (Yorkshire), 398
Shetland Isles, 47–8, 198, 219–20, 447
ship(s), 70, 71, 81, 232, 234, 242; *see also* fleets; navies
shire (*scīr*), 92–3, 448; court, 448–9; reeve, 448–9; *see also* Mercia/Mercians; Northumbria/Northumbrians
Shottery (Warwickshire), 62
shrines, 407–8; pre-Christian, 161
Siefrid, Scandinavian king, 206
Sigebert, king of the East Angles (fl.630), 86, 153
Sigeric, archbishop of Canterbury, 358, 372
Sighelm, ealdorman, 421
Sigulf, abbot of St.-Josse, 236
Sigurd Hlödvisson, earl of Orkney, 289–90
Sigurd Jerusalem-farer, king of Norway (d.1130), 296
Sihtric, grandson of Ímar, king of York (d.927), 217, 256
silk, 236, 366
silver, as currency, 119; *see also* coins/coinage

Simy Folds (Co. Durham), 214
Sitric/Sihtric son of Amlaíb, king of Dublin, "Silkbeard" (d.1042), 262, 275, 277–8, 279, 281, 289, 290,
Siward, earl of Northumbria, 262, 310, 327, 399
Sixtus, saint, 146
Skaill (Deerness, Orkney), 220
Skreen (Ireland), 403
Skye (Hebrides), 196
Slane (Co. Meath), 199, 278
slave, 97, 115; in *Domesday Book*, 116; female, as currency, 96, 119; raiding/ raids, 107, 308
slavery, 45, 52–3, 66, 81, 147, 231, 434, 447; and intensive lordship,119–20; and plowing, 120
Slavs, 127
Slige Dála, routeway, 61
social divisions, 68, 416, 432; *see also* class and status; ranked societies; status
sokes, 311
Solway, river, 309
Solway Firth, 61
Somerset, 291, 349, 448
Somerton (Somerset), 448
Somme, river, 232
songs, 233, 243
sources, written volume of, 4, 26, 28, 127–8, 252–3, 304–5, 358–9, 416; factors in survival, 25–7; patterns of survival, 28–31, 358, 416–17; prescriptive, 170–1; primary, 10; problems of definition, 25; record, 31
souterrain, 433
South Newbald (Humberside), 62
South Saxons, 77
South Shields (Tyne and Wear), 44
Southampton (Hampshire), 448
Southumbria, 6, 233, 235, 251, 255, 309, 417
spiritual kinship, 115
spolia, 235
Springfield Lyons (Essex), 438
Sprouston (Roxburghshire), 435
stable isotope analysis, 216, 221
Stafford, 448
Staffordshire, 448
Staindrop (Co. Durham), 310
Stamford (Lincolnshire), 216

Stamford Bridge (Yorkshire), battle, 312, 369
stapulae, 238
state, 5; English, 13, 31–2; formation, 128, 323–34, 416
status, 96–8, 100, 115–18, 446–7; and buildings, 423; legally prescribed, 96–8, 414, 416–17, 423–4, 447; and settlement form, 432
Staunch Meadow, Brandon (Norfolk), 440
Stephen, monk of Ripon, 162, 166, 183; *Life of Bishop Wilfrid*, 73
Stephen V, pope, 241
Stigand, archbishop of Canterbury, 378, 381–2
stones, inscribed memorial, 96, 145–6, 168, 180; *see also* sculpture/stone-carving
Strathclyde, kingdom of, 49–50, 78, 201, 255, 257–8, 262–3, 303, 308, 344, 352
Strathearn (Perthshire), 253, 260, 261
subkings, *see* underkings
"submission" to southern English kings, 251–2, 255–6, 259, 263, 308–9
succession, royal, 82–3, 459, 463–4, 465–7, 472; designation, 262, 467; English, 83, 323–4, 326, 329–32, 369, 420–1, 466–7; Irish, 82–3, 272–3, 466, 470; Pictish, 83, 463; royal women and, 83, 257, 262, 276–7, 462–3, 466, 472; Scottish, 254, 256–62, 463; study of, 11, 33–4; *tanáiste*, 262; Welsh, 344, 463; West Saxon, 239–40; *see also aetheling*; marriage; matriliny, Pictish
Suffolk, 388, 448
Sulien (*Sulgenus*), bishop of St. Davids (d.1091), 347, 353
surety, 102
Surrey, 448
Sussex, 68, 149, 152, 448–9
Sutton Hoo (Suffolk), 58, 66, 130, 151, 161, 185
Swale, river, 167
Swegn Forkbeard, Danish king (d.1014), 289, 310, 311, 323, 365
Swifne, Irish scholar, 242
swine, 62
Swithun, saint, 406–7
sword/sword-belt, 236
Swords (Dublin), 403
Syagrius, 49

symbol stones, Pictish, *see* sculpture/stone-carving
Symeon of Durham, chronicler, 304, 314
synods, 165, 293–4; *see also* councils
"systems collapse," 49

Tacitus, Roman historian, 100, 150, 151
Taghmon (Co. Wexford), 109
Táin Bó Cúailnge, 24, 418–19, 424
Talacre (Flintshire), 222
Talorcan, king of the Picts (d.657), 83
Tamar, river, 343, 351
Tamworth (Warwickshire), 217, 342–3
Taprain Law, 43
Tara (Temair, Co. Meath), 85, 257, 270–2, 275, 286, 469; "king of Tara," 271, 286
Tara brooch, 187
Tating ware, 439
tattoos, 47–8
taxation, 78–9, 84, 232; *see also* geld; toll(s); tribute/tribute-taking
Tay, river, 253
Tees, river, 304, 306, 308, 309, 310, 311, 313
Teesmouth (Cleveland), 59
Teilo, St., *alias* Eiludd, 109, 397
temples, 44; *see also* pagans/paganism
Terryglass (Co. Tipperary), 275
Tewdwr ab Elise, king of Brycheiniog (d. after 973), 343
Thames, river, 62, 68, 254
thanages, 434
Thanet (Kent), 198
thegn, 401, 418, 432, 437, 447; development of meaning of, 112–13
Thelwall (Cheshire), 330
Theodore of Mopsuestia, author of Greek Psalter-Commentary, 242
Theodore of Tarsus, archbishop of Canterbury, 101, 134, 165, 169, 177, 182; *Penitential*, 155
theology, 23, 30, 233
Theophanu, empress, 364
Thetford (Norfolk), 216
Thietmar of Merseburg, chronicler, 364–5
Thomas of Bayeux, archbishop of York, 382
Thorney (Cambridgeshire), monastery, 329
Thundersley (Essex), 150
Thunor, pagan god, 150
Thurbrand Hold, 453

Thurstable (Essex), 449
tin, 70
Tintagel (Cornwall), 70, 128, 145, 255
Tipperary, county, 67
Tírechán, 32, 147, 166, 169
tithe(s), 231, 398; *see also* church dues
tithing, 450
Tiw, pagan god, 150
Tlachtga (Hill of Ward, Co. Meath), 272
Tofig the Proud, thegn, 327
Toirdelbach Ua Briain, king of Munster (d.1086), 291–6, 382
toll(s), 232, 234, 334
Torquay (Devon), 59
Tostig, earl of Northumbria, 263, 311, 312, 313, 332, 345
towns, 44, 49, 63, 64, 82, 215–16, 269, 292–3, 305, 333–4, 350–1, 441–2, 446, 448; church in, 399, 406; monastic proto-, 385; *see also* Ostman towns; urban settlement
Toxandria, 137
trade/traders, 43, 45–6, 59, 64, 70, 72, 82, 128, 129, 131, 135, 162, 222–3, 232, 234, 278, 341, 344, 351, 366–7, 422, 439; embargo, 298; *see also* gifts/gift-giving; *negotiatores*; *wics*
"transformation of the Roman world," 16, 126
transhumance, 68
Treaty of Alfred and Guthrum, 205
tref (Welsh, "small settlement"), 350
Trent, river, 28; battle of (679), 111, 113
Tribal Hidage, 66, 78, 92, 137
tribe/tribal, 11, 416
tribute/tribute-taking, 61, 66, 67, 79–80, 343, 351, 433
Trumwine, bishop for the Picts, *alias* Tumma, 108
túath/túatha, 78, 92–3, 129, 164–5, 166, 169, 170, 270, 379, 441
Tuathal, abbot of Dunkeld, 165
Tuirbe, kingdom, 270
Tunberht, abbot of Gilling, 163
Turgot, chaplain of Margaret of Scotland and monk of Durham, 367, 371, 459
Turonensian order, 389
Tuscany, 231
Tweed, river, 263, 314, 315
Tyne, river, 61, 306, 310, 312, 313, 314

Tynemouth (Tyne and Wear), 389
Tysoe (Warwickshire), 150
Tywi, river, 349

Ubbe, leader of the Great Army, 403
Uchtred/Uhtred, lord of Bamburgh, earl of Northumbria, 310, 453
Udal (North Uist, Hebrides), 220
Uhtred, son of Eadwulf, 254
Uí Áeda Odba, 277
Uí Briain, 275, 281, 292, 294, 296, 297
Uí Chennselaig, 290, 291
Uí Dúnchada, 385
Uí Dúnlainge, 61, 387
Uí Fhiachrach Aidne, 277
Uí Néill, 61, 83, 85, 92, 148, 201–2, 257, 268–9, 271–2, 277, 280–1, 286, 292, 293, 294, 298, 384, 418, 466
Uí Néill, Southern, 201, 286
Uí Sinaig/Sínaich, 280, 386
Uinniau, see Finnian
Uisnech (kingship), 271–2
Ulaid Ulster (kingship), 271, 454
Ulf, bishop of Dorchester, 368
Ulster, 79, 83, 297
Ultan, Irish exile, 132
underkings, 80, 81, 342, 343 (subreguli); see also client kings; overlordship
Uraicecht Becc, Irish law tract, 96–7
urban settlement, 223, 437, 441–2; see also towns
Urien, king of Rheged (fl. late sixth century), 49, 61
Utrecht, 135

vegetables, 237
veiled woman, 110
Venicones, 165
Verdun, 238
vernacular language, 14, 24, 27–30, 326, 399; literature, 424
verse-forms and metrics, Latin, 181, 182, 183
vici, 164
vikings, 6, 31, 61, 195–230, 233, 237, 234, 237–42, 259, 268–2, 274–5, 277–9, 285, 288, 289, 291, 293, 296, 298, 304–9, 322–4, 333, 352, 365, 383–6, 402–3, 446–7, 449; definition, 195; impact on church, 376–7, 383–6 (see also conversion); impact on settlement and

social structure, 434, 439; Scandinavians or vikings, 345, 351
village, 68, 434; nucleated, 118, 333
villani, in Domesday Book, 116
villas (Roman), 44, 63, 71
Vindolanda (Northumberland), 64
vineyards, 438
violence, and the free male, 110
Vitalian, pope, 134
Vortigern, British ruler, 49
Vortipor, king of Dyfed, 46, 48
Votadini, 43, 49, 165
Voteporix, 46
Voyage of Máel Dúin, 422

Walafrid Strabo, abbot of Reichenau, 198
Walcher, bishop of Durham, 313, 314
Wallingford (Oxfordshire), 333
Walter Bower, prior of Inchcolm, 254
Waltham (Essex), 407
Waltheof, earl of Northumbria (d.1076), 313, 314, 371, 454
Waltheof of Bamburgh, earl, 259, 310
wapentakes, 311, 449–50
Wareham (Dorset), British inscriptions, 117
warehouse(s), 232
warfare, 46, 77, 79–82
"warland," 119–20
warlords, 66
Waterford, 96, 269, 275, 277–8, 292, 295, 297
watermills, 71
Waulsort, 362
Weald, the, 62
wealh/wealas/walas, 66, 94, 117
weapons, 50, 81, 217–18; see also sword/sword-belt
Wear, river, 306
Wearmouth (Tyne and Wear), 187, 384, 388–9; see also Monkwearmouth-Jarrow
weaving, 69, 184–5
Wednesbury (Staffordshire), 150
Wells (Somerset), see of, 349, 380
Welsh tractates (laws of court), 464, 471
Wensley (Yorkshire), 204
Wer, 456
wergild (wergeld), 67, 96, 100–1, 109–10, 131, 447, 454
West Heslerton (North Yorkshire), 58, 62, 69
West Highlands (Scotland), 400

West Saxons/Wessex, 52, 58, 77, 84, 98, 100, 114, 149, 165, 200, 205–7, 237, 240, 251, 253, 255, 257, 258, 290, 303, 304, 305, 307, 308, 309, 310, 315, 322–3, 329–31, 341, 342, 343, 352, 380, 447–9, 451

Westbury (Gloucestershire), 398

Western Isles, 253, 385

Westminster (Middlesex), 313, 380

Westness (Rousay, Orkney), 221

Wexford, 291, 292

Wharram Percy (Yorkshire), 215

Whitby (Yorkshire), monastery (double house), 154, 161, 166, 168, 388–9; daughter houses, 169; synod, 86, 149, 165

Whitford (Flintshire), 222

Whithorn (Dumfries & Galloway), 61, 128, 129, 148, 165, 166

wics, 70–1, 82, 131

widows, 257, 421, 462, 463, 466

Wight, Isle of, 51, 77, 109, 149, 152, 406

Wigmund, archbishop of York, 238

Wihtred, king of Kent (d.725), 63, 66, 109; laws, 97–8, 154, 155

Wilfrid, bishop and saint, 83, 97, 113, 133, 135, 154, 162, 165, 166, 167, 187, 406

William I "the Conqueror," king of the English (d.1087), 263, 294, 295, 312, 313, 314, 324, 332, 347, 351, 359, 368–72, 381, 389, 459, 465, 468, 472

William I of Warenne, 390

William II, Rufus, king of English (d.1100), 263, 294, 324, 370

William fitz Osbern, earl of Hereford, 346, 389

William of Jumièges, chronicler, 369

William Longsword, Norman duke (d.942), 369

William of Malmesbury, chronicler, 297–8, 329, 343, 351, 397, 404

William of Saint-Calais, bishop of Durham, 314, 368

William of Volpiano, 390

Willibrord, missionary archbishop, 135, 137

Wilton (Wiltshire), 448, 387; nunnery, 329

Wiltshire, 448

Winchcombe (Gloucestershire), 405, 448

Winchcombeshire, 448

Winchester (Hampshire), 166, 215, 293, 309, 378, 380–1, 387, 399, 406–7; Council of (1070), 381, 399; New Minster, 328

Windsor (Berkshire), Council of (1070), 399

Winwaed, battle, 80

Witham, river, 216

witness lists, 255, 331, 343, 344, 461, 467–8

Woccingas, 93

Woden, pagan god, 85, 127, 130, 150, 151, 152, 154

Woking (Surrey), 93

woman/women, 7–8, 27, 69, 70, 220–1, 231, 269, 276–7, 462, 468; dress and identity, 51; female slavery, 66, 96, 119; and inheritance, 420; paternity and identity, 108; and religious authority, 161–2; study of, 18; symbolic, 18, 461–2; woman/spouse as opposed to maiden, 110

women, royal: sources for, 460–2; *see also* queens

woodland, 62

Worcester, 62, 71, 293, 309, 315, 329, 330, 380, 387, 389, 397

work and identity, 422

writing, 26–7

written sources, 41–2, 46, 57–8, 62, 76–8, 127–8; lack of, 252–3

Wroxeter (Salop), 44, 63

Wuffa, ancestor of East Anglian kings, 116

Wuffingas, East Anglian dynasty, 116, 130

Wulfhere, archbishop of York, 203

Wulfhere, king of the Mercians (d.675), 109, 152

Wulfric Spott, thegn, 330

Wulfrun, Mercian noblewoman, 330

Wulfstan I, archbishop of York, 305, 306, 309

Wulfstan II, bishop of London, bishop of Worcester and archbishop of York, 304, 309, 311, 328, 381–2, 398–9, 404, 451, 469

Wulfstan II, bishop of Worcester, 293, 378, 381, 397–8, 408

Wye, river, 62, 451

Wynfrith, *see* Boniface (Wynfrith), saint

Wyre Forest, 62

Y Gododdin, 24, 48, 81
yardland, 118
Yarnton (Oxfordshire), 439
Yeavering (Northumberland), 161, 306, 435
York, 3, 62, 70, 201, 205, 215–16, 238–9, 295, 305, 307, 312, 313, 314, 446; archbishops, 165–6, 203, 215–16, 236, 238, 304, 305, 307, 309, 311, 378, 380; Church of St. Peter, 166, 305, 307; churches, 167, 399; earldom, 310; kingdom, 203, 277–9, 305, 308, 332; library, 27, 239; Minster/cathedral 168, 313, 381, 399; mint, 206, 308; prince-bishops, 305, 306; school, 183–4, 233
Yorkshire, 311, 448
Youghal (Co. Cork), 199
youth, 81, 112
Ystrad Tywi, 347, 348

Zosimus, Byzantine historian, 44–5

CPSIA information can be obtained
at www.ICGtesting.com
Printed in the USA
BVHW090819160122
626332BV00017B/202

9 781118 425138